FREEDOM RIDERS

**PIVOTAL MOMENTS
IN AMERICAN HISTORY**

Series Editors
David Hackett Fischer
James M. McPherson

James T. Patterson
*Brown v. Board of Education:
A Civil Rights Milestone and Its Troubled Legacy*

Maury Klein
Rainbow's End: The Crash of 1929

James McPherson
Crossroads of Freedom: The Battle of Antietam

Glenn C. Altschuler
All Shook Up: How Rock 'n' Roll Changed America

David Hackett Fischer
Washington's Crossing

John Ferling
Adams vs. Jefferson: The Tumultuous Election of 1800

Joel H. Silbey
*Storm over Texas:
The Annexation Controversy and the Road to Civil War*

FREEDOM RIDERS
1961 and the Struggle for Racial Justice

RAYMOND ARSENAULT

OXFORD

UNIVERSITY PRESS

2006

OXFORD
UNIVERSITY PRESS

Oxford University Press, Inc., publishes works that
further Oxford University's objective of excellence
in research, scholarship, and education.

Oxford New York
Auckland   Cape Town   Dar es Salaam   Hong Kong   Karachi
Kuala Lumpur   Madrid   Melbourne   Mexico City   Nairobi
New Delhi   Shanghai   Taipei   Toronto

With offices in
Argentina Austria Brazil   Chile Czech Republic France Greece
Guatemala Hungary Italy Japan Poland Portugal Singapore
South Korea Switzerland Thailand Turkey Ukraine Vietnam

Copyright © 2006 by Raymond Arsenault

Published by Oxford University Press, Inc.
198 Madison Avenue, New York, NY 10016
www.oup.com

Oxford is a registered trademark of Oxford University Press

Library of Congress Cataloging-in-Publication Data
Arsenault, Raymond.
Freedom riders : 1961 and the struggle for racial justice / Raymond Arsenault.
p. cm. — (Pivotal moments in American history)
Includes bibliographical references and index.
ISBN-13: 978-0-19-513674-6
ISBN-10: 0-19-513674-8
1. African American civil rights workers—History—20th century.
2. Civil rights workers—United States—History—20th century.
3. African Americans—Segregation—Southern States—History—20th century.
4. Segregation in transportation—Southern States—History—20th century.
5. African Americans—Civil rights—Southern States—History—20th century.
6. Civil rights movements—Southern States—History—20th century.
7. Southern States—Race relations—History—20th century. I. Title. II. Series.
E185.61.A69 2006   323'.0975'09046—dc22   2005018108

9 8 7 6 5 4 3 2 1
Printed in the United States of America
on acid-free paper

For
John Hope Franklin—the Freedom Writer

Parts of this book previously appeared in a different form and are republished with permission: "'You Don't Have to Ride Jim Crow': CORE and the 1947 Journey of Reconciliation," in *Before* Brown*: Civil Rights and White Backlash in the Modern South*, ed. Glenn Feldman, 21–67 (Tuscaloosa: University of Alabama Press, 2004); "You Don't Have to Ride Jim Crow," *Stetson Law Review* 34 (Winter 2005): 343–411; "One Brick at a Time: The Montgomery Bus Boycott, Nonviolent Direct Action, and the Development of a National Civil Rights Movement," in *Sunbelt Revolution: The Historical Progression of the Civil Rights Struggle in the Gulf South, 1866–2000*, ed. Samuel C. Hyde Jr., 153–189 (Gainesville: University Press of Florida, 2003); and "Taking the Road to Freedom," *Forum* 28 (Spring 2004): 30–35.

Contents

Maps

Editors' Note

MANY AMERICANS who were alive on May 4, 1961, will remember the Freedom Riders. On that day, thirteen activists climbed aboard buses in Washington, with tickets for New Orleans. Their purpose was to challenge racial segregation in interstate travel, which the Supreme Court had declared an unconstitutional violation of human rights.

They had little trouble in Virginia and North Carolina, but as the buses rolled deeper into the South, the hostility increased. In South Carolina, the beatings began. In Georgia, Martin Luther King met them and warned, "You will never make it through Alabama." He had learned of a conspiracy by the Ku Klux Klan, the police, and local officials to stop them by brute force. The Freedom Riders pressed on with great courage, even as they knew what lay ahead. In Anniston, Alabama, one bus was stopped and set ablaze. As the Freedom Riders ran from the smoke and flames, a mob tried to murder them, while other southerners sought to save them. The other bus reached Birmingham, and the Freedom Riders were dragged off and beaten nearly to death.

These savage scenes were recorded by journalists and photographers, who were attacked as viciously as the Freedom Riders themselves. Their reports flashed around the world and inspired hundreds of Americans to make more than sixty Freedom Rides through the Deep South in 1961, which brought out more mobs and caused more violence.

The images of these events remain fresh and vivid, but the history has grown faint and hazy, and much of it was never understood. Scarcely anyone remembers the story as it actually happened. Now at last we have the first full-scale book on the Freedom Riders, by a professional historian. Raymond Arsenault is one of the most gifted scholars of his generation. He has devoted many years of deep research to this subject.

The result is truly a definitive work, which draws on unpublished writings of Freedom Riders that have never been used before. The author has also studied the papers of their mortal enemy Bull Connor, their dubious friends in Washington, John and Robert Kennedy, and forty other manuscript collections. Much of the book is based on more than two hundred personal interviews of participants, the records of more than two dozen court cases, and many film, video, and sound recordings.

The author has brought together these materials with consummate skill. He also has a southern gift for story-telling. From the moment when the Freedom Riders climb aboard the bus, his narrative carries the reader along with an intensity and pace that few works of fiction are able to achieve.

The story is full of surprises. We meet the Freedom Riders as individuals, 436 of them in a fascinating appendix which is in itself a major contribution. They were very diverse. No novelist could have invented Albert Bigelow, a retired captain in the U.S. Navy who became a Quaker, a pacifist, and a Freedom Rider; or Walter Bergman, a retired teacher from Michigan and a Norman Thomas socialist; or Genevieve Hughes, a beautiful young woman who worked on Wall Street at Dun and Bradstreet and was a capitalist with a social conscience. All three were severely wounded on the first Freedom Ride.

Most Freedom Riders were students, black and white, some as young as thirteen, and all with their own stories to tell. Others were men and women past retirement. Many were divinity students and clergy of various denominations. The Freedom Ride to Jackson, Mississippi, on September 13, 1961, called "the Prayer Pilgrimage," consisted entirely of Episcopal ministers.

In this book we learn much that is new about the major civil rights organizations, which were deeply divided over tactics and goals, but most found a way to work together on the Freedom Rides. The reactions of the South are also full of surprises. The author finds that every southern town responded in its own way, and the range was as broad as the limits of possibility. In one town we meet southern white women who were so consumed with insane rage that they shoved their way through a mob of men to claw the faces of the Freedom Riders, and then held up their babies so that they could claw the Riders too. In other towns we meet white southerners who gave aid and comfort and every quality of kindness. The active roles of black southerners are among the most interesting of all, and very different from what has been written.

Raymond Arsenault's book will be deeply engaging to younger readers who don't remember the event. And the more one learns about the subject, the more absorbing it becomes. Readers who think they know President John Kennedy, and Robert Kennedy, will be continually amazed by their attitudes and acts. Opinion polls throughout the country are very startling. And the outcome of the event is full of unexpected twists and turns. This was so for the Freedom Riders themselves, for the people of the South, for others in many nations whose minds and hearts were touched by these events.

David Hackett Fischer
James M. McPherson

FREEDOM RIDERS

Introduction

The plan . . . was simplicity itself. In any sane, even half-civilized society it would have been completely innocuous, hardly worth a second thought or meriting any comment at all. CORE would be sending an integrated team—black and white together—from the nation's capital to New Orleans on public transportation. That's all. Except, of course, that they would sit randomly on the buses in integrated pairs and in the stations they would use waiting room facilities casually, ignoring the white/colored signs. What could be more harmless . . . in any even marginally healthy society?

—Stokely Carmichael[1]

MAY 21, 1961. It was Sunday night on the New Frontier, and freedom was on the line in Montgomery, Alabama. Earlier in the evening more than a thousand black Americans, including the Reverend Martin Luther King Jr. and several other nationally prominent civil rights leaders, had gathered at the First Baptist Church (Colored) to show their support for a visiting band of activists known as Freedom Riders. Located just a few blocks from the state capitol where President Jefferson Davis had sworn allegiance to the Confederate cause in 1861, First Baptist had been the setting for a number of dramatic events over the years, but the historic church had never witnessed anything quite like the situation unfolding both inside and outside its red-brick walls. For several hours the Freedom Riders and the congregation sang hymns and freedom songs and listened to testimonials about courage and commitment. But as the spirit of hope and justice rose inside the crowded sanctuary, a wholly different mood of defiance and outrage developed outside.

By nightfall the church was surrounded and besieged by a swelling mob of white protesters determined to defend a time-honored system of racial segregation. Screaming racial epithets and hurling rocks and Molotov cocktails, the protesters threatened to overwhelm a beleaguered group of federal marshals who feared that some members of the mob were intent on burning the church to the ground. When it became obvious that the marshals were overmatched, the governor of Alabama deployed a battalion of National Guardsmen to disperse the crowd, and tragedy was averted. But it would be early morning before the surrounding streets were secure enough for the Freedom Riders and their supporters to leave the church. Loaded into a convoy of military trucks and looking much like wartime refugees, the troublesome visitors and their hosts were escorted back to a black community that must have wondered what other indignities and challenges lay ahead. The battle of May 21 was over, but the centuries-old struggle for racial justice would continue.

How the Freedom Riders came to be at First Baptist, why they inspired so much hope and fear, and what happened to them—and the hundreds of other Americans who joined their ranks—are the questions that drive this book. As the epigraph from Stokely Carmichael suggests, these are important and perplexing questions that should engage anyone concerned with freedom, justice, and the realization of America's democratic ideals. With characters and plot lines rivaling those of the most imaginative fiction, the saga of the Freedom Rides is an improbable, almost unbelievable story. In 1961, during the first year of John F. Kennedy's presidency, more than four hundred Americans participated in a dangerous experiment designed to awaken the conscience of a complacent nation. Inspired by visions of social revolution and moral regeneration, these self-proclaimed "Freedom Riders" challenged the mores of a racially segregated society by performing a disarmingly simple act. Traveling together in small interracial groups, they sat where they pleased on buses and trains and demanded unrestricted access to terminal restaurants and waiting rooms, even in areas of the Deep South where such behavior was forbidden by law and custom.

Patterned after a 1947 Congress of Racial Equality (CORE) project known as the Journey of Reconciliation, the Freedom Rides began in early May with a single group of thirteen Riders recruited and trained by CORE's national staff. By early summer the Rides had evolved into a broad-based movement involving hundreds of activists representing a number of allied local, regional, and national civil rights organizations. Attracting a diverse assortment of volunteers—black and white, young and old, male and female, religious and secular, Northern and Southern—the Freedom Rider movement transcended the traditional legalistic approach to civil rights, taking the struggle out of the courtroom and into the streets and jails of the Jim Crow South. Empowered by two U.S. Supreme Court decisions mandating the desegregation of interstate travel facilities, the Freedom Riders brazenly flouted state and local segregation statutes, all but daring Southern officials to arrest them.[2]

Deliberately provoking a crisis of authority, the Riders challenged federal officials to enforce the law and uphold the constitutional right to travel without being subjected to degrading and humiliating racial restrictions. Most amazingly, they did so knowing that their actions would almost certainly provoke a savage and violent response from militant white supremacists. Invoking the philosophy of nonviolent direct action, they willingly put their bodies on the line for the cause of racial justice. Openly defying the social conventions of a security-conscious society, they appeared to court martyrdom with a reckless disregard for personal safety or civic order. None of the obstacles placed in their path—not widespread censure, not political and financial pressure, not arrest and imprisonment, not even the threat of death—seemed to weaken their commitment to nonviolent struggle. On the contrary, the hardships and suffering imposed upon them appeared to stiffen their resolve, confounding their white supremacist antagonists and testing the patience of even those who sympathized with their cause.

Time and again, the Riders seemed on the verge of defeat, but in every instance they found a way to sustain and expand their challenge to Jim Crow segregation. After marauding Alabama Klansmen used bombs and mob violence to disrupt and disband the original CORE Freedom Ride, student activists from Nashville stepped forward to organize a Ride of their own, eventually forcing federal officials to intervene on their behalf. Later, when Mississippi officials placed hundreds of Freedom Riders in prison and imposed bond payments that threatened the financial solvency of CORE, the net effect was to strengthen rather than to weaken the nonviolent movement. On a number of other occasions, too, attempts to intimidate the Freedom Riders and their supporters backfired, reinvigorating and prolonging a crisis that would not go away.[3]

It is little wonder, then, that the Freedom Rides sent shock waves through American society, evoking fears of widespread social disorder, racial polarization, and a messy constitutional crisis. In the mid-1950s the Montgomery Bus Boycott and its leader Martin Luther King Jr. had familiarized Americans with the tactics and philosophy of Gandhian nonviolent resistance, and in 1960 the sit-in movement conducted by black college students in Greensboro, North Carolina, and scores of other Southern cities had introduced direct action on a mass scale. But nothing in the recent past had fully prepared the American public for the Freedom Riders' interracial "invasion" of the segregated South. With the Freedom Rides, the civil rights struggle reached a level of intensity that even the sit-ins, potentially the most disruptive episode of the pre-1961 era, had managed to avoid. Loosely organized by local student activists and only tangentially connected to federal court mandates, the sit-in movement had skirted the potentially explosive issues of states' rights and outside agitation by Northern-based civil rights organizations.

The closest thing to a national civil rights crisis prior to the Freedom Rides was the school desegregation fight following the *Brown v. Board of Education* implementation decision of 1955, but the refusal of the Eisenhower administration to press for anything more than token integration had seemingly defused the crisis by the end of the decade. Even in Little Rock, Arkansas, where Eisenhower had dispatched troops to enforce a court order in 1957, the spirit of intense confrontation had largely subsided by the time of the Freedom Rides.[4] By then John Kennedy's New Frontier was in full swing, but there was no indication that the new administration was willing to sacrifice civic peace or political capital in the interests of school desegregation or any other civil rights issue, despite periodic pledges to abide by the Supreme Court's "with all deliberate speed" implementation order. Indeed, with public opinion polls showing little interest in civil rights among white Americans, there was no compelling reason, other than a personal commitment to abstract principles of freedom and justice, for any national political leader to challenge the racial orthodoxies and mores of Jim Crow culture.

During and after the fall campaign, Kennedy proclaimed that his New Frontier policies would transcend the stolid conservatism of the Eisenhower era; and in a stirring inaugural address he declared that the United States would "pay any price, bear any burden, meet any hardship, support any friend, oppose any foe to assure the survival and success of liberty." In the winter and early spring of 1961, however, the New Frontier manifested itself primarily in an assertive presence abroad, not in enhanced social justice at home. As civil rights leaders waited for the first sign of a bold initiative on the domestic front, superheated rhetoric about "missile gaps" and Soviet expansionism heightened Cold War tensions, fostering a crisis mentality that led to the ill-fated Bay of Pigs invasion in April. Marginalizing all other issues, including civil rights, the military and diplomatic fiasco in Cuba only served to sharpen the administration's focus on international affairs.[5]

The president himself set the tone, and by early May there was no longer any doubt, as the journalist Richard Reeves later observed, that the Cold Warrior in the White House regarded civil rights matters as an unwelcome "diversion from the priority business of promoting and winning freedom around the world." Father Theodore Hesburgh, the chairman of the U.S. Civil Rights Commission, was one of the first to learn this sobering truth. During an early briefing held two weeks after the inauguration, Kennedy made it clear that he considered white supremacist transgressions such as the Alabama National Guard's illegal exclusion of black soldiers to be a trivial matter in the grand scheme of world affairs. "Look, Father," he explained, "I may have to send the Alabama National Guard to Berlin tomorrow and I don't want to have to do it in the middle of a revolution at home."[6] Neither he nor Hesburgh had the faintest suspicion that in three months' time these same Alabama Guardsmen would be called not to Berlin but rather to a besieged black church in Montgomery where Freedom Riders required protection from a white supremacist mob. In early February neither man had any reason to believe that a group of American citizens would deliberately place themselves in jeopardy by traveling to Alabama, counting "upon the racists of the South to create a crisis, so that the federal government would be compelled to enforce federal law," as CORE's national director Jim Farmer put it.[7]

To many Americans, including the president, the rationale behind the Freedom Rides bordered on madness. But Farmer and other proponents of direct action reasoned that they could turn the president's passion for Cold War politics to their advantage by exposing and dramatizing the hypocrisy of promoting freedom abroad while maintaining Jim Crow in places like Alabama and Mississippi. With the onset of decolonization, the "colored" nations of Africa and Asia had emerged as important players in the escalating struggle between the United States and the Soviet Union, and it was no secret that America's long and continuing association with racial discrimination posed a potential threat to the State Department's continuing efforts to secure the loyalty and respect of the so-called Third World. If movement leaders could find some means of highlighting the diplomatic costs of Jim Crow, the administration would be forced to address civil rights issues as a function of national security.

Putting this strategy into practice, however, was extremely risky in a nation still conditioned by a decade of McCarthyism. To embarrass the nation on the world stage, for whatever reason, was to invite charges of disloyalty and collusion with Communist enemies. Even though a growing number of Americans acknowledged the connection between civil rights and the legitimacy of America's claims to democratic virtue and moral authority, very few, even among self-professed liberals, were willing to place the nation's international stature at risk for the purpose of accelerating the pace of social change. Such considerations extended to the civil rights movement itself, where internecine Red-baiting and periodic purges had been common since the late 1940s. In varying degrees, every civil rights organization from the NAACP to CORE had to guard against charges of subversion and "fellow-traveling," and even the most cautious advocates of racial justice were sometimes subject to Cold War suspicions.[8]

Civil rights activists of all persuasions faced an uphill struggle in the Cold War context of 1961. For the Freedom Riders, however, the challenge of mounting an effective protest movement was compounded by the fundamental conservatism of a nation wedded to consensus politics. As earlier generations of radical activists had discovered, enlisting support for direct action, economic boycotts, and other disruptive tactics was a difficult task in a society infused with the mythology of superior national virtue and equal access to legal redress. While a majority of Americans endorsed the goal of desegregating interstate transportation, a much smaller proportion supported the use of direct action, nonviolent or otherwise. According to a Gallup Poll conducted in late May and early June 1961, 66 percent of Americans agreed with the Supreme Court's recent ruling "that racial segregation on trains, buses, and in public waiting rooms must end," but only 24 percent approved "of what the 'freedom riders' are doing." When asked if sit-ins, Freedom

Rides, and "other demonstrations by Negroes" would "hurt or help the Negro's chances of being integrated in the South," only 27 percent of the respondents thought they would help.[9]

In many communities, public opposition to the Rides was reinforced by negative press coverage. Editorial condemnation of CORE's intrusive direct action campaign was almost universal in the white South, but negative characterizations of the Freedom Rides as foolhardy and unnecessarily confrontational were also common in the national press. Although most of the nation's leading editors and commentators embraced the ideal of desegregation, very few acknowledged that Freedom Rides and other disruptive tactics were a necessary catalyst for timely social change. Indeed, many journalists, like many of their readers and listeners, seemed to accept the moral equivalency of pro- and anti-civil-rights demonstrators, blaming one side as much as the other for the social disorder surrounding the Rides. In later years it would become fashionable to hail the Freedom Riders as courageous visionaries, but in 1961 they were more often criticized as misguided, if not dangerous, radicals.

The Freedom Riders' negative public image was the product of many factors, but two of their most obvious problems were bad timing and a deeply rooted suspicion of radical agitation by "outsiders." Set against the backdrop of the Civil War Centennial celebration, which began in April 1961, the Freedom Rides evoked vivid memories of meddling abolitionists and invading armies. This was especially true in the white South, where a resurgent "siege mentality" was in full force during the post-*Brown* era. But "outside agitators" were also unpopular in the North, where Cold War anxieties mingled with the ambiguous legacy of Reconstruction. When trying to comprehend the motivations behind the Freedom Rides, Americans of all regions and of all political leanings drew upon the one historical example that had influenced national life for nearly a century: the allegedly misguided attempt to bring about a Radical Reconstruction of the Confederate South. While some Americans appreciated the moral and political imperatives of Reconstruction, the dominant image of the tumultuous decade following the Civil War was that of a "tragic era" sullied by corruption and opportunism.

Among black Americans and white liberals the *Brown* decision had given rise to the idea of a long-overdue Second Reconstruction, but even in the civil rights community there was some reluctance to embrace a neo-abolitionist approach to social change. Some civil rights advocates, including Thurgood Marshall and Roy Wilkins of the NAACP, feared that Freedom Riders and other proponents of direct action would actually slow the process of change by needlessly provoking a white backlash and squandering the movement's financial and legal resources. To Wilkins, who admired the Riders' courage but questioned their sanity, the CORE project represented "a desperately brave, reckless strategy," a judgment seconded by Leslie Dunbar, the executive director of the Southern Regional Council. "When I heard about all those Northerners heading south I was sure they were going to catch hell and maybe even get themselves killed," Dunbar recalled many years later.[10]

Dunbar had good reason to be concerned. In a nation where the mystique of states' rights and local control enjoyed considerable popularity, crossing state lines for the purpose of challenging parochial mores was a highly provocative act. The notion that Freedom Riders were outside agitators and provocateurs cast serious doubt on their legitimacy, eliminating most of the moral capital that normally accompanied nonviolent struggle. Freedom Rides, by their very nature, involved physical mobility and a measure of outside involvement, if only in the form of traveling from one place to another. But the discovery—or in some cases, the assumption—that most of the Freedom Riders were Northerners deepened the sense of public anxiety surrounding the Rides. Judging by the national press and contemporary public commentary, the archetypal Freedom Rider was an idealistic but naive white activist from the North, probably a college student but possibly an older religious or labor leader. In actuality, while many Freedom Riders resembled that description, many others did not. The Freedom Riders were much more diverse than most Americans realized. Black activists born and raised in the South accounted for six of the original thirteen Freedom Riders and approximately 40 percent of the four-hundred-plus Riders who later joined the movement.[11] The Freedom Rider movement was as interregional as it was interracial, but for some reason the indigenous contribution to the Rides did not seem to register in the public consciousness, then or later. Part of the explanation undoubtedly resides in the conventional wisdom that Southern blacks were too beaten down to become involved in their own liberation. Even after the Montgomery Bus Boycott and the 1960 sit-ins suggested otherwise, this misconception plagued popular and even scholarly explanations of the civil rights struggle, including accounts of the Freedom Rides.

Redressing this misconception is reason enough to write a revisionist history of the Freedom Rides. But there are a number of other issues, both interpretative and factual, that merit attention. Chief among them is the tendency to treat the Freedom Rides as little more than a dramatic prelude to the climactic events of the mid- and late 1960s. In the rush to tell the stories of Birmingham, Freedom Summer, the Civil Rights Acts of 1964 and 1965, the Black Power movement, and the urban riots, assassinations, and political and cultural crises that have come to define a decade of breathless change, the Freedom Rides have often gotten lost. Occupying the midpoint between the 1954 *Brown* decision and the 1968 assassination of Martin Luther King, the events of 1961 would seem to be a likely choice as the pivot of a pivotal era in civil rights history. But that is not the way the Rides are generally depicted in civil rights historiography. While virtually every historical survey of the civil rights movement includes a brief section on the Freedom Rides, they have not attracted the attention that they deserve. The first scholarly monograph on the subject was published in 2003, and amazingly the present volume represents the first attempt by a professional historian to write a book-length account of the Freedom Rides.[12]

The reasons for this scholarly neglect are not altogether clear, but in recent years part of the problem has been the deceptive familiarity of the Freedom Rider story. Beginning with Taylor Branch's *Parting the Waters: America in the King Years, 1954–63*, published in 1988, several prominent journalists, including Diane McWhorter and David Halberstam, have written long chapters that cover significant portions of the Freedom Rider experience. Representing popular history at its best, both Branch's book and McWhorter's *Carry Me Home: Birmingham, Alabama: The Climactic Battle of the Civil Rights Revolution*, published in 2000, attracted wide readership and won the coveted Pulitzer Prize for their authors. Halberstam's 1998 bestseller, *The Children*, has also been influential, bringing the Nashville Movement of the early 1960s back to life for thousands of Americans, including many historians. Written in vivid prose, these three books convey much of the drama and some of the meaning of the Freedom Rides.[13]

Yet, as good as they are, these books do not do full justice to a historical episode that warrants careful and sustained attention from professional scholars. The Freedom Rides deserve a comprehensive and targeted treatment unhampered by the distraction of a broader agenda. Every major episode of the civil rights struggle merits a full study of its own, but none is more deserving than the insistent and innovative movement that seized the attention of the nation in 1961, bringing nonviolent direct action to the forefront of the fight for racial justice. Foreshadowed by Montgomery and the sit-ins, the Freedom Rides initiated a turbulent decade of insurgent citizen politics that transformed the nature of American democracy. Animated by a wide range of grievances, from war and poverty to disfranchisement and social intolerance, a new generation of Americans marched, protested, and sometimes committed acts of civil disobedience in the pursuit of liberty and justice. And many of them did so with the knowledge that the Freedom Riders had come before them.[14]

As the first historical study of this remarkable group of activists, *Freedom Riders* attempts to reconstruct the text and context of a pivotal moment in American history. At the mythic level, the saga of the Freedom Riders is a fairly simple tale of collective engagement and empowerment, of the pursuit and realization of democratic ideals, and of good triumphing over evil. But a carefully reconstructed history reveals a much more interesting story. Lying just below the surface, encased in memory and long-overlooked documents, is the real story of the Freedom Rides, a complicated mesh of commitment and indecision, cooperation and conflict, triumph and disappointment. In an attempt to recapture the meaning and significance of the Freedom Rides without sacrificing the drama of personal experience and historical contingency, I have written a book that is chronological and narrative in form. From the outset my goal has been to produce a "braided narrative" that addresses major analytical questions related to cause and consequence, but I have done so in a way that allows the art of storytelling to dominate the structure of the work.

Whenever possible, I have let the historical actors speak for themselves, and much of the book relies on interviews with former Freedom Riders, journalists, and government officials. Focusing on individual stories, I have tried to be faithful to the complexity of human experience, to treat the Freedom Riders and their contemporaries as flesh-and-blood human beings capable of inconsistency, confusion, and varying modes of behavior and belief. The Freedom Riders, no less than the other civil rights activists who transformed American life in the decades following World War II, were dynamic figures. Indeed, the ability to adapt and to learn from their experiences, both good and bad, was an essential element of their success. Early on, they learned that pushing a reluctant nation into action required nimble minds and subtle judgments, not to mention a measure of luck.

While they sometimes characterized the civil rights movement as an irrepressible force, the Freedom Riders knew all too well that they faced powerful and resilient enemies backed by regional and national institutions and traditions. Fortunately, the men and women who participated in the Freedom Rides had access to institutions and traditions of their own. When they boarded the "freedom buses" in 1961, they knew that others had gone before them, figuratively in the case of crusading abolitionists and the black and white soldiers who marched into the South during the Civil War and Reconstruction, and literally in the case of the CORE veterans who participated in the 1947 Journey of Reconciliation. In the early twentieth century, local black activists in several Southern cities had staged successful boycotts of segregated streetcars; in the 1930s and 1940s, labor and peace activists had employed sit-ins and other forms of direct action; and more recently the Gandhian liberation of India and the unexpected mass movements in Montgomery, Tallahassee, Greensboro, Nashville, and other centers of insurgency had demonstrated that the power of nonviolence was more than a philosophical chimera. At the same time, the legal successes of the NAACP and the gathering strength of the civil rights movement in the years since the Second World War, not to mention the emerging decolonization of the Third World, infused Freedom Riders with the belief that the arc of history was finally bending in the right direction. Racial progress, if not inevitable, was at least possible, and the Riders were determined to do all they could to accelerate the pace of change.[15]

Convincing their fellow Americans, black or white, that nonviolent struggle was a reliable and acceptable means of combating racial discrimination would not be easy. Indeed, even getting the nation's leaders to acknowledge that such discrimination required immediate and sustained attention was a major challenge. Notwithstanding the empowering and instructive legacy left by earlier generations of freedom fighters, the Freedom Riders knew that the road to racial equality remained long and hard, and that advancing down that road would test their composure and fortitude.

The Riders' dangerous passage through the bus terminals and jails of the Jim Crow South represented only one part of an extended journey for justice that stretched back to the dawn of American history and beyond. But once that passage was completed, there was renewed hope that the nation would eventually find its way to a true and inclusive democracy. For the brave activists who led the way, and for those of us who can only marvel at their courage and determination, this link to a brighter future was a great victory. Yet, as we shall see, it came with the sobering reminder that "power concedes nothing without a demand," as the abolitionist and former slave Frederick Douglass wrote in 1857.

The story of the Freedom Rides is largely the story of a single year, and most of this book deals with a rush of events that took place during the spring and summer of 1961. But, like most of the transformative experiences of the 1960s, the Freedom Rides had important antecedents in the midcentury convulsions of depression and war. Though frequently associated with a decade of student revolts that began with Greensboro and ended with a full-scale generational assault on authority, the Rides were rooted in earlier rebellions, both youthful and otherwise. Choosing a starting point for the Freedom Rider saga is difficult, and no single individual or event can lay claim to its origins. But perhaps the best place to begin is 1944, the year of D-Day and global promise, when a young woman from Baltimore named Irene Morgan committed a seminal act of courage.[16]

1

You Don't Have to Ride Jim Crow

You don't have to ride jim crow,
You don't have to ride jim crow,
Get on the bus, set any place,
'Cause Irene Morgan won her case,
You don't have to ride jim crow.

—1947 freedom song[1]

WHEN IRENE MORGAN BOARDED A GREYHOUND BUS in Hayes Store, Virginia, on July 16, 1944, she had no inkling of what was about to happen—no idea that her trip to Baltimore would alter the course of American history. The twenty-seven-year-old defense worker and mother of two had more mundane things on her mind. It was a sweltering morning in the Virginia Tidewater, and she was anxious to get home to her husband, a stevedore who worked on the docks of Baltimore's bustling inner harbor. Earlier in the summer, after suffering a miscarriage, she had taken her two young children for an extended visit to her mother's house in the remote countryside near Hayes Store, a crossroads hamlet in the Tidewater lowlands of Gloucester County. Now she was going back to Baltimore for a doctor's appointment and perhaps a clean bill of health that would allow her to resume work at the Martin bomber plant where she helped build B-26 Marauders. The restful stay in Gloucester—where her mother's family had lived and worked since the early nineteenth century, and where she had visited many times since childhood—had restored some of her physical strength and renewed a cherished family bond. But it had also confirmed the stark realities of a rural folk culture shouldering the burdens of three centuries of plantation life. Despite Gloucester's proximity to Hampton Roads and Norfolk, the war had brought surprisingly few changes to the area, most of which remained mired in suffocating poverty and a rigid caste system.

Irene Morgan, ca. 1943.
(Courtesy of Sherwood Morgan)

As Irene Morgan knew all too well, Baltimore had its own problems related to race and class. Still, she could not help feeling fortunate to live in a community where it was relatively common for people of "color" to own homes and businesses, to vote on election day, to attend high school or college, and to aspire to middle-class respectability. Despite humble beginnings, Irene herself had experienced a tantalizing measure of upward mobility. The sixth of nine children, she had grown up in a working-class black family that had encountered more hardships than luxuries. Her father, an itinerant house painter and day laborer, had done his best to provide for the family, but the difficulty of finding steady work in a depression-ravaged and racially segregated city had nearly broken him, testing his faith as a devout Seventh-Day Adventist. Although a strong-willed mother managed to keep the family together, even after one of her daughters came down with tuberculosis, hard realities had forced Irene and several of her brothers and sisters to drop out of high school long before graduation. As a teenager, she worked long hours as a laundress, maid, and babysitter. Yet she never allowed her difficult economic circumstances, or her circumscribed status as a black female, to impinge on her sense of self-worth and dignity. Bright and self-assured, with a strong sense of right and wrong, she was determined to make her way in the world, despite the very real obstacles of prejudice and discrimination. As a young wife and mother preoccupied with her family, she had not yet found the time to join the National Association for the Advancement of Colored People (NAACP) or any other organization dedicated to racial uplift, but in many ways she exemplified the "New Negro" that the NAACP had been touting since the 1930s. Part of a swelling movement for human dignity and racial equality, she was ready and willing to stand up—or, if need be, sit down—for her rights as an American citizen.[2]

The Greyhound from Norfolk was jammed that morning, especially in the back, where several black passengers had no choice but to stand in the aisle. As the bus pulled away from the storefront, Morgan was still searching for an empty seat. When none materialized, she accepted the invitation of a young black woman who graciously offered her a lap to sit on. Later, when the bus arrived in Saluda, a county-seat town twenty-six miles north of Hayes Store, she moved to a seat relinquished by a departing passenger. Although only three rows from the back, she found herself sitting directly in front of a white couple—an arrangement that violated Southern custom and a 1930 Virginia statute prohibiting racially mixed seating on public conveyances.

Since she was not actually sitting next to a white person, Morgan did not think the driver would ask her to move. And perhaps he would not have done so if two additional white passengers had not boarded the bus a few seconds after she sat down. Suddenly the driver turned toward Morgan and her seatmate, a young black woman holding an infant, and barked: "You'll have to get up and give your seats to these people." The young woman with the baby complied immediately, scurrying into the aisle near the back of the bus. But Irene Morgan, perhaps forgetting where she was, suggested a compromise: She would be happy to exchange seats with a white passenger sitting behind her, she calmly explained, but she was unwilling to stand for any length of time. Growing impatient, the driver repeated his order, this time with a barely controlled rage. Once again Morgan refused to give up her seat. As an uneasy murmur filled the bus, the driver shook his head in disgust and rushed down the steps to fetch the local sheriff.[3]

Irene Morgan's impulsive act—like Rosa Parks's more celebrated refusal to give up a seat on a Montgomery bus eleven years later—placed her in a difficult and dangerous position. In such situations, there were no mitigating circumstances, no conventions of humanity or even paternalism that might shield her from the full force of the law. To the driver and to the sheriff of Middlesex County, the fact that she was a woman and in ill health mattered little. Irene Morgan had challenged both the sanctity of segregation and the driver's authority. She had disturbed the delicate balance of Southern racial etiquette, endangering a society that made white supremacy the cornerstone of social order.

The sheriff and his deputy showed no mercy as they dragged her out of the bus. Both men claimed that they resorted to force only after Morgan tore up the arrest warrant and threw it out the window. According to the deputy's sworn testimony, the unruly young woman also kicked him three times in the leg. Morgan herself later insisted that propriety and male pride prevented him from telling what really happened. "He touched me," she recalled in a recent interview. "That's when I kicked him in a very bad place. He hobbled off, and another one came on. He was trying to put his hands on me to get me off. I was going to bite him, but he was dirty, so I clawed him instead. I ripped his shirt. We were both pulling at each other. He said he'd use his nightstick. I said, 'We'll whip each other.' " In the end, it took both officers to subdue her, and when she complained that they were hurting her arms, the deputy shouted: "Wait till I get you to jail, I'll beat your head with a stick." Charged with resisting arrest and violating Virginia's Jim Crow transit law, she spent the next seven hours slumped in the corner of a county jail cell. Late in the afternoon, after her mother posted a five-hundred-dollar bond, she was released by county authorities confident that they had made their point: No uppity Negro from Baltimore could flout the law in the Virginia Tidewater and get away with it.

As Morgan and her mother left the jail, Middlesex County officials had good reason to believe that they had seen the last of the feisty young woman from Baltimore. In their experience, any Negro with a lick of sense would do whatever was necessary to avoid a court appearance. If she knew what was good for her, she would hurry back to Maryland and stay there, even if it meant forfeiting a five-hundred-dollar bond. They had seen this calculus of survival operate on countless occasions, and they didn't expect anything different from Morgan. What they did not anticipate was her determination to achieve simple justice. "I was just minding my own business," she recalled many years later. "I'd paid my money. I was sitting where I was supposed to sit. And I wasn't going to take it." The incident in Saluda left her with physical wounds, but it did not diminish her sense of outrage or her burning desire for vindication. As she waited for her day in court, discussions with friends and relatives, some of whom belonged to the Baltimore branch of the NAACP, brought the significance of her challenge to Jim Crow into focus. Her personal saga was part of a larger story—an ever-widening struggle for civil rights and human dignity that promised to recast the nature of American democracy. Driven, as one family member put it, by "the pent-up bitterness of years of seeing the colored people pushed around," she embraced the responsibility of bearing witness and confronting her oppressors in a court of law.[4]

On October 18 Morgan stood before Middlesex County Circuit Judge J. Douglas Mitchell and pleaded her case. Although she represented herself as best she could, arguing that Virginia's segregation laws did not apply to interstate passengers, the outcome was never in doubt. Pleading guilty on the resisting arrest charge, she agreed to pay the hundred-dollar fine assessed by Judge Mitchell. The conviction on the segregation violation charge was, however, an altogether different matter. To Mitchell's dismay, Morgan refused to pay the ten-dollar fine and court costs, announcing her intention to appeal the second conviction to the Virginia Supreme Court. Adamant that she had been within her rights to challenge the driver's order, she vowed to take her case all the way to Washington if necessary.[5]

Morgan's appeal raised more than a few eyebrows in the capital city of Richmond, where it was no secret that the NAACP had been searching for suitable test cases that would challenge the constitutionality of the state's Jim Crow transit law. Segregated transit was a special concern in Virginia, which served as a gateway for southbound bus and railway passengers. Crossing into the Old Dominion from the District of Columbia, which had no Jim Crow restrictions, or from Maryland, which, unlike Virginia, limited its segregationist mandate to local and intrastate passengers, could be a jarring and bewildering experience for travelers unfamiliar with the complexities of border-state life. This was an old problem, dating back at least a half century, but the number of violations and interracial incidents involving interstate passengers had multiplied in recent years, especially since the outbreak of World War II. With the growing number of black soldiers and sailors and with the rising militancy of the Double V campaign, which sought twin victories over enemies abroad and racial discrimination at home, Virginia had become a legal and cultural battleground for black Americans willing to challenge the dictates of Jim Crow.

The struggle was by no means limited to the Virginia borderlands, of course. All across the South segregated buses, trains, and streetcars provided blacks with a daily reminder of their second-class status. As early as 1908 a regional survey of the "color line" by the journalist Ray Stannard Baker had revealed that "no other point of race contact is so much and so bitterly discussed among Negroes as the Jim Crow car." This was still true thirty-six years later when Gunnar Myrdal, the author of the monumental 1944 study *An American Dilemma: The Negro Problem and American Democracy*, observed "that the Jim Crow car is resented more bitterly among Negroes than most other forms of segregation." From Virginia to Texas—where Lieutenant Jackie Robinson faced a wartime court-martial for refusing to move to the back of a bus—segregated transportation facilities, including terminal waiting rooms and lunch counters, remained an indelible though not uncontested fact of Southern life. During the early and mid-1940s, the NAACP received hundreds of complaints about the indignities of Jim Crow transit, and reports of individual challenges to the system were common throughout the black press.[6]

NAACP attorneys, both in Virginia and in the national office, knew all of this and did what they could to chip away at the legal foundations of Jim

Segregated transit facilities in Durham, North Carolina, 1940. (Library of Congress)

Crow transit, but they were frustrated by their inability to attract the attention of the United States Supreme Court. *Plessy v. Ferguson*, the cornerstone of the "separate but equal" doctrine that had sustained segregationist law since 1896, had validated a Louisiana segregated coach law, and through the years the Court had been reluctant to revisit the issue in any fundamental way. In 1910, with former Ku Klux Klansman Edward White of Louisiana serving as chief justice, the Court ruled in *Chiles v. Chesapeake and Ohio Railway* that state segregation laws could be applied to interstate passengers. Four years later, in *McCabe v. Atchison, Topeka, and Santa Fe Railroad*, the Court showed some openness to the argument that black travelers had a legal right to equal accommodations, citing the equal protection clause of the Fourteenth Amendment and rejecting the railroad's argument that the paucity of black travelers requesting Pullman sleeping berths justified the absence of black accommodations on Pullman cars. But this tantalizing decision only served to divert attention from the underlying reality of racial separation. According to Catherine Barnes, the leading historian of transit desegregation, for the next three decades "Southern blacks attempted only to equalize accommodations, not to undo segregation."[7]

During the 1920s and early 1930s, when conservative Republicans dominated the Court, few NAACP attorneys questioned this pragmatic strategy. From the mid-1930s, however, the increasingly liberal "Roosevelt" Court encouraged a reformulation of the organization's approach to the interrelated problems of racial discrimination and segregation, especially in cases involving segregated transit. In 1941 the campaign for equal travel accommodations finally brought a measure of victory in *Mitchell v. Arkansas*—a unanimous decision that affirmed Illinois congressman Arthur Mitchell's claim to the same first-class service accorded white travelers. Thurgood Marshall, William Hastie, and other NAACP legal theorists were convinced that the practice of applying state laws to interstate passengers was especially vulnerable to legal challenge. Citing the interstate commerce clause and *Hall v. DeCuir*—a long-forgotten 1877 decision that, ironically, had invalidated a state law *prohibiting* racial segregation among interstate steamboat passengers—they felt confident that they could persuade the Roosevelt Court to restrict legally mandated segregation to intrastate passengers. This strategy called for a reversal of the 1910 *Chiles* decision and allowed the NAACP to move forward without risking defeat by a premature reconsideration of *Plessy*. Since pushing the Court too fast or too far would almost certainly lead to a setback for the cause of civil rights, a careful and cautious selection of test cases was essential. To counter the inertial presumptions of law based on precedent, the NAACP needed the right defendant in the right place at the right time.[8]

In 1942 the state legal committee of the Virginia NAACP, led by three Howard University–trained attorneys—Spottswood Robinson, Oliver Hill, and Martin A. Martin—began the search for a case that would bring the interstate issue before the Court. Working closely with Marshall and the national legal staff, the committee considered and rejected a number of potential clients before discovering Irene Morgan in the fall of 1944. Almost immediately they sensed that this was the case and the defendant they needed. Not only was the basis of her conviction clear, but she also had the makings of an exemplary client. She was young, attractive, articulate, and, judging by her poised performance in Saluda, strong enough to withstand the pressures of a high-profile legal battle.[9]

With Thurgood Marshall's blessing, the Virginia NAACP filed a carefully crafted appellate brief emphasizing the interstate commerce clause and *Hall v. DeCuir.* But, as expected, the seven justices of the Virginia Supreme Court unanimously affirmed Morgan's conviction. In a rambling sixteen-page opinion issued on June 6, 1945, the court upheld the constitutionality of the 1930 Jim Crow transit law, reiterating the wisdom and legality of segregating all passengers, regardless of their origin or destination. Speaking for the court, Justice Herbert Gregory did not deny that *Hall v. DeCuir* established a legal precedent for invoking the commerce clause as a barrier to state statutes that interfered with interstate commerce, but he summarily dismissed the NAACP's claim that the 1930 law involved such interference. "Our conclusion," he declared at the end of the opinion, "is that the statute challenged is a reasonable police regulation and applies to both intrastate and interstate passengers. It is not obnoxious to the commerce clause of the Constitution."[10]

Gregory's forthright words were just what the NAACP wanted to hear. With a little help from the Virginia Supreme Court, *Morgan v. Commonwealth of Virginia* had become a near-perfect test case. When the Virginia court denied the NAACP's petition for a rehearing in September, Spot Robinson could hardly wait to file an appeal to the U.S. Supreme Court. In January 1946 the Court agreed to hear the case, and two months later Robinson joined Marshall and Hastie for the oral argument in Washington. Even though he was the NAACP's leading authority on segregated transportation law, Robinson could not actually argue the case because he was not yet certified to appear before the Court. But during the argument he sat at the table with Marshall and Hastie. Although this was the first time that the NAACP had argued a segregated transit case in front of the Court, the organization's talented team of attorneys made short work of Virginia attorney general Abram Staples's predictable arguments on behalf of the status quo. Focusing on the Virginia statute's broad reach, they argued that forcibly segregating interstate passengers violated the commerce clause, infringed upon congressional authority, and threatened the nation's tradition of free movement across state lines. Insisting that this misuse of state segregation laws placed an unnecessary and unconstitutional burden on individuals as well as interstate bus companies, the NAACP gave the Court a compelling rationale for overruling the Virginia court's judicial and racial conservatism. "Today, we are just emerging from a war in which all of the people of the United States were joined in a death struggle against the apostles of racism," the NAACP brief reminded the justices. Surely it was time for the Court to declare that federal law no longer sanctioned "disruptive local practices bred of racial notions alien to our national ideals, and to the solemn undertakings of the community of civilized nations as well."[11]

Since this was essentially the same Court that had struck down the Texas "white primary" electoral system in the *Smith v. Allwright* decision of April 1944, NAACP leaders were cautiously optimistic. But in the unsettled atmosphere of postwar America, no one could be certain how the Court would rule—or how white Americans would respond to an NAACP victory over Jim Crow transit. The year 1946 had already brought a number of surprises, both bitter and sweet, ranging from the brutal repression of black veterans in Columbia, Tennessee, to the signing of Jackie Robinson by the Brooklyn Dodgers. Although change was in the air, it was not entirely clear which way the nation was headed on matters of race. Two years earlier, in the wake of the Texas decision, Marshall had urged delegates to the national NAACP convention to accelerate the pace of the movement for civil rights. "We must not be delayed by people who say, 'The time is not ripe,' " he had declared, "nor should we proceed with caution for fear of destroying the status quo. People who deny us our civil rights should be brought to justice now." It was in this spirit that he had encouraged his Virginia colleagues to file the *Morgan* appeal. Now, as he nervously awaited the Court's ruling, he could not help wondering if he had acted precipitously. Adding to his nervousness was the knowledge that Staples, Virginia's sharp-tongued attorney general, had never lost a case in nine appearances before the Court.[12]

When the Supreme Court announced its decision on June 3, 1946, Marshall was both relieved and elated. With only one dissenting vote—that of Harold Burton, a former Republican senator from Ohio appointed to the Court in 1945—the justices sustained Morgan's appeal. In a carefully worded opinion delivered by Associate Justice Stanley Reed, a Kentucky Democrat who had spoken for the Court in *Smith v. Allwright*, six justices (in June 1946 the recent death of Chief Justice Harlan Fiske Stone and the assignment of Associate Justice Robert Jackson to the Nuremberg Trials had reduced the size of the Court to seven members) accepted the NAACP's argument that segregating interstate passengers violated the spirit of the interstate commerce clause. "As there is no Federal act dealing with the separation of races," Reed explained, "we must decide the validity of this Virginia statute on the challenge that it interferes with commerce, as a matter of balance between exercise of the local police power and the need for National uniformity in the regulations for interstate travel. It seems clear to us that seating arrangements for the different races in interstate motor travel requires a single uniform rule to promote and protect national travel."

The ruling affirmed the NAACP's claim that the Virginia statute requiring segregation of interstate bus passengers was unconstitutional. But the opinion, cast in narrow terms, said nothing about intrastate passengers, its applicability to other means of conveyance such as railroads, or how and when desegregation of interstate buses might be implemented, and it offered no clear sign that the Court was moving closer to an outright rejection of the *Plessy* doctrine of separate but equal. As a *Time* reporter put it, "This week seven nimble Justices ducked the racial question and settled everything on the basis of comfortable traveling." None of this surprised Marshall and the other NAACP attorneys, who had maintained modest expectations throughout the *Morgan* proceedings. For the time being, they were satisfied that in their first appearance before the Court on a segregated transit issue, pragmatic reasoning had given them a solid victory. In the aftermath of the decision, their greatest concern was not with the narrowness of the ruling but rather with the prospects of enforcement by federal and state authorities. As with all legal controversies involving social mores or public behavior, the true value and meaning of the decision would depend on the reactions to it.[13]

On June 4 the *Morgan* decision was front-page news throughout the nation, and by the end of the day the NAACP's national office was flooded with congratulatory telegrams. Many hailed the *Morgan* decision as a legal milestone comparable to *Smith v. Allwright*, but NAACP officials knew that praise from friends and allies, however welcome, was less important than the responses of editors, reporters, public officials, and bus company executives. Marshall and his colleagues hoped for the best, but no one was surprised when the press coverage followed racial, regional, and political lines, offering a wide range of explanation and speculation about the decision's probable impact on segregated travel. In the black press, the headlines and stories tended to be expansive and even jubilant, suggesting that *Morgan* represented a landmark decision. In the major dailies of the Northeast, Midwest, and West, most of the coverage was favorable but restrained. In the white South, with few exceptions, editors and reporters downplayed the significance of the Court's ruling. Anyone who scanned the pages of the *Baltimore Afro-American*, the *New York Times*, and the *Birmingham Post-Herald*, for example, would have come away with more questions than answers. Had the Court issued a minor legal clarification that would affect a few border-state travelers in northern Virginia? Or had it struck a major blow against Jim Crow? In the days and weeks following the decision, no one could be sure.[14]

In this atmosphere of confusion and conflicting signals, most politicians, North and South, lay low. Former secretary of the interior Harold Ickes and ex-governor of New York Herbert Lehman lauded the decision, and Representative Adam Clayton Powell Jr., a black Democrat representing Harlem, called *Morgan* "the most important step toward winning the peace at home since the conclusion of the war." But the rest of the political establishment, from President Truman on down, had little or nothing to say about the Court's ruling. Even in the Deep South, the political response was muted. One exception was Mississippi congressman Dan McGehee, who insisted

the decision proved that "the Supreme Court judges are a bunch of medio-
cre lawyers with no judicial training, and limited experience in the practice
of the law." In "taking away the rights of the States of this great republic to
regulate the affairs within their borders," he added, "they did so unmindful
of the trouble and bloodshed that may be caused in the future." Foreshad-
owing the attacks on Chief Justice Earl Warren following the 1954 *Brown*
school desegregation decision, McGehee called for judicial impeachment
proceedings "against each and every one of those who have handed down
such decisions."[15]

In the immediate aftermath of the *Morgan* decision, most of the public
officials in a position to implement the ruling adopted a wait-and-see attitude. Though clearly worried about the days ahead, NAACP leaders initially
regarded this restraint as a hopeful sign. "Despite intemperate attacks . . . by
a few professional southerners," executive secretary Walter White announced
on June 5, "we have indications [an] overwhelming majority of southerners
will approve and abide by [the] decision." As time passed, however, it became
increasingly clear that the vast majority of Southern officials had no intention of facilitating the desegregation of interstate bus passengers. Stanley
Winborne, North Carolina's utilities commissioner, admitted that the "re-
grettable" decision would require bus companies to "halt the practice of Jim
Crowing" on interstate runs. Officials in other parts of the South were not so
sure. Speaking for the Louisiana Public Service Commission, Clayton
Coleman vowed that segregation among intrastate passengers "will continue
to be enforced" and that even among interstate passengers no racial mixing
would be allowed until the Interstate Commerce Commission (ICC) validated the *Morgan* ruling. Alabama governor Chauncey Sparks castigated the
decision as "fertilizer for the Ku Klux Klan" and as an unconstitutional interference with states' "rights to conduct their internal affairs." In Georgia, gubernatorial candidate Eugene Talmadge, one of Dixie's most notorious racial
demagogues, claimed that, regardless of the justices' intentions, the ruling
could be easily nullified. Under his plan, black passengers passing south
through Georgia would "have to get off 50 feet from the Florida line and buy
another ticket," which he insisted "would make them intrastate passengers
and outside the protection of the decision." Mississippi governor Thomas
Bailey expressed his defiance in simpler terms: "Segregation will continue
down here. Neither the whites nor the Negroes want it any other way."[16]

Tentative and often conflicting responses of bus company executives
compounded the confusion. In the wake of the decision, some companies
promptly ordered the desegregation of interstate buses, others all but ignored the decision, and still others waffled. In several cases, desegregation
orders were issued but later reversed after state officials pressured executives
to maintain traditional arrangements. Since there were no counter-pressures
from the ICC or the Justice Department, the sense of urgency and the likelihood of actual desegregation soon faded. By midsummer there were few

signs of progress and a growing realization among civil rights advocates that the *Morgan* decision was a paper tiger. Strict segregation remained the norm on the vast majority of interstate buses, and the number of racial incidents related to interstate travel actually increased. Fueled by unmet expectations, complaints and misunderstandings multiplied, particularly in the Upper South. The result was bewilderment and frustration among interstate travelers on buses—and on trains, where there was uncertainty about the ruling's applicability.[17]

All of this left the NAACP in a legal and political bind. The initial trumpeting of the decision placed Marshall and his colleagues in an "awkward position," according to the legal historian Mark Tushnet. Scaling down their expectations, "the legal staff had to urge Walter White to make it clear how limited the victory was," something White did not want to do. By late summer, NAACP attorneys had concluded that Justice Reed's opinion was far more problematic than they had realized in the heady days immediately following the decision. As Tushnet has written, "*Morgan* cast doubt on Northern antidiscrimination statutes, which the NAACP surely could not have welcomed. And, by apparently leaving decisions about passenger seating to carriers themselves, *Morgan* drew the NAACP in the direction of attempting to devise a constitutional challenge to decisions by private operators of buses rather than decisions by state legislatures."

In other words, the decision lost most of its meaning when the primary defense of segregation no longer involved "state action," the activating principle of the Fourteenth Amendment. Marshall, Robert Carter, and other NAACP legal theorists tried to devise a new strategy that would attack privately enforced segregation, but their deliberations proved unsuccessful. As Carter later confessed, they didn't "know just how to proceed in this type of situation." In the end, they retreated to a political strategy of lobbying Congress for legislation outlawing private discrimination and of applying "extra-legal . . . pressures to get the carriers to abolish their private rules and regulations requiring segregation of the races." What this really meant, of course, was that the end of Jim Crow travel was nowhere in sight.[18]

Immediately following the *Morgan* decision, the NAACP's victorious legal strategy drew praise from a wide variety of civil rights activists, including Morgan herself. Having left Baltimore for New York City, where she found work as a practical nurse, Morgan expressed confidence that the Court's decision would "abolish jim crow for northerners going south." "Jim-crow tension has been removed by the edict," she proclaimed, "and the insult and degradation to colored people is gone." Unfortunately, the situation looked much different two months later. Segregated transit, with all its insults and degradation, remained firmly in place; Morgan herself was all but forgotten; and the leadership of the NAACP was ready to move on to new challenges. Despite their disappointment, Marshall and his colleagues were not about to let the *Morgan* case disrupt their long-term plan to dismantle the

legal structure of Jim Crow. After more than a decade of careful legal maneuvering, they remained committed to a patient struggle based on the belief that American constitutional law provided the only viable means of
achieving civil rights and racial equality. Confident that they were slowly but
surely weakening the legal foundations of prejudice and discrimination, they
were determined to press on in the courts.[19]

Within the NAACP, some local activists—especially in the Youth
Councils—felt constrained by this narrow, legalistic approach, but their restlessness had little impact on the organization's national leaders, who maintained tight control over all NAACP activities. Alternative strategies such as
economic boycotts, protest marches, and picketing were anathema in the
national office, which saw itself as the guardian of the organization's respectability. In the midst of the Cold War, NAACP leaders did not want to do
anything to invite charges of radicalism or subversion. Even though the
NAACP prided itself on being a militant organization, public association
with direct action tactics or with groups that might be termed "red" or even
"pink" was to be avoided at all costs. In the Cold War context such caution
was understandable, but in a number of instances, including the *Morgan* case,
it placed severe limits on the NAACP's capacity to represent the interests of
black Americans. Other than counseling patience, the nation's largest civil
rights organization had no real answer to the white South's refusal to take
Morgan seriously.[20]

In the fall of 1946 the NAACP's disengagement from the fading, unresolved controversy over the *Morgan* decision created an opening for the radical wing of the civil rights movement. Though no one realized it at the time,
this opening represented an important turning point in the history of the
modern American freedom struggle. When the NAACP fell by the wayside,
a small but determined group of radical activists seized the opportunity to
take the desegregation struggle out of the courts and into the streets. Inspired by an international tradition of nonviolent direct action, this response
to segregationist intransigence transcended the cautious legal pragmatism
of the NAACP. In the short run, as we shall see, their efforts to breathe life
into the *Morgan* decision failed, but in the long run, their use of direct action
in the late 1940s planted the seeds of a larger idea that bore remarkable fruit
a decade and a half later. Although called a "Journey of Reconciliation," this
nonviolent foray into the world of Jim Crow represented the first formal
"freedom ride."

To most Americans, then and now, the pioneer freedom riders were
obscure figures, men and women who lived and labored outside the spotlight
of celebrity and notoriety. During the immediate postwar era, the radical
wing of the civil rights struggle was small, predominantly white, and fragmented among several organizations. Concentrated in New York, Chicago,
and other large Northern cities, the radicals included followers of Mohandas

Gandhi, Christian socialists, labor and peace activists, Quaker pacifists, Communists, and a varied assortment of left-wing intellectuals. Though ideologically diverse, they shared a commitment to militant agitation aimed at bringing about fundamental and even revolutionary change. Like India's Gandhi, they dreamed of a world liberated from the scourges of racial prejudice, class oppression, and colonialism. Open to a variety of provocative tactics—economic boycotts, picketing, protest marches, sit-ins, and other forms of direct action—they operated on the radical fringe of American politics. With perhaps a few thousand adherents, the radical approach constituted something less than a mass movement, but the social and political turmoil of the Great Depression and the Second World War had produced a vanguard of activists passionately committed to widening the scope and accelerating the pace of the struggle for civil and human rights.

In 1946 the most active members of this radical vanguard were affiliated with two interrelated organizations, the Congress of Racial Equality (CORE) and its parent organization, the Fellowship of Reconciliation (FOR). It was within these groups that the idea of the Freedom Ride was born. Founded in Chicago in 1942, CORE drew inspiration from the wartime stirrings of decolonization in Africa and Asia and from the recent success of nonviolent mass resistance in Gandhi's India. It also drew upon a somewhat older tradition of nonviolent protest nurtured by FOR.[21]

Founded in 1914 at an international gathering of Christian pacifists in London, FOR maintained a steady course of dissent through war and peace. During the 1920s and 1930s the American branch of FOR included some of the nation's leading social justice advocates, including radical economist Scott Nearing, socialist leader Norman Thomas, American Civil Liberties Union founder Roger Baldwin, and eminent theologians such as Reinhold Niebuhr, Harry Emerson Fosdick, and Howard Thurman. Representing the interests of such a diverse group was never easy, but with the approach of the Second World War the organization found it increasingly difficult to satisfy both "radical" pacifists, who insisted on an absolutist commitment to nonviolence, and "pragmatic" pacifists, who acknowledged the necessity of waging war against totalitarian oppression. In 1940 the selection of an absolutist, A. J. Muste, as executive director drove most of the pragmatists out of FOR, leaving the American branch with a small but dedicated core of radical activists. Muste was a former Dutch Reformed and Congregationalist minister who passed through Trotskyism and militant trade unionism before embracing radical pacifism and Gandhianism. Determined to make FOR more than a left-wing debating society, he urged his followers to dedicate their lives to the cause of nonviolence. Countering the evils of militarism and social injustice required moral discipline, personal courage, and a willingness to suffer for one's beliefs, and nothing less than a total commitment to pacifist activism would do. Convinced that American society needed a radical overhaul, especially in the area of race relations, he welcomed the creation of CORE as a natural extension of FOR's reform program.

Muste's prescriptive model was not for everyone, even in faithful pacifist circles. Nevertheless, his impassioned calls for engagement and sacrifice attracted a number of remarkable individuals. During the early 1940s the FOR national office in New York became the nerve center of American Gandhianism. Crammed into a small building on upper Broadway near Columbia University, the FOR staff of twelve shared ideas, plans, and soaring dreams of social justice. Young, well educated, and impoverished—most made less than twenty dollars per week—they lived and worked in the subterranean fringe of American life.[22]

Among the FOR/CORE stalwarts were three men destined to play pivotal roles in the Freedom Rider saga: Bayard Rustin, James Peck, and James Farmer. A founding member of CORE and the co-secretary of FOR's Racial-Industrial Department, Rustin—along with co-secretary George Houser—organized and led the Journey of Reconciliation of 1947, and would later serve as an advisor to Dr. Martin Luther King Jr. He played no direct role in the Freedom Rides of 1961, spending most of the early 1960s in Africa and Europe. Yet, perhaps more than anyone else, Rustin was the intellectual godfather of the Freedom Rider movement. Peck, a radical journalist who acted as CORE's chief publicist, was the only person to participate in both the Journey of Reconciliation and the 1961 Freedom Rides. Severely beaten by Klansmen in Alabama in May 1961, he later wrote a revealing memoir of his experiences as a Freedom Rider. Farmer, like Rustin, was one of the founders of CORE. Although personal circumstances prevented him from participating in the Journey of Reconciliation, he was the guiding spirit behind CORE's 1961 Freedom Rides. As national director of CORE from 1961 to 1966, he presided over the organization's resurgence, crafting and sustaining the legacy of the Freedom Rides. Together, these three activists provided a critical link between the nonviolent civil rights initiatives of the 1940s and the full-blown movement of the 1960s. While none of these men achieved national fame in the manner of King or Rosa Parks, each in his own way exerted a powerful influence on the development of nonviolence in the United States. Their personal stories reveal a great deal about the origins and context of the Freedom Rides and about the hidden history of the civil rights struggle—especially the complex connections between North and South, blacks and whites, liberalism and radicalism, and religious and secular motivation.[23]

Rustin, the oldest of the three, was born in 1912 in West Chester, Pennsylvania. The child of Florence Rustin, an unwed black teenager, and Archie Hopkins, an itinerant black laborer who barely acknowledged his son's existence, he was adopted by Florence's parents, Julia and Janifer Rustin, and raised by an extended family of grandparents, aunts, and uncles who collectively eked out a living by cooking and catering for the local Quaker gentry.

Julia Rustin was a member of the local Quaker meeting before joining her husband's African Methodist Episcopal (AME) church following their marriage in 1891, and she remained a Quaker "at heart," naming her grandson for Bayard Taylor, a celebrated mid-nineteenth-century Quaker leader. A woman of substance and deep moral conviction, Julia was the most important influence in Bayard's upbringing and the primary source of the pacifist doctrines that would anchor his lifelong commitment to nonviolence. Indulged as the favorite child of the Rustin clan, he gained a reputation as a brilliant student and gifted singer and musician, first as one of a handful of black students at West Chester High School, where he also excelled as a track and football star, and later at all-black Wilberforce University in Ohio, where he studied history and literature and toured as the lead soloist of the Wilberforce Quartet. Despite these accomplishments, he eventually ran afoul of the Wilberforce administration by challenging the school's compulsory ROTC program and by engaging in homosexual activity (he reportedly fell in love with the son of the university president). Expelled in December 1933, he returned to Pennsylvania and enrolled at Cheyney State Teachers College the following fall.

At Cheyney, where he remained for three years, Rustin gained a reputation as a multitalented student leader, distinguishing himself as a singer, a keen student of philosophy, and a committed peace activist. When Cheyney's president, Leslie Pinckney Hill, a devout black Quaker, invited the American Friends Service Committee to hold an international peace institute on the campus in the spring of 1937, Rustin was a willing and eager participant. Inspired by the dedicated pacifists who attended the institute and already primed for social action by his family and religious background, he soon accepted a position as a "peace volunteer" with the American Friends Service Committee's Emergency Peace Campaign. During a training session, he received further inspiration from Muriel Lester, a noted British pacifist and Gandhi protégé. After listening to Lester's eloquent plea for pacifism and nonviolent struggle, he threw himself into the peace campaign with an uncommon zeal that would later become his trademark. Along with three other volunteers—including Carl Rachlin, who would later serve as a CORE and Freedom Rider attorney—he spent the summer of 1937 in the upstate New York town of Auburn, where he honed his skills as a lecturer and organizer.

At the end of the summer, he returned to West Chester and Cheyney, but not for long. In the early fall, propelled by a growing disenchantment with southeastern Pennsylvania's political and cultural scene, and by a second scandalous (and interracial) homosexual incident, he moved northward to the alluring uncertainties of metropolitan Harlem, the unofficial capital of black America. Cast adrift from the relatively secure world of college life and facing the vagaries of the Great Depression, Rustin embarked on a remarkable odyssey of survival and discovery that took him through a labyrinth of radical politics and bohemian culture. Along the way, he became a professional singer, a dedicated Communist, and an uncloseted homosexual. During the late thirties, he sang backup for Josh White and Huddie "Leadbelly" Ledbetter, worked as a recruiter for the Young Communist League, preached revolution and brotherhood on countless street corners, and even squeezed in a few classes at City College, all the while gaining a reputation as one of Harlem's most colorful characters.

In early 1941 the Young Communist League asked Rustin to organize a campaign against segregation in the American armed forces, but later in the year, following the unexpected German attack on the Soviet Union, league leaders ordered him to cancel the campaign in the interests of Allied military solidarity. With this apparent shift away from racial and social justice agitation, Rustin became deeply disillusioned with the Communist Party. "You can all go to hell," he told his New York comrades. "I see that the Communist movement is only interested in what happens in Russia. You don't give a damn about Negroes." In June 1941 he left the Communist fold for good and transferred his allegiance to A. Philip Randolph, the legendary black socialist and labor leader who was busy planning a mass march on Washington to protest the Roosevelt administration's refusal to guarantee equal employment opportunities for black and white defense workers. Randolph appointed Rustin the youth organizer for the march, but the two men soon had a serious falling-out. After Roosevelt responded to Randolph's threatened march with an executive order creating the Fair Employment Practices Committee (FEPC), Randolph agreed to call off the march, but many of his young supporters, including Rustin, thought the protest march should continue as planned. Later in the war Rustin and Randolph resumed their friendship and collaboration, but the temporary break prompted the young activist to look elsewhere for a political and spiritual home. Consequently, in the fall of 1941, he accepted a staff position with A. J. Muste's Fellowship of Reconciliation.

As FOR youth secretary, Rustin returned to the pacifist track that he had followed as an American Friends Service Committee volunteer, immersing himself in the writings and teachings of Gandhi and pledging his loyalty to nonviolence, not just as a strategy for change but as a way of life. Muste encouraged and nurtured Rustin's determination to apply Gandhian precepts to the African American struggle for racial equality, and in the spring of 1942 the two men joined forces with other FOR activists to found the Committee (later Congress) of Racial Equality. "Certainly the Negro possesses qualities essential for nonviolent direct action," Rustin wrote prophetically in October 1942. "He has long since learned to endure suffering. He can admit his own share of guilt and has to be pushed hard to become bitter. . . . He is creative and has learned to adjust himself to conditions easily. But above all he possesses a rich religious heritage and today finds the church the center of his life."[24]

As a CORE stalwart, Rustin participated in a number of nonviolent protests, including an impromptu refusal to move to the back of a bus during a
trip from Louisville to Nashville in the early summer of 1942. This particular episode earned him a roadside beating at the hands of the Nashville police, who later hauled him off to jail. A month after the incident, Rustin offered
the readers of the FOR journal *Fellowship* a somewhat whimsical description
of his arrest:

> I was put into the back seat of the police car, between two policemen. Two
> others sat in front. During the thirteen-mile ride to town they called me
> every conceivable name and said anything they could think of to incite me
> to violence. . . .When we reached Nashville, a number of policemen were
> lined up on both sides of the hallway down which I had to pass on my way
> to the captain's office. They tossed me from one to another like a volley-
> ball. By the time I reached the office, the lining of my best coat was torn,
> and I was considerably rumpled. I straightened myself as best I could and
> went in. They had my bag, and went through it and my papers, finding
> much of interest, especially in the *Christian Century* and *Fellowship*. Finally
> the captain said, "Come here, nigger." I walked directly to him. "What can
> I do for you?" I asked. "Nigger," he said menacingly, "you're supposed to
> be scared when you come in here!" "I am fortified by the truth, justice, and
> Christ," I said. "there's no need for me to fear." He was flabbergasted and,
> for a time, completely at a loss for words. Finally he said to another officer,
> "I believe the nigger's crazy!"

In the end, the timely intervention of a sympathetic white bystander who had
witnessed the roadside beating and the restraint of a cool-headed assistant
district attorney (Ben West, a future Nashville mayor who would draw widespread praise for his moderate response to the student sit-ins of 1960 and
1961) kept Rustin out of jail, reinforcing his suspicion that even the white
South could be redeemed through nonviolent struggle.[25]

Soon after his narrow escape from Nashville justice, Rustin became a
friend and devoted follower of Krishnaial Shridharani, a leading Gandhian
scholar and the author of *War Without Violence*. This discipleship deepened
his commitment to nonviolent resistance and noncooperation with evil, and
in 1943 he rejected the traditional Quaker compromise of alternative service
in an army hospital. Convicted of draft evasion, he spent the next twenty-
eight months in federal prison. For nearly two years, he was imprisoned at the
penitentiary in Ashland, Ohio, where he waged spirited if futile campaigns
against everything from the censorship of reading materials to racial segregation. In August 1945 a final effort to desegregate the prison dining hall led to
solitary confinement, but soon thereafter he and several other pacifist mal-
contents were transferred to a facility in Lewisburg, Pennsylvania.

Following his release from Lewisburg in June 1946, Rustin returned to
New York to accept an appointment as co-secretary (with George Houser)
of FOR's Racial-Industrial Department, a position that he promptly turned
into a roving mission for Gandhian nonviolence. Though physically weak

and emaciated, he took to the road, preaching the gospel of nonviolent direct action to anyone who would listen. As his biographer Jervis Anderson has noted, during the critical postwar year of 1946 Rustin "functioned as a one-man civil disobedience movement in his travels across the United States. He occupied 'white only' railroad compartments; sat in at 'white only' hotels; and refused to budge unless he was forcibly ejected." All of this reinforced his dual reputation as a fearless activist and a Gandhian sage. He was both irrepressible and imaginative, and no one who knew him well was surprised when he, along with Houser, came up with the provocative idea of an inter-racial bus ride through the South. After the Journey of Reconciliation proposal was hatched, Rustin acted as a relentless advocate, eventually winning over, or at least wearing down, those who thought the plan was too dangerous. Without his involvement, the Journey—and perhaps even the Freedom Rides of 1961—would never have taken place.[26]

Jim Peck followed a somewhat different path to the Journey of Reconciliation. Three years younger than Rustin, he grew up in one of Manhattan's most prosperous households. The son of Samuel Peck, a wealthy clothing wholesaler (who died when his son was eleven years old), he spent the early years of the Great Depression at Choate, an elite prep school in Wallingford, Connecticut. Despite his family's conversion from Judaism to Episcopalianism, Peck was a social outsider at Choate, which used a strict quota system to limit the number of religious and ethnic minorities on campus. The primary factor separating him from his fellow students was not religion or ethnicity, however. Politically precocious, he cultivated a reputation as an independent thinker who espoused idealistic political doctrines and who preferred the company of bookish intellectuals.

In the fall of 1933 he enrolled at Harvard, where he honed his skills as a writer while assuming the role of a campus radical. At Harvard, he missed few opportunities to challenge the social and political conventions of the Ivy League elite and shocked his classmates by showing up at the freshman dance with a black date. As he recalled, this particular act of defiance was directed not only at "the soberly dressed Boston matrons on the sidelines," who "stared at us, whispered, and then stared again," but also at his own mother, who "referred to Negroes as 'coons' " and "frequently remarked that she would never hire one as a servant because 'they are dirty and they steal.' " By the end of his freshman year, he was a pariah, and his alienation from his family and the American establishment was complete. Dropping out of school, he emigrated to Paris, where he lived as an avant-garde expatriate for two years. His years in Europe, where he witnessed the ascendance of authoritarian and totalitarian regimes, deepened his commitment to activism and social justice. In the late thirties a severe case of wanderlust and a desire to identify with the working class led to a series of jobs as a merchant seaman, an experience that eventually propelled him into the turbulent world of radical unionism. His years at sea also reinforced his commitment to civil rights. "Living and working aboard ships with interracial crews," he later wrote, "strengthened my beliefs in equality."

Returning to the United States in 1938, Peck helped to organize the National Maritime Union, which made good use of his skills as a writer and publicist. During these years he also became a friend and follower of Roger Baldwin, the strong-willed founder of the American Civil Liberties Union (ACLU). Baldwin encouraged him to become involved in a number of social justice organizations, including the War Resisters League, and helped him find work with a trade union news syndicate. By the end of the decade, Peck was an avowed pacifist who spent much of his time publicizing the activities of the War Resisters League. Like Rustin, he refused to submit to the draft and was imprisoned for his defiance in 1942. He spent almost three years in the federal prison in Danbury, Connecticut, where he helped to organize a work strike that led to the desegregation of the prison mess hall. After his release in 1945 he rededicated himself to pacifism and militant trade union-ism, offering his services to a number of progressive organizations. For a time he devoted most of his energies to the War Resisters League and to editing the Workers Defense League *News Bulletin*, but in late 1946 he be-came increasingly absorbed with the race issue, especially after discovering and joining CORE. Recent events had convinced him that the struggle for racial equality was an essential precondition for the transformation of Ameri-can society, and the direct action philosophy of CORE provided him with a means of acting upon his convictions. With the zeal of a new recruit, he embraced the idea of the Journey of Reconciliation, which would be his first venture as a CORE volunteer.[27]

Jim Farmer shared Peck's passion for direct action and nonviolent pro-test, but in most other respects, from style and temperament to racial and regional background, the two men represented a study in contrasts. Born in Marshall, Texas, in 1920, Farmer was a black Southerner who had firsthand experience with the institutions of the Jim Crow South. Raised in a middle-class family, he was fortunate enough to avoid the degrading economic inse-curities of the rural poor. But as the aspiring son of educated parents, he was forced to endure the painful psychological and social indignities of a racial caste system that warped and restricted his prospects. His mother, Pearl Houston Farmer, was a graduate of Florida's Bethune Cookman Institute and a former teacher; his father, James Leonard Farmer Sr., was a learned Methodist minister who had earned a Ph.D. in theology at Boston Univer-sity. One of the few blacks in early twentieth-century Texas to hold a doc-toral degree, Farmer's father spoke seven languages and held academic positions at a number of black colleges, including Rust College in Holly Springs, Mississippi, and Samuel Houston College in Austin, Texas. A tow-ering figure in black academic circles, he was nonetheless cautious and defer-ential in his dealings with whites. This inconsistency troubled his young son, who idealized his father's moral and intellectual stature but who eventually recoiled from what he came to see as a cringing hypocrisy that perpetuated racial injustice.[28]

A brilliant student, young Jim Farmer entered school at the age of four and graduated from Wiley College at eighteen. At Wiley he came under the influence of Melvin Tolson, an English professor and debating coach who nurtured his young protégé's oratorical skills. Farmer possessed a deep, mellifluous voice that was perfectly suited to a dramatic style of oratory, and by the time Tolson got through with him, his studied intonations carried the barest hint of an East Texas twang. This remarkable speaking voice became Farmer's trademark and the cornerstone of a grand manner that struck some observers as pretentious and condescending. Even as a teenager, he was a large and imposing figure with an ego to match. Ambitious and articulate, he felt constrained by the small-town, segregated culture of Marshall. His first taste of the outside world came in 1937 when he represented Wiley at a National Conference of Methodist Youth at Miami University in Oxford, Ohio. Although there were only a handful of black delegates in attendance, Farmer emerged as one of the stars of the conference, persuading his fellow Methodists to approve a resolution urging Congress to pass anti-lynching legislation. "Everyone here wants to stop lynching," he informed the assembled delegates. "The only question is how long do we have to wait? How long, oh, Lord, how long? The purpose of this motion is not to damn the South and the many decent people who live there. . . . The purpose of this motion is to *stop lynching now*." The audience responded with a standing ovation and approval by acclamation, providing him with the "first taste of the heady wine of public acclaim." The conference later elected him to its governance committee, a remarkable achievement for a seventeen-year-old black boy from East Texas.[29]

The exhilarating triumph in Ohio reinforced Farmer's determination to become involved in the widening struggle for racial justice, and a few weeks later he accepted an invitation to attend a joint meeting of the National Negro Congress and the Southern Negro Youth Conference. Held in Richmond, Virginia, the meeting attracted some of the nation's most prominent black leaders, including A. Philip Randolph, Howard University president Mordecai Johnson, and Howard political scientist Ralph Bunche. Traveling the twelve hundred miles to Richmond by car, Farmer and two companions, one of whom was a white delegate from the University of Texas, encountered the inevitable frustrations of finding food, shelter, and restroom facilities along the Jim Crow highways of the Deep South. By the time the young travelers arrived at the conference, they had seen and experienced enough to fuel a growing sense of outrage. The conference itself was even more eyeopening. Here Farmer received his first exposure to the passionate militance of left-wing politics. He also got more than a glimpse of the sectarian intrigue and political infighting between Communists and socialists that threatened to tear the National Negro Congress apart. Founded in 1936 as a national clearinghouse for civil rights and labor organizations concerned about fair employment issues, the National Negro Congress had elected Randolph as its first chairman. But during the organization's first two years, the black socialist leader had grown increasingly suspicious of Communist activists who were reportedly exploiting the congress for selfish political purposes. Randolph's anger boiled over at the Richmond conference, where his explosive resignation speech both shocked and thrilled Farmer.[30]

To his conservative father's dismay, Farmer was never quite the same after the Richmond conference. The dream of becoming a theologian and following in his father's footsteps was still alive, and in the fall of 1938 he dutifully entered the Howard University School of Theology, where his father had recently accepted a position as a professor of Greek and New Testament studies. During his years at Howard, though, the young divinity student continued to gravitate toward radical politics. Inspired by Howard Thurman, a charismatic professor of social ethics and dean of the chapel whom he later described as a "mystic, poet, philosopher, preacher," Farmer became intrigued with Gandhianism, pacifism, and radical versions of the social gospel. Under Thurman's direction, he wrote his thesis on "A Critical Analysis of the Interrelationships Between Religion and Racism." Thurman also helped him secure a position as a part-time secretary in the Washington office of the Fellowship of Reconciliation, and by the time he graduated in 1941 he was completely captivated by FOR's philosophy of nonviolent interracial activism. Refusing ordination as a Methodist minister—a decision clinched by the news that his choice of pastorates was limited to all-black congregations—he accepted a full-time position as FOR's race relations secretary. Assigned to FOR's regional office in Chicago, he arrived in the Windy City in August 1941, ready, as he put it, to lead "an assault on the demons of violence and bigotry."[31]

For the next two years he spearheaded a series of direct action campaigns in Chicago and also traveled throughout the Midwest spreading the FOR gospel of pacifism and nonviolent resistance to social injustice. Though barely old enough to vote, he exuded an aura of confidence and command that belied his youth. Some found him arrogant and a bit overbearing, but no one doubted his intelligence or his passionate belief in the struggle for racial justice. At the University of Chicago, he organized an interracial study group on Gandhianism and encouraged students and others to engage in sit-ins and picketing campaigns at segregated coffeehouses, restaurants, roller rinks, and theaters. Working closely with both Rustin and George Houser, FOR's white field secretary, he also created Fellowship House, "an interracial men's cooperative" designed to challenge a restrictive covenant that segregated the neighborhood surrounding the university. In the spring of 1942 these efforts led to the formation of the Chicago Committee of Racial Equality, which Farmer conceived as part of a national direct action network known as the "Brotherhood Mobilization." By 1943 the organization had evolved into the

Committees of Racial Equality, and a year later the name was changed to Congress of Racial Equality. At first, A. J. Muste resisted Farmer's insistence that CORE should be allowed to have an identity largely independent of FOR, but the FOR chairman eventually relented. Adopted at the organization's first annual meeting, the CORE charter stated that "the purpose of the organization shall be to federate local interracial groups working to abolish the color line through direct non-violent action." With Muste's blessing, Farmer became CORE's first national chairman, though not for long.[32]

Muste's acceptance of CORE's partial autonomy came at a price, one that eventually proved too costly for Farmer to bear. In June 1943 he received a "promotion" that required relocation to New York. "I knew at once what it all meant," he later wrote. "New York, where they could watch me closely, and full-time so I would have less time to freewheel for CORE. I was being given bigger wings, but they would be clipped wings." Muste was not unsympathetic to the aims and activities of CORE, but his primary loyalty was to pacifism and FOR. He expected the same from Farmer, whose primary job, in his view, was to organize and recruit new members for FOR. As long as FOR was paying Farmer's salary, the interests of the parent organization, not CORE, had to come first. Moreover, Farmer was a notoriously inattentive administrator who preferred public speaking to the background work of building and maintaining an organization. Well aware of Muste's concerns, Farmer made a valiant effort to satisfy his obligations to FOR and to pay more attention to administrative matters, but by the spring of 1945 it was clear to both men that the dual arrangement was not working. In May, following an awkward meeting in Muste's office, Farmer resigned from his FOR staff position—and from his cherished unpaid position as CORE's national chairman.

Following Farmer's departure, CORE reorganized its leadership structure, creating an executive directorship filled by Houser. But the troubled relationship between FOR and CORE continued to plague both organizations in the postwar years. While the split between Muste and Farmer was largely personal and organizational in nature, the nonviolent movement also harbored persistent philosophical and ideological divisions, including disagreements over the connection between pacifism and social justice and the competing claims of morality and pragmatism as the primary rationale for nonviolent direct action.[33]

Farmer himself would later participate in these ongoing debates, especially during and after the Freedom Rides of 1961, but in the immediate postwar era he found himself somewhat removed from the world of FOR and CORE. In late 1945 he accepted a position with the Upholsterers International Union of North America (UIU), which sent him to Virginia, and later to High Point, North Carolina, to organize furniture workers. Throughout his stay in the Piedmont he maintained contact with Houser, who kept him abreast of CORE affairs, including the Journey of Reconciliation. As soon as Farmer heard about the idea of the Journey, which he considered "exciting and intriguing," he was sorely tempted to abandon the frustrations of union organizing and join the ride, but with a new wife to support, he could not afford to leave a steady-paying job. Turning down a chance to take part in the Journey of Reconciliation was a difficult decision that isolated him from the cause that still excited his deepest passions, and when the UIU transferred him to Cincinnati, he felt even farther removed from the action. Later, after learning that Rustin and several other old friends had been arrested in North Carolina, he "felt pangs of guilt for not having been there." This failure to take part in the Journey would bother him for many years, and only in 1961— when he returned to CORE as national director and the leader of the Freedom Rides—would he begin to feel that he had atoned for his absence from CORE's first great adventure below the Mason-Dixon line.[34]

THE PLAN FOR AN INTERRACIAL BUS RIDE through the segregated South grew out of a series of discussions between Bayard Rustin and George Houser held during the summer of 1946. Like Rustin, Houser was a Northerner with little firsthand experience in the South. Born in Cleveland, he traveled to the Philippines with his white Methodist missionary parents and later lived in New York, California, China, and Colorado before entering Union Theological Seminary in 1939. At Union he became a committed pacifist and refused to register for the draft. Convicted of draft evasion, he served a year in federal prison. Following his release in the fall of 1941, Muste hired him to run FOR's Chicago office. During the early days of CORE, he collaborated with Farmer but developed an even closer relationship with Rustin, whom he came to admire greatly. Later, as the newly appointed co-secretaries of FOR's Racial-Industrial Department and as members of CORE's executive committee, the two young friends were eager to boost CORE's profile by demonstrating the utility of nonviolent direct action.[35]

For them the timing of the *Morgan* decision and the ensuing controversy over compliance and enforcement could not have been better. During its first four years, CORE had operated as "a loose federation of local groups which were united mostly by their aim of tackling discrimination by a particular method—nonviolent direct action." "This put emphasis almost completely on local issues and organization," Houser recalled many years later. "Thus it was difficult to get a sense of a national movement or to develop a national strategy. One of the results of this reality was that it was almost impossible for CORE to raise funds to establish itself as a separate entity." In addition to enhancing CORE's national stature and autonomy, a project like the Journey of Reconciliation also promised to provide "an entering wedge for CORE into the South." As Houser explained, "We had no local groups in the South and it wasn't easy to organize them at this point, especially with the two words 'racial equality' in our name. Those were fighting words in the

South. But with a definite project around which to rally, we felt there was a possibility of opening up an area seemingly out of reach." Rustin and Houser were confident that the issue of Jim Crow transit—which, in Houser's words, "touched virtually every black person, was demeaning in its effect and a source of frequent conflict"—represented a perfect target for CORE's first national project. Even if the project failed to desegregate interstate buses, "challenging discrimination in transportation, by striking a raw nerve, would get public attention."[36]

During the summer of 1946, as expectations of compliance with the *Morgan* ruling faded, the idea of a CORE-sponsored freedom ride became a frequent topic of conversation among CORE stalwarts in New York. Some predicted that the proposed ride would reveal a liberalizing trend in the postwar South, but others were less hopeful. Indeed, judging by the experiences of individual travelers who had challenged Jim Crow in recent months, the prospects for a smooth ride seemed dim. The most troubling incident was the brutal beating of Isaac Woodard in mid-February. Brought to national attention by NAACP executive secretary Walter White in July, the Woodard case involved a recently discharged black veteran returning to his North Carolina home from a Georgia military base. Traveling on an interstate Greyhound, Woodard was arrested in Batesburg, South Carolina, after he and the bus driver "exchanged words over some minor point of racial etiquette." Dragged from the bus and beaten by Batesburg police chief Linwood Shull and a deputy, the twenty-seven-year-old soldier suffered massive injuries, including the blinding of both eyes. Having survived fifteen months fighting the Japanese in the Pacific, he had run afoul of two white men who saw fit to gouge out his eyes with the blunt end of a billy club. Such treatment was egregious enough to prompt an FBI investigation and a federal indictment of Shull in the fall of 1946. But even the sworn testimony of army doctors was not enough to secure a conviction from an all-white Columbia, South Carolina, jury.

A second and equally revealing case involved Wilson Head, a courageous black World War II veteran who undertook his own personal freedom ride from Atlanta to Washington in July 1946. Traveling on the Greyhound line and insisting on his right to sit in the front of the bus, he braved angry drivers, enraged passengers, and menacing police officers—one of whom threatened to shoot him during a brief detention in Chapel Hill, North Carolina. Somehow Head managed to make it to Washington without injury or arrest, suggesting that testing compliance with the *Morgan* decision was possible if not altogether safe. To the dismay of many white Southerners, individual acts of defiance on segregated buses and trains were becoming increasingly common in the postwar years, especially in the Upper South and even among local and intrastate passengers. The black historian John Hope Franklin, for example, successfully defied a Richmond bus driver who ordered him to the back of a local bus in 1947. Having just given a blood transfusion for his older brother Buck, who lay dying in a veterans' hospital, Franklin was distracted by shock and grief as he took a seat in the "white" section of the bus. In no mood to submit to white authority, he told the driver that he planned to remain in the front no matter what. With several black passengers in the back urging Franklin to stand his ground, the driver ultimately backed down, but the young historian was fortunate he did not end up in a Richmond jail cell.

Widely publicized in the black press, the Woodard and Head episodes provided concrete examples of what CORE activists were likely to face if they ventured into the South as freedom riders. But these and other cautionary tales had no apparent impact on the resolute organizers of the proposed project. By the time CORE's executive committee met in Cleveland in mid-September, Rustin and Houser had developed a full-scale plan for the ride. After a lengthy discussion of the risks and dangers of a Southern foray, the committee endorsed the idea and authorized Rustin and Houser to seek approval and funding from FOR. With a little coaxing, the FOR staff soon embraced the plan, although Muste insisted that the ride should be a joint project of FOR and CORE.[37]

Over the next few months, FOR's Racial-Industrial Department worked out the details, adding an educational component and ultimately limiting the scope of the ride to the Upper South. The revised plan called for "a racially mixed deputation of lecturers" who would speak at various points along the route, giving "some purpose to the trip outside of simple tests and experimentation with techniques." The riders would not only test compliance with the *Morgan* decision; they would also spread the gospel of nonviolence to at least part of the South. The original plan involved a region-wide journey from Washington, D.C., to New Orleans, Louisiana, but after several of CORE's Southern contacts warned that an interracial journey through the Deep South would provoke "wholesale violence," Rustin and Houser reluctantly agreed to restrict the ride to what was perceived as the more moderate Upper South. "The deep South may be touched later," they explained, "depending on what comes out of this first experience." After much debate, they also agreed that all of the riders would be men, acknowledging "that mixing the races and sexes would possibly exacerbate an already volatile situation." This decision was a grave disappointment to several women—including the veteran black activists Ella Baker and Pauli Murray—who had been actively involved in planning the trip. Many of the planning meetings took place in the New York apartment of Natalie Mormon, who, like Baker and Murray, had considerable experience traveling through the South. But the women's plaintive protests against paternalism fell on deaf ears. Less controversially, Rustin and Houser also came up with an official name for the project: the Journey of Reconciliation. This redemptive phrase pleased Muste and lent an air of moral authority to the project.[38]

For reasons of safety and to ensure that the compliance tests would be valid, CORE leaders did not seek any advance publicity for the Journey.

Within the confines of the movement, though, they quietly spread the word that CORE was about to invade the South. The proposed ride received enthusiastic endorsements from a number of black leaders—most notably Howard Thurman, A. Philip Randolph, and Mary McLeod Bethune—and from several organizations, including the Fellowship of Southern Churchmen, an interracial group of liberal Southern clergymen. The one organization that expressly refused to endorse the ride was, predictably, the NAACP. When CORE leaders first broached the subject with national NAACP officials in early October, Thurgood Marshall and his colleagues were preoccupied with a recent District of Columbia Court of Appeals decision that extended the applicability of *Morgan* to interstate railways. In *Matthews v. Southern Railway*, the court ruled that there was "no valid distinction between segregation in buses and railway cars." For a time, this ruling gave NAACP attorneys renewed hope that the *Morgan* decision would actually have an effect on interstate travel. In the aftermath of the ruling, however, only one railway—the Richmond, Fredericksburg, and Potomac Railroad—actually desegregated its interstate trains. The vast majority of Southern railways continued to segregate all passengers, interstate or not. Several railroad officials insisted that the ruling only applied to the District of Columbia, but to protect their companies from possible federal interference they also adopted the same "company rules" strategy used by some interstate bus lines. The basis for segregation, they now claimed, was not state law but company policy. Racial separation in railroad coaches was thus a private matter allegedly beyond the bounds of public policy or constitutional intrusion. Because the *Chiles* decision, rendered by the U.S. Supreme Court in 1910, sanctioned such company rules, NAACP attorneys were seemingly stymied by this new strategy.[39]

In mid-November Marshall and the NAACP legal brain trust held a two-day strategy meeting in New York to address the challenge of privatized segregation. No firm solution emerged from the meeting, but the attorneys did reach a consensus that CORE's proposal for an interracial ride through the South was a very bad idea. The last thing the NAACP needed at this point, or so its leaders believed, was a provocative diversion led by a bunch of impractical agitators. A week later Marshall went public with the NAACP's opposition to direct action. Speaking in New Orleans on the topic "The Next Twenty Years Toward Freedom for the Negro in America," he criticized "well-meaning radical groups in New York" who were planning to use Gandhian tactics to breach the wall of racial segregation. Predicting a needless catastrophe, he insisted that a "disobedience movement on the part of Negroes and their white allies, if employed in the South, would result in wholesale slaughter with no good achieved." He did not mention FOR or CORE by name, nor divulge any details about the impending Journey of Reconciliation, but Marshall's words, reprinted in the *New York Times*, sent a clear warning to Muste, Rustin, and Houser. Since the Journey would inevitably lead to multiple arrests, everyone involved knew that at some point CORE would require the assistance and cooperation of NAACP-affiliated attorneys, so Marshall's words could not be taken lightly. The leaders of FOR and CORE were in no position to challenge the supremacy of the NAACP, but, after some hesitation, they realized that Marshall's pointed critique could not go unanswered.[40]

The response, written by Rustin and published in the *Louisiana Weekly* in early January 1947, was a sharp rebuke to Marshall and a rallying cry for the nonviolent movement.

> I am sure that Marshall is either ill-informed on the principles and techniques of non-violence or ignorant of the processes of social change.
>
> Unjust social laws and patterns do not change because supreme courts deliver just opinions. One need merely observe the continued practices of jim crow in interstate travel six months after the Supreme Court's decision to see the necessity of resistance. Social progress comes from struggle; all freedom demands a price.
>
> At times freedom will demand that its followers go into situations where even death is to be faced. . . . Direct action means picketing, striking and boycotting as well as disobedience against unjust conditions, and all of these methods have already been used with some success by Negroes and sympathetic whites. . . .
>
> I cannot believe that Thurgood Marshall thinks that such a program would lead to wholesale slaughter. . . . But if anyone at this date in history believes that the "white problem," which is one of privilege, can be settled without some violence, he is mistaken and fails to realize the ends to which man can be driven to hold on to what they consider privileges.
>
> This is why Negroes and whites who participate in direct action must pledge themselves to non-violence in word and deed. For in this way alone can the inevitable violence be reduced to a minimum. The simple truth is this: unless we find non-violent methods which can be used by the rank-and-file who more and more tend to resist, they will more and more resort to violence. And court-room argumentation will not suffice for the activization which the Negro masses are today demanding.[41]

Rustin's provocative and prophetic manifesto did not soften Marshall's opposition to direct action, but it did help to convince Marshall and NAACP executive secretary Walter White that CORE was determined to follow through with the Journey of Reconciliation, with or without their cooperation. CORE leaders had already announced that the two-week Journey would begin on April 9, and there was no turning back for activists like Rustin and Houser who believed that the time for resolute action had arrived. For them, all the signs—including Harry Truman's unexpected decision, in December 1946, to create a President's Commission on Civil Rights—suggested that the movement for racial justice had reached a crossroads. It was time to turn ideas into action, to demonstrate the power of nonviolence as Gandhi and others were already doing in India.[42]

With this in mind, Rustin and Houser left New York in mid-January on
a scouting expedition through the Upper South. During two weeks of recon-
naissance in Virginia and North Carolina, they followed the proposed route
of the coming Journey, scrupulously obeying the laws and customs of Jim
Crow transit so as to avoid arrest. At each stop, they met with local civil
rights and black community leaders who helped to arrange lecture and rally
facilities and housing, as well as possible legal representation for the riders to
come. Some dismissed the interracial duo as an odd and misguided pair of
outside agitators, but most did what they could to help. In several communities, Rustin and Houser encountered the "other" NAACP: the restless branch
leaders and Youth Council volunteers (and even some black attorneys such
as future CORE leader Floyd McKissick) who were eager to take the struggle
beyond the courtroom. After Rustin returned to New York in late January,
Houser traveled alone to Tennessee and Kentucky, where he continued to
be impressed with the untapped potential of the black South.

In the end, the four-state scouting trip produced a briefcase full of commitments from church leaders and state and local NAACP officials, a harvest
that pushed Marshall and his colleagues toward a grudging acceptance of the
coming Journey's legitimacy. Soon Roy Wilkins, Spot Robinson, Charles
Houston, and even Marshall himself were offering "helpful suggestions" and
promising to provide CORE with legal backup if and when the riders were
arrested. Most national NAACP leaders still considered the Journey to be a
foolhardy venture, but as the start of the Journey drew near, there was a
noticeable closing of the ranks, a feeling of movement solidarity that provided the riders with a reassuring measure of legal and institutional protection. As Houser put it, with the promise of Southern support and with the
NAACP more or less on board, "we felt our group of participants would not
be isolated victims as they challenged the local and state laws."[43]

Even so, the Journey remained a dangerous prospect, and finding sixteen qualified and dependable volunteers who had the time and money to
spend two weeks on the road was not easy. The organizers' determination to
enlist riders who had already demonstrated a commitment to nonviolent direct action narrowed the field and forced CORE to draw upon its own staff
and other seasoned veterans of FOR and CORE campaigns. When it proved
impossible to find a full complement of volunteers who could commit themselves to the entire Journey, Rustin and Houser reluctantly allowed the riders to come and go as personal circumstances dictated. In the end, fewer than
half of the riders completed the entire trip.[44]

The sixteen volunteers who traveled to Washington in early April to
undergo two days of training and orientation represented a broad range of
nonviolent activists. There were eight whites and eight blacks and an interesting mix of secular and religious backgrounds. In addition to Houser, the
white volunteers included Jim Peck; Homer Jack, a Unitarian minister and

founding member of CORE, who headed the Chicago Council Against Racial and Religious Discrimination; Worth Randle, a biologist and CORE stalwart from Cincinnati; Igal Roodenko, a peace activist from upstate New York; Joseph Felmet, a conscientious objector from Asheville, North Carolina, representing the Southern Workers Defense League; and two FOR-affiliated Methodist ministers from North Carolina, Ernest Bromley and Louis Adams. The black volunteers included Rustin; Dennis Banks, a jazz musician from Chicago; Conrad Lynn, a civil rights attorney from New York City; Eugene Stanley, an agronomy instructor at North Carolina A&T College in Greensboro; William Worthy, a radical journalist affiliated with the New York Council for a Permanent FEPC; and three CORE activists from Ohio—law student Andrew Johnson, pacifist lecturer Wallace Nelson, and social worker Nathan Wright.[45]

Most of the volunteers were young men still in their twenties; several were barely out of their teens. Lynn, at age thirty-nine, was the oldest. Nearly all, despite their youth, had some experience with direct action, and seven had been conscientious objectors during World War II. But with the exception of Rustin's impromptu freedom ride in 1942, none of this experience had been gained in the Jim Crow South. No member of the group had ever been involved in a direct action campaign quite like the Journey of Reconciliation, and only the North Carolinians had spent more than a few weeks in the South.

Faced with so many unknowns and the challenge of taking an untried corps of volunteers into the heart of darkness, Rustin and Houser fashioned an intensive orientation program. Meeting at FOR's Washington Fellowship House, nine of the riders participated in a series of seminars that "taught not only the principles but the practices of nonviolence in specific situations that would arise aboard the buses." Using techniques pioneered by FOR peace activists and CORE chapters, the seminars addressed expected problems by staging dramatic role-playing sessions. "What if the bus driver insulted you? What if you were actually assaulted? What if the police threatened you? These and many other questions were resolved through socio-dramas in which participants would act the roles of bus drivers, hysterical segregationists, police— and 'you.' Whether the roles had been acted correctly and whether you had done the right thing was then discussed. Socio-dramas of other bus situations followed. In all of them, you were supposed to remain nonviolent, but stand firm," Jim Peck recalled. Two days of this regimen left the riders exhausted but better prepared for the challenges to come.[46]

Leaving little to chance, Rustin and Houser also provided each rider with a detailed list of instructions. Later reprinted in a pamphlet entitled *You Don't Have to Ride Jim Crow*, the instructions made it clear that the task at hand was not, strictly speaking, civil disobedience but rather establishing "the fact that the word of the U.S. Supreme Court is law":

WHEN TRAVELING BY BUS WITH A TICKET FROM A POINT IN ONE STATE TO A POINT IN ANOTHER STATE:

1. If you are a Negro, sit in a front seat. If you are a white, sit in a rear seat.
2. If the driver asks you to move, tell him *calmly and courteously*: "As an interstate passenger I have a right to sit anywhere in this bus. This is the law as laid down by the United States Supreme Court."
3. If the driver summons the police and repeats his order in their presence, tell him exactly what you told the driver when he first asked you to move.
4. If the police ask you to "come along" without putting you under arrest, tell them you will not go until you are put under arrest. Police have often used the tactic of frightening a person into getting off the bus without making an arrest, keeping him until the bus has left and then just leaving him standing by the empty roadside. In such a case this person has no redress.
5. If the police put you under arrest, go with them peacefully. At the police station, phone the nearest headquarters of the National Association for the Advancement of Colored People, or one of their lawyers. They will assist you.
6. If you have money with you, you can get out on bail immediately. It will probably be either $25 or $50. If you don't have bail, anti-discrimination organizations will help raise it for you.
7. *If you happen to be arrested, the delay in your journey will only be a few hours. The value of your action in breaking down Jim Crow will be too great to be measured.*[47]

Additional instructions assigned specific functions to individuals or subgroups of riders, distinguishing between designated testers and observers. "Just which individual sat where on each lap of our trip," Peck recalled, "would be planned at meetings of the group on the eve of departure. A few were to act as observers. They necessarily had to sit in a segregated manner. So did whoever was designated to handle bail in the event of arrests. The roles shifted on each lap of the Journey. It was important that all sixteen not be arrested simultaneously and the trip thus halted." Throughout the training sessions, Rustin and Houser kept reiterating that Jim Crow could not be vanquished by courage alone; careful organization, tight discipline, and strict adherence to nonviolence were also essential. An unorganized and undisciplined assault on segregation, they warned, would play into the hands of the segregationists, discrediting the philosophy of nonviolence and postponing the long-awaited desegregation of the South.[48]

WHEN THE RIDERS GATHERED at the Greyhound and Trailways stations in downtown Washington on the morning of April 9 for the beginning of the Journey, the predominant mood was anxious but upbeat. As they boarded the buses, they were accompanied by Ollie Stewart of the *Baltimore Afro-American* and Lem Graves of the *Pittsburgh Courier*, two black journalists

Nine Journey of Reconciliation volunteers pose for a photograph in front of the Richmond, Virginia, law office of NAACP attorney Spottswood Robinson, April 10, 1947. From left to right: Worth Randle, Wallace Nelson, Ernest Bromley, Jim Peck, Igal Roodenko, Bayard Rustin, Joseph Felmet, George Houser, and Andrew Johnson. (Swarthmore College Peace Collection)

who had agreed to cover the first week of the Journey. Joking with the reporters, Rustin, as always, set a jovial tone that helped to relieve the worst tensions of the moment. There was also a general air of confidence that belied the dangers ahead. Sitting on the bus prior to departure, Peck thought to himself that "it would not be too long until Greyhound and Trailways would 'give up segregation practices' in the South." Years later, following the struggles surrounding the Freedom Rides of 1961, he would look back on this early and unwarranted optimism with a rueful eye, but during the first stage of the Journey, his hopeful expectations seemed justified.[49]

The ride from Washington to Richmond was uneventful for both groups of riders, and no one challenged their legal right to sit anywhere they pleased. For a few minutes, Rustin even sat in the seat directly behind the Greyhound driver. Most gratifying was the decision by several regular passengers to sit outside the section designated for their race. Everyone, including the drivers, seemed to take desegregated transit in stride, confirming a CORE report that claimed the Jim Crow line had broken down in northern Virginia

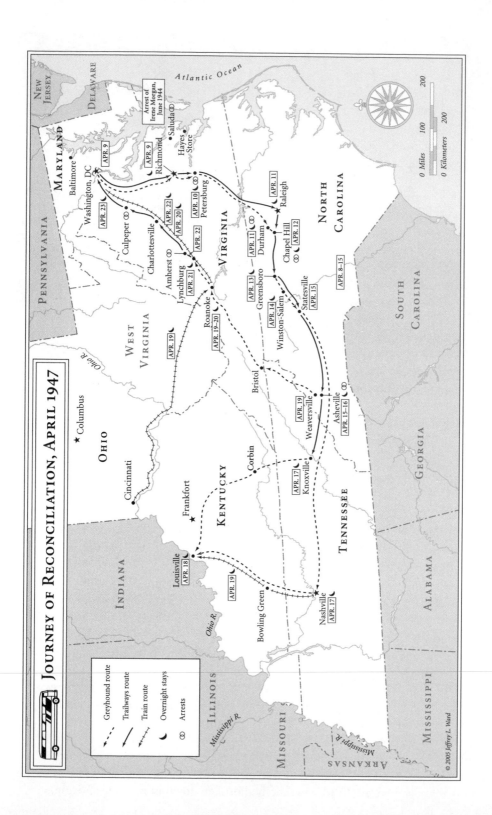

JOURNEY OF RECONCILIATION, APRIL 1947

Greyhound route
Trailways route
Train route
Overnight stays ☽
Arrests ⊗

© 2005 Jeffrey L. Ward

in recent months. "Today any trouble is unlikely until you get south of Richmond," the report concluded. "So many persons have insisted upon their rights and fought their cases successfully, that today courts in the northern Virginia area are not handing down guilty verdicts in which Jim Crow state laws are violated by interstate passengers."

At the end of the first day of the Journey, the CORE riders celebrated their initial success at a mass meeting held at the Leigh Avenue Baptist Church. Prior to their departure for Petersburg the following morning, Wally Nelson delivered a moving speech on nonviolence during a chapel service at all-black Virginia Union College. At the church the enthusiasm for desegregation among local blacks was palpable, suggesting that at least some Southern blacks were more militant than the riders had been led to believe. But the mood was decidedly different among the predominantly middle-class students at Virginia Union, who exhibited an attitude of detachment and denial. During a question-and-answer session, it became clear that many of the students were "unwilling to admit that they had suffered discrimination in transportation." As Conrad Lynn, who joined the Journey in Richmond, observed, the students simply "pretended that racial oppression did not exist for them."[50]

The prospects for white compliance and black militance were less promising on the second leg of the Journey, but even in southern Virginia, where most judges and law enforcement officials had yet to acknowledge the *Morgan* decision, the riders encountered little resistance. During the short stint from Richmond to Petersburg, there were no incidents other than a warning from a black passenger who remarked that black protesters like Nelson and Lynn might get away with sitting in the front of the bus in Virginia, but farther south things would get tougher. "Some bus drivers are crazy," he insisted, "and the farther South you go, the crazier they get." As if to prove the point, a segregationist Greyhound driver had a run-in with Rustin the following morning. Ten miles south of Petersburg, the driver ordered the black activist, who was seated next to Peck, to the back of the bus. After Rustin politely but firmly refused to move, the driver vowed to take care of the situation once the bus reached North Carolina. At Oxford the driver called the local police, but after several minutes of interrogation the officer in charge declined to make an arrest. During the wait most of the black passengers seemed sympathetic to Rustin's actions, but a black schoolteacher boarding the bus at Oxford scolded him for needlessly causing a forty-five-minute delay. "Please move. Don't do this," he pleaded. "You'll reach your destination either in front or in back. What difference does it make?" This would not be the last time that the CORE riders would hear this kind of accommodationist rhetoric.[51]

While Rustin was dealing with the Greyhound driver's outrage, a more serious incident occurred on the Trailways bus. Before the bus left the Petersburg station, the driver informed Lynn that he could not remain in the front section reserved for whites. Lynn did his best to explain the implications of *Morgan*, but the driver—unaccustomed to dealing with black lawyers—"countered that he was in the employ of the bus company, not the Supreme Court, and that he followed company rules about segregation." The unflappable New Yorker's refusal to move led to his arrest on a charge of disorderly conduct, but only after the local magistrate talked with the bus company's attorney in Richmond. During a two-hour delay, several of the CORE riders conducted a spirited but largely futile campaign to drum up support among the regular passengers. A white navy man in uniform grumbled that Lynn's behavior merited a response from the Ku Klux Klan, and an incredulous black porter (who reminded Houser of a fawning "Uncle Tom" character in Richard Wright's *Black Boy*) challenged Lynn's sanity. "What's the matter with him? He's crazy. Where does he think he is?" the porter demanded, adding: "We know how to deal with him. We ought to drag him off."

As a menacing crowd gathered around the bus, Lynn feared that he might be beaten up or even killed, especially after the porter screamed: "Let's take the nigger off! We don't want him down here!" In the end, he managed to escape the vigilantism of both races. Released on a twenty-five-dollar bail bond, he soon rejoined his comrades in Raleigh, where a large crowd of black students from St. Augustine's College gathered to hear Nelson and Roodenko hold forth on the promise of nonviolent struggle. Thanks to Lynn's composure, a relieved Nelson told the crowd, the Journey had experienced its first arrest without disrupting the spirit of nonviolence.[52]

New challenges awaited the riders in Durham, where three members of the Trailways group—Rustin, Peck, and Johnson—were arrested on the morning of April 12. While Rustin and Johnson were being hauled off for ignoring the station superintendent's order to move to the black section of the bus, Peck informed the police: "If you arrest them, you'll have to arrest me, too, for I'm going to sit in the rear." The arresting officers promptly obliged him and carted all three men off to jail. When Joe Felmet and local NAACP attorney C. Jerry Gates showed up at the jail a half hour later to secure their release, the charges were dropped, but a conversation with the Trailways superintendent revealed that there was more trouble ahead. "We know all about this," the superintendent declared. "Greyhound is letting them ride. But we are not." Even more disturbing was the effort by a number of local black leaders to pressure Gates and the Durham NAACP to shun the riders as unwelcome outside agitators. A rally in support of the Journey drew an unexpectedly large crowd, and the local branch of the NAACP refused to abandon the riders. Still, the rift within Durham's black community reminded the riders that white segregationists were not the only obstruction to the movement for racial equality.[53]

The next stop was Chapel Hill, the home of the University of North Carolina. Here, for the first time, the CORE riders would depend on the hospitality of white Southerners. Their host was the Reverend Charles M. Jones, the courageous pastor of a Presbyterian congregation that included

the university's president, Frank Porter Graham—a member of President
Truman's Committee on Civil Rights—and several other outspoken liberals.
A native Tennessean, Jones was a member of the Fellowship of Southern
Churchmen, a former member of FOR's national council, and a leading figure among Chapel Hill's white civil rights advocates. Despite the efforts of
Jones, Fellowship of Southern Churchmen activist Nelle Morton, and others, life in this small college town remained segregated, but there were signs
that the local color line was beginning to fade. Earlier in the year, the black
singer Dorothy Maynor had performed before a racially integrated audience
on campus, and Jones's church had hosted an interracial union meeting sponsored by the Congress of Industrial Organizations (CIO). These and other
breaches of segregationist orthodoxy signaled a rising tolerance in the university community, but they also stoked the fires of reaction among local
defenders of Jim Crow. By the time the CORE riders arrived, the town's
most militant segregationists were primed and ready for a confrontation that
would serve warning that Chapel Hill, despite the influence of the university
and its liberal president, was still white man's country.[54]

The riders' first few hours in Chapel Hill seemed to confirm the town's
reputation as an outpost of racial moderation. Jones and several church elders welcomed them at the station, and a Saturday night meeting with students and faculty at the university went off without a hitch. On Sunday
morning most of the riders, including several blacks, attended services at
Jones's church and later met with a delegation representing the Fellowship
of Southern Churchmen. At this point there was no hint of trouble, and the
interracial nature of the gatherings, as Houser later recalled, seemed natural
"in the liberal setting of this college town." As the riders boarded a Trailways
bus for the next leg of the journey, they could only hope that things would
continue to go as smoothly in Greensboro, where a Sunday night mass meeting was scheduled. Since there was no Greyhound run from Chapel Hill to
Greensboro, the riders divided into two groups and purchased two blocks of
tickets on Trailways buses scheduled to leave three hours apart.[55]

Five of the riders—Johnson, Felmet, Peck, Rustin, and Roodenko—
boarded the first bus just after lunch. But they never made it out of the station. As soon as Felmet and Johnson sat down in adjoining seats near the
front of the bus, the driver, Ned Leonard, ordered Johnson to the "colored"
section in the rear. The two riders explained that they "were traveling together to meet speaking engagements in Greensboro and other points south"
and "that they were inter-state passengers . . . 'covered' by the Irene Morgan
decision." Unmoved, Leonard walked to the nearby police station to arrange
for their arrest. While he was gone, Rustin and Roodenko engaged several of
the passengers in conversation, creating an "open forum" that revealed that
many of the passengers supported Felmet's and Johnson's protest. When
Leonard later passed out waiver cards that the bus company used to absolve
itself from liability, one woman balked, declaring: "You don't want me to

sign one of those. I am a damn Yankee, and I think this is an outrage." Shaking her hand, Roodenko exclaimed: "Well, there are two damn Yankees on the bus!" By this time Felmet and Johnson had been carted off to the police station, and Peck had followed them to the station to arrange bail. But Leonard soon discovered that he had two more protesters to deal with. Encouraged by the sympathetic reaction among the regular passengers, Rustin and Roodenko moved to the seat vacated by the arrested riders, which prompted a second round of arrests. Having already paid fifty dollars each for Felmet's and Johnson's release, Peck called Houser, who was still at Jones's parsonage, to bring down another hundred dollars to get Rustin and Roodenko out of jail.[56]

While the four men waited for Houser and Jones to arrive with the bail money, Peck shuttled back and forth from the police station to the bus, checking on his colleagues' bags and trying to keep tabs on the situation at the bus station. By this point the bus had been delayed almost two hours, and it was obvious to everyone at the scene that a group of "outside agitators" had provoked an incident. One bystander, a white cabdriver, vowed, "They'll never get a bus out of here tonight," and a few minutes later Peck found himself surrounded by five angry cab drivers as he crossed the street. Snarling, "Coming down here to stir up the niggers," one of the drivers punched Peck in the side of the head. When Peck refused to retaliate and simply asked, "What's the matter?" the man gave him "a perplexed look and started to walk away awkwardly." Moments later, two men—an unidentified local white minister and Eugene Stanley, the black rider who taught at North Carolina A&T—urged the driver to leave Peck alone but were told to mind their own business. Thinking that both men were part of the CORE group, the cab drivers rushed toward them menacingly, but after learning that both were North Carolinians, they let them go. Returning to the police station, Peck warned Jones and Houser, who had finally arrived with the bail money, that trouble was brewing.[57]

After surveying the situation, Jones concluded that the riders would have to travel to Greensboro by car. Once bond had been posted for the arrested riders, the group piled into Jones's car and headed to the parsonage for a brief stop before leaving town. Unfortunately, two cabs filled with irate whites sped after them. As Peck recalled the harrowing scene: "We succeeded in getting to Reverend Jones's home before them. When we got inside and looked out the window, we saw two of the drivers getting out with big sticks. Others started to pick up rocks by the roadside. Then, two of the drivers, apparently scared, motioned to the others to stop. They drove away. But a few minutes later Reverend Jones, who since the CIO meeting in his church had been marked as a 'nigger lover,' received an anonymous phone call. 'Get the niggers out of town by midnight or we'll burn down your house,' threatened a quivering voice." Determined to get the riders out of Chapel Hill before nightfall, Jones rounded up three university students willing to drive the group to Greensboro and also called the police, who reluctantly agreed to provide an escort to the county line.[58]

As soon as the riders left, Jones took his wife and two children to a friend's house for protection, a precaution that seemed warranted by subsequent events. When Jones returned home Sunday evening accompanied by a friend, Hilton Seals, he found a crowd of angry white protesters in his front yard. The two men tried to ignore the crowd's taunts, but as they walked to the door Seals was struck with a rock. On Monday morning Jones received a second anonymous call threatening him with death. Later in the day several cabdrivers milling around the bus station attacked Martin Walker, a disabled white war veteran and university student, after he was seen "talking to a Negro woman." A second university student, Ray Sylvester, "was knocked unconscious by a cabdriver for 'being too liberal.' " During the next few days, Jones received additional death threats by mail, and several anonymous calls threatened his church, prompting an emergency meeting of the congregation. When they learned of the threats, several university students volunteered to guard Jones's home and church, but this proved unnecessary, thanks in part to President Frank Graham's forceful consultation with the local police. By the end of the week the wave of intimidation had subsided, even though the controversy surrounding the bus station incident continued to simmer.[59]

Speaking to an overflow crowd at the university's Memorial Hall four days after the arrests, Jones defended the Journey of Reconciliation as the work of true Christians who had made "a thorough and exhaustive study of law as related to transportation in order that Christians and others might understand the law and practice it." But several students in the audience criticized the Journey's provocative tactics. "When you consider the general attitudes and practices in the South," one student insisted, "it is stupid to raise a point which can bring only friction, a crusade of going about and raising such questions cannot be merely trying to bring about reconciliation. It has as its end the creation of dissensions not here before. I cannot but damn all connected with bringing a group here merely to stir up dissension." Unmoved, Jones, along with a few other local dissenters, continued to speak out on behalf of CORE and the struggle for racial justice.

For most of the Chapel Hill community, the restoration of an uneasy truce between "university liberals" and the local segregationist majority represented an acceptable resolution of the crisis, but for some the unsettling influence of the CORE riders persisted. In late April, after Rustin returned to Chapel Hill to deliver two lectures on nonviolence, one in the basement of a Methodist church and a second in a university lecture hall, one local liberal, William McGirt, wrote a letter to the *Daily Tar Heel* praising Rustin as a "prophet" who had turned "a non-violent example of resistance" into "a dramatic symbol upon which racial minorities can seize to find their freedoms courageously but without debasing their spirits with anger." "These

Fellows of Reconciliation, many of whom have been in prison for their convictions," McGirt added, ". . . are the genuine creators of a new age."[60]

In the wake of the Chapel Hill incident, the CORE riders were somewhat apprehensive about the remaining ten days of the Journey. But whatever doubts they may have had about the wisdom of continuing the trip disappeared during a rousing mass meeting in Greensboro on Sunday evening. At the Shiloh Baptist Church—the same church that would welcome the Freedom Riders fourteen years later—the congregation's emotional embrace reminded them of why they had come south seeking justice. "The church was crowded to capacity and an atmosphere of excitement prevailed," Peck recalled in 1962. "Word had spread about what had happened to us and why we were late. . . . After the usual invocation, hymn-singing, scripture-reading, and prayer, Rustin, who is a particularly talented speaker, told our story. He interrupted it only to get one or another of us to rise and tell about a specific incident or experience. Then he continued. When he finished, the people in the crowded church came forward to shake hands and congratulate us. A number of women had tears in their eyes. A few shook my hand more than once."[61]

The mass meeting in Greensboro was the emotional high point of the Journey, and for most of the riders the last ten days on the road represented little more than a long anticlimax. There were, however, a few tense moments— and a few surprises—as the riders wound their way through the mountains of western North Carolina, Tennessee, Kentucky, and Virginia. No two bus drivers—and no two groups of passengers—were quite the same. On the way from Greensboro to Winston-Salem, a white passenger from South Carolina expressed his disgust that no one had removed Lynn from a front seat. "In my state," he declared, "he would either move or be killed." The following day, during a Greyhound run from Winston-Salem to Statesville, Nelson occupied a front seat without incident, but after the riders transferred to a Trailways bus in Statesville, the driver ordered him to the rear. Nelson explained that he was an interstate passenger protected by the *Morgan* decision, and the driver relented, but this did not satisfy several white passengers, including a soldier who demanded to know why Nelson had not been moved or arrested. "If you want to do something about this," the driver responded, "don't blame this man [Nelson]; kill those bastards up in Washington." Following several stops north of Asheville, the white section of the bus became so crowded that two white women had to stand in the aisle. When they asked why Nelson had not been forced to give up his seat, the driver cited the *Morgan* decision. Although the women later moved to the Jim Crow section in the back, the atmosphere on the bus remained tense. "It was a relief to reach Asheville," Houser recalled many years later.[62]

Asheville was the hometown of Joe Felmet, the young Southern Workers Defense League activist who had been arrested in Chapel Hill, and several of the riders spent the night at his parents' house. This did not please at least one neighbor, who shouted, "How're your nigger friends this morning?" as Felmet and the other riders left for the station. After the riders boarded a Trailways bus headed for Knoxville, Tennessee, a white woman complained to the driver that Dennis Banks, a black musician from Chicago who had just joined the Journey, was sitting in the whites-only section. When Banks, who was sitting next to Peck, politely refused to comply with the driver's order to move, the police were summoned. Twenty minutes of haggling over the law ensued before Banks was finally arrested. The police also arrested Peck, but only after he moved to the Jim Crow section, insisting that he be treated the same as his black traveling companion.

Brought before Judge Sam Cathey, a blind and notoriously hard-edged Asheville politician, the two defendants created a sensation by hiring Curtiss Todd to represent them in court. Neither Cathey nor the local prosecutor had ever heard of *Morgan*, and they had to borrow Todd's copy of the decision during the trial. An NAACP-affiliated attorney from Winston-Salem, Todd was the first black lawyer ever to practice in an Asheville courtroom. Despite this breach of local racial etiquette, Judge Cathey—who reminded the defendants that "we pride ourselves on our race relations here"—made sure that other shibboleths of Jim Crow justice remained in force. "In the courtroom where we were tried," Peck later declared, "I saw the most fantastic extreme of segregation in my experience—Jim Crow Bibles. Along the edges of one Bible had been printed in large letters the words 'white.' Along the page edges of the other Bible was the word 'colored.' When a white person swore in he simply raised his right hand while the clerk held the Bible. When a Negro swore in, he had to raise his right hand while holding the colored Bible in his left hand. The white clerk could not touch the colored Bible."[63]

The Jim Crow ethos did not prevent the white and black defendants from receiving the same sentence: thirty days on the road gang, the maximum under North Carolina law. But during a long night in the white section of the city jail, Peck discovered that many of his fellow inmates bore a special animus toward white agitators from the North. "Defending the niggers?" one oversized man bellowed, moving toward the rail-thin activist with his fists clenched. "They should have given you thirty years." Bracing himself for a blow, Peck blurted out: "I was just traveling with my friend and I happen to believe that men are equal." After an awkward silence, another inmate, playing the role of peacemaker, interjected: "Well, it's too bad that all men can't get along together, but they can't." With this puzzling statement the mood shifted, and the inmates decided to leave Peck alone. Banks had less trouble among the black inmates, some of whom regarded him as a hero. But both riders were relieved when Todd arrived with the required eight-hundred-dollar bail bond a few hours later.[64]

While Peck and Banks were detained in Asheville, the rest of the riders went on to Knoxville, where they welcomed three new riders: Homer Jack,

Nathan Wright, and Bill Worthy. A seasoned veteran of Chicago direct action campaigns, Jack could hardly wait to join the Journey, but he found the "taut morale" of his CORE colleagues a bit unnerving. "The whites were beginning to know the terror that many Negroes have to live with all the days of their lives," he noted. "All members of the party were dead-tired, not only from the constant tenseness, but also from participating in many meetings and conferences at every stop."[65]

Jack himself soon experienced the emotional highs and lows of direct action in the South. After a full day of interracial meetings in Knoxville, he and Wright tested compliance on the night Greyhound run to Nashville. With Houser serving as the designated observer, they sat in adjoining seats four rows behind the driver. "Slowly heads began to turn around and within five minutes the driver asked Wright to go to the back of the bus," Jack recalled. "Wright answered, 'I prefer to sit here.' I said I and Wright were friends, that we were riding together, that we could legally do so because of the *Morgan* decision. The bus driver then pleaded, 'Wouldn't you like to move?' We said we would like to stay where we were. The driver left the bus, apparently to talk to bus officials and police. After much ogling by passengers and bus employees . . . the driver finally reappeared and started the bus, without any more words to us." *So far so good*, Jack thought to himself, but as the bus left the outskirts of Knoxville he started to worry "that the hard part of the Journey was still ahead." Unaccustomed to the isolation of the rural South, he began to conjure up images of impending doom. "Ours was the first night test of the entire Journey," he later noted. "The southern night, to Northerners at least, is full of vigilante justice and the lynch rope from pine trees if not palms. We wondered whether . . . the bus company—or one of its more militant employees—would telephone ahead for a road block and vigilantes to greet us in one of the Tennessee mountain towns. Neither of us slept a moment that night. We just watched the road." When nothing of this sort actually happened, Jack felt more than a little foolish, concluding that the South, or at least Tennessee, was less benighted than he had been led to believe. "The reaction of the passengers on the trip was not one of evident anger," he observed, "and certainly not of violence. It was first surprise, then astonishment, and even tittering. On that bus, anyway, there was only apathy, certainly no eager leadership in preserving the ways of the Old South."

In Nashville, Jack and Wright—having arrived "early in the morning, exhausted, relieved, and with a bit of the exhilaration of the adventurer"—regaled several college classes with tales of nonviolent struggle. At the end of the day, just before midnight, they resumed their journey of discovery, boarding a train for Louisville. This was "the first train test" attempted by the CORE riders, and no one knew quite what to expect. When a conductor spied Jack and Wright sitting in adjoining reserved seats in a whites-only coach, he collected their tickets without comment, but he soon returned, whispering to Jack: "He's your prisoner, isn't he?" After Jack responded no, the incredulous conductor ordered Wright to "go back to the Jim Crow coach." Wright refused, citing *Morgan*, which prompted the conductor to mutter "that he never had had to face this situation before and that if we [Jack and Wright] were riding back in Alabama he wouldn't have to face it: the passengers would throw us both out the window." Despite this bluster, the conductor did not follow through with his threat to have them arrested when the train stopped in Bowling Green, and Wright remained in the white coach all the way to Louisville.[66]

A second team of riders traveled from Knoxville to Louisville by Greyhound, and they too escaped arrest. Worthy and Roodenko shared a seat in the front of the bus, and no one commented on the arrangement until they reached the small town of Corbin, a hundred miles north of Knoxville. When the young black journalist refused to move to the back, the driver called the police and "hinted that there would be violence from the crowd if Worthy did not move." However, the driver and the local police relented after one of the white passengers, a woman from Tennessee, defended Worthy's legal right to sit wherever he pleased. Once again there was hard evidence that at least some white Southerners were willing to accept desegregated transit.[67]

Several of the riders, including Jack and Wright, left the Journey in Louisville on April 19, but approximately half of the riders participated in the final four days of testing, as three small groups of riders converged on Washington. Although most of these concluding bus and train trips were uneventful, there were two arrests in western Virginia, Nelson in Amherst and Banks in Culpepper. In both cases, the drivers and law enforcement officers involved displayed confusion about the law and some reluctance to follow through with actual arrests, suggesting that Virginia officials were still trying to sort out the implications of *Morgan*. And, despite the arrests, the behavior of several bystanders indicated that race relations in Virginia were changing. In Culpepper, one courageous black woman who sold bus tickets at a local concession stand boarded the bus and offered to help Banks in any way she could, and two local whites spoke out on Banks's behalf. "If I had been you I would have fought them before letting them take me off the bus," one of them told Banks, as the young musician calmly went off to jail.[68]

FOR THE RIDERS, the return to Washington on April 23 brought a sense of relief—and a measure of pride in their perseverance. To their disappointment, however, there was no public event to mark the conclusion of a remarkable collective experience. "At the end of our Journey," Peck recalled in 1962, "there were no reporters flocking around us to ask whether it had been worth it or whether we would do it again—as they did after the Freedom Ride fourteen years later. If there had been, most of us would have answered yes." The Journey's official balance sheet, as reported by CORE, listed twenty-six tests of compliance, twelve arrests, and only one act of violent resistance, but the project's accomplishments drew little attention from the mainstream press in the spring of 1947. Even among white reporters interested in racial matters, the Journey could not compete with the unfolding drama of Jackie Robinson's first few weeks in a Brooklyn Dodgers uniform.[69]

In the black press, the Journey fared much better, of course, especially in the columns of the two black reporters who accompanied the riders during the first week of the trip. Ollie Stewart of the *Baltimore Afro-American*, who witnessed the confrontation in Chapel Hill and the mass meeting in Greensboro, hailed the Journey as a watershed event. "For my part, I am glad to have had even a small part in the project—even that of an observer," he wrote in late April. "History was definitely made. White and colored persons, when the whole thing was explained to them as they sat in their seats on several occasions, will never forget what they heard (or saw). The white couple who went to the very back seat and sat between colored passengers, the white marine who slept while a colored woman sat beside him, the white Southern girl who, when her mother wouldn't take a seat in the rear, exclaimed 'I do not care, I'm tired'—all these people now have an awareness of the problem. The Journey of Reconciliation, with whites and colored traveling and sleeping and eating together, to my way of thinking, made the solution of segregation seem far simpler than it ever had before. I heard one man refer to the group as pioneers. I think he had something there. They wrote a new page in the history of America."[70]

In the weeks and months following the Journey, several riders published reports on their recent experiences in the South. Rustin and Houser—in CORE's official report, *We Challenged Jim Crow*—offered both a day-by-day narrative and general commentary on what the Journey had revealed. "The one word which most universally describes the attitude of police, of passengers, and of the Negro and white bus riders is 'confusion,' " they concluded. "Persons taking part in the psychological struggle in the buses and trains either did not know of the *Morgan* decision or, if they did, possessed no clear understanding of it." Yet there were clear indications that the confusion could be alleviated. "Much was gained when someone in our group took the lead in discussion with bus drivers or train conductors and when police appeared," they reported, adding: "As the trip progressed it became evident that the police and the bus drivers were learning about the Irene Morgan decision as word of the 'test cases' was passed from city to city and from driver to driver." To Rustin and Houser, the Journey demonstrated "the need for incidents as 'teaching techniques.' " "It is our belief that without direct action on the part of groups and individuals, the Jim Crow pattern in the South cannot be broken," they insisted. "We are equally certain that such action must be nonviolent." Homer Jack, writing in the Unitarian magazine *Common Ground*, offered a similar assessment. "What, finally, did the Journey of Reconciliation accomplish?" he asked rhetorically, answering: "It showed progressive Americans that the *Morgan* decision must be implemented by constant 'testing'—in the spirit of goodwill—and by subsequent law enforcement. The Journey helped implement the decision at least by spreading knowledge of it to bus drivers and some law-enforcement officers (both policemen and judges) in the upper South. The Journey also showed whites and Negroes living in that area that the *Morgan* decision could be enforced without disastrous results, if the proper psychological and legal techniques were used. The Journey gave these techniques—and accompanying inspiration—to thousands of whites and Negroes in the South."[71]

As they wrote these and other reflections, Rustin, Houser, and Jack were well aware of the unfinished business in the courts. Six separate incidents during the Journey had produced twelve arrests, the legal and financial consequences of which were still looming in late April 1947. Fortunately, local officials had already dropped the charges against the three men arrested in Durham, and in May the district attorney in Asheville did the same when Curtiss Todd appealed the convictions of Peck and Banks. The three Virginia arrests were under review by the state supreme court, which would eventually rule in favor of the riders. Thus CORE's major concern was the fate of the four men arrested in Chapel Hill.[72]

On May 20 two of the four defendants—Rustin and Roodenko—went on trial in the Chapel Hill Recorder's Court. Judge Henry Whitfield, a hard-line segregationist, made no effort to hide his contempt for the defendants' three NAACP attorneys: C. Jerry Gates, Herman Taylor, and Edward Avant. After the local prosecuting attorney, T. J. Phipps, delivered "a lengthy argument to show that the Negroes really want jimcrow," the judge approvingly issued a guilty verdict, assessing Rustin court costs and sentencing Roodenko to thirty days on a road gang. Explaining the differential treatment, he termed Rustin "a poor misled nigra from the North" who bore less responsibility than white agitators who should know better, and later added a dash of anti-Semitism to his admonition. "I presume you're Jewish, Mr. Rodenky," drawled the judge. "Well, it's about time you Jews from New York learned that you can't come down here bringing your nigras with you to upset the customs of the South." NAACP attorneys immediately filed an appeal with the superior court in nearby Hillsboro, but a month later Felmet and Johnson received even harsher sentences from Judge Whitfield. Johnson was fined fifty dollars and court costs, while Felmet, as a native Southerner and latter-day scalawag, was sentenced to six months on the road gang, six times the maximum allowed by law. When the prosecutor pointed out the error, Whitfield reluctantly reduced Felmet's sentence to thirty days, remarking: "I can't keep all these things in my little head."[73]

In March 1948, after summarily rejecting the defendants' claimed status as interstate passengers, Superior Court Judge Chester Morris ruled that all four deserved uniform thirty-day sentences. NAACP attorneys quickly filed an appeal with the North Carolina Supreme Court, but ten months later, in January 1949, the state's highest court, as expected, upheld the convictions and ordered the four men to return to North Carolina to serve their sentences.

Rustin and Houser welcomed this ruling as the basis for an appeal to the United States Supreme Court—an appeal that would clarify and extend the nearly three-year-old *Morgan* decision—but it soon became all too apparent that NAACP leaders had no interest in filing any further appeals. Financially strapped and preoccupied with school desegregation cases and other legal challenges to Jim Crow—including the high-profile case of Norvell Lee, an Olympic boxer and Howard University student who had tried to desegregate a whites-only railway coach in northern Virginia—the NAACP national office informed CORE and FOR leaders that it could neither fund nor participate in an appeal of the North Carolina Supreme Court's decision. The NAACP claimed that a further appeal was useless because defense attorneys could no longer prove that the defendants were interstate travelers. "The black lawyer who had the ticket stubs, proving that you were interstate passengers, now claims he has lost the stubs," Roy Wilkins, the NAACP's assistant executive secretary, confessed to Rustin, "although we believe he was paid to destroy them." Rustin and others suspected that the NAACP's recalcitrance involved much more than lost ticket stubs, but there was nothing they could do to remedy the situation.[74]

NAACP attorneys had never been easy to work with, and earlier disagreements over funding and strategy had prompted FOR to form an internal committee to oversee the Chapel Hill case. Some members of the committee had actually welcomed the NAACP's disengagement, preferring to keep the struggle outside the courts. Thus they were relieved when the defendants' options were reduced to three choices: seeking a gubernatorial pardon, fighting extradition, or surrendering voluntarily to North Carolina authorities. After it became clear that a pardon was highly unlikely, the committee decided that the best means of demonstrating CORE's commitment to nonviolence was to accept the sentences. Although Andrew Johnson, who was then finishing his senior year at the University of Cincinnati, declined to return to North Carolina, confessing that he was "both mentally and physically unprepared to serve thirty days on the road gang," the other three defendants embraced the committee's decision. Having just returned from a three-month tour of Europe and India, where he lectured on nonviolence and American race relations and met with Gandhi's son Devadas, Rustin predicted that his impending imprisonment would help to expose the hypocrisy of America's democratic pretensions. "Our conviction, unfortunately, is one more demonstration to the colored majority of the world of the failure of American democracy," he declared upon arriving in New York. "America cannot maintain its leadership in the struggle for world democracy as long as the conditions exist which caused our arrest and conviction. We don't fool anybody. People abroad know and are losing faith."[75]

On March 21, 1949, Rustin, Felmet, and Roodenko surrendered to authorities at the Orange County Courthouse in Hillsboro, North Carolina. Assigned to the state prison camp at Roxboro, they braced themselves for thirty days of harsh punishment and humiliation. The actual sentence turned out to be only twenty-two days, thanks to an early release for good behavior, and all three men survived the ordeal. But their experiences with inhumane conditions and brutal guards at Roxboro, especially Rustin's, soon became the stuff of legend among movement activists. Following his release in mid-April, Rustin wrote "Twenty-two Days on a Chain Gang," a searing memoir of his incarceration that was later serialized in the *New York Post* and the *Baltimore Afro-American*. Laced with dark humor—including an account of Rustin's dealings with a prison guard who kept reminding him, "You ain't in Yankeeland now. We don't like no Yankee ways"—the piece shocked many readers and eventually led to a legislative investigation of conditions in North Carolina's prison camps.[76]

This unexpected benefit pleased Rustin and his CORE colleagues, but as the decade drew to a close it was all too obvious that the Journey of Reconciliation's primary objective remained unfulfilled. While the first freedom ride had demonstrated the viability of nonviolent direct action in the Upper South, it had not precipitated wholesale desegregation or even protest on a mass scale. With few exceptions, company rules and social inertia still kept the races apart on interstate buses and trains, and no one, other than a few die-hard optimists, expected the situation to change anytime soon. As it had done so many times in the past, the shape-shifting monster known as Jim Crow had adapted to changing legal and political realities without sacrificing the cold heart of racial discrimination. Irene Morgan and the CORE activists who followed her lead would have to wait a bit longer for the day of jubilee.[77]

2

Beside the Weary Road

And ye, beneath life's crushing load, Whose forms are bending low,
Who toil along the climbing way With painful steps and slow,
Look now! For glad and golden hours Come swiftly on the wing:
O rest beside the weary road, And hear the angels sing.

   —from the hymn "It Came Upon the Midnight Clear"[1]

DESPITE THE STUBBORN PERSISTENCE of segregated travel in the late 1940s, most CORE activists regarded the Journey of Reconciliation as a qualified success. Some even talked of organizing a series of interracial rides and other direct action challenges to Jim Crow in the Deep South. Speaking at an April 1948 Council Against Intolerance in America dinner in New York, Bayard Rustin hailed the Journey as the first of many interracial bus rides and "a training ground for similar peaceful projects against discrimination in employment and the armed services." At the time, neither he nor anyone else in CORE suspected that more than a decade would pass before even one more "freedom ride" materialized.

During the early 1950s CORE and the broader nonviolent movement entered a period of steady decline. As Jim Peck later recalled, "These were CORE's lean years—the years when social consciences throughout the United States were numbed by the infection of McCarthyism." In the 1960s civil rights advocates of all persuasions would become adept at turning the Cold War to their advantage by pointing out the international vulnerability of a nation that failed to practice what it preached on matters of race and democracy. But this was not the case in the 1950s, before the decolonization of Africa and Asia heightened State Department sensitivity to public opinion in the "colored" nations of the Third World. Plagued by anti-radical repression, an uncertain relationship with the Fellowship of Reconciliation, and nagging factionalism,

CORE lost its momentum and most of its active membership by mid-decade. As the cautious optimism of the immediate postwar era dissolved into a struggle for organizational and ideological survival, several of CORE's early stalwarts, including Rustin and Farmer, redirected their energies elsewhere. Outside of the Baltimore and St. Louis chapters there was little activity or enthusiasm, and to make matters worse, the beleaguered FOR withdrew most of its financial support in 1953, forcing the resignation of executive director George Houser, technically an FOR staff member on loan to CORE.[2]

Following Houser's departure in early 1954, the burden of leadership fell upon the shoulders of Peck, the editor of the organization's newsletter *CORE-lator*, and Billie Ames, a talented and energetic St. Louis woman who served as CORE's national group coordinator. In the summer of 1954, Ames tried to revive CORE's flagging spirit by proposing a "Ride for Freedom," a second Journey of Reconciliation that would recapture the momentum of the organization's glory days. Ames planned to challenge segregated railway coaches and terminals as far south as Birmingham, but the project collapsed when the NAACP, which had provided legal support for the original 1947 freedom ride, refused to cooperate. Arguing that an impending Interstate Commerce Commission ruling made the "Ride for Freedom" unnecessary, NAACP leaders advised CORE to devote its attention "to some other purpose." This disappointment, combined with continuing factionalism and dissension, brought CORE to the verge of dissolution. After personal problems forced Billie Ames to leave in March 1955, some wondered if the organization would last the year. In desperation, the delegates to the 1955 national convention voted to hire a national field organizer with experience in the South. Encouraged by the formation of a small student chapter in Nashville earlier in the year, many regarded the South as CORE's last best hope. Even though the potential for successful nonviolent direct action in the region was unproven, the organization had few options at this point.[3]

In early December 1955, during the same fateful week that witnessed the arrest of Rosa Parks—a forty-three-year-old black seamstress and NAACP leader who refused to give up her seat on a Montgomery, Alabama, bus— LeRoy Carter became CORE's first national field organizer. A former NAACP field secretary with twenty years of experience in the civil rights struggle, Carter seemed well suited to the task of spreading the CORE philosophy to the South. Soft-spoken and deliberate, yet full of determination, he could have been an important asset to the cause of nonviolent resistance in the Deep South, especially during the early weeks of the bus boycott triggered by Parks's arrest. Led by Dr. Martin Luther King Jr.—the charismatic twenty-six-year-old minister of Montgomery's Dexter Avenue Baptist Church and newly elected president of the Montgomery Improvement Association (MIA)—the boycotters faced an uphill struggle against local white supremacists and were in desperate need of help. Unfortunately for King and the MIA, the national leadership of CORE was slow to react to the unexpected events in Alabama and did not dispatch Carter to Montgomery until late March 1956. Despite its obvious affinity for what was happening in Alabama, CORE did not rush to embrace the Montgomery movement and made no attempt to associate itself with the MIA during the first three months of the boycott. Convinced that the Montgomery protest would soon collapse, CORE activists worried that the boycotters' untutored efforts would do more harm than good by seemingly demonstrating the futility of direct action in the Deep South. When James Robinson, CORE's finance secretary, composed a fund-raising letter in early February highlighting the potential for direct action in the South, he avoided any mention of the controversial bus boycott in Montgomery.[4]

Such disdain all but disappeared in late February, of course, when the mass arrest of boycott leaders, including King and several dozen other black ministers, turned the Montgomery protest into front-page news and a national cause célèbre. Realizing that they had misjudged the situation, embarrassed CORE leaders scurried to make up for lost time. On February 22 a group of local CORE enthusiasts organized a Montgomery chapter, and a month later the national council of CORE adopted a resolution commending the boycotters "for their vision, courage, and steadfastness of purpose in

Rosa Parks is fingerprinted by a Montgomery, Alabama, policeman in February 1956, following the mass indictment of MIA leaders. (Library of Congress)

sustaining a significant struggle against a great evil, and at the same time pioneering in the mass use in this country of a technique and spirit which holds unlimited promise for use elsewhere against oppression." The council also voted to send Carter to Montgomery.

In early April, Carter spent several days conferring with King and other MIA leaders, but it soon became evident that he had arrived too late to exert any measurable influence on the Montgomery movement. While the boycotters welcomed CORE's support, they were understandably wary of an organization that presumed to teach them the "rules" of nonviolent protest. Even King, who knew something about CORE's long-standing commitment to direct action, had mixed feelings about what appeared to be a belated and opportunistic attempt to capitalize on the boycotters' struggle. To his surprise, when the spring 1956 issue of *CORE-lator* ran a picture of MIA officials standing on the steps of the Holt Street Baptist Church, it identified them as the "leaders of the CORE-type protest in Montgomery." In the accompanying story, editor Jim Peck proclaimed that "the CORE technique of non-violence has been spotlighted to the entire world through the effective protest action which the Montgomery Improvement Association has been conducting since December 5." And in an adjoining column, Peck proudly quoted a *New York Post* article that reminded the world that CORE had employed Gandhian techniques "long before Montgomery joined the passive resistance movement."[5]

For Peck, as for most CORE veterans, the "miracle of Montgomery" was a bittersweet development. Having suffered through the lean years of the early 1950s, when nonviolent resistance was routinely dismissed as an irrelevant pipe dream, they could not help viewing the boycott with a mixture of pride and jealousy. "I had labored a decade and a half in the vineyards of nonviolence," Jim Farmer explained in his 1985 memoir. "Now, out of nowhere, someone comes and harvests the grapes and drinks the wine." He, along with most of his colleagues, eventually overcame such feelings, acknowledging that Montgomery gave nonviolence a new legitimacy and probably saved CORE from extinction. As he put it: "No longer did we have to explain nonviolence to people. Thanks to Martin Luther King, it was a household word." But such graciousness was the product of years of reflection and common struggle. In the uncertain atmosphere of the mid-1950s, charity did not come so easily, even among men and women who had dedicated their lives to social justice.[6]

The Montgomery Bus Boycott was an important connecting link between the nonviolent movement of the 1940s and the freedom struggle of the 1960s. And it was also part of a great historical divide. Along with the *Brown* decision, the rise of massive resistance in the white South, and other related developments of the 1950s, the boycott and the subsequent emergence of the Southern Christian Leadership Conference (SCLC) radically altered the context of racial and regional conflict. Even more important, the 1950s was an era of broad and deep social change. In the international arena, the passing of the Stalinist regime, the escalating tensions of the Cold War, the nuclear arms race, the economic recovery of Europe, and the decolonization of the Third World brought a new tone to world affairs. The pace of change was equally dramatic on the domestic front, as significant shifts in political, legal, and popular culture transformed the nature of American life. The anti-Communist excesses of McCarthyism, the "rights revolution" initiated by the Warren Court, the proliferation of television, the growing influence of consumerism and corporate power, the emergence of a distinct youth culture that found expression in the racially subversive medium of rock 'n' roll, the desegregation of professional sports and the entertainment industry, and the massive postwar migration of blacks to the North and whites to the suburbs all contributed to this transformation. In many cases, the full impact of these changes did not become manifest until the mid-1960s, but the relative calm of the Eisenhower years should not obscure the shifting realities that the fifties represented—realities that helped to lay the groundwork for the social upheavals of the following decade.

As difficult as they are to unravel, the themes of continuity and discontinuity are an important part of the Freedom Rider story. The celebrated Freedom Rides of 1961 represented a reprise of the lesser-known Journey of Reconciliation of 1947, and the tactics, guiding philosophy, organizational roots, and goals of these two experiments in nonviolent resistance were strikingly similar. Yet the impact—and the ultimate meaning—of the two historical episodes could hardly have been more different. While the Journey brought about little change and was soon forgotten by all but a handful of nonviolent activists, the Freedom Rides triggered a major political crisis that forced the federal government to fulfill an unkept promise to desegregate public transit, revitalizing the nonviolent movement and bringing direct action to the forefront of a widening struggle. This contrast in consequences can be traced to a number of factors, including chance and a web of contingency, but the relative success of the Freedom Rides was largely a function of historical context. America—and the world—was a different place in 1961, especially with respect to expectations of racial and social change. For those who dreamed of a nonviolent transformation of American race relations, there were new strands of experience and hope that subverted the moral authority of white culture—strands from which the fabric of the modern civil rights movement was woven. To understand how the seemingly overmatched activists of CORE marshaled enough courage and conviction to launch the Freedom Rides, we need to take a close look at what happened to the civil rights struggle between 1955 and 1961—first in Montgomery, and later in other centers of racial insurgency.[7]

CORE's FORMAL INVOLVEMENT in the Montgomery Bus Boycott never amounted to much, but this was not the case with CORE's parent organization. Largely through the efforts of Bayard Rustin, FOR exerted a powerful influence on the emerging historical, political, and ideological consciousness of King and other MIA leaders. The first national civil rights leader to grasp the full significance of what was happening in Montgomery, Rustin thrust himself into the center of the struggle. He wanted the boycotters to broaden their philosophical horizons and to feel the pride and responsibility of being part of a worldwide movement for human rights. Styling himself a Gandhian sage, he became convinced that he was the one person who could show them how to make the most of an extraordinary opportunity. Though virtually unknown to the general public, he was a revered figure in the international subculture of Gandhian intellectuals. No one who met him could fail to be impressed by the quality of his mind and his deep commitment to nonviolence, not to mention his boundless energy. Those who knew him well, however, were painfully aware of another side of his life. In an age when homosexuality was associated with social and political subversion, his personal life was a source of concern and embarrassment for FOR, a fragile organization that could ill afford a major scandal. After several encounters with the vice squad and a stern reprimand from the normally placid A. J. Muste, Rustin promised to behave, but in June 1953 an arrest for lewd and lascivious behavior in Pasadena, California, led to a thirty-day jail term and his resignation from the FOR staff. By the time he returned to New York to pick up the pieces of his life, even some of his closest friends had concluded that the nonviolent movement might be better off without him. Although he soon found a haven at the War Resisters League, which offered him a position as executive secretary, Rustin's career as an influential activist appeared to be over. He, of course, felt otherwise. All he needed was a chance to redeem himself, an opportunity to use his hard-earned wisdom to demonstrate the liberating power of nonviolence. Amazingly, he would soon find what he was looking for—not in New York or Chicago or any of the other cities that had witnessed the courage of FOR and CORE activists, but rather in the faraway streets of Montgomery.[8]

Soon after the boycott began, the radical white Southern novelist Lillian Smith, who had once served on the national board of FOR, wired Rustin and urged him to offer his assistance to King and the MIA. If someone with experience in Gandhian tactics could bring his knowledge to bear on the situation, she suggested, the boycotters might have a real chance to sustain their movement. Rustin had never been to Alabama, but as he pondered Smith's suggestion and mulled over the early news reports on the boycott, a bold plan began to take shape. If he could find a sponsor, he would "fly to Montgomery with the idea of getting the bus boycott temporarily called off"; then, with the help of FOR, he would organize "a workshop or school for nonviolence with a goal of 100 young Negro men who will then promote it not only in Montgomery but elsewhere in the South." In early January he shared his thoughts with several friends at FOR but found little enthusiasm for his plan. Charles Lawrence, FOR's national chairman, not only questioned the wisdom of suspending an ongoing protest but also worried "that it would be easy for the police to frame him [Rustin] with his record in L.A. and New York, and set back the whole cause there." FOR executive director John Swomley shared Lawrence's concern, as did the socialist leader Norman Thomas, who thought Rustin was "entirely too vulnerable on his record." "This young King is doing well. Bayard is considered a homosexual, a Communist and a draft dodger. Why do you put such a burden on King?" Thomas asked.[9]

Eventually Rustin found a more sympathetic audience in Phil Randolph and Jim Farmer, but even they had strong misgivings about dispatching a homosexual ex-Communist to a conservative Deep South city. Though he admired Rustin's bravado, Randolph agreed to fund the trip only after it became clear that his old friend was prepared to hitchhike to Montgomery if necessary. After a telephone call to King confirmed that the MIA would welcome Rustin's visit, only the details needed to be worked out. Rustin wanted Bob Gilmore of the American Friends Service Committee to accompany him and to act as a liaison with the white community in Montgomery. Randolph and Farmer, fearing that an interracial team would be too conspicuous, turned instead to Bill Worthy, a thirty-four-year old black reporter for the *Baltimore Afro-American*. A seasoned activist, Worthy had participated in a number of FOR and CORE campaigns, including the Journey of Reconciliation. Nevertheless, the decision to send him to Montgomery as Rustin's unofficial chaperone was one that Randolph and Farmer would later regret. In 1954 Worthy had raised the hackles of the State Department with a series of sympathetic stories on the Soviet Union, and his presence in Montgomery only served to exacerbate the fear that Communists had infiltrated the MIA.[10]

As fate would have it, Rustin and Worthy arrived in Montgomery on Tuesday, February 21, the day of the mass indictments. The MIA office was in chaos. Rustin asked to speak to King but was told that the MIA president was in Nashville, preaching at Fisk University. At this point no one in the MIA, other than King, had the faintest idea who Rustin was. Nevertheless, he soon talked his way into the office of King's close friend, the Reverend Ralph Abernathy, who after a brief conversation warned his visitor that Montgomery was a dangerous place for an unarmed black activist. Undaunted, Rustin found his way to E. D. Nixon, a longtime and seemingly fearless NAACP and Brotherhood of Sleeping Car Porters activist, who became an instant ally after Rustin produced a letter of introduction from Randolph. For more than an hour, Nixon briefed Rustin on the boycotters' situation, which was obviously growing more perilous by the day. "They can bomb us out and they can kill us," he vowed, "but we are not going to give in." For a time Rustin simply listened, but when Nixon confessed that he was not sure how the boycotters should respond to the mass indictments, the veteran activist promptly suggested the Gandhian option of voluntarily filling the jails. As Rustin laid out the rationale for nonviolent martyrdom, Nixon became intrigued, and the next morning he became the first boycott leader to turn himself in. "Are you looking for me?" he asked a stunned sheriff's deputy.

"Well, here I am." Once the news of Nixon's arrest got out, there was a virtual stampede at the county courthouse, as scores of black leaders joined in the ritual of self-sacrifice. Through it all Rustin was on the scene, dispensing advice and encouragement and basking in the knowledge that, although he had been in Montgomery for less than a day, he had already made a difference. Even Worthy, who had seen his friend in action many times before, was impressed, though he worried that this early triumph would feed Rustin's reckless spirit and ultimately lead to trouble.[11]

Trouble was not long in coming. On Wednesday evening, after attending a rousing prayer meeting at Dexter Avenue Baptist Church, Rustin decided to pay a visit to Jeanette Reece, who a week earlier had been frightened into dropping her legal challenge to segregated buses. To Rustin's surprise, Reece's home was under police surveillance. As he approached the front door, he was immediately accosted by gun-waving white policemen who demanded to know who he was. Rustin assured them that he just wanted to talk to Reece and that he meant her no harm. The officers continued to press him for some identification. On the verge of being arrested, he blurted out: "I am Bayard Rustin; I am here as a journalist working for *Le Figaro* and the *Manchester Guardian*." This seemed to satisfy the policemen, who granted him a brief interview with Reece, but the impromptu cover story would later come to haunt him.

Having narrowly escaped arrest, a somewhat chastened Rustin finally met Dr. King on Thursday morning, following the boycott leader's booking at the county courthouse. Surrounded by dozens of reporters and a throng of cheering supporters, King had little time to greet visitors, but at Nixon's urging he invited Rustin to a late-morning strategy session of the MIA executive committee. At the session, Rustin was impressed by King's intelligent, forthright leadership, and he was thrilled when the committee voted to turn the MIA's traditional mass meetings into prayer meetings. After King and his colleagues agreed that all future meetings would center around five prayers, including "a prayer for those who oppose us," he knew that he had underestimated his Southern hosts.

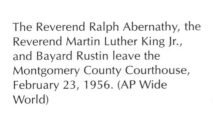

The Reverend Ralph Abernathy, the Reverend Martin Luther King Jr., and Bayard Rustin leave the Montgomery County Courthouse, February 23, 1956. (AP Wide World)

In their own untutored way, he now realized, the boycotters had already begun to master the art of moral warfare. Although he still had doubts about the depth of the MIA's commitment to nonviolence, his original plan for a temporary suspension of the boycott no longer seemed realistic or necessary. As he told King later that afternoon, in all his travels, even in India and Africa, he had never witnessed anything comparable to the Montgomery movement. The boycotters' accomplishments were already remarkable. With a little help from the outside—with the proper publicity, with a disciplined and carefully constructed long-range strategy, and with enough funds to hold out against the die-hard segregationists—the Montgomery story could become a beacon for nonviolent activists everywhere. To this end, he and his friends at FOR were ready to help in any way they could. Though still a bit puzzled by this strange visitor from New York, King thanked Rustin for his gracious offer and invited him to the MIA's Thursday evening prayer meeting at the First Baptist Church.

What Rustin witnessed that evening confirmed his growing optimism. The meeting at First Baptist was the first mass gathering since the arrests, and the spirit that poured out of the overflow crowd was like nothing Rustin had ever seen. When the ninety indicted leaders gathered around the pulpit to open the meeting, the sanctuary exploded with emotion. As Rustin later described the scene:

> Overnight these leaders had become symbols of courage. Women held their babies to touch them. The people stood in ovation. Television cameras ground away, as King was finally able to open the meeting. He began: "We are not struggling merely for the right of Negroes but for all the people of Montgomery, black and white. We are determined to make America a better place for all people. Ours is a non-violent protest. We pray God that no man shall use arms."

Near the close of the meeting, one of the speakers seized the moment to declare that Friday would be a "Double-P Day," a time for prayer and pilgrimage; the car pools would be suspended, private cars would be left at home, and everyone would walk. This gesture was almost too much for Rustin, who after years of lonely struggle could hardly believe what he was witnessing. Later that evening he called John Swomley in New York and breathlessly related what he had seen. The Montgomery movement had unlimited potential, he reported, but the boycotters were in desperate need of assistance— not only money for legal fees but also veteran activists who could teach them the finer points of nonviolence. In the short run, he would do what he could, but he urged Swomley to alert Muste and Randolph that a full mobilization of resources was in order.

True to his word, Rustin maintained a hectic schedule in the days that followed. On Friday and Saturday, he discussed strategy with the executive committee, sat in on a meeting of the car pool committee, survived an awkward interview with Robert Hughes, the executive director of the Alabama

Council on Human Relations, and even helped a group of volunteers design a new logo for the MIA. The climax of his whirlwind tour came on
Sunday, when he spent most of the day with King. The day began with
morning services at Dexter, where the young minister preached a moving
sermon on the philosophy of nonviolence. "We are concerned not merely
to win justice in the buses," King explained, "but rather to behave in a new
and different way—to be non-violent so that we may remove injustice itself, both from society and from ourselves." Later, during a private dinner
at the parsonage, King briefed Rustin on the boycott. Rustin listened attentively, but as the evening progressed he began to regale his hosts with
tales of Harlem and the Northern underground. Coretta Scott King, who
suddenly recalled that she had heard Rustin speak at Antioch College in
the early 1950s, was utterly charmed, and her husband was captivated by
his guest's sweeping vision of social justice. For several hours Rustin and
the Kings discussed religion, pacifism, nonviolent resistance, and other moral
imperatives, and by the end of the evening a deep philosophical and personal bond had been sealed. Despite periodic disagreements over strategy
and a serious falling-out in the early 1960s, they would remain close friends
until King's assassination in 1968.[12]

Not everyone in the MIA was so enamored with the strange visitor from
New York. Within hours of Rustin's arrival, there were complaints about
"outside agitators" and rumors that subversives were trying to take over the
Montgomery movement. Even those who dismissed these fears as ground-
less worried about the MIA's credibility and public image. Despite the recent
eclipse of Senator Joseph McCarthy, fear of Communist infiltration was still
rife in the United States, even among black Americans. No popular movement could afford the taint of Communism, especially in a state where the
Scottsboro case was a relatively recent memory. In Deep South communities
like Montgomery, smooth-talking outsiders like Rustin were always a little
suspect, but any chance he had of gaining broad acceptance ended when he
posed as a European correspondent. When word got around that the editors
of *Le Figaro* and the *Manchester Guardian* had never heard of him, Rustin's
situation in Montgomery became precarious. Several of the national reporters covering the mass indictment story knew the true identity and background
of both Rustin and Worthy, and the inevitable murmurings soon alerted the
local press and police. Rustin was having the time of his life and was determined to hang on as long as he could, but by the end of his first week in town,
there were enough cold stares and wary handshakes to convince him that his
days in Montgomery were numbered. Reluctantly he informed Swomley and
the FOR staff that sooner or later he would need a replacement. Swomley,
who had opposed Rustin's venture from the outset, needed no prodding to
send one. Indeed, Glenn Smiley, FOR's national field secretary, was already
on his way to Montgomery.[13]

Smiley and Rustin were old friends and compatriots, but they were strikingly different in style and temperament. Though he was roughly the same

age as Rustin and shared his colleague's pacifist faith, Smiley came from a radically different world. A soft-spoken Texan with a wry smile, he grew up in the cattle country west of Fort Worth, attended an all-white Methodist college in Abilene, and entered the ministry in his early twenties. A strong belief in pacifism and a commitment to the social gospel led him to the FOR in 1942, and for the next twelve years he worked as FOR's southwestern field secretary, operating mostly in southern California and Arizona. Like Rustin, he served a federal prison term for draft evasion during World War II, emerging from the ordeal with a renewed faith in nonviolent resistance. After the war he worked with pacifists, labor organizers, and civil libertarians across the Southwest, lectured for FOR in Mexico and Europe, and barely survived the ravages of Cold War inquisition. Named FOR's national field secretary in 1954, he redirected his attention to the East Coast. His first foray into the Deep South came in November 1955, when he went to Orangeburg, South Carolina, to aid a black boycott of local white businesses. Unfortunately, his experience in Orangeburg, where a counter-boycott by the White Citizens' Council threatened blacks with unemployment and starvation, was a sobering introduction to the repressive atmosphere of the post-*Brown* South and a preview of what he would encounter in Montgomery.[14]

By the time Smiley arrived in Montgomery on February 27, Rustin's situation had become untenable. The FBI, the local police, and several suspicious reporters were following his every move, and there were rumors that he would soon be arrested for inciting to riot. *Le Figaro* had offered a reward to anyone who could identify the impostor posing as its correspondent, and there was increasing pressure from Emory Jackson, a black newspaper editor from Birmingham who knew about Rustin's—and Worthy's—background. Appalled by King's apparent lack of concern about left-wing infiltration, Jackson threatened to publish an exposé if MIA leaders failed to expel the Northern intruders. All of this alarmed E. D. Nixon, who phoned Phil Randolph for an explanation. Randolph assured Nixon that Rustin was a trusted associate and an asset to the movement, but he was deeply troubled by Nixon's call. The following morning a hastily assembled group of twenty civil rights leaders met in Randolph's New York office to decide what to do about Rustin's maverick crusade. Thomas, Swomley, Farmer, and nearly everyone else present concluded that Rustin had outlived his usefulness in Montgomery. The crisisborn meeting also forced the leaders to reevaluate their potential role in the Montgomery protest. As Swomley wrote to Smiley on February 29: "It was the conviction yesterday that we should not try from the North to train or otherwise run the non-violent campaign in Montgomery, as Bayard had hoped to do, but rather to expect them to indicate ways in which we could be of help. Only Bayard's roommate argued for his staying in the South. Phil Randolph indicated that the Montgomery leaders had managed thus far more successfully than any of our 'so-called non-violence experts' a mass resistance campaign and we should learn from them rather than assume we know it all."

Smiley had strict instructions to avoid public association—or even private contact—with Rustin while he was in Montgomery; no one, not even the leadership of the MIA, was to know that they shared the same organizational sponsors. But on Wednesday morning Smiley ran into Rustin and Worthy at MIA headquarters. This chance encounter gave Rustin the opportunity to brief Smiley on his activities. To Smiley's relief, King was the only MIA leader to witness the meeting. Nevertheless, when FOR officials learned of the encounter later in the day, the pressure to get Rustin and Worthy out of Montgomery took on a new urgency. After consulting with representatives of FOR and several other civil rights organizations, Randolph phoned Rustin and begged him to leave. At first Rustin pleaded for a few more days in Montgomery, but in the end, realizing that he had pushed his patron to the limit and confident that Smiley would carry on in his absence, he relented. After a round of bittersweet good-byes, he and Worthy set out for Birmingham, where the trial of Autherine Lucy, a young black woman seeking admission to the University of Alabama, was about to begin. Rustin's role in the boycott was far from over, as he continued to advise King and the MIA, both by phone and in periodic meetings in Birmingham. but it would be several weeks before he returned to Montgomery. With King's blessing, he spent most of the spring and summer of 1956 in New York publicizing the boycott and trying to raise funds for the MIA.[15]

FOLLOWING RUSTIN'S DEPARTURE, Smiley worked tirelessly to expand FOR's role in the bus boycott. During the remainder of the boycott, he shuttled in and out of Montgomery, sometimes staying for weeks at a time. At first some boycott leaders were understandably suspicious of the inquisitive white stranger with the Texas twang, but it did not take him long to endear himself to the MIA staff. He grew especially close to King and Abernathy, whom he engaged in lengthy discussions of movement strategy and moral philosophy, and his wry humor and gentle prodding on behalf of nonviolence eventually disarmed even his toughest critics.[16]

Smiley, in turn, came to respect and admire his MIA hosts, though he often fretted about what he perceived as ideological naïveté. Soon after his arrival in Montgomery, he informed the FOR office in New York that King was "a grand guy" who "had Gandhi in mind when this thing started." But he warned his superiors that King and the boycotters had a lot to learn about the moral strictures of nonviolence: "[King] is aware of the dangers to him inwardly, wants to do it right, but is too young and some of his close help is violent. King accepts, as an example, a body guard, and asks for permits for them to carry guns. This was denied by the police, but nevertheless, the place is an arsenal. King sees the inconsistency, but not enough. He believes and yet he doesn't believe. The whole movement is armed in a sense, and this is what I must convince him to see as the greatest evil. At first King was merely asked to be the spokesman of the movement, but as sometimes happens, he has really become the real leader and symbol of growing magnitude. If he can *really* be won to a faith in non-violence there is no end to what he can do." Despite this caveat, Smiley communicated an almost breathless enthusiasm for the boycott, which, thanks to his and Rustin's influence, was now officially known as a "non-violent protest" among MIA leaders. "The story is not a clear one, not nearly as clear as we would like," he admitted, "but potentially it is the most exciting thing I have ever touched."[17]

The more Smiley saw of King and the boycotters, the more he was impressed, even awed, by their raw courage and spiritual strength. "Strange," he wrote Swomley on March 2. "Whites are scared stiff and Negroes are calm as cucumbers. It is an experience I shall never forget. The mass meeting last night was like another world. 2500 people, laughing, crying, moaning, shouting, singing. . . . Not once was there an expression of hatred towards whites, and the ovation I received when I talked of Gandhi, his campaign, and then of the cross, was tremendous. They want to do the will of God, and they are sure this is the will of God."

Even so, he continued to insist that the boycott could not succeed without increased support and counsel from movement leaders in the North. The brief involvement of FOR had already made a difference; in the short span of ten days he and Rustin had helped to give the Montgomery protest a new image and a renewed sense of purpose. Now that he was on the scene, he was convinced that Randolph, who had been arguing for several weeks that the boycotters needed little help or advice from the outside, was "wrong in several respects." As he told Swomley:

> Montgomery leaders have managed a mass resistance campaign, but it was petering out until (1) the indictments & arrests, (2) King suddenly remembered Gandhi and what he had heard from Chalmers and others. Although the protest had been going on for 9 weeks, little help, if any of consequence, had come from the outside until the announcement of the non-violent features, and the quotation of King's magnificent address. When that hit the press, simultaneous with the arrests, handled with a non-violent response, help began to pour in. Hundreds of telegrams, letters, checks, etc. poured in. . . . The non-violent method has caught the imagination of people, especially negroes everywhere. No one will know how much pacifism through the FOR has had to do with this. All I can say is that we have had a lot, and can have more. Secondly, we can learn from their courage and plain earthy devices for building morale, etc., but they can learn more from us, for being so new at this. King runs out of ideas quickly and does the old things again and again. He wants help, and we can give it to him without attempting to run the movement or pretend we know it all.[18]

Smiley's skills as an interracial organizer and his ability to lend a helping hand without being condescending or controlling proved invaluable to the MIA during the spring and summer of 1956. He was seemingly everywhere: addressing the weekly mass meetings on the relevance of nonviolence to the Southern freedom struggle, organizing workshops on the tactics of direct action and passive resistance, distributing pacifist literature, encouraging white ministers to take a public stand against segregation, and overseeing the production of a fifteen-minute documentary film entitled *Walk to Freedom*. On occasion, he even served as an intelligence agent: Posing as a segregationist sympathizer, he attended several Citizens' Council meetings and one Klan rally. These periodic forays into the segregationist camp provided the MIA with important information, but Smiley spent most of his time, and made his greatest contributions, either cultivating local white liberals or strengthening the bond between the MIA and movement leaders in the North.

At his suggestion, in early March the national office of FOR drew up a statement of support for the boycott and mailed it to sixteen hundred clergymen around the country. The statement, which began with the words "As Christian ministers we rejoice in the leadership our brother pastors in Montgomery are giving in the nonviolent campaign for racial brotherhood," received the endorsement of several hundred ministers, more than two hundred of whom expressed "their own willingness to go personally to Montgomery to supply the pulpits of any of the defending ministers who were jailed." To Smiley's dismay, none of the signees lived in the state, but he refused to abandon his efforts to awaken the Christian conscience of white Alabama.

On March 10, just prior to the mass mailing, he had convened a secret meeting of ten white Alabama ministers, who agreed to hold a larger meeting of sixty-five ministers on April 6. The second gathering, held at a YMCA camp ten miles outside of Montgomery, included religious leaders from seven denominations, and even though the participants did not feel comfortable enough to publicize the meeting, Smiley was heartened by what transpired. "It was the first meeting of this sort that has been held in Alabama since the crisis began," he wrote Swomley, "and the men were tremendously encouraged to learn that there were this many standing out, and it could very easily be the start of something most exciting. Since the meeting was to be held without publicity, there were no statements issued. . . . But they did set up another meeting in a month, at which time they planned to make a general announcement inviting men to attend and would issue a public statement. This is the thing that we need, for if we could get 100 men who would issue a statement, it is inconceivable to me that the 100 men could be fired, even in Alabama." Although the plans for a public mass meeting of liberal white ministers never materialized, Smiley continued to search for potential supporters in the white community. With the help of Abernathy and Wilson Riles, a black FOR field secretary and former head of the Arizona NAACP who spent most of April in Montgomery, he organized a series of interracial prayer meetings, which strengthened the lines of communication between the city's black and white ministers. The vast majority of the white ministers remained cautious in their dealings with the MIA, but the resolute courage of a small group of FOR converts who met periodically with the Reverend Bob Graetz, the white minister of the all-black Trinity Lutheran Church, gave Smiley some hope for the future.[19]

During the spring of 1956, Smiley and Riles constituted the official FOR presence in Montgomery. However, throughout this pivotal period their efforts were reinforced by Rustin's increasingly close relationship with King. Although operating out of New York after March 8, Rustin was in frequent contact with the MIA president, who had come to regard him as a trusted advisor and who seemed untroubled by his radical past or maverick ways. In a series of meetings held in Birmingham in early March, the two men continued their ongoing philosophical discussion of nonviolence and also addressed practical matters such as fund-raising, publicity, and coalition building. Most important, facing a dilemma that would later bedevil the Freedom Riders, they tackled the difficult problem of determining how movement leaders in the North could help the MIA without exacerbating fears of meddling and outside agitation. Since even some MIA leaders were extremely wary of outside interference, King and Rustin agreed that all "communications, ideas, and programs" should be funneled through King or Nixon and that publicly the MIA "must give the appearance of developing all of the ideas and strategies used in the struggle." Whatever the real source, the MIA was to be given credit. In this spirit, Rustin asked Randolph and other movement leaders to provide "ghostwriters for King, who cannot find time at present to write articles, speeches, etc., himself." Rustin himself soon wrote an article under King's byline that was published in the April 1956 issue of *Liberation*. Entitled "Our Struggle," it was King's first published work.[20]

The MIA's growing dependence on Rustin, Smiley, and FOR represented an important turning point in the history of the boycott, and perhaps in the history of the civil rights movement as well. Despite its haphazard beginnings, this historic alliance established a pattern of collaboration and interdependence that would be repeated and expanded upon in the months and years that followed. No one can be sure what would have happened if these nonviolent missionaries had not become actively involved in the boycott during the crucial months of February and March, but it is highly unlikely that either the movement-building process or the evolution of the perceived meaning of Montgomery would have proceeded as rapidly, or as creatively, without them. Thanks in large part to FOR's influence, the leaders of the MIA adopted an increasingly self-conscious identification with Gandhian nonviolence, an identification that magnified and deepened the national and international impact of the boycott, presaging an ideological connection that would influence the Freedom Rides five years later.

Several factors contributed to this fortunate turn of events, but none was more important than King's leadership. To some degree, the MIA's receptiveness to outside help was born of necessity. During the tense days of late February and early March, the boycotters' resources were pressed to the limit, and the MIA was in no position to refuse any reasonable offer of assistance. With or without King, the MIA eventually would have forged some kind of relationship with national civil rights organizations. However, it was by no means inevitable that this relationship would involve anything more than a one-way pipeline propelling funds and advice into the benighted South. Fortunately for the future of the movement, King's presence encouraged a true collaboration between local and national leaders. Among the leaders of the MIA, he alone possessed enough intellectual sophistication and charisma to deal with Rustin and Smiley on a more or less equal plane. While he lacked their experience, his broad educational background, especially his years at Crozer Theological Seminary and Boston University, gave him the self-confidence to advance his own ideas about the strategic and moral implications of nonviolence. From the outset he was able to mediate between Gandhianism and African American evangelism—and between the protest traditions of North and South—because, unlike most Southern Baptist ministers, he was already familiar with the language and political culture of Northern intellectuals and activists. Although his deliberative style and intellectual stubbornness did not always sit well with his older and more experienced Northern allies, King's ability to grasp the subtleties of both movement politics and nonviolent philosophy inspired confidence and loyalty, convincing Rustin, Smiley, and many others that this young Alabama preacher had the potential to become an American Gandhi. With King's help, they were able to look beyond the traditional stereotypes of the black South and to appreciate the largely untapped intellectual resources of a people long burdened by condescension and neglect.

Of course, even King had his limitations. Contrary to popular hagiography, his advanced understanding of nonviolent philosophy did not spring forth full blown; rather it emerged from months of careful nurturing and reflective deliberation. Even his basic commitment to nonviolence came later than myth now suggests. "Quite contrary to what many people think," Rustin recalled in a 1976 interview, "Dr. King was not a confirmed believer in nonviolence, totally, at the time that the boycott began." To prove his point, Rustin related a troubling incident during an early visit to the Dexter parsonage. When Worthy "went to sit down in the King living room," he encountered a loaded gun resting on the seat of a chair. Later in the evening, Rustin pressed King for an explanation: How could the leader of a nonviolent movement be so casual about firearms? King explained that he and his colleagues had no intention of using their weapons except in cases of self-defense, a response that hardly assuaged Rustin's fears. For several hours that night, and in the weeks that followed, Rustin tried to persuade King that any association with weapons negated the spirit of nonviolence. At first King rejected Rustin's argument as impractical, but "within six weeks, he had demanded that there be no armed guards" in the MIA.

Smiley's recollections offer a similar picture of King's conversion to nonviolence. "He didn't even use the word at first. He used 'passive resistance' almost entirely," Smiley recalled. During their first meeting, Smiley presented King with a pile of books on Gandhianism, hoping to engage the young minister in a discussion of the finer points of nonviolent theory, but after an awkward silence King sheepishly confessed that, although he admired Gandhi, he knew "very little about the man." Undaunted, Smiley pledged to do what he could to remedy the situation, an offer King gratefully accepted and Smiley more than made good on in the weeks that followed. "The role that I played," he told sociologist Aldon Morris in 1978, ". . . was one in which I literally lived with him hours and hours and hours at a time, and he pumped me about what nonviolence was." Blessed with a talented and willing student, Smiley had a profound influence on King's "pilgrimage to nonviolence." When King took the first integrated bus ride following the boycott's successful conclusion in December 1956, he fittingly gave Smiley the honor of sitting by his side, though then and later the always gracious Texan insisted that Rustin deserved most of the credit for nurturing the MIA leader's maturation as a proponent of nonviolent resistance.[21]

Whatever its sources, by late spring King's pilgrimage had progressed to the point where Rustin and Smiley were eager to show off their protégé's progress. To this end, Smiley invited King and Abernathy to Atlanta to meet with Muste, Swomley, Lawrence, and a handful of FOR activists from across the South. In late March 1956, following a speaking engagement in New York City, King had met briefly with an FOR-sponsored group known as the Committee for Nonviolent Integration, but the Atlanta meeting represented the first real opportunity for the nation's leading pacifists to engage the MIA president in a face-to-face dialogue. Held at Morehouse College on May 12, the daylong meeting focused on the racial crises in Alabama, South Carolina, and Mississippi and on "the future of nonviolence in the South." Specifically, FOR leaders wanted to know how other potential centers of nonviolent resistance could "achieve the unity of Montgomery." After listening to depressing reports on Orangeburg, South Carolina, where white segregationists were on the offensive and where black leaders were squabbling among themselves, and on the situation in Mississippi, where the FOR movement had been driven underground, the leaders looked to King for a measure of solace. He did not disappoint them. Flanked by Abernathy and Martin Luther King Sr., the young minister presented a moving account of how thousands of seemingly ordinary citizens had become infused with the extraordinary power of nonviolent direct action. As Muste and his colleagues listened with rapt attention, King insisted that a successful nonviolent movement required both personal resistance, which was "a day-by-day affair," and collective passive resistance, which "must be used with care in a controlled situation." To Smiley's relief, the eloquence and thoughtfulness of King's words dispelled the gloom of the earlier reports, and at the close of the meeting the participants endorsed a proposal for two subregional conferences to be held in mid-July. Under the proposal each Southern city would send two representatives to compare notes and exchange ideas, with the expectation that a coordinated network of protest would emerge.

Despite its brevity and bittersweet quality, the Morehouse conference represented a major step forward in FOR's fledgling Southern campaign. Muste, in particular, left the meeting with renewed hope. This was his first encounter with the young Alabama preacher, though King had been in the audience when Muste had given a speech at Crozer Seminary in 1949. As Muste later told his friends in New York, King was even more impressive than he had been led to believe, and the idea that the boycott leader could become an American Gandhi no longer seemed far-fetched. For more than half a century, Muste had dreamed of spreading the FOR message to the American masses. Now it appeared he had found an ideal messenger, one who could not only prick the conscience of white Americans but could also demonstrate the transformative power of nonviolence. From Muste's perspective, the boycotters had to do more than win the struggle in Montgomery; they also had to win it in the right way, creating a model of nonviolent resistance that others could follow. One false step, one act of violence, he feared, could sully the MIA's image and halt the nonviolent movement's newfound momentum. With this in mind, he urged Smiley and Rustin to stay close to King and to redouble their efforts to mold the MIA president in the Gandhian image.[22]

OTHER MOVEMENT LEADERS, including Muste's old friends Norman Thomas and Phil Randolph, saw things somewhat differently. In late March, Thomas warned King that "the intrusion of Northerners in Montgomery will do more harm than good." As a socialist who had barely survived the ravages of McCarthyism, he was sensitive to the realities of the Cold War and did not want the MIA to take any unnecessary chances. To him, collaborating with individuals who might taint the Montgomery movement with the appearance of left-wing infiltration or, as in the case of Rustin, with personal scandal was not worth the risk. Randolph shared Thomas's fears, but he also had concerns of a broader nature: white infringement on an indigenous black movement, elite manipulation of a grassroots protest, the likelihood of organizational squabbling, and an unhealthy preoccupation with ideology. In his calculation, allowing outsiders to set unrealistic goals—to measure the boycotters' moral progress with an absolutist ideological or philosophical yardstick that made sense in New York or New Delhi but not necessarily in Montgomery—would almost certainly doom the boycott to failure. Although he had great respect for Muste, whom he had known and admired for nearly twenty years, Randolph questioned the wisdom of subjecting local leaders to indoctrination and extended debate on the finer points of nonviolent theory.[23]

Despite his misgivings about the FOR campaign, Randolph never wavered in his support of the boycott. More than any other nationally prominent black leader, he welcomed the appearance of nonviolent direct action in the Deep South. A longtime critic of the NAACP's legalistic approach to social change, he had been one of the first African American leaders to advocate direct action on a mass scale. As the organizer of the 1941 March on Washington Movement, he had been instrumental in forcing President Franklin Roosevelt to issue an executive order creating the Fair Employment Practices Committee. Although Roosevelt's capitulation rendered the Washington march unnecessary, Randolph continued to press for nonviolent resistance during and after World War II. He called in 1942 for "a fusion of Gandhi's Satyagraha with the sit-down strike of the industrial union movement" and later lent his support to Rustin, Farmer, and other CORE activists who staged sit-ins in Chicago and other Northern cities. None of this activity drew much enthusiasm from the black masses, and unsympathetic observers chided him for presuming to be "a kind of Gandhi of the Negroes," but Randolph never lost his conviction that "nonviolent mass activity" was destined to be "an important part of the future strategy and technique of the Negro."[24]

The Montgomery movement thus brought a measure of redemption to Randolph, who was especially proud of the role his old friend E. D. Nixon had played in the creation of the boycott. From the beginning of the protest, Nixon's frequent phone calls and letters kept his mentor abreast of what was happening in Montgomery, and Randolph responded with increasing enthusiasm as the boycotters sustained and extended their defiance of Jim Crow. Although he needed little prodding, the old socialist's interest in the boycott took on a new urgency in early February after white supremacists bombed Nixon's home. When the Eisenhower administration all but ignored his telegrams demanding federal protection for MIA leaders, an angry but determined Randolph stepped up his efforts to aid and encourage the boycotters. This new determination led to the funding of Rustin's pilgrimage to Montgomery and to renewed cooperation with FOR, but Randolph devoted most of his energy to the difficult task of raising money for the MIA.[25]

Since early January 1956 he had been a leading supporter of In Friendship, a new relief organization dedicated to "aiding those who are suffering economic reprisals because of their fight against segregation." Originally conceived as a response to "race terror" in Mississippi and South Carolina, In Friendship was the brainchild of Rustin and two remarkable behind-the-scenes activists, Stanley Levison, a socialist gadfly and professional fund-raiser for the liberal American Jewish Congress, and Ella Baker, a transplanted black Virginian who had lived in New York since 1927. During the 1940s Baker had worked as a field secretary and as national director of branches for the NAACP, and since 1954 she had served as president of the organization's New York City branch. Known in movement circles as a courageous truth-teller, this "tiny woman with a booming voice" had long been a vocal inside critic of the NAACP's preoccupation with legal and organizational matters. A forceful advocate of direct action, she helped plan the 1947 Journey of Reconciliation—even though, as we have seen, she was not allowed to participate in the all-male campaign. Surely no one was surprised when, with Levison's help, she brought together a number of New York City's most prominent religious leaders, labor organizers, and liberal and radical activists for In Friendship's founding meeting on January 5, or when she later persuaded Randolph to serve as the organization's first chairman.[26]

In a February 17 letter inviting sympathetic leaders to In Friendship's first "Action Conference," Randolph emphasized the plight of black Mississippi farmers being squeezed by the White Citizens' Councils, which had "succeeded in choking off loans and other credits on which farmers depend." Following the mass indictments in Montgomery, however, he wasted no time in redirecting In Friendship's activities toward the struggle in Alabama. For the remainder of the year, the organization's primary focus was raising funds for the MIA.[27]

In early March, in an effort to depoliticize In Friendship's image, Randolph resigned as chairman and was replaced by three distinguished religious co-chairmen: Rabbi Edward Klein, Monsignor Cornelius Drew, and Dr. Harry Emerson Fosdick. Even after his resignation, though, Randolph continued to serve as the organization's principal sponsor. When In Friendship held a mass rally and fund-raiser in Madison Square Garden on May 24, Randolph's involvement was a key element of the event's success. In large part, it was his stature that enabled Baker and Levison to enlist a star-studded array of celebrities, including Eleanor Roosevelt, Tallulah Bankhead, Sammy Davis Jr., Pearl Bailey, Cab Calloway, and Josh White, who brought down the house with a throbbing rendition of "Free and Equal Blues." King, Rosa Parks, and Autherine Lucy were also on hand, but Bankhead, the daughter of a former U.S. senator from Alabama, stole the show when she kissed Parks and Lucy onstage. "Prejudice is so stupid," the actress told the crowd in her best Alabama drawl. "I'm a Bankhead and there have been generations of Bankheads in Alabama, but I'm not proud of what's happening there today." To Randolph's delight, the rally drew sixteen thousand participants and, despite Congressman Adam Clayton Powell Jr.'s financial shenanigans, raised more than eight thousand dollars, half of which went to the MIA.[28]

Unfortunately, the May rally proved to be the high-water mark of In Friendship's fund-raising activities. With Randolph's blessing, Baker and Levison continued to work feverishly through the summer and fall, but their efforts were hampered by stiff competition from political fund-raisers— particularly after the contest between Dwight Eisenhower and Adlai Stevenson took shape—and by lukewarm support from the national leadership of the AFL-CIO and the NAACP. Even though In Friendship's publications repeatedly pledged that the organization would "limit itself to programs of economic aid and will not attempt to duplicate the legal, legislative, and other phases of civil rights which are now being carried on by other appropriate organizations," AFL-CIO chief George Meany, NAACP executive director Roy Wilkins, and others remained wary of the new organization's intentions. For this reason, In Friendship's activities were essentially limited to the New York area and never became national in scope. On December 5 the organization celebrated the boycott's first anniversary with a benefit concert at Manhattan Center featuring a performance by Calypso star Harry Belafonte, a vocal solo by Coretta King, and jazz accompaniment by Duke Ellington; even so, the $1,863 raised for the MIA represented only a small fraction of what might have been raised if Baker and Levison had enjoyed the backing of a unified civil rights movement.[29]

Randolph had worked long and hard to foster such a movement, but in 1956 not even he could overcome the organizational rivalries and ideological divisions that had plagued civil rights advocates for decades. Even though Randolph, Wilkins, and other civil rights leaders developed close personal friendships, were in frequent communication with one another, and sometimes even shared resources, true cooperation eluded them. Ironically, the situation had gotten worse in the wake of the NAACP's victory in the *Brown* decision, which simultaneously reinforced and undermined a legalistic approach. The victory elevated the NAACP's status, but it also unleashed expectations and feelings that inevitably led to impatience, dissatisfaction, and experimentation with direct action. An event like the bus boycott, which ideally should have served as a rallying point for the movement, actually complicated the task of organizational cooperation. In the long run the boycott helped to create a unifying movement culture, but in the short run it probably created more confusion than solidarity.

This unfortunate reality became apparent when Randolph convened a "private" conference on "The State of the Race" in Washington on April 24, 1956. Originally conceived as a counterpoint to the pro-segregation "Dixie Manifesto" signed by Southern congressmen in February, the conference attracted scores of black leaders representing religious, civic, business, and labor organizations from across the nation. It was Randolph's hope that in framing a response to the segregationists' manifesto the gathering would move toward the creation of an omnibus organization that could coordinate the civil rights movement on a national level. But it was not to be. The discussions among the black leaders were generally civil, and at the end of the day the participants approved a statement calling for an end to segregation, the strengthening of the NAACP's legal and educational programs, the passage of federal legislation ensuring voting rights and fair employment, and an immediate meeting with President Eisenhower to discuss the dangerous state of race relations in the South. Yet the conference took no stand on the need for an omnibus organization or the advisability of direct action. Worst of all, following adjournment the leaders went their separate ways as if nothing had happened. As one historian put it, whatever unity the conference inspired soon "dissolve[d] into competition for funds, membership, and publicity," leaving Randolph "deeply discouraged by his inability to unite black leadership."[30]

Randolph's frustrations serve as a reminder that the creation of the modern civil rights movement was neither simple nor preordained. Montgomery provided a focal point for the movement in the critical year of 1956, but it did not eliminate the difficulties of bridging long-standing ideological, regional, organizational, and personal divisions. Years of negotiation, compromise, sacrifice, and struggle lay ahead. The bus boycott forced the issue, accelerating the evolution of the idea—and to some extent the reality—of a national civil rights movement, and the lessons learned on the streets of Montgomery clearly encouraged African Americans to quicken their steps on the road to freedom. But, as movement leaders soon discovered, the road itself remained long and hard. In the absence of a fully developed, cohesive national movement, the task of turning a small step into a meaningful "stride toward freedom," to borrow Martin Luther King's apt phrase, would prove far more difficult than he or anyone else realized during the heady days of the bus boycott.

The boycott itself ended triumphantly in December 1956, following the Supreme Court's unanimous ruling in *Gayle v. Browder*. Applying the same logic used in *Brown*, the Court struck down Montgomery's bus segregation ordinance and by implication all similar local and state laws. But the decision did not address the legality of segregating interstate passengers, and it did not challenge mandated segregation in bus or train terminals. Indeed, its immediate impact was limited to local buses in Montgomery and a handful of other Southern cities. Predictably, political leaders in most Southern communities insisted that *Gayle* only applied to Montgomery, forcing local civil rights advocates to file a series of legal challenges. Armed with the legal precedent set in *Gayle*, NAACP attorneys were "virtually assured . . . ultimate victory in any legal contest over segregated carriers," as one legal historian put it, but the actual process of local transit desegregation was often painfully slow and limited in its effect. By 1960 local buses had been desegregated in forty-seven Southern cities, but more than half of the region's local bus lines remained legally segregated. In the Deep South states of Alabama, Mississippi, Georgia, and Louisiana, Jim Crow transit prevailed in all but three communities. And, despite *Gayle*, there was no sign that local and state officials in these states recognized the inevitability of bus desegregation. On the contrary, their resistance to change gained new life in November 1959, when Federal District Judge H. Hobart Grooms upheld the legality of the Birmingham city commission's strategy of sustaining segregation with a law authorizing bus companies to establish "private" segregation rules designed to maintain public order on buses. Asserting that private discrimination was sanctioned by the Fourteenth Amendment, Grooms's ruling virtually ensured that the legal struggle over segregated buses would continue into the next decade.[31]

The battle in the courts ultimately proved to be only one part of a wider struggle against the indignities of Jim Crow transit, but this wider struggle took much longer to develop than anyone anticipated in the immediate aftermath of the victory in Montgomery. In early 1957 King and others predicted that the Montgomery experience would serve as a catalyst for a region-wide movement of nonviolent direct action. To the dismay and puzzlement of those who had come to believe that Southern blacks were on the verge of self-liberation, however, the spirit of Montgomery did not spread readily to other cities. Indeed, in Montgomery itself the local movement atrophied as factional and internal strife weakened the MIA's hold over the black community. While nearly every Southern city boasted a local civil rights movement of some kind by the late 1950s, there was little momentum and no expectation of successful mass protest. Even in Birmingham, where the Reverend Fred Shuttlesworth and the Alabama Christian Movement for Human Rights (ACMHR) were engaged in a valiant and long-standing struggle against local white supremacists, mass support for nonviolent direct action appeared to be slipping away. Despite the recent victory in Montgomery, the black South at large, it seemed, harbored little interest in direct action and even less interest in the abstract philosophy of nonviolence.[32]

Part of the explanation resides in the politics of massive resistance. In the aftermath of Montgomery, civil rights activists faced an increasingly militant white South. The signs of white supremacist mobilization were everywhere: in the resurgence of the Ku Klux Klan; in the spread of the White Citizens' Councils; in the angry rhetoric of demagogic politicians; and especially in the taut faces of white Southerners who seemed ready to challenge even the most minor breaches of racial etiquette. As the voices of moderation fell silent, a rising chorus of angry whites ready to defend the "Southern way of life" gave the appearance of regional and racial solidarity. Not all

The Reverend Fred Shuttlesworth and parishioner Elizabeth Bloxom ride an integrated city bus in Birmingham, Alabama, on December 26, 1956, five days after the desegregation of buses in Montgomery. (Library of Congress)

white Southerners were comfortable with the harsh turn in race relations, and some even harbored sympathy for the civil rights movement. Still, as the decade drew to a close the liberal dream that the white South would somehow find the moral strength to overcome its racial fears faded from view. This temporary loss of faith forced civil rights activists to reevaluate their plans and strategies for desegregation. In the long run, white intransigence left black Southerners with little choice but to take to the streets, but in the intimidating atmosphere of the late 1950s even the most committed proponents of direct action must have wondered about its viability in the Deep South.[33]

Ironically, the paucity of direct action in these years also stemmed from an unfounded but expectant faith in the Eisenhower administration's commitment to civil rights. For a brief period in 1957 and 1958, federal enforcement of *Brown* and other aspects of civic equality appeared imminent. In August 1957 Congress approved the first federal civil rights act in eighty-two years, creating the U.S. Commission on Civil Rights and confirming the Fifteenth Amendment's guarantee of black voting rights. A threatened filibuster by white Southern senators and opposition from conservative Republicans weakened the enforcement provisions of the bill, reducing its meaning to symbolic proportions, but disappointment with the final version did not prevent civil rights leaders from hailing the 1957 act as a step in the right direction. This cautious optimism received further encouragement during the tumultuous school desegregation crisis in Little Rock, Arkansas. On September 24, two weeks after signing the 1957 Civil Rights Act, President Eisenhower answered the defiant challenge of Governor Orval Faubus and an angry white mob by federalizing the Arkansas National Guard and dispatching soldiers of the 101st Airborne Division to Little Rock's Central High School. The soldiers remained in Little Rock for nearly a year, protecting the rights of the nine black children at Central High while asserting the preeminence of federal law. The belief that this show of federal force heralded a new attitude in the White House eventually turned into disillusionment, as the pace of school desegregation ground to a halt during the final two years of the Eisenhower era, but for a time the clash in Little Rock provided support for those who advocated a legalistic approach to social change. Even among advocates of nonviolent resistance, Little Rock confirmed the suspicion that the streets of the Jim Crow South were mean and dangerous, especially for unarmed civil rights activists.[34]

This confusing combination of fear and hope produced an understandable wariness that inhibited risk-taking and innovation. As movement leaders watched and waited, organizational and ideological inertia set in, perpetuating the dominance of the NAACP and delaying the dreams of those who hoped to infuse the civil rights struggle with the spirit of Montgomery. For better or for worse, the NAACP, which celebrated its fiftieth anniversary in 1959, continued to steer the movement toward a legalistic resolution of social injustice. Despite its willingness to represent the MIA in court, the national leadership of the NAACP had mixed emotions about the emergence of Martin Luther King and his philosophy of nonviolence. Among the rank-and-file members of the NAACP local branches and Youth Councils, King enjoyed considerable popularity. This was not the case at the national NAACP office in New York, however, where Roy Wilkins and others resented King's fame and regarded him as an unwelcome rival for funds and influence.

During the bus boycott, the national office had allowed local NAACP branches to raise funds for the MIA, but this sharing of resources ended in early 1957, when King became the leader of a rival national organization, the Southern Christian Leadership Conference. Wilkins, Thurgood Marshall, and other NAACP leaders felt that they had already paid an exorbitant price (including the virtual dissolution of the Alabama NAACP, which was driven underground by the state legislature) for what Wilkins's assistant John Morsell called "the hullabaloo of the boycott." Suspicious of anything that complicated their carefully designed program of litigation and legislation, they were determined to avoid the emotional diversions of mass protest and the risk of being tarnished with charges of radicalism and civil disobedience. As Wilkins later explained: "My own view was that the particular form of direct action used in Montgomery was effective only for certain kinds of local problems and could not be applied safely on a national scale. Although there was a great deal of excited talk about adapting the tactics of Gandhi to the South, the fact remained that the America of the Eisenhower era and the Silent Generation was not the India of Gandhi and the Salt March. . . . The danger I feared was that the Montgomery model would lead to a string of unsuccessful boycotts . . . at a time when defeats could only encourage white supremacists to fight all the harder."[35]

In the short run, NAACP leaders had little to worry about, as King and others struggled with the problem of getting a new organization off the ground. Planning and logistical details consumed most of SCLC's energy during the late 1950s. In 1957 King visited the new nation of Ghana, helped organize a "Prayer Pilgrimage" to Washington to commemorate the third anniversary of *Brown*, and headlined a four-day institute on "Non-Violence and Social Change" held in Tallahassee, Florida, where SCLC vice president C. K. Steele was trying to fend off white backlash following a local bus boycott that had driven the municipal bus company into bankruptcy. In 1958 SCLC established an Atlanta office run by Ella Baker, a Nashville affiliate (Nashville Christian Leadership Council, or NCLC) spearheaded by the Reverend Kelly Miller Smith, and a modest voting rights project known as the "Crusade for Citizenship"; and in 1959 King visited India, hired Rustin as a part-time public relations director, and moved from Montgomery to Atlanta. But none of this did much to rekindle the fires of nonviolent resistance. By the end of the decade, the notion that King possessed the capacity or the will to lead a liberation movement in the Deep South had all but disappeared, and even he had begun to wonder if the spirit of Montgomery would ever return.[36]

The organizational obstacles to nonviolent direct action were formidable, but, as King and his colleagues at SCLC knew all too well, the greatest challenge to nonviolence was cultural. No amount of lofty rhetoric could disguise the hard truth that proponents of nonviolent struggle were operating in an inhospitable cultural environment. Reliance on force, gun ownership, and armed self-defense were deeply rooted American traditions, especially in the South, where the interwoven legacies of slavery, frontier vigilantism, and a rigid code of personal honor held sway. The classic form of Southern violence was most evident among whites, but the regional ethos of life below "the Smith and Wesson line" extended to black Southerners as well. Weapons and armed conflict were an accepted fact of life, and even among the most religious members of Southern black society the philosophy of nonviolence cut across the grain of cultural experience and expectation. According to white regional mythology, the uneasy racial peace that had existed since the collapse of Radical Reconstruction rested almost exclusively on the twin foundations of white resolve and black accommodation. In reality, however, historic patterns of racial negotiation involved a complicated mix of accommodation and resistance. If knowing one's "place" was an important survival skill in the Jim Crow South, in certain circumstances so was the willingness to engage in what Robert Williams called "armed self-reliance."[37]

As the militant leader of the Monroe, North Carolina, branch of the NAACP, Williams created a storm of controversy in October 1957 when he and other local blacks engaged in a shoot-out with marauding Klansmen. Openly brandishing a shotgun and carrying a .45 pistol on his hip, the thirty-two-year-old U.S. Army and Marine Corps veteran urged all black Southerners to do whatever was necessary to defend themselves and their families from white violence and oppression. Defying local whites as well as national NAACP leaders, he refused to disarm or to eschew violence as a means of taming "that social jungle called Dixie." In May 1959, expressing outrage over the acquittal of a white man who had beaten and raped a local black woman, he told reporters: "We must be willing to kill if necessary. . . .We cannot rely on the law. We get no justice under the present system. If we feel injustice is done, we must right then and there on the spot be prepared to inflict punishment on these people." Horrified by Williams's angry outburst, Wilkins suspended him as president of the Monroe branch, and Thurgood Marshall even urged the FBI to investigate his role as a "communist" provocateur. But Williams refused to back down.[38]

In July 1959 he began to disseminate his views in a weekly newspaper called *The Crusader*, attracting the attention of everyone from an admiring Malcolm X of the Nation of Islam to Martin Luther King, who felt compelled to speak out against him. In September the pacifist magazine *Liberation* featured a debate between King and Williams, in which Williams expressed "great respect" for pacifists but insisted that nonviolence was something "that most of my people" cannot embrace. "Negroes must be willing to defend themselves, their women, their children and their homes," he declared. "Nowhere in the annals of history does the record show a people delivered from bondage by patience alone." King countered with an eloquent distillation of nonviolent philosophy but acknowledged that even Gandhi recognized the moral validity of self-defense. The exchange, later reprinted in the *Southern Patriot*, left editor Anne Braden and many other nonviolent activists with the uneasy feeling that Williams spoke for a broad cross-section of the black South. As Braden conceded, Williams's views on armed self-reliance were not only common, they were likely to spread "unless change comes rapidly." The dim prospects for such change in the absence of direct action on a mass scale underscored the dilemma that all civil rights activists faced in the late 1950s. As the decade drew to a close, no one seemed to have a firm grasp on how to turn social philosophy into mass action, or how to awaken the black South without risking mass violence.[39]

DURING THE FALLOW YEARS OF THE LATE 1950s, local NAACP Youth Councils, and in one case SCLC, conducted sit-ins protesting discrimination in stores and restaurants in several Southern or border-state communities. However, none of these early efforts garnered much organizational or popular support. Initiated by local leaders at the grassroots level, these short-lived precursors of the famous 1960 Greensboro, North Carolina, sit-in received little attention in the press and only grudging recognition from the regional and national leaders of the NAACP and SCLC. Consequently, they produced meager results, leaving their participants isolated, frustrated, and vulnerable. During these years, the only national organization that evidenced a clear determination to translate the philosophy of nonviolence into action on behalf of civil rights was CORE. And, unfortunately for the nonviolent movement, CORE's resolve was tempered by the limitations of a small organization hampered by inadequate funding and limited experience in the South. Despite lofty goals, CORE activity in the late 1950s was restricted to a handful of communities where local chapters, generally consisting of a few brave individuals, mustered only occasional challenges to the institutional power of Jim Crow. Most of this activity took place in the border states of Missouri, West Virginia, and Kentucky, where several CORE chapters organized brief but sometimes successful picketing and sit-in campaigns directed at discrimination in employment and public accommodations. Farther south, in the ex-Confederate states, early efforts at direct action were much rarer and seldom successful, though not entirely unknown.

In Nashville, a group led by Anna Holden, a white activist originally from Florida, established an interracial committee that pressured the local school board to comply with *Brown*. In Richmond, CORE volunteers organized a 1959 New Year's Day rally that brought two thousand people to the Virginia capital to protest against the state's "massive resistance" plan. In Miami, a newly organized CORE chapter staged a series of sit-ins at segregated downtown lunch counters in the spring and summer of 1959, hosted a two-week-long Interracial Action Institute in September that brought the national staff to the city and forced the closing of a segregated lunch counter at Jackson-Byron's department store, and later joined forces with the local NAACP branch in an effort to desegregate a whites-only beach. In Tallahassee, a chapter organized by students at Florida A&M University in October 1959 anticipated the Freedom Rides by conducting observation exercises that documented segregated seating on city and interstate buses, as well as segregation patterns at downtown department stores, restaurants, and other public accommodations. In South Carolina, CORE's Southern field secretary, Jim McCain, led a statewide black voter registration project and presided over several local protests, including one that desegregated an ice-cream stand in Marion in 1959. Taken together, these activities constituted a vanguard, giving the Southern nonviolent movement a handhold on the towering cliff of desegregation. But few if any CORE activists held out much hope that such activities would actually take the movement to the proverbial mountaintop, much less to the promised land on the other side.[40]

At CORE headquarters in New York—a tiny office on Park Row "not much bigger than a closet"—executive secretary Jimmy Robinson presided over a small but dedicated staff that included *CORE-lator* editor Jim Peck, field secretaries Jim McCain and Gordon Carey, and community relations director Marvin Rich. Peck had been a CORE stalwart since the 1940s, and Carey and Rich had been active in the organization for nearly a decade. Born in Michigan in 1932, Carey grew up in a movement household in Ontario, California, where his father, the Reverend Howard Carey, was active in FOR. After serving a year in prison as a conscientious objector during the Korean War, he became the head of the Pasadena chapter of CORE and later a national CORE vice president. In 1958 he joined the CORE staff as the organization's second roving field secretary. McCain, CORE's first field secretary and for several years the organization's only black staff member, was hired in 1957. A former teacher and high school principal from Sumter, South Carolina, where he was head of the local NAACP branch, McCain was fired in 1955 after local white officials grew tired of his movement activities. Before becoming active in CORE, he worked for the South Carolina Council on Human Relations, an interracial group committed to a gradualist approach to desegregation. Rich, a white activist with a strikingly different background, was involved in the labor movement before joining the CORE staff in October 1959. Born in St. Louis in 1929, he first became active in CORE as an undergraduate at Washington University, where he met Charles Oldham, a law student who spearheaded the development of the vibrant St. Louis CORE chapter. During the late 1940s Rich was the founding president of the Student Committee for the Admission of Negroes (SCAN), an organization that successfully promoted the desegregation of Washington University. In 1956, after working as a fund-raiser and organizer for the Teamsters Union, Rich moved to New York with his new wife, a black woman also active in CORE. Later in the year, after Oldham was elected CORE's national chairman, Rich became a member of the organization's National Council, a position that eventually led to a staff appointment.

During the late 1950s Robinson and the staff worked closely with the National Council in an effort to raise CORE's profile, but the absence of a mass following continued to limit the organization's influence. While CORE claimed more than twelve thousand "associated members" by early 1960, only a small fraction of this following was actively involved in direct action campaigns. Despite recent gains in membership, the number of available volunteers remained well below the threshold needed to effect broad social change, especially in the South. To have any hope of transforming the region most in need of change, CORE would have to provoke a general crisis of conscience among white Southerners. And for that they would need an army of nonviolent insurgents, a mass of men and women willing to put themselves at considerable risk, including the very real possibility of going to jail for their beliefs. Where this hypothetical nonviolent army might come from was unclear, and none of the most likely sources, from organized labor to the black churches of SCLC, looked very promising as the new decade began. Rebellious and impatient students would soon fill the void, but when the student sit-in movement burst upon the scene in the late winter of 1960, it took almost everyone by surprise.[41]

Ignited by the unexpected daring of four black freshmen at North Carolina A&T College in Greensboro—Ezell Blair Jr., Joseph McNeil, Franklin McCain, and David Richmond—the shift to mass protest was sudden and dramatic. Unlike the scattered and short-term sit-ins of the 1950s, the Woolworth's lunch counter sit-in that began on February 1, 1960, drew the rapt attention of national civil rights leaders, especially after the scale of the protest widened beyond anyone's expectations. As the number of participants multiplied, from twenty-nine on the second day to more than three hundred on the fifth, the Greensboro students realized that they needed help. Hoping to keep the situation under control, they turned to Dr. George Simkins Jr., the president of the Greensboro NAACP, and to Floyd McKissick and the Reverend Douglas Moore, two black activists who had been experimenting with direct action in nearby Durham since 1957. After McKissick agreed to serve as legal counsel for the original four participants, he and Moore began to contact local activists in several other cities, including Nashville, where Moore's old friend and SCLC colleague Jim Lawson had been conducting nonviolent workshops in preparation for a sit-in campaign even more ambitious than Greensboro's. The student activists who had been attending his NCLC-sponsored workshops were eager to follow Greensboro's lead, he assured Moore. Other SCLC leaders, including King and the Reverend C. K. Steele in Tallahassee, shared Lawson's enthusiasm for the unexpected developments in North Carolina. This was not the case among national

NAACP leaders, however. When Simkins informed the national office that the Greensboro branch had endorsed the student sit-ins at its February 2 meeting, he was rebuked for violating organizational policy. Unmoved by the revelation that the originators of the Greensboro sit-ins were all NAACP Youth Council veterans, the national staff left Simkins with no choice but to look elsewhere for support.

Simkins's plaintive call to Jimmy Robinson on February 4—an action that, as Jim Farmer later commented, "did not endear him" to his NAACP superiors—sent shock waves through the CORE office. Sensing that this was the break they had been waiting for, CORE leaders immediately turned all of their attention to sustaining and publicizing the Greensboro sit-in. By February 5 both of CORE's field secretaries were on their way to the Carolinas, Carey to Greensboro and McCain to Rock Hill; back in New York, Peck and Rich were initiating negotiations with Woolworth and Kress executives and planning a nationwide campaign of sympathy demonstrations. Within a week the first sympathy demonstration was held in Harlem, and before long CORE chapters were picketing dime stores across the country. All of this elicited considerable press attention, especially after the sit-ins spread to other North Carolina cities and beyond. By February 14 the ever-widening sit-in movement stretched across five states and fourteen cities, involving hundreds of young black demonstrators. Over the next three months it spread to more than a hundred Southern towns and cities, as thousands of students experienced the bittersweet combination of civil disobedience and criminal prosecution. By July nearly three-fourths of these local movements had achieved at least token desegregation, dispelling the myth that the Jim Crow South was invulnerable to direct action. The fact that virtually none of this desegregation took place in the cities and towns of the Deep South was disturbing, but the partial victories in the Upper or "rim" South represented an empowering development to a regional movement that had been virtually moribund six months earlier.[42]

CORE's early involvement in the sit-ins brought the organization unprecedented notoriety, particularly among white segregationists, who rushed to protect the South from "outside agitators." Following his arrest at a Durham sit-in on February 9, an almost giddy Carey informed his New York colleagues that "CORE has been on the front page of every newspaper in North Carolina for two days. CORE has been on radio and TV every hour. . . . I can't move without the press covering my movement." Later, as Carey and McCain shuttled from sit-in to sit-in, it appeared to some that CORE had assumed control of the student movement. In actuality, however, CORE activists made little headway in their campaign to provide the movement with ideological and organizational discipline. Most student demonstrators exhibited only a passing interest in the subtleties of Gandhian philosophy, and many were suspicious of any effort to check the spontaneous and largely untutored nature of the sit-ins.[43]

Following a series of sit-ins, four student activists become the first blacks to eat lunch at the Post House Restaurant in the Nashville, Tennessee, Greyhound terminal, May 16, 1960. The Post House was the first downtown lunch counter in Nashville to be desegregated. From left to right: Matthew Walker Jr., Peggy Alexander, Diane Nash, and Stanley Hemphill. Walker and Nash became Freedom Riders in 1961. (Courtesy of the *Nashville Tennessean*)

This spirit of independence became manifest when nearly two hundred student activists—including 126 black students representing fifty-six colleges and high schools across the South—met at Shaw University in Raleigh in mid-April. The Raleigh conference was the brainchild of fifty-six-year-old Ella Baker, who after years of false starts and dashed hopes had grown disenchanted with the cautious policies of SCLC and the NAACP. Representatives of all the major civil rights organizations were present, but Baker made sure that the students themselves ran the show. Though still an employee of SCLC, she urged the student activists to plot their own course and to avoid the controlling influence of any existing organization. Just before the opening of the Raleigh meeting, King issued a lengthy press-conference statement outlining a proposed strategy for the student movement. But the speaker who aroused the most interest among the delegates was Jim Lawson, recently expelled from Vanderbilt University's School of Divinity for his leadership role in the Nashville sit-ins.

Born in western Pennsylvania in 1931 and raised in Massillon, Ohio, Lawson was an articulate and sophisticated student of Gandhian philosophy who had already served a year in prison as a conscientious objector during the Korean War and three years as a Methodist missionary in India. After meeting King at Oberlin College in 1956, Lawson took the Montgomery minister's advice to postpone his divinity studies and head south to spread the word about nonviolence. Subsequent conversations with A. J. Muste and Glenn Smiley, whom he had known for years, led to his appointment as FOR's Southern field secretary. At Smiley's suggestion, he soon moved to Nashville, Tennessee, where he helped organize the Nashville Christian Leadership Conference and where his nonviolent workshops eventually attracted a dedicated following of young disciples, including John Lewis, Diane Nash, Bernard Lafayette, and others who would later gain prominence as Freedom Riders. Grounded in a mixture of social-gospel Methodism and insurgent Gandhianism, Lawson's intellectual and moral leadership gave the local Nashville movement a strength of purpose that no other student group could match. With the blessing of the Nashville Christian Leadership Council (NCLC) president Kelly Miller Smith, Lawson's increasingly restless disciples had recently formed a Student Central Committee to mediate the relationship between local student activists and the older and generally more cautious ministers of the NCLC. Together, the students and the NCLC constituted a powerful if sometimes uneasy tandem that made the Nashville Movement the most effective local direct action organization since the early Montgomery Improvement Association. Speaking at Fisk University in the immediate aftermath of the Raleigh conference, an admiring King called the Nashville Movement "the best organized and most disciplined in the Southland," a judgment later confirmed by Nashville's critical role in the Freedom Rides.

In Raleigh, Lawson and the Nashville delegation dazzled King and many of the student activists with concrete visions of social justice and the "beloved community." To some, Lawson's sermon-like keynote speech seemed long on religion and a bit short on practical politics, but even the most secular delegates applauded when he warned established movement leaders that the sit-ins represented a "judgment upon middle-class conventional, halfway efforts to deal with radical social evil." In an obvious slap at the NAACP, he insisted that the civil rights struggle could no longer tolerate a narrow reliance on "fund-raising and court action." Instead, it had to cultivate "our greatest resource, a people no longer the victims of racial evil who can act in a disciplined manner to implement the constitution." Baker later echoed these words in a stirring speech that called for a broad assertion of civil rights, rights that involved "more than a hamburger," as she put it. All of this inspired the young delegates to take themselves seriously, and on the second day of the conference they voted to form an independent organization known as the Student Nonviolent Coordinating Committee (SNCC). Marion Barry, a twenty-two-year-old Fisk University chemistry graduate student and future mayor of Washington, D.C., won election as SNCC's first chairman, solidifying the Nashville group's influence.[44]

In May, SNCC reaffirmed its independence at an organizational meeting held in Atlanta, but at this point the student organization constituted little more than a "clearinghouse for the exchange of information about localized protests." With no permanent staff and no financial backing to speak of, SNCC leaders had little choice but to draw upon the resources of older organizations such as SCLC, which allowed them to establish a small office at SCLC headquarters. The national leadership of the NAACP, despite serious misgivings about the sit-in movement, provided SNCC activists with free legal representation and even hired the Reverend Benjamin Elton Cox, an outspoken, courageous black minister and future Freedom Rider from High Point, North Carolina, to serve as a roving ambassador of nonviolence. Paralleling the efforts of CORE field secretaries Carey and McCain, Cox traveled across the South during the spring and summer of 1960, spreading the gospel of nonviolence to as many students as possible. Most student activists were receptive to the nonviolent message, if only for pragmatic reasons, and despite numerous provocations by angry white supremacists, the sit-ins proceeded without unleashing the violent race war that some observers had predicted. At the same time, however, the students were unwilling to sacrifice the intellectual and organizational independence of their movement, even when confronted with elders who invoked religious, moral, or paternal authority. All of this led historian and activist Howard Zinn to marvel that "for the first time in our history, a major social movement, shaking the nation to its bone, is being led by youngsters."[45]

CORE's failure to absorb the student movement was a disappointment, but the organization took pride in the fact that a number of the movement's most committed activists gravitated toward CORE's demanding brand of nonviolence. In Tallahassee, Florida A&M coed Pat Stephens and seven other young CORE volunteers became the first sit-in demonstrators of their era to acknowledge the importance of "unmerited suffering." By refusing to accept bail and remaining behind bars for sixty days in the spring of 1960, they introduced a new tactic known as the "jail-in." In an eloquent statement composed in her cell, Stephens reminded her fellow activists of Martin Luther King's admonition that "we've got to fill the jails in order to win our equal rights." At the time, it was standard practice for arrested demonstrators to seek an early release from jail. Most demonstrators, as well as most movement leaders, agreed with Thurgood Marshall, who insisted that only a fool would refuse to be bailed out from a Southern jail. "Once you've been arrested," he told a crowd at Fisk on April 6, 1960, "you've made your point. If someone offers to get you out, man, get out."[46]

Convincing arrested demonstrators to ignore such advice soon became a cornerstone of CORE policy, and one of the activists most responsible for this new emphasis was Tom Gaither, another rising star among CORE recruits. When he first met McCain in March 1960, Gaither was a biology major and student leader at all-black Claflin College in Orangeburg, South Carolina. Following a mass protest in Orangeburg, he was one of more than 350 students "arrested and herded into an open-air stockade." This was the largest number of demonstrators arrested in any Southern city up to that point, and McCain couldn't help being impressed with the courage of the Orangeburg students. Gaither's leadership in the face of tear gas and fire hoses prompted CORE to offer him a staff position, and by September he found himself in the midst of a major sit-in campaign in Rock Hill. Working closely with McCain and student leaders at Friendship Junior College, he helped to turn Rock Hill into one of the movement's most militant battlegrounds. In February 1961 Rock Hill became the site of the movement's first widely publicized "jail-in." A month later, following his release from a county road gang, Gaither agreed to serve as an advance scout for a new CORE project known as the Freedom Ride—a fitting assignment for someone who had been one of the first to promote the idea of such a ride earlier in the year.[47]

The youthful dynamism of Stephens, Gaither, and other recruits helped to revitalize CORE, which was brimming with optimism by the summer of 1960. At the national CORE convention in July, Carey—recently promoted to the position of field director—claimed that the organization was on the verge of becoming "a major race relations group." In August CORE's expanding staff gathered in Miami for a second "interracial action institute," during which they experimented with the tactic of "jail–no bail." Following a sit-in at a Miami lunch counter, seven participants, including Gaither, Stephens, executive director Jimmy Robinson, and future Freedom Rider Bernard Lafayette, spent ten days in jail. Such actions enhanced CORE's reputation for militance and boosted expectations of increased activity. By September CORE's field staff had grown to five "field secretaries": McCain; Gaither; Joe Perkins, a black graduate student at the University of Michigan; Richard Haley, a Chicago-born black Tallahassee activist and former music professor at Florida A&M; and Genevieve Hughes, a twenty-eight-year-old white stockbroker who had spearheaded the New York City chapter's dime-store boycott.[48]

In October 1960 the CORE field staff fanned out across the South looking for new centers of struggle. What they found—especially in New Orleans, where a committed band of activists was engaged in an all-out assault on Jim Crow, and in South Carolina, where more and more students were responding to McCain and Gaither's organizing efforts—demonstrated that the spirit of nonviolent resistance was still on the rise. But, at the time, none of CORE's advances into the Southern hinterland drew much attention. In the movement at large, all eyes were on Atlanta. Part of the excitement was the reorganization of SNCC, which, during a fateful meeting at Atlanta University, moved toward a more secular orientation that placed "a greater emphasis on political issues." The influence of Lawson and the Nashville Movement on SNCC was declining, and Orangeburg sit-in veteran Chuck McDew, a black Ohioan who had converted to Judaism, soon replaced Marion Barry as SNCC chairman. The biggest news, however, was the arrest and imprisonment of Martin Luther King following a sit-in at Rich's department store on October 19.

The first of eighty demonstrators to be arraigned, King refused Judge James Webb's offer to release him on a five-hundred-dollar bond. "I cannot accept bond," the SCLC leader proclaimed. "I will stay in jail one year, or ten years." This was the kind of courageous leadership that the militants of SNCC and CORE had been advocating, but they got more than they had bargained for when Georgia authorities dropped the charges against all of the defendants but King. The apparent singling out of the nation's most celebrated civil rights leader raised doubts about his safety, a concern that turned into near panic after he was moved from the relative security of his Atlanta jail cell, first to the DeKalb County Jail and later to the maximum security prison at Reidsville. Fearing that King's life was in danger, SCLC and other movement leaders urged the Justice Department to intervene but got no response—a development that set the stage for one of the most fateful decisions in modern American political history.[49]

Harris Wofford, a liberal campaign aide to Democratic presidential candidate John Kennedy, had known King since 1957 and had even raised funds for the SCLC leader's trip to India, where Wofford had spent several years studying Gandhian philosophy. Frustrated by Kennedy's reluctance to take a forthright stand on civil rights, he sensed that King's endangerment provided his candidate with a golden opportunity to make up for past mistakes. After receiving a phone call from an obviously desperate Coretta King, Wofford made the political and ethical case for an expression of sympathy. "If the Senator would only call Mrs. King and wish her well," he told his boss Sargent Shriver, "it would reverberate all through the Negro community in the United States. All he's got to do is say he's thinking about her and he hopes everything will be all right. All he's got to do is show a little heart." While campaigning with Kennedy in Chicago, Shriver relayed Wofford's suggestion, which, to the surprise of the entire campaign staff, led to an impulsive late-night phone call. Startled and touched by Kennedy's expression of concern, Mrs. King later made it clear to the press that she appreciated the senator's gesture, which stood out in stark contrast with Vice President Richard Nixon's refusal to comment on her husband's situation.

Nixon's inaction widened the opening for the Kennedy campaign, allowing the Democratic candidate's younger brother Bobby to exploit the situation. Though initially opposed to any public association with King, he soon matched his brother's impulsiveness by calling Georgia judge Oscar Mitchell to demand King's release from prison. Following some additional prodding from Atlanta's progressive mayor, William Hartsfield, Mitchell complied, and after eight harrowing days behind bars King was out on bail. Following a joyful reunion with his family, King expressed his gratitude to the Kennedy brothers—and his intention to vote Democratic, something he had not done in previous presidential elections. Coming during the final week of the campaign, this delighted Kennedy's staff. But the best was yet to come. On the Sunday before the election, more than two million copies of a pro-

Kennedy pamphlet entitled *The Case of Martin Luther King: "No Comment" Nixon Versus a Candidate with a Heart* appeared in black churches across the nation, thanks in part to the efforts of Gardner Taylor, a leading figure in the National Baptist Convention who also served on the National Council of CORE. Later known as the "blue bomb," the brightly colored comic-book-style pamphlet produced a groundswell of support for Kennedy, who received approximately 68 percent of the black vote, 8 percent more than Adlai Stevenson had garnered in 1956. Some observers even went so far as to suggest that Kennedy, who defeated Nixon by a mere 114,673 votes in the closest presidential election to date, owed his victory to a late surge in black support.[50]

Kennedy's election brought renewed hope of federal civil rights enforcement. Even though he said relatively little about race or civil rights during the fall campaign, and the calls to Coretta King and Judge Mitchell were not much to go on, most civil rights advocates reasoned that the young president-elect could hardly be worse than Dwight Eisenhower. Personally conservative on matters of race and preoccupied with the Cold War and foreign affairs, Eisenhower had allowed the executive branch's commitment to civil rights to lag far behind that of the federal courts. While Kennedy, too, was an inveterate Cold Warrior with a weak civil rights record, the soaring rhetoric of the New Frontier suggested that the new president planned to pursue an ambitious agenda of domestic reform that included civil rights advances. Despite his reluctance to make specific promises, he often talked about the moral imperatives of a true democracy, and on one occasion he even alluded to the need for a presidency that would "help bring equal access to public facilities from churches to lunch counters and . . . support the right of every American to stand up for his rights, even if on occasion he must sit down for them." This implicit endorsement of the sit-ins did not go unnoticed in the civil rights community, though by inauguration day there were increasing

Presidential candidates John F. Kennedy and Richard M. Nixon, with moderator and CBS newsman Howard K. Smith, following a presidential debate held in Chicago in September 1960. (Getty Photos)

suspicions that Kennedy's commitment to social change was more rhetorical than real. Civil rights leaders were disappointed when he passed over Wofford and appointed Burke Marshall, a corporate lawyer with no track record on civil rights, as the assistant attorney general for civil rights, and they were stunned when he failed to mention civil rights in his inaugural address—or to include Martin Luther King in the list of black leaders invited to the inauguration. These mixed signals left King and others in a state of confusion, though most activists remained hopeful that the arc of American politics was at least tilting toward racial justice.[51]

As Washington and the nation weathered the transition to the Kennedy administration, CORE experienced its own administrative overhaul. A staff revolt against executive secretary Jimmy Robinson, who left on an extended European vacation in October, prompted a general bureaucratic reorganization and a search for someone to fill the newly created position of national director. "Jimmy Robinson was skilled at fund raising, a tiger on details, and as fiercely dedicated as anyone alive," Jim Farmer recalled many years later. "But he was unprepossessing and could not lead Gideon's army, nor sound the call for battle. Furthermore he was white. If CORE was to be at the center of the struggle, its leader and spokesperson had to be black."

The search for a national director quickly focused on King, who briefly entertained an offer tendered by search committee chair Val Coleman. At first King agreed to consider the offer if CORE would consent to a formal merger with SCLC, but the obvious impracticality of combining a secular, Northern-based organization with a group of devout, Southern black ministers soon convinced him to withdraw his name from consideration. The committee's second choice was Farmer, who had been languishing as a minor official at the national NAACP office since 1959. Frustrated by the cautious policies and bureaucratic inertia of Roy Wilkins and other NAACP leaders, Farmer leaped at the chance to rejoin and lead the organization that he had helped to found nineteen years earlier. When Wilkins heard about the offer, he urged Farmer to take it and even acknowledged a bit of envy. "You're going to be riding a mustang pony," he confessed to his departing assistant, "while I'm riding a dinosaur."[52]

3

Hallelujah! I'm a-Travelin'

Stand up and rejoice! A great day is here!
We're fighting Jim Crow and the victory's near!
Hallelujah! I'm a-travelin', Hallelujah, ain't it fine.
Hallelujah! I'm a-travelin' down freedom's main line!

—1961 freedom song[1]

TRUE TO WILKINS'S PREDICTION, Farmer's directorship of CORE began with a gallop. His first day on the job, February 1, 1961, was the first anniversary of the Greensboro sit-in, and all across the South demonstrators were engaging in commemorative acts of courage. As Farmer sat at his desk that first morning waiting for reports from the Southern front, he made his way through a stack of accumulated correspondence. Among the letters that caught his attention were several inquiries about *Boynton v. Virginia*, a recent Supreme Court decision involving Bruce Boynton, a Howard University law student from Selma, Alabama, arrested in 1958 for attempting to desegregate the whites-only Trailways terminal restaurant in Richmond. In December 1960 the Court overturned Boynton's conviction by ruling that state laws mandating segregated waiting rooms, lunch counters, and restroom facilities for interstate passengers were unconstitutional. With this ruling, the Court extended the 1946 *Morgan* decision, which had outlawed legally enforced segregation on interstate buses and trains. But, according to the letter writers, neither of these decisions was being enforced. Why, they asked, were black Americans still being harassed or arrested when they tried to exercise their constitutional right to sit in the front of the bus or to drink a cup of coffee at a bus terminal restaurant?

At a late-morning meeting, Farmer relayed this troubling question to his staff. To his surprise, two staff members had already come up with a tentative plan to address the problem of nonenforcement. As Gordon Carey explained, during an unexpectedly long bus trip from South Carolina to New York in mid-January he and Tom Gaither had discussed the feasibility of a second Journey of Reconciliation. Adapting the phrase "Ride for Freedom" originated by Billie Ames in the mid-1950s, they had come up with a catchy name for the project: "Freedom Ride." Thanks to a blizzard that forced them to spend a night on the floor of a Howard Johnson's restaurant along the New Jersey Turnpike, they had even gone so far as to map out a proposed route from Washington to New Orleans. Patterned after Gandhi's famous march to the sea—throughout the bus trip Carey had been reading Louis Fisher's biography of Gandhi—the second Journey, like the first, would last two weeks. But, taking advantage of the Southern movement's gathering momentum, it would also extend the effort to test compliance with the Constitution into the heart of the Deep South. Despite the obvious logistical problems in mounting such an effort, everyone in the room—including Farmer—immediately sensed that Carey and Gaither were on the right track. By the end of the meeting there was a consensus that the staff should seek formal approval of the project at the next meeting of CORE's National Action Committee, scheduled for February 11–12 in Lexington, Kentucky. There was also general agreement that, unlike the more staid "Journey of Reconciliation," the name "Freedom Ride" was in keeping with "the scrappy nonviolent movement that had emerged" since the Greensboro sit-ins. As a symbol of the new CORE, the project, in Farmer's estimation, required a name that expressed the organization's determination to put "the movement on wheels . . . to cut across state lines and establish the position that we were entitled to act any place in the country, no matter where we hung our hat and called home, because it was our country."[2]

Later in the day, as the news of sit-ins and mass arrests reached the CORE office, Farmer became even more convinced that the time was right for a bold initiative in the Jim Crow South. In Nashville, James Bevel, Diane Nash, and dozens of other local black activists celebrated the Greensboro anniversary by picketing downtown movie theaters, and in Rock Hill, South Carolina, Gaither and nine others ended up in jail after staging a sit-in at a segregated McCrory's lunch counter. When nine of the ten Rock Hill defendants chose thirty days on a road gang rather than a hundred-dollar fine, the "jail–no bail" policy that CORE had been advocating for nearly a year took on new life. As Farmer later recalled, he and his staff "felt that one of the weaknesses of the student sit-in movement of the South had been that as soon as arrested, the kids bailed out. . . . This was not quite Gandhian and not the best tactic. A better tactic would be to remain in jail and to make the maintenance of segregation so expensive for the state and the city that they would hopefully come to the conclusion that they could no longer afford it. Fill up the jails, as Gandhi did in India, fill them to bursting if we had to."

The courage of the Rock Hill Nine was a major topic of conversation when SNCC leaders met in Atlanta on February 3. Jim Lawson had always encouraged his Nashville followers to refuse bail—both as a matter of principle and as an effective tactic—but to date no one in SNCC had chosen to remain behind bars. A heated discussion of the Rock Hill situation and other topics engaged the SNCC leaders well into the night but seemed to be going nowhere until a phone call from Gaither focused their attention. Speaking from a York County Jail phone, Gaither promised them that the Rock Hill Nine were committed to serving out their thirty days of hard labor, but he pleaded for reinforcements that would magnify the impact of the Rock Hill jail-in. He wanted SNCC's student activists to put their own bodies on the line. They could stage jail-ins in other cities, or they could come to Rock Hill to share the pleasures of the York County road gang, but they had to do something dramatic to sustain the momentum of the movement.

Following the call, four students—Diane Nash of Fisk, Charles Jones of Johnson C. Smith University in Charlotte, Ruby Doris Smith of Atlanta's Spelman College, and Charles Sherrod of Virginia Union Seminary—vowed to join the Rock Hill Nine. The next day the four volunteers were on their way to South Carolina and jail. A SNCC press release urging other nonviolent activists to join the second wave of Rock Hill inmates found no takers, but the jail-in movement soon spread to Atlanta and Lynchburg, Virginia, raising the total number of students choosing jail over bail to nearly one hundred. As the Rock Hill Thirteen served out their month in jail, the bond between SNCC and CORE tightened, creating a legend of solidarity and sacrifice that would inspire later activists. On February 12, Abraham Lincoln's Birthday, more than a thousand marchers, some local and some from as far away as Florida, demonstrated their support with a "pilgrimage to Rock Hill," suggesting that Gaither and CORE had started something big.[3]

After his release on March 2, Gaither traveled to New York, where he was greeted as a hero by his CORE colleagues. By this time the office was abuzz with tentative plans for a Freedom Ride scheduled for early May. Three weeks earlier, on the same day as the Rock Hill pilgrimage, the Ride had received the official endorsement of CORE's National Action Committee. Several members of the committee were old enough to remember the excitement surrounding the Journey of Reconciliation, and the gathering in Lexington embraced the staff's proposal as a welcome reprise of CORE's most celebrated project. Prior to the meeting, Farmer had been unsure about the committee's receptivity to such a daring and costly project, so he and his staff came away from the Lexington meeting with a mixture of relief and elation. The committee's decision was especially gratifying to *CORE-lator* editor Jim Peck, the only veteran of the Journey still active as a CORE leader. Having waited fourteen years for a second freedom ride, he felt a sense of vindication, and his only regret was that neither George Houser nor Bayard Rustin was close at hand to witness the rebirth of their dream. Both men, of course, shared Peck's pride once they learned about the Freedom Ride, though neither would play any direct role in planning or implementing the project. Preoccupied with the American Committee on Africa, which had consumed his activist life since 1953, Houser wished CORE well from afar, as did Rustin, who spent most of 1961 in India, England, and various European countries representing the War Resisters League, lobbying for nuclear disarmament, and organizing international peace marches. Cast aside by image-conscious NAACP and SCLC leaders who considered him a political liability, Rustin was temporarily disconnected from the civil rights movement that he had helped to create. He did not return to the United States until the fall of 1961, too late to have any further influence on the Freedom Rides that he had helped to inspire.

The Freedom Ride sanctioned by the National Action Committee followed the basic outline of Rustin and Houser's original 1947 Washington-to–New Orleans plan, which had been adapted by Carey and Gaither in January. In Farmer's words, CORE planned to "recruit from twelve to fourteen persons, call them to Washington, D.C., for a week of intensive training and preparation, and then embark on the Ride. Half would go by Greyhound and half by Trailways." The Riders would leave Washington on May 4, travel through Virginia, North and South Carolina, Georgia, Alabama, and Mississippi, and arrive—it was hoped—in New Orleans on May 17, the seventh anniversary of the *Brown* decision. Realizing that the trip posed a series of potential dangers and logistical challenges, Farmer asked Gaither to act as the Riders' advance scout, just as Rustin and Houser had done in 1947. With his recent experiences in Rock Hill and his hard-earned knowledge of the Southern scene, Gaither was the logical choice for this dangerous mission. But no one—not even Gaither—could be certain how much resistance he would encounter once he returned to the South.

Setting out in early April, Gaither scouted the entire route from Washington to New Orleans. At each stop, he surveyed the layout of terminal facilities, met with black leaders to arrange housing and speaking engagements for the Riders, and assessed the tenor of local race relations. As he made his way across the region, news of the impending Freedom Ride drew a mixed response among Southern blacks. Some weren't sure how they felt about CORE or the Ride, and others wanted nothing to do with the troublemakers from the North, but in virtually every black community along the route Gaither found some support for the Riders. In the end, he was able to secure local sponsors in a dozen communities from Virginia to Louisiana. Representing the scattered local movements that had dotted the black South since the 1940s, the organizations willing to host the Riders ranged from small Baptist congregations in Petersburg and Lynchburg to private black colleges in Richmond, Charlotte, Rock Hill, and Atlanta. In each case, the decision to associate with the Riders involved considerable risk, and Gaither could not be sure that the promised arrangements would be honored once

the Freedom Riders actually arrived. But on balance he was encouraged by
the prospects for cooperation and insurgency among black Southerners.

Especially encouraging was the enthusiasm that he encountered at a SNCC
meeting in Charlotte on April 21. With SNCC advisor Ella Baker and representatives from SCLC, the National Student Association, the Southern Conference Education Fund, and the American Friends Service Committee present
as observers, the fifteen student leaders at the meeting embraced the idea of
direct action on buses and trains. While there was no formal endorsement of
the CORE Freedom Ride, the students approved a "Summer Action Program"
that included a plan to urge black college students to exercise the rights guaranteed by the *Morgan* and *Boynton* decisions. "With the closing of the school
year and with thousands of students traveling across state lines on public
conveyances en route to their homes," a SNCC memorandum explained, "they
offer and provide the manpower for a really massive realization of the promise
made in these decisions. Many of these students, of course, will not be the
hard-core activists who are ready to continue sitting when refused service and
to be jailed in a strange city or town, but such students can still be useful if they
will simply request service, stressing their rights as interstate passengers."
Gaither agreed and left the Charlotte meeting with renewed hope that the
black freedom struggle was widening.

His assessment of the white South was less sanguine, however. In the
Upper South states of Virginia and North Carolina, the prospects for compliance with *Morgan* and *Boynton* looked promising, but from South Carolina
on down Gaither didn't like what he saw. He already had firsthand experience with the harshness of segregationist resistance in Rock Hill and other
South Carolina communities, but the belligerence and defiance that he encountered in Alabama and Mississippi shocked him. If the Freedom Riders
challenged the ultra-segregationists of the Deep South without benefit of
police protection, he concluded, they would be lucky to escape with their
lives. In his report, he identified the white supremacist strongholds where
the Riders would be most likely to encounter violence, including Birmingham and Anniston, which he termed "a very explosive trouble spot without a
doubt." Confirmed by the Reverend Fred Shuttlesworth and other embattled
movement leaders in Birmingham and Montgomery, Gaither's warning about
the volatile situation in Alabama was also consistent with the experiences of
several recent visitors to the state, including Journey of Reconciliation veteran Bill Worthy. While en route to Tuskegee in January, Worthy encountered stiff resistance from local authorities who did not appreciate his attempt
to test compliance with the *Boynton* decision. "At the Greyhound terminal in
Birmingham and Montgomery, and at the Birmingham airport restaurant,"
he reported, "I was involved in five separate incidents, was twice held by the
police, and several times threatened with violence."[4]

While Gaither was checking out the route, other CORE staffers were
busy recruiting and selecting the dozen or so Riders with the requisite skills

and courage to survive. More than anything else, CORE wanted recruits who had already demonstrated a strong commitment to nonviolence and who knew what was being asked of them. Recruitment material made no attempt to hide the potential dangers of the Ride or to minimize the difficulty of fulfilling the responsibilities of nonviolent resistance. Only the most committed and the stoutest of heart were encouraged to apply. Freedom Riders could expect to be harassed and arrested, as sixteen members of the St. Louis and Columbia, Missouri, CORE chapters discovered in mid-April when they participated in what the *CORE-lator* later dubbed a "Little Freedom Ride." Setting out by bus from East St. Louis, the interracial band only made it as far as the southeastern Missouri town of Sikeston, 150 miles down the road, before being arrested at a whites-only terminal restaurant for "disturbing the peace." With their cases still pending in late April, the "little" Freedom Riders provided potential recruits with a sobering preview of what the "big" Freedom Ride might entail. As Carey warned in a letter sent to CORE leaders on May 1, "If bus protests end in arrest in Missouri, what can be expected when the Freedom Ride gets to Georgia and points South?"[5]

CORE solicited applications from outside the organization and even placed an ad in the *Student Voice*, SNCC's monthly newsletter, but from the outset Farmer and Carey intended to rely heavily on CORE veterans and word-of-mouth recruitment. The first Freedom Riders selected were Farmer himself and Peck. As a veteran of the Journey of Reconciliation, Peck was an obvious choice. But Farmer's decision to put himself in harm's way raised more than a few eyebrows. Known more as an office and idea man than as a hands-on activist, CORE's forty-one-year-old leader had never exhibited much interest in risking arrest and imprisonment. Those who knew him well, however, understood his motivation. The Freedom Ride was Farmer's personal ticket to glory, his best chance to join King, Randolph, and Marshall in the front rank of civil rights heroes. Having missed the 1947 ride, he wasn't about to miss this one. At the very least, participating in the Ride would help dispel his reputation for elitist disengagement, or so he hoped.

In selecting the remaining Riders, Farmer and his staff tried to come up with a reasonably balanced mixture of black and white, young and old, religious and secular, Northern and Southern. The only deliberate imbalance was a lack of women. Although, unlike the Journey of Reconciliation, the Freedom Ride would not be limited to men, Farmer and Carey were reluctant to expose women, especially black women, to potentially violent confrontations with white supremacists. Their decision to limit the number of female Freedom Riders to two was undoubtedly rooted in patriarchal conservatism, but they also feared that a balanced contingent of men and women might be interpreted as a provocative pattern of sexual pairing. The situation was dangerous enough, they reasoned, without taunting the segregationists with visions of interracial sex. Later in the summer, when the Freedom Rides involved a large number of women, white Southern fixations on interracial couplings and other perceived threats to sexual orthodoxy confirmed the CORE leaders' fears. But CORE's original decision would remain a subject of controversy, within both the organization and the broader movement, for years to come.

CORE asked each applicant to include a recommendation from a teacher, pastor, or co-worker and to write an essay outlining his or her commitment to nonviolence and the struggle for civil rights. Volunteers under the age of twenty-one also had to submit proof of parental permission. By late April the CORE office had received several dozen applications, all filled with testimonials of courage and conviction and eagerness to serve the cause. From this pool, Farmer and Carey chose fourteen riders. Three of those chosen were unable to make it to Washington in time for the Ride: the Reverend J. Metz Rollins, a veteran of the 1956 Tallahassee bus boycott who had become the Nashville-based field director of the United Presbyterian Church; and Julia Aaron and Jerome Smith, two members of New Orleans CORE who were languishing in a Louisiana jail. But those who did show up provided CORE with an experienced and committed band of activists.[6]

THE ELEVEN FREEDOM RIDERS who joined Farmer and Peck in Washington on May 1 represented a wide range of backgrounds and movement experiences. Two of the eleven, Genevieve Hughes and Joe Perkins, were CORE staff members. A tall, attractive twenty-eight-year-old white woman, Hughes was a relative newcomer to the movement who had spent most of her life in the prosperous Washington suburb of Chevy Chase. Following her graduation from Cornell, she had moved to New York City to work as a stockbroker at Dunn and Bradstreet. During the late 1950s she became active in the local chapter of CORE, eventually helping to rejuvenate the chapter by coordinating a boycott of dime stores affiliated with chains resisting the sit-in movement in the South. Exhilarated by the boycott and increasingly alienated from the conservative complacency of Wall Street, she gravitated toward a commitment to full-time activism, accepting a CORE field secretary position in the fall of 1960. The first woman to serve on CORE's field staff, she made a lasting impression on everyone who met her. Years later, fellow Freedom Rider John Lewis wistfully recalled that she was "as graceful and gentle as her name," yet "not at all afraid to speak up when she had strong feelings about something." When asked to explain her decision to join the Freedom Ride, she replied: "I figured Southern women should be represented so the South and the nation would realize all Southern people don't think alike."[7]

At twenty-seven, Perkins was a year younger than Hughes, and he too had been on the CORE staff for less than a year. Born and raised in Owensboro, Kentucky, as the oldest of six children, he spent four years at Kentucky State University in Frankfort before enlisting in the army in 1954. After serving two years as a medical technician, he left the army and enrolled at Howard University as a music education major. He later transferred to the University of Michigan, where he and several other black graduate students became passionately involved in the activities of the Ann Arbor Direct Action Committee in the spring of 1960. As a demonstration of support for the Southern sit-in movement, he picketed Woolworth's and Kresge department stores and later organized a "stand-in" at the Newport Beach on Lake Erie. Recruited by Ann Arbor CORE in August, he attended the Interracial Action Institute in Miami as a trainee and served ten days in jail after he and several others were arrested during a sit-in at Shell's Supermarket. Following his release, he took a leave of absence from the University of Michigan to work full-time for CORE as a field secretary in the borderlands of Kentucky and West Virginia. During the fall and winter prior to the Freedom Ride, he spearheaded successful direct action campaigns in Louisville, Covington, and several other cities, earning a reputation as a skilled and fearless organizer. Perkins's outspoken manner and sometimes impatient approach to activism clashed with the more deliberate style of his supervisor, national field director Gordon Carey, and disagreements with Carey and Marvin Rich led to his resignation in June 1961. But during the Freedom Ride he was at his best, prompting one admiring observer to call him "one of the smoothest operators on the tour."[8]

Rounding out the Michigan contingent were the Bergmans, Walter and Frances, two white activists who brought a unique set of experiences to the Freedom Ride. At sixty-one, Walter Bergman was the oldest of the Freedom Riders, and Frances, a former elementary school teacher and assistant principal, was the second oldest at fifty-seven. A retired school administrator who had taught part-time at the University of Michigan and Wayne State University, Walter had been a leading figure in the teachers' union movement of the 1930s and 1940s, serving as the first president of the Michigan Federation of Teachers. In the mid- and late 1940s, following military service in the European theater, he spent several years in Germany as a civilian educational specialist, first for the United Nations Relief and Rehabilitation Administration, and later for the U.S. government's de-Nazification program in Bavaria. In 1948 he returned to the United States to become director of research for the Detroit Board of Education, but his wife Isabel remained in Europe as a UN relief worker. Divorce and remarriage to Frances soon followed, and by the early 1950s he had resumed his leadership role with the Michigan Federation of Teachers, a position that drew him into the academic freedom and civil liberties controversies of the McCarthy era. Both Bergmans were committed socialists and admirers of Norman Thomas, as well as leaders of the Michigan affiliate of the ACLU. Since 1958 they had become increasingly active in CORE picketing campaigns against segregated hotels, chain stores, and swimming pools in Detroit. By the time they volunteered for the Freedom Ride, they were veteran civil rights activists, though virtually all of their movement experience was in the North. While they had recently attended a CORE conference in Lexington, Kentucky, the Freedom Ride would be their first journey to the Deep South.[9]

The Bergmans were not the only Freedom Riders to have limited experience in the South. Four others—Albert Bigelow, Jimmy McDonald, Ed Blankenheim, and John Moody—were unmistakably Northern in background. A fifty-five-year-old former navy captain and World War II veteran, Bigelow had earned an architecture degree at Harvard and served as the state housing commissioner of Massachusetts before moving to Connecticut in the 1950s. Repulsed by the dropping of atomic bombs on Hiroshima and Nagasaki, he became a devout Quaker and pacifist who opened his home to Hiroshima survivors undergoing plastic surgery in American hospitals. A founding member of the Committee for Non-Violent Action (CNVA), he gained an international reputation as a militant anti-nuclear activist in 1958 when he captained the *Golden Rule*, a protest ship sponsored by CNVA and the National Committee for a Sane Nuclear Policy (SANE). Sailing the thirty-foot ketch into a drop zone in the Pacific to protest America's scheduled testing of nuclear weapons near the island of Eniwetok, he warned President Eisenhower that even though "our voices have been lost in the massive effort of those responsible for preparing this country for war . . . we mean to speak now with the weight of our whole lives." Arrested in Honolulu before they could enter the test zone, Bigelow and his Quaker crew served sixty days in prison but drew international attention to their cause. A square-shouldered, imposing man with a commanding presence, he did not fit the stereotypic image of a peace crusader. But no one who knew him well doubted the depth of his commitment to pacifism and nonviolent direct action.[10]

Jimmy McDonald was a twenty-nine-year-old black folk singer from New York City known for his vast repertoire of labor and freedom songs. As a precocious seventeen-year-old, he had campaigned for Progressive Party presidential candidate Henry Wallace in 1948, inspired in part by a Wallace rally featuring the radical black activist and singer Paul Robeson. Asked to perform at a CORE fund-raiser in Brooklyn in 1956, McDonald later participated in a number of New York CORE direct action campaigns, and for a brief period in 1960 he worked at CORE headquarters as a part-time clerk. "A very playful, bohemian, Greenwich Village kind of guy," as John Lewis later described him, he added comic relief and a touch of whimsy to the band of Freedom Riders. Though street-smart, he was something of a loose cannon and unquestionably the least disciplined of the Riders. Somewhat uncomfortable with the interracial nature of CORE and generally dismissive of nonviolence as a viable philosophy, he viewed the bus journey through the South as a chance for adventure and "a great ride," as he later put it. "I was not sent because I had a lot of intellect," he recalled in 1969; ". . . certainly I was not in there because I wanted to be like Gandhi." They wanted "me to go . . . to lead the singing."[11]

Two years younger than McDonald, Ed Blankenheim was a carpenter's apprentice and part-time chemistry student at the University of Arizona in Tucson. Feisty and full of resolve, he had talked his way into the Marine Corps in 1950, at the age of sixteen. Eleven years later, as a Korean War veteran and father of two, he traveled more than two thousand miles to join the Freedom Ride. Born in Minnesota and raised in Illinois, he moved to Arizona in the late 1950s, after spending two years at Wright Junior College in Chicago. Befriending fellow chemistry student Tom Burroughs and several other black student activists, he became one of the few whites to participate in local civil rights activities, first as a member of Tucson's NAACP Youth Council, and later as a leader of a local CORE chapter known as Students for Equality. The CORE affiliation came after Blankenheim and Burroughs called the New York office for help. Eager to establish a foothold in the Southwest, Jim Farmer dispatched pacifist leader David McReynolds, a War Resisters League official who frequently donated his services to CORE, to Tucson to help organize the local student movement. McReynolds stayed for two weeks, enthralling the students with discussions of Gandhian wisdom and strategy.

Blankenheim, in particular, embraced McReynolds as a friend and mentor worth following. "His belief in mankind and the human potential for kindness," he later recalled, "changed Students for Equality and changed me." The feeling of respect was mutual, and when the Freedom Ride project emerged a few weeks later, McReynolds unhesitatingly recommended the wiry young man with the sardonic wit and impish grin. Farmer had asked him "to keep an eye out for potential Freedom Riders," and he felt he had found a good prospect in Arizona. Blankenheim had seen enough of the South as a young marine recruit at Parris Island, South Carolina, to be wary of directly challenging the region's racial shibboleths, and he knew full well that he "was being invited on a trip into the Deep South as part of a mixed-race bomb." After a little prodding from Farmer, though, he could not resist joining the Ride. "I was no less concerned about the danger of my commitment," he later explained, "but all that I had seen in the South and all that I had learned from Dave stared me down. I had come too far and I couldn't turn back."[12]

John Moody was a thirty-year-old student at Howard University and an active member of the SNCC-affiliated Nonviolent Action Group (NAG), which had staged a series of successful sit-ins in Washington, Maryland, and northern Virginia. Born and raised in Philadelphia, where he was a leader of the local NAACP Youth Council, Moody threw himself into student and movement politics soon after transferring to Howard from Lincoln University. Self-conscious about his Northern background, he was both fascinated and frightened by images of black life in the Jim Crow South. As a young boy in Philadelphia, he listened with rapt attention to a transplanted North Carolina–born cousin who often reminisced about violent encounters with white Southern racists. Such stories, combined with his experiences at Howard, helped to draw him into the movement, but he remained very apprehensive about actually visiting the Deep South. As he confessed to his roommate in late April, even though he had volunteered to join the Freedom Ride, he didn't really want to go. This ambivalence and an untimely case of the flu soon plunged Moody into a mental and physical crisis that forced him to drop out on the last day of orientation. Three weeks later, after regaining his health and composure, he would take part in a Freedom Ride from Montgomery to Jackson, serving six weeks in a Mississippi jail cell for his trouble. But in early May he was in no condition to head south with the original Riders.[13]

Realizing this, Farmer and Carey accepted Moody's young roommate, Hank Thomas, as a last-minute replacement. Although Thomas did not have the chance to go through the early orientation sessions, the strapping nineteen-year-old sophomore was well prepared for the challenges of the Ride. Like Moody, Thomas had been active in the NAG protests, but he also had the benefit of years of firsthand experience in the Jim Crow South and had even attended the founding conference of SNCC in April 1960. A native Floridian with rural roots, he grew up in an impoverished and troubled family headed by an abusive stepfather. One of eleven children, he chopped cotton in southern Georgia before moving to St. Augustine at the age of eight. As a Deep South migrant, he never felt completely comfortable at Howard, an institution dominated by the sons and daughters of the black bourgeoisie. For him, the Freedom Ride provided a welcome escape from the stuffy complacency and condescension of privileged students who displayed little concern for the plight of their vulnerable Southern cousins. "When folks ask me what incident led me to ride," he explained many years later, "I can't say it was one. When you grow up and face this humiliation every day, there is no one thing. You always felt that way."[14]

The rest of the Riders, like Thomas, were young black Southerners raised in the midst of rigidly segregated institutions. The youngest was eighteen-year-old Charles Person, a freshman at Atlanta's Morehouse College. Born and raised in Atlanta, where his father worked as an orderly at the Emory University Hospital, Person was a gifted math and physics student who dreamed of a career as a scientist. After being denied admission to the all-white Georgia Institute of Technology, he enrolled at Morehouse in the fall of 1960. Person had been a member of the local NAACP Youth Council during his senior year in high school, and he and several other Morehouse students, including future Freedom Riders Frank Holloway and Harold Andrews, became active in a student protest organization known as the Atlanta Committee on Appeal for Human Rights. In early 1961 one sit-in earned him a sixteen-day jail sentence, an experience that deepened his commitment to the struggle and drew the attention of CORE recruiters looking for a Freedom Rider who could represent the Atlanta sit-in movement. Since he was still a minor, he had to talk his father (his mother refused) into signing a CORE permission form, but his persistence ultimately prevailed. As he left his tearful parents in Atlanta to embark on the long bus ride to Washington, he reluctantly took a seat in the back of the bus—perhaps, he hoped, for the last time.[15]

The oldest of the "Southern" Freedom Riders (aside from Farmer) was the Reverend Benjamin Elton Cox. Though only twenty-nine, he had packed a lot of living—and talking—into his three decades of existence. A native of Whiteville, Tennessee, Cox was a loquacious and eloquent preacher who earned the nickname "Beltin' Elton" during the course of the Freedom Ride. The seventh of sixteen children, he moved to Kankakee, Illinois, at the age of five. A high-school dropout, he shined shoes for eighteen months before completing the work for his diploma at the age of twenty. He later attended Livingstone College, an AME Zion institution in Salisbury, North Carolina, before studying for a divinity degree at Howard, and even spent a year as a visiting student at a seminary in Cambridge, Massachusetts. Following his ordination in 1958, he became the pastor of the Pilgrim Congregational Church in High Point, North Carolina, a small city fifteen miles southwest of Greensboro. In High Point he quickly gained a reputation as a militant civil rights advocate by spearheading local school desegregation efforts, serving as an advisor for the local NAACP Youth Council, and acting as an observer for the American Friends Service Committee. Following the early Greensboro sit-ins in February 1960, he encouraged local students to stage their own sit-ins, but only if they were willing to keep them nonviolent. Forceful in his public commitment to nonviolence, he soon drew the attention of national NAACP leaders, including Farmer, who hired him to stump the South. Later, after Farmer became executive director of CORE, Cox received a call from his former boss, who wanted at least one ordained minister to join the Freedom Ride. Cox agreed without hesitation and, honoring the spirit of Farmer's request, showed up in Washington wearing a formal clerical collar, just in case anyone doubted that the Ride was blessed with divine guidance.[16]

The roster of Freedom Riders originally included two ordained ministers, in fact: Cox and the Reverend J. Metz Rollins of Nashville. Rollins was also one of two Riders recruited from Nashville, but in late April he had to bow out, leaving Cox as the lone preacher and John Lewis as the sole representative of the Nashville Movement. Destined to be the most celebrated Freedom Rider of them all, Lewis first learned about the Freedom Ride when Rollins showed him a CORE advertisement in the *Student Voice*. At twenty-one, the future Georgia congressman was one of the youngest Freedom Riders, but with five arrests he was already a jail-tested veteran of the nonviolent movement. Born on a hardscrabble tenant farm in Pike County, Alabama, a few miles outside the town of Troy, Lewis was a dedicated student who dreamed of being the first person in his family to go college. Despite a natural shyness, he wanted to be a preacher, especially after listening to a stirring radio sermon by Martin Luther King Jr. in 1955. Two years later he enrolled at American Baptist Theological Seminary (ABT), a small, unaccredited college in Nashville, Tennessee. At ABT he became a student and protégé of the Reverend Kelly Miller Smith, the founder of the Nashville Christian Leadership Council, and by the fall of 1958 he had been drawn into the orbit of Jim Lawson and the emerging Nashville Movement. Along with several ABT classmates, including his close friends Bernard Lafayette and Jim Bevel, Lewis eagerly absorbed the lessons of Lawson's weekly workshops on nonviolence. In November his commitment to nonviolent struggle deepened during a memorable weekend at the Highlander Folk School in Monteagle, Tennessee, where Septima Clark, Myles Horton, and other movement veterans shared their experiences and ideas. "I left Highlander on fire," he recalled.

Over the next year, Lawson's workshops deepened his young disciple's religious and moral faith with visions of "redemptive suffering," "soul force," and the "beloved community," concepts that would inform and animate Lewis's long and influential career as a civil rights leader. Instrumental in the founding of the Nashville Student Central Committee in October 1959, Lewis found an opportunity to put his evolving philosophy into action the following winter when downtown Nashville became a center of sit-in activity. Arrested along with scores of other student demonstrators during a February 1960 sit-in, he underwent what he later characterized as a conversion-like experience, "crossing over . . . into total, unquestioning commitment." More arrests followed, pushing thoughts of the ministry and school and family ties farther and farther into the background of his life. By the spring of 1961, when he volunteered for the Freedom Ride, the movement had become his surrogate "family." "At this time," he wrote revealingly on his application, "human dignity is the most important thing in my life. This is [the] most important decision in my life, to decide to give up all if necessary for the Freedom Ride, that Justice and Freedom might come to the Deep South." The depth of his commitment was already a source of inspiration for other Nashville activists, and those who knew him well realized that the CORE initiative would not be his first freedom ride.[17]

In late December 1959, while traveling home for the Christmas break, Lewis and Bernard Lafayette impulsively decided to exercise their rights as interstate passengers by sitting in the front section of a bus from Nashville to Birmingham. Lafayette sat right behind the driver, and Lewis sat a few rows back on the opposite side. When the driver ordered them to the rear, they refused to budge. The driver then left the bus to call the Nashville police, but later returned in a rage after the police refused to intervene. At one point, he pushed his seat backward, crushing Lafayette's suitcase, but the two "freedom riders" stubbornly remained in the front as the bus headed southward. At several stops the driver left the bus to use the phone, convincing Lewis and Lafayette that he was alerting the Klan. No Klansmen actually appeared, but when the two friends parted company later that night in Troy, they nervously joked that they might not see each other again. For Lafayette, who still had five hundred miles to travel before reaching his home in Tampa, the situation seemed especially dangerous. In the end, both students arrived home safely, suffering no more than the broken suitcase and the driver's scowls in the process. The whole experience filled them with a strange mixture of exhilaration and outrage, and after their return to Nashville a discussion of their narrow escape led to the idea of a second and more ambitious ride.

For more than a year they let the idea simmer, but in March 1961 they sent a letter to the Reverend Fred Shuttlesworth, Birmingham's leading civil rights activist, proposing a test of both the *Morgan* and *Boynton* decisions. As Lewis recalled many years later, "Our idea was to have a core group of us ride the bus down to Birmingham and test the waiting areas, rest rooms and eating facilities in the Greyhound station there—perhaps the most rigidly segregated bus terminal in the South—applying the same tactics we'd used with our sit-ins and stand-ins in Nashville." Though appreciative of their bravery, Shuttlesworth urged the Nashville insurgents to find some other way to serve the cause. Birmingham, he warned, was a racial powder keg that would explode if local white supremacists were unduly provoked, especially by outsiders. This was not what Lewis and Lafayette wanted to hear, but their disappointment turned to vindication a few days later when they discovered CORE's plan for a Freedom Ride. Lafayette, like Lewis, was determined to join the Ride, but he was not yet twenty-one and needed his parents' permission. Already exercised over her son's role in the Nashville sit-ins, Lafayette's mother refused to sign the permission form, reminding him that she had sent him "to Nashville to study, not to aggravate white folks." Lafayette's father, an itinerant carpenter who had spent most of his life in the tough Ybor City section of Tampa, was even more emphatic, thundering: "Boy, you're asking me to sign your death warrant." Three weeks later young Lafayette would ignore his parents' wishes and join an NCLC-sponsored Freedom Ride that would land him in Mississippi's Parchman Prison. But at this point the best he could do was to accompany Lewis and Bevel on a wild car ride to Murfreesboro, where Lewis—who had missed his connection in Nashville—caught the morning bus to Washington.[18]

Lewis arrived in Washington on the morning of April 30, just in time to join the other Freedom Riders for three days of intensive preparation and training in nonviolence. All thirteen Riders stayed at Fellowship House, a well-known Quaker meetinghouse and dormitory on L Street that had served generations of pacifists and social activists. "Inside was room after room filled with books and posters and pieces of art," Lewis later recalled, "all centered around the themes of peace and community." To many of the Riders, such a scene was familiar, but the young Alabamian "had never been in a building like this," nor "among people like this." In this enclave of interracial brotherhood, the beloved community that Lawson had conjured up suddenly seemed less abstract and more achievable, at least until Farmer's rather heavy-handed welcoming speech complicated this ethereal vision.

In greeting his fellow Riders, Farmer made it clear that he was in charge and that the Freedom Ride was first and foremost a CORE project. Anyone unwilling to abide by CORE's strict adherence to nonviolence should withdraw from the project, he informed them in his best stentorian voice. He then went on to outline the proposed Ride, providing "an overview of what we were going to do, how we were going to do it, and the most optimistic and pessimistic outcomes possible." After several minutes of sobering orientation, he turned the podium over to Carl Rachlin, a forty-two-year-old New York labor and civil rights lawyer who served as CORE's general counsel. Rachlin gave the Riders a short course in constitutional law, focusing on federal and state laws pertaining to discrimination in interstate transportation, and told them what to do if and when they were arrested. Two additional speakers, a sociologist and an experienced social activist, briefed the Riders on what to expect from the white South. The sociologist, Farmer later recalled, "elaborated on the mores and folkways of the areas through which we would be riding and described the lengths to which the local populace probably would go to force compliance with their sacrosanct racial customs," and the activist followed with a description of "what really was going to happen to us, including clobberings and possibly death." In the discussions that followed, several of the Riders shared personal stories about the dangers of nonviolent protest and their experiences with Jim Crow, and later in the day they were all encouraged to read and re-read classic texts by Gandhi, Thoreau, and other celebrated exponents of nonviolence and civil disobedience.[19]

All of this was a prelude to what CORE leaders considered to be the most important part of the Riders' training: "intense role-playing sessions" designed to give them a sense of what they were about to face. Coordinated by Carey, the sessions were carefully constructed "sociodramas—with some of the group playing the part of Freedom Riders sitting at simulated lunch counters or sitting on the front-seats of a make-believe bus. Others acted out the roles of functionaries, adversaries, or observers. Several played the role of white hoodlums coming to beat up the Freedom Riders on the buses or at lunch counters at the terminals." The sessions, which at times became "all too realistic," according to Farmer, went on for three grueling days, as the participants swapped and reswapped places. After each session they evaluated the role players' actions and reactions, and over the course of the training each Rider got the chance to experience the full range of emotions and crises that were likely to emerge during the coming journey. "It was quite an experience," Ben Cox recalled. "We were knocked on the floor, we poured Coca-Cola and coffee on each other, and there was shoving and calling each other all kinds of racial epithets, and even spitting on each other, which would inflame you to see if you could stand what was going to come." As a veteran of Lawson's Nashville workshop, Lewis had already undergone this kind of training, but for most of the Riders the sessions represented a new and somewhat disconcerting ordeal. For John Moody, suffering from the flu and already unnerved by images of Southern violence, the training was intense enough to prompt withdrawal from the Ride. And he was not the only recruit to have second thoughts about subjecting himself to such abuse.[20]

By the afternoon of May 3, the day before their scheduled departure, all of the Riders were emotionally drained. During the final hours of preparation, as pride and anticipation mingled with fear and apprehension, Farmer realized that he had to do something to break the tension. Following a few freedom songs from Jimmy McDonald, he took the Riders downtown for an elaborate Chinese dinner at the Yen Ching Palace, an upscale Connecticut Avenue restaurant managed by NAG activist Paul Dietrich. The owner of the restaurant, Van Lung, a close friend of Dietrich's since their childhood in upstate New York, was also a longtime associate of General Claire Lee Chennault, the famed Louisiana-born leader of the World War II "Flying Tigers" Asian fighter squadron. Prior to his death in 1958, Chennault had been a frequent visitor to the Yen Ching Palace, and for several years, at the close of duck-hunting season, the restaurant had hosted the Louisiana congressional delegation's annual Peking duck banquet. None of the Louisiana politicos was present when the Freedom Riders filed into the restaurant on the evening of May 3, but the dinner episode was exotic nonetheless. Many of the younger Riders, including John Lewis, had never eaten Chinese food before, and the whole scene somehow seemed appropriate for men and women about to explore the unknown. "As we passed around the bright silver containers of food," Lewis recalled, "someone joked that we should eat well and enjoy because this might be our Last Supper." This gallows humor seemed to break the ice, and the gathering settled into a mood of genuine fellowship. By the time the steamed rice and stir-fried vegetables gave way to fortune cookies, it was clear that the experiences of the last three days had created a family-like bond among the Riders.

As the cookies and pots of tea were making their way around the table, Dietrich and several other NAG activists joined the group, just in time to hear a soul-searching speech by Farmer. Obviously pleased with what had transpired since the Riders had arrived in Washington, he wanted them to know that he had faith in their ability to meet any challenge, but he went on to insist that he was the only "one obligated to go on this trip," that "there was still time for any person to decide not to go." If one or more of them chose not to go, "there would be no recrimination, no blame, and CORE would pay transportation back home." After Farmer closed his remarks and settled back into his chair, Cox offered to lead the Riders in prayer. Farmer, in deference to the atheists and agnostics present, suggested that a moment of silence was more appropriate. The "moment" went on for a full five minutes as the Riders mulled over the CORE leader's offer. Finally, he broke the silence by telling them that they did not have to make an immediate decision;

they could tell him "later that night or just not show up at the bus terminal in the morning, whichever was easiest." With this unsettling benediction, the Riders filed out of the restaurant in near silence. Back at Fellowship House, a few nervous conversations ensued, but most chose to wrestle with their consciences individually and in private. Although the long-awaited Freedom Ride was scheduled to leave in a few hours, no one knew how many Riders would actually appear at the bus station in the morning.

Farmer's escape clause reminded the Riders of the gravity of the situation. Most were well aware of the dangers ahead, and earlier in the week each would-be Rider had signed a waiver releasing CORE from any liability for injuries suffered during the Ride, but Farmer's final warning virtually guaranteed a night of wide-eyed restlessness. Some of the Riders made last-minute calls to friends and family before retiring. Others stayed up late completing their wills or just jotting down their thoughts and reflections. A few never went to bed at all. There was so much to think about, and even among the most hardened veterans of the struggle so many unknowns to contemplate, so many mysteries of the human condition to ponder.

Farmer received several calls that evening, including one from his old boss Roy Wilkins, who asked, somewhat facetiously, if CORE was actually going to go through with its "joy ride." Farmer was not amused, but, knowing that the Riders might need the NAACP in the days ahead, he bit his tongue. He assured Wilkins that everything was set, though in truth he was beginning to have his doubts. During the long, hard night before the departure, as he replayed the evening's events in his mind, he began to worry that he had unwittingly sown the seeds of failure with his offer to let the volunteers back out. He was not one to wallow in self-doubt, but this time he could not help but second-guess himself. Why hadn't he left well enough alone? Had he come this far only to see his dream dissolve in a torrent of needless panic fostered by his own well-meaning but careless words? What would happen to CORE and the movement if word got out, as it surely would, that the Freedom Riders had lost their nerve? These questions haunted him as he awoke on the most important morning of his life.

Only when Farmer arrived at the breakfast table and saw the determination in the eyes of his fellow Riders did he realize that his fears were unfounded. "They were prepared for anything, even death," he later insisted. No one had withdrawn, and individually and collectively they appeared ready to do what had to be done, not in a spirit of selfless or reckless heroism but as a vanguard of ordinary citizens seeking simple justice. The time had come to challenge the hypocrisy and complacency of a nation that refused to enforce its own laws and somehow failed to acknowledge the utter indecency of racial discrimination.[21]

THE SCENE AT THE DOWNTOWN TRAILWAYS AND GREYHOUND STATIONS that morning gave little indication that something momentous was about to unfold. There were no identifying banners, no protest signs—nothing to signify the start of a revolution other than a few well-wishers representing CORE, NAG, and SCLC. Despite a spate of CORE press releases, the beginning of the Freedom Ride drew only token coverage. No television cameras or radio microphones were on hand to record the event, and the only members of the national press corps covering the departure were an Associated Press correspondent and two local reporters from the *Washington Post* and the *Washington Evening Star*.

The only other journalists present were three brave individuals who had agreed to accompany the Riders to New Orleans: Charlotte Devree, a fifty-year-old white freelance writer and CORE activist from New York who hoped to publish a firsthand account of the Freedom Ride (and who frequently would be misidentified as a Freedom Rider); Simeon Booker, a forty-three-year-old black feature writer originally from Baltimore representing Johnson Publications' *Jet* and *Ebony* magazines; and Ted Gaffney, a thirty-three-year-old Washington-based photographer and Johnson stringer. A fourth journalist, Moses Newson, the thirty-four-year-old city editor of the *Baltimore Afro-American*, would later join the Ride in Greensboro, North Carolina. All four were seasoned journalists, especially Booker, a former Nieman Fellow who had attracted considerable attention for his riveting coverage of the sensational 1955 Emmett Till murder case. But only Newson—a native of Leesburg, Florida, who had worked for the *Memphis Tri-State Defender* in the early 1950s and who had covered both the 1956 Clinton, Tennessee, and 1957 Little Rock, Arkansas, school desegregation crises—had extended experience in the Deep South. Gaffney had relevant experience of a different kind, however. In June 1946, as a young soldier traveling by bus from Washington to Fort Eustis, Virginia, he had conducted a personal test of the recent *Morgan* decision. Although the driver "turned red and trembled with rage," Gaffney ignored the order to move to the back of the bus and rode all the way to Fort Eustis on a front seat. Fifteen years later memories of this "first freedom ride" came flooding back as he boarded the bus that would take him on the ride of his life.

Two weeks earlier the CORE office had sent letters describing the impending Freedom Ride to President Kennedy, FBI director J. Edgar Hoover, Attorney General Robert Kennedy, the chairman of the ICC, and the presidents of Trailways and Greyhound. But no one had responded, and as the Riders prepared to board the buses there was no sign of official surveillance or concern. At Farmer's request, Simeon Booker, who was known to have several close contacts in the Washington bureaucracy, called the FBI to remind the agency that the Freedom Ride was about to begin, and on the eve of the Ride Booker had a brief meeting at the Justice Department with Attorney General Kennedy and his assistant John Seigenthaler. Booker warned Kennedy that the Riders might need protection from segregationist thugs, but the young attorney general did not seem to appreciate the gravity of the situation. After telling the black journalist to "call" him if trouble arose,

B4   Friday, May 5, 1961   THE WASHINGTON POST

Pilgrimage Off On Racial Test

By Elsie Carper
Staff Reporter

Thirteen men and women, Negro and white, boarded Greyhound and Trailway buses here yesterday to begin a two week pilgrimage through the deep South testing racial segregation in buses, eating facilities and rest stops.

The trip, called "Freedom Ride 1961," is sponsored by the Congress of Racial Equality (CORE) and is a repeat of the "Journey of Reconciliation," a trip made into border states 14 years ago.

The 13, divided into two groups, will visit Richmond, Petersburg and Lynchburg, Va.; Greensboro and Charlotte, N. C.; Rock Hill and Sumter, S. C.; Augusta and Atlanta, Ga.; Birmingham and Montgomery, Ala.; Jackson, Miss.; and New Orleans.

They plan to arrive in New Orleans May 17 to take part in a freedom rally marking the seventh anniversary of the Supreme Court school desegregation decision.

college teacher from Detroit and his 57-year-old wife.

The 13 were selected by CORE from about 50 volunteers and spent three days in training in Washington before setting out. The training consisted of discussions on meeting situations that may develop during the trip, Farmer said. The participants are committed to the doctrine of non-violence.

Others taking part include Albert Bigelow, 55-year-old artist from Cos Cob, Conn., who, as a Naval officer, commanded combat ships during World War II. He was captain of the Golden Rule, a ketch that three years ago, sought to enter the Pacific bomb detonating area in protest of the continuation of nuclear tests.

Shown looking over a map of the route they will follow on a 2-week pilgrimage through the South testing racial segregation, are (from left) Edward Blankenheim of Tucson, Ariz.; James Farmer, New York City; Genevieve Hughes, Chevy Chase, Md.; the Rev. B. Elton Cox, High Point, N. C., and Henry Thomas, St. Augustine, Fla. The trip is called "Freedom Ride 1961."

Written by staff reporter Elsie Carper, this article on the CORE Freedom Ride appeared on page B4 of the *Washington Post*, May 5, 1961. (Courtesy of the *Washington Post*)

Kennedy quipped: "I wish I could go with you." All of this left Booker wondering if Kennedy had been paying full attention to their conversation, a suspicion confirmed when the attorney general later claimed that he had been blindsided by the Freedom Ride.

Once all of the Freedom Riders had arrived at the bus stations, Farmer held a brief press conference, during which he tried to explain both the philosophy of nonviolence and CORE's "jail–no bail" policy. "If there is an arrest, we will accept that arrest," he told the handful of reporters, "and if there is violence we will accept that violence without responding in kind." Accepting bail was contrary to the spirit of noncooperation with evil, he added: "We will not pay fines because we feel that by paying money to a segregated state we would help it perpetuate segregation." Leaving the reporters to puzzle over the implications of this declaration, he turned to the Riders themselves, whom he divided into two interracial groups. Six Riders lined up at the Greyhound ticket counter, and the other seven did the same at the Trailways station across the street.

After checking their bags, the Riders received last-minute instructions about seating arrangements. A proper test of the *Morgan* decision required a careful seating plan, and Farmer left nothing to chance. Each group made sure that one black Freedom Rider sat in a seat normally reserved for whites, that at least one interracial pair of Riders sat in adjoining seats, and that the remaining Riders scattered throughout the bus. One Rider on each bus served as a designated observer and as such remained aloof from the other Riders; by obeying the conventions of segregated travel, he or she ensured that at

CORE Freedom Riders (left to right) Charles Person, Jim Peck, and Frances Bergman board a southbound Trailways bus in Washington, D.C., May 4, 1961. (Photograph by Theodore Gaffney)

least one Rider would avoid arrest and be in a position to contact CORE officials or arrange bail money for those arrested. Most of the Riders, however, were free to mingle with the other passengers and to discuss the purpose of the Freedom Ride with anyone who would listen. Exercising the constitutional right to sit anywhere on the bus had educational as well as legal implications, and the Riders were encouraged to think of themselves as teachers and role models. Farmer imposed a strict dress code—coats and ties for the men and dresses and high heels for the women—and all of the Riders were asked to represent the cause of social justice openly and honestly without resorting to needlessly provocative or confrontational behavior. As Farmer reminded them just before the buses pulled out, they could be arrested at any time, so they had to be prepared for the unexpected. Accordingly, he urged each Rider to bring a carry-on bag containing a toothbrush, toothpaste, and an inspiring book or two that would help fill the hours behind bars. Many years later, Lewis remembered packing three books in the bag that he placed under his seat: one by the Roman Catholic philosopher Thomas Merton, a second on Gandhi, and the Bible.[22]

All of these precautions and warnings took on new meaning as the buses actually headed south on Route 1. At first the regular passengers, both black and white, paid little attention to the Freedom Riders. No one, including the drivers, voiced any objection to the Riders' unusual seating pattern. This was encouraging and somewhat unexpected, but the first true test of tolerance did not come until the Greyhound stopped at Fredericksburg, fifty miles south of Washington. A small river town with a rich Confederate heritage and the site of one of the Union Army's most crushing defeats, Fredericksburg had a long tradition of strict adherence to racial segregation and white supremacy. Gaither's scouting report had warned the Riders that the facilities at Fredericksburg's bus terminals featured the all too familiar WHITE ONLY

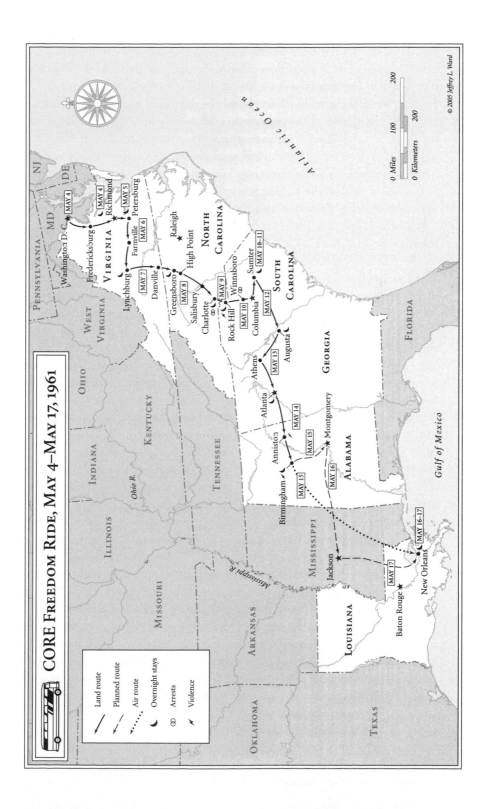

CORE FREEDOM RIDE, MAY 4–MAY 17, 1961

Land route
Planned route
Air route
Overnight stays
Arrests
Violence

© 2005 Jeffrey L. Ward

PENNSYLVANIA
NJ
MD
DE
OHIO
WEST VIRGINIA
INDIANA
ILLINOIS
KENTUCKY
TENNESSEE
MISSOURI
Ohio R.
Mississippi R.
ARKANSAS
OKLAHOMA
TEXAS
LOUISIANA
MISSISSIPPI
ALABAMA
GEORGIA
FLORIDA
SOUTH CAROLINA
NORTH CAROLINA
VIRGINIA

Washington D.C. MAY 4
Fredericksburg MAY 4
Richmond MAY 5
Petersburg MAY 5
Farmville MAY 6
Lynchburg MAY 7
Danville
Greensboro MAY 8
Salisbury
Charlotte MAY 10
Rock Hill
Raleigh
High Point
Winnsboro MAY 9
Sumter MAY 10–11
Columbia MAY 12
Augusta MAY 13
Athens
Atlanta
Anniston MAY 14
Birmingham MAY 15
Montgomery MAY 15
MAY 16
Jackson
Baton Rouge MAY 17
New Orleans MAY 16–17

Atlantic Ocean
Gulf of Mexico

0 Miles   100   200
0 Kilometers   200

and COLORED ONLY signs. When they arrived at the Greyhound terminal, the Jim Crow signs were prominently displayed above the restroom doors. Nevertheless, someone in a position of authority had decided that there would be no trouble in Fredericksburg on May 4. Peck used the colored restroom, and Person, the designated black tester for the day, used the white restroom and later ordered a drink at the previously whites-only lunch counter, all without incident. To the Riders' surprise, the service was cordial, and not a harsh word was spoken by anyone. This apparent lack of rancor in the state that had spawned the "massive resistance" movement only a few years earlier was almost eerie, and as the Riders reboarded the bus, they couldn't help wondering what other surprises lay ahead.[23]

The next stop was Richmond, where the Riders were scheduled to spend the night at Virginia Union College, a black Baptist institution located a few blocks north of the city's downtown business district. Understandably wary of a city that had served as the capital of the Confederacy for four years, they did not expect a warm welcome, especially after Farmer informed them that local NAACP leaders had urged their followers to avoid any association with the Freedom Ride. Even so, the fear that local whites would try to prevent them from desegregating the city's bus terminals proved unfounded. As Lewis later recalled, the Riders encountered "No signs. No trouble. Nothing but a few cold stares." There were, however, a few disheartening moments, at least for Peck. As he wandered through the Greyhound terminal—the same terminal that he had visited fourteen years earlier—he realized that the absence of Jim Crow signs had not led to any apparent changes in behavior. Unaware of or unmoved by the *Boynton* decision, "Negroes were sticking to the formerly separate and grossly unequal colored waiting rooms and restaurants." The same was true at the nearby Trailways station, where traditional patterns of separation and deference still prevailed. Such scenes were profoundly discouraging to a man who had devoted his entire adult life to the struggle for racial equality. Peck knew that, as a white man and a Northerner, he had no right to pass judgment on the frailties of black Southerners. Later that evening, however, as he sat through a sparsely attended meeting at the Virginia Union chapel, he felt a twinge of sadness, not only for the blacks still ensnared in the indignities of Jim Crow but also for the Freedom Riders who were taking such grave risks for a potentially empty victory. After interviewing several apathetic Virginia Union students, the New York writer Charlotte Devree shared some of Peck's concerns. But a late-night conversation with Charles Sherrod, a campus hero from Petersburg who had just gained his release from the Rock Hill jail, restored some of her faith in the black student movement. Speaking with a "cold fury" that stunned Devree, Sherrod insisted: "Some of us have to be willing to die."[24]

Sherrod's words were enough to give anyone pause, especially a New Yorker facing her first visit to the Deep South. But when it came time to board the bus for the second day of the Freedom Ride, Devree overcame her fears and headed south with the rest of the group, realizing full well that the Freedom Riders, like Sherrod, were prepared to make the ultimate sacrifice for the cause of freedom. Fortunately, no such sacrifice was expected any time soon. Still in the Upper South, the Riders did not foresee much resistance in towns like Petersburg, where they disembarked for an overnight stay on May 5. Only twenty miles south of Richmond, Petersburg was a rough-and-tumble railroad town that had witnessed more than its share of carnage during the Civil War, including the final collapse of Robert E. Lee's army. In the modern era the town had evolved into an important processing center for the tobacco and peanut farmers of the Virginia Southside. Over 40 percent black and the home of Virginia State University, Petersburg, like many lowcountry Virginia communities, practiced an ambiguous mix of hard-edged segregation and paternalistic pretense. As Gaither's scouting report had promised, despite recent tensions the town had seen relatively few manifestations of ultra-segregationist extremism. On the contrary, it had become a major center of movement activity and one of the few communities in the South where sit-ins had already led to desegregated bus terminals. In August 1960, after the Petersburg Improvement Association (PIA) sponsored a series of sit-ins at the local Trailways terminal, the president of Bus Terminal Restaurants agreed to desegregate lunch counters in Petersburg and several other cities. Thus, when the Freedom Riders arrived in the city nine months later, the successful testing of local facilities was almost a foregone conclusion. As expected, the testing went off without incident, and the Riders received an enthusiastic welcome from a crowd that included some of the fifty-five sit-in veterans arrested at the Trailways terminal the previous summer.

Ironically, the one Petersburg civil rights activist who was not there to greet them was the Reverend Wyatt Tee Walker, the strong-willed thirty-one-year-old Baptist minister who had led the PIA since its founding. Having replaced Ella Baker as executive secretary of SCLC the previous spring, Walker was in Atlanta, where he and other SCLC leaders would meet with the Riders on May 13. A native of New Jersey who as a teenager had joined the Communist Party after attending a lecture by Paul Robeson, Walker was one of the movement's most flamboyant characters. After attending Virginia Union and moving to Petersburg in 1953 to become pastor of Gillfield Baptist Church, he became active in the NAACP and eventually came under the influence of Vernon Johns, the legendary black preacher who preceded Martin Luther King Jr. as pastor of Montgomery's Dexter Avenue Baptist Church. With Johns's blessing, Walker caused quite a stir in 1958 when he and several others tried to desegregate the Petersburg Public Library—a protest that included a cheeky attempt to check out Douglas Southall Freeman's admiring biography of Robert E. Lee. This and other acts of defiance drew the admiring attention of King, who both encouraged the formation of the PIA and eventually invited Walker into SCLC's inner circle. At the same time, Walker developed a working relationship with CORE, first as the coordinator of a January 1959 "Emancipation Day" march in Richmond and later as the keynote speaker at CORE's national convention in July 1960.

The head of the welcoming committee on May 5, the Reverend W. Lloyd James of Bethany Baptist Church, lacked Walker's near legendary status, but, as the Freedom Riders soon discovered, he was both a gracious host and a powerful exponent of faith-based activism. Accompanied by a half dozen deacons, James escorted the Riders to a group of waiting cars that whisked them off to dinner and a mass meeting at Bethany Baptist. The joyous meeting at the tiny red-brick church was the first of many such gatherings for the Freedom Riders. CORE's plan called for a mass meeting at every nightly stop along the route to New Orleans. Gaither had prearranged most of the meetings, but in a few instances, where local leaders were reluctant to commit themselves, the Riders had to improvise. At each meeting, one or more of the Riders spoke to the crowd about the goals and implications of the Freedom Ride. Through a mixture of preaching and teaching, they tried to engage the men and women and children of the black South in the widening struggle for freedom. As Lewis later recalled, the primary message was that "no place was too small and no people were too powerless to do what we on those buses were doing." At the Petersburg meeting, the spokesperson for the Riders was Bert Bigelow, who had the unenviable task of following the Reverend James at the pulpit. Surrounded by a sea of black faces, the former navy captain, who had never been in a Southern church before, spoke from the heart. The Freedom Riders were committed not only to the fight for equal justice, he insisted, but also to the redemptive spirit of nonviolence. Later, as the Riders split up to join the families that had agreed to put them up for the night, Bigelow's words reverberated in thoughts and conversations that had been all too rare even in movement towns like Petersburg.[25]

Bigelow's words might have had even greater impact if another navy captain had not already made history that day. At 9:32 in the morning, just as the Freedom Riders were packing up to leave their dormitory rooms at Virginia Union, astronaut Alan B. Shepard became the first American to rocket into space. As the nation watched and waited and later celebrated, the Riders, like everyone else, wondered how Shepard's flight would affect the space race and the broader Cold War. One thing was clear, however: They wouldn't have to worry about too much press attention in the days to come. It would take something pretty spectacular, the likes of which they did not want to think about, to bring the press and the public back to earth anytime soon. Petersburg did not worry them, but Farmville, their first scheduled rest stop on Saturday morning, was the kind of place where almost anything could happen. The seat of Prince Edward County, the small farming and college town was the birthplace of Virginia's Massive Resistance campaign. In 1959 local officials had closed the county's public schools rather than submit to desegregation, establishing Farmville as a symbol of white supremacist defiance. The white children of Prince Edward County attended an array of private segregationist academies, but most local black children had no affordable options, a situation that didn't seem to bother county school officials or other local whites. The Freedom Riders expected trouble in Farmville, but to their surprise the signs designating segregated terminal facilities were hidden under a fresh coat of paint. Although the Riders could still make out the letters that had traditionally directed "white" and "colored" where to go, they met no resistance when they violated the color line in the restrooms and at the lunch counter. Farmville's white establishment clearly wanted nothing to do with the Freedom Riders and was willing to overlook a momentary lapse in racial etiquette to ensure the Riders' quick departure.[26]

The next stop was Lynchburg, where the Riders hoped to find true compliance with the law rather than the cynical maneuvering they had encountered in Farmville. Despite its foreboding name, Lynchburg had a reputation for moderate race relations. Nestled in the foothills of the Blue Ridge Mountains, the city of fifty thousand was home to two private colleges, Randolph-Macon Woman's College and Lynchburg College, and a busy tobacco market. Although blacks accounted for only one-fifth of the local population, Lynchburg boasted a black seminary—the Virginia Theological Seminary and College—and a small, homegrown movement that had hosted an SCLC "Institute on Nonviolence" and sustained a brief jail-in earlier in the year. Upon their arrival, the Freedom Riders were pleased to discover that the city's bus terminals were free of Jim Crow signs, but at the Trailways lunch counter they encountered a towering partition "making persons on one side virtually invisible to those on the other." Whether the absence of signs represented social progress or merely white supremacist cunning was a subject of debate and some puzzlement as the Riders mingled with their hosts later that evening.

In Lynchburg, local leaders dispersed the Riders among eight black churches, an arrangement that led to varied experiences. For many of the Riders there was a welcome reprise of the powerful emotions that had erupted in Petersburg the night before. Indeed, for Frances Bergman, who spoke at one of the churches, Lynchburg provided "the warmest reception thus far." But for others, including Ben Cox, Lynchburg turned out to be a strange and disturbing stop. At the Court Street Baptist Church, where Cox was the designated speaker, the Riders drew a small and unenthusiastic crowd, plus a stern admonition from the host preacher, who was clearly having second thoughts about the wisdom of associating with outside agitators. "If God had wanted us to sit in the front of the bus," the preacher exclaimed, "he would have put us there." Flabbergasted, Cox did his best to salvage the evening, but the preacher's rebuke served as a warning that unabashed racial accommodation was still a powerful force in many areas of the black South. More than anything else, his words reminded them of how far they had come in three days of traveling. Though still within two hundred miles of Washington, they were worlds away from the restless energy and relative freedom of the capital's black community. In the isolated hill country of southwest Virginia, the paradox-laden Southern mystique seemed to be drawing them into a divided and almost surreal world of faith-based hope and mind-numbing resignation. If the quickening spirit of the movement was palpable even in Lynchburg, so too were the lingering effects of decades of white intimidation and black accommodation. The raw emotionalism and political contradictions of the black South were familiar to the Southern-born Freedom Riders, especially to Lewis and Cox, but among the more secular Northern volunteers the Ride was turning out to be quite an educational experience. All this, and the Freedom Ride had yet to penetrate the Deep South. Indeed, as the buses headed toward Danville on Sunday morning, even the most experienced of the Southern Riders must have wondered what unexpected lessons and ironic twists were waiting for them down the road.[27]

The Freedom Riders' experience in Danville, a mill town sixty-five miles south of Lynchburg, represented a milestone of sorts. Here for the first time the Riders encountered open hostility and resistance. At the combined Greyhound-Trailways station, a black waiter refused to serve Ed Blankenheim when he insisted on sitting at the "colored counter." After several minutes of waiting and after the waiter explained that his white boss had promised to fire him if he served a Freedom Rider on the wrong side of the color line, Blankenheim gave up and reboarded the bus. An hour or so later, three white Riders from the second bus—Jim Peck, Genevieve Hughes, and Walter Bergman—renewed the challenge. Following a curt refusal and a brief standoff, Peck convinced the station manager to relent. While the seeming irrationality of insisting on eating at an inferior facility undoubtedly puzzled the manager and his staff, the Freedom Riders knew they had won a small but significant victory.[28]

By mid–Sunday afternoon, both buses had crossed the North Carolina border, leaving proud but perplexed Virginia to its own devices. The day's final destination was Greensboro, the birthplace of the 1960 sit-in movement. Prior to the sit-ins, Greensboro had been one of the first communities in the South to initiate voluntary compliance with *Brown*, and local white leaders had taken great pride in the city's reputation for progressive politics and enlightened paternalism. But more than a year of militant civil rights agitation had shaken the white community, which had great difficulty coping with Greensboro's new image as a center of the Southern freedom struggle. By the time the Freedom Riders arrived, the city's "civil" approach to racial accommodation had long since given way to the politics of racial polarization and white backlash. While a few local white leaders continued to push for moderate gradualism, the dominant mood was anything but conciliatory. The result was a curious mix of lingering moderation and rising defiance. This confusion was obvious at the Greensboro Trailways station, where the Riders encountered huge signs pointing to a "colored" lunch counter that had been closed down earlier in the week. One local black told Peck that "he was amazed when upon entering the colored lunch room one day, he was advised to walk around to the formerly white restaurant." Two years earlier this same restaurant had refused to serve Joseph McNeil, one of the four students who later initiated the Greensboro sit-ins. Some friends even speculated that the episode, which followed a long bus ride from New York, had triggered McNeil's decision to join the sit-in.

Still enrolled at North Carolina A&T, McNeil was among those who escorted the Freedom Riders to Bennett College for an afternoon meeting with student leaders and later to Shiloh Baptist Church for an eight o'clock mass meeting. This was the same church that had welcomed CORE riders in 1947, following the beatings at Chapel Hill. Shiloh's pastor, the Reverend Otis Hairston, was a fearless activist who had spearheaded a local NAACP membership drive in 1959 and turned his church into an unofficial command center during the early stages of the sit-in movement. He was proud that two of the four students who participated in the original February 1, 1960, sit-in were Shiloh members, and he was equally pleased to host the Freedom Riders. After a rousing invocation, he turned the meeting over to Dr. George Simkins Jr., the NAACP leader who had urged CORE to become involved in the Greensboro sit-ins. Perhaps more than any other NAACP official, Simkins had been an active supporter of the Freedom Ride, beginning with his insistence to Gaither that the Riders spend at least one night in Greensboro. He could hardly contain himself as he introduced the Riders to an overflow crowd of well-wishers.

Nothing, not even the mass meeting in Petersburg, had prepared the Riders for the warm reception they received at Shiloh. When Farmer expressed both his fear that the desegregation fight had lost some of its "steam" and his determination to make segregation "so costly the South can't afford it," the sanctuary reverberated with amens and other words of encouragement. "Life is not so dear and sweet," Farmer added, "that we must passively accept Jim Crow and segregation. . . . If our parents had gone to jail we wouldn't have to go through the ordeal now. Our nation cannot afford segregation. Overseas it gives Uncle Sam a black eye. Future generations will thank us for what we have done." On and on he went, crying out for a resurgence of the spirit that had nurtured and sustained the city's famous sit-ins. By the end of the evening, both Farmer and the audience were emotionally spent, but as the Freedom Riders and their hosts filed out of the sanctuary, the dual message of empowerment and responsibility was clear. Before they could hope to redeem the white South, Farmer and the Freedom Riders felt, they had to embolden the black South, to stir things up to a point where a critical mass of activists demanded fundamental change. Although they realized that mobilizing and sustaining such a critical mass would not be easy, the warm welcome that the Riders received in Greensboro suggested that at least one local movement was poised to take an unequivocal stand for freedom.[29]

THE UPPER NORTH CAROLINA PIEDMONT was as far south as CORE's 1947 Journey of Reconciliation had dared to go, so when the Freedom Riders headed down Highway 29 on Monday morning, May 8, they were entering uncharted territory. Gaither's report—and in a few cases their own experiences—gave the Riders some sense of what to expect, but they were understandably apprehensive about the dangerous days ahead. In Salisbury, fifty-two miles southwest of Greensboro, the Riders encountered Jim Crow signs at both bus terminals but were able to desegregate the restrooms and lunch counters without incident. Even more encouraging was the unexpected bravado of two black women, both regular passengers on the bus, who followed the Riders' example of demanding service at the white counter. They, too, received prompt and reasonably courteous service, which was more than the Riders had expected from a town that had once housed one of the Confederacy's most notorious prison camps. Ben Cox, who had spent four years at Salisbury's Livingstone College in the mid-1950s and who had vivid memories of the town's rigid color line, was as surprised as anyone.[30]

From Salisbury, the buses continued southward, through Rowan Mill, China Grove, and Kannapolis, and on to Charlotte. The largest city in the Carolina Piedmont, Charlotte was a banking and textile center with a flair for New South commercialism. The "Queen City," as North Carolinians often called it, was 28 percent black and almost 100 percent segregated in 1961. As in Greensboro, city leaders cultivated an image of moderation and urbane paternalism, but they did so with the expectation that all local citizens, black and white, knew their place. The immutability of racial segregation, even in the most mundane aspects of life, was a given, and anyone who crossed the color line in Charlotte or Mecklenburg County was asking for trouble. Charles Person discovered just how true this was when he tried to get a shoeshine in Charlotte's Union Station. As Jim Peck later explained, the young Atlanta student "didn't even think of it as a test. He simply looked at his shoes and thought he needed a shine." But after being rebuffed, he decided to remain in the whites-only shoeshine chair until someone either changed the policy or arrested him. Within minutes, a policeman arrived and threatened to handcuff him and haul him off to jail if he didn't move. At this point, Person decided to avoid arrest and scurried back to tell the other Riders what had happened.

After an impromptu strategy session, the Riders designated Joe Perkins as the group's official shoeshine segregation tester. The whole scene carried a touch of the absurd—the Riders later referred to the incident as the South's first "shoe-in"—but Perkins agreed to sit in the shoeshine chair until somebody came and arrested him. A few minutes later, the young CORE field secretary became the first Freedom Rider to be arrested. The formal charge was trespassing, and bail was set at fifty dollars. Ed Blankenheim, the designated observer in Charlotte, was on hand with the required bail money, but Perkins bravely chose to spend two nights in jail instead. On Monday evening, while the rest of the Riders met with Charles Jones and other Johnson C. Smith University student activists—including twenty-year-old Gus Griffin of Tampa, Florida, who volunteered to replace Perkins on the Freedom Ride to Rock Hill, South Carolina—Perkins was at the city jail. On Tuesday Perkins was transferred to the county jail, where he remained until his trial on Wednesday morning.

With Blankenheim looking on, Perkins went before Judge Howard B. Arbuckle expecting the worst. To his surprise, and to the amazement of his NAACP attorney, Thomas Wyche, Arbuckle promptly rendered an acquittal based on the *Boynton* decision. Elated, Perkins and Blankenheim headed for Union Station, but as they left the courthouse the same police officer who had arrested Perkins on Monday confronted them. The officer advised the interracial duo "to get the hell out of town" and declared that he wasn't about "to let no New York nigger come down here and make trouble for us and our good nigras." Though tempted to argue the point, Perkins and Blankenheim decided to let the comment pass and proceeded on to the terminal, where they caught a late-morning bus to Rock Hill. Arriving in the South Carolina mill town just in time to rejoin the other Riders for the trip to Sumter, the two stragglers soon discovered that a great deal had happened during their absence.[31]

Rock Hill, which had been seething with racial tension since the celebrated jail-in three months earlier, turned out to be the first serious trouble spot for the Freedom Ride. Gaither, who had spent considerable time there, both in and out of jail, warned the Riders that the town was literally crawling with Klansmen and other hard-line white supremacists. But the relative ease of the journey through Virginia and North Carolina left many of the Riders unprepared for the rude welcome they encountered during their first stop in South Carolina. A cotton mill town with a chip on its shoulder, Rock Hill harbored a large contingent of what Senator Ben Tillman once called "the damned factory trash," displaced farmers who had been pushed off the land by declining cotton prices and a brutal crop-lien system. Over the years their economic and cultural grievances spawned a hardy tradition of racial scapegoating that sustained political demagogues such as Cole Blease and "Cotton Ed" Smith. The fact that the local white elite continued to tolerate all-black Friendship Junior College suggested that Rock Hill may not have been the most Negrophobic town in South Carolina, but it was still a tough place to discuss the fine points of constitutional law. As Lewis, who had traveled to Rock Hill earlier in the year to visit his jailed SNCC colleagues, put it, "I could tell we were in trouble as soon as I stepped off the bus."[32]

In his 1998 memoir *Walking with the Wind*, Lewis reconstructed the disturbingly simple origins of what turned out to be the first of many assaults against nonviolent Freedom Riders:

> As Al Bigelow and I approached the "WHITE" waiting room in the Rock Hill Greyhound terminal, I noticed a large number of young white guys

hanging around the pinball machines in the lobby. Two of these guys were leaning by the door jamb to the waiting room. They wore leather jackets, had those ducktail haircuts and were each smoking a cigarette.

"Other side, nigger," one of the two said, stepping in my way as I began to walk through the door. He pointed to a door down the way with a sign that said "COLORED."

I did not feel nervous at all. I really did not feel afraid. "I have a right to go in there," I said, speaking carefully and clearly, "on the grounds of the Supreme Court decision in the *Boynton* case."

I don't think either of these guys had ever heard of the *Boynton* case. Not that it would have mattered.

"Shit on that," one of them said.

The next thing I knew, a fist smashed the right side of my head. Then another hit me square in the face. As I fell to the floor I could feel feet kicking me hard in the sides. I could taste blood in my mouth.

At that point Al Bigelow stepped in, placing his body between mine and these men, standing square with his arms at his sides.

It had to look strange to these guys to see a big, strong white man putting himself in the middle of a fistfight like this, not looking at all as if he was ready to throw a punch, but not looking frightened either.

They hesitated for an instant. Then they attacked Bigelow, who did not raise a finger as these young men began punching him. It took several blows to drop him to one knee.

At that point several of the white guys by the pinball machines moved over to join in. Genevieve Hughes stepped in their way and was knocked to the floor.

Whether out of chivalry or just plain common sense, a white police officer who had witnessed the entire assault finally intervened and grabbed one of the assailants. "All right, boys," he stated with some authority. "Y'all've done about enough now. Get on home." After a few parting epithets, the boys retreated to the street, leaving the Freedom Riders and the policeman to wait for several other officers who had been called to the scene. To Lewis's surprise, one of the officers appeared to be sympathetic to the injured Riders and asked them if they wanted to file charges against their attackers. They declined the offer. Though still shaken, Lewis, Bigelow, and Hughes then staggered into the terminal restaurant to join the rest of the Riders. Lewis, who had suffered bruised ribs and cuts around his eyes and mouth, was in need of medical attention, but he stubbornly insisted on remaining at the restaurant until he finished his hard-earned cup of coffee. Several hours later, after someone at Friendship Junior College fetched a first-aid kit, he allowed a friend to place Band-Aids over the wounds on his face. Throughout the whole ordeal he downplayed his injuries; no bones had been broken, he insisted, displaying the quiet courage for which he would later become famous. Most important, he pointed out, no pledges had been violated: The Freedom Riders had passed their first major test, refusing to strike back against an unprovoked assault.

The Trailways Riders who arrived later in the afternoon faced a similarly threatening situation but were able to avoid a violent confrontation, thanks to the intervention of the Reverend C. A. Ivory, the courageous leader of the Rock Hill movement. Upon their arrival, the Trailways group discovered that the Rock Hill Trailways terminal was locked shut and that the terminal's restaurant had been closed for weeks, a casualty of the Friendship Junior College students' sit-in campaign. As the Riders stepped off the bus, a welcoming committee of drivers rushed up to inform them about the assault on the Greyhound group—and to protect them from essentially the same gang of white "thugs" responsible for the earlier attack. Across the street was a line of cars filled with tough-looking young white men hoping for a second shot at the outside agitators who had dared to invade their town. Several of the men shouted epithets and motioned menacingly at the Riders, but Ivory told the Riders not to worry, that he was not afraid of these cowardly "hoodlums." He soon proved his point by glaring at the whites as he and the rest of the welcoming committee hustled the Riders into several waiting cars. As they drove to Friendship Junior College, where the Riders were scheduled to spend the night, the threatening whites followed for a few blocks but eventually turned off without attacking their prey. Later in the evening, both groups of Riders gathered at Ivory's home to share the details of what had happened earlier in the day. While they all had stories to tell, Lewis, Bigelow, and Hughes drew most of the attention. From the outset, the Riders had known that violent resistance to the Freedom Ride was almost inevitable. Now, as the three Riders told and retold the story of their confrontation with the young toughs, the dangers of challenging Jim Crow—and the responsibilities of nonviolent protest—took on a new and unsettling specificity.

At the mass meeting held at the college that night, the Reverend Ivory and others praised the courage and restraint of the bloodied but unbowed Freedom Riders. Confined to a wheelchair and in poor health, Ivory himself was no stranger to threats of violence or acts of courage. For four years—ever since he had led a successful boycott of Rock Hill's local bus company—the outspoken minister had been a primary target of militant segregationists who hoped to drive him out the community. But nothing seemed to faze him—not hate mail, not death threats, not even a recent phone call that pledged to bomb his home and family. "The other night the person on the other end threatened to plant a bomb under my house," he told the Riders. "'Why don't you plant two while you're at it?' I asked. Nothing ever came of it." Six months later, Ivory would die of natural causes, but those who knew him well placed part of the blame on the extraordinary burden of leadership he had agreed to bear.

Ivory's eloquent tribute to the injured Riders touched everyone in the hall, and Jimmy McDonald, joined by nine veterans of the Rock Hill jail-in, capped off the evening with a joyous round of freedom songs. The exuberance of the students was just what Lewis and the Freedom Riders had hoped to discover in the recesses of the Deep South, though Lewis himself had other things to think about that night. Within minutes of his arrival at the college, he had received a telegram from the American Friends Service Committee (AFSC) notifying him that he been selected as a finalist for a two-year foreign service internship—the same internship that his mentor Jim Lawson had held in the mid-1950s. It had taken the AFSC a while to track him down, but there was still enough time for him to make the required final interview in Philadelphia. Accompanying the telegram was a money order that would buy him a plane ticket, but if he wanted to pursue the internship he would have to leave the Freedom Ride almost immediately. Following a long night of soul-searching, Lewis decided to fly to Philadelphia for three days, after which he planned to rejoin the Ride. Barring any unforeseen problems, he would be back on the bus by Monday, May 15, the day the Riders were scheduled to leave Birmingham, Alabama.

The next morning, as the rest of the Riders prepared to head south toward Chester and Winnsboro, a Friendship Junior College student drove Lewis to the Charlotte airport, where he caught a plane to Philadelphia. Before leaving Rock Hill, the remaining Riders desegregated the waiting rooms in both bus terminals without incident. As a relieved Peck put it, "the hoodlums did not stage a repeat performance," though as the Riders left the scene of their first violent confrontation they had no illusions about the hard road to freedom in towns like Rock Hill. Just how hard this road could be became increasingly obvious as the day progressed. The Riders had planned to stop for lunch in Chester, a mill town and county seat twenty-three miles southwest of Rock Hill. Chester's closest brush with notoriety had occurred in 1807, when former vice president Aaron Burr, while under arrest for acts of treason, momentarily escaped from his guards while passing through the town. But the Riders did not get the chance to stay long enough to see the famous rock from which Burr "harangued a curious crowd before he was recaptured." Having learned that troublemakers were on their way, local officials had locked the doors of the Chester bus terminal. Over the doors several makeshift signs announced that the terminal was "closed" until further notice. Shaking off this lapse in Southern hospitality, the Trailways and Greyhound drivers changed the lunch stop to Winnsboro, twenty-eight miles farther down the road.[33]

The seat of hilly Fairfield County, Winnsboro was a conservative community with a deep Confederate heritage. On his march north from the capital city of Columbia in February 1865, General William Tecumseh Sherman had stopped in Winnsboro just long enough to burn most of the town, an act that was not soon forgotten. Later in the nineteenth century, local patriots constructed one of the state's largest Confederate monuments, which stood guard against any transgressions of the "Southern way of life." Nearly 60 percent black in 1961, Winnsboro had earned a reputation as an ultrasegregationist stronghold, a place where the local White Citizens' Council invariably got its way. Challenging the white supremacist traditions of Winnsboro would have been dangerous under any circumstances, but in the wake of the Rock Hill incident it was especially so.

As the Freedom Riders rolled into the sand hills of central South Carolina on the morning of the tenth—which happened to be Confederate Memorial Day—newspapers all across the nation ran a wire story describing the beatings of the previous day. Thanks in part to the hoopla surrounding Shepard's space flight, the Rock Hill story generally appeared on the back pages far removed from the front-page limelight. Still, much of South Carolina, not to mention the rest of the South, now knew that Riders were coming their way, which helped to explain the locked doors in Chester. Officially CORE welcomed the publicity, but from this point on the Riders would have to deal with an awakened white South. Suddenly the potential for confrontation had ratcheted upward.

In Winnsboro, the first sign of trouble came when Hank Thomas, the young Howard student from St. Augustine, sat down at a whites-only lunch counter. Accompanied by Peck, who later recalled that they had hardly settled in their seats when "the restaurant owner dashed away from the counter to call the police," Thomas soon found himself in a conversation with a brawny "police officer who was a stereotype for such a role in Hollywood." "Come with me, boy," the officer drawled. At this point Peck tried to explain that Thomas had a constitutional right to eat lunch wherever he pleased. This didn't seem to faze the policeman, who promptly arrested both men. Within minutes, the two Freedom Riders were behind bars in the city jail—in separate Jim Crow cells. After several hours of confusion and indecision, local officials charged Thomas with trespassing and Peck with "interfering with arrest." By this time the rest of the Riders—with the exception of Frances Bergman, the designated observer for the Winnsboro lunch counter test—had gone on to Sumter, where they were scheduled to spend the night. For several hours, Bergman, as a grateful Peck later put it, "braved the hate-filled town alone trying to find out what the authorities intended to do" with the two arrestees. She got little cooperation from the local police, who seemed pleased that Winnsboro's unwelcome visitors had gotten more than they had bargained for in the heart of Dixie. One officer, after calling her a "nigger lover" and an "outside agitator," told her "to get out of town," adding: "We have no use for your kind here."

Following a CORE policy agreed upon at the beginning of the Ride, Farmer left Thomas, Peck, and Bergman behind, hoping that they would be able to rejoin the Ride in Sumter. But he did so reluctantly. Farmer knew from his conversations with field secretary Jim McCain that Winnsboro— like Rock Hill—was a dangerous town, especially for an assertive young black man like Thomas. As a white woman, Bergman, despite her lack of experience in the South, would probably be all right, and Peck—a veteran civil disobedient who had served three years in prison as a young man—could probably take care of himself. Thomas, though, was young and full of pent-up emotion left over from a troubled boyhood. A last-minute replacement for his roommate, he was an unknown quantity compared to most of the other Riders. With some justification, Farmer worried that the untried re-cruit might not be able to hold his tongue or his fists if provoked. Fortu-nately, while Farmer was still mulling over his options, the Winnsboro police dropped all charges against Thomas, releasing him around midnight.

While Peck was still languishing in his cell, two policemen drove Thomas to Winnsboro's partially closed and virtually empty bus station. As the police sped off, Thomas noticed several white men standing in the parking lot, look-ing to his eyes very much like a potential lynch mob. One of the men, upon seeing him, ordered him to "go in the nigger waiting room." Somehow the young Freedom Rider summoned up enough courage to enter the white wait-ing room, purchase a candy bar, and stroll past "gaping segregationists" who seemed stunned by his defiance. Before the whites could react, a local black minister whom Frances Bergman had called earlier in the day drove up to the waiting room entrance and literally screamed at Thomas to "get in the car and stay down." As Thomas recalled years later: "We expected gunshots, but they didn't come. He saved my life that night, because they were going to kill me." After the rescue, the minister drove Thomas twenty-five miles south to Co-lumbia, where the Freedom Rider found refuge in the home of a local NAACP leader. The next day Thomas took a bus to Sumter to rejoin the other Riders— including Peck, who had his own tale to tell.

The Winnsboro police had planned to release Peck and Thomas at roughly the same time, but after dropping the original arrest-interference charge against Peck, local officials immediately rearrested him for violating a state liquor law. Though unsure of their legal standing on the matter of seg-regation, they found a way to extend Peck's ordeal by turning to an obscure South Carolina statute that prohibited the importation of untaxed liquor into the state. Two days earlier, just prior to crossing the South Carolina line, Peck and the Trailways group had stopped for a few minutes at a small ter-minal attached to a liquor store. Thinking that some alcoholic sustenance might come in handy during the difficult days ahead, Peck purchased a bottle of imported brandy, which he promised to share with his fellow Riders. This produced a few wry comments from Farmer and others familiar with Peck's fondness for hard liquor, but no one realized that he was about to violate South Carolina law.

Two days later, as Peck was about to be released from the Winnsboro jail, a police officer spied the bottle of whiskey and proudly informed his superiors that the bottle lacked the required South Carolina state liquor stamp. Within minutes Peck was back in jail, charged with illegal possession of un-taxed alcohol. Upon learning of Peck's second arrest, Farmer and a carload of CORE supporters—including Jim McCain and a local black attorney, Ernest Finney Jr.—drove from Sumter to Winnsboro, arriving just before dawn. Securing Peck's release with a fifty-dollar bail bond, Farmer and McCain whisked their old friend back to Sumter, knowing full well that they could not afford to wait for his day in court. Although jumping bail violated

CORE Freedom Riders (left to right) Hank Thomas, Jim Farmer, Mae Frances Moultrie, Albert Bigelow, Ed Blankenheim, Joe Perkins, Jim Peck, and Charles Person attend a mass meeting at the Emmanuel AME Church in Sumter, South Carolina, May 11, 1961. (Photograph by Theodore Gaffney)

CORE policy, Peck, for once, was in no mood to argue the finer points of legal and organizational responsibility. When Peck and the rescue party arrived safely at McCain's house—CORE's unofficial headquarters in Sumter—everyone was relieved to be back in the fold. Thomas and Bergman's reappearance later in the day completed the reunion, as the returnees swapped jail stories and regaled the other Riders with tales of "friendly" Winnsboro.[34]

The safe return of Thomas, Peck, and Bergman buoyed the spirits of the Riders, all of whom were thankful that the schedule called for two days of rest in Sumter. Aside from a brief test of a bus terminal waiting room—the small Sumter terminal had no restaurant—the stay in Sumter afforded them a chance to relax, reflect upon the experiences of the first week on the road, and gather their strength for the expected challenges to come. At a mass meeting on Thursday evening at the Emmanuel AME Church, Farmer talked about the significance of the Freedom Ride, and Peck and Thomas recounted their harrowing experiences in Winnsboro. But the highlight of the meeting, according to Moses Newson of the *Baltimore Afro-American*, was a testimonial by Frances Bergman, who "hushed" the audience with a moving account of her rude introduction to the Deep South. "For the first time I felt that I had a glimpse of what it would be like to be colored," she confessed. "This thing made me realize what it is to be scorned, humiliated and made to feel like dirt. . . . The whole thing was such an eye-opener for me. . . . It left me so filled with admiration for the colored people who have to live with this all their lives. It seems to me that anything I can do now, day or night, would not be enough. . . . Somehow you feel there is a new urgency at this time. You see the courage all about you." Rededicating herself to the cause of racial justice, she praised the activism of young black students but warned that "older persons" should not "sit back and wait for them to do it." Despite its hint of presumption, this admonition struck a responsive chord in the crowd, which included a number of students from nearby Morris College, a black Baptist institution that had been a hotbed of sit-in and boycott activity since the establishment of a campus CORE chapter in March 1960. Here, as in many other Southern communities, student activists had fashioned a militant local movement that went far beyond anything that their parents or most other black community leaders were willing to endorse.

Jim McCain was justifiably proud of the Morris College CORE chapter, especially after several of the chapter's stalwarts volunteered to join the Freedom Ride. Earlier in the week Farmer had politely brushed off such offers, but that was before the Ride faced a temporary personnel crisis. Soon after the Riders' arrival in Sumter, Cox took a leave of absence to return to High Point, where he was obliged to deliver a Mother's Day sermon on Sunday morning. Thus, with Lewis already gone, the number of Riders was suddenly down to eleven, only five of whom were black. Both Lewis and Cox planned to rejoin the Ride in Birmingham on Monday morning, but CORE needed at least two substitute Riders for the pivotal three-day journey from Sumter to Birmingham. Fortunately, with McCain's help, Farmer not only found replacements for Lewis and Cox but also added two extra recruits for good measure. One of the four new Freedom Riders was Ike Reynolds, a twenty-seven-year-old black CORE activist and Wayne State University sophomore who had been awakened on Wednesday morning by a 7:00 A.M. phone call from Gordon Carey. The next thing Reynolds knew, he was on a midmorning plane from Detroit to Atlanta, where he was picked up and driven to Sumter. The other recruits—Jerry Moore, Herman Harris, and Mae Frances Moultrie—were students at Morris College. Moultrie was a twenty-four-year-old senior from Dillon, South Carolina, and Harris, twenty-one, and Moore, nineteen, were Northern transplants—Harris from Englewood, New Jersey, and Moore from the Bronx. Harris was president of the local CORE chapter and a campus football star, and Moultrie and Moore had been actively involved in several sit-ins and marches. Trained by McCain, all three were seasoned veterans of the Southern freedom struggle.

With the new recruits in hand, Farmer, McCain, and the other CORE staff members spent most of the second day in Sumter assessing the experiences of the previous week and refining the plan for the remainder of the Ride. In gauging the future, they had to deal with a number of unknowns, including the attitudes of black leaders and citizens in Deep South communities that would inevitably be affected by the Ride. Would the Freedom Riders be welcomed as liberators? Or would they just as likely be shunned as foolhardy provocateurs by black Southerners who knew how dangerous it was to provoke the forces of white supremacy? How many black adults were ready to embrace the direct action movement that their children had initiated? And how would the student activists themselves respond to an initiative directed by an organization associated with white Northern intellectuals and an exotic and secular nonviolent philosophy? CORE leaders were hopeful, but after a week on the road they still regarded the black South as something of a puzzle.

Equally perplexing, and far more threatening, was the unpredictability of white officials in the Deep South—and in Washington. What would the police do if the Freedom Riders were physically attacked by segregationist thugs? Would the mayors of cities like Augusta, Birmingham, and Montgomery set aside their avowed segregationist beliefs and instruct their police chiefs to uphold the law? Would Southern officials enforce the *Morgan* and *Boynton* decisions, now that they knew that at least some members of the public were aware of the Freedom Ride? Perhaps most important, what would the Kennedy administration do if white Southerners brazenly violated the law as interpreted by the Supreme Court? How far would the Justice Department go to protect the Freedom Riders' constitutional rights, knowing that direct intervention would be politically costly for the administration? The probable answers to all of these questions remained murky as the Riders set out on the second week of their southward journey, but with each passing day CORE leaders felt they were getting a better grasp of what they were up against, and of what they could expect from friends and foes alike. In particular, they were fortunate to have the benefit of a remarkable and illuminating civil rights address delivered earlier in the week by Attorney General Robert Kennedy.[35]

ON SATURDAY, MAY 6, in a Law Day speech at the University of Georgia, Robert Kennedy issued the first major policy statement of his attorney generalship. Since no prior attorney general in the post-*Brown* era had dared to speak about civil rights in the Deep South, Kennedy's appearance attracted considerable press attention, as well as an overflow crowd of students, faculty, and invited guests. Noticeably absent from the gathering in Athens were the state's leading politicians, including Georgia's governor, Ernest Vandiver. Kennedy knew, as he reminded the audience, that Georgia had given his brother the second largest electoral majority in the nation during the recent election. But he also knew that most of his listeners were segregationists who would bristle at even the slightest suggestion that the Justice Department planned to force the white South to desegregate any time soon. Of the sixteen hundred persons present, only one—Charlayne Hunter, one of two students who had desegregated the university the previous January—was black. It was in this context that Kennedy faced the ominous task of convincing white Southerners that he intended to enforce the law in a firm but conciliatory manner. Knowing that he had to choose his words carefully, he and his staff had been working on the speech for more than a month.

The result was a clever blend of disarming humor, patriotic rhetoric, and well-placed candor. After reminding the audience that "Southerners have a special respect for candor and plain talk," he got right to the point. "Will we enforce the civil rights statutes?" he asked rhetorically. "The answer is yes, yes we will." His motivation for upholding the civil rights of all Americans was rooted in his commitment to equal justice, he told the crowd, but he was also concerned about the realities of the Cold War: "We, the American people, must avoid another Little Rock or another New Orleans. We cannot afford them. . . . Such incidents hurt our country in the eyes of the world." Later in the speech he endorsed the *Brown* decision, condemned the closing of Prince Edward County's schools, hailed the first two black students at the University of Georgia as courageous freedom fighters, and, with an eye to Southern sensitivity to Northern hypocrisy, promised to put his own house in order by hiring black staff members at the Justice Department. He also made it clear that he had no intention of following the lead of the Eisenhower administration's passive approach to civil rights. "We will not stand by and be aloof," he assured the crowd. "We will move."

After a few closing remarks, he sat down, hoping that the crowd would accord him at least a smattering of polite applause. To his surprise, a moment of awkward silence soon gave way to a long and loud ovation. Whether the audience was applauding the substance of his remarks or just his courage was unclear, but most observers judged the speech to be a diplomatic triumph. According to Ralph McGill, the liberal editor of the *Atlanta Constitution*, "Never before, in all its travail of by-gone years, has the South heard so honest and understandable a speech from any Cabinet member." While other Southern editors were somewhat more restrained in their enthusiasm, there was little negative reaction, even among hidebound conservatives. In the civil rights community, the speech drew rave reviews; congratulations poured in from every major civil rights leader, including Roy Wilkins, who expressed the NAACP's "profound appreciation" for the attorney general's forthright stand.

CORE, too, sent a congratulatory note to Attorney General Kennedy. In truth, though, Farmer and other CORE staff members harbored serious reservations about the tone and content of the speech. They were disappointed that he had failed to mention CORE or the Freedom Ride. Even more troubling was his avowed determination "to achieve amicable, voluntary solutions without going to court." Far too often, in their experience, the word "voluntary" had served as a code word for foot-dragging noncompliance. For Kennedy to say, as he did in the speech, that "the hardest problems of all in law enforcement are those involving a conflict of law and custom" seemed tantamount to saying that continued segregationist resistance was inevitable and even legitimate. They wanted the Kennedy administration to take an unequivocal stand on the immediate and uncompromising enforcement of the law. Nothing less would satisfy the freedom fighters of CORE, especially those who were about to test the waters of resistance in the Deep South.

The Freedom Riders' uneasy feeling about the Kennedy administration's position on civil rights deepened on Tuesday morning, May 9, when a White House press release distanced the president from two civil rights bills that he had previously promised to support. Later the same day, Governor Vandiver issued a statement claiming that during the recent campaign Senator Kennedy had promised that his administration would never use federal troops to enforce desegregation in Georgia. When the expected White House denial failed to materialize, civil rights leaders began to worry that the Kennedy brothers were talking out of both sides of their mouths. At the very least, the Freedom Riders had renewed cause for concern as they said their good-byes to McCain and boarded the buses to Augusta on the morning of the twelfth.[36]

The 120-mile trip from Sumter to Augusta took the Freedom Riders through the historic midsection of South Carolina—east across the Wataree River to the capital city of Columbia, then southwest through the heart of agrarian Lexington and Aiken counties, and finally to the banks of the Savannah River. Along the way, they skirted the edge of notorious Edgefield County—reputed to be the most violent county in the South, and celebrated in Southern political lore as the spawning ground of such notables as the antebellum Fire Eater James Henry Hammond, the late nineteenth- and early twentieth-century white supremacist demagogue "Pitchfork Ben" Tillman, and the 1948 Dixiecrat standard-bearer Strom Thurmond.[37]

Though only a short ride from "bloody" Edgefield, Augusta—where the Freedom Riders were scheduled to spend Friday night—fancied itself as a genteel enclave epitomizing the finest traditions of the Old South. Situated on the west bank of the river, the city exuded an aura of stolid confidence that matched the graceful Victorian homes lining its streets. Augustans, black and white, seemed to live their lives at an unhurried pace, well within the confines of a paternalistic ethos. Like most "Old South" communities, the city had a rough underside that belied the pretense of complacent serenity, but the Riders did not expect much trouble during their first stop in Georgia. Earlier in the year the Augusta police had arrested a black soldier for trying to desegregate one of the city's terminal lunch counters, but the Riders encountered no such resistance at either terminal. Although the black Riders were the first nonwhites to break the color line at the Augusta bus stations, no one seemed to care, except for one white waitress who refused to serve Joe Perkins, forcing a black co-worker to do so. It all seemed too easy, and later that evening Walter Bergman and Herman Harris, one of the Morris

College students who had joined the Ride in Sumter, returned to the Trailways restaurant for a second test. Once again they "were served courteously" and without incident. One thing the Riders had learned during their first week on the road was that each community had its own peculiarities where matters of race and segregation were concerned. Regional and even statewide generalizations, it appeared, were untrustworthy and often misleading. This revelation was not altogether reassuring, since it suggested that the struggle for civil rights would have to be waged in a bewildering array of settings. But the variability of Jim Crow culture across time and space certainly added to the adventure of the Freedom Ride, which was turning out to be far less predictable than expected.[38]

On Saturday morning, May 13, the Freedom Riders set out for Atlanta by way of Athens, the college town that had recently hosted Attorney General Kennedy. The surprisingly warm reception accorded to the attorney general indicated that Athens was a fairly progressive community compared to Rock Hill or Winnsboro, but as the Freedom Riders pulled into Athens for a short rest stop, they could not help remembering the news reports of the ugly scenes that had accompanied the desegregation of the University of Georgia in January. Charlayne Hunter and Hamilton Holmes had gained admission, but only after braving a mob of angry whites and overcoming the machinations of university administrators and politicians. To their relief, the Freedom Riders encountered no such problems when they sat down at the Athens lunch counter. The terminal staff, as well as the regular passengers, seemed to take everything in stride. Noting that "there were no gapers," Peck marveled that "a person viewing the Athens desegregated lunch counter and waiting room during our fifteen-minute rest stop might have imagined himself at a rest stop up North rather than deep in Georgia." Later in the day the Riders enjoyed a similar episode in Atlanta, leading Peck to conclude that "our experiences traveling in Georgia were clear proof of how desegregation can come peacefully in a Deep South state, providing there is no deliberate incitement to hatred and violence by local or state political leaders." Civil rights activists who lived in Georgia knew all too well that this sanguine observation gave their state far too much credit, but Peck's appreciation for the importance of political leadership was clearly on the mark, as events in Alabama and Mississippi would later confirm.[39]

The welcoming scenes at the Atlanta bus stations provided a moving affirmation of the civil rights movement's rising spirit. As the Trailways Riders stepped off the bus, a large gathering of students—nearly all veterans of lunch counter sit-ins and picketing campaigns—broke into applause. Rushing forward, the students greeted the road-weary Riders as conquering heroes. Pleased but a little bit flustered by all of this attention, the Riders, after gathering their bags, found it impossible to extricate themselves from the throng for a brief test of the terminal's facilities. The test would have to wait until their departure the next morning. There was a similar scene at the Greyhound station, though there the Riders managed to test the waiting rooms and restrooms. Finding the Greyhound restaurant closed, they headed for a row of waiting cars, which took them to Atlanta University, where they were scheduled to spend the night. The reception in Atlanta could hardly have been better, though the Riders were disappointed to learn that Dr. King was in Montgomery attending an SCLC board meeting. Fortunately, he and SCLC executive director Wyatt Tee Walker were expected back in Atlanta late in the afternoon.

To the Riders' delight, King and Walker returned to Atlanta in time to join them for dinner. Having just received a surprisingly glowing report on SCLC's financial situation, King was in a celebratory mood. Accompanied by several aides, he met the Riders at one of Atlanta's most popular black-owned restaurants. This was the first time that the Riders had eaten in a real restaurant since their "Last Supper" in Washington ten days earlier, and the belief that King planned to pick up the tab—an assumption that, to Farmer's consternation, later proved false—added a festive touch to the occasion. During the dinner, the SCLC leader was at his gracious best, repeatedly praising the Freedom Riders for their courage and offering to help in any way he could. As he listened to the Riders, who one by one related personal stories of commitment and restraint, he interjected words of encouragement and reassurances that their behavior represented "nonviolent direct action at its very best." He told them that he was proud to serve on the national advisory board of CORE, and before saying good night he made a point of shaking hands with each Rider.

Some of the Riders were so moved by King's show of support and affection that they began to hope that he might join them on the bus the following morning, but they soon learned that King had no intention of becoming a Freedom Rider. At one point during the dinner, King privately confided in Simeon Booker, the reporter covering the Freedom Ride for *Jet* and *Ebony*, warning him that SCLC's sources had uncovered evidence of a plot to disrupt the Ride with violence. "You will never make it through Alabama," the SCLC leader predicted, obviously worried. Booker did his best to laugh off the threat, facetiously assuring King that he could always hide behind Farmer, who presented attackers with a large and slow-moving target. Later, when Booker told Farmer what King had said, he discovered that the CORE leader had already been apprised of the situation. Unnerved by what he had learned earlier in the evening, Farmer took both Jimmy McDonald and Genevieve Hughes aside and tried to convince them to leave the Ride in Atlanta. He did not want McDonald in Alabama because he did not think he could trust the young folk singer to remain nonviolent, and he did not want Hughes along because he feared that the presence of a young white woman might provoke additional violence among white supremacists obsessed with the threat of miscegenation. To Farmer's dismay, both adamantly refused to leave the Ride, and Hughes even vowed to buy her own ticket to Birmingham if she had to.[40]

Farmer's growing sense of apprehension became clear when the Freedom Riders gathered for a late-night briefing at their Atlanta University dormitory. The Riders were accustomed to Farmer's assertive style of leadership, but they had never seen him quite so solemn or peremptory. He alone would "lead the testings" for the Trailways group, and Jim Peck would do the same for the trailing Greyhound group. They were entering "the most ominous leg of the journey," and there was no room for error. "Discipline had to be tight," he told them, and "strict compliance" with Gandhian philosophy would have to be maintained. The coming journey through Alabama would pose daunting challenges, but it would also give them the opportunity to prove to the world that nonviolent resistance was an idea whose time had come. Surely this was the time when their rigorous training in nonviolence would pay off. By the end of the meeting, all of the Riders appeared ready, if not altogether eager, to face the challenges that awaited them. Huddling together, they linked arms and sang a few choruses of "We Shall Overcome" before retiring to their rooms. What dreams and nightmares followed can only be imagined.[41]

Later that night, a dormitory counselor awakened Farmer from a deep sleep. His mother was on the phone, and he rushed down to the first floor to receive what he knew was bad news. Prior to leaving Washington, he had paid a tearful visit to his father's bedside at Freedman's Hospital. Suffering from acute diabetes and recovering from a recent cancer operation, James Farmer Sr. was near death when his son first told him about the Freedom Ride. Realizing that it was unlikely that he would ever see his son again, the old man offered his blessing, plus a few words of warning: "Son, I wish you wouldn't go. But at the same time, I am more proud than I've ever been in my life, because you are going. Please try to survive. . . . I think you'll be all right through Virginia, North Carolina, South Carolina, and maybe even Georgia. But in 'Bama, they will doubtless take a potshot at you. With all my heart, I hope they miss." As Farmer's mother informed him of his father's passing, these final words came flooding back to him. He knew that his father would want him to finish the Ride, but he also knew that his distraught mother expected him to return for the funeral. As Farmer later confessed, in making the choice to return to Washington he had to overcome an almost unbearable "confusion of emotions." "There was, of course, the incomparable sorrow and pain," he recalled. "But, frankly, there was also a sense of reprieve, for which I hated myself. Like everyone else, I was afraid of what lay in store for us in Alabama, and now that I was to be spared participation in it, I was relieved, which embarrassed me to tears."

During and after the funeral, Pearl Farmer insisted that her husband had actually "willed the timing of his death" in order to save his son from the coming ordeal in Alabama. But no explanation, real or imagined, made it any easier for Farmer to tell his fellow Riders that he was abandoning them. As they gathered around the breakfast table on Sunday morning, May 14, the embarrassed and emotionally drained leader stunned his charges with the news that his father's death required him to fly to Washington later in the morning. He would rejoin the Ride as soon as possible, he assured them, probably within two or three days. Until then, they could communicate with him by phone, and Joe Perkins would take over his duties as "captain" of the Greyhound group. Perkins appreciated Farmer's vote of confidence, but he—like most of the Freedom Riders—did not know quite how to respond to Farmer's announcement. They could hardly begrudge their grieving leader the chance to bury his father. After all, it was Mother's Day, and they couldn't help thinking of their own families as Farmer said his good-byes. They were confident that he would keep his word and rejoin the Ride, but some of the more nervous Riders weren't sure what shape they would be in after several leaderless days in the wilds of Alabama.[42]

Farmer was the third Rider to take leave of the group, following John Lewis and Ben Cox, who was in High Point polishing his Mother's Day sermon. Lewis had been gone the longest—four days—and a great deal had happened since his departure. The trip to Philadelphia, his first journey to the Northeast, was a qualified success. He weathered the American Friends Service Committee interview with ease and even passed the physical, despite the cuts and bruises received during the Rock Hill beating. On Friday, while the other Riders were en route from Sumter to Augusta, he learned that he had won a fellowship, but the overseas assignment, which would begin in the late summer, was to India, not to Tanganyika, where he had hoped to explore his African roots. Though somewhat disappointed, he accepted the India fellowship, which would allow him to follow in the footsteps of Jim Lawson—and Gandhi.

On Sunday he caught a plane to Nashville, with the hope that he could find a ride to Birmingham on Sunday evening. Arriving in Nashville on Saturday night, he had just enough time to spend a few hours with Bernard Lafayette, Jim Bevel, and his other friends in the Nashville Movement. Earlier in the weekend, Nashville's civil rights leaders had received word that the city's white theater owners had agreed to desegregate. For fourteen weeks the Nashville Movement had applied almost constant pressure in the form of stand-ins and picketing campaigns, vowing to continue the protests until every black activist in the city was in jail if necessary. The theater owners' surrender represented a great victory, and movement leaders planned to celebrate their triumph with a "big picnic" on Sunday afternoon. Against all odds, Lewis was there to help his friends celebrate, but not even a victory of this magnitude could take his mind off his fellow Freedom Riders for very long. "The Freedom Ride," he later confessed, "was once again all I was thinking about."[43]

ALTHOUGH LEWIS DID NOT KNOW IT AT THE TIME, he was not the only person fixated on the Freedom Ride. While he was in Nashville making plans to rejoin the Ride, the leaders of the Alabama Knights of the Ku Klux Klan

were finalizing plans of their own. The Klansmen had known about the Freedom Ride since mid-April, thanks to a series of FBI memos forwarded to the
Birmingham Police Department. Police Sergeant Tom Cook—an avid Klan
supporter and anti-Communist zealot who worked closely with Eugene "Bull"
Connor, Birmingham's ultra-segregationist sixty-three-year-old commissioner of public safety—provided the organization with detailed information
on the Ride, including a city-by-city itinerary. Thus, even though press reports on the Freedom Ride were sketchy and the Klansmen knew next to
nothing about Jim Farmer or CORE, they knew enough to sound the alarm
among the stalwart defenders of white supremacy. In a flurry of secret meetings in April and early May, the Klansmen—with Cook's help—prepared a
rude welcome for the invading "niggers" and "nigger-lovers" who were about
to violate the timeworn customs and laws of the sovereign state of Alabama.

On April 17, more than two weeks before the Freedom Ride began, Sergeant Cook met with Gary Thomas Rowe, a member of the Eastview Klavern
#13, the most violent Klan enclave in Alabama. W. W. "Red" Self, a police
detective and Eastview collaborator who had befriended Rowe while moon-
lighting as a bouncer at a local VFW hall, arranged the meeting. A rough-
edged, loud-talking bully from Savannah, Georgia, Rowe was a dairy worker
whose fixation with guns and power sometimes led him to pose as a police
officer. Unbeknownst to Cook and Self, Rowe also happened to be an FBI
informer, having been recruited by Special Agent Barrett Kemp in April 1960.
Unaware that Rowe planned to relay his words to the Birmingham FBI office, Cook laid out an elaborate plot to bring the Freedom Ride to a halt in
Birmingham. He assured Rowe that other members of the Birmingham Police Department, as well as officials of the Alabama Highway Patrol, were
privy to the plan and could be counted on to cooperate. "You will work with
me and I will work with you on the Freedom Riders," he promised. "We're
going to allow you fifteen minutes. . . .You can beat 'em, bomb 'em, maim
'em, kill 'em. I don't give a shit. There will be absolutely no arrests. You can
assure every Klansman in the country that no one will be arrested in Alabama
for that fifteen minutes."

During the following week, Cook and Rowe held several additional meetings to refine the plan, and after each meeting Rowe reported to his FBI
contacts, who relayed the information to Washington. On May 3, the day
after Connor was reelected public safety commissioner, FBI headquarters
"instructed the Birmingham field office to use care in furnishing information
to the Birmingham police department, and discretion in its contacts with
Bull Connor and Tom Cook in light of Cook's contacts with Rowe." According to Rowe, Connor had recently held a secret rendezvous with Bobby
Shelton, a Tuscaloosa tire salesman who served as the Imperial Wizard of
the Alabama Knights, Knights of the Ku Klux Klan, Inc., a rapidly expanding
and politically well-connected "invisible empire" that had broken off from
the Atlanta-based U.S. Klans in May 1960. The meeting was arranged by

Rowe and the North Alabama region's Grand Titan, Hubert Page, a local electrician who often acted as a covert liaison between the Klan and both Cook and Connor. Actively involved in a tight mayoral race between the moderate Thomas King and the militant white supremacist Arthur Hanes, Connor could not afford an open association with the Klan, but his behind-the-scenes role was a crucial element of the evolving plan to teach the Freedom Riders a lesson they would never forget. As Cook had with Rowe, he reportedly promised Shelton that "he would see to it that 15 or 20 minutes would elapse before the police arrived," plenty of time for a squad of Klansmen to beat the Freedom Riders into submission. "By God," he insisted, "if you're going to do this thing, do it right."[44]

On Thursday night, May 4, while the Freedom Riders were at Virginia Union in Richmond, several Alabama klaverns conducted closed discussions of the Freedom Riders. At the Warrior Klavern meeting, an FBI informant learned that when the Riders headed west out of Atlanta, they would be accompanied by "three unidentified Klansmen." At the meeting of the Eastview Klavern #13, which Rowe attended, Hubert Page placed local Klan leaders on special alert in preparation for the Freedom Riders' arrival. Rowe promptly relayed all of this to the FBI, including Page's comment that "the best way to handle the situation was to get all of the CORE representatives out of Alabama, as soon as possible." The FBI informer also told the Birmingham field office that Shelton had drafted a press release claiming that "it was up to the constituted authorities of Alabama to stop any demonstrations by CORE, but if state authorities did not do their duty, the Alabama Knights, KKK, Inc. would do all they could to force the CORE representatives to leave Alabama." Shelton, like most Klansmen, did not trust the state's political leaders. Even Governor John Patterson, who had swept to victory in 1958 on a stridently white supremacist platform and who often had worked with Shelton behind the scenes, did not seem to understand the gravity of the civil rights crisis. Bull Connor—who had been knocking heads since the 1930s—was, of course, the exception, but even he could not hold back the tide of integration and mongrelization all by himself. Protecting the sanctity of white supremacy required vigilante justice dispensed by red-blooded Klansmen willing to give the do-gooders from the North an old-fashioned Alabama-style welcome.

On May 5 the Birmingham field office wired a summary of Rowe's assessment of Shelton's plans to FBI director J. Edgar Hoover, who forwarded some, though apparently not all, of this information to Attorney General Kennedy, Deputy Attorney General Byron White, and other Justice Department officials four days later. The field office also sent word of the plot to Birmingham police chief Jamie Moore, even though they suspected that Moore was a Klan sympathizer who already knew more about the plot than they did. However, as the circle of informed parties widened, no one said a word to the Freedom Riders themselves. SCLC sources in Alabama picked up vague rumors of the Klan's intentions and passed them along to Martin

Luther King, but the specific information that was accumulating in the FBI's files remained hidden from movement leaders. As the FBI monitored the situation during the last days before the Freedom Riders' arrival in Alabama, there were numerous opportunities to warn the Riders of impending violence, but FBI agents simply watched and waited as a final series of Klan conclaves sealed the Freedom Riders' fate.

When asked to explain this apparent negligence, J. Edgar Hoover and other FBI officials placed the blame on the Justice Department's failure to issue "special instructions" regarding the Birmingham situation. According to Hoover, if the attorney general wanted the bureau to go beyond its standard fact-finding function in matters related to local law enforcement, he should have said so. Robert Kennedy, along with many other Washington insiders, knew full well that this explanation sidestepped the director's and the agents' obvious disdain for civil rights agitation. But neither he nor anyone else in the administration felt secure enough to challenge Hoover's rather lame defense of the bureau's inaction.[45]

On Thursday, May 11, Rowe attended a meeting in Birmingham during which Klan leaders assigned individual duties and responsibilities and advised their troops "to bring ball bats and clubs with them to greet the Freedom Riders." The next day the Eastview klavern entertained Imperial Wizard Shelton, who presided over a special meeting of Klan leaders—including Page and Eastview's Exalted Cyclops, Robert Thomas, one of Alabama's most rabid white supremacists. Though excited by the prospect of a bloodletting, Shelton insisted that the Birmingham assault force would be limited to sixty handpicked men, thirty assigned to the bus depots and thirty waiting in reserve at a nearby hotel. This limitation disappointed some members of the Eastview klavern who were afraid that they would miss out on the chance of a lifetime, but Page and Thomas had no choice but to obey Shelton's order. With this taken care of, Shelton and the Alabama Klan's board of directors held a Saturday meeting in Tuscaloosa, where they ratified the plot to attack the "outside agitators" from CORE.

The final plan, which resembled a full-scale military operation, called for an initial assault in Anniston, the Riders' first scheduled stop in Alabama, followed by a mop-up action in Birmingham. As an FBI informant reported to the Birmingham field office, the Anniston klavern was responsible for blocking the Riders' access to the local bus stations, but Birmingham Klansmen, working in conjunction with Connor and Cook, were calling most of the shots. Led by Kenneth Adams, a notorious bigot who had ordered the beating of black singer Nat King Cole at the Birmingham Municipal Auditorium in 1956, the Anniston klavern did not belong to Shelton's Alabama Knights, KKK confederation. But Adams and his boys needed little encouragement when Shelton asked them to help out with the welcoming party. No one in Birmingham trusted Adams, and on Friday, the day before the Tuscaloosa meeting, Connor dispatched Cook to Anniston to make sure that everything was in order. From there Cook went on to Atlanta to survey the bus stations where the unsuspecting Freedom Riders were scheduled to arrive the following afternoon.

Connor, of course, was primarily concerned with what was about to happen in his own city, and he left few details unattended as the hour of the Freedom Riders' arrival approached. "If the Negroes go into the restaurant of the depot," he told a Klan contact, "the Klansmen should start an incident of some sort, such as a Klansman pouring coffee on himself and blaming it on the Negro, thus starting a fight. Also, if the Negroes attempt to use the restroom in the depot, Klansmen are to beat them in the restroom and 'make them look like a bulldog got a hold of them'; then remove the clothing of the victim and carry the clothing away. If the nude individual attempts to leave the restroom, he will be immediately arrested and it will be seen that this person is sent to the penitentiary." This particular bit of advice did not merit much attention, since neither Connor nor the Klan had any intention of allowing the Freedom Riders to see the inside of an Alabama bus station, or at least not for very long. Mother's Day or not, the loyal sons of Alabama would show their weak sisters in Virginia, Georgia, and the Carolinas how to deal with outside agitators who challenged the Southern way of life. If the Klansmen did their duty on Sunday afternoon, the Freedom Riders and others would be forced to recognize the power and passion of men who regarded massive resistance as something more than idle talk.[46]

4

Alabama Bound

We had most trouble, it turned into a struggle,
Half way 'cross Alabam,
And that 'hound broke down, and left us all stranded,
In downtown Birmingham.

—Chuck Berry[1]

JIM FARMER'S UNEXPECTED DEPARTURE placed a heavy burden on Jim Peck, who suddenly found himself in charge of the Freedom Ride. As Farmer left for the Atlanta airport, Peck could not help wondering if he would ever see his old friend again. They had been through a lot together—surviving the depths of the Cold War and CORE's lean years, not to mention the first ten days of the Freedom Ride. Now Peck had to go on alone, perhaps to glory, but more likely to an untimely rendezvous with violence, or even death. When Peck phoned Fred Shuttlesworth, the outspoken pastor of Birmingham's Bethel Baptist Church and the leader of the Alabama Christian Movement for Human Rights, to give him the exact arrival times of the two "Freedom Buses," the normally unflappable minister offered an alarming picture of what the Freedom Riders could expect once they reached Birmingham. The city was alive with rumors that a white mob planned to greet the Riders at the downtown bus stations. Shuttlesworth was not privy to FBI surveillance and did not know any of the details, but he urged Peck to be careful. Peck, trying to avoid a last-minute panic, relayed Shuttlesworth's warning to the group in a calm and matter-of-fact fashion. He also repeated Tom Gaither's warning about Anniston, a rest stop on the bus route to Birmingham. But he quickly added that he had no reason to believe the Riders would encounter any serious trouble prior to their arrival in downtown Birmingham. Barring any unforeseen problems, the four-hour ride would give them plenty of time to prepare a properly nonviolent response to the waiting mob—if, in fact, the mob existed.[2]

Faced with staggered bus schedules, the two groups of Freedom Riders left Atlanta an hour apart. The Greyhound group, with Joe Perkins in charge, was the first to leave, at 11:00 A.M. The bus was more than half empty, unusual for the Atlanta-to-Birmingham run. Fourteen passengers were on board: five regular passengers, seven Freedom Riders—Genevieve Hughes, Bert Bigelow, Hank Thomas, Jimmy McDonald, Mae Frances Moultrie, Joe Perkins, Ed Blankenheim—and two journalists, Charlotte Devree and Moses Newson. Among the "regular" passengers were Roy Robinson, the manager of the Atlanta Greyhound station, and two undercover plainclothes agents of the Alabama Highway Patrol, Corporals Ell Cowling and Harry Sims. Both Cowling and Sims sat in the back of the bus, several rows behind the scattered Freedom Riders, who had no inkling of who these two seemingly innocuous white men actually were. Following the orders of Floyd Mann, the director of the Alabama Highway Patrol, Cowling carried a hidden microphone designed to eavesdrop on the Riders. Unsure of the Freedom Ride's itinerary, Mann—and Governor John Patterson—wanted Cowling to gather information on the Riders and their plans.

During the ninety-minute trip to Tallapoosa, the last stop in Georgia, on Highway 78, none of the passengers said very much, other than a few words of nervous small talk. Around one o'clock the bus crossed the Alabama line and followed the road in a southwesterly arc to Heflin, a small country town on the edge of the Talladega National Forest. After a brief rest stop in Heflin, the Greyhound continued west through De Armanville and Oxford before turning north on Highway 21 toward Anniston. The largest city in Calhoun County and the second largest in east-central Alabama, Anniston was a no-nonsense army town that depended on nearby Fort McClellan and a sprawling ordnance depot for much of its livelihood. Known for its hard-edged race relations, Anniston boasted a relatively large black population (approximately 30 percent in 1961), a well-established NAACP branch, and some of the most aggressive and violent Klansmen in Alabama.[3]

Just south of Anniston, the driver of a southbound Greyhound motioned to the driver of the Freedom Riders' bus, O. T. Jones, to pull over to the side of the road. A white man then ran across the road and yelled to Jones through the window: "There's an angry and unruly crowd gathered at Anniston. There's a rumor that some people on this bus are going to stage a sit-in. The terminal has been closed. Be careful." With this message the Riders' worst fears seemed to be confirmed, but Joe Perkins—hoping that the warning was a bluff, or at least an exaggeration— urged the driver to keep going. A minute or two later, as the bus passed the city limits, several of the Riders couldn't help but notice that Anniston's sidewalks were lined with people, an unusual sight on a Sunday afternoon in a Deep South town. "It seemed that everyone in the town was out to greet us," Genevieve Hughes later commented.[4]

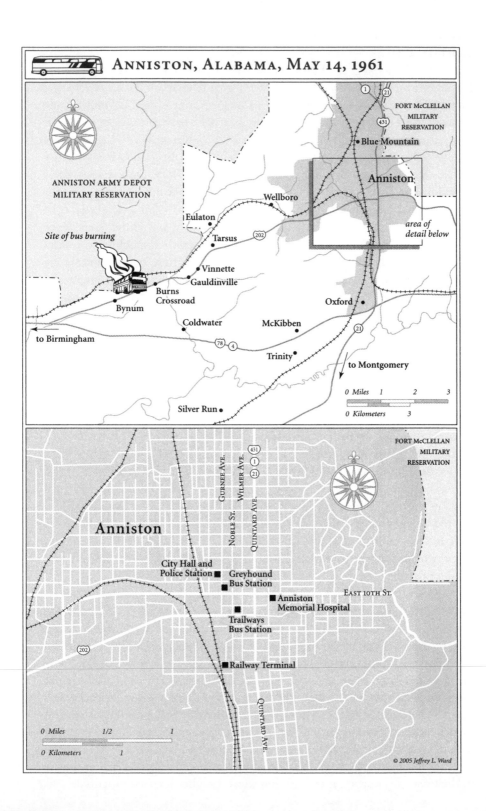

Anniston, Alabama, May 14, 1961

FORT McCLELLAN
MILITARY
RESERVATION

• Blue Mountain

ANNISTON ARMY DEPOT
MILITARY RESERVATION

Anniston

*area of
detail below*

Site of bus burning

Wellboro

Eulaton

Tarsus

• Vinnette
Gauldinville

Burns
Crossroad

Bynum

Oxford

Coldwater   McKibben

to Birmingham

78 4

Trinity

to Montgomery

Silver Run •

0 Miles   1   2   3

0 Kilometers   3

FORT McCLELLAN
MILITARY
RESERVATION

GURNEE AVE.
WILMER AVE.
NOBLE ST.
QUINTARD AVE.

Anniston

City Hall and
Police Station ■
■ Greyhound
Bus Station

■ Anniston
Memorial Hospital

EAST 10TH ST.

Trailways
Bus Station

■ Railway Terminal

QUINTARD AVE.

0 Miles   1/2   1

0 Kilometers   1

© 2005 Jeffrey L. Ward

Amazingly enough, Hank Thomas did not recall seeing anyone on the streets. He did remember the strange feeling that he and the other Riders experienced as the bus eased into the station parking lot just after 1:00 P.M. The station was locked shut, and there was silence—and then suddenly, as if out of nowhere, a screaming mob led by Anniston Klan leader William Chappell rushed the bus. Thomas thought he heard Jones encourage the attackers with a sly greeting. "Well, boys, here they are," the driver reportedly said with a smirk. "I brought you some niggers and nigger-lovers."[5] But it all happened so fast that no one was quite sure who was saying what to whom.

As the crowd of about fifty surrounded the bus, an eighteen-year-old Klansman and ex-convict named Roger Couch stretched out on the pavement in front of the bus to block any attempt to leave, while the rest—carrying metal pipes, clubs, and chains—milled around menacingly, some screaming, "Dirty Communists" and "*Sieg heil!*" There was no sign of any police, even though Herman Glass, the manager of the Anniston Greyhound station, had warned local officials earlier in the day that a potentially violent mob had gathered around the station. After the driver opened the door, Cowling and Sims hurried to the front to prevent anyone from entering. Leaning on the door lever, the two unarmed investigators managed to close the door and seal the bus, but they could not stop several of the most frenzied attackers from smashing windows, denting the sides of the bus, and slashing tires. "One man stood on the steps, yelling, and calling us cowards," Hughes noticed, but her attention soon turned to a second man who "walked by the side of the bus, slipped a pistol from his pocket and stared at me for some minutes." When she heard a loud noise and shattering glass, she yelled, "Duck, down everyone," thinking that a bullet had hit one of the windows. The projectile turned out to be a rock, but another assailant soon cracked the window above her seat with a fist full of brass knuckles. Joe Perkins's window later suffered a similar fate, as the siege continued for almost twenty minutes. By the time the Anniston police arrived on the scene, the bus looked like it had been in a serious collision. Swaggering through the crowd with billy clubs in hand, the police officers examined the broken windows and slashed tires but showed no interest in arresting anyone. After a few minutes of friendly banter with members of the crowd, the officers suddenly cleared a path and motioned for the bus to exit the parking lot.[6]

A police car escorted the battered Greyhound to the city limits but then turned back, once again leaving the bus to the mercy of the mob. A long line of cars and pickup trucks, plus one car carrying a news reporter and a photographer, had followed the police escort from the station and was ready to resume the assault. Once the entourage reached an isolated stretch of Highway 202 east of Bynum, two of the cars (one of which was driven by Roger Couch's older brother Jerome) raced around the front of the bus and then slowed to a crawl, forcing the bus driver to slow down. Trailing behind were thirty or forty cars and trucks jammed with shrieking whites. Many, like

Chappell and the Couches, were Klansmen, though none wore hoods or robes. Some, having just come from church, were dressed in their Sunday best— coats and ties and polished shoes—and a few even had children with them. The whole scene was darkly surreal and became even more so when a pair of flat tires forced the bus driver to pull over to the side of the road in front of the Forsyth and Son grocery store six miles southwest of town, only a few hundred yards from the Anniston Army Depot. Flinging open the door, the driver, with Robinson trailing close behind, ran into the grocery store and began calling local garages in what turned out to be a futile effort to find replacement tires for the bus. In the meantime, the passengers were left vulnerable to a swarm of onrushing vigilantes. Cowling had just enough time to retrieve his revolver from the baggage compartment before the mob surrounded the bus. The first to reach the Greyhound was a teenage boy who smashed a crowbar through one of the side windows. While one group of men and boys rocked the bus in a vain attempt to turn the vehicle on its side, a second tried to enter through the front door. With gun in hand, Cowling stood in the doorway to block the intruders, but he soon retreated, locking the door behind him. For the next twenty minutes Chappell and other Klansmen pounded on the bus demanding that the Freedom Riders come out to take what was coming to them, but they stayed in their seats, even after the arrival of two highway patrolmen. When neither patrolman made any effort to disperse the crowd, Cowling, Sims, and the Riders decided to stay put.

Eventually, however, two members of the mob, Roger Couch and Cecil "Goober" Lewallyn, decided that they had waited long enough. After returning to his car, which was parked a few yards behind the disabled Greyhound, Lewallyn suddenly ran toward the bus and tossed a flaming bundle of rags through a broken window. Within seconds the bundle exploded, sending dark gray smoke throughout the bus. At first, Genevieve Hughes, seated only a few feet away from the explosion, thought the bomb-thrower was just trying to scare the Freedom Riders with a smoke bomb, but as the smoke got blacker and blacker and as flames began to engulf several of the upholstered seats, she realized that she and the other passengers were in serious trouble. Crouching down in the middle of the bus, she screamed out, "Is there any air up front?" When no one answered, she began to panic. "Oh, my God, they're going to burn us up!" she yelled to the others, who were lost in a dense cloud of smoke. Making her way forward, she finally found an open window six rows from the front and thrust her head out, gasping for air. As she looked out, she saw the outstretched necks of Jimmy McDonald and Charlotte Devree, who had also found open windows. Seconds later, all three squeezed through the windows and dropped to the ground. Still choking from the smoke and fumes, they staggered across the street. Gazing back at the burning bus, they feared that the other passengers were still trapped inside, but they soon caught sight of several passengers who had escaped through the front door on the other side.[7]

They were all lucky to be alive. Several members of the mob had pressed against the door screaming, "Burn them alive" and "Fry the goddamn niggers," and the Freedom Riders had been all but doomed until an exploding fuel tank convinced the mob that the whole bus was about to explode. As the frightened whites retreated, Cowling pried open the door, allowing the rest of the choking passengers to escape. When Hank Thomas, the first Rider to exit the front of the bus, crawled away from the doorway, a white man rushed toward him and asked, "Are you all okay?" Before Thomas could answer, the man's concerned look turned into a sneer as he struck the astonished student in the head with a baseball bat. Thomas fell to the ground and was barely conscious as the rest of the exiting Riders spilled out onto the grass.[8]

By this time, several of the white families living in the surrounding Bynum neighborhood had formed a small crowd in front of the grocery store. Most of the onlookers remained safely in the background, but a few stepped forward to offer assistance to the Riders. One little girl, twelve-year-old Janie Miller, supplied the choking victims with water, filling and refilling a five-gallon bucket while braving the insults and taunts of Klansmen. Later ostracized and threatened for this act of kindness, she and her family found it impossible to remain

"Freedom bus" in flames, near Forsyth and Son Grocery, six miles southwest of Anniston, Alabama, Sunday, May 14, 1961. (Birmingham Public Library)

in Anniston in the aftermath of the bus bombing. Even though city leaders were quick to condemn the bombing, there was little sympathy for the Riders among local whites. Indeed, while Miller was coming to the Riders' aid, some of her neighbors were urging the marauding Klansmen on.

At one point, with the Riders lying "on the ground around the bus, coughing and bleeding," the mob surged forward. But Cowling's pistol, the heat of the fire, and the acrid fumes wafting from the burning upholstery kept them away. Moments later a second fuel tank explosion drove them back even farther, and eventually a couple of warning shots fired into the air by the highway patrolmen on the scene signaled that the would-be lynching party was over. As the disappointed vigilantes slipped away, Cowling, Sims, and the patrolmen stood guard over the Riders, most of whom were lying or sitting in a daze a few yards from the burned-out shell of the bus. But no one in a position of authority showed any interest in identifying or arresting those responsible for the assault. No one wrote down the license numbers of the Klansmen's cars and pickup trucks, and no one seemed in any hurry to call an ambulance. Several of the Riders had inhaled smoke and fumes and were in serious need of medical attention, but it would be some time before any of them saw a doctor. One sympathetic white couple who lived nearby allowed Hughes to use their phone to call for an ambulance, and when no one answered, they drove her to the hospital. For the rest of the stricken Riders, getting to the hospital proved to be a bit more complicated. When the ambulance called by one of the state troopers finally arrived, the driver refused to transport any of the injured black Riders. After a few moments of awkward silence, the white Riders, already loaded into the ambulance, began to exit, insisting they could not leave their black friends behind. With this gesture—and a few stern words from Cowling—the driver's resolve weakened, and before long the integrated band was on its way to Anniston Memorial Hospital.[9]

Unfortunately, the scene at the hospital offered the Riders little solace. The first to arrive, Hughes found the medical care in Anniston almost as frightening as the burning bus:

> There was no doctor at the hospital, only a nurse. They had me breathe pure oxygen but that only burned my throat and did not relieve the coughing. I was burning hot and my clothes were a wet mess. After awhile Ed and Bert were brought in, choking. We all lay on our beds and coughed. Finally a woman doctor came in—she had to look up smoke poisoning before treating us. They brought in the Negro man who had been in the back of the bus with me. I pointed to him and told them to take care of him. But they did not bring him into our emergency room. I understand that they did not do anything at all for Hank. Thirteen in all were brought in, and three were admitted: Ed, the Negro man and myself. They gave me a room and I slept. When I woke up the nurse asked me if I could talk with the FBI. The FBI man did not care about us, but only the bombing.[10]

Hughes's general distrust of the FBI's attitude toward civil rights activists was clearly warranted, but—unbeknownst to her—the FBI agent on the

The burned-out shell of the bus disabled and bombed by white supremacists near Anniston, Sunday, May 14, 1961. Journalist Moses Newson (far left, partially obscured) and Alabama Highway Patrol investigator Ell Cowling stand near the bus. Freedom Riders (left to right) Jimmy McDonald and Hank Thomas and regular passenger Roberta Holmes can be seen sitting in the foreground. (Library of Congress)

scene had actually intervened on the Freedom Riders' behalf. At his urging, the medical staff agreed to treat all of the injured passengers, black and white, though in the end they failed to do so. When the ambulance full of Freedom Riders arrived at the hospital, a group of Klansmen made an unsuccessful attempt to block the entrance to the emergency room. Later, as the crowd outside the hospital grew to menacing proportions, hospital officials began to panic, especially after several Klansmen threatened to burn the building to the ground. With nightfall approaching and with no prospect of adequate police protection, the superintendent ordered the Riders to leave the hospital as soon as possible.[11]

Hughes and several other Riders were in no shape to leave, but Joe Perkins, the leader of the Greyhound group, had no choice but to comply with the evacuation order. Struggling to conceal his rage, he told the Riders to be ready to leave in twenty minutes, though it actually took him well over an hour to arrange safe passage out of the hospital. After both the state troopers and the local police refused to provide the Riders with transportation—or even an escort—Bert Bigelow called friends in Washington in a vain effort to get help from the federal government. A few minutes later Perkins placed a frantic call to Fred Shuttlesworth in Birmingham. A native of the Alabama Black Belt, Shuttlesworth knew enough about towns like Anniston to know that the Freedom Riders were in serious danger. Mobilizing a fleet of eight cars, he planned to lead the rescue mission himself until his longtime bodyguard, Colonel Stone "Buck" Johnson, persuaded him to remain in Birmingham with the Trailways Riders, who had arrived in the city earlier in the afternoon. Just before the cars left for Anniston, Shuttlesworth reminded Johnson and the other volunteers that this was a nonviolent operation. "Gentlemen, this is dangerous," he admitted, "but . . . you mustn't carry any weapons. You must trust God and have faith." All of the "deacons" nodded in assent, but as soon as they were safely out of sight, several of the faithful pulled out shotguns from beneath their seats. Checking triggers and ammunition, they made sure they would be able to defend themselves if the going got rough.[12]

While the Riders waited for Shuttlesworth's deacons to make their way across the back roads of the Alabama hill country, the Anniston hospital superintendent grew impatient and reminded Perkins that the interracial group would not be allowed to spend the night in the hospital. Perhaps, he suggested with a wry smile, they could find refuge in the bus station. Fortunately, the superintendent's mean-spirited suggestion became moot a few minutes later when the rescue mission pulled into the hospital parking lot. With the police holding back the jeering crowd, and with the deacons openly displaying their weapons, the weary but relieved Riders piled into the cars, which promptly drove off into the gathering dusk. "We walked right between those Ku Klux," Buck Johnson later recalled. "Some of them had clubs. There were some deputies too. You couldn't tell the deputies from the Ku Klux." [13]

As the convoy raced toward Birmingham, the Riders peppered their rescuers with questions about the fate of the Trailways group. Perkins's conversation with Shuttlesworth earlier in the afternoon had revealed that the other bus had also run into trouble, but few details had been available. The deacons themselves knew only part of the story, but even the barest outline was enough to confirm the Riders' worst fears: The attack on the bus in Anniston could not be dismissed as the work of an unorganized mob. As the deacons described what had happened to the Trailways group, the true nature of the Riders' predicament came into focus: With the apparent connivance of law enforcement officials, the organized defenders of white supremacy in Alabama had decided to smash the Freedom Ride with violence, in effect announcing to the world that they had no intention of letting the law, the U.S. Constitution, or anything else interfere with the preservation of racial segregation in their sovereign state.[14]

THE TRAILWAYS RIDERS' ORDEAL began even before the group left Atlanta. As Peck and the other Riders waited in line to purchase their tickets, they couldn't help noticing that several regular passengers had disappeared from the line after being approached by a group of white men. The white men themselves—later identified as Alabama Klansmen—eventually boarded the bus, but only a handful of other regular passengers joined them. The Klansmen were beefy, rough-looking characters, mostly in their twenties or thirties, and their hulking presence gave the Riders an uneasy feeling as the bus pulled out. There were seven Freedom Riders scattered throughout the bus: the Bergmans, Jim Peck, Charles Person, Herman Harris, Jerry Moore, and Ike Reynolds. Simeon Booker and his *Jet* magazine colleague, photographer Ted Gaffney, were also on board. Seated in the rear of the bus, the two journalists had a close-up view of the entire harrowing journey from Atlanta to Birmingham. "It was a frightening experience," Booker later reported, "the worst encountered in almost 20 years of journalism."[15]

He was not exaggerating. The bus was barely out of the Atlanta terminal when the Klansmen began to make threatening remarks. "You niggers will be taken care of once you get in Alabama," one Klansman sneered.[16] Once the bus passed the state line, the comments intensified, giving the Riders the distinct impression that something might be brewing in Anniston. Arriving at the Anniston Trailways station approximately an hour after the other Riders had pulled into the Greyhound station, Peck and the Trailways Riders looked around warily before leaving the bus. The waiting room was eerily quiet, and several whites looked away as the unwelcome visitors walked up to the lunch counter. After purchasing a few sandwiches, the Riders walked back to the bus. Later, while waiting nervously to leave, they heard an ambulance siren but didn't think much of it until the bus driver, John Olan Patterson, who had been talking to several Anniston police officers, vaulted up the steps. Flanked by eight "hoodlums," as Peck later called them, Patterson gave them the news about the Greyhound riot. "We have received word that a bus has been burned to the ground and passengers are being carried to the hospital by the carloads," he declared, with no hint of compassion or regret. "A mob is waiting for our bus and will do the same to us unless we get these niggers off the front seats." His bus wasn't going anywhere until the black Freedom Riders retreated to the back of the bus where they belonged.[17]

After a few moments of silence, one of the Riders reminded Patterson that they were interstate passengers who had the right to sit wherever they pleased. Shaking his head in disgust, he exited the bus without a word. But one of the white "hoodlums" soon answered for him: "Niggers get back. You ain't up north. You're in Alabama, and niggers ain't nothing here." To prove his point, he suddenly lunged toward Person, punching him in the face. A second Klansman then struck Harris, who was sitting next to Person in the front section of the bus. Both black Freedom Riders adhered to Gandhian discipline and refused to fight back, but this only encouraged their attackers. Dragging the defenseless students into the aisle, the Klansmen started pummeling them with their fists and kicking them again and again. At this point Peck and Walter Bergman rushed forward from the back to object. As soon as Peck reached the front, one of the attackers turned on him, striking a blow that sent the frail, middle-aged activist reeling across two rows of seats. Within seconds Bergman, the oldest of the Freedom Riders at sixty-one, suffered a similar blow, falling to the floor with a thud. As blood spurted from their faces, both men tried to shield themselves from further attack, but the Klansmen, enraged by the white Riders' attempt to protect their "nigger" collaborators, proceeded to pound them into a bloody mass. While a pair of Klansmen lifted Peck's head, others punched him in the face until he lost consciousness. By this time Bergman was out cold on the floor, but one frenzied assailant continued to stomp on his chest. When Frances Bergman begged the Klansman to stop beating her husband, he ignored her plea and called her a "nigger lover." Fortunately, one of the other Klansmen—realizing that the defenseless Freedom Rider was about to be killed—eventually called a halt to the beating. "Don't kill him," he said coolly, making sure that no one on the bus mistook self-interested restraint for compassion.[18]

Although Walter Bergman's motionless body blocked the aisle, several Klansmen managed to drag Person and Harris, both barely conscious, to the back of the bus, draping them over the passengers sitting in the backseat. A few seconds later, they did the same to Peck and Bergman, creating a pile of bleeding and bruised humanity that left the rest of the passengers in a momentary state of shock. Content with their brutal handiwork, the Klansmen then sat down in the middle of the bus to block any further attempts to violate the color line. At this point a black woman riding as a regular passenger begged to be let off the bus, but the Klansmen forced her to stay. "Shut up, you black bitch," one of them snarled. "Ain't nobody but whites sitting up here. And them nigger lovers . . . can just sit back there with their nigger friends."

Moments later, Patterson, who had left during the melee, returned to the bus, accompanied by a police officer. After surveying the scene, both men appeared satisfied with the restoration of Jim Crow seating arrangements. Turning toward the Klansmen, the police officer grinned and assured them that Alabama justice was on their side: "Don't worry about no lawsuits. I ain't seen a thing." The officer then exited the bus and motioned to Patterson to head out onto the highway. Realizing that there was a mob waiting on the main road to Birmingham, the driver kept to the back roads as he headed west. When none of the Klansmen objected to this detour, the Freedom Riders were puzzled but relieved, thinking that perhaps there were limits to the savagery of the segregationists after all, even in the wilds of eastern Alabama. What they did not know, of course, was that the Klansmen were simply saving them for the welcoming party already gathering in the shadows of downtown Birmingham.

During the next two hours, as the bus rolled toward Birmingham, the Klansmen continued to taunt and torment the Riders. One man brandished a pistol, a second threatened the Riders with a steel pipe, and three others served as "sentries," blocking access to the middle and front sections of the bus. As Booker recalled the scene, one of the sentries was "a pop-eyed fellow

who kept taunting: 'Just tell Bobby [Kennedy] and we'll do him in, too.' "
When one of the Klansmen approached Booker threateningly, the journalist
nervously handed him a copy of *Jet* that featured an advance story on CORE's
sponsorship of the Freedom Ride. Over the next few minutes, as the article
was passed from Klansman to Klansman, the atmosphere became increasingly
tense. "I'd like to choke all of them," one Klansman confessed, while others
assured the Riders that they would get what was coming to them when they
arrived in Birmingham. By the time the bus reached the outskirts of the city,
Peck and the other injured Riders had regained consciousness, but since the
Klansmen would not allow any of the Riders to leave their seats or talk among
themselves, there was no opportunity for Peck to prepare the group for the
impending onslaught. He could only hope that each Rider would be able to
draw upon some combination of inner strength and past experience, some res-
ervoir of courage and responsibility that would sustain the Freedom Ride and
protect the viability and moral integrity of the nonviolent movement.[19]

Though battered and bleeding, and barely able to walk, Peck was determined to set an example for his fellow Freedom Riders. As the designated
testers at the Birmingham stop, he and Person would be the first to confront
the fully assembled power of Alabama segregationists. The terror-filled ride
from Atlanta was a clear indication that they could expect some measure of
violence in Birmingham, but at this point Peck and the other Trailways Riders had no detailed knowledge of what had happened to the Greyhound group
in Anniston two hours earlier. They thought they were prepared for the worst.
In actuality, however, they had no reliable way of gauging what they were up
against, no way of appreciating the full implications of challenging Alabama's
segregationist institutions, and no inkling of how far Birmingham's ultra-
segregationists would go to protect the sanctity of Jim Crow. This was not
just the Deep South—it was Birmingham, where close collaboration between
the Ku Klux Klan and law enforcement officials was a fact of life. The special
agents in the Birmingham FBI field office, as well as their superiors in Washington, possessed detailed information on this collaboration and could have
warned the Freedom Riders. But they chose to remain silent.[20]

The dire consequences of the bureau's refusal to intervene were compounded by the active involvement of FBI informant Gary Thomas Rowe.
In the final minutes before the Trailways group's arrival, Rowe helped ensure that the plot to "welcome" the Freedom Riders would actually be carried out. The plan called for Rowe and the other Klansmen to initiate the
attack at the Greyhound station, where the first group of Freedom Riders
was expected to arrive, but news of the Anniston bombing did not reach
Birmingham until midafternoon, just minutes before the arrival of the
Trailways bus. A frantic call from police headquarters to Rowe, who quickly
spread the word, alerted the Klansmen waiting near the Greyhound station
that a bus of Freedom Riders was about to arrive at the Trailways station,
three blocks away. The "welcoming committee" had just enough time to

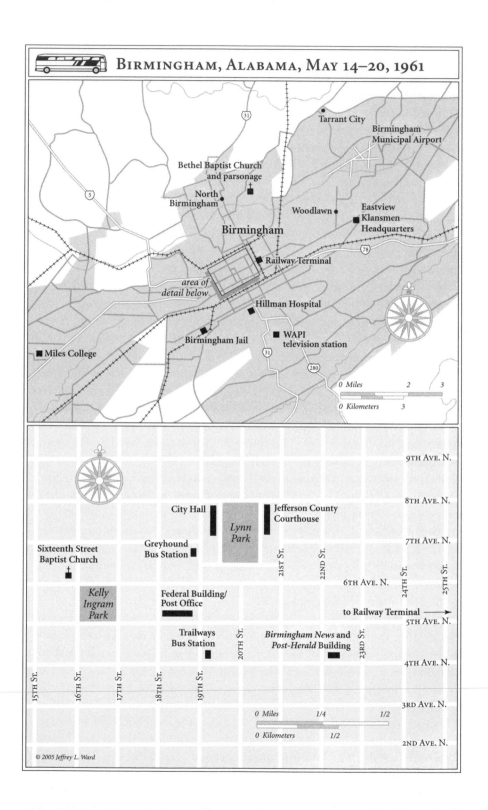

BIRMINGHAM, ALABAMA, MAY 14–20, 1961

Tarrant City

Birmingham
Municipal Airport

Bethel Baptist Church
and parsonage

North
Birmingham

Woodlawn

Eastview
Klansmen
Headquarters

Birmingham

Railway Terminal

area of
detail below

Hillman Hospital

Birmingham Jail

WAPI
television station

Miles College

0 Miles   2   3

0 Kilometers   3

9TH AVE. N.

8TH AVE. N.

City Hall

Jefferson County
Courthouse

Lynn
Park

Greyhound
Bus Station

Sixteenth Street
Baptist Church

7TH AVE. N.

21ST ST.

22ND ST.

24TH ST.

25TH ST.

6TH AVE. N.

Kelly
Ingram
Park

Federal Building/
Post Office

to Railway Terminal →

5TH AVE. N.

Trailways
Bus Station

20TH ST.

Birmingham News and
Post-Herald Building

23RD ST.

4TH AVE. N.

15TH ST.

16TH ST.

17TH ST.

18TH ST.

19TH ST.

3RD AVE. N.

0 Miles   1/4   1/2

0 Kilometers   1/2

2ND AVE. N.

© 2005 Jeffrey L. Ward

regroup at the Trailways station. Years later Rowe recalled the mad rush across downtown Birmingham: "We made an astounding sight . . . men running and walking down the streets of Birmingham on Sunday afternoon carrying chains, sticks, and clubs. Everything was deserted; no police officers were to be seen except one on a street corner. He stepped off and let us go by, and we barged into the bus station and took it over like an army of occupation. There were Klansmen in the waiting room, in the rest rooms, in the parking area."[21]

By the time Peck and company arrived, the Klansmen and their police allies were all in place, armed and ready to do what had to be done to protect the Southern way of life. Police dispatchers, following the agreed-upon plan, had cleared the "target" area: For the next fifteen minutes there would be no police presence in or near the Trailways station. The only exceptions were two plainclothes detectives who were in the crowd to monitor the situation and to make sure that the Klansmen left the station before the police arrived. Since it was Sunday, and Mother's Day, there were few bystanders, aside from a handful of news reporters who had been tipped off that something big was about to happen at the Trailways station. Despite the semisecret nature of the operation, the organizers could not resist the temptation to let the outside world catch a glimpse of Alabama manhood in action.

One of the reporters on hand was Howard K. Smith, a national correspondent for CBS News who was in Birmingham working on a television documentary titled *Who Speaks for Birmingham?* Smith and his CBS colleagues were investigating *New York Times* columnist Harrison Salisbury's charges that Alabama's largest city was consumed by lawlessness and racial oppression. "Every channel of communication, every medium of mutual interest, every reasoned approach, every inch of middle ground," wrote Salisbury in April 1960, "has been fragmented by the emotional dynamite of racism, reinforced by the whip, the razor, the gun, the bomb, the torch, the club, the knife, the mob, the police and many branches of the state's apparatus." After several days of interviews, Smith was still trying to decide if Salisbury's claims were exaggerated. A Louisiana native with considerable experience in the Deep South, Smith was more than intrigued when he received a Saturday night call from Dr. Edward R. Fields, the president of the ultra-conservative National States Rights Party (NSRP), an organization known to promote a virulent strain of white supremacist and anti-Semitic extremism. Identifying himself simply as "Fields," the arch segregationist urged Smith to hang around the downtown bus stations "if he wanted to see some real action."

A gun-toting Birmingham chiropractor with close ties to the infamous Georgia extremist J. B. Stoner, Fields himself had every intention of taking part in the action. Along with Stoner, who had driven over from Atlanta for the occasion, and several other NSRP stalwarts, Fields showed up at the Greyhound station on Sunday afternoon armed and ready for the bloodletting— even though Klan leader Hubert Page warned him to stay away. Page and his police accomplices were having enough trouble controlling their own forces without having to worry about Fields and his crew of professional trouble-makers. With Police Chief Jamie Moore out of the city and Connor lying low in an effort to distance himself from the impending violence, Detective Tom Cook was in charge of the operation, but Cook did not share Page's concern. When Rowe called Cook to complain that the NSRP was compli-cating the Klan's plans, the detective told him to relax. "You boys should work together," Cook suggested.[22]

Connor—who spent Sunday morning at city hall, barely a stone's throw away from the Greyhound station—was probably the only man in Birming-ham with the power to call the whole thing off. But he was not about to do so. Resisting the entreaties of several friends, including his Methodist pastor, John Rutland, who warned him that joining forces with the Klan was a big mistake, he cast his lot with the extremists. He knew that the welcoming party might backfire—that it could complicate the mayoral campaign of his political ally Art Hanes, that Birmingham might even become a second Little Rock, a city besieged by federal troops—but he simply could not bring himself to let the Freedom Riders off the hook. He had been waiting too long for an opportu-nity to confront the Yankee agitators on his own turf. It was time to let Earl Warren, the Kennedys, the Communists, and all the other meddling South-haters know that the loyal sons of Alabama were ready to fight and die for white supremacy and states' rights. It was time for the blood to flow.[23]

At 4:15 on Sunday afternoon, Connor got all the blood he wanted—and then some. As soon as the bus pulled into the Trailways terminal, the Klansmen on board raced down the aisle to be near the front door. Follow-ing a few parting taunts—one man screamed, "You damn Communists, why don't you go back to Russia. You're a shame to the white race"—they hustled down the steps and disappeared into the crowd. They had done their job; the rest was up to their Klan brethren, several of whom were waiting expectantly in front of the terminal. The Klansmen's hurried exit was a bit unnerving, but as Peck and the other Freedom Riders peered out at the crowd there was no sign of any weapons. One by one, the Riders filed off the bus and onto the unloading platform, where they began to retrieve their luggage. Although there were several rough-looking men standing a few feet from the platform, there was no clear indication that an attack was imminent. After a few mo-ments of hesitation, Peck and Person walked toward the white waiting room to begin testing the terminal's facilities. In his 1962 memoir, Peck recalled the intensity of the scene, especially his concern for the safety of his black colleague. "I did not want to put Person in a position of being forced to proceed if he thought the situation was too dangerous," he remembered, but "when I looked at him, he responded by saying simply, 'Let's go.' "[24] This bravery was not born of ignorance: Person had grown up in the Deep South; he had recently served sixteen days in jail for his part in the Atlanta sit-ins, and he had already been beaten up earlier in the day. Nevertheless, neither he nor Peck was fully prepared for what was about to happen.

Ku Klux Klansmen beat black bystander George Webb in a back
corridor of the Birmingham
Trailways bus station, Sunday,
May 14, 1961. The man with his
back to the camera (center right)
is FBI undercover agent Gary
Thomas Rowe. The man being
beaten was initially misidentified
by the press as Freedom Rider
Jim Peck. The photographer,
Tommy Langston, was assaulted
by Klansmen moments after the
photograph was taken. (Photograph by Thomas Langston,
Birmingham Post-Herald;
Bettmann-CORBIS)

Moments after the two Freedom Riders entered the waiting room and
approached the whites-only lunch counter, one of the waiting Klansmen
pointed to the cuts on Peck's face and the caked blood on his shirt and
screamed out that Person, who was walking in front of Peck, deserved to die
for attacking a white man. At this point, Peck tried to explain that Person was
not the man who had attacked him, adding: "You'll have to kill me before
you hurt him." This blatant breach of racial solidarity only served to incite
the crowd of Klansmen blocking their path. After an Eastview Klansman
named Gene Reeves pushed Person toward the colored waiting room, the
young black Freedom Rider gamely continued walking toward the white lunch
counter but was unable to sidestep a second Klansman who shoved him up
against a concrete wall. Standing nearby, NSRP leader Edward Fields pointed
toward Peck and yelled: "Get that son of a bitch." Several burly white men
then began to pummel Person with their fists, bloodying his face and mouth
and dropping him to his knees. When Peck rushed over to help Person to his
feet, several Klansmen grabbed both men by the shoulders and pushed them
into a dimly lit corridor leading to a loading platform. In the corridor more
than a dozen whites, some armed with lead or iron pipes and others with
oversized key rings, pounced on the two Riders, punching and kicking them
repeatedly. Before long, the assault turned into a chaotic free-for-all with
"fists and arms . . . flying everywhere." In the ensuing confusion, Person
managed to escape. Running into the street, he staggered onto a city bus and
eventually found his way to Fred Shuttlesworth's parsonage. In the meantime Peck bore the brunt of the attack, eventually losing consciousness and
slumping to the floor in a pool of blood.

The fracas had been moved to the back corridor in an effort to avoid the
reporters and news photographers roaming the white waiting room, but several newsmen, including Howard K. Smith, witnessed at least part of the

attack. Smith, who had only been in Birmingham for a few days, could hardly believe his eyes as the rampaging Klansmen and NSRP "storm troopers" swarmed over the two Freedom Riders. But he soon discovered that this was only the beginning of one of the bloodiest afternoons in Birmingham's history.[25]

While Peck and Person were being assaulted in the corridor, the other Riders searched for a refuge. Jerry Moore and Herman Harris avoided detection by losing themselves in the crowd and slipping away just before the assaults began. Frances Bergman, at her husband's insistence, boarded a city bus moments after their arrival, but Walter himself was unable to escape the mob's fury. Still woozy from his earlier beating, with blood still caked on his clothing, he bravely followed Peck and Person into the white waiting room. After witnessing the initial assault on his two colleagues, he searched in vain for a policeman who could help them, but soon he too was knocked to the floor by an enraged Klansman. When Simeon Booker entered the terminal a few seconds later, he saw the bloodied and defenseless professor crawling on his hands and knees. Recoiling from the grisly scene, Booker retreated to the street, where he found a black cabdriver who agreed to whisk him and Ted Gaffney away to safety.[26]

Others were less fortunate. Several white men attacked Ike Reynolds, kicking and stomping him before heaving his semiconscious body into a curbside trash bin. In the confusion, the mob also attacked a number of bystanders misidentified as Freedom Riders. One of the victims was actually a Klansman named L. B. Earle, who had the misfortune of coming out of the men's room at the wrong time. Attacked by fellow Klansmen who failed to recognize him, Earle suffered several deep head gashes and ended up in the hospital. Another victim of the mob, a twenty-nine-year-old black laborer named George Webb, was assaulted after he entered the baggage room with his fiancée, Mary Spicer, one of the regular passengers on the freedom bus from Atlanta. The last person to leave the bus, Spicer was unaware of the melee inside the station until she and Webb encountered a group of pipe-wielding rioters in the baggage area. One of the men, undercover FBI informant Gary Thomas Rowe, told Spicer to "get the hell out of here," and she escaped harm, running into the street for help. But Rowe and three others, including an NSRP member, immediately surrounded Webb and proceeded to pummel him with everything from their fists to a baseball bat. Webb fought back but was soon overwhelmed as several more white men joined in. Dozens of others looked on, some yelling, "Kill the nigger." But moments later the assault was interrupted by Red Self, one of the plainclothes detectives on the scene, who grabbed Rowe by the shoulder and told him it was time to go. "Get the boys out of here," he ordered. "I'm ready to give the signal for the police to move in."[27]

During the allotted fifteen minutes, the violence had spread to the sidewalks and streets surrounding the Trailways station, making it difficult to get the word to all of the Klansmen and NSRP members involved in the riot. But by the time the police moved in to restore order, virtually all of the rioters had left the area. Despite Self's warning, Rowe and those attacking Webb were among the last to leave. "Goddamn it, Tom," Self finally screamed at Rowe, "I told you to get out of here! They're on the way." Rowe and several others, however, were preoccupied with Webb and continued the attack until a news photographer snapped a picture of Rowe and the other Klansmen. As soon as the flashbulb went off, they abandoned Webb and ran after the photographer, Tommy Langston of the *Birmingham Post-Herald*, who made it to the station parking lot before being caught. After one man grabbed Langston's camera and smashed it to the ground, Rowe and several others, including Eastview klavern leader Hubert Page, kicked and punched him and threatened to beat him with the same pipes and baseball bats used on Webb. In the meantime, Webb ran into the loading area, where he was recaptured by a pack of Klansmen led by Gene Reeves. With the police closing in, Webb, like Langston, was released after a few final licks, though by this time both men were bleeding profusely. Stumbling into the parking lot, Webb somehow managed to find the car where his terrified fiancée and aunt had been waiting. As they drove away to safety, Langston, whose life had suddenly become intertwined with the beating of a man whom he had never met, staggered down the street to the *Post-Herald* building, where he collapsed into the arms of a shocked colleague. Later in the afternoon, another *Post-Herald* photographer returned to the scene of the assault and retrieved Langston's broken camera, discovering to his and Langston's amazement that the roll of film inside was undamaged.

The graphic picture of the Webb beating that appeared on the front page of the *Post-Herald* the next morning, though initially misidentified as a photograph of the attack on Peck, turned out to be one of the few pieces of documentary evidence to survive the riot. Immediately following the attack on Langston, Rowe and Page grabbed *Birmingham News* photographers Bud Gordon and Tom Lankford and promptly destroyed all of the unexposed film in their cameras. Neither photographer was beaten, but Clancy Lake, a reporter for WAPI radio, was not so lucky. As Rowe and two other Eastview Klansmen, Billy Holt and Ray Graves, walked toward the Greyhound station parking lot to retrieve their cars, they spied Lake sitting in the front seat of his car broadcasting an eyewitness account of the riot. Convinced that Lake had a camera and had been taking photographs of the scene at the Trailways station, the Klansmen smashed the car's windows with a blackjack, ripped the microphone from the dashboard, and dragged the reporter onto the pavement. Although Lake noticed a passing police car and screamed for help, the officer drove on, leaving him at the mercy of attackers. At one point the three men pushed him into a wall, but after Holt swung at him with a pipe and missed, Lake bolted into the Trailways station, where he was relieved to discover that a squad of police had just arrived. With the police on the scene, the gritty reporter was able to resume his broadcast via telephone, as Rowe and his companions called off the pursuit and once again headed toward their cars.

Along the way, they encountered a smiling Bobby Shelton, who congratulated them for a job well done and offered them a ride to the Greyhound parking lot in his Cadillac. Upon their arrival, the Imperial Wizard and his passengers were shocked to discover several local black men writing down the license plate numbers of the Klansmen's cars. Following a brief struggle—at least one of the overmatched blacks was in his mid-sixties—the Klansmen ripped up the pages with the incriminating numbers before heading to Rowe's house for a victory celebration. Arriving at the house around five o'clock, they stayed there only a few minutes before a phone call from Sergeant Tom Cook sent them back downtown to intercept another bus full of Freedom Riders. The Greyhound freedom bus, having been burned in Anniston, never actually arrived, but Rowe and Page had too much blood lust to return home without getting some action. Wandering into a black neighborhood on the north side of downtown, they picked a fight with a group of young blacks who gave as good as they got. The battle put one Klansman in the hospital and left Rowe with a knife wound in the neck serious enough to require immediate attention from a doctor. None of this, however, dampened the sense of triumph among the Klansmen and their police collaborators.

At a late-night meeting with Rowe, Red Self suggested that the shedding of a little blood was a small price to pay for what they had accomplished. After weeks of anticipation and careful planning, they had done exactly what they set out to do. Carried out in broad daylight, the assault on the Freedom Riders had turned a bus station into a war zone, and the Klansmen involved had come away with only minor injuries and little likelihood of criminal prosecution. In the coming days and weeks, the publication of Langston's photograph would be a source of concern for those who were identifiable as Webb's attackers—and for Rowe's FBI handlers, who were furious that one of their informants had allowed himself to be captured on film during a criminal assault. But as Self and Rowe congratulated each other in the waning hours of May 14, there was no reason to believe that anything had gone wrong. Backing up words with action, the white supremacists of the Eastview klavern and their allies had demonstrated in no uncertain terms that they were ready to use any means necessary to halt the Freedom Rides.[28]

The late-afternoon scene at the Trailways station testified to the success of the operation. Within twenty minutes of the Freedom Riders' arrival, the mob had vanished, leaving surprisingly little evidence of the riot and few witnesses with a clear sense of what had just happened. When Peck regained consciousness a few minutes after the assault, he was alone in the corridor. Staggering into the waiting room, he encountered a white soldier who asked if he needed help. Before Peck could answer he was surrounded by smirking policemen who made a mock show of concern for his welfare. Waving them off, he slumped on a bench, where he was soon joined by Walter Bergman, the only other Rider still inside the station. With the help of Howard K. Smith, Bergman tried to hail a cab for himself and Peck, but no driver was willing to take them. Fearing that Peck might bleed to death if he remained at the station much longer, Smith offered to transport the two Riders in the station wagon being used by CBS producer David Lowe and his camera crew. But by the time Smith retrieved the car, Peck and Bergman were gone, having finally found a black cabdriver brave enough to drive them to Shuttlesworth's parsonage.

Minutes later, as he watched the police make a belated show of force outside the station, Smith ran across three injured black men sitting on the curb, "bleeding and uncared for." One was Ike Reynolds, and the other two were bystanders caught in the melee. Though dazed and a bit shaken, they all agreed to talk with the CBS newsman about what they had just seen and experienced. Seizing an opportunity to make television history, Smith promptly "piled them" into the station wagon and took them to his motel for a series of "on-camera interviews." Conducted within an hour of the riot, the interviews would have made for spectacular viewing if Smith had been able to show them to a national audience on Sunday evening. Throughout the afternoon, he issued live hourly radio broadcasts on the riot over his motel telephone, but when he tried to file an eyewitness report for the *CBS Evening News* that night the WAPI television floor director informed him that "we aren't getting any signals." Technical difficulties aside, Smith suspected that the real problem was the ultra-conservative politics of Vincent Townsend, the influential owner of the *Birmingham News*, WAPI radio, and WAPI television, which served as the local television affiliate for both CBS and NBC. But at the time, neither he nor the disappointed anchorman of the *CBS Evening News*—Troy, Alabama, native Douglas Edwards—could do anything about it. [29]

Following the late-afternoon interviews, one of Smith's cameramen delivered Reynolds to the Bethel Baptist Church parsonage, where the rest of the Riders had already gathered. An hour or so earlier, a bleeding and battered Charles Person had arrived on Shuttlesworth's doorstep, followed a few minutes later by Bergman and Peck, who stumbled out of a cab looking "as bloody as a slaughtered hog." Peck's condition, in particular, was cause for considerable alarm. Shuttlesworth, who had already spent several minutes frantically trying to find a doctor to tend to Person's wounds, called for an ambulance. It took nearly an hour to locate an ambulance company willing to have anything to do with the Freedom Rides, and during the delay Peck was moved to the parsonage guest room, where he and the other Riders had a brief reunion. Doubled up with pain, Peck struggled to find the right words to buoy their spirits. He wanted to tell them that the Freedom Ride would continue no matter what, that they couldn't give up. But as he drifted in and out of semiconsciousness, it became clear that such serious talk would have to wait. Before long the blood from his wounds saturated a white bed-spread, prompting a worried Shuttlesworth to wonder if his injured guest would even make it to the hospital.

To make matters worse, several police cars soon descended on the parson-age. After surveying the interracial group, one of the officers threatened to arrest the Freedom Riders for violating local segregation laws. But Shuttlesworth stood his ground. "You can't arrest these men. They are sick!" he told the officer, who seemed unnerved by the minister's bravado. "They are going to the hospital, or they can stay at my house." A few minutes later, Bull Connor himself phoned to repeat the threat, but once again Shuttlesworth refused to be intimidated. "If you provide them a hotel downtown, I will be glad to re-lease them," he insisted. "Otherwise, they stay here." Realizing that news re-porters would have a field day when they learned that the commissioner of public safety had cast the injured Freedom Riders into the street, Connor re-lented, but he never forgave Shuttlesworth for this act of impertinence.[30]

Within minutes of the police's departure, an ambulance arrived to take Peck to Carraway Methodist Hospital, but the injured Freedom Rider's ordeal was far from over. After Carraway officials refused to treat him, Peck was taken to Jefferson Hillman Hospital, where he underwent emergency surgery to re-pair several deep gashes in his head. As soon as the press discovered that he was at Hillman, curious reporters swarmed around his bedside, snapping pictures of his wounds—which required fifty-three stitches—and asking him what it felt like to be a martyr. Despite considerable grogginess and weakness, Peck did his best to field the reporters' questions. Speaking almost in a whisper, he told the press—and the nation—exactly what had happened in the mean streets of Birmingham and Anniston. When asked about his plans for the future, he raised his voice just enough to make sure that everyone in the room heard his pledge. "The going is getting rougher," he admitted, "but I'll be on that bus tomorrow headed for Montgomery." With this declaration, he clearly sur-prised the reporters, nearly all of whom had expected CORE to throw in the towel. As they ran to the phones to file their stories, some may have doubted Peck's sanity, but none doubted his courage.[31]

While Peck was holding his remarkable impromptu press conference, the rest of the Freedom Riders were huddling at the parsonage. In the early evening the convoy from Anniston had finally arrived, prompting a joyous reunion of the Trailways and Greyhound survivors. Though some of the Riders were still in a state of shock, there were handshakes and embraces all around. As they swapped tales of narrow escapes and close encounters with rampaging white bigots, the bonds of common struggle became apparent. All had been battered by the events of the day, and all were fearful of the future. But somehow they had survived, psychologically as well as physically. No one had collapsed under the pressures of the moment, and no one had broken or dishonored the nonviolent code they had pledged to uphold. Al-though the Freedom Ride itself was clearly in jeopardy, they were still hopeful that their willingness to put their bodies on the line would inspire others to do the same.

At a mass meeting held at Bethel Baptist Church that evening, several of the Freedom Riders spoke in emotional tones about what they had experienced during ten days on the road. Sitting in chairs placed alongside the altar, looking like an array of accident victims in a hospital waiting room, they told their stories one by one. Although fear of the police and the suspicion that the violence was not yet over kept the audience small, the fifty or so who were there witnessed an amazing outpouring of movement culture. Despite a badly swollen eye, cracked ribs, and deep facial cuts, Walter Bergman spoke the longest, presenting an eloquent explanation of CORE's philosophy and hopes for the future. He and others pleaded with the crowd to join the nonviolent movement, to redeem the land of Jim Crow with acts of commitment and sacrifice. For more than an hour the sanctuary reverberated with amens and shouts of encouragement, until Shuttlesworth rose to cap off the evening with a brief sermon. "This is the greatest thing that has ever happened to Alabama," he insisted, momentarily puzzling some of his listeners, "and it has been good for the nation. It was a wonderful thing to see these young students—Negro and white—come, even after the mobs and the bus burning. When white and black men are willing to be beaten up together, it is a sure sign they will soon walk together as brothers. . . . No matter how many times they beat us up, segregation has still got to go. Others may be beaten up, but freedom is worth anything." As the Freedom Riders and the faithful roared their approval, Shuttlesworth was almost overcome with emotion, but he regained his composure in time to lead a final round of hymns and prayers before ending the meeting. He and the Riders then retired to the parsonage to share a meal and some sober discussion of what to do next.[32]

By midnight an unforgettable Mother's Day was mercifully over, and most of the Freedom Riders soon left the parsonage with the Alabama Christian Movement for Human Rights members who had volunteered to put them up for the night. Four of the white Riders, plus the late arrival Gordon Carey, stayed at the parsonage, most curling up on

The Reverend Fred Shuttlesworth and injured Freedom Rider Walter Bergman at Bethel Baptist Church in Birmingham, Sunday evening, May 14, 1961. (Photograph by Theodore Gaffney)

couches and chairs. When Carey finally arrived, Shuttlesworth graciously gave up his own bed, perhaps realizing that he would have little need for it himself. Despite the late hour, he had at least one more duty to perform before calling it a night. Just after 2:00 A.M., he received word that Peck had been released from Hillman Hospital. After ordering the injured CORE leader to stay put until he got there, Shuttlesworth—along with one of his deacons—rushed to the hospital. Waiting at the entrance, a still woozy Peck managed to stagger to the car. As the three men headed back to the parsonage, two policemen on motorcycles pulled them over. When one of the officers accused the deacon of stealing the car, Shuttlesworth identified himself and eventually talked his way out of the situation, but this additional round of harassment did not bode well for the Freedom Riders' future in Birmingham. By four o'clock the three men were back at the parsonage, where Shuttlesworth found a place for his injured guest on the living room couch. After watching Peck drift off to sleep, Shuttlesworth tried to get some sleep himself, but as he thought about what he and the Riders were likely to face the next day, the exhausted minister found that he was too "keyed up" to close his eyes for very long.[33]

On Monday morning the sight of Peck's heavily bandaged body reminded the Riders of their predicament. Clearly, they could not continue the Freedom Ride without some form of police protection. But who could provide such protection? The Anniston and Birmingham police had demonstrated that they had no intention of upholding the civil rights of "outside agitators," and, aside from Ell Cowling's individual bravery in Anniston, there was no reason to believe that the state police could be counted on to fill the void. Indeed, Governor Patterson had already made it clear during a radio broadcast that the Freedom Riders should not expect police protection in Alabama. In December 1960, long before the Freedom Riders appeared on the scene, Patterson had predicted that "you're going to have rioting on your hands if they try forced integration" in Alabama, assuring a group of reporters that, even though he was opposed to mob violence, he would have to side with the defenders of segregation if Northern agitators forced a showdown. "I'll be one of the first ones stirring up trouble, any way I can," he declared.

The Riders' only hope, it seemed, was federal intervention. Surely, once they learned about the lawlessness and violence in Alabama, the Kennedy brothers would have no choice but to intervene, either with federal marshals, federalized national guardsmen, or, as Eisenhower had done in Little Rock, federal troops. But such intervention had to be timely—almost immediate, in fact—for the Freedom Riders to have any hope of reaching New Orleans by May 17.

To this end, Simeon Booker, who had established contact with the Justice Department two weeks earlier on the eve of the Ride, tried to call the attorney general's special assistant John Seigenthaler within minutes of the attack at the Birmingham Trailways station. After several failed attempts,

Booker finally got Seigenthaler on the phone late Sunday afternoon. Offering a blow-by-blow account of the violence in both Anniston and Birmingham, Booker reminded him of their earlier conversation in Washington. He
had warned Justice Department officials that something like this might happen, and no one had believed him. Now there was no longer any question
that the Freedom Riders' civil rights had been violated—indeed, their very
lives were in danger. Stunned, Seigenthaler jotted down a few notes and promised to call back after speaking to the attorney general, which he did a few
minutes later. By this time early radio reports and FBI communications had
confirmed Booker's account, and Seigenthaler knew he had to do something
to calm the Freedom Riders' fears. The Justice Department was committed to
protecting the Freedom Riders' civil rights, he assured Booker, and department officials would work out the particulars as soon as possible. In the meantime, however, it was essential, according to Seigenthaler, to defuse the situation
by keeping the most sensational aspects of the story out of the press. In response, Booker bluntly reminded Seigenthaler that reporters had been among
those attacked in Birmingham. No one could or should put a lid on such a
story, he insisted. The Freedom Riders needed protection, not a cover-up.[34]

Seigenthaler's initial response to Booker's plea for help was mildly reassuring. But could he be trusted? He claimed to speak for the attorney general, who, eight days earlier in his celebrated speech at the University of
Georgia, had vowed to enforce the law in the Deep South, but at this point
neither man had a clear track record on civil rights. A native Tennessean
who had earned a considerable reputation as a forward-looking reporter with
the liberal *Nashville Tennessean*—especially as a probing investigator of labor
racketeering by Jimmy Hoffa and the Teamsters Union in the late 1950s—
Seigenthaler had been with the Justice Department less than six months.
Prior to his appointment as Robert Kennedy's special assistant, he helped
Kennedy—then chief counsel for the Senate Permanent Subcommittee on
Investigations, sometimes known as the "Rackets Committee"—to write a
book on labor racketeering, and during the 1960 presidential race he served
as a John Kennedy campaign aide. But he had never been called upon to
address so sensitive an issue as the Freedom Rides. Friends and colleagues
knew him as a man of integrity with liberal racial views, but, along with the
other key Southerners in the Justice Department, Ramsey Clark and Louis
Oberdorfer, he sometimes exaggerated his "Southernness" for political effect. Paired with Assistant Attorney General Burke Marshall, as part of a
good cop–bad cop duo, he played the role of a sympathetic Southern moderate in the administration's behind-the-scenes effort to prepare the white South
for school desegregation. As he once confessed, "I'd go in, my Southern ac-
cent dripping sorghum and molasses, and warm them up." Though understandable in a political sense, this was just the kind of posturing that made
the Freedom Riders and other civil rights activists nervous.[35]

If the Freedom Riders had been privy to the inner workings of the Kennedy administration, which they were not, their anxiety level would have been even higher. In the White House, and even in the Justice Department, administration leaders viewed civil rights primarily as a political issue, not as a moral imperative. There were exceptions, of course, most notably Harris Wofford, Sargent Shriver, and Louis Martin. Indeed, with the help of the Freedom Riders, the list would soon expand to include several other administration "liberals" who could not resist the spirit of the movement—most obviously Seigenthaler and John Doar, a Minnesota-born attorney hired by the Justice Department's Civil Rights Division in 1959. In mid-May 1961, though, the political calculus of the administration allowed little room for interracial provocateurs, however well-meaning they might be. To the Kennedy brothers, taking the civil rights movement into the streets, where uncontrolled conflict was inevitable, was an embarrassing luxury that the United States could not afford in the context of the Cold War. The president was first and foremost a Cold Warrior, and his focus on world affairs was never more intense than during the troubled spring following the Bay of Pigs fiasco. In the midst of getting ready for his first presidential trip abroad— to England and France—he had just learned that Soviet premier Nikita Krushchev had agreed to a June summit meeting in Vienna. As Wofford recalled the mood in the White House on that fateful Mother's Day, the embattled president "was busy preparing for his forthcoming encounter with Krushchev and concentrating on the impending crisis in Berlin; he did not appreciate the crisis CORE had deliberately precipitated in Alabama." From the administration's perspective, the timing of the confrontation in Alabama couldn't have been much worse, as the president told Wofford in no uncertain terms after reading the Monday morning headlines. "Can't you get your goddamned friends off those buses?" Kennedy exploded. "Stop them."[36]

Part of President Kennedy's anger lay in the fact that the Freedom Rider crisis appeared to have come out of nowhere. Why hadn't anybody told him about this crazy band of civil rights agitators? No one, including his brother in the Justice Department, had uttered a word of warning. Interestingly enough, Robert Kennedy also claimed to have been blindsided by the crisis, apparently forgetting that he had met with Booker on the eve of the Freedom Ride. Whether or not the attorney general was feigning ignorance to avoid his brother's wrath is unclear, but there is a large measure of truth in his claim that he too was surprised by the events in Alabama. The FBI, the agency that should have kept him informed about such matters, had detailed advance information on the Klan plot to disrupt the Freedom Ride, but no one in the bureau saw fit to relay this information to anyone in the Justice Department. Although Robert Kennedy never knew the full extent of the FBI's advance knowledge of the Alabama plot, he and other Justice Department officials suspected that the FBI was partly responsible for the crisis. After all, it was no secret that J. Edgar Hoover was a racial conservative who firmly believed that the civil rights movement was riddled with Communist sympathizers, or that official FBI policy directed agents to limit their involvement in civil rights crises to observation and note taking. Thus, when rumors and reports from Alabama suggested that local FBI agents had done little or nothing to avert the present crisis—indeed, when some even suggested FBI complicity—the Kennedy brothers began to worry that they could no longer depend on the director for assistance in civil rights matters.[37]

At this point, of course, the Kennedys had little time to focus on Hoover and the FBI. As Seigenthaler's Sunday afternoon conversation with Booker indicated, they were more concerned with the press. While there is no reason to doubt the sincerity of Seigenthaler's concern for the Freedom Riders' safety, the administration's primary goal, at least initially, was to downplay the significance of what had happened in Anniston and Birmingham. To the White House's dismay, the first radio reports of the attacks on the Freedom Riders were as sensational as they were unwelcome, especially Howard K. Smith's gripping eyewitness account broadcast over the CBS radio network. "One passenger was knocked down at my feet by twelve of the hoodlums," Smith told the nation, "and his face was beaten and kicked until it was a bloody pulp." Obviously shaken by what he had seen, the veteran reporter insisted that "the riots have not been spontaneous outbursts of anger but carefully planned and susceptible to having been easily prevented or stopped had there been a wish to do so." Later in the broadcast, he talked about a dangerous "confusion in the Southern mind" about the sanctity of law and order and went on to suggest that the "laws of the land and purposes of the nation badly need a basic restatement, perhaps by the one American assured of an intent mass hearing at any time, the President."[38]

Smith's remarkable broadcast opened the floodgates of public reaction. By early Sunday evening, hundreds of thousands, perhaps even millions, of Americans were aware of the violence that had descended upon Alabama only a few hours before. At this point few listeners had ever heard of CORE, and fewer still were familiar with the term "Freedom Rider." But this would change in a matter of minutes. The dramatic words and images of martyrdom coming out of Alabama proved irresistible beyond anything the civil rights struggle had yet produced. Earlier confrontations—in Montgomery, Little Rock, and elsewhere—had pierced the veil of public complacency, and white supremacist violence in the Deep South was hardly news in a nation that had grieved over the battered body of Emmett Till in 1955.[39] But somehow the beating of the Freedom Riders was different. Nothing, it seems, had prepared Americans for the image of the burning bus outside of Anniston, or of the broken bodies in Birmingham. Even those who had little sympathy for the Freedom Riders could not avoid the disturbing power of the photographs and accounts of the assaults. Citizens of all persuasions found themselves pondering the implications of the violence and dealing with the realization that a group of American citizens had knowingly risked their lives to assert the right to sit together on a bus.

Whatever chance the Kennedy administration had of downplaying the events in Alabama ended on Monday morning when hundreds of newspapers, including the *New York Times* and the *Washington Post*, ran front-page stories describing the carnage in Anniston and Birmingham. Later in the day several television news broadcasts featured brief but dramatic interviews with the injured Riders. In a televised interview conducted at the Bethel parsonage by CBS correspondent Robert Schakne, the camera provided shocking close-ups of Peck's heavily bandaged face as he told the nation of his two beatings by "hoodlums." Many accounts, both in print and on the air, featured a riveting photograph of the burned-out shell of the Greyhound, the newest icon of the civil rights struggle. After gazing at the photograph in the *Post*, Jim Farmer sensed that the Anniston Klansmen had unwittingly given CORE a powerful and potentially useful image of Southern oppression. "I called my staff in New York," he recounted many years later, "and directed them to superimpose that photograph of the flame on the torch of the Statue of Liberty immediately, and to use that composite picture as the symbol of the Freedom Ride."[40] This proved to be a good idea, but at the time, Farmer's New York colleagues must have wondered if there was a Freedom Ride left to symbolize.

Farmer himself was racked with doubt. Since being notified of the attacks on Sunday afternoon, he had been an emotional basket case. Dealing with his father's death—and his mother's grief—was difficult enough, but now he had to face the most threatening crisis in the history of CORE, one that involved not only pressing strategic concerns but also the safety of colleagues who looked to him for leadership. In trying to sort out his emotions, he inevitably passed through a range of feelings—from pride and hope to guilt and fear, all bound up in a sense of personal responsibility for what had happened. He had led the Freedom Riders to a dangerous place, only to abandon them on the eve of their greatest challenge. Now, as he tried to figure out how to salvage the situation, he couldn't help but second-guess the decisions that had placed the Freedom Riders in harm's way. On Sunday evening he had dispatched Gordon Carey to Birmingham, but the plucky field secretary could not be expected to work miracles in a city that had already demonstrated its contempt for law and order. After his father's funeral on Tuesday, Farmer himself would be in a position to travel to Alabama to resume leadership of the Ride. But, judging from what he had learned from press reports and hurried conversations with Shuttlesworth and others in Birmingham, there was no guarantee that the Riders would be in any condition to continue the journey even if he managed to join them. All of this pushed Farmer toward the reluctant conclusion that it was probably too risky to continue the Ride. While he still held out some hope that the Riders could travel on to New Orleans by bus, he began to consider a retreat to safer ground—to a war of words that CORE had at least some chance of winning.[41]

IRONICALLY, IF FARMER HAD ACTUALLY BEEN IN BIRMINGHAM, rather than 750 miles away in Washington, he might have been more hopeful. When the Freedom Riders—including Cox, who flew in from North Carolina to rejoin the Ride—gathered at the parsonage on Monday morning, the situation appeared less desperate than it had only a few hours earlier. Having survived the initial shock of the attacks, the Riders had regained at least some of the spirit that had brought them to the Deep South in the first place. Suffering from severe smoke inhalation, Mae Frances Moultrie had decided to return directly to South Carolina, but the other Riders were more or less ready to travel on to Montgomery. By a vote of eight to four, the group decided to continue the Freedom Ride. While even those in the majority expressed concern about the lack of police protection in Alabama, Peck's resolute determination to carry on seemed to steel their courage. As Peck himself recalled the scene: "I must have looked sick for . . . some of the group insisted that I fly home immediately. I said that for the most severely beaten rider to quit could be interpreted as meaning that violence had triumphed over nonviolence. It might convince the ultrasegregationists that by violence they could stop the Freedom Riders. My point was accepted and we started our meeting to plan the next lap, from Birmingham to Montgomery. We decided to leave in a single contingent on a Greyhound bus leaving at three in the afternoon."[42]

A second source of inspiration was the courage of Shuttlesworth and the local activists of the Alabama Christian Movement for Human Rights. The crusading minister and his deacons had stood by the Riders in their hour of need, refusing to cower in the face of the Klan and its powerful allies in the Birmingham police department. Having placed the local movement at considerable risk, CORE's vanguard could not, in good conscience, turn back now—unless Shuttlesworth himself advised them to do so. Several of the Riders, including Peck and Joe Perkins, warned their colleagues that the nonviolent movement had reached a critical juncture and that it was no time to retreat, but even the most resolute Riders recognized the wisdom of consulting with Shuttlesworth before deciding on a definite course of action. After a decade of struggle against Bull Connor and Birmingham's white supremacist establishment, he, more than anyone else, knew what the Riders were up against. Thus, when he voiced a cautious optimism that they had a reasonable chance of resuming the Freedom Ride, the determination to finish what they had started gained new life.

Part of the basis for Shuttlesworth's optimism was the surprisingly evenhanded response of the local press to the events of the previous day. The city's staunchly segregationist morning newspaper, the *Birmingham Post-Herald*, carried two front-page stories on the attacks, complete with Langston's photograph of Webb's beating and the graphic image of the burned Greyhound. A companion story on page four featured an interview with Charlotte Devree, who recounted her escape from the burning bus, and the editorial page included a biting commentary entitled "Where Were the Police?" "Prompt arrest and prosecution of the gang of hoodlums who took the law in their own hands yesterday afternoon at the Trailways Bus Terminal is extremely important," the *Post-Herald*'s editors declared. "Failure of the police to preserve order and to prevent violence is deeply disturbing. . . . The so-called 'Freedom Riders' came looking for trouble and they should have been handled just as all other law violators are handled. But they should have been protected against assault by a gang of thugs who also should been jailed promptly. . . . To let gangs get away with what happened here yesterday not only will undermine respect for the law but will invite more serious trouble. That must not happen." Shuttlesworth had no illusions about the meaning of the *Post-Herald*'s criticism of police complicity; the wording in the paper's front-page headline—"Gangs Beat Up Photographer, And Travelers In Bus Clashes"—gave a telling indication of the editors' priorities. But the criticism was encouraging nonetheless, a sign that the segregationist front was cracking ever so slightly. Perhaps this time Bull Connor and his rogue police force had gone too far.[43]

There were many unknowns to ponder that Monday morning, and Shuttlesworth and the Riders were not quite sure what the day would bring. But the mood at the parsonage brightened considerably around ten o'clock when Booker received a call from Robert Kennedy. The fact that the attorney general himself was on the line was reassuring, the first clear sign that the administration recognized the seriousness of the crisis in Alabama. As the Freedom Riders gathered around the phone, Booker breathlessly told Kennedy that the situation remained critical: Gangs of Klansmen were still roaming the downtown in anticipation of the next attempt to desegregate the bus terminal. "We are trapped," he reported, before passing the phone to a couple of the Riders, who assured the attorney general that Booker was not exaggerating. Finally, Shuttlesworth went on the line to tell Kennedy what had to be done to ensure the Riders' safe passage to Montgomery and beyond. After the two men agreed that the Riders would continue the Freedom Ride on a single bus, Kennedy offered to arrange police protection and promised to call back with the details. True to his word, he was back on the line a few minutes later with the news that the local police had agreed to provide protection. "Mr. Connor is going to protect you at the station and escort you to the city line," he declared. Alarmed by Kennedy's naïveté, Shuttlesworth reminded him that a similar police escort had done nothing to stop the mob in Anniston. The Riders required police protection all the way to the Mississippi line, he insisted. Though disappointed, Kennedy realized that the Birmingham preacher was right. Promising to consult with his staff, as well as with local and state officials in Alabama, he asked Shuttlesworth to hold tight until a proper escort could be arranged.[44]

During the next two hours, as the Freedom Riders waited nervously at the parsonage, the attorney general and his staff made a flurry of phone calls, including several to Governor John Patterson in Montgomery. Widely known as an outspoken segregationist, Patterson was nonetheless a long-standing supporter of President Kennedy, having boosted his national political ambitions as far back as 1956. Even before he picked up the phone, Robert Kennedy knew Patterson well enough to know that the Alabama governor would do everything he could to avoid the appearance of supporting "outside agitators." He felt confident, though, that he could convince Patterson that protecting the Freedom Riders from violent assaults was essential, not only from a legal or moral perspective but also as a deterrent to federal intervention. Thus, when Patterson stubbornly refused to cooperate, Kennedy was both surprised and disappointed. In a series of heated conversations, the governor lectured Kennedy and Burke Marshall on the realities of Southern politics and blasted the Freedom Riders as meddling fools. By midday, the best that the Justice Department officials could get out of the governor was a vague promise to maintain public order.[45]

Early in the afternoon, after being informed that the "personal diplomacy" between Patterson and the Justice Department was still in progress with no clear resolution in sight, the Freedom Riders decided to force the issue. At their morning meeting, they had agreed to board the three o'clock Greyhound to Montgomery, and, even in the absence of guaranteed police protection, it was now time to follow through with their commitment. Although they knew full well that a mob was waiting for them at the Greyhound terminal, the Riders calculated that city, and perhaps even state, officials would do whatever was necessary to prevent a recurrence of the previous afternoon's violence. National publicity and attention had inoculated them, or so they hoped. This time there would be a full complement of reporters and television cameras at the station and an inescapable awareness that the outside world was watching. With this in mind, but with little else to calm their fears, the Riders somehow mustered the courage to follow Shuttlesworth out of the parsonage and into a caravan of waiting cars assembled to take them downtown to an uncertain fate.

When the Riders arrived at the Greyhound station, they were relieved to see that both the police and the press were out in force. Although a crowd of menacing-looking white men tried to block the entrance to the station, the police managed to keep the protesters at bay. As the Riders filed into the white waiting room, some of the protesters—including a number of Klansmen who had been at the Trailways station the previous afternoon—shouted racial epithets and lunged forward, but all of the Riders made it safely inside, where several reporters were waiting to conduct impromptu interviews. When one reporter asked Peck how he was faring, the veteran activist repeated the refrain from his bedside news conference the night before. "It's been rough, he declared, "but I'm getting on that bus to Montgomery."[46] At that moment, it appeared that he might be right, that the Riders would actually board the three o'clock bus and be on their way. All of the Riders—including Shuttlesworth, who was forced to buy a ticket to Montgomery after a policeman insisted that he could not remain in the waiting room without one—had their tickets and were ready to go. But in the next few minutes whatever chance they had of leaving Birmingham on their own terms slipped away.

As they waited in vain for a boarding announcement, Shuttlesworth, Peck, and the other Riders discovered just how cruel and efficient segregationist politics could be. Suddenly the station was abuzz with a radio report that Governor Patterson had refused to guarantee the Freedom Riders "safe passage." "The citizens of the state are so enraged," claimed Patterson, "that I cannot guarantee protection for this bunch of rabble-rousers." According to the state police, all along the route from Birmingham to Montgomery angry segregationists were lying in wait for the Freedom Riders. The only solution, Patterson declared, was for the Riders to leave the state immediately; he might provide them with an escort to the state line, but certainly not to Montgomery, where they were sure "to continue their rabble-rousing."[47]

As news of the governor's statement spread, panic and confusion set in. Claiming that the Teamsters Union had issued an order prohibiting its members from driving the Freedom Riders to Montgomery or anywhere else, George Cruit, the manager of the Birmingham Greyhound station, canceled the three o'clock run. Hearing this, the Riders and Shuttlesworth gathered in a corner of the waiting room to decide what to do. After a few moments of confusion, Shuttlesworth counseled the Riders to be patient and to adopt a wait-and-see approach to their apparent predicament. After all, he reminded them, "now that the station is integrated we can stay here and wait them out. They are bound to put a bus through sooner or later."[48] Peck and the other CORE staff members on the scene agreed, but they also remained convinced that their best hope was federal intervention.

Earlier in the day Attorney General Kennedy had given Shuttlesworth his private number and had urged the minister to contact him if the Freedom Riders found themselves in need of federal assistance. But, as Shuttlesworth stood by the waiting-room pay phone dialing the numbers, he wasn't sure what to expect, or what he would actually say to the attorney general. In the brief conversation that followed, Kennedy tried to put the Birmingham minister at ease, assuring him that the Justice Department would do whatever it took to get the Freedom Riders on the road. Furious at Patterson and determined to keep his promise, Kennedy immediately mobilized his staff to deal with the situation. After rousting Burke Marshall, who was still recovering from a two-week bout with the mumps, he made a series of calls to Alabama officials. Unfortunately, during several minutes of frantic activity he and Marshall encountered one frustrating obstacle after another. Governor Patterson was not in his office, and when a call to Floyd Mann, the head of the state police, revealed that Patterson had reneged on a promise to have Mann accompany the bus to Birmingham, Kennedy exploded, vowing to teach the Alabamians not to trifle with the Justice Department.

At 3:15, as Shuttlesworth and the Riders waited anxiously for some sign of progress, the attorney general was on the phone with George Cruit, demanding that Greyhound find a replacement driver. When Cruit insisted that no regular driver was willing to take the assignment, Kennedy suggested that Greyhound could hire "a driver of one of the colored buses" or perhaps "some Negro school bus driver." After Cruit brushed aside the black driver option, Kennedy was incredulous, refusing to believe that the company couldn't find someone to drive the bus. "We've gone to a lot of trouble to see that they [CORE Freedom Riders] get to [take] this trip, and I am most concerned to see that it is accomplished," he explained, using words that would later come back to haunt him. "Do you know how to drive a bus?" Kennedy asked plaintively. "Surely somebody in the damn bus company can drive a bus, can't they? . . . I think you should . . . be getting in touch with Mr. Greyhound or whoever Greyhound is and somebody better give us an answer to this question." Before hanging up in exasperation, he reminded Cruit that "under the law" the Freedom Riders "were entitled to transportation provided by Greyhound." "The Government is going to be very much upset if this group does not get to continue their trip," he warned. ". . . Somebody better get in the damn bus and get it going and get these people on their way."[49]

As the afternoon progressed, there were more calls and more frustrations. At one point, Kennedy even threatened to send an air force plane to Birmingham to pick up the Freedom Riders, but without the cooperation of Patterson and Connor—both of whom made themselves scarce that day— there wasn't much he could do. By four o'clock it was clear that the Freedom Riders weren't going anywhere by bus anytime soon. For the time being, they appeared to be safe, thanks to the protective custody of Connor's police. But no one, other than perhaps Connor himself, knew what mean-spirited mischief was in the making. In an interview appearing in the Monday afternoon edition of the *Birmingham News*, Connor made no attempt to hide his contempt for the Freedom Riders, who, he insisted, had no one but themselves to blame for their predicament. "I have said for the last twenty years that these out-of-town meddlers were going to cause bloodshed if they kept meddling in the South's business," he declared, adding that surely he and his police force could not be blamed for the outside agitators' foolish decision to arrive on Mother's Day, "when we try to let off as many of our policemen as possible so they can spend Mother's Day at home with their families." This tongue-in-cheek explanation of the police's absence was a telling reminder that Birmingham was still Bull's town, and after thirty years of holding the line against integrationists and limp-wristed moderates he wasn't about to change his ways. Birmingham's image-conscious businessmen could criticize his methods all they wanted, but he was the one who protected the white people of Alabama from the Communist-inspired designs of the Yankee invaders.[50]

This siege mentality was all too familiar to Shuttlesworth, who feared that Kennedy had little chance of outmaneuvering Connor and Patterson on their own turf. Throughout the afternoon he held out some hope that the combination of federal power and national publicity would force state and local officials to accept a compromise that gave the Freedom Riders much of what they wanted. As the impasse continued into the late afternoon, however, both he and the Freedom Riders began to question the wisdom of prolonging the crisis. By five o'clock, after several minutes of spirited discussion, the Riders had reached a consensus that it was time to break the stalemate at the Greyhound station. Rather than risk further bloodshed and a complete collapse of the project, they decided to leave Birmingham by plane. The only remaining question was whether they should fly to Montgomery or directly to New Orleans. Some of the Riders had seen enough of Alabama and had no interest in resuming the Freedom Ride in Montgomery. Others reasoned that it was still possible to finish the trip by bus and reach New Orleans in time to attend the *Brown* commemoration rally on May 17. Since no one could be sure what they would encounter at the Birmingham airport, the choice of destination remained open as the Riders made arrangements to leave the bus station. Many of the Riders suspected that the choice was beyond their control and that in all likelihood they would end up on the first available southbound flight out of the city. Whatever their destination, they were sure to face some criticism for abandoning the struggle in Birmingham, but Shuttlesworth's sympathetic reaction to their decision gave them some hope that their departure from the troubled city would be seen as a strategic retreat and not as a surrender. Privately, Shuttlesworth could not help worrying that the Freedom Riders' retreat would embolden the Klan and perhaps slow the momentum of the local civil rights movement. But as he assembled a convoy of cars to take the Riders to the airport, he kept such concerns to himself.

Coming at the end of a long and frustrating afternoon, this sudden turn of events elicited sighs of relief from Robert Kennedy and his staff. In addition to resolving the immediate crisis in Birmingham, the decision to bypass the bus link to Montgomery indicated that the Freedom Riders were finally coming to their senses. While they were afraid to wish for too much, Justice Department officials now had some hope that the beleaguered Riders would soon abandon the buses altogether and fly directly to New Orleans. Moving the crisis to Montgomery would buy Kennedy and his staff a little time, but from their perspective the best solution was to get the Freedom Riders to Louisiana as soon as possible, preferably by air. With the very real possibility that more violence was waiting down the road in central Alabama and Mississippi, the prospect of putting the Riders back on the buses represented a frightening scenario for federal officials, who had come to regard CORE's project as a reckless, almost suicidal experiment.[51]

When the Freedom Riders filed out of the Greyhound waiting room a few minutes after five, the idea of resuming the Ride in Montgomery was still very much alive. As the fourteen Riders—plus Carey, Shuttlesworth, Booker, Newson, Gaffney, and Devree—hustled to the curb and into a line of cars, they were relieved to see that the crowd outside the station had thinned. Only later would they discover that part of the crowd, having been tipped off by the police or reporters, was already on its way to the airport. After hours of waiting for a chance to get at the Riders, the Klansmen of the Eastview klavern, along with dozens of other hard-core white supremacists, had no intention of letting them leave the city without a few parting shots. Although the scene at the airport was tense, the police managed to keep the Klansmen in check as the convoy unloaded. Earlier in the afternoon, Police Chief Jamie Moore had assured the FBI that his men would take care of any potential troublemakers who threatened the Freedom Riders, and the large police presence at the airport suggested that he intended to honor his pledge. Shuttlesworth, satisfied that there would be no repeat of the previous day's assaults, led the Riders into the terminal before saying good-bye. Scheduled to lead the weekly mass meeting of the Alabama Christian Movement for Human Rights, he only had time for a quick round of embraces before racing back to the crowd of 350 waiting patiently at the Kingston Baptist Church.

The first evening flight to Montgomery was scheduled to leave approximately an hour after the Riders arrived at the airport—but in that hour, a bomb threat phoned in by Klan leader Hubert Page effectively ended the Riders' hopes of actually making it to Montgomery. After purchasing a block of seats at the Eastern Airlines ticket counter, Peck led the Riders onto a plane that would remain on the tarmac until the following morning. "No sooner had we boarded it," Peck later recalled, "than an announcement came over the loudspeaker that a bomb threat had been received, and all passengers would have to debark while luggage was inspected. Time dragged on and eventually the flight was canceled."[52] During the wait, Booker called Robert Kennedy and told him about the developing situation at the airport. "It's pretty bad down here and we don't think we're going to get out," Booker explained. "Bull Connor and his people are pretty tough." This discouraging report was enough to convince Kennedy that he needed a personal representative on the scene, preferably someone who had some familiarity with the Deep South. Even though it would take several hours to fly from Washington to Alabama, and with any luck the Freedom Riders would be gone by the time his representative arrived, Kennedy immediately dispatched John Seigenthaler to Birmingham.

As a native Southerner and a member of the team that had been monitoring the Freedom Riders' situation for the past twenty-four hours, Seigenthaler had a good idea of what he was likely to encounter in Alabama, but before he left for National Airport, there were no firm instructions from

Kennedy other than to "let them know that we care." Later, while changing planes in Atlanta, he phoned his boss for an update. Informed that the crisis seemed to be getting worse by the minute and that someone had threatened to blow up the Freedom Riders' plane, he began to wonder what he or anyone else could do in the face of such lawlessness.[53]

In his darkest moments, Shuttlesworth had harbored similar thoughts, but as he surveyed the overflowing throng at Kingston Baptist, he knew that the local movement in Birmingham had come too far to let Bull Connor have his way. Chasing the Freedom Riders out of town might represent a victory of sorts for the hard-core segregationists, but only in the most limited sense. The real victory, he assured the crowd, could be found in the courage of the Freedom Riders, who had exposed Birmingham's Klan-infested police force, forcing the Kennedy administration to pay attention to the white supremacist terror in the Deep South. The Freedom Ride might be over, but the nonviolent movement was here to stay—a movement that now had direct access to the president's brother. With undisguised pride, Shuttlesworth told the faithful that the attorney general had given him a personal phone number, assuring him that he could call anytime he needed help. After noting that he had already "talked to Bob Kennedy six times," he temporarily excused himself from the pulpit to accept a seventh "long-distance call from Bob." Returning a few minutes later, he proudly reported: "They got plenty of police out at the airport tonight simply because Bob talked to Bull." As a host of amens rose from the pews, he repeated Kennedy's words—"If you can't get me at my office, just call me at the White House"—punctuating an extraordinary moment in the history of the local movement.[54]

While Shuttlesworth was spreading hope at Kingston Baptist, the realities of the siege at the airport were closing in on the Freedom Riders. Despite a vigorous dissent by Joe Perkins, a solid majority of the Riders concluded that flying to Montgomery was no longer a viable option. Following an informal vote that effectively ended the Freedom Ride, Perkins unloaded on his close friend Ed Blankenheim, who had voted with the majority. "You can go back to being white anytime you want to," Perkins complained. "You have no right to make decisions where black people are involved unless you are prepared to go the distance. In this case, stay with the Freedom Ride plan which dictates going to Montgomery even if it means you might lose your life." Although he shared some of Perkins's concerns, Peck promptly booked eighteen seats on a Capital Airlines flight to New Orleans via Mobile. The flight, however, was canceled after an anonymous caller threatened to blow up the plane. It was now past eight o'clock, the increasingly dispirited Riders had suffered through two bomb scares, and the chance of leaving Birmingham before morning seemed to be slipping away. When Seigenthaler arrived on the scene a few minutes later, Perkins was still fuming. But everyone else seemed resigned to the fact that the Freedom Ride was over.

As Seigenthaler introduced himself to the Riders, he could see right away that a long day of indignities and threats had exacted a heavy toll. Their downcast eyes told him that they were fed up with Alabama and its hate-mongering white majority; they just wanted out. At least five of the Riders—Jim Peck, Walter Bergman, Charles Person, Ike Reynolds, and Genevieve Hughes—were still weak from the attacks and had no business being out of bed, but there they were, huddled in a corner trying to cope in the face of both physical and emotional pain. As Seigenthaler listened to Booker's account of the events of the past few hours—the bomb threats, the taunts from the police and passengers, the airport staff's refusal to serve the Freedom Riders food, the threats from the mob outside the terminal—he knew he had to find a way to get the Riders out of Birmingham as soon as possible. Three members of the group, according to Booker, had already cracked under the strain and were acting irrationally. "This is a trap," one panic-stricken Rider had whispered to the reporter. "We'll all be killed." Clearly the situation called for immediate action.

A frantic round of phone conversations with airline officials produced nothing but frustration, even after Seigenthaler reminded them that he was a personal representative of the attorney general. Fortunately—with the help of a police officer who assured him that his boss, Bull Connor, was as anxious as anyone to see the last of the Freedom Riders—he eventually convinced the airport manager to cooperate with a plan to sneak the Riders on board a flight to New Orleans. Many years later, in an interview with journalist David

Halberstam, Seigenthaler recalled his instructions to the manager: "Just pick a plane, get the baggage of everyone else on it, then get the Freedom Riders' baggage on it, slip the Freedom Riders on, then at the last minute announce the plane, and from the moment you announce it, don't answer the phone because all you'll do is get a bomb threat." Somehow the plan went off without a hitch, and at 10:38 P.M. an Eastern Airlines plane carrying Seigenthaler, Carey,

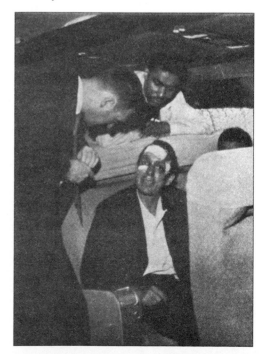

Department of Justice representative John Seigenthaler (standing in aisle), Ben Cox, and Jim Peck (seated) on the "freedom plane" to New Orleans, Monday evening, May 15, 1961. (Photograph by Theodore Gaffney)

fourteen Freedom Riders, and the four accompanying journalists lifted off the runway. One hour later they were in New Orleans—still in the Deep South but far removed from the angry, tormented city that had nearly cost some of them their lives.[55]

At the New Orleans airport, several reporters, photographers, and television cameramen were on hand to document the Freedom Riders' arrival. But the presence of the press did not stop the New Orleans police from putting the unwelcome fugitives from Alabama through a few moments of gratuitous harassment. Forming a cordon along the tarmac, a long line of white police officers dressed in riot gear surrounded the Riders as they walked towards the terminal. When some of the officers shouted racial epithets, Seigenthaler became concerned and more than a little angry. Only after he identified himself as a Justice Department official did the police reluctantly back off, allowing the Riders to make their way to a small but deliriously relieved welcoming committee of CORE volunteers. Several of the Riders, with tears of joy streaming down their faces, looking much like returning prisoners of war, collapsed into the outstretched arms of their comrades. Against all odds they had made it to New Orleans after all. The great CORE Freedom Ride of 1961 was over.[56]

5

Get on Board, Little Children

Get on board, little children, Get on board, little children,
Get on board, little children, Let's fight for human rights.
Can't you see that mob a-comin', Comin' 'round the bend.
If you fight for freedom, They'll try to do you in.

—1960s freedom song[1]

THE JOYOUS LATE-NIGHT RENDEZVOUS in New Orleans captured the raw emotion of the moment, but in the cold light of day on Tuesday the complex realities of the situation swept over the Freedom Riders like a dense cloud. Morning conversations among the Riders and their hosts revealed considerable confusion about the implications of what had just happened. At the home of Oretha and Doris Jean Castle—the unofficial headquarters of New Orleans CORE, where several of the Riders spent the night—there was nervous speculation about the future of the nonviolent movement in the Deep South. Even in cosmopolitan New Orleans, the political atmosphere was more threatening than anyone had expected. Within hours of the Riders' arrival, the South Louisiana White Citizens' Council asked Mayor deLesseps Morrison to "rid the community of these agitators before violence erupts." And later in the day, during a press briefing held at Xavier University (where some of the Riders were housed until a bomb threat forced an evacuation of their dormitory), Gordon Carey and Ben Cox were bombarded by questions from hostile reporters who seemed to accept the Citizens' Council's claim that CORE was "a lawless, radical group." When one reporter suggested that the violence-plagued Freedom Ride had failed, Cox countered: "It proved what we set out to prove—that American citizens cannot travel freely in the United States. Laws are on the books, but they are not being enforced." Before flying home to New York for medical care, Jim Peck tried to reassure his fellow

Freedom Riders Jim Peck and Jimmy McDonald are interviewed by reporter Bill Cook after arriving at the New Orleans Airport, Tuesday morning, May 16, 1961. (Bettmann-CORBIS)

Riders that the Freedom Ride had indeed accomplished much of what it had been designed to do. But, in truth, he too was worried. With much of the CORE staff out of commission due to injuries and with Jim Farmer still in Washington at his father's funeral, the organization was in obvious disarray, despite Carey's and Marvin Rich's best efforts to hold things together.

Farmer himself was overcome with a jumble of conflicting emotions in the immediate aftermath of the Ride. He was proud of CORE's partial victory, relieved that his colleagues were safe, a little ashamed that he had not been with them during the hours of crisis, and more than a little concerned about how all of this would play in the national media. While he welcomed the national publicity generated by the Ride, he worried about mainstream America's visceral fear of direct action. To his dismay, most of the press reports on Tuesday morning characterized the decision to end the Ride as a triumph of pragmatic realism over misguided idealism. Although many observers acknowledged and admired the Freedom Riders' courage, virtually everyone expressed serious reservations about a style of protest that courted martyrdom. Even in the wake of the Montgomery Bus Boycott and the more recent sit-in movement, few Americans, it seemed, had anything more than a superficial understanding of the theory and practice of Gandhian nonviolence. In a nation committed to nuclear superiority and Cold War posturing—a nation that promoted the individual pursuit of happiness above all else—the concept of progress through unmerited suffering was simply too alien to take seriously.[2]

Even in black America, where the idea of Christian martyrdom had long been a powerful force and where Martin Luther King's image as an American Gandhi had some currency, nonviolent struggle remained a novel idea. The lone exception was the black student movement that had taken hold in a number of Southern communities. Here there were clear signs that nonviolence was on the verge of becoming a mass movement, especially in Nashville, where Jim Lawson and a growing band of student activists had launched wave after wave of stand-ins, sit-ins, and other acts of nonviolent resistance. Widely regarded as the leading edge of the student movement, the Nashville group had played a pivotal role in the founding of SNCC, producing an extraordinary number of dedicated activists, including the Freedom Rider John Lewis. Thus, when Nashville became the flash point that reignited the Freedom Ride, few close observers of the movement were surprised. As the legendary SNCC organizer Bob Moses would later put it, "Only the Nashville student movement had the fire to match that of the burning bus."[3]

While the rest of the nation breathed a collective sigh of relief that the Freedom Ride was over, the young activists of the Nashville Movement cried out for continued sacrifice and commitment. Indeed, Nashville's student activists were already talking about mobilizing reinforcements for the Freedom Ride on Sunday afternoon, a full day before the CORE Riders retreated to New Orleans. One of the key figures in this early effort was Lewis, who, by a strange twist of fate, was in Nashville, not Birmingham, when the Freedom Ride collapsed. Sitting among several dozen friends and fellow activists who had gathered at a picnic ground to celebrate the successful conclusion of a five-week campaign to desegregate Nashville's downtown movie theaters, he could hardly believe his ears when the first reports of the Anniston bombing came on the radio. It had been four days since he had said good-bye to the Freedom Riders in South Carolina, promising them that he would return to the fold as soon as was humanly possible. Now he had to face the possibility that there might not be a Freedom Ride to rejoin, that some of his colleagues might not even be alive by the end of the day. Though almost overcome by feelings of pain and guilt, he soon regained enough composure to help Diane Nash, Bernard Lafayette, and other members of the Nashville student movement's central committee sound the alarm. Interrupting a speech by committee chairman Jim Bevel, who was holding forth on the theological implications of the Nashville Movement's victory, Lewis, Nash, and Lafayette rounded up the rest of the committee and rushed to the First Baptist Church for an emergency meeting.[4]

Within minutes Bevel and the committee were huddled around a church radio waiting for additional reports from Alabama. Before long they learned that the Trailways Riders had been attacked by a mob in Birmingham and that some of the Riders had sustained serious injuries. Desperate for more information, Nash tried to reach Jim Farmer by phone, but there was no answer at his Washington number. For the time being, she and the others would have to proceed without any firm knowledge of what had actually happened in Anniston and Birmingham. Fearing the worst, they moved to a nearby conference room to discuss their options. For the remainder of the afternoon and evening, and into the early morning hours, the students examined and reexamined every aspect of the situation. From the outset, Nash, Lewis, and several others argued that the civil rights community could not afford to let the Freedom Ride fail. The nonviolent movement had reached a critical juncture, they insisted, a moment of decision that in all likelihood would affect the pace of change for years to come. If the movement allowed segregationist thugs to destroy the Freedom Ride, white supremacist extremists would gain new life, violent attacks on civil rights activists would multiply, and attracting new recruits to the nonviolent cause would become much more difficult. The violence in Alabama had forced the movement to face a soul-testing challenge: Did those who professed to believe in nonviolent struggle have the courage and commitment to risk their lives for the cause of simple justice? The original Freedom Riders had done so willingly and without self-pity, Lewis assured his friends. Could the members of the Nashville Movement be satisfied with anything less from themselves?

When no one in the room disagreed with the logic of this rhetorical question, the die was cast: The Nashville Movement would do whatever was necessary to sustain the Freedom Ride. At this point they did not know how many Freedom Riders had been injured or disabled, but the situation seemed to call for reinforcements. As they began to map out a precise plan of action, the excitement and nervous energy in the room became palpable. Young student activists who had previously focused their attention on the limited goals of a local movement were about to stride onto the national stage—if they could work out the logistics. As Lewis recalled the scene, there were suddenly so many questions to consider: "How many of us would go? When? And where would the money come from to pay our way? There were dozens of details to iron out, and just as many opinions on each one."[5]

In typical student movement fashion, the meeting was democratic in tone and structure, with little sense of hierarchy. Some opinions, however, clearly carried more weight than others. Although Bevel was technically in charge, Lewis and Nash came closest to embodying the spirit of soul power that Lawson, who was away visiting family in Ohio, had prescribed. They were able to exert a quiet but firm leadership among their peers. Despite his unassuming demeanor, Lewis's status as a Freedom Rider gave his carefully chosen words a special force, and the beautiful and poised Nash, already something of a local movement icon, relied on her reputation as the most effective organizer among Nashville's student activists. Light-skinned enough to be mistaken for a white woman and, according to Lewis, "just about the most gorgeous woman any of us had ever seen," Nash had worked hard to overcome suspicions that she was miscast as a movement leader. As Lewis recalled, other women active in the Nashville movement "couldn't help being envious in the beginning at all the attention Diane was getting. But none of this turned Diane's head. She was dead serious about what we were doing each week, very calm, very deliberate, always straightforward and sincere. As time passed, she came to be seen more as our sister than as an object of lust."[6]

Born and raised in Chicago, where she grew up in a middle-class Catholic family, Nash transferred to Fisk University in the fall of 1959 after spending two years at Howard. Sheltered from the worst indignities of Jim Crow for most of her life, she became interested in the local movement after being forced to use segregated restroom facilities at the Tennessee State Fair. By the end of her first semester at Fisk, she had become one of Lawson's most devoted disciples, and when the Nashville sit-in movement took off in February 1960 she quickly emerged as one of the local movement's most visible leaders. In mid-April, at the founding meeting of SNCC in Raleigh, she was the only woman to receive serious consideration as a candidate for SNCC chairperson. Her Nashville colleague Marion Barry got the nod as SNCC's first official leader, but soon after her return from Raleigh the soft-spoken but determined woman from Chicago almost single-handedly transformed the local movement by challenging Mayor Ben West during a rally on the courthouse steps. With the press looking on, she extracted a grudging admission from West, a moderate trying to navigate the dangerous political waters of gradual desegregation, that he had no personal objection to the desegregation of Nashville's downtown lunch counters. Later seen as a pivotal turning point in the decline of local white resistance, Nash's ability to outmaneuver West into a breach of segregationist solidarity added to her growing reputation as a rising star in the student movement. In February 1961, her stature rose even higher after she became one of four SNCC activists to join the "jail–no bail" protest in Rock Hill, South Carolina. Following her release from jail in April, she withdrew from Fisk and accepted a joint staff position with SNCC and SCLC. Working out of a rented room at the Nashville YWCA, she told friends that the movement had become her life.[7]

Local stature aside, Nash remained largely unknown outside of SNCC and SCLC circles. When she finally reached Farmer on Monday afternoon to discuss the Nashville Movement's plan to resume the Freedom Ride, he wasn't quite sure who she was or what to make of the students' offer to help. Farmer later claimed that Nash had called to see if he "had any objections to members of the Nashville Student Movement . . . going in and taking up the Ride where CORE left off." But Nash, Lewis, and others insisted that the call was simply a means of letting "him know our intent and to ask for his support—not his permission." Whatever her intention, Nash clearly caught Farmer off guard. "You realize it may be suicide," he stammered into the phone. These words of warning only served to steel her nerves and to confirm her suspicion that Farmer was out of touch with the spirit of the student movement. "We fully realize that," she replied, brushing off his objection, "but we can't let them stop us with violence. If we do, the movement is dead."

When it became clear that Nash was undeterred by his prediction that the students faced a probable "massacre" in Alabama, he wished her well and promised that CORE would do what it could to help. He also made it clear that he still considered the Freedom Ride to be a CORE project, regardless of any Nashville student involvement. As soon as his father's funeral was over, he would return to Alabama, presumably to resume control of the Ride. "I'll fly down and join you wherever you are," he vowed.[8]

All of this took on a somewhat hollow ring a few hours later when the CORE Riders actually flew to New Orleans. "I couldn't believe it," Lewis later wrote. "I understood the thinking behind the decision, but it defied one of the most basic tenets of nonviolent action—that is, there can be no surrender in the face of brute force or any form of violent opposition." This and other arguments reinvigorated the ongoing meeting of the central committee, which was moving toward concrete action by Monday evening. As the discussions progressed, the idea of sending a new wave of Freedom Riders to Alabama and beyond took on a seemingly irreversible momentum, especially after a call to Jim Lawson in Ohio drew a ringing endorsement from the one person who could have nixed the students' plan. Far from reining in his disciples, Lawson promised to join the Freedom Ride as soon as he returned to the South.[9]

By CONTRAST, the reaction of the more senior members of Nashville's civil rights community was anything but encouraging. As word of the students' plan spread, several members of the Nashville Christian Leadership Council—the Nashville Movement's semiofficial sponsoring organization—expressed serious reservations about putting the city's young activists in harm's way. By early Tuesday morning someone in Nashville, either inside or outside the movement, had contacted the Justice Department in Washington, identifying Nash as the ringleader of a proposed new Freedom Ride. The reaction in the attorney general's office, which less than two hours earlier had learned that Seigenthaler and the CORE Freedom Riders were safely on the ground in Louisiana, was one of shock and dismay. Fearing that the crisis was being resurrected, Robert Kennedy placed a frantic call to Seigenthaler, who had just drifted off to sleep in his New Orleans motel room. A new Freedom Ride was about to be launched, he informed his half-conscious assistant, and something had to be done to stop it. At 4:00 A.M. Seigenthaler received a second call, this time from Burke Marshall, Kennedy's special deputy for civil rights. After reiterating the seriousness of the situation, Marshall gave Seigenthaler Nash's phone number and a few additional words of advice: "You come from that goddam town. . . . If you can do anything to turn them around, I'd appreciate it."

Seigenthaler knew enough about Nash, Lewis, and the Nashville student movement to know that he had been given a nearly impossible task. But, after two hours of fitful tossing and turning, he placed a call to George

Barrett, an old Nashville friend, labor lawyer, and white liberal with close ties to the local movement, the Highlander Folk School, and the Southern Regional Council. At Seigenthaler's urging, Barrett phoned Nash, whom he knew well, and later spent several minutes at her office trying to persuade her to abandon the proposed Alabama Freedom Ride. He got nowhere, however. A few minutes later Seigenthaler called Nash directly, with the same result. After describing the explosive atmosphere in Birmingham, he asked her to consider a temporary postponement of the Ride. She refused, insisting that delaying the hour of freedom was out of the question. Exasperated, Seigenthaler predicted: "You're going to get your people killed." Once again, she was unmoved. If the first wave of Nashville Freedom Riders were to die, she calmly informed him, "then others will follow them."[10]

This first encounter with Nash left Seigenthaler a bit shaken, but, with Robert Kennedy and Burke Marshall waiting expectantly for a quick resolution to the Nashville crisis, he was not about to give up. On Tuesday morning John Kennedy was en route to Canada for a two-day visit, and Seigenthaler knew that his superiors expected him to clean up the mess in Nashville before the president's return. Throughout the morning—before boarding a plane for Birmingham—he placed call after call to friends and contacts in Nashville, imploring them to do whatever they could to deter the would-be Freedom Riders' plans. By midafternoon, this campaign—along with the growing concern among NCLC ministers, the students' parents, and others who had seen press reports of the violence in Birmingham—began to take its toll on the small group of activists meeting at the First Baptist Church. Working out the details of the Ride—especially finding enough money to pay for bus tickets—was proving to be more difficult than the students had anticipated, and the frequent interruptions by frightened relatives and other naysayers added a heavy burden to an already difficult enterprise. With the exception of John Lee Copeland, Grady Donald, C. T. Vivian, and J. Metz Rollins, four combative and fearless ministers who had won the respect of the students with their willingness to join the Nashville sit-ins, the NCLC members who drifted in and out of the central committee deliberations counseled patience. "As always," Lewis recalled, "there was caution and resistance from several of the older NCLC members taking part in our meetings. We needed their support, at least in terms of money, and they were using that as a lever for their position."

The generational struggle reached a climax that evening when the students met with the NCLC's executive board. As students and ministers alike strained to keep their emotions in check and to remember that they were all part of the same movement, Nash announced that the committee planned to send Freedom Riders to Alabama within twenty-four hours. All they needed was a few hundred dollars from the NCLC, but she assured the board that even if the money did not materialize, the students would find some way to resume the Freedom Ride. When it became clear that virtually all of the student leaders shared Nash's determination to follow through with the Ride, the NCLC executive board, by a vote of nine to one, reluctantly authorized a nine-hundred-dollar check to fund the project. But they did so knowing that the students could not cash the check without two signatures. Since only one board officer was available to sign the check at the meeting, the NCLC leaders went home with some hope that the Freedom Ride would be delayed at least a day and that there was still time for the students to come to their senses. This hope was soon dashed, however, when a local "numbers man" agreed to cash the check despite the missing signature, proving, as one of the students later put it, that "there's no price tag on freedom."[11]

With the funds safely in hand, an elated Nash telephoned Fred Shuttlesworth in Birmingham to let him know that a new batch of Freedom Riders would soon be on their way. Prior to this point, Shuttlesworth had heard only vague rumblings that something was afoot in Nashville, so he was more than a little surprised when Nash informed him that the Freedom Riders might be coming to Birmingham as early as the next morning. "The students have decided that we can't let violence overcome," she declared. "We are going to come into Birmingham to continue the Freedom Ride." Intrigued, but not sure that the Nashville students knew what they were getting themselves into, Shuttlesworth responded sternly: "Young lady, do you know that the Freedom Riders were almost killed here?" Nash assured him that she did, adding: "That's exactly why the ride must not be stopped. If they stop us with violence, the movement is dead. We're coming. We just want to know if you can meet us." After he agreed, she promised to call back with further details.[12]

The next step was to select the students who would actually participate in the Ride. At a late-night meeting, the central committee calculated that it had enough funds to support ten Freedom Riders, but the gathering momentum of the previous two days had produced far more than ten volunteers. While the entire committee discussed the possible choices, it was agreed that Bevel, as the temporary chairman, would have the final say as to who would board the buses on Wednesday morning. Somewhat surprisingly, Bevel's ten choices did not include Nash, who was deemed too crucial to the entire operation to be placed in jeopardy, or himself. As Bevel explained, rather lamely to some, he had already promised a close friend that he would drive to New York to pick up a load of furniture. If there were later Freedom Rides, he would be eager to join them, but he would not be available for at least a week. Trying to avoid a split and realizing that the eccentric Bevel was too stubborn to change his plans, Nash and others did their best to conceal their disapproval. With only a few hours to go before the Riders' departure, it was essential to maintain a solid front. Besides, everyone agreed that Bevel's selections were all good choices. While there was disappointment among the volunteers who had not been chosen, even they were consoled by the likely prospect that a second wave of Nashville Freedom Riders would be dispatched later in the week.

The chosen included two whites—Jim Zwerg and Salynn McCollum—and eight blacks: John Lewis, William Barbee, Paul Brooks, Charles Butler, Allen Cason, Bill Harbour, Catherine Burks, and Lucretia Collins. Zwerg was a twenty-one-year-old exchange student from Wisconsin who had joined the Lawson workshops and the theater stand-ins soon after his arrival at Fisk in early 1961; preparing for a career as a Congregational minister, he had grown close to Lewis in the months leading up to the Freedom Ride. McCollum, also twenty-one, was a transplanted upstate New Yorker attending George Peabody College; active in the sit-in movement, she would later work for SNCC in Atlanta. Barbee, nineteen, was a theology student at American Baptist Theological Seminary, as was Brooks, a twenty-two-year-old East St. Louis, Illinois, native who had become one of Nashville's most outspoken activists.

The remaining five Riders were all students at Tennessee Agricultural and Industrial (A&I) State University, an all-black public institution that had recently gained fame as the home campus of Olympic track star Wilma Rudolph. Tennessee State, as the university was commonly known, had also provided the Nashville Movement with many of its most committed participants. Butler was a twenty-year-old sophomore from Charleston, South Carolina, and Cason was a bookish nineteen-year-old freshman from Orlando, Florida, who insisted on taking his typewriter on the Freedom Ride. Harbour, also nineteen, was from Piedmont, Alabama, where his father worked in a yarn factory. Like fellow Alabamian John Lewis, Harbour was the first member of his family to go to college, and earlier in the year he and Lewis had struck up a friendship during a long bus ride to the jail-in rally in Rock Hill, South Carolina. Burks was an outgoing and vivacious Birmingham native, who, like Nash, posed for *Jet* magazine. A twenty-one-year-old senior, she would marry fellow Freedom Rider Paul Brooks later in the year. Collins, who had lived on an army base in El Paso, Texas, before coming to Nashville, was also a twenty-one-year-old in her last semester at Tennessee State. Tall and strikingly attractive, with a soft voice that masked a steely determination to confront the white supremacist power structure, she always seemed to be on the front lines of the local freedom struggle. While the ten Riders represented a range of personalities and class backgrounds, all were seasoned veterans of the Nashville Movement. None had yet reached the age of twenty-three.[13]

Once the lineup of Freedom Riders was set, Nash placed a call to Shuttlesworth. This time much of their conversation was relayed in a prearranged code. Realizing that his phone had been tapped by local police, the Birmingham minister had worked out a set of coded messages related to, of all things, poultry. "Roosters" substituted for male Freedom Riders, "hens" for female Riders, "pullets" for students, and so on. What the eavesdropping police thought of all this can only be imagined, but when Nash called Shuttlesworth again on Wednesday morning to tell him "the chickens are boxed," he knew that the Freedom Riders were on their way.

The decision to put the Riders on an early-morning Greyhound reflected the students' determination to seize the moment. "As far as I was concerned," Lewis later insisted, "it was time to go. . . . Time was wasting. This was a crisis, and we needed to act." Unfortunately, as Lewis realized all too well, acting with such haste left the Riders and their families with little time to prepare for what was about to unfold. After the steering committee broke up around 10:00 P.M., many of those chosen to participate in the Ride made emotional calls to friends and relatives, most of whom were shocked to learn that someone they knew and cared about would soon be at risk. Some of the students notified teachers and deans that they weren't sure they would be around to take final exams or finish the semester. Others, in what was becoming a movement tradition, composed last-minute wills or letters to loved ones. Several solemnly handed Nash sealed letters "to be mailed if they were killed." "We thought some of us would be killed," Collins explained years later. "We certainly thought that some, if not all of us, would be severely injured."

While all of this was going on, Nash was busy placing calls to SNCC and SCLC leaders in Atlanta, and to Justice Department officials in Washington, who pleaded with her to cancel the Ride. Unmoved, she placed a final call to Shuttlesworth just before dawn. The shipment of ten "chickens"—seven "roosters" and three "hens"—was scheduled to leave Nashville at 6:45 A.M., she reported, and would arrive in Birmingham by late morning. Responding in code, Shuttlesworth promised that he would be at the bus station to accept the shipment. As Shuttlesworth later explained, the code was designed to hide the details of the operation, not the operation itself. He wanted Bull Connor and the Birmingham police to know that the Riders were coming. Whatever else happened, he did not want a repeat of the Mother's Day massacre, when the absence of police protection nearly got the CORE Freedom Riders killed. Accordingly, he sent an early-morning telegram to Connor informing him that the Birmingham police would soon be given a second chance to protect the constitutional rights of visiting Freedom Riders. Suspecting a trick, Connor asked his daughter Dora Jean to phone Shuttlesworth's house to see if the information in the telegram was true. Pretending to be a sympathetic white liberal, she was able to confirm that a new Freedom Ride was indeed imminent.[14]

SHUTTLESWORTH ALSO ALERTED THE PRESS that the Freedom Riders were coming, but by that time the "freedom bus" had already left the Nashville terminal. When the students boarded the bus there were no reporters present, and neither the bus driver—E. S. Lane—nor any of the other passengers had any idea that a new Freedom Ride had begun. Nash and Lewis, the designated leader on the bus, had counseled the students to behave like normal passengers and to avoid any overt challenges to Jim Crow during the Nashville-to-Birmingham run. If all went well, the actual Freedom Ride would begin later in the day when they boarded the bus to Montgomery. But all did not go well. Salynn McCollum, the only white female Rider, missed the bus, although after a frantic seventy-mile car chase she managed to join the other Riders when the bus stopped at Pulaski, a small town in south central Tennessee that had served as the birthplace of the original Ku Klux Klan in 1866. With McCollum safely on board, the bus crossed the Alabama line without incident by midmorning. The only hint of trouble was the impatience of Jim Zwerg and Paul Brooks, who insisted on sitting as a conspicuously interracial duo near the front of the bus. Somewhat surprisingly, according to Lewis, "no one, not the white passengers nor the driver" seemed to object to this seating arrangement. "It was not until we reached the Birmingham city limits, two hundred miles south of Nashville, that the trouble began," he recalled.

Waiting at the city line were several police cars and a boarding party of police officers who promptly arrested Zwerg and Brooks for violating Alabama law. The officers then checked all of the passengers' tickets, revealing that nine passengers held identical tickets marked Nashville–Birmingham–Montgomery–Jackson–New Orleans. The only Freedom Rider to escape the dragnet was McCollum, who had purchased her ticket in Pulaski. Confident that he had apprehended a band of agitators, the officer in charge ordered the driver to head for the Birmingham Greyhound terminal under police escort. The bus arrived at the terminal at 12:15, too late for the Riders to be transferred to the noon bus to Montgomery. But a late arrival was the least of the Riders' problems. At the terminal, the police temporarily sealed the bus, taping newspaper over the windows to conceal what was going on inside. After reexamining each passenger's ticket before letting anyone off, the police maintained an armed guard over the seven remaining "suspects." By this time Zwerg and Brooks had already been carted off to the city jail, and McCollum, avoiding identification as a Freedom Rider, had disembarked with the other passengers. Rushing undetected through the crowd, she called Nash from a pay phone. Trying not to panic, Nash immediately phoned Burke Marshall in Washington. Why, she asked, were the Freedom Riders being forcibly detained by the Birmingham police? Caught off guard, Marshall promised to investigate, but he couldn't resist reminding Nash that she and the Nashville students had been warned that Birmingham was a dangerous place.

As news of the Freedom Riders' arrival spread, a large crowd began to gather at the terminal, providing the police with a rationale for protective custody. The only way to safeguard the Riders' safety, the officer in charge insisted, was to keep them on board. For more than an hour, the Riders pleaded with the police to respect their constitutional rights, but whenever one of them made a move for the door, a billy-club-wielding officer blocked

The Reverend Fred Shuttlesworth (standing with arm extended) offers counsel to Nashville Freedom Riders (seated, from left to right) Charles Butler, Catherine Burks, Lucretia Collins, and Salynn McCollum in the white waiting room at the Birmingham Greyhound bus station, Wednesday afternoon, May 17, 1961. The man standing on the right wearing a coat and tie is the Reverend Nelson Smith, a Birmingham ACMHR leader. (Courtesy of the *Nashville Tennessean*)

the aisle. The only place the Riders were likely to go, one guard suggested, was back to the Tennessee line with a police escort. Outside of the bus, the press was being told that the Riders were being detained so that they could be safely transferred to the three o'clock bus to Montgomery. At one point, the police actually allowed the Riders' luggage to be transferred to the Montgomery bus. But a telephoned bomb threat and the driver's insistence that the Montgomery-bound Greyhound would not move from its bay if the Freedom Riders were permitted to board ended any chance that they would actually leave at three.

In the meantime, Shuttlesworth, accompanied by two aides and Emory Jackson of the *Birmingham World*, was trying to find out what was going on. Arriving at the terminal just before noon, he managed to have a few guarded words with McCollum, but there wasn't much he could do until the Riders were allowed to leave the bus. Finally, at five minutes after four, Police Chief Jamie Moore shepherded the Riders through two rows of police officers and into the terminal building. With the crowd straining to get a piece of them, the seven students made their way to the white waiting room, where they were welcomed by McCollum and a relieved and defiant Shuttlesworth. Ignoring Moore's warning that interracial mingling would incite the crowd, Shuttlesworth led the Riders, white and black, to the terminal's whites-only restaurant, but the door was locked. Cordoned off by the police, the Riders retreated to the terminal's white restrooms, which, to their relief, were open.

Preoccupied with the surging crowd, the police made no move to prevent this historic desecration of segregated toilets. Later, back in the waiting room, Shuttlesworth and the Riders celebrated their small victory with round after round of freedom songs. Seemingly unfazed by either the police or the protesters, they invited reporters and other onlookers to join them on the next "freedom bus" to Montgomery.

As the drama at the Greyhound station unfolded, the Birmingham police—and Alabama officials in general—found themselves in a delicate position. Simultaneously restraining the crowd and intimidating the Freedom Riders was turning out to be a difficult proposition, especially with the press looking on. Everyone in a position of authority, from Governor Patterson to Chief Moore, had been under intense scrutiny since Sunday afternoon, and it was becoming increasingly obvious in the wake of the Mother's Day riot that neither Birmingham nor Alabama could afford another round of mob violence and bloodshed. Indeed, on Tuesday, in the face of mounting criticism, the Birmingham police had made a show of arresting Melvin Dove, Jesse Thomas Faggard, and his son Jesse Oliver Faggard—three Tarrant City Klansmen involved in the beating of George Webb. Associates of Dr. Edward Fields, the National States Rights Party leader who defied the Birmingham police order to keep his followers away from the terminal area on Sunday afternoon, the three men were clearly identifiable in the Langston photograph that appeared on the front page of the *Birmingham Post-Herald* on Monday morning. Other assailants, including several Birmingham Klansmen, could also be identified from the photograph, but the police conveniently limited the initial arrests to the three suburban "outsiders" from Tarrant City. The token prosecution of Dove and the Faggards, combined with the later arrests of Howard Thurston Edwards, an Irondale Klansman who can be seen wielding a lead pipe in the photograph, and Herschel Acker, a Klansman from Rome, Georgia, took at least some of the pressure off of the Birmingham police, countering the charge that the riot was the result of collusion between local vigilantes and public officials. In the end, the Tarrant City Klansmen escaped with nothing more than misdemeanor disorderly conduct convictions, small fines, and brief jail terms. Acker and Edwards faced the more serious charge of assault with intent to murder, but both men ultimately walked away without serving a day in prison—Acker after being acquitted by an all-white jury in November, and Edwards after three separate trials ended with hung juries.

This calculated blend of defiance and legal pretense was on full display as state and local officials tried to outmaneuver the Nashville Riders on May 17. Ignoring the larger issue of constitutional rights, Alabama authorities restored "law and order" by branding the Tennessee students as troublemakers and criminals. In a midafternoon statement to the press, an exasperated Governor John Patterson declared that no one could "guarantee the safety of fools." And a few minutes later, just as the Riders were contemplating a move

Birmingham commissioner of public safety Theophilus Eugene "Bull" Connor, 1963. (Photograph by Bob Adelman, Magnum)

to the loading platform where the five o'clock bus to Montgomery was scheduled to depart, Bull Connor strode into the terminal waiting room. Lewis later claimed that he knew who Connor was, even "though I'd never seen him before in my life. He was short, heavy with big ears and a fleshy face. He wore a suit, his white hair was slicked straight back above his forehead, and his eyes were framed by a pair of black, horned-rimmed glasses." At first Connor seemed content to mingle with the police guards, but as soon as the Riders began to move toward the loading platform he stepped in and ordered his officers to place the unwanted visitors from Nashville in "protective custody." Pointing to the unruly crowd, he assured the students that he was arresting them for their "own protection." When Shuttlesworth stepped forward to object, Connor directed Chief Moore to arrest him for interfering with and refusing to obey a police officer. All nine "agitators" were then led to a line of waiting paddy wagons that whisked them off to Birmingham's notorious Southside jail.

At the jail, guards separated the detainees by gender. As the only white female, McCollum was placed in a special facility, and Collins and Burks were put in a cell with several other black women. With the exception of Shuttlesworth, all of the men ended up in a dark and crowded cell that Lewis likened to a dungeon: "It had no mattresses or beds, nothing to sit on at all, just a concrete floor." At ten o'clock Shuttlesworth was released on bond, but the other prisoners remained in jail, even though no formal charges had been brought against them. Isolated from the outside world with no access to the press—or to Nash, who was desperately trying to find out what had happened to them—Lewis and his cellmates adopted a strategy of Gandhian noncooperation. Although they had not eaten since morning, the students defiantly refused to eat or drink anything. And, since sleeping under these conditions was difficult at best, they decided to pass the time singing freedom songs, a morale booster that had served them well during the Nashville sit-ins. After all, they informed the guards, it was May 17—the seventh anniversary of *Brown*, a day worth celebrating in or out of jail. "We went on singing," Lewis later confessed, "both to keep our spirits up and—to be honest—because we knew that neither Bull Connor nor his guards could stand it."[15]

While the Nashville students were singing and shouting their way into Bull's doghouse, CORE was orchestrating a drama of its own in more than a score of cities and college towns across the nation. With the help of the

Freedom Riders Hank Thomas and Jim Peck picket the New York Port Authority bus terminal, May 17, 1961. (Bettmann-CORBIS)

National Student Association and several labor unions, CORE chapters simultaneously commemorated the May 17 anniversary of the *Brown* decision and protested the violence in Alabama by setting up picket lines in front of bus terminals from Boston to Los Angeles. In the South the demonstrations were limited to small groups of college students in Nashville, Chapel Hill, Austin, and Lynchburg, but in several Northern cities picket lines stretched around the block. The largest demonstration took place in New York, where more than two thousand people gave up their lunch hour to march in front of the Port Authority bus terminal. Walking at the head of the New York picket line were Jim Peck and Hank Thomas, who had flown in from New Orleans the night before. Carrying signs declaring that "segregation is morally wrong," and that they were victims "of an attempt at lynching by hoodlums in Anniston, Ala.," Peck and Thomas later joined the activist author Lillian Smith for an emotional postmarch press conference. Straining to keep her composure, Smith offered Peck's bruised and bandaged face as proof that "the dominant group in Alabama seems to care more for their color than they care for the survival of our nation," adding: "They don't believe much in the dignity and freedom of all men, their belief is in white supremacy."

Wednesday was also an emotional day in New Orleans, where most of the CORE Freedom Riders attended a private banquet followed by a mass meeting at the New Zion Baptist Church. Frances Bergman was still too shaken to attend, Genevieve Hughes was in a New Orleans hospital ward recovering from smoke inhalation and nervous exhaustion, and Jerry Moore was in New York attending his grandfather's funeral. But Carey and the rest of the Riders, with the exception of the Port Authority picketers Peck and Thomas, were on hand to help their New Orleans hosts commemorate the judicial death of Jim Crow education. With Rudy Lombard, the chair of New Orleans CORE, serving as master of ceremonies, and with CORE stalwart and sit-in leader Jerome Smith making a surprise appearance after his release from jail earlier in the day, the overflow crowd of fifteen hundred at New Zion listened with rapt attention for more than two hours as, one by one, the "survivors" of the Alabama Freedom Ride came forward to say a few words. After Blankenheim and Bigelow described the bus-burning scene in Anniston, and Person and Bergman described the Birmingham riot, Ben Cox nearly brought down the house when he urged the audience to stage "sit-ins, kneel-ins, vote-ins, ride-ins, motor-ins, swim-ins, bury-ins, and even marry-ins." In a similar vein, Carey explained that the Freedom Ride "was also meant to challenge you, to ask you, 'please don't segregate yourselves.' " According to Moses Newson, the *Baltimore Afro-American* correspondent who had been with the Riders for more than a week, the crowd "roared approval" of Carey's admonition, providing a fitting climax to CORE's campaign to arouse the black masses by exposing "Deep South lawlessness." At the rally's end, New Zion's pastor, the Reverend Abraham Lincoln Davis Jr., collected nearly seven hundred dollars in donations, which Carey gratefully and tearfully accepted on CORE's behalf.[16]

EIGHT HUNDRED MILES TO THE NORTH, the mood was a bit more somber as Justice Department officials puzzled over how to deal with the latest crisis in Alabama. At a Wednesday night dinner party hosted by Birmingham native Louis Oberdorfer, the head of the department's tax division, the conversation inevitably turned to the legal and political dilemmas posed by the new Freedom Ride. Two of Oberdorfer's guests, Birmingham attorney Douglas Arrant and Deputy Attorney General Byron "Whizzer" White, a former classmate of Oberdorfer's at Yale Law School and a future Supreme Court justice, had good reason to turn their attention to the developing situation in Alabama. Arrant voiced concerns that a full-scale race war was brewing in his hometown, and White was scheduled to meet with Burke Marshall on Thursday morning to discuss the Kennedy administration's response to the recent arrests and Governor Patterson's apparent refusal to guarantee the Freedom Riders' safety. When White remarked that the administration had "to get those people out of there and keep them moving somehow," and that the use of federal soldiers might be the only way to do it, Oberdorfer suggested the politically more palatable alternative of a civilian force made up of federal marshals. By relying on a limited number of marshals, the administration could protect the Riders and also continue to disavow any plan of imposing a second military Reconstruction on the South. A political moderate, White was willing to consider any plan that promised to avoid the heightened tensions that had plagued Eisenhower's handling of the Little Rock crisis. By the end of the evening, the three men had roughed out a proposal to send several dozen marshals to Alabama.[17]

The next morning, as the Nashville students completed their first night in jail, White met with Marshall and Robert Kennedy, who decided to interrupt his brother's breakfast with an emergency meeting. With the president still in his pajamas, the attorney general launched into an impromptu briefing on the deteriorating situation in Birmingham. A new group of Freedom Riders was in jail and conducting a hunger strike, the bus company was demanding police protection for any bus carrying Freedom Riders, and John Patterson was waffling on his earlier pledge to provide the Riders with safe passage through the state. The reports from John Seigenthaler and John Doar, the most reliable federal officials on the scene in Alabama, were increasingly discouraging. Seigenthaler's plea for the students' release had gotten nowhere. "Well, sonny boy," Connor had drawled, "they violated the law, so they're going to have to pay the price. You just tell all your friends up in Washington that." In sum, the crisis that seemingly had been resolved just before the president's departure for Ottawa had reappeared with a vengeance. Clearly, something had to be done before the situation got completely out of control.

As the president nodded in agreement, his younger brother proceeded to unveil a tentative plan for federal intervention that stopped short of military engagement. White then filled in the details, describing potential sources of federal paramilitary personnel such as the U.S. Marshal Service, the Border

Patrol, the Bureau of Prisons, and the revenue agents of the Bureau of Alcohol, Tobacco, and Firearms. Under White's plan the army would only be used as a means of transport and logistical coordination, and, if all went well, even this limited deployment would prove unnecessary. The idea was to create a credible force that would convince Patterson that the threat of federal intervention was real. Once the governor realized that federal marshals and army support staff were poised to invade Alabama, White reasoned, he would have little choice but to use the state's police power to protect the Freedom Riders. While no one could be certain that the bluff would work, in all likelihood the proposed peacekeeping force would never actually be used.

With this reassurance, and with the president still sitting in front of his uneaten breakfast, White gave way to Marshall, who outlined the legal requirements and ramifications of authorizing the use of a federal peacekeeping force in Alabama. According to Marshall, using the army or the National Guard would require a presidential proclamation, but the civilian alternative proposed by White could be legalized with a simple note to the attorney general. And since federal law did not require public notification of presidential involvement, the president retained the option of distancing himself from the decision to send in the marshals. As added insurance, the Justice Department also planned to seek two federal court injunctions, one against the Alabama Klansmen threatening the Freedom Riders and a second ordering the local police to do whatever was necessary to protect the Riders. Judge Frank Johnson Jr., Marshall insisted, could be trusted to issue the necessary injunctions. When this would occur, if ever, depended on the pace of events in Alabama, but the legal basis for limited federal intervention was secure.

John Kennedy's preference, as he soon made clear, was to avoid the use of even a civilian federal force; somehow Patterson had to be coaxed into doing the right thing and lifting the burden from the Kennedy brothers' shoulders. To this end, he asked the White House operator to call Patterson's office. Confident that his "old friend" and political ally would listen to reason if the personal touch were administered, he was surprised and a bit miffed when Patterson dodged his call. The governor, according to his secretary in Montgomery, was away on a fishing trip in the Gulf of Mexico and could not be reached by phone. Kennedy, who suspected otherwise, now realized what he was up against. Eisenhower had been forced to deal with Orval Faubus, and now four years later Patterson seemed to be following the same path of states'-rights demagoguery. Reluctantly Kennedy ordered White and Marshall to begin preparations for sending the marshals to Alabama. Still hoping to avoid federal intervention, he counseled his aides to proceed as discreetly as possible without mentioning his involvement. But he was determined to be ready if the crisis in Alabama exploded.[18]

John Kennedy was not the only leader mapping strategy on that fateful Thursday morning. Back at the Bethel parsonage after his four-hour stint behind bars, Fred Shuttlesworth convened a meeting of SCLC leaders to decide what to do about the jailed Freedom Riders and the slow pace of desegregation in Birmingham. Joining him were SCLC executive director Wyatt Tee Walker, Joseph Lowery from Mobile, J. Metz Rollins from Nashville, and Len Holt, a black lawyer from Norfolk, Virginia, who had agreed to represent the Nashville students after Arthur Shores, Birmingham's most prominent black lawyer, and other local NAACP attorneys made it clear that they disapproved of the Freedom Ride. To Shuttlesworth's dismay, the visiting SCLC leaders, with the exception of Rollins, shared many of Shores's concerns about the nature and timing of the Freedom Riders' campaign. Speaking for Martin Luther King and the SCLC executive committee, Walker suggested that it might be best for all concerned if Shuttlesworth could work out a compromise similar to the one that King had recently endorsed in Atlanta. The tentative agreement there called for a cessation of sit-ins and other protests once city leaders agreed to desegregate lunch counters and other public accommodations at the same time that the public schools were desegregated. After listening politely to the suggestion that this might work in Birmingham, Shuttlesworth did his best to bury the idea. Unwilling to postpone the day of reckoning, he eventually convinced his reluctant colleagues to stand behind the students. As he told the press later in the day: "These students came here to ride out on a regularly scheduled bus and that's what they still hope to do. That is our irrevocable position. The challenge has to be made." Shuttlesworth chose his words carefully, realizing that Holt had already muddied the waters during negotiations with the police department on Wednesday evening by suggesting that the students might accept alternative means of leaving the city. Concerned that Connor and other local white leaders had been given the wrong impression, Shuttlesworth ordered Holt to go back to the police with the clear message that "we are not going anyplace until we ride out on the bus."

By Thursday afternoon, at least one thing was already clear: Bull Connor had decided to use the Freedom Rider crisis to discredit both Shuttlesworth and the local civil rights struggle. Brandishing the minister's telegram announcing the arrival of the outside agitators from Nashville, Connor claimed that Shuttlesworth had masterminded a conspiracy to breach the peace. "As early as 9 a.m.," Connor declared, "he began precipitating trouble by making statements to newspapers and radio stations and sending telegrams and otherwise warning people." This was proof, he insisted, that Shuttlesworth was a rabble-rouser who deserved prosecution for inciting a riot. The editors of the *Birmingham News*, among others, agreed, arguing in a special front-page editorial that Shuttlesworth's actions were equivalent to shouting "fire" in a crowded auditorium.

Shuttlesworth already faced charges of interfering with the Freedom Riders' arrests, and in a brief but raucous trial on Thursday evening he was convicted. Connor, on hand to watch his nemesis squirm, appeared smug as Shuttlesworth stood in the dock, but any thought that the troublesome preacher would break under pressure disappeared as soon as he was released on bail. At a posttrial press conference held at the Bethel parsonage, Shuttlesworth was as defiant as ever, repeating his vow that neither he nor the students in the Southside jail would abandon the Freedom Ride. As the students themselves had been telling Chief Moore throughout the day, they were prepared to remain in jail indefinitely. Moore, who had offered to release the students if they promised to leave the city in private cars, seemed baffled by their apparent attraction to martyrdom. He couldn't decide which was crazier, the hunger strike or the incessant clamor of their freedom songs. Nothing in his long career as a police officer had prepared him for such utter disregard for authority and intimidation. What was the world coming to when a band of kids, black kids at that, could threaten the peace of an entire city, bringing its customs and most hallowed beliefs into question in front of the entire nation?[19]

Moore's concern, like that of many white Birminghamians, was heightened by the broadcast that evening of the CBS documentary *Who Speaks for Birmingham?* Aired at 9:00 P.M., just as Shuttlesworth's press conference was coming to a close, the program featured a series of interviews with black and white citizens, including Shuttlesworth and John Temple Graves, a columnist for the *Birmingham Post-Herald*. The dean of Birmingham journalists, Graves was a onetime pro–New Deal moderate who had grown conservative in his declining years. On screen, he presented an image of white-haired civility and reason that belied his militant defense of white supremacy and racial and class privilege. Asked to speak as the unofficial voice of the Birmingham establishment, he vehemently disputed journalist Harrison Salisbury's statement that the city was hopelessly "fragmented by the emotional dynamite of racism." "We are guilty of all sorts of sins," Graves acknowledged, but "no more proportionately than other parts of the country." Certainly there was no "reign of terror," as Salisbury had charged in the *New York Times*, and Graves challenged the press to produce evidence to the contrary. After Shuttlesworth countered with the claim that he had firsthand knowledge that "a person can be terrorized," the camera turned to a young white student who echoed Graves's defense: "If we're afraid of anything, perhaps it's that outside agitators, attempting to sell newspapers, will cause trouble that actually doesn't exist."

With producer David Lowe and reporter Howard K. Smith interjecting questions and occasional commentary, the back-and-forth dialogue continued for nearly an hour. Stories of cultural and educational progress alternated with tales of Klan violence and white supremacist intransigence. But the overall depiction of the city was less than flattering. At one point Bill Pritchard, one of Birmingham's leading attorneys, offered an embarrassingly frank explanation of the city's troubles. "I have no doubt," he declared, "that the Negro basically knows that the best friend he's ever had in the world is the Southern white man. He'd do the most for him—always has and will continue to do it, but when they, from Northern agitators, are spurred on to believe that they are the equal to the white man in every respect and should be just taken from savagery, and put on the same plane with the white man in every respect, that's not true. He shouldn't be." Pritchard went on to offer a segregationist parable, insisting that "even the dumbest farmer in the world knows that if he has white chickens and black chickens, that the black chickens do better if they're kept in one yard to themselves."

Shuttlesworth, the creator of the poultry code that had signaled the Freedom Riders' departure from Nashville, was not asked what he thought of Pritchard's segregated chicken yards. But near the end of the broadcast he had his say, coolly recounting several beatings and two attempts to bomb his church and parsonage, the first on Christmas night 1956. "I have to have somebody guard my home at night . . . ," he explained. "The police won't do it. It causes your family—wife and children—to go through severe strain. . . . But we've learned to make out on it. We found out that if you can't take it, you can't make it. . . . Life is a struggle, here, for me in Birmingham," he added, "but it's a glorious struggle." When asked about Bull Connor, Shuttlesworth didn't mince words: "He wants the white people to believe that just by his being in office, he can prevent the inevitable, so he has to talk loud, he has to be loud, because when the sound and fury is gone, then there'll be nothing. There'll be emptiness." The program closed with a brief but powerful epilogue on the May 14 beatings. After replaying his eyewitness report from Sunday, Smith—standing in front of a sprawling photograph of Connor—described the Freedom Riders' airborne exodus to New Orleans and ended by quoting from the *Birmingham News* May 15 editorial acknowledging that "fear and hatred did stalk Birmingham's streets yesterday." Smith had wanted to end the broadcast with a quotation from the philosopher Edmund Burke: "The only thing necessary for the triumph of evil is for good men to do nothing." But CBS executives, fearing a barrage of criticism from white Southerners, insisted that he drop it from the script.[20]

CONNOR NEVER ACKNOWLEDGED that the combination of Shuttlesworth's barbs and Smith's epilogue pushed him into action. But at 11:30 P.M., an hour and a half after the show's sign-off, he appeared at the city jail, grim-faced and barking orders at people on both sides of the bars. Accompanied by five police officers and *Birmingham News* reporters Tom Lankford and Bud Gordon, he announced that he was tired of listening to freedom songs. It was time for the students to go back to Nashville where they belonged. "You people came in here from Tennessee on a bus," he shouted through the bars. "I'm taking you back to Tennessee in five minutes under police protection." Waiting outside were two black unmarked police cars and a hearse-like limousine ready to transport the students out of the state. As the police began rounding up the seven students (Zwerg and Brooks were later released separately, and Salynn McCollum, released into her father's custody, was already on her way back to New York; before boarding an 11:30 P.M. flight, Walter McCollum told reporters: "I sent her to Nashville to get an education, not to get mixed up in this integration mess"), they demanded to speak with their attorney Len Holt but were told he couldn't help them because he wasn't licensed in Alabama. Though not sure what to make of the situation, Lewis and the others decided to rely on the training they had received in Lawson's seminars. "We refused to cooperate," Lewis recalled with pride many years later. "We let our bodies go limp, forcing the officers to drag us from the jail and out into the night."

Eventually the police loaded the students into two of the cars, jamming all of their luggage into the limousine. With Lankford and Gordon along for the ride as observers, Connor himself took the wheel of the lead car and guided the convoy northward to Highway 31, the same road that the students had traveled by bus on Wednesday morning. As they left the jail, he ordered the students to keep all of the windows closed for their own protection, prompting a defiant Lucretia Collins to remind him that the windows might "keep bullets out, but they can't keep God out." Later, after leaving the city lights behind, Connor tried to engage several of the students in friendly small talk but made no effort to reveal his exact plans for them. At first the students feared that they were headed for some sort of staged ambush, but as Connor continued his jovial chatter they began to relax. Most of the conversation was between Connor and the feisty Birmingham native Catherine Burks, who refused to be intimidated by a man she later claimed "was a powerful dictator but didn't have any power over me." After Connor hinted that he planned to take the students all the way back to Nashville, Burks suggested that in the spirit of Christian fellowship he should join them for breakfast before returning to Alabama. At one point she even offered to cook for him.

To Lewis, who was sitting directly behind the driver's seat, this unexpected banter was somewhat reassuring, but the strained joviality came to an abrupt halt when the convoy reached the small border town of Ardmore, Alabama. "This is where you'll be gettin' out," Connor informed them, adding: "There is the Tennessee line. Cross it and save this state and yourself a lot of trouble." While the officers unloaded the luggage, stacking it alongside the road, the seven students climbed out of the cars to an uncertain fate. Before driving off, Connor pointed to a railroad track that led to a nearby depot from which, he assured them with a wry smile, they could catch a train to Nashville. "Or maybe a bus," he said with a laugh.

It was four o'clock in the morning, and for a while they "just stood there in the dark" wondering whether they were about to be ambushed or even lynched, but before long they headed down the tracks in search of help. Failing to find the railroad depot, they stumbled on a pay phone and placed a collect call to Nash. Stunned that they had been released from the Birmingham jail, she tried to gather her thoughts about what to do next. She could send a car to bring them to Nashville, or she could find some way to send them back to Birmingham. The choice was up to them, she declared, but the situation was complicated by the fact that eleven new Freedom Riders would soon be on their way to Alabama. Since this was the first they had heard of the second wave of Nashville Riders, the weary students decided to seek food and shelter before making any commitments. Promising to call Nash back as soon as they found a safe haven, they resumed their trek down the tracks.

After walking nearly a mile, they approached a cluster of houses that Lewis later described as "broken-down shacks." Reasonably certain that they were in an all-black neighborhood, the students summoned the courage to knock on the front door of one of the houses, awakening an elderly black couple who, after a bit of coaxing, reluctantly let them in. As Lewis recalled: "They had heard about the Freedom Ride and . . . were very frightened, but they put us all in the back room of their house. . . . By this time we were very, very hungry, because we didn't eat anything during the hunger strike, and the elderly man went to three different stores to buy food for our breakfast, so that no one would get suspicious." The couple also allowed Lewis to use their phone to call Nash, who was anxiously awaiting their decision. All seven, he assured her, were determined to go on to New Orleans as planned. Relieved but hardly surprised, she promised to send a car that would have them back in Birmingham by midafternoon.[21]

Leo Lillard, a recent graduate of Tennessee State and a close friend of Nash's, had already volunteered to pick up the Freedom Riders in Ardmore and drive them to Birmingham. As a sit-in veteran and devoted Lawson disciple, the irrepressible twenty-two-year-old jumped at the chance to play an important role in the Freedom Ride. Later in the summer, he would prove to be an invaluable organizer as he, along with Nash and several others, trained and dispatched the scores of Freedom Riders who passed through the Nashville office. But on that Friday morning, the things that mattered most were his driving skills and his passion for speed. Racing southward, he managed to reach the state line by late morning, bragging to his seven grateful friends that he had made the ninety-mile trip from Nashville in a little over an hour. Piling into the large four-door sedan that Lillard had borrowed for the rescue mission, the students thanked the elderly couple for their help before roaring down the same highway that had seemed to seal their fate only a few hours earlier.

The car was crowded, and whenever they passed another vehicle they took the precaution of "squeezing ourselves down in the seats, out of sight," just in case the Alabama police or Klan vigilantes were looking for them. Nevertheless, the mood in the car was upbeat, even jubilant, especially after they heard a radio report that Connor had boasted that he had resolved the crisis by personally returning the would-be Freedom Riders to their college campuses in Tennessee. As Burks and several others mused about how shocked Bull was going to be when he discovered the truth, gales of laughter filled the car. Minutes later, however, the mood was broken when a second radio bulletin corrected the first. According to United Press International, the Freedom Riders were not back in Nashville after all but rather in a private car headed for Birmingham. The source, the students later discovered, was Nash herself who had inadvertently spilled the beans in a series of telephone conversations with movement contacts. In trying to counter the notion that the students had given up, she couldn't resist predicting that Connor was in for a big surprise.

During the remainder of the journey, Lillard nervously guided the "freedom car" through the back roads hoping to escape detection. For a time every approaching car seemed menacing, but finally, just a few minutes before three—a mere fifteen hours after being rousted from their jail cells—the students pulled into the driveway of the Bethel parsonage. Back at Ardmore, Burks had promised the departing Connor that she would be back in Birmingham by noon, and she had almost done it. As Shuttlesworth rushed out to greet the lost Riders, other familiar faces began to appear in the background. All eleven of the reinforcements that Nash had mentioned on the phone were at the parsonage. Of the original ten Nashville Riders, only Brooks and Zwerg—who would be released from jail later in the afternoon—and McCollum were missing; and, as the arriving students soon discovered during a rollicking reunion on the lawn, McCollum had already been replaced by Ruby Doris Smith, a Spelman student and SNCC stalwart who had shared a jail cell with Diane Nash in Rock Hill. In all there were nineteen volunteers ready to board the next "freedom bus" to Montgomery. In addition to Smith, the new recruits included Bernard Lafayette and Joe Carter of American Baptist Theological Seminary, seven sit-in veterans from Tennessee State, and two white women: eighteen-year-old Susan Wilbur of George Peabody College and twenty-year-old Susan Hermann of Fisk, an exchange student from Whittier, California. Most had traveled to Birmingham by train, with Lafayette in charge of the group. A few, at Nash's suggestion, had straggled in by other means in an effort to ensure that at least some of the students would avoid interception by Alabama authorities. When Lewis called to tell her that nineteen "pullets" had arrived at Shuttlesworth's coop, she could hardly believe it, though she continued to worry that the police might close in at any minute. Not wishing to press their luck, she and Lewis decided to put the Riders on the first available bus to Montgomery.[22]

Following a hurried lunch, Shuttlesworth organized a car pool to transport the Riders to the Greyhound terminal and once again sent word to law enforcement officials that a new Freedom Ride was about to begin. By late afternoon news of the Ride had spread across town and even to Montgomery and Washington. The reaction at all levels was a combination of surprise and head-shaking frustration. Despite their differences, local, state, and federal officials shared a common resolve to bring the Freedom Rider crisis to a close. In downtown Birmingham, Connor and the police were growing tired of a cat-and-mouse game with troublemakers who didn't seem to respond to the traditional forms of control and intimidation. Under increasing political pressure to maintain law and order, they knew they could not afford another public relations disaster like the Mother's Day riot. Yet they were not about to let the Freedom Riders run roughshod over the hallowed strictures of racial segregation. At the governor's office in Montgomery, Patterson was playing an equally difficult game, trying to extract political capital out of the crisis without having it blow up in his face. Dodging federal entreaties that he guarantee the Freedom Riders' safety, he was determined to defend the shibboleths of states' rights and to teach the Freedom Riders, the Kennedys, and other potential meddlers from the North a lesson. But to do so, especially with new Freedom Riders popping up all over the place, was proving to be more challenging than he or anyone in his circle had anticipated.

The situation was no less frustrating for the Justice Department officials who spent most of Thursday working out the preliminary organization of a federal peacekeeping force. Faced with a politically unpalatable scenario, Kennedy and his staff continued to search for some means of ending the crisis before the peacekeeping force was deployed. Hoping for a miracle, they privately welcomed Connor's attempt to take the situation in hand. Despite the initial fear that Connor had snapped—"Jesus Christ, Bull has kidnapped them. He's going to kill them," a panic-stricken Seigenthaler had reported early Friday morning—Marshall, White, and Kennedy were actually relieved to learn that Connor had driven the jailed Riders back to Tennessee. Their only major concern now seemed to be how the impulsive public safety commissioner would explain his actions to the press. When Connor quipped that he planned to tell reporters that he just couldn't stand the students' singing any longer, they weren't sure that he was serious, but even this strained attempt at humor was a welcome change from the threatening mood of a few hours earlier.

For a brief period on Friday morning, Justice Department officials believed that the day of reckoning in Alabama had been postponed. As the morning progressed, however, they were forced to confront the rumor and later the reality that not one but two groups of Freedom Riders were about to invade Birmingham. By early afternoon the vulnerability of the administration's position—not to mention the vulnerability of the Freedom Riders themselves—had become all too clear. Earlier in the day a breaking news story from South Africa, where white police officers and soldiers were in the process of arresting thousands of black anti-apartheid protesters concerned about the reactionary implications of South Africa's impending withdrawal from the British Commonwealth, had reminded federal officials of just how explosive racial crises could become. Indeed, the likely prospect of parallel headlines linking Johannesburg and Birmingham compounded the administration's problems.

With the Freedom Riders mobilizing, Connor raging, Patterson hiding, and crowds of angry whites gathering, the prospects for a timely resolution of the crisis seemed to be slipping away. And with only Seigenthaler and a token force of FBI agents on the ground in Birmingham, there wasn't much that the Justice Department could do about it, at least in the short run. As the federal officials entrusted with the task of resolving the crisis, Kennedy and his lieutenants could only hope that the Nashville Freedom Riders would come to their senses before it was too late. But even this faint hope began to fade later in the afternoon as word spread that a caravan of Riders had left the parsonage heading in the direction of the downtown Greyhound terminal.[23]

BY THE TIME SHUTTLESWORTH AND THE FREEDOM RIDERS arrived at the terminal, a dozen police officers, a number of newspaper and television reporters, and several hundred onlookers were already at the scene. For the fourth time in six days a large crowd had gathered to protest the Freedom Riders' presence in Alabama. Later in the day the size of the crowd would grow to three thousand and beyond, and the rising anger of the most militant protesters would eventually force the police to use its new K-9 corps to maintain order. But as the Riders piled out of the cars and headed toward the loading platform to board the three o'clock bus to Montgomery, the protesters seemed more stunned than anything else. "They pushed in at us as we entered the terminal," Lewis recalled, "but no one touched us." Although the bus was already idling in preparation for its departure and there were enough empty seats to accommodate all nineteen Freedom Riders, Greyhound officials promptly canceled the run, claiming that no driver was available. With the police holding back the crowd, the Riders retreated to the white waiting room, where they vowed to remain until the bus line found a driver to take them to Montgomery. After waiting for more than an hour, the Riders returned to the loading platform, but once again they were told that no Greyhound driver was willing to take them to Montgomery or anywhere else. Later, back in the waiting room, they sang freedom songs and prayed as the police strained to keep the swell of protesters from getting completely out of hand.

Most of the protesters remained outside the terminal, but the police made a point of allowing some, including several men dressed in Klan robes, to wander around the waiting room with impunity. Standing smugly only a few feet from the Riders was Imperial Wizard Robert Shelton, decked out in a black robe with an embroidered snake on the back. For nearly three hours the police stood by and watched as Shelton's Klansmen indulged in petty acts of provocation, such as "accidentally" stepping on the Riders' feet, spilling drinks on their clothes, and blocking access to the restrooms. But as darkness approached, Chief Moore decided to clear the room of everyone but the Riders. At the same time, in an effort to reassure the crowd that the police were not coddling the outside agitators, Moore—acting upon orders from

Nashville Freedom Riders wait to board a Montgomery-bound bus at the Birmingham Greyhound bus station, Friday afternoon, May 19, 1961. From left to right: Joseph Carter, Susan Hermann, Susan Wilbur, Catherine Burks, Lucretia Collins, and Bernard Lafayette. John Lewis is the partially obscured figure standing behind Lafayette. (AP Wide World)

Connor—also disconnected the waiting room's public telephones, closed the terminal restaurant, and dispatched two officers to the Bethel parsonage to arrest Shuttlesworth, who had returned to the church to lead a mass meeting. The charge, Connor later explained to reporters, was conspiracy to incite a riot. Who else, he asked, had done more to instigate the civil disorder that had plagued the city since Mother's Day?

By nightfall the scene in and around the terminal had taken on an eerie tone. Emboldened by the cover of darkness, the crowd grew increasingly restless as it became clear that the Riders were prepared to spend the night at the terminal. "We could see them through the glass doors and streetside windows," Lewis remembered, "gesturing at us and shouting. Every now and then a rock or a brick would crash through one of the windows near the ceiling. The police brought in dogs and we could see them outside, pulling at their leashes to keep the crowd back." The brusqueness of the police, and the absence of food and working phones, added to the siege-like atmosphere, but the entire group—which swelled to twenty-one when Brooks and Zwerg arrived at the terminal around eight o'clock—was determined to outlast both the mob and local authorities. As the night progressed, the students began to wonder what was happening in the outside world. Did the public know what was going on in downtown Birmingham? Was anyone working to break the stalemate? "The only reality we were sure of," Lewis recalled, "was the crowd of hateful faces outside those windows." Later in the evening, after the police permitted a handful of reporters to reenter the waiting room, the students learned that Robert Kennedy and other Justice Department officials were in the process of negotiating with Greyhound executives. Shuttlesworth, who rejoined the students after being released on bond, confirmed that federal authorities were well aware of the standoff at the terminal and actively seeking a solution. Although he knew few details, he did know that Seigenthaler had been dispatched to work out a deal with Patterson.[24]

Seigenthaler's mission to Montgomery followed repeated attempts to reach Patterson by phone, including a call from John Kennedy himself. After Patterson declined to take the president's call, this time without resorting to the subterfuge of a fishing trip, Kennedy phoned Lieutenant Governor Albert Boutwell, but Boutwell, a loyal Patterson crony, pleaded ignorance of the governor's whereabouts and intentions. By midafternoon the Kennedy brothers knew that they had to do something dramatic to force Patterson to the bargaining table. Infuriated by an obvious snub of his brother, Robert Kennedy informed Patterson's aides that the president was now ready to issue a public ultimatum that would lead to federal intervention in Alabama. This threat brought an immediate response from Patterson, who grabbed the phone to explain why he wanted nothing to do with the Freedom Riders. In the long conversation that followed, Kennedy urged Patterson to cooperate and predicted dire consequences if he didn't, but the recalcitrant governor stubbornly resisted making any commitment to protect the Freedom Riders. At one point, after Patterson indulged in a gratuitous outburst about the sanctity of segregation, Kennedy nearly lost his temper. Regaining his composure, he continued the jawboning effort until Patterson, sensing that he was being boxed into a corner, abruptly ended the conversation with the demand that the Justice Department send someone to Montgomery to discuss the situation with his staff.[25]

By the time Seigenthaler arrived at the state capitol in Montgomery on Friday evening, the Alabama crisis seemed to be spiraling out of control. Flanked by his entire cabinet, Governor Patterson sat stony-faced at the head of a long polished table. When he learned that Seigenthaler was a Southerner from Tennessee, the governor cracked a smile and welcomed his noticeably nervous visitor to Montgomery, but such niceties soon gave way to a long tirade on states' rights and the Southern way of life. "There's nobody in the whole country that's got the spine to stand up to the goddamned niggers

except me," he proclaimed, adding that he had a desk full of mail "congratu-
lating me on the stand that I've taken against what's going on in this country." Bragging that he was "more popular in this country today than John
Kennedy," he vowed to hold the line "against Martin Luther King and these
rabble-rousers" who had breached the peace. "I want you to know," he added,
"that if schools in Alabama are integrated, blood's gonna flow in the streets,
and you take that message back to the President and you tell the Attorney
General that."

Seigenthaler, who had heard this kind of political bombast before, politely sidestepped Patterson's demagogic posturing and eventually managed
to move the conversation toward a consideration of realistic options. After
several false starts, he began to make headway with the argument that it was
in Alabama's interest to hand the Freedom Rider problem over to Mississippi as soon as possible. When Patterson insisted that no one could guarantee the Riders' safe passage from Birmingham to the Mississippi border, Floyd
Mann, Alabama's director of safety, surprised the governor with the calm
assertion that the state highway patrol was up to the task. Over the next few
minutes, Mann, with Seigenthaler's encouragement, guided Patterson toward a reluctant acceptance of the responsibility for the Riders' safety. Although many of the details would not be worked out until later in the evening,
Mann's plan called for a combined effort of local and state officials: The
Birmingham and Montgomery police would protect the Riders within city
limits, and the state police would provide protection on the open highways,
with Mann himself on the bus as added insurance.

To this end, Patterson and Seigenthaler hammered out a mutually acceptable public statement, and the suddenly cooperative governor even allowed Seigenthaler to use his phone to call Robert Kennedy with the news
that an agreement had been reached. With Patterson and the Alabama cabinet listening in the background, Seigenthaler read the agreed-upon statement over the phone: "The State of Alabama has the will, the force, the men,
and the equipment to give full protection to everyone in Alabama, on the
highways and elsewhere." When Kennedy asked if the pledge was genuine,
Patterson yelled out, "I've given my word as Governor of Alabama." Still
skeptical, Kennedy asked if Patterson was willing to repeat the pledge to
H. Vance Greenslit, the president of Southern Greyhound. Once again the
governor said yes, and moments later he was on the phone assuring Greenslit
that there would be no more bus burnings in the state of Alabama.[26]

By late afternoon Seigenthaler was confident that the end of the Freedom Rider crisis was in sight. Even though the situation remained volatile,
Patterson's apparent change of heart and Mann's professionalism had convinced him that the Riders could be protected without the direct involvement of federal law enforcement officers. Events would soon prove him wrong,
but as he settled into his Montgomery motel room later that evening, he had
no way of knowing that Patterson was having second thoughts about the

wisdom of letting the Freedom Riders slip from his grasp. While Mann was busy conferring with local and state police commanders in a legitimate effort to live up to the agreement forged earlier in the day, Patterson was effectively undercutting the agreement with some last-minute political maneuvering. Before leaving his office for the night, the governor directed state attorney general MacDonald Gallion to track down Circuit Judge Walter B. Jones. Earlier in the week Gallion had approached Judge Jones about the need for an injunction that would bar the Freedom Riders from traveling in Alabama, and now he and Patterson wanted to make it official. An arch-conservative who had been grousing about civil rights agitators since the days of the Montgomery Bus Boycott, Jones was happy to oblige, though he reminded Gallion that the draft of the injunction that he was being asked to sign named Jim Farmer and the CORE Riders, not the Nashville Riders, as the offending parties to be enjoined. Unfazed, Gallion insisted that he and the governor wanted the injunction anyway. If nothing else, he reasoned, the resulting confusion could be used as a legal delaying mechanism. The longer the Freedom Riders were tied up in court, the longer they could be kept off Alabama's highways.[27]

By Saturday morning Alabama officials essentially had two plans in place, one that tacitly recognized the Freedom Riders' right to travel and another that branded them as outlaws. If the agreement with the feds fell apart or became too costly politically, they could simply revert to hard-line resistance. Seigenthaler, upon learning of the injunction, felt betrayed, but the knowledge that his own department was hedging its bets tempered his indignation. Even though Robert Kennedy had sanctioned the highway patrol's preparations for the Riders' trip to Montgomery, he continued to pressure the Riders to abandon the Freedom Ride altogether. In an early-morning conversation with Shuttlesworth, Kennedy insisted that the students' best option was to follow the CORE Riders' example and fly to New Orleans. Alabama was dangerous enough, but traveling through Mississippi would be even worse, Kennedy declared, facetiously reminding Shuttlesworth that even "the Lord hasn't . . . been to Mississippi in a long time." Never one to miss a preaching opportunity, Shuttlesworth shot back: "But we think the Lord *should* go to Mississippi, and we want to get him there."

These words dredged up Kennedy's worst fear—that Shuttlesworth himself had decided to join the Freedom Ride. When asked directly if he planned to be on the bus, Shuttlesworth did not hesitate: "Mr. Kennedy, would I ask anybody else to do what I wouldn't do? I'm a battlefield general. I lead troops into battle. Yes, sir, I'm goin' to ride the bus. I've got my ticket." After a brief but futile effort to change the minister's mind, Kennedy realized that he was wasting his time. Shuttlesworth and the Riders were about to put themselves— and the well-being of the nation—at risk, and there was nothing he could do to stop them. Even worse, he had been forced to entrust their lives and the civic order to a group of law enforcement officers that in all probability would let him down and embarrass his brother's administration, all for the sake of an outmoded belief in racial privilege and states' rights.[28]

Despite his misgivings about the Alabama police, Kennedy believed that it was essential to remove the Freedom Riders from the Birmingham Greyhound terminal as soon as possible. Bull Connor's city, he was now convinced, was every bit as dangerous as Harrison Salisbury had said it was. During the night much of the crowd surrounding the terminal had dispersed, but Kennedy expected it to build up again after daylight. Thus he urged Shuttlesworth to put the Riders on the first available bus to Montgomery. Wasting no time, Shuttlesworth made sure that the students were ready to ride by 6:00 A.M. Though stiff from a night of trying to sleep on the waiting room's hard benches, the Riders gathered at the loading platform, where they, along with several reporters, waited expectantly for a driver to appear. At five minutes after six a uniformed driver named Joe Caverno approached the bus. Turning to the Riders, he asked if any of them were members of CORE or the NAACP. When no one responded affirmatively, he became flustered and seemed to lose his nerve. "I'm supposed to drive this bus to Dothan, Alabama, through Montgomery," he stammered, barely audible over the clamor of the crowd behind the police lines, "but I understand there is a big convoy down the road. And I don't have but one life to give. And I don't intend to give it to CORE or the NAACP." After Caverno walked away, several onlookers yelled out that Greyhound would never find a driver crazy enough to take the Freedom Riders to Montgomery. Though fearing that this was the case, the Riders decided to stay on the loading platform until another driver materialized. Standing there in front of the press and the police, they began singing freedom songs and spirituals. Years later Jim Zwerg recalled the poignancy of the scene, how the huddled Riders greeted the dawn with song, and how he, the only white boy among them, summoned enough courage to sing a few bars in solo. Clearly, this was a movement with the power to push individuals beyond the limits of ordinary experience.

The drama unfolding on the loading platform was hardly what Justice Department officials had expected following the negotiations with Patterson and Mann on Friday. After Patterson reassured Southern Greyhound president Greenslit that state and local law enforcement officers were determined to avoid a repeat of the Mother's Day violence, everything seemed set. Connor and the Birmingham police had agreed to escort the bus to the city line, and Mann and the highway patrol would take over from there. Highway patrol cars would surround the bus during the ninety-mile trip to Montgomery, and the Montgomery police would see to it that nothing happened to the bus or the Freedom Riders during what was expected to be a brief stay in the state capital. Once the bus left Montgomery, the highway patrol would resume responsibility during the westward link to the Mississippi state line. What would happen in Mississippi and Louisiana was anybody's guess, but Justice Department officials were hopeful that Governors Ross Barnett and Jimmie Davis would provide the Riders with safe passage through Jackson and on to New Orleans. While both Barnett and Davis were outspoken segregationists, neither had given any indication that he would tolerate anything akin to the violent disruptions that had plagued Anniston and Birmingham. All of this seemed to satisfy Greenslit, who assured Justice Department officials that Greyhound was prepared to do its part. Finding a driver for the Birmingham-to-Montgomery run would not be easy, but he was confident that a volunteer could be found by Saturday morning.

Caught off-guard by the early-morning decision to take the first bus, Seigenthaler was still in his motel room when a Birmingham FBI agent called with the alarming news that the Freedom Riders were stranded on the loading platform. Before rushing to a breakfast meeting with John Doar, Seigenthaler placed a frantic call to Greenslit in Atlanta. Professing shock that Caverno had refused to drive the bus, Greenslit vowed to get the bus out of Birmingham "at the earliest possible moment" and "to come over there and drive it myself" if no one else would do it. Greenslit then called George Cruit, the top Greyhound official in Birmingham, demanding to know why the bus was still at the loading platform. When Cruit explained that no driver was willing to take the wheel, Greenslit threatened to fire him if he didn't get the bus on the road. Cruit promised to do what he could, and within minutes Bull Connor strode into the terminal to take personal charge of the situation. Moments later Caverno reappeared on the loading platform, flanked by a dispatcher and a local Teamsters Union leader. Stepping onto the bus, the stone-faced driver settled in behind the wheel and motioned to the Riders to board.

Most of the Riders were too startled to say anything, but as the police closed ranks around the bus Shuttlesworth could not resist commenting on the irony of the situation. "Man, what's this state coming to!" he shouted to the police. "An armed escort to take a bunch of niggers to a bus station so they can break these silly laws." After a few parting taunts directed at the line of officers—including the jibe "we're gonna make a steer out of Bull"—he attempted to board the bus along with the other Riders. But Chief Moore stepped in front of the door and ordered him to go home. Although Shuttlesworth produced a ticket, Moore repeated the order, and when the minister once again failed to back away from the bus he was arrested for refusing to obey a police officer.

As Shuttlesworth was being led away, a phalanx of police cruisers and motorcycles pulled in front of the loading platform, signaling to Caverno that the escort was assembled and ready to leave. Afraid of being left behind, several reporters made a mad dash for their cars, just in time to join the convoy that was soon barreling down the streets of Birmingham. After five days of turmoil and delay, the Freedom Ride was back on track and moving southward toward Montgomery, an historic capital city with a divided heritage. Having served as both "the cradle of the Confederacy" and the unwilling nurturer of nonviolent struggle, Montgomery presented the Freedom Riders with a unique set of challenges no less daunting than those encountered in Bull Connor's Birmingham.[29]

6

If You Miss Me from the Back of the Bus

If you miss me from the back of the bus, And you can't
    find me nowhere,
Come on up to the front of the bus, I'll be
    riding up there.

—1960s freedom song[1]

THE FREEDOM RIDERS' DEPARTURE from Birmingham resembled a staged Hollywood chase scene—but the high-speed drama was all too real. Since none of the Riders had been briefed on the plan to protect them, there was high anxiety on the bus, at least in the early going. When the Greyhound reached the southern edge of the city, there was a moment of panic as the police escort pulled to the side of the road, but within seconds several highway patrol cars appeared in front of the bus. Overhead a low-flying highway patrol plane tracked the bus's progress down Highway 31, with the rest of the convoy—the cars carrying FBI observers, Floyd Mann's plainclothes detectives, and several reporters—following close behind. Additional highway patrol cars were stationed all along the route at intervals of fifteen miles, and at each checkpoint a new patrolman took the lead. All of this was reassuring, and by the time the bus passed over the Shelby County line and approached the town of Jemison, thirty miles south of Birmingham, many of the Riders had begun to relax. State officials had promised the Justice Department that the bus run to Montgomery would include all of the normal stops, so there was some surprise when the bus did not stop in Jemison—or in any of the other towns along the route. No one on the bus, however, voiced any objection to the express-like pace of the trip. For the first time in days the Nashville students felt relatively safe. "No one on the bus said much," recalled John Lewis, but "the mood was very relaxed." Exhausted from several sleepless nights, some of the students "actually dozed off" during the last half of the journey.[2]

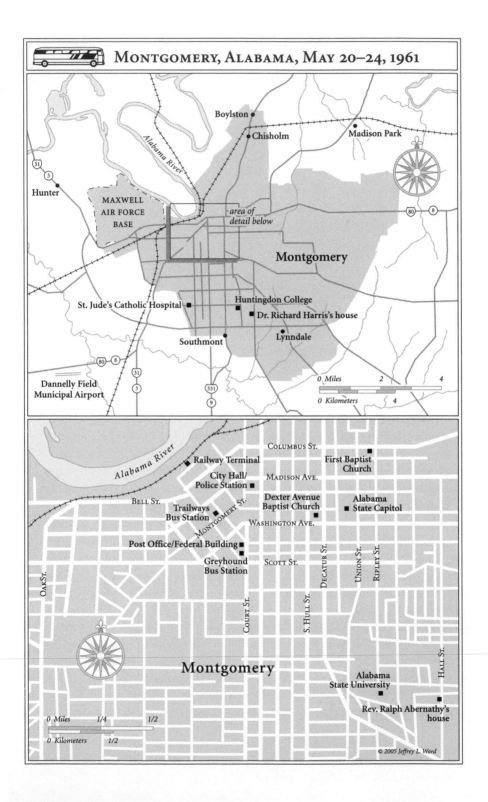

MONTGOMERY, ALABAMA, MAY 20–24, 1961

Boylston

Chisholm

Madison Park

Alabama River

31
3

Hunter

MAXWELL AIR FORCE BASE

area of detail below

Montgomery

St. Jude's Catholic Hospital

Huntingdon College

Dr. Richard Harris's house

Southmont

Lynndale

80 8

31
3

331
9

Dannelly Field Municipal Airport

0 Miles 2 4

0 Kilometers 4

Alabama River

COLUMBUS ST.

Railway Terminal

City Hall/ Police Station

MADISON AVE.

First Baptist Church

BELL ST.

Trailways Bus Station

MONTGOMERY ST.

Dexter Avenue Baptist Church

WASHINGTON AVE.

Alabama State Capitol

Post Office/Federal Building

Greyhound Bus Station

SCOTT ST.

DECATUR ST.

UNION ST.

RIPLEY ST.

OAK ST.

COURT ST.

S. HULL ST.

HALL ST.

Montgomery

Alabama State University

Rev. Ralph Abernathy's house

0 Miles 1/4 1/2

0 Kilometers 1/2

© 2005 Jeffrey L. Ward

After passing through the rural Black Belt counties of Chilton and Autauga, the convoy crossed over the Alabama River and entered Montgomery County around 10:00 A.M. With the capital city of Montgomery lying just a few miles to the southeast, everything seemed set for a safe arrival. When a message from the pilot of the patrol plane confirmed that the bus was only fourteen miles from the city, Mann relayed the news to Montgomery's public safety commissioner, L. B. Sullivan, the local official responsible for the final leg of the Freedom Riders' escort. A notoriously hard-line segregationist, Sullivan had already gained national attention as the plaintiff in an April 1960 libel suit against the *New York Times*, Shuttlesworth, and three other SCLC leaders who had signed an advertisement in that paper condemning Alabama officials for intimidating and persecuting Martin Luther King. Realizing that Sullivan was potentially the weakest link in the chain of security, Mann reminded the commissioner that he and other city officials had promised to protect the Riders inside the city limits of Montgomery. Unruffled, Sullivan calmly assured Mann that a large contingent of police was waiting at the Montgomery Greyhound terminal. Earlier in the morning both Sullivan and Montgomery's acting police chief, Marvin Stanley (Chief G. J. Ruppenthal was out of town), had given a similar assurance to FBI agents, who passed the information on to Justice Department officials in Washington and Birmingham.

When Seigenthaler and Doar left their motel, they had every reason to believe that state and local officials would provide the Riders with safe passage through Montgomery. Confident that everything was proceeding according to plan, they felt secure enough to enjoy a leisurely breakfast before heading for the Greyhound terminal. Expecting the bus to make several stops, they calculated that the Riders would arrive at the Montgomery terminal sometime around eleven o'clock. After finishing breakfast around 10:15, Seigenthaler dropped Doar off at the Federal Building before finding a parking place near the Greyhound terminal just a few yards away. As Doar made his way to a third-floor office to resume work on a Selma voting rights case, Seigenthaler circled the block, unaware that the bus had already arrived.

Like Seigenthaler, the arriving Freedom Riders expected to find the terminal area crawling with police, but when Caverno eased the bus into its arrival bay at 10:23, there were no policemen in sight. A few minutes earlier, at the Montgomery city line, the Riders had discovered that their police escort was limited to a lone patrolman on a motorcycle. Now, as they prepared to leave the bus, there was an unsettling quiet, not unlike the situation that had greeted the CORE Riders in Birmingham the previous Sunday. "The only people I could see," Lewis recalled, "were a couple of taxi drivers sitting in their cabs, a small group of reporters waiting on the platform and a dozen or so white men standing together over near the terminal door."

In actuality, there were as many as two hundred protesters in the immediate area waiting to strike a blow for segregation. Lookouts in parked cars had been posted in the streets around the terminal since Friday evening, and some of central Alabama's most notorious Klansmen—including more than a dozen of those involved in the Birmingham Mother's Day riot—were on hand to lead the mob. The ringleader of the "welcoming" party was Claude Henley, a local car salesman and former highway patrolman who had served on Montgomery's volunteer reserve police force since 1956. A close friend of Captain Drue Lackey, the commander of the city's patrol division, Henley had been promised that the police would not interfere with his plan to teach the Freedom Riders a lesson. Although Commissioner Sullivan later tried to justify the absence of police protection by claiming that he had feared that sending patrolmen to the terminal would draw a crowd, both he and Lackey were aware of Henley's intentions well before the Riders' arrival.

After a few moments of hesitation, Lewis, Catherine Burks, Bill Harbour, Jim Zwerg, and several other Riders exited the bus, stepping onto a loading platform where a group of reporters waited with notepads and microphones in hand. Before turning to the reporters to make a statement, Lewis, who had passed through the Montgomery terminal many times before, warned Harbour that things didn't look right. Seconds later, a group of white men armed with lead pipes and baseball bats rushed toward them. Norman Ritter, a writer for *Life* magazine, had just asked the first question, but Lewis, distracted by the advancing mob, never finished his answer. After wheeling around to see what was happening, Ritter attempted to shield the Riders with his outstretched arms. The mob brushed him aside, forcing the Riders to back away toward a low retaining wall that overlooked the post office parking lot eight feet below. For a few moments, the focus of the frenzy was on the reporters, as several attackers clubbed and kicked Ritter, *Life* photographer Don Uhrbrock, Herb Kaplow and Moe Levy of NBC, and *Time* magazine correspondent Calvin Trillin. Other members of the mob began to smash television cameras and sound equipment before turning on the Freedom Riders themselves.

By this time, most of the Riders had left the bus, and several pairs of seatmates had joined hands, forming a human chain on the loading platform. Following nonviolent protocol, Lewis counseled the Riders to hold their ground and "stand together," but the surging mob quickly overwhelmed them. As he remembered the scene: "Out of nowhere, from every direction, came people. White people. Men, women, and children. Dozens of them. Hundreds of them. Out of alleys, out of side streets, around the corners of office buildings, they emerged from everywhere, from all directions, all at once, as if they'd been let out of a gate. . . .They carried every makeshift weapon imaginable. Baseball bats, wooden boards, bricks, chains, tire irons, pipes, even garden tools—hoes and rakes. One group had women in front, their faces twisted in anger, screaming, '*Git them niggers, GIT them niggers!*' "[3]

Pressed against the retaining wall, most of the Riders either jumped or were pushed over the railing into the parking lot below. Some landed on the hoods or roofs of cars before scrambling to their feet and staggering toward the street in front of the terminal. With most of the attackers still on the loading platform, the Riders fortunate enough to make it to the lower level gained at least some chance of escape. As the mob concentrated its fury on the reporters and the half-dozen Riders who remained on the platform, the Riders on the street either ran from the area or frantically tried to find someone willing to drive them to Ralph Abernathy's First Baptist Church or some other safe haven. After briefly huddling on the curb, the seven female Riders spied a parked taxicab with a black driver at the wheel. Catherine Burks begged the driver to take them to First Baptist, but he balked—protesting that the law would not allow him to carry more than four passengers, or to carry white passengers at all. Burks, seeing the fear in his face, told him to move over so she could drive the cab herself. Realizing that she meant business, the driver motioned to the five black women to get in, but he wouldn't budge on the segregation issue. Moments later, as the cab pulled away, the two white female Riders, Susan Wilbur and Susan Hermann, found a second cab; once again the driver was black. As the two women climbed into the backseat, the driver started to object, but before he could press his case a screaming white man grabbed his keys and pulled him out of the car. Other members of the mob, including several women, then dragged Wilbur and Hermann onto the sidewalk and proceeded to beat them with swinging pocketbooks and other makeshift weapons.[4]

In the meantime, Seigenthaler was circling the block looking for a parking place. After slowly steering his way through the throng in front of the terminal, he began to realize that a full-scale riot was in progress. To his amazement and horror, white protesters were smashing luggage and tossing it into the street, and several young Freedom Riders appeared to be running for their lives. All of this was bad enough, but as he drew closer to the terminal he saw Susan Wilbur being punched repeatedly by a teenage boy, "a young, skinny kid who looked about fifteen years old . . . facing her and dancing like a boxer and smacking her in the face." On impulse, Seigenthaler jerked the wheel to the right and drove onto the sidewalk. He jumped out of the car and raced over to help but arrived just as Wilbur was slammed against his front fender. Pulling the young woman to her feet, he urged her to get into the car. Not knowing who he was, she pushed him away, screaming: "Mister, this is not your fight! Get away from here! You're gonna get killed!" In the meantime, Hermann had crawled into the backseat, but Seigenthaler hardly noticed her as he pleaded with Wilbur. Suddenly, two rough-looking men dressed in overalls blocked his path to the car door, demanding to know who "the hell" he was. Seigenthaler replied that he was a federal agent and that they had better not challenge his authority. Before he could say any more, a third man struck him in the back of the head with a pipe. Unconscious, he fell to the pavement, where he was kicked in the ribs by other members of the mob. Pushed under the rear bumper of the car, his battered and motionless body remained there until discovered by a reporter twenty-five minutes later.[5]

Somehow Wilbur and Hermann managed to escape their tormentors before being seriously injured. Others were less fortunate. The worst of the carnage was back on the loading platform, where Zwerg, Lewis, and several others found themselves cornered by the mob. The first Rider to be assaulted was Zwerg, who bowed his head in prayer as a group of attackers closed in. Attracting special attention as the only white male Rider, he was knocked to the pavement amid screams of "filthy Communists, nigger lovers, you're not going to integrate Montgomery!" According to Fred Leonard, who was standing only a few feet away when Zwerg went down: "It was like those people in the mob were possessed. They couldn't believe that there was a white man who would help us. . . . It's like they didn't see the rest of us for about thirty seconds. They didn't see us at all." As the other Riders looked on in horror, Claude Henley and several other Klansmen kicked Zwerg in the back before smashing him in the head with his own suitcase. Dazed and bleeding, Zwerg struggled to get up, but one of the Klansmen promptly pinned the defenseless student's arms back while others punched him repeatedly in the face. To Lucretia Collins, who witnessed the beating from the backseat of a departing taxicab, the savagery of Zwerg's attackers was sickening. "Some men held him while white women clawed his face with their nails," she recalled. "And they held up their little children—children who couldn't have been more than a couple years old—to claw his face. I had to turn my head because I just couldn't watch it." Eventually Zwerg's eyes rolled back and his body sagged into unconsciousness. After tossing him over a railing, his attackers went looking for other targets.

Turning to the black Freedom Riders huddled near the railing, several of the Klansmen rushed forward. The first victim in their path was William Barbee, the only Rider who had not traveled to Montgomery on the Greyhound. Sent ahead "to arrange for cars and other necessities," he was at the terminal to welcome his friends when the riot broke out. Standing next to his ABT classmates, Lewis and Lafayette, Barbee had only a moment to shield his face before the advancing Klansmen unleashed a flurry of punches and kicks that dropped him to the pavement. While one Klansman held him down, a second jammed a jagged piece of pipe into his ear, and a third bashed him in the skull with a baseball bat, inflicting permanent damage that shortened his life. Moments later, Lewis went down, struck by a large wooden Coca-Cola crate. "I could feel my knees collapse and then nothing," he recalled. "Everything turned white for an instant, then black." Lying unconscious on the pavement, he missed the drama that followed, as Leonard, Lafayette, and Cason escaped from the mob by jumping over the retaining wall and running into the post office, where, to their amazement, postal employees and customers were "carrying on their business, just like nothing was happening outside." As he ran through the mail-sorting room, Lafayette heard the sound of gunfire, which he feared was coming from the Klansmen on the loading platform. "I thought they were shooting Freedom Riders," he recalled years later. The shots actually came from the gun of Floyd Mann, who had arrived just in time to protect the three unconscious Freedom Riders from further injury.[6]

Unsure of Sullivan's commitment to protect the Riders, Mann had stationed a force of highway patrolmen a few blocks from the terminal. Although he had no jurisdiction inside the city limits, he was prepared to intervene if the Montgomery police abandoned their responsibility. What he was not prepared for, however, was the massive disorder that he encountered at the terminal. Arriving five minutes after the melee began, he wandered helplessly through the chaos until he reached the scene at the loading platform. Moments earlier, a local black man named Miles Davis had tried to rescue Barbee, but by the time Mann arrived both men were under attack. After trying but failing to pull several attackers off of Barbee, he instinctively pulled out his pistol, fired two warning shots, and shouted, "I'll shoot the next man who hits him. Stand back! There'll be no killing here today." To prove that he meant business, Mann then arrested one of the attackers, a Montgomery Klansman named Thurman Ouzts. This seemed to break the spell, and most of the rioters on the loading platform drifted away, though one man continued to attack James Atkins, a Birmingham television reporter, until Mann threatened to shoot him if he didn't stop.[7]

In other areas of the terminal, the rampage continued unabated for several minutes, much of it in full view of reporters, FBI agents, and other witnesses. Looking down from a third-floor window in the Federal Building, John Doar saw enough to make him heartsick. After witnessing the first part of the riot from the street, he had raced upstairs and placed a frantic call to Burke Marshall. "Oh, there are fists punching," the normally soft-spoken attorney shouted into the phone, "A bunch of men led by a guy with a bleeding face are beating them. There are no cops. It's terrible. . . . There's not a cop in sight. People are yelling 'Get 'em, get 'em. It's awful." For several minutes Doar provided Marshall with a running commentary, though he did not witness the attack on Seigenthaler.

Also watching from a nearby office building was Virginia Durr, the wife of liberal attorney Clifford Durr and the sister-in-law of U.S. Supreme Court Justice Hugo Black. A longtime radical activist with close ties to the Highlander Folk School and various voting rights organizations, Durr had been relegated to near pariah status since her open support of the bus boycott. In the wake of the Mother's Day riot in Birmingham, she had warned Marshall that the same thing could happen in Montgomery. "The Greyhound station is right across the street from our office," she wrote, "and it is full of hard faced, slouchy men waiting for them to 'come in.' I doubt if the police here will give them any protection either." Now, on Saturday morning, she saw her prediction come true, and to make matters worse, one of her closest friends, the British author Jessica Mitford, was somewhere down on the street and possibly caught in the melee. Eventually another friend, Bob Zellner—a white student activist at Montgomery's Huntingdon College who would become a Freedom Rider himself later in the year—retrieved an unharmed Mitford from the mob. But the whole scene left Durr shaken and despairing for the future of her city.[8]

Closer to the action on the street, Fred and Anna Gach, a local white couple with liberal views, tried to intervene on the Freedom Riders' behalf. This only seemed to inflame the mob. Later in the day, the Montgomery police arrested the Gaches for disorderly conduct. Eventually fined three hundred dollars by a city judge, they were among only a handful of persons arrested that Saturday, even though the police arrived in time to apprehend at least part of the mob. When Commissioner Sullivan and the police appeared on the scene, approximately ten minutes after the bus's arrival, the initial phase of the riot was still in progress. But there was no effort to detain or arrest anyone involved in the beatings. Nor was there any attempt to clear the area, even though the crowd continued to grow. Most of the officers simply stood by and watched as the rioters got in a few more licks. Indeed, according to several observers, the realization that the police were openly sympathetic actually emboldened some members of the crowd, turning gawkers into active rioters. "I saw whites and negroes beaten unmercifully while law officers calmly directed traffic," Tom Lankford of the *Birmingham News* reported, adding: "I was an eye-witness to the mob attack last Sunday on the so-called 'freedom riders' in Birmingham. But with all its terror, it didn't compare with this. . . . Saturday was hell in Montgomery."

Although the police were officially on hand to restore order, Sullivan's primary concern was clearly a reassertion of local authority. As soon as he learned that Mann was on the loading platform, he rushed over to take charge. To his dismay, however, he was soon upstaged by the arrival of several state and county officials, including Judge Walter Jones and Attorney General MacDonald Gallion. Walking over to Lewis, who was still lying half-conscious on the pavement, Gallion asked a deputy sheriff to read the injunction that Jones had issued earlier in the morning. The Freedom Riders, Lewis now learned, were outlaws in the state of Alabama.

That the Freedom Riders were also victims of vigilante violence did not seem to trouble Jones and Gallion, or the police officers nearby who made a point of fraternizing with members of the mob. Other than Mann, no one in a position of authority showed any interest in helping the injured Riders. Although Zwerg was bleeding profusely and passing in and out of consciousness, the police refused to call an ambulance. Convinced that Zwerg was near death, Lewis and Barbee, with the help of a reporter, carried the young divinity student over to an empty cab, but the white driver grabbed the keys and stormed off. Still sitting in the back seat but barely conscious, Zwerg soon attracted the attention of the deputy sheriff, who sauntered over to read

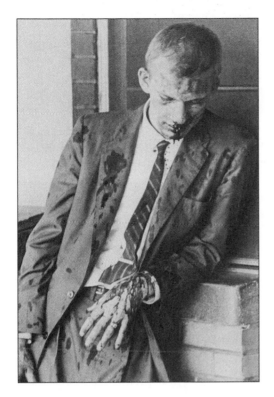

Freedom Rider Jim Zwerg after being attacked by Klansmen at the Montgomery Greyhound bus station, Saturday, May 20, 1961. (Bettmann-CORBIS)

Freedom Riders John Lewis and Jim Zwerg after they were beaten at the Montgomery Greyhound bus station, Saturday, May 20, 1961. (Library of Congress)

the injunction for a second time. A few minutes later, Lewis and Barbee found a black cabdriver willing to drive them to a doctor's office, but the police would not allow Zwerg to go with them, insisting that he would have to wait for a white ambulance. When reporters asked Sullivan why no such ambulance had appeared, he claimed that all of the city's white ambulances were in the repair shop. Eventually Mann intervened, ordering one of his young patrolmen, Tommy Giles, to transport Zwerg to St. Jude's Catholic Hospital by car. But Sullivan's intended message was unmistakable: The outside agitators, especially the "nigger loving" white ones, had gotten what they deserved.[9]

By the time Mann and Giles put Zwerg in the car, all of the other Riders had left the bus terminal, and most had found at least a temporary refuge. The five female Riders in the taxicab—all of whom witnessed the beatings of Zwerg, Lewis, and Barbee before leaving—found a phone booth a few blocks from the terminal and called Fred Shuttlesworth, who relayed their whereabouts to Diane Nash. Others called Nash directly, blurting out the shocking news of what had just happened, including the injunction that seemed to make them all fugitives. Fearing that all of the Riders were now subject to arrest, Nash advised them to stay out of sight and away from the police. Unfortunately, this plan had already been compromised by Wilbur and Hermann, who had called the police after fleeing from the terminal area. After retrieving them from a downtown church, police officers promptly made arrangements to send the two women back to Nashville by train. The rest of the Freedom Riders, however, got the word in time to lay low. When he heard about the Riders' plight, the Reverend Solomon S. Seay Sr., one of the heroes of the bus boycott, offered his home as a safe house, and by early afternoon the Riders began to gather there.[10]

Back at the terminal, the crowd hardly seemed to notice that the Freedom Riders were no longer there. With the police making only a token effort to restore order, several of the rioters gathered up the Riders' belongings and constructed a bonfire in the middle of the street. Others continued the attacks on newsmen and anyone else who looked like an outsider. Although the size of the crowd had swelled to several hundred, Sullivan and the handful of officers dispatched to the terminal seemed content to let the riot run its course with a minimum of interference. At 11:30 a disgusted Floyd Mann called in sixty-five highway patrolmen to the scene, and a few minutes later they were joined by several deputy sheriffs on horseback. But the city police did not respond in force until one o'clock, nearly three hours after the riot had begun. Sensing the reporters' disapproval, Sullivan belatedly ordered his men to make a few arrests and even authorized the use of tear gas to disperse the crowd. Nevertheless, sporadic violence continued for more than two hours as the mob broke up into small gangs that spread the mayhem into surrounding streets. Several parked cars were overturned and set ablaze, and less than a block from the terminal a band of whites assaulted two black bystanders—dousing one with kerosene and setting him on fire, and breaking the other's

Mounted deputy sheriffs arrive at the riot scene outside the Montgomery Grey-hound bus station at 11:45 A.M., more than an hour after the attack on the Freedom Riders, May 20, 1961. (Courtesy of the *Nashville Tennessean* and AP Wide World)

leg. Both survived, but their attackers avoided arrest or even passing notice from the police. By the time the rioting ended around four o'clock, twenty people had been seriously injured.

Once order was restored, Sullivan held an impromptu press conference in the terminal parking lot. "I really don't know what happened," he told the reporters. "When I got here, all I saw were three men lying in the street. There was two niggers and a white man." Obviously pleased with what had transpired, he made little effort to hide his disregard for the victims, though later in the day he became a bit more cautious as he and other city leaders began to worry about how all of this would play in the press. "We all sincerely regret that this happened here in Montgomery," he declared, insisting "it could have been avoided had outside agitators left us alone. . . . Providing police protection for agitators is not our policy, but we would have been ready if we had had definite and positive information they were coming." Federal and state officials would later put Sullivan on the defensive by disputing the claim that he had been unaware of the Freedom Riders' impending arrival. Indeed, many observers, including Judge Richard Rives, eventually concluded that Sullivan had followed the lead of Birmingham's Bull Connor. Several days after the beatings, Rives overheard a local Klansman praise Sullivan for cooperating with the mob. "Sully kept his word," the Klansman chortled. "He said he'd give us half an hour to beat up those God-damned sons of bitches and he did." Even John Patterson, in a 1988 interview, acknowledged that he was fairly certain that Sullivan "had let the Klan know that he'd give them a few minutes to work on the riders a little bit."

Some members of the press suspected as much from the outset, but in the absence of hard evidence of complicity most were content, for the time being at least, to focus on the most sensational episode of the day—the attack on John Seigenthaler. At first Sullivan himself paid little attention to the news that a man claiming to be a personal representative of the president had been beaten by the mob, but the apparent seriousness of Seigenthaler's injuries and the rumor that Sullivan had initially refused to call an ambulance for the stricken federal official made the incident an unavoidable issue by late Saturday afternoon. Following a brief conversation with a police lieutenant, Seigenthaler had lapsed back into unconsciousness before being rushed to a local hospital. Listed in serious condition, he later woke up in an X-ray room as his doctor talked to a stunned Byron White on the phone. Seigenthaler had a fractured skull and several broken ribs, the doctor told White, but with a little luck he would make a full recovery. To prove his point, the doctor then handed the phone to Seigenthaler, who managed to say a few words before drifting off to sleep. Relieved, White assured his groggy colleague that the attorney general already had been apprised of the situation.[11]

Before calling the hospital, White had tracked Robert Kennedy down at an FBI baseball game. Visibly shaken by White's sketchy but graphic report of the riot, Kennedy called an emergency meeting of his senior staff. By late Saturday afternoon he was cloistered with White, Marshall, and several others who were still trying to determine exactly what had happened. When it became clear that the Montgomery police had done little or nothing to protect the Freedom Riders or anybody else who got in the mob's way, Kennedy called John Patterson for an explanation. Patterson, who had not spoken to Kennedy since Thursday evening, dodged the call. For Kennedy this was the final straw. No governor could be allowed to thumb his nose at the federal government while countenancing the wanton disruption of civil order. The force of federal marshals that he and his brother had hoped would never be used, he now realized, was the only available deterrent to continued disorder and disrespect.

After a brief conversation with his brother, who was away on a weekend retreat, the attorney general ordered Marshall and White to activate the mobilization plan. Declaring that he wanted the marshals on the ground in Alabama within twenty-four hours, he asked White to assume operational command of the force and Marshall to handle the legal side of the operation through John Doar. Within minutes Marshall was on the phone with Doar finalizing the language of a proposed federal court injunction prohibiting the Klan and the National States Rights Party from interfering with interstate transit. And within an hour, James McShane, the head of the U.S. Marshal Service, and twenty of his deputies were on their way to National Airport to catch a flight to Montgomery. Other marshals from the various parts of the South and Midwest soon followed, and by midnight more than a hundred had arrived at Montgomery's Maxwell Air Force Base, two miles from the site of the riot.

As the preparations began to take shape on Saturday afternoon, Robert Kennedy called Seigenthaler's hospital room and was pleased to discover that the patient was doing better than expected, despite "a terrible headache." When Kennedy informed him that the marshals were on the way, Seigenthaler expressed regret and apologized for his inability to defuse the crisis. Kennedy assured him that it was not his fault. The federal-state showdown was bound to happen "sooner or later," the attorney general insisted, adding: "Don't feel bad about it, it's just what you had to do, and I'm glad you're alright." Before hanging up, Seigenthaler thanked Kennedy for his understanding, though he couldn't resist offering a few parting words of advice: "Don't run for governor of Alabama; you're not too popular down here." A few minutes later, an unexpected visit from a tearful Floyd Mann reminded Seigenthaler that not all white Alabamians were Kennedy haters. But the hard truth of his quip seemed unassailable as the most harrowing afternoon of his life came to a close.[12]

ROBERT KENNEDY did not like the idea of alienating the voters of a state that had just given his brother five electoral votes, but he was running out of patience—and options. Though politically expedient, relying on state and local officials to preserve civic order was proving too risky. While Kennedy planned to do everything he could to minimize the political damage, he now saw no alternative to a show of federal force in Alabama. With the summit in Vienna less than two weeks away, he simply could not allow the image and moral authority of the United States to be undercut by a mob of racist vigilantes, or, for that matter, by a band of headstrong students determined to provoke them. Like it or not, he had to do something dramatic to bring the Freedom Rider crisis to a close. The decision to send in the marshals was also personal. As several administration insiders later acknowledged, the Kennedy brothers were furious at Patterson. Either out of incompetence or in outright connivance—and the Kennedys suspected the latter—he had presided over a needless escalation of violence that included a shameless attack on federal authority. Allowing a gang of white supremacist roughnecks to beat up a bunch of kids in front of the press was bad enough. Standing by while a personal representative of the president of the United States was assaulted in the street was unforgivable.

Neither the attorney general nor the president would ever trust Patterson again, but by late Saturday afternoon both men had worked through enough of their anger to draft carefully worded public statements outlining the federal government's response to the Montgomery riot. Realizing that the national wire services and radio and television networks were bound to treat a riot that included attacks on newsmen and a presidential envoy as a major news story, the Kennedys hoped to preempt what they feared would be an alarmist press response. The president's brief statement, released directly to the press, conveyed a mixture of concern and reassurance and implicitly criticized Alabama officials as well as the Freedom Riders:

> The situation which has developed in Alabama is a source of the deepest concern to me as it must be to the vast majority of the citizens of Alabama and all America. I have instructed the Justice Department to take all necessary steps based on their investigation and information. I call upon the Governor and other responsible state officials in Alabama as well as the Mayors of Birmingham and Montgomery to exercise their lawful authority to prevent any further outbreaks of violence. I would also hope that any person, whether a citizen of Alabama, or a visitor there, would refrain from any action which would in any way tend to provoke further outbreaks. I hope that state and local officials will meet their responsibilities. The United States Government intends to meet its.

Longer and more explicit than his brother's effort, the attorney general's statement took the form of a personal telegram to Patterson, the text of which was immediately released to the press. Robert Kennedy wanted the world to know the exact circumstances that had prompted the decision to send a federal peacekeeping force to Alabama: the failure of state and local officials to live up to the agreement worked out by Seigenthaler and Mann on Friday evening; the repeated and largely futile attempts to communicate directly with the governor by phone; the unexpected and inexcusable absence of police protection at the Montgomery terminal; the "severe beating" of "several of the travelers"; and the unwarranted attack on the "President's personal representative, Mr. Seigenthaler, who attempted to rescue a young white girl." According to Kennedy, Patterson had assured "the President and the Federal Government" that state and local officials had the "will, the force, the men, and the equipment to protect everyone in Alabama." Through Seigenthaler, the federal government had offered "to provide marshals and any other assistance in order to assure that interstate commerce was unimpeded." But the governor had rejected the offer of help, insisting that "local authorities would be completely able to handle any contingency." "It was based on this assurance of safe conduct," the telegram continued, "that the students boarded the bus in Birmingham on their trip to Montgomery." Indeed, the Justice Department had taken "the additional precautionary step of having the F.B.I. notify the Police Department that these students were coming and ask the police to take all necessary steps for their protection. The F.B.I. was informed and in turn notified us that all necessary steps had been taken and that no action on our part was necessary." That the riot ensued nonetheless was proof that the federal government now had "no alternative but to order . . . United States officers to begin to assist state and local authorities in the protection of persons and property and vehicles in Alabama." The telegram also informed Patterson that the Justice Department planned to send a team of FBI investigators to Montgomery and to seek an injunction against the Klan and any other groups "interfering with interstate travel by buses."[13]

As it turned out, Kennedy received a call from Patterson a few minutes before the telegram was actually sent. After being assured that "everything seemed to be under control in Alabama," Kennedy read the text of the telegram over the phone. Caught off guard by the announcement that federal intervention was imminent, Patterson insisted that Alabama needed no "outside help," prompting Kennedy to ask him to prove it. "Why don't you call out the National Guard and make it unnecessary for us to take any outside action?" Kennedy asked. Alarmed by this suggestion, Patterson stammered: "This is unnecessary. This will be a matter of embarrassment to me. I will have to take steps to defend myself politically." Kennedy responded, with some sympathy, that he understood the political constraints of Alabama politics, but he added that the Justice Department could not allow political considerations to interfere with a timely resolution of the crisis. "You are going to have to paddle your own boat," he warned.[14]

Later in the evening, Patterson issued a public response to Kennedy's telegram. After claiming that he had "no sympathy for lawbreakers whether they be agitators from outside Alabama or inside-the-state troublemakers," he stated that Alabama law enforcement officials needed "no help—from the Federal Government, from 'interested citizens,' or anyone else." He then went on to qualify his pledge of protection. "While we will do our utmost to keep the public highways clear and to guard against all disorder," he declared, "we cannot escort bus loads or carloads of rabble rousers about our state from city to city for the avowed purpose of disobeying our laws, flouting our customs and traditions, and creating racial incidents. Such unlawful acts serve only to further enrage our populace. I have no use for these agitators or their kind." While acknowledging that Alabama officials had "the duty and the desire to protect human lives no matter who is involved," he insisted that "how we do it is a matter for us to determine."[15]

The full text of the statements, detailed accounts of the riot, and graphic pictures of injured newsmen and Freedom Riders appeared in newspapers across the nation on Sunday morning. What did not appear, however, was any hint of the behind-the-scenes drama being played out among movement activists in Montgomery, Nashville, Atlanta, New Orleans, and Washington. For the Freedom Riders themselves, the biggest story of May 20 was the unreported transformation of a limited project into a full-fledged movement. The seeds of this transformation had been planted the previous Tuesday when the Nashville students had stepped in for the CORE Riders, but it was not until Saturday afternoon that a true movement culture began to take hold among the Riders.

As the survivors of the riot gathered at the Reverend Seay's house, the scene began to resemble a religious revival. Far from scaring the Riders off, the riot seemed to have forged a renewed sense of common purpose and solidarity. Surviving a trial by fire had somehow dispelled the mystique of massive resistance, and despite fears of future violence, as well as concern for those who had already been injured, the importance of sustaining the Freedom Ride was clearer than ever. The presence of John Lewis and other bandaged martyrs only served to reinforce the growing realization that the stakes had been raised and that there could be no turning back in the face of danger. Indeed, even for the Riders who missed the movement revival at Seay's house, the necessity of carrying on was becoming an article of faith. Speaking from his hospital bed at St. Jude's, Jim Zwerg assured reporters that "these beatings cannot deter us from our purpose. We are not martyrs or publicity-seekers. We want only equality and justice, and we will get it. We will continue our journey one way or another. We are prepared to die. " Lying one floor below, in St. Jude's black ward, William Barbee echoed Zwerg's pledge: "As soon as we're recovered from this, we'll start again. . . . We'll take all the South has to throw and still come back for more."[16]

This collective resurrection of the spirit sprang from many sources, some intensely personal, others largely contextual, but no element of the Freedom Riders' resolve was more important than the network of support sustained by Nash and the movement volunteers back in Nashville. In the critical hours following the riot, the Nashville office was a beehive of activity, dispensing words of comfort and encouragement to the Riders and mobilizing a broad coalition of supporters. Delivered in a flurry of phone calls, Nash's message to the national civil rights community was unequivocal: The movement could not afford a second failed Freedom Ride. If the white supremacist vigilantes and irresponsible officials in Alabama got their way, the entire movement would lose momentum and credibility. Surely it was time for movement leaders to put aside whatever reservations they had about the wisdom of the Freedom Ride and rally behind the students in Montgomery.

By late afternoon Nash's personal appeals had brought several key organizations and individuals on board. In Nashville, Jim Lawson promptly volunteered to go to Montgomery to join the Ride, as did Nash herself. In Birmingham, Shuttlesworth, who had tried to join the Ride earlier in the day, also agreed to travel to Montgomery to help the students regroup. In Atlanta, Ella Baker and other SNCC leaders promised to recruit a new batch of Freedom Riders if needed; and in Washington, NAG, the SNCC affiliate that had contributed Hank Thomas to the original CORE Ride, made a similar pledge. Indeed, several NAG stalwarts, including John Moody and Paul Dietrich, were already on their way to Alabama. Remorseful about his earlier recalcitrance, Moody was determined to be in the thick of things this time. Thomas himself was in New York recovering from his injuries, but as soon as he heard the news reports of the Saturday morning riot, he too made plans to fly to Montgomery.

All of this support was welcome, but Nash knew that none of it would matter if she failed to enlist the Southern Christian Leadership Conference and King in the cause. To this point, King and his advisors had been wary of supporting the second Freedom Ride, as the May 17 SCLC meeting at Shuttlesworth's parsonage had revealed. Thus she was greatly relieved to discover that King agreed with her assessment of the seriousness of the situation. The SCLC president was in Chicago to deliver a speech, but after conferring with Nash, Abernathy, and Walker he decided to cancel his engagement and return to Atlanta. By late Saturday afternoon Nash and the three SCLC leaders had worked out a plan to hold a mass meeting at Abernathy's church in Montgomery on Sunday evening. King, who had been in Montgomery as recently as May 11, would fly in to deliver the keynote address, and other movement leaders, including Shuttlesworth, would also speak. The purpose of the mass meeting was simple. By presenting a show of solidarity and commitment, the nonviolent movement would seize the initiative, demonstrating that it could not be intimidated by segregationist hooligans. Other, more difficult matters—such as the advisability of mobilizing a whole wave of Freedom Rides—could be decided later. But the message that the Nashville students were not alone had to be delivered immediately and forcefully.[17]

Realizing that SCLC's approach to nonviolent direct action was more cautious than SNCC's, Nash had some misgivings about bringing King to Montgomery. Indeed, using his prestige and celebrity to shore up the Freedom Ride was hardly in keeping with SNCC's or the Nashville student movement's democratic ethos. She could only hope that King and other SCLC leaders would come to see the wisdom of SNCC's grassroots philosophy instead of trying to co-opt the students' energies. To some extent, she faced the same problem with Jim Farmer and CORE. When she called Farmer to enlist his support and cooperation, he too promised to fly to Montgomery, adding that he would immediately dispatch additional CORE Riders to Alabama, but, as she suspected, his motives involved more than concern for the future of the Freedom Ride. "Quite frankly," Farmer acknowledged in his autobiography, "although I welcomed the intervention of SNCC, a concern burned within me. I could not let CORE's new program slip from its grasp and be taken over by others." Consequently, he wasted no time in ordering his staff to "recruit, train, and send to Montgomery a contingent of young CORE members from New Orleans." Much of Farmer's competitive drive was, of course, directed at King. Still smarting from the SCLC leader's usurpation of the nonviolent movement during the bus boycott, Farmer was determined to share the spotlight in Montgomery.[18]

Farmer was not the only person perplexed by King's decision to interject himself into the Montgomery crisis. At the Justice Department, Robert Kennedy nearly exploded when he received word that King had agreed to lead a rally at First Baptist. The decision to send in the marshals was risky enough, but King's involvement presented Kennedy with a nightmare scenario. Already the subject of intense news coverage, the Montgomery situation would become a media circus if King were allowed to take center stage. Considering the probable threat to King's safety, the federal government would have no choice but to offer him protection, a development that was bound to add fuel to the fire of massive resistance. In an effort to forestall this escalation of the crisis, Kennedy called King in Chicago to plead with him to stay away from Montgomery. To Kennedy's dismay, King refused to change his plans. After a follow-up call from Burke Marshall produced similar results, Kennedy, in desperation, turned to Seigenthaler for help, hoping that a plea from his injured assistant might change King's mind. Kennedy arranged for Seigenthaler to make the call, but before Seigenthaler actually talked to King, Kennedy called back to say it was no use. The SCLC leader had made it clear that nothing could dissuade him from appearing at the rally.

The near certainty that King was coming to Montgomery erased any doubts at the Justice Department about the wisdom of mobilizing a force of federal marshals. Convinced that the crisis was deepening, Kennedy summoned his staff, set up a round-the-clock command center in his office, and established an open phone line to his brother's weekend retreat at Glen Ora, Virginia. While the Kennedys and other administration officials still held out some hope that state authorities—perhaps with the help of the National Guard—could keep things in hand, King's involvement dramatically increased the likelihood that the marshals would actually be used. Even if no actual rioting ensued, marshals would still be needed to escort King to and from the church—an unwelcome development that would provide Alabama segregationists with a convenient symbol of federal encroachment. All of this weighed heavily on Robert Kennedy's staff as they proceeded with the mobilization of the marshals. But by early Saturday evening there was no turning back. White, Oberdorfer, and several other Justice Department officials had already boarded a plane to Montgomery provided by Najeeb Halaby, the head of the Federal Aviation Administration and White and Oberdorfer's former classmate at Yale Law School.

Arriving at Maxwell Air Force Base at eight o'clock, White and his staff set up headquarters in a vacant Quonset hut that soon became a processing center for hundreds of newly deputized marshals. McShane and other experienced marshals from the District of Columbia, who had arrived earlier in the day, provided a core of professionalism, but White soon discovered that most of his makeshift civilian army was a motley assortment of revenue agents, prison guards, and border patrolmen. As Marshall later acknowledged, "the border patrol were the only ones that could shoot. . . . Most of them," he admitted, "were the product of senatorial patronage, middle-aged, fat, le-thargic people with no law enforcement experience. Many of them came from the South and really thought they were being asked to protect black people whom they considered Communists, or worse. We weren't sure which side they would be on." White himself, of course, was no general, though he had served in the navy during World War II. His sense of command stemmed primarily from his years as an All-American football star at the University of Colorado, where he had earned the nickname "Whizzer." Renowned for his bulldog demeanor, he was a self-professed political realist who, as head of Citizens for Kennedy during the 1960 campaign, had counseled against ide-alistic involvement in civil rights matters. He was also politically ambitious. On the flight down, he and Oberdorfer had speculated about the likely po-litical fallout from their mission to Montgomery, wondering aloud whether the expected ire of Southern conservatives would doom his chances of mov-ing up the ladder at the Justice Department. White's own conservatism was one of the reasons why Robert Kennedy had entrusted him with command of the marshals, but whether he could survive the counter-pressures of duty and practical politics remained to be seen.[19]

Across town John Doar faced pressure of a different kind. While White and Oberdorfer were busy assembling their peacekeeping force, Doar was running out of time in his efforts to secure a temporary restraining order against the Klan and other groups determined to break the peace. Although he was confident that Judge Frank Johnson would sign the order, Doar had to find him first. Johnson, as it turned out, was spending the weekend at his summer cottage fifty miles north of Montgomery. Fortunately, Lee Dodd, a lifelong friend of Johnson's who also served as his marshal, agreed to guide Doar to the cottage. After driving through the Alabama woods and crossing a small lake by boat, Doar and Dodd finally reached Johnson's cottage a few minutes after midnight. As expected, the judge promptly granted the restrain-ing order, though he surprised Doar by limiting the order's scope to the alleged perpetrators of the Montgomery riot. For the time being, the Klans-men responsible for the previous week's violence in Birmingham were off the hook. Though disappointed, Doar realized that granting even a limited order was an act of courage for an Alabama judge. Accordingly, as soon as he returned to Montgomery he quietly arranged for a band of federal marshals to protect Johnson's life.[20]

Along with the marshals' arrival, the granting of the temporary restrain-ing order set the stage for a dramatic political showdown between state and federal authorities. By Sunday morning Governor Patterson, who seemed to relish his new role as the South's leading defender of states' rights, was fulmi-nating against Washington's unwarranted invasion of Alabama. Pushed into a dangerous but politically promising corner, he demanded a meeting with White in full view of the press. When White arrived at the capitol, the governor was flanked by the entire Alabama cabinet and a gaggle of reporters. Wasting no time, Patterson immediately took the offensive. "We consider you interlopers here," he declared, "and we feel that your presence here will only serve to agitate and provoke the racial situation. We don't need your marshals, we don't want them, and we didn't ask for them. And still the Federal Government sends them here to help put down a disturbance which it helped create." Declining to take the bait, White remained calm. But Patterson refused to let up, warning White that the federal marshals risked arrest if they challenged state sovereignty. "Make especially certain," he counseled, "that none of your men encroach on any of our state laws, rights or functions, because we'll arrest them just like anybody else." Patterson went on to grill White about the motives and location of the Freedom Riders, who he claimed were Communist-inspired agitators. After denying that there was any evidence of Communist infiltration into the Freedom Rider movement, White bravely added that "no matter what this group's connection may be, if any, that is no reason why they shouldn't be assured of the right to travel peacefully by bus." Undeterred, Patterson demanded to know if federal marshals were willing to help state authorities enforce Judge Jones's injunction against outside agitators. Caught off guard, White pleaded ignorance of the injunction—and of the Freedom Riders' exact whereabouts. No, he would not arrest the

Deputy Attorney General Byron "Whizzer" White (seated on left) discusses the Freedom Rider crisis with Governor John Patterson (seated at the head of the table) and his cabinet at the Alabama State Capitol in Montgomery, Sunday, May 21, 1961. (Getty Photos)

Freedom Riders or even help state authorities to apprehend them. Satisfied with this admission, Patterson allowed the forty-five-minute ordeal to end. The political battle lines had been drawn, though neither side was quite sure how far the other was willing to go to make its point.

Deeply discouraged by his meeting with Patterson, White took the risky step of bypassing the chain of command with a late-morning call to the White House. Although the attorney general was his immediate superior, he felt more comfortable speaking directly with the president, whom he had known since their navy days in the Pacific. The marshals' presence in Alabama seemed to be making matters worse, he told John Kennedy, adding that it might be prudent to have them withdrawn. Wisely, Kennedy sidestepped White's suggestion with a gentle admonition and a plea for fortitude. But White's momentary crisis of confidence would later prove embarrassing when word of the proposed withdrawal reached Patterson via an eavesdropping telephone operator.[21]

After assuring the president that he would do his best, White steeled his nerves and turned his attention to the crisis of the moment. A plane carrying Martin Luther King was scheduled to arrive around noon, and White had dispatched an armed guard of fifty marshals to the Montgomery airport to make sure that no one got hurt. Fortunately, the scene at the airport was quiet, and the marshals safely escorted King to a brief private meeting with Nash, Lewis, and Lafayette at an outlying black church before proceeding on to Abernathy's downtown parsonage. Later in the afternoon twelve of the marshals returned to the airport to provide an escort for Shuttlesworth, who soon joined the Freedom Riders who had gathered in the basement library at First Baptist, where they were hiding as fugitives from the injunction issued by Judge Jones. Zwerg and Barbee were still in the hospital, and Wilbur and Hermann were already back in Nashville, but the rest were on hand to welcome a procession of rallying friends and allies that included Shuttlesworth, Nash, Walker, Len Holt, and NAG volunteers Paul Dietrich and John Moody. The reunion with Nash was especially emotional. For nearly a week she had been physically removed from the action in Alabama, trying to maintain a steady hand without actually confronting what she and the Freedom Riders were up against. Now she was in the thick of things, trying to comprehend the drama that was unfolding before her.[22]

ALTHOUGH THE MASS MEETING was scheduled to begin at eight o'clock, the faithful began to arrive at First Baptist as early as five. At that point only a few protesters were in sight of the church, and the early-comers had no trouble making their way to the sanctuary. Outside, a dozen marshals wearing yellow armbands stood quietly by, warily observing the surrounding streets. Then, and for several hours thereafter, the only other law enforcement officers present were a handful of FBI agents and two plainclothes state detectives sent to monitor the situation. Indeed, the most striking aspect of the scene

was who was not there. Throughout the day local radio stations had broadcast "the news that Negroes would hold a mass meeting that night at the
First Baptist Church," virtually ensuring that a large crowd of white protesters would eventually descend upon the church; and "all day long," according
to one observer, "carloads of grim-faced whites converged on Montgomery." Yet there were no city policemen, no uniformed highway patrolmen,
and no National Guardsmen on the scene. As events would soon prove, this
was a formula for mob violence. At the time, though, authorities on all sides
seemed determined to play a dangerous guessing game of holding back and
waiting for their counterparts to make the first move. Sullivan and the police
wanted nothing to do with protecting the Freedom Riders, and among state
officials only Mann showed any inclination to accept responsibility for keeping the peace—and even he wasn't much help, hamstrung as he was by
Patterson's stubborn determination to extract as much political capital out of
the affair as possible.

Despite all the rhetoric of the past twenty-four hours, federal authorities
in Washington and at Maxwell Field were also reticent to do anything beyond the minimum effort needed to forestall disaster. Even as dusk approached
and the crowd outside the church swelled to two thousand and beyond, Justice Department officials stuck to the plan of waiting for Patterson's call for
assistance. Unless the situation got completely out of hand, they would not
reinforce the small band of marshals at the scene until officially asked to do
so. This hesitancy to act reflected political sensitivity to Patterson's charges
of federal encroachment, but more than politics was involved. The scene at
Maxwell Field on Saturday afternoon bordered on chaos as White and his
staff readied the marshals for duty. Although William Orrick, an assistant
attorney general with some military experience, did his best to organize the
nearly four hundred marshals into workable units, severe organizational and
logistical problems persisted. Not only did properly arming the marshals prove
to be a challenge, but for a time the marshals even lacked a means of getting
downtown. When local army officials unexpectedly refused to allow the marshals to use military trucks, White and Orrick had no choice but to comman-
deer an assortment of air force vehicles and mail trucks borrowed from the
Montgomery post office. By nightfall both the marshals and the trucks were
more or less ready for action, though White still held out some hope that
they would not be needed.[23]

Despite the sense of foreboding that dominated the marshals' periodic
reports, so far the crowd outside First Baptist had limited its protests to name-
calling and occasional jostling. By eight o'clock fifteen hundred people were
inside the sanctuary, and the rising sound of hymns and amens signaled the
beginning of the program. The vast majority of the crowd inside the church
was black—the only whites being news reporters and television cameramen,
plus a few white liberals such as Jessica Mitford. Many of those present were
veterans of the mass meetings that had sustained the bus boycott five years

earlier, but nothing quite like this had been seen in Montgomery for a long time. With King still downstairs polishing the speech that he had written on the plane, the Reverend Seay opened the program with a description of how the Freedom Riders, who had gathered at his home to restore their energies for the coming struggle, had inspired him with their courage. The Freedom Riders were in the sanctuary, he told the crowd, but he did not dare introduce them because an unjust law had made them fugitives. The only "Freedom Rider" that he could safely identify was Diane Nash, who had been given a seat of honor near the front of the church. Eventually, without naming names, he asked a couple of the Riders to make a brief statement, but the fear of arrest kept them in the background for most of the evening. As an extra precaution, all of the Riders were dressed in choir robes to make them more difficult to identify.

While Seay presided over the emotional opening of the mass meeting, a drama of a different sort was developing downstairs, where a conclave of ministers—including King and Abernathy—was growing increasingly concerned about the size and mood of the crowd outside. The last few parishioners who had straggled into the church had encountered screamed epithets and a shower of rocks, and some protesters were beginning to smash the windows of cars parked along Ripley Street. Even more alarming to King was the rumor that a group of armed black taxicab drivers was planning to confront the white protesters. No one had been hurt, and so far the cabdrivers had kept their distance from the mob, but the situation was serious enough to prompt King to venture outside to see for himself. Ignoring the strong objections of his aides, he and a few volunteers spent several minutes circling the church and eyeing the crowd across the street. At first the protesters seemed stunned by the scouting party's audacity, but eventually someone recognized the famous Atlanta preacher and began screaming, "Nigger King!" Before long, rocks and other missiles were being thrown in King's direction—including a metal canister that one of his aides feared was a bomb. As the aide tossed aside what turned out to be an empty tear gas canister, King and the others scurried back inside the church.[24]

A few minutes later Shuttlesworth had his own brush with the mob. Earlier in the evening, before the crowd had grown unruly, he had volunteered to pick up Farmer at the airport. Now, as he and Farmer approached the church, the scene was much more menacing. Surrounded by a group of angry whites who began to rock their car, the two men fled on foot through a nearby cemetery. Before reaching the church, they encountered an even larger mass of protesters. To Farmer's amazement, Shuttlesworth simply plowed through them, screaming, "Out of the way! Come on! Let him through! Out of the way!"—as if he were escorting a visiting dignitary. With Shuttlesworth waving his arms wildly above his head, the protesters in front of him stepped aside just long enough to allow the two civil rights leaders to make it to the church's basement door. "That Shuttlesworth, who's just a little fellow, was either insane or the most courageous man I've ever met," Farmer recalled with a chuckle years later. "I tried to hide behind him, but I didn't fit. Fortunately, those people didn't know who I was. Shuttlesworth just walked through them, cool as a cucumber."

Once inside, Farmer and Shuttlesworth were taken upstairs to the sanctuary, where King introduced the CORE leader to a congregation that was growing increasingly concerned about what was going on outside. Following his encounter with the tear gas canister, King had tried to reassure the men, women, and children inside the church that the marshals had everything under control; and now the safe arrival of Shuttlesworth and Farmer served as proof that all was well. As Farmer embraced Lewis, whom he had grown fond of during the first week of the original Freedom Ride, and Nash, whom he had never met, a rush of amens filled the sanctuary. Farmer then stepped to the pulpit for a few salutary words before retiring to the basement to join King, Abernathy, and the other movement leaders, who were busily assessing the situation.[25]

It was now a few minutes past eight, and the crisis of the moment was an overturned car. The car, it was later discovered, was an ancient Buick that the Durrs had loaned to Jessica Mitford. Ignoring Virginia Durr's advice to park no closer than "three or four blocks," Mitford had left the car directly in front of the church. As King and others watched through a half-open window,

Ministers and other civil rights leaders address the Freedom Rider rally at the besieged First Baptist Church in Montgomery, Sunday evening, May 21, 1961. The Reverend Martin Luther King Jr. is standing in the center of the group at the pulpit. Jim Farmer is the figure on the far right of the pulpit. (Getty Photos)

the crowd torched the car's gas tank, causing an explosion that seemed to signal an assault on the church itself. Up to this point, the marshals had managed to keep the protesters off of church property and on the far side of Ripley Street, but now the mob was closing in amid screams of "Let's clean the niggers out of here!" Regrouping along the near side of Ripley Street, the marshals, with the encouragement of Mann's two detectives, used their nightsticks to keep the mob at bay. But, as they soon informed White by radio, it was only a matter of time before the thin shield of marshals was pushed aside. White immediately relayed this alarming message to Robert Kennedy, who reluctantly gave the go-ahead for the deployment of the nearly four hundred marshals at Maxwell Field. Within minutes McShane, an ex–New York cop who had served as John Kennedy's bodyguard and chauffeur during the 1960 campaign, was back on the road, this time leading a convoy of postal trucks and air force vehicles toward First Baptist. With the marshals jammed in the back and with black drivers at the wheel of several of the red, white, and blue postal trucks, the convoy made for a strange sight as it careened through the streets of west Montgomery. Not since the Reconstruction era of the 1870s had Montgomerians seen anything quite like this.[26]

While McShane and the reinforcements were en route, the situation outside the church grew increasingly ominous. As rocks, bricks, and Molotov cocktails rained down on the church grounds, the hopelessly outnumbered marshals—led by William Behen, a revenue agent from Florida—bought a few minutes of time by firing several rounds of tear gas into the crowd of protesters, some of whom waved Confederate flags in defiance. With each round the crowd fell back for a moment, only to advance again as soon as the air cleared. Inside the church, the Reverend Seay led the congregation through several rousing choruses of "Love Lifted Me" in a spirited attempt to stem a full-scale panic. "I want to hear everybody sing," Seay roared from the pulpit, "and mean every word of it." Sing they did, but the stanzas of faith and hope did not stop them from preparing to defend themselves and their families. Anticipating trouble, many of the men—and some of the women—had come to the church armed with knives and pistols, and there was little doubt that they would use them against the white mob if necessary. "We riders were nonviolent, steeped and trained in the teachings of Gandhi," Lewis later explained, "but most of the people of Montgomery were not."[27]

All of this, plus the news that some members of the mob had broken through the line of marshals and were banging on the church door, prompted King to ask Wyatt Tee Walker to call Robert Kennedy in Washington. Seconds earlier Kennedy had received an ominous report from White, who had been monitoring the assault via an open radio line, so he was not surprised when Walker, and then King, described the situation as desperate. Dispensing with formalities, Kennedy immediately assured King that a large contingent of marshals was on its way. After Walker and Abernathy rushed upstairs to deliver the good news, King pressed Kennedy for details. Unsure of the

Freedom Rider supporters choke on tear gas as they step outside the First Baptist Church in Montgomery, Sunday evening, May 21, 1961. The man standing nearest the right-hand door is CORE attorney Len Holt. (Bettmann-CORBIS)

marshals' exact location, Kennedy responded that they would be there soon. When King pressed him again a few seconds later, Kennedy tried to change the subject. Wasn't it time to call off or at least postpone the Freedom Ride? he asked. Would the Freedom Riders agree to some sort of "cooling-off period" that would give federal and state authorities the opportunity to work out a solution? Not quire sure how to respond to this request, King explained that he could not speak for the Freedom Riders; he would, however, broach the idea with Jim Farmer and Diane Nash. Satisfied that he had at least planted the idea of a cooling-off period, Kennedy tried to ease the tension with a nervous quip: "As long as you're in church, Reverend King, and our men are down there, you might as well say a prayer for us." Unimpressed with this strained attempt at gallows humor, King respectfully reminded Kennedy that the mob was closing in. If the marshals "don't get here immediately," King exclaimed, "we're going to have a bloody confrontation." Fortunately, the marshals' arrival soon brought what was becoming an awkward conversation to a close. Before signing off, a greatly relieved King thanked Kennedy for his intervention and promised to call back as soon as the crisis had subsided. They would not talk again until 12:10 A.M. Montgomery time, three long hours later.[28]

Before making his way upstairs, King quickly briefed Abernathy, Nash, and Farmer on the essentials of his conversation with Kennedy. Turning first to Farmer, the organizer of the original Freedom Ride, King relayed the suggestion about the cooling-off period. Though obviously pleased to be consulted, Farmer did not think much of Kennedy's suggestion. "I won't stop it now," he replied. "If I do, we'll just get words and promises." After King hinted that he was inclined to agree with the attorney general's conclusion that "the Freedom Ride has already made its point and now should be called off," Farmer asked Nash what she thought of the idea. "No," she responded, with a flash of irritation. "The Nashville Student Movement wants to go on. We can't stop it now right after we've been clobbered." Buoyed by her certainty, Farmer gave King a definitive answer. "Please tell the attorney general that we've been cooling off for 350 years," he declared in a voice loud enough to be heard throughout the basement. "If we cool off any more, we will be in a deep freeze. The Freedom Ride will go on." Nash was relieved when King agreed to deliver the message, but as the group of leaders walked upstairs to see what was happening, she couldn't help wondering what might have happened if the decision had been left to the great men of the movement. In the days ahead, she and other members of the Nashville Movement would have to keep vigilant watch over their nervous elders, or so she feared.[29]

King and his colleagues had no idea how many marshals had been dispatched, but as they peered out the church windows, the situation seemed to be improving. After pushing part of the mob back with their nightsticks, the marshals lobbed a massive round of tear gas that momentarily cleared the church grounds. Unfortunately, the retreat proved to be short-lived, and several members of the mob were soon back pounding on the church's front door. To make matters worse, the besieged congregation had to contend with a cloud of tear gas that had drifted into the sanctuary. The marshals, most without gas masks, also found themselves gasping for air. Forced to withdraw from the area in front of the church, they temporarily lost whatever tactical advantage they might have enjoyed. Suddenly an aroused vanguard of protesters was on the verge of breaking into the front of the church. Cutting through the church basement, a rescue squad of marshals managed to block the intruders with nightsticks and an additional round of tear gas, but not before one of the rioters shattered a large stained-glass window with a brick. The brick also struck the forehead of an elderly parishioner, who was soon being attended by several nurses. Most of the congregation, however, sought refuge on the sanctuary floor. At Seay's urgent request, the children were evacuated to the basement, just in time to escape a volley of rocks that broke several windows. Before long, however, no one in the church, not even those in the basement, could avoid the sickening fumes of the tear gas that had seeped through the building's exterior. Despite the marshals' good intentions, the rescue was turning into a fiasco.

Even so, there was no wholesale panic in the church. Over the next thirty minutes, as the outnumbered marshals struggled to keep the mob at bay, the besieged parishioners at First Baptist continued to tap an inner strength that defied the logic of their precarious position. Even in the face of tear gas and surging rioters, freedom songs reverberated through the sanctuary. Earlier the mood had dictated the singing of traditional hymns of hope and praise, But now the hymns were interspersed with the "music of the movement"—songs such as "Ain't Gonna Let Nobody Turn Me 'Round" and "We Shall Overcome." In some cases the Freedom Riders themselves led the singing, as the fear of being arrested was overwhelmed by the emotion of the moment. Like most of those who had mustered the courage to attend the rally, they believed that it was time to stand up and be counted, whatever the consequences.[30]

To Federal authorities, few of whom shared the Riders' faith in direct action, the consequences of standing up for freedom in a Montgomery church seemed very grave indeed. By 9:30, with the crisis at First Baptist showing no signs of letting up, Justice Department officials were preparing for the worst. After releasing a public statement urging "all citizens of Alabama and all travelers in Alabama to consider their actions carefully and to refrain from doing anything which will cause increased tension or provoke violence or resistance," Robert Kennedy began to contemplate the previously unthinkable. Moved by the force of his own words, he asked the Pentagon to place army units at Fort Benning, ninety-five miles east of Montgomery, on high alert. The troops would only be used as a last resort, he assured White, but the inability of the marshals to disperse the mob and the lack of response from state officials left the federal government with few options.

Unbeknownst to Kennedy and White, Patterson, with the help of a Maxwell telephone operator, was listening in on this and other Justice Department conversations. Officially, though, Patterson was out of the loop. After several futile attempts to contact the governor, Kennedy and White turned to Floyd Mann as the only reachable—and reasonable—state official. A native of Alexander City, Alabama, Mann considered himself a segregationist, but not to the point of countenancing violence or disrespect for the Constitution or the law. "He was Southern," Bernard Lafayette recalled years later, "but I don't think he had the same kind of passion for preserving segregation at any cost as some of his colleagues. I think he was . . . caught in a system where he had to perform certain duties, but he wanted to do it in the most humane way." Although there was little Mann could do without firm authorization from Patterson, he took it upon himself to urge White to send in additional marshals. White, interpreting this request as the first indication that state officials were beginning to recognize the seriousness of the situation, offered to place the marshals already on the scene at Mann's disposal, but he had to confess that he had no additional marshals in reserve. This admission was not what Mann wanted to hear, although, as he later admitted, he secretly hoped that the marshals' weakness would force Patterson's hand.[31]

Meanwhile, the violence in the streets around First Baptist was intensifying. Marshals were being attacked by brick-throwing rioters, and some of the federal peacekeepers were too scared to get out of their vehicles. There were reports of guns being fired randomly into black homes in the vicinity of the church, and a Molotov cocktail had nearly set the church roof on fire. Gangs of marauding whites were roaming the streets at will and appeared to be converging on the church for a massive, coordinated assault. At one point things looked so bleak that Abernathy and King suggested that they and the other high-profile ministers should consider surrendering themselves to the mob in order to save the men, women, and children in the sanctuary. No one was quite sure whether King and Abernathy were serious, and Walker later confessed that his first thought was that King had lost touch with reality, but for a few moments there was a soul-searching silence as the leaders contemplated the advisability of sacrificial redemption. Shuttlesworth, in characteristically impulsive fashion, cut through the tension with a straightforward "If that's what we have to do, let's do it." But no one actually moved toward the door. Fortunately, events beyond the ministers' control soon rendered martyrdom unnecessary.

After McShane informed White that he was not sure that his marshals could hold out much longer, the bad news was relayed to the attorney general, who finally had heard enough. Following a brief consultation with Marshall, he decided to ask the president to sign a proclamation authorizing the immediate deployment of the soldiers at Fort Benning. As it turned out, however, the attorney general was not the only one who had heard enough. While Justice Department staff members puzzled over the logistics of acquiring the vacationing president's signature (he was a helicopter ride away in northern Virginia), Patterson, who had been eavesdropping on the phone communications between Washington and White's office at Maxwell Field, decided to act. At ten o'clock, he placed the city of Montgomery under what he called "qualified martial rule." Almost immediately, a swarm of city policemen rushed down Ripley Street, closely followed by fifteen helmeted members of the Alabama National Guard. Within five minutes, more than a hundred Guardsmen had formed a protective shield in front of the church. By that time, the police, with Commissioner Sullivan making a show of his authority, had cleared the immediate area of rioters. Nearby a greatly relieved McShane, with White's approval, offered to place his marshals under the command of the National Guard. Accepting McShane's offer, the colonel in charge of the Guardsmen promptly ordered the marshals to leave the scene. As the overall commander of the Guard, Adjutant General Henry Graham announced a few minutes later that the sovereign state of Alabama had everything under control and needed no further help from federal authorities.[32]

In actuality, dispersing the mob proved more difficult than Graham or anyone else had anticipated. While the worst of the mayhem was over by 10:15, sporadic violence continued for several hours. Indeed, for the besieged gathering inside the sanctuary the joyous news of the soldiers' arrival was soon tempered by the realization that their rescuers were Alabama segregationists, not federal troops. This disappointment did not stop them from proceeding with the mass meeting, however. Despite lingering fumes and frazzled nerves, the celebration of freedom went forward almost as if nothing had happened. As several of the reporters covering the rally—and the Freedom Riders themselves—later remarked, the spirit inside the sanctuary was difficult to explain to anyone who was not there. "I don't think I've ever seen a group of people band together as the crowd did in the church that night," Nash marveled, during a conference on "The New Negro" a few weeks later. The soulful music, the presence of the Freedom Riders and so many other movement veterans, the sight of women and children sitting amid broken glass, the soaring rhetoric from the pulpit—everything conspired to create an emotion-filled experience.

King and others did not mince words that evening. As the television cameras whirred, one speaker after another juxtaposed praise for the Freedom Riders with condemnation of the state and local authorities who had incited a week of lawlessness. After urging the audience to launch "a full scale nonviolent assault on the system of segregation in Alabama," King insisted that "the law may not be able to make a man love me, but it can keep him from lynching me. . . . Unless the federal government acts forthrightly in the South to assure every citizen his constitutional rights, we will be plunged into a dark abyss of chaos." Departing from his prepared text, he placed much of the blame on Patterson, who bore the "ultimate responsibility for the hideous action in Alabama." "His consistent preaching of defiance of the law," King claimed, "his vitriolic public pronouncements, and his irresponsible actions created the atmosphere in which violence could thrive. Alabama has sunk to a level of barbarity comparable to the tragic days of Hitler's Germany." Shuttlesworth agreed. "It's a sin and a shame before God," he declared, "that these people who govern us would let things come to such a sad state. But God is not dead. The most guilty man in this state tonight is Governor Patterson." For nearly two hours expressions of outrage alternated with impassioned calls for continued struggle and sacrifice until everyone in the sanctuary, as Farmer put it, "was ready at that moment to board buses and ride into the Promised Land." Following a final hymn and an emotional benediction, the exhausted preachers dismissed the congregation a few minutes before midnight.[33]

Despite some concern about what they would encounter outside the church, most of the audience wasted no time in heading for the exits. Some had been in the sanctuary since late afternoon, and even those who had arrived late were eager to get home to reassure friends and family that they were safe. To their surprise, however, the exits were blocked by National Guardsmen with drawn bayonets. The only person allowed outside the church was King, who demanded an explanation from General Graham. Moments earlier Graham had received word that Robert Kennedy had officially sanctioned the placing of federal marshals under state control, and he was in no mood to relinquish any of his expanded authority, especially to a meddling black preacher from Georgia. An arch-segregationist who worked as a Birmingham real estate agent in his civilian life, Graham turned a deaf ear to King's appeal for compassion. Some members of the congregation were at the breaking point and desperately needed to go home, King explained. But Graham would not relent, insisting that the situation outside the church was too unstable. Though disappointed, King urged Graham to deliver this message directly to the men and women inside the sanctuary. After some hesitation, he agreed.

Marching into the church with several of his aides, Graham presided over a formal reading of Patterson's declaration of martial law, which predictably began with the hostile phrase "Whereas, as a result of outside agitators coming into Alabama to violate our laws and customs." Farther down, the proclamation claimed that the federal government had "by its actions encouraged these agitators to come into Alabama to foment disorders and breaches of the peace." As a murmur of indignation spread through the sanctuary, Graham stepped forward to inform the crowd that the siege was not over, that in all likelihood they would have to remain in the church and under the protection of the National Guard until morning. Technically it was already morning, but the meaning of his words was clear: Liberation had turned into protective custody.

To the Freedom Riders, who had already experienced the protective custody provided by Bull Connor, the scene was all too familiar. "Those soldiers didn't look like protectors now," Lewis later commented. "Their

rifles were pointed our way. They looked like the enemy." From the perspective of those in the sanctuary, martial law looked a lot like continued intimidation and harassment, especially after they realized that the forces surrounding the church were all controlled by Patterson, a governor who had branded the Freedom Riders as outlaws. King, in particular, felt betrayed by the federal government's apparent abdication

Attorney General Robert F. Kennedy awaits the resolution of the church siege in Montgomery, Sunday evening, May 21, 1961. (Getty Photos)

of authority. In a fit of anger, he called Robert Kennedy to complain, but Kennedy, who had just come from an upbeat interview with a magazine reporter, was not interested in listening to King's lament. "Now, Reverend," he retorted, "don't tell me that. You know just as well as I do that if it hadn't been for the United States marshals, you'd be as dead as Kelsey's nuts right now!" The allusion to Kelsey's nuts—an old Boston Irish aphorism—meant nothing to King, but the tone of Kennedy's voice gave him pause. Before hanging up, King handed the phone to Shuttlesworth, who echoed his colleague's complaint about the marshals' withdrawal. Kennedy would have none of it. "You look after your end, Reverend, and I'll look after mine," he scolded. Clearly, on this night at least, the attorney general had done about all that he was going to do on behalf of the Freedom Riders. As King and Shuttlesworth explained to Seay a few moments later, they now had no choice but to make the best of a bad situation.[34]

While King and others reluctantly turned First Baptist into a makeshift dormitory, the National Guard, aided by Sullivan's police and Mann's highway patrolmen, conducted a mopping-up operation in the surrounding streets. By this time almost all of the marshals had returned to Maxwell Field, leaving the downtown battleground in the hands of state and local forces. After Graham assured Patterson that everything was under control, the formerly recalcitrant governor called Robert Kennedy to vent his anger. Patterson's tone was abusive from the start, as the pent-up hostilities and emotions of the past week burst forth. "Now you've got what you want," Patterson literally shouted over the phone. "You got yourself a fight. And you've got the National Guard called out, and martial law, and that's what you wanted. We'll take charge of it now with the troops, and you can get out and leave it alone." Kennedy protested that he had only sent in the marshals reluctantly after state and local officials had abrogated their responsibilities, but Patterson refused to accept this or any other explanation that let the federal government off the hook.

Later in the conversation Kennedy tried to get beyond recriminations by quizzing Patterson about his plans to evacuate First Baptist, but when he asked specifically if the governor and the National Guard could guarantee the safety of the Freedom Riders and their hosts once they left the church, he did not get the answer he was looking for. The state could offer a guarantee to everyone but King, Patterson declared. Stunned, Kennedy shot back: "I don't believe that. Have General Graham call me. I want to hear a general of the United States Army say he can't protect Martin Luther King." Patterson later explained his reticence to protect King as a simple matter of common sense. Kennedy, he complained, "really didn't understand the problem. . . . When you've got a man running all over this town that will not do what you say, and people all over town wanting to kill him, how can you personally guarantee that man's protection?" At the time, however, Patterson freely admitted to Kennedy that his decision was largely a matter of political survival, a confession that drew little sympathy. "John," Kennedy responded, "it's more important that these people in the church survive physically than for us to survive politically." To Patterson, this final insult was too much to bear, and the conversation ended in a curt exchange of strained salutations.[35]

It was now one o'clock in the morning, and back at First Baptist the exhausted congregation was reluctantly settling in for the night. Some were still lined up to use the church's only phone, but most had sprawled out among the pews in an attempt to get some sleep. As Frank Holloway, a SNCC volunteer from Atlanta, described the scene, there "were three or four times as many people as the church was supposed to hold, and it was very hot and uncomfortable. Some people were trying to sleep, but there was hardly room for anybody to turn around. Dr. King, other leaders, and the Freedom Riders were circulating through the church talking to people and trying to keep their spirits up." Fortunately, there was room in the basement

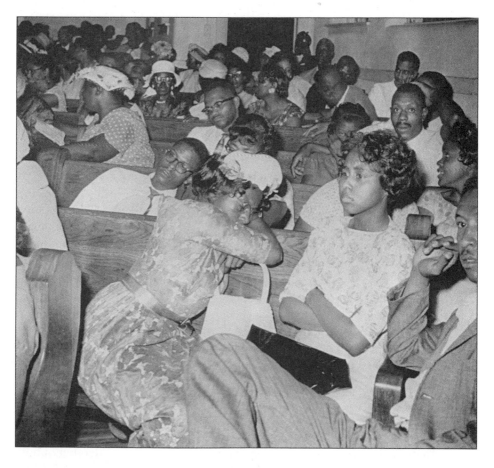

In the early hours of Monday morning, May 22, 1961, the pews of Montgomery's First Baptist Church were transformed into a makeshift dormitory. (Courtesy of the *Nashville Tennessean* and AP Wide World)

to accommodate the children, and most of the reporters had already slipped out of the church to file their stories, but the air inside the sanctuary, still smelling of tear gas, made the quarters seem even tighter than they actually were. Even so, many inside the church were grateful to be alive, having survived what Jessica Mitford called "the most terrifying evening of my life."

Adding to the terror was the sullen presence of Graham and the National Guardsmen—many of whom made no secret of their contempt for the outside agitators who had provoked the Montgomery crisis—and the gnawing uncertainty about what was going on outside the church. As the long night of protective custody stretched on, the gathering at First Baptist was kept in the dark literally and figuratively about the implications of state authority. Only later did they learn that White and other Justice Department officials were engaged in frantic behind-the-scenes negotiations with the National Guard to end the siege once and for all. By four o'clock White's growing frustration with Graham had prompted him to send William Orrick to the National Guard armory to see what could be done to get the church evacuated sometime before dawn. What followed was an almost surreal combination of Southern Gothic and Cold War drama. As Orrick recalled the scene: "I was treated like I might have been treated in Russia and taken over to Dixie division . . . where there wasn't a sign of an American flag . . . just the Confederate flags."

After being escorted to Graham's office, Orrick declared that he had been sent by the Justice Department to "negotiate" a timely evacuation of First Baptist. "We want to know whether your troops are going to leave that church and let the people go home," Orrick explained, "and whether they're going to keep the peace here tomorrow." Busy polishing his boots, Graham raised his eyes slowly and grunted: "Well, I'm not about to decide either matter." When Orrick pressed him further, Graham claimed he couldn't make any commitments without talking to the governor first. Only after an exasperated Orrick threatened to send the marshals back to the church did Graham begin to come around. Despite the suspicion that Orrick was bluffing and speaking without clear authority, Graham eventually agreed to begin the evacuation as soon as he could arrange a proper escort. Within minutes a convoy of National Guard trucks and jeeps pulled up in front of the church, and over the next hour the Freedom Riders and the faithful parishioners of First Baptist finally left the scene of a confrontation that none of them would ever forget.[36]

By that time the morning newspapers were already hitting the streets of New York and other Eastern cities, as the nation awoke to the news that Montgomery had once again been plunged into chaos. To the relief of both federal and state officials, most of the initial press coverage gave the impression that, as bad as it was, the situation in Montgomery could have been much worse. Despite the threat of mass violence, the damage to persons and

The evacuation of parishioners and Freedom Riders from Montgomery's First Baptist Church by the Alabama National Guard, Monday morning, May 22, 1961. The men wearing armbands and straw hats are federal marshals. The three evacuees on the far left are (left to right) Bill Harbour, John Lewis, and Joseph Carter. (Getty Photos)

property apparently had been kept to a minimum. Accounts differed as to the relative contributions of federal, state, and local law enforcement, with conservative and Southern papers emphasizing the latter two, but the dominant story line was cooperation. Faced with an unfortunate confrontation between militant civil rights activists and white supremacist vigilantes, federal, state, and local authorities reportedly had put aside their differences in the interest of restoring civil order. Even a *New York Times* editorial that excoriated Patterson for encouraging mob violence went on to express the opinion that "the Constitutional issue between the Federal and the state authorities may have actually reached its climax yesterday and may already be moving toward a solution." Interestingly enough, the *Times* editorial also tried to strike a delicate balance between defending the Freedom Riders' constitutional rights and warning about the dangers of provocative agitation. "The issue in Montgomery," the editors insisted, ". . . is the right of American citizens, white and Negro alike, to travel in safety in interstate commerce, without being segregated in contravention of the Constitution. This right is now being tested by the so-called 'Freedom Riders,' a racially mixed group consisting primarily of students, who are waging their campaign for civil rights in the

South in a Gandhian spirit of idealism and of non-violent resistance to an evil tradition. But it is also being waged with loud advance publicity and in deliberate defiance of state laws and local customs. There can be no question that in the Freedom Riders' completely legal action there is an element of incitement and provocation in regions of high racial tension."

This tenuous endorsement reinforced the Kennedy administration's preferred position on the Freedom Ride, sanctioning the legality but not the advisability of forcing the issue of desegregated transit. On Monday morning, however, administration spokesmen did their best to push this vexing inconsistency—along with the Freedom Riders themselves—into the background. Political damage control called for an uplifting cover story of intergovernmental harmony that downplayed the specter of constitutional crisis. White and others denied that the administration had been on the verge of sending in the army, and Robert Kennedy made a point of praising Floyd Mann as an exemplary law enforcement officer who put professionalism ahead of personal interest. If there was a villain in the official account of the Montgomery crisis—other than the mob itself—it was Patterson, but even he got off fairly lightly considering the hard feelings of the night before. While still angry at Patterson for flouting federal authority, Kennedy did not want to provoke another war of words with a member of his own party. The administration was already on shaky political ground in the Deep South, and turning Patterson into another Orval Faubus would only make matters worse.[37]

As expected, Patterson wasted no time in putting his own spin on the events of May 21. Though relatively unconcerned about the national and international reactions to the crisis, he was determined to protect his political reputation among white Southerners. At a carefully staged Monday morning press conference, he took full credit for his dual defense of segregation and state sovereignty. Pointing to a stack of telegrams that endorsed his actions and condemned the meddling Freedom Riders and their federal accomplices, he defiantly contradicted the claim that federal and state authorities were working in harmony. The deployment of the marshals was an affront to the principle of states' rights and to Alabama's proud tradition of capable law enforcement. The marshals were no more welcome in Alabama than the Freedom Riders, he insisted, and the sooner they left the state the better. Other state officials, including Attorney General Gallion and the entire Alabama congressional delegation, promptly echoed Patterson's call for an immediate withdrawal of the marshals. By early afternoon an emergency meeting of thirty business and professional leaders convened by Montgomery mayor Earl James had approved a resolution calling the marshals' presence "more inflammatory than tranquilizing," and as the day wore on white public opinion in the state seemed to be lining up behind the governor's anti-federal position.

There were, however, several notable exceptions. Former governor Jim Folsom phoned Robert Kennedy to express his support for the marshals' deployment, and the Alabama Press Association, meeting in Tuscaloosa, while taking no explicit stand on the marshals or the Freedom Rides, had already passed a resolution attributing the "breakdown of civilized rule" on Saturday to "the failure on the part of law enforcement officers in parts of Alabama to provide protection to and insure basic freedom to citizens in general and to newspaper, wire service, radio, and television representatives in particular." Grover Hall Jr., the editor of the *Montgomery Advertiser*, spoke for many of the state's journalists when he questioned Patterson's leadership in a biting Monday morning editorial. "Patterson started out by saying that he would not nursemaid the agitators and he might arrest the U. S. marshals," Hall reminded his readers. "But before it was over Patterson was baby-sitting the agitators all night in a church and the highway patrol was working in harness with the federal troops." While Hall had little sympathy for either the Freedom Riders or the federal government, he could not resist asking why the crisis had occurred in Alabama and not elsewhere. In the days ahead, this nagging question would spell political trouble for Patterson and other Alabama officials who found themselves riding an unpredictable wave of reaction.[38]

For federal officials the public mood in Alabama was only one of several unpredictable factors complicating the situation in the immediate aftermath of the Sunday night siege. Despite Judge Johnson's temporary restraining order, the legal position of the Freedom Riders remained in doubt. Under martial law the warrants issued by Judge Jones had been turned over to Colonel Herman Price of the Alabama National Guard, but as yet Price had made no arrests. During a tense afternoon press conference at Maxwell Field, White deflected questions about the Freedom Riders' whereabouts and denied that federal officials were working in close cooperation with local "Negro groups or Negro leaders." Indeed, he indicated that federal marshals would not intervene if local or state authorities attempted to arrest the Freedom Riders. "That would be a matter between the Freedom Riders and local officials," he insisted, adding: "I'm sure they would be represented by competent counsel." White also tried to reassure the reporters that the decision to deploy two hundred additional marshals earlier in the day was a simple logistical maneuver aimed at replacing "men who are headed home for various reasons." "Our present intentions are to remain here for a few days," he declared. If additional trouble arose, federal authorities would "take cooperative action" with General Graham and the National Guard, but the marshals had "no desire to push aside local officers." When asked if federal authorities planned to prosecute any of the rioters, White hedged, explaining that "if we can turn up evidence that any Federal violations have been committed, we will make some arrests." Still, the overall message was one of conciliation and deference to local sensibilities.[39]

White's statement to the press reflected the administration's growing misgivings about the decision to use federal marshals to protect the Freedom Riders. Earlier in the day Robert Kennedy had spent forty-five minutes at the White House briefing his brother on the events of the weekend and the political and legal dilemmas posed by the Freedom Riders' unexpected persistence. Despite public pronouncements to the contrary, many of the marshals had not performed well under pressure, the attorney general confessed, and the events of the weekend had cast serious doubt on their reliability as peacekeepers in the Deep South. Reliance on the state police and the National Guard also involved a certain amount of risk, but it did not present the serious problems of political liability provoked by the deployment of marshals. While the marshals had been a necessary means of forcing Patterson to mobilize the National Guard, their continued presence in Alabama was politically problematic and even dangerous. The decision to deploy the marshals had already drawn considerable fire from conservative politicians in both parties, including non-Southerners such as Senator Barry Goldwater of Arizona, and such criticism was likely to increase dramatically if the marshals remained in Alabama much longer. The task at hand, the Kennedy brothers concluded, was to arrange for a graceful retreat without weakening the integrity of federal authority or appearing to abandon the Freedom Riders. The latter challenge was especially acute in view of the Freedom Riders' continuing vulnerability to arrest and intimidation by state and local officials. Robert Kennedy, in particular, agonized over the prospect of standing by while Alabama authorities carted the Freedom Riders off to jail. But by late Monday afternoon no one in the White House or the Justice Department had come up with a plan that would get both the marshals and the Freedom Riders safely out of Alabama.

One of the most frustrating aspects of the administration's unenviable position had been the ambiguous role of the FBI in Alabama. In the week since the initial riots in Anniston and Birmingham, FBI officials at all levels had kept a respectful distance from the developing crisis. At this point no one outside of the bureau was aware of Gary Thomas Rowe's involvement in the Birmingham riot, but the inevitable grousing in the attorney general's office about the FBI's apparent failure to keep tabs on the Alabama Klan had already pushed J. Edgar Hoover into preemptive action. On Monday morning, May 15, Hoover informed Burke Marshall and Robert Kennedy that the Birmingham office of the FBI had begun an investigation of the Anniston bus-burning incident. Given the code name FREEBUS, the investigation initially drew plaudits from both Marshall and Kennedy, who made a point of thanking the notoriously thin-skinned Hoover for giving the matter prompt attention. As the week progressed, however, it became clear to Seigenthaler, Doar, and other Justice Department officials in Alabama that Hoover and his agents were more interested in enhancing the bureau's public image than in protecting the Freedom Riders' constitutional rights. Although there were several special agents at the Montgomery riot scene on Saturday morning, none made any attempt to intervene on behalf of the men and women under attack. Instead, they seemed content to conduct motion picture surveillance through the windows of several parked vans, an activity that later took on a farcical touch when it was discovered that all of their film was defective. Less comically, the reluctance of the bureau's Alabama agents to provide the marshals with logistical support during the Sunday evening siege led a frustrated William Orrick to complain to Robert Kennedy, who promptly relayed the criticism to the White House. Sometime after midnight the president forwarded the complaint to Director Hoover's office, which immediately ordered the Alabama agent in charge to give Orrick whatever he wanted in the way of support.

Later that morning, around 9:30, Robert Kennedy received an uncharacteristically solicitous call from Hoover himself. After pledging his cooperation, the director delivered the welcome news that the bureau had just arrested four of the men responsible for the Anniston bus burning. All four, including an unemployed teenager, were active members of the Klan. To Kennedy, who had just returned to his office after a few hours of fitful sleep, the arrests could not have been more timely. After thanking Hoover for the bureau's good work, he immediately issued a press release declaring that the case against the four Klansmen would "be pursued with utmost vigor."

Hoover was also pleased, having relieved some of the pressure on the bureau. After hanging up, though, he complained to his staff that he wasn't sure that the attorney general understood the nature of the real danger in Alabama. Outside agitators like King and the Freedom Riders, he was convinced, were actually more dangerous than the Klan. As radical provocateurs and Communist fellow-travelers, they represented a serious threat to civic order and national security, and they were certainly not the kind of people that deserved a special FBI escort, which he feared was part of the Justice Department's plan. Throughout the Freedom Rider crisis, Hoover reiterated his long-standing insistence that the FBI was an investigative agency and "not a protection agency," but he wasn't sure that he could trust the new attorney general to respect its time-honored prerogatives. Realizing that he might need hard evidence of Communist infiltration to head off such an unpleasant assignment, Hoover ordered an immediate investigation of King, the one agitator he was fairly certain had close ties to subversive groups. Later in the day, he received a preliminary report that noted several suspicious connections, including King's ties to the Highlander Folk School, which was described as a "Communist Party training school." Intrigued, Hoover urged his staff to dig deeper into what he suspected was a sinkhole of subversion and unsavory activity.[40]

Back in Montgomery, King and the Freedom Riders had no way of knowing that Hoover and the FBI had launched an investigation that would become an important part of a decade-long effort to discredit the civil rights movement. But they had few illusions about the support that federal officials were prepared to offer. King's early-morning conversation with Robert Kennedy about the danger of placing the marshals under state control had ended badly, and nothing had happened since to indicate that the Justice

Department was ready to provide the kind of protection that would guarantee the Freedom Riders' safe passage to New Orleans. Even more important, despite the rhetoric coming out of Washington about the sanctity of interstate commerce, the administration's commitment to upholding the Freedom Riders' constitutional rights seemed hollow in the light of Kennedy's plea to postpone the Ride. All of this weighed heavily on the hearts and minds of the Riders in the hours following the evacuation of First Baptist. In the early-morning confusion the Riders had scattered throughout Montgomery's black community, but by late Monday afternoon virtually the entire contingent had regrouped at the home of Dr. Richard Harris, a prominent black pharmacist and former neighbor of King's. Joined by an array of movement leaders—including King, Abernathy, Walker, Farmer, CORE attorney Len Holt, Nash, and Ed King of SNCC—the Riders turned Harris's luxurious three-story brick home into a combination refuge and command center.

During the next two days, Harris's sprawling den became the backdrop for a marathon discussion of the future of the Freedom Ride. The conversation ultimately touched on all aspects of the Freedom Riders' situation, from narrow logistical details to broad philosophical considerations of nonviolent struggle. The first order of business was finding a solution to the Riders' legal problems. In an ironic twist, Patterson's declaration of martial law had suspended normal civil processes, temporarily negating Judge Jones's injunction within the city limits of Montgomery, but the Riders were still subject to arrest everywhere else in Alabama. In an effort to remedy this situation, movement attorneys Fred Gray and Arthur Shores went before Judge Frank Johnson on Monday afternoon seeking to vacate the injunction. Held at the federal court house adjacent to the Greyhound terminal, the hearing required John Lewis and the other Riders accompanying Gray and Shores to pass by the scene of the Saturday morning riot. This time the streets were patrolled by National Guardsmen, and the courtroom was ringed with federal marshals. The atmosphere was tense nonetheless.

As the Riders' designated plaintiff and primary witness, Lewis—still bruised and heavily bandaged—was called upon to explain the motivations behind both the original CORE Ride and the Nashville Ride. It was a simple question of exercising legal and constitutional rights, the young Freedom Rider told Johnson, in a quavering voice that betrayed both his nervousness and his passion for equal justice. After a brief deliberation, Johnson issued a ruling affirming that very point: Judge Jones's injunction represented an unconstitutional infringement of federal law. The Freedom Riders were no longer fugitives, Johnson declared, though he could not help questioning the wisdom of continuing the Ride at the risk of civic disorder.

With the immediate threat of arrest eliminated by Judge Johnson's ruling, the Riders and their advisors began to consider an expanded range of options. While virtually all of the Riders spoke out in favor of resuming the Freedom Ride, the large contingent from Tennessee State faced a special dilemma. Threatened with expulsion by Tennessee governor Buford Ellington, who had ordered state education commissioner Joe Morgan to investigate the recent protest activities of public university students, the twelve Tennessee State Riders were under heavy pressure to return to Nashville to attend the final week of spring semester classes. In the end, all but one—Lucretia Collins, a senior who had already fulfilled the requirements for graduation—reluctantly decided to head back to school, forfeiting their chance to be among the first Riders to travel to Mississippi. With their departure, the number of available Nashville Riders fell to less than a dozen, including Lawson and four other NCLC ministers—C. T. Vivian, John Lee Copeland, Alex Anderson, and Grady Donald—who had offered to reinforce the students. Nash, however, had already enlisted additional reinforcements from other movement centers, some from Atlanta and New Orleans and others from as far away as Washington and New York. Although several were still en route as late as Tuesday evening, she expected to have at least twenty volunteers in Montgomery by the time the Freedom Ride departed for Mississippi on Wednesday morning.

Before anyone could actually board the buses, however, there were a number of important matters to attend to, including working out clear lines of organizational authority and responsibility. Complicated by generational and ideological divisions, the ongoing discussion among students and older movement leaders took several unexpected turns on Monday evening. Ignoring the democratic sensibilities of the students, Farmer took immediate charge of the meeting, to the obvious consternation of Nash, Lewis, and others. Farmer, Lewis recalled years later, began and ended with self-serving pronouncements on CORE's centrality. "He talked loud and big," Lewis remembered, "but his words sounded hollow to me. His retreat after the attacks in Anniston and Birmingham had something to do with it, I'm sure, but he just struck me as very insincere. It was clear to everyone that he wanted to take the ride back now, when we all knew that without our having picked it up, there would have been no more Freedom Ride. It didn't matter to me at all who got the credit; that wasn't the point. But from where Farmer stood, that seemed to be all that mattered. He saw this ride in terms of himself. He kept calling it 'CORE's ride,' which amazed everyone." Some students openly challenged the CORE leader's proprietary claims, while others quietly wrote him off as an organization man hopelessly out of touch with the spirit of the modern movement. But most of the attention ultimately focused on King rather than Farmer.

King's personal participation in direct action had been a major topic of discussion since the time of the Greensboro sit-ins, and his recent support of the CORE and Nashville Freedom Rides had triggered speculation that at some point he might become a Freedom Rider himself. Earlier in the week Diane Nash had broached the subject during a phone conversation with King, suggesting that his presence on one of the freedom buses was essential to the

movement, but prior to the Monday night meeting there was no organized
or collective effort to persuade him to join the Freedom Ride. Though discouraged by King's noncommittal response to her initial entreaties, Nash
decided to try again in the more public setting in Montgomery. After consulting with SNCC advisor Ella Baker, who encouraged her to press King on
the matter, the young Nashville activist steeled her courage and asked King
directly if he were willing to join the coming ride to Mississippi. By setting a
personal example of commitment, she explained, he could advance the cause
of nonviolent struggle to a new level. Momentarily caught off guard, King
responded that Nash was probably right, but he needed time to think about
it. As several other students seconded Nash's suggestion, Walker, Abernathy,
and Bernard Lee—a young SCLC staff member from Montgomery who had
been active in the student movement at Alabama State—moved to quash the
idea with a series of objections: King was too valuable a leader and too critical to the overall movement to be put at risk. He had already put his body on
the line at First Baptist and elsewhere, they argued, and did not need to
prove his courage by engaging in a reckless show of solidarity. When it became clear that King was uncomfortable with this line of reasoning, Walker
offered a more specific objection, reformulating a legal argument that SCLC
attorneys had advanced in anticipation of such a debate. Since King was still
on probation for a 1960 Georgia traffic citation, Walker declared, he could
not risk an additional arrest, which might put him in prison for as much as six
months.

    For a moment this seemed to provide King with a graceful means of
deflecting Nash's suggestion, but several of the students quickly pointed out
that they too were on probation. With King wavering, Nash and others pressed
for an answer. King's response, tempered by his obvious discomfort with
being put on the spot, was a qualified no. As much as he would like to join
them on the Ride, he informed the students, he could not allow himself to be
forced into a commitment that threatened the broader interests of the movement. Resorting to a biblical allusion to Christ's martyrdom, he brought the
discussion to an abrupt end with the insistence that only he could decide the
"time and place" of his "Golgotha." He then left the room for a private conversation with Walker, who returned a few minutes later with the word that
further discussion of the matter was off-limits. For the moment, at least, the
face-to-face tension was broken, though many in the room resented Walker's
admonition as a violation of movement democracy. While virtually all of the
students recognized King's dilemma, the abrupt suspension of debate was a
rude jolt, especially to those inclined to reject the stated rationale for the
SCLC leader's decision. As the meeting broke up, one disappointed student
muttered, "De Lawd," a mocking reference to King's assumption of Christ-
like status, and others were visibly upset by what they had witnessed.

    Later in the evening, Lee and Abernathy, along with Lewis, did their
best to smooth things over with the most disillusioned students, but for some

King's mystique was permanently broken. Paul Brooks was reportedly so upset that he called Robert Williams, the radical NAACP leader in Monroe, North Carolina, to vent, prompting an acerbic telegram from Williams to King. "The cause of human decency and black liberation demands that you physically ride the buses with our gallant Freedom Riders," Williams insisted. "No sincere leader asks his followers to make sacrifices that he himself will not endure. You are a phony. Gandhi was always in the forefront, suffering with his people. If you are a leader of this nonviolent movement, lead the way by example."[41]

ON TUESDAY MORNING the movement conclave at Dr. Harris's house continued to wrestle with the issues of organizational harmony and personal commitment, but the scene inside the house was calm compared to what was going on elsewhere. On Monday evening sporadic violence, multiple bomb threats, and "roving gangs of white youths" had forced General Graham to dispatch 150 National Guardsmen to reinforce the fifty Guardsmen patrolling the area around the Greyhound terminal, and the fear of additional disruption was still palpable the next morning. Most of the action, however, was in the corridors of power in Montgomery, Jackson, and Washington. With martial law still in effect and with the resumption of the Freedom Ride scheduled for Wednesday morning, Tuesday was a time for public posturing and behind-the-scenes negotiation. All through the day there were signs of rising apprehension and mobilization, especially in Mississippi.

In a morning telegram to Robert Kennedy, Governor Ross Barnett warned: "You will do a great disservice to the agitators and the people of the United States if you do not advise the agitators to stay out of Mississippi." At the same time, Barnett—an outspoken sixty-three-year-old white supremacist with close ties to the White Citizens' Councils—assured the attorney general that the Magnolia State would not tolerate the kind of mob violence that had erupted in Alabama. "The people of Mississippi are capable of handling all violations of law and keeping peace in Mississippi," he insisted. "We . . . do not want any police aid from Washington, either marshals or federal troops." To prove his point, Barnett placed the Mississippi National Guard on alert and authorized state troopers to search for Freedom Riders at checkpoints along the Alabama-Mississippi border. Later in the day, Barnett's plan of action received the endorsement of John Wright, the head of the Jackson White Citizens' Councils, who declared: "Mississippi is ready. . . . Our Governor, the Mayor of Jackson and other state and city officials have already stated plainly that these outside agitators will not be permitted to stir up trouble in Mississippi." Pointing out that "the vast majority of our public officials are Citizens' Council members," Wright urged his fellow Mississippians to let "our Highway Patrolmen, policemen and other peace officers handle any situation which may arise. . . .You and I can help by letting our public officials and police officers know that we're behind them all the way—and by not adding to their problems in time of crisis."[42]

Such calls for restraint buoyed the spirits of Justice Department officials and others who had worried that Mississippi segregationists were even more prone to vigilantism and violence than their Alabama cousins. Earlier in the week former Mississippi governor James Coleman had warned Burke Marshall that he feared that the Freedom Riders would "all be killed" if they tried to cross the state without a military escort, and other sources had confirmed the seriousness of the threat. Thus Barnett's call for law and order was a welcome sign. The implication that Mississippi was determined to avoid Alabama's mistakes did not sit well, however, with John Patterson, who lashed out at his critics in a Tuesday afternoon press conference. Meddling federal authorities, he declared, not local or state officials, were to blame for the mayhem and rioting in the streets of Montgomery. As he had predicted, the unwarranted intrusion of federal marshals had fanned the flames of interracial violence, making it impossible for local and state law enforcement officers to maintain civic order. "If the marshals want to contribute to law and order they should go home," he insisted. From the outset of the Freedom Rider crisis, he had maintained that respecting state sovereignty was the best way—indeed, the only way—to insure law and order in Alabama, but the president and the attorney general had refused to listen to him. While he still considered the president "a friend of mine," he urged the Kennedy administration to use its "prestige and power" to persuade the so-called Freedom Riders to leave Alabama as soon as possible. "If they want to go to the state line we will see that they get there," he assured the reporters, adding: "I'm opposed to agitation and mob violence no matter who does it. But it's just as guilty to provoke an incident as to take part in one."[43]

Patterson's bombastic performance made good copy, but it could not compete with the drama of another press conference held earlier in the day. Determined to sustain the momentum of the Freedom Ride and eager to demonstrate the solidarity of the coalition that had formed over the past week, King and several other movement leaders abandoned the security of Dr. Harris's house to brief the press on their plans. Surrounded by federal marshals and a crush of local, national, and international reporters, Farmer, Abernathy, and Lewis explained why they and their organizations—CORE, SCLC, and SNCC—were committed to resuming the Freedom Ride. King then read a joint declaration vowing that the Freedom Riders would soon board buses for Mississippi, with or without guarantees of police protection. Prior to their departure the Freedom Riders would participate in a nonviolent workshop led by Nashville Movement leader Jim Lawson, King announced. And to make sure that the reporters understood the implications of extending the nonviolent movement into Mississippi, he put down the prepared text and spoke from the heart. "Freedom Riders must develop the quiet courage of dying for a cause," he declared, his voice cracking with emotion.

Freedom Riders and civil rights leaders hold a press conference in Montgomery, Tuesday, May 23, 1961. From left to right: Jim Farmer, Wyatt Tee Walker (standing in background), Ralph Abernathy, Martin Luther King Jr., and John Lewis. (Photograph by Bruce Davidson, Magnum)

Freedom Riders Julia Aaron, David Dennis, Paul Dietrich, and John Lewis participate in a planning session at the Montgomery home of Dr. Richard Harris, Tuesday, May 23, 1961. (Photograph by Bruce Davidson, Magnum)

"We would not like to see anyone die. . . . We all love life, and there are no martyrs here—but we are well aware that we may have some casualties. . . . I'm sure these students are willing to face death if necessary."[44]

King's dramatic statement cleared the air and clarified the Freedom Riders' sense of purpose. But it also reinforced the public misconception that he was the supreme leader and chief architect of the Freedom Rides. In truth, he had never been a central figure in the Freedom Rider saga, and his refusal to join the Mississippi Ride had further marginalized his position among the student activists in Montgomery. To the outside world the celebrated founder of SCLC inevitably represented the moral compass of the movement, but to the students themselves his moral authority was uncertain at best. That evening, when they gathered to finalize preparations for Wednesday morning, the question of King's participation in the Mississippi Freedom Ride came up again. This time the discussion included Jim Bevel, who had driven down from Nashville earlier in the day with three new recruits: Rip Patton of Tennessee State, and LeRoy Wright and Matthew Walker Jr. of Fisk. Lawson was also on hand, having arrived a few hours later in a second carload of NCLC reinforcements.

Before leaving Nashville, Lawson dismissed the importance of his role as workshop coordinator, graciously insisting to reporters that King was "in over-all charge" of the Montgomery gathering, and during the discussion of King's proper role in the Freedom Rides, he and Bevel, among others, defended the SCLC leader's decision to serve as a spokesperson and fund-raiser rather than as an actual Freedom Rider. Though well-intentioned, the campaign to enlist King as a Freedom Rider had become problematic in their eyes. In practical terms, it threatened the fragile alliance between SCLC and the student movement; perhaps even more important, pursuing the effort after King's reluctance became clear violated the philosophical principles of nonviolent struggle, in which individual conscience was the only proper arbiter of bodily and spiritual commitment. Many others in the room, regardless of their position on King's involvement, had reached the same conclusion and were relieved when the center of attention shifted to Lawson's nonviolent workshop.

For several hours, Lawson led the Riders through a reprise of the sessions that had been instrumental to the Nashville Movement. Nearly half of the Riders were from Nashville and had seen Lawson work his magic before, but others were encountering his quiet intensity for the first time. While everyone in the room had practical experience with sit-ins and other forms of direct action, Lawson's presentation of nonviolence as an all-encompassing way of life provided some with a new philosophical grounding for their activism. Indeed, several of the Freedom Riders would look back on the final hours in Dr. Harris's den as a life-changing experience, one that deepened their theoretical understanding of nonviolent struggle and sacrifice, preparing them as nothing else had for the difficult challenges ahead.

Among those present at the workshop were three Riders representing New Orleans CORE and four SNCC activists representing Washington's Nonviolent Action Group. Jail terms had forced two members of the New Orleans group—Julia Aaron and Jerome Smith—to miss the original May 4 CORE ride, and they were anxious for a second chance to become active Freedom Riders. The journey to Alabama also represented a second chance for John Moody, who, along with Paul Dietrich, had left Washington by car on Saturday. Driving as far as Atlanta, they had flown in on the same plane as King on Sunday morning. Also on hand were two other NAG stalwarts, Dion Diamond, a Howard student from Petersburg, Virginia, who had taken final exams early so that he could join the Freedom Ride in Montgomery, and Hank Thomas, who had flown to Montgomery after several days of recuperation in New York. Some of the new volunteers did not arrive in Montgomery until Tuesday evening and missed the early part of the workshop, but by the time the gathering broke up around midnight, the number of potential Freedom Riders had risen to almost thirty, enough for two freedom buses, one Greyhound and one Trailways. While no one knew exactly how many Riders would actually board the buses in the morning, the stage was set for the nonviolent movement's first major project in Mississippi.[45]

The nonviolent workshop and the camaraderie that surrounded it produced moments of exhilaration and renewal. But, as several of the Riders later acknowledged, the final hours in Montgomery also brought feelings of dread, including fearful thoughts of what might actually happen in Mississippi. Making an interracial foray into Mississippi had always been a frightening prospect, but earlier in the day the Riders learned that even Medgar Evers, the Mississippi NAACP's state field secretary, had confessed to reporters that he hoped the Freedom Riders would postpone their trip to Jackson. In his words, under the present circumstances it was simply "too dangerous" to force a confrontation with Mississippi segregationists. During the workshop, Lawson, Holt, and others urged the Riders to ignore Evers's warning. But they did not deny the seriousness of the situation. "Although the law is on your side, you don't have any rights that any Southern state is bound to respect," Holt reminded the Riders during a discussion of the legal obstacles to nonviolent protest in Mississippi. "Please try to remember that, so that you'll be prepared for anything." He insisted that "participants in the Freedom Ride must go stripped for action. I know some of you may be tense and upset from what you've experienced for the past few days, but don't take any sleeping pills or aspirins with you that could be labeled as narcotics. . . . Don't even carry any medicine containing alcohol. . . . Get rid of any long hair pins, fingernail files or necklaces which could be called dangerous weapons. These people will be trying to find anything they can to arrest you for. . . . Whatever happens, be firm but polite. Remember you have no rights. . . . You can't fight back."

Holt's sobering advice focused on the perils of protest in Mississippi, but the Riders also had to face the possibility that they might not make it out of Montgomery. Indeed, much of the discussion during and after the workshop focused on the likelihood of more mob violence at the local bus stations. Federal and state officials had promised to protect them from white vigilantes, but few of the Riders were confident that these promises would be kept. Considering the events of the past week and the continuing public banter about state sovereignty, the intentions of law enforcement officials at all levels were open to question. As the Sunday night siege had demonstrated, there was even some doubt about the federal government's *ability* to protect the Riders. Could the limited number of federal marshals and National Guardsmen on the ground in Alabama and Mississippi muster enough force to hold back a large and determined mob? None of the Riders could be sure, since, aside from a few general and mildly comforting assurances, the details of the government's plans were unknown to them. Many of the Riders had decided to go to Mississippi no matter what the risk, but, as several of them sat down to write wills and final letters to loved ones before drifting off to bed, the uncertainties of the situation tested their already frayed nerves.[46]

Had the Freedom Riders been privy to the government's planned security measures, they might have slept a little easier. Although some of the details were still being worked out on Tuesday evening—and even into the morning hours—several days of close collaboration between federal and state authorities in Mississippi and Alabama had produced a consensus that a massive show of force was needed to forestall any chance of violence. In a final flurry of phone calls, Byron White and Governor Ross Barnett put the finishing touches on a military operation "worthy of a NATO war game," as one historian later put it. Unfortunately, the close collaboration also produced a tacit understanding that once the Freedom Riders arrived in Jackson there would be no federal interference with local law enforcement. Earlier in the week Barnett had promised "nonstop rides" for the Freedom Riders. Now it appeared that Barnett was contemplating mass arrests and a declaration of martial law. Unbeknownst to White and other federal officials, the governor was even considering an alternate and more extreme plan that would put the Freedom Riders in a state mental hospital.

While White stated emphatically that the Justice Department hoped that the Freedom Riders would be allowed to travel on to New Orleans, he did not insist upon it—in part because his superiors at the Justice Department and the White House had decided that it was too risky to use federal marshals or military personnel in Mississippi, but also because Robert Kennedy had already struck a deal with the state's senior senator, James O. Eastland. After ex-governor James P. Coleman warned Marshall that Barnett was a rank demagogue who "could not be trusted," Kennedy turned to Eastland, whom he considered to be a political and even personal friend. Unlike many Northern senators, Eastland had been an enthusiastic supporter during

Kennedy's confirmation hearings, and despite the obvious ideological gulf between them, the two men had developed a mutual trust during the early months of the new administration. Over the course of three days and several dozen phone conversations, this trust deepened as Eastland convinced the young attorney general that he would see to it that Mississippi's response to the Freedom Rides served the best interests of the nation. Despite his unwavering commitment to segregation, Eastland promised Kennedy that no harm would come to the Freedom Riders in Mississippi; however, he could not guarantee that they would escape arrest. Indeed, Eastland hinted that any attempt to violate Mississippi's segregation laws would result in mass arrests. Though hardly pleased with the prospect of jailed Freedom Riders, Kennedy assured Eastland that the federal government's "primary interest was that they weren't beaten up."

While he did not say so on the phone, Kennedy knew all too well that he was in no position to press Eastland on this point. If the Jackson police chose to put the Freedom Riders in jail, there wasn't much that he or any other federal official could do about it. In effect, the rioting in Alabama had convinced the Kennedy brothers, along with White and Marshall, that almost anything was preferable to mob violence—including unconstitutional arrests of interstate travelers. Ironically, a tentative show of force in one state had undercut federal authority in a second. As events would soon demonstrate, the situation was made to order for Barnett, a militant segregationist eager to cement his ties to the White Citizens' Councils. Realizing that he had been handed a scenario that would allow him to take credit for maintaining both order and segregation, he was almost giddy by the time the arrangements were complete. Inviting White to accompany the Freedom Riders to Jackson, Barnett promised that the Mississippi Highway Patrol would see to it that he had "the nicest ride." "You'll be just as safe as you were in your baby crib," Barnett added with a chuckle.[47]

In later years, some members of the administration—prompted by civil rights leaders and historians who condemned the negotiations with Eastland as a betrayal of democratic ideals—would acknowledge that the agreement to defer to state authorities was a mistake. At the time, however, Robert Kennedy and his colleagues regarded the deal as an unpleasant but necessary resolution to a crisis that had already taken up too much of the administration's time and energy. In their eyes, the decision to accede to Eastland's demands was simply a postponement of the day of reckoning and not a surrender. Sometime in the future the federal government would find a way to guarantee the right to travel from state to state without accommodating outdated segregationist laws and customs. But under the current conditions of Cold War politics, administration leaders did not feel that they could afford a prolonged crisis that would almost certainly weaken the Democratic Party and embarrass the nation in front of the world. In their view, the realities of both domestic and international political life dictated a moderate course of action.

As the government official shouldering the ultimate responsibility for the Freedom Riders' arrests, John Kennedy could take comfort in the knowledge that he was following a long tradition of presidential pragmatism. Like many presidents before him, including Thomas Jefferson and Abraham Lincoln, he could claim that he was simply doing the best he could with a difficult situation. Indeed, against the dual backdrop of the Civil War Centennial and the civil rights movement, the comparison with Lincoln was inevitable. In the wake of Kennedy's assassination in November 1963, pointing out the parallels between the two martyred presidents became a popular pastime, with some observers noting the broad and substantive similarities between the historical challenges of the Lincoln and Kennedy eras.

A century before the Freedom Rider crisis, Lincoln had faced a similarly wrenching dilemma involving the competing interests of political realism and moral urgency. As a moderate Republican candidate in 1860, he committed his party to the twin goals of saving the Union and excluding slavery from the territories. But, as he freely admitted, the two goals were not yet equal, or even compatible. If forced to choose between partial abolition and the preservation of the Union, he would choose the latter. It would take two years of armed conflict and abolitionist ferment to push Lincoln toward a more humane and democratic resolution of this dilemma. Only in September 1862 did he and the nation reach what the historian James McPherson has labeled the "crossroads of freedom." By issuing the Emancipation Proclamation in the aftermath of the Union victory at Antietam, Lincoln established the immediate abolition of slavery in the seceded states and a perpetual Union as complementary war aims. Even though nearly three years of brutal warfare—not to mention a century of largely unfulfilled promises—lay ahead, the road taken from Antietam led African Americans to eventual, if incomplete, freedom.

In late May 1961, John Kennedy faced the Lincolnesque challenge of extending that road through the Deep South. By sending federal marshals to Alabama and affirming the constitutionally protected rights of all Americans, Kennedy had taken an important first step toward the implementation of racial justice. But on the morning of the twenty-fourth, as the Freedom Riders prepared to hack out a path of progress through the magnolia jungle of Mississippi, no one could be quite sure how far or fast the young president was willing to travel.[48]

7

Freedom's Coming and It Won't Be Long

We took a trip on a Greyhound bus,
Freedom's coming and it won't be long.
To fight segregation where we must,
Freedom's coming and it won't be long.
Freedom, give us freedom,
Freedom's coming and it won't be long.

—1961 "calypso" freedom song[1]

THE FEDERAL PRESENCE in Alabama and Mississippi was both everywhere and nowhere on Wednesday morning, May 24. Having asserted the power and authority of the national government, the Kennedy administration had withdrawn, at least temporarily, to the sidelines. The short-term, if not the ultimate, fate of the Freedom Ride had been placed in the hands of state officials who, paradoxically, had promised to protect both the safety of the Riders and the sanctity of segregation. When the Trailways group of Freedom Riders left Dr. Harris's house at 6:15 A.M., they were escorted by a half-dozen jeeps driven by Alabama National Guardsmen. This unimpressive show of force raised a few eyebrows among the Riders, who knew next to nothing about the details of the plan to protect them. But as the convoy approached the downtown Trailways terminal, the familiar outline of steel-helmeted soldiers came into view. In and around the terminal, more than five hundred heavily armed Guardsmen stood watch over several clusters of white bystanders. Although the Freedom Riders did not know it, there were also several FBI agents and plainclothes detectives nervously wandering through the crowd.

As the Freedom Riders filed out of their cars, the scene was tense but quiet until the crowd spotted King, who, along with Abernathy, Shuttlesworth, and Walker, had agreed to accompany the Riders to the terminal. Still uncomfortable with his refusal to join the Ride, King was determined to provide the disappointed students with as much visible support as possible. During an early-morning prayer meeting at Harris's house, he and Abernathy had blessed the Riders; and in a show of solidarity his brother, A. D., had flown in from Atlanta to help desegregate the Montgomery terminal's snack bar. With some members of the crowd screaming words of indignation, King led the combined SCLC–Freedom Rider entourage through the white waiting room and up to the counter, where he and the others ordered coffee and rolls. As several reporters and cameramen pressed forward to record the moment, "the white waitresses removed their aprons and stepped back," but, with the approval of the terminal's manager, black waitresses from the "Negro lunch counter stepped up and took the orders," thus breaking a half-century-old local color bar. Local and state officials, it seemed, had put out the word that nothing—not even the sanctity of Jim Crow dining—was to get in the way of the Freedom Riders' timely departure from Montgomery. Pleased, but wary of this unexpected politeness, some of the Riders began to wonder what other surprises were in the offing. They did not have to wait for very long to find out.

Upon arriving at the Trailways loading bay, the Freedom Riders discovered that there were no regular passengers waiting for the morning bus to

Prior to their departure for Mississippi, Freedom Riders hold a prayer breakfast in Dr. Richard Harris's kitchen in Montgomery, Wednesday morning, May 24, 1961. The man in the dark suit standing behind the table is A. D. King, brother of Martin Luther King Jr. The man at the left corner of the table is the Reverend Joe Boone of SCLC. The woman standing on the left is Diane Nash. The man in the right foreground wearing a T-shirt is Hank Thomas. (Getty Photos)

Jackson. Alabama Guardsmen, on orders from General Graham, were only allowing Freedom Riders and credentialed reporters to enter the bus. More than a dozen reporters were already on board, and several others soon joined them, as the Riders sized up the situation. Not all of the Riders were comfortable with the prospect of traveling to Jackson under such artificial conditions, and others were simply scared to death, but eventually all twelve of the Trailways Riders agreed to board the bus. Each, according to David Dennis, a twenty-year-old Louisiana CORE activist and student at Dillard College, "was prepared to die." In addition to Dennis, the group included two Southern University students from New Orleans, Julia Aaron and Jean Thompson; Harold Andrews, a student at Atlanta's Morehouse College; Paul Dietrich of NAG; and seven members of the Nashville Movement—Jim Lawson, Jim Bevel, C. T. Vivian, Bernard Lafayette, Joseph Carter, Alex Anderson, and Matthew Walker Jr. Three of the Nashville Riders—Lawson, Vivian, and Anderson—were practicing ministers, and three others—Bevel, Lafayette, and Carter—were divinity students. Dietrich was the only white. Walker and Thompson were the youngest at age nineteen, and Vivian was the oldest at thirty-six. Lawson, the third oldest at thirty-two, was the consensus choice as the group's designated leader and spokesperson.[2]

Soon after the twelve Freedom Riders took their seats, General Graham, the movement anti-hero of the Sunday night siege, stepped onto the bus to say a few words. Flanked by several Guardsmen, he warned the Riders—and the newsmen scattered throughout the bus—that they were about to embark on "a hazardous journey." Seconds later, however, speaking in a reassuring

Accompanied by a military and police escort, the first group of Mississippi-bound Freedom Riders leaves the Montgomery Trailways bus station, Wednesday morning, May 24, 1961. (Courtesy of *Nashville Tennessean* and AP Wide World)

voice, he insisted that "we have taken every precaution to protect you," adding: "I sincerely wish you all a safe journey." This was not what the Riders had come to expect from Alabama-bred officials, and several of the Riders thanked him for humanizing their last moments in Montgomery. After Graham departed, six Guardsmen remained on board, as an array of jeeps, patrol cars, and police motorcycles prepared to escort the bus northward to the city limits, where a massive convoy of vehicles was waiting. Once the bus reached the city line, the magnitude of the effort to get the Freedom Riders out of Alabama without any additional violence became apparent. In addition to several dozen highway patrol cars, there were two helicopters and three U.S. Border Patrol planes flying overhead, plus a huge contingent of press cars jammed with reporters and photographers. As the Riders would soon discover, nearly a thousand Guardsmen were stationed along the 140-mile route to the Mississippi border. Less obtrusively, there were also several FBI surveillance units placed at various points along Highways 14 and 80. While Graham, Mann, and other state officials were in the foreground running the show, federal officials were in the background monitoring as much of the operation as they could.

Leaving Montgomery a few minutes before eight, the convoy headed west toward Selma, the first scheduled stop on the 258-mile trip to Jackson. During the hour-long, fifty-mile journey to Selma, the Riders chatted amiably with reporters, but when the bus arrived in the town that four years later would become the site of the movement's most celebrated voting rights march, the National Guard colonel in charge of the bus announced that there would be no rest stops on the journey to Jackson. Motioning to the crowds lining the streets of Selma, the colonel did not have to explain why. But Lawson and several of the other Riders made it clear that they did not appreciate the heavy-handed style of protection being imposed on a Freedom Ride that was supposed to test the constitutional right to travel freely from place to place. "This isn't a Freedom Ride, it's a military operation," Bevel yelled out, a sentiment echoed by Lafayette, who confessed: "I feel like I'm going to war." At the same time, they couldn't help wondering what kind of specific threats had precipitated such extreme caution.

As the bus passed through Uniontown, thirty miles west of Selma, the sight of fist-shaking whites on the side of the road was unnerving, but the first sign of serious trouble came near Demopolis, where three cars of screaming teenagers started weaving through the convoy in an attempt to chase down the bus. After a brief stop, during which a nauseated Alex Anderson momentarily left the bus to vomit on the side of the road, the teenagers were detained long enough to allow the convoy to continue unimpeded to the state line. The bus did not stop again until it reached the tiny border town of Scratch Hill, Alabama. A few minutes later, the bus passed through the slightly larger town of Cuba, prompting several of the Riders to serenade their companions with what one reporter called "impromptu calypso rhythms." One

Freedom Riders Julia Aaron and David Dennis, with National Guardsmen, on the first freedom bus to Mississippi, Wednesday morning, May 24, 1961. The man sitting on the back seat is Jim Lawson. (Photograph by Bruce Davidson, Magnum)

Alabama National Guardsmen protect the Freedom Riders' Trailways bus near the Mississippi border, Wednesday morning, May 24, 1961. (Photograph by Paul Schutzer, Getty Photos)

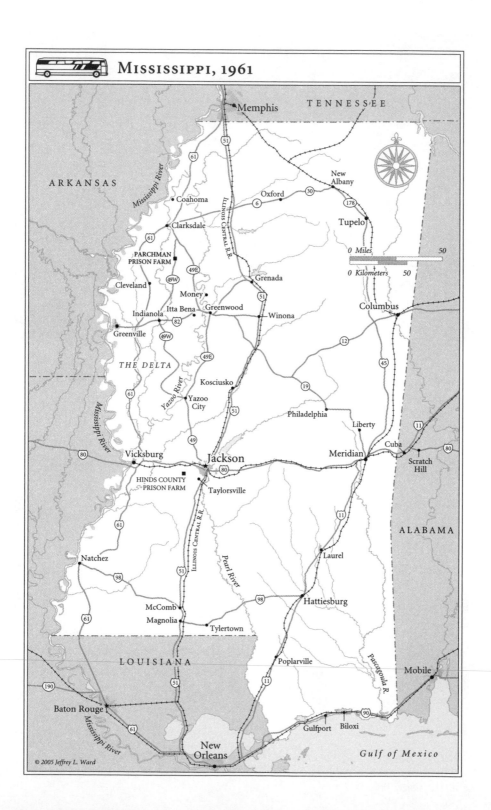

MISSISSIPPI, 1961

TENNESSEE

Memphis

ARKANSAS

New Albany

Coahoma
Oxford
Tupelo

Clarksdale

PARCHMAN PRISON FARM

Cleveland
Grenada

Money
Columbus

Indianola   Itta Bena   Greenwood
Winona

Greenville

THE DELTA

Kosciusko

Yazoo City

Philadelphia
Liberty

Vicksburg
Jackson
Meridian   Cuba
Scratch Hill

HINDS COUNTY PRISON FARM
Taylorsville

ALABAMA

Natchez
Laurel

McComb
Magnolia   Tylertown
Hattiesburg

LOUISIANA
Poplarville
Mobile

Baton Rouge

Gulfport   Biloxi

New Orleans
Gulf of Mexico

Mississippi River
Illinois Central R.R.
Yazoo River
Pearl River
Pascagoula R.

0 Miles 50
0 Kilometers 50

© 2005 Jeffrey L. Ward

of the songs, improvised by the Riders earlier in the journey, was an adaptation of Harry Belafonte's popular calypso ballad "The Banana Boat Song," sometimes known as "Day-O." "We took a trip on the Greyhound bus, freedom's coming and it won't be long. To fight segregation where we must, freedom's coming and it won't be long. Freedom, give us freedom, freedom's coming and it won't be long," the Freedom Rider chorus sang over and over again, as waves of laughter rippled through the bus. Moments later, however, both the music and the laughter gave way to the sobering reality of the martial spectacle at the state line.[3]

Matching their Alabama cousins, Mississippi authorities had assembled a small army of National Guardsmen and highway patrolmen, enough to escort half a dozen freedom buses into the state. If this was not bracing enough, word soon came that Mississippi authorities had uncovered a plot to dynamite the bus as soon as it crossed the state line. This and other unconfirmed threats caused an hour's delay, during which Mississippi Guardsmen searched the nearby woods and General Graham and his Mississippi counterpart, Adjutant General Pat Wilson, assessed the situation. While Wilson and Graham worked out the details of the transfer, an impatient Jim Lawson decided to hold an impromptu press briefing. To the amazement of the reporters encountering Lawson for the first time, the young minister complained that the Freedom Riders had not asked to go to Mississippi in the equivalent of an armored vehicle. As disciples of nonviolence, they "would rather risk violence and be able to travel like ordinary passengers" than cower in the shadow of protectors who neither understood nor respected their philosophy of countering "violence and hate" by "absorbing it without returning it in kind." With the reporters still puzzling over what seemed to be a foolhardy embrace of martyrdom, the bus resumed its journey around 11:30 A.M., nearly four hours after leaving Montgomery.

As soon as the bus crossed over the state line, Graham turned over control of the convoy to Mississippi's commissioner of public safety, T. B. Birdsong, and General Wilson, who promptly replaced the Alabama Guardsmen on board with six Mississippi Guardsmen under the command of Lt. Colonel and future congressman G. V. "Sonny" Montgomery. After Wilson informed the Freedom Riders and reporters on the bus there would be no rest stops on the one-hundred-mile trip to Jackson, C. T. Vivian complained to Montgomery that this decision was "degrading and inhumane," considering that there was no restroom on the bus. Montgomery's only response was to order Vivian to sit down and be quiet. Stunned by this curt dismissal, Vivian was unable to restrain himself. "Have you no soul?" he plaintively asked Montgomery. "What do you say to your wife and children when you go home at night? Do you ever get on your knees and pray for your inhumanity to your fellow man? May God have mercy on you." Staring ahead, Montgomery did not answer. While Vivian and others seethed, Birdsong directed the motorcade toward Meridian, where the bus stopped briefly for

The Reverend C. T. Vivian pleads with Lt. Colonel Sonny Montgomery to make a rest stop along the route to Jackson, Mississippi, Wednesday, May 24, 1961. The man on the right is a news reporter. (Photograph by Lee Lockwood, Getty Photos)

an exchange of drivers. A colorful character who sported dark glasses, a plaid shirt, and a matching plaid-banded hat that made him look like he had just come from the racetrack, Birdsong planned to lead the convoy all the way to Jackson. However, after learning that a second and unexpected band of Free-dom Riders had just left Montgomery, he peeled off from the caravan a few miles outside of Meridian and headed back to the Alabama line.[4]

Among the Freedom Riders themselves, the decision to send a second group to Mississippi on Wednesday morning was a simple one in keeping with CORE's original plan to conduct bus desegregation tests on both major carriers. But among officials in Montgomery, there was considerable sur-prise when fifteen Freedom Riders purchased tickets for the late-morning Greyhound run to Jackson. While rumors were rampant that hordes of Free-dom Riders were descending upon the Deep South, the governmental ar-rangements for the group that had congregated at Dr. Harris's house had assumed that the Wednesday morning Freedom Ride would involve only one bus. The second group, like the first, included only one white Rider—Peter Ackerberg, a student at Antioch College in Yellow Springs, Ohio—and only two women: Lucretia Collins and Doris Castle. Six of the male Riders—John Lewis, Rip Patton, John Lee Copeland, Grady Donald, Clarence Thomas, and LeRoy Wright—were veterans of the Nashville Move-ment, and three—Hank Thomas, John Moody, and Dion Diamond—were Howard students and members of NAG. The remaining three Riders were Frank Holloway, representing the Atlanta chapter of SNCC; Jerome Smith of New Orleans CORE; and Jim Farmer. Copeland was the oldest at age forty-four, and Castle the youngest at eighteen.

The Greyhound group bypassed the most obvious choices and selected Collins as their designated leader. Farmer, despite his prominence, was not considered because no one was quite sure he actually intended to join the Ride. Indeed, as he later acknowledged, he had no intention of going to Jackson until Castle shamed him into it. "I was frankly terrified with the knowledge that the trip to Jackson might be the last trip any of us would ever take," he wrote in 1985. "I was not ready for that. Who, indeed, ever is? . . . It was only the pleading eyes and words of the teenage Doris Castle that persuaded me to get on that bus at the last minute."

With Farmer finally on board, the bus left the terminal at 11:25 amid the jeers of a crowd that had swelled to more than two thousand. Before the bus pulled out, several National Guardsmen and reporters rushed forward to fill some of the unoccupied seats near the Riders, as a much larger force of Guardsmen strained to control the crowd. Out on the highway, a hastily organized escort of highway patrol cruisers and helicopters shadowed the bus's westward track, and the National Guardsmen along the route were once again put on full alert. But, in general, the carefully arranged military procession that had accompanied the first bus was missing. Though hardly on their own, the Greyhound Riders knew nothing of the fate of the first bus and were clearly more vulnerable to assault, or at least to feelings of insecurity, than the Trailways Riders. "There was a lot of tension on the ride to Jackson," Collins recalled. "We didn't know what would happen when we got to the Mississippi line. Whether they were going to implement federal and Alabama 'state' protection or turn us over to the Mississippi state police."

When the bus reached the border and stopped for an exchange of drivers and Guardsmen, a rumor of an impending ambush convinced all but one of the reporters to travel the rest of the way by car. Mississippi officials waved the bus onward anyway. Years later Farmer recalled the sight of Mississippi Guardsmen flanking the highway with "rifles pointed toward the forests." To him the scene conjured up images of "runaway slaves a century ago, sloshing through water and hiding behind trees as they fled pursuing hounds. Visions of Harriet Tubman and the Underground Railroad. Visions, too, of black bodies swinging, with bulging eyes and swollen tongues."

To boost morale, and perhaps to calm her own fears, Collins conducted an on-board workshop on nonviolence, and others sang freedom songs. But there was no real antidote to the heart-stopping tension that Farmer claimed was "greater than that felt by troops being dispatched to a battlefront where bombs were bursting and comrades were dying." That the Riders refused to crack under the strain was, in Farmer's words, a testament to their "indomitable human spirit." As the bus rolled westward, Hank Thomas began singing a new version of the 1947 freedom song "Hallelujah! I'm a-Travelin'" —creating an instant anthem by inserting the words "I'm taking a ride on the

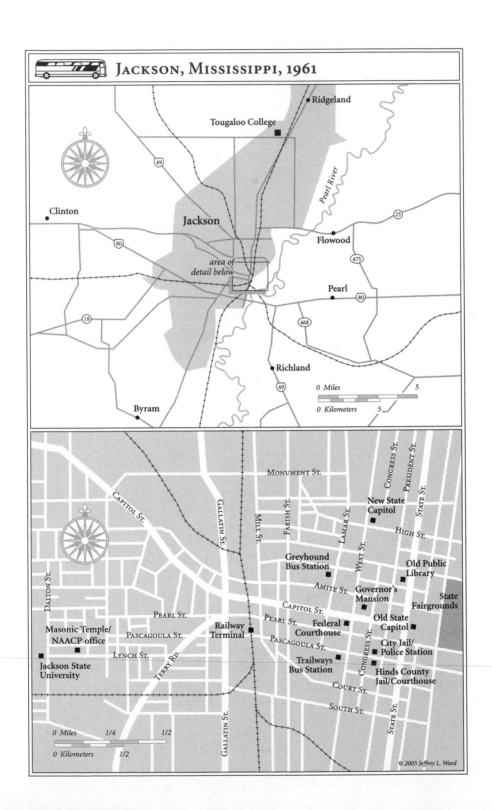

Greyhound bus line, I'm-a-riding the front seat to Jackson this time." By the time the Greyhound pulled into the Jackson terminal, every Rider on the bus was singing about traveling "down freedom's main line," convincing even the most skeptical among them that somehow the journey to Mississippi would turn out all right.[5]

OFFICIALS IN MONTGOMERY AND WASHINGTON, not surprisingly, saw things differently. From the perspective of those concerned about civil order and national or regional image, the spirit that propelled the Riders onward looked a lot like misguided fanaticism. For Robert Kennedy, in particular, the news of a second bus inspired feelings of rage, betrayal, and even denial. The supposed leaders of the Freedom Rider movement had said nothing about a second bus, and Kennedy initially claimed that the Greyhound group had "nothing to do with the Freedom Riders." A few minutes later, when it became clear to everyone that this was patently false, he issued a formal statement praising the law enforcement efforts of Alabama and Mississippi authorities and warning potential Freedom Riders that they would not be accorded federal protection. No federal marshals had accompanied the Freedom Riders, he declared, and there were no plans to deploy marshals in the future. After reiterating that "our obligation is to protect interstate travelers and maintain law and order only when local authorities are unable or unwilling to do so," he claimed that "there is no basis at this time to assume that the people of Mississippi will be lawless or that the responsible state and local officials in Mississippi will not maintain law and order with respect to interstate travel." Even so, he urged "all persons in Alabama and elsewhere to use restraint and weigh their actions carefully." For the good of the nation, he insisted, the disruptive behavior by individuals and organizations on both sides of the segregation controversy must be halted. "I think we should all keep in mind," he explained, "that the President is about to embark on a mission of great importance. Whatever we do in the United States at this time which brings or causes discredit on our country can be harmful to this mission."[6]

This appeal to Cold War patriotism would be repeated by Kennedy and many others later in the day, but it came too late to have any effect on the immediate situation in Alabama and Mississippi. By noon Kennedy's hopes for a quick resolution to the crisis had all but disappeared, and the reports from the Deep South only got worse as the afternoon progressed. Five minutes after the second bus left the Montgomery terminal, a third group of Freedom Riders departed from Atlanta. The leader of the group was Yale University chaplain William Sloane Coffin Jr., a thirty-six-year-old graduate of Union Theological Seminary who had served as a military liaison to the Russian army during World War II and as a CIA operative during the Korean War. A nephew of the distinguished theologian Henry Sloane Coffin and a member of the Peace Corps Advisory Council, the Reverend Coffin represented the leftward-leaning wing of the Northeastern intellectual elite.

Prior to flying south, Coffin defended the Freedom Riders at a rally on the New Haven green, arguing that "the time for moderation may be coming to an end." Later, in Atlanta, before boarding a Greyhound bus to Montgomery, he and six other Riders held a press conference to announce their intention to test facilities all along the route from Georgia to Louisiana. In addition to Coffin, the group included three white professors of religion— Gaylord Noyce of Yale, and David Swift and John Maguire of Wesleyan University; a black Yale law student, George Smith; and two black students from Johnson C. Smith University in Charlotte, North Carolina, Clyde Carter and Charles Jones, both of whom had been active in SNCC and the Rock Hill sit-ins. Coffin's group would not arrive in Montgomery until mid-afternoon, but their looming presence confirmed Kennedy's fear that the Freedom Rider movement was on the verge of enlisting a whole new crop of well-meaning but misguided agitators. Although Georgia detectives were on board the bus monitoring the situation, there was little anyone could do to stop this latest challenge to civil order.

While Robert Kennedy and others were speculating about the implications of the Connecticut-based Freedom Ride, word came that the first bus had reached Jackson. To Kennedy's relief, the Freedom Riders had arrived

Yale University chaplain William Sloane Coffin Jr. (wearing glasses, walking toward an armed National Guardsman) and six other Freedom Riders arrive at the Montgomery Greyhound bus station, Wednesday afternoon, May 24, 1961. Standing on the far left, partially hidden by the Guardsman, is Dr. David Swift. Standing behind him nearest the bus, and wearing glasses, is Dr. John Maguire. The three black Freedom Riders standing behind Coffin are (left to right) George Smith, Charles Jones, and Clyde Carter. (Photograph by Perry Aycock, AP Wide World)

safely a few minutes before two. But otherwise the news was not good. As soon as the bus arrived at the Jackson Trailways terminal, the Riders, black and white, filed into the white waiting room. Several also used the white restroom, but when the Riders ignored police captain J. L. Ray's order to "move on," all twelve were placed under arrest. As several reporters, a contingent of National Guardsmen, and a small but cheering crowd of protesters looked on, the police jammed the Riders into a paddy wagon and hauled them off to the city jail. To make matters worse, Kennedy soon learned that the arrested Riders had refused an offer by NAACP attorneys to post a thousand-dollar bond for each defendant. The Riders would remain in jail at least until their scheduled trial on Thursday afternoon. The formal charges against the Riders were inciting to riot, breach of the peace, and failure to obey a police officer, not violation of state or local segregation laws.

Later in the day the Jackson police dropped the riot incitement charge, but that was cold comfort for federal officials who, despite fair warning from Senator Eastland that the Freedom Riders would be arrested, had continued to hope for an uninterrupted and uneventful journey to New Orleans. In a 1964 interview, Robert Kennedy reluctantly acknowledged his complicity, conceding that he had, in effect, "concurred to the fact that they were going to be arrested." Eastland, he recalled, had told him "what was going to happen: that they'd get there, they'd be protected, and then they'd be locked up." But for some reason the near certainty of the arrests escaped him and others in May 1961.

While the Trailways Riders were settling in at the Jackson city jail, rumors of an impending invasion from the east were precipitating a volatile situation at the downtown Montgomery Greyhound terminal. By the time Coffin's group arrived, a crowd of unruly protesters—some of whom had been at the scene since early morning—was ready for a fight. As Wyatt Tee Walker and Fred Shuttlesworth stepped forward to welcome the seven new recruits, the crowd began pelting them with rocks and bottles. For twenty minutes a cordon of National Guardsmen strained to keep the protesters at bay, as officials puzzled over how to get the nine civil rights activists out of harm's way. Fortunately, the siege was broken when the Guardsmen cleared a path through the crowd large enough to accommodate two cars, one of which was driven by Ralph Abernathy. With the Guardsmen holding back the crowd, the grateful Riders and their hosts climbed into the cars, though it took a minute or two to find a safe exit. In the meantime, several reporters approached the cars to get a statement from Abernathy. Asked what he thought about Robert Kennedy's complaint that the Freedom Riders were embarrassing the nation in front of the world, Abernathy responded tartly: "Well, doesn't the Attorney General know we've been embarrassed all our lives?"[7]

What the attorney general knew, or did not know, about black life would ultimately have a profound bearing on the evolution of the Freedom Rider crisis. But on the afternoon of May 24—in Washington no less than in

Montgomery and Jackson—pure emotion seemed to be driving much of the official reaction to the Freedom Riders' exasperating commitment to nonviolent direct action. Although Robert Kennedy was angry at Ross Barnett for allowing the Jackson police to put the Trailways group in jail, he was even angrier at the obstinacy of the Riders themselves. Mostly he was worried about the apparent widening of the crisis, and he said so in blunt terms in a late afternoon press release. In a thinly veiled reference to Coffin's group and others contemplating the mobilization of Northern sympathizers, he condemned "curiosity seekers, publicity seekers, and others who are seeking to serve their own causes." Considering the "confused situation" in Alabama and Mississippi, travel in these states was inadvisable, according to Kennedy. Indeed, he had received word that a bomb threat had forced the evacuation of the Montgomery Greyhound terminal just minutes after Abernathy and Coffin's group had driven away. Making a public plea for "a cooling-off period," he claimed that "it would be wise for those traveling through these two states to delay their trips until the present state of confusion and danger has passed and an atmosphere of reason and normalcy has been restored." Otherwise, he suggested, "innocent people may be injured," adding: "A mob asks no questions."

Judging by the earlier rejection of his private plea for a cooling-off period, Kennedy knew that movement leaders, not to mention the Freedom Riders themselves, were unlikely to respond favorably to his request for what amounted to a moratorium on activism. Indeed, he was disappointed but not surprised when one of the first responses, a telegram from the Reverend Uriah J. Fields, representing the Montgomery Improvement Association, chastised him for ignoring a century of delayed justice. "Had there not been a cooling-off period following the Civil War," Fields insisted, "the Negro would be free today. Isn't 99 years long enough to cool off, Mr. Attorney General?" Nevertheless, with the crisis deepening, Kennedy felt that he had little choice but to put the Freedom Riders on the moral defensive. If they were unwilling to listen to reason, they would have to suffer the consequences of abandoning the sensible restraint of Cold War liberalism. While he had considerable and rising sympathy for their goals, he could not understand their stubborn adherence to a means of protest that put themselves and the nation at risk. With nothing less than the national image at stake, he had few if any qualms about pointing out their lack of patriotism. And he was hardly the only one who felt that way. Speaking on NBC television's evening news broadcast, commentator David Brinkley, a native of North Carolina, editorialized that the Freedom Riders "are accomplishing nothing whatsoever and, on the contrary, are doing positive harm." While acknowledging that the "bus riders are, of course, within their legal rights in riding buses where they like," he maintained that "the result of these expeditions are of no benefit to anyone, white or Negro, the North or the South, nor the United States in general. We think they should stop it."[8]

The Greyhound group of Freedom Riders arrives in downtown Jackson, Mississippi, where local policemen and police dogs stand guard, Wednesday afternoon, May 24, 1961. (Library of Congress)

Robert Kennedy was heartened by Brinkley's commentary, and the subsequent arrest of the second group of Freedom Riders following their late-afternoon arrival in Jackson only reinforced his willingness to sacrifice immediate justice in the interests of national security. The second round of arrests followed the same pattern as the first, with the Jackson police swooping in and apprehending all fifteen Riders within three minutes of their arrival. As Farmer recalled the scene: "As soon as we walked out of the door, they [the Jackson police] parted, and they knew precisely where I was going, to the white waiting room and not to the colored waiting room. So they parted and made a path for me leading right to the white waiting room [laughing], and I thought maybe I could have pled entrapment when we got to court, because we couldn't go anyplace else." Walking behind Farmer, Lewis had just enough time to make it to the white men's room, where he was unceremoniously arrested while standing at a urinal. When the arresting officer told him to move, Lewis said: "Just a minute. Can't you see what I'm doing?" That only angered the officer, who barked: "I said *move! Now!*"

Kennedy was unaware of this and other indignities until much later, but his mood was such that only a full-scale beating, which the Jackson police were careful to avoid, would have garnered any sympathy. His patience with

Jim Farmer leads a group of Freedom Riders into the white waiting room at the Jackson Greyhound bus station, Wednesday afternoon, May 24, 1961. The Freedom Rider walking behind Farmer is Frank Holloway. The man wearing a hat and standing in front of the bus is T. B. Birdsong, head of the Mississippi Highway Patrol. (Photograph by Lee Lockwood, Getty Photos)

the Freedom Riders was growing thin, especially after he learned that the second group, like the first, had refused bail and was even talking about remaining in jail following their expected convictions on Friday. On the way to jail, they had serenaded the paddy wagon driver with chorus after chorus of "We Shall Overcome," which included the line "We are not afraid"; and they seemed to mean it. If Kennedy had thought that having the Freedom Riders in jail would put an end to the crisis, he would have been all for it. But he knew better, realizing that in the upside-down world of movement culture the incarceration of twenty-seven activists would only encourage others to put their bodies on the line. While he admired their courage, he questioned their sanity. He could only hope that a few hours in a Mississippi jail cell would change their minds. To this end, he asked Marshall and White to see if any of the jailed Riders would reconsider the decision to remain behind bars. When they could not find anyone willing to discuss the matter, much less agree to an early release, Kennedy decided to call King directly to see if he could be persuaded to intervene on behalf of a more reasonable approach to nonviolent protest.

The resultant exchange between the two young leaders did not go well. Transcribed by Kennedy's aides, the conversation testified to the wide ideological gap between nonviolent activists and federal officials—even those who had considerable sympathy for the cause of civil rights:

> *King*:   It's a matter of conscience and morality. They must use their lives and bodies to right a wrong. Our conscience tells us that the law is wrong and we must resist, but we have a moral obligation to accept the penalty.

Kennedy: That is not going to have the slightest effect on what the government is going to do in this field or any other. The fact that they stay in jail is not going to have the slightest effect on me.

King: Perhaps it would help if students came down here by the hundreds—by the hundreds of thousands.

Kennedy: The country belongs to you as much as to me. You can determine what's best just as well as I can, but don't make statements that sound like a threat. That's not the way to deal with us. [a pause]

King: It's difficult to understand the position of oppressed people. Ours is a way out—creative, moral and nonviolent. It is not tied to black supremacy or Communism, but to the plight of the oppressed. It can save the soul of America. You must understand that we've made no gains without pressure and I hope that pressure will always be moral, legal and peaceful.

Kennedy: But the problem won't be settled in Jackson, but by strong federal action.

King: I'm deeply appreciative of what the Administration is doing. I see a ray of hope, but I am different from my father. I feel the need of being free now.

Kennedy: Well, it all depends on what you and the people in jail decide. If they want to get out, we can get them out.

King: They'll stay.[9]

Despite King's strained attempt to salvage the conversation, the call left both men shaken and angry. After hanging up, King complained to Coffin and others who had gathered in Abernathy's living room: "You know, they don't understand the social revolution going on in the world, and therefore they don't understand what we're doing." Kennedy, meanwhile, feeling that he knew all too well what was going in Montgomery and Jackson, immediately called Harris Wofford, the only administration official with close ties to the nonviolent movement. "This is too much," an exasperated Kennedy told Wofford. "I wonder whether they have the best interest of their country at heart. Do you know that one of them is against the atom bomb—yes, he even picketed against it in jail. The President is going abroad and this is all embarrassing him."

Back at Abernathy's house, the postmortem on the Kennedy call was evolving into a long and wrenching discussion of whether the group should go on to Jackson in the morning. Stung by the suggestion that joining a Freedom Ride was unpatriotic, Coffin and the others asked King for guidance. Should they go on in the face of Kennedy's plea for a moratorium? King answered the question by leading them in prayer, after which a vote was taken by secret ballot. Despite considerable anguish, the vote was unanimous. All agreed that they had come too far to turn back, and one of the most adamant was John Maguire, a Montgomery native who had been shocked by the tumultuous scene at the Trailways terminal. Later in the evening Coffin placed a call to McGeorge Bundy, an old friend and fellow Yale graduate who was serving as a presidential advisor on foreign policy. The purpose of the call was to convince Bundy to talk directly to the president about the need for a clear-cut moral statement denouncing racial prejudice and segregation, a statement that would implicitly endorse the Freedom Rides. To Coffin's dismay, he got nowhere with Bundy, who offered a few words of stern advice before going back to bed. Refusing to give up, Coffin called Wofford, who, though much more sympathetic than Bundy, expressed doubt that "the President would take further action." With his ears still burning from Robert Kennedy's earlier fulmination against the Riders, Wofford had to report that the likelihood of a presidential endorsement was slim. If Coffin and his friends continued their Freedom Ride, they would have to do so without the approval of the administration.[10]

THERE WERE MANY REASONS for the Kennedy brothers' determination to keep the Freedom Rider movement from spreading. One of their most pressing concerns was the apparent polarization of the struggle over racial segregation. The Freedom Rides had attracted the attention of extremists at both ends of the political spectrum, including the Arlington, Virginia–based American Nazi Party. On Wednesday evening, just minutes before Kennedy's emotional call to King, George Lincoln Rockwell, the Fuehrer of the American Nazi Party, and nine of his uniformed storm troopers were arrested outside of a New Orleans movie theater where the pro-Israeli film *Exodus* was playing. Earlier in the evening they had tried to disrupt a local NAACP membership rally, but the New Orleans police had ordered them to leave the area. Rockwell and his bodyguard had flown to New Orleans from Washington on Tuesday afternoon, but the rest of the troopers had traveled south in a two-vehicle caravan that included a blue and white Volkswagen van dubbed the "Hate Bus." Signs emblazoned on the van advertised LINCOLN ROCKWELL'S HATE BUS and slogans such as WE DO HATE RACE MIXING and WE HATE JEW-COMMUNISM. Pledging solidarity with the Klansmen who had attacked the Freedom Riders in Alabama, Rockwell hoped to confront the Riders when they arrived in New Orleans. "Anybody that doesn't hate communism and doesn't hate race-mixers," he explained to reporters, "there's something wrong with them." On Tuesday the Hate Bus stopped briefly in Montgomery, but National Guardsmen promptly escorted them out of town. In New Orleans, Rockwell and the troopers carried signs with the words "America for Whites, Africa for Blacks" and "Gas Chamber for Traitors," which they made clear included the "Communist, nigger-loving" Freedom Riders.[11]

Not wanting to call attention to Rockwell's grotesque parody of the Freedom Ride, administration officials at first tried to downplay the significance of the Hate Bus, but on Wednesday evening Rockwell's antics became entwined in a senatorial discussion of the wisdom of the Freedom Rides. Al-

American Nazi Party storm troopers and their "Hate Bus" in Montgomery en route to New Orleans, Tuesday, May 23, 1961. (AP Wide World)

ready embroiled in a battle over the advisability of attaching an anti-segregation rider to the administration's aid-to-education bill, liberals and conservatives squared off in a fight over the civil and moral equivalency of Rockwell and the Freedom Riders. After Senator John Stennis of Mississippi insisted that by employing "the same reason and logic as the Freedom Riders," Rockwell's neo-Nazis "could well claim they are merely exercising their constitutional rights," Senator Jacob Javits, a liberal Republican from New York, called for a full Senate debate on his colleague's outrageous defamation of the civil rights movement. Ignoring the fact that the administration had already taken a public position that, while not going as far as Stennis's equivalency argument, had implicitly challenged the moral authority of the Freedom Riders, Javits also announced plans to offer a Senate resolution supporting the president's intervention in the South. Despite Javits's good intentions, none of this pleased the president or any of the other administration officials who just wanted the crisis to pass quietly from the scene.[12]

The Freedom Riders would later appreciate Javits's effort to mobilize bipartisan support for racial justice and desegregation, but at the moment they were more concerned with the challenge of surviving their first night in a Mississippi jail. Of the twenty-seven incarcerated Riders, only Bevel, a native of Itta Bena, had significant firsthand experience with Mississippi's special brand of segregation. Prior to their arrival on Wednesday afternoon, the others could only imagine what indignities awaited them. For black Americans, and even for many white Americans, the Mississippi of myth and legend was a terrifying place. Lewis, for example, was unnerved on the road to Jackson by the sight of Mississippi Guardsmen who "wore big bushy beards that made them look like Confederate soldiers." Only later did he discover that the menacing-looking Guardsmen were actually Confederate reenactors suitably groomed for upcoming participation in a Civil War Centennial celebration—and even this discovery was only mildly reassuring in a state where blacks had good reason to fear the worst.

As the state with the highest concentration of black population (42.3 percent in 1960), Mississippi boasted a rich tradition of African American folk culture, including the artistry of down-home blues. But among white Mississippians, both inside and outside the Black Belt Delta region, an unforgiving and often brutal form of white supremacist repression held sway. In 1890 the state legislature had spearheaded a region-wide trend toward codification of black disfranchisement and Jim Crow with the so-called Mississippi Plan, and in the seventy years since disfranchisement the state had not relinquished its reputation as the home of the South's most vigilant defenders of racial control and white privilege. Noting that Mississippi led the nation in lynching, poverty, political demagoguery, and social backwardness, the pundit H. L. Mencken dubbed it "the worst American state" in the 1920s. Sadly, in 1961 there was little reason to challenge this unenviable designation; indeed, the recent lynchings of Emmett Till (1955) and Mack Charles Parker (1959) seemed to confirm Mississippi's benighted status as a land apart.[13]

As the Freedom Riders would soon discover, many white Mississippians were uncomfortable with the state's image as a lawless home of Negrophobic vigilantes. There was much talk of a new Mississippi, still proudly segregated but dedicated to the peaceful coexistence and well-being of all of its citizens. Many white Mississippians were proud that, unlike Klan-infested Alabama, Mississippi was a White Citizens' Council (WCC) state. Founded in the Mississippi Delta town of Indianola in 1954, the White Citizens' Councils advocated economic and political pressure, not violence, as the best means to preserve segregation and white supremacy. Even though critics sometimes referred to the councils as "the Klan in the grey flannel suit," most WCC chapters in Mississippi and elsewhere were determined to counter the Deep South's reputation for violent repression. It was in this spirit that Mississippi officials, virtually all of whom were WCC members, accorded the Freedom Riders a firm but polite reception. To the surprise of the national press and the Freedom Riders themselves, the arresting officers and jailers in Jackson went about their business with cool efficiency. The show of courtesy and professionalism had actually begun on Wednesday morning when local officials led visiting reporters on an upbeat public-relations tour of the "new" Jackson. Prior to the tour,

Mayor Allen Thompson presented each reporter with an honorary police badge and a brochure detailing recent improvements in housing, schools, and recreation facilities open to the city's black population. Separate but equal was a reality in Jackson, he assured them, even in the city jail.[14]

One New York reporter, who found Mississippi officials "excruciatingly polite," claimed that the Freedom Riders had been "upstaged and virtually smothered by cordiality." But the reality at the Jackson city jail was less pleasant than the carefully crafted public image implied. From the outset, most of the jailed Riders refused to cooperate with their jailers. In an effort to boost morale, Bevel, blessed with a beautiful voice, led round after round of freedom songs, an irritant that nearly drove the guards to distraction. Others— though not Bevel—engaged in a hunger strike that caused considerable controversy among the Riders. Still others infuriated police interrogators by refusing to end their "Yes" and "No" answers with the word "Sir." Just after his arrival at the city jail, Vivian admonished a guard for calling him "boy." "My church generally ordains *men*, not boys," Vivian informed him, whereupon the guard, with billy club in hand, screamed: "I'll knock yo' fuckin' black nappy head through that goddamn wall if you don't shut yo' goddamn mouth, nigger." Vivian escaped this particular encounter without injury, but not everyone agreed that such symbolic challenges to authority were a good idea. Nor was there any consensus on the proper limits of noncooperation or on the best means of expressing the nonviolent creed. Indeed, many of the Riders—even some of those who had spent time in Tennessee and Alabama jails—had difficult moments either dealing with their fears or maintaining a composure that reconciled protest with common decency. There was, however, solid agreement that as many of the Riders as possible should remain in jail. When Len Holt, who had flown to Jackson with Diane Nash, visited the Riders on Wednesday evening, the commitment to the "jail–no bail" policy was still strong.[15]

Back in Montgomery, where Coffin's group was preparing to depart for Jackson, there was also an unmistakable spirit of movement solidarity. Accompanied to the Trailways terminal by four SCLC leaders—Shuttlesworth, Walker, Abernathy, and Bernard Lee—Coffin and his six colleagues held a preboarding press conference to explain why they had decided to travel on to Mississippi against the Kennedy administration's wishes. Rejecting the argument that the Freedom Rides were embarrassing the nation in front of the world and endangering President Kennedy's stature on the eve of a critical summit meeting, Coffin declared: "We can't drag the name of the United States in the mud. The name of the United States is already in the mud. It is up to us to get it out."

Following the press conference, the seven Riders and their SCLC hosts moved to the Trailways lunch counter for a brief breakfast—the same counter that the Lawson group had desegregated the day before. This time, however, on orders from Governor Patterson, the Montgomery County sheriff, Mac

Sim Butler, arrested all eleven of the offending activists for disorderly conduct and conspiring to breach the peace. Although General Graham had agreed to provide Coffin's group with an armed escort of fifty National Guardsmen and thirty-two highway patrolmen, he did not interfere with the arrests. Indeed, he seemed relieved that the escort to the Mississippi border was no longer necessary. "Now everyone is happy," he told reporters. "This is what they wanted and we have accommodated them. They've been arrested quietly, like they wanted to be, and now I'm happy too."[16]

Graham's not-so-subtle suggestion that this new batch of Freedom Riders was a band of publicity seekers who did not really want to travel on to Mississippi reflected a deliberate strategy to delegitimize the hordes of outside agitators that he and others feared were about to descend upon the Deep South. Based on a combination of misinformation and wishful thinking, it was a strategy that appealed to a wide variety of government leaders, including officials at the Justice Department and the White House. In his initial reaction to the Greyhound group on Wednesday morning, Robert Kennedy had drawn a sharp distinction between real and phony Freedom Riders, and in desperation he returned to this specious line of reasoning on Thursday afternoon. This time, however, he distinguished between the original CORE Freedom Riders and the pretenders that followed. "It took a lot of courage for the first group to go," he told a Washington reporter, "but not much for the others." He even suggested that the Freedom Riders who insisted on remaining in a Mississippi jail should be shunned for irresponsibly producing "good propaganda for America's enemies." Earlier in the afternoon, he had ordered the demobilization of all but one hundred of the federal marshals in Alabama, and now he appeared to be assuming a position of constitutional neutrality with respect to the Freedom Riders' right to travel. At this point he was acting more out of anger and frustration than calculated decision-making, and he would soon draw back from his implied surrender to parochial and political interests. But in the midst of what amounted to a temporary failure of nerve at the Justice Department, it is little wonder that some liberal administration supporters became confused and a bit dispirited.

One casualty was Jacob Javits's effort to garner a Senate resolution endorsing the use of federal marshals in Alabama. Without clear-cut signals from the White House, there was no way to counter the threat of a Southern filibuster, and the resolution died before ever coming to a vote. Emboldened by this turn of events, Mississippi's Senator Eastland immediately went on the attack, claiming that the Freedom Rides were "Communist-inspired" and "devised deliberately . . . as a propaganda method to embarrass the President and the United States." Reaching back to the original CORE Ride, he denounced Jim Peck as "a Communist agitator and organizer of the most dangerous kind" and CORE as a subversive organization whose "creed has been lawlessness" and whose "tactics have followed the pattern set by Communist agitators the world over."[17]

Eastland's unrestrained Red-baiting played better in Jackson than in Washington, and the Kennedy administration quickly distanced itself from this and other intemperate attacks on the Freedom Riders. Clearly, the position of the defiant white South provided no refuge for administration officials, who had received an even more telling reminder of this fact earlier in the day when a carload of gun-toting white teenagers wounded the Reverend Solomon Seay outside of his parsonage. Fortunately, Seay escaped with only a wrist wound, but the drive-by incident reminded the Kennedy brothers of why they had sent the marshals to Alabama. If administration officials were somewhat uncomfortable with associating with the Freedom Riders, they were even more uncomfortable tying themselves to the antics and attitudes of cowardly gunmen or white supremacist zealots like Eastland. Even so, when John Kennedy delivered a special State of the Union address to Congress on Thursday evening, he avoided any reference to the Freedom Riders or the domestic civil rights struggle. After declaring that he had come to the Capitol "to promote the freedom doctrine," he identified "the whole southern half of the globe" as "the great battleground for the expansion of freedom today." The more immediate battleground in the southern half of the United States received no mention. Most of the speech focused on foreign aid, national defense, and the space program, and the most memorable line was the president's daring pledge to put a man on the moon by the end of the decade. This implicit slight to the cause of civil rights did not go unnoticed in movement circles, prompting one New York rabbi to comment that "it seems strange to discuss trips to the moon when it is impossible for white and colored Americans to travel together on a bus and use the same facilities in 'the land of the free and the home of the brave.' "[18]

Politically speaking, Kennedy's omission of the domestic freedom struggle may have made sense, but neither his silence nor Eastland's bombast did anything to slow the momentum of the Freedom Rider movement. On Thursday afternoon, several hours before the State of the Union address, Pauline Knight, speaking for the Nashville Movement, announced that there was no shortage of available reinforcements for the Riders arrested in Jackson. "If the people there have to stay in jail—if they are convicted," Knight promised, "then there will be another busload from Nashville." Not to be outdone, the CORE office in New York issued a field order expanding its nonviolent campaign to railroad and airline terminals. Written by Farmer earlier in the week, the order declared that "the time to act is now." On Friday morning the *New York Times* reported that the CORE office "had the appearance of a combat field headquarters," as more than a dozen staff members and volunteers "frantically answered batteries of telephones, dispatched telegrams and mimeographed statements and bulletins." According to CORE spokesperson Marvin Rich, "more than 100 Freedom Riders" were "standing by at strategic locations in the South to train others in nonviolent techniques or to take places on buses themselves." When reporters pressed him for a statement on where all this was headed, Rich suggested that the movement was poised to "end segregation by the end of this year."

Rich's heady prediction was part hyperbole, but it also reflected a growing confidence that the entire civil rights movement was lining up behind the Freedom Riders. On Thursday even the leaders of the NAACP and the National Urban League, two organizations that generally steered clear of direct action, summarily rejected the attorney general's plea for a cooling-off period. "There can be no cooling-off period in the effort to obtain one's citizenship rights," Roy Wilkins declared. "The effort must go on continuously by all feasible methods. . . . We further reject the contention that Negro citizens should voluntarily declare a moratorium on their efforts to challenge the denial of their rights, and should permit segregation-as-usual in the interest of lessened tension." Accordingly, he urged the student members of the NAACP's 123 college chapters to insist on nonsegregated travel when they returned home at the end of the spring semester. Putting the matter more succinctly, a National Urban League spokesperson insisted that "this is no time for the nation to compromise with freedom."[19]

On Friday morning the Freedom Rider movement received another unexpected boost when Jim Peck was interviewed by Dave Garroway on the NBC network's *Today Show*. Speaking in a calm and reasoned voice and looking much like an ordinary citizen, Peck defended the Freedom Rides in front of a national audience, a good part of which had seen pictures of his bandaged head ten days earlier. Although Peck's television appearance triggered a storm of protest in the Deep South—especially in Mississippi, where editors characterized the CORE leader as "Garroway's latest anti-Southern hero"—for many Americans it matched a sympathetic human face with a movement that sometimes seemed too abstract and exotic to comprehend.

Perhaps even more important, Friday morning also marked an organizational milestone in the brief history of the Freedom Rider movement. At Ebenezer Baptist Church in Atlanta, King convened an organizational meeting of the Freedom Ride Coordinating Committee (FRCC). On hand were representatives of five organizations interested in sustaining and expanding the Freedom Rider movement: King and Bernard Lee of SCLC; Gordon Carey of CORE; Ed King of SNCC; two preachers representing the NCLC in the absence of the arrested Freedom Riders Bevel and Lawson; and a delegate from the National Student Association. At the founding meeting, the group agreed to establish recruitment centers in Nashville, Atlanta, New Orleans, and Jackson; to coordinate fund-raising for an all-out assault on Jim Crow transportation; to seek a meeting with the president; and to push for unambiguous endorsements of desegregated travel from both the Justice Department and the Interstate Commerce Commission. This was a tall order for a movement that had seen a majority of its leaders arrested in the preceding forty-eight hours, but the founding members of the FRCC were determined to make a statement, both to themselves and the world, that the

Freedom Rider movement could not be broken by arrests, demagogic Red-baiting, or even federal equivocation. As the FRCC's first press release put it, they felt compelled to "fill the jails of Montgomery and Jackson in order to keep a sharp image of the issue before the public."[20]

Predictably, King and the Freedom Riders also faced mounting criticism from Southern white liberals and moderates who either endorsed a cooling-off period or questioned the entire strategy of relying on "outside agitators." In an interview published in the Friday, May 26, issue of the *New York Times*, an unnamed "white leader who has played a prominent role in the civil rights struggle" scolded the Freedom Riders for alienating potential allies and en-dangering the hard-earned progress that the civil rights movement had al-ready achieved. "It is one thing for persons to demand equal treatment in the towns where they live or for persons to insist on it in the course of their normal travel," he pointed out. "But for persons just to test and challenge is too much like baiting. They don't appeal to any underlying sympathy among Southerners. This becomes a dare, not a protest. I agree with the Attorney General that it is time for the freedom rides to end." The article went on to quote an "equally well known Negro," also unnamed, who shared the white liberal's views. "What concerns me," the Negro leader declared, "is what may happen to Southern Negroes after the Freedom Riders return to the safety of their homes outside the Deep South." This particular complaint, which would find wide currency in the press in the days and weeks to come, drew more than a few wry smiles from the Freedom Riders themselves, many of whom had been born and bred in the South.[21]

ON FRIDAY AFTERNOON, while administration officials and Southern liberals continued to tiptoe across the minefield of Cold War politics and public opinion, the focus of movement and media attention shifted to the Freedom Riders' pending legal problems. In Montgomery, five members of Coffin's group, after deciding that one night in a Southern jail was enough, posted bond and prepared to return to Connecticut. Of the seven Freedom Riders who had come in from Atlanta, only Jones and Carter, the two SNCC activ-ists from Charlotte, remained in jail with their SCLC hosts to await trial. Prior to leaving Montgomery, Coffin and Maguire spent two hours with *Life* correspondent Ronald Bailey, who later published their comments under Coffin's byline. In "Why Yale Chaplain Rode: Christians Can't Be Outside," Coffin, with Maguire's help, explained why he felt compelled to become a Freedom Rider. "Many people in the South have criticized the Freedom Riders as 'outsiders' who went there to stir up trouble," Coffin acknowledged. "But if you're an American and a Christian you can't be an outsider on racial dis-crimination, whether practiced in the North or in the South. Discrimination has always been immoral and now, as it undermines U.S. foreign policy, it is a matter of national concern, not of local mores. Here was a group of fellow Americans striving for rights that were legally and morally theirs. As

Christians and Americans, we couldn't *not* go on the Freedom Ride. On this issue all Americans are insiders." Coffin went on to explain that "by joining the Freedom Riders we hoped to dramatize the fact that this is not just a student movement. We felt that our being university educators might encourage the sea of silent moderates in the South to raise their voices. . . . I've heard it said that 60% of white Southerners take a neutral attitude on the race question. But only the extremists are heard. As always, it has been the listless, not the lawless, who are the deciding factor." Closing with the rhetorical question "Would we do it again?" he counseled that "every man must finally do what he believes is right."

Later in the day, before boarding a plane for New York, Coffin condemned the arrest and confinement of the eleven movement activists as "blatantly illegal" and "a travesty of justice," while Maguire warned "that our fellow faculty members and students across the nation are poised to continue riding these buses if that is the only way we can obtain our goal of civil rights." Adding that he and his colleagues were only going back north because of compelling teaching responsibilities and final exams, Maguire assured reporters that they had not seen the last of academic Freedom Riders. Earlier in the afternoon General Graham, on hand to arrange a National Guard escort for the departing professors, had condemned the plan to send in additional Freedom Riders as "immoral, stupid, and criminal." Infuriated by a hunger strike being staged by the five activists still in jail, Graham and other Alabama officials insisted that Abernathy and his fellow inmates were being treated well and in accordance with the law. Indeed, if anyone wanted proof of Montgomery's commitment to equal justice, he only had to visit the county courthouse, where earlier in the day five white men had been convicted and sentenced for their involvement in the rioting of May 20 and 21.[22]

In Jackson, Mississippi officials were making similar claims as twenty-seven jailed Freedom Riders were brought before Municipal Judge James L. Spencer. With the courtroom under tight security and with no photography allowed, the trial began at four o'clock. At the outset, the proceedings were strictly segregated, according to Mississippi law and custom, but after Wiley Branton, one of the Freedom Riders' four attorneys, objected to the racial separation of his clients, Judge Spencer allowed Paul Dietrich and Peter Ackerberg to join their black co-defendants. Though known as a hard-line segregationist, Spencer also made a point of welcoming Branton—a well-known black civil rights attorney from Pine Bluff, Arkansas—and the Riders' other out-of-state lawyer, Charles Oldham, the St. Louis–based national chairman of CORE. Spencer was noticeably less respectful toward the defendants' two black Mississippi lawyers, R. Jess Brown of Vicksburg and Jack Young of Jackson. As several national reporters later acknowledged, though, the overall mood in the courtroom was unexpectedly civil. Following Spencer's lead, the local prosecutor, Jack Travis, began with a gesture of compassion by dropping the second charge of disobeying a police officer. City officials did not want to "be harsh," he explained. Nodding his head in approval, Judge Spencer then asked the defendants to enter a plea to the remaining charge of breaching the peace. When all twenty-seven defendants pleaded not guilty and defense attorneys followed with a request for a directed verdict of acquittal, both Travis and Spencer seemed a bit miffed, but, realizing that Mississippi justice was also on trial, they made a concerted effort to keep their composure.

The city's first and only prosecution witness was J. L. Ray, the police captain who had rounded up both groups of Riders on Wednesday. After acknowledging that he had been given a standing order to arrest the Riders if they tried to enter the terminal's white waiting room, Ray explained that he and his superiors were aware of "what happened in Montgomery" and "didn't want a similar incident to happen here." When defense attorneys cross-examined him on the legal and racial implications of arresting interstate passengers for simply entering a white waiting room, he replied with the maxim "When in Rome, do as the Romans do." And when asked where he wanted the offending Freedom Riders to go, he replied: "Out, just keep going." With this explanation in the record, a confident Travis rested his case. The defense then called three of the defendants to the stand as witnesses. The first was Jim Lawson, who, after describing his background as a pacifist and conscientious objector, proceeded to excoriate Mississippi authorities for escorting the Freedom Riders to Jackson against their will. Taking Lawson's testimony as a cue, Branton interjected the assertion that the state of Mississippi was guilty of "entrapment," having "deliberately brought these defendants from the state line to Jackson to arrest them." This line of reasoning seemed to catch Travis and Judge Spencer off guard, and during the testimony of the last two defense witnesses, Vivian and Farmer, there was a noticeable edge to the back-and-forth between defense attorneys and the prosecution. Following a question from Travis about the philosophy of nonviolence, Vivian gave the prosecutor more than he had bargained for, launching into a detailed discussion of Gandhi and Thoreau. After a minute or two, Travis yelled, "Stop! Stop!"—prompting Vivian to shoot back: "Well, you asked the question." "I won't make that mistake again," Travis replied, providing the trial with one of its few lighthearted moments.

After nearly two hours of listening to Travis's warnings and the Freedom Riders' apostasy, Judge Spencer had heard enough. Within seconds of Branton's closing statement—which reminded the judge that he and other Mississippi officials had taken an oath to uphold the United States Constitution—Spencer found all twenty-seven defendants guilty as charged. After informing the audience that "we're not here trying any segregation laws or the rights of these people to sit on any buses or to eat in any place," he scolded the Freedom Riders for seeking recourse in the streets instead of the courts. "Their avowed purpose," he insisted, "was to inflame the public." Finding them "in open defiance of the laws of Mississippi," he sentenced each defendant to a two-hundred-dollar fine and a suspended sixty-day jail term. Whether he regarded the suspension of jail time as leniency or simply as an efficient means of ridding the state of unwelcome visitors was unclear, but the look on his face suggested that he never wanted to see them or their kind again.[23]

Prior to the trial, the Freedom Riders had announced their intention to remain in jail until Mississippi authorities agreed to recognize the legality of desegregated interstate transit, but Spencer and other Mississippi officials held out some hope that at least some of the Riders were bluffing. In truth, there were those among the Riders who questioned the strategy of "jail–no bail." For some, spending sixty days, or even one more night, in a Mississippi jail was a frightening prospect. Nevertheless, when the convicted Freedom Riders met with their attorneys on Friday evening, no one spoke in favor of a mass bail-out. Some, like Lucretia Collins, who had promised to return to Nashville for the May 29 graduation exercises at Tennessee State, had personal reasons for paying her two-hundred-dollar fine and accepting a suspended sentence, and CORE officials decided that the four Freedom Riders from Louisiana—David Dennis, Jerome Smith, Doris Castle, and Julia Aaron—were needed in New Orleans to set up an FRCC recruitment and training center. But there was general agreement that the rest of the Riders could serve the cause best by remaining in jail. Later in the evening, while the Jackson NAACP held a mass meeting at a black Masonic temple to protest the convictions, local authorities transferred the Riders across the street to the Hinds County Jail. With reports circulating that at least two new groups of Nashville-based Freedom Riders were about to leave for Jackson, the defenders of white Mississippi's most cherished traditions wanted to be ready for the next invasion.[24]

On Friday afternoon, following the organizational meeting of the FRCC, King had told reporters that there would be a "temporary lull" in the Freedom Rides while movement organizers set up recruiting and training centers around the South. But the predicted lull did not last long. Hoping to sustain the movement's momentum, Nash returned to Nashville on Saturday morning to help Leo Lillard and Pauline Knight finalize the arrangements for a new round of Rides. By Saturday afternoon, thirteen new Freedom Riders were ready to go. Just after lunch, Knight, Allen Cason (who had narrowly escaped serious injury in Montgomery the previous Saturday), and two other Riders boarded a bus for Montgomery, with plans to travel on to Jackson. At 5:15 a second group of nine Riders—all students at Tennessee State—boarded a Greyhound headed for Jackson via Memphis. Like Cason, six of the nine Tennessee State Greyhound Riders had participated in the recent Birmingham-to-Montgomery Ride, and even though they had returned to Nashville earlier in the week to take their final exams, all still faced the possibility of expulsion for their participation in the Freedom Rides.

While the new Riders were en route, Lillard issued a deliberately confusing statement that puzzled many observers. After refusing to confirm that the Riders planned to conduct desegregation tests once they arrived in Jackson, he coyly suggested to reporters that both groups were "just normal college students going home from schools here." Their behavior was simply in keeping with the national NAACP's call, issued the day before, for college students "to return home at the end of the school year on a 'nonsegregated transportation basis.' " Speaking in New York, Roy Wilkins had urged students to "sit where you choose on trains and buses" and to "use terminal restaurant and other facilities without discrimination." Anxious officials in Alabama and Mississippi did not know what to make of Lillard's suggestion that the Nashville students were not necessarily "Freedom Riders," especially when a SNCC spokesperson in Atlanta was calling for a mass of volunteers to join the Freedom Rider movement. Representing both SNCC and FRCC, Ed King told reporters on Saturday afternoon that three interracial groups of Freedom Riders were on their way to Jackson, and many others would soon follow. According to King, SNCC members in sixteen states and the District of Columbia were mobilizing for an all-out assault on segregated transit. Before long, King predicted, there would be hundreds of new Freedom Riders committed to "jail–no bail," students picketing Greyhound and Trailways terminals across the South, and a flood of telegrams to President Kennedy and the Justice Department "demanding protection for interstate passengers from arrests by local law-enforcement officers on segregation charges." Like Lillard, King refused to provide confirmation that the Riders presently headed for Jackson planned to violate local segregation laws, but he hinted that desegregation tests would begin as soon the Riders could coordinate their plans with local movement leaders "on the scene."[25]

In the case of Knight's group, such coordination led to the addition of four more Freedom Riders. Arriving in Montgomery at 8:25 P.M., the four Nashville students soon joined forces with two members of the Washington-based Nonviolent Action Group, William Mahoney and Franklin Hunt, and two white students from Wilberforce, Ohio, David Fankhauser and David Myers. After spending the night as the guests of Montgomery Improvement Association leaders, the eight Riders made their way to the Trailways terminal, which was still under heavy guard. In contrast to the riotous scene of the previous weekend, the terminal was almost empty, and the Riders had no trouble desegregating the terminal's restaurant and restrooms. When Sheriff Butler was later asked why he had not arrested the most recent violators of Montgomery's segregated facilities ordinance, he replied: "None of us saw it. We were getting some sleep when the call came." In truth, local and state officials, eager to escort the Riders out of Montgomery, had made sure that there would be no arrests, and no trouble. "It's so calm," Knight remarked, "it's almost unbelievable in comparison with what happened [last] Saturday. I just hope people are peaceful in their hearts." When Knight and the others boarded the bus for Jackson a few minutes later, Sheriff Butler, General Graham, and a line of highway patrol cars moved into position to escort the bus to the Mississippi border. Though more modest than Wednesday's operation, the Sunday morning convoy reached the border without incident and proceeded on to Jackson, arriving at 1:30 P.M.

By the time the Trailways group arrived in Jackson, the Greyhound group was already in jail. After a late-night stop in Memphis, the Greyhound departed for Mississippi around 1:15 in the morning and arrived in Jackson just before dawn. Although the Greyhound Riders, unlike the Trailways Riders, traveled without a police escort, local authorities were waiting for them at the terminal. As soon as they walked into the white waiting room, the nine students were arrested for breaching the peace and led to a waiting paddy wagon. Before entering the wagon, one of the students handed a pile of pamphlets on "Fellowship and Human Rights in America" to a detective who jokingly promised to distribute them. Otherwise the arrests followed the same pattern as those of the previous Wednesday. "They passed us right on through the white terminal, into the paddy wagon, and into jail," Fred Leonard recalled. "There was no violence in Mississippi." Eight hours later, Knight and the Trailways group suffered a similar fate, bringing the total number of arrested Mississippi Freedom Riders to forty-four. Arresting Freedom Riders, as one local editor complained on Monday morning, was becoming "monotonous."[26]

Freedom Riders are placed under arrest at the Jackson Greyhound terminal, Sunday, May 28, 1961. From left to right: Frances Wilson, Fred Leonard, Catherine Burks, Lester McKinnie, and Clarence Wright. (Bettmann-CORBIS)

He was not alone in his feelings. Even before news of the latest arrests hit the papers, there were signs that many Americans—and not only white Mississippians—were growing tired of the Freedom Riders. In a stinging Sunday morning editorial, the *New York Times* declared that "the battle against segregation will not be won overnight nor by any one dramatic strategy. The Freedom Riders, for all their idealism, now may be overreaching themselves. There is a danger that if their offensive is continued at the present pace, exacerbated feelings on both sides could lead to tragic results in which the extremists could overwhelm the men of moderation on whom the real solution will ultimately depend. . . . The Freedom Riders have made their point. Now is the time for restraint, relaxation of tension and a cessation of their courageous, legal, peaceful but nonetheless provocative action in the South." The *Times* certainly did not speak for all white Americans, and there were still many voices urging the Freedom Riders to press their case, including an unrepentant William Sloane Coffin, who reminded his Sunday morning congregation at Yale that "any return to normalcy means a return to injustice." In the nation as a whole, however, the tide of public opinion seemed to be running against the Riders. Many Americans, particularly outside the South, felt conflicted, as sympathy for civil rights vied with disapproval of the Freedom Riders' tactics. Even among those who were strongly sympathetic to the civil rights movement, there seemed to be a rising wave of sentiment in favor of a moratorium or cooling-off period. Indeed, with the president's departure for Paris scheduled for Tuesday evening, the argument for national solidarity seemed especially compelling.[27]

ON MONDAY, MAY 29, the prospects for a cooling-off period did not look good. On the contrary, the situation appeared to be heating up on all fronts. In Jackson, the day began with the pre-dawn transfer of twenty-two Freedom Riders to the Hinds County Penal Farm, seventeen miles south of the city. Judging by the smiles on the faces of their guards, the Riders had good reason to fear the move. As one black inmate at the county jail told Farmer: "That's where they're gonna try to break you. They're gonna try to whip your ass." After Jack Young seconded the inmate's warning—"That place is rough. You're going to have trouble there," he predicted—Farmer asked him to let the FBI know what was going on. The actual scene at the penal farm turned out to be even worse than the Riders had anticipated. "When we got there," Frank Holloway recalled, "we met several men in ten-gallon hats, looking like something out of an old Western, with rifles in their hands, staring at us as if we were desperate killers about to escape." This sight drew a sardonic smile from Holloway, but what happened next was anything but humorous. As he described the scene: "Soon they took us out to a room, boys on one side and girls on the other. One by one they took us into another room for questioning before they gave us their black and white stripes. There were about eight guards with sticks in their hands in the second room, and the Freedom Rider being questioned was surrounded by these men. Outside we could hear the questions, and the thumps and whacks, and sometimes a quick groan or cry when their questions weren't answered to their satisfaction. They beat several Riders who didn't say 'Yes, sir,' but none of them would Uncle-Tom the guards. Rev. C. T. Vivian . . . was beaten pretty bad. When he came out he had blood streaming from his head."

This was more than enough to convince Holloway, Harold Andrews (Holloway's classmate at Morehouse), and Peter Ackerberg, the white Freedom Rider from Antioch College, to post bond and accept a police escort to the Jackson airport. However, nineteen of the Riders decided to stick it out, to the obvious satisfaction of farm superintendent Max Thomas and his boss, Sheriff J. R. Gilfoy. "We are not going to coddle them," promised Gilfoy. "When they go to work on the county roads this afternoon they are going to work just like anyone else here." The Freedom Riders would also wear "black and white striped prison uniforms," just like the other prisoners, though he couldn't resist pointing out that so far the regular inmates had refused to "have anything to do with them." This would not be the last time that a Mississippi official would suggest that outside agitators were the lowest of the low, deserving the contempt of even hardened criminals. Despite his pledge to treat the Riders like the other prisoners, Gilfoy soon decided that it was too risky to put them to work on the roads or in the fields, where they might encounter meddling journalists. Instead he kept them confined to their cells, which many of the Riders came to view as a greater hardship than anything that might have awaited them beyond the bars.[28]

In Montgomery, Monday morning brought excitement of a different sort. Praising the Alabama National Guard for "restoring public confidence in law and order" and proving to "the world that this state can and will continue to maintain law and order without the aid of Federal force," John Patterson announced that martial law in Montgomery would end at midnight. With most of the federal marshals already withdrawn, Patterson's announcement seemed to signal a lessening of the tension between state and federal authorities. But any notion that the Alabama phase of the crisis was completely over was dispelled by the continuing hunger strike at the county jail, where, to the dismay of their jailers, Abernathy and company had organized the Montgomery County Jail Council for the purpose of encouraging other prisoners to sing freedom songs and "join in the spirit" of the movement. Even more alarming was the legal drama unfolding in Judge Frank Johnson's courtroom. On Wednesday, May 24, the Justice Department had filed a request to expand the injunction against Alabama Klansmen and other vigilantes to include local police officials in Birmingham and Montgomery, and Judge Johnson had agreed to begin hearings on the matter on Monday. With John Doar handling the government's case and federal marshals standing guard, and with L. B. Sullivan, Jamie Moore, Bull Connor, riot leader Claude Henley, and Imperial Wizard Robert Shelton in the audience, the scene in Johnson's courtroom was one of the most dramatic in the city's history.

The opening witness, a Tennessee State student named Patricia Jenkins, identified Henley as one of the leading assailants during the May 20 riot and testified that she had seen a policeman leave the scene as soon as the bus arrived at the terminal. Other witnesses—including Fred Gach, FBI Special Agent Spender Robb, and John McCloud, a black postal employee—confirmed the general absence of police protection and the refusal of sheriff's deputies and other local authorities to intervene on behalf of reporters and Freedom Riders under attack. Even more damning was the testimony of Stuart Culpepper, a reporter for the *Montgomery Advertiser*, who testified that Jack Shows, a local police detective, had told him before the riot began that the police "would not lift a finger" to protect the Freedom Riders. By the time the hearing recessed just after six o'clock, the government's case for an expanded injunction appeared to be a lock. but there were still more witnesses waiting to testify, and Johnson had yet to hear from the defense. To the dismay of those who had hoped to put the episode behind them, the hearing would go on for three more days.[29]

In Louisiana, the ultimate destination of the Freedom Rides, the scene was only slightly less charged. On May 29 George Lincoln Rockwell was spending his last day in jail before being released on bond, but the rest of the Hate Bus contingent planned to remain behind bars and to continue a four-day hunger strike. Across town, the four CORE Freedom Riders who had posted bond on Saturday—Dennis, Smith, Aaron, and Castle—were busy helping set up a Freedom Rider "school." According to Rudy Lombard, the president of New Orleans CORE, the school boasted two visiting instructors, CORE field secretary Jim McCain and Dr. Walter Bergman, one of the victims of the May 14 riots in Alabama. The first class of ten students— which included five white students from Cornell University in upstate New York—began studying nonviolence on Monday morning, in preparation for an upcoming trip to Jackson. Although Lombard would not disclose when the group planned to leave for Mississippi, the announcement that the school had opened put Louisiana law enforcement on full alert. The anxiety was so high on Monday afternoon that New Orleans policemen began stopping any vehicles carrying suspicious-looking passengers who might be Freedom Riders. One group caught in the dragnet turned out to be fifteen college-age students (only one of whom was black) who had come to Louisiana to sell magazine subscriptions. Police officials, who considered the city to be under attack, made no apologies for their misplaced vigilance. In the wake of the Alabama and Mississippi Freedom Rides, traveling in interracial groups had become a suspicious activity all across the Deep South, regardless of the circumstances. No one was above suspicion, as popular rhythm-and-blues singers Clyde McPhatter and Sam Cooke had discovered earlier in the week when their charter bus with a New York license plate pulled into Birmingham. Misidentified as Freedom Riders by vigilant local whites, McPhatter, Cooke, and several white backup musicians were forced to leave town in a hurry.[30]

Racial tensions were also rising in Washington, where there was a lot of tough talk on both sides of the Freedom Rider issue on the Monday following the Mississippi arrests. While Senator Philip Hart of Michigan and other prominent liberals continued to defend the Freedom Rides, the demise of the Javits resolution endorsing the deployment of federal marshals encouraged a number of conservative senators and congressmen to unleash verbal assaults on outside agitators. One militant segregationist, Senator Olin D. Johnston of South Carolina, even sent a public letter to his constituents insisting that the Freedom Riders "should be stopped in their tracks at the place of origin and not allowed to prey upon the religious, racial, and social differences of our people." The biggest political story to come out of the nation's capital on May 29, however, was Robert Kennedy's decision to file a petition asking the Interstate Commerce Commission to adopt "stringent regulations" prohibiting segregation in interstate bus travel. Citing the recent experiences of the Freedom Riders, he declared that ICC action was needed to end the legal confusion that had contributed to mob violence in the South.

Six years earlier the ICC had issued an order mandating the desegregation of interstate train travel, including terminal restaurants, waiting rooms, and restrooms. The November 1955 order had also directed interstate bus companies to discontinue the practice of segregating passengers, but said nothing about segregated bus terminals. Even more confusing was the commission's subsequent decision to forego any real effort to enforce the order. When the ICC won a judgment against Southern Stages, Inc. in April 1961, it was the first instance of even token enforcement of bus desegregation. And even in the Southern Stages case, which involved the segregation of a black interstate passenger in Georgia in the summer of 1960, the hundred-dollar fines levied against the company and a driver represented little more than a slap on the wrist. While a number of other cases were pending, the ICC's overall record of enforcement was, in the words of one historian, "a sorry one," thanks in part to the willingness of Justice Department officials to look the other way.

In submitting a detailed, seven-section petition to the ICC, Kennedy was attempting to end the confusion. He was also sending a clear signal that his own department would no longer tolerate nonenforcement of the law. Why he waited so long to do so is something of a mystery, but there is no evidence that he thought much about the ICC's potential role until the Freedom Ride Coordinating Committee called for the commission's involvement on May 26. As he surely knew, the ICC had enjoyed jurisdiction over interstate buses since the passage of the Motor Carrier Act of 1935, yet had done next to nothing to combat discrimination; but he also knew that, as a newly appointed attorney general still adjusting to the realities of bureaucratic life, he had little hope of summarily countermanding decades of inaction and neglect. Considering the ICC's notorious reputation for political conservatism and glacial deliberation, his lack of confidence was well founded, which suggests that his decision to turn to the ICC on May 29 was more an act of desperation than the result of a carefully rendered strategy.

When Kennedy first broached the subject with Burke Marshall and others on Friday, there was no hint that he actually planned to follow through with a formal appeal to the ICC. But on Monday morning, after a weekend of alarming reports about impending Freedom Rides and racial polarization, he could think of nothing else, ordering his staff to produce a fully developed document by the end of the day. The resulting "petition," a novel form of appeal suggested by Justice Department attorney Robert Saloscin, was a hodgepodge of legal and legislative citations mixed with moral and political imperatives. Nevertheless, the message to the lumbering ICC was clear. "Just as our Constitution is color blind, and neither knows nor tolerates classes among citizens" the petition advised, "so too is the Interstate Commerce Act. The time has come for this commission, in administering that act, to declare unequivocally by regulation that a Negro passenger is free to travel the length and breadth of this country in the same manner as any other passenger."

Kennedy's enthusiasm for the egalitarian platitudes in the petition confirmed what many on his staff already knew: Despite his growing impatience with the Freedom Riders' confrontational tactics and his lack of experience in civil rights matters, the attorney general was ideologically and emotionally committed to racial equality. Even when concern for his brother's vulnerability on the world stage pushed him to lash out at the Freedom Riders' intransigence, he could not bring himself to abandon the basic principle of equal justice. On Friday afternoon, while he was still fuming over the civil rights community's rejection of a cooling-off period, he delivered an apparently unscripted Voice of America radio address that trumpeted the nation's commitment to equality. Speaking to an international audience spread across sixty countries, he attempted to put the recent troubles in Alabama and Mississippi in the context of a nation that was trying to overcome the violent and white supremacist excesses of a lawless minority. Most of his speech was a predictable rejoinder to Communist insinuations that the mobs in Alabama represented the interests and attitudes of a racially repressive capitalist regime, but at times he went much farther down the freedom road than Cold War rhetoric or political discretion dictated, even suggesting the possibility that the American electorate would elect a black president before the end of the century. Pointing out the contrast between his brother's status as an Irish-Catholic president and the anti-Irish discrimination that his grandfather had faced in the early-twentieth century, he insisted that a similar transformation would soon come to black America. Such talk was no substitute for action, as several liberal commentators pointed out. In the politically and racially constrained atmosphere of May 1961, though, even a single moment of idealistic indiscretion was newsworthy.

None of this, of course, proves or even suggests that idealism was the driving force behind Kennedy's decision to petition the ICC on May 29. On

Members of the Washington Freedom Riders Committee display protest signs as they depart Times Square in New York for Washington, D.C., where they plan to picket the White House and demand federal intervention in the South, May 30, 1961. (Library of Congress)

the contrary, all available evidence indicates that he embraced the petition as a pragmatic solution to a short-term political problem. Although he knew that it would take weeks and even months to obtain a definitive ICC ruling on the regulations themselves, he recognized the immediate symbolic value of the petition. Having failed in his jawboning effort to convince the Freedom Riders to accept a cooling-off period, he hoped that the petition would at least take some of the steam out of the movement. That it did not do so was a profound disappointment for him and his staff, not to mention a clear sign that, for all his good intentions, the attorney general did not yet understand the depth of feeling that was driving young Americans, black and white, onto the freedom buses.[31]

THE RISING SPIRIT OF THE MOVEMENT was much in evidence on Tuesday morning as the first press accounts of the ICC petition vied with radio and television reports of new activity among Freedom Riders and their supporters. In Washington, more than a hundred pro–Freedom Rider demonstrators—most of whom were college or high school students from New York and Philadelphia—marched back and forth in front of the White House to protest the administration's lukewarm support of the Riders. Carrying signs that read "End Segregation, the Shame of Our Nation" and "Attention Robert Kennedy—There's Been a 95-Year Cooling-Off Period," the picketers denied reports that they were Communist sympathizers, although one spokesperson acknowledged that the biracial group "was left of center by all traditional political definitions."

Similar suspicions greeted the first "graduates" of the New Orleans Freedom Rider school when they arrived at the Illinois Central railway station in downtown Jackson later in the morning. The newest group of Freedom Riders—the first to conduct tests at a railway terminal—included four white male students from Cornell; Bob Heller, a white Tulane sophomore and CORE member originally from Long Island; and three black students—Sandra Nixon of Southern University in Baton Rouge, and Glenda Gaither and Jim Davis of Claflin College in Orangeburg, South Carolina. Both Gaither, the younger sister of CORE field secretary Tom Gaither, and Davis, her boyfriend and future husband, were veterans of the South Carolina sit-in movement. An all-conference football star and the son of a prominent Methodist preacher, the towering Davis served as the group leader during the May 30 Freedom Ride.

On the Ride itself, Davis and the others were pleased to discover that seating on the train was fully integrated. It was a different story, however, when he, Nixon, and Gaither tried to use the white restrooms at the Illinois Central terminal. Once again police captain Ray was on the scene. After disobeying his order to "move on," the three restroom invaders—along with the rest of the Riders—were arrested for disorderly conduct. Within an hour all eight found themselves in front of a noticeably irritated Judge Spencer, who, after a five-minute trial, meted out the expected sentence of a two-hundred-dollar fine and a sixty-day jail term. By midafternoon the five whites were in the city jail and the rest were in the county jail, which was already crowded with the fifteen black Riders convicted on Monday as well as most of the first batch of Riders convicted on Friday. On Monday evening, after reporters, federal officials, and CORE field secretary Richard Haley had begun to inquire about Vivian's beating by county penal farm guards, Sheriff Gilfoy had moved Vivian and most of the other Riders back to the county jail. As a result, the conditions at the jail were declining by the hour.

By Tuesday evening—with the exception of eight white Riders incarcerated in the city jail—the first five groups were all packed into a county jail that was Spartan even by Mississippi standards. Even without the overcrowding the county jail was a miserable place, as Frank Holloway's experience earlier in the week had demonstrated. "When we went in," Holloway recalled, "we were met by some of the meanest looking, tobacco-chewing lawmen I have ever seen. They ordered us around like a bunch of dogs, and I really began to feel like I was in a Mississippi jail. Our cell was nasty and the beds were harder than the city jail beds, hardly sleepable, but the eight of us in our cell had to lie down somewhere." Later, after Holloway and others disobeyed an order to stop singing freedom songs, several Riders were put in a sweat box; and when even that didn't stop the singing, at least one jailer warned them that he "could get rid of a nigger in Mississippi, and nobody could do anything about it."[32]

The wretched conditions at the Hinds County Jail should have been enough to force at least some of the Freedom Riders to reconsider their commitment to the "jail–no bail" policy. Most observers, including government officials at all levels, certainly expected the policy to unravel as the Freedom Riders began to realize what it was actually like to spend hard time in a Mississippi jail. Even among movement supporters, there was a common expectation that sooner or later most of the Riders would agree to be released on bond. Only among the Freedom Riders themselves, it seems, was there a full appreciation of the strange but powerful seductiveness of meaningful sacrifice and unmerited suffering. The greater the hardship, the more committed they seemed to be, a dynamic that could not be explained away as a mere manifestation of peer pressure or youthful illusions of invulnerability. Something deeper was at work, something that remained hidden from all but the most perceptive observers. As Farmer recalled, reflecting on the Riders' response to their unexpected return to the county jail: "A half-dozen new occupants were there, having arrived during our absence. They had been informed of our transfer to the county farm by the trusties and the upstairs prisoners—those non–Freedom Riders who now sang Freedom Rider songs. The homecoming was celebrated with more singing, joined by the other three Rider groups and, occasionally, by the upstairs inmates. Some in our group swaggered triumphantly, like conquering heroes. We had met the enemies at the dreaded county farm, and they were *ours*. We had survived it with a minimum of brutalization. We had forced them to retreat. Our tormentors were tormented. We had twisted the tail of the lion and lived to tell the story. Even the upstairs fellows were impressed."

One of the first to detect the special character of the Freedom Rider experience was the veteran journalist Walter Lippman. "It would be vain for anyone to expect that there can be a quick and easy end to the kind of courage and determination which has been shown in the bus rides and in the lunch-counter sit-ins," he wrote on May 25. "No one should expect this kind of thing to disappear." A second observer who shared Lippman's viewpoint was Leslie Dunbar, the executive director of the Southern Regional Council and the author of a special Freedom Ride report authorized by the council and released on Tuesday, May 30. "The Freedom Ride will continue," Dunbar predicted. "If not in its present form, in some other similar style, and soon. There is in it momentum too great to be held back. The South and the nation are now critically dependent on the quality of Negro leadership, and its ability to direct that momentum and not be overrun by it." Nevertheless, in keeping with the traditions of white Southern liberalism, Dunbar went on to insist that "the big problems . . . can be tackled only by the South itself: by white Southerners coming to deserve the trust of Negro Southerners." "There would be no Freedom Ride," the Southern Regional Council report declared, "if there were compliance with law and decency in the South."[33]

The overlapping issues of legal compliance and public decency were also the focus of attention in Montgomery on Tuesday morning. In one courtroom, the Alabama Court of Appeals upheld the conviction of twelve Birmingham blacks arrested during a series of sit-ins in March 1960. Ten of those arrested were students, and two, including Fred Shuttlesworth, were leaders charged with inciting the sit-ins. Just down the street, in a second courtroom, Judge Johnson was presiding over the second day of the injunction hearing. Throughout the day Doar grilled a series of witnesses, including Imperial Wizard Shelton and Cecil "Goober" Lewallyn, the Klansman suspected of tossing the firebomb into the Trailways bus outside of Anniston. Lewallyn, along with two other Klan suspects, avoided giving detailed testimony by pleading the Fifth Amendment, and Shelton's testimony came only after Johnson threatened him with a contempt of court citation. Other witnesses offered scattered evidence of Klan involvement and police inaction in Anniston and Birmingham, but by the end of the day there was no clear picture of the perpetrators of the May 14 attacks. For a frustrated Doar, the only real highlight of the day occurred during a brief recess when Calvin Whitesell, the attorney representing Montgomery police officials, informed him that he planned to call Robert Kennedy to the witness stand. Implying that the attorney general was a suspected co-conspirator, Whitesell wanted to know "what, if anything, he [Kennedy] had to do with the segregation-challenging 'freedom riders.' " Incredulous, Doar informed the earnest but naive Alabama attorney that he was fairly certain that the attorney general would respectfully decline to testify.

Whitesell's request provided a moment of comic relief, but Doar was not amused when the subject of Kennedy's collusion with the Freedom Riders came up again on Wednesday afternoon. Earlier in the day, after Doar had rested his case, Judge Johnson had rejected the federal government's motion to include the Birmingham police in the injunction and, even more surprising, had lifted a temporary restraining order against a Montgomery-based Klan group, the Federated Ku Klux Klan, Inc. From then on, as defense attorneys for the Montgomery police and two Klan groups still subject to injunctive restrictions sensed an opening, the proceedings turned into a counter-attack against meddling Justice Department officials. The star witness for the defense of Alabama's sovereignty was George Cruit, the Birmingham Greyhound superintendent who had haggled with the attorney general by phone on May 15 and again on May 20. Reading from a transcript of the first conversation, Cruit quoted Kennedy's declaration that the "Government is going to be very much upset if this group does not get to continue their trip." To Cruit, to most of the white Southerners in the courtroom, and to thousands of others who read the attorney general's words in news accounts, this declaration was proof that the federal government had conspired with the Freedom Riders to attack the Southern way of life. Even more damning for some was Kennedy's insistence that Cruit recruit a black driver after white bus drivers refused to drive to Montgomery. By the end of the afternoon, this and other alleged violations of racial etiquette had put Doar and the Justice Department on the defensive, so much so that a beaming Whitesell filed a counter-motion seeking a temporary restraining order against CORE, SCLC, SNCC, and Abernathy's newly organized Montgomery County Jail Council. Somewhat taken aback, Johnson took the counter-motion under advisement, promising a ruling by the end of the week.[34]

On Thursday, June 1, the fourth and final day of the hearing, Commissioner Sullivan offered a predictable and anticlimactic litany of excuses for the Montgomery police department's failure to protect the Freedom Riders, producing yawns from reporters and other spectators. Elsewhere, however, there were new wrinkles in the Freedom Rider story. In Birmingham, Circuit Judge Francis Thompson ruled that Fred Shuttlesworth was guilty on two counts of inciting a breach of peace, at the Trailways station on May 14 and at the Greyhound station three days later. Fined a total of a thousand dollars and sentenced to six months in jail, Shuttlesworth immediately posted bond and appealed the conviction. The next morning, the minister announced that he would be leaving Alabama in August for a pastorate at the Revelation Baptist Church in Cincinnati, Ohio. The move to a larger congregation, he explained, would make it easier to support his family. Though sad to leave Bethel Baptist, he promised to make frequent visits to Birmingham and remain active in the local civil rights struggle that he had fostered for nearly a decade.

Meanwhile, in Jackson, the seven white Freedom Riders (the eighth white Rider, Peter Sterling, a Cornell student scheduled to be married on June 27, paid his fine and left for home on Thursday morning) at the city jail initiated a hunger strike that soon spread to the black Riders incarcerated in the county jail across the street. And in Chicago, seven former Freedom Riders—Walter and Frances Bergman, Ike Reynolds, Jerome Smith, Dave Dennis, Doris Castle, and Julia Aaron—announced a drive to recruit "hundreds or thousands" of new Riders. Dismissing the call for a cooling-off period, Bergman urged his fellow activists to strike "while the iron is hot." "American students are going to strike, strike, strike and ride, ride, ride," he predicted, "until we achieve our goal of an open country." In Ithaca, New York, a group of Cornell students promised to reinforce the student Riders already arrested in Mississippi; in Cambridge, Massachusetts, Harvard students formed an Emergency Public Integration Committee (EPIC) that sponsored end-of-the-semester "freedom parties" as a means of raising funds for CORE; and in New Haven, Connecticut, a petition of support for the Freedom Riders signed by 307 members of the Yale faculty and administration, including Yale Law School dean Eugene Rostow, was on its way to the White House. Farther afield, in

San Francisco, a group of clergymen announced the founding of "Freedom Writers," an organization pledged to gather funds and a million signatures in support of the Freedom Rides. To the dismay of those who had hoped for an early resolution of the crisis, the Freedom Rider movement was becoming national in scope.[35]

Nevertheless, on Friday morning the focus of attention returned to Montgomery, where Judge Johnson issued an unexpectedly sweeping set of injunctive rulings. As expected, Johnson formally enjoined Alabama Klansmen from interfering with interstate travel and ordered the Montgomery police to protect all interstate travelers regardless of race. Citing Klan-inspired violence and the "willful and deliberate failure" of Montgomery police officials to do their duty, he issued a preliminary injunction against Robert Shelton's Alabama Knights of the Ku Klux Klan, Alvin Horn's Talladega-based U.S. Klans, Montgomery Klansmen Claude Henley and Thurman Ouzts, Commissioner Sullivan, Police Chief Ruppenthal, and "their officers, agents, employees, members, and all persons acting in concert with them." But he did not stop there. To the surprise of almost everyone in the courtroom, he also granted a temporary restraining order prohibiting CORE, SNCC, SCLC, and the Montgomery City Jail Council from "sponsoring, financing, assisting or encouraging any individual or group of individuals in traveling in interstate commerce through or in Alabama for the purpose of testing the state or local laws as those laws relate to racial segregation." The order also specifically restrained the activities of several movement leaders, including King, Abernathy, Walker, and Shuttlesworth. In effect, he had placed at least a temporary ban on future Freedom Rides in the state of Alabama. On June 12 he would convene a hearing to determine whether the order should be vacated or turned into a full-fledged injunction. Until then, he warned, the anti–Freedom Ride ruling, like the injunction against the Klan and the Montgomery police, would be rigidly enforced. "If there are any such incidents as this again," he declared, "I am going to put some Klansmen, some city officials and some Negro preachers in the Federal penitentiary."[36]

In a lengthy, fifteen-page preamble and in a stern-voiced statement from the bench, Johnson surveyed the evidence of incitement and dereliction of duty and explained the logic of his double-edged ruling. "Those who sponsor, finance, and encourage groups to come into this area, with the knowledge that such trips will foment violence," he argued, "are just as effective in causing an obstruction to interstate travel as mobs themselves." Even though he conceded that the sponsoring organizations and individuals had engaged "in agitation within the law of the United States," he maintained that such agitation constituted "an undue burden upon the free flow of interstate commerce at this particular time and under the circumstances that exist." While acknowledging that organizing bands of Freedom Riders "may be a legal right," he insisted that "the right of the public to be protected from the evils of their conduct is a greater and more important right." Anticipating legal and constitutional objections, he reminded potential critics that "the right of the public to be protected from evils of conduct, even though the constitutional rights of certain persons or groups are thereby in some manner infringed, has received frequent and consistent recognition from the courts of the United States." Individuals traveling through Alabama "on bona-fide trips" deserved full constitutional protection, but civil rights activists, at least in the short run, would have to sacrifice some of their freedom for the greater good.[37]

Predictably, Johnson's bold ruling elicited a wide range of reactions. In Alabama, the mainstream white press hailed the paired injunctions as an even-handed rebuke to violent Klan-led extremists and provocative outside agitators. Earlier in the morning, two Alabama legislators, one in the senate and one in the house, had introduced anti–Freedom Rider bills that imposed three-hundred-dollar fines and sixty-day jail terms on anyone who willfully violated the state's "social customs." Now, in the wake of Johnson's ruling, some observers were no longer sure that the emergency legislation was necessary. "With one stroke of the pen," one Montgomery editor wrote, the "upstart Republican" judge from Winston County "ceased to be the villain and became the hero of the hour." James Free, a columnist with the *Birmingham News*, agreed, pointing out that Johnson was "the first federal official of real stature and influence to crack down on both sides of the freedom rider hullabaloo." According to Free, Johnson was on "the way to becoming a national hero and there are backstage predictions that he may wind up on the Supreme Court, Republican appointee though he be." Other local and regional commentators were less effusive, but virtually all of the white Southerners who commented publicly on the ruling were supportive. "Judge Johnson," the editor of the *Huntsville Times* exclaimed, "deserves the thanks of the South and the nation."[38]

Most civil rights activists, of course, felt otherwise. From the perspective of those who saw the Freedom Rides as a necessary step down the road to desegregation, Johnson's ruling was an unexpected slap in the face. Within minutes of Johnson's injunctive decree, Marvin Rich announced that CORE had asked Montgomery attorney Solomon Seay Jr., the son of one of the leaders named in the restraining order, to seek a stay in federal court. "Every person has the right to travel on the public highways with dignity," Rich insisted, "and this is what we in CORE have been trying to do. There is no justification for this temporary injunction." In Atlanta, Martin Luther King initially refused to comment on Johnson's decision to include the names of specific civil rights leaders in the order, but he expressed serious doubt that the ruling would halt the Freedom Rides. "I think we have revealed through many experiences," King reminded Johnson and the nation, "that we have no fear of going to jail and staying to serve time when necessary. We have transformed jails and prisons from dungeons of shame to havens of freedom and justice." Others voiced their objections more bluntly, and some even put their words into action.[39]

At 11:30 A.M., a little over an hour after Johnson issued his injunction, eight Freedom Riders left the Montgomery Trailways terminal on a bus bound for Jackson. An eclectic assortment of activists, the group included three young white men from Chicago, a forty-five-year-old white woman from New York City, a twenty-eight-year-old black male laborer from Corinth, Mississippi, a female nurse from Nashville's Meharry Medical School, a male Howard student representing the Nonviolent Action Group, and Cordell Reagon, a Tennessee State freshman who would soon gain fame as a leader of the Albany Movement in southwestern Georgia. Before leaving, the eight "post-injunction" Riders tested the station's restrooms and waiting rooms. Even after a bomb threat delayed their departure, local authorities did not attempt to stop them from boarding the bus (as a federal district court spokesman later explained, the injunction did not apply to anyone who did not have prior knowledge of it). When the bus stopped near Selma, Sheriff Jim Clark, who would achieve national notoriety in 1965 for his persecution of civil rights demonstrators, arrested one of the white Riders, Ralph Fertig of Chicago, for allegedly bothering a white female passenger. But the other seven Riders made it safely to Jackson, where they were promptly arrested for trying to desegregate the Trailways terminal.

The first Freedom Riders to leave Montgomery after the injunction, they were actually the second group to be arrested in Jackson on June 2. At 7:30 A.M., two and a half hours *before* Johnson's ruling, another group of Mississippi-bound Freedom Riders had departed from the Montgomery Trailways terminal. Led by SNCC veteran and Montgomery-riot survivor Ruby Doris Smith, the group of six Riders included three white male volunteers from Long Island and two black students from Nashville, Charles Butler and Joy Reagon. On Friday afternoon, when a frightened but defiant Reagon was arrested in Jackson along with Smith and the others, she was taken to the Hinds County Jail. Four hours later her younger brother Cordell joined her there, the sixty-fifth Freedom Rider to enter the strange world of Mississippi justice. With the exception of C. T. Vivian, Hank Thomas, and Jean Thompson—all of whom were struck in the face by penal farm superintendent Max Thomas for failing to address him as "sir"—none of the jailed Riders had yet seen the violent side of that world. But no one could be sure how long the show of restraint would last. Earlier in the day, following a perfunctory investigation, Mississippi authorities had exonerated Max Thomas, ruling that Vivian's injuries had occurred during an assault on the superintendent and not, as Vivian claimed, during a beating. Even more ominously, there were signs that the hunger strikes and freedom songs were beginning to wear on the nerves of the guards, particularly at the overcrowded county jail where the black Riders were imprisoned.[40]

For Justice Department officials in Washington, the increasingly unstable situation in Mississippi was a matter of great concern, but on Friday afternoon and on through the weekend their most pressing problem was formulating a response to Judge Johnson's temporary restraining order. From the outset Marshall, Doar, and others expressed grave doubts about the constitutionality of the order. Earlier in the week, after Whitesell had requested the order, Doar had presented Johnson with a memorandum explaining why the Justice Department opposed such an extreme measure. In the wake of the Friday morning ruling, department officials publicly reiterated their objections, pointing out that the Supreme Court had already closed the option of restoring civil order through constitutionally questionable judicial orders. In the 1958 Little Rock case, the Court had ruled that no such shortcuts would be allowed, and the department had no interest in reopening the question three years later. Privately, however, many department officials welcomed the order as a judicial substitute for the voluntary cooling-off period requested by the attorney general. While they felt compelled to challenge the order in court, they were pleased that the ban on Alabama Freedom Rides would be in effect for at least two weeks, and perhaps even longer if the Fifth Circuit Court of Appeals took its time to rule on a motion to vacate the order.

Of course, no one in the Justice Department could be sure how the FRCC would react to Johnson's high-handed judicial intervention. As an act of faith, the department went ahead with its withdrawal of the marshals at Maxwell Field, announcing on Friday that the remaining fifty marshals had received demobilization orders. Even so, the likelihood of additional Freedom Rides was a continuing concern. On Saturday King announced that the FRCC planned to sidestep Judge Johnson's improper ruling by sending Freedom Riders into Mississippi through states other than Alabama, and he even hinted that the present plan to comply with the order might change in the future. "There are legal remedies to the order," he declared, "and we intend to exhaust them all." But he also warned that the option of civil disobedience was still open. "If a law is unjust," he told reporters, "we have a moral responsibility to disobey the unjust law."[41]

This kind of talk made Justice Department officials, and many other observers, very nervous. While editorial and public opinion outside of the South was sharply divided on the question of the restraining order's legality, there was widespread agreement that mass disorder offered no solution to the problem of racial discrimination. On Friday, during a visit to New York City, former president Harry Truman took time out from his morning walk to excoriate "meddlesome intruders" from the North. "They stir up trouble," he declared. ". . . They ought to stay here and attend to their own business." Likening the Freedom Riders to William Lloyd Garrison, Harriet Beecher Stowe, and other abolitionists who provoked a bloody civil war, Truman argued that the nation should let the South solve its own problems. "Goodwill and common sense," not agitation or civil disobedience, he insisted, represented the best approach to social change. In upbraiding the Freedom Riders, Truman undoubtedly spoke for many, if not most, white Americans. But there were some, perhaps even a growing number, who were willing to speak out for a broader vision of participatory democracy. One such voice was that of Rabbi David Seligson, whose Saturday sermon on June 3 applauded the Freedom Riders' commitment to nonviolent direct action. "The Gandhian spirit is written all over them . . . ," he told his midtown Manhattan congregation. "While the faces of the whites are distorted with hatred and rage, the Negroes radiate a kind of spiritual dignity and inner peace, a quality of the soul that is slowly and surely teaching Americans a moral lesson. . . . The world of Gandhi and that of the segregated South may be worlds apart. But the confrontation between physical force and the power of the spirit, between evil and good, is essentially the same."

Although Rabbi Seligson did not mention him by name, the example set by William Barbee in a Montgomery courtroom on Friday morning testified to the integrity and raw moral courage described in the sermon. Brought back to Montgomery to sign a warrant against Thurman Ouzts, one of the Klansmen who had nearly beaten him to death on May 20, Barbee decided that signing the warrant violated "the principles of nonviolence." "I feel that the violence perpetrated against me was prompted by the general evil of segregation to our society," he later explained. "Therefore, no one person should be punished." One month after the original CORE Freedom Riders boarded a bus to destiny, the message of hope and redemption was still alive.[42]

8

Make Me a Captive, Lord

Make me a captive, Lord, And then I shall be free;
Force me to render up my sword, And I shall conqueror be.
                    —from the hymn "Make Me a Captive, Lord"[1]

DELIVERING THE MESSAGE OF HOPE AND REDEMPTION required a sustained campaign of personal commitment and nonviolent fortitude. In and of themselves, however, the actions and experiences of the Freedom Riders could not topple or even seriously challenge the Jim Crow regime. To be an effective agent of historical change, the moral drama of the Freedom Rides needed a broad and attentive audience—an audience that could only be reached through the mass media. Without widespread press coverage, the 1961 Freedom Rides would have suffered the same obscure fate as the 1947 Journey of Reconciliation. In the early going, as we have seen, the 1961 CORE Ride garnered few headlines. But that situation changed dramatically in the wake of the May 14 riots in Anniston and Birmingham. During the second half of May, the Freedom Rider crisis was front-page news in newspapers across the nation and throughout much of the world, and a source of riveting images for local and network television reporters. Indeed, following the formation of the FRCC on May 26, nourishing and sustaining press interest in the Freedom Rides was a key element of movement strategy.

In early June, maintaining the Freedom Rides' status as a media event became more challenging as President Kennedy's visit to Paris and Vienna overshadowed all other news stories. But FRCC leaders did their best to keep the movement in the public eye, resorting to press conferences, television and radio interviews, and even staged publicity stunts. On June 5, for example, Jim Peck interrupted Harry Truman's Monday morning walk in an effort to obtain a retraction of Friday's anti–Freedom Rider remarks. Although Truman refused to oblige, the confrontation between the former president and the injured Freedom Rider became a national news story. Later in the day Martin Luther King, who was also in New York, held a press conference during which he called for "a second Emancipation Proclamation." "The time has now come," King declared, "for the President of the United States to issue a firm Executive Order declaring all forms of racial segregation illegal. . . . There is a mighty stirring in this land. The sit-ins at lunch counters and Freedom Riders on buses are making it palpably clear that segregation must end and that it must end soon."[2]

King and other FRCC leaders feared that some headline-hunting journalists would lose interest in the Rides as the threat of violence subsided and the daily arrests in Jackson became routine; and the daily coverage of the movement did indeed drop off in early June. Nevertheless, the developing story in the Deep South continued to attract considerable media attention, especially among magazine editors. As the Freedom Rider saga entered its second month, several major magazines ran cover stories or lengthy features on the Rides. Displaying a cover picture of John Patterson standing in front of a Confederate monument, the June 2 issue of *Time* featured a five-page article on "The South and the Freedom Riders." While most of the article focused on recent events in Montgomery and Jackson, it also included a legal primer on the statutory confrontation between federal and state officials, as well as profiles of four Freedom Riders: Diane Nash, Jim Lawson, Jim Farmer, and William Sloane Coffin. Openly sympathetic to the Freedom Riders' cause, the article, after reporting that "the boldness and bravery of the Freedom Riders" had "won over most of the old-line, conservative leaders," concluded with a quotation from Howard University president James Nabrit's recent commencement address at Benedict College, a black institution in Columbia, South Carolina. "Swifter than you can imagine," Nabrit predicted, "you will have all the rights and privileges of every other citizen in the U.S." "That time," the *Time* reporter interjected, "cannot come too swiftly for young Negroes of 1961—and the John Pattersons of the South can do little to stop them."[3]

Taking an equally sympathetic stance, the editors of *Life* chose the Freedom Rides as the "Story of the Week" in the June 2 issue. Under the title "Asking for Trouble—and Getting It: The Ride for Rights," the editors ran ten pages of photographs framed by straightforward captions and intermittent commentary. Several of the most captivating pictures showed the Freedom Riders during the May 21 siege at First Baptist, which *Life* characterized as a near tragedy that "might have been the most shocking racial attack in U.S. history—a riot within the holy precincts of a church." The photo essay included snapshots of Robert Kennedy and John Patterson and of bayonet-wielding National Guardsmen, but the primary focus was the Freedom Riders themselves. One photograph captured several fresh-faced students raising their hands during a discussion session at Dr. Harris's house, and another showed a wary Matthew Walker Jr. poking his head out of a bus window to scan the scene as Alabama National Guardsmen protected the first freedom bus to Mississippi. The last two pages were devoted to William Sloane Coffin and his eloquent defense of Freedom Riding.[4]

Later in the week, a number of other magazines—including *Nation, U.S. News and World Report, New Republic*, and *Newsweek*—ran feature stories on the Freedom Rides. Though generally sympathetic to the civil rights struggle, some commentators, such as Gerald Johnson in the *New Republic*, were critical of the Freedom Riders' provocative tactics. Nevertheless, among nationally circulated magazines, only the ultra-conservative *National Review* offered an outright defense of Southern segregationists, and even the *National Review* based its argument on states' rights, not racial bigotry. At the other end of the spectrum, the June 5 issue of *Newsweek* presented three captioned photographs on its cover: one of Robert Kennedy accompanied by the quotation "We stand for human liberty"; a second of Martin Luther King with the caption "We must be prepared to suffer . . . even die"; and a third of John Patterson, with the defiant quotation "The Federal government encourages these agitators." The five-page cover story focused on the journey from Montgomery to Jackson but also included two long sidebars. The first, entitled "A New Breed—The Militant Negro in the South," presented profiles of SNCC, CORE, and the Nashville Movement, plus thumbnail sketches of Lawson, Nash, Ed King, and Wyatt Tee Walker. "The white South has not seen such Negroes before," the sidebar proclaimed. "Impatient at the slow course of racial integration, they are mostly young people who have emerged from the Negro colleges and churches to take up battle with their own complex mystique of religious fervor and Gandhi-like passive resistance—all of it summed up in the word non-violence."

The second sidebar, "How the World Press Viewed the Days of Tension," offered a far-flung sample of international editorial opinion, including comments from editors in Egypt, India, Kenya, France, and the Soviet Union. "As if written on the wind," *Newsweek* concluded, "the Freedom Rider story swept around the globe last week." Noting the Cold War implications of the crisis, the sidebar cited no less an authority than Edward R. Murrow, the distinguished journalist and newly appointed director of the U.S. Information Agency (USIA), who declared: "There are no more domestic issues." As the reaction to the Freedom Rides had demonstrated, significant events in the United States were inevitably "absorbed, debated, and pondered on all shores of every ocean." Fortunately, according to *Newsweek*, many "overseas editors" had stressed not only the "racial bigotry" of Southern segregationists but also "the complex issues involved and the Federal government's efforts to calm and correct the situation." Predictably, the pro-administration sidebar ended with a summary of Robert Kennedy's May 26 Voice of America broadcast, and at the close of the general article the editors allowed him to have the last word. Re-creating the late-night scene at the Justice Department on May 24—the Freedom Riders' first day in Jackson—the editors portrayed a weary but resolute attorney general pouring himself "a nightcap of Old Grand-Dad over ice." "Well, it's still a step forward," Kennedy mused. "But these situations are something we're going to have to live with. This is going on and on."[5]

KENNEDY WAS RIGHT, of course. But for a brief period in early June some observers wondered if the Rides would continue. During the weekend of June 3–4, and on Monday the fifth, there were no new Rides in Mississippi or anywhere else. With the attention of the nation and the world focused on the summit in Vienna, it is unlikely that additional Riders would have drawn much media coverage, but the three-day respite had little to do with the public's preoccupation with the Cold War parley between Kennedy and Krushchev. In movement circles, the matter of greatest concern was Judge Johnson's restraining order. Until Johnson rendered a final injunctive decision on June 12, the FRCC had little choice but to bypass Alabama. Circumventing Johnson's order required an unexpected and complicated rerouting of several planned Freedom Rides, as well as a temporary relocation of FRCC recruiting and training centers. For the time being, at least, Montgomery could no longer serve as a major center of Freedom Rider activity. New Orleans, Nashville, and Atlanta would have to pick up the slack as new travel patterns were developed. Jackson, FRCC leaders agreed, would remain the primary target, but the Freedom Rides would now converge on the city from the north and the south, not the east.

The situation also prompted a partial reorganization of the FRCC. Working in close collaboration but with separate strengths, the four primary participating organizations—CORE, SNCC, SCLC, and the Nashville Movement—divided up the movement's responsibilities along geographical lines. While CORE concentrated its energies in New Orleans and on various recruiting and fund-raising efforts outside the South, SCLC and SNCC volunteers jointly maintained a recruiting and communications command center in Atlanta. At the same time, the Nashville student movement remained the emotional nerve center of the struggle. Despite the persistence of ideological disagreements—especially over the role of religion in the movement— representatives of the four organizations held weekly meetings in an effort to maintain their common commitment to nonviolent struggle. The result was a loose but surprisingly effective coalition that sustained the Freedom Rider movement without stultifying the creativity of an eclectic band of volunteers. Striking a balance between nonviolent discipline and individual freedom was never easy, but as a general rule the Freedom Riders came closer than most movement activists to achieving this ideal.[6]

Even among the Freedom Riders, however, a unifying common cause could only do so much. As a social movement with hundreds of participants, the Freedom Rider campaign reflected the diverse experiences, as well as the strengths and weaknesses, of individual personalities. Following the CORE model, the FRCC relied on brief but intensive training and group leaders to maintain adherence to nonviolent discipline. And as long as the Freedom Riders were conducting tests in buses or trains, or in terminals, the system worked well. In the jails of Mississippi, it was not always so effective. For the most part, imprisoned Riders remained true to the principles of nonviolent self-sacrifice, but there were enough exceptions to cause considerable concern among movement leaders. Even with Farmer, Lewis, and Lawson on the scene, there were troubling breaches of movement solidarity. CORE field secretary Richard Haley was also in Jackson, but he had little access to the jailed Riders and could do little to influence their behavior. Once the Riders were behind bars and dispersed among various cell blocks, they were essentially on their own. Under such conditions, individual proclivities and factional loyalties sometimes outweighed collective ties and responsibilities. This became painfully evident during the first week of the Jackson jailings, as personal grievances and disagreements over the etiquette of nonviolent struggle became commonplace.

The split between devoutly religious and largely secular activists was the most persistent source of conflict, but in early June the most publicized issue dividing the Riders was the pressure to participate in hunger strikes. Some of the Riders opposed the idea of a hunger strike from the beginning, and on Saturday, June 3, thirty of the fifty jailed Riders decided to end a three-day fast. Among the twenty who continued to fast, there were feelings of disappointment and even betrayal, and some relationships never fully recovered from the controversy. Earlier in the day Jim Lawson and Grady Donald, after growing tired of the squabbling, had posted bond and returned to Nashville, but Lewis and other valiant peacemakers remained on the scene.

On most issues the stresses and strains within the movement were kept hidden from the outside world. On June 5, however, as FRCC leaders were making final preparations for the resumption of the Rides, a jailed white Freedom Rider from Chicago publicly broke ranks. After posting bond, Richard Gleason, a twenty-four-year-old minister and social worker, held a thirty-minute news conference during which he criticized the background and behavior of several of his fellow Riders. Claiming that some of the jailed Riders were not the "high caliber people" that he had expected to encounter in a movement for racial justice, Gleason said he had become "alarmed when I found out about the police records of others in my cell." "I told them I didn't want to have anything to do with a questionable group," he declared, "and they thought I was a traitor." After disclosing that his disillusionment had crystallized after other Riders had criticized him for refusing to fast, and that the guards had moved him to another cell for his own protection, Gleason advised "anyone thinking of joining the rides to look them over carefully before deciding." Even more sensationally, he insisted that some of the Riders had expressed support for the Communist Party and were planning to disrupt their Monday afternoon trial. "There was all sorts of Yoga and other exercises going on in the cells," he reported, "and they were talking about 'passive resistance' moves where people fall in their places and refuse to move."

After returning to Chicago, Gleason held a second news conference during which he repudiated much of what he had said in Jackson, but the damage had already been done. Fortunately, the Gleason incident taught movement leaders an important lesson that would serve them well in the weeks and months to come. Discovering that Gleason had joined a June 2 Ride at the last minute after impulsively flying to Atlanta, where a brief conversation with Ed King led to his recruitment, FRCC organizers decided to pay closer attention to the process of selecting future Freedom Riders. With a half-dozen Rides planned for the coming week, there was some nervousness that another Gleason might have slipped through the cracks, but a quick check of the roster of new Riders failed to uncover any obvious problems.[7]

The next group scheduled to arrive in Jackson represented an eclectic assortment of activists, ranging from Ernest Weber, a fifty-two-year-old white photographer from Orange, New Jersey, to Shirley Thompson, an eighteen-year-old student at New Orleans's all-black George Washington Carver High School. The other five Riders included two white college students from New York, a white student from Madison, Wisconsin, a black student from Chicago's Marion College, and Terry John Sullivan, the editor of *Awareness*, a monthly alternative newspaper published in Chicago. Despite her youth, Shirley Thompson was a movement veteran, and all of the others arrived in the city in time to undergo the rigorous nonviolent training offered by New Orleans CORE. Shirley was also the sister of Jean Thompson, who was among the first group of Riders to be arrested in Jackson. After being struck by Mack Thomas at the Hinds County Penal Farm on May 31, Jean posted bond and returned to New Orleans, where she filed a complaint against Thomas with the FBI. When her younger sister boarded a bus for Jackson almost a week later, the investigation of the incident—which Hinds County Sheriff Gilfoy described as "funny"—was still in progress.

The arrests at the Jackson Trailways station on Tuesday afternoon, June 6, followed the same pattern as those of the previous week, with one exception. At a Monday afternoon trial, Judge Spencer had announced that future Freedom Riders would face stiffer penalties than the sentences handed out during the first week of arrests. The new policy, which mandated four-month rather than two-month sentences, was prompted by the discovery that some of the Freedom Riders had "served time in Federal prisons for refusing to bear arms in defense of their country." "Some have discharges other than honorable conditions," Spencer explained. "Some have atheistic beliefs, and three . . . have beliefs, learnings and ideologies contrary to the principles on which this country was founded." While he didn't elaborate on what those principles were, his message to the press and the Freedom Riders was clear: Mississippi was cracking down on outside agitators. In a brief trial held minutes after their arrival, the seven new Riders received four-month jail terms, two months of which were suspended, and two-hundred-dollar fines. Unfazed, all seven declined to post bond and announced that they planned to join the hunger strikes at the county and city jails.[8]

The onslaught continued on Wednesday as two groups of Riders converged on the city. At the Trailways terminal in the early afternoon, the Jackson police arrested six Riders—three black students from Virginia Union, two white Yale Divinity School students, and Carol Ruth Silver, a twenty-two-year-old white secretary from New York City. Four hours later three more Freedom Riders were apprehended at the city airport. To the dismay of local officials, the second group—all black activists from St. Louis—had staged the movement's first "fly-in." After trying to desegregate the airport's white restrooms, they were charged with breaching the peace. In a separate incident, Michael Audain, a white Canadian student at the University of British Columbia, was arrested at the Greyhound terminal after entering a black restroom. Visiting the United States to conduct research on housing discrimination in Memphis and New Orleans, Audain decided to conduct a one-man protest during a rest stop in Jackson, an impulsive act that led to a two-week stint in the notorious Parchman Prison Farm.[9]

By Wednesday evening there was no doubt that the Freedom Rides were once again in full swing and gaining momentum. Within the civil rights movement, there were still those who had serious reservations about the use of provocative direct action in the Deep South. Indeed, Roy Wilkins voiced such reservations during a visit to Jackson that evening. Speaking to an overflow crowd of twelve hundred at the Lynch Street Masonic Hall, Wilkins acknowledged that the NAACP believed that the best "way to make progress . . . is to set up a test case, carry it through the courts and get a determination. We do not believe you can test a law and get it thrown out by staying in jail. After one spends 20 or 60 days in jail, the law is still on the books and still constitutes a support for segregation." Nevertheless, even Wilkins seemed resigned to the reality that the Freedom Riders' tactics had energized the movement. The NAACP does "not sneer at those who choose to stay in jail," he told the crowd, adding that "even though methods may differ there is basic agreement among Negro leaders and organizations in the overall goals and objectives. All methods should be used." Wilkins went on to pay what the *Jackson Daily News* characterized as "a back-handed tribute" to Ross Barnett for avoiding the violence that had erupted in Alabama. But the overall gist of his remarks provided little comfort for Mississippi officials.[10]

The next morning Wilkins made an unannounced visit to the county jail. Two weeks earlier he had warned Farmer that Mississippi was a perilous place for Freedom Riders, but now he came to comfort his old friend and colleague. Bearing two books, including Harper Lee's popular novel *To Kill a Mockingbird*, as a peace token, he embraced a startled Farmer through the bars, quipping: "You look all right, Jim, but you need a shave." Both men smiled, and as Farmer's cellmates came forward to shake the hand of a man whom they had often criticized but whom they now welcomed as a comrade, Wilkins graciously acknowledged the Freedom Riders' achievements. "You've really shaken them up, fellow," declared the NAACP leader. "I'm watching closely and if I can be of any help, if you need anything at all, just have Jack Young give me call." Moments later he was gone, off to catch a plane to the North, but to Farmer and his cellmates even a brief visit signaled a new spirit of cooperation within the movement.

As Farmer later recalled, Wilkins's visit triggered "an explosion of song" that reverberated through the cell block. "We sang and sang," he remembered, "and then we paused to catch our breath." During the pause, a seemingly remarkable thing happened: A voice from the floor above, where the regular black prisoners were housed, cried out: "Freedom Riders, if you teach us your songs, we'll teach you ours." To this point there had been no contact between the Riders and the other prisoners, but with the ensuing exchange of songs the worst fears of Mississippi officials were confirmed. The impudent spirit of agitation, which most Mississippi whites regarded as a deadly and alien virus, was beginning to spread. Soon after the first arrests, Farmer had urged the guards to put the Freedom Riders in cells with the regular prisoners, but, as one guard told him, such an arrangement was out of the question. "No, we can't do that," the jailer explained. "Them other nigras would kill y'all. They know their place and they hate y'all for coming down here stirrin' up trouble." Farmer, of course, knew better. "The real fear," as he later put it, "was that we might contaminate the convicts, turning them into Freedom Riders." During an interview with Franklin Hunt, a *Baltimore Afro-American* correspondent who spent two weeks in the Hinds County Jail after being arrested as a Freedom Rider on May 28, Farmer put it even plainer. "We are prisoners of war," he told Hunt. "This is, in a very real sense, a battle to the death . . . the death of segregation."[11]

The successful recruitment of local Freedom Riders would rattle the nerves of Mississippi officials in the weeks to come, but in early June their most pressing concern was the daily tide of Riders from other parts of the nation. Virtually every day brought at least one new group of Riders to Jackson. On Thursday, June 8, the day Wilkins made his morning visit to the county jail, two groups of Riders descended upon the city. The first—a two-man delegation from New York—arrived on an early-morning plane from Montgomery. Mark Lane, a white New York state assemblyman, and Percy Sutton, a black attorney recently elected president of the Manhattan branch of the NAACP, told reporters that they were "deeply concerned" about recent arrests of New Yorkers visiting Mississippi. Their fact-finding mission took on a new dimension when Sutton tried to use the airport's white restroom. Charged with breaching the peace, both men were behind bars by noon.

A few hours later, the police arrested nine Riders at the Illinois Central railway station. Before boarding a train in New Orleans, the Riders had been jostled and in several cases pummeled by white protesters who tried to block their way. "They were shouting. Throwing cans and lit cigarettes at us. Spitting on us," Howard student Stokely Carmichael later recalled. "And swinging, actually fighting each other to get in a good lick at us. . . . To this day I don't know how we got through and onto the train. Some of us were bleeding, but we all got on, wiped off the spit and blood, and the train set out." Led by Carmichael's NAG colleague Travis Britt, a twenty-seven-year-old cafeteria worker and part-time student, the New Orleans group brought together a provocative combination of four black men, one black woman— Howard student Gwendolyn Greene, Britt's future wife and a future Maryland state senator—and four young white women, including Joan Trumpauer, a nineteen-year-old secretary who worked in the Washington office of Senator Clair Engle of California. Even so, there was no violence once they arrived in Jackson, as Captain Ray and the police quickly ushered them to a waiting paddy wagon. Unlike Lane and Sutton, who immediately posted bond and returned to New York on Thursday afternoon, all nine refused bail. Two weeks after the first Jackson arrests, the total number of jailed Riders had risen to more than seventy; and there was no end in sight.[12]

For the most part, Mississippi officials denied that the growing number of jailed Riders was putting a strain on the state's police and penal facilities. But there were signs that at least some were beginning to worry about the seemingly endless stream of outside agitators willing to go to jail. On Friday, June 9, several speakers at the annual convention of the Mississippi Municipal Association, meeting in Biloxi, warned that the Freedom Riders represented an unprecedented challenge to the Mississippi way of life. After Lieutenant Governor Paul Johnson told the gathering of municipal leaders that "we in Mississippi and this nation of ours are facing some frightening years," Attorney General Joe Patterson acknowledged that "the very soul and fiber of every city in Mississippi is being tested." They had good reason to worry. Earlier in the day, just before dawn, a new group of Freedom Riders had been arrested at the Illinois Central terminal. After undergoing nonviolence training in Nashville, five white college students—three from Ohio and two from New York—had boarded a train for Jackson determined to demonstrate their solidarity with earlier Riders.

Mississippi officials were also troubled by a sweeping desegregation petition filed with the federal district court in Jackson later in the morning. Presented on behalf of three local blacks by NAACP attorneys R. Jess Brown, Constance Baker Motley, and Derrick Bell, the petition initiated a class action suit to enjoin the police from enforcing state and local transit segregation statutes. Although the petition did not mention the Freedom Riders by name, the NAACP also sought an injunction against the breach-of-peace ordinances used to "arrest, harass, and intimidate" travelers exercising "their federally protected right to use interstate and intrastate facilities and services without segregation or discrimination against them solely because of race or color." Several weeks earlier the NAACP had asked the court to overturn the convictions of several black students arrested for sitting in the front section of a local bus, but the new petition represented a significant escalation of the legal campaign to dismantle the state's Jim Crow transit system.[13]

On Saturday the district court forwarded the petition to Judge Elbert P. Tuttle, the chief judge of the Fifth Circuit Court of Appeals in New Orleans. Empowered to convene a three-judge panel to rule on the petition, Tuttle promised to begin hearings on the matter sometime in July. In the meantime, the Freedom Riders would continue to face arrest and imprisonment. Six Riders arrived in Jackson on Saturday, followed by six more on Sunday. Arrested at the Greyhound terminal, the Saturday group demonstrated the growing diversity of the Freedom Rider movement. All six underwent three days of nonviolent training in Nashville, but otherwise they represented a wide variety of backgrounds. The two black Riders were Lowell Woods, a thirty-four-year-old police reporter for the *Chicago Crusader News*, and Leon Horne, a troubled twenty-four-year-old student and part-time waiter who had drifted from his home in Madison County, Mississippi, to Florida before settling briefly in Chicago. Down on his luck and homesick, Horne later claimed that for him the Freedom Ride "was just a way to come home." With "no friends and no money" in Chicago, he pretended to be a Freedom Rider and accepted CORE's offer to buy him a ticket to Jackson. "I'd rather be in jail here than free in Chicago," he told reporters on Monday, adding that he had found the Freedom Riders to be "demoralized characters" who associated with Communists and other radicals. "They say God is on their side, but he's not," Horne insisted.

The rest of the group, though diverse, consisted of legitimate Freedom Riders. The four white Riders included two young women from Chicago—Katherine "Kit" Pleune, a twenty-one-year-old mimeograph operator, and Leora Berman, an eighteen-year-old high school student—and two men: Richard Griswold, a thirty-four-year-old social worker from Brooklyn, and Steve Green, a twenty-one-year-old junior at Middlebury College in Vermont. Though drawn together in a common quest for social justice, each Rider brought a unique perspective to the Freedom Ride. Green, for example, had grown up in a privileged family in Kentucky and had only recently embraced the civil rights movement. In early May, while serving as chairman of a campus lecture series committee, he took William Sloane Coffin on a campus tour that prompted a stinging comment from the Yale chaplain. "What a wonderful place to go to sleep for four years," Coffin intoned. Two weeks later, after brooding about Coffin's remark and after reading the shocking accounts of the Anniston and Birmingham riots, Green informed his father that he had decided to become a Freedom Rider. Canceling a much-anticipated summer trip to Norway, he soon left for Nashville and the movement that would transform his life. When he returned to Middlebury in the fall, after surviving several weeks at Parchman prison, he was, by his own estimation, an entirely different person, saddened but energized by what he had seen. Propelled toward a stint in the Peace Corps and ultimately a forty-year career as a crusading journalist and international relief specialist, he, like so many others, became in effect a Freedom Rider for life.[14]

While not everyone followed such a dramatic path to the movement, the Freedom Riders' personal stories of awakening and commitment were as diverse and complex as the society they were trying to transform. Even when they came from the same locale, as the six arrested on June 11 did, individual decisions and experiences reflected a wide range of choice and contingency. All six were white Minnesotans, and five were current or former students at the University of Minnesota. Several were longtime friends who had been part of a local bohemian subculture that existed on the fringes of Dinkytown, the sprawling student ghetto in Minneapolis.

Marv Davidov, the oldest of the group at twenty-nine, was a transplanted New York Jew who had become active in anti-war and anti-nuclear protests in the mid-1950s. An art dealer, he was politically and culturally sophisticated and the most radical member of the Minnesota group. To him, becoming a Freedom Rider was a natural and connecting link in an activist career that led to regional and even national notoriety in the 1970s and 1980s. A tireless proponent of nonviolent civil disobedience, he eventually helped to organize movements against the draft, nuclear power plants, high-voltage power lines, and the Honeywell Corporation's production of military technology.

Zev Aelony, a native Californian who moved to Minnesota as a child in the 1940s, was a political science major who had spent time on an Israeli kibbutz and at Koinonia, an experimental biracial religious cooperative in Americus, Georgia. Horrified by what he witnessed in Georgia, where there was a concerted campaign to destroy the Koinonia farm, Aelony attended the CORE direct action workshop in Miami in 1959. While in Miami, he was arrested with Pat and Priscilla Stephens during a sit-in at a Royal Castle hamburger restaurant, an experience that brought him in contact with Tobias Simon, Florida's most celebrated civil rights attorney and a distant relative of Aelony's mother. All of this reinforced his dual commitment to CORE and racial justice, preparing him for the Freedom Rides and later civil rights struggles in Florida, Georgia, and Alabama. In 1963 he would suffer a savage beating after an arrest in Dunnellon, Florida, and later in the year he and three SNCC voting rights workers arrested in Sumter County, Georgia, would become the first such activists to be charged with a capital offense by local officials intent on stifling voting rights agitation. Eventually acquitted, he remained active in CORE until 1965.

The other four Minnesota activists had less experience with the movement but were no less committed to the Freedom Rides. Bob Baum was a nineteen-year-old college dropout whose attraction to existential philosophy led him to a deep and abiding distrust of social and political complacency. Quiet and introspective, and a self-described "mystic," he viewed the Freedom Ride as an opportunity to test the applicability of ideas that challenged the conventional limits of the American mainstream. Gene Uphoff was a nineteen-year-old premedical student and Quaker who also performed as a folk and rock guitarist in several Minneapolis coffee houses. After the Freedom Rides, he attended the University of Colorado Medical School and later opened a series of government-sponsored "storefront" clinics for the poor. Dave Morton, a Unitarian and self-styled "mountain man" who spent part of 1961 in Jackson Hole, Wyoming, was, like Uphoff, a talented musician who expressed his dissatisfaction with the American mainstream through folk ballads and protest songs. An occasional sideman for a rising Minnesota folk singer named Bob Zimmerman (aka Bob Dylan), Morton added a lyrical and quixotic touch to the growing community of Freedom Riders.

To some extent the same could be said of Claire O'Connor, a twenty-two-year-old Boston-born Catholic who worked as a practical nurse at the University of Minnesota Hospital. The daughter of a politically active mother and a deceased father who had worked as a union organizer, O'Connor had little experience with racial issues. As she explained years later, though, there was something irresistible about the Freedom Rides, something that drew her into a world that she could hardly imagine before leaving the safe and secure atmosphere of Minneapolis. Later, after her experiences as a Freedom Rider, she became active in anti-poverty work, wrote a master's thesis on the plight of battered women, and served as the executive director of a health clinic for teenagers. But why this relatively naive young woman became involved in the Freedom Rides in the first place when so many others like her refused to put themselves at risk remains a mystery. In her words, she simply accepted "a one-way ticket" to the movement and never looked back.[15]

THE "MINNESOTA SIX," as they came to be known, were part of a widening circle of engagement that troubled Mississippi authorities and many other white Southerners. Despite the obvious fact that the Freedom Rides were disrupting civic order and providing Soviet publicists with propaganda material, the ongoing frontal assault on segregated transit had now achieved a measure of respectability in certain quarters. During the same weekend that the Minnesota Six arrived in Jackson, the noted Broadway theatrical team of Elaine May and Mike Nichols hosted a benefit concert in New York to raise funds for Freedom Riders, and the general board of the National Council of Churches approved a resolution endorsing nonviolent direct action as a legitimate means of attacking racial segregation. Even worse, from the perspective of conservative white supremacists, on Monday, June 12, Judge Frank Johnson allowed the temporary restraining order against the Freedom Riders to lapse. Ruling that there was no justification for a permanent injunction, Johnson, in effect, reopened Alabama and Mississippi's eastern flank to future Freedom Rides. Almost immediately, jubilant FRCC and CORE officials announced plans to open an office in Montgomery where Tom Gaither and Ralph Abernathy would recruit and train Mississippi-bound Freedom Riders.[16]

These and other related developments were more than enough to convince Mississippi authorities that the Freedom Rider onslaught would continue for the foreseeable future. As far as they were concerned, the only good news on the horizon was an FRCC decision to send at least some of the impending Freedom Rides to locations other than Mississippi. During a four-day hiatus, from June 12 to 15, the only Freedom Rider to arrive in the state was Danny Thompson, a white college student from Cleveland, Ohio, who had missed a connecting bus in Memphis. After straggling into Jackson on Wednesday morning and conducting a one-man test of the segregated facilities at the Greyhound terminal, he ended up in the city jail with the other white Riders.

By that time, both the city and county jails were jammed with Freedom Riders, and local officials had already made plans to transfer some of the Riders to the state prison farm at Parchman, 120 miles northwest of Jackson. On Monday, June 12, the Hinds County Board of Supervisors authorized Sheriff Gilfoy to transfer as many prisoners to Parchman "as he may deem necessary to relieve and keep relieved the crowded conditions in the county jail." White supremacist leaders immediately hailed the prospect of transferring the Freedom Riders to the dreaded confines of Parchman, where the Riders would finally encounter the full force of Mississippi justice. The editor of the *Jackson Daily News* even penned an invitation sarcastically touting the benefits of spending time at the state's most notorious prison:

ATTENTION: RESTLESS RACE MIXERS
Whose Hobby is Creating Trouble.

Get away from the blackboard jungle.
Rid yourself of fear of rapists, muggers, dopeheads, and
switchblade artists during the hot, long summer.

FULFILL THE DREAM OF A LIFETIME
HAVE A "VACATION" ON A REAL PLANTATION

Here's All You Do

Buy yourself a Southbound ticket via rail, bus or air.

Check in and sign the guest register at the Jackson City Jail. Pay a nominal fine of $200. Then spend the next 4 months at our 21,000-acre Parchman Plantation in the heart of the Mississippi Delta. Meals furnished. Enjoy the wonders of chopping cotton, warm sunshine, plowing mules and tractors, feeding the chickens, slopping the pigs, scrubbing floors, cooking and washing dishes, laundering clothes.

Sun lotion, bunion plasters, as well as medical service free. Experience the "abundant" life under total socialism. Parchman prison fully air-cooled by Mother Nature.

(We cash U.S. Government Welfare Checks.)

By Wednesday, June 14, it appeared that the transfer to "the most fabled state prison in the South" was imminent. Parchman superintendent Fred Jones had already made room for more than a hundred Freedom Riders by clearing out the prison's maximum security unit, and he assured Hinds County officials that he could accommodate four hundred more as soon as a new first offenders' camp was completed in late June. After learning that the first transfer might come as early as Thursday morning, Jones insisted that he and his guards were eager to "welcome" the Freedom Riders to Parchman.[17]

As Mississippi officials prepared for the transfer to Parchman, the Freedom Rides also took a new turn in Washington, where CORE field secretary Genevieve Hughes held a press conference on Monday, June 12. Still recovering from her harrowing experiences in Alabama, but now flanked by more than thirty volunteers sporting large blue and white buttons identifying themselves as "Freedom Riders," Hughes announced that two special groups of Riders would depart from the nation's capital within twenty-four hours. The

The Reverends Perry A. Smith and Robert J. Stone speak to reporters before departing from Washington on the Interfaith Freedom Ride, June 13, 1961. The other Interfaith Freedom Riders standing in front of the bus are (left to right) the Reverends Arthur L. Hardge, Robert McAfee Brown, Donald Alstork, George Leake, A. McRaven "Mack" Warner, and John W. Collier. (Bettmann-CORBIS)

first group, consisting of eighteen clergymen—fourteen Protestant ministers and four rabbis—had agreed to undertake an "Interfaith Freedom Ride"
from Washington to Tallahassee, Florida. The second group, numbering
fourteen—seven blacks and seven whites—represented an eclectic assortment
of teachers, students, doctors, and representatives of organized labor. Taking a more easterly route than the Interfaith Ride, they planned to conduct
tests along the Atlantic seaboard, stopping in Wilmington, North Carolina,
Charleston, South Carolina, and Jacksonville, Florida, and ending up in
the Gulf Coast city of St. Petersburg. It had been more than five weeks
since the original CORE Freedom Ride had left Washington, but now the
Southeastern states would get a second chance to demonstrate compliance
with federal law. Flashing her effervescent smile, Hughes optimistically
predicted that the new Riders would "be given service at all stops but Tallahassee and Tampa."

On Tuesday both groups did indeed reach their first-night stopovers in
North Carolina without any major problems. The Interfaith group spent the
night at Shaw University in Raleigh, where SNCC had been founded fourteen months earlier, and the second group stayed at a black hotel in the coastal
city of Wilmington. "We have been treated with the utmost courtesy," the
Reverend Gordon Negen, pastor of Manhattan's Christian Reformed Church,
told reporters in Raleigh: "We hope it will be that way all the way." When
the second group arrived in Wilmington, there was a surly crowd of 150
whites waiting outside the local bus station, but a strong police presence kept
the crowd at bay. On Wednesday morning the Wilmington Riders split into
two groups that planned to reunite in Charleston after conducting tests in
Myrtle Beach and other low-country communities. In Charleston, and elsewhere in South Carolina, the Riders received what one reporter called "a
cool but orderly reception," and the Riders spent the night in the city of
secessionist memories without incident.[18]

Meanwhile, the Interfaith Riders made their way to Sumter, South Carolina, where they were greeted by several local CORE stalwarts, including the
veteran Freedom Rider Herman Harris. Before arriving in Sumter, the Riders
were warned that the town was fraught with tension stemming from Harris's
claim that he had been abducted by four white Klansmen after returning
from New Orleans. Blindfolded and taken to an isolated clearing in the woods,
he was subjected to a night of terror. After forcing him to strip, his assailants
carved crosses and the letters "KKK" into his legs and chest and threatened
to castrate him for challenging white supremacist orthodoxy. Even though
his abductors vowed to kill him if he reported what had happened, Harris
eventually asked the Justice Department to conduct an investigation. When
the Interfaith Riders arrived in Sumter on Wednesday, June 14, the matter
was still pending. But a dismissive response from state and local officials—
South Carolina Governor Fritz Hollings called Harris's story "a hoax"—had
all but invited local white supremacists to stand guard against any additional
civil rights agitation.

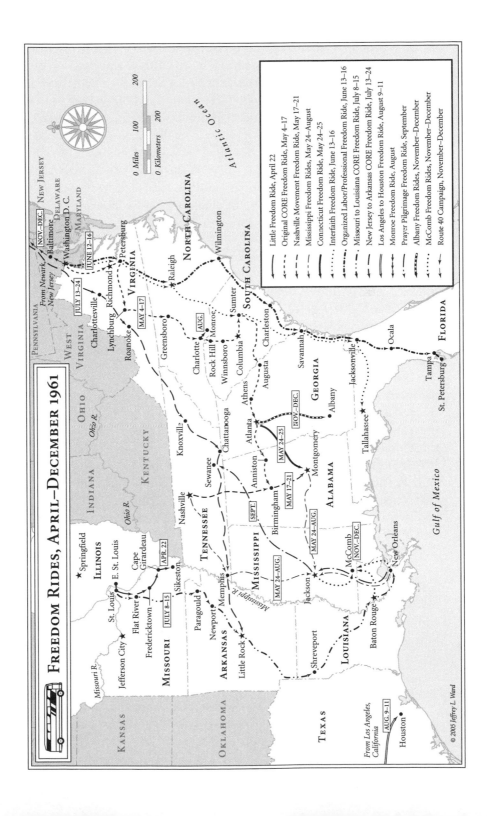

FREEDOM RIDES, APRIL–DECEMBER 1961

Little Freedom Ride, April 22
Original CORE Freedom Ride, May 4–17
Nashville Movement Freedom Ride, May 17–21
Mississippi Freedom Rides, May 24–August
Connecticut Freedom Ride, May 24–25
Interfaith Freedom Ride, June 13–16
Organized Labor/Professional Freedom Ride, June 13–16
Missouri to Louisiana CORE Freedom Ride, July 8–15
New Jersey to Arkansas CORE Freedom Ride, July 13–24
Los Angeles to Houston Freedom Ride, August 9–11
Monroe Freedom Ride, August
Prayer Pilgrimage Freedom Ride, September
Albany Freedom Rides, November–December
McComb Freedom Rides, November–December
Route 40 Campaign, November–December

© 2005 Jeffrey L. Ward

In this atmosphere, some form of confrontation was virtually inevitable, as the Riders' first stop in Sumter demonstrated. Stopping for lunch at the Evans Motor Court a few miles north of town, the Riders encountered "twenty or thirty toughs" and an angry proprietor who blocked their path. Informing them that he had "no contract with Greyhound" and that he was "not subject" to any Supreme Court decisions, he drawled: "We been segregated, and that's the way we gonna stay." Moments later the local sheriff stepped forward to back him up, literally shouting: "You heard the man. Now move along. I'm ready to die before I let you cross this door." As the stunned Riders quickly considered their options, another local man bragged: "I got a snake in my truck over there I'm just dyin' to let loose among them nigger lovin' Northerners." Even this threat did not faze some members of the Interfaith group, but the majority prevailed and all eighteen Riders reboarded the bus. Later, at the Sumter bus terminal, the Riders had no trouble desegregating the white waiting room and restrooms, and their spirits were further renewed at an extended mass meeting at the same black church that had welcomed the original CORE Riders in mid-May. Nevertheless, the earlier retreat continued to bother many in the group, including one minister who vowed to return someday to complete the unfinished business at the motor court.[19]

Just before midnight the Riders left Sumter behind and pressed on to Savannah and Jacksonville, where they found the local bus terminals fully integrated, at least for the moment. In the latter city, the Riders shared a breakfast with an interracial group of five NAACP activists. Sponsored by the Florida NAACP, these self-styled "fact-finders" were essentially local Freedom Riders who had been traveling around the state testing various facilities. The unexpectedly cordial reception that they and the Interfaith Riders received in Jacksonville reflected days of behind-the-scenes maneuvering by Florida governor Farris Bryant. Earlier in the week Robert Kennedy had called Bryant to urge him to avoid any unnecessary confrontations with the Riders, and Bryant had taken the advice to heart. Accordingly, he dispatched personal representatives to each of the major communities along the Riders' scheduled route. In Florida, unlike Alabama, the official policy was polite indifference, a strategy plotted by a governor who did not want his state to end up in the national headlines. Much of the state, particularly northern Florida, was rigidly segregated by law and custom, but Bryant and others decided that the best way to preserve that segregation was to make sure that the Freedom Riders traversed the state without provoking open hostility or violence.

This goal seemed well in reach on Thursday morning as the Interfaith Riders headed west toward Tallahassee and the Florida Panhandle on the final leg of their journey. Along the way they ran into a bit of trouble in the county-seat town of Lake City, where waitresses at a snack bar refused to serve a racially mixed group of clergymen, but they encountered less hostility than was expected at the Tallahassee Trailways terminal, where they once again shared a meal with the NAACP fact-finders. The situation was tenser later in the day at the Greyhound terminal, where the Riders had to sidestep a crowd of angry protesters, two of whom attacked an interracial testing team trying to desegregate a white restroom; with the grudging assistance of the Tallahassee police, a second attempt to desegregate the restroom proved successful. In the terminal restaurant, the management saw to it that black Freedom Riders were served by black waiters and white Riders by white waiters, but the fact that all of the Riders were served in the same room took at least some of the sting out of what was clearly a halfhearted effort at compliance with federal law. Satisfied that they had established an integrationist beachhead in the capital of the Sunshine State, the eighteen Interfaith Riders decided to fly home that afternoon.[20]

Accompanied by several local black activists, the Riders arrived at the Tallahassee airport in time to conduct a test at the airport's white restaurant. A relatively new facility constructed with the help of federal funds but managed by a private company, the restaurant had never served black patrons, as a black CORE staff member turned away in April had discovered. That segregated dining was still the rule on June 15 became abundantly clear when local authorities stymied the proposed test by simply closing the restaurant as soon as the Riders arrived at the airport. Tired and disgusted, eight of the Riders soon flew home as planned. The other ten, however, decided to remain at the airport until the restaurant reopened and served them in compliance with federal law. Among the ten were Robert McAfee Brown, a distinguished Presbyterian theologian who held a chaired professorship at Union Theological Seminary; Ralph Roy, a longtime CORE member and pastor of the Grace Methodist Church in New York City; three black ministers—John W. Collier Jr. of Newark, New Jersey, Arthur Hardge of New Britain, Connecticut, and Petty McKinney of Springfield, Massachusetts; and two young reform rabbis from northern New Jersey—Martin Freedman, a friend and protégé of Bayard Rustin's, and Israel "Si" Dresner, an outspoken Brooklyn-born activist later dubbed "the most arrested rabbi in America."[21]

The press initially reported the Riders' action as a hunger strike, but from the outset their common goal was to break the local color bar by eating together at the airport restaurant. Before they were through they discovered just how difficult this seemingly simple task could be. As Burke Marshall had conceded in a lengthy interview on June 11, enforcing desegregation at aviation facilities was a "knotty problem" complicated by clever uses of private funding and the fact "that the Federal Aviation Agency was not a regulatory agency in the sense that the I.C.C. was." But, as several members of the group explained to reporters, such legalisms were of little concern to ten clergymen who knew right from wrong. Even so, they sent a telegram to the chairman of the ICC urging federal intervention. By nightfall their stubborn protest had drawn a large crowd of angry whites, but they refused to budge until the airport itself closed at midnight. Taken to a black Baptist church in downtown Tallahassee, they spent an emotional hour discussing racial and social justice with a gathering of local civil rights activists, many of whom were veterans of the 1956 Tallahassee bus boycott and other civil rights campaigns. Later the Riders slept on the floor as two of the state policemen who had escorted the Riders from the airport stood guard across the street.

At 7:30 the next morning, they returned to the airport to resume the vigil outside the terminal restaurant. Joined by several local activists and surrounded by police and a bevy of reporters, they remained there for nearly five hours. After nervously monitoring the situation throughout the morning, Governor Bryant called Robert Kennedy to ask for help. "You've got to get these people out of here," Bryant pleaded. "I've done all I can do." Concerned about the Riders' safety and fearful that he had another white supremacist siege on his hands, Kennedy asked Bryant to hold things together for an hour or two while he tried to persuade the Riders to suspend their protest. Minutes later, around 12:30, Burke Marshall was on the phone with John Collier, but their brief conversation ended abruptly when Tallahassee city attorney James Messer ordered the Riders to leave the airport within fifteen seconds. When Collier and the others stood their ground, the police moved in and arrested them for unlawful assembly. The police also arrested three local civil rights leaders—CORE veteran Priscilla Stephens, the Reverend Stephen Hunter, and Jeff Poland, a student sit-in organizer at Florida State University. When Stephens—who along with Poland had only recently been released from jail—objected to the arrests, the police charged her with interfering with an officer and resisting arrest.

By midafternoon all thirteen defendants were ensconced in the city jail, a run-down and overcrowded facility that shocked those who had never seen the inside of a Southern lockup. "The conditions in the jail were foreboding," Ralph Roy wrote later. "Our black colleagues were separated from us, of course, though we could communicate by yelling through a wall dividing us by race. They were received as heroes among their fellow prisoners. In contrast, inmates with us were initially hostile. We were, to most of them, interlopers from the north, even damnable traitors to the white race. . . .We were crowded into an area designed to house twenty-four and there were, altogether fifty-seven. There was one sink, one toilet, and one shower. . . . The food was slop. After a twenty-four hour fast, our supper Friday evening was a piece of gingerbread and a cup of cold, weak coffee."[22]

While Stephens, Hunter, Poland, and the "Tallahassee Ten," as they came to call themselves, were dealing with the miserable conditions at the capital city jail, other Freedom Riders were running into trouble in the central Florida community of Ocala, Governor Bryant's home town. When several black Riders tried to enter a white cafeteria at the Ocala Greyhound station, two white men shoved them backward. The police immediately intervened, ordering the Riders to return to the bus. Three of the seven Riders involved—Leslie Smith, a black minister from Albany, New York; Herbert Callender, a black union leader from the Bronx; and James O'Connor, a white economics instructor at Barnard College in Manhattan—refused to comply with the order. Charged with unlawful assembly and failure to obey a police officer, they were released on bond later in the day. By that time their fellow Riders, after successfully desegregating the Ocala terminal's white restrooms, had proceeded southward to Tampa and St. Petersburg, the final destination for many of the Florida-bound Freedom Riders. Before the day was over the two Gulf Coast cities had weathered three different Freedom Rides with less difficulty than most local observers had anticipated.

In St. Petersburg, a fabled resort and retirement center that had recently been rocked by a controversy over the proposed desegregation of accommodations for Major League baseball players during spring training, one white man was arrested for harassing the Reverend Macdonald Nelson, a local black minister who was part of a welcoming committee at the downtown Greyhound station. Otherwise the city took the arrival of the Freedom Riders in stride, thanks in part to the prodding of the *St. Petersburg Times*, the South's most liberal daily newspaper. After eating lunch at the Greyhound station without incident, four of the Riders participated in an afternoon workshop at a local black Baptist church. During the workshop Ralph Diamond, a black labor leader from New York City, urged local activists to build upon the Freedom Riders' positive experience in St. Petersburg. "We will lose what we've gained if this is not followed up locally," Diamond declared. "It must get to the point where it will become a natural thing for the two races to sit together at counters. When the tenseness wears off, you'll find there will be no problem."

Speaking to an integrated audience at a mass meeting that evening, the Reverend William Smith, the president of the biracial St. Petersburg Council on Human Relations, repeated Diamond's warning. "Unless we continue the work of these courageous people by using all the facilities of our bus stations," the black minister exhorted, "I'm afraid the freedom riders' trip may have been in vain." Two days later, after the Riders had flown back to New York, the *St. Petersburg Times* offered a congratulatory editorial. "We did not expect any trouble here," the editors insisted. "We didn't get it. And had it come, law enforcement was ready. This is a healthy situation of which we can all be proud. . . . We can't afford, for our own good, to permit unconstitutional practices, head-turning law enforcement, discrimination and violence anywhere in this country." Such rhetoric was an encouraging sign for movement leaders, but at the same time they knew all too well that St. Petersburg was a long way from Jackson—and Tallahassee.[23]

The conclusion of the Florida Freedom Rides was less satisfying for the Tallahassee Ten, who were arraigned at a city court on Saturday morning. Released on bond, they flew to Newark for a four-day respite before returning to Tallahassee for a June 22 trial. During the trial, the three local

defendants—Stephens, Poland, and Hunter—were acquitted of unlawful assembly, but Judge John Rudd was unmoved by attorney Tobias Simon's defense of the Freedom Riders' determination to desegregate the airport
restaurant. Offering the Riders a choice between thirty days in jail and a five-
hundred-dollar fine, Rudd scolded them for coming "here for the whole purpose of forcing your views on the community." "If I thought for one minute
that you came here on a noble, Christian purpose and acted accordingly,"
Rudd continued, "you would not be here now. Stop and think when you go
back home and check the records of crime, prostitution and racial strife there
compared to Tallahassee. Then clean up your own parishes, and you'll find
you have more than you can take care of." Stephens also received a tongue-
lashing and even harsher punishment. Though acquitted on the unlawful
assembly charge, she was convicted of resisting arrest and sentenced to five
days in jail, plus thirty more for violating probation related to a 1960 sit-in
conviction. Stephens appealed her conviction, as did the Tallahassee Ten,

Nine members of the Tallahassee Ten hold a press conference after returning
to Florida to serve out their sentences, August 4, 1964. Seated, from left to right:
the Reverends Robert McAfee Brown and John W. Collier and Rabbi Martin
Freedman. Standing, from left to right: Rabbi Israel Dresner and the Reverends
Petty D. McKinney, Robert J. Stone, A. McRaven "Mack" Warner, Arthur L.
Hardge, and Wayne Hartmire. (Florida State Archives)

and the legal wrangling over the airport arrests continued for years. Although a state circuit court overturned Stephens's conviction in 1962, the Freedom Riders' case dragged on until 1964, when the same circuit court judge and the Florida Supreme Court denied their appeal. The United States Supreme Court refused to overrule the Florida courts, which sent the case back to Judge Rudd for final disposition and sentencing. In the end, one of the ten defendants avoided jail by agreeing to pay a fine. But the other nine returned to Tallahassee in August 1964 to serve brief jail terms—and, following their release, to eat triumphantly at the same airport restaurant that had refused to serve them in 1961.[24]

IN THE EARLY HOURS of Thursday, June 15, only minutes before the Interfaith Riders left Sumter, a new and dark chapter of the Freedom Rider saga opened in Mississippi. The first transfer of Freedom Riders to Parchman began just after midnight as forty-five male prisoners—twenty-nine blacks and sixteen whites—were loaded into a convoy of trucks. After the Riders were herded into what amounted to "airless, seatless containers," in John Lewis's words, "the doors were closed, locked, and in utter darkness we were driven away, bracing ourselves against one another, as the trucks lurched around turns, the drivers doing the best they could to slam us into the walls. We had no idea where we were going." As the convoy lurched northward, however, at least some of the Riders began to suspect that they were on Highway 49, the road to the Delta and the dreaded Parchman farm. It was a road that thousands of unfortunate Mississippians had taken since the prison's construction in 1904, and very few had survived the experience without suffering lasting physical and emotional scars. Many, of course, did not survive at all. "Throughout the American South, Parchman Farm is synonymous with punishment and brutality . . ." historian David Oshinsky observed in 1996, and the farm's gruesome reputation for unfettered violence was, if anything, even more widespread and deserved in 1961 when the Freedom Riders were there. As a character in William Faulkner's 1955 novel *The Mansion* put it, Parchman was "destination doom."[25]

When the Riders arrived at the prison at dawn, there was just enough light to see the outlines of their new home—a world bounded by "a barbed-wire fence stretching away in either direction." There were also "armed guards with shotguns," Lewis recalled. "And beyond the guards, inside the fence, a complex of boxy wooden and concrete buildings. And beyond them, nothing but dark, flat Mississippi delta." As the Freedom Riders' eyes adjusted to the light, the imposing figure of Superintendent Fred Jones appeared at the gate. "We have some bad niggers here," Jones drawled. "We have niggers on death row that'll beat you up and cut you as soon as look at you." Moments later the guards began pushing the Riders toward a nearby processing building, but the forced march was soon interrupted by a scuffle in the rear of the line. Terry Sullivan and Felix Singer, two white Freedom Riders who had remained in the back of one of the trucks and then gone limp in defiance of the guards, were being dragged toward the processing center by their feet. "We refuse to cooperate, because we've been unjustly imprisoned," Sullivan cried out. The guards were unimpressed. "What you actin' like that for?" one guard asked. "Ain't no newspaper men out here."

Taken to the basement of the concrete-block processing center, the Riders soon found themselves under the control of a man who introduced himself as Deputy Tyson. Later described by Stokely Carmichael as "a massive, red-faced, cigar-smoking cracker in cowboy boots," Tyson would become an all too familiar figure to the Riders during their stay at Parchman. Without any explanation other than a smirk, he ordered them to remove all of their clothes. When Sullivan and Singer refused, a guard shocked them with an electric cattle prod. But even this did not bring compliance, forcing the frustrated guards to rip off the resisters' clothes before throwing them into a holding cell. The rest of the Riders remained in the room for more than two hours as a crowd of curious white guards gawked at them through barred basement windows. The whole scene was both frightening and demeaning, and the Riders did not know what to expect next. "We were consumed by embarrass-ment," Farmer recalled. "We stood for ages—uncomfortable, dehumanized. Our audience cackled with laughter and obscene comments. They had a fixa-tion about genitals, a preoccupation with size." Finally, they were led, two by two, down a long corridor to a shower room, where they were ordered to shave off all facial hair. To John Lewis, the shower room evoked images of Nazi Germany and concentration camps. "This was 1961 in America," he later reflected, "yet here we were, treated like animals." From the shower room, they marched to their cells in Parchman's maximum security wing, where, still naked, they waited for the distribution of prison clothes. The clothes, when they finally arrived, were meager—a T-shirt and boxer shorts, but no shoes or socks. Understandably some complained, but Bevel, for one, responded philosophically. "What's this hang-up about clothes?" he bel-lowed, "Gandhi wrapped a rag around his balls and brought the whole Brit-ish Empire to its knees!"[26]

A few hours later, on Thursday evening, Governor Ross Barnett and Colonel T. B. Birdsong, the head of the Mississippi Highway Patrol, paid a visit to Parchman to see how the prisoners were doing. In a meeting with the prison staff, Barnett warned that "it will be hard for you men to take what they may say to you," and Birdsong predicted that the Freedom Riders would be "different than any other prisoners you have handled before." Accord-ingly, Barnett announced, the Freedom Riders would not be put to work in the fields with the other prisoners, at least for the time being. "If they re-fused to work, what could we do?" he explained. "It would upset the whole prison routine." By keeping the Freedom Riders locked up and isolated, the dual threat of a sit-down strike and unsettling contact between outside agita-tors and regular inmates could be avoided. As he told reporters before returning to Jackson, everything was under control, and the Freedom Riders whom he had visited had assured him that they had been "well treated." Indeed, they were "resigned to serving their sentences."[27]

The prospect of scores, and eventually hundreds, of Freedom Riders spending the rest of June and July at Parchman was appealing to Barnett and many other white Mississippians. But this scenario held no such charm for federal officials in Washington. A world unto itself, Parchman was almost impossible to monitor; and, while the terrors of the South's most infamous prison might deter some prospective Freedom Riders from actually coming to Mississippi, others almost certainly would be drawn by the lure of real danger and meaningful sacrifice. On Friday, June 16, President Kennedy returned to Washington after ten days in Palm Beach, Florida, where he was vacationing and receiving treatment for a painful back condition. Like his personal ailments, the ongoing Freedom Rider crisis presented him with a seemingly inexhaustible set of irritations. In addition to the Parchman transfers and the arrests in Tallahassee and Ocala, a new set of five Freedom Riders was arrested in Jackson on Friday afternoon. Four of the five were college students, and one, Elizabeth Hirschfeld, was a laboratory technician who worked for the Atomic Energy Commission in Ithaca, New York, adding a new wrinkle to the argument that the Freedom Riders represented a security risk.

One of the four students, Bob Filner, was an eighteen-year-old engineering student at Cornell and the son of Joseph Filner, a left-wing labor organizer who had been active in civil rights fund-raising circles since the early 1950s. A founding member of the Cornell Liberal Union, Filner later taught at the Tuskegee Institute, participated in the 1965 Selma-to-Montgomery March, and beginning in 1992 served seven terms as a liberal Democratic congressman representing a predominantly Hispanic district in San Diego, California. "The Freedom Ride changed my whole life, personally and politically," he insisted forty years after his arrest. A political ally of Senator Ted Kennedy in the 1990s, Filner as a teenager was emblematic of the idealistic college students who pushed the senator's older brother to accelerate the pace of social change.

As President Kennedy was well aware, such acceleration posed political and physical risks. Indeed, while Filner was en route to Jackson, two Freedom Rider–related bombings rocked the city of Washington during the night of June 15–16. At 11:00 P.M. on Thursday evening, a homemade bomb exploded in front of the Veterans Administration building, and nine hours later a second bomb exploded in a Massachusetts Avenue phone booth. No one was injured by either blast, but later in the day an anonymous caller informed the FBI that he had planted six bombs in the capital city as a protest against the Freedom Rides and racial integration. Although there were no additional explosions, and a police search of downtown Washington failed to locate the other four bombs, local citizens and federal officials were on edge for days.[28]

In the midst of this turmoil, Robert Kennedy presided over a memorable meeting at the Justice Department. A week earlier Burke Marshall had met with a small group of civil rights activists during a conference held at a York River plantation house near Capahosic, Virginia. For several weeks Justice Department officials had been looking for a chance to nudge student activists toward a greater emphasis on voting rights agitation, and the Capahosic conference represented the first opportunity for Marshall to make his pitch. A voter registration campaign, Marshall argued, had distinct advantages over confrontational direct action campaigns such as sit-ins and Freedom Rides, not the least of which was the administration's willingness to fund the former but not the latter. Among those at the Capahosic conference were several black student leaders favorably disposed to the idea, including the incoming SNCC chairman, Chuck McDew, Charles Jones of Johnson C. Smith (and the recent Freedom Ride led by William Sloane Coffin), Charles Sherrod of Virginia Union, and Tim Jenkins, a recent Howard graduate who served as vice president of the National Student Association. Encouraged by their receptiveness, Marshall invited them, along with several FRCC leaders, to a June 16 meeting at the Justice Department.

Student leaders and Freedom Ride Coordinating Committee representatives at the Justice Department prior to their meeting with Attorney General Robert Kennedy, June 16, 1961. From left to right: Chuck McDew, Wyatt Tee Walker, Diane Nash, New Orleans attorney Lolis Elie, Jim Lawson, Gordon Carey, and Charles Sherrod. The partially obscured figure cannot be identified. (Getty Photos)

To Nash, Lawson, Walker, and the other FRCC representatives present, the primary purpose of the meeting was to urge the federal government to intervene on behalf of the Freedom Riders unjustly arrested in Mississippi. But, from the outset, Marshall and Kennedy tried to steer the conversation toward a discussion of voting rights. After making the administration's preferences clear, Kennedy all but promised to provide movement leaders with tax exemptions, foundation grants, and legal and physical protection if they agreed to shift their attention to voting issues. To several of the students, including the voting rights enthusiast Sherrod, Kennedy's offer sounded too much like a bribe, and the meeting nearly broke up when Sherrod jumped to his feet to scold the attorney general. "You are a public official, sir," Sherrod reminded Kennedy. 'It's not your responsibility before God or under the law to tell us how to honor our constitutional rights. It's your job to protect us when we do." At this point Walker and others interceded to calm Sherrod down, and Kennedy, after a brief pause, continued to press the argument for a voting rights campaign. Ignoring the gathering's emotional ties to direct action, he outlined an ambitious region-wide voter education project similar to one proposed earlier in the year by Stephen Currier of the Taconic Foundation and Harold Fleming, the founder of the Potomac Institute and the former director of the Southern Regional Council. All of this was food for thought, and by the time the meeting adjourned even the most skeptical of the young leaders had a heightened sense of the attorney general's interest in civil rights. For better or for worse, the Freedom Rides had certainly gotten his attention.[29]

Kennedy left the June 16 meeting with the distinct impression that he had witnessed the beginnings of a move toward voting rights and away from direct action. Even though he realized that the Freedom Rider crisis was far from over, the long-term prospects for a less confrontational approach to civil rights activism seemed to be improving. His faith in such a reorientation rested on a rather simplistic dichotomy of orderly voting rights campaigns versus provocative direct action struggles that would lead inexorably to disorder and violence in the streets. But on June 17, less than twenty-four hours after the meeting with the student leaders, the validity of this dichotomous conception was challenged by Martin Luther King. During a Saturday afternoon press conference at the Los Angeles airport, King predicted that the Freedom Rides would be followed by an all-out nonviolent campaign for black voting rights. "We are going to win the transportation fight through passive resistance," he told reporters. "Then we will tackle the problem of Negro voting in Dixie. We will make a nonviolent assault on all phases of all segregation. But our big move will be to intensify voter registrations through stand-ins at places of registration and polling, and anything else we can do to emphasize the degree to which the negro is denied his right of franchise."

Such an open-ended, multifaceted approach to voting rights activism was not, of course, what Kennedy or the Taconic Foundation had in mind.

The gap between the movement's view of things and Kennedy's became even more apparent on Sunday when King—followed by Sammy Davis Jr., Mahalia Jackson, Dick Gregory, and a string of other celebrities—reiterated his commitment to direct action during a mass rally at the Los Angeles Sports Arena. The rally, which drew a crowd of nearly twenty thousand and raised a substantial amount of money for Freedom Rides and other civil rights causes, signaled that the restless spirit of grassroots insurgency was still rising. Whether the target was disfranchisement or segregated bus terminals, getting the struggle out of the streets was not going to be easy.[30]

Even so, voting rights remained the strategy of choice at the Justice Department, in most intellectual circles, and for many movement activists. For Robert Kennedy, in particular, the effort to accelerate the transition from protest to politics was a high priority throughout the summer of 1961. On Saturday, June 17, while King was raising funds in Los Angeles, Kennedy interrupted a dinner party to lobby Harry Belafonte on the matter. Even though it was his tenth wedding anniversary, Kennedy found time to urge the singer-activist to use his influence on behalf of political action. Ten days later Belafonte, who was in Washington for a series of concerts, met with a select group of SNCC leaders in an effort to convince them to form a political action vanguard within the Freedom Rider movement. At the close of the meeting, the students agreed to do so, and a grateful Belafonte promised to give them ten thousand dollars to initiate the project. Led by Tim Jenkins and Charles Jones, the Harry Belafonte Committee, as the group came to be known, would play a pivotal role in SNCC's turn toward political action later in the summer.[31]

IN THE MEANTIME, however, the direct action tactics of the FRCC continued to draw new recruits into the movement. During the week following the Sunday rally in Los Angeles, four groups of Freedom Riders arrived in Jackson. On Monday, June 20, nine more jailed Freedom Riders were transferred from Jackson to Parchman, but later in the day their former cells were filled by fifteen new Riders. One of those arrested was Eugene Levine, a thirty-four-year-old English instructor at Oklahoma State University, who, after traveling to Jackson by car, conducted a "lone wolf" desegregation test at the Greyhound terminal. The other fourteen were northern Californians who attempted to desegregate the Illinois Central railroad depot after arriving on a train from New Orleans. Eleven of the fourteen were white, and eleven were college students, six at the University of California, Berkeley. According to one disapproving reporter, following their long trip from the West Coast "most of the group wore wrinkled clothes and the men needed haircuts." Described as "amateurish," they "didn't even know the tune to the 'Freedom Song' " that earlier Freedom Riders had sung on their way to jail. Only one of the Riders, Paul McConnell, a Pennsylvania native who had attended both the University of Mississippi and the University of Alabama in the mid-1950s, had spent any time in the Deep South, and he reportedly had been dismissed from both universities because of poor grades.[32]

The nine Riders who arrived from Montgomery on Tuesday provoked less scorn from the Mississippi press but ended up in the same courtroom facing the same unsympathetic judge. The Tuesday group included Wyatt Tee Walker and his wife, Theresa; two Northern white college students, Judith Frieze of Smith and Miriam Feingold of Swarthmore; Henry Schwarzchild, a German-born Jewish official from Chicago; and Margaret Burr Leonard, a nineteen-year-old student at Sophie Newcomb College in New Orleans. Blonde, blue-eyed, and fair-skinned, Leonard presented Mississippi officials with a disturbing development in the evolution of the Freedom Rides. The daughter of Margaret Long "Maggie" Leonard, a liberal-minded columnist for the *Atlanta Journal*, she was the first unmistakably Southern white student to participate in the Mississippi Freedom Rides. Fearful that other white Southern dissidents would follow her lead, white Mississippians would have been even more anxious if they had known that a second Southern white girl had tried to join the June 21 Freedom Ride.

Mary Little, Margaret Leonard's best friend and the daughter of the noted Atlanta columnist and writer Celestine Sibley, traveled alone to Montgomery a day early in an effort to accompany Margaret and the other Riders to Mississippi. While Sibley privately supported nonviolent direct action, she thought that her precocious seventeen-year-old daughter was too young to become a Freedom Rider, especially considering the situation that the Walker group was likely to encounter in Montgomery. When the group arrived in Montgomery on Tuesday afternoon, it became clear that Sibley's fears were justified. Minutes before the group's arrival, the police stationed at the terminal received two bomb threats, and despite heavy rain a "sullen crowd" of five hundred whites was on hand to protest against the first batch of Freedom Riders to visit Alabama since the issuance of Judge Johnson's June 2 restraining order. Protected by sixty heavily armed police officers, the Riders avoided contact with the protesters and eventually made their way to the Dexter Avenue Baptist Church, where a BBC film crew was waiting to record the group's final preparations for the next day's journey to Mississippi.

That night, amidst the whir of BBC cameras, Little, along with Leonard and the other Riders, participated in a socio-drama performed in the church basement. However, on Wednesday morning, just as the Riders were preparing to leave for the terminal, Walker told Little that Martin Luther King wanted to speak with her. Prompted by a call from an overwrought Sibley, King informed the wide-eyed high school student that she needed parental permission to go on the Ride. Crestfallen, she reluctantly returned to Atlanta, where she defiantly lived with the Leonards for several weeks before making up with her "hypocritical" mother. Later in the summer, when she picked up Leonard at the airport following Leonard's release from Parchman,

Little finally achieved her goal of being arrested—albeit for driving without a license. But the sting of not becoming a full-fledged Freedom Rider bothered her for years, fueling the compensating passion that drove her later activities as a SNCC, CORE, and SCLC volunteer.[33]

June 21, the day the Freedom Rides resumed along the Montgomery-to-Jackson stretch of Highway 80, was the summer solstice, the official dividing line between spring and summer. Coincidentally, it was also a day of deep contextual change for the Freedom Rider movement. While the Walker group was on the way to Jackson, U.S. District Judge Sidney Mize was presiding over a hearing that would determine the legality of the Freedom Rider arrests by Mississippi authorities. The plaintiff was Elizabeth Wyckoff, a forty-five-year-old freelance writer—and former professor of Greek at Bryn Mawr, Vassar, Wells, and Mount Holyoke Colleges—from Greenwich Village. The first white woman to participate in a Mississippi Freedom Ride, she had been arrested for breaching the peace on June 2. Declaring that the arrest was unconstitutional and a "disgrace in the eyes of the rest of the world," her attorney William Kunstler, a feisty New York civil liberties lawyer, made a plea for a writ of habeas corpus, which if granted would free not only Wyckoff but all of the other jailed Freedom Riders. Opposing the writ was Hinds County prosecutor Jack Travis, who maintained that the arrests had rescued the state from an outbreak of interracial violence. After listening to two hours of testimony, Judge Mize took the matter under advisement and promised to render a decision before the end of the month.[34]

On the same day, there were two other potentially important legal developments. In New Orleans, Judge Elbert Tuttle, the chief judge of the U.S. Fifth Circuit Court of Appeals, ordered a three-judge panel to convene in Jackson on July 10 to consider an NAACP motion challenging transit segregation in Mississippi. Meanwhile, in Nashville, Burke Marshall clarified the federal government's position on the Mississippi arrests in a speech at the annual Fisk University Race Relations Institute. Speaking to more than a hundred race relations specialists from around the nation, Marshall confessed that the Justice Department was "powerless" to prevent the arrest of Freedom Riders by local or state authorities. Describing the government's unfortunate position as "one of the frustrations" of federalism, he nonetheless predicted that segregated transit would soon be a thing of the past. Noting the hearing held in Biloxi earlier in the day, he endorsed Kunstler's habeas corpus motion and expressed hope that Judge Mize would invalidate the Freedom Riders' arrests.[35]

The legal maneuvering in Biloxi, New Orleans, and Nashville was significant and newsworthy, but the day's most important development related to the Freedom Rides did not take place in a courtroom or any other public arena. In a run-down dormitory at Jackson's Tougaloo College, hidden from the gaze of judges and reporters, four black students were plotting a minor revolution. To this point all of the Freedom Riders arrested in Mississippi had come from somewhere else, and many editors and politicians from around the state had boasted that black and white Mississippians shared a common disregard for disruptive outside agitators. Hardly a day passed without an editorial or speech reminding the public that the Freedom Riders were all outsiders, and even the *Jackson Advocate*, the state's most widely read black newspaper, lent its editorial voice to the anti–Freedom Rider campaign. According to *Advocate* columnist Percy Greene, "a vast majority of the rank and file of Jackson Negroes view the Freedom Riders as doing more harm than good in visiting the city. . . . Most point to a sharp change in the attitude of their employers, and most noticeable change in the attitude of the white employees with whom and by whose direction they perform the duties of their daily work. A large number of those among the unemployed have been heard to blame the Freedom Riders for their continued unemployment and their failure to find a new job. Many have been heard to express the opinion that Negroes of the city would be better off if the Freedom Riders had never come to Jackson."

Whatever truth there was in Greene's assessment, it did not apply to many of the city's students, including four Tougaloo students who set out to dispel the image of local black complacency. One of the four, Mary Harrison, was a twenty-one-year-old Asian-American from San Antonio, Texas, and another, Joe Ross, was a visiting student from Tennessee State who had helped recruit and train Freedom Riders in Nashville. Along with Elnora Price, a twenty-five-year-old from nearby Raymond, Mississippi, and Tom Armstrong, a nineteen-year-old sophomore from the Delta town of Silver City, Harrison and Ross decided that it was time to organize a home-grown Freedom Ride. Accordingly, on Friday afternoon, June 23, they entered the Jackson Trailways station, bought tickets to New Orleans, and sat down in the white waiting room. Disregarding a police order to leave, they were arrested and carted off to jail, making them the first Freedom Riders to be apprehended while trying to *leave* Mississippi.[36]

The full implications of the first local Freedom Ride would not become apparent until early July, when scores of black Mississippians followed the lead of the "Tougaloo Four." But the episode raised deep concerns among local and state authorities. Publicly they dismissed the Tougaloo Four as little more than misguided pranksters, but privately they began to brace themselves for what they feared was an inevitable coupling of local and national movements.

To many white Mississippians, the public fiction of local black complacency was still an article of faith. But, for at least a decade and perhaps longer, that faith had coexisted with the reality of an emerging indigenous freedom struggle. Despite the persistence of white supremacist violence and intimidation, local civil rights initiatives and organized resistance to the status quo had become a fact of life in Mississippi. Although SNCC and CORE were new to the state, the NAACP had maintained a strong presence in Jackson and several other communities since the 1940s. With the rise of the White Citizens' Councils and the reemergence of the Klan in the mid-1950s, some black Mississippians retreated into heightened accommodationism and political and social conservatism. But others became increasingly assertive and even militant, especially after the brutal lynching of Mack Charles Parker in Poplarville in April 1959.[37]

As in other areas of the South, this new spirit was most evident among high school and college students, who exhibited both the impatience of youth and the bravado of those who were relatively invulnerable to the economic intimidation tactics employed by the White Citizens' Councils. In the spring of 1960, for example, more than two hundred Jackson college students distributed leaflets announcing an "Easter boycott" of downtown stores that had discriminated against or failed to hire black citizens. Organized by NAACP field secretary Medgar Evers, the boycott met with limited success, but it helped to set the stage for other protests, including the April 1960 Biloxi "wade-ins." The attempt to desegregate Mississippi's Gulf Coast beaches provoked a determined response from the police and led to a shootout that injured eight blacks and two white vigilantes. Indirectly, it also prompted a change of leadership in the state NAACP. In September, Aaron Henry, a militant activist from Clarksdale, replaced Charles Darden, a conservative critic of direct action, as state president. "Our actions will probably result in many of us being guests of the jails of the state," Henry predicted in his inaugural speech as president. "We will make these jails Temples of Freedom."

True to his word, in collaboration with Evers and a somewhat reluctant Roy Wilkins, Henry launched "Operation Mississippi" in early April 1961, a direct action desegregation initiative designed to enlist black students. Ten days earlier a sit-in by nine Tougaloo students at the main branch of the Jackson Public Library had led to a mass meeting at Tougaloo, a student boycott at Jackson State College, and a march on the city jail where the "Tougaloo Nine" were incarcerated. Using tear gas and nightsticks, the police intercepted the march before it reached the jail, which was probably fortunate since the streets in the area of the jail were filled with white Mississippians—including three thousand Confederate reenactors—celebrating the centennial of the state's secession from the Union. This near miss scared even Henry, but it did not stop him from pushing for Operation Mississippi or from organizing a Freedom Rider support committee in May that evolved into the Council of Federated Organizations (COFO)—a movement "umbrella" group that later coordinated the freedom struggle in Mississippi.[38]

To the dismay of white officials, interaction between the Freedom Riders and local activists began as soon as the first group of Riders arrived in Mississippi. When the first group was brought into Judge Spencer's courtroom, several local civil rights leaders were on hand to lend support, including Claire Collins Harvey. The owner of a Jackson funeral home and the daughter of one of the founding members of the local NAACP, Harvey did not hesitate to identify with the Freedom Riders. Noticing that several of the female defendants were shivering inside the courtroom, she rushed over to inquire "if they needed sweaters or something." That evening she and Aurelia Young, the wife of attorney Jack Young, delivered an assortment of warm clothing to the city jail, and several days later she canvassed three local churches to plead for support for the Freedom Riders. Over the next few weeks her personal campaign evolved into Womanpower Unlimited (WU), a broad network of more than three hundred volunteers who donated and collected "food, sheets, clothes, magazines, and books, blankets and everything to help minister to the needs of the Freedom Riders." Whatever the Freedom Riders asked for, from something as simple as a toothbrush to the often complicated task of relaying messages to outside contacts, Harvey and the women of WU did their best to provide it. And they did so without the support of the majority of the city's black leaders, many of whom considered close identification with the Freedom Riders to be foolhardy and even dangerous. In the face of both criticism and apathy, they carried on and later in the summer even expanded their activities to include voter registration, economic boycotts, and the sponsorship of pro–Freedom Rider rallies.[39]

THE LOCAL SUPPORT SYSTEM created by activists such as Henry, Evers, and Harvey was part of a growing national network that boosted the Freedom Rider movement during the critical days of late June and early July. In addition to the substantial financial contributions solicited by CORE, SCLC, and the NAACP, there were numerous expressions of support from a wide range of groups and influential individuals. On June 17, for example, the Episcopal Society for Cultural and Racial Unity announced that it would sponsor a "Prayer Pilgrimage" from New Orleans to Detroit, where the Episcopal Church was scheduled to convene its triennial convention on September 17. In a show of solidarity with the Freedom Riders, a busload of thirty-seven clergymen would conduct desegregation tests along the route while "penitently admitting our own involvement in the sinful system of separation and segregation at so many levels." On June 20 Rabbi Bernard Bamberger, the president of the Central Conference of American Rabbis, endorsed "the great ethical principle" of the Freedom Rides by contrasting it with the morally bankrupt pageantry of the Civil War Centennial. "The war was in vain, the celebration is a blasphemy and a disgrace," Bamberger insisted, "if a century later the Negro's right to full equality may still be limited by prejudice enacted into law or perpetuated by custom." In Mississippi and most other areas of the South, rabbis and other Jewish leaders were either too conservative or too fearful to speak out in favor of the Freedom Rides. But in the North, many Jewish leaders and congregations were active and vocal supporters of the incarcerated Riders, a growing number of whom were Jewish.[40]

In many Northern communities, religious authorities were the Freedom Riders' most vocal supporters, but there was also considerable support among secular leaders, especially among labor union officials, academic intellectuals, and liberal politicians such as New York governor Nelson Rockefeller. Speaking at a CORE rally in Washington in mid-June, United Auto Workers leader Victor Reuther characterized the Freedom Riders as "America's Peace Corps to America," and several other noted speakers, including the novelist James Baldwin, echoed his praise for the young idealists languishing in Mississippi jails. "I don't see how we can blame these young people," Rockefeller reasoned in a conversation with reporters. "In fact, I think we can't help but admire them."

In the June 18 issue of the *New York Times Magazine*, Eric Goldman, a prominent Princeton University historian, defended the Freedom Riders' use of direct action by placing it in historical context. "The buses that have been carrying the Freedom Riders into the South," Goldman argued, "have confronted Americans with an old and endlessly tortuous problem: How do you achieve genuine social progress in a democracy? Is it better simply to pass the laws and let them grind away or should the legal processes be supplemented, and run ahead of, by the fire of dramatic agitation and direct action?" Goldman's answer, grounded in an understanding of successful reform movements such as abolitionism and woman's suffrage, was that real progress frequently comes from a combination of "moderation *and* agitation." While he acknowledged that not all agitation is productive, he concluded that the "Freedom Riders and the whole present-day movement of passive resistance seem likely to prove one of those agitations which genuinely pushes ahead the cause." Citing the Riders' identification with a rising international spirit of freedom and democracy, he argued that "the Freedom Riders not only have behind them a solid foundation; they also represent the clear trend of affairs. . . . Plainly, incontestably, the Freedom Riders have the great strength of riding with history."[41]

Eugene Rostow—the dean of the Yale Law School and brother of Walt Rostow, one of John Kennedy's leading economic advisors—expressed similar sentiments in the June 22 issue of the *Reporter*. In a provocative essay entitled "The Freedom Riders and the Future," Rostow challenged the popular argument, common even "among Northern liberals," that the Freedom Riders were "provocative intruders, needlessly agitating a situation already well on its way to solution." "This criticism is mistaken, for basic reasons," he declared. "First, the South is not making rapid progress in the civil rights field. Second, judicious intervention from outside is needed now, as it has always been needed, to help Southerners who believe in enforcing the Constitution to overcome the resistance of those who do not. Indeed, outside help is now more needed than ever in the South, for the Ku Klux spirit has not been more active or more effective since Reconstruction days." Saving his most provocative argument for last, Rostow noted a "third reason why this criticism of the Freedom Riders is unconvincing. By openly challenging the final bastion of segregation in the Deep South, the Freedom Riders chose the most dramatic theater in the struggle for civil rights. But their protest was national, not regional. It was addressed as much to New York and Chicago as to Mississippi."

Like Goldman, Rostow went on to point out that the significance of the Freedom Rides transcended not only regional but national borders. Nevertheless, he rejected the argument, sometimes advanced in less than subtle terms by the State Department, that the primary objective of the civil rights struggle was or should be "to please public opinion in Africa and Asia and score a point in the cold war." "We are struggling to accomplish these social changes," Rostow insisted, "because we know they are right." Two days after Rostow's article appeared, Edward R. Murrow made the same point in a cover letter introducing a United States Information Agency report on the Freedom Rider crisis's "harmful effect" on America's international image. "I think it would be a mistake to base our action against discrimination mainly on the ground that our image abroad is being hurt," wrote Murrow. "We should attack this problem because it is right that we should do so. To do otherwise, whatever the overseas reaction might be, would violate the very essence of what our country stands for." Whether Murrow's lofty rhetoric represented the views of the State Department or the White House remained to be seen, but the reiteration of Rostow's moral stance was regarded as a hopeful sign by FRCC leaders and other movement activists.

Two weeks earlier Vice President Lyndon Johnson, in a commencement address at Howard University, had condemned "mob rule" and affirmed the administration's commitment to "the fundamental belief that before the law all stand equal and all are entitled to their full Constitutional rights, regardless of race, creed, color, or section of birth." Yet he, like Murrow, had stopped short of an explicit endorsement of the Freedom Rides. Despite the pressures of world opinion, no one within the administration was willing to go as far as Ralph Bunche, the celebrated black diplomat, Nobel Peace Prize laureate, and undersecretary of the United Nations, who told reporters: "I have great sympathy for the Freedom Riders, because in effect I have been a freedom rider all my life." According to Bunche, he "had never respected 'colored' signs on restaurants and rest rooms in the South and had never been challenged."[42]

Outside the narrow world of movement activists and black diplomats, forthright endorsements of nonviolent direct action were rare, even in the North. And they were rarer still in the white South, where support for the Freedom Rides was limited to the goal of racial equality and almost always stopped short of encouraging direct action. One of the few exceptions was Ralph McGill, the liberal editor of the *Atlanta Constitution*. Speaking to a gathering of editors and media union officials in Manhattan on June 22, McGill simultaneously defended the Freedom Riders and castigated white segregationists, who "reveal the folly of those who, in our times, are trying to keep the past upon a throne." "The real agitators," he declared, "are the states involved," especially those that tolerate political demagoguery and mob action. In retrospect McGill's sentiments may seem self-evident, but at the time his open sympathy for the Freedom Riders was tantamount to treason in most of the white South. In other areas of the nation, there was broader support for direct action, but even outside the South, Freedom Rider supporters were in the minority.

According to a June 21 Gallup Poll, only 63 percent of those polled responded that they were familiar with the activities of the Freedom Riders; and of that group, 24 percent approved of the Rides, 64 percent disapproved, and 12 percent had no opinion. By contrast, 70 percent of the respondents to a June 18 poll approved of the Kennedy administration's decision to send federal marshals to Alabama, with only 13 percent expressing disapproval. Among Southern respondents the comparable figures were 50 percent approval and 29 percent disapproval, suggesting that law and order was a powerful national ideal. When asked "Do you think integration should be brought about gradually or do you think every means should be used to bring it about in the near future?" only 23 percent favored the "near future" option, as opposed to 61 percent favoring "gradually," 7 percent responding "never," and 9 percent with no opinion. Even though a solid majority of Americans supported integrated transportation, Gallup researchers concluded that "many persons had misgivings about the way in which the Freedom Riders were attempting to bring an end to segregation in buses, trains and in waiting rooms, chiefly on the grounds that it was causing too much trouble. The public has also been found to be pessimistic about the racial outlook in the South in the year ahead. As Freedom Riders continue to move into that region Americans are fearful that racial relations in the South will get worse rather than better in the next twelve months." All of this stood in sharp contrast to a June 8 *Jet* magazine reader poll, in which 96 percent of the respondents, presumably almost all black, said yes when asked if the Freedom Rides should continue. But this simply underscored the wide gulf between black and white Americans on matters of civil rights strategy.

While the Gallup figures were neither authoritative nor easily interpretable, they reinforced the general impression that many whites continued to resent the Freedom Riders' disruptive tactics long after the mobs in Anniston and Birmingham had dispersed. In late June, as the second month of Freedom Rides drew to a close, the general public's acceptance of nonviolent direct action was still very much in doubt. Indeed, the rift between the attitudes of ordinary citizens and those of movement activists and their religious and intellectual supporters seemed to be widening.[43]

Even within the movement some leaders had begun to question the advisability of continuing the Rides indefinitely. For some, the strategy of filling the jails of Mississippi was a dangerous gambit that threatened to monopolize and squander the broader movement's energies and funds. With the Justice Department leaning on the ICC, with the entire administration pressing for a systemic reorientation toward voting rights, and with the national and international press losing interest in the crisis, the need for additional Rides became questionable. As a dramatic construct, the daily arrests in Jackson and elsewhere were still newsworthy and useful to the movement. But the nerve-shattering sense of crisis that had followed the confrontations in Alabama was gone, replaced by the grinding routine of prison life and legal wrangling. The human dramas being played out in the minds of new Riders, in Southern courtrooms, and in the cells of Parchman were often extraordinary and compelling, but for the most part they were only accessible to those directly involved. While almost everyone involved in the freedom struggle would eventually recognize the relationship between the Freedom Rides and the emergence of a powerful movement culture, the significance of this connection was not so obvious in the summer of 1961.

In this context of doubt and uncertainty, the Freedom Rider movement—despite its growing support among religious leaders and intellectuals—nearly came unraveled during the last week of June. Ironically, the strands of unity came undone not in Parchman, where the Freedom Riders were withstanding severe physical and psychological strain, but in Nashville, where the Freedom Rider movement had been reborn six weeks earlier. The trouble developed during the annual two-week-long Fisk Race Relations Institute, where the Freedom Rides were a major topic of discussion. Anticipating the discussion, FRCC leaders had scheduled a strategy meeting in Nashville to coincide with the gathering of many of the nation's most influential black scholars.

The institute also attracted several reporters, including Claude Sitton, a Georgia-born *New York Times* columnist who had been covering the Freedom Rides since late May. For three years Sitton had served as the *Times*'s primary Southern correspondent, but in the wake of Harrison Salisbury's controversial article on Birmingham, his superiors in New York had ordered him to stay clear of Alabama. At Sitton's insistence, this order was shelved on May 21, the day following the riot at the Montgomery Greyhound terminal, and he rushed from Atlanta to Montgomery to write the first of what would become almost daily stories on the Freedom Rider crisis. Sitton's coverage of the crisis was reliable and comprehensive, and by early June he had assumed a special position among the journalists writing about the Freedom Rides. As a Georgian who had known Martin Luther King since 1957, he was especially close to the leaders of SCLC, who regularly provided him with what was purported to be inside information on the Freedom Rides and other movement issues.

For the most part this special access served Sitton well, but on at least one occasion it led him astray. While covering the Fisk Institute, he held a series of conversations with various contacts—conversations that convinced him that established movement leaders were about to pull the plug on the Freedom Rides. Even though both Nash and Carey assured him that this was not the case, Sitton wrote a front-page story that gave the clear impression that the Freedom Rides were about to end. Under the headline "Negro Leaders Seek Halt in Freedom Ride Testing," he reported that "powerful forces within the Negro protest movement against segregation have thrown their support behind a proposal to de-emphasize the Freedom Rides." Citing "sources among the movement's top leaders," the article went on to explain that the change in strategy had been precipitated by a combination of factors: the Justice Department's request for an ICC order, the depletion of movement financial coffers, and the failure of Southern blacks "to volunteer for the demonstrations." While Sitton also reported that "considerable sentiment still exists among a handful of the more militant student leaders for continuing the Freedom Rides," he made it clear that neither he nor anyone else expected this militant minority to prevail. "Some might ignore any decision to suspend the activity and carry on independently," he wrote, but the general decision to disengage from the Freedom Rides had already been made and would likely be ratified at an upcoming meeting of the FRCC. The article ended with a parting shot at the FRCC, reporting that "leaders of the movement were said to feel that the demonstrations had suffered from a lack of coordination and planning."

Even though the exact identity of these leaders was never revealed, the primary source of the story leaked to Sitton was hardly a mystery. As the Freedom Rides had evolved into a movement priority, some of King's lieutenants at SCLC had grown increasingly uncomfortable with the emerging influence of student and secular activists, and with the heightened organizational profiles of CORE and SNCC. After privately urging King to keep his distance from the Freedom Rides, they, in effect, decided to force the issue by planting a story in the nation's most influential newspaper. At the risk of exacerbating organizational and generational tensions within the movement, this strategy represented a calculated attempt to restore SCLC's regional dominance. And it almost worked. Immediately following the FRCC meeting on June 24, Bernard Lee, SCLC's representative at the meeting, told Sitton that Nash's statement on the future of the Freedom Rides was misleading. According to Lee, there had been sharp disagreement at the meeting over the continued viability of the Freedom Rides, and the committee's next meeting would probably see a decision to suspend the Rides, at least temporarily.[44]

On Tuesday, June 26, the committee did indeed meet again to reconsider the question of continuing the Rides, but the result was hardly what Lee predicted. Held at a black Masonic hall in Jackson, the four-hour meeting yielded a unanimous decision to continue the Rides indefinitely and without interruption. This time King, Lee, Abernathy, and Walker—who along with his wife posted bond minutes before the meeting started—represented

SCLC. They were joined by Carey and McCain representing CORE, Sherrod and Marion Barry of SNCC, and the Nashville Movement's Bevel and Nash, who chaired the meeting. Although King was the center of attention and Carey was the designated liaison to the press, the "kids" did most of the talking. Taking full advantage of King's personal commitment to nonviolent direct action, they talked about the sacrifices being made at Parchman, about the awakening freedom struggle in Mississippi, and about the gathering momentum of nonviolent protest across the nation and the world. Predictably, King quickly concluded that there was no turning back. Indeed, as he listened to the passionate arguments of Nash and others, whatever reservations he had about the organization of the Rides suddenly seemed insignificant and irrelevant to the larger issues at hand. Pledging his support to the aggressive policies spearheaded by CORE and SNCC, he made one of the most important decisions of his career. Within the movement he alone had the power to cast the students adrift, but he refused to do so.

Following the close of the meeting, a joyous and almost breathless Carey informed reporters that there was unanimous agreement among FRCC leaders that there could be no suspension of the Freedom Rides as long as "segregation is still a living factor." When the reporters turned to Sherrod to ask whether the FRCC planned to step up its recruiting activities among Southern blacks, the young SNCC activist replied: "No one can say where the next people will come from." Even so, Sherrod's sly smile suggested that, wherever they came from, future Freedom Riders would descend upon the Jim Crow South in unprecedented numbers. Moments later, when Carey was asked about the likelihood of Communist recruits, he deflected the reporter's question by insisting that the recruiting centers in Nashville, Atlanta, Montgomery, and New Orleans made a practice of "screening out" all "undesirables." In the future, as in the past, the Freedom Riders would represent a cross-section of Americans committed to the nonviolent exercise of "moral pressure."[45]

Despite the unfortunate diversion precipitated by Sitton's pronouncement that the Freedom Rides were all but over, Carey and Sherrod had good reason to be optimistic. Two days earlier, on June 25, twenty Freedom Riders—the largest single group to date—had arrived in Jackson by train. Ten of the Riders were black, nine were women, and fourteen were from California. Several were Jewish, others were Catholic or Protestant, and still others were completely secular. The oldest, Marian Kendall, a social worker from San Leandro, California, was thirty-five. The youngest, Bob Mason, was a seventeen-year-old high school student from Los Angeles. Among the twenty Riders arrested, there were nine students, two clerks, a housewife, a painter, a civil engineer, a social worker, a freelance writer, a teacher, a secretary, a model, and a professional boxer. In the local press, all were dismissed as cranks and misfits. In private, though, even the most zealous segregationists must have wondered what was unfolding in the hearts and minds of a new generation of Americans. Mississippi, along with much of the nation, was still rigidly segregated, but intrusions such as the June 25 Freedom Ride made many white Mississippians feel that their once comfortable world was shrinking and under siege. And they were right. Despite the misgivings of politicians and public concern about the implications of direct action, an impatient vanguard of young Americans had finally brought the struggle for racial liberation and democratic renewal to the one state widely considered beyond redemption.[46]

9

Ain't Gonna Let No Jail House Turn Me 'Round

Ain't gonna let no jail house, Lordy, turn me 'round,
I'm gonna keep on a-walkin', Lord, keep on a-talkin', Lord,
Marching up to freedom land.

—1960s freedom song[1]

DIVERSITY WAS THE HALLMARK OF THE FREEDOM RIDES. No previous move-ment campaign—not even the sit-ins of 1960—had attracted such a variety of participants. Transcending organizational, regional, and racial boundaries, Freedom Riders became emblematic symbols of a movement that extolled the virtues of political inclusion and social equality. While many Freedom Riders were Southern black college students in their late teens or early twen-ties, others were white, Northern, or middle-aged. While many were deeply religious, others were largely or completely secular. Men were in the major-ity, but more than a quarter of the Riders were women. This diversity, so fitting for an idealistic cause, was one of the strengths of the Freedom Rider campaign, one of the reasons why so many men and women were willing to join the Rides even after it became clear that they were headed for Parchman. Nevertheless, in the social and political context of Cold War America, diver-sity was a decidedly mixed blessing. In 1961 the tensions and suspicions that had given rise to McCarthyism, the Red Scare, and consensus ideology were still very much alive in the American mainstream. In many communities, especially in the South, intolerance of difference and unorthodox behavior was a reflexive reality, and anyone who strayed from the common channels of national or regional life was subject to intense criticism and even ostra-cism. Activists of any kind engendered suspicion, but activists such as the Freedom Riders, many of whom were unconventional even by civil rights movement standards, inevitably provoked the public's deepest fears. Even in the early going, when the campaign was limited to a small vanguard of CORE activists, the Freedom Rides encountered a certain amount of criticism. But once the campaign evolved into a mass movement, the Riders' individual and collective vulnerability to charges of social and political subversion became a serious liability for the entire civil rights movement.[2]

This vulnerability, manifested in both external criticism and internal conflict, was one of the costs of success. As the scope of the Freedom Rides expanded, movement leaders lost a measure of control over the recruiting process and inevitably faced the problem of maintaining cohesion and focus. Like any movement with hundreds of participants, the Freedom Rides attracted a range of individuals representing a wide spectrum of personalities, backgrounds, and ideologies. For the most part, these differences did not pose a serious threat to the common purpose of the Rides, but the personal histories of individual Riders did provide critics with ammunition that could be used to discredit the entire movement. Once the Riders were arrested and identified, investigating and exposing their flawed characters and unsavory backgrounds became a popular pastime among segregationist politicians and law enforcement officers. In Mississippi, and to a lesser extent in other Deep South states, investigators pored over arrest records, college transcripts, and public statements in an effort to uncover patterns of social and political subversion. Presented in daily press installments, these tales of personal infamy, antisocial behavior, and racial and political conspiracies became an important part of the Freedom Rider story. In the white Southern version of this story— and sometimes even in the version propagated by national columnists—the Freedom Riders were social and political misfits. Some were juvenile delinquents, others were beatniks or miscegenationists, and still others were Communist fellow-travelers. Regardless, the clear implication was that all of the Riders were pathological in some fundamental way.

Though common throughout the South, rhetorical attacks on the Freedom Riders reached epic proportions in Mississippi, especially in Jackson. Headlines and articles in the *Jackson Daily News* and the *Jackson Clarion-Ledger* routinely referred to the Freedom Riders as "crackpots," "mixers," "mix riders," "friction riders," or "freedom raiders," and local editors and columnists took advantage of every opportunity to ridicule the individuals and organizations involved in the movement. Jimmy Ward, a columnist for the *Daily News*, excoriated Jim Peck as a "draft-dodger and professional hate monger" and delighted in quoting a Brookhaven man who coined the phrase "FREE-DUMB-RIDERS." After Ward referred to the Riders as "invading CORE crumbs" in early June, other reporters and editors tried to match his mix of invective and dismissive humor. On June 16, for example, the *Daily News* published an anti-Freedom Rider diatribe written by the conservative syndicated columnist Westbrook Pegler. After interviewing David Myers, a white Freedom Rider from Ohio incarcerated in the Jackson city jail, Pegler complained "that bands of insipid futilities of the type called bleeding hearts" had foolishly invaded "a really fine American city" arousing a "bawling national uproar of indignation, disgust, pity and shame." Myers, Pegler reported, "had sprigs of wispy whiskers and the start of beatnik sideburns" and confessed to being "a Quaker whose soul suffered at the thought that someone (God, of necessity) had created a difference between him and his dark brethren." In a follow-up article published a week later, Pegler added that Myers and a second white Rider, David Fankhauser, "were pallid fellows with pallid voices and the watery passiveness of the conscientious objector. They wouldn't fight anybody for anything, but they didn't think it wrong of them to affront a local social system and kick up riots and civil war with painful, even fatal, results to men and women to them unknown." Openly questioning their manhood, he concluded that both men "were negative weaklings who have hit upon this nuisance as a momentary career."[3]

The notion that the Freedom Riders were socially maladjusted found frequent reinforcement in editorials and letters to the editor. To one irate Jackson segregationist the Freedom Riders were "muddled punks and crackpots," while to a man writing from Missouri they were simply "Northern Negroes and trash whites." Indeed, according to Marvin Mobley of Decatur, Georgia, even the financial backers of the Freedom Riders were social misfits. "These troublemakers seem to have the lush funds in unlimited supply," Mobley insisted, "sluiced into their treasuries from Foundations" led by "those who are in a liquor-cure when not on a psychiatrist's couch." Other observers emphasized the criminality of the Freedom Riders, encouraged by revelations that many of the Riders had been arrested before. Cataloging both major and minor transgressions, Southern newspapers often portrayed the Riders as habitual lawbreakers who warranted vigilant surveillance. Though laughable in retrospect, these charges were serious business to many segregationists, including F. James Dabney, an Eastland, Texas, businessman and former military intelligence officer who founded an organization called RAPE—an acronym for "Resist All Pressures Endlessly." According to Dabney, it was "about time someone, or some well-organized group, dug into the background and true purposes of each 'rider' and disclose the findings to the public, so they will know just what kind of people these self-appointed rabble-rousers are." "We intend to make complete background checks, using whatever sources are available, on each and every participant in these riding groups," he declared. "We feel the public should know the true facts about these individuals—who they are, who pays their fares, for their food, their fines, their bail, why they aren't working at regular jobs instead of cavorting all over the countryside causing trouble, their political connections, and their complete police records."[4]

Dabney's call for scrutiny was, of course, unnecessary. In Mississippi, the task of uncovering the criminal backgrounds of the Freedom Riders had already been delegated to the State Sovereignty Commission, an investigative and propaganda agency established in 1956. Working in close cooperation with the highway patrol and the White Citizens' Councils, the commission was empowered "to do and perform any and all acts and things deemed necessary and proper to protect the sovereignty of the State of Mississippi, and her sister states." Like the Georgia Bureau of Investigation (GBI) and Florida's Legislative Investigation Committee, also known as the Johns Committee, the Sovereignty Commission patterned itself after the FBI, targeting alleged subversives and troublemakers. Even before the first group of Freedom Riders arrived in Mississippi, the commission was on the case, compiling information on CORE, SNCC, and movement leaders. Once the rounds of arrests began, investigators monitored every aspect of the Freedom Rides, amassing files on each Rider and scrutinizing anyone who publicly supported the Rides.[5]

Although the stated rationale for this massive effort was the preservation of civic order, the driving force behind the Sovereignty Commission's investigative activities was the deeply held conviction that the civil rights movement, including the Freedom Rides, was connected to an international Communist conspiracy. The sense of panic that spread across much of the Deep South in the summer of 1961 was, first and foremost, a reaction to what appeared to be an impending loss of racial privilege and social control. But the intensity of the resistance to the Freedom Riders had a lot to do with the widespread perception that they were "outside agitators" in the truest sense of the term, that they represented forces alien and hostile to American values. The notion that the Freedom Rides were part of a Communist plot first emerged in Alabama in mid-May when Bull Connor, Attorney General MacDonald Gallion, and others played upon Cold War suspicions of a grand conspiracy to subvert the Southern way of life. Later, after the focus of the Rides moved to Jackson, the Communist linkage became the stock-in-trade of Mississippi politicians and editors attempting to discredit the campaign.

On June 9, for example, the *Jackson Daily News* printed an exposé of CORE and FOR under the headline "Record Reveals Close Ties of Leftwing Organizations—'Freedom-Riding' CORE Linked with Conspiratorial Outfits." Increasingly sensational exposés followed, and the *Daily News* and other local papers printed scores of articles and letters to the editor reinforcing the themes of conspiracy and subversion. One letter from a Camden, South Carolina, man insisted that "the so-called 'freedom riders' were really backed by the Communists and their dupes, the NAACP, CORE, and others," adding: "When you fight to stop these 'Riders' you are also fighting communism." Speaking in Memphis on June 20, Robert Welch, the head of the ultra-conservative John Birch Society, claimed that Communists were "behind the Freedom Rides," and two days later Alabama congressman Michael Huddleston asked the House Un-American Activities Committee to launch a full-scale investigation of the Freedom Rides. Mississippi's Senator James Eastland, the chairman of the Senate Subcommittee on Internal Security, had already hinted that he was considering a similar investigation, and in late June the momentum for a congressional probe continued to build.[6]

Despite rising concerns, the political and editorial Red-baiting of the Freedom Riders remained unfocused until June 29, when General T. B. Birdsong, the head of the Mississippi Highway Patrol, revealed that his investigators had discovered that at least two white Freedom Riders had attended a "Communist planning workshop" in Havana, Cuba, three months before the start of the Rides. Under the sensational headlines "Soviets Planned 'Freedom Rides'" and "No God, Non-Christian—FR's Learn Trade in Red School," the *Jackson Daily News* and the *Jackson Clarion-Ledger* reported that Katherine Pleune, a twenty-one-year-old Chicago woman, and Jim Wahlstrom, a twenty-four-year-old graduate student at the University of Wisconsin, were among 202 American students who had traveled to Cuba to meet with "nine officials of Soviet Russia." According to Birdsong, the purpose of the meeting was "to teach the students how to make sit-ins, walk-ins, kneel-ins, and Freedom Rides." Both Pleune and Wahlstrom freely admitted that they had gone to Havana in February as part of a student "Fair Play for Cuba" tour. But after Pleune refused to divulge whether she was a member of the Communist Party, Birdsong concluded that she was an active conspirator, especially after she revealed that she was an atheist who "did not receive a Christian upbringing" and that she had been arrested dozens of times for picketing racially segregated facilities, including the CIA headquarters in Washington.

Even more disturbing, according to Birdsong, was the mounting evidence that Pleune's unsavory background was typical of the Freedom Riders. In addition to a record of convictions for auto theft, burglary, and grand larceny, as well as "undesirable discharges from military service," some Riders were clearly "Communist backed, pawns in the hands of Communist powers that be." Art Richardson, the highway patrol's public relations chief, issued an even bolder charge, announcing that the Freedom Rides had been "planned and directed by the communists." "We have known for some time the communist party is behind the freedom rider movement," Richardson added. "Now we're getting some proof." This statement drew an angry denial from Gordon Carey, who, after terming such accusations "so ridiculous as to merit no reply," replied anyway "because the reputation of scores of imprisoned Freedom Riders is at stake." "The Freedom Rides have no connection whatsoever with the Communist party in this nation or any other," Carey declared.[7]

Such denials carried little weight in a state where many prominent editors and politicians regarded the connection between civil rights agitation and Communist subversion as self-evident. For many white Mississippians, the most trusted source of information on public affairs was the White Citizens' Councils' monthly newsletter, *The Citizens' Council*, which made frequent reference

to the conspiratorial designs of "CORE and its Communist-tinged supporters" and which repeated even the most outlandish accusations against the
Freedom Riders and other movement activists. Quoting Senator Eastland,
the June 1961 issue of the *Citizens' Council* reported that "CORE is known as
the war department of the U.S. integration movement. Since its inception,
its creed has been lawlessness and its tactics have followed the pattern set by
Communist agitators the world over." Not to be outdone, Mississippi congressman John Bell Williams, quoted in the same issue, stated flatly that the
Freedom Riders were "part of the Communist conspiracy to destroy America."
Such rhetoric was also featured in a widely syndicated radio program, *The
Citizens' Council Forum*. In mid-July, a Citizens Council spokesman boasted
that three special programs focusing on the subversive nature of the Freedom Rides had been distributed to more than four hundred stations in forty-
two states. On one program, Mississippi attorney general Joe Patterson assured
an interviewer that "there is not a bit of doubt in the world that Communist
influence is behind the freedom rides. The Communists have endorsed the
program, and it is in direct keeping with their plan of activity in the South, to
go in and create chaos, confusion, strife and discontent among the races."

Though generally speculative, these assertions were sometimes grounded
in what appeared to be hard evidence, such as the supposed exposé of Pleune
and Wahlstrom or pro–Freedom Rider statements in the Soviet press. Equally
alarming were the periodic reports that Communist activists in Northern
cities were openly agitating on behalf of the Freedom Riders. Under the
headline "Communists Mount Soapboxes in NYC to Back Riders," the *Citizens' Council* described the sinister activities of party leaders, including James
Jackson, the editor of the *Daily Worker*, and Benjamin Davis, the national
secretary of the CPUSA, both of whom were black. At a series of rallies in
midtown Manhattan, Jackson and others used sound trucks to incite the public to exert pressure on behalf of the Freedom Riders in "the union, in your
shops, and in your neighborhoods." Such activities, which undoubtedly raised
a few eyebrows even among politically jaded New Yorkers, communicated a
frightening message to white Mississippians—and perhaps to many other
Americans as well.

While the practice of tar-brushing the Freedom Riders with the Communist label was most evident in the Deep South, it was not unknown in
other parts of the country. Northern conservatives such as the columnist
Walter Winchell also tried to discredit the Riders by linking them to Communists and other political subversives. "The Communist Party, always anxious to exploit our racial problems," Winchell reported on July 4, "is busy
turning out stickers focusing attention on the Freedom Riders. Some of the
commy-written slogans are: 'Action, Yes. Cool Off, No' . . . 'Ride the South
the Freedom Way,' etc." Winchell, like most cosmopolitan conservatives,
characterized the Freedom Riders as Communist dupes rather than as active

conspirators, but one suspects that this distinction did little to calm the fears of Americans caught in the throes of Cold War hysteria. At the very least, the Freedom Riders had powerful and brazen allies who were bent on the destruction of the American way of life, and for many Americans this was more than enough justification to withhold support from a movement that they might otherwise endorse.[8]

THE GROWING DIVERSITY of the Freedom Riders also affected the internal dynamics of the movement. Any movement that involved multiple organizations, hundreds of participants, and thousands of active supporters was bound to have a measure of inconsistency and internal conflict. This was especially true in a protest movement that faced the emotional and physical challenges of mass incarceration. Beginning in late May, prison life was the dominant reality for most of the Freedom Riders, including many of the movement's leaders. The fact that Farmer, Lewis, Bevel, Walker, and hundreds of others shared the Parchman experience provided a certain commonality, a bond of sacrifice and struggle that fostered a sense of solidarity. Yet, at the same time, the intensity and uncertain outcome of the experience sometimes reinforced and even accentuated existing differences of perspective, political ideology, and philosophical conviction. While Parchman often brought people together in ways that they could not have imagined before entering the prison's walls, it sometimes had the opposite effect. Like most closed authoritarian institutions, Parchman exerted a powerful influence over everyone in its grasp. But for a group as diverse and determined as the Freedom Riders it was an imperfect and unpredictable crucible of personal survival, collective engagement, and movement culture.

The depth and variety of the Freedom Riders' prison experiences had a lot do with the special conditions created for them at Parchman. For the Riders, even more than for regular inmates, Parchman was a world unto itself. While beatings and acts of outright brutality were rare, the world of isolation and deprivation mandated by Mississippi authorities tested the limits of the Riders' resilience. By order of Governor Barnett, the Freedom Riders did no prison labor and were confined to their cells "throughout each day, never going outside, even for exercise." Spread out through the prison's large U-shaped maximum security wing, the Freedom Riders' two-person cells made group conversation and community life extremely difficult. In early August, when the number of Freedom Riders in Parchman became too large for the maximum security wing, many of the white male Riders were transferred to the prison's first offenders' unit, where they lived barracks-style in two large rooms filled with cots. During the first six weeks, though, there was little or no opportunity for communal living, beloved or otherwise. With a few exceptions, interaction beyond adjoining cells was limited to singing, which became a treasured lifeline for many of the Riders.

"The monotony was tremendous," John Lewis recalled. "We had no reading material other than the Bible, a palm-sized copy of the New Testament, which was given to each of us by the local Salvation Army. . . .We each had our own metal-frame bed with a mattress made by the inmates. That, a commode and a small washbowl completed the cell's furnishings. There were walls between the cells, so we could not see one another. Only when we were taken out to shower, which was twice a week, did we see anyone but our cellmate and the guards. Once a week we could write a letter." The biweekly shower, as Steve Green recalled many years later, "was easily the highlight of each week" and a ritual that the Riders tried to make the most of:

> We were instructed to strip the sheet off the beds and bring it with us. The cell doors were opened one by one, and naked, two of us at a time could proceed to the end of the hallway where we handed over our dirty sheet, and were given a towel. In front of the guard door, we could shower and shave with no mirror and, as the evening passed, an increasingly dull razor. We then returned our towel, were issued a clean sheet, and told to return to our cells. . . . It was the only time we could actually see each other, but the trip down the hallway became an occasion for rude comments, heard by all, and even a crude form of competitive theater. A bed sheet, we discovered, could become a judge's robe, or a hanging rope, or a cop's club, or a slave's head dress and pants, or a pasha's turban, or any number of costumes. The performances were more than entertainment—they also became a form of "communication" with the guards who gathered around the ward door at the end of the hallway, glaring at our depictions of the traditions of the South.

The shower ritual provided a brief respite from the loneliness and isolation of cell life. But the dominant reality for Green, Lewis, and hundreds of others was an involuntary personalization of time and space. Cut off from family, friends, and worldly institutions, separated from the regular prisoners, constricted by the limits of cells and cellmates, and deprived of most of life's chosen pleasures, the Riders had no choice but to fall back upon themselves. Consigned to seemingly endless hours of reflection, introspection, and contemplation, they lived primarily in interior worlds dominated by matters of mind and spirit. Freedom songs, hunger strikes, and other provocations provided a semblance of community life. For the most part, though, the individual Freedom Riders were on their own.[9]

It was in this context that Farmer, Lewis, and other leaders tried to maintain a modicum of unity and collective purpose. From the beginning of the Freedom Rides, few had doubted the difficulty of building the beloved community. But doing so under these conditions was especially daunting, given the wide differences of opinion among the Riders on matters of faith and philosophy. Despite a common commitment to nonviolent direct action, the philosophical distance between secular and religious activists involved persistent and even fundamental disagreements. At one end of the spectrum, the Nashville students led by Bevel, Lewis, and Lafayette pressed for a deep and mystical commitment to a philosophy grounded in the principles of the Christian social gospel and Gandhianism. To them, nonviolent struggle was an all-encompassing way of life and the challenges of Parchman were a welcome spur to greater sacrifice and commitment. By contrast, at the other end of the spectrum avowedly secular and worldly activists such as the streetwise New Yorker Stokely Carmichael saw the Freedom Riders' predicament primarily in terms of power and political realism. To them nonviolent direct action was a tactical initiative that carried no meaning beyond its social and political utility. Many others, of course, fell somewhere between these two poles, and with so much time for thought and reflection nearly everyone was engaged in some form of reformulation or reassessment. Consequently, there was more dynamism than order, and for some, more confusion than clarity.

These swirling emotional and intellectual currents did not promote consistent factionalism or submit to easy categorization, but there were discernible patterns of thought and behavior that both divided and unified the jailed Riders. According to Bill Mahoney, a Nonviolent Action Group activist from Washington who spent forty days in cell 13, most of the Freedom Riders at Parchman fell into three broad categories—"political, emotional, and moral." Drawing upon conversations with his cellmate and the Freedom Riders housed in adjoining cells, Mahoney offered Marv Davidov, the radical Jewish art dealer from Minnesota, as an example of the political group. To Davidov, the Freedom Rides were essentially a "way of fighting a system which not only hurts the Negro but is a threat to world peace and solidarity." The men who defend segregation, he told Mahoney, serve the same interests as those who develop "war industries[,] . . . recklessly speculate in other countries, and in general . . . meticulously exploit masses of people." Representing the second group was Mahoney's cellmate, a young black musician from Nashville who was relatively uninterested in politics but nonetheless passionately committed to the Freedom Rides. A close friend of William Barbee's, he had decided to become a Freedom Rider after Barbee suffered serious injuries during the Montgomery bus station riot. Living next door, in cell 12, was an example of the third group—"the son of a well-to-do businessman who had come because it was his moral duty." Politically moderate, "he spoke proudly of his father who had fought hard and 'made it,' and was constantly defending North America's economic and political system from the attacks made upon it by myself and the art dealer."

In this particular microcosm of the Parchman experience, there was little movement toward consensus, but in the broader population of jailed activists, Mahoney detected a powerful common denominator that provided a basis for intellectual dialogue if not convergence. "The name of Gandhi was constantly on the minds and lips of most of the imprisoned riders," he recalled in an article published a few months after his release. "Anything Gandhi had said or done was interpreted and reinterpreted to be applied to the situation in Mississippi." Despite considerable disagreement on the meaning and implications of the Indian philosopher's life and teachings, Gandhianism served as a touchstone for deliberation and debate. Competing versions of Gandhian orthodoxy justified a wide range of positions on everything from hunger strikes to the choice of freedom songs. Even within the ranks of the Nashville group—generally the most experienced Gandhian activists at Parchman—there were doctrinal disagreements. On balance, however, the desire to stay on the right side of the Mahatma was a unifying force among the jailed Riders.[10]

In effect, the Freedom Riders turned a prison into an unruly but ultimately enlightening laboratory where competing theories of nonviolent struggle could be discussed and tested. In the darkest corners of Parchman, where prison authorities had hoped to break the Riders' spirit, a remarkable mix of personal and political education became the basis of individual and collective survival. Even though fear and insecurity remained an integral part of the Parchman experience throughout the summer, it did not take long for the Riders to make the best of a bad situation. Once they realized that Mississippi authorities did not dare resort to Parchman's traditional means of intimidation and control—namely, brutal, life-threatening violence—the Riders, despite numerous indignities and aggravations, had the upper hand.

If federal officials and the national press had not been hovering over the situation in Mississippi, the guards might have been given the authority to unleash the full force of Parchman's infamous brutality, but political and cultural realities left Barnett and his lieutenants with a limited range of options. They could make the jailed Riders miserable by withholding privileges, restricting movement, or serving inedible food. And, as John Lewis recalled, they could keep the lights on "around the clock, making it difficult to sleep," or keep the windows closed as the Riders "baked in the airless heat." Indeed, they could even spray the Riders with fire hoses, as they did on one occasion, and then bring in giant fans to blow cold air over shivering bodies. But none of this was enough to slow the momentum of a nonviolent movement that embraced unmerited suffering. While a few individual Riders buckled under the strain and abandoned their "jail–no bail" pledges, the vast majority came to view the Parchman experience as an eminently survivable rite of passage. Unwittingly, Mississippi authorities had provided them with a means of achieving a higher stage of Gandhian consciousness, and most of the Riders took full advantage of this ironic situation.[11]

On occasion prison authorities resorted to the extreme measure of placing an offending Freedom Rider inside a six-foot by six-foot metal box known as "the hole." This horrific creation, located in the basement of the maximum security wing, offered its unlucky inhabitants "no light, no food," and only "an open hole in the floor for defecation." But even the hole did not always have the intended effect on those subjected to its dungeon-like aura. A case in point was the unforgettable "concert" sung by a black Freedom Rider from California with operatic training. Described by Steve Green in his Parchman memoir, the Californian's response to being put in the hole was to take advantage of the discovery "that the metal walls of his box made a perfect reverberator." "That evening," Green recalled, "as we began our usual sing-along of protest songs, there rose from the bowels of the Parchman Prison maximum security unit the notes of a beautiful spiritual. The volume was incredible—his deep baritone could be clearly heard in every room of the building, by prisoners and guards alike. In silence, with tears of joy in some eyes and rage in others, we listened to the most moving concert I have ever heard, to this day."[12]

The Riders' ability to turn almost any situation to their advantage also became clear during the so-called mattress war that began on June 24. After a week of exuberant singing and preaching, the Riders had pushed their jailers to the limits of endurance, prompting Deputy Tyson, the head of the maximum security unit, to threaten to remove all of the mattresses in the cell block if the Riders didn't quiet down. Though ultimately a subject of dark humor, the idea of taking away the Riders' mattresses and forcing them to sleep either on a concrete floor or on the cold metal coils of a box spring was hardly a trivial matter at the time. As Jim Farmer recalled: "The mattresses were the only convenience we had in those little cells. They were our link to civilization, so to speak. Everything else was cold and hard and the mattress was no more than an inch and a half thick, and straw, but at least it was something." Already sleep-deprived, many of the Riders soon fell silent in an effort to keep their mattresses. But others could not resist transforming the threatened removal into a test of moral fortitude.

Speaking in his best preacher's voice, Jim Bevel yelled out: "What they're trying to do is take your soul away. It's not the mattress, it's your soul. . . . Satan put us in here for forty days and forty nights. To tempt us with the flesh. He's sayin' to us, 'If you'll just stop your singin' and bail outta there, I'll give you anything you want—soft, thick, cotton mattresses and down pillows and everything. Be good boys and I'll let you keep your mattresses.' " This call to righteousness elicited a round of concurring amens, especially among Bevel's Nashville colleagues, but the first Rider to turn Bevel's words into action was, surprisingly, Hank Thomas, a predominantly secular activist who loved to sing. After bellowing, "Come get my mattress, I'll keep my soul," Thomas propped his mattress up against the cell bars and urged the other Riders to follow suit. Soon all but two had done so.

The only holdouts were cellmates Fred Leonard and Stokely Carmichael, but when the guards and trustees came to collect the mattresses a few minutes later no exceptions were allowed, and they too lost their bedding. This apparent injustice left Leonard and Carmichael fuming, but the rest of the Riders broke into song, intoning the choruses of "Ain't Gonna Let Nobody Turn Me 'Round" and placing special emphasis on the lines "Ain't gonna let no jail house, Lordy, turn me 'round, I'm gonna keep on a-walkin', Lord, keep on a-talkin', Lord, marching up to freedom land." The forceful singing continued for hours, as the Riders worked their way through a medley of freedom songs before falling asleep on their mattress-less box springs. The next day Deputy Tyson returned the mattresses but warned that he would take them away permanently if the Riders didn't tone down their incessant singing. Accepting the challenge, Thomas and several other Riders were soon singing louder than ever, and Tyson promptly ordered the trustees to re- trieve the mattresses, this time for good. As the trustees went through the cell block, there was little resistance—until they reached Leonard and Carmichael's cell. After a brief struggle Carmichael surrendered his mat- tress, but Leonard fought on, defying both Deputy Tyson and his fellow Riders, the majority of whom had decided that voluntarily relinquishing the mattresses was the best way to demonstrate moral authority. Undaunted, Leonard clung to his mattress with a determination that he later recalled with pride:

> They drug me out into the cellblock. I still had my mattress, I wouldn't turn it loose. They were using black inmates to come and get our mat- tresses, and I mean *inmates*. And there was this guy, Peewee they called him, short and muscular. They said, "Peewee get him." Peewee came down on my head. *Whomp, whomp*—he was crying. Peewee was crying. And I still had my mattress. Do you remember when your parents used to whup you and say, "It's going to hurt me more than it hurts you"? It hurt Peewee more than it hurt me. I still wouldn't turn my mattress loose, and they had these things they put on my wrists like handcuffs, and they started twisting and tightening them up—my bones start cracking and going on and finally I turned my mattress loose.[13]

After vanquishing Leonard, Deputy Tyson returned to the cell block to gloat and to see if the Riders were ready to acknowledge his authority. As he strutted along the cell bars, he was sorely disappointed by what he heard. Instead of bowing down, the Riders mocked him. "Since those mattresses are so valuable," Lafayette yelled out, "why don't you auction them off and tell people that the Freedom Riders slept there. In that way, you can get back some of the money the Freedom Rides are costing you. And we'll sing a little song at your auction." Unaccustomed to such insolence from black prison- ers, Tyson shot back: "You shut yo' mouth, boy." Realizing that he had struck a nerve, Lafayette couldn't resist following up with a question about the deputy's use of the word "boy." "Deputy Tyson," Lafayette asked, straining to keep a straight face, "do you mean anything derogatory when you call us boy?" Caught off guard, Tyson lost whatever composure he had left. "I don't know nuthin' 'bout no *'rogatory*," he insisted. "All I know is if you boys don't stop that singin', y'all gon' be singin' in the rain." What he meant by this was unclear, but within minutes Hank Thomas was singing a new stanza of the old labor song "Which Side Are You On?" that went: "Ole *big* man Deputy Tyson said, I *don'* wanna cause you pain, But *if* you don't stop that singin' now, You'll be singin' in the rain."

Hearing this taunt, Tyson ordered his guards to spray the cell block with a high-pressure fire hose. Later, as the drenched Riders sat in their cells wondering what other indignities Tyson was planning, the cell block windows were opened and exhaust fans were turned on to confirm the message of intimidation. During the long, cold night that followed, there was more shivering and sniffling than singing in the cell block. But once they dried out, the Riders returned to their singing as if nothing had happened. Indeed, though the mattresses were gone, the struggle had left many of the Riders with a new sense of collective purpose and pride. For a growing number of Riders, the mystique of sacrifice and unmerited suffering was evolving into an article of faith and a powerful source of individual and common resolve.[14]

In a few cases, this evolution led to a blanket rejection of worldly concerns. At some level, though, most of the Riders continued to struggle with the competing concerns of mind and body. Most obviously, the nagging issues of dealing with prison food and a lack of exercise were serious problems for almost everyone. In early July, several days after the removal of the mattresses, Jim Farmer discussed both issues with prison superintendent Fred Jones. Granted a brief appointment in Jones's office, Farmer, barefoot and dressed only in a flimsy T-shirt and a pair of shorts, found himself straining to keep his composure, desperately trying, as he later recalled, "to salvage what dignity I could." Avoiding any discussion of the mattresses, he made only one request: that the Freedom Riders "be allowed to go outside and work, along with the other prisoners." Before he could elaborate on why he felt this was so important, Jones summarily dismissed the suggestion as too dangerous. "You all wouldn't last two minutes out there," he declared with a sly smile. "The other nigras'd kill you. If you want to get y'selves killed, it's all right with me. But y'ain't goin' to do it here." Undeterred, Farmer replied that he and the other Riders "would gladly take our chances with the other prisoners." But Jones, turning deadly serious, made it clear that he had no intention of providing the Riders with exercise, fresh air, or any other form of comfort. "We ain't goin' to let y'all go no place," he bellowed. "We didn't tell you all t' come down here, but y' came anyhow. Now, we want y' to stay in there an' *rot!* We've got to feed ya, but we can put so much salt in y' food that y' won't be able to eat it. And that may be just what we're gonna do." Later, back in the cell block, a dejected Farmer reported that the meeting had been a waste of time and that the barely edible food the Riders had been forcing down might get even worse.[15]

During the following week Jones made good on his threat, instructing the prison kitchen staff to lace the Riders' food with mounds of salt. But, like the removal of the mattresses, the salt episode turned out to be a minor physical irritant that, at least for some, could be added to the lore of sacrifice and resistance. Dealing with prison slop was never easy, of course, and from their first days at Parchman the Riders had squabbled among themselves over how to respond to the food issue. While complaints about the quality of the food were frequent and undoubtedly justified, some of the Riders, especially those from poor or working-class backgrounds, felt that such complaints smacked of bourgeois privilege and were inappropriate in a movement of mass liberation. On several occasions individuals or groups of Riders called for a general hunger strike and total noncooperation with prison authorities "until the food gets better," but no such strike ever materialized, even during the salt episode. Interestingly enough, the hunger strikes that did occur had more to do with individual conscience and Gandhian strategy than inedible food. And even the philosophically based hunger strikes led to disagreements about the etiquette and timing of prison-constricted protest. "Those who went on long fasts," Bill Mahoney recalled, "justified Gandhi's remark that at times he had to fast in spite of his followers' refusal to join him; others, who would fast only when there were numbers large enough to be politically effective, said that they took this stand in accord with Gandhi's practice of only making meaningful sacrifices."

Most of the hunger strikes at Parchman—unlike the earlier fasts at the Jackson and Hinds County jails—were short-lived and unpublicized, but there were a few exceptions. After Ken Shilman, an eighteen-year-old white Freedom Rider from Long Island, posted bond on June 20, he told the press that three of his fellow inmates were conducting a prolonged hunger strike to protest the inhumane conditions at Parchman. One of the hunger strikers, Price Chatham, a twenty-nine-year-old white Rider from East Rockaway, New York, had begun his fast in Jackson on June 2 and had not eaten for nearly three weeks. According to Shilman, Chatham's weight had dropped from 150 to 120 pounds, endangering his health. Prison authorities disputed Shilman's claim, insisting that Chatham was actually sneaking food from other prisoners and had lost only two and a half pounds during his so-called fast. To prove their point, they placed Chatham in solitary confinement on June 23, a move that brought his fast to an end three days later. Whatever the truth of Shilman's claims on behalf of his friend, the episode demonstrated the difficulty of using a hunger strike to send a message from Parchman to the outside world.[16]

Fortunately, there were other means of reaching beyond the prison's walls. While personal visitors were prohibited, carefully monitored contact with visiting ministers, rabbis, and priests was allowed. And even though letters to and from the Freedom Riders were routinely censored by prison authorities, some Riders developed elaborate codes to foil the censors. Others relied on the periodic release of individual Riders as a means of delivering messages to friends and family members or of publicizing what was going on at Parchman. Shilman's description of the inhumane conditions in the maximum security wing was only the first of several exposés offered by recently released Freedom Riders. After posting bond on June 29 and returning to his home in Victoria, British Columbia, Michael Audain gave the press a detailed briefing on the treatment being dispensed at Parchman, including the removal of the mattresses and the use of "wrist breakers," viselike metal clamps that administered excruciating pain when tightened. "I would not describe it as torture," Audain told reporters, with a touch of sarcasm, "because I do not know the precise definition of that word, but I would at least say it was very brutal treatment."

After posting bond on July 3, Jim Farmer issued similar charges during an emotional Independence Day press conference in Jackson. Joined by CORE field secretary Jim McCain, Farmer held forth on the situation at Parchman and on the movement's plans for the future—and he did not hold back on either front. After predicting that his experiences at Parchman would prove valuable to CORE's efforts "to orient new riders about what to expect there," he confessed that his time in prison had "tried my faith in human nature." Judging by what he had seen and experienced, "the policy of the prison is the dehumanization of the riders, to make us as animals." Prison authorities had violated the Riders' civil rights at every turn, Farmer insisted, and Superintendent Fred Jones was well aware of what was going on. When asked to respond to the charges by Farmer and others, Jones simply grinned and said he had never intended "to turn the prison into a country club." Referring to the mattress episode, he declared that "a penitentiary must have some order and discipline. . . . This is a bunch of trouble makers . . . who came here to make trouble. They thought they could come down here and take over, but they're not going to take over as long as I'm here."[17]

Such explanations drew wry smiles from local reporters and other white Mississippians, but they did not dispel the growing suspicion that the Freedom Riders were being systematically mistreated at Parchman. On the day of Farmer's release, Minnesota governor Elmer Andersen ordered the head of the state Human Rights Commission, Wright Brooks, to conduct an investigation of the conditions at Parchman. Two weeks earlier the families of the six Minnesota Freedom Riders arrested and jailed in Mississippi had asked Anderson to help them gain access to their children, but Anderson's appeal on their behalf had gotten nowhere. Frustrated by Ross Barnett's seeming indifference to the parents' concerns, he eventually decided to send Brooks and Assistant Attorney General John Casey Jr. to Mississippi for a "firsthand look at the situation."

When the two Minnesota officials arrived in Jackson on July 6, a defiant Barnett placed severe restrictions on the investigation. While the Minnesotans "would be permitted to view jail facilities in Jackson, Hinds County and at Parchman" and talk with the jailed Minnesota Riders for "about five minutes," they would not be allowed to conduct an extended inspection of penal conditions. Mississippi had nothing to hide, Barnett assured Brooks and Casey, pointing out that earlier in the week a local judge had asked a Hinds County grand jury to visit Parchman on a fact-finding mission. Indeed, Barnett even arranged for the Minnesotans to take a tour of Jackson State College and other "Negro facilities" to demonstrate how much racial progress had been made in recent years. Nevertheless, when the two officials arrived at Parchman they were given only a cursory look at the prison's cell blocks and only a brief, tightly monitored visit with their fellow Minnesotans. With most of their scheduled time at Parchman taken up by a lavish dinner with Superintendent Jones and his wife, they had little chance to gather the kind of detailed information that they had been told to gather. Predictably, their subsequent report was noticeably lacking in specifics and of little value to Governor Anderson or the worried parents back in Minnesota. In fact, to the dismay of movement leaders, the report all but absolved Mississippi prison officials of any wrongdoing. Brooks told reporters upon her return to Minnesota: "A tour of the prison facilities has convinced me that there have been no examples of mistreatment or abuse." Other than a few complaints about the food and requests for more exercise, there were allegedly no problems to report. Claire O'Connor, who posted bond and returned to Minnesota just prior to Brooks's visit, presented a darker version of Parchman to anyone who would listen. But her personal testimony had little impact on the official response to the plight of the Minnesota Six.[18]

BOTH THEN AND LATER SOME OBSERVERS suspected that the Brooks Report was a whitewash. But others concluded that the report accurately reflected the treatment accorded *white* Freedom Riders. The treatment of *black* Riders, it was commonly assumed, was far worse—not an unreasonable assumption considering Parchman's unrivaled reputation for racial oppression. Notorious for breaking both the spirit and the flesh of black men, Parchman epitomized a criminal justice system dedicated to the interests of racial control and exploitation. Forged in the image of Mississippi's caste system, it was a plantation masquerading as a prison, a place where the state's least fortunate black laborers went to suffer and die. Thus, even though whites also suffered and sometimes died there, the mystique of Parchman was generally more intense for black prisoners. This is not to say that the white Freedom Riders who spent time at Parchman felt safe and secure. On the contrary, in the aftermath of the assaults in Birmingham and Montgomery there was no longer any doubt that under certain conditions white segregationist rage could fixate just as easily on white transgression as on its black equivalent. Indeed, the brutal beatings of Jim Peck, Jim Zwerg, and Walter Bergman indicated that at least some segregationists were capable of a special rage when confronted by white civil rights activists. Still, not even these harrowing events could overturn the conventional wisdom that the institutional manifestations of white supremacy were more dangerous for blacks than whites.

This was certainly true of the Freedom Riders themselves, many of whom felt extremely uncomfortable about the imposed racial segregation in Mississippi jails and prisons. At Parchman, all of the Freedom Riders, black and white, lived in the same maximum security unit, but the unit's individual cells were rigidly segregated. While blacks and whites sometimes found themselves in adjoining cells, they were not allowed to share the same living quarters. In such a Jim Crow setting, differential treatment of some kind was virtually inevitable, even though the basic physical conditions of food, clothing, and shelter seem to have been the same for both races. How meaningful these differences were to those who suffered relative deprivation probably varied from individual to individual, and from cell to cell, but the racialized nature of the overall Parchman experience was, at the very least, an unfortunate reality that interrupted the rising interracialism of the nonviolent movement. Denied the opportunity to practice racial integration in prison, black and white Riders were prevented from practicing what they preached.[19]

The separation of male and female Freedom Riders was an additional source of guilt and anxiety. Both in the Hinds County and Jackson jails and at Parchman, the female Riders faced many of the same problems and conditions as the men—racial segregation, bad food, monotony, and even the removal of their mattresses—but they also had to deal with persistent fears related to gender and sexual vulnerability. While several had been arrested before, none had spent more than a few days behind bars. Nor did any of them have any extended experience with an artificial environment detached from the traditional world of men and women. Virtually all of the female Riders, black or white, had been reared in families where some man or woman, either a father or a mother, or perhaps an older brother or sister, assumed the role of custodian; and most had an array of other protectors, friends both male and female, who constituted an extended support system that could be called upon in time of need. None of this was available to them in the jails of Mississippi, where normal patterns of both "feminine" and dependent behavior lost meaning and relevance. At one time or another, insecurity and anomic disorientation plagued almost all of the jailed Freedom Riders, male or female. But, in the pre-sexual-revolution context of the early 1960s, problems related to privacy, hygiene, and personal security often held a special significance for women.

Of course, what made them especially vulnerable was not so much gender per se as it was the assumption that they had crossed the boundaries of racial and sexual decency. In the Deep South, women often found themselves on a cultural pedestal of affection and sentimental deference, but there was no room on this pedestal for women who abandoned the shibboleths of regional orthodoxy. In the calculus of patriarchal traditionalists, white women who collaborated with black men to attack the cultural mores of the South did not deserve to be treated as women, much less ladies. Neither did black women who violated Southern conventions from the opposite direction. Female transgressions, even when they were essentially political, could seldom be separated from the broader assault on white supremacy. To many white segregationists, women riding on buses with men of another race was a sexually provocative act that could not be ignored or forgiven. To them, the very fabric of civilization was at stake, and the women involved deserved punishment harsh enough to deter other women from straying from the fold. Such attitudes seemed to be especially common among white Mississippians, who could turn even the most casual conversation about the Freedom Rides into a discourse on miscegenation. William Kunstler had been in the state less than a week when he encountered this fixation during a visit to Governor Barnett's office. After learning that Kunstler was both an ardent integrationist and the father of two daughters, Barnett could not resist asking the question: "Mr. Kunstler, what would you think if your daughter married a dirty, kinky-headed, fieldhand nigger?" Stunned by Barnett's language, Kunstler shot back that his daughter, like all American women, had "the right to select her own husband." Unmoved, Barnett warned the New York lawyer that the real goal of the civil rights movement was intermarriage. "That's all the niggers want," the governor insisted.

From the moment they arrived in Mississippi, the female Riders had to deal with variations of this theme, including the insinuation that they were fallen women who had joined the movement as a sexual lark. Whatever their actual behavior, they were treated as little more than civil rights whores. While there is no evidence that any of the women were raped—a violation that was probably precluded by the glare of publicity surrounding the Freedom Riders—other sexual indignities were common. For Carol Ruth Silver, a white Freedom Rider from New York who kept a detailed diary during her six weeks of incarceration in Mississippi, the undercurrent of sexual suspicion became palpable when detectives interrogated her the day after her arrest. With no apparent justification, she was bombarded with questions about interracial sex. Had she ever dated "Negro boys"? Would she be willing to marry a Negro? Over the next few weeks, such questions would become almost routine for Silver and the other female Riders.

Insulting and unwelcome questions represented only a small part of the sexually related intimidation that the women were forced to endure. After their arrival at Parchman, the female Riders had to deal with male guards who could not resist watching them undress and shower and with a prison doctor who conducted invasive and unnecessary vaginal examinations. The strong suspicion that the doctor used the same cloth glove for all the women he examined added to the feeling of victimization and served as a symbol of the prison staff's contempt for the female Riders. During most of their stay at Parchman, the female Riders were placed under the collective supervision of one male guard, one matron, and a staff of female trusties. In actuality, though, they received little attention from prison authorities, other than the delivery of daily rations. On several occasions the guards and trusties all but ignored requests for medical attention, including one instance in which a young California Freedom Rider, Janice Rogers, suffered a miscarriage.

This was Parchman at its worst. Fortunately, there was another side to the women's saga. As one of the first female Riders to be transferred to Parchman, Silver was able to experience—and to chronicle—not only the hardships and indignities of prison life but also the evolution of resistance and community in the women's section of the maximum security unit. Like the male Freedom Riders who lived at the opposite end of the unit, the women were racially segregated and housed in small six-foot by nine-foot cells. Unlike the men, however, the women were crowded into a tight cluster of thirteen cells that provided opportunities for considerable interaction and collaboration. Thus for them the Parchman experience took on a more collective cast than the cell-by-cell pairings that dominated prison life among the men. Perhaps for this reason, the women, even more than the men, were able to turn Parchman into a makeshift school of political education and cultural enrichment. In addition to endless rounds of freedom songs, female Freedom Riders organized nonviolent workshops, political seminars, ballet lessons, French classes, and even a series of lectures on Roman history and Greek mythology. Not all of the women participated in these activities, and prison life was never easy for the female Riders. But the stories of resilience and ingenuity that appear in Silver's diary and other sources stand as a testament to the female Riders' determination to make the best of a difficult situation. While some of the women found Parchman unbearable and posted bond as soon as bail money became available, many others stuck it out for a month or more, creating a saga of survival that became a staple of movement lore. Often condescended to as the "weaker sex," they very nearly proved the opposite during the first "freedom summer" at Parchman.[20]

At the same time, women prisoners, like their male counterparts, discovered the difficulty of reaching a consensus in a group that spanned a wide range of cultural backgrounds and personal philosophies. Even before they arrived at Parchman, the cancellation of a planned hunger strike caused hard feelings among several of the female Riders. On June 14, after learning that many of the male Riders were about to be transferred to Parchman, eleven of the women at the Hinds County Jail agreed "to go on a hunger strike until the boys come back or we are sent there." Selecting Pauline Knight, a twenty-year-old black student from Nashville, as their designated spokesperson, the eleven women began a fast that within a day caused one of them, Winonah Beamer—a nineteen-year-old white Rider from Ohio—to faint and others to question how long they could hold out. Though several of the hunger strikers were determined to make good on their pledge, the strike quickly collapsed when attorney Jack Young persuaded Knight that fasting in a Mississippi jail was a waste of time and energy. Before the end of the second day, Knight had announced that as far as she was concerned the strike was over, a decision immediately seconded by Ruby Doris Smith and at least two other black Riders. Among several of the white hunger strikers, however, Knight's statement engendered considerable resentment. As Silver chronicled in her diary: "All eleven of us had considered very carefully the value, implications, etc., of this strike, its objectives and purpose and how it should be run. We felt a great deal of resentment against Pauline for not having consulted with us in the first place. . . . We had all felt very strongly that the spokesman for the strike and the leadership of it should come from one of the Negro girls rather than from one of us in this cell, but we also felt that as individuals equally with them involved in a democratic movement, we had at least the right to be treated equally."[21]

This was not the last time that hard feelings and misunderstandings would disrupt the solidarity of the women Riders, and the necessity of compromise and cultural negotiation became one of the prime lessons of the prison experience. But with the women, as with the men, the problem of bridging racial and philosophical gaps never reached the level of a true crisis. While several incidents foreshadowed the deep divisions that would plague the movement later in the decade, the newness of the experience and the relative innocence of the Riders, male and female, seemed to foster a spirit of cooperation that eliminated the worst manifestations of suspicion and distrust. Though the Riders were flesh-and-blood human beings and hardly infallible, the common ground of the emerging freedom struggle provided a foundation for generosity and forgiveness that few movements, before or since, have been able to match. On a number of occasions strong feelings and tactless statements led to frayed nerves and even angry outbursts, but with few exceptions the Riders seemed to be able to absorb whatever barbs came their way with a measure of disarming grace or humor.

Even the acerbic Stokely Carmichael generally produced more comic relief than meanness when he tangled with other Riders. Steve Green, for one, discovered the comic side of Carmichael during his first week at Parchman. After Green introduced himself as a student at Middlebury and offered an "exuberant" prediction that "hundreds if not thousands of college students . . . would head to Jackson when the school year ended," Carmichael, the son of struggling West Indian immigrants, yelled out: "Hey, guys, did you hear that? We just need to hold on here until Harvard, Yale, and Princeton let out, and then there's going to be an invasion of the Deep South by rich white kids." Momentarily stung by Carmichael's sarcasm, Green managed only a perfunctory response that was drowned out by gales of laughter. But it didn't take him long to develop respect for Carmichael's hard-earned cynicism. "Stokely was a bit rough," Green acknowledged in a candid memoir of his Parchman experience, "but then, as later, he was mostly right." In John Lewis's memory, Carmichael was the most argumentative of the Freedom Riders in Parchman. With his strong views and sharp tongue, he could be an unsettling influence, and his challenges to what he viewed as a misguided faith in Gandhian sacrifice often irritated Lewis and others. Carmichael's dissent did not, however, lead to serious disruption or consistent factionalism. During the mid-1960s his fervent advocacy of "Black Power" would have major consequences and effectively split the movement, but in 1961 there was no such cleavage.

For Green, Lewis, and Carmichael, as for Silver and Knight, prison was not so much a battleground as it was a testing ground where generalizations and stereotypes related to race, class, region, and religion could be examined and reconsidered. As Carmichael later recalled: "What with the range of ideology, religious belief, political commitment and background, age, and experience, something interesting was always going on. Because, no matter our differences, this group had one thing in common, moral stubbornness. Whatever we believed, we really believed and were not at all shy about advancing. We were where we were only because of our willingness to affirm our beliefs even at the risk of physical injury. So it was never dull on death row." For many of the Riders, the time at Parchman represented their first extended experience with exotic allies—movement activists who had grown up in places that they had read about but never visited. Freedom Riders of all descriptions—blacks and whites, Northerners and Southerners, Christians and Jews, working-class laborers and relatively privileged students—discovered firsthand that the freedom struggle was a movement of multiple and shifting perspectives. In such a setting, they could not help but learn from each other. Indeed, despite the artificial constraint of racially segregated cells, they all shared enough of the dangers and challenges of mass incarceration to develop a level of mutual respect that would have been impossible under less authoritarian circumstances.

This was not, of course, what Ross Barnett and his lieutenants had intended. But, like the imposed institutionalization of Jim Crow in the early twentieth-century South, the mass incarceration of Freedom Riders at Parchman had unintended consequences for a movement that had long suffered from organizational disunity and fragmentation. Not only did the unresolved crisis at Parchman provide a temporary focus for the movement at large, but also the personal dynamics of the drama being played out in the cells and corridors of the prison acted as a unifying force among the Freedom Riders themselves. Organizationally, the Freedom Rider coalition remained a fragile entity. Indeed, the cooperative spirit among the Riders at Parchman suggested that a meaningful convergence of CORE, SNCC, SCLC, and the Nashville Movement was more likely to take place inside the walls of a prison than outside. Why this was so is difficult to explain, but in a state renowned for paradox and irony the prison-based maturation of a democratic social movement somehow seems fitting.[22]

WHATEVER THEIR ULTIMATE SIGNIFICANCE, the unexpected benefits derived from the gathering at Parchman were not apparent enough at the time to alter the movement's strategy of challenging the constitutionality of the Freedom Riders' arrests and imprisonment. Having already proven that they could mobilize hundreds of activists willing to go jail for their beliefs, movement leaders saw little advantage in prolonging the struggle. In addition to the obvious injustice involved, Mississippi's policy of fining Freedom Riders and sentencing them to long jail terms placed a heavy legal and financial burden on CORE, which continued to bear the primary responsibility for underwriting and sustaining the Freedom Rider movement. In effect, Mississippi's decision to arrest the Freedom Riders had initiated a war of attrition, a contest between the state's ability to accommodate wave after wave of Riders and the movement's capacity to sustain them, financially and otherwise. As of early July the outcome of this struggle was still very much in doubt, and Farmer and others worried that the movement's greatest challenges lay ahead. To this point much of the financial cost had been postponed by the Riders' decision to forgo bail, but this favorable situation was about to end, thanks to a provision of Mississippi's disorderly conduct statute that required the jailed Riders to post bond within forty days of conviction. Riders who missed this deadline lost their right of appeal and any alternative to serving out their entire sentence. In this context, posting bond on the thirty-ninth day became an essential part of the Riders' legal challenge to Mississippi's Jim Crow system. The day of reckoning varied depending on the date of conviction, but for the first group of Riders—those convicted on May 26—the thirty-ninth day was Tuesday, July 4. While more than a third of the first group had already posted bond, fifteen remained in jail as the deadline approached.

The first mass bailout, which actually took place on July 7 due to procedural delays, brought joy and liberation to the Freedom Riders involved. But it also represented an ominous development for a movement perpetually short of funds. For each Freedom Rider, bond was set at five hundred dollars, but that was only the beginning of the financial burden imposed by litigation. In addition to the bond payment, CORE had to come up with enough money to provide each Freedom Rider with a defense attorney, transportation back home, and, at some time later in the summer, transportation back to Mississippi for an appellate trial. When combined with court costs, housing costs, the purchase of bus and train tickets for the actual Freedom Rides, and other miscellaneous outlays, the average cost per Freedom Rider was well over a thousand dollars. CORE had raised a considerable amount of money since late May, prompting Marvin Rich, the organization's financial coordinator, to exclaim in a letter to Farmer in early June: "More and more freedom riders should be moving toward Jackson in the next two weeks—and we have the money to get them there!" But CORE leaders felt less flush by early July. With more than a hundred Freedom Riders already in jail and the prospect of hundreds more by the end of the summer, the projected budget required to sustain the Freedom Rider movement had risen to more than a half million dollars.[23]

At his postrelease press conference in Jackson, Farmer was careful to avoid any mention of CORE's precarious financial situation. He was equally discreet when he arrived at New York's LaGuardia Airport the next day. Greeted by his pregnant wife, Lula, his two-and-a-half-year-old daughter, Tami, and more than a hundred friends and colleagues sporting buttons proclaiming "Freedom Now–CORE," he was all smiles as he entered the terminal. Standing in front of a large banner that read "Welcome Home, Big Jim," the crowd erupted into song as he rushed to embrace his family. "We Shall Overcome," they sang over and over again, giving reporters and other on-lookers a glimpse of the movement's soaring spirit. Later, after one of the well-wishers in the crowd began singing a special version of the spiritual "We Shall Not Be Moved," the entire gathering joined in. "Farmer is our leader, We shall not be moved," they chanted. "Just like a tree that's planted by the waters, We shall not be moved." Years later Farmer described the scene as one of the high points of his life and a "dizzying" introduction to national fame. As soon as he stepped off the plane, he felt as if he had been thrust into an "Alice-in-Wonderland world." "I was blinded by flashbulbs." he recalled. "Microphones were shoved into my face as newspersons jock-eyed for position. Television cameras recorded my walk to the terminal as if each step were a stride into history." During his six weeks of isolation at Parchman, he had developed some sense of the Freedom Rides' widening impact, but the realization that the project had already exceeded his wildest expectations did not hit him with full force until he returned to New York. As he told the reporters at LaGuardia, the Freedom Rides had unleashed a transcendent feeling of hope and redemption that was stronger than any force wielded by demagogic politicians or prison wardens. Despite the desperate efforts of men like Ross Barnett and Fred Jones, the nonviolent movement

This picture was taken in July 1961 in Chicago, where these six Freedom Riders—all Nashville Movement veterans—had gathered to raise funds for CORE. From left to right: Bill Harbour, Lucretia Collins, Jim Zwerg, Catherine Burks, John Lewis, and Paul Brooks. (Courtesy of Bill Harbour)

was alive and well and poised to expand its influence into every corner of the Jim Crow South.[24]

Though undoubtedly genuine, Farmer's lofty rhetoric represented the public face of the movement. The behind-the-scenes reality at CORE headquarters was, as might be expected, considerably more complicated. Despite its recent notoriety, CORE remained a relatively small organization with a limited staff and modest financial resources. During Farmer's absence the number of volunteers and chapters, and the general level of activity, had all increased, but it was a constant struggle for the organization to keep pace with expanding responsibilities. As the scale of the Freedom Rides reached well beyond anything that CORE leaders had anticipated, Marvin Rich, Jim Peck, and others scrambled to find new sources of funding. The level of contributions was never substantial enough—and the flow of funds never steady enough—to allow CORE leaders to feel confident that they could cover all of the expenses related to the Rides.

Part of the problem resided in the inability of the other organizations affiliated with the FRCC to raise their share of the funds. SNCC and the Nashville Movement had no money to speak of, and SCLC had already committed most of its small budget to sustaining King's activities in Atlanta. In 1961 most of the movement's money resided in the coffers of older and more conservative organizations such as the NAACP, the NAACP Legal and Educational Defense Fund, and the National Urban League, and none of these organizations was inclined to transfer funds to a risky and controversial project that did not square with its established set of priorities. Consequently, CORE had to look elsewhere for funding—primarily to individual donors in New York and other Northern cities. Unfortunately, few of these donors were in a position to contribute more than a modest sum to the cause, and CORE was eventually forced to rely on personal loans to keep afloat financially. The largest of these loans came from Andy Norman, a Sears and Roebuck heir who agreed to bankroll the Freedom Rides with several installments of fifty thousand dollars. With his help, CORE was able to meet most of its obligations during the lean weeks of July and August, but the unusual nature of this arrangement underscored the organization's financial vulnerability. By the end of July CORE had already spent $138,500 on the Freedom Rides, and there was no end in sight to the spiraling costs of fighting for freedom in the Deep South.[25]

For this and other reasons, movement leaders—especially those at CORE—favored a timely settlement of the legal stalemate in Mississippi. Somehow they had to find a way to extract the Freedom Riders from the legal morass concocted by Mississippi's white segregationists; and they had to do so without sacrificing the principles and objectives that had brought the Riders to the state in the first place. The challenge, in effect, was to secure freedom for the Riders as individuals without abandoning the broader goal of bringing freedom to Mississippi and the rest of the Jim Crow South.

A difficult challenge under any circumstances, it was especially so during the early summer of 1961 when movement attorneys had to deal with an unpredictable legal context that reflected the uncertainties of federal authority. At this point no one could be sure how far the Kennedy administration was willing to go to protect the Freedom Riders' constitutional rights, or whether the Riders could gain meaningful access to the federal court system. Ironically, some of this uncertainty stemmed from Robert Kennedy's decision to petition the ICC. Though promising in the abstract, the petition essentially put the administration on the sidelines until the notoriously slow-moving regulatory agency got around to responding to the attorney general's request. On June 19 the ICC announced that it had begun a preliminary investigation of the issues raised by the Justice Department's petition, but it also announced that formal hearings on the matter would not begin until August 15.[26]

In the meantime, movement attorneys were left with limited legal options. In mid-June the filing of a habeas corpus motion on behalf of Betsy Wyckoff held out some hope that all of the Freedom Rider arrests would be nullified, but on June 27 District Judge Sidney Mize ruled against the motion, arguing that the plaintiff had not yet exhausted potential remedies in state courts. Ignoring William Kunstler's insistence that the racially biased Mississippi courts were of no value to Wyckoff or any other Freedom Rider, Mize declared that the federal courts had no valid interest in the case until the state courts rendered a judgment on the legality of the arrests. A week later, Jack Young, Wyckoff's other attorney, asked for a reconsideration of the ruling, but on July 6 Mize denied the appeal. Refusing to give up, Kunstler, backed by the national office of the ACLU, applied for a certificate of probable cause, a document that would allow Wyckoff's case to be heard by the Fifth Circuit Court of Appeals. On July 12, Judge Minor Wisdom, the most racially liberal member of the Fifth Circuit Court, granted the certificate, but ten days later Wisdom and his four colleagues issued a unanimous decision rejecting Kunstler's appeal. The final blow came two weeks later, on July 26, when Associate Justice Hugo Black, speaking for the U.S. Supreme Court, upheld the Fifth Circuit's denial of a writ of habeas corpus. In private, Black, like Wisdom, expressed considerable sympathy for the Riders' precarious legal situation, but as a matter of law he felt compelled to rule against Kunstler's unproven allegation that Wyckoff could not get a fair hearing in the courts of Mississippi.[27]

The Wyckoff case represented a major setback for movement leaders who had hoped to circumvent the costly and potentially debilitating process of appealing the Freedom Riders' convictions in state court. Fortunately for the movement, it was only one of several important legal developments to emerge in late June and July. Most were favorable to the cause of racial equality, and for the first time in years civil rights advocates detected a quickening in the legal assault on Jim Crow. For more than a decade the trajectory of civil rights law and federal policy had been tilting toward desegregation, but now it appeared that both the Justice Department and the federal courts were zeroing in on specific violations of social justice and equal protection. Most obviously, there was a noticeable shift in the Justice Department's approach to enforcement. The first sign of this shift was the petition sent to the ICC in late May, but the new attitude became even more obvious in mid-June when Robert Kennedy testified before a largely hostile Senate appropriations subcommittee. Asked to justify the funds expended on federal marshals in Alabama, Kennedy was immediately put on the defensive by two ultra-segregationist senators, John McClellan of Arkansas and Allen Ellender of Louisiana. Turning the hearing into a debate on the Freedom Rides, McClellan and Ellender subjected Kennedy to a withering attack. To their surprise, Kennedy not only stood his ground, defending the federal government's actions in Alabama, but also hinted that the Justice Department was gearing up for broader civil rights initiatives in the Deep South. After Ellender insisted that the Freedom Riders "were deserving of their reception and got exactly what was to be expected," the attorney general responded coolly but forcefully: "I have a tough time accepting that this should be determined in the streets and that people should be beaten."

One week later, on June 26, his words took on added significance when Justice Department attorneys filed a suit to end racial discrimination at New Orleans's Moisant International Airport. This was the first time that the federal government had actually gone to court to challenge segregated air terminal facilities. Normally stymied by complicated private leasing arrangements that seemed to place airport restaurants beyond the reach of federal authority, the department's attorneys had decided that, as a new facility, the New Orleans terminal offered a good test case for emerging interpretations of the Federal Aviation Act. As the Tallahassee Ten had recently discovered, segregation at air terminals was a tough nut to crack, but the Justice Department's new resolve in this difficult area of civil rights law suggested that even here Jim Crow's days were numbered. Less surprising was the department's increased activity on behalf of voting rights. On July 6 the department filed voter registration suits against two Mississippi counties, Forrest and Clarke, and a week later it filed a similar suit against the city of New Orleans.[28]

All of these suits were encouraging, but for the Freedom Riders the most promising legal development in late June and early July was the Justice Department's decision to join an existing NAACP suit seeking a permanent injunction barring the city of Jackson, the state of Mississippi, and several bus and railroad lines from arresting Freedom Riders. Certified by a three-judge federal panel on July 11, the Justice Department's petition to serve as "a friend of the court" declared that "the United States is concerned when Federal civil rights are violated on a massive scale and a continuing basis." Insisting that Mississippi officials had no legal basis to arrest passengers for violating state segregation laws, the petition contended that "the state and its officials are acting beyond the scope of their lawful power if they make such arrests and obtain such convictions." Accepted over the strong objections of the state's attorney, the petition was especially alarming to segregationists because the NAACP's brief made no distinction between interstate and intrastate passengers. For the first time the Justice Department appeared to be sanctioning an all-out assault on segregated transit laws, even laws that did not affect interstate commerce.

The legality of intrastate bus segregation had been successfully challenged as early as 1956, when the Supreme Court had ordered the desegregation of Montgomery's local buses in *Gayle v. Browder*, but the Justice Department had demonstrated little interest in applying *Gayle* to other cities. If the department's attorneys recognized the significance of the unprecedented challenge to states' rights in Mississippi, they did not say so in the petition. Still, everyone involved had some sense that the Federal government was sailing into uncharted waters. Whatever their intentions, department attorneys soon discovered that they would have to wait for their day in court. Overruling Judge Elbert Tuttle's objections, the two Mississippi judges on the panel—Sidney Mize of Gulfport and Claude Clayton of Tupelo—voted to postpone hearings on the injunction until August 7, one week before the Freedom Riders' appellate trials were scheduled to begin.[29]

The apparent liberalization of the Justice Department's civil rights policies gave movement leaders a measure of hope, but few observers had any illusions about the source of the change. Like the rest of the Kennedy administration, the leadership of the Justice Department appeared to be more political than ideological, and the department's response to the Freedom Rider crisis still bore all the earmarks of an exercise in political damage control. Despite the recent legal maneuvering, this was the same group of men that had struck a bargain with Ross Barnett and James Eastland, agreeing to stand by while the Mississippi police violated the Freedom Riders' constitutional rights. As a means of resolving the crisis, the bargain had backfired, forcing the department to deal with the politically embarrassing situation at the Hinds County Jail and Parchman. But there was no evidence that the new attitude in Washington represented anything more than a frantic attempt to calm the passions that threatened to overtake the administration's low-key approach to the issue of civil rights.

IN THIS CONTEXT, continued pressure from the movement was essential. Despite financial difficulties, the FRCC was determined to maintain a steady flow of Freedom Riders into Mississippi. And, for the most part, the recruiting and training centers in Nashville, New Orleans, Atlanta, and Montgomery did just that, drawing a wide range of college students, ministers, labor leaders, and other volunteers into the struggle. The one notable exception was the first week in July when a temporary shortage of recruits dictated a shift in strategy. Faced with a potentially embarrassing lull in movement activity, the FRCC turned to Mississippi's home-grown activists for help. Cultivating

Jackson's local movement was nothing new, but the decision to recruit local Freedom Riders represented a significant escalation of the campaign to foment a wide-scale internal rebellion. Even though the vast majority of the state's black citizens remained aloof from the movement, the exceptions had grown too numerous and too vocal to ignore. Despite protestations to the contrary, this was cause for considerable concern among white Mississippians, particularly in Jackson, where the connection between the Freedom Rides and the recent upsurge in local activism was obvious. Led by CORE field secretaries Tom Gaither and Richard Haley, the campaign to embolden Jackson's local activists became a significant factor in the larger struggle when it became clear that a number of students at Tougaloo, Jackson State, and several local high schools were eager to become Freedom Riders. Taking advantage of the notoriety surrounding the June 23 arrest of the Tougaloo Four, Gaither and Haley, with the approval of the FRCC, recruited more than a score of local Freedom Riders by the end of the month, setting the stage for a new round of Rides that would soon shake the state to its foundations. Giddy with anticipation, the FRCC authorized Haley to announce the formation of the Jackson Non-Violent Movement, an organization that was sure to arouse the ire of local segregationists.

Three days later, on July 6, Martin Luther King flew into the city to formalize the new arrangement with a mass meeting. But by the time he arrived, the new movement had already rocked the city of Jackson. On Wednesday afternoon, July 5, four black students were arrested after attempting to desegregate a downtown park, and a few minutes later three others—all high school students—were taken into custody after trying to desegregate the white waiting room at the Trailways terminal. That evening six more young protesters—the oldest of whom was nineteen—made a second attempt to use the same waiting room, and they too were arrested. The assault continued on Thursday morning when six local blacks, including a seventeen-year-old high school student, attempted to test the facilities at the Illinois Central railway terminal. All of this prompted Mayor Allen Thompson to repeat an earlier vow that there would be "no mixing" in Jackson as long as he was in charge and to offer some stern words of advice to his white constituents. "Let's start right now emphasizing what I've said about getting over to the colored people their responsibility in this matter," he declared, sounding very much like a spokesman for the White Citizens' Councils. "There is no threat, no economic reprisal involved, but just show them how lucky they are to be living and working here in this fine city. Then have them talk to their fathers and mothers and their neighbors about controlling their children who may be causing trouble. Our colored people are not to be afraid, but they must get out and emphasize to everyone they want things to be left as they are." Reinforcing the seriousness of the situation, Thompson added that "now is the time to stand up and be counted and I want to hear a response from the colored preachers here who believe in this."

Thompson never revealed whether he was pleased with the response to his thinly veiled threat, but what he read in the Friday morning papers could not have been very reassuring. On Thursday evening, with several white reporters in attendance, King spoke to an overflow crowd of fifteen hundred that did not appear to be intimidated by the mayor's challenge. Declaring that "segregation is dead," he insisted that the only question left to be answered was "how expensive the segregationists will make the funeral." Offering words of exhortation seldom heard in Mississippi, by blacks or whites, he praised the local heroes arrested during the past two days and proclaimed: "Let the Negroes fill the jail houses of Mississippi." Participating in nonviolent protest, he maintained, had become the best available means of forcing government officials to move toward equal justice under the law. Chiding Ross Barnett and other segregationist demagogues who claimed that the primary goal of the movement was intermarriage, he assured the crowd that "our basic aim is to be the white man's brother, not his brother-in-law." "We are not agitators and rabble-rousers," he added, "but in a true sense the saviors of democracy. We must learn to live together as brothers or die together as fools." With this benediction, the crowd erupted. Some, with tears rushing down their cheeks, came forward to shake his hand, while more than a few stood motionless in the aisles, temporarily stunned by a message of hope that they could hardly believe was real.

Others wasted no time in acting upon the message. Less than an hour after listening to King's speech, six black high school students descended upon the white waiting room at the Greyhound station. The oldest of the six, Earl Vance, was nineteen, and the youngest, Hezekiah Watkins, was a thirteen-year-old eighth grader at Rowan Junior High School. Asserting the right to purchase a ticket at a window in the white section of the terminal, Vance, Watkins, and their four friends soon found themselves in the back of a paddy wagon singing freedom songs and promising to remain in jail until true freedom came to Mississippi.[30]

The sudden upsurge of the Jackson Non-Violent Movement was a shocking development for many white Mississippians. Time and again they had been assured by state and local officials that everything was under control and that the Freedom Rides were a temporary annoyance concocted by outside agitators. Now it appeared that the Freedom Rides had tapped a wellspring of dissent inside Mississippi itself. Although many wary segregationists had suspected as much for some time, the events of early July confirmed their worst fears. Buffeted on all sides, they faced the prospect of an ever-widening and seemingly permanent challenge to their authority. Almost every day brought new intrusions, some in the form of perceived breaches of racial etiquette that reflected subtle but disturbing changes in racial behavior. Mostly they had to endure the continued invasion of Freedom Riders from far and near.

In the four days following King's speech, the Jackson police arrested forty-nine Freedom Riders, twenty-three of whom were from Mississippi. One group of eight, led by CORE veteran Ike Reynolds, came by bus from Montgomery, arriving at the Jackson Trailways station on the afternoon of July 7, just hours after six local blacks had been arrested at the Greyhound station. Two days later, a group of nine Riders—including seven from California—came in on the late-morning train from New Orleans, and three hours later eight more Riders from Montgomery arrived at the Trailways station. By nightfall all seventeen were behind bars. The most alarming event of the day, from the perspective of white Mississippians, took place at the Greyhound station, where eleven young members of the Jackson Non-Violent Movement attempted to desegregate the white waiting room. When it was discovered that seven of the students were under the age of eighteen, the police promptly arrested not only the students but also the three organizers who recruited them: Diane Nash, Jim Bevel, and Bernard Lafayette. Although Nash was granted a continuance until November, Bevel and Lafayette—only recently released from Parchman—once again found themselves in front of Judge Spencer, this time charged with multiple counts of contributing to the delinquency of a minor. Shaking his head in disbelief and vowing to meet the latest challenge to civil order with the full force of the law, Spencer presided over a two-day show trial on July 18 and 19.

The determination of state and local officials to crush the Jackson Movement was on full display throughout the trial. As the prosecuting attorney made clear, the issue of greatest concern was Bevel's and Lafayette's decision to remain in Mississippi after their release from Parchman. With scores of Freedom Riders scheduled to be released during the coming weeks, Mississippi authorities wanted to make sure that potential agitators left the state as soon as possible. Accordingly, the prosecutor offered to drop the charges against Bevel and Lafayette if they agreed to leave Mississippi immediately. After both men refused to accept the offer, an angry Judge Spencer sentenced them to a five-hundred-dollar fine and six months in jail on each count. Although an immediate appeal allowed Bevel and Lafayette to return to their organizing activities, the trial delivered a chilling message: Any Freedom Rider foolish enough to follow the lead of the two agitators from Nashville could expect stiff penalties and an eventual return to Parchman.[31]

For the vast majority of the Freedom Riders awaiting release, this message of intimidation was probably unnecessary. After nearly six weeks in Parchman, they were eager to return home, and, despite the fears of white officials, movement organizers never encouraged them to do otherwise. The few who stayed in Mississippi did so as carefully selected volunteers or staff members. While the FRCC wanted a small vanguard of released Freedom Riders to remain in the state as organizers, the situation was much too volatile to risk a full-scale provocation of the white power structure—or the alienation of indigenous black leaders. Mississippi was an extremely dangerous place where even the most courageous of activists had to weigh the pluses and minuses of every action, a place where the realities of movement politics generally dictated a relatively cautious approach to mass mobilization. As the NAACP's Medgar Evers pointed out on several occasions, building a movement in Mississippi required patience as well as courage. Wary of overly aggressive activists who did not seem to comprehend the racial realities of Mississippi, Evers was never entirely comfortable with the Freedom Riders' invasion of the state. In public he often lauded the Riders as valiant freedom fighters, but in private he expressed strong reservations about the FRCC's reliance on direct action. To some degree, his complaints stemmed from organizational considerations, and it was no secret that he resented the FRCC's challenge to the NAACP's control of the civil rights struggle in Mississippi. But his objections also reflected a sincere concern for the future of a state-wide movement that could ill afford a serious misstep. Whatever his motivations, FRCC leaders knew that they would lose his support and the cooperation of the NAACP if they stepped too far in front of the veterans of the Mississippi movement.[32]

With so much at stake, Evers had good reason to feel as he did, and many other NAACP leaders, both in Mississippi and elsewhere, shared his ambivalent attitude toward the Freedom Rides. The relationship between the NAACP and the organizations affiliated with the FRCC was troubled from the outset, but during the first two months of the Freedom Rider campaign there was little public discussion of the NAACP's concerns about the wisdom of placing so much emphasis on a new and untried form of direct action. Indeed, in the early weeks of the campaign many Americans, especially in the Deep South, mistakenly believed that the NAACP, not CORE, had organized and masterminded the Freedom Rides. For many observers, white and black, the first sure sign that this assumption was incorrect did not appear until mid-July, when the delegates to the NAACP's annual convention, meeting in Philadelphia, debated the organization's position on the Rides. In the convention's keynote address, delivered on Monday, July 10—the day after Nash, Bevel, and Lafayette were arrested—the Reverend Stephen Spottswood questioned the ultimate significance of the Freedom Rides. "The dramatic exposure of segregation practices and of law enforcement procedures is useful in awakening a complacent public opinion among white and colored Americans," he conceded, "but to suggest that its function is much beyond this is to confuse a signal flare with a barrage." Referring to the NAACP's long-standing leadership of the civil rights struggle, he added: "We are too old in the ways of the long struggle that has engaged our fathers and forefathers not to realize that wars are won by using every available military resource and not by the employment of raiding parties."

The next day, when puzzled reporters asked Roy Wilkins to comment on Spottswood's statement and to explain the NAACP's role in the Freedom Rides, the executive secretary responded tersely that his organization "had nothing to do with the Freedom Rides." "They are run by CORE," he pointed out, adding that the rumor that the NAACP planned to take over the management of the Rides had no basis in fact. Suggesting that the NAACP had better things to do with its time and resources, Wilkins soon found an ironic way to prove his point. On Wednesday morning, he joined more than a thousand delegates on a twenty-two-car "Freedom Train" to Washington. While Wilkins and sixty other NAACP leaders met with President Kennedy in the White House, the rest descended upon Capitol Hill to lobby state representatives and senators. Following the meeting with Kennedy, Wilkins expressed regret that the President apparently had no plans to introduce a new civil rights bill, but in general he and the rest of the NAACP delegation were pleased with the administration's respectful response to the organization's mass lobbying effort. If nothing else, the trip to Washington reinforced the NAACP's commitment to working within the rule of law and legislation, drawing the administration's attention away from the confrontational tactics of the Freedom Riders. For Wilkins and his colleagues, as for the administration, the Freedom Rider crisis had gone on too long, evolving from an unexpected curiosity to a chronic diversion that threatened to undermine civil society and the gradualist paradigm of reform politics. Within the NAACP, as in the broader American society, the Freedom Riders were often regarded as extremists and provocateurs, or, more specifically, as unrestrained idealists who refused to acknowledge the necessity of moderation and compromise.

The conservatism that dominated the national leadership of the NAACP did not always reflect the views of the organization's rank and file, especially among younger members. On the fourth day of the conference, the Youth Councils mounted a near revolt against their elders' reluctance to grant high school and college students a larger voice in the making of policy. One of the major points at issue was their desire to become more involved in the Freedom Rides and to expand and formalize the NAACP's support for the Rides. "I would have the NAACP join in the Freedom Rides," future Freedom Rider Charles Sherrod told reporters. "The courts alone cannot do the work, cannot alone fulfill our dream. . . . We must engage in these moral struggles to push the courts so our cases won't keep being postponed." This and similar statements kept the issue alive, and two days later the convention adopted a compromise resolution explicitly endorsing direct-action techniques such as sit-ins, Freedom Rides, and boycotts. The compromise involved the inclusion of a controversial statement on the dictates of nonviolent strategy. "In supporting the principle of the Freedom Rides," the statement explained, "we do not require our members who participate in them to choose jail rather than bail, but we leave that decision to each individual member concerned."[33]

By defeating an effort to delete this restriction, the NAACP's old guard demonstrated that it was still in control of the organization, but the passage of even a watered-down resolution endorsing direct action reflected the changing realities of movement politics. In many of the NAACP's local branches, there was considerable grassroots support for the Freedom Rides, not to mention a growing restlessness that produced a number of local direct action campaigns. During the first two weeks of July alone, NAACP members were involved in several sit-ins protesting segregated parks, "wade-ins" on the beaches of Ft. Lauderdale and Lake Michigan, an attempt to desegregate a river steamer in St. Louis, and a successful boycott of downtown merchants in Savannah. And, while no branch went so far as to organize its own Freedom Ride, a number of NAACP activists joined the FRCC-sponsored Rides.

In many cases, of course, individual Freedom Riders held memberships in several civil rights organizations. Indeed, as the summer progressed, the Riders' commitment to nonviolent direct action tended to supersede loyalty to any particular organization. For many, an attachment to the broader movement became primary, sometimes to the dismay of leaders grounded in the traditional organization-based approach to activism. To the leaders of CORE, this ecumenism added an ironic twist to the organization's recent success. By sponsoring the Freedom Rides, CORE had greatly expanded its membership and influence. At a broader level, however, the organization had actually weakened the institutional basis of the movement by inadvertently promoting a style of activism rooted in individual acts of conscience and belief. Even though the successful practice of nonviolence required a certain amount of discipline and cooperation, the Freedom Riders were essentially free moral agents. Driven by personal codes of conduct and commitment, they were more inclined to listen to an inner voice than to follow orders from above.[34]

This largely noninstitutional approach, when combined with the unpredictability of state and local officials confronted with an unprecedented assault on white authority, gave the Freedom Rider saga an unscripted quality. Despite careful planning, movement organizers, government officials, and the Freedom Riders themselves never knew what to expect next. As we have seen, this was certainly true during the early weeks of the campaign. But it is striking that the element of surprise never seemed to give way to a predictable routine. As the crisis moved into the summer months and beyond, individual acts of conscience and the responses they provoked continued to produce unexpected complications and situations that sometimes bordered on the bizarre.

ONE SUCH EPISODE took place in mid-July when Ben Cox led a Freedom Ride from St. Louis, Missouri, to New Orleans, Louisiana. Something of a marked man since his May 17 "marry-in" speech in New Orleans, Cox found himself at the center of an unforeseen drama that tested his courage as well as his ability to orchestrate a public demonstration of nonviolent commitment. Sponsored by the St. Louis chapter of CORE, Cox and four other Riders— John Curtis Raines, a white Methodist minister from Long Island; Janet Reinitz, a white artist from New York City; and two black activists from St.

Louis, Bliss Anne Malone, a twenty-three-year-old teacher, and Annie Lumpkin, an eighteen-year-old high school student—encountered little resistance as they conducted desegregation tests at a series of rest stops in Missouri and northern Arkansas. Their smooth ride came to an abrupt end, however, when they arrived in the troubled city of Little Rock on the afternoon of July 10.

Met by a surly crowd of several hundred white protesters, the five Riders managed to make their way into the terminal with the help of the police. Once inside, they discovered that local authorities had divided the terminal into two areas, one designated for interstate passengers and a second for white intrastate passengers. In effect, local officials had taken steps to bring the facility into technical compliance with the *Boynton* decision without capitulating to the demand for complete desegregation. In this way, they hoped to avoid a major incident, but, as often happened with the halfway measures employed by segregationists, it didn't work. Following a brief discussion, Cox and the other Riders simply sauntered into the waiting room reserved for white intrastate passengers, essentially daring the authorities to arrest them. This turned out to be too much provocation for Little Rock's police chief, Paul Glascock, who, despite clear orders to avoid a confrontation, promptly invoked a breach-of-peace statute and carted four of the five Riders off to jail. Fearing bad publicity, Glascock decided to release the youngest of the five Riders, Annie Lumpkin, whom he ordered to return to St. Louis on the first available bus. But this gesture did not stop the *Little Rock Arkansas Gazette* from sharply criticizing the chief's decision to delay the other Riders' departure from the city. "The quicker the defendants can be freed," the *Gazette* editorialized, "the better for the community."

Although many local citizens agreed with the *Gazette*'s position, and even Governor Orval Faubus urged his followers to ignore the Riders' provocations, getting rid of the Little Rock Four proved to be easier said than done. In an emotional trial held on Wednesday, July 12, the Riders' attorney, Thaddeus Williams, maintained that the arrests constituted an abridgement of interstate commerce. Judge Quinn Glover countered that the case was a matter of state, not federal, law. Under Arkansas's breach-of-peace statute the Riders were guilty, and Glover wasted no time in handing out the maximum sentence of six months in jail and a five-hundred-dollar fine to each defendant. He did, however, offer to suspend their sentences if they promised to "leave the state of Arkansas and proceed to their respective homes." At first Williams and the Riders did not know what to make of Glover's offer, but after consulting with CORE officials in St. Louis they reluctantly decided to accept the suspended sentences. A few hours later, however, the deal fell apart when it became clear that the Riders had no intention of returning home. As Williams explained to Glover, the Riders were willing to leave the state, but only if they were allowed to proceed to Louisiana by bus. Unmoved, Glover declared that the Riders had only two options: to return home or to return to jail. To the Riders, of course, there was only one legitimate option, and by nightfall they were once again behind bars. From his jail cell, a defiant Cox told reporters that he was contemplating a hunger strike and that he "would much rather be dead and in my grave" than submit to a system that made him a "slave to segregation."

By the morning of July 13, what was fast becoming known as the "second Little Rock crisis" was in its fourth day, and the local business community was beginning to fear that things were getting out of hand. Forming an ad hoc organization called the Civic Progress Association, thirteen civic and business leaders issued a public statement expressing their gratitude to Chief Glascock and Judge Glover for upholding the law. Privately, however, they pressured Glover to do whatever it took to bring the crisis to a close. Later in the day an obviously conflicted Glover reluctantly conceded that he could not legally prevent the Riders from continuing their trip to Louisiana. Before releasing the defendants, he issued an order prohibiting them from conducting any additional desegregation tests in Arkansas. Still, there was little doubt in anyone's mind that the Riders had successfully challenged the authority of a powerful die-hard segregationist. When the four Riders boarded an afternoon bus for Pine Bluff, Texarkana, and Shreveport, they left behind a still segregated city, but they also left a city that had could not afford to ignore the resolute and disruptive power of the movement.

Even so, whatever satisfaction Cox and the others could take from their partial victory in Little Rock was soon dispelled by the reception they received in the notoriously tough town of Shreveport. Prior to the Riders' arrival, the local police had sealed off the terminal, precluding any test of local facilities. With police snipers placed along the edge of the terminal roof, there would be no protests or arrests in Shreveport, at least on this day; and it would be several weeks before the Freedom Rider movement returned to the city. Despite this intimidating scene, Dave Dennis, a Shreveport native and Freedom Rider recently released from Parchman, met the Riders at the terminal and took them to a meeting with several local clergymen who had promised to put them up for the night. But the extreme nervousness of their hosts led to a change of plan, and the Riders quietly boarded a night bus for Baton Rouge. Refused service at the Baton Rouge terminal, they proceeded to New Orleans, where they used the Greyhound terminal's whites-only facilities without incident. Relieved that the weeklong journey was over, the four weary Riders were greeted by Jim McCain and members of New Orleans CORE, several of whom organized a joyous Saturday night party to celebrate the survival and fortitude of their heroic colleagues.[35]

As the episodes in Arkansas and Louisiana demonstrate, the one thing the Freedom Riders came to expect was the unexpected. What happened in one city was rarely repeated in another. While Ben Cox was confronting and confounding the authorities in Little Rock, Hank Thomas, his friend and fellow veteran of the original CORE Freedom Ride, was undergoing an entirely different experience on a Ride from New York to Chattanooga, Tennessee. Only recently released from Parchman, Thomas led four other Riders—two New Jersey rabbis, a black psychologist, and a twenty-year-old white Michigan State student—on a Ride that deliberately retraced part of the 1947 Journey of Reconciliation. Conducting tests in Roanoke and other communities in western Virginia and eastern Tennessee, they encountered little resistance to transit desegregation in this part of the South. In contrast to the situation in the Deep South, there were no mobs at any of the terminals, and compliance with the *Boynton* decision, though grudging, seemed genuine. After eating lunch at a Greyhound lunch counter in Chattanooga, Thomas told reporters that his group appreciated the hospitality and planned to stay in the city "for two or three days, and see the sights." When asked what they planned to do after that, he simply smiled and said, "We may go on back home or we may go farther south."[36]

As Thomas knew all too well, traveling farther south could lead to serious trouble, and in this instance the Riders decided to head west through Tennessee and Arkansas with the ultimate goal of retesting the same Little Rock facilities that had foiled Cox's group. In general, though, there was no letup in the Rides' southward push into the heart of the Deep South. On Saturday, July 15, the same day Cox's group arrived in New Orleans, twelve Freedom Riders were arrested at the Jackson Greyhound terminal, and on Sunday eight more, including five white Riders from New York City, joined them in the city and county jails. In Jackson such arrests had become routine, and local and state officials felt that they had developed a firm and effective way of dealing with the Freedom Riders. Yet, at the same time, they were becoming increasingly concerned about what was happening in the rest of the South. Governor Ross Barnett, in particular, was convinced that an inconsistent response was weakening the South's defense of segregation. Fearful that many Southern officials had let down their guard, he invited the region's governors to a special conference held in Jackson on July 19.

Billed as a wake-up call for the leaders of the segregationist South, the meeting turned out to be a major disappointment, drawing only the governors of Alabama, Arkansas, South Carolina, and Mississippi, plus lower-level representatives from Florida, Georgia, Louisiana, and Kentucky. Barnett had hoped to demonstrate that the white South constituted a solid bloc, but he accomplished exactly the opposite by convening a rump meeting of extremists. Obviously bitter at being snubbed, he opened the conference with a public complaint against "the lack of unity among the leaders of the South," many of whom he found to be "soft" and "timid" in their defense of the Southern way of life. Several hours of segregationist posturing followed, including suggestions that Barnett was ready to form a third party based on resistance to segregation. But neither he nor any of the other delegates could hide the fact that the conference had failed to rally the region's political elite.[37]

To make matters even worse, the timing of Barnett's gathering coincided with several other newsworthy events related to the Freedom Rides. In addition to the two-day trial of Bevel and Lafayette, there was a competing interracial conference at Tougaloo College that attracted thirty-five prominent ministers and theologians, including Martin Luther King Jr. Organized by Dr. Charles McCoy of the Pacific School of Religion in San Francisco, the Tougaloo conference was advertised as an opportunity for "religious leaders from all parts of the nation and from varying religious backgrounds to search for constructive steps to relieve racial tensions." In truth, it was also a means of buttressing the moral authority of the Freedom Rides, and, as it turned out, of recruiting a new and distinguished group of Riders. After a day of discussing the beloved community, nine of the attendees—seven whites and two blacks—felt inspired to conduct a segregation test before departing from the airport. Ignoring Captain Ray's familiar order to "move on," they soon found themselves on the way to jail. Singing freedom songs and praying for the souls of their oppressors, they reveled in the opportunity to act upon their beliefs, inviting comparison with the earlier experiences of the Tallahassee Ten. Eight of the nine arrested at the airport were from northern California, including one professor (the historian of the antebellum South, Charles G. Sellers Jr.) and two chaplains from the University of California at Berkeley.[38]

To Barnett's dismay, July 19 was also an unusually busy day in Washington, where a White House press conference revealed the president's newfound determination to use the interstate commerce clause as a guarantor of the right to travel freely from state to state. In his most forceful statement to date, Kennedy insisted that "there is no question of the legal rights of the freedom travelers, freedom riders, that move in interstate commerce." Drawing an analogy with freedom of the press, he reasoned: "We may not like what people print in a paper, but there is no question about their constitutional right to print it. So that follows, in my opinion, for those who move in interstate commerce." While he stopped short of endorsing the Freedom Riders' reason for traveling, he maintained that all Americans, regardless of "the purpose for which they travel[,] . . . should enjoy the full constitutional protections given to them by the law and by the Constitution." Alluding to the Justice Department petition awaiting consideration by the ICC, he added that he was "hopeful" that the administration's position would eventually "become the generally accepted view" and that "any legal doubts about the right of people to move in interstate commerce" would soon disappear.[39]

To the editors of the *New York Times*, the president's long-awaited statement on the Freedom Rides "had no precise meaning" and fell far short of "a profile in political courage." But the president's words communicated an entirely different message to the besieged segregationists of the Deep South. To them, Kennedy's oblique language represented a semantic smoke screen for the administration's aggressive advocacy of civil rights and social equality. Earlier in the year, many white Southerners had held out hope that political considerations would force the administration to adopt a cautious approach to civil rights matters, and for a time administration leaders actively reinforced this view through legislative inaction and the appointment of racial conservatives to the federal judiciary. Despite repeated entreaties from civil rights lobbyists, the administration steadfastly refused to introduce any new civil legislation. And as late as June, the president, ignoring the strong objections of virtually every civil rights leader in the nation, appointed W. Harold Cox, one of Mississippi's most outspoken white supremacists, to the federal bench. Yet none of this seemed to matter very much by midsummer. Unable to avoid the constitutional questions posed by the Freedom Rider crisis, the administration, despite its strong political ties to the white South, edged closer and closer to actual enforcement of equal protection under the law.

Politics still mattered, of course, but as the summer progressed the administration's civil rights policy-makers seemed to be increasingly concerned with the international politics of the Cold War as opposed to the traditional domestic variety. While the Kennedy brothers did not want to alienate Southern conservatives such as James Eastland and John Patterson, the goal of securing the trust of the Third World often took priority over efforts to maintain existing domestic political arrangements. Clearly, the Kennedys did not want to have to choose between white Southern votes and the approval of the dark-skinned masses of Africa, Asia, and Latin America. But, with the eyes of the world watching, the administration simply could not afford to repudiate the basic principles of racial equality and equal protection affirmed in *Boynton* and other Supreme Court decisions. In this context, the rhetoric, if not the reality, of social justice prevailed, and desegregation took on an air of inevitability. To this point the administration's accomplishments in the field of civil rights had been modest and largely symbolic, but the white supremacists of the South were increasingly fearful that this situation was about to change and that it was only a matter of time before the federal government launched an all-out assault on segregation. Such fears were exacerbated in late July, when administration supporters in the Senate overcame stiff opposition from Southern senators and pushed through the appointment of NAACP attorney and Howard University Law School dean Spottswood Robinson to the Civil Rights Commission. And there were even rumors that the president had decided to appoint Robinson's longtime NAACP colleague Thurgood Marshall to a federal judgeship.[40]

The suspicion that the Kennedy administration was actively encouraging the civil rights movement was especially strong in Alabama, where Governor Patterson and others were still fulminating about the unwarranted federal invasion of Montgomery. In the two months since the confrontation over the use of federal marshals, Patterson had done his best to sustain a running feud with the attorney general, the favorite whipping boy of Alabama politics. But this was not always easy. Unlike the situation in Mississippi, most of the action in Alabama during June and July took place behind the scenes as FBI agents and other investigators gathered evidence against the Anniston bombers and the Birmingham rioters. On June 16, in an obvious attempt to stir things up, Patterson announced that he was prepared to fire any Alabama highway patrolman who cooperated with the FBI, which he depicted as a meddling agency that sympathized with outside agitators. To most civil rights activists, the notion that the FBI was actively working on behalf of the movement was laughable, but this notion was almost an article of faith in Alabama, where many whites were convinced that they were up against a broad federal conspiracy led by the Justice Department.

According to Patterson, the continuing assault on the state's segregation laws reflected a special animus toward Alabama. When the Justice Department filed a discrimination suit against Montgomery's Dannelly Field on July 26, Patterson charged that Robert Kennedy was "picking on Alabama," even though the governor was well aware that the suit was identical to an earlier action brought against airport segregation in New Orleans. "This must be his way of getting even with us for the humiliation which came from his support of the so-called Freedom Riders," Patterson explained. "These rabble rousers really took Mr. Kennedy for a ride, and now he is trying to vent his ire again on the Southern people." Upon hearing this, Kennedy once again vehemently denied that he had encouraged the Freedom Riders to travel through the South, though he could not resist reminding the public that Patterson, not the federal government, was to blame for the breakdown of law and order in Alabama. In predictable fashion, Patterson responded with another round of personal invective, but Kennedy, sensing that he was being used for political purposes, allowed the matter to drop. Faced with a troubling and uncertain situation in Mississippi, where the Freedom Riders' appellate trials were scheduled to begin in three weeks, he saw no advantage in fanning the flames of sectional discord in a state that had already tested the limits of his patience.[41]

10

Woke Up This Morning with My Mind on Freedom

Woke up this morning with my mind stayed on freedom,
Walkin' and talkin' with my mind stayed on freedom,
Ain't no harm to keep your mind stayed on freedom,
Everybody's got his mind stayed on freedom.

—1960s freedom song[1]

THE MIDSUMMER EXCHANGE between John Patterson and Robert Kennedy drew surprisingly little reaction from the national press, suggesting that the two-month-old Freedom Rider crisis had lost much of its novelty. Despite the periodic arrests in Jackson and the fulminations coming out of Montgomery, the Freedom Rides were no longer front-page news outside of Mississippi and Alabama. For most Americans, the Rides had receded into the background of national life, taking their place alongside school desegregation suits and sit-ins as manifestations of a continuing struggle. With no easy resolution in sight, the controversy surrounding the Rides appeared to be a virtual stalemate. After interviewing representatives of both the Freedom Rider movement and the white supremacist resistance in mid-July, Associated Press staff writer Hugh Mulligan concluded that "oddly enough, in the absence of any racial progress either way both sides are claiming victory in Mississippi. Meanwhile, the buses continue to arrive, the patrol wagon still waits, and the rest of the South, and the country, watches to see how long either philosophy can hold out."

What Mulligan detected, more than anything else, was the willingness of both sides to prolong the struggle indefinitely, regardless of the consequences. "It is now plain to even the few so-called moderates in our midst," insisted White Citizens' Councils leader William Simmons, "that the integrationists will stop at nothing in their efforts to force the South to integrate.

There is now a clearer public understanding of the tactics of the integrationists and of the steps necessary to defeat them. The issue has finally been joined, and the white South has tasted victory. Our appetites are whetted." Speaking for the Freedom Riders, Jim Lawson was no less resolute in his determination to engage the enemy, albeit nonviolently. Acknowledging that he and other nonviolent activists had broken an unjust peace, he warned Mulligan that it was all but impossible "to solve the problem" of racial injustice "without people being hurt." "Only when this hostility comes to the surface," he advised, "as it did in Montgomery and Birmingham, will we begin to see that the system of segregation is an evil which destroys people and teaches them a contempt for life. We are trying to reach the conscience of the South. Brutality must be suffered to show the true character of segregation."[2]

In this combative context, with the result still very much in doubt, momentum was a precious commodity. Neither side could afford to let up or to give even the appearance of weakness or doubt. For the segregationists of Mississippi, the situation dictated an open-ended commitment to the arrest and prosecution of Freedom Riders, while for movement leaders it underscored the necessity of maintaining a steady flow of Riders into Jackson. This calculus tested the human and logistical resources of both sides, but in late July and early August the FRCC and CORE faced the special challenge of rounding up and preparing the released Freedom Riders for trial. Making sure that all of the appellate defendants returned to Mississippi in time for the legal proceedings scheduled to begin in mid-August was an enormous task. Indeed, the staff members and volunteers at the CORE office in New York and at the FRCC recruiting centers in the South soon discovered that they had time for little else. This realization, combined with financial considerations, forced movement leaders to suspend the Mississippi Freedom Rides for the month of August. However, they did so only after orchestrating a burst of new Rides in late July.

Designed to convince Mississippi authorities that there was no shortage of Freedom Riders willing to come to Jackson, the four groups that descended upon the city during an eight-day period raised the total number of Riders arrested since May 24 to nearly three hundred. On Sunday morning, the twenty-third, seven white Riders—six from California and one from New York City—were arrested at the Jackson train depot. And on Monday afternoon four Riders who had flown to Jackson from Montgomery were arrested at the city airport after trying to desegregate the airport restaurant. Three of those arrested were members of the Petway family: the Reverend Matthew Petway, pastor of the AME Zion Church in Montgomery; his sixteen-year-old son, Alphonso; and his twenty-year-old daughter, Kredelle, a student at Florida A&M in Tallahassee. The fourth was Cecil Thomas, a white college student from Ohio who had spent a year at Fisk. Jailing three Freedom Riders from the same family was a new experience for the Jackson police, but this was only the first of several unusual arrests that punctuated the week.[3]

On Saturday, July 29, the police apprehended ten white Riders at the Greyhound terminal, including Wollcott Smith, a Michigan State student who had participated in the Newark–to–Little Rock Freedom Ride earlier in the month and who would later co-author a cartoon guide to racial discrimination in Mississippi; Byron Baer, a thirty-one-year-old special effects technician from Englewood, New Jersey, who would eventually become the majority leader of the New Jersey State Senate; Hilmar Pabel, a fifty-year-old photo-journalist from Munich, West Germany; Widjonarko Tjokroadisumarto, a graduate student at the University of Washington and the son of the former Indonesian ambassador to Pakistan; and Norma Wagner, a forty-four-year-old blind woman from Rochester, New York. Wary of bad publicity and fearing an international incident, the police reluctantly arrested Pabel, later engineering his acquittal, and they refused to arrest Tjokroadisumarto and Wagner. "We're more humane than to arrest a blind woman," Chief of Detectives M. B. Pierce explained, adding that the Indonesian student was accorded special courtesy as "a guest of this country."

Earlier in the week, both the State Department and the Indonesian Embassy had urged Tjokroadisumarto to stay away from the Freedom Rides, either as a participant or as an observer, but the young student ignored their entreaties. In a telegram sent to the embassy, he cited "the Supreme Court decision on interstate travel, and President Kennedy's opinion on the exercise of the individual to travel" as proof that his participation in a Freedom Ride was "neither illegal nor political." Adding to the drama, the Jackson police confessed that they were not sure whether their dark-complexioned visitor was "black" or "white." "I do not intend to change Mississippi customs," Tjokroadisumarto explained with a grin. "That's for Mississippians to do. In my opinion, however, the customs of segregation and discrimination are wrong, ethically and otherwise."[4]

On Sunday morning, while local officials were still pondering the implications of racial ambiguity and international scrutiny, not to mention the special challenges posed by handicapped Riders, the largest single group of Freedom Riders to date arrived at the Jackson railroad terminal. Accompanied by Richard Steward, a Dillard student and New Orleans CORE activist, fourteen Riders from southern California filled several paddy wagons after challenging the terminal's segregated facilities. Most of the California Riders were student activists affiliated with UCLA. Ten were white, and four were black: Lonnie Thurman, a Montgomery native and Alabama State College graduate; Michael Grubbs, the nephew of the noted black historian John Hope Franklin; Helen Singleton, an art student at Santa Monica City College; and her husband, Bob, a twenty-five-year-old graduate student in international economics at UCLA.

The primary organizer of the Los Angeles–to–Jackson Freedom Ride, Bob Singleton had served as the chairperson of UCLA's NAACP chapter during a controversial picketing campaign in 1960. Targeting discrimination at Woolworth's stores in Santa Monica and Hollywood, he and other picketers raised the ire of a disapproving Roy Wilkins as well as university administrators. Evicted from its campus office, the chapter was reorganized first as the Southern California Boycott Committee and later as a CORE chapter. In the early summer of 1961 Henry Hodge, a black social worker and CORE vice president who had moved to Los Angeles from St. Louis in the late 1950s, encouraged Singleton and other local activists to become Freedom Riders. But not even he could have foreseen how useful and timely the Los Angeles Ride would be. By bringing Southern California into play just prior to the August hiatus, the FRCC sent a clear message that the movement had more Freedom Riders in reserve than Mississippi officials had imagined.[5]

The mass arrest of the Los Angeles Riders on July 30 was the last major confrontation between the Jackson police and Freedom Riders prior to the trials. However, the last individual arrest took place the next day when Jim Wahlstrom tried to use the telephone in the "Negro" waiting room at the Greyhound terminal. The arrest and conviction of the twenty-four-year-old University of Wisconsin student represented a milestone of sorts, since he was the first Freedom Rider to be rearrested. Originally arrested on June 6, he was out on bond and awaiting his appellate trial when a patrolman apprehended him in the phone booth. Wahlstrom's second arrest caused a considerable stir, not only because it set a precedent but also because state investigators had identified him as a "Soviet trained" Freedom Rider. Having traveled to Havana with the Fair Play for Cuba Committee in 1960, he was especially suspect in the eyes of vigilant Mississippians. "Moscow is still interested in Mississippi's race problem," the *Jackson Daily News* had recently reminded its readers, after learning that Governor Barnett had just received a telephone call "from behind the Iron Curtain seeking information on the 'freedom riders.' " Although no one could be sure that Wahlstrom's call entailed similarly subversive activity, the many white Mississippians who considered their society to be under siege were ready to believe it.

The air of extreme suspicion surrounding the Wahlstrom episode reflected white Mississippi's long-standing fixation with Communist subversion, but it was also indicative of a noticeable intensification of the Cold War during the summer of 1961. Centering around the crisis in Berlin, where Soviet and East German officials were threatening to prohibit migration from the eastern to the western zone of the city, the tense relationship between the United States and the Soviet Union appeared to be approaching a breaking point by late July. The Berlin crisis had been building since early spring, but now things were coming to a head, threatening to push all other issues, including the civil rights struggle, into the background. In most areas of the United States this is exactly what happened, especially after the East Germans began to construct the Berlin Wall on August 13. In the white South, however, a different dynamic often prevailed. Here civil rights and Cold War crises tended to merge into a single confrontation between outside forces and the Southern way of life. For many segregationists the local and regional struggle against Freedom Riders and other "outside agitators" was inextricably bound to the international struggle against Soviet tyranny. And nowhere was the mutual reinforcement of segregationist anxieties and Cold War tensions more obvious than in Jackson, especially in the weeks leading up to the Freedom Rider trials.[6]

With the temporary suspension of the Freedom Rides, Jackson's bus and train terminals entered a period of relative calm in early August. But this hiatus did not extend to the city's courtrooms, where a series of heated legal confrontations created a warlike atmosphere. Fought on segregationist soil, the legal war between local prosecutors and movement attorneys was a decidedly unequal struggle skewed by powerful racial and regional traditions. Initially, Jackson city officials "had agreed to the customary procedure in mass arrests, requiring only one or two typical cases to show for arraignment and trial and applying the findings in those cases to all the others," but in late July, in an obvious attempt to ensnare CORE and the FRCC in a financially burdensome legal tangle, the city's attorneys reneged on the agreement. Instead of a few representative defendants, all of the Freedom Riders out on bail would now be required to return to Jackson by August 14, the designated arraignment date, "on pain of forfeiting the five-hundred-dollar bond CORE had put up on each." City prosecutor Jack Travis and other local officials made no secret of their intentions. "We figure that if we can knock CORE out of the box, we've broken the back of the so-called civil rights movement in Mississippi," Travis informed CORE attorney Jack Young, "and that's what we intend to do." Dragging out the trials, making them as costly as possible, and generally keeping the defendants and their attorneys off balance were all part of a strategy designed to sap the movement's energies and resources.[7]

Bringing nearly two hundred defendants back to Jackson by mid-August was a daunting task, but movement leaders had no other way of avoiding a financially crippling forfeiture of one hundred thousand dollars or more. At an emergency meeting on Thursday, August 3, the FRCC authorized Carl Rachlin and William Kunstler to meet with Hinds County Judge Russel Moore in the hope that he would overrule the decision to require all of the Riders to appear in court both on the day of arraignment and on their individual trial dates. On the following Wednesday, during a special conference with Moore, the two attorneys argued that representative proceedings were not only fairer but safer than the proposed mass return. "We are here to try to assure an orderly trial," Rachlin insisted, suggesting that a mass return of Freedom Riders "might spark an 'irresponsible act' by white Mississippians." When Judge Moore turned them down, Rachlin and Kunstler filed an appeal with Circuit Judge Leon Hendrick, urging a compromise that would eliminate the requirement to appear at the August 14 arraignment. "All are ready and willing to come back for their trials as they come up," Kunstler maintained, but "to make them come when the calendar is called and again for their trials is a harassment on the part of the state." Forcing the defendants to appear twice would cost CORE an estimated twenty thousand dollars in unnecessary expenses, he explained. Unmoved, Judge Hendrick advised the Freedom Riders to be in court on August 14 or suffer the consequences. Later in the day, after Judge W. N. Ethridge of the Mississippi State Supreme Court turned down a request to overrule the lower court judges, Kunstler threw in the towel. "This is it," he informed the press. "There are no more appeals. I've called and told them to have all the defendants here for the opening of the term."[8]

The rebuff from Mississippi's highest court on August 10 capped off a week of legal setbacks for the Freedom Riders. Earlier in the week the Justice Department had refused CORE's request for the placement of federal marshals at the upcoming trials in Jackson, and on Monday, August 7, Judge Robert Rives, speaking for a three-judge panel of the Fifth Circuit Court of Appeals, had granted a six-week delay in the NAACP's suit against Jackson's municipal breach-of-peace law. Dismissing the objections of NAACP attorney Constance Baker Motley, who had asked for a temporary injunction that would forestall any further arrests under the law, the court scheduled the next hearing on the matter for September 25. Motley's co-counsel in the suit, Justice Department attorney Robert Owens, was present in the court room when the ruling was handed down, but neither he nor any other federal official offered an opinion on the wisdom of the delay. Once again it appeared that the Justice Department was eager to avoid any precipitous or provocative action that might be construed as a challenge to the integrity of the legal process in the Deep South.[9]

FRCC leaders had no such reservations and continued to question the fairness of a legal system that harassed and intimidated anyone who challenged the segregationist order—a system that they hoped would soon disappear. For the time being, however, they had no choice but to comply with the requirements of that system. Anticipating the unfavorable court rulings, Jim Farmer and the staff of the CORE office had been preoccupied with the task of rounding up the Freedom Riders since the beginning of August. "I put the organization on an emergency basis," he later recalled, "canceling all leave and ordering that staff, including myself, be on call for duty around the clock and reachable by phone. Many of the Riders were mobile persons of tenuous roots. . . . Tracking them down would be no small task. Yet, locating the scattered army was perhaps the least of our problems. There was also the matter of getting them to central checkpoints, onto chartered buses to Jackson, where we would have to feed and house them for an indeterminate stay, and then get them back to their homes. The cost of that operation would be staggering and as open-ended as Mississippi chose to make it."

Although Farmer and other movement leaders were reluctant to say so publicly, much more than money was at stake. The Freedom Riders' public image and the integrity of the nonviolent movement were also on the line. If a substantial number of Freedom Riders failed to return to Mississippi for trial, there would be widespread speculation that the missing Riders were afraid to return, that fear or other personal considerations had outweighed their commitment to the struggle. Whatever the real reasons for the failure to appear, the suspicion that the Freedom Riders lacked faith or courage was potentially devastating to a movement that trafficked in moral capital. No element of the movement's mystique was more compelling than the drama of personal sacrifice, and no aspect of nonviolent direct action was more essential than individual accountability. Thus there was no allowance for ex-

Freedom Riders arrive in Jackson for their arraignment on August 14, 1961. The man with his arm around a young woman is John Moody Jr. The man sticking his head out of the bus window is Clarence Thomas. (AP Wide World)

cused absences. Realizing this simple truth, Farmer and his colleagues spared no effort in the campaign to retrieve the scattered Freedom Riders. With Marvin Rich skillfully coordinating an emergency fund raising effort and with the rest of the staff and volunteers focusing on the logistics of contacting and transporting the defendants, CORE was able to retrieve 192 of the released Freedom Riders. Only nine Riders failed to appear for arraignment on August 14, and three of those arrived a day late after being detained by the New Orleans police, leaving only six actual forfeitures. One of the six could not be found, and two others—one in northern Saskatchewan and a second in Turkey—were simply too far away to return to Jackson in time.

The sheer number of returning Freedom Riders was impressive, but CORE's greatest accomplishment was the orderly and uneventful nature of the mass return. Following a carefully orchestrated plan, the vast majority of the Riders arrived in Jackson either on the Saturday or Sunday just prior to the Monday arraignment. Instructed to avoid individual acts of conscience or other provocative acts, the Riders slipped into the city as quietly as possible before being whisked away to their overnight accommodations at Tougaloo College or in private homes. Fortunately, local and state officials were equally determined to maintain the peace. Deployed in full force, the Jackson police, sheriff's deputies, and state troopers kept any potential attackers away from the terminals and from Tougaloo. The only violent incidents marring the mass return occurred outside of Mississippi.

In New York City, Marvin Rich and Marvin Doolittle, a reporter for the *New York Post*, were struck by a white assailant on Friday morning after Rich put Farmer and thirty other returning Riders on a southbound bus. Later the same day, in Houston, Texas, eighteen new Freedom Riders were arrested after trying to desegregate a railway terminal coffee shop. Eleven were Californians who had just arrived on a train from Los Angeles, and seven were members of the Progressive Youth Association, a local black protest group that had been trying to break the color line at the coffee shop and other downtown Houston restaurants for several months. Some of the Riders were roughed up by the police, and four of the Californians—Bob Kaufman, Steve McNichols, Steve Sanfield, and Joe Stevenson—ended up in a "white male misdemeanor tank" that, according to McNichols, "was dominated by a small band of hardened criminals who shared common homosexual and sadomasochistic bonds." "You must be those fuckin' nigger lovers," one inmate shouted as the four Riders entered the cell block. Two days of intimidation and intermittent terror followed, and by the time they bailed out on Sunday they had seen enough of the Texas penal system to last a lifetime. The other fourteen Riders remained in jail until the following week, and all eighteen were eventually convicted of unlawful assembly, a judgment later nullified by the Texas Court of Criminal Appeals.

To the surprise of many, there were no such violent episodes or mass arrests in Jackson. When two new Freedom Riders— a young British woman named Pauline Sims and George Raymond of New Orleans—were arrested in the white waiting room of the Jackson Trailways terminal on Sunday morning, both the local police and the press tried to downplay the incident. Earlier in the week the blind activist Norma Wagner, accompanied by Earl Bohannon Jr., a black Freedom Rider from Chicago, had made a second attempt to get arrested at the same terminal, but once again the police refused to arrest her. Frustrated after sitting at the black lunch counter for several hours, she caught a bus to New Orleans, where she was finally arrested two days later for distributing CORE leaflets in a black neighborhood. Trumpeted by the Mississippi press, this story symbolized the surprising calm that Jackson enjoyed in the days leading up to the mass arraignment.[10]

On Sunday evening the mood in Jackson was calm enough to allow movement leaders to hold a mass "freedom rally" at the same black Masonic Temple where Martin Luther King had spoken five weeks earlier. Sponsored by the Jackson Non-Violent Movement, the rally drew more than a thousand supporters, including virtually all of the returning Freedom Riders. Following an afternoon planning session at Tougaloo, the Riders traveled to the downtown temple in a caravan of cars, avoiding any unnecessary stops, and they were ushered into the hall through a cordon of police officers who kept the surrounding area clear of white demonstrators. Once inside, they were greeted by waves of applause from an overwhelmingly black audience dominated by young student activists, some still in their early teens. During the next two hours the Riders and their hosts "clapped, sang, and shouted" as a series of speakers representing the NAACP, CORE, SLCL, and the Jackson Movement held forth. With several national reporters looking on, Farmer told the crowd that they were part of a growing national movement for freedom. The morning after he had left New York, more than three hundred CORE supporters had gathered at the foot of the Statue of Liberty to praise the Freedom Riders, and later in the day many of the same activists, black and white, had joined a twenty-four-hour "Fast for Freedom" in Battery Park. This was the spirit that had propelled the Freedom Rides into the national limelight, he insisted, a spirit that was alive and well in Jackson. By forcing the mass return of the Freedom Riders, Mississippi officials had unwittingly saved a movement that had almost "run out of steam." The return to Jackson had pumped new life into the Freedom Rides, "which now must continue no matter how much it costs."

Representing SCLC, Wyatt Tee Walker followed Farmer's speech with a special greeting from Martin Luther King. Dr. King wished that he could be there with them, Walker declared, but the needs of the movement required him to be in New York to deliver a "freedom" sermon at the Riverside Church. As a round of amens filled the hall, Walker went on to hail the Freedom Riders as heroes and later entertained the crowd with a revised "movement" version of the minstrel song "Old Black Joe." The new words, according to Walker, were "I'm coming, I'm coming, And my head ain't bending low. I'm coming, I'm coming, I'm America's new Black Joe." Although he did not explain the song's relevance in so many words, the message was clear: The Freedom Riders had come to Jackson, and they were not leaving until both Jim Crow and Old Black Joe were dead and gone. Carried along by Walker's booming voice, this ringing expression of hope and purpose capped off an emotional evening of individual and collective renewal. For the Freedom Riders themselves, these feelings of emotional uplift would soon be tested by the challenges of a hostile courtroom. For their local supporters, there would be even greater tests imposed by a rigidly segregated society. But no one present at the Masonic Temple that evening left the hall without at least some appreciation for the rising power of the movement.[11]

One index of the civil rights movement's rising power was its ability to draw national and international press coverage, but in this instance the coverage was relatively thin, largely because much of the nation and the world was preoccupied with the construction of the Berlin Wall earlier in the weekend. In Jackson and a few other Deep South communities, the mass return and arraignment of the Freedom Riders earned front-page headlines. Elsewhere, however, the story was buried in the back pages, robbing Judge Russel Moore of his chance for worldwide celebrity.

The scene at the Hinds County Courthouse on Monday, August 14, was rife with tension, but the soft-spoken judge did his best to maintain legal decorum and the appearance, if not the reality, of judicial neutrality. Early in the day, he convened a special arraignment for Percy Sutton and Mark Lane, two high-profile Freedom Riders scheduled to return to New York on an early afternoon plane. Both men pleaded not guilty, as did all of the defendants who later appeared at the regular 2:00 P.M. arraignment. At the beginning of the afternoon session, Kunstler filed several defense motions, including a declaration that the local statutes involved in the Freedom Rider arrests "were unconstitutional on their face and a violation of the U.S. Constitution," a call for a "class action" streamlining of the court's appellate procedures, and a demand for a change of venue to the "furtherest county in the state from Hinds." After swiftly rejecting all of Kunstler's motions, Judge Moore brought the defendants forward in pairs to register their pleas and assign trial dates. Following a prearranged agreement grudgingly accepted by Kunstler, the judge scheduled two appellate trials a day, beginning with Hank Thomas and Julia Aaron on August 22. Collectively, the scheduled trials filled twenty-two weeks of the court's docket, stretching into mid-January 1962. By five o'clock the mass arraignment was over, bringing temporary relief to the defendants who now knew when they had to return to Mississippi. Having seen enough of Mississippi justice for one day, most filed out of the courtroom as quickly as possible, and many left the state before nightfall.[12]

JUDGE MOORE'S RULINGS set a difficult course for CORE and the Freedom Riders. In the short term, the scheduled appellate trials would consume virtually all of CORE's resources, making it all but impossible to extend the

Freedom Rides to other areas of the South. And, with more than a hundred additional Freedom Riders languishing in Mississippi jails, there would almost certainly be many more trials to follow. Barring timely intervention by the federal courts, the legal tangle related to the Jackson arrests would take months, and even years, to unravel. To CORE stalwarts, this burden was an unfortunate but necessary part of conducting nonviolent direct action on a mass scale. But to many others, both inside and outside the movement, the mounting costs and uncertain future of the Freedom Rides seemed to confirm the wisdom of less disruptive approaches to social change. Publicly, the leaders of the NAACP and SCLC pledged their support to the legal battle being waged in Jackson. Privately, however, they expressed grave doubts about any strategy that placed the fate of the movement in the hands of segregationist judges.

Officials at the Justice Department were even less sanguine about the legal situation in Mississippi. Earlier in the summer Robert Kennedy and his colleagues had placed their faith in the Interstate Commerce Commission, and the events of July and early August had done nothing to alter their belief that the long-neglected but potentially powerful regulatory agency would eventually provide a politically and legally palatable solution to the Freedom Rider crisis.

Most movement leaders doubted that the present ICC commissioners had either the will or the capacity to desegregate public transit facilities. But, whatever their expectations, they recognized the symbolic and political importance of the ICC hearings that opened in Washington on Tuesday, August 15, less than twenty-four hours after the mass arraignment in Jackson. On the Sunday afternoon following his speech at the Riverside Church, King challenged the ICC to issue a sweeping ruling that included a "blanket order" against segregation in bus, rail, and air terminals. "The Freedom Rides have already served a great purpose," he told reporters, highlighting "the indignities and injustices that the Negro people still confront as they attempt to do the simple thing of traveling as interstate passengers." He acknowledged, though, that a clear and broad ICC mandate held the power to go even further. If strict compliance were enforced for interstate travelers, all segregated travel would "almost inevitably end," even among intrastate travelers. "This will be the point where Freedom Rides will end," he predicted.

The ICC had already received similar advice from hundreds of CORE supporters who had either signed petitions or submitted letters endorsing the Justice Department's proposal for a comprehensive desegregation order. To make sure that the commissioners realized what was at stake, CORE set up a line of sign-carrying "Freedom Riders" outside the ICC building on the first morning of the hearings. Inside the building, CORE's chief counsel, Carl Rachlin, was one of thirteen witnesses testifying before the commission. Following the lead of Justice Department attorney St. John Barrett, who insisted that the ICC had the power and the duty "to halt discrimination in this field," Rachlin urged the commissioners to "apply a little moral force" to the "wonderful, decent people" of the white South. "You must help them to get rid of a tradition which is morally wrong," he declared, with a wink, "even though they oppose change at the moment."[13]

The oral arguments that began on August 15 initiated the public phase of the ICC's deliberations, but most of the groundwork for the deliberations had already been laid in lengthy behind-the-scenes negotiations held in June, July, and early August. The procedures established by the ICC in mid-June set aside a month for the submission of written briefs and three additional weeks for rebuttal statements. Representing the Justice Department, Burke Marshall urged the commissioners to act with dispatch, and the department's brief filed on July 20 reiterated the comprehensive demands outlined in the attorney general's extraordinary May 29 petition. The attorney general wanted nothing less than a broadly enforceable order that would supersede the indefinite mandates of the Motor Carrier Act of 1935 and the obvious limitations of the *Morgan* and *Boynton* decisions. Historically, the conflicting provisions of state and federal laws on matters of Jim Crow transit had tilted toward segregation, in part because only the state statutes included specific commands. Thus meaningful desegregation would require a detailed and directive order along the lines proposed by the attorney general. Although the opposition of state and local officials to such an order was a given, Justice Department officials hoped to persuade private bus companies and other interstate carriers to support the administration's position. After the briefs submitted in July indicated that the carriers had serious reservations about the scope and coercive nature of the attorney general's plan, Marshall invited several transit industry executives to a closed-door meeting in Washington.

At the meeting the executives listened politely to what Marshall and other Justice Department officials had to say, but in the end they were unwilling to accept a comprehensive plan. The best they could do was to offer to withdraw their opposition if the administration agreed to limit the plan's regulatory power to vehicles and facilities specializing in interstate travel. Leaving most of the Jim Crow transit system intact, this limitation was, as Marshall explained, totally unacceptable to an administration looking for a way to end rather than perpetuate the Freedom Rider crisis.

The failure to convert the transit executives was disappointing, but the most important lobbying effort, the one that really mattered, was directed at the ICC commissioners themselves. Since most of the commissioners were Republicans appointed during the Eisenhower era, and only one—a Massachusetts Democrat named William Tucker—was a Kennedy appointee, the administration faced an uphill political struggle in its dealings with the notoriously prickly commission. Having Tucker on the commission was a plus, but the others had to be approached with great care through essentially nonpolitical channels. Consequently, the administration mounted a broad-gauged appeal that emphasized the national security aspects of the struggle for civil rights. According to Marshall and several other high-ranking members of the administration, the immediate need for a sweeping ICC desegregation order transcended considerations of racial equity or legal precedent. In a letter to the commissioners, Secretary of Defense Robert McNamara argued that the enforcement of segregation on buses and trains posed a serious threat to the morale of black military personnel assigned to Southern bases. A similar letter submitted by Secretary of State Dean Rusk, a native Georgian familiar with Southern laws and customs, insisted that the persistence of segregated transit facilities was a major embarrassment for a nation promoting democracy and freedom in a largely nonwhite world.[14]

Reiterated by other administration officials throughout the summer of 1961, Rusk's point received timely reinforcement from a series of diplomatic incidents related to the recent proliferation of black African envoys to the United States. As recently as 1959 the sub-Saharan diplomatic corps in Washington and New York had consisted of a small number of envoys representing Ethiopia, Liberia, and Ghana, but with the arrival of representatives from more than two dozen newly independent African nations in 1960 and 1961, the treatment of African diplomats by their American hosts became a subject of intense interest and controversy. Most obviously, the racial segregation that dominated the greater Washington area became an embarrassing reality for the new Kennedy administration. The segregated housing patterns of the District of Columbia, suburban Maryland, and northern Virginia proved to be a major irritant for visiting African families. The primary flash point, though, was the segregated facilities along the Route 40 corridor between Washington and the New Jersey border. When traveling back and forth between Washington embassies and the United Nations headquarters in New York, black Africans discovered that virtually all of the restaurants and other public accommodations were for whites only.

After receiving a number of complaints from African delegations, the State Department created the Special Service Protocol Section (SPSS) of the Office of Protocol in March 1961. Headed by Pedro Sanjuan, a thirty-year-old Cuban emigré and former Kennedy campaign worker with a Russian studies degree from Harvard, the SPSS initially worked quietly behind the scenes to smooth over any hard feelings. But, following a denial of service to Adam Malik Sow, the new ambassador from Chad, in late June, Sanjuan discussed the Route 40 problem directly with President Kennedy, who authorized an organized effort to convince restaurant owners and Maryland officials that discrimination along Route 40 was harming the national image. By the end of July several White House aides, including Harris Wofford and Fred Dutton, had been enlisted in the effort to promote the desegregation of Route 40, setting the stage for a major public controversy that would eventually involve CORE and a recalcitrant Maryland legislature. At the time of the August ICC hearings, the public struggle over what was later known as the

Route 40 campaign had not yet begun, but it would soon become an important part of the political backdrop that both the ICC and the Justice Department had to take into account.[15]

The increasingly obvious diplomatic implications of segregation provided administration officials with a degree of leverage in the effort to secure
an ICC desegregation order. The effort itself, however, was not something
that many officials relished. Although Marshall and others would eventually
come to appreciate the political and moral growth that the Freedom Rider
crisis forced upon them, the usefulness and advisability of nonviolent direct
action escaped them at the time. While recognizing the need for social change,
they strongly preferred less disruptive forms of civil activism such as bringing test cases before the courts or conducting voter registration drives. Encouraging movement leaders to deemphasize direct action techniques had
been on the administration's agenda since the earliest days of the Kennedy
presidency, but the effort to make the civil rights movement more "civil"
took on a new urgency after the Freedom Rides provoked massive resistance
in the Deep South. As we have already seen, several meetings held in the
early summer brought black student leaders, white liberals, and Justice Department representatives together for an ongoing discussion of the prospects
for a region-wide voting rights campaign funded by private foundations. Although the discussion angered Diane Nash and other direct action advocates
who suspected that the administration was trying to blunt the radicalism of
the student movement with the promise of voting rights funding, a growing
number of student activists appeared willing to consider the proposed shift.

As the summer progressed, it became clear that the likelihood of such a
shift rested upon the organizational and ideological evolution of SNCC. When
SNCC's central committee hired Charles Sherrod as the organization's first
field secretary in June, it took an important step toward the actualization of a
voting rights project. Even though Sherrod was a strong advocate of direct
action, he also believed that SNCC should be actively involved in promoting
the registration of black voters. Less than a month after becoming field secretary, he met with Amzie Moore, a veteran NAACP activist who had been
calling for a voting rights campaign since the late 1940s, and Bob Moses, a
twenty-five-year-old black teacher from Harlem who had befriended Moore
the previous summer. Meeting in Moore's hometown of Cleveland, Mississippi, in the heart of the Delta, the three men discussed the viability of establishing a pilot voting rights project in Cleveland and nearby Black Belt
communities. After assessing the local situation, they agreed that Cleveland
was not quite ready for an infusion of SNCC volunteers, but with Moore's
help Sherrod and Moses soon found another site for the project in Pike
County, two hundred miles to the south. C. C. Bryant, the president of the
Pike County NAACP, shared Moore's belief that voting rights held the key
to the liberation of black Mississippians. So when Bryant learned that SNCC
was interested in voter registration, he invited Moses and SNCC to McComb,

the southwestern Mississippi town where he worked as a crane operator for the Illinois Central Railroad.[16]

In mid-July, while Moses was in the process of moving to McComb, more than a dozen SNCC leaders met in Baltimore to discuss the organization's progress and priorities, including the implications of the impending Pike County project. During the three-day meeting, Charles Jones and other voting rights enthusiasts associated with the "Belafonte Committee" took the initiative, calling for the establishment of an extensive voting rights project headed by an executive director and staffed by at least eight full-time employees. Jones's argument that the project should be SNCC's "top priority" gained some support, but a majority of those present opposed the project on either ideological or practical grounds. Deferring a final decision on the voting rights proposal until the next monthly meeting—scheduled for August 11–14 at the Highlander Folk School, in Monteagle, Tennessee—the students asked Jones and the Belafonte Committee to prepare a more precise description of the project's logistical and financial requirements.[17]

During the four weeks between the Baltimore and Highlander meetings, the SNCC leaders witnessed the anxious preparations for the Freedom Rider trials and the growing apprehensions about the movement's ability to sustain direct action in the Deep South. To the dismay of the Justice Department, however, their willingness to elevate voting rights over direct action as an organizational priority remained very much in doubt. In late July and early August a number of SNCC leaders—including Sherrod, Jones, Chuck McDew, Diane Nash, John Lewis, Jim Bevel, and Stokely Carmichael—participated in a student leadership seminar organized by voting rights enthusiast Tim Jenkins and funded by the New World Foundation. Held in Nashville, the seminar focused on the problem of "Understanding the Nature of Social Change" and featured presentations by the psychologist Kenneth Clark, the sociologist E. Franklin Frazier, the historian Rayford Logan, and several other distinguished black scholars. John Doar of the Justice Department and Herbert Hill of the NAACP were also on hand, adding to the seminar's orientation toward the institutional context of social change.

The seminar's primary objective, according to Jenkins, was to give the student leaders "a solid academic approach to understanding the movement." More specifically, he wanted to expand their appreciation for the institutional "power of the Justice Department and its potential to help and protect us in the political revolution." As Jenkins later explained his motivation, in a conversation with Carmichael: "Even before the Freedom Rides I didn't think we could allow the energy of the sit-ins simply to dissipate. After the rides, it was even clearer that the student movement, if it were to survive at all, would need a new, sustainable program and focus. And I certainly wanted to nudge it down off that lofty, ethereal plane of 'the beloved community' and the excessive zeal of the pain-and-suffering school of struggle. . . I felt what the movement really needed at that point was not idealism or inspiration but information. Hard, pragmatic information about how the political system actually worked . . . or failed to work. Where the pressure points were. What levers were available that students could push. Where allies might be found. Who the real enemies were. What exactly was the nature of the beast we were up against? That was the purpose in Nashville." Thus, despite the pretense of academic detachment, the prescribed necessity of deferring to the federal government's wishes hovered behind many of the presentations and discussions.

Predictably, the Nashville seminar yielded mixed results. According to Carmichael, "Folks were, depending on their inclinations, in turn suspicious, flattered, surprised, confused, or all of the above simultaneously." For some of the student participants, mingling with academic stars and government officials had the desired effect. For others, the experience only reinforced the suspicion that the administration and its allies were bringing undue pressure to bear on the student movement. This suspicion was most apparent among the Freedom Riders, "all of whom," according to John Lewis, "spoke firmly in defense of sticking to our roots." To Lewis and the others awaiting trial in Jackson, "the matter was simple. We had gotten this far by dramatizing the issue of segregation, by putting it onstage and *keeping* it onstage. I believed firmly that we needed to push and push and not stop pushing. . . . I believed in drama. I believed in *action*. Dr. King said early on that there is no noise as powerful as the sound of the marching feet of a determined people, and I believed that. I *experienced* it. I agreed completely with Diane and the others, at least at that time, that this voter registration push by the government was a trick to take the steam out of the movement, to slow it down."[18]

When the SNCC leaders gathered at Highlander on Friday, August 11, it became clear that the factional line between direct action and voting rights advocates had hardened since the Baltimore meeting. Convened on the eve of the mass return to Jackson, the Highlander meeting promised to live up to its dramatic setting in the mountains of southeast Tennessee. Founded in 1932 by labor activists Myles Horton and Don West, the legendary folk school had hosted scores of important meetings over the years, including several interracial workshops for student activists in 1960 and early 1961. But none was more significant than the SNCC showdown of August 1961. Several of the SNCC leaders had been to Highlander before, and they knew that it was a place for open discussion and honest disagreement. As the discussions deepened over the weekend, some worried that SNCC was in danger of dividing into two separate organizations or of disappearing altogether. Jones and Jenkins were adamant that voting rights should be SNCC's first priority, while Nash, Lewis, and the Freedom Rider faction were no less certain that direct action represented the heart and soul of the organization and the movement. Fortunately, Ella Baker was on hand to serve as a mediating influence, just as she had done at SNCC's founding conference in Raleigh fourteen months earlier. On Sunday, after nearly three days of wrangling, Baker, the

one veteran organizer trusted by both factions, fashioned a workable compromise that divided SNCC into two equal "wings." Nash, everyone agreed,
would lead the direct action wing, and Jones would lead the voter rights wing.
Though no one was completely satisfied with this division, most, including
Bernard Lafayette, tried to make the best of the situation. Assuming his usual
calming role, Lafayette reminded his departing colleagues that "a bird needs
two wings to fly."[19]

The creation of SNCC's voting rights wing would have a profound impact on the student movement in the months and years to come, but for
Sherrod and Moses the decision at High-
lander simply formalized what they had
already begun. After meeting with
Moses and Amzie Moore in Mississippi,
Sherrod traveled to southwest Georgia
to lay the groundwork for a multicounty
voter registration project. Moses, following Moore's suggestion, set up shop
in McComb, establishing a voter registration school on the second floor of a
black Masonic temple. Moses's "educational" experience included a childhood
in Harlem, four years at Hamilton College in upstate New York, summer in-
ternships in France and Japan, a stint at
Harvard, where he earned an M.A. degree in philosophy, two years of teaching high school math in suburban

Bob Moses, 1962. (Photograph by
Danny Lyon, Magnum)

Westchester County, and participation in the Atlanta sit-in movement. But
nothing in his background had fully prepared him for the challenge of bringing democracy to southwestern Mississippi.

Joined by John Hardy, a Tennessee State student from Nashville, and
Reggie Robinson, a SNCC activist from Baltimore, Moses spent two weeks
combing the local countryside for prospective students before opening the
school on August 7. Only a handful of students showed up that first night,
but four of them bravely agreed to try to register at the county courthouse in
Magnolia the next day. To their and Moses's surprise, three of the four were
allowed to register. After a second night of classes, two more gained registered voter status. Encouraged, Moses accompanied nine more potential registrants to the courthouse on August 10, but this time only one new voter was
registered. Alarmed by this unusual surge of interest in voting, the registrar
contacted the editor of the *McComb Enterprise-Journal*, who promptly ran a
story informing local segregationists that something sinister was afoot.

Over the next few days, news of Moses's school spread throughout the
local white community. Ironically, the story in the *Enterprise-Journal* also

alerted hundreds of local blacks, most of whom had been unaware of Moses's recruitment activities. Suddenly, Moses found his citizenship classes swelling with new recruits, including a number of black farmers from the neighboring counties of Amite and Walthall, areas that had even fewer black voters than McComb. Compared to the semi-urban setting of Pike County, Amite and Walthall were rural backwaters that posed an even more daunting challenge to Moses's fledgling voting rights project. Extending the project beyond Pike County was both dangerous and logistically difficult, but, after consulting with C. C. Bryant, Moses concluded that his credibility rested upon his willingness to tackle even the toughest challenges. Thus, less than a week after opening the school in McComb, he temporarily moved his base of operations to Amite, where there was only one black voter in the entire county and where the local NAACP branch had been driven underground by the local sheriff. When E. W. Steptoe, the fearless leader of the defunct Amite NAACP, offered Moses room and board at his farmhouse, the SNCC organizer gratefully accepted. And by Tuesday morning, August 15, the same morning that saw the opening of the ICC hearings in Washington, Moses found himself accompanying three prospective black voters—an elderly man and two middle-aged women—to the Amite County Courthouse in Liberty.

The four black visitors caused quite a stir at the historic courthouse that had graced the Liberty town square since 1840. Constructed of bricks "fired by slaves" and flanked by a twenty-foot-high Confederate monument, the building symbolized the white power structure of a Black Belt county that was unaccustomed to contact with outsiders of any kind. To the registrar and the other county officials who came to gawk at Moses and his three local charges, the notion of a black voter registration project led by a New Yorker was almost beyond comprehension. Still, after making his visitors wait for several hours, the registrar allowed the three applicants to fill out the necessary registration forms. While there was no suggestion that their applications would actually be approved, they left the courthouse with the satisfaction that they had recaptured a certain amount of dignity just by applying. Unfortunately, their sense of accomplishment was soon dispelled by a state trooper who forced their car to the side of the road and then ordered them to follow him back to McComb. Once there the three applicants were released and allowed to return home, but Moses was placed under arrest, charged with interfering with the trooper's discharge of his duties. After a brief phone conversation with John Doar of the Justice Department, who had assured him in mid-July that the federal government would protect voting rights workers and potential registrants from intimidation and interference, Moses was taken before a local justice of the peace, who quickly rendered a guilty verdict carrying a fifty-dollar fine. Refusing on principle to pay a fine levied for unjust purposes, Moses was taken to the Pike County Jail in Magnolia, where he remained until an NAACP attorney from Jackson paid the fine three days later.

After grudgingly accepting the NAACP's intercession on his behalf, Moses returned to McComb to discover that his arrest had triggered a flurry of activity among his SNCC colleagues. During his brief imprisonment, Sherrod, Ruby Doris Smith, and several other Freedom Riders had rushed to McComb, and others, including Charles Jones and Marion Barry, were on the way. Coming on the heels of the Highlander meeting and the mass arraignment in Jackson, Moses's arrest had prompted an immediate response from student activists determined to sustain SNCC's widening involvement in voting rights activity. Intent on sending a clear message that arrests and attempts at intimidation would only strengthen SNCC's resolve to register black voters, Sherrod and the other new arrivals turned McComb into a full-fledged movement center. While Moses himself shuttled back and forth between Pike and Amite Counties over the next few days, others greatly expanded the activities of the McComb citizenship school—planning sit-ins, recruiting high school students, and all but daring local white supremacists to try to stop them.[20]

With Steptoe's help, Moses set up a makeshift citizenship school in a black Baptist church hidden deep in the woods of Amite County. But, following the arrest, it was difficult to find volunteers brave enough to face the registrar in Liberty. Each night Moses held forth on the responsibilities of citizenship and the necessity of challenging the white stranglehold on county politics, but it took almost two weeks for him to find anyone willing to accompany him to Liberty. On the morning of August 29, he escorted two applicants, a respected middle-aged farmer named Curtis Dawson and an elderly man known locally as Preacher Knox, to the courthouse. Waiting on the sidewalk outside the entrance were three white men, including Billy Jack Caston, the son-in-law of Amite County's most outspoken white supremacist, State Representative E. H. Hurst. After demanding to know why three black men wanted to enter the courthouse, Caston struck Moses in the face with a knife handle, knocking him to the pavement. After getting in a few more blows, Caston ran off, leaving a dazed and bleeding Moses with three gashes in his head. Undaunted, Moses led Knox and Dawson in to see the registrar, who, upon seeing the blood pouring from Moses's wounds, promptly closed the office.

Following a brief stop at Steptoe's farm, Dawson drove Moses back to McComb, where they found a black doctor willing to stitch up Moses's wounds, and where they discovered that the town was about to experience its first mass meeting. Earlier in the day two local students, Hollis Watkins and Curtis Hayes, had been arrested during a sit-in at a Woolworth's lunch counter, prompting Marion Barry to call a meeting to take advantage of the rising outrage among the town's black citizens. The featured speaker was Jim Bevel, who inspired a crowd of nearly two hundred with resounding pleas for righteous struggle. The high point of the evening, however, proved to be Moses's plaintive and powerful testimony relating the events at the Liberty

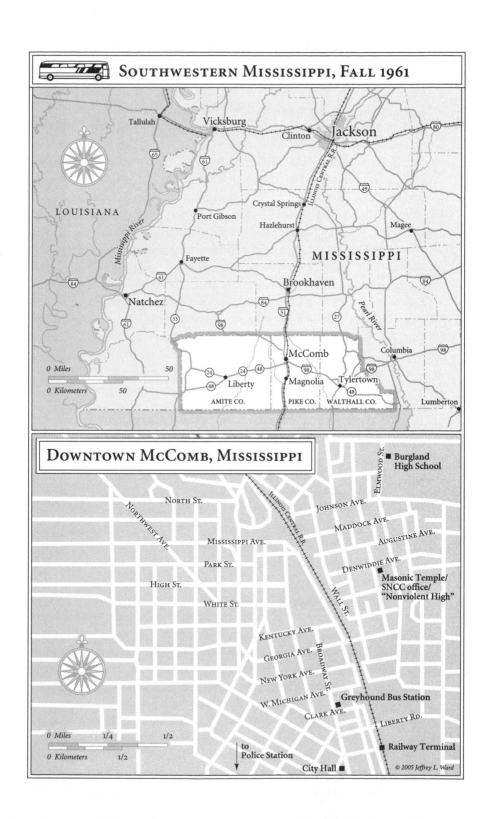

SOUTHWESTERN MISSISSIPPI, FALL 1961

Tallulah
Vicksburg
Clinton
Jackson

LOUISIANA

65
61
80
49

Crystal Springs
Port Gibson
Hazlehurst
Magee

Fayette

MISSISSIPPI

61
84
84

Brookhaven

Natchez

33
84
51
27
98

Columbia
98

McComb

0 Miles 50
0 Kilometers 50

24 24 48
98
98

48 Liberty Magnolia Tylertown

48

AMITE CO. PIKE CO. WALTHALL CO.

Lumberton

DOWNTOWN McCOMB, MISSISSIPPI

Burgland
High School

ELMWOOD ST.

NORTH ST.

JOHNSON AVE.

NORTHWEST AVE.

ILLINOIS CENTRAL R.R.

MADDOCK AVE.

AUGUSTINE AVE.

MISSISSIPPI AVE.

PARK ST.

DENWIDDIE AVE.

HIGH ST.

WALL ST.

Masonic Temple/
SNCC office/
"Nonviolent High"

WHITE ST.

KENTUCKY AVE.

GEORGIA AVE.

BROADWAY ST.

NEW YORK AVE.

W. MICHIGAN AVE.

Greyhound Bus Station

CLARK AVE.

LIBERTY RD.

0 Miles 1/4 1/2
0 Kilometers 1/2

to
Police Station

City Hall

Railway Terminal

© 2005 Jeffrey L. Ward

courthouse. Urging the audience to bear witness to the power of the movement, he vowed to continue the fight, a pledge he promptly fulfilled the next
morning. Filing a formal complaint against Caston with the Amite County
prosecutor, he soon found himself testifying in front of an all-white jury and
an angry white crowd that not only filled the courtroom but also spilled out
onto the same sidewalk where he had been assaulted two days earlier. Following the trial—which had little impact on the jury, judging by the acquittal
rendered the next day—Moses walked down the hall to greet Freedom Rider
Travis Britt, who had accompanied an elderly black farmer named
Weathersbee to the registrar's office. Just as Moses was about to shake Britt's
hand, the sound of a shotgun blast forced everyone in the hallway to duck for
cover. While no one was injured, the incident convinced the sheriff that it
was wise to hustle Moses out of the county before someone got killed.

Moses and his companions made it back to McComb in one piece, but
the situation there was only slightly less threatening. The white community
was outraged over an attempt to desegregate the lunch counter at the city's
Greyhound terminal. The day after the mass meeting, three local students—
Bobbie Talbert, Ike Lewis, and Brenda Travis—had put Bevel's words into
action, and the police had responded by putting all three in the city jail. The
fact that Travis was only fifteen years old was cited as proof that the Freedom
Rider–inspired protest was both irresponsible and dangerous, and that the
movement had taken advantage of the community's children. At the same
time, her incarceration in an adult facility infuriated local black leaders who
feared that this was the beginning of a no-holds-barred defense of segregation. Both sides, it appeared, were preparing for a protracted struggle over
desegregation, something that had been almost unthinkable in McComb prior
to the arrival of Moses and SNCC. It was a scenario that C. C. Bryant had
dreamed about for years but had never really expected to see. Now that the
movement whirlwind had descended upon Pike County, Bryant was not sure
that he or anyone else was completely ready for the revolution that loomed
on the horizon. But he was confident that Pike and the neighboring counties
of southwestern Mississippi would never be quite the same again.

The shift had begun with Moses's arrival in McComb, but the proximate
catalyst of the new era was the critical mass of outsiders who had turned
Moses's voting rights project into the Pike County Nonviolent Movement.
Although Moses himself had doubts about the viability of the makeshift movement initiated in his absence, there was no turning back. Even in the remot-
est corner of the state, the fallout from the arrest and imprisonment of
hundreds of committed activists had penetrated the previously impenetrable
walls of segregationist complacency. Here, as elsewhere, the involvement of
Freedom Riders added volatility to the situation, confounding traditional patterns of accommodation and compromise. Wherever the Freedom Riders
showed up during the late summer and fall of 1961—from McComb, Mississippi, to Albany, Georgia, to Monroe, North Carolina—the spirit of nonvio-

lent direct action empowered and energized local black movements, creating an interlocking chain of movement centers. Both before and after their appellate trials in Jackson, restless Riders offered their services as nonviolent shock troops, confirming the suspicion that the Freedom Rides represented the opening campaign of an all-out assault on the Jim Crow South.[21]

BY THE END OF THE YEAR the diffusion of Freedom Riders would help to turn Mississippi and southwestern Georgia into major civil rights battlegrounds, but nothing demonstrated the widening impact of the Freedom Rides more clearly than the developing situation in the North Carolina Piedmont town of Monroe. Destined to be the most controversial episode of the Freedom Rider saga, the Monroe Freedom Ride was the by-product of a personal mission undertaken by two of the movement's most independent activists, Paul Brooks and Jim Forman. Born in East St. Louis, Illinois, to parents who had migrated from DeKalb, Mississippi, Brooks was a divinity student at American Baptist in Nashville before becoming a full-time activist in the spring of 1961. After participating in the Birmingham and Montgomery Freedom Rides, he moved to Chicago to coordinate the FRCC's Midwestern fund-raising efforts. Soon after his arrival in late May, he met Forman, a thirty-three-year-old ex-schoolteacher who had become active in a campaign to provide relief for black voting rights advocates in two counties in western Tennessee, Fayette and Haygood. Though born in Chicago, Forman had spent part of his childhood in Mississippi. After graduating from Roosevelt University, where he was elected student body president in 1956, he did graduate work in African studies at Boston University before returning to Chicago to teach at an elementary school. Along the way he worked as a reporter for the *Chicago Defender* during the 1957 Little Rock crisis, wrote an unpublished novel depicting an interracial nonviolent movement, and acquired a growing reputation as a an outspoken and freewheeling black intellectual.

In November 1960 Forman visited western Tennessee as part of a two-person fact-finding team. His companion was Sterling Stuckey, a young folklore scholar and Chicago CORE leader who had spearheaded the formation of the Emergency Relief Committee, a CORE project organized as a response to a White Citizens' Councils effort to starve black voting rights advocates into submission. The desperate situation in Fayette County, where many black families were living in tents after being displaced from their homes by white landlords, shocked Forman and Stuckey, but after their return to Chicago an effort to expand the Emergency Relief Committee led to personal and political bickering and the eventual dissolution of the committee. Disgusted with the internal politics of Chicago CORE but determined to continue the relief effort, Forman organized a new relief organization, the National Freedom Council, in March 1961. Comprised primarily of Forman's friends and fellow teachers, the National Freedom Council had some success in gathering funds and supplies, and in raising awareness about the economic plight of western Tennessee's voting rights activists. By midsummer the situation seemed to be improving, though hundreds of evicted black farmers were still living in a sprawling tent city. In January the Justice Department had obtained a temporary restraining order prohibiting such evictions, and the department had subsequently filed voting rights suits in both counties. But the ultimate economic and political fate of those involved in the Fayette and Haygood movements was still very much in doubt in early July, prompting Forman to return to Tennessee to see for himself.[22]

The night before he boarded a train for Memphis, Forman paid a visit to Brooks and Catherine Burks, who had just arrived in Chicago after her release from Parchman. Both Brooks and Burks, his girlfriend and future wife, were staying at the home of a friend of Forman's—University of Chicago professor Walter Johnson—and Forman was eager to meet the young woman who had refused to be intimidated by Bull Connor in Birmingham. For a few minutes Forman talked about the National Freedom Council and what he expected to encounter in Tennessee, but mostly he listened attentively as the two Freedom Riders described their recent experiences in the nonviolent movement in the Deep South. Both were sharply critical of the majority of black Southerners, most of whom refused to join or openly endorse the struggle for desegregation and social justice. Brooks and Burks were especially critical of middle-class blacks, including some who "are always ready to talk about civil rights but who seldom, if ever, commit themselves to positive acts to end segregation." To Forman's surprise, they also expressed strong reservations about the viability of nonviolence as an all-encompassing movement strategy. Brooks, in particular, seemed open to the argument that Southern blacks should not rule out armed self-defense as a necessary part of the struggle for freedom. This argument was anathema to many of Brooks's closest friends in the movement—including his American Baptist Theological Seminary classmates John Lewis, Jim Bevel, and Bernard Lafayette—but in recent weeks Brooks had grown increasingly disillusioned with both the philosophy and the leadership of the nonviolent movement. Profoundly disappointed by Martin Luther King's refusal to become a Freedom Rider, he had undertaken a personal search for a less hypocritical and more realistic model of movement leadership—a search that ultimately led him to the South's most controversial black leader, North Carolina's Robert Williams.[23]

Brooks's fascination with Williams demonstrated just how far he had traveled in a few short weeks, from the inner circle of Jim Lawson's nonviolent apostles to a flirtation with the outer fringe of radical politics. For more than two years, Williams and the Monroe NAACP had been engaged in an ongoing and high-profile struggle with both local segregationists and national civil rights leaders alarmed by his advocacy of "armed self-reliance." Since his celebrated censure by a large majority of the delegates to the 1959 NAACP national convention, he had grown even more militant, openly challenging the Jim Crow system at every opportunity and roundly condemning moderate leaders for their empty words and lack of resolute action. Refusing to abide by the conventional rules of practical and Cold War politics, he attracted a loyal following among black radicals, especially in Harlem, where community activists such as Mae Mallory and black intellectuals such as novelist Julian Mayfield and historian John Henrik Clarke welcomed his unabashed militance as a refreshing alternative to liberal inaction and caution. In 1960 Williams became a key figure in the radical Fair Play for Cuba Committee, defending Fidel Castro as a visionary exponent of social and racial democracy; and by the spring of 1961 he was punctuating his speeches with revolutionary rhetoric that came dangerously close to a call to arms. "I am going to meet violence with violence," he told a Harlem crowd on May 17, the seventh anniversary of *Brown*. "It is better to live just thirty seconds, walking upright in human dignity, than to live a thousand years crawling at the feet of our oppressors."

Those who knew Williams well recognized that such rhetoric was less a celebration of violence than a reflection of his continuing frustration with local officials who refused to protect him and other Monroe blacks from marauding Klansmen. As Brooks explained to Forman in mid-July following a phone conversation with Williams, the Klan had tried to kill the Monroe civil rights leader after he had led an attempt to desegregate a public swimming pool in the summer of 1960. The local police knew the identity of the assailant, Williams insisted, but refused to make an arrest. Feeling vulnerable and alone, Williams asked Brooks and other outsiders for help. Intrigued, the young Freedom Rider decided to conduct a personal investigation of the situation in Monroe. After further conversations with Williams, Forman, and movement friends in Nashville, Brooks sought and received an endorsement for the trip from both SCLC and the National Freedom Council. The leaders of the Freedom Council urged Forman to accompany Brooks, and on Friday, July 21, the two men set out for Monroe via Nashville and Atlanta.[24]

In Nashville, where they stopped off for more than a week, Brooks and Forman found themselves in the midst of a movement hothouse. At the Nashville Movement office, they spent several days discussing movement philosophy and strategy with Nash, Bevel, Lafayette, and several other SNCC and SCLC activists who had recently returned from Mississippi. Much of the discussion, Forman recalled, revolved around a series of interrelated issues: the difficulty of provoking and sustaining a mass movement among Mississippi blacks; the necessity of overcoming the relative timidity and organizational inertia of groups such as the NAACP and SCLC; the future of SNCC and the central role of student activists in the expanding struggle for freedom and social justice; the tactical and philosophical viability of nonviolence; and the advisability of shifting the movement's focus from direct action to voting rights. This last issue was currently the major topic of conversation at the student movement workshop convened at Fisk on July 30, and before leaving town on August 2, Forman and Brooks participated

in several workshop sessions. Listening to and interacting with seasoned activists such as McDew, Sherrod, Bevel, Lewis, Nash, and Ruby Doris Smith
was exhilarating, and both men came away from the experience with a new
sense of the movement's potential to transform the South. This was a fitting
prelude to their upcoming meeting with a man who made no effort to disguise his revolutionary aims, and they could hardly wait to meet Williams in
person to see how far he had actually traveled on the road to revolution.

Before proceeding eastward to Monroe, however, Brooks and Forman
traveled southward by car to Atlanta. Offered a ride by Nash and Bevel, who
were on their way to an FRCC meeting, the two men visited the adjoining
headquarters of SNCC and SCLC, where they picked up a letter of endorsement signed by Martin Luther King. At the SNCC office, they met Ed King,
who seemed "lonely" and "dejected." As Forman later recalled the scene:
"He was leaving [to return to school at Kentucky State] and did not know
who would replace him. No decision had been made; it was not his problem,
but he was worried. SNCC faced serious problems as an organization, he
said. It should have developed more staff and instigated more activity in its
name. It had not developed a fund-raising base and had to rely heavily upon
contributions from the Southern Christian Leadership Conference, which
was like pulling teeth. In addition, it was identified in many eyes as an arm of
SCLC rather than as an independent organization. King seemed to feel frustrated on many levels." All of this was sobering news, but a visit with Ella
Baker that evening went a long way toward restoring the two travelers' spirits. Neither man had met Baker before, but she more than lived up to her
image as a movement sage. After a frank discussion of the problems and prospects of the student movement, she gave her blessing to the Monroe expedition, leaving her two visitors, as Forman put it, "more wise about the history
of civil rights organizations in this country and with that deepened sense of
perspective which was Miss Baker's constant gift to people."[25]

This whirlwind education continued the next evening when Brooks and
Forman arrived at the Monroe railway depot. Befriending a porter who warned
them that Monroe was "a rough town" but who nonetheless offered to drive
them to Williams's house, they soon found themselves walking through a
living room arsenal cluttered with "forty rifles lying on the floor, stacked on
top of each other." Following a hearty welcome, Williams explained that the
guns were a necessary deterrent to marauding Klansmen who had threatened to kill him and torch his house. That evening, after visiting a local black
civil rights leader who claimed that he too feared for his life, Brooks and
Forman helped guard Williams's house. Sitting on the porch until four in
the morning with rifles in hand, Williams and the two visitors heard loud
gunfire in the neighborhood. But, to their relief, no Klansmen appeared.

Over the next three days Brooks and Forman talked to a number of
Monroe residents, including the police chief and the city manager, and came
away with the sense that the city was a racial tinderbox. They also had lengthy

discussions with Williams about "the difference in connotation between meeting violence with violence and self-defense." "It is the latter they are doing," Forman wrote in a field report to the National Freedom Council, "a right guaranteed in the Constitution and practiced by many other civil rights fighters. People and organizations ought to try to understand the historical context of the struggle here and the necessity to formulate courses of actions predicated upon given situations at given times in history. *Monroe is not Nashville nor Montgomery.*" At the end of the report, Forman offered the sobering warning that "there is growing support for Williams throughout the South, for the Negro is becoming impatient and *he is not always going to turn the other cheek.*"[26]

On Tuesday, August 8, Brooks and Forman boarded a train for Jackson, but before they left they promised to return to Monroe later in the month accompanied by a group of Freedom Riders. Despite his misgivings about nonviolence, Williams was open to the idea of using Freedom Riders to bring attention to the situation in Monroe. The tentative plan was to place the Riders on an interracial picket line surrounding the county courthouse, with the goal of forcing the city police to issue a warrant for the arrest of the Klansman who had tried to kill Williams in June. After explaining the plan to a gathering of Freedom Riders in Jackson, Brooks and Forman were able to recruit seventeen Riders—fifteen whites and two blacks—willing to travel to Monroe. Among the seventeen were Fred Leonard, two of the Minnesota Riders, and NAG veterans Paul Dietrich and Bill Mahoney. The motivations of the volunteers, all of whom had just experienced the mass arraignment, were not altogether clear or consistent, but many claimed that they hoped to steer Williams toward nonviolence and to effect some sort of reconciliation between his supporters and detractors. Unlike Brooks and Forman, they had no intention of joining or rationalizing Williams's armed defense of the Monroe civil rights struggle. Instead, they hoped to demonstrate the power and moral authority of nonviolence.

This rationale made little difference to white North Carolinians, who regarded the Freedom Riders' visit to Monroe as a needless and dangerous provocation. When the Riders arrived at Charlotte's Union Station on August 17, they discovered that little had changed since Joe Perkins had been arrested at the station three months earlier. While there was no obvious threat of violence in Charlotte, local officials made it clear that they did not want the Riders to remain in the city any longer than was absolutely necessary. Fortunately, the Riders had already arranged to stay in Matthews, a farming town located ten miles southeast of Charlotte, halfway between Charlotte and Monroe. Matthews was the home of Harry and Janet Boyte, two SCLC supporters who had been active in the effort to desegregate Atlanta's schools in the late 1950s. Eager to provide the Riders with a safe refuge, the Boytes turned their farmhouse into a movement encampment and staging ground for the project in Monroe.

Despite an uneasy and ambiguous relationship with Williams, the Riders wasted no time in launching the project, establishing the Monroe Nonviolent Action Committee (MNAC) and opening a headquarters, which they named "Freedom House," just down the street from Williams's home. Publicly Williams welcomed the Riders as allies and urged his followers to adhere to nonviolent discipline when participating in demonstrations sponsored by the MNAC, but in private he told friends that the Riders' nonviolent efforts were bound to fail. As he wrote to William Worthy, the veteran journalist who had participated in both the Journey of Reconciliation and Bayard Rustin's 1956 mission to Montgomery, "I am not a pacifist and don't believe their philosophy will work with conscienceless racists."[27]

Amidst rising fears among local whites, the MNAC organized its first demonstration on Monday, August 21, when ten activists—six Freedom Riders, three local blacks, and Constance Lever, a young English anti-apartheid activist—set up a picket line outside the Union County Courthouse in downtown Monroe. Carrying signs proclaiming "Freedom for All," the picketers remained at the courthouse for several hours without incident. When they returned the next day, however, a small but angry crowd of whites provoked a melee that resulted in several beatings and the arrest of four picketers, including Richard Griswold, a white Freedom Rider from Brooklyn who took an "unauthorized" picture of Paul Dietrich being beaten. On Wednesday a second confrontation at the courthouse led to the arrest of a white protester who assaulted Danny Thompson, a white Freedom Rider from Cleveland, Ohio. Despite the arrest, the police at the scene made it clear that they sympathized with the attackers. The MNAC, angered by the police's refusal to protect the right to protest against city officials, returned to the downtown on Friday to establish a new picket line outside the dentist office of Mayor Fred Wilson. In response, Wilson ordered city workers to tear up and resurface the sidewalk in front of the office, and before the afternoon was over several picketers "had been roughed up." One of those assaulted, Ed Bromberg, a white Freedom Rider from New York, suffered a flesh wound from a high-powered air rifle fired by an unidentified sniper.[28]

Despite the escalating violence, MNAC picketers returned to the courthouse on Saturday morning. This time they encountered the largest and most aggressive crowd to date, and by mid-afternoon the local police were forced to call in highway patrolmen to keep the situation from getting completely out of hand. After several assaults and arrests, Forman asked the police to escort the picketers back to Freedom House and the black section of town. As the picketers marched in double file away from the courthouse, two policemen accompanied them. But so did hundreds of angry whites. "Seeing us prepare to leave," Forman recalled years later, "the racists began to line up in their cars. . . . Car after car of whites passed—some loaded with guns, some with occupants throwing stones at us, all hurling insults and threats." As the marchers left the downtown and entered a white neighborhood, one woman wielding a large knife ran toward them screaming: "I told you niggers not to come past my house singing those damn songs." Other white bystanders threw rocks, bricks, and Coke bottles at the advancing marchers, some of whom were injured.

For several blocks the marchers maintained a tight nonviolent discipline, refusing to respond in kind and channeling their anger into louder and louder singing, but as they approached Boyte Street, the main thoroughfare of Williams's neighborhood, the discipline began to break down. After several neighborhood blacks tried to protect the marchers by returning "stone for stone," two of the marchers—both local supporters of Williams—rushed over to one of the cars that had been following them, pulled out the driver, and began beating him. Soon a second car was being pummeled with rocks, prompting Danny Thompson, who was still recovering from the beating he had received on Wednesday, to jump in front of the car in an effort to shield the driver from harm. In the heat of the moment not all of the marchers approved of Thompson's intervention, but, fortunately for the driver, the entire confrontation came to an abrupt end a few seconds later when a black sentry fired his rifle into the air, "sending the whites fleeing back toward downtown Monroe."[29]

That evening the MNAC held an emergency strategy session that revealed sharp differences of opinion about the implications of what had just happened in the streets of Monroe. While Williams and other local activists reiterated the black community's right to an armed defense, the visiting Freedom Riders condemned the acts of retaliation that had placed civil rights advocates and white segregationists on the same moral plane. After much debate, and with Williams reluctantly agreeing to go along with the majority's wishes, the group adopted a two-part plan for the following day. In the morning the MNAC would send interracial delegations to several of Monroe's white churches, and in the afternoon the picketers would return to the courthouse square. Although Williams warned them not to expect too much from the city's religious leaders, the church visits went off surprisingly well, with only one interracial team being forced to conduct a kneel-in on the steps of an all-white Episcopal church. As one Freedom Rider recalled: "We were received rather warmly everywhere. In most churches, the minister greeted us personally after the service and invited us to return the following week."

This encouraging experience raised the expectations for the afternoon demonstration at the courthouse, but the picketers soon discovered that the churches' openness represented only one side of a sharply divided and volatile white community. When the picketers arrived at the courthouse around two o'clock, they encountered a shrieking, unruly crowd of more than two thousand white protesters. Waving Confederate flags and carrying signs condemning "nigger lovers" and proclaiming "Open Season on Coons," the protesters included hundreds of Klansmen who had descended upon Monroe from as far away as central Georgia. To make matters worse, a group of young blacks loyal to Williams soon joined the throng. Though unarmed, they immediately attracted the attention of the Klansmen, who moved menacingly in their direction. Although the police managed to keep the Klansmen and the rest of the crowd at bay for more than two hours, the standoff collapsed as soon as the picketers and the group of black teenagers tried to leave the scene.

Earlier in the day the MNAC had arranged for four taxicabs to pick up the picketers at 4:30, but the organizers had not counted on the presence of the black teenagers. As the designated leader at the scene, Forman decided to fill the cabs with the teenagers and as many of the picketers as could be jammed in. That left twenty picketers waiting for a second set of cabs. In the meantime, one of Williams's lieutenants, Woodrow Wilson, rushed to the courthouse square accompanied by several armed colleagues. By the time Wilson arrived, the crowd had broken through the police lines, attacking several of the picketers, including Constance Lever. At this point Forman managed to shepherd Lever to Wilson's car, but before he could put her inside, a police officer screamed: "You ain't going to put a white woman in a car with a bunch of niggers!" Advancing toward the car, the officer noticed that several of the black men inside were armed with shotguns. After grabbing one of the guns, he handed it to a white protester, who promptly turned to Forman, threatening to kill him if he didn't move away from the car. "If you move one step," the man warned, "I'm going to blow your black brains back to Africa." Seconds later the crowd closed in around Forman and began chanting: "Kill him! Kill him! Kill the nigger."

Sure that he was going to die, Forman stood motionless for several minutes before deciding to make a run for the car. Pushing Lever into the front seat, he scrambled in after her, but not before the man who had threatened to kill him struck him in the head with a gun barrel. As blood poured from a deep gash in Forman's forehead, three of the policemen at the scene decided that they had seen enough. Commandeering Wilson's car, they drove Forman, Lever, and the others to the police station, leaving the crowd screaming for more blood. For the next twenty minutes the crowd surged out of control, roughing up Heath Rush and several other Freedom Riders and eventually forcing the police to place all of the picketers under "protective custody." By the end of the afternoon the Union County jail was jammed with twenty-six picketers and one newsman, all arrested for inciting a riot.[30]

During the next five hours, the real perpetrators of the riot spread mayhem across the city. After roving bands of armed whites, including some uniformed policemen, drove through black neighborhoods firing at innocent bystanders, Williams began to mobilize the black community for armed resistance. One gun battle between four of Williams's lieutenants and two police officers left one of the officers with a bullet wound in the thigh, and before the night was over rumors of an unrestrained race war were rampant. By ten o'clock the worst of the fighting was over, but fear of an all-out assault on the black community had already led Williams to order the construction of barricades at both ends of Boyte Street. Placing armed sentries in the trees overlooking the barricades, he urged his followers to prepare for the worst. While he counseled them to stay at home and avoid contact with the roving whites, he passed out enough weapons to ensure that the community could defend itself if the Klan forced a showdown. Earlier in the day Williams's wife, Mabel, had called Harry Boyte in Manning, hoping that he could convince federal or state officials to provide protection for local blacks and their MNAC allies. Boyte was able to relay the message to Governor Terry Sanford through an intermediary, and by late afternoon several dozen state troopers had set up roadblocks in the streets surrounding the black Newtown neighborhood.

Unfortunately, the troopers' effort to keep all whites out of the neighborhood proved less than foolproof. Just after six o'clock Charles and Mabel Stegall, a white couple from the nearby town of Marshville, drove toward the crowd that had filled the stretch of Boyte Street near Williams's home. Assuming that the Stegalls were part of a Klan raiding party, several members of the crowd rushed forward with rifles at the ready. After being pulled out of the car— which to their misfortune closely resembled a known Klan car that had been seen downtown the day before—the two frightened visitors tried to explain that they had simply driven down the wrong street and that they harbored no ill feelings toward "niggers." This patronizing explanation only made matters worse, prompting several angry onlookers to suggest that the Stegalls should be killed on the spot. Others objected, and Williams soon emerged from his house to rescue the couple.

Assuring them that no one planned to harm them, Williams offered the Stegalls a temporary refuge in his home and even allowed Bruce Stegall to phone the chief of police, A. A. Mauney. But when the Stegalls begged Williams to provide an escort out of the neighborhood, he refused, advising them that they could leave of their own accord anytime they wished. A few minutes later they did just that, returning safely to Marshville. Before leaving Monroe, however, they spoke to two policemen, who relayed their story to members of the sheriff's department and the highway patrol, some of whom began to refer to the incident as a "hostage situation." Despite the absence of any firm confirmation from the Stegalls, the rumor soon spread that Williams had kidnapped the couple, held them at gunpoint, and threatened to kill them.

Even before this rumor exacerbated the situation, Williams, convinced that Chief Mauney and the police planned to kill him before the night was over, had arranged for a possible escape. But any chance of remaining in Monroe ended with the Stegall incident. To save himself and his family, not to mention the lives of his loyal supporters, Williams slipped out the back door into the darkness sometime before midnight. Accompanied by his wife, his two young sons, and Mae Mallory, he made his way to a prearranged rendezvous, where Julian Mayfield was waiting with a getaway car. Both Mayfield and Mallory had come down from New York the previous week to help Williams cope with the worsening situation in Monroe, but Mallory, a fiery and sometimes bitter woman, had lost her composure, urging Williams to kill any white segregationists who challenged his authority. At one point she apparently threatened to kill the Stegalls, an indiscretion that angered Williams and implicated her in the alleged kidnapping. Fearing that she would get herself and others killed if he left her behind, Williams wisely took her with him to the rendezvous with Mayfield, though this decision would later contribute to the case for a grand conspiracy.

Dodging an army of law enforcement officers, Mayfield drove all night through the back roads of North Carolina, Virginia, Maryland, and New Jersey. Arriving at a safe house in Harlem on Monday morning, August 28, the band of fugitives soon discovered that they were the object of a national manhunt. Within minutes of the escape, local and state law enforcement officers had ransacked Williams's house, uncovering a cache of weapons but no clues as to where he had gone. When early-morning interrogations of several Williams lieutenants failed to reveal his whereabouts, the officers turned their attention to the Stegalls, who were brought before a grand jury on Monday afternoon. As the all-white jury listened with rapt attention, the Stegalls told a lurid story of kidnapping and murderous threats, insisting they had been held hostage by a madman. According to Mabel Stegall, the kidnapping represented a desperate attempt to force the authorities to release the picketers arrested at the courthouse square. After narrowly escaping death at the hands of a black mob, she and her husband had been taken to Williams's home to serve as human bargaining chips. Showing no mercy, Williams had called Chief Mauney and threatened to kill both of his captives if the picketers were not released within thirty minutes. Although Williams and others would later dispute this version of events, the Stegalls' testimony was more than enough to convince the grand jury to issue an indictment for kidnapping.[31]

By Monday evening Monroe was swarming with FBI agents. Dispatched by J. Edgar Hoover, who firmly believed that Williams was part of a Communist-inspired plot to incite violence among disgruntled Southern blacks, the agents searched for weapons and other evidence that would confirm the director's suspicions. Monroe remained a powder keg of racial tension and animosity, and Hoover and many others feared that renewed violence might break out at any time. The greatest fear, of course, was that the violence and racial polarization in Monroe would spread to other Southern communities if Williams's extremist behavior went unpunished. Indeed, the Monroe incident had already provoked segregationist politicians and other white supremacists across the South, several of whom wasted no time in exploiting the situation. Even before the grand jury returned its indictment, Governor John Patterson sent telegrams to Governor Terry Sanford

WANTED BY THE FBI

INTERSTATE FLIGHT — KIDNAPING
ROBERT FRANKLIN WILLIAMS

Photograph taken May, 1961

FBI No. 84,275 B

Aliases: Bob Williams, Robert F. Williams.

DESCRIPTION

Age:	36, born February 26, 1925, Monroe, North Carolina		
Height:	6'	Complexion:	dark brown
Weight:	240 pounds	Race:	Negro
Build:	heavy	Nationality:	American
Hair:	black	Occupations:	free lance writer, freight
Eyes:	brown		handler, janitor, machinist

Scars and Marks: scar left eyelid, scar left nostril, scar on calf of right leg.

Fingerprint Classification: 19 L 1 R 100 8 Ref: T R T
                                     M 1 T 10   A A T

CAUTION

WILLIAMS ALLEGEDLY HAS POSSESSED A LARGE QUANTITY OF FIREARMS, INCLUDING A .45 CALIBER PISTOL WHICH HE CARRIES IN HIS CAR. HE HAS PREVIOUSLY BEEN DIAGNOSED AS SCHIZOPHRENIC AND HAS ADVOCATED AND THREATENED VIOLENCE. WILLIAMS SHOULD BE CONSIDERED ARMED AND EXTREMELY DANGEROUS.

A Federal warrant was issued on August 28, 1961, at Charlotte, North Carolina, charging Williams with unlawful interstate flight to avoid prosecution for kidnaping (Title 18, U. S. Code, Section 1073).

IF YOU HAVE INFORMATION CONCERNING THIS PERSON, PLEASE NOTIFY ME OR CONTACT YOUR LOCAL FBI OFFICE. TELEPHONE NUMBER IS LISTED BELOW.

DIRECTOR
FEDERAL BUREAU OF INVESTIGATION
UNITED STATES DEPARTMENT OF JUSTICE
WASHINGTON 25, D. C.
TELEPHONE, NATIONAL 8-7117

Wanted Flyer No. 290
September 6, 1961

Robert Williams was the subject of a national FBI manhunt during the fall of 1961.

and Mayor Fred Wilson offering the services of Alabama National Guards-men and state troopers. Eager to expose the Freedom Riders who had be-come entangled with Williams, he also wired Robert Kennedy to express his outrage against the "lawless elements" from the North who had fo-mented the violence and racial strife in Monroe.

To Patterson's delight, the Freedom Riders' involvement in the Monroe crisis was a source of considerable embarrassment for the nonviolent move-ment. With the early press reports depicting Williams as a violent criminal who trafficked in conspiracy and political subversion, CORE, SCLC, and SNCC leaders took immediate steps to disassociate themselves from his com-mitment to armed self-defense. Since Brooks had gone to Monroe with a letter of endorsement from King, SCLC felt especially vulnerable to criti-cism. On Monday evening SCLC executive board member Kelly Miller Smith released a statement deploring the situation in Monroe and condemning both blacks and whites for resorting to violence. "There are considerable wrongs on both sides of the situation," he acknowledged, after talking to several of the Monroe Freedom Riders by phone, adding: "Violence is never a final solution to any problem. Any perpetrator of violence, regardless of his stated purpose, contributes to the shame of America and to the frustration of hu-man decency." Several CORE and SNCC leaders also publicly reiterated their commitment to nonviolence, but there were no detailed comments on the situation since at this point no one outside of Monroe had much sense of what had actually happened to the Freedom Riders.[32]

Even among the Freedom Riders themselves there was considerable con-fusion about the unfolding drama in Monroe. Five of the Riders—including Paul Brooks and Danny Thompson—escaped arrest on Sunday afternoon, but Forman and the rest spent the night in the county jail. When they first arrived at the police station, it was unclear whether they and the other pick-eters were under arrest or simply in protective custody, but after inquiring about a police escort back to Boyte Street, they learned that they had been charged with inciting a riot. Bail was a thousand dollars each, they were told, with the trial set for September 11. Only Constance Lever, who was sched-uled to fly back to England on September 9, seemed concerned about the trial date or the prospect of spending two weeks in jail. Later, after being transferred to the county jail, they serenaded the guards with freedom songs and protested their unwarranted incarceration by declaring a hunger strike. Still bleeding from his head wound, Forman was treated at a local hospital before rejoining his fellow prisoners, all of whom were jammed into a cell block designed for less than half their number. Sleeping three abreast on the concrete floor, they survived the night without any contact with the outside world and without knowing anything about Williams's escape or the alleged kidnapping. They had no inkling of the seriousness of the situation until a police captain filled them in on Monday afternoon. Earlier in the day, unbe-knownst to them, Thompson had vowed that the Freedom Riders would remain in Monroe until "something is done" about the discriminatory and inhumane conditions forced upon the local black community. But Forman and the jailed Riders had no real opportunity to discuss their options until CORE attorney Len Holt visited the jail on Tuesday morning.

Holt made it clear that the situation was too volatile for the Freedom Riders to remain in Monroe any longer than necessary. For the good of the movement, he urged Forman and the others to forgo the normal strategy of "jail–no bail." Although the bail figure was hefty and the trial date was nearly two weeks away, he was confident that he could convince the authorities to arrange for reasonable bail and an earlier trial. Later in the day, SCLC's executive director, Wyatt Tee Walker, also paid a visit to the jail, and he too confirmed the movement's desire to get the Riders out of Monroe as soon as possible. Walker had only been in town for a few hours, but any doubts he might have harbored about the poisonous nature of race relations in Monroe had disappeared earlier in the afternoon during a confrontation with an enraged white supremacist. When Walker and two black reporters tried to enter the county courthouse, Vann Wickery, a towering three-hundred-pound restaurant manager, picked the diminutive SCLC leader up and threw him down a flight of concrete steps into a bed of ivy surrounding a granite Civil War monument. Picking himself up, Walker reclimbed the steps only to be thrown down a second time, and moments later a third. Finally, the police intervened, placing Wickery in handcuffs and carting him off to jail, where he was charged with public drunkenness and resisting arrest. In the end, Walker escaped serious injury and entered the courthouse, but the incident—especially the symbolism of Walker's landing place—quickly became a staple of movement lore.

At a hearing later in the afternoon, a local judge reduced the picketers' bail to twenty-five dollars and moved the trial date to September 1, setting the stage for a mass bailout. By midnight all but five of the picketers were out on bond. The remaining five—Forman, Paul Dietrich, Ken Shilman, Richard Griswold, and William Mahoney—were all movement veterans who felt uncomfortable about accepting bail. At one point on Tuesday evening they reluctantly agreed to post bond, but all five changed their minds and decided to remain in jail for at least one more night after discovering that the warrant for their release contained several new charges, including the charge that they had carried concealed weapons. Though still concerned about the implications of the new charges, Forman and Griswold accepted bail on Wednesday morning, leaving only three Freedom Riders behind bars. As Forman later explained, with so much uncertainty about what had happened to Williams and with the unpredictable Danny Thompson making provocative statements to the press, there was even more concern about what was happening back on Boyte Street.[33]

"Monroe seemed like a ghost town when I emerged from the police station that Wednesday afternoon, and Newtown was like a ghost that had died,"

Forman recalled. "Robert's house, where I went to stay until the trial on Friday, had the atmosphere of an ancient monument." Although it had been three days since the alleged kidnapping, most of Monroe's black population remained indoors as the police and FBI investigators conducted a house-to- house search for weapons and collaborators. Forman himself spent part of Wednesday afternoon fending off an FBI agent who badgered him with questions about the missing black leader and the Freedom Riders' involvement in the Stegall affair. He also talked with two of Williams's lieutenants, Harold Reape and Richard Crowder, and urged them to leave town as soon as possible. But both were arrested before nightfall, charged as accessories to kidnapping. The previous evening the police had arrested and filed similar charges against John Lowry, a white Freedom Rider from New York who had moved the Stegalls' car from the middle of the street to the curb in front of Williams's house.

Even the slightest connection to the events of Sunday evening, it seemed, could lead to arrest and incarceration, and movement leaders began to fear that the dragnet would eventually implicate all of the Freedom Riders through guilt by association. At the very least, the movement faced a public relations nightmare, especially after the police discovered several large caches of weapons, including a case of dynamite buried in Williams's back yard. Recognizing the seriousness of the situation, Wyatt Tee Walker asked William Kunstler, who had just returned to New York following the initial trials in Jackson, to come to Monroe to represent the Freedom Riders at the trial scheduled for Friday, September 1. Kunstler arrived on Thursday afternoon, just in time for a pretrial meeting with Walker and the defendants. At the meeting Walker advised against Len Holt's participation in the trial, but after a protracted discussion all agreed that Kunstler and Holt would act as co-counsels.

When the Freedom Riders arrived at the Union County Courthouse on Friday morning, they encountered a crowd that included some of the same men who had attacked them the previous Sunday. But this time there was no bloodshed, and the trial began without incident. Faced with an unusually large number of defendants, the presiding judge, J. Emmett Griffin, bowed to practicality and allowed the white Freedom Riders to sit in the black section of the courtroom. Once the proceedings began, however, he made no effort to hide his contempt for the defendants and their interracial team of attorneys. Striking down motion after motion by the defense, he was unmoved by the argument that picketing the courthouse was a legally protected form of expression. After Kunstler pointed out that the state had provided no proof that the defendants had carried weapons of any kind, Griffin struck the concealed weapons charge from the warrant. The inciting-to-riot charge remained, despite an eloquent closing argument by Holt, who bravely pointed out the moral and political implications of segregationist intolerance.

In the end, Griffin found all of the defendants guilty and pronounced stiff sentences ranging from six months to two years in prison. To nearly everyone's surprise, however, he immediately offered to suspend the sentences if the defendants agreed "not to picket or to violate the laws of Union County or the state of North Carolina for a period of two years." Given thirty minutes to decide whether to accept the offer, the Freedom Riders huddled, first with Holt, and then with Kunstler, to discuss the alternative of rejecting the suspended sentences, which would allow them to file an appeal that would challenge the constitutionality of their prosecution. When both attorneys advised against an appeal, the Riders reluctantly accepted Griffin's offer. But some, including Forman, regarded the decision as a sacrifice of principle. Although he did not say so publicly, Kunstler privately acknowledged that the urge to disengage the Freedom Riders from Monroe and the violent images attached to Williams superseded all other considerations. As he wrote to Walker on September 5: "It was a grievous error for the Riders to associate themselves with Williams, but I feel we did the best we could with a difficult situation."[31]

To the relief of Walker and other movement leaders, virtually all of the Freedom Riders left town immediately after the trial. But for some the Monroe episode was not quite over. Although CORE, SCLC, and other nonviolent organizations tried to distance themselves from Williams and the Monroe fugitives, individual Freedom Riders and some CORE chapters became involved in the various Monroe defense groups that sprang up during the fall of 1961. Dave Morton, the independent-minded Freedom Rider and folk singer from Minnesota, picketed the White House in September before going on to New York to help organize the Committee to Aid the Monroe Defenders (CAMD). Other Freedom Riders, including Journey of Reconciliation veterans Conrad Lynn and William Worthy, later raised funds and spoke at CAMD rallies in New York, Cleveland, and other Northern cities. Part of their motivation was the defense of fellow Freedom Rider John Lowry, who went on trial in September for being an accessory to the Stegall kidnapping. Represented by Kunstler, the young New Yorker survived the nine-day trial, but this was only the beginning of a long legal ordeal. After several appeals, his conviction was upheld by a North Carolina appellate court in 1964, and he, along with several other Monroe defendants, received a long jail sentence.[35]

For Williams himself the ordeal was even longer, although the trials that he faced turned out to be those of exile, not legal prosecution. Despite the best efforts of the FBI, he and his family made their way from Harlem to Long Island, and eventually across the Canadian border to Toronto, where they found refuge with Vernal and Anne Olsen, two white socialist activists involved in the Fair Play for Cuba Committee. After six weeks in Toronto, the Williamses traveled on to Nova Scotia and then to Gander, Newfoundland, where they boarded a plane for Cuba. Welcomed by the Castro regime, Williams soon resurfaced as the host of a weekly radio show provocatively named *Radio Free Dixie*. Mixing jazz and soul music with biting social commentary on the freedom struggle, Williams could be heard throughout the southeastern United States, to the dismay of the federal and state authorities who still hoped to see him behind bars. After several years in Cuba, Williams continued his international odyssey in North Vietnam and China, witnessing the Vietnam War and Mao's Cultural Revolution from a firsthand perspective. Although these experiences made him a cult figure among leftist intellectuals and Black Power advocates, he eventually grew tired of the ideological strictures and racial hypocrisies of the Communist world. After offering to brief American officials on the situation in China, he was allowed to return to the United States in 1969 without fear of federal prosecution. Still subject to local and state prosecution in North Carolina, he settled in Michigan, where he was able to avoid extradition. After North Carolina authorities dropped all charges against him in 1976, he made frequent visits to Monroe, but Michigan remained his primary home until his death in 1996. Though controversial to the end, Williams was laid to rest in Monroe by a large crowd of mourners that included Rosa Parks, a fellow Michigan transplant and longtime friend, who did not always share his views on violence but who nonetheless eulogized "his courage and his commitment to freedom."[36]

FOR SHEER DRAMA, nothing could match the story of Robert Williams. But, as a key episode of the lengthy legal struggle between the Freedom Riders and the State of Mississippi, the trial of Hank Thomas had a special excitement of its own. With both sides anticipating a pivotal contest, the tension began to build in the days leading up to the August 22 trial. Earlier in the month Kunstler had deliberately muddied the legal waters by filing a special appeal on behalf of five Freedom Riders. By asking that the Riders' cases be remanded from the county court to state court, he automatically triggered an appeal at the federal district level. On Saturday, August 19, the matter went before District Judge Harold Cox, the extreme segregationist who had recently been appointed to a federal judgeship over the strong objections of civil rights leaders. Arguing that the local breach-of-peace statute under which his clients had been convicted was actually "a segregation law—pure and simple," Kunstler hoped to circumvent the county court appellate proceedings scheduled to begin the following Tuesday. Since the Freedom Riders had come to Mississippi "to dramatize the segregation in interstate commerce," he insisted that 'the federal court is the proper place for these cases." After questioning Kunstler about CORE's motives, Cox promised to issue a ruling on the removal issue, but not before the beginning of the trials in Judge Moore's court. Hank Thomas and the other early defendants would have their day in court, Mississippi style.[37]

Mississippi was not the only state where authorities were determined to maintain the legal pressure on the Freedom Riders. On Monday, the day before the opening of Thomas's trial, a Shreveport, Louisiana, district judge convicted six Riders of breaching the peace during an August 4 attempt to desegregate a Trailways waiting room. Among those convicted were CORE's Dave Dennis and the Reverend Harry Blake, a courageous Shreveport activist who had been serving as an SCLC field secretary since 1960. On Tuesday an Ocala, Florida, county judge convicted Herbert Callender, a black Freedom Rider from New York City, sentencing him to six months in jail and a three-hundred-dollar fine. And pressure of a different kind surfaced a few hours later in Maryland, when George O'Dea, the superior general of the St. Joseph's Society of the Sacred Heart, ordered two Louisiana priests, Richard Wagner and Philip Berrigan, to cancel their plan to become Freedom Riders. On Monday afternoon, after consulting with CORE officials in New York, Wagner and Berrigan had flown to Jackson with the intention of conducting desegregation tests at local airport and bus terminals; O'Dea's order forced both men to return to New Orleans, where Wagner worked as a chaplain at Xavier University and Berrigan taught at St. Augustine High School. Though failing in their effort to become the first Catholic priests to be arrested as Freedom Riders, Wagner and Berrigan would gain considerable notoriety as anti-war and human rights activists later in the decade.[38]

On Tuesday morning, August 22, as the supporting dramas in Louisiana, Florida, North Carolina, and Maryland were still unfolding, Hank Thomas's trial began at the Hinds County Courthouse. Flanked by four defense attorneys—Rachlin, Kunstler, Jack Young, and Carsie Hall—the strapping nineteen-year-old Freedom Rider stood silently as Judge Moore's bailiff called the court to order. After a few opening remarks from Moore, who acknowledged the reporters in the gallery and noted that this was the only the first of approximately 190 trials to come, the selection of the jury commenced. As expected, the defense attorneys promptly challenged the selection process, which all but guaranteed an all-white jury. Although Mississippi law prohibited women from serving on juries, it was technically possible for black jurymen to be selected from the registered voter list. In this instance, fifty-one of the fifty-three members of the jury pool were white, and with six peremptory challenges the prosecution could easily exclude the two black members of the pool. After Kunstler pointed this out and introduced testimony from several longtime black voters who had never been asked to serve on a jury, the prosecution countered with evidence from "several Jackson white city employees and newsmen that they, too, had been registered voters for many years and had never been called for jury duty." Such assurances proved good enough for Judge Moore, who dismissed Kunstler's motion to quash the venire. Later, when Kunstler questioned the impartiality of prospective jurors, asking specifically about their attitudes toward racial integration and CORE, Moore upheld state attorney Jack Travis's objection to this line of questioning. And when Travis himself alluded to the racial implications of the trial, Moore issued a stern reprimand to both sides. "This is not a racial issue," the judge insisted, "it is a breach of the peace trial. CORE is not on trial here."[39]

Despite Moore's protestations, the proceedings quickly turned into a racial show trial on Wednesday afternoon. Parading a string of witnesses in front of the all-white jury, Travis tried to prove that the arrest of Thomas and the other Freedom Riders who had invaded Jackson on May 24 had prevented an outbreak of violence and rioting. Among the dozen witnesses called to confirm both the seriousness of the threat and the Freedom Riders' provocative behavior were Chamber of Commerce officials, Alabama and Mississippi law enforcement officers, and reporters who covered the Freedom Riders' journey from Montgomery to Jackson. The first to take the stand was Ell Cowling, the Alabama Public Safety Commission investigator who had witnessed the assaults on the Freedom Riders in Anniston. Describing the mob that met the bus at the Anniston terminal, Cowling recalled that several angry whites had beaten "on the side of the bus with heavy instruments" and screamed "Communist Niggers" at the Riders. He then went on to describe the roadside bombing of the bus several minutes later. When asked on cross-examination if he had seen Thomas "do anything illegal from Atlanta to Anniston," Cowling said no. But this admission did nothing to diminish the image of rioting segregationists that Travis hoped to convey to the jury.

Birmingham police sergeant Tom Cook added to this image with a vivid depiction of the rioting at the Birmingham bus station, which he claimed was exacerbated by the fear of Communist-inspired agitators. Following Kunstler's objection to the interjection of the Communist issue into the trial, Judge Moore ordered the jury to disregard Cook's statement. But even with this caveat, Cook's testimony reminded everyone in the courtroom that the Alabama Freedom Rides, unlike the Mississippi Rides, had provoked violent conflict. Later in the day the memory of Alabama's civil disorder received further reinforcement when a news bulletin reported that Governor Patterson had just signed a state law mandating jail terms and fines for Freedom Riders or anyone else committing an act "calculated to . . . outrage the sense of decency and morals or . . . violate or transgress the customs, pattern of life and habits of the people of Alabama."[40]

An array of white Mississippians followed the Alabama witnesses, and in each case they told the same story: The arrest of the Freedom Riders by the Jackson police had forestalled a riot. The monotonous marathon of examination and cross-examination continued into the evening until Judge Moore finally called a recess a few minutes before midnight. When the trial resumed the next morning, Travis was at it again, bringing the total number of prosecution witnesses to fifteen before resting his case. By the time Travis sat down it was early afternoon, and nearly everyone in the room expected Thomas's attorneys to fill the rest of the day with an examination of defense witnesses. But when Kunstler rose to speak he announced that the defense had decided to rest its case without calling any witnesses of its own. Instead, he offered a motion to place the text of the *Boynton* decision into the trial record, a motion summarily rejected by Judge Moore, who had already ruled that *Boynton* was irrelevant to the case.

Surprised and a bit flustered by Kunstler's maneuver, Travis launched into a rambling closing argument that reminded the members of the jury of their duty to uphold law and order. The police and the prosecution had done their part; now it was time for the jury to send a clear message to anyone who dared to challenge the laws and customs of Mississippi. Pointing to Thomas, Travis declared: "Turn him loose . . . and blood will flow. . . . If you want your property protected from riff-raff and subversives, you must return a guilty verdict." In response, Kunstler offered a brief closing statement praising Travis's rhetorical flair but questioning whether the prosecution had presented any proof that the Freedom Riders had breached the peace. Forty-five minutes later a unanimous jury returned the expected guilty verdict. After granting Kunstler's request for an individual poll of the jurors, Judge Moore sentenced Thomas to four months in jail and a two-hundred-dollar fine, a somewhat stiffer penalty than the two-month sentence (plus two months suspended) imposed by the municipal court in May. Kunstler immediately announced that the defense would appeal the verdict to the state courts, and ultimately to the United States Supreme Court if necessary. Moments later Thomas was released pending payment of a two-thousand-dollar bond, bringing what one observer called "the hardest contested misdemeanor case in the annals of Mississippi jurisprudence" to a close.[41]

In actuality, of course, Thomas's trial involved no real closure. On Friday morning, while he was en route to Washington to discuss his future at Howard University, Julia Aaron became the second Freedom Rider to face Travis and Judge Moore. Like Thomas, Aaron was a college student who had become a movement veteran at a young age. As a student activist at Southern University, she had been a mainstay of New Orleans CORE and one of the first to volunteer for the Mississippi Freedom Rides. Petite and attractive, she did not fit the image of a disruptive subversive. But that did not stop Travis from portraying her as a dangerous "rabble-rouser." "What did she want here?" he asked the jury rhetorically, answering: "The same thing they had in Montgomery—bloodshed. She wouldn't be sitting there today if those policemen hadn't been there. We would have had martial law and lots of other things this city doesn't want if we hadn't had the police protection." This time it took only three witnesses and six hours to bring the case to the jury, which needed only fifteen minutes of deliberation to agree on a guilty verdict. The streamlining of the trial eased the burden on those in the courtroom, but it brought little comfort to movement leaders, who were more concerned with the mounting cost of the appeals process. While Aaron announced that she planned to forgo bail and return to jail, defense attorneys did not expect many of the Freedom Riders to follow her lead. With bail set at two thousand dollars per defendant, it wouldn't take long to exhaust CORE's coffers. Indeed, there was nothing to stop Judge

Moore from raising the bail figure even higher as the trials progressed. Barring intervention by the federal courts or a massive infusion of funds, the State of Mississippi's goal of bankrupting CORE now loomed as a realistic possibility.[42]

The likelihood of federal intervention had never been high, but the slight hope that the appellate trials would be removed to the federal courts disappeared on August 26, the day after Aaron's trial. Refusing to invoke the Reconstruction-era civil rights act cited in Kunstler's request for removal, District Judge Cox ruled that the federal courts had no interest in the breach of peace trials. Prior to his appointment in June, movement leaders had warned the Kennedy administration that Cox was a white supremacist ideologue, and now they saw just how right they had been. Insisting that the Freedom Riders' arrests had nothing to do with "integration or segregation," Cox characterized the statute in question as "a pure and simple peace law enacted by the Legislature in good faith to assure peace and tranquility among its people." "This court may not be regarded as any haven for any counterfeit citizens from other states deliberately seeking to cause trouble here," he declared, using language that might have been appropriate at a White Citizens' Council rally but seemed unnecessarily harsh in the context of a federal court order. Claiming that the "petitioners heralded their arrival in Jackson from other states for provocative purposes," he argued that "their status as interstate passengers is extremely doubtful." Although most legal observers, including those at the Justice Department, failed to see the logic of this last statement, Cox's intemperate ruling was not subject to a timely legal challenge. For the foreseeable future, the Freedom Riders' legal fate would remain in the hands of white Mississippians who shared the judge's contempt for the civil right struggle.[43]

Coming on the heels of the first two appellate convictions, Cox's ruling gave pause to the Freedom Riders awaiting trial. Even though CORE policy expressly prohibited the paying of fines in cases of unjust prosecution, some of the Riders began to consider the wisdom of dropping their appeals and accepting the option of paying the remainder of their fines plus three dollars per day for unserved jail time. The third and fourth trials were scheduled for Monday, August 28, but just prior to the opening of court Judge Moore announced that both defendants—John Moody, Hank Thomas's roommate at Howard, and Matthew Walker Jr., a nineteen-year-old black Freedom Rider from Nashville—had withdrawn their appeals and paid their fines. Speaking for CORE, field secretary Tom Gaither made it clear that the two Riders had done so without organizational approval. "We feel it is an admission of guilt," Gaither explained, pointing out that both Moody and Walker had paid the fines with their own funds.[44]

Before the day was over, there would be more bad news for CORE, as the manhunt for Robert Williams widened and the hunger strike at the Monroe jail went into its second day. On Tuesday the assaults on Bob Moses in

McComb and Wyatt Tee Walker at the Union County Courthouse added a sobering message to a nonviolent movement that suddenly seemed to be under physical attack on all fronts. And on Wednesday, New Orleans CORE activists Doris Castle and Jerome Smith became the third and fourth Freedom Riders to drop their appeals, prompting speculation that most or all of the 184 Freedom Riders awaiting trial would soon follow suit. Unlike Moody and Walker, Castle and Smith chose to return to jail rather than pay their fines, an option endorsed by Jim Farmer the next day. In a hastily prepared press release, Farmer predicted that "a significant number of freedom riders will drop their appeals and return to jail to serve out their terms." When pressed for an exact number, Farmer and other CORE officials admitted that they had not yet polled all of the defendants, but they made it clear that the decision to return to jail was a matter of individual conscience. Despite CORE's strong opposition to paying fines, the organization accepted the "moral responsibility to do so in case of extreme emergency." For "students and others who would suffer personal inconvenience by remaining in jail," CORE would find a way to fund their release.

At this point, not even Farmer—who was busy preparing for CORE's annual convention, scheduled to open in Washington the next day—had a firm sense of the Freedom Riders' willingness to return to jail. But he worried that relatively few would follow the lead of Aaron, Castle, and Smith, the three New Orleans CORE stalwarts who always seemed to put the needs of the movement ahead of personal considerations. With the beginning of the fall semester only days away, many student activists were preparing to return to school, and others had jobs and families to consider. Earlier in the summer, many Freedom Riders had vowed to remain in jail for as long as it took to bring down the walls of segregation. Now, as the long season of sacrifice drew to a close, the harsh realities of Mississippi prison life began to take their toll. During the tumultuous final week of August, seven Freedom Riders, including Jim Wahlstrom and Bob Singleton, posted bond before serving the full thirty-nine days recommended by movement attorneys. On the last day of the month, even CORE field secretary Richard Haley, who had been languishing in the Hinds County Jail since his arrest for picketing Ross Barnett's segregationist governors' conference in late July, accepted bail. For the native Chicagoan, as for many of the Freedom Riders, August in Mississippi had proven to be the cruelest month.[45]

11

Oh, Freedom

Oh, Freedom, Oh, Freedom, No More Jim Crow Over Me.
And before I'll be a slave, I'll be buried in my grave,
And go home to my Lord and be free.

—1960s freedom song[1]

JIM FARMER woke up on the morning of September 1 with a troubled mind. He had been national director of CORE for exactly seven months and was proud of what he and the Freedom Riders had accomplished. But, as he contemplated the mounting challenges to the nonviolent movement, he couldn't escape the thought that Roy Wilkins, Thurgood Marshall, and other critics of the Freedom Rides might be right after all. With the appellate trials in Jackson bogged down in confusion, with the escalation of violence in McComb and Monroe, and with no apparent movement in the Interstate Commerce Commission's deliberations, there was little reason for optimism. Despite all of the sacrifices, and despite many inspiring acts of courage, the Freedom Rides appeared to be headed for failure. After four months of Rides and the mobilization of hundreds of activists, the crisis had evolved into a war of attrition that seemed to favor the defenders of segregation. Having set out to prove the viability of direct action in the Deep South, CORE was in danger of proving exactly the opposite. Confounded by the ambiguous response of the Kennedy administration, a strategy designed to guarantee federal protection of constitutional rights had actually put the Freedom Riders at the mercy of unreconstructed state and local officials. Perhaps worst of all, by inadvertently revealing the movement's financial and legal vulnerability, the Freedom Rides had placed the entire civil rights struggle in jeopardy.

Later that day, as Farmer made his way to a staff planning meeting at a Washington church, several reporters pressed him for a statement on the deteriorating situation in Jackson. With the CORE convention scheduled to open in a few hours, there was widespread speculation that the organization's attorneys had decided to withdraw all of the pending appeals. After insisting that there "will be no definite word" on the matter until after the convention delegates had deliberated in closed session, Farmer hinted that CORE had little choice but to shift tactics. "Our feeling is that the authorities of Mississippi are merely harassing us," he declared, predicting that each Freedom Rider would "receive a maximum sentence in the appeal trial regardless of the sentence previously received." Farmer himself was ready to return to jail if the only alternative was to pay an extortionist fine levied by an all-white Mississippi jury, or so he said as he walked away from the reporters. In truth, Farmer had no desire to serve the remaining twenty-seven days of his sentence and desperately hoped that some force would intervene before he had to make good on his pledge.[2]

Timely intervention by the federal judiciary was Farmer's best hope, but the probability of such intervention was difficult to gauge in the wake of recent district and circuit court decisions. He and other movement leaders had been looking for a clear indication from the federal courts that legal and physical harassment of civil rights activists would no longer be tolerated. Fortunately for Farmer, who was ready for a bit of good news, one of the earliest signs that the federal judiciary was moving in this direction surfaced just hours before the opening of the CORE convention. Speaking at a press conference across town, Attorney General Kennedy announced that a federal grand jury meeting in Birmingham had issued indictments against nine of the men involved in the May 14 Anniston bus burning. Charged with violating section 33 of the United States motor vehicle code on two counts— "interfering with the safety and welfare of persons in interstate commerce and with conspiring to interfere with interstate commerce"—the defendants faced a maximum penalty of twenty years imprisonment and a ten-thousand dollar fine on the first count and five years and an additional ten-thousand-dollar fine on the second. All nine were members of the Anniston Klan, including Cecil "Goober" Lewallyn, the twenty-two-year-old hothead who had tossed the firebomb into the bus. Lewallyn was in the Anniston hospital recovering from injuries suffered in an August 13 automobile accident, and a second Klansman, Roger Couch, was already in jail awaiting trial on a burglary charge. The other seven were taken into custody by the FBI and brought before U.S. Commissioner Ruby Price Robinson for arraignment. A tenth conspirator, Dalford Roberts, escaped indictment after agreeing to testify against his fellow Klansmen.[3]

Although the indictment of the Anniston Klansmen represented only the first step toward conviction, Kennedy's announcement was welcome news to the embattled leaders of CORE. Faced with a number of challenges, including an internal revolt led by former executive director Jim Robinson and other members of New York CORE, Farmer, Carey, and Rich would need all the good news they could muster during the next three days. Tensions related to a perceived power grab by the national staff reinforced the sense of crisis as the convention's 160 delegates considered a series of resolutions crafted to deal with the legal and financial ramifications of direct action. At several points during the weekend it appeared that the staff might lose control of the situation. In the end, however, Farmer's growing stature as a movement hero prevailed.

Moments after the conference's closing on Monday, a beaming Farmer told reporters that CORE was not only alive and well but ready to expand the struggle for freedom. After confirming CORE's plan to withdraw the Freedom Rider appeals and after urging all of the defendants to return to Mississippi to serve the remainder of their sentences, he called for a series of new nonviolent initiatives. "It would be easy for us to get bogged down in litigation," he explained, "and that is just what the state of Mississippi would like to see. We have resolved to resume direct nonviolent action instead." Not only would there be new Freedom Rides, but squads of "Freedom Dwellers" would soon fan out across the country to combat racial discrimination in the housing industry. "Negro motorcades" would be sent to housing developments to ensure that "open houses" were truly open; real estate offices refusing to serve blacks could expect sit-ins; and developers who enforced restrictive covenants would be picketed. At the same time, CORE's existing campaign against employment discrimination by chain stores would receive new emphasis. In particular, CORE planned to target the retail giant Sears Roebuck, which generally restricted its black employees to menial positions. Finally, in a gesture that did not go unnoticed at the Justice Department, Farmer also announced an expansion of CORE's involvement in voter registration.[4]

Designed to restore momentum, Farmer's press briefing reflected CORE's continuing commitment to direct action and the Freedom Rides, but it remained to be seen whether the embattled organization could put any of its ambitious plans into operation. Even within the movement there was widespread skepticism about CORE's capacity to sustain a broad program of direct action; and back in Mississippi many local and state officials dismissed Farmer's declarations as empty bluster. Noting that five hundred dollars in bail money would be returned to each Freedom Rider who decided to serve out his or her sentence, one assistant city prosecutor claimed that CORE's decision to drop the appeals was a desperate gambit "to get their hands on the appeal bond money." In Jackson, CORE's change in tactics was widely interpreted as a sign of weakness and impending defeat. "Mississippians are beginning to feel they have licked the 'Freedom Rider' movement," an Associated Press story in the *Jackson Daily News* reported on Wednesday, September 6. Quoting unnamed local observers, the story suggested that the Freedom Riders' "prolonged attack" on Mississippi had "backfired." The American public, one observer insisted, had concluded that outside agitators "were taking unfair advantage" of a state that had "bent over backward being fair to them, within the framework of segregation."[5]

Farmer and other movement leaders were quick to dispute this assessment of public opinion, but in the days following the CORE convention they could not deny that the movement's image was in need of restoration. If the Freedom Riders' association with Robert Williams and the Monroe fugitives was not enough to worry about, there was also renewed violence in southwestern Mississippi. When Bob Moses and Travis Britt accompanied four local blacks to the Liberty courthouse on Tuesday morning, September 5, they were intercepted by an angry crowd of white protesters. While the four applicants were inside trying to register, Britt was assaulted by an enraged white man who kept shouting "Why don't you hit me, nigger?" Refusing to fight back, the veteran Freedom Rider and NAG activist was nearly unconscious after being slammed to the ground, but with Moses's help he managed to stagger to their car and escape serious injury.

Both Moses and Britt were safely back in McComb before nightfall, but more movement-related violence occurred on Wednesday, this time in a highly unlikely setting. When nonviolent leaders learned that a riot had broken out at the annual convention of the nation's largest association of black Baptists, some were convinced that a hex had been placed on the movement. Meeting in Kansas City, Missouri, the leaders of the National Baptist Convention, including Martin Luther King, allowed a tense September 6 plenary session to turn into a brawl that sent several delegates to the hospital. One prominent minister, the Reverend A. G. Wright of Detroit, suffered a fractured skull and a brain hemorrhage, and when Wright died two days later King and the entire nonviolent movement shared the shame and embarrassment.[6]

As damaging as Wright's death was for the overall image of the movement, CORE had even more pressing concerns to address. On Tuesday, the day before the brawl in Kansas City, two white Freedom Riders, Elizabeth Adler and Peter Ackerberg, elected to go ahead with their appeals. Convicted and released on a fifteen-hundred-dollar bond, they were joined on Wednesday morning by the Minnesota Freedom Rider Zev Aelony, who became the fifth defendant to go to trial. Coming on the heels of Farmer's press conference, the three appeals called CORE's influence into question. To add to the confusion, the defendant scheduled for trial on Wednesday afternoon—Alex Anderson, a thirty-three-year-old black Methodist minister from Nashville—tried to withdraw his appeal at the last minute but was told he could not do so. Sustaining an objection by Jack Travis, Judge Moore ruled that Mississippi law did not allow for the withdrawal of an appeal following arraignment. A defendant could change his plea, Moore later advised, but dropping the appeal altogether was not an option. Although Jack Young pointed out that several defendants had already done so, Moore refused to alter his interpretation of state law.

Shocked by this sudden turn of events, Young soon turned to the only viable option left open to him—counseling his clients to plead *nolo contendere*. On Friday, Frank Ashford, a twenty-two-year-old black student from Chicago, became the first Freedom Rider to enter such a plea, and Judge Moore responded by assessing a two-hundred-dollar fine and a four-month suspended sentence. Later in the day, Tom Armstrong, a nineteen-year-old Tougaloo student, adopted a different strategy and entered a not guilty plea, but after he was convicted by the jury, Moore pronounced a punitive sentence, including release on a fifteen-hundred-dollar bond. This sent a clear signal to financially strapped CORE officials, who advised Young and other movement attorneys to encourage their clients to follow Ashford's lead. Although worthless as a basis for appeal to a higher court, a mass of no contest pleas would save CORE and the Freedom Riders a great deal of money over the coming weeks.[7]

While CORE leaders were mulling over their limited options, the struggle over voting rights in Pike and surrounding counties took a new turn. On Thursday, the day after Judge Moore's ruling, John Hardy's attempt to register two black voters at the Walthall County courthouse in Tylertown led to a beating at the hands of the county registrar, John Wood. Accompanied by MacArthur Cotton, a Tougaloo student who had been helping him run a voter registration school for Walthall's black farmers, Hardy stood quietly outside Wood's office until it became clear that neither of the applicants would be allowed to register. After inquiring about the situation, the Nashville SNCC activist caught the full fury of Wood's ire. "What right do you have coming down here messing in these people's business? Why don't you go back where you came from?" the registrar asked, before pulling a pistol out of a drawer and pointing it at Hardy. Frightened, Hardy turned to leave but was struck on the back of the head with the pistol butt before he could get out the door. Staggering into the street, he soon encountered Sheriff Ed Kraft, who all but laughed at his request that the registrar be arrested for assault. Instead, Sheriff Kraft hauled Hardy off to the Tylertown jail, charging him with resisting arrest and inciting a riot. After several hours of interrogation by local prosecuting attorneys, Hardy was told that he was being transferred to the Magnolia jail for his "own protection"; and by nine o'clock that evening he found himself in the same cell block that had housed Bob Moses three weeks earlier.

After Hardy was released on bond the next morning, Moses phoned John Doar to see if the Justice Department was willing to follow through with the promise to protect the rights of voter registration activists. Following his call to Doar from the Magnolia jail in mid-August, Moses had sensed that the man who witnessed the attack on the Freedom Riders in Montgomery was a cut above the normal Justice Department bureaucrat, but he was still surprised when Doar actually dispatched two staff attorneys to Mississippi to investigate Hardy's confrontation with John Wood. Even more surprising was the Justice Department's effort to block Hardy's prosecution by Mississippi authorities. With Burke Marshall's approval, Doar sought a temporary restraining order that would delay a scheduled September 22 trial. Citing a provision of the 1957 Civil Rights Act prohibiting intimidation of voters on racial grounds, Justice Department attorneys pleaded their case before District Judge Cox but came away with nothing but a judicial scolding from the segregationist stalwart. Undaunted, Doar immediately flew to Montgomery to make a personal appeal to Circuit Judge Richard Rives, who agreed to convene a three-judge Fifth Circuit Court of Appeals panel. When the panel met in Montgomery later in the month, Marshall himself argued the government's case in *U.S. v. Wood*, and by a vote of two to one the court granted his request to overrule Cox, setting an important legal precedent for federal intervention in voting rights cases.

Although Marshall's successful appeal to the Fifth Circuit was good news for Hardy, Justice Department leaders had no intention of asserting such authority when issues other than voting rights were involved. Within the Civil Rights Division, there was considerable sympathy and growing admiration for the Freedom Riders and other student activists challenging the status quo in the Deep South, but in the political context of 1961 these sentiments did not lead to broad-based or sustained legal intervention. Beginning with the first arrests in Jackson in late May, the intimidation of Freedom Riders by state and local officials had drawn little public comment from federal officials. And, despite the civil rights rhetoric that animated the attorney general's ICC petition, there was no indication that the events of the late summer had altered the administration's essentially neutral position on the prosecution of nonviolent dissenters. Detecting little or no political pressure to intervene on behalf of the Freedom Riders and judging public opinion to be sharply divided on the issue, administration leaders from the president on down were unwilling to undertake risky or radical initiatives that might endanger existing political arrangements.[8]

Aside from a few maverick politicians and left-leaning commentators, those who spoke out most forcefully for the right to agitate were either the Freedom Riders themselves, student activists on college campuses, or liberal religious leaders. During the late summer and early fall of 1961, recent veterans of the Freedom Rides delivered lectures and testimonials at scores of churches and colleges across the nation. Virtually all of the original CORE Riders participated in this makeshift speakers bureau, and Ed Blankenheim, Hank Thomas, and Ben Cox—all of whom had joined the CORE staff— were especially active as recruiters and fund-raisers. Almost all of this activity took place in carefully selected venues where a sympathetic audience was guaranteed, namely college lecture halls and chapels. While the vast majority of students and faculty at predominantly white institutions Sremained too conservative to embrace the Freedom Rides, movement lecturers attracted significant attention and support on campuses from Cornell to UCLA. Even in the South there were signs that at least some white students harbored sympathy for the Riders. One notable expression of support surfaced on September 8, when several dozen students gathered at the Tennessee state capitol in Nashville to protest the expulsion of fourteen Freedom Riders from Tennessee State. While an interracial group of twenty-five picketed outside the capitol, eleven others, including John Lewis, formed a double line in front of Governor Buford Ellington's office. Although Ellington managed to scurry out a side door without confronting the protesters, the boldness of the students' action did not go unnoticed in a nation unaccustomed to such assertive behavior. The sit-ins and the Freedom Rides had involved private businesses and a few public terminals, but now the student invasion had spread to a seat of state government.[9]

Most of the students involved in the Tennessee capitol protest were black, and much of the student movement resided on black campuses in the South.

John Lewis (second from right) and other student activists stand at the entrance to Tennessee governor Buford Ellington's office to protest the expulsion of fourteen Tennessee State University Freedom Riders, September 8, 1961. (Courtesy of *Nashville Tennessean*)

As Martin Luther King pointed out in a timely essay published in the *New York Times Magazine* on September 10, the new contrasting symbols of the civil rights struggle were the black student activist—"college-bred, Ivy League-clad, youthful, articulate and resolute"—and the segregationist "hoodlum stomping the bleeding face of a Freedom Rider." Quoting the novelist Victor Hugo's assertion that "there is no greater power on earth than an idea whose time has come," King credited the black student vanguard with delivering the message that "the time for freedom for the Negro has come." "The young Negro is not in revolt, as some have suggested, against a single pattern of timid, fumbling, conservative leadership," King insisted. "Nor is his conduct to be explained in terms of youth's excesses. He is carrying forward a revolutionary destiny of a whole people consciously and deliberately. Hence the extraordinary willingness to fill the jails as if they were honors classes and the boldness to absorb brutality, even to the point of death, and remain nonviolent." While acknowledging that "not long ago the Negro collegian imitated the white collegian," he proclaimed: "Today the imitation has ceased. The Negro collegian now initiates. Groping for unique forms of protest, he created the sit-ins and Freedom Rides. Overnight his white fellow students began to imitate him."

Such claims were more than enough to set most American parents on edge, but King went on to expose the international roots of student activism. "Many of the students, when pressed to express their inner feelings, identify themselves with students in Africa, Asia, and South America," he reported. "The liberation struggle in Africa has been the greatest single international influence on American Negro students. Frequently I hear them say that if their African brothers can break the bonds of colonialism, surely the American Negro can break Jim Crow." The students, King warned, were "not after 'mere tokens' of integration." "Theirs is a revolt against the whole system of Jim Crow," he declared, "and they are prepared to sit-in, kneel-in, wade-in and stand-in until every waiting room, rest room, theatre and other facility throughout the nation that is supposedly open to the public is in fact open to Negroes, Mexicans, Indians, Jews or what-have-you. Theirs is a total commitment to this goal of equality and dignity. And for this achievement they are prepared to pay the costs—whatever they are—in suffering and hardship as long as may be necessary."

King expressed the hope that the students' spirit of commitment and sacrifice would soon spread to other segments of the American population. "These students are not struggling for themselves alone," he reminded his readers. "They are seeking to save the soul of America. They are taking our whole nation back to those great wells of democracy which were dug deep by the Founding Fathers in the formulation of the Constitution and the Declaration of Independence. In sitting down at the lunch counters, they are in reality standing up for the best in the American dream." Predicting that "one day historians will record this student movement as one of the most significant epics of our heritage," he asked plaintively if it made any sense for the rest of the nation to "sit by as spectators when the social unrest seethes." Since "most of us recognize that the Jim Crow system is doomed . . . ," he reasoned, "would it not be the wise and human thing to abolish the system surely and swiftly? This would not be difficult, if our national Government would exercise its full powers to enforce Federal laws and court decisions and do so on a scale commensurate with the problems and with an unmistakable decisiveness." [10]

DESIGNED TO PRICK THE CONSCIENCE of the American intellectual and political elite, King's essay appeared at a critical moment in the Freedom Rider saga. Despite the essay's declarative title—"The Time for Freedom Has Come"—in reality the timing of freedom's arrival in the Jim Crow South was still very much in doubt. To bring the Freedom Rides to a successful and timely conclusion, movement leaders would need every influential ally they could muster, especially in the legal arena. On Monday, September 11, the arraignment of seventy-eight additional Freedom Rider defendants in Jackson intensified the legal and financial pressure bearing down on CORE. After each defendant pleaded not guilty, the Hinds County court scheduled appellate trials for the spring of 1962, ensuring that the legal struggle in Mississippi would continue for at least nine more months. The movement's prospects for a quick legal victory were no more promising in Alabama, where white officials announced on Tuesday that the U.S. Fifth Circuit Court of Appeals had upheld Judge Frank Johnson's ruling that William Sloane Coffin, Wyatt Tee Walker, Fred Shuttlesworth, Ralph Abernathy, and six other Freedom Riders must stand trial on the breach-of-peace charges filed on May 25. This and other recent developments drew cheers that evening at a raucous White Citizens' Council rally in Montgomery. As more than 800 WCC members looked on, the special guest speaker, Governor Ross Barnett, reported that the "ruthless actions" of the Freedom Riders, the NAACP, and meddlers such as Chief Justice Earl Warren had backfired. Outside agitators were on the run, Barnett declared, and even in the North the integrationist cause was losing ground. Back in Jackson, according to the governor, the Freedom Riders were finally learning the full meaning of Mississippi justice.[11]

On Wednesday morning Barnett's words took on added weight when Jim Bevel went on trial for contributing to the delinquency of a minor. Charged with enticing four local high school students to demonstrate in support of the Freedom Rides, Bevel refused Judge Russel Moore's offer of a light sentence in exchange for a no-contest plea. Acting as his own counsel, the twenty-four-year-old minister was eloquent in defending the young students' right to bear witness against the evil of Jim Crow, but not even Bevel, the most mystical of the Nashville Freedom Riders, could make any headway against the flow of racial tradition. Following a swift conviction, Moore issued the maximum sentence of two thousand dollars in fines and six months in jail. Bevel, who for the time being chose not to appeal, was behind bars by early afternoon. And he was not alone. Earlier in the day, while Bevel was standing trial, the Jackson police had arrested fifteen new Freedom Riders at the Trailways terminal.[12]

All of those arrested—twelve whites and three blacks—were Episcopal priests affiliated with the Episcopal Society for Cultural and Racial Unity, an Atlanta-based group of racially liberal clergymen and lay leaders. Led by the Reverend John B. Morris of Atlanta, they were part of a twenty-eight-member "prayer pilgrimage" that had originated in New Orleans on Tuesday. Traveling to Jackson via Vicksburg by chartered bus, all twenty-eight spent Tuesday night at Tougaloo College, to the consternation of the Reverend John Allin, the bishop of the Mississippi Episcopal Diocese. Informed that the pilgrims were headed for Detroit, where the sixtieth General Convention of the Episcopal Church was scheduled to open on Thursday, Allin urged them to move on in "a quiet and orderly manner" without disrupting the social peace of Mississippi. While he saw "no value" in the strategy of nonviolent resistance, fifteen of the priests felt otherwise. Piling into three black taxicabs, the interracial band of brothers rode to the Trailways terminal with the intention of desegregating the white waiting room. Intercepted by Captain Ray and two other policemen, the priests became the thirty-seventh group of Freedom Riders arrested in Jackson. Since six weeks had passed since the last round of arrests on July 31, the priests' arrival at the city jail caused quite a stir, especially after the police and the press discovered that one of the arrested Freedom Riders was Robert L. Pierson, the thirty-five-year-old son-in-law of Nelson Rockefeller, the liberal Republican governor of New York.

While Pierson and his colleagues were being processed at the jail, the other participants in the pilgrimage sent a telegram to Robert Kennedy. "In view of your request to American clergymen to exert leadership in these areas," the message read, "we urge you immediately to apply your influence to resolve problems of interstate travel for Americans." The clergymen also "called upon the nation to say special prayers for their fifteen colleagues and the cause of integration daily at 7 a.m., noon, and 7 p.m." Speaking for the entire group, the Reverend Malcolm Boyd, an Episcopal chaplain at Wayne State University in Detroit, vowed that the pilgrimage would continue; and on Thursday he and five other priests made good on the promise by traveling to Sewanee, Tennessee, home of the partially desegregated University of the South. While the Episcopal seminary at the University was racially integrated, the staunchly traditional undergraduate student body remained all white. Encouraged by the interracialism of the nearby Highlander Folk School, local seminarians had been pressing for a full desegregation of the campus for several years, but university and church officials had refused to confront the issue, including a strict color bar at a popular on-campus restaurant leased to a local segregationist. As soon as Boyd and the other pilgrims arrived on campus and discovered that the restaurant remained segregated, he announced plans for a sit-in and a hunger strike. By Friday morning, however, Boyd had received assurances from church and campus officials that all of the university's facilities would be desegregated in the near future. After the presiding Episcopal bishop of the United States, the Right Reverend Arthur C. Lichtenberger, issued a strong public statement endorsing the prayer pilgrimage and condemning racial discrimination, Boyd and his colleagues canceled the planned protests and departed for the convention in Detroit.

Several other Episcopal leaders—including the bishop of Rhode Island, who wired five hundred dollars of bail money to one of the jailed priests— spoke out in defense of the prayer pilgrimage. But such support had no discernible effect on the situation in Jackson. On Friday, after two nights in jail, the fifteen defendants went on trial in the municipal court of Judge James Spencer. A lifelong Episcopalian, Spencer felt an obligation to scold the wayward priests on religious as well as legal grounds. Unmoved by Carl Rachlin's impassioned defense of the priests' actions, Spencer explained his special responsibility to discipline the defendants. "As a judge of Episcopal faith," he declared, "I find my position especially grievous and as I read the articles of religion of my faith and what I reasoned to be their faith, I find in Article 37 . . . the short paragraph which says—'and we hold it to be the duty of all men who are professors of the Gospel to pay respectful obedience to the civil authority.' I find my duty clear as a judge. I believe these definitely have violated the laws of the State of Mississippi as well as those of the Episcopal law of the articles of religion as I read them." Accordingly, he sentenced each defendant to a two-hundred-dollar fine and four months in jail.

The next morning the press reported that the fifteen clergymen were back in the city jail praying "for the segregationists whose policies had led to their imprisonment." In Detroit, where the national Episcopal convention was still in session, and in many other Northern cities, there were signs of sympathy for the jailed priests. Locally, any feelings of remorse were tempered by a wire service story detailing a pretrial conversation between Mayor Allen Thompson and the Reverend Lee Belford of New York. According to Thompson, Belford told him that the prayer pilgrimage "would have been worth it" even if it had led to violence. "Our church has a history of martyrdom," Belford proudly explained.[13]

The wide philosophical gulf between white Christian segregationists and social gospel activists such as Belford became increasingly clear in the fall of 1961, as segregationist officials demonstrated their willingness to mete out harsh punishment to clergymen who violated the South's racial mores. On September 15, the same day that the fifteen priests faced Judge Spencer in Jackson, the Reverend William Sloane Coffin and nine other ministerial Freedom Riders charged with breaching the peace were assessed hundred-dollar fines and sentenced to jail terms ranging from ten to fifteen days by Montgomery County Judge Alex Marks. The two local defendants, Ralph Abernathy and Bernard Lee, received ten-day sentences, but all the others, including Shuttlesworth, received fifteen days. An eleventh defendant, Wyatt Tee Walker, was actually acquitted on the breach-of-peace charge, but conviction on a related charge of unlawful assembly resulted in a ninety-day sentence. Explaining the severity of Walker's sentence, Judge Marks reasoned that the SCLC executive director's role as a liaison to the press made him especially dangerous. "There would have been very little trouble in Montgomery if there hadn't been so much publicity," Marks insisted. All of the defendants, including Walker, filed immediate appeals and accepted bail, but as they left the courthouse they could not help wondering how far Alabama officials were willing to go in their effort to ensnare the movement in a tangle of legal prosecutions.[14]

For Shuttlesworth, who had faced the hard edge of the Alabama legal system more times than he could count, the question was particularly troubling. A year earlier almost to the day, W. W. Rayburn, a juvenile court judge in Gadsden, had placed Shuttlesworth's three teenaged children—Patricia, Ricky, and Fred Jr.—on indefinite probation after they occupied the front seats on a Greyhound bus traveling from Chattanooga to Birmingham. Returning from an interracial nonviolence workshop at Highlander, they tried to act out the principles that they had learned but were thwarted by a vigilant bus driver and a police officer who later claimed that he arrested them "for their own protection." After hearing someone in a crowd outside the bus yell, "Get those damned niggers off the bus, or we'll throw them off!" the officer carted the children off to jail, where they encountered more threats from their guards. By the time Shuttlesworth arrived to retrieve his children, Fred Jr. had been roughed up by a guard who put him in a choke hold, and all three had been warned that their "cotton-pickin' nigger" father was unwelcome in Gadsden. After several hours of tense negotiation, Shuttlesworth managed to free his children, and three days later Judge Rayburn put them on probation. But the mean-spirited prosecution in Gadsden elicited cries of outrage from the NAACP and SCLC, both of which called for a Justice Department investigation. When the brief FBI investigation that followed went nowhere, Shuttlesworth filed a $9 million damage suit in federal court alleging that the Southeastern Greyhound driver had provoked an incident leading to false arrest and imprisonment. Originally filed in Atlanta, the suit was eventually transferred to the U.S. District Court in Birmingham, where it was still pending in September 1961.[15]

Shuttlesworth's effort to extract justice from the federal courts suggested a measure of faith in American democracy. For more than a decade the Birmingham minister had served as a model of assertive citizenship—a black man undeterred by bombs, beatings, and legal harassment. Encouraged by the *Brown* decision and the promise of a Second Reconstruction, he preached and practiced a gospel of rising expectations for black Americans. During the first eight months of the Kennedy presidency, the expansive rhetoric of the

"New Frontier" boosted such expectations, and Shuttlesworth stepped up his demands for a realization of democratic ideals. Nevertheless, as the summer of the Freedom Rides came to a close, he and other movement leaders began to wonder if the new administration was capable of taking an unequivocal stand on matters of racial justice. Repeating the same pattern of mixed signals that had delayed the implementation of school desegregation during the Eisenhower years, the administration had adopted a policy of temporization that unintentionally sustained white supremacist resistance to social change. Indeed, by mid-September some segregationist leaders were declaring victory in the war against the Freedom Riders.

On Monday, September 18, the *Jackson Daily News* smugly trumpeted that local and state officials had rejected a desperate overture from CORE, which had "offered to halt their Freedom Rider program into Jackson" if Mississippi authorities agreed to withhold further prosecutions and let 250 pending appeal cases be adjudicated by the circuit and state supreme court justices. Quoting a weekend television interview with Mayor Allen Thompson, the *Daily News* reported that Jackson officials did not intend "to yield one inch in prosecuting those who violate our local laws." "There will be no letup in a single case," Thompson declared, "nor will we permit any other type of disturbance here which violates our laws. We feel we have completely broken the Freedom Rider movement here." The threat to the Mississippi way of life had been turned back, he insisted, adding: "If anything, things have improved in Jackson since the advent of the first Freedom Rider group here four months ago." Mississippians were allegedly more convinced than ever that "our way of life here is best for us, and for the most part, no one pays any attention to them anymore since our splendid police department is handling the situation."[16]

Thompson's growing confidence rested on a sanguine but credible assessment of the situation. On the surface, at least, the Freedom Riders' prospects appeared to be declining on all fronts, from public opinion and politics to legal decisions and the financial condition of the movement. For several weeks the American public had been preoccupied with the home-run race between two New York Yankees sluggers, Mickey Mantle and Roger Maris. The pursuit of Babe Ruth's record of sixty home runs, set in 1927, had eclipsed all other stories, including the pursuit of freedom in Mississippi and Alabama. However, on Tuesday evening, September 19, some Americans were momentarily distracted by two remarkable television documentaries. Shown on the NBC network as part of its White Paper series, *Angola: Road to War* profiled the "indescribable brutality, hate and suffering that have accompanied the revolt against Portuguese colonial rule in Angola." The second documentary, entitled *Walk in My Shoes*, aired on the rival ABC network, though many Southern affiliates refused to broadcast the program. Billed as an exploration of black America "told purposely from the standpoint of the Negro" and co-produced by the black journalist Louis Lomax, the program included an interview with Percy Sutton, the black New York lawyer arrested in Jackson, along with New York state representative Mark Lane, on June 8. In a moving sequence, Sutton explained the guilt that he had felt after not joining the early Freedom Rides, the feelings of both fear and satisfaction that he later experienced as a Freedom Rider, and the sense of triumph and liberation that came over him after "being served orange juice at a 'white' counter in Alabama." After hearing Sutton's testimonial and other "chant[s] of freedom" featured in the two programs, one New York television critic reminded his readers that freedom's "insistency transcends geography." "Its denial," he insisted, "is the West's major shame."

How other Americans responded to the documentaries' "searing indictment" of racial oppression and exploitation was unclear, but the paucity of similar broadcasts in the following months suggests that the networks received little encouragement from the viewing public. As Thompson and others detected, the dominant attitudes among white Americans reflected complacency and a visceral distrust of radical reform. Even among liberals there was a strong preference for gradualism and a hesitance to embrace confrontational activism. Despite all that had happened during the past four months, there was no groundswell of public support for the Freedom Rides; indeed, the popular basis for altering long-standing political arrangements and legal traditions seemed to be slipping away. Most obviously, the legal strategy had revealed the movement's financial vulnerability. When all but two of the "prayer pilgrimage" defendants filed appeal bonds and flew to Detroit on September 19, the Jackson press explained that high-ranking Episcopalians had come up with the bail money, the implication being that this was a special case. Run-of-the-mill Freedom Riders who depended on CORE for financial resources were presumably much more vulnerable to economic pressure.[17]

The common assumption that CORE stood on the verge of financial collapse by mid-September was understandable, but the organization's actual financial condition was less grave than Thompson and many other white Mississippians believed. Although Marvin Rich's effort to find a bail-bond company willing to underwrite CORE's growing obligations proved futile (one Connecticut company agreed to advance the bond money but withdrew the offer the next day when Mississippi officials threatened to cancel its license to do business in the state), Jim Farmer found an unlikely angel at the NAACP Legal Defense and Educational Fund, Inc., commonly known as the "Inc. (or Ink) Fund." Despite his strong misgivings about the wisdom of the Freedom Rides, Thurgood Marshall, who would soon leave his position as head of the fund to take a seat on the U.S. Second Circuit Court of Appeals, magnanimously offered to step into the breach. "What the hell!" he told Farmer, after learning of CORE's plight. "The Ink Fund has about $300,000 in bail-bond money. It's not doing anything but sitting there. You might as well use it as long as it lasts."

Stunned by Marshall's offer, Farmer "could hardly wait" to relay the good news to his CORE colleagues. But at a staff meeting the next morning he was surprised to discover that Rich was reluctant to accept the money. The fear that there would be strings attached to the loan and the suspicion that Marshall's organization planned to take partial credit for the Freedom Rides made Rich more than a little uncomfortable. Indeed, in light of the public criticism of the Rides by Marshall, Wilkins, and other national NAACP leaders, he found the offer galling, if not insulting. Earlier in the summer, one NAACP leader had jibed to reporters that "CORE gets people in jail and we have to get them out," but now for some reason the Inc. Fund was willing to put itself in financial jeopardy to save CORE. Rich smelled a rat. Farmer himself was mindful of the danger of becoming a junior partner to an organization that did not share CORE's commitment to direct action. But, having run out of viable alternatives, he waved off Rich's objections and accepted Marshall's offer.

Whatever Marshall's motivations, acceptance of the offer was, as Rich predicted, only a prelude to even greater Inc. Fund involvement in the Freedom Rider campaign. Following several weeks of discussion and negotiation between Farmer and Marshall, CORE's policy-making body, the National Action Committee, agreed to let the Inc. Fund take over the responsibility of representing the Mississippi Freedom Riders in court. By the end of November the transfer of responsibility was complete, lessening CORE's legal and financial burden but confirming the widespread suspicion among white Southerners that the NAACP had been masterminding the Freedom Rides all along.[18]

Even with this infusion of funds, CORE faced a difficult road ahead. The only real solution to the organization's financial and legal problems was federal intervention on a massive scale, and the probability of such intervention was still in doubt as the summer of 1961 came to an official end on September 22. More than a month had passed since the members of ICC had listened to the oral arguments for and against Attorney General Kennedy's desegregation petition, and it had been almost four months since the filing of the petition itself. "The time has come for this commission to declare unequivocally by regulation," Kennedy had declared on May 29, "that a Negro passenger is free to travel the length and breadth of this country in the same manner as any other passenger." But time, it seemed, was marching on with no unequivocal resolution in sight. Growing increasingly impatient, CORE leaders in New York, as well as SNCC activists in Nashville, began to look for some means of forcing the ICC to issue a favorable ruling. In early September tentative plans for a mass demonstration known as the "Washington Project" took shape. Patterned after A. Philip Randolph's planned 1941 March on Washington, the project would bring hundreds, perhaps even thousands, of nonviolent demonstrators to the capital city to apply pressure on the ICC and the Kennedy administration. The exact date of the march was yet to be determined, and movement leaders were still working out the logistical details as the summer drew to a close. But among the members of the FRCC there was general agreement that situation required a "spectacular" demonstration of nonviolent commitment and solidarity. As Farmer declared in a September 5 press release, the Washington project would transfer "the struggle for dignity on the nation's highways from the courts to the conscience of America."[19]

WHETHER THE FINANCIALLY STRAPPED nonviolent movement could have pulled off a march of this magnitude in the fall of 1961 remains an open question. The proposed demonstration that seemed so critical as late as September 21 became moot a day later when the eleven commissioners of the ICC issued a unanimous ruling prohibiting racial discrimination in interstate bus transit. Endorsing virtually every point in the attorney general's petition, the commission announced that, beginning on November 1, 1961, all interstate buses would be required to display a certificate that read: "Seating aboard this vehicle is without regard to race, color, creed, or national origin, by order of the Interstate Commerce Commission." Displaying the signs would be mandatory until January 1, 1963, but the commission reserved the right to extend the requirement indefinitely. Beginning in 1963, federal law would require the same text to be printed on all bus tickets "sold for transportation in interstate or foreign commerce." This provision, which made an allowance for the thousands of tickets already printed, was the only delay granted by the commission. As of November 1, all terminals serving interstate buses would be required to post and abide by the new ICC regulations. Interstate carriers were forbidden to use racially segregated terminal facilities, which, according to the commissioners, were still common "in a substantial part of the United States." "In many motor passenger terminals," they reported, with a suggestion of feigned surprise, "Negro interstate passengers are compelled to use eating, rest room and other facilities which are segregated."

In an important point of clarification that raised more than a few eyebrows in movement circles, the commissioners indicated that their desegregation order "would not be applicable . . . to every independently operated roadside restaurant at which a bus stops solely to pick up or discharge passengers, or to every independently operated corner drug store which sells tickets for a motor carrier. Where a carrier's ticket agent does nothing more for the benefit of the carrier's passengers than sell tickets and post schedules, we would not consider his place of business to be a terminal facility." However, the commissioners made it clear that the new rules applied to any ticket agent who "offers or provides facilities for the comfort and convenience of passengers, such as a public waiting room, rest room, or eating facilities." The ICC order also required bus operators to report any attempts to interfere with the new regulations and provided fines of up to five hundred dollars for each violation. The obligation to report interference within fifteen days of an incident pertained to governmental as well as individual violators, a provision that would prove crucial to enforcement in the months to come.[20]

The ICC ruling applied only to interstate bus transportation and did not extend to air or train travel, but within these limitations the commissioners had gone about as far anyone in the Kennedy administration could have reasonably expected. William Tucker, the Kennedy appointee to the commission, had consulted with Burke Marshall and other Justice Department officials throughout the deliberations, and those same officials had encouraged Tucker to press for a sweeping ruling that would resolve the Freedom Rider crisis and ensure meaningful desegregation. Still, until the ruling was actually announced there was concern within the Administration that the conservative bent of the other commissioners would foil Tucker's efforts. Since anything short of a complete endorsement of the attorney general's petition would have sustained or even exacerbated the conflict over bus segregation, Marshall and his colleagues regarded the ruling as a major accomplishment.

"This was a much more imaginative and controversial step than the commission was used to taking," Marshall insisted in a 1964 interview. "And it was our judgment, my judgment, after we heard the oral argument that there was a good chance the commission wouldn't issue any rules, or that if it did issue rules they would cut way back and they wouldn't be effective and the commission wouldn't deal with the problem. . . . I think on the whole it was really rather incredible for anyone that had experience with the commission that the commission came out unanimously with the rules suggested by the Department of Justice." As Marshall conceded, part of the explanation for the commission's surprising display of leadership rested in the administration's behind-the-scenes efforts—both formal and informal—to nudge the commissioners toward a forthright advocacy of desegregation. A political promise to one commissioner interested in a federal court appointment and the assurances given to others concerned about reappointment were an important part of the story, even though such considerations remained hidden from public view.[21]

Whatever its origins, the ICC ruling drew considerable praise from the national press. Even editors who had expressed serious misgivings about the Freedom Rides hailed the ruling as a legal and administrative milestone. Although many expressed surprise at the scope of the ruling, outside of the South there was a strong current of editorial support for the commission's advanced position. Almost everyone credited the attorney general with precipitating the ruling, but there was also widespread recognition that the Freedom Rides had been a crucial factor in both the timing and character of the ICC's deliberations. "Much of the credit for overcoming the inertia and political resistance that hamstrung the I.C.C. before on this issue must obviously go to the Freedom Rider movement of last spring," a *New York Times* editorial declared two days after the ruling. "Though, as we argued at the time, the movement raised dangers when it continued beyond the realization of its point of focusing attention on the need for integrated interstate bus transportation, nevertheless that demonstration started the chain of events which resulted in the new I.C.C. order."

The notion that the Freedom Rides had catalyzed the ruling was even stronger among white Southern editors, the vast majority of whom rejected the rationale for the commission's newfound activism. Repeating the pattern established in the mid-1950s following the *Brown* decision, many segregationist editors tried to downplay the significance of the ruling. Some made passing references to a minor adjustment in administrative policy, and others ignored the ruling altogether. But, other than the expected expressions of outrage by Citizens' Council stalwarts, there were few calls for outright defiance or massive resistance.

Among the more thoughtful segregationists, this restraint reflected a spirit of resignation, a sense that desegregation was inevitable. For many others, however, an entirely different set of expectations was at work. To most white Southerners, the ICC ruling appeared to be just another unenforceable edict. In May 1955 the Supreme Court had ordered the implementation of school desegregation "with all deliberate speed," yet six years later all but a handful of Southern schools remained segregated. In November 1955 the ICC had ordered the desegregation of interstate railway travel, yet racial segregation was still the general rule on Southern trains in 1961. Perhaps this time it would be different, but historical experience suggested that there was no reason for segregationists to panic.

Such skepticism was also prevalent among black Americans. In the black press, as in the broader black community, past disappointments tempered the response to the ICC ruling. Virtually all of the editorials and public statements praising the ruling included a word or two of warning. The true value of the ruling, black editors and civil rights leaders pointed out, depended on the degree of enforcement—a condition that would only be revealed in the weeks and months following implementation on November 1. Every major civil rights organization, from CORE to the NAACP, sent telegrams of congratulation to the Justice Department, but in private conversations, and in some cases in press releases, these same organizations expressed concerns about the likelihood of effective enforcement. Farmer went even further, reminding the attorney general that, in and of itself, the ICC ruling did not solve the legal problems of the Freedom Riders convicted in Jackson. Although Farmer promised that "no additional riders would be recruited and sent to Mississippi," he informed Kennedy that "those already in jail would continue serving their forty days." Beginning on November 1, Farmer added, CORE "would send out interracial teams to crisscross the South and test the enforcement of the order." If enforcement proved lacking or haphazard, he warned, the Freedom Rides "would resume immediately."[22]

The ICC ruling had an immediate impact on the Freedom Rider movement. Suspending the preparations for the Washington Project, movement leaders began to plan a new wave of Freedom Rides designed to test enforcement of the ruling. At the CORE office in New York and at the FRCC recruitment centers in the South, the next six weeks would be a time of feverish activity and hopeful speculation about the future. A decade after *Brown* and fourteen years after *Morgan v. Virginia*, a major federal agency other than the Justice Department had finally weighed in on the side of racial justice, mandating desegregation as something more than an unrealized ideal. Whether the rhetoric of equal treatment could be translated into something tangible remained to be seen. But this time, unlike the "with all deliberate speed" waffling of the 1955 *Brown* implementation decision, there was a firm date for compliance. Government officials had set a date for desegregation, and Farmer and other movement leaders were determined to hold them to it.[23]

The prospects for enforcement depended upon a number of unknowns, including the level of commitment at the Justice Department, the response of local and state officials, and the willingness of white Southerners to obey federal law and to eschew violence. The last of these was perhaps the most difficult to predict, but the initial signs following the ruling were not encouraging, at least as far as John Doar was concerned. Just hours before the announcement of the ICC decision, Doar arrived in Mississippi to conduct an investigation of the situation in Amite, Pike, and Walthall counties. For three days he roamed around McComb and Liberty, gauging both the status of the voting rights campaign and the mood of local white supremacists. By Sunday morning he was convinced that southwestern Mississippi was a racial time bomb that could explode at any time, but the seriousness of the situation did not become fully apparent until he met with E. W. Steptoe and Bob Moses at Steptoe's farm that afternoon. Shocked by the sight of Moses's unhealed wounds, Doar was even more troubled after listening to descriptions of the repeated threats of violence against SNCC voter registration activists. Several local black volunteers had also received threats, including Herbert Lee, a fifty-two-year-old father of nine who had helped to found the Amite branch of the NAACP. According to Steptoe, State Representative E. H. Hurst, Billy Jack Caston's father-in-law, had made threatening statements after learning that Lee had offered to drive Moses around the county. Alarmed, Doar asked to be driven over to Lee's farm. Although Lee was not at home when they got there, Doar, who was scheduled to return to Washington later in the day, urged Moses to do what he could to keep Lee out of harm's way.

Twelve hours later Moses received a chilling message from a black mortuary in McComb: A hearse from Amite County had just delivered an unidentified black corpse with a bullet wound above the left ear. Rushing over from his makeshift office at the Masonic Temple, Moses had his worst fears confirmed: The corpse was Herbert Lee. Earlier in the morning, Hurst had shot Lee after following the black farmer to a cotton gin on the outskirts of

Liberty. According to two eyewitnesses, one black and one white, Lee lunged at Hurst with a tire iron forcing Hurst to fire his gun in self-defense. On Tuesday, the day after the incident, a coroner's jury ruled that the white legislator's response was justifiable homicide. Moses suspected otherwise and soon found three black witnesses who confirmed that Hurst had committed cold-blooded murder. One of Moses's informants was Louis Allen, a forty-three-year-old timber worker who had been forced to corroborate Hurst's story in front of the coroner's jury. Although he was afraid to say so publicly, Allen told Moses that prior to the shooting Lee had tried to reason with Hurst, asking him to put down his gun. Angered by Lee's insolence, Hurst screamed, "I'm not playing with you this morning!" and fired a fatal shot at Lee's head. According to Allen and the other black witnesses, Hurst was the aggressor throughout, and the tire iron found at the scene was put there just prior to the arrival of the sheriff. A close friend of Hurst's and a cousin of Caston's, the sheriff unhesitatingly accepted Hurst's story and made sure that the local press reported the incident as "the routine dispatch of a crazed Negro."

After Moses relayed all of this to Washington by phone, Doar ordered the FBI to "examine Lee's body and photograph the wounds before burial." But Lee was in the ground by the time the assigned agent arrived in McComb. Hampered by the absence of a physical report on the remains, Doar reluctantly postponed the investigation until a federal grand jury could be convened sometime in October. In the meantime, he promised Moses, the federal government would continue to push for meaningful desegregation and the protection of constitutional rights. With the implementation of the ICC order looming, such promises were more credible than in the past, though the likelihood of real change still hinged on the government's ability to bring people like Hurst to justice. As both Doar and Moses knew all too well, the power and arrogance of Mississippi's white supremacists continued to dominate the state, and an all-encompassing cradle-to-grave racial segregation remained in force.[24]

The determination of state and local officials to maintain the status quo was on full display in a Jackson courtroom on the morning of Lee's death. After a fifteen-week delay, the NAACP's lawsuit challenging the legality of segregated public transportation in Mississippi finally gained a hearing from a three-judge federal panel headed by Circuit Judge Richard Rives of Montgomery. Flanked by two conservative Mississippi jurists, Sidney Mize of Gulfport and Claude Clayton of Tupelo, the liberal Rives made a valiant effort to give the NAACP suit a fair and proper hearing, but no amount of judicial decorum could dampen the tension and hostility that filled the courtroom. A close friend of Justice Hugo Black's, Rives was widely regarded as a traitor to the white South, and Mize and Clayton made no effort to conceal their disdain for his heretical views.

During the four-day hearing, NAACP attorney Constance Baker Motley presented a string of witnesses, including several bus and railway company representatives and NAACP field secretary Medgar Evers. All testified to the pervasiveness of segregated transit in Mississippi, and Evers described a harrowing personal incident that had taken place on a Trailways bus in Meridian in March 1958. Prior to the Jackson-bound bus's departure, Evers took a seat in the front section reserved for whites and refused the driver's order to move to the back. Removed from the bus by the Meridian police, Evers endured twenty minutes of interrogation before being allowed to return to his original seat. Though clearly disgusted with the police's decision to ignore Evers's defiance, the driver reluctantly put the bus in gear and headed toward Jackson. Moments later, however, the driver stopped to discuss the situation with a white taxicab driver who had followed the bus out of the terminal. "If you can't get him out, I can," the cabdriver vowed before entering the bus. After striking Evers in the face, he tried to drag the feisty field secretary into the aisle. Evers, a World War II combat veteran, fought back, forcing his stunned attacker to flee from the bus. With Evers still sitting in the front seat, the bus continued on to Jackson without any additional confrontations. Although Evers later reported the incident to NAACP officials in New York and to the ICC, neither the bus driver nor the cabdriver suffered any consequences other than the humiliation of being bested by a black man.[25]

Evers's testimony was disturbing to white supremacists on several counts, including the suggestions that native black Mississippians were dissatisfied with the present system of racial segregation and that even the police were sometimes uncertain about their authority to enforce Jim Crow laws. Even so, several witnesses for the state did their best to reassure the court that racial separation and social order were still synonymous in Mississippi. "It has been a policy of mine and the city council, the police department and the people," Mayor Allen Thompson of Jackson declared on Tuesday morning, "to maintain what has worked for the past 100 years to bring happiness, peace and prosperity. That has been to maintain a separation of the races—not segregation, we don't call it segregation—to maintain peace and order and to keep down disturbances. . . . Laws can come and laws can go and laws can change. But the policy we have adopted here has been to maintain happiness and contentment between the races and to live together in peace and quiet."

The notion that Mississippi's traditions fostered tranquility drew a strong objection from Motley, who countered with several witnesses who had been arrested or beaten for challenging Jim Crow transit. Noting that most of the incidents in question occurred outside of Jackson, Attorney General Joe Patterson and city attorneys reiterated an earlier objection to the statewide scope of the NAACP suit. Since the court had already ruled that the attorney general could not be held responsible for the breach-of-peace arrests in Jackson, Motley was in a difficult position, but she continued to press for an injunction that would invalidate segregated transit throughout the state. Later in the day Patterson himself took the stand to defend the state's and the city's response to the Freedom Riders' provocations. After commending Mississippi's citizenry for allowing "constitutional authority [to] deal with the matter rather than have incidents occur like those which did occur in Alabama," he expressed "amazement and surprise that the Attorney General of the United States seems to find himself on the side of those who would create these disorders and troubles rather than on the side of the State of Mississippi."[26]

On Wednesday morning Patterson renewed his attack on the federal government, objecting to a courtroom conversation between Motley and Justice Department attorney Howard Glickstein. After Rives ruled that the Justice Department had "entered the case as a friend of the court and the conference was not improper," Glickstein assured Patterson that he would "be happy to confer with any parties in this hearing." "We prefer to confer with friendly parties," Patterson shot back, prompting an admonition from Glickstein that "the Justice Department is friendly to anyone interested in justice." For Patterson and others interested in preserving segregation in Mississippi, Glickstein's mere presence was unnerving. Since the NAACP's class action suit extended to intrastate transit, the federal government's interest and involvement in the case was both surprising and potentially significant. Accordingly, defense attorneys for the city and state tried to refocus the court's attention on the Freedom Riders' role as interstate provocateurs. Three Alabama law enforcement officers—including Ell Cowling—testified as defense witnesses, recalling the violence in Anniston, Birmingham, and Montgomery. During cross-examination, Motley pointed out that "violence is no excuse for maintaining segregation" and urged the court to issue a sweeping injunction that addressed issues related to both intrastate and interstate transit. Before adjournment on Wednesday afternoon, her request received support from a surprising source.

Abandoning the strategy employed by the other defense attorneys, J. Will Young, the attorney for Jackson City Lines, pleaded for an immediate decision that would resolve the conflict between local and state ordinances and the impending ICC order. Describing the situation in Jackson as "explosive," Young predicted that, unless the court intervened, his company would be forced to cease operations within twenty-four hours. At issue was the legality of the posted signs designating separate seating areas for blacks and whites. According to Young, if local blacks challenged the color barrier on city buses en masse, as he expected they would, the company would have no choice but to halt all of its runs. After Patterson and Jackson city attorney Tom Watkins registered their opposition to an immediate decision, Judge Rives ruled that all parties would be given twenty days to file written briefs, a decision that pleased not only Patterson and Watkins but also Judge Mize. "Nobody has yet prosecuted anybody," Mize reminded Young, "and if you want to go and take the signs down that is your privilege."[27]

Following closing arguments on Thursday morning, the four-day hearing came to an end, though not without a measure of confusion. Catching almost everyone off guard, Judge Rives announced that he saw no need to wait twenty days before issuing a ruling on the NAACP's request for injunctive relief. Although a permanent injunction could only come after the filing of written briefs, he was ready to issue a preliminary injunction "removing segregation signs from all waiting rooms," prohibiting the arrest of Freedom Riders under breach-of-peace statutes, and directing the Jackson City Lines to cease enforcement of racial segregation on city buses. While he stopped short of advocating an injunction against Greyhound, Trailways, or Attorney General Patterson, Rives's announcement sent a shudder through the courtroom. Suddenly all eyes turned to Mize and Clayton, either one of whom could turn Rives's revolutionary proposal into a legal mandate. Those familiar with the two Mississippi jurists had no reason to believe that Rives's judgment would be sustained, but some segregationists were disappointed when Clayton refused to comment and Mize offered only a curt statement that he was "not prepared to express any opinion or give any views at this time."[28]

In the days following Rives's announcement, there was considerable speculation about the likelihood and implications of a preliminary injunction. In Nashville, where SCLC was wrapping up its annual three-day convention, even a slight chance that such an injunction might be granted was greeted as welcome news. Three days earlier, on the eve of the convention, Martin Luther King had hailed the ICC ruling as proof that the Freedom Riders' struggle "had not been in vain." The desegregation of buses and terminals was imminent, he insisted, and the nonviolent movement would soon move on to other challenges, including the goal of doubling the number of black voters in the South by the end of the year. "We are willing to suffer, sacrifice and die, if necessary, to make that freedom a reality," he declared, adding that the struggle for racial equality was actually a fight "to save the soul of the nation."

Sadly, by the time the convention opened on Wednesday, the shocking news of Herbert Lee's death had already tempered the optimism and euphoria of the day before. Over the next two days conflicting reports about the developing situations in Jackson and McComb only added to delegates' anxieties. On Wednesday evening, during the intermission of an SCLC benefit concert featuring Harry Belafonte, Miriam Makeba, and the Chad Mitchell Trio, the convention paid tribute to the Freedom Rides by awarding five-hundred-dollar scholarships to ten student Riders—including John Lewis, Jim Zwerg, and six of the students expelled from Tennessee A&I. But not even the beaming faces of the young Riders and the congratulatory rhetoric that washed over the crowd could disguise a growing apprehension about the future of the nonviolent movement.[29]

The mixed signals coming out of Mississippi complicated SCLC's plans for an expanded program of direct action. In a report delivered to the SCLC board just prior to the opening of the convention, executive director Wyatt Tee Walker proposed two major changes in organizational activity. The first proposal suggested that SCLC might be more effective as an organization made up of individual members, as opposed to its present status as a regional confederation of local groups. Avoiding direct competition with the NAACP had been SCLC policy since its founding in 1957, but Walker urged the board to reconsider its decision to forgo the financial and programmatic benefits of mass membership. The second proposal was to add a "Special Projects Director" to the SCLC staff, someone who could develop direct action into a "Southwide mass movement." The obvious choice for this position, according to Walker, was Jim Lawson, the architect of the Nashville Movement.

After King endorsed the proposal, the board authorized Walker to hire Lawson, who soon found himself explaining SCLC's new initiative to reporters. Although he and Walker had not yet had time to work out the details of the initiative, Lawson decided to provide the reporters with an expansive vision of SCLC's plans. Over the coming months, he declared, the organization planned to recruit a nonviolent army of ten thousand committed activists, each willing to put his or her body on the line, or in jail if need be. In the tradition of Gandhi's followers, SCLC's nonviolent soldiers would attack social injustice wherever they found it, including the darkest recesses of the Deep South. Until white Americans repudiated their attachment to racial privilege and discrimination, sit-ins, stand-ins, and other acts of nonviolent resistance would be an unavoidable fact of life. When asked to confirm Lawson's lofty prediction, Walker hedged, acknowledging that the goal of ten thousand activists would take several years to achieve. In the short run, he suggested, a cadre of 100 to 150 would suffice.

The disagreement over numbers reflected something more than a miscommunication between Lawson and Walker. The Tennessee preacher's conception of the SCLC project represented the most ambitious and idealistic version of nonviolent direct action. Unlike Walker and most other movement leaders, Lawson viewed nonviolence as an all-encompassing philosophy. For him the strategic objectives of legal and political leverage were less important than the search for the "beloved community." Sending several hundred Freedom Riders into Mississippi was an instructive exercise in nonviolent discipline and a means of forcing politicians to pay attention to the freedom struggle, but Lawson envisioned the nonviolent movement of the future on a much grander scale. Effecting a moral revolution in America would require the direct participation of thousands of activists and a deeper and broader experience with sacrifice and unmerited suffering. Nothing less than filling and refilling the jails over and over again and bringing the normal activities of the nation to a halt would do.

How the nation would respond to nonviolent activity of this magnitude was unclear, but many movement activists regarded Lawson's ambitious proposal as a formula for mass suicide, or at the very least as a strategic blunder that would reduce the movement's effectiveness. In private conversations with members of the SCLC board, Lawson himself expressed doubts about the current viability of mass direct action in the Deep South, especially in Mississippi. The murder of Herbert Lee and the general spirit of massive resistance among white Mississippians made him wonder if the state was ready for nonviolence on a mass scale. As committed as he was to the strategy of nonviolent confrontation, he did not want to squander the movement's resources in a premature effort that had little or no chance of success. Replicating the nonviolent workshops that had worked so well in Nashville required a degree of social space that many parts of Mississippi had yet to achieve. With this in mind, even Lawson began to shy away from an unhealthy emphasis on Mississippi.[30]

The intractable nature of white supremacy in Mississippi was also a major topic of discussion at a SNCC meeting held in Atlanta during the last weekend of September. The gathering in Atlanta was the first general meeting of SNCC leaders since the retreat at Highlander in mid-August, and the first since Ed King had stepped down as SNCC's executive secretary in mid-September. Virtually the entire coordinating committee, as SNCC's leaders loosely called themselves, was on hand, including a carload of weary activists from McComb. SNCC's chairman, Chuck McDew, decided to stay in McComb and skip the meeting, but Jim Forman, who had recently moved to Atlanta to fill in for the departing King, was there to act as an informal coordinator. The first order of business was to replace King as executive secretary, and after Ella Baker declined the position Forman agreed to take it, even though he had serious misgivings about SNCC's organizational structure and prospects. As Forman later revealed, the reorganization at Highlander had not eliminated the "factional fights over direct action versus voter registration" or the radical democratic ethos that gave SNCC meetings a discursive and disorderly quality. While the students' commitment to the cause of civil rights was undeniable and impressive, Forman found their free-form discussions of philosophy and strategy to be unproductive and even a bit unnerving.

Some, including Bob Moses, had little patience for organizational niceties. Early in the meeting Moses announced that he was ready to return to McComb, where he felt he was needed. Although he eventually agreed to stay for at least another day, the volatile situation back in Mississippi weighed on his mind. As he, Charles Sherrod, and other members of the McComb group explained, the struggle in southwestern Mississippi was like nothing they had ever experienced before. The responsibility of asking a poor black farmer to put his life on the line for the right to register to vote was proving to be a heavy burden. Everyone had expected Mississippi to be tough, but no one had anticipated a scene such as the one that Moses and McDew encountered at Herbert Lee's funeral when a distraught widow looked them in the eye and screamed: "You killed my husband! You killed my husband!"

This and other stories related to the ongoing struggle in Mississippi had a noticeable impact on the deliberations in Atlanta. In the end, however, the students refused to be cowed either by violent resistance or their own fears. Shelving a plan to dispatch field secretaries to various movement centers across the South, they formulated a long-range project known as Operation MOM, March (or Move) on Mississippi. For the foreseeable future, SNCC's entire direct action wing would be assigned to Mississippi. Headquartered in Jackson, Operation MOM would include local projects in McComb and other targeted communities where SNCC volunteers could develop "a locally based attack on the state power structure." The students also agreed to expand the efforts of the voting rights wing, especially in southwestern Georgia, where Sherrod had already explored the prospects for a pilot project. Sherrod and Cordell Reagon, a Freedom Rider from Nashville, would relocate to the city of Albany, which had little experience with civil rights activism but nonetheless had the potential to become a major center of movement activity, according to Sherrod. Others were not so sure about Albany's prospects, but the enthusiasm and renewed sense of purpose that emerged from the Atlanta meeting gave a measure of hope even to the most pessimistic among them.[31]

For Sherrod and Reagon, as for many of the SNCC activists, this spirit of optimism would be sorely tested during the first week of October. On Monday, October 2, they drove back to McComb with Moses, not knowing exactly what had transpired there over the weekend. Upon arriving at the SNCC Masonic Temple office in McComb, they learned that the five students arrested during the Woolworth's sit-in on August 26 were about to be released on bond. Two of the students, Brenda Travis and Ike Lewis, were still enrolled at Burgland High, McComb's all-black junior and senior high school. But when they tried to return to their classes on October 4, the principal expelled them for participating in an illegal demonstration. Other students at Burgland, anticipating the principal's decision, had already made preparations for a mass walkout, and within minutes of the expulsion more than a hundred students were walking down the street with the intention of marching the full eight miles to the county courthouse in Magnolia. Along the way they stopped at the Masonic Temple to pick up protest signs they had made the night before; while at the temple, they sought counsel from several SNCC workers, including Moses, McDew, Reagon, and Marion Barry. Concerned that the students' parents would blame SNCC if the march led to mass arrests or violence, Moses and McDew urged the marchers to disband. But Reagon and Barry advised the students to march on regardless of the consequences. When it became clear that the students were determined to march, Moses and McDew agreed to accompany them to Magnolia, even though they had grave doubts about the wisdom of provoking local authorities with a hastily planned protest. Ironically, Reagon and Barry, the two SNCC leaders who enthusiastically supported the march, remained at the temple office.

Moses's fear of losing most of his staff in a single round of arrests was reason enough to limit the number of SNCC marchers, but the students' plan to walk all the way to the county courthouse also posed a daunting physical challenge to potential volunteers. To Moses's relief, the students abandoned the original plan once they reached the outskirts of McComb; turning back toward downtown, they headed for the McComb city hall, where they hoped to find someone who could overrule the expulsion of Travis and Lewis. Along the way the marchers tried to ignore the taunts of white bystanders, but by the time the march reached city hall a swelling crowd of angry protesters had surrounded the building. Although the McComb police were also out in force, the officers on duty refused to intervene when several members of the mob began to beat Bob Zellner, the only white participant in the march.

A recent graduate of Huntingdon College, a small Methodist school in Montgomery, Zellner had joined the SNCC staff on September 1 after being recruited by Anne Braden and Jim Dombrowski of the Southern Conference Education Fund (SCEF). Braden and Dombrowski had been looking for a talented organizer who could recruit liberal white students on Southern campuses, and Zellner ably fulfilled their expectations, visiting more than twenty campuses during his first month on the road. McComb, however, proved to be a costly diversion. Having witnessed the attack on Jim Zwerg and other Freedom Riders in Montgomery in May and fearing that his presence might exacerbate an already volatile situation, Zellner was initially reluctant to join the October 4 march. As Moses and the students departed, though, he could not resist the temptation to join them. This decision nearly cost him his life. During the confrontation at city hall, Moses and McDew tried to shield him from the advancing mob, but the police pulled them away, leaving him at the mercy of several attackers who gouged his eyes and eventually kicked him into unconsciousness. In the end, the only thing that saved him was a belated police order to arrest all of the marchers, many of whom had climbed the city hall steps to pray. By nightfall the police had carted 116 students and 3 SNCC workers off to jail, including a stunned and bleeding Zellner.

Although the police quickly dropped the charges against 97 students who were under the age of eighteen, 19 "adult" students and Moses, McDew, and Zellner were prosecuted for breach of peace and contributing to the delinquency of minors. The next morning the police arrested Reagon, Sherrod, and C. C. Bryant as accomplices, temporarily leaving Charles Jones as the only SNCC worker remaining free. Thanks to a five-thousand-dollar contribution by Harry Belafonte, all of the defendants were soon released on bond, but bail brought no relief from the wrath of black parents who blamed SNCC for leading their children astray. When the Burgland principal threatened to expel any student demonstrator who refused to sign a pledge promising to refrain from additional protests, some parents supported their children's decision to join a second walkout, but most felt that the walkouts were counterproductive and dangerous. SNCC, they believed, had exploited and incited their children for political purposes. Before long, even Bryant concluded that the SNCC visitors had worn out their welcome. Convinced that SNCC campaign was doing more harm than good, he asked Medgar Evers and the NAACP to assume control of the McComb voting rights project.

Despite serious misgivings about SNCC's aggressive tactics, Evers politely deflected Bryant's request, preferring to limit the NAACP's involvement to legal representation of the defendants. At an October 10 rally held at the Masonic Temple, Evers endorsed the students' continued defiance. But he had second thoughts about the wisdom of the students' actions after an October 11 march provoked a violent response from local whites. While the marchers themselves escaped injury, two college journalists covering the march, *National Student News* correspondent Paul Potter and future anti-war activist and recent University of Michigan graduate Tom Hayden, were dragged from their car and beaten. Evers and other NAACP leaders also grew concerned when the SNCC workers organized an alternative "freedom school" known as "Nonviolent High." Recruiting many of the expelled students, Moses, McDew, and Dion Diamond taught classes for three weeks until their efforts were cut short by a trial that put all twenty-two defendants behind bars.[32]

On the last day of October, the day before the ICC order was scheduled to go into effect, Moses, McDew, Zellner, and the student defendants re-

ceived jail sentences ranging from four to six months. During the trial the presiding judge had characterized the students as "sheep being led to the slaughter" by "outside agitators," and he and other local white leaders showed no sympathy when the defendants were unable to raise bail. It took SCEF president Jim Dombrowski more than a month to raise the required thirteen thousand dollars in bond money, and the three SNCC leaders and most of the convicted

Freelance reporter and University of Michigan student activist Tom Hayden struggles to get up after being assaulted by Carl Hayes (standing) and other local whites protesting a pro-integration march in McComb, Mississippi, October 11, 1961. (Bettmann-CORBIS)

students languished in the Magnolia jail until early December. By then the McComb movement was in shambles, having run "head-on into the stone wall of absolute police power," as historian Howard Zinn later put it.

While Moses and his colleagues were behind bars in Magnolia, the black community in nearby McComb retreated behind the familiar walls of racial accommodation, which in turn encouraged the local white community to reassert its traditional dominance. When six Freedom Riders traveled to McComb in early November to test compliance with the ICC order, they were fortunate to escape with their lives. Soon even Moses reluctantly conceded that the town was not quite ready for SNCC's assertive approach to direct action. Following his release on December 5, he relocated to Jackson, partly because several of the Burgland students had moved there to attend classes at Campbell Junior College, but primarily because there was no longer much that he could do in McComb. Philosophical in defeat, he proposed a shift from the "dusty roads" of southwestern Mississippi to the "dusty streets" of Jackson. As he put it, having gotten their "feet wet" in McComb, the young activists of SNCC "now knew something of what it took to run a voter registration campaign in Mississippi." [33]

Among the many valuable lessons learned in McComb was the realization that voting rights agitation was just as dangerous as other forms of direct action. Contrary to the expectations of Justice Department officials, most white segregationists seemed to put black voter registration efforts in the same category as sit-ins and freedom rides. Regardless of the specific issue at hand, a fixation on a broad-based conspiracy of "outside agitators" invalidated the claim to legitimate dissent. Later in the decade—following the 1963 March on Washington, the Civil Rights Acts of 1964 and 1965, and other expressions of movement strength and solidarity—the notion of the civil rights movement's legitimacy would become a grudgingly accepted fact of life among white Southerners. In 1961, however, such acceptance was rare, especially in the Deep South, where racial demography and the dictates of caste and class kept open dissent to a minimum. Unbeknownst to all but a few whites, and to many blacks as well, there were untapped sources of movement strength, even in the most remote black communities. But the conditions had to be right, as they were in the wake of the Freedom Rides, for this unrealized potential to become a meaningful part of the political landscape.

The movement that emerged in Albany, Georgia, during the fall of 1961 demonstrated just how quickly an external provocation could energize internal dissent. Within days of their arrival in a seemingly placid community of sixty thousand, Sherrod and Reagon turned a series of church prayer meetings at Shiloh Baptist Church into an insurgent revolt against racial complacency. With the black proportion of the local population hovering around 40 percent and a tradition of nonconfrontational race relations, Albany supported a struggling NAACP branch with a declining membership. At the height of its influence, in the years following World War II, the Albany branch had

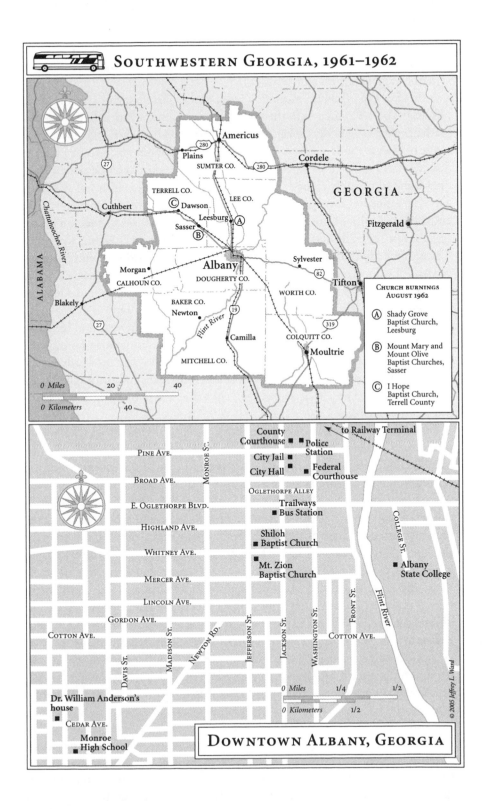

SOUTHWESTERN GEORGIA, 1961–1962

Americus
280
Plains
SUMTER CO.
280
Cordele

GEORGIA

TERRELL CO.
LEE CO.
27
Cuthbert
Ⓒ Dawson
Leesburg Ⓐ
Sasser
Ⓑ
Fitzgerald •

Chattahoochee River

Morgan •
CALHOUN CO.
Albany
DOUGHERTY CO.
Sylvester
82
Tifton •

ALABAMA

Blakely •
BAKER CO.
Newton
WORTH CO.
27
Flint River
19
Camilla
COLQUITT CO.
319
Moultrie

MITCHELL CO.

0 Miles   20   40
0 Kilometers   40

CHURCH BURNINGS AUGUST 1962

Ⓐ Shady Grove Baptist Church, Leesburg

Ⓑ Mount Mary and Mount Olive Baptist Churches, Sasser

Ⓒ I Hope Baptist Church, Terrell County

---

to Railway Terminal

County Courthouse ■ ■ Police Station

PINE AVE.
City Jail ■
City Hall ■ ■ Federal Courthouse

BROAD AVE.

OGLETHORPE ALLEY

E. OGLETHORPE BLVD.
Trailways ■ Bus Station

HIGHLAND AVE.
Shiloh ■ Baptist Church

WHITNEY AVE.

Mt. Zion ■ Baptist Church

MERCER AVE.

LINCOLN AVE.

GORDON AVE.

COTTON AVE.

■ Albany State College

COTTON AVE.

MONROE ST.
DAVIS ST.
MADISON ST.
NEWTON RD.
JEFFERSON ST.
JACKSON ST.
WASHINGTON ST.
FRONT ST.
COLLEGE ST.
Flint River

0 Miles   1/4   1/2
0 Kilometers   1/2

Dr. William Anderson's house ■

CEDAR AVE.

Monroe ■ High School

DOWNTOWN ALBANY, GEORGIA

© 2005 Jeffrey L. Ward

mounted a successful voter registration drive that produced an expectation of black participation in local public life, but a decade and a half later the city remained rigidly segregated.

In May 1961 Tom Chatmon, a local black businessman, organized an NAACP Youth Council with the intention of nudging white officials toward gradual reform. Like Martin Luther King, Chatmon had attended Morehouse College during the late 1940s, but he did not share King's faith in militant direct action. Instead, he counseled Albany's black youth to be patient and ever mindful of their elders' vulnerability. Alarmed by rumors of SNCC's growing influence among the Youth Council members, who were reportedly enthralled by tales of Freedom Rides and sit-ins, Chatmon warned local and regional NAACP leaders that Sherrod and Reagon were playing with fire. Though not unmindful of Chatmon's limitations, Vernon Jordan, Georgia's NAACP field secretary, shared the Youth Council leader's concerns and did what he could to discourage any further SNCC interference. In mid-October several local NAACP leaders informed the two troublesome SNCC workers that they were no longer welcome in the city, but Sherrod and Reagon, confident that something significant was stirring among their young followers, had no intention of leaving. Indeed, several of the most adventurous Youth Council members had already informed Chatmon that they planned to participate in a desegregation test at the Albany Trailways terminal on November 1.

Fearing that he was about to lose all credibility with his charges, Chatmon reluctantly agreed to consider the idea, and in late October he met with Sherrod and Reagon to work out a compromise that would protect both the students and the local reputation of the NAACP. All agreed that there would be no mention of NAACP involvement, and that the students would suspend the test if and when arrests became imminent. Though somewhat uncomfortable with the latter restriction, Sherrod and Reagon decided not to force the issue. Despite the NAACP's foot-dragging, their organizational efforts were progressing much faster than they had hoped, and they were eager to share the good news with their colleagues in Mississippi. On October 30 they boarded a bus for a whirlwind trip to McComb, where they planned to discuss the situation in Albany and to attend the trial of Moses, McDew, and Zellner. Two days later, if all went well, they would return to Albany as Freedom Riders testing the ICC order. The students, Chatmon promised, would meet them in the white waiting room of the Trailways station for a joint test.

Sherrod and Reagon returned to Albany via the SNCC office in Atlanta, where they met with Forman and Charles Jones on Halloween night. Forman and Jones were busy making final preparations for their own ICC test—an early-morning visit to Jake's Fine Foods Restaurant at the downtown Atlanta Trailways station—but they offered Sherrod and Reagon an official observer for the four-hour bus run to Albany. Salynn McCollum, the veteran Freedom Rider from Nashville's Peabody College who had been hired as one of

SNCC's first white staff members, was eager to go along, and when the morning bus to Albany left the Trailways station she was on it. Avoiding any direct contact with Sherrod and Reagon, she sat quietly among the white passengers as the drama of Georgia's first compliance test unfolded. Halfway along the route, the bus was pulled over to the side of the road by Georgia state troopers who walked up and down the aisle before waving the driver on. Although Sherrod and Reagon were sitting in the front section behind the driver, there were no arrests, but it was clear that authorities in Atlanta and Albany knew that a Freedom Ride was in progress. Arriving at the Albany Trailways station at 6:30 in the morning, Sherrod and Reagon, with McCollum trailing well behind, strolled into the waiting room expecting to see the familiar faces of the Youth Council volunteers. To their surprise and dismay, however, not a single volunteer was there to greet them. Fearing that the students were already in jail, they looked warily at the police patrolling the waiting room, then quietly exited the station in search of their missing disciples. After a few frantic phone calls, they learned that there had been no arrests and no attempt to desegregate the station. The students had stayed away because they had become convinced that local white supremacists planned to beat or even kill them if they tried to test compliance with the ICC order.

In actuality, Albany's police chief, Laurie Pritchett, had convinced Mayor Asa Kelley and the city commission that the best way to handle Freedom Riders was to avoid violence at all costs. At a special closed meeting of the city commission on October 30, Pritchett had outlined a strategy patterned after that of the Jackson police: Vigilante violence would be preempted by timely arrests, and the basis for all Freedom Rider arrests would be the maintenance of public order, not the violation of segregation laws. That the rumor mill in the black community suggested just the opposite spoke volumes about the underlying insecurities and fears that dominated race relations in the city. How Sherrod and Reagon were able to quiet such fears is not altogether clear, but by midafternoon they had convinced nine Youth Council members to violate the sanctity of the same white waiting room they had been afraid to enter only hours before.

With the two SNCC workers watching from a nearby street corner, and with McCollum observing from an even closer vantage point, the nine students walked into the waiting room to confront the unjust power of the white establishment. "The bus station was full of men in blue," Sherrod later wrote, "but up through the mass of people, past the men with guns and billies ready, into the terminal they marched, quiet and clean. They were allowed to buy tickets to Florida but after sitting in the waiting room they were asked to leave under threat of arrest." Although they did so immediately, the significance of what they had already accomplished soon became apparent. By standing up for their constitutional rights, however briefly, they had broken the spell of unchallenged dominance. As Sherrod put it, "From that moment on, segregation was dead." In the aftermath of the November 1 confrontation, the black community in Albany seemed to take on a new spirit of assertiveness and pride. Indeed, despite persistent disputes over organizational authority and the advisability of outside involvement in the local struggle, the expectation of direct and even militant action would soon become a widely accepted fact of life in Albany.[34]

BY THE END OF THE YEAR the gathering movement in Albany would become one of the freedom struggle's most visible manifestations, but in early November it was still a minor sideshow in the larger drama prompted by the implementation and testing of the ICC order. At the CORE and NAACP offices in New York, at SCLC's headquarters in Atlanta, and at the FRCC recruiting stations around the South, the focus of attention was the systematic testing of the order by several hundred volunteers. After weeks of careful preparation, CORE, acting on behalf of the FRCC, dispatched several dozen bands of Freedom Riders during the first week of November. With Gordon Carey and Marvin Rich serving as the primary coordinators, teams of testers traveled designated routes in sixteen states, from the Deep South to the border regions of Oklahoma, Kentucky, Maryland, and Delaware. The goal was to get a comprehensive picture of compliance and noncompliance that could be reported to the press and forwarded to the ICC and the Justice Department.

Publicly CORE and other FRCC leaders predicted near universal compliance, but privately they conceded that there was no way of knowing how the white South would respond to the ICC order. In truth, they expected a mixed response, ranging from gracious acceptance to grudging acknowledgment to outright resistance. Since the mass testing represented the most ambitious short-term project ever attempted by CORE or any other civil rights organization, there were also concerns about logistical shortcomings and possible lapses in nonviolent discipline. While some of the testers were veterans of earlier Freedom Rides, most were new and untested volunteers— a less than ideal situation for a movement that could ill afford a misstep. Since CORE wanted the tests to replicate the experiences of normal travelers, local volunteers were essential, but this strategy carried obvious risks. Whatever the degree of compliance, getting to the end of the day without suffering an embarrassing incident or losing anyone along the way would be an accomplishment in itself.

Fortunately for CORE, as the reports trickled in during the first week of testing, it became clear that even the unseasoned testers were living up to the high standards of poise and discipline that had characterized the Freedom Rider movement since early May. Perhaps even more important, the reports indicated that most of the testers were encountering less resistance than expected. The best news came out of Virginia, Kentucky, Texas, and West Virginia, where the tests found total compliance. In Florida, where tests were conducted at bus stations in Jacksonville and the Panhandle communities of Tallahassee and Marianna, there was compliance but no sign of the required ICC postings; the same was true in Arkansas, where Freedom Riders were served at bus stations in six cities. In Tennessee there was compliance in four of the five bus stations tested, with mandated segregation persisting only in the small town of Linden. In North Carolina the only community to enforce transit segregation on the first day of the new order was the tiny Piedmont town of Wadesboro, just down the road from Monroe. And in Oklahoma noncompliance was limited to McAlester, a remote hill town in the southeastern part of the state.

The reports from the Deep South, though decidedly mixed, were more troubling. In South Carolina testers were served without incident in Charleston, Columbia, Greenville, Rock Hill, Spartanburg, and Sumter, but segregated facilities persisted in Camden, Florence, and Lancaster. In some South Carolina communities—in Camden, where a follow-up test revealed compliance, and in Greenville, where the manager of the Trailways station endorsed compliance but insisted that many black passengers were confused by the ICC order and "didn't know where to sit"—the situation was difficult to evaluate. Similar inconsistencies appeared in Louisiana, where compliance was generally limited to New Orleans and the southern Cajun parishes. When a group of Freedom Riders arrived in the southwest Louisiana town of Crowley, they were greeted by "policemen armed with sawed-off shotguns and tear gas guns." Though fearing the worst, the Riders soon learned that the somewhat overzealous local sheriff simply "wanted to avoid an Alabama or Mississippi incident." Adding to the confusion, the waiting room at the Crowley Greyhound terminal complied with the ICC order, but the adjacent terminal restaurant remained closed to black patrons. There was more consistency in the northern and central part of the state, where Freedom Riders encountered stiff resistance from police determined to maintain segregated facilities. In Shreveport, Monroe, Alexandria, and Lafayette, black Riders were barred from entering white waiting rooms, and in Baton Rouge a terminal restaurant was closed. When the manager of the Shreveport Trailways terminal defied a police order and removed several WHITES ONLY signs, he ended up in jail. And when Trailways officials removed segregation signs in Alexandria, a state judge immediately ordered the installation of new signs.

The situation was no less confusing in Georgia, where state officials had taken preliminary steps to challenge the legality of the ICC order in federal court but where Freedom Riders also found compliance in a number of communities, including Thomasville, Valdosta, Macon, and Augusta. At this point the only sign of active noncompliance outside of Albany was an ugly incident at the Atlanta Trailways station, where Jim Forman, Charles Jones, Bernard Lafayette, and Jim Bevel were arrested after trying to desegregate the whites-only lunch counter at Jake's Fine Foods. The Atlanta arrests surprised some

movement observers who had expected more from a city that had taken the
first steps toward school desegregation earlier in the year. But no one was
surprised by the turmoil that ensued when CORE testers attempted to desegregate bus station facilities in Birmingham, Alabama.[35]

Hoping to avoid violence, CORE leaders scheduled a minimal number
of tests in Alabama. The symbolic importance of Birmingham, however, was
impossible to ignore, and Freedom Riders were sent into the city on November 3. Two days earlier, on the day the ICC order went into effect, the trial
of the Anniston bus burners had opened in the courtroom of U.S. District
Judge H. Hobart Grooms, an unfortunate coincidence that concerned both
government and movement observers. Almost simultaneously Grooms's colleague in Montgomery, Judge Frank Johnson, had issued an injunction enjoining Trailways and Greyhound officials, as well as state and local officials,
from maintaining segregation among interstate passengers at any of the terminals located in the twenty-three counties of the Middle District of Alabama. Unfortunately, this injunction did not apply to Birmingham or Bull
Connor, who promised to arrest anyone who violated the city's segregation
ordinances. Though somewhat less specific, Governor Patterson appeared
to endorse Connor's threat, labeling Johnson's ruling an "insult to every citizen of Alabama." If the Freedom Riders "continue to invade our state and
continue to try to run over us," Patterson warned, "we want to serve notice
that we are going to defend ourselves and we are not going to take it lying
down." This bluster did not prevent compliance in several Alabama towns
and cities, including Anniston, where CORE testers successfully desegregated the lunch counters at both of the city's bus terminals. But Connor's
Birmingham was another matter.

When the testers arrived at the Birmingham Greyhound station, the required ICC posting was, predictably, nowhere in sight. But Ralph Sizemore,
the thirty-four-year-old manager of the Greyhound cafeteria, agreed to serve
the testers anyway. Moments later, a Birmingham policeman stepped forward
to arrest Sizemore for violating a city ordinance outlawing mixed dining. While
the Freedom Riders themselves escaped arrest, Sizemore was carted off to jail
before being released on a hundred-dollar bond. On November 5, when Freedom Riders made a second attempt to desegregate the cafeteria, Sizemore was
rearrested along with two waitresses. And over the next three days the plucky
manager was arrested two more times. Caught in the middle, Greyhound officials urged the Justice Department to intervene, but department officials in
Washington were reluctant to do so, fearing that a precipitous attempt to enforce the ICC order would only make matters worse. The only "official" response from the Federal government came from Malcolm Weaver, the U.S.
attorney in Birmingham, who worked out a tentative compromise with city
attorney John Breckinridge. If the city called a halt to the arrests, Weaver
promised, the Justice Department would not contest state court jurisdiction
over the Sizemore case. Summarily rejected by Bull Connor, the proposed

agreement had little discernible effect on a legal impasse that would bedevil lawyers and politicians for several months. But the Justice Department's timidity did not go unnoticed among movement leaders awaiting confirmation of the department's determination to enforce the ICC order.[36]

Judging by the early reports from Mississippi, the ICC was going to need all the help it could get. Although there was an encouraging report from the Delta town of Greenville, where a group of interracial testers was served without incident, Mississippi Freedom Riders met stiff resistance everywhere else. In Hamilton and Tupelo testers were told that the local bus stations had been closed "for repairs," and in a dozen other communities the ICC order was simply ignored. In Grenada city officials challenged the order with a new ordinance prohibiting race mixing in all public facilities, and in Meridian the police installed new signs directing passengers to separate waiting rooms. In the Vicksburg station the ICC order was prominently displayed, but that did not stop the local police from escorting two black Freedom Riders out of the white waiting room.

Although the Vicksburg testers avoided arrest, three Freedom Riders who tried to desegregate the Jackson Trailways terminal were not so fortunate. The first tester arrested was the Reverend Charles Jones, dean of Campbell Junior College, the institution that had welcomed the McComb students expelled from Burgland High School. Entering the white waiting room at the Trailways terminal just after dawn, Jones was promptly arrested for breaching the peace. An hour later a policeman patrolling the same waiting room arrested Levert Taylor and Glenda Jackson, two veterans of Shreveport CORE who had just arrived on an overnight bus. In Jackson, as in McComb, bus company officials had posted the ICC order and had even painted over the WHITE and COLORED door signs that identified separate waiting rooms. But just before the order went into effect, city officials in both cities countermanded these actions by placing temporary Jim Crow signs on the sidewalks adjacent to the cities' bus and railway stations. When asked to explain this apparent inconsistency, Mayor Thompson told reporters that he had consented to the ICC posting and the sign removal because he "didn't want to embarrass the bus and train people." Denying that the arrests at the Trailways station constituted a violation of the ICC order, he repeated the familiar refrain that he was simply trying to keep the peace. "We're going to see that there's no violence from these agitators coming from the outside," he declared with a hint of a smile, "even if we have to have policemen for each one."[37]

Though not unexpected, the situation in Mississippi posed a difficult problem for movement leaders, who did not want to give the impression that white Southerners were defying the ICC order with impunity. Allowing stories of resistance to overshadow evidence of compliance would not serve the interests of the movement, but neither would ignoring or glossing over outright acts of defiance. Somehow Farmer, Carey, and Rich had to find a way to accentuate the positive while simultaneously pointing out the need for continued pressure from activists and governmental officials. In a November 4 interview with *New York Times* reporter Claude Sitton, Rich made a valiant attempt to provide a balanced assessment, stressing reports of successful desegregation but also listing several troubling examples of noncompliance. CORE leaders adopted a similar strategy a few days later when they forwarded a more systematic report to the Justice Department and the ICC. In this and other communications, the message was clear: Timely enforcement of the ICC order was crucial. Straightforward and prescriptive, the order presented a welcome alternative to the "all deliberate speed" syndrome that had slowed the pace of school desegregation. But it also carried a sobering responsibility to assert the authority and legitimacy of federal law. If the Justice Department allowed a defiant minority to ignore the order, the consequences could be catastrophic, not only for the cause of desegregation but also for the broader interests of the Kennedy administration. After six months of involuntary zigzagging across the political landscape, the Freedom Rider crisis had finally brought the administration to a crossroads. Like it or not, federal authorities entrusted with enforcement of the ICC order faced a clear choice that would influence the course of American democracy for months or even years to come.

Despite the foot-dragging in Birmingham, proof of federal resolve came almost immediately. In fact, the Justice Department's first request for an injunction enjoining local officials from obstructing compliance actually preceded the ICC order by several hours. On October 31 department attorneys asked District Judge Claude Clayton to overrule a state circuit court order forbidding the removal of Jim Crow signs at the Greenwood, Mississippi, bus station. Clayton refused to grant an immediate restraining order, but he scheduled a November 20 hearing to discuss the matter. Though disappointed with Clayton's response, Department officials decided to take even bolder action three days later. Responding to both the Greenwood situation and the obstructionist actions of city officials in McComb, a suit filed with the federal district court in Jackson requested the convening of a three-judge federal panel that could rule on the constitutionality of Mississippi's bus segregation laws. The suit targeted McComb and named Mayor C. H. Douglas and Police Chief George Guy as defendants. On November 3 a similar suit was filed against officials in Monroe, Louisiana, and department officials promised additional actions would be forthcoming in other non-compliant communities. Almost simultaneously, the ICC district office announced that it had opened an investigation of complaints by Levert Taylor and Glenda Jackson, the two Louisiana Freedom Riders arrested in Jackson on November 1.

The balance sheet at the end of the first week of implementation was mixed but generally encouraging. Although several Deep South communities were resisting the order, there were signs of hope almost everywhere—even in Birmingham. On November 7 an unidentified high-level official at the Justice Department hinted to one Birmingham reporter that additional arrests at the Trailways café would force the government to seek relief in the federal courts. The attorney general, the official was careful to add, preferred to avoid such action, but the department was ready to add Birmingham to the growing list of communities under a court order to desegregate. Adding force to this threat, on the following day Judge Grooms issued an injunction prohibiting the city of Birmingham from enforcing segregation in public parks, theaters, and auditoriums.[38]

Despite these promising developments, CORE and other movement leaders were wary of putting too much faith in federal power. Even though outright defiance of the ICC order was limited to the Deep South, resistance to the spirit of the law clearly extended to all parts of the segregated South. Segregation in intrastate transit and other public accommodations remained almost universal across the region, and even in the border states the color line was, with few exceptions, still in force. The extent and persistence of discrimination became painfully clear during the second week of November when CORE activists stepped up the pressure along Route 40 in an action designed to complement an ongoing federal desegregation initiative. Seven weeks earlier, on September 13, State Department protocol officer Richard Sanjuan had addressed the Maryland legislature on the importance of eliminating segregation along the diplomatic corridor from Washington to New York. Couched in the rhetoric of Cold War patriotism, Sanjuan's appeal stressed the international implications of discrimination. "When an American citizen humiliates a foreign representative or another American citizen for racial reasons," he insisted, "the results can be just as damaging to his country as the passing of secret information to the enemy." Stunned by the bluntness of Sanjuan's words, and more incensed than chastened, the Maryland legislators promptly dug in their heels on the Route 40 desegregation issue. CORE, however, seized upon the Sanjuan episode as a rationale for organizing a formal campaign to desegregate Route 40.

In mid-October Washington CORE leader Julius Hobson announced plans for a massive Freedom Ride to be held on Saturday, November 11. Hoping to dramatize the issue in a way that would force Maryland governor Millard Tawes to call a special legislative session for the purpose of passing an equal access public accommodations law, CORE recruited a large number of Riders willing to stage sit-ins at restaurants along the route. Behind the scenes, Hobson and others, including Sanjuan, tried to persuade the restaurant owners to desegregate voluntarily. But there were few signs of cooperation until early November, when the ICC order gave added force to the effort. On November 8, just three days before the scheduled sit-ins, fortyseven restaurants (thirty-five in Maryland and twelve in Delaware) agreed to desegregate. Although this left approximately half of the restaurants outside of the agreement, CORE leaders decided to suspend the scheduled protest. Declaring a partial victory, Hobson congratulated the compliant restaurant owners and managers but warned that CORE would conduct a series of de-segregation tests later in the month.

Though the Route 40 campaign was far from over, its trajectory provided movement leaders with a measure of encouragement. While no one expected limited progress in the borderlands to resolve the impasse in the Deep South, the State Department's unofficial alliance with Maryland CORE reinforced the expectation that the Justice Department would do whatever was necessary to enforce the ICC order. Reaching beyond bus terminals and the ICC mandate, the Route 40 campaign also demonstrated the broadening sweep of the Freedom Rider movement. Even universal compliance with the ICC order, it now seemed, would not bring the crisis to a close. As many segregationists had feared, partial desegregation had unleashed a revolution of rising expectations that virtually ensured a recurring cycle of movement and resistance. For movement activists, the Freedom Rides, along with sit-ins and other forms of nonviolent direct action, had confirmed the power of public protest, signaling the emergence of a new democratic ethos. Thus, even though the desegregation of interstate transportation was far from complete in November 1961 and federal officials remained reluctant to force the issue in the absence of outright violence, observers close to the action were confident that the ICC order was propelling the Freedom Riders towards the promised land.[39]

IN SOUTHERN BUS TERMINALS, as in other areas of regional life, old ways died hard even in the face of a clear federal mandate. Here, as elsewhere, the power of law to effect social change was limited and uncertain, as many communities along the Southern front continued to embrace the traditional institutional arrangements and customs that discouraged blacks and whites from intermingling. All of these communities, in varying degrees, would eventually adapt to the implications of the ICC order. But ironically, among the first to do so were the noncompliant Deep South towns and cities that initially defied the order. In McComb and Albany, for example, institutional and social inertia gave way to racial polarization and creative disorder during the final weeks of 1961. In both of these troubled communities, Freedom Rides produced dramatic confrontations that demonstrated the potential volatility of Southern race relations.

In the case of McComb, the common determination of movement activists and white supremacists to force a showdown tested the resolve of federal authorities and helped to dispel any lingering doubts about the wisdom of timely intervention. Emerging at a critical moment, the McComb crisis simplified the normally complex calculus of decision-making at the Justice Department, where policy makers struggled to balance legal and political considerations. In a department run by the president's brother, there was normally a strong sensitivity to the political price of legal interference in local and state affairs, but such considerations fell by the wayside when the

McComb police chief George H. Guy poses beside the new WHITE WAITING ROOM signs placed on the sidewalk outside the McComb Greyhound bus station, November 2, 1961. (AP Wide World)

attorney general and other high-level officials became convinced that resolute action was the only way to prevent massive civil disorder in McComb and other areas of Mississippi. As soon as the Justice Department learned that a group of Freedom Riders planned to conduct a compliance test in the troubled southwest Mississippi town, some level of federal involvement became almost inevitable. But the decision to place new Jim Crow signs on the sidewalk outside the McComb bus and railway terminals on November 1 pushed the department to intervene before the situation got out of hand.

After the request for a federal injunction was filed on November 2, department officials waited for nearly three weeks before the court responded favorably. In a November 21 ruling, Judge Elbert Tuttle, the chief judge of the Fifth Circuit Court of Appeals, and his liberal colleague, Judge Richard Rives, granted an injunction against McComb's noncompliant officials over the objection of Judge Sidney Mize. At the same time, Tuttle and Rives ruled that three Mississippi laws requiring racial segregation among intrastate passengers were unconstitutional. Both of these rulings carried broad implications and were a welcome relief to department officials still smarting from a November 17 federal district court ruling that effectively nullified an NAACP

suit seeking to overturn the convictions of the Freedom Riders arrested in
Jackson earlier in the year. Overriding a sharp dissent by Rives, Claude Clayton
and Sidney Mize informed NAACP attorneys that they "must first seek recourse through state courts." Tantamount to an endorsement of segregation, the two-to-one decision convinced John Doar and others that resistance
to the ICC order was hardening in Mississippi, even among some judges
who had sworn to uphold constitutional authority.[40]

With this in mind, Justice Department attorneys began to view McComb
as a crucial test case in the campaign to convince Mississippi authorities that
continued resistance to the ICC order was futile. Although targeting the ultra-
segregationist community of McComb carried obvious risks, aiming at the
heart of the beast made the move toward enforcement even more emphatic.
The move, when it came, was swift and decisive. On Monday, November 27,
department attorneys filed official papers at the federal courthouse in Jackson, and on Tuesday a federal marshal delivered copies to Mayor Douglas,
Police Chief Guy, and the McComb city selectmen. At the same time, several FBI agents were dispatched to the city as observers. In response, Mayor
Douglas issued a public statement assuring federal authorities that the city
would abide by the court order: "There are no two ways about it. That means
no attempt will be made to separate as far as race is concerned." With Freedom Riders expected in the city as early as Wednesday, Douglas ordered the
police to remove the Jim Crow signs outside the local Greyhound and Illinois Central terminals, though he made sure they did so "during the night
when there's nobody around." Despite this move toward compliance, he could
not resist making the prediction that "our local people are going to respect
the color line whether the signs are there or not." What he did not say was
that no amount of careful maneuvering could quell the rising anger in a white
community that had already proven its segregationist mettle by putting several SNCC volunteers and many of the Burgland student rebels behind bars.
As news of the federal presence and rumors of an impending Freedom Ride
spread throughout the city and into the surrounding countryside, some of
southwestern Mississippi's roughest characters began to organize a rude welcoming party.

Even before the Freedom Riders arrived on Wednesday morning, a small
but angry crowd outside the McComb bus station assaulted Johann Rush, a
freelance television cameraman from Jackson. A few minutes later, five Riders led by Jerome Smith, only recently released from Parchman, stepped off
a Greyhound from New Orleans and walked toward the white waiting room.
All five—including two eighteen-year-old students, Doratha Smith and
George Raymond—were veterans of New Orleans CORE. Turned away from
the waiting room by a station agent who claimed that a gas leak made the
station unsafe to enter, the Riders piled into a taxi that whisked them away to
the black section of town. Returning later in the morning, they made a second attempt to enter the waiting room. This time they succeeded, sidling

through a crowd of scowling whites to a lunch counter in the rear of the waiting room. Refused service and ordered to leave by the station manager, who informed them that "Greyhound does not own this building," they soon found themselves being attacked by several enraged white onlookers. Raymond was struck in the head with a half-filled coffee cup, and Jerome Smith was assaulted by a man screaming, "I'll kill him." Other assailants soon jumped in, shoving and kicking all five Riders onto the sidewalk, and slamming Smith into the pavement. Though bloodied, Smith, along with the others, managed to stagger to a waiting cab and escape. No one at the scene, including the FBI observers, made any attempt to intervene on the Riders' behalf. The local police, though headquartered only a block away, did not arrive at the station until after the Riders had left. To Claude Sitton, who witnessed the melee from a few yards away, the combination of mob behavior and negligent law enforcement "repeated on a smaller scale the riots that greeted Freedom Riders last May in Anniston, Birmingham, and Montgomery, Ala."

After belatedly clearing the streets surrounding the station and arresting four of the assailants, Chief Guy joined Mayor Douglas for an impromptu news conference, during which both men assured reporters that they were determined to maintain civil order and enforce the law. While no one who had followed the recent course of events in McComb put much stock in this pledge, city officials and other civic leaders held an extended discussion of the situation on Thursday, prompting Douglas to issue a second public statement calling for compliance with the desegregation order. "The law regarding our bus and railroad terminals is a Federal law," he declared. "We did not make it at the local level, but it is our purpose to enforce it. We are determined to this end." The previous night, the police had escorted the injured Riders to the station, where they boarded a bus for New Orleans. But the ability of local officials to maintain order in the difficult days ahead seemed questionable.

On Friday afternoon, when a group of six Freedom Riders from Baton Rouge arrived at the McComb station, the police had to hold back a mob of more then five hundred white protesters. Finding the lunch counter closed, the Riders sat in the waiting room for a short time before leaving the station. When they returned two hours later, roughly half of the crowd had slipped away. Still, after putting the Riders on an outbound bus, the police had to deal with a minor riot that injured a *Time* reporter and two photographers, one of whom was "knocked through a plate glass window." While no one was bold or foolish enough to attack any of the forty FBI agents at the scene, several members of the crowd could not resist the opportunity to take out their frustrations on some of the prying newsmen assumed to be movement supporters.

Though alarmed by the rising resistance in McComb, CORE officials soon authorized a third attempt to desegregate what was fast becoming the most notorious small-town bus terminal west of Anniston. This time the

Freedom Rider Jerome Smith (with bandaged ear) arrives in New Orleans after being assaulted by white protesters at the McComb Greyhound bus station on November 29, 1961. The well-wishers surrounding him in the doorway are (left to right) Patricia Smith, Jean Thompson, Doris Castle, Carlene Smith (dark coat), and Frank Nelson. (Bettmann-CORBIS)

Freedom Riders were all local activists: Jerome Byrd, James Burnham, and Joe Lewis—three of the expelled Burgland students who had enrolled at Campbell Junior College in Jackson. Arriving on Saturday morning "with no advance notice," they managed to enter the white waiting room and remain there for several minutes. With the police almost outnumbering the small number of whites at the scene, the three Riders exited the station to report their success to CORE field secretary Tom Gaither and his assistant, Tougaloo student MacArthur Cotton, who were sitting nearby in a car after driving down from Jackson. Following a brief conversation, Cotton left the car and walked over to a ticket window, where he tried to buy a ticket to Jackson. At this point a group of whites who had been playing pool at a billiard parlor across the street noticed what was happening and rushed over to the station. Moments later a white man punched Cotton twice in the jaw, and several others began beating and kicking the windows of the car. The police pulled the attackers away before the car or its occupants suffered any serious harm, and there were no arrests, but the incident deepened the sense of crisis. After consulting with Farmer, Gaither reluctantly agreed to grant the city a "breathing spell" before any additional Rides were undertaken.[41]

To Judge Sidney Mize, the situation in McComb called for more than a brief moratorium. On Saturday afternoon, just hours after Cotton's narrow escape, he issued a temporary ten-day restraining order prohibiting any additional Freedom Rides in the city. Acting upon a joint request from panicky city officials and the bus station operator, he set a hearing date for December 7 to determine if the temporary order should be extended or made permanent. Even though CORE officials pointed out that Judge Frank Johnson had already overruled a similar order in Alabama, Mize insisted that it would be irresponsible to allow any further provocations to threaten civil order in McComb. Outside interference, in his view, had disrupted the peaceful course of local life, a judgment seemingly confirmed on Sunday morning when John Oliver Emmerich Sr., the sixty-one-year-old editor of the *McComb Enterprise-Journal*, was attacked on his way to church. A self-styled moderate who had encouraged Mayor Douglas to comply with the ICC order, Emmerich angered many local white supremacists when he allowed visiting newsmen to use his office as their unofficial headquarters. Confronted on the street by Melton Stayton, a forty-three-year-old oil worker who claimed that the editor was "responsible for these out-of-town newspaper men being here," the physically frail World War I veteran was knocked to the ground with a gash in his head. After several bystanders interceded, saving him from further injury, Emmerich was more perplexed than angry. "The problem is historic," he later explained to reporters "The cause of it is not in this generation. That's why I take a tolerant view of it. All of the people on the scene are like pawns moved by destiny." Others, including a local judge who sentenced Stayton to thirty days in jail, were less philosophical. But, for many, the incident underscored the volatility of race and class relations in one of the Deep South's most conservative communities.

At the December 7 hearing Judge Mize, as expected, extended the Freedom Rider restraining order for two weeks. Although CORE attorneys immediately filed an appeal, there was little hope of overturning Mize's ruling, at least in the short run. To the dismay of CORE and the Justice Department, the federal district judge assigned to rule on the appeal was Harold Cox, the arch-segregationist who had recently foiled the attempt to protect John Hardy's right to register black voters in southwestern Mississippi. On December 22 Cox upheld Mize's ruling by granting an open-ended temporary injunction enjoining CORE from sponsoring any further Freedom Rides to McComb. Stretching the limits of what one historian later called "blatant sophistry," Cox argued that the injunction was justified because it applied only to outside agitators and not to blacks as a general racial grouping. There was, he contended, no conflict with the ICC desegregation order. At the urging of Burke Marshall, the Fifth Circuit Court of Appeals would eventually nullify the injunction, after summarily rejecting the conservative jurist's logic. But, for the time being, the McComb Freedom Rides, along with the broader movement that Bob Moses and others had brought to the area, were over. For movement leaders, as for the Justice Department, the irony of the situation was inescapable. Of the seven communities placed under court order by the Justice Department in 1961, McComb probably did the most to tip the balance in favor of decisive federal action. Yet at the end of the year, it was the only community where Freedom Rides were barred by law.[42]

The developing situation in Albany was no less ironic. Here the Freedom Rides helped to inspire a local civil rights struggle that provided the national movement with organizational opportunities and strategic dilemmas in almost equal measure. Before the year was over, the Albany Movement, as the local struggle came to be known, would enlist thousands of black citizens in a community-wide effort to hasten the demise of Jim Crow in one of the nation's most segregated cities. But it would also draw SNCC, SCLC, and to a lesser extent the NAACP into a factional quagmire that would teach Martin Luther King and other movement leaders a painful lesson about the difficulties of mass protest in the Deep South. With Sherrod and Reagon lighting the fuse, Albany became one of the first communities to feel the explosive force, both positive and negative, of sustained mass participation in nonviolent struggle. The sequence of events fueling this explosion began on November 17, when representatives of several black community groups decided to form an umbrella organization known as the Albany Movement. Announcing a broad civil rights program calling for fair employment, an equitable legal justice system, and desegregation of all public accommodations, including transit facilities, the Albany Movement soon entered into preliminary negotiations with city leaders. At the same time, however, the organization began planning mass demonstrations designed to push those same leaders towards acceptance of movement demands.

As encouraging as it was, this adult activity could not keep pace with the youthful rebellion fostered by Sherrod and Reagon. On November 22, the day before Thanksgiving, three of Albany's most impatient black activists—all members of the NAACP Youth Council—attempted to desegregate the white waiting room at the downtown Trailways station. Promptly arrested by Chief Pritchett for breaching the peace, they spent less than an hour at the city jail before being bailed out. But later in the day two Albany State College students, Bertha Gober and Blanton Hall, made their own attempt to violate the waiting room color line. Following their arrest, however, there was no immediate release on bail. Over the next three days, as the two students spent the Thanksgiving holiday in jail far away from their families, their plight attracted considerable attention in the local black community, especially among the leaders of the Albany Movement. On Saturday night, when the movement convened a mass meeting at the Mount Zion Baptist Church to protest the arrests, all five of the students were on hand to bear witness to the spirit that had moved them. Both before and after the testimony, Reagon and two talented young singers, Rutha Harris and Bernice Johnson, led the faithful through stanza after stanza of a capella freedom songs, inaugurating the "Albany Singers" tradition that would become the hallmark of the local civil rights struggle. By the end of the evening the emotional surge in the Mount Zion sanctuary had surpassed Reagon and Sherrod's wildest expectations, spiritualizing the Albany Movement before their very eyes.

This new spirit was very much in evidence two days later when more than five hundred demonstrators appeared outside the county courthouse during the students' trial. With a nervous Chief Pritchett monitoring their every move, the demonstrators joined Charles Jones, recently dispatched from the SNCC office in Atlanta, on a "prayer pilgrimage" from the courthouse to Shiloh Baptist Church. Although Jones and his followers escaped arrest, city leaders, including the conservative black administrators at Albany State, warned the Albany Movement that it was courting danger. When Sherrod tried to speak to a group of students on the Albany State campus the next day, he was promptly arrested on a trespassing warrant. Over the next two weeks there were no further arrests, but the pressure and excitement continued to build in the black community.

By early December Sherrod and his SNCC colleagues were pleased with the local movement's gathering momentum but concerned that the city remained rigidly segregated with no real breakthrough on the horizon. Feeling that both local communities, black and white, needed a little push, they asked Jim Forman to organize a high-profile Freedom Ride from Atlanta to Albany. On Sunday, December 10, Forman himself, along with seven other Riders and one designated observer—Bernard Lee, Lenora Taitt, Norma Collins, Bob Zellner, Joan Browning, Per Laursen, Tom Hayden, and his wife, Casey Hayden (the observer)—traveled to Albany by train. Beginning in mid-October—when Robert Kennedy had personally negotiated the desegregation of trains and depots operated by three large railways systems, the Southern, the Louisville and Nashville, and the Illinois Central—most of the nation's railways, including the Central of Georgia line that served Albany, had recently agreed to desegregate their facilities. So, as expected, Forman and the other Riders encountered little trouble en route to Albany, even though they made a point of sitting together as an interracial group. At one point an indignant conductor tried to separate the black and white Riders, but the real trouble did not begin until they entered the Albany railway terminal.

Arriving in the early afternoon, they were met by a grim-faced Chief Pritchett backed up by a squad of police. Earlier in the day Pritchett had sealed off the white waiting room, and by his order the Albany Movement welcoming party inside the station was limited to Charles Jones, Bertha Gober, and A. C. Searles, a local black journalist. Out on the street, however, a large crowd of movement enthusiasts was waiting for the Riders to emerge. After hustling the Riders through the waiting room, Pritchett became unnerved as the crowd surged forward to greet them. When an order to clear the sidewalk went unheeded, he placed all eight Riders and three members of the crowd, including Jones, under arrest.

With this impulsive act, Pritchett produced eleven martyrs and a black community seething with outrage. Following an emotional mass meeting on Sunday evening, the Albany Movement went into action as never before. On Monday several movement supporters were arrested during a prayer vigil on the city hall steps; and on Tuesday, the day the eleven defendants went on trial, Sherrod led more than four hundred marchers through the heart of downtown Albany. Undeterred by a steady rain and the taunts of disapproving white onlookers, the singing and shouting marchers circled the city hall block twice before Pritchett had seen enough. Herding the marchers into a nearby alley, Pritchett ordered his officers to arrest the entire group for unlawful assembly. By early afternoon 267 protesters were in custody. Although nearly half of those arrested soon posted bond, 150 others, including Sherrod, remained in jail overnight, in many cases for several days. Most, like Sherrod, ended up at prison farms in nearby towns and counties that had agreed to accept the overflow from Albany's small city jail. By Wednesday morning the Albany arrests were front-page news all across the nation, and even Pritchett began to have second thoughts about the wisdom of calling national attention to the city's troubles. Nevertheless, he found himself arresting 202 more protesters later in the day. Many of those arrested were high school students that Pritchett soon released to the custody of parents, but the youthful innocence of the demonstrators did not weaken his resolve to maintain control of the situation. As he explained to reporters: "We can't tolerate the NAACP or the Student Nonviolent Coordinating Committee or any other 'nigger' organization to take over this town with mass demonstrations."

Sherrod and the local leaders of the Albany Movement were no less determined to carry on the fight. In addition to demanding the release of all prisoners and good-faith negotiation with city leaders on all matters related to desegregation, they called for a boycott of twelve downtown stores operated by white segregationists. On Wednesday evening city officials quietly agreed to indirect negotiations filtered through six mediators, three of whom were black; and on Thursday Marion Page, the secretary of the Albany Movement, announced that "some progress has been made," primarily on the issue of desegregated transit facilities. For at least some of Albany's white leaders, maintaining the color line at the city's bus and rail terminals appeared to be less important than restoring order. But there was more confusion than clarity, both inside and outside of the negotiating room.

After facing charges for disorderly conduct, SNCC executive director Jim Forman and other Freedom Riders (from left to right, Bertha Gober, Bernard Lee, Forman, Lenora Taitt, Charles Jones, unidentified, Norma Collins) leave the Albany, Georgia, city hall while supporters kneel in prayer along the sidewalk, December 13, 1961. (Bettmann-CORBIS)

Earlier in the day, Norma Anderson—the wife of Dr. William G. Anderson, the president of the Albany Movement—had led twenty demonstrators, mostly high school students, to the white waiting room at the Trailways terminal. After purchasing tickets to Tallahassee, Mrs. Anderson and nine others sat down at a previously whites-only lunch counter and ordered coffee, which, to their surprise, was promptly served by a black waitress. Ten minutes later, however, Chief Pritchett ordered their arrest. Carted off to jail, they expected to be behind bars before noon. But to their amazement, a police spokesman soon informed them that the charges had been dropped. They were free to return to the bus station, by police escort if they wished. Relieved but not quite sure what to make of this reversal, Anderson led her charges back to the station waiting room, where they remained for nearly an hour, the first Albany blacks to experience at least partial compliance with the ICC order.[43]

Though somewhat encouraging, the developing situation at the Trailways lunch counter did little to cool the fires of racial discord in Albany. While Norma Anderson and the students were still at the terminal, Governor Ernest Vandiver fulfilled Albany mayor Asa Kelley's request to put 150 National Guardsmen on alert at the local armory. And later in the day the negotiations were temporarily suspended when Albany Movement leaders received a report that Sherrod had been "brutally beaten" by guards at a Terrell County prison farm. Tempers cooled and the negotiations resumed only after Pritchett allowed an obviously healthy Sherrod to appear at a mass meeting that evening. "They slapped me a couple of times" and "cut my lip," Sherrod told the crowd, but there had been no beating. Relieved, the audience filled the hall with amens and shouts of praise. Before the night was over, however, the Albany crisis would take a strange and unexpected turn.

Reviving an idea floated earlier in the week, Dr. Anderson invited Martin Luther King to speak to an Albany Movement mass meeting on Friday evening, December 15. Although apologizing for the short notice, Anderson insisted that the Albany crisis had reached a critical stage and King's presence was needed to push the negotiations to a successful conclusion. Unaware that Jim Forman, Marion Page, and others were opposed to SCLC involvement in Albany, King accepted the invitation, in part because Ralph Abernathy, a college classmate of Anderson's, urged him to do so. Accompanied by Abernathy, Wyatt Tee Walker, and NAACP regional secretary Ruby Hurley, King arrived in Albany on Friday afternoon to discover that Anderson had arranged two mass meetings, one at Shiloh Baptist and a second at Mount Zion.

The speeches King gave that evening and the emotional procession that followed him from Shiloh to Mount Zion drove a crowd of fifteen hundred to near hysteria. After Hurley admonished the faithful to "keep your feet on the ground although your heads are in the air," King urged them to draw upon the sustaining power of nonviolent struggle: "Say to the white man, 'We will win you with the power of our capacity to endure,' " he advised. Soulful spirituals, Albany-style freedom songs, and nearly two hours of eloquent testimony followed, and by the end of the evening nearly everyone was overcome with emotion, including King and Dr. Anderson. When Anderson rose to thank the SCLC leader, he could not resist adding an invitation to spend the weekend marching for freedom in Albany. After a brief conference in the pastor's office, King agreed to stay in the city for at least another day—an impulsive decision that had an immediate and unfortunate effect on the ongoing negotiations with white leaders. Sometime after midnight Anderson, without consulting any of his colleagues, sent a brief telegram to Mayor Kelley that sounded like an ultimatum: Frustrated with the slow pace of negotiations, the Albany Movement expected a favorable response to its demands by 10:00 A.M. Saturday. Although the telegram did not say so explicitly, Kelley and other city officials interpreted the message as a thinly veiled threat to return to the strategy of mass protest. Angered by Anderson's perceived bluster, Kelley announced that the Albany Movement had broken off negotiations with the city.

In the ensuing confusion, recriminations and factional suspicions threatened to tear the Albany Movement apart. With some of its leaders noticeably absent, the Andersons joined King, Abernathy, Walker, and 260 other march-

ers on a Saturday afternoon prayer pilgrimage to city hall. None of the marchers, however, actually made it to the city hall steps. Intercepted by a large
force of local police and state troopers, all 265 marchers, including King,
were herded into an alley behind the city jail and placed under arrest. By
nightfall their arrests had swelled the number of movement demonstrators
behind bars to more than four hundred. As SCLC's designated spokesman
on the Albany crisis, Abernathy accepted bail and returned to Atlanta on
Sunday morning. But King remained in jail as a symbol of SCLC commitment to the Albany cause. "I will not accept bond," he explained to reporters
from his cell at the Sumter County Jail. "If convicted, I will refuse to pay the
fine. I expect to spend Christmas in jail. I hope thousands will join me."

Determined to take full advantage of King's pledge, Abernathy announced
that SCLC was ready to spearhead a mass pilgrimage to Albany, and behind
the scenes Walker was busy soliciting funds and mobilizing local and national support for the SCLC initiative. Both men, however, were soon rebuffed by a coalition of SNCC and Albany Movement leaders who resented
SCLC's presumptuous declarations of authority and command. At a Sunday
press conference organized by Charles Jones and SNCC advisor Ella Baker,
Marion Page issued a firm denial that SCLC or any other outside group had
assumed leadership of the Albany Movement. Local movement leaders, he
insisted, had no plans to participate in an SCLC-sponsored pilgrimage or
any other mass demonstration that would prevent the Albany Movement from
resuming negotiations with city leaders.

This public rebuke would poison relations between SNCC and SCLC
in the coming months, but an unexpected development inside the Sumter
County Jail took some of the sting out of the situation. Minutes before Page's
statement, King had changed his mind about remaining in jail. Worried that
his cellmate, Dr. Anderson, was on the verge of a nervous breakdown, King
told Walker "to get us out of here." How Walker could do so without damaging King's reputation among movement stalwarts was unclear, but forces
beyond his or King's control soon brought a timely if imperfect solution of
their dilemma. By Monday, December 18—the day of King's trial—local,
state, and federal officials had reached a consensus that the only way to defuse the crisis was to get King and the other demonstrators out of jail as soon
as possible. With James Gray, the conservative editor of the *Albany Herald*,
acting as a mediator, Robert Kennedy and Burke Marshall assured Mayor
Kelley that the Justice Department would refrain from interfering in the
Albany situation as long as it remained nonviolent. Encouraged by the resumption of negotiations on Sunday evening, Kennedy and Marshall urged
Kelley to forge a compromise before King's trial and conviction pushed the
crisis to a new level. After a frantic round of communications, movement and
city leaders worked out a preliminary settlement, just in time for Judge Abner
Israel to order a sixty-day postponement of King's trial.

Under the terms of the agreement, King and all of the breach-of-peace defendants were to be released immediately, most without the burden of posting bond. Although the Freedom Riders and other "outside agitators" were required to post hefty bail bonds, King endorsed the mass release of prisoners as a precondition for future progress. The rest of the settlement, which amounted to a verbal commitment to form a biracial desegregation commission, was more difficult to assess, he told reporters gathered on the courthouse steps. But for now he felt that he could leave town with the comforting knowledge that the city of Albany was finally moving in the right direction.

Unfortunately for King and the Albany Movement, this sanguine interpretation of the situation was promptly contradicted by Chief Pritchett, who denied that white leaders had agreed to anything beyond a willingness to consider creating a biracial commission. Speaking for Mayor Kelley and the city commission, Pritchett gave the distinct impression that King had decided to leave Albany with or without a satisfactory settlement. Although King and others later disputed Pritchett's claim, the ensuing confusion put King's departure from Albany in a bad light. Coinciding with the collapse of negotiations, his apparent retreat created a public relations disaster for SCLC. Most reporters interpreted his involvement in Albany as a mistake; the *New York Herald Tribune*, for example, labeled it "a devastating loss of face." Many movement leaders agreed, suggesting serious dissension within the movement. Excluded from King's postrelease press conference, Reagon and other SNCC leaders could not hide their disdain for the cult of personality that had prompted SCLC's high-handed interference in Albany.

Although CORE officials tried to stay clear of the rising feud between SNCC and SCLC, they too were concerned about the deteriorating situation in Albany. For them, however, the most troubling aspect of the Albany crisis was the federal government's tacit acceptance of Pritchett's strategy of indirection and delay. His insistence that the arrests at the Albany terminals were designed to keep the peace, not to maintain segregation, was a transparent attempt to justify non-compliance with the ICC order. Yet Justice Department officials had not sought a Federal court implementation order for Albany as they had in seven other recalcitrant communities. The fact that the State of Georgia had filed a federal court suit challenging the ICC order would, in all likelihood, eventually provide the Justice Department with a legal lever to enforce desegregation in Albany and other Georgia cities. But the department's apparent willingness to treat the Albany situation as a special case was still a troubling reminder of the political constraints that had delayed civil rights enforcement in the past.[44]

As the year of the Freedom Rides drew to a close, the unresolved crises in Albany and McComb confirmed that, despite a general pattern of compliance with the ICC order, there was a great deal of desegregation work left to be done in the Deep South. "A well-advertised group of Freedom Riders may receive police protection," columnist Anthony Lewis wrote in the *New York Times* on December 3, "but it would probably still be a brave, indeed foolhardy local Negro who sat down at the 'white' restaurant in an Alabama or Mississippi bus terminal." While he predicted "that acceptance of Federal law is only a matter of time—in short, inevitable," Lewis warned his readers that "ending the deep-seated tradition of racial discrimination will be a long and difficult process," especially in places like Mississippi where "one should beware of false optimism." Indeed, even in the Upper South and border states, where virtually all terminals, buses, and trains were desegregated, there were pockets of dogged segregationist resistance, as a series of arrests at several Route 40 restaurants demonstrated on December 16.

For the most part, however, movement leaders and administration officials were pleased with the overall response to implementation of transit desegregation. In most areas outright resistance had been replaced by a spirit of resignation, and evidence of real progress could be seen in some of the South's toughest white supremacist strongholds. Even in Birmingham, where Bull Connor sustained a spirited rear-guard political action against desegregation of bus terminal restaurants, there was some grudging movement toward compliance by mid-December. After Connor urged the city commission to revoke the Trailways restaurant's license because it violated the city's segregated dining ordinance, an influential local businessmen's group countered with a call for compliance with federal law. On December 14 the Justice Department tried to preempt Connor's action by seeking a federal injunction against any further interference with the ICC order in Birmingham. But five days later—following a public hearing—the city commission voted unanimously to revoke the license, all but forcing the federal courts to intervene. In early January 1962 Federal District Judge Seybourn H. Lynne, a conservative segregationist, surprised many local observers by issuing a temporary injunction that nullified the commission's action. Left with no legal alternative, Connor and the commissioners conceded defeat on the narrow issue of segregated transit facilities and transferred their energies to other fronts in the war against desegregation and federal encroachment. While the broader struggle to preserve Alabama's white supremacist traditions went on, the battle of the Birmingham bus terminals was over.[45]

The prospects for compliance with the ICC order were also improving in Mississippi, though here the situation was muddled by mixed signals from the federal courts and by continued reliance on local breach-of-peace ordinances. Even though the traditional Jim Crow signs had been removed from the bus and rail terminals in Jackson and other cities, the threat of arrest remained for anyone who attempted to desegregate white waiting rooms and lunch counters. Lacking Pritchett's political and diplomatic skills, and burdened with the stigma of the Freedom Rider trials, Jackson officials made little effort to conceal their segregationist intentions. Consequently, on December

14, the Justice Department joined the NAACP's appeal of the federal district court's refusal to grant an injunction enjoining the use of segregationist breach-of-peace statutes in Mississippi. In a written brief filed with the United States Supreme Court Associate Justice Hugo Black, Solicitor General Archibald Cox complained that "hundreds of American citizens" had been "arrested and convicted for merely claiming their constitutional rights."

Two days later, a long-awaited Supreme Court ruling on a Baton Rouge sit-in case that involved similar misuse of breach-of-peace statutes temporarily raised hopes that the Court would grant at least a temporary stay of the ongoing prosecution of more than three hundred Mississippi Freedom Riders. Reversing the convictions of sixteen blacks arrested for causing civil disorder in Baton Rouge, the Court's reasoning seemed to open the door for the ultimate dismissal of charges against all of the Riders convicted in Jackson. But on Monday, December 18, the Court stunned NAACP attorneys and Justice Department officials with a unanimous ruling rejecting the request for a stay. Although the stated basis of the rejection was narrow and hinged on a technical interpretation of legal standing—the three defendants representing the class action had not been arrested for breach of peace—the Court's ruling sent a chill through movement and government leaders already weary from several months of seemingly unnecessary and gratuitous complications. "It is important not to read too much into the Supreme Court's refusal," a *New York Times* editorial counseled. But among those who had grown accustomed to victory at the highest level of judicial review, this was not easy advice to follow. Coming one week before the most cherished day of the Christian faith, the unexpected twist of legal defeat provided yet another reminder that unmerited suffering was the chosen fate of those who embraced the philosophy of nonviolence. For many of the Freedom Riders, the trials and tests of tolerance would continue, literally and figuratively, for years to come. And for some, even legal triumph and racial desegregation would bring little satisfaction as long as the beloved community remained an unrealized ideal.[46]

Epilogue: Glory Bound

Yes, we are the Freedom Riders,
And we ride a long Greyhound.
White or black, we know no difference, Lord,
For we are Glory bound.[1]

DURING THE WINTER OF 1961–1962, the Freedom Riders exited from the center stage of American public life. But they did not go quietly. If 1961 was the year of the Freedom Rides, encompassing the heart of the drama, 1962 was the denouement. For the movement, and for the Freedom Riders themselves, the weeks and months following the initial implementation of the ICC order were filled with legal, tactical, and other matters related to the Rides. Indeed, for much of the nation—especially for white Southerners—1962 proved to be a challenging period of adaptation and adjustment, a transitional era that saw the passing of old myths and the birth of new realities of race, region, and democracy. In Washington, Justice Department officials spent much of the year scrambling to meet—or in some cases deflect—the rising expectations of movement activists, while the president and other administration leaders dealt with the political fallout from the federal government's recent tilt toward constitutional enforcement and social justice. And in New York and Atlanta, civil rights leaders faced similar challenges as they strained to maintain momentum and a spirit of cooperation in the face of new organizational realities—chiefly, the enhanced power and vitality of CORE and SNCC.

The Freedom Rides had compounded and accelerated the changes initiated by the 1960 sit-ins, and the reconfigured world of civil rights activism—in which students generally took the lead while lawyers, ministers, and other elders struggled to keep up—looked radically different from the late-1950s movement led by the NAACP and SCLC. By the end of 1962 virtually all matters related to the movement—from generational and organizational lines of authority to ideological considerations of nonviolence and interracialism—were in flux or undergoing serious reexamination. Not all of this could be attributed to the success of the Freedom Rides, of course. But, as Diane McWhorter later put it, the Rides seemed to be "one of history's rare alchemical phenomena, altering the structural makeup of everything they touched."[2]

The aftershocks from the Freedom Rides could be felt everywhere, but the most obvious seismic shifts were in the Deep South, where the active phase of the crisis lasted the longest. This was especially true in Mississippi, where the weekly Freedom Rider appellate trials continued until late May 1962, and where the rumblings of black unrest and white resistance were amplified by the unsettling influence of student activists affiliated with SNCC and CORE.

Despite the removal of Jim Crow signs across the state, compliance with the ICC order was haphazard at best, and in many Mississippi communities anyone asserting the constitutional right to equal access to transit facilities risked arrest for breach of peace. NAACP attorney and future Harvard Law School professor Derrick Bell discovered this on January 10, when he was arrested for loitering in the white waiting room of the Jackson railroad terminal, and three weeks later the police arrested Ernest McBride, a black soldier from Los Angeles, for a similar infraction at the Jackson Greyhound station.

Such arrests became less common after February 26, when the U.S. Supreme Court issued a unanimous and definitive ruling in *Bailey v. Patterson*, the NAACP class-action desegregation case filed by the NAACP on behalf of Samuel Bailey and three other Jackson blacks in June 1961. Annulling the two-to-one decision of the three-judge federal district panel, the Court stated plainly: "We have settled beyond question that no state may require racial segregation of interstate or intrastate transportation facilities." Once again, however, the situation was muddied by the Court's refusal to issue an injunction staying the prosecution of the Freedom Riders arrested in Jackson. According to the Court, since the plaintiffs were not actually Freedom Riders and had never been arrested as such, Bailey and the others had no standing to enjoin the prosecutions. Though technically correct, this decision created confusion and ensured continued resistance on the part of Mississippi segregationists interested in preserving Jim Crow transit.[3]

Part of the problem was a poisonous statewide political atmosphere that implicitly sanctioned vigilante and extralegal enforcement of segregated mores. Emboldened by defiant White Citizens' Council leaders and demagogic politicians, individual bus drivers, station agents, and police officers routinely ignored federal mandates, dismissing them as illegitimate infringements of local control and states' rights. Believing that intimidation and even violence were acceptable means of maintaining segregation, many white Mississippians felt empowered to do whatever was necessary to counter the efforts of perceived troublemakers. On April 26, for example, a policeman in the southern Mississippi town of Taylorsville shot and killed Corporal Roman Duckworth after the young black soldier failed to move to the back of a bus. Although Duckworth was unarmed and had the legal right to sit wherever he pleased, there were no legal consequences for the policeman, and the local and state press all but ignored the incident. The fact that Duckworth was a Mississippi native returning home to visit a sick wife did not seem to evoke much sympathy among white segregationists, who saw him as just another good Negro gone bad. In the wake of the Freedom Rides, any black Mississippian with experience outside the state was suspect, and Duckworth's violation of segregationist traditions simply confirmed the suspicion that virtually all of the state's racial problems could be attributed to outside influences.[4]

During the weeks and months following the Rides, Mississippi segregationists felt that they were still under siege from outside agitators, and to some extent they were right. Even though the vast majority of Freedom Riders had long since left the state, the dozen or so who remained were part of a growing movement presence in Mississippi. Though modest in comparison to Freedom Summer 1964, when nearly a thousand student activists descended upon the state, the rising spirit of the "Move on Mississippi," as SNCC called it, was palpable in 1962. Even in Jackson, where the concentration of visiting activists was greatest and where CORE field secretary Tom Gaither returned in January to reorganize the Jackson Non-Violent Movement, the number of those involved was small. But the mere presence of "professional agitators" such as Gaither was unnerving to white Mississippians, many of whom were beginning to realize that the state was no longer off-limits to the national movement. Martin Luther King drove this point home in early February when he chose Clarksdale, Mississippi, in the heart of the Delta, as the first stop in a region-wide "People to People" tour aimed at recruiting a "nonviolent army" known as the SCLC "Freedom Corps." Visiting seven communities and delivering a dozen speeches in three days, King served notice that the local activists who had been struggling for years to bring change to the Delta were no longer alone.[5]

SCLC's profile in Mississippi never quite matched the promise of King's speeches, but an emerging alliance of SNCC, CORE, and the NAACP picked up at least some of the slack. Less than a week after King's speaking tour, Bob Moses of SNCC, Tom Gaither of CORE, and Medgar Evers and Aaron Henry of the state NAACP conference met in Jackson to reorganize the Council of Federated Organizations established the previous May. Searching for "a unifying force," as former Freedom Rider Dave Dennis later put it, and anticipating the distribution of Voter Education Project (VEP) funds through the Southern Regional Council, the new COFO founders crafted an umbrella organization to coordinate voter registration projects and other movement initiatives across the state. With Henry as president, Moses as program director, and Dennis as assistant program director, COFO soon put the VEP funds to good use, establishing or expanding existing voting rights projects in ten communities spread across six counties. Four of the counties were in the Delta, where SNCC and NAACP organizers took the lead, and two were in southeastern Mississippi, where CORE was given primary responsibility.

All of the projects involved collaboration between local and visiting student activists, and several were staffed by former Freedom Riders, including Lester McKinnie in Laurel and the newly married Jim and Diane Nash Bevel in Cleveland. Even when Freedom Riders were not involved, many local whites and blacks assumed otherwise. In Greenwood, for example, project leader Sam Block was routinely misidentified as a Freedom Rider, a mistake that compounded the difficulty of organizing fearful black citizens. "People would just get afraid of me," Block later explained to Jim Forman. "They said, 'He's a Freedom Rider.' " They didn't want "to have anything to do with me . . . because I was a Freedom Rider. I was there to stir up trouble, that's all." As Block and many others discovered, being identified as—or even associating with—an outside agitator could have severe consequences in Mississippi. Arrested seven times during his first eight months in Greenwood, Block suffered several beatings at the hands of white vigilantes or policemen, one of whom characterized him as "the most dangerous nigger in Mississippi."[6]

At one time or another, similar characterizations were applied to other militant activists, including Moses, Medgar Evers, and Dave Dennis, who became CORE's Mississippi field secretary in the summer of 1962. But for many white Mississippians the most unsettling and confounding activists of them all were the Bevels, a husband-and-wife team that symbolized the continuing influence of the Freedom Rides. Indeed, Diane Nash Bevel's status as the most visible female "agitator" in the state was especially perplexing to white supremacists unaccustomed to tongue-lashings and moral challenges from twenty-three-year-old pregnant women. After spending several frustrating weeks in Jackson and Laurel, and facing an upcoming appellate trial for her alleged corruption of underage activists the previous summer, she confounded prosecutors and other white officials on April 30 by abandoning her appeal. Surrendering herself to authorities, who promptly arrested her for sitting in the white section of the Hinds County courtroom, she released a public statement explaining why she was ready to begin serving a two-year term in jail:

> To appeal further would necessitate my sitting through another court trial in a Mississippi court, and I have reached the conclusion that I can no longer cooperate with the evil and unjust court system of this state. I subscribe to the philosophy of nonviolence; thus to one of the basic tenets of nonviolence—that you refuse to cooperate with evil. The only condition under which I will leave jail will be if the unjust and untrue charges against me are completely dropped. Some people have asked me how I can do this

when I am expecting my first child in September. I have searched my soul about this and considered it in prayer. I have reached the conclusion that in the long run this will be the best thing I can do for my child. Since my child will be a black child, born in Mississippi, whether I am in jail or not, he will be born in prison. I believe that if I go to jail now it may help hasten that day when my child and all children will be free, not only on the day of their birth, but for all of their lives.

Though destined to become a part of movement lore, this eloquent testimonial did not have the intended effect among black or white Mississippians. After three weeks of private consultation with local and state leaders, Judge Russel Moore stymied Bevel's attempt at martyrdom by denying her right to drop the appeal. Even more discouraging was the lack of reaction from the local black community. Two student activists, Luvaghn Brown and Jesse Harris, expressed their support by challenging the segregated seating patterns in Moore's courtroom, an infraction that earned them forty days at the Hinds County prison farm. And four others were arrested in downtown Jackson on June 2 during a protest against Brown's and Harris's treatment. But the general failure of the Jackson Non-Violent Movement to rise up in protest convinced the Bevels that their energies might be better spent in other areas of the state. Moving to the Delta town of Cleveland, where they joined forces with longtime activist Amzie Moore, the determined couple spent most of the summer and fall coordinating voter registration among rural blacks.

With Moses overseeing a general movement of SNCC operations into the Delta and with Jim Bevel serving as SCLC's state field secretary, the Voter Education Project in Cleveland, along with those in the nearby counties of Coahoma, Leflore, and Sunflower, made a valiant effort to bring a measure of democracy to a benighted region during the second half of 1962. But, in the absence of a solid guarantee from the Justice Department to shield civil rights workers and black registrants from white supremacist intimidation and violence, it was all but impossible for a small vanguard to accomplish much beyond the symbolic victory of survival. By the end of the year the lack of progress in the face of determined, often violent, white resistance had forced COFO leaders to scale down their expectations and to suspend operations in several of the most dangerous counties. Like the Freedom Riders of the previous year, the Mississippi Voter Education Project workers and their local allies had demonstrated their willingness to put their bodies on the line. This time, however, the sacrifices of committed nonviolent activists did not lead to a timely government mandate for racial progress.[7]

In Mississippi the ICC mandate yielded relatively little in the way of actual desegregation by the end of 1962. Here, more than anywhere else, movement leaders had to deal with a ferocious form of white supremacist resistance paradoxically fueled by a combination of outside intervention and the apparent futility of that intervention. In the long run the ICC order would lead to grudging desegregation and ultimately to new social mores, but in the short run, the perceived emptiness of the Freedom Riders' victory encouraged continued resistance on all fronts, including voting rights and school desegregation. With the help of meddling federal officials, outside agitators had invaded the state, yet the Mississippi way of life remained intact. Among white Mississippians in 1962, this was the primary lesson conveyed by the Freedom Rides.

For some, this delusional sense of invulnerability to fundamental change began to fade in the fall of 1962 following the court-ordered integration of the University of Mississippi by James Meredith, a plucky air force veteran and Jackson State student who had enlisted the support of the NAACP Legal Defense Fund during a long legal struggle to breach the barriers of Mississippi's most hallowed bastion of white privilege. For many others, though, the fact that Meredith's arrival at Ole Miss precipitated a major riot later known as the Battle of Oxford—that the enrollment of a single black student required the deployment of more than three thousand federal troops—simply reinforced the notion that Mississippi was a land apart and beyond the reach of effective outside intervention. With military guards shadowing his every move, Meredith remained at Ole Miss for a full academic year, graduating in the spring of 1963. But the Battle of Oxford and its aftermath left a legacy of racial polarization and distrust that heightened white Mississippi's sense of alienation. Most tragically, as the historian John Dittmer has observed, the backlash from the Meredith crisis struck the disfranchised and dispossessed blacks living in "movement" communities such as Greenwood with special force. Economically and physically vulnerable, without the benefit of political power or constitutional protection, they "would bear the brunt of white rage over the defeat suffered at the hands of the federal government."[8]

At the close of 1962, the same could have been said of the Freedom Rides, which seemingly had produced more resistance than progress, leaving local blacks in a precarious position once the mass of Freedom Riders had left the state. In the case of transit desegregation, however, the balance sheet soon shifted toward compliance and genuine progress, providing even Mississippi blacks with tangible gains that justified the provocations and intrusions of 1961. Despite the federal government's continuing reluctance to interfere in other areas of public life, the combined efforts of the Justice Department, the ICC, and the federal courts to desegregate the state's bus, rail, and air terminals proved successful by the summer of 1963. Early in the year the Justice Department filed lawsuits against the police departments of Greenwood and Winona, which had persisted in enforcing segregation at local terminals, but in June the department reported that its investigators "knew of no rail, bus, or airline facility still maintaining segregation," in Mississippi or anywhere else. While *de facto* and self-segregation remained common, especially in communities where unmarked but duplicate waiting rooms and other facilities survived, and many Mississippi blacks were still wary of asserting the right to sit where they pleased, the age of systemic, legally enforced transit segregation was over. Nearly two years after the Mississippi Freedom Rides, the results could be seen as a civil rights milestone, despite a rear-guard legal action to punish the individuals and organizations involved. For at least some of the Riders arrested in Jackson and McComb, and for the attorneys who represented them, the legal ordeal of appeals, continuances, and court appearances continued until 1965. But by that time the first major civil rights victory in the nation's most hidebound state was secure, suggesting that the Rides were only a prelude to further struggle and ultimate triumph.[9]

NO OTHER STATE MATCHED Mississippi's general and persistent pattern of defiance and delay in the aftermath of the Freedom Rides, but for a time there were pockets of determined resistance in the nearby states of Louisiana, Alabama, and Georgia. As the intended final destination of the original Freedom Ride, Louisiana harbored more than its share of angry white supremacists, many of whom felt that their state had been singled out for abuse. Most of the active resistance to the ICC order was in the northern and central parts of the state, especially in Shreveport and Baton Rouge, where local CORE chapters were pressing for enforcement. During the Freedom Rides, the Shreveport police had been among the most aggressive in the South, maintaining strict segregation in all city facilities and arresting anyone who challenged their right to do so. This spirit of outright defiance continued well into 1962, making Shreveport one of the last cities in the region to comply with the ICC mandate. Only after a Justice Department suit and a June 4 Supreme Court decision setting aside the convictions of six Freedom Riders did the police force and the white community begin to countenance even token desegregation. And it would be several years before local blacks could comfortably exercise the rights guaranteed by the ICC without risking economic retaliation or police harassment.

The situation was not much better in Baton Rouge, where the effort to test compliance with the ICC order became entangled with a broader movement to desegregate Baton Rouge's downtown business district. Led by former Freedom Riders Dave Dennis and Ben Cox, a series of mass demonstrations by Southern University students in December 1961 resulted in hundreds of arrests and several confrontations between marchers and police squads armed with tear gas and attack dogs. After university administrators expelled seven students affiliated with CORE and temporarily closed the school, the demonstrations ceased, but in late January a Baton Rouge judge sentenced Cox and fellow Freedom Rider Dion Diamond to long jail terms. In Diamond's case, the conviction was for "criminal anarchy," since, according to the prosecutor, the young SNCC veteran was a member of "an organization known to teach, practice, and advocate the overthrow of the government of the State of Louisiana by unlawful means." When SNCC chairman Chuck McDew and field secretary Bob Zellner visited Diamond in jail in mid-February, they too were charged with criminal anarchy. All were eventually released on bail, and after SNCC mounted a national campaign to protest harassment of its leaders, the charges were reduced to the standard breach-of-peace variety. But officials in Louisiana's capital city had served notice that they were not going to coddle activists who challenged their authority to enforce local or state Jim Crow laws. In the end, the prominence of the capital ensured that transit desegregation would come earlier than in Shreveport, but this achievement was cold comfort for an embattled black community with a long history of civil rights activity that included a 1953 bus boycott predating the struggle in Montgomery.[10]

The pace of change was also disappointingly slow in New Orleans, where both the Freedom Rides and a bitter struggle over school desegregation had reinvigorated a tradition of racial extremism. With a moderate mayor, a large and vigilant local movement, and the judges of the Fifth Circuit on hand as observers, city police and transit employees had little choice but to comply with the letter of the law. But the overall tone of the white community's response to the Freedom Rides and the ICC order suggested that nonviolent activists had failed to dispel the fear and parochialism that had plagued the city during the school crisis of 1960. To the dismay of the city's outnumbered moderates and liberals, the New Orleans metropolitan area became a center of symbolic resistance to the Freedom Rides during the spring and summer of 1962. Long known as a unique center of creativity, the city and its environs produced an imaginative but gratuitously cruel countermovement known as the Reverse Freedom Rides.

The brainchild of George Singelmann—the head of the Greater New Orleans Citizens' Council and a close associate of the infamous Plaquemines Parish demagogue Judge Leander Perez—the proposal for Reverse Freedom Rides created a sensation when it was first announced in mid-April. Singelmann's original plan, advertised on handbills distributed throughout southeastern Louisiana, offered "Free Transportation plus $5.00 for Expenses to any Negro Man or Woman, or Family (No limit to size) who desire to migrate to the Nation's Capital, or any city in the north of their choosing." On the back of the flyer, Singelmann printed a list of the addresses and phone numbers of welfare departments and NAACP and Urban League offices in Washington and four other Northern cities, ostensibly to help the Reverse Freedom Riders find a job after they arrived. Although he and other Citizens' Council leaders claimed that they were acting in the best interests of Louisiana's black citizens, they did not deny that their primary aim was to tell "the North to put up or shut up." Decrying the hypocrisy of Northern liberals, they predicted, often with a wink and a smirk, that the northward migration of unemployed blacks would promote interregional understanding and confirm the benefits of racial segregation for all Americans.[11]

Louis and Dorothy Boyd and their eight children, the first family to take advantage of the Citizens' Council offer, arrived in New York City on April 20. An unemployed longshoreman, Louis Boyd soon found work as a handyman for a Jersey City electronics firm and told reporters he "couldn't be happier" with his decision to relocate in the North. Many of those who arrived later in the year would have an entirely different experience, but this initial success encouraged Singelmann to expand his proposal to include a one-way "freedom train" that would transport "1,000 Negroes" northward. Claiming that he had secured twenty thousand dollars from local philanthropists to underwrite the train, the jubilant Citizens' Council leader soon received an enthusiastic endorsement from Louisiana's senior senator, Allen Ellender. Responding to an NAACP official's criticism of the plan, Ellender defended the idea of Reverse Freedom Rides as a legitimate response to the provocations of the past year. "Now the Freedom Riders are North-bound and they are Freedom Riders in the truest sense of the phrase," he told reporters on April 24, "for not only are they riding free but of their own free will. Why doesn't the NAACP want these free people in the North? Is it possible the NAACP has no genuine interest in the advancement of colored people?" Angered by this sophistry and outraged by the Citizens' Councils plans, Senator Jacob Javits of New York immediately denounced the "casting off of destitute Negroes" as "a shocking and shameful act," predicting that the "American people will be aroused by this heartless display of theatricalism at the expense of the innocent."

Javits's prediction was accurate, and most of the national press and public commentary on the Reverse Freedom Rides was sharply critical, including a May 9 press conference statement by President Kennedy characterizing them as "a rather cheap exercise . . . in publicity." In some areas of the white South, however, the Reverse Rides attracted considerable support. While the freedom train did not materialize and the actual number of Reverse Riders never quite matched Singelmann's grand projections, the countermovement soon spread beyond greater New Orleans and Louisiana. On April 27 the Mississippi legislature passed a resolution urging the state's White Citizens' Councils to follow Singelmann's lead; and on May 19, delegates to the Citizens' Councils of America's annual conference, meeting in New Orleans, formally endorsed the Reverse Rides. But by that time several local Citizens' Councils—including the councils of Shreveport, Baton Rouge, Birmingham, Montgomery, Selma, and Jackson—had already announced plans to sponsor groups of black migrants.[12]

Among the first to send Reverse Riders northward was the Capitol Citizens' Council of Little Rock, which came up with a notorious variation of Singelmann's plan later copied by the Baton Rouge and other chapters. Beginning in mid-May, virtually all of the Reverse Riders from Little Rock were sent to Hyannis, Massachusetts, the Cape Cod summer home of the Kennedy family. Hoping to embarrass not only the president and the attorney general but also their younger brother, Ted, who was in the midst of a race for a seat in the U.S. Senate, Capitol Council president Amos Guthridge distributed recruitment posters indicating that "President Kennedy's brother assures you a grand reception to Massachusetts. Good jobs, housing, etc. are promised." When, as expected, the actual reception accorded the scores of black migrants to Hyannis proved to be something less than grand, Guthridge declared that his experiment had confirmed the immutable nature of racial segregation. Here, as elsewhere, there were individual acts of kindness that belied the Citizens' Councils' sweeping claims that all white Northerners were racially prejudiced. But the generally inhospitable response of Northern officials—which included Massachusetts governor John Volpe's request for federal legislation outlawing the Reverse Rides—allowed the Citizens' Councils to score propaganda points that were trumpeted by conservative commentators north and south. "Listen to them squirm!" advised the Chicago-based columnist Paul Harvey. "The hypocrisy of pompous Northern do-gooders has never been more apparent." More sympathetic observers pointed out that factors other than racism were involved—that Volpe and others were understandably worried that a flood of impoverished migrants would overwhelm an already overburdened welfare system in unprepared Northern communities—but it was difficult to counter the general impression that Northern hypocrisy had been exposed.

The deteriorating situation in Hyannis was especially embarrassing: Most of the black migrants moved on as soon as they found an alternative, and only one family of Reverse Riders remained there three years later. But the experiences of the Reverse Riders sent to other communities—from Concord, New Hampshire, to Pocatello, Idaho—were not much better. By midsummer, the negative publicity surrounding the general disillusionment of the approximately two hundred blacks who had joined the Reverse Freedom Rides had convinced almost everyone, including most Citizens' Council leaders, that the program had run its course. Strapped for funding, the participating councils quietly withdrew their offers to sponsor additional Riders. In September Singelmann promoted a desperate plan to revive the program by dispatching unemployed black Southerners to the hometowns of Hubert Humphrey and other liberal politicians during the Christmas season, and for several months thereafter he continued to solicit funds for the expressed purpose of resuming the Rides. But mercifully his efforts proved futile. The sordid affair that the *New York Times* had aptly labeled "a cheap trafficking in human misery" was over.[13]

THE REVERSE FREEDOM RIDES never quite caught on in Georgia, where the White Citizens' Councils were less powerful than in Louisiana or Mississippi. Only the chapter in Macon—where a bus boycott forced the desegregation of local transit facilities in March 1962—came forward to sponsor black migrants, and fewer than a dozen Reverse Riders actually left the state. While many white Georgians undoubtedly sympathized with the effort to embarrass Northern liberals, few seemed willing to engage in public manifestations of revenge or defiance in the wake of the Freedom Rides. In many areas of the state, this spirit of restraint turned out to be a temporary flirtation, and later in the decade a powerful political backlash against moderates perceived to be soft on segregation put the race-baiting demagogue Lester Maddox in the governor's mansion. But in 1962 political moderation was on the upswing in Georgia, which appeared to be moving away from its more truculent Deep South neighbors on matters of race and resistance. Led by an image-conscious Atlanta business community and propelled by *Baker v. Carr*, a landmark March 1962 Supreme Court decision that struck down a long-standing county unit system giving unfair advantage to rural voters, the state had reached a "turning point," as former president Jimmy Carter later put it.

Elected to the state senate in the fall of 1962, in his first race for public office, Carter was just one of the moderates to come to the fore in that pivotal year. In the Democratic gubernatorial primary, reform-minded Carl Sanders of Augusta defeated the arch-segregationist former governor Marvin Griffin, thanks to strong support from both white and black voters in metropolitan Atlanta. In the capital city as a whole, Mayor Ivan Allen Jr. presided over an increasingly progressive political culture, and in one downtown district Leroy Johnson became the first black since Reconstruction to be elected to the state senate. Die-hard segregationists and conservative politicos remained dominant throughout rural and small-town Georgia, and even in Atlanta the desegregation process had barely begun. But with a cluster of Atlanta-based civil rights organizations—notably SCLC, SNCC, and the Southern Regional Council—providing close scrutiny and steady pressure, and with Ralph McGill's *Atlanta Constitution* taking a stand against racial extremists, the prospects for future progress in the state looked bright in the year following the Freedom Rides.[14]

There was, however, one major exception to this optimistic forecast—one white community hell-bent on countering the overall trend toward moderation and desegregation. If Atlanta represented the progressive end of the spectrum in Georgia, Albany stood at the opposite end as a symbol of white intransigence and black frustration. Here, in the wiregrass lowlands of southwestern Georgia, there was no letup in the bitter struggle between an ultra-segregationist local power structure and the determined Albany Movement. Though hobbled by dissension following King's embarrassing departure in December 1961, Albany's black activists regrouped in early January, coalescing around an effort to overturn the dismissal of forty student demonstrators from Albany State College. Issues related to the Freedom Rides and segregated transit facilities continued to simmer, and on January 12 the arrest of eighteen-year-old Ola Mae Quarterman for refusing a driver's order to move to the back of a city bus prompted the Albany Movement to extend its month-old boycott of downtown stores to the city's private municipal bus line. Sustained by a car pool similar to the one used by the Montgomery Improvement Association in 1956, the boycott soon forced the financially strapped bus company to ask the city commission for a subsidy.

In the meantime, segregation remained in force, and on January 18 Charles Sherrod and Charles Jones were arrested for "loitering" after a brief sit-in at the Trailways station's lunch counter. Five days later, at the first meeting of the newly elected city commission, Dr. William Anderson and Marion Page appeared before the commissioners to request a written reaffirmation of the December 18 oral agreement, which had authorized the creation of a biracial committee and the complete desegregation of local transit facilities. But Mayor Asa Kelley adjourned the meeting without committing to the reaffirmation. Subsequent negotiations between the Albany Movement and the bus company produced promises to maintain integrated seating and to hire black drivers, but on January 29 the city commission refused to endorse the agreement and rejected the request for a subsidy. Two days later the hardliners on the commission went even further, formally repudiating the December 18 agreement and reprimanding Mayor Kelley for coddling the Albany Movement. At a second meeting later in the day, the commission, with only Mayor Kelley dissenting, reiterated its refusal to allow the bus company to desegregate its facilities. Facing bankruptcy and caught in the whipsaw of political posturing, the company suspended all operations at midnight.

The hardening of the city commission's position and the suspension of bus service on January 31 initiated a series of confrontations that kept the city in turmoil until late summer. But Chief Laurie Pritchett, the main architect of Albany's response to movement activists, made sure that the turmoil stopped short of mass violence. Throughout the spring and summer of 1962, he maintained a consistent strategy of obstructing desegregation with breach-of-peace arrests that avoided outright defiance of the ICC order. In late March, during the trial of the Freedom Riders arrested on December 10, the Albany police dragged Sherrod, Bob Zellner, Tom Hayden, and Per Laursen out of the courtroom after they tried to sit together as an integrated group, but for the most part Pritchett and his men used as little force as possible when arresting and controlling demonstrators. Armed with weekly and sometimes daily briefings on Gandhian discipline, the uniformed defenders of Albany's white supremacist status quo tried to offset the moral force of nonviolent struggle by responding in kind—by enforcing segregation with as much courtesy and restraint as the situation allowed.

In this way, Pritchett kept both the Kennedy administration and the Albany Movement off balance, forestalling federal intervention and disrupting the momentum of mass protest. In neighboring Terrell County, where Sheriff Zeke Mathews tried to intimidate Sherrod and other voting rights work-

The arrest of Martin Luther King Jr. by Police Chief Laurie Pritchett in Albany, Georgia, July 27, 1962. (AP Wide World)

ers with thinly veiled threats of violence, the administration was much more assertive, filing a formal complaint against Mathews after a *New York Times* reporter quoted one of his deputies exclaiming, "We're going to get some of you," to a group meeting in a black church. And in both Terrell and nearby Lee County, a series of black church burnings during the summer of 1962 triggered an ongoing FBI investigation and several arrests. But in Albany itself Pritchett and his men were able to maintain an aura of peaceful, if firmly segregated, coexistence.[15]

The effective and confounding nature of Pritchett's strategy became obvious in July, when King and Abernathy returned to Albany to serve forty-five-day jail terms. Choosing jail instead of paying $178 fines, the SCLC leaders hoped that their incarceration would re-energize the local movement, refocus media attention on Albany, and perhaps force the Kennedy administration to intervene on the movement's behalf. The drama surrounding the sentencing and King and Abernathy's first night in jail was all that movement leaders hoped it would be. But the Albany saga took a strange turn during the next two days—first when a movement march and rally deteriorated into a violent confrontation between the police and brick-throwing teenagers, and later when an "unidentified black man," later discovered to be an agent of Pritchett's, paid King's and Abernathy's fines. With the SCLC leaders' un-expected release, the fragile coalition of local and national civil rights organi-zations began to unravel.

After several days of confusion and indecision, and after SNCC activists questioned his motives as well as his courage, King reluctantly agreed to lead a demonstration that would almost certainly put him back in jail, but on July 20 District Judge Robert Elliott, a conservative Kennedy appointee and ar-dent segregationist, issued an injunction banning any additional civil rights marches in Albany. While this was hardly the federal intervention that he had sought, King promptly announced that he would abide by Elliott's rul-ing and call off the planned marches. This decision infuriated Charles Jones, Jim Forman, and several other SNCC activists who confronted King in an emotional meeting that revealed deep divisions between SCLC and the stu-dent movement. Tempers cooled, however, four days later when Federal Circuit Judge Elbert Tuttle rescinded Elliott's injunction.

Rearrested with ten others following a July 27 march, King spent the next two weeks in jail, still hoping that his high-profile arrest would force the Justice Department to exert enough legal pressure to break the stalemate in Albany. By this time, however, the Albany Movement was losing steam, and city officials were growing increasingly confident that they were on the verge of winning a "war of attrition." On August 10, with the number of available marchers dwindling and with little prospect of federal intervention, move-ment leaders announced the suspension of demonstrations. In return, city officials arranged for the immediate release of King and Abernathy, both of whom returned to Atlanta the next day.

Later in the month, after white leaders made it clear that they had no interest in any further negotiations with the Albany Movement, demonstra-tions resumed on a limited scale. And on August 28, an SCLC-sponsored "Prayer Pilgrimage" brought seventy-five clerical leaders—including several former Freedom Riders—to the city in an effort to dramatize the plight of Albany blacks. All 75 were arrested following a prayer vigil on the city hall steps, and 11 remained in jail for several days after refusing to accept bail. But not even the incarceration of nearly a dozen nationally prominent minis-ters and rabbis could move the Kennedy administration to action—or regen-erate the flagging spirit of the Albany Movement. In southwestern Georgia, the era of mass protest was essentially over, even though cradle-to-grave seg-regation remained in force. While Sherrod and the SNCC voting rights project remained active in the area for another year, the broad-based Albany Movement went into permanent decline during the fall of 1962. In 1963 the Albany Movement secured a Federal court injunction ordering the desegre-gation of all municipal facilities, including bus terminals, but full implemen-tation of the order did not come for several years. Indeed, in the case of transit desegregation, the injunction proved useless because the municipal bus system was no longer in operation.

Of all the civil rights projects related to the Freedom Rides, Albany probably produced the fewest tangible gains. Observers inside and outside the movement, both then and later, often characterized the Albany Movement's collapse as the national civil rights struggle's first major defeat. At the same time, however, there has been widespread and justified appreciation of the intangible benefits of the Albany episode. In Albany's black community, where individual empowerment and bold assertions of equal rights had been rare prior to 1962, sustaining eleven months of demonstrations and capturing the nation's attention brought a collective sense of pride, even in the face of defeat. Most significantly, in the broader context of an evolving national civil rights movement Albany prompted a searching self-evaluation that took the movement—especially SCLC and SNCC—to a higher level of tactical and strategic consciousness. Outlined in an influential Southern Regional Council report and discussed at numerous movement gatherings in late 1962 and early 1963, the lessons learned in Albany—notably, the limitations and vulnerability of nonviolent protest, the difficulty of melding local and national civil rights organizations, the pitfalls of being drawn into a campaign without careful advance planning and well-defined goals, the indispensability of federal support, and the capacity of shrewd segregationist leaders to undercut the movement's moral imperatives in the eyes of reporters and politicians—would prove valuable to King and other movement leaders in the months and years to come.[16]

THE ALBANY EPISODE was also instructive to white segregationists, especially in Alabama, where the unintended consequences of mob violence and heavy-handed political resistance were becoming apparent. For all but the most myopic extremists, the sharp contrast between Albany's Laurie Pritchett and Birmingham's Bull Connor was revealing. Unlike Pritchett, Connor had played into the hands of nonviolent civil rights activists by turning himself into a symbol of segregationist lawlessness and unrestrained racial hatred. By relinquishing the moral high ground to martyred Freedom Riders, he and his Klan accomplices forfeited whatever chance they had of persuading the outside world that segregation was essential to liberty and civic order. In the glare of unfavorable media attention and with the pressure of the Kennedy administration and the federal courts bearing down on Alabama, die-hard segregationists had seen the balance of political and legal power shift in the Freedom Riders' favor. Even though many white Alabamians seethed with resentment against outside agitators in the aftermath of the Freedom Rides, the crisis had not led to white solidarity on matters of politics and racial control. On the contrary, the use of violence to maintain segregation had convinced some Alabama segregationists that the irresponsibility of politicians such as Connor was actually jeopardizing the future of segregation.

And in a few cases, notably among image-conscious businessmen, opposition to extremism had led to doubts about the viability of segregation itself. In a sense, the outbreak of violence early in the crisis had put Alabama on the spot, effectively inoculating the state from further official complicity with violence. By early 1962 the battle of the Freedom Rides was essentially over, and even Connor realized that there was no politically acceptable alternative to compliance with the ICC order.

Echoes of the Freedom Rider struggle continued to reverberate through-out Alabama, however, as Connor and other hard-core white supremacists pursued the wider war against desegregation. Frequently targeting the local activists who had collaborated with the Freedom Riders, they mounted an aggressive counter-attack that put the movement on the defensive in many areas of the state. Indeed, despite the successful desegregation of transit fa-cilities, 1962 would prove to be a year of frustration for those who had hoped that the Freedom Riders' victory would accelerate the pace of change in Ala-bama. The disappointments began on New Year's Day when Birmingham officials circumvented a federal district court desegregation order by simply closing all of the city's parks; not even a petition signed by more than twelve hundred "moderate" whites could convince the city commission to reopen the parks on an integrated basis. On January 8 the local movement suffered a second setback when the U.S. Supreme Court, citing a legal technicality in-volving a filing deadline, refused to set aside the convictions of Fred Shuttles-worth and his Alabama Christian Movement for Human Rights colleague, the Reverend J. S. Phifer, on a 1958 disorderly conduct charge. Even though their convictions were based on an unconstitutional enforcement of a local bus segregation statute, Shuttlesworth and Phifer served thirty-six days in jail before pressure from a national sympathy campaign organized by SCLC secured their release on bail.

In the meantime, Federal District Court Judge Hobart Grooms dealt the movement another blow on January 16, when he sentenced five of the Anniston bombers to one-year probation terms and allowed a sixth to serve time concurrently with a sentence for burglary. The blatant inconsistency with the treatment of Shuttlesworth and Phifer was disheartening to move-ment leaders, who had expected long jail terms for the Anniston bombers, all of whom had pleaded guilty. That night, things got even worse when Klansmen dynamited three of Birmingham's black churches. In the after-math of the bombings, Connor cynically told reporters: "We know the Ne-groes did it." Even more upsetting was the FBI's refusal to investigate the bombings, compounded by Burke Marshall's confession that he couldn't force Hoover and his agents to do so. The inability of government officials at any level to protect movement activists from violent retribution was also evident in Huntsville, where CORE field secretaries Hank Thomas and Richard Haley were trying to organize a local CORE chapter. After Thomas helped a group of Alabama A&M students launch a series of sit-ins at downtown lunch counters in early January, the police made forty-nine arrests and refused to intervene when local white supremacists sprayed the former Freedom Rider and a local white CORE supporter with caustic mustard oil. Despite these and other forms of harassment, and declining support from a frightened local black community, Thomas and Haley hung on for a nearly a month. But they were forced to withdraw in early February, when a state court issued a sweeping injunction prohibiting CORE from conducting operations anywhere in Alabama.

Although it proved to be temporary, CORE's expulsion from Alabama was alarming. When Martin Luther King visited Birmingham on February 12 to address a mass meeting honoring Shuttlesworth and Phifer, he could not conceal his concern for the future of the movement in the state. "I wish I could tell you our road ahead is easy," he told the crowd at the Sixteenth Street Baptist Church, the future site of a senseless 1963 bombing that took four innocent lives. "That we are in the promised land, that we won't have to suffer and sacrifice anymore, but it is not so. We have got to be prepared. The time is coming when the police won't protect us, the mayor and commissioner won't think with clear minds. Then we can expect the worst." As any of the Alabama Freedom Riders could have attested, King's concern was well-founded; indeed, the physical vulnerability of movement activists or anyone associated with them had been confirmed in a Montgomery courtroom earlier in the day when Claude Henley, after being convicted of assaulting two NBC cameramen during the Montgomery riot, escaped with a fine of only one hundred dollars.[17]

None of these concerns or disappointments seemed to faze Shuttlesworth, however. When he emerged from jail on March 1, he was full of bluster. "Whites can't stop us now," he asserted. "Negroes are beginning to realize Birmingham is not so powerful after all—not in the face of a federal edict. ... There was no peace for 'Bull' when I was in jail and certainly there will be no peace for him now that we are out." Other movement leaders were also eager to project an image of confidence, and later in the week King and Roy Wilkins attended an Alabama Christian Movement for Human Rights banquet to celebrate Shuttlesworth's and Phifer's release. In a show of solidarity at a mass meeting following the banquet, Wilkins declared that "the courage and persistence of these men and of their people reveal the shame of this city," and he went on to encourage local activists to attack the entire range of segregated institutions. At the banquet itself, Shuttlesworth stole the show when he expressed relief that Connor had survived a recent traffic accident. "I am glad it didn't kill him," he told the crowd, with a smile. "I want to pester him some more. I am glad it did not put his eye out, for I want him to see me some more when I ride the buses with Negro drivers later on." To make his point, Shuttlesworth promptly offered his help to a group of militant Miles College activists planning a boycott of Birmingham's segregated department stores. By mid-March the boycott was in full swing, with leaflets urging black citizens to "Wear Your Old Clothes for Freedom."

Shuttlesworth's involvement in the boycott led to yet another arrest and conviction in early April, but less than two weeks later he and his Alabama Christian Movement for Human Rights colleagues reaffirmed their determination to withstand intimidation by hosting a major civil rights conference co-sponsored by the Southern Conference Education Fund, SCLC, and SNCC. Advertised as a series of workshops designed to explore "Ways and Means to Integrate the South," the racially integrated gathering attracted some of the movement's most prominent activists, including Ella Baker, Kelly Miller Smith, Anne Braden, and the former Freedom Riders C. T. Vivian and Jim Forman. During the two days of meetings, Connor dispatched a pack of police photographers to record the presence of known subversives, but he made no attempt to disrupt the proceedings.

To Shuttlesworth, Connor's restraint was added confirmation of white supremacists' propensity to back off in the face of resolute action. As he had told a mass meeting in late March: "When the white people see you mean business, they will step aside." Others, however, were convinced that only the politics of the moment had kept the conference delegates out of jail and prevented Shuttlesworth's provocative strategy from backfiring. At the time, Connor was a struggling gubernatorial candidate trying to broaden his narrow political base. Having already created a furor by curtailing the local distribution of surplus food to poor blacks, as an indirect retaliation against the downtown boycott, he could ill afford another incident that reinforced his image as an extremist. Once he was eliminated from the field of Democratic candidates in the May 8 primary, he faced fewer constraints, but by then the provocation of the integrated conference had passed.[18]

Connor's poor showing in the primary—he received fewer than twenty-five thousand votes statewide and finished a distant fifth behind the front-runner, Judge George C. Wallace, moderate Tuscaloosa lawyer Ryan deGraffenreid, the liberal-leaning two-time former governor Jim Folsom, and Attorney General MacDonald Gallion—was a clear indication that even a muted form of his violence-tinged politics did not play well outside of Klan circles and a few Birmingham neighborhoods. But, to the dismay of movement activists, Connor's defeat did not bring a turn toward moderation. On the contrary, with Wallace's victory over deGraffenreid in the runoff primary, the movement faced a more sophisticated and powerful version of what historian and biographer Dan Carter later called "the politics of rage." Having lost to John Patterson in the 1958 gubernatorial primary, "Alabama's Fighting Judge," as Wallace liked to call himself, had vowed that "no other son-of-a-bitch will ever out-nigger me again." And he more than kept his promise four years later. With Patterson ineligible to succeed himself under Alabama law, Wallace emerged as the state's most popular defender of sovereignty, states' rights, and segregation. Appropriating and capitalizing on

Patterson's feud with the Kennedys, he invoked the specter of invading Freedom Riders throughout the primary campaign.[19]

Although Wallace never went quite as far as Connor, who began his campaign in January with a pledge to purchase "one hundred new police dogs for use in the event of more Freedom Rides," he went far enough to garner the Birmingham commissioner's support in the run-off. On May 17, the eighth anniversary of *Brown*, Connor endorsed Wallace as the best man to protect Alabama from "the filthy hands of the NAACP and CORE." Wallace did his best to live up to this billing, stopping just short of violent resistance and punctuating his speeches with vivid rhetorical attacks on outside agitators. While he ultimately focused on the school desegregation issue, promising to "stand in the schoolhouse door" if necessary, much of his rage during the spring and summer of 1962 was directed at the Freedom Riders and their meddling federal accomplices, especially Judge Frank Johnson, whom he labeled "a low-down, carpet-baggin', scalawagin', race-mixin' liar." He also singled out SNCC as a menace to the state, particularly after field secretary and former Freedom Rider Bob Zellner became involved in a series of sit-ins and mass marches conducted by Talladega College students, some of whom had traveled to nearby Anniston the previous spring to protest the burning of the CORE freedom bus. Following a cross-burning on campus, dozens of arrests, and several confrontations between students and police in April, Attorney General Gallion obtained a temporary injunction from a state judge prohibiting further demonstrations. But Zellner's continued presence in Alabama provided Wallace and others with a convenient scapegoat in an atmosphere of escalating tension.[20]

In Talladega and many other communities, there was an unmistakable air of intimidation and impending violence, and Zellner was just one of many activists who were either threatened or assaulted by Alabama vigilantes in 1962. Prior to a planned attempt to desegregate the Birmingham airport restaurant in July, the FBI informed Shuttlesworth that they had uncovered a conspiracy to assassinate him during the sit-in. Two months later SCLC's annual conference, meeting for the first time in Birmingham, was disrupted by Roy James, a twenty-four-year-old neo-Nazi from Alexandria, Virginia, who rushed onto the stage and struck Martin Luther King in the face. Prior to the attack, the convention had gone smoothly and preconvention negotiations between Shuttlesworth and a committee of white businessmen had yielded an informal agreement to remove Jim Crow signs from downtown businesses in exchange for a promise to suspend the six-month-old boycott. But the assault reminded the SCLC delegates that Birmingham remained a violent and inhospitable place for movement activists—a reality confirmed in early October when Connor ordered the signs to be reinstalled and even more dramatically in December when Klansmen bombed Bethel Baptist Church for the third time.

Throughout the fall, these and other incidents, plus a renewal of the boycott, fueled an effort by moderate and image-consciousness businessmen to wrest control of local politics from Connor's grasp by replacing Birmingham's commission form of government with a more open mayor-council system. But the November referendum victory of the group known as Citizens for Progress did not lead directly to desegregation or to Connor's political demise. Even though Connor lost to former lieutenant governor Albert Boutwell in the spring 1963 mayoral race, he retained his position as police commissioner long enough to stymie the movement's efforts to crack what some called the most segregated city in America.[21]

Connor's defeat in the April 2 runoff primary was part of a larger drama that placed Birmingham at the center of the civil rights struggle during the spring of 1963. This was the unforgettable season that brought SCLC's Project C (for "Confrontation") to the city; that saw thousands of nonviolent demonstrators march in the streets, only to be pushed back by police dogs and high-pressure fire hoses; that produced King's "Letter from a Birmingham Jail," the controversial children's marches, and the movement's greatest victory to date. To a nation and a world shocked by searing images of police brutality and mass marches, the scale and intensity of Project C represented something new and unprecedented, an escalation of conflict that overshadowed earlier crises, including the Freedom Rides. But to close observers of the freedom struggle in Alabama, the 1963 Birmingham crisis also evoked memories of the 1961 Freedom Rides. The provocative combination of national and local movements, the personal duel between Connor and Shuttlesworth, and the involvement of several former Freedom Riders all suggested an element of continuity. When King balked at supplementing the depleted supply of adult marchers with younger activists, it was the Bevels and CORE Freedom Rider Ike Reynolds who forced the issue by organizing the first children's march. Employing the same brinksmanship that they had displayed during the Freedom Rides, the Bevels, along with Shuttlesworth and the anti-hero Connor, did more than anyone else to push the crisis to a point where there was no turning back from confrontation and climactic resolution.[22]

The legacy of the Alabama Freedom Rides was also apparent in the concurrent Freedom Walkers episode. On April 20, just as Project C was heating up, William Moore, an eccentric twenty-five-year-old white Baltimore postman and CORE member, hand-delivered a letter to the White House announcing his intention to conduct a one-man "Freedom Walk" from Chattanooga, Tennessee, to Jackson, Mississippi, where he hoped to deliver a second letter to Governor Ross Barnett. A veteran of the Route 40 sit-in campaign and a friend and admirer of Jim Peck's, Moore had sought funding and formal endorsement from the Baltimore chapters of CORE and the NAACP. But both groups turned him down, arguing that his insistence on traveling alone and wearing provocative signboards with the words "End Seg-

Former Freedom Riders Jim Lawson (center) and Jim Bevel (right) confer with the Reverend Kelly Miller Smith (left) prior to a civil rights march in Birmingham, May 7, 1963. (Courtesy of *Nashville Tennessean*)

regation in America," "Eat at Joe's—Both Black and White," and "Equal Rights for All Men (Mississippi or Bust)" made the proposed trip much too dangerous. Peck counseled Moore to "get a group to walk with you," but Moore was determined to set out by himself.

After traveling to Chattanooga by bus, he started walking down Highway 11 on the morning of April 21, adorned with a front-and-back sandwich board and pushing a small postal cart containing a satchel of clothes and mimeographed copies of letters to President Kennedy and Governor Barnett, which he hoped to distribute to passersby. Two days of walking took him out of Tennessee, across a narrow corner of northwestern Georgia, and into northeastern Alabama, where he spent the night in the town of Fort Payne. On the morning of the twenty-third, he resumed his lonely journey, heading southward toward Birmingham, where his hero Peck had been beaten two years earlier. While passing through the village of Collbran, he had a disturbing encounter with a local Klansman and grocery store owner named Floyd Simpson, who, along with a second Klansman, jumped in a pickup truck and began following Moore down Highway 11. In Collinsville, Moore had a second confrontation with Simpson, who called him an atheistic Communist and warned him that he wouldn't "make it past Birmingham." Less than two hours later, Moore's freedom walk ended when he was gunned down just outside the village of Keener. The two .22-caliber rifle bullets that killed him were promptly traced to Simpson's gun, and the Klansman was arrested for murder.

In the immediate aftermath of Moore's death, the national press treated the incident as a major story with obvious connections to the Freedom Rides, but both press and public attention soon shifted to the more compelling daily confrontations in Birmingham. In a press conference held the day after the shooting, President Kennedy characterized Moore's murder as "an outrageous crime" and offered "the services of the FBI in the solution of the crime," even though he admitted that the federal government did "not have direct jurisdiction." The promised help never materialized, however, and any hope of conviction ended five months later when a local grand jury refused to issue an indictment.[23]

In the meantime, movement activists made several attempts to memorialize Moore's sacrifice by completing his Freedom Walk. On April 26 John Lewis and more than a hundred students carrying signs pronouncing that Moore "Died for Love" and asking "Who Will Be Next?" marched from Fisk to a downtown Nashville federal building. On the following morning CORE and SNCC—the same two organizations that had taken the lead during the Freedom Rides—issued a joint statement declaring their intention to collaborate on a Moore Memorial Trek. Four days later two groups of Freedom Walkers were on the road, despite Governor Wallace's warning to Jim Forman that "your apparent desire to bally-hoo this tragic incident for political and selfish reasons would be an affront to the dignity of the people of Alabama and to the family of the deceased." "I strongly urge you to abandon your project," he added. "If you persist, the laws of Alabama will be strictly enforced." One group of Freedom Walkers—an interracial and interregional band of ten experienced CORE and SNCC activists that included CORE field secretary Richard Haley and former Freedom Riders Bob Zellner, Zev Aelony, and Bill Hansen—set out from Chattanooga; and a second group of eight black Alabama Christian Movement for Human Rights activists led by Diane Nash Bevel gathered in Keener, at the scene of the murder, before heading southward. At a premarch press conference, Haley described the Freedom Walkers' goal of reiterating Moore's simple notion that "the idea of human brotherhood" could be expressed "by a peaceful walk through the American countryside." But there would be no peaceful walk for either group.

The Nash group was arrested in Gadsden, barely ten miles into their journey, and the Haley group did not fare much better. Surrounded by hecklers in Tennessee and Georgia during the first two days of the trek, they were arrested on the afternoon of the third day as soon as they crossed the Alabama line. As state troopers rounded them up, using electric cattle prods on at least two of the Freedom Walkers, a crowd of angry whites shouted racial epithets. One man shrieked, "Get the goddamn communists," and another yelled, "Throw them niggers in the river. Kill the white men first." Taken to the county jail, all ten Freedom Walkers refused bail and were later transferred to Kilby State Prison, where they were kept on death row for several weeks. On May 16, the day after the transfer to Kilby, a new group of eleven Freedom Walkers took to the road in Keener, but they too were arrested. In early June, following the release of the Haley group, several Freedom Walkers joined with other CORE, SNCC, and SCLC activists to organize a short-lived coalition known as the Gadsden Freedom Movement. Following a series of sit-ins and marches, the Gadsden Freedom Movement made an attempt to resume Moore's march on a mass scale on June 18, and this time more than 450 Freedom Walkers ended up in jail. Though somewhat weakened, the Gadsden Freedom Movement continued to organize sporadic demonstrations for another six weeks, and on August 3 a fifth and final attempt to sponsor a Freedom Walk led to a staggering 683 arrests.

Hoping to draw national attention to this and other episodes of escalating police repression in Gadsden, Jim Farmer assembled a celebrity-packed delegation that included actors Marlon Brando and Paul Newman, but a planned march to dramatize the situation was called off when CORE attorneys advised Farmer not to defy a local court injunction prohibiting additional demonstrations. Indeed, when it became clear that neither the Justice Department nor the federal judiciary was willing to intervene on behalf of the Gadsden demonstrators, both the Gadsden Freedom Movement and the broader Freedom Walker campaign collapsed. Although legal wrangling over the Gadsden cases would continue for another year, movement leaders, realizing that the Freedom Walks were not going the way of the Freedom Rides, quietly moved on to other, more promising projects before the end of the summer.[24]

As the last chapter of a two-year-long saga initiated by the Alabama Freedom Rides, the ill-fated Freedom Walker campaign was a major disappointment for the movement. But, like the Albany campaign, it provided local as well as national movement leaders with a refined sense of the realities of struggle in the Deep South. Most important, it confirmed the nonviolent movement's vulnerability in the absence of meaningful legal and constitutional protection. Without resolute federal intervention, there was only so much that even the bravest of activists could accomplish in a state like Alabama, where legal and extralegal retribution and white supremacist extremism were a fact of life long after the bus stations were desegregated. One telling barometer of this climate of fear was the inability of Alabama's homegrown Freedom Riders to return to their native state without endangering themselves and their families. For John Lewis, Catherine Burks Brooks, John Maguire, Bill Harbour, and others, it would be years before being a "Freedom Rider" was detached from social ostracism, economic intimidation, and potential violence. "Be best for you not to come," Harbour's mother advised in May 1961, and with the exception of one brief and furtive visit later in the year, he stayed away from Piedmont, where he was born and raised, until mid-decade. Despite pressure from the White Citizens' Councils, his extended family remained in Piedmont, and Harbour eventually reconnected with kin and community in Alabama. But in the early 1960s the minimum price of radical dissent in Alabama was temporary exile. For Harbour, who lived to see substantial progress in his home state, including the election of both his younger brother Jerry and a cousin to the Piedmont city council, this price ultimately proved bearable, justifying the sacrifices that he and others had made. But, in the dark and difficult period following the Freedom Rides, few Alabamians, black or white, would have predicted such a positive outcome.[25]

IN THE HEART OF THE DEEP SOUTH, as we have seen, the Freedom Rides inadvertently spawned an era of racial polarization and political resistance. Here, with the notable exception of metropolitan Atlanta, the pace of social change actually slowed for a time, and the quality of life for many blacks got worse before it got better, triggering widespread disillusionment and despair. Indeed, if the situation in Mississippi, Louisiana, Alabama, and southwestern Georgia had been the only measure of the Freedom Rides' impact, the non-violent movement's claim to victory would have been in some jeopardy. Fortunately for the movement, this pattern of reactionary defiance did not hold in other areas of the South and its borderlands. While there was plenty of grousing about black militants, outside agitators, and federal meddling in local affairs, the dominant reality in most of the region was slow but steady progress toward desegregation. Not only was compliance with the ICC order all but universal outside the Deep South by early 1962, but the suddenness of transit desegregation, however grudging or involuntary, seemed to foster a growing resignation that desegregation of other institutions was inevitable and even imminent. Unlike the Deep South, where the threat of massive and even violent resistance remained an integral part of regional culture, the rest of the area below the Mason-Dixon line seemed to be moving toward political moderation and away from the sectionalist siege mentality associated with the "Solid South." As early as November 1961 public opinion polls revealed that, outside of Mississippi and Alabama, an overwhelming majority of Southern whites had concluded that it was only a matter of time before all public accommodations were desegregated. And the proportion of Southern respondents who felt this way continued to rise in 1962.

This was especially true in border states such as Missouri, Kentucky, and Maryland, where two-party political dynamics and racial demographics promoted a more open atmosphere, and where both school desegregation and black voting had proceeded beyond the stage of tokenism. But even in the so-called Rim South states of Florida, Texas, and Arkansas, as well as in the Upper South states of Virginia, North Carolina, and Tennessee—all states where the dual school system was still intact and black voting was still rare—

the Freedom Rides failed to produce the kind of backlash that forestalled progress. In South Carolina, a state often accorded Deep South status, the situation was less promising, especially in communities such as Rock Hill and Winnsboro, where the Freedom Riders had encountered stiff resistance in 1961. Yet, in general, the Palmetto State did not live up to its longstanding reputation for sectionalist defiance. Movement activity in the state quickened noticeably in 1962, as Jim McCain spearheaded an ambitious Voter Education Project that registered 3,700 new black voters by the end of the year. And both CORE and an increasingly active NAACP led by state field secretary I. DeQuincey Newman organized a series of desegregation campaigns that extracted significant gains without provoking widespread violence. While segregated institutions remained in force throughout most of the state, the tone of public reaction and political discourse suggested something less than massive resistance.[26]

The ability of McCain to operate in the open, despite his close association with the Freedom Rides, and his continuing success in recruiting local volunteers were welcome signs that encouraged CORE to expand its operations in neighboring states, especially in North Carolina. During the spring of 1962 the organization launched an ambitious campaign to create "Freedom Highways" all along the southeastern seabord. Conceived as "a natural southward extension of the Route 40" campaign," which was still active in Maryland, the Freedom Highways project targeted the popular but

A Maryland policeman and a restaurant proprietor confront Bayard Rustin during the 1962 Route 40 desegregation campaign. (Photograph by Bob Adelman, Magnum)

segregated Howard Johnson's restaurants that dotted tourist routes from Baltimore to Miami. The campaign attracted a number of veteran activists, including Jim Peck and Bayard Rustin, and by the end of May almost all of the chain's restaurants in Maryland and Florida had capitulated to CORE's pressure. Some locally owned franchises in other states resisted, however, prompting the organization to refine its strategy. Concentrating its efforts on North Carolina, CORE dispatched field secretaries and former Freedom Riders Ben Cox and Jerome Smith to the state to organize local chapters and mobilize demonstrators in several key cities. Aided by many of the same local activists who had hosted and supported the original Freedom Riders in May 1961, Cox and Smith developed strong CORE chapters in Greensboro, Raleigh, and Burlington that initiated mass protests at several Howard Johnson's restaurants in August and September.

During four weeks of sit-ins and marches, more than two thousand demonstrators participated and nearly one hundred were arrested. After an initial round of arrests in Durham, Farmer, Peck, and Roy Wilkins flew in from New York to lead a protest march, and at a subsequent march in Statesville, Farmer and a local minister spoke to more than six hundred supporters in the town square amidst "a thick fog of insecticide laid by the police." In other communities, the police were more restrained, and Peck—whose gripping memoir *Freedom Ride* would soon be published by Harper and Row—came away from the Durham march with the sense that both official intimidation and white resistance were diminishing. Comparing his recent experience with his first visit to Durham in 1947, he concluded that "this type of protest in a place like Durham would have been inconceivable 15 years ago." Perhaps even more telling was the successful desegregation of more than half of the state's Howard Johnson's restaurants by the end of August, along with Governor Terry Sanford's willingness to meet with Farmer and other movement leaders to discuss ways of accelerating the pace of desegregation in North Carolina. Desegregating the remaining restaurants would require eight more months of negotiation and mass protest. But, as Peck observed, North Carolina officials, unlike their Mississippi and Alabama counterparts, seemed to be embracing a more tolerant attitude toward dissent.[27]

This trend was also evident in Tennessee, where two liberal Democratic senators, Estes Kefauver and Albert Gore, maintained close ties with the Kennedy administration, and where, for the most part, segregationist ferment was on the wane following the Freedom Rides. Unlike its neighbors to the south, Tennessee boasted a highly competitive two-party political system that inhibited racial demagoguery and extremist rhetoric. And, despite the Nashville Movement's prominent role in the Freedom Rides, relatively few white Tennesseans exhibited the kind of reactionary fervor that gripped much of Mississippi and Alabama. Although many communities, particularly in the lowlands of western and central Tennessee, retained a strong commitment to racial separation, the state as a whole lacked ideological consistency.

In late January 1962 the noted black journalist Carl Rowan, who had recently accepted an appointment as a deputy assistant secretary of state, was refused service at a Memphis airport restaurant, but thoroughly desegregated transit facilities were the norm almost everywhere else. Aside from a few marginal Klansmen, there was no public interest in challenging or defying the ICC order, and the overall tenor of race relations was noticeably calmer in Tennessee than in many areas of the South.

This relative calm, as proud Tennessee moderates liked to point out, was partly a function of reasoned political dialogue and interracial cooperation, but it also reflected the weakness of the movement in Tennessee. In the western counties of Fayette and Haygood, the bitter three-year-old voter registration struggle that had attracted national attention and legal intervention by the Justice Department continued with no resolution in sight. But outside of Nashville and the nearby town of Lebanon, where CORE established a small chapter in July, there was little civil rights activity in the state in 1962. Even the Nashville Movement was only a shadow of what it had been earlier in the decade. Despite the best efforts of John Lewis, who returned to the city in September 1961 to enroll at Fisk, the number of local students willing to engage in nonviolent direct action fell below the level of a true mass movement; and the student central committee never quite regained its momentum, even after Lewis's former American Baptist Theological Seminary roommate, Bernard Lafayette, joined him at Fisk in the winter of 1962. Bill Harbour and Fred Leonard and several other former Tennessee State students remained active, but following the collective expulsion of the Tennessee State Freedom Riders the campus had ceased to be a reliable source of nonviolent foot soldiers.

At the same time, the Nashville student movement was becoming a victim of its own success. Not only had partial victory bred a measure of complacency and dispelled a messianic sense of urgency in the city recently dubbed the "Best City in the South for Negroes" by *Jet* magazine, but the central committee had turned out to be a training ground for regional leadership. The Bevels, Lester McKinnie, and others had long since moved on to continue the struggle in other parts of the South, and by the end of 1962 Lafayette was also gone, having agreed to lead a SNCC voting rights initiative in Selma. Even Lewis spent the summer of 1962 as a SNCC organizer in Cairo, Illinois, and after his election as SNCC national chairman in June 1963, he too moved on, relocating in Atlanta, where voters would elect him to Congress twenty-three years later.[28]

LADEN WITH IRONY, the situation in Tennessee was emblematic of the nonviolent movement's dilemma in the wake of the Freedom Rides. The Rides had led to the desegregation of Jim Crow transit facilities, but the meaning of the victory was subject to a wide range of interpretation and manipulation, both inside and outside the movement. For a majority of the Freedom Riders, achieving compliance with the *Morgan* and *Boynton* decisions was essentially a means to an end rather than an end in itself, a way of exercising rights of citizenship that would not only challenge the status quo but also reveal the stifling limitations of gradualist reformism. By demonstrating the moral power of nonviolence as well as the resolute determination of ordinary citizens to achieve simple justice, the Riders hoped to transform the civil rights movement into a broad-based and insistent freedom struggle. For some, nothing short of Jim Lawson's "beloved community" would do, but even those activists who set their sights on a less revolutionary goal saw the Rides as a progenitor of radical and accelerated change.

Many other observers, however, viewed the Freedom Riders' victory quite differently, either as an anomaly or as confirmation that governmentally administered gradualism was the key to civil order and social progress. Emphasizing the Kennedy's administration's capacity to respond to the crisis, while downplaying the catalyzing role of the Freedom Riders themselves, the mainstream viewpoint tended to focus on the ICC order, not on the provocations that brought it about. Predictably, this perspective became stronger over time. While detailed memories of the Rides inevitably faded, the effects of the order became clearer and more tangible, especially after the official validation of the order's importance by administration and supporting media sources.

Reformulated to fit both the general myths of reformist politics and the more specific conditions of an election year, the story of the Freedom Rides became the story of transit desegregation in 1962. Among nonviolent activists and in some black communities, particularly along the route of the Freedom Rides, there was consternation that recent history was being recast to serve the interests of a centrist administration. But most Americans, then and later, had little appreciation for the clash between movement and establishment lore. Even though it had great difficulty resolving the Freedom Rider crisis, the Kennedy administration demonstrated its ability to put a self-serving spin on the Rides as early as May 1961, during the immediate aftermath of the Anniston and Birmingham riots. And this effort continued off and on for the better part of a year. In December an official press release summarizing "the Administration's accomplishments in the civil rights field" hailed the ICC order and the government's role in bringing about "substantial progress" in transit desegregation but barely mentioned the Freedom Riders. Indeed, at a press conference held in January 1962, the president failed to mention the Freedom Riders at all in a statement citing the order as one of three significant civil rights achievements accomplished during his first year in office.

Whether this particular statement represented a failure of understanding or a deliberate misappropriation of credit is unclear, but one suspects that such slights often reflected a purposeful political or ideological strategy. For a variety of reasons, administration officials did not want to encourage or legitimize direct action, especially by naive and radical provocateurs who operated outside the bounds of political consensus. Later in the decade, government authorities would freely acknowledge the heroism and sacrifices of the Freedom Riders. And even the original architects of the dismissive interpretation of the Freedom Rides, including Burke Marshall and Robert Kennedy, eventually admitted that the crisis provided the federal government with an "education" and a much-needed push toward constitutional enforcement. But as long as the Kennedys were in power, there would be no White House receptions, or even public statements, honoring the risk-takers who had forced a reluctant administration to act.[29]

This policy was grounded in practical politics, and administration leaders thought they had a strong electoral rationale for distancing themselves from the Freedom Riders, even though liberal contemporaries and later historians and political scientists accused them of excessive timidity. Operating without a strong public mandate or a solid Democratic majority in Congress and facing the prospect of losing congressional seats to the Republicans in the fall 1962 elections, the Kennedys calculated that they could ill afford to alienate powerful conservatives within their own party. As early as July 1961 one aide, after concluding that "the dynamics both here and abroad compelling desegregation are accelerating," advised that providing "leadership for those forces and to moderate Southern difficulties without destroying the Congressional coalition at mid-term is the nub of the problem." This problem loomed even larger in the wake of the Freedom Rides and the ICC order. After disappointing the civil rights community in January 1962 with the announcement that he had no immediate plans to "put forward . . . major civil rights legislation," the president tried to assuage the feelings of blacks and liberals by letting it be known that he intended to appoint a black man, Robert Weaver, as the first secretary of a new Department of Urban Affairs. But this gesture backfired when a conservative bipartisan coalition promptly rejected the bill authorizing the new department.

At the same time, Kennedy endorsed a moderately progressive bill prohibiting the use of literacy tests for federal election registration, but even this fairly innocuous challenge to the political status quo in the white South went down to defeat in May. By summer he and other chastened Northern Democrats were in full retreat on legislative issues related to civil rights, and the elevated priority of avoiding sectional disharmony remained in force until well after the fall elections sustained a Democratic majority in both houses of Congress. Only the federal intervention at the University of Mississippi in September interrupted this strategy, but for many white Southerners this anomaly was an acceptable response to violent extremism.[30]

Justified or not, political considerations alone cannot explain the administration's rude treatment of the Freedom Riders, or its continuing inattention to pressing civil rights matters. Ideological commitments also dictated an official postmortem that reduced the Riders to bit players in a government drama. While the crisis provoked by the Freedom Rides seized the Kennedy brothers' attention, forcing them to address an expanded range of issues related to race and democracy, it did not persuade either of them that ending Jim Crow was a moral imperative requiring immediate and uncompromising action. They did not celebrate the achievements of nonviolent direct action in 1962 and 1963, in large part, for the same reason that prevented them from embracing the Freedom Riders in 1961: They did not believe that radical or disruptive change was in the best interests of the nation or the world.

Robert Kennedy was more receptive to the Freedom Riders' tactics and ideas than was his brother, but neither leader was ready to jettison his commitment to what the political scientist David Niven has labeled "glacial change." In the case of John Kennedy, the attachment to glacialism was as broad as it was deep. But, as Niven has pointed out, the young president's response to the Freedom Rides was also guided by a traditional interpretation of Reconstruction that convinced him "that moderation was always a more successful course than coercion." Encumbered by this simplistic model of regional and national history, he had difficulty absorbing the lessons that the Freedom Riders might have taught him. The concept of "freedom now" struck him, as it struck many Americans of moderate and conservative leanings, as an unreasonable expectation that threatened both civic order and evolutionary progress. "Quixotic crusades," the historian Harvard Sitkoff once wrote of Kennedy, "interfered with his careful plans and cautious timetables." Indeed, John Dittmer probably came closest to the truth when he observed that "in the short run, at least," both Kennedy brothers "preferred order to justice."

In the long run, the Kennedys—especially Robert, who had five more years than his brother to rethink his views on race and radicalism—gained some appreciation for the insistent and compelling nature of the civil rights agenda. And when the president finally went before the nation in June 1963 to make the case for a comprehensive civil rights bill, he insisted that Americans were "confronted primarily with a moral issue," not a mere legislative or political problem. In 1962, though, there was little indication that administration leaders had acquired anything more than a superficial and detached understanding of the nonviolent movement's passions and frustrations. The president's continuing preoccupation with the Cold War—both before and after the Cuban Missile Crisis of October—relegated civil rights issues to secondary status in Washington, and even the attorney general seemed more interested in J. Edgar Hoover's relentless search for subversive elements within the movement than in the movement itself. The mixed signals from the top influenced all levels of the federal government. Thus, despite the legal advances of the previous year, federal agencies were still more adept at nurturing moderates and consoling conservatives than at protecting the constitutional rights—and the lives—of grassroots activists.[31]

Appalled by the collective inability of the federal courts, the FBI, and the Justice Department to provide the movement—especially Voter Education Project volunteers and potential registrants in the Deep South—with even a semblance of justice or security, CORE convened a special Commission of Inquiry into the Administration of Justice in the Freedom Struggle, chaired by former first lady Eleanor Roosevelt. Meeting in Washington on May 25 and 26, 1962, on the first anniversary of the initial Jackson Freedom Rider trials, the commission collected 300 pages of testimony from a long list of activists critical of federal officials. The Justice Department, however, displayed little interest in the commission's findings, and the situation on the Southern front remained perilous. By midsummer Farmer and other CORE leaders were so frustrated that they began to discuss the idea of bringing "aggressive nonviolent action" to Washington in an effort to highlight the administration's failings. But the national board scotched the idea, arguing that directly challenging the White House was too risky in a volatile pre-election atmosphere. Alienating the president or putting more Republicans in Congress might make matters even worse, they concluded, indicating that memories of the lean Eisenhower years placed certain limits on anti-Kennedy sentiment within the movement. Such limits did not preclude expressions of profound disappointment, however. In a September letter to the novelist Lillian Smith, Marvin Rich acknowledged that Kennedy had "done ever so much more than Eisenhower" for the cause of civil rights, but he also offered the telling qualifier that "when measured against our expectations and against the awesome rush of events he has done little."[32]

RICH'S LAMENT captures the bittersweet quality of movement life in the aftermath of the Freedom Rides. Caught in the throes of a classic revolution of rising expectations, civil rights activists chafed at the restrictions imposed by the inertial power of institutions and individuals. As the Freedom Riders and others watched and waited for signs of fundamental change, it became clear that neither the American public nor the Kennedy administration could keep pace with the new expectations. But equally clear was the realization that the civil rights movement had undergone a thoroughgoing transformation during the past year. While the barriers of racism remained formidable, the struggle against those barriers had acquired new sources of strength and energy. Most obviously, the various organizations that made up the movement had established a precedent of working together, building a coalition that crossed regional, racial, and ideological lines. Though loose and uneasy at times, and subject to the full range of problems related to organizational competition and diversity, the coalition that emerged during the Freedom Rides initiated the nationalization of a movement that would later oversee massive mobilizations such as the March on Washington, Freedom Summer, and the Selma-to-Montgomery voting rights campaign later in the decade. The collective efforts of 1961 also exposed deep ideological and personal conflicts within the movement and revealed the difficulty of coordinating local and national initiatives, as in Albany and Monroe. But even the worst of these problems contributed to the maturation of a movement that eventually found ways to offset the negative influence of rivalries and disagreements.

Notwithstanding the trend toward cooperation and collaboration, most of the movement's growth and activity in 1962 took place within the confines of individual organizations. As we have seen, the Freedom Rides had an immediate though differential impact on CORE, SNCC, SCLC, and the NAACP, both at the local and national level. Reshaping the organizational contours of the freedom struggle, the Rides altered the traditional hierarchy that had prevailed since the 1940s. CORE and SNCC gained the most, establishing themselves as major players in an unfolding civil rights drama previously dominated by the NAACP and, since 1957, by SCLC.

As the originator and chief financial sponsor of the Rides, CORE had the closest organizational identification with the elimination of segregated transit facilities, a victory that brought unprecedented attention and influence to a group of activists unaccustomed to visibility or notoriety. Despite the continuing legal responsibilities and debts associated with the Rides, CORE emerged from the crisis in good shape, with an expanded budget and staff, thousands of new members, and an expansive sense of its new role as a leading force within the nonviolent movement. The enhanced stature of Farmer and other former Freedom Riders gave the organization credibility and standing, even in the arena of popular culture, where musicians such as Chuck Berry and Phil Ochs paid tribute to them in song. "Jim Farmer was a hard fightin' man," Ochs's 1962 folk ballad "Freedom Riders" intoned, "decided one day that he had to make a stand. He led them down to slavery town, and they threw Jim Farmer in the can." Buoyed by this and other public tributes, the national office in New York, along with local CORE chapters around the nation, was brimming with proposals for direct action. By the end of the year several of these proposals had become operational, from the Freedom Highways campaign in the Southeast to a national recruiting project known as Task Force Freedom. And, unlike in the past, there was no sense that such projects were limited to a small vanguard or constrained by organizational inertia. Despite the continuing challenges of public complacency and political backsliding, CORE—the organization that had put the movement on wheels—was on the move.[33]

Aside from CORE, SNCC had the greatest structural and emotional investment in the Freedom Rides. As the organization that saved the Rides at several critical junctures, that through its local "affiliates" in Nashville, Washington, and Atlanta provided many of the participating student activists, and that helped to turn a two-week project into a six-month-long mass movement, SNCC deservedly received much of the credit for vanquishing Jim Crow from the buses, trains, and terminals of the South. And, like CORE, SNCC was able to turn this experience into the equivalent of a functional rebirth. Having first emerged during the 1960 sit-ins, the scattered clusters of students associated with SNCC barely constituted an organization at the beginning of the Freedom Rides. But by early 1962 SNCC's status as the foundation of a burgeoning student movement was undeniable. While SNCC's profile remained hazy among the general public, within the civil rights movement itself the small bands of student activists that had spread across the South had earned an unparalleled reputation for selfless commitment to the struggle. In Albany, McComb, and several other Deep South communities, SNCC activists pushed the limits of protest, often traveling beyond what their elders, both inside and outside the movement, viewed as the boundaries of prudence. With fewer than twenty staff members and a meager budget, the organization retained an unimposing skeletal structure, but this lack of structure only reinforced the organization's mystique, helping it to attract some of the region's most independent-minded grassroots organizers.

Unfortunately, maintaining this mystique of openness had its costs, and by the spring of 1962, when SNCC held its third annual conference in Atlanta, the untrammeled emotional intensity that would later destroy the organization was already in evidence. With the noticeable absence of Lawson, Lafayette, and the Bevels, and with many of the delegates openly questioning the utility and viability of nonviolent struggle, SNCC's leadership seemed to be heading in a new direction. "Our cause remained the same, of course," John Lewis recalled many years later, "but our methods were all in question. You heard the term 'revolution' more than the term 'integration.' The spirit of redemptive love was being pushed aside by a spirit of rage. And the whole idea of nonviolence was up for debate." To Lewis, as to several other former Freedom Riders, the 1962 conference marked the beginning of a long and troubling retreat from "beloved community" idealism. Even so, with considerable effort, he and his fellow proponents of nonviolent interracial struggle were able to mobilize enough support to keep much of the organization within the "beloved" orbit for several years.[34]

SCLC also experienced growing pains following the Freedom Rides, but the unifying figure of Martin Luther King kept the organization relatively free of fractious debate. Even though his reputation was on the decline among student activists disappointed first by his refusal to become a Freedom Rider and later by his alleged grandstanding in Albany, and despite the FBI's success in reducing his moral and political capital in the eyes of some Washington insiders, King remained an immensely popular leader within SCLC and among black Americans in general. The fact that he missed few opportunities to speak out on behalf of the Riders muted public criticism of his decision to stay off the freedom buses, and the power of his words continued to inspire civil rights activists across the nation. King's periodic "People to People" tours, the creation of a support group known as the Gandhi Society, and a high-profile campaign calling for a "Second Emancipation Proclamation" kept him in the public eye, countering the image of frustration coming out of Albany. At the same time, both King and his organization benefited from the direct participation in the Freedom Rides by Fred Shuttlesworth, Wyatt Tee Walker, Ralph Abernathy, and several Nashville Christian Leadership Council ministers. By the spring of 1962 the SCLC staff was loaded with former Freedom Riders, including Jim Lawson and the Bevels, and in June John Lewis was added to the SCLC board of directors for good measure. The election of Lewis, who had spurned an offer to join the SCLC staff the previous fall, was especially gratifying to King, who recognized that student activism was the key to the movement's future. Already impressed by the critical role that students had played in the sit-ins and the Freedom Rides, he would discover just how critical young activists could be when Jim Bevel's "children's crusade" came forth to save the Birmingham campaign in 1963.[35]

Unlike King, Roy Wilkins and the national leaders of the NAACP were not inclined to collaborate with or trust the instincts of this new generation of activists. Drawn into the Freedom Rides as a reluctant partner, the NAACP had eschewed membership in the FRCC and had tried to limit its involvement in the crisis to legal representation and fund-raising. Yet even the relatively staid NAACP found the Freedom Rides to be a liberating influence. Not only did the organization have to share the spotlight with a broader range of activists, but the internal balance between local branches and the national headquarters, and between legal and direct action advocates, had shifted noticeably since 1959, when delegates to the NAACP national conference had celebrated a fifty-year-old commitment to keeping the struggle in the courtroom. After resisting the entreaties of impatient Youth Councils and radical branches for decades, the national office could not withstand the centrifugal and democratic forces unleashed by the student movement and the Freedom Rides. In communities from the Deep South and the Carolinas— where, as we have seen, Wilkins himself manned the barricades on one occasion—to the Northwest and the Pacific Coast, local NAACP involvement in direct action spoke volumes about the growing militancy within the organization. Even in areas where the NAACP was not involved, the organization often served as a convenient target for white supremacists who assumed that all outside agitation could ultimately be traced to Wilkins's office. Whatever its actual policies, the NAACP was symbolically out in the streets with CORE, SNCC, and SCLC—a reality that further eroded the cautionary legalistic tactics of the past. By 1962 all civil rights organizations, whether their leadership was fully aware of it or not, were being drawn into the vortex of a new insurgent style of protest that would become the trademark of the decade ahead.[36]

The Freedom Rides offered important lessons to anyone willing to acknowledge the gap between democratic ideals and the many imperfections of American life. Not everyone paid attention to the unfolding drama below the Mason-Dixon line, and much of the nation was slow to absorb the full implications of nonviolent direct action. But it did not take long for the Rides to alter the consciousness of citizen activists or to inspire related acts of organized protest, both in the United States and around the world. Indeed, thanks to an almost universally sympathetic international press, the impact of the Rides was nearly as great abroad as it was at home. As United Nations Secretary-General U Thant observed in November 1961: "The Freedom Riders journeying to the South are looked upon in Asia and Africa as the Champions for the colored American's holy war for freedom." Just as American civil rights activists had drawn inspiration from the emerging decolonization of the Third World, insurgents in nations as far away as South Africa and Australia saw the Freedom Riders as instructive role models. In South Africa blacks challenging the hated "pass laws" that restricted their mobility often referred to themselves as Freedom Riders, and in Australia Aborigines chafing under the restrictions of racial discrimination organized a full-scale Freedom Ride.

In 1965 Charles Perkins, a twenty-nine-year-old Aboriginal student at the University of Sydney and the leader of Student Action for Aborigines (SAFA), led an interracial group of twenty-nine students on a Freedom Ride through the province of New South Wales. Hoping to gather information on and draw attention to racial discrimination against Australian Aborigines, Perkins and the other Riders encountered considerable resistance from whites who forced their bus off the road in one Outback town and from local police in a second community where they tried to desegregate a public swimming pool. Though only two weeks long, the Australian Freedom Ride attracted considerable press attention and was later credited with launching the modern Aboriginal freedom struggle. Many of the Australian Freedom Riders remained active in Aboriginal and other social justice causes, and Perkins, the first Aborigine to graduate from an Australian university, went on to become the secretary of the national Department of Aboriginal Affairs in the 1980s.[37]

In the United States, as in Australia, the Freedom Rides exerted an impact that transcended tangible, quantifiable changes in institutional behavior or public policy. Within six months of the first Ride, travelers of all races were sitting side by side on buses and trains all across the nation without fear of arrest, the WHITE and COLORED signs that had blighted the walls of Southern bus and train stations for decades were gone, the nation's major civil rights organizations had undergone significant transformations, and the Justice Department had been pushed into a deepening engagement in civil rights matters. But even this impressive list of accomplishments does not capture the full effect of the Freedom Rides. The most important and lasting consequence—the one that confirmed the Rides' status as a pivotal moment in American history—was a revolutionary change in the character of citizen politics. In the course of six months, the nation's first mobile nonviolent army expanded the realm of the possible in American political and social insurgency, redefining the limits of dissent and setting the stage for the escalating demands and rising expectations of the mid- and late 1960s.

While the Freedom Riders ultimately failed in their effort to bring the nation, or even most of the civil rights movement, into the confines of the "beloved community," they, more than any other activists of their day, fore-shadowed the grassroots "rights revolution" that would transform American citizenship over the next four decades. The rising movements for women's rights, military withdrawal from Southeast Asia, environmental reform, gay and lesbian rights, and the rights of the disabled all built upon the foundation of legitimacy and success established by Freedom Riders and other nonvio-lent activists in the early 1960s. By demonstrating the power of personal commitment and sacrifice in a new and dramatic way, the Freedom Riders countered traditional assumptions of institutional authority and top-down politics, pushing American democracy to what the journalist Malcolm Gladwell has called a "tipping point," and beyond. Reflecting on his experi-ences as a Freedom Rider, Stokely Carmichael used a different metaphor, characterizing the Rides as a "great leap forward" that superseded the ortho-doxy of slow and steady gradualism. But whatever the words used to the de-scribe the change, the conclusion that the Rides created a new context for social activism seems inescapable.[38]

The sociologist James Laue came to this conclusion as early as 1962, after interviewing a wide array of movement activists. Detecting a profound change in the scope and intensity of the movement, Laue identified national-ization as the most obvious effect of the Rides. "The national mobilization of conscience which had begun in Montgomery and grown in 1960," he ob-served, "reached full bloom with the Freedom Rides." Paradoxically, a cru-cial aspect of the nationalization process was shifting the focus to the Deep South, or, as he put it, carrying "the protest squarely to the most recalcitrant and dangerous areas of the nation." By bringing a measure of radical change to the most hidebound corner of American society, the Freedom Rides "broke the charade of silence and with it the monolithic hold of the racist ethos on many Deep South communities."

At the same time, the Rides also nationalized the movement by drama-tizing, "to any who remained doubters, that segregation was a national con-cern, rather than a series of local problems," as the journalist Milton Viorst once wrote. Forcing the Kennedy administration to take a belated but ulti-mately forthright stand on one aspect of racial discrimination, the Rides has-tened the day when the federal government would embrace a broader agenda of promoting integrated schools and neighborhoods, equal access to public accommodations, affirmative action in hiring policies, and black voting rights. Although one unintended consequence of the Freedom Rider crisis was the government's turn to voting rights advocacy as a means of diverting move-ment energies away from additional direct action campaigns, that too was a tribute to the power and influence of the Rides. Indeed, without the pressure exerted by the crises of 1961, the Voter Education Project that led to Freedom Summer, Selma, and the 1965 Votings Right Act might not have been part of the historical equation.

Looking back after four decades of uneven progress, it is evident that this hard-won alliance with federal authorities imposed certain limits on the movement, virtually guaranteeing an emphasis on civil reform, not moral revolution. For some Americans, the Freedom Rides and the nonviolent direct action campaigns that followed brought about a direct transformation of heart and mind. But for most, the lesson of the Rides was the ability of ordinary citizens to affect public policy. Both inside and outside the movement, the primary legacy was the efficacy of direct action, not the moral rectitude of nonviolence. This was not what many Freedom Riders had intended, but such are the ironies of history forged by real people in real time.[39]

Though ultimately problematic, these limitations were barely visible in the immediate aftermath of the Freedom Rides. When James Laue talked with several of the Freedom Riders in 1962, he discovered that they were proud of what they had accomplished. They felt they had proven that even a small vanguard of activists could initiate fundamental change through righteous action and moral discipline. All that was needed, they believed, was the physical and moral courage to express their passion for social justice through the medium of nonviolent struggle. And that was what they had done, experiencing unmerited suffering and demonstrating their willingness to "give a little bit of blood to redeem the soul of America," as John Lewis recalled in a 2001 speech. "We allowed the spirit of history to use us," Lewis explained, invoking the sense of destiny that propelled him and so many others down the road to freedom.[40]

Destiny, however, meant something less than determinism. Even with history on their side, the Freedom Riders had faced difficult choices at every turn in the road. At several points during the spring, summer, and fall of 1961, seemingly insurmountable challenges had threatened to push the movement backward, forcing even the most resilient Riders to contemplate retreat or compromise. In every instance movement activists and organizers had found a way to push on, but they had done so with a growing appreciation for the difficulty and magnitude of the task before them. The original CORE Freedom Riders came to the South to teach and preach and spread the gospel of nonviolence, which they did in full measure. But in the process of delivering the movement's message, they, and the other Freedom Riders who followed them, became experiential learners, acquiring essential truths about themselves, the human condition, and the nature of historical agency. Wherever they found themselves—on buses, in terminal waiting rooms, in mass meetings, in the jails and prisons of the benighted South—Freedom Riders absorbed the concrete lessons of struggle. Some were hard and sobering lessons about the intractability of racial hatred and entrenched privilege. Others were hopeful and inspiring, demonstrating the expansive possibilities

of individual and collective action and the transformative power of movement culture.

Disseminating these lessons to the American public proved difficult, and
the nonviolent movement never realized its full potential, but for a time the
Freedom Riders' victory over fear and violence became an object lesson in
itself. During the remainder of the Kennedy era and into the mid-1960s, the
term "Freedom Rider" took on a special mystique, providing black Southerners and many others with an empowering example of engaged citizenship. Indeed, by 1964, when nearly a thousand college students traveled to
Mississippi to participate in the Freedom Summer equal rights campaign,
the term had morphed into a generic and iconic symbol only loosely connected to the events of 1961. For a time, the simple phrase "the Freedom
Riders are coming" invoked hope among those seeking change and dread
among those defending the racial status quo. Later in the decade, as the freedom struggle moved through the stages of Black Power, urban rioting, and
ideological fragmentation, memories of both the Freedom Rides and Freedom Summer faded, and the term lost some of its force. But it did not disappear entirely.[41]

Speaking at the 2000 Democratic National Convention, President Bill
Clinton lauded vice-presidential candidate Joseph Lieberman as a former
"Freedom Rider" who had risked his life "to register black voters in the then
segregated South." After a bit of checking, several observers pointed out that
the president was mistaken—that Lieberman's experiences as a civil rights
activist had actually taken place in 1963, two years after the Freedom Rider
campaign. But, judging by the lack of public reaction to the correction, few
Americans had enough historical background to appreciate the significance
of the president's error. Four years later a scene in the popular film *Ladykillers*
added to the confusion. Speaking to a native black Mississippian named
MacSam, Garth Pancake, a former "Freedom Rider" now living in Mississippi, explains how he first came to the state: "I wasn't born here you know.
I'm from Scranton, Pennsylvania. . . . Came down here in 1964. Greyhound
bus. With the Freedom Riders. Do you know who the Freedom Riders were,
MacSam? . . . The Freedom Riders, my fine young man, were a group of
concerned liberals from up north, all working together just like we are here—
involved citizens who came down here so that local black people could have
their civil liberties, so that people like you could have the vote."[42]

SUCH MISINFORMATION IS UNFORTUNATE, not only because it violates the
integrity of the historical record but also because it obscures the special
nature of the experiences and contributions of the 436 men and women
who actually were Freedom Riders. The saga of the Freedom Rides deserves
to be remembered in all of its meaning and nuance and, within the limits of
human memory and the historian's craft, to be faithfully reconstructed for a

society still grappling with the confounding issues of race, prejudice, and inequality.

The Freedom Riders themselves have done their best to keep the record straight. For the past forty years, participation in the Rides has been a continuing source of identity, pride, and fellowship. Bound by ties of friendship, memory, and shared sacrifice, many former Freedom Riders have protected and sustained a common legacy. Among the ex-Riders there are distinct subgroups—the original CORE Riders, those who survived the burning bus in Anniston, those who spent time in Parchman, the Interfaith Riders, and so forth—each with its own set of experiences and lore. But there is also a commonality of perspective that binds them all together, setting them apart from everyone else, including the rest of the movement.

Forged in the fires of nonviolent struggle, this sense of common purpose and experience has persisted through the decades, despite the inevitable physical dispersion of the Riders. During the tumultuous years of the 1960s and 1970s, the Riders went their separate ways, passing into a wide variety of careers and private lives. Some either became disillusioned or moved too far to the right or left to remember the Freedom Rides without a measure of embarrassment or regret. And, against the increasingly violent backdrop of the Vietnam War and the Johnson and Nixon eras, many abandoned the nonviolent philosophy that had propelled the Freedom Rides during the relatively innocent years of the early 1960s. Some went to Vietnam as soldiers or sailors, some became anti-war activists, and others filled both functions, turning against a war that ultimately seemed ill-conceived and morally unjustifiable. Most embraced the liberating themes of 1960s counter-culture, but as the politics of reform and revolution became darker and more complicated, there was an inevitable divergence of opinion and belief, symbolized by Stokely Carmichael's strident advocacy of Black Power and Jim Farmer's unexpected endorsement of Richard Nixon in the 1972 presidential campaign. And yet, even with this divergence, a large majority continued to identify with a broad-based struggle for human rights and social justice that inevitably drew them into a variety of new movements from environmentalism to gay and lesbian liberation. An inordinate number went on to distinguished careers as social workers, community organizers, health care providers, labor leaders, lawyers, jurists, politicians, writers, journalists, theologians, teachers, college professors and administrators, entrepreneurs, or corporate executives. But whatever their professional experiences or private enthusiasms, they were still Freedom Riders, still part of a select group of activists that had changed the course of American history.

In the immediate aftermath of the Freedom Rides and for several years thereafter, many of the Riders maintained intermittent contact through the natural interplay of their lives and careers, but as time went on some felt the need to enhance the maintenance of old ties through formal reunions and other planned gatherings. The first event of this kind occurred in May 1981, on the twentieth anniversary of the Rides, when Jim Farmer and John Lewis co-hosted a small gathering in Atlanta. Prior to the reunion, Lewis and Hank Thomas traveled the route of the original CORE Ride, from Washington to Montgomery, before joining their old friends in Atlanta. Farmer, an ailing sixty-year-old diabetic who had just lost the sight in his right eye, was not up to the bus trip. But at the reunion he proudly reflected on the Riders' experiences, describing the Rides as "one of the most important, if not the most important single project of the civil rights movement in the early '60s." Recalling the controversies and challenges of 1961, he maintained that the Riders not only "established the principle that the federal government has a duty to enforce federal laws over and against conflicting state laws" but also "drove the nail in the coffin of the carpetbagger idea, the idea that unless you live in a certain community you have no right to be concerned about what happens in that community." An aspiring politician who would be elected to the Atlanta city council later in the year, Lewis emphasized the fear and dread that had shadowed the Freedom Riders, confessing: "When I was beaten in Montgomery, I thought it was the end."[43]

Similar recollections surfaced in July when Lewis's old friend Bernard Lafayette led a tour of students and several former Freedom Riders through Mississippi, Alabama, and Georgia. Sponsored by the Atlanta-based Martin Luther King Jr. Center for Nonviolent Social Change and Lindenwood College in St. Louis, where Lafayette served as an administrator, the tour attracted more than thirty participants and an ABC television documentary film crew. After brief stops in McComb and Jackson, the group traveled to Philadelphia, Mississippi, the site of the 1964 murder of three Freedom Summer volunteers, before heading east toward Montgomery and Atlanta. "We're doing this to expose young people to the movement of the 1960's," Lafayette told reporters before leaving Mississippi—to take a nation under the sway of the conservative Reagan revolution back to a time when "ordinary people did extraordinary things," when Freedom Riders "had the commitment and courage to stand up for their principles and were willing to give their lives." In this same spirit, Lafayette himself would later help found both the U.S. Institute for Peace, headquartered in Washington, and the Center for Nonviolence and Peace Studies at the University of Rhode Island. After establishing a nonviolence training center in Colombia and leading a 120-mile peace march to a Medellín guerrilla stronghold in the mountains of Antioquia Province in 2002, he would be kidnapped and briefly held hostage. Several others in his group, including the governor of Antioquia, remained in captivity and later died in a failed rescue attempt by government forces. But none of this deterred Lafayette from continuing his effort to bring peace and nonviolence to a war-torn region a continent away.[44]

In 1982 and 1983 reunions of a different sort took place in Michigan, where veteran newsman Howard K. Smith, Ike Reynolds, Hank Thomas, and several other Riders served as witnesses in a trial involving eighty-two-year-old Walter Bergman. Outraged by testimony given by former under-cover FBI informer Gary Thomas Rowe to the Senate Select Committee to Study Governmental Operations with Respect to Intelligence Activities in 1975, Bergman and Jim Peck filed separate civil damage suits alleging FBI complicity in the 1961 Birmingham beatings that left both men severely in-jured. Filed in 1976 and 1977 with the help of the ACLU, the suits sought damages from the FBI and six of its agents. Initially dismissed by a New York judge on a technicality in 1979, Peck's suit ultimately yielded twenty-five thousand dollars in damages on appeal. Bergman's suit went to trial in De-cember 1982, and six months later, Judge Richard Enslen of the federal dis-trict court in Kalamazoo ruled in his favor, issuing an eloquent decision that closed with a stirring quotation from the nineteenth-century black abolition-ist Frederick Douglass: "Those who profess to favor Freedom and yet depre-cate agitation are men who want crops without plowing up the ground. They want rain without thunder and lightning. They want the ocean without the awful roar of its many waters. This struggle may be a moral one, or it may be a physical one, but it must be a struggle. Power concedes nothing without a demand. It never did and it never will."

Judge Enslen ultimately limited Bergman's award to fifty thousand dol-lars (fifteen thousand of which was awarded to the estate of Frances Bergman, who died in 1979), only a fraction of the two million dollars sought, conclud-ing that the injured party's "condition might have resulted in part from an appendectomy he had four months after the beating." But the victory was sweet nonetheless, correcting "the essential history of the period," as Howard Simon, the executive director of the Michigan ACLU and Bergman's close friend, later put it. While the modest award did not bring much monetary benefit to an ag-ing and infirm Bergman—who somehow managed to live an-other sixteen years—the decision, in Simon's judgment, "proved the Federal Government was not an ally of the civil rights worker, but in fact was in league with local law enforcement and the K.K.K." Though reasonable, this judgment

Michigan ACLU executive director Howard Simon wheels former Free-dom Rider Walter Bergman into a federal courtroom in Grand Rapids, Michigan, February 28, 1983. (Courtesy of *Kalamazoo Gazette*)

was not what had been communicated to a national television audience four years earlier in a controversial film entitled *Undercover with the KKK*. Based on Gary Thomas Rowe's self-serving memoir and co-produced by NBC and Columbia Pictures, the 1979 film depicted Rowe as a heroic, freedom-loving FBI informant. With former Dallas Cowboys quarterback Don Meredith playing the lead role, the script gave the impression that Rowe and the FBI were blameless not only in Bergman's 1961 beating but also in the 1965 murder of Detroit housewife Viola Liuzzo, for which Rowe had recently been indicted.[45]

Fortunately, a more accurate and less mythic video history of these and other episodes in Alabama's violent past appeared in 1986 with the release of the documentary film series *Eyes on the Prize*, the third episode of which focused on the Freedom Rides. Featuring riveting interviews with Jim Farmer, John Lewis, and Fred Leonard, the *Eyes on the Prize* segment reached a large public television audience and introduced the Rides to a generation largely unfamiliar with what had happened in Alabama and Mississippi during the early 1960s. Nineteen eighty-six was the twenty-fifth anniversary of the Freedom Rides, and several former Riders commemorated this milestone by participating in a partial re-creation of their experiences filmed by the Canadian Broadcasting Company. Bergman and Peck were too frail to attend the mini-reunion, but those returning to Alabama included John Lewis and Jim Zwerg, a quarter century removed from the adventure of his life but still plagued by periodic bouts of pain from the beating he had received in Montgomery. A business executive and former United Church of Christ minister who had moved from Wisconsin to Arizona in the 1970s, Zwerg agreed to retrace the steps that had left him crumpled and bleeding on a bus station ramp. En route to Montgomery, he sat next to a fifteen-year-old black boy who had never heard of the Freedom Rides and who was puzzled by his assertion that there was a time, not so long ago, when they could not have shared a seat on an Alabama bus. Captured on film by cameramen who had been children themselves during the Rides, this intergenerational exchange added poignancy to an already emotional exercise in historical reconnection. Although he had remained active in matters of social and racial justice, Zwerg had not been back to the Deep South or seen many of his fellow Freedom Riders since the 1960s. Reconnected, he returned again four years later to participate in a nonviolent workshop commemorating the thirtieth anniversary of the Nashville sit-ins.[46]

A year later, in 1991, a group of Freedom Riders convened a similar gathering in Jackson. The thirtieth anniversary celebration combined a monthlong bicycle tour—called the Unity Tour—that attracted eleven bicyclists (but no Freedom Riders) eager to retrace the route of the Freedom Rides from Washington to New Orleans, and an elaborate four-day conference held at Tougaloo College in mid-July. Featuring sessions on a variety of social justice issues, the conference explored the theme "A Look

Back—A Leap Forward." Two hundred conference participants—including Lewis, Farmer, Hank Thomas, Ben Cox, Ed Blankenheim, and several other former Freedom Riders—spent part of the time recalling the horrors of the Jim Crow era, but much of the focus was on contemporary problems and challenges. When the Unity Tour had arrived in the city in late June, local and state officials had rolled out the red carpet in an effort to demonstrate that times had changed in Mississippi. Greeted first by David Walker, Jackson's black police chief, and later by former governor William Winter, the bicyclists joined several veterans of the Jackson Non-Violent Movement at a special symposium on the legacy of the Freedom Rides, moderated by Justice Reuben Anderson, the first black to serve on the state supreme court.

A month later the conference participants received the same warm welcome, prompting several Riders to comment on the sharp contrast with their earlier visits to Mississippi. But this did not stop Lewis, a liberal third-term congressman, from lamenting that "thirty years later, the scars and stains of racism are still deeply embedded in American society." Noting persistent discrimination and inequality and commenting on the bitter irony of President George Bush's selection of ultra-conservative Clarence Thomas to replace Justice Thurgood Marshall on the Supreme Court, Lewis insisted that "we've seen the Berlin Wall tumble, but the wall of racism is still up in America." Jim Farmer, wearing an eye patch and virtually sightless in both eyes, was somewhat more conciliatory, arguing that the progress since the Freedom Rides had shown that "this nation is capable of great and rapid change, if enough people work with diligence to that end." But he too pointed out that the nation still had a ways to go before civil rights activists could rest on their laurels. "As long as I have breath in my body," he told the gathering, "I want to be active in the struggle for equality." The presence of Hank Thomas, who had parlayed a string of fast food franchises into a considerable fortune following his return from combat in Vietnam, was an object lesson that for some black Americans things really had improved. Yet Thomas himself, in a speech on economic empowerment, warned that a whole series of problems, from discriminatory loan policies and governmental neglect to drugs and black-on-black crime, continued to inhibit economic uplift among black Americans.

Fittingly, the conference ended with a bittersweet comedy monologue by longtime activist Dick Gregory. In one of his more serious moments, Gregory metaphorically reminded the audience that "the freedom riders had a power in being a light in a dark room." "What did the freedom riders do?" he asked, cupping his hands as if to cover a flaming candle. "The early civil rights activists," he explained, were nothing less than "the shields against the wind that would snuff the light of freedom." Now, thanks to the Freedom Riders and their legacy, "there are so many wicks out there that no one could ever blow them out."[47]

This legacy grew stronger in the decade following the 1991 reunion, as the Clinton administration refocused attention on race and civil rights and as the Freedom Riders themselves gained a renewed sense of their historical importance. Propelled by a rising interest in civil rights history—manifested in the appearance of popular books such as Taylor Branch's *Parting the Waters* (1988) and in the opening of major civil rights museums in Memphis and Birmingham—the Freedom Rides reentered both the consciousness of the American public and the private lives of movement veterans. Throughout the decade Lewis's political success was a major source of pride and a rallying point for former Freedom Riders, some of whom sought out their colleagues for the first time since the 1960s. Lewis himself missed few opportunities to expound on the meaning and legacy of the Rides. Speaking to anyone who would listen to his message on nonviolence and the beloved community, he proclaimed the continuing relevance of both the tactics and the goals of the Freedom Rides. And to prove his point he organized a weeklong Immigrant Workers Freedom Ride in the fall of 2003, mobilizing eight hundred immigrant Riders who traveled on buses to New York and Washington to protest the withholding of civil rights from noncitizens. "Like the Freedom Rides of 1961," Lewis insisted, "Freedom Ride 2003 calls on ordinary people to do extraordinary things; to put their bodies on the line at a moment in American history when immigration is a volatile issue everywhere; to stand up for their rights and the rights of many others; to call attention to bad laws that harm good people; and to challenge the federal government to act where it seems determined not to." In the end, the organizers of the Immigrant Workers Freedom Ride could only claim a modest impact on the second Bush administration's immigration policies, but the scope of the Ride served notice that Lewis and his allies were still a vital force in American politics.[48]

Seven years earlier, in a 1996 cover story in the *New Republic*, historian Sean Wilentz had facetiously characterized Lewis as "The Last Integrationist," emphasizing his importance as "the strongest link in American politics between the early 1960s—the glory days of the civil rights movement—and the 1990s." Leaving the overall impression that Lewis was "black America's most powerful politician," Wilentz suggested that the former Freedom Rider was perhaps the only member of Congress capable of leading a liberal renaissance. While the renaissance did not materialize, there were continuing signs that the spirit of the Freedom Rides was very much alive. In November 1996 Lewis was reelected for a sixth term, and Bob Filner, a white Freedom Rider and Democratic congressman from San Diego, was reelected to a third. Eight months later, at the urging of Lewis and others, President Bill Clinton launched a national Initiative on Race and Reconciliation, appointing the renowned eighty-two-year-old African American historian John Hope Franklin as chairman of an advisory board that included Mississippi's William Winter. Over the course of fifteen months, the advisory board held a series of hearings that highlighted the continuing challenges and dilemmas facing America's multiracial society, including many of the issues raised by the Freedom Riders in 1961.[49]

Throughout the 1990s the legacy of the Freedom Rides also gained currency from the speeches and appearances of former Riders at community events, academic symposia, and college campuses—all of which piqued the curiosity of an emerging generation too young to fathom the compulsions of the Jim Crow past. Testimonials and public reminiscences by Freedom Riders became common, and one documentary filmmaker even brought four surviving Journey of Reconciliation participants to Washington for a taping in 1993. Touted as movement celebrities, the Riders gained a new visibility, especially after several enterprising writers and teachers rediscovered and amplified the story of the Freedom Rides. Two children's books on the Freedom Rides, including one by the noted black author James Haskins, were published in the mid-1990s, and during the following decade several schools and community theaters staged plays that recalled the experiences of 1961. In 1996 Simon and Schuster published a novel by Vicki Covington that focused on the relationship between Bull Connor and two white teenagers who witnessed the attack on the Freedom Riders at the Birmingham Trailways station. And at the University of Wisconsin an imaginative professor organized an entire course around the history of the Freedom Rides, allowing students to spend part of a semester visiting civil rights sites along some of the routes traveled in 1961.[50]

Even more ambitiously, Gary Younge, a twenty-eight-year-old black journalist from Britain, spent three months in the fall of 1997 retracing the entire route of the original CORE Freedom Ride from Washington to New Orleans. Traveling by Greyhound, Younge conducted scores of interviews along the way while recording his personal impressions of "familiar places to which I had never been." As he later explained in his revealing 1999 book, *No Place Like Home: A Black Briton's Journey Through the American South*: "I had seen its battles unfold in black and white and heard its speeches and screams from over the Atlantic. Now I needed to see it in colour. I had to feel the fear, taste the food and ride at the front of the bus. I wanted to breathe life into the legend of my formative years."[51]

For Younge and many others born in the aftermath of the Freedom Rides, the legends and exploits of the early 1960s were finally taking concrete form, as movement veterans found increased opportunities to reflect on the meaning and relevance of the Rides, especially after the publication of Lewis's captivating memoir *Walking with the Wind* and David Halberstam's monumental study of the Nashville movement, *The Children*, in 1998. Both books provoked new interest in the Freedom Rides, taking advantage of public curiosity primed earlier in the year by a long overdue tribute to Jim Farmer.

In January 1998, Bill Clinton awarded Farmer the prestigious Presidential Medal of Freedom, providing the ailing seventy-seven-year-old wheelchair-bound warrior with a token of the recognition that he had long craved but was now too blind to see. "I have had great anxiety that my people would forget me, forget my work. I was hoping the day would come when I would be remembered," he observed a few weeks after the White House ceremony. "They know my name now. I think that medal, which they tell me is quite beautiful, will preserve my place in history." Fourteen months later, he died at his home in Fredericksburg, Virginia, surrounded by few possessions other than memorabilia from a lifetime of struggle. Following the deaths of Ella Baker in 1986, Bayard Rustin in 1987, and Jim Peck in 1993, Farmer's passing marked the closing of an era in civil rights history. In the end, even many of those who had shrunk from his vanity or condemned him for his Republican apostasy in the 1970s shed a tear or two in remorse and memory of his undeniable passion for justice.[52]

Farmer's death was a reminder that all of the Freedom Riders—men and women who had once seemed so young—were getting older. Some were already in their sixties and approaching retirement, and even the youngest had passed mid-life by century's end. While many remained actively engaged in professional life and other pursuits, thoughts of mortality and a reflective attitude born of age inevitably brought at least some of the Riders closer together. Lewis, for one, believed that it was time to renew historical and personal connections in a dramatic way. In 2000 he began to organize an elaborate fortieth anniversary reunion commemorating the "Ride to Freedom." After securing funding from Greyhound and several other corporate

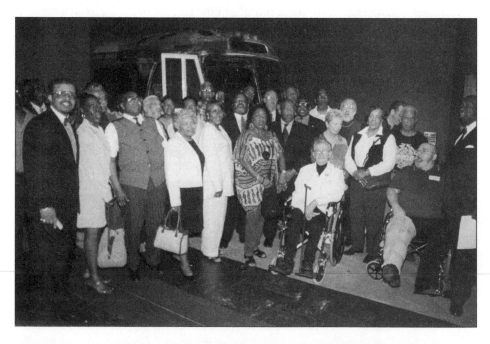

Gathered in front of the burned bus exhibit at the Birmingham Civil Rights Institute, former Freedom Riders and friends sing freedom songs to help commemorate the fortieth anniversary of the Freedom Rides, May 12, 2001. (Courtesy of Greyhound Corporation)

sponsors, he hired a special congressional staff liaison to mobilize a select group of CORE and SNCC veterans for a three-day celebration and partial reenactment of the original Freedom Ride.

The reunion began in Washington on May 10, 2001, with a ceremony featuring speeches by Lewis and D.C. congresswoman Eleanor Holmes Norton, the presentation of a "Greyhound Award" to each Freedom Rider in attendance, and a Chinese buffet dinner commemorating the famous "Last Supper" of May 3, 1961. Five of the original CORE Riders—Lewis, Thomas, Cox, Blankenheim, and Person—were on hand, as were Marvin Rich, Moses Newson, several Nonviolent Action Group Riders, and two veterans of the 1947 Journey of Reconciliation, George Houser and Bill Worthy.

On May 11, most of the group, plus a number of other movement veterans, gathered in Atlanta for a series of ceremonial events before boarding buses for Alabama the following morning. Accompanied by a C-SPAN film crew, several journalists, and two historians conducting onboard interviews, the caravan of freedom buses traveled to Anniston, Birmingham, and Montgomery, where local officials and black community leaders went out of their way to welcome the entourage—but where the returning Freedom Riders dredged up haunting memories nonetheless. In Anniston, where he had been beaten forty years earlier, the normally gregarious Hank Thomas was overcome with conflicting emotions and could barely find words to express his feelings. In Birmingham, during a stop at the downtown bus station and a tour of museum exhibits at the Civil Rights Institute, others encountered similar difficulties. "In a sense this is holy ground," Lewis told the crowd at the bus station, his voice cracking with emotion as he reminded them that this was the very place where "you planted the seeds of a mighty movement." Minutes later, upon seeing a museum replica of the burned bus, Ed Blankenheim, confined to a wheelchair following a disabling stroke, broke down into sobs and had to be wheeled away from the exhibit. But somehow he was able to regain his composure, joining with his fellow Riders to sing a chorus of "Keep Your Eyes on the Prize" before leaving the museum.

Later in the day, after the group gathered for a final event at the First Baptist Church in Montgomery—the scene of the 1961 siege that had changed not only their lives but the lives of millions of Americans—there was more singing, and more reminiscing, both solemn and soulful. By the time they reboarded the buses for the return trip to Atlanta, everyone was emotionally spent, confirming to Lewis and everyone else on board that at least the dream, if not the broader reality, of the beloved community was still alive. And if this was not enough to prove the point, Lewis soon added a postscript to the commemoration. Traveling to Boston with several of his closest friends on May 21, he was awarded the first Profiles in Courage Lifetime Achievement Award by the John F. Kennedy Library Foundation. Coming forty years to the day after the famous siege of the First Baptist Church in Montgomery, the ceremony at the Kennedy Library was a fitting end to a week of renewal and remembrance.[53]

The ideals of interracial harmony and social justice were once again on full display six months later when an even larger group of former Freedom Riders gathered in Jackson, Mississippi. Organized by a band of California-based Freedom Riders who had kept in contact over the decades, the reunion attracted more than sixty Riders, many of whom had spent time in Parchman prison and other Mississippi jails in 1961. Only one of the original CORE Riders—Charles Person—attended, and aside from Jim Forman there were no movement celebrities at the gathering. But those who were there represented the full range of activists who had turned the Freedom Rides into a mass movement forty years earlier. In 1961 they had been college or high school students, ministers, rabbis, professors, artists, secretaries, nurses, long-shoremen, and day laborers. Some had traveled thousands of miles to become Freedom Riders, and others had simply moved to the front of a local bus, confronting Jim Crow in their hometown of Jackson. Whatever their origins, they all shared a proud heritage of being among the first Americans to take a ride for freedom. Many, as the events and speeches of the reunion weekend demonstrated, were still on the road to freedom, still struggling to bring civil and human rights to the nation and the world.

Captured in a series of oral history interviews conducted by researchers from the University of Mississippi—the same university where violent white supremacists had tried to bar James Meredith's admission in 1962—the individual stories of continuing struggle and sacrifice provided a link between past and present, and between hope and partial fulfillment. Tom Gaither, the scout for the original CORE Freedom Ride, had gone on to become a distinguished professor of biology and environmental activist. Claire O'Connor, one of the Minnesota Six, had moved from practical nursing to directing a clinic for impoverished and at-risk teenagers. The Parchman diarist Carol Ruth Silver had turned a legal career into a seat on the San Francisco Board of Examiners, where she fought for all manner of progressive causes. John Maguire, the Alabama-born associate of Martin Luther King Jr., had divided the forty years since the Freedom Rides between Connecticut and California, first as a professor of theology and later as a college president. The founding chairman of the Martin Luther King, Jr. Center for Nonviolent Social Change, he had spent his entire adult life refining and acting upon the moral truths raised by his famed seminary roommate. Steve Green, once Stokely Carmichael's verbal sparring partner, had passed through a long and successful tenure as a writer and editor for the *Christian Science Monitor* to become a specialist in emergency relief for the United Nations. Bob Singleton, the onetime leader of the UCLA Freedom Riders, had gone from graduate school to an influential career as an economist specializing in issues of poverty and employment discrimination.

No less inspiring was Singleton's wife, Helen, an accomplished artist and lifelong activist who had been with him every step of the way from California to Parchman and back again. Fittingly, she was accorded the honor of accepting a commemorative plaque on behalf of all of the returning Riders. Issued by Governor Ronnie Musgrove, once an avowed segregationist, the plaque proclaimed November 10, 2001, as "Freedom Riders Day" in Mississippi. Hailing those who had taken "the long, often perilous road to end segregation," the gubernatorial proclamation saluted "the heroic efforts" of the Freedom Riders, many of whom had never expected to live long enough to witness such a gesture by a white Mississippi politician. For those who had returned to the benighted state of Mississippi with mixed emotions and modest expectations, the governor's implicit apology was perhaps the most redeeming story of all.[54]

There was, however, at least one redemptive Freedom Ride story that went unnoticed and unrecorded in Jackson. Twelve hundred miles to the north, in the Long Island town of Roosevelt, a long-forgotten eighty-four-year-old woman named Irene Morgan Kirkaldy lived quietly with her daughter. Though technically not a veteran of the Freedom Rides, she was perhaps the one indispensable person in the long saga that stretched back to the summer of 1944. The gray-haired great grandmother had come a long way since the fateful moment when she refused to move to the rear of a Virginia bus, but in many respects she was the same woman who had manifested a resolute courage almost six decades earlier. Her life had taken her to widowhood at the young age of thirty-two, to a second marriage and a career providing maid service and child care to several generations of New York families, and belatedly to college. While in semi-retirement during the 1980s, she won a college scholarship in a radio contest and entered St. John's University, where she majored in

Irene Morgan Kirkaldy and several generations of her family pose with President Bill Clinton following the Presidential Citizens' Medal award ceremony at the White House, January 8, 2001. (Courtesy of Sherwood Morgan)

communications. Graduating in 1985 at the age of sixty-eight, she went on to Queens College, where she earned an M.A. degree in urban studies in 1990. Along the way, she maintained a keen interest in issues of racial equality and social justice, demonstrating her concern in numerous ways, from writing letters to officials on behalf of victims of discrimination to an annual gesture of inviting homeless persons to her home for Thanksgiving dinner.

Shunning her status as a historic figure, Irene Kirkaldy sought and received no public attention until 1995, when she made a brief appearance in a documentary film on the Journey of Reconciliation. Five years later, during the summer of 2000, she was rediscovered a second time by a *Washington Post* journalist and a Gloucester County Historical Society committee conducting research for the county's upcoming 350th anniversary. Eager to include at least one black hero in its list of historical personages, the committee invited Kirkaldy to attend the anniversary celebration as an honored guest. Establishing a scholarship fund in her name and feting her with a special "Homecoming for Irene Morgan" day in early August, the local establishment that had treated her so harshly in the 1940s went out of its way to make amends. Kirkaldy's response to all of this attention was both gracious and measured. As a frequent visitor to the county where most of her mother's family had lived and worked since the time of slavery, she knew all too well that racial and economic discrimination still burdened the poorest and darkest citizens of the Virginia Southside. But she was also touched by the genuinely warm reception that she received from both blacks and whites in the new Gloucester.

On balance, the experience was more than enough to revive a long-suppressed idea of moving south, and six months later her sense that both the white South and the entire nation had changed for the better was confirmed by a public tribute from a Southern-born president born the same year as the landmark Supreme Court decision bearing her name. Invited to the White House by President Clinton, she—along with twenty-seven others, including Fred Shuttlesworth, sports stars Muhammad Ali and Hank Aaron, and NAACP attorneys Jack Greenberg and Constance Baker Motley—was awarded the coveted Presidential Citizens Medal. "When Irene Morgan boarded a bus for Baltimore in the summer of 1944," the medal citation proclaimed, "she took the first step on a journey that would change America forever."

Whether this apparent transformation will prove to be as fundamental or as permanent as the citation implies remains an open question. But even the most skeptical among us should take some comfort from Irene Kirkaldy's recent decision to live out her days in Gloucester. Since January 2004 she and her daughter have shared a home just down the road from the bus stop where she was once denied simple justice. Surrounded by friends and family members who see her as a righteous symbol of redemption and promise, she lives peacefully, secure in the knowledge that her life—like the lives of the Freedom Riders who came after her—made a difference. For her, at least, the long-awaited day of jubilee has arrived.[55]

Acknowledgments

THIS IS PRIMARILY A BOOK OF INTERRELATED STORIES, and I fear that my personal story pales in comparison with the lives and experiences of the Freedom Riders. Nevertheless, I feel that I owe my readers at least a few words of autobiographical explanation, a brief reflection on how and why I came to write this book. Though born on Cape Cod in Massachusetts, I spent much of my childhood in Virginia, Maryland, and northern Florida. During the 1950s and early 1960s, several alternating stints in the North and South left me with a measure of confusion on matters of regional identity and culture. By my teenage years, making sense of race and civil rights across time and space had become both a personal passion and a survival skill. In 1961, the year of the Freedom Rides, I was a junior high school student living in suburban Maryland a few miles from the Washington bus stations that launched the first Freedom Ride. I have only vague memories of the headlines that followed and my reactions to the burning bus and the senseless beatings in Birmingham and Montgomery. I remember having sympathy for the Riders but also wondering why they had chosen such a provocative and dangerous means of protest. Like many other young Americans during the Kennedy years, I had hopeful expectations about the future of American democracy and generally trusted the administration to do what was right. This optimism was reinforced during a high school field trip in the spring of 1963 when I spent several hours in a Senate hearing room listening to Attorney General Robert Kennedy defend civil rights while withstanding a withering assault by several reactionary Southern segregationists.

Later that year, just as my family was preparing to move to northern Florida, I had a chance encounter with a group of black civil rights activists on the eve of the March on Washington. For more than two hours they explained why they had come to Washington, and when I responded sympathetically they urged me to join the march, even though I was only fifteen. The next day, as I rode southward though Virginia and the Carolinas with my parents, I was consumed with guilt and the suspicion that I had just squandered my first opportunity to witness history in the making. Over the next two years, as I navigated my way around the social conservatism of a segregated high school, this lost opportunity nagged at my conscience, though for the most part I did not act upon these feelings until later.

My interest in civil rights and civil rights history took on new life during my undergraduate years at Princeton, thanks to the inspiring teaching and engaged scholarship of Sheldon Hackney. I have often wondered what my life and career would have been like if I had not had the good fortune to become Sheldon's research assistant in the summer of 1967. A native of Birmingham with close personal and intellectual ties to the civil rights movement, he introduced me to a cast of historical characters and a hidden world of activism and struggle that I could have scarcely imagined a year earlier. Under his mentorship, I confronted the dark history of race and region while trying to deal with the confounding realities of contemporary political polarization and social fragmentation. The civil rights movement itself was fragmenting, as hope struggled against disillusionment, and the entire tumultuous scene was both fascinating and disturbing, providing me with enough puzzling questions to sustain a lifetime of inquiry and intellectual and political engagement.

Later, as a graduate student at Brandeis University, I learned a great deal more about social movements—and the broader study of social and political history—from a remarkable interdisciplinary faculty that included David Hackett Fischer, John Demos, Morton Keller, Marvin Meyers, and Jim Green. Set against the unpredictable social and political backdrop of the 1970s, this historical education deepened my interest in the interconnected realties of political power, grassroots democracy, and social justice. Understanding these interconnections was the central concern of my dissertation and first book, a case study of early twentieth-century Southern demagoguery, and this same concern later propelled me to write *Freedom Riders*.

During thirty years of teaching and research, first at the University of Minnesota and later at the University of South Florida, I have tackled an eclectic list of historical topics, from air-conditioning and hurricanes to baseball and the Bill of Rights. But no topic has ever engaged my attention as deeply as the Freedom Rides. It has been a long and wonderful ride, and I want to thank the many people who helped and guided me along the way. During the past decade I have been the beneficiary of so many acts of kindness, generosity, and consideration that I hardly know where to begin my thanks and acknowledgments.

Most obviously, I owe an incalculable debt to the scores of former Freedom Riders and civil rights activists, journalists, government officials, and other contemporary observers who shared their memories, experiences, and perspectives. Some did so in casual conversations, others in extended oral history interviews. But each reminiscence, however brief or impromptu, added something significant to my knowledge of the text and context of the Freedom Rides. In the field of civil rights scholarship, oral history is an essential tool, and I could not have written this book without the help and cooperation of Peter Ackerberg, Zev Aelony, Thomas Armstrong III, Michael Audain, Aleah Bacquie, George Barrett, Abraham Bassford, Scott Bates, Robert Baum, Charles Berrard, Ed Blankenheim, Jorgia Siegel Bordofsky, Clark Bouwman, Harry Boyte Jr., Ellen Kleinman Broms, Catherine Burks Brooks, Joan Browning, Gordon Carey, Clyde Carter, Judge Robert L. Carter, William Sloane Coffin Jr., John Collier, Lucretia Collins, Norma Collins, Ben Cox, Margaret Crowder, Marv Davidov, Glenda Gaither Davis, James K. Davis, David Dennis, James Emerson Dennis, Dion Diamond, John Doar, Paul Abdullah Dietrich, John Dolan, Israel Dresner, Patricia Stephens Due, Leslie Dunbar, W. McKee Evans, Bob Farrell, Walter Fauntroy, Robert Filner, John Hope Franklin, Martin Freedman, Winston Fuller, Tom Gaither, Joe Gerbac, William Goodman, Jacquelyn Grant, Reginald Green, Steve Green, Joe Griffith, Michael Grubbs, Herbert Hamilton, Bill Hansen, Bill Harbour, Harry Harvey, Bob Heller, Burton Hersh, Holly Hogrobrooks, George Houser, Mae Frances Moultrie Howard, Charles Jones, Irene Amos Morgan Kirkaldy, Pat Kovner, Bernard Lafayette, Barbara Lawrence, Belford Lawson III, Margaret Leonard, Alan Levine, John Lewis, Norma Libson, Claude Liggins, Chela Lightchild, Kwame Leo Lillard, Morton Linder, Mary Little-Vance, Leon Litwack, Rudy Lombard, Lenore Taitt Magubane, John Maguire, Salynn McCollum, Mikki McCray, Steve McNichols, Beverly Mill, John Moody Jr., Jerry Moore, Sherwood Morgan, Dave Morton, Joan Trumpauer Mulholland, Charles David Myers, Diane Nash, Frank Nelson, Juanita Nelson, Moses Newson, Sandra Nixon, Claire O'Connor, Gene Patterson, Max Pavesic, Charles Person, Alphonso and Kredelle Petway, Philip Posner, Grady Wilson Powell Sr., Laura Randall, Janet B. Reinitz, Marvin Rich, Ralph Roy, Steve Sanfield, Shirley Saunders, John Seigenthaler, Sidney Shanken, Rick Sheviakov, Fred Shuttlesworth, Carol Ruth Silver, Benjamin Simms, Howard Simon, Robert Singleton, Jerome Smith, Woolcott Smith, Doratha Smith-Simmons, Bill Svanoe, John Swomley, John Taylor, Hank Thomas, Gene Uphoff, C. T. Vivian, Matthew Walker Jr., Wyatt Tee Walker, Hezekiah Watkins, Frank Wilkinson, Mike Wolfson, Virgil Wood, William Worthy, Ellen Ziskind, Lewis Zuchman, and Jim Zwerg.

Several of these interviewees—Charles Berrard, Ed Blankenheim, Joan Browning, John Dolan, Steve Green, Steve McNichols, Francis and Laura Randall, Ralph Roy, Rick Sheviakov, and Carol Ruth Silver—deserve special thanks for allowing me to make use of their written memoirs. And several others—including Ed Blankenheim, Catherine Burks Brooks, Gordon Carey, Ben Cox, Si Dresner, Bill Harbour, Bernard Lafayette, Marvin Rich, and John Seigenthaler—went well beyond what is normally expected of an oral history subject, providing me with photographs and other memorabilia, fact-checking parts of the manuscript, and responding to my numerous queries about what must have seemed to be arcane details. Collectively, they saved me from making an embarrassingly long list of mistakes; my gratitude to them cannot be overstated, and I hope they recognize and take pride in their positive impact on the book. As the unofficial archivist of the Freedom Rides, Bill Harbour was especially generous in sharing his vast knowledge and collected artifacts related to the Rides, and I want him to know how much I appreciate his many kindnesses.

I also owe a special debt to Sherwood Morgan for providing me with photographs and other documentary evidence related to his mother's remarkable life, and to John Lewis and

Carol Ruth Silver for encouraging me to participate in two memorable Freedom Riders reunions in 2001. Thanks also to Nicole Young and David Lisker for organizing the reunions and facilitating my participation, and to Susan Glisson for graciously arranging for the reproduction of the Freedom Rider interviews conducted in Jackson in November 2001. I am also grateful to Jerry Eisterhold for inviting me to take part in the development of the Rosa Parks Museum in Montgomery and the International Civil Rights Center and Museum in Greensboro.

Attempting to reconstruct the history of the Freedom Rides sometimes made me feel like an overmatched child tackling a massive jigsaw puzzle. But fortunately I never had to face the puzzle alone. From start to finish, I was able to draw upon the talents and insights of others, including a long list of imaginative and dedicated civil rights historians who have turned this once neglected area into one of American history's most vital subfields. Several of these pioneering civil rights historians have provided me with much-needed assistance, friendship, and intellectual stimulation during the long gestation of this book; I want to express my sincere appreciation to Tony Badger, Bud Bartley, Jack Bass, Fitz Brundage, Clay Carson, Dan Carter, Derek Catsam, Bill Chafe, David Chalmers, David Chappell, Jim Cobb, David Colburn, Connie Curry, Jane Dailey, Pete Daniel, Jack Davis, John D'Emilio, John Dittmer, Charles Eagles, John Egerton, Glenn Eskew, Sara Evans, Adam Fairclough, Lee Formwalt, John Hope Franklin, Kari Frederickson, David Garrow, Paul Gaston, David Goldfield, Jim Grossman, Steve Hahn, Jackie Hall, Wesley Hogan, Walter Jackson, Betsy Jacoway, Maxine Jones, Richard King, John Kirk, Bob Korstad, Steve Lawson, Jama Lazerow, Len Lempel, George Lewis, Peter Ling, Ralph Luker, Neil McMillen, Vivien Miller, Kay Mills, Geoff Norrell, Gail O'Brien, David Oshinsky, Greg Padgett, Jim Patterson, Charles Payne, Larry Powell, John Salmond, Harvard Sitkoff, Lara Smith, Pat Sullivan, Mills Thornton, Stephen Tuck, Tim Tyson, Brian Ward, Clive Webb, and Steve Whitfield. I am especially grateful to John Dittmer for reading the original book proposal, to Lee Formwalt for assisting me with the Albany material, to Ralph Luker for helping me on several occasions with research leads, to Lara Smith for tracking down Irene Morgan, to Pat Sullivan for arranging an interview with Judge Robert Carter, and to Mills Thornton for all of his help during our long collaboration on Alabama history.

I am also indebted to several journalists who helped me with various aspects of my research. Sincere thanks to Carol Morello and Leonard Downie Jr. of the *Washington Post*, Craig Colgan of the *Charlotte Observer*, Bill Maxwell of the *St. Petersburg Times*, Mark Strassmann of CBS News, and Roy Peter Clark of the Poynter Institute.

I would also like to thank Michael O'Brien, Bert Wyatt-Brown, Vernon Burton, Jim Farmer, Drew Faust, Sarah Gardner, Chaz Joyner, Steve Kantrowitz, John Mayfield, David Moltke-Hansen, Houston Roberson, Mitch Snay, Steve Stowe, and the other "usual suspects" who have turned the annual meetings of the Southern Intellectual History Circle into an unparalleled community of scholars. I like to think that my many experiences with the "Circle" have sharpened my critical facilities and made this a better book, even though my narrative approach to history may still fall short of "intellectual history" standards.

I also owe a huge debt of gratitude to another circle—a small group of close friends whom I have known since my graduate school days at Brandeis in the early 1970s. Despite geographic dispersal and frequent humiliations and disappointments on and off the tennis court (and inside Fenway Park), we have remained close and more or less sane for more than thirty years, sharing the joy of true friendship and an uncommon bond of intellectual curiosity and personal commitment. Notwithstanding the side bets that this book would never see the light of day, Steve and Lee Whitfield, Jim and Lois Horton, Fred Hoxie, Dave and Elaine Gould, Ted and Nan Hammett, David Oshinsky, and Mitch Snay are still the most cherished of friends. As always, Steve, the toughest and sharpest of critics, was willing to read my work at a moment's notice, despite his rigorous schedule as an international pundit. And Jim took time out from his presidential labors at the OAH to provide wise counsel about how to bring a long-overdue book to closure. The others did even more important work, sharing my blind faith in the Red Sox even when they were seemingly down to their last out.

Several other close friends provided critical support during the writing of this book. Even though they faced the daunting challenge of finishing their own weighty tomes, my University of South Florida colleagues Gary Mormino and John Belohlavek never missed an opportunity to lend a hand or to offer timely words of encouragement. Both are master teachers and talented scholars, but most of all they are two of the finest human beings on the planet. Jack Davis, a former student who turned himself into a first-rate historian and more recently into a happily married man and proud father, assumed most of the burden of completing our co-edited book on Florida's environmental history, allowing me to concentrate on the Freedom Riders. And, despite an overwhelming array of professional commitments, he accompanied me to two Freedom Rider reunions and was the first to volunteer to read large portions of the manuscript. I am deeply grateful for his insightful comments and continuing friendship. I would also like to thank three other friends who offered expert commentary on portions of the manuscript: Sheldon Hackney of the University of Pennsylvania; and Richard King and Peter Ling, both of the University of Nottingham.

Many other friends offered advice and encouragement at critical points during the writing of this book. Sincere thanks to Jean Agnew, Merle Allshouse, Charles Arnade, Chris Arsenault, Bill and Marion Ballard, Ron Bayor, Bill Belleville, Laurie Berlin, Peter and Susan Betzer, Bob Bickel, Pam Blankenheim, Jim Bledsoe, Jeannie Blue, Sarah Boyer, Alan Brinkley, Mark Brown, Sally Brown, Seville Brown, Tom Brown, Rus Buchan, Fran Cary, Robert Cassanello, Lloyd and Louise Chapin, Tim Clemmons, Beverly Coyle, Goliath Davis, Jack Day, Erig Deggans, Bob Devin-Jones, Arnette Doctor, Carol and Justus Doenecke, Paul Dosal, Don Doyle, Tom and Vicky Dunn, Susie Erenrich, Rebecca Falkenberry, Charlotte Fellonius, Janine Farver, Robert Ford, Steve Forman, Ron Formisano, Gaines Foster, Winnie Foster, Larry Friedman, Matt Gallman, Jennifer Gallop, Thavolia Glymph, Sid Goetz, Peter Golenbock, Don and Marika Gordon, Ed Griffin, Mike Grossberg, Ira Grupper, Lucy Hackney, Bill Harris, Dirk Hartog, Harry Harvey, Leland Hawes, Adrien Helm, Ben Houston, Mark Huddle, Andy Huse, Allen and Bobbie Isaacman, Carolyn Johnston, Jackie Jones, Walter Kalaf, Jon Kile, Susan King, Jack Temple Kirby, Jeff Klinkenberg, Peter Kuryla, Jane Landers, Reed and Glenna Letsinger, Anthony Lewis, Riley L. Lewis Jr., Susan Lockwood, Rob Lorei, John C. Meehan, Jeanne and Peter Meinke, Tyna Middleton, Randall Miller, Ray Mohl, Jerry Moore, Meredith Morris-Babb, Lynne Mormino, Bill Murray, Harvey and Nancy Nelsen, Roby O'Brien, Barbara O'Reilley, Kathleen Paul, Paul Pohlman, Patricia Putnam, Bob Randolph, John Shelton Reed, Rene Reno, Larry Rivers, Randy Roberts, Sonya Rudenstine, Ann Schoenacher, Stuart Schwartz, Ken Scott, Joyce Seltzer, Perkins Shelton, Mike Slicker, John David Smith, Herb Snitzer, Diane Sommerville, Rhonda Sonnenberg, David Stamps, David Starr, Ward Stavig, Bob and Carol Steele, Ted and Bill Steger, Betty Jean Steinshouer, Jim Stewart, John and Sheila Stewart, Bill Stokes, Marian Strobel, Tom Terrill, Brenda Thornton, Susan Turner, Ruth Uphaus, Don Vappie, Maria Vesperi, Bill and Sally Wallace, Nigel Watson, Vibert White, Lee Whitfield, and Randall Williams.

Janine Farver, director of the Florida Humanities Council, deserves special mention for pulling off one of the cruelest April Fools' jokes in living memory. I am sure that if he had wanted to, David Garrow could have written *No Easy Ride to Freedom*, the definitive account of the Freedom Rides based on more than seven hundred interviews. But it was something of a relief to learn that the splashy HarperCollins press release announcing Garrow's forthcoming book was a concoction of Janine's devious mind.

During the past decade, a number of institutions and individuals have provided me with opportunities to present various aspects of my research on the Freedom Rides. I am grateful to Dean Frank Wetta and Daytona Beach Community College for asking me to kick off their spring 2000 lecture series on "America in the Sixties" with a lecture on the Freedom Rides; to Jim Horton and the Smithsonian Institution's National Museum of American History for inviting me to speak at its February 2001 symposium "Created Equal: African Americans and the Presidency"; to David Moltke-Hansen of the Historical Society of Pennsylvania for inviting me to participate in a session on "Liberty and Equality: The Civil Rights Years" at the April 2001 conference commemorating the 225th anniversary of the Pennsylvania Abolition Society; to Sylvia Frey and Larry Powell for allowing me to organize and moderate the Freedom Rider session at the April 2001 Tulane–Cambridge University Conference on Freedom Struggles in the Atlantic World; to Vernon Burton and Bo Moore for organizing the 2003 Citadel Conference on the Civil Rights Movement in South Carolina, where I presented a paper on the Freedom Riders' experiences in South Carolina; to Clive Webb for organizing a session on the Freedom Rides at the 2003 British Association of American Studies conference at Aberstwyth, Wales; to Chaz Joyner for asking me to deliver the 2003 Phi Alpha Theta Lecture at Coastal Carolina University; to Bob Bickel and the Stetson University College of Law for asking me to moderate a symposium on civil rights and the *Brown* decision at the February 2004 Law and Higher Education Conference held in Clearwater, Florida; and to John Kirk and Mara Keire for inviting me to present a paper on the Freedom Rides to the American History Research Seminar at the University of London's Institute for Historical Research in February 2005.

I would like to thank Ed Blankenheim, Ben Cox, Diane Nash, and Hank Thomas for making the session at the Tulane–Cambridge conference so inspiring, and Ed and Ben once again for joining me at the University of Illinois in May 2004 for an equally memorable Freedom Rider mini-reunion. Ben, John Hope Franklin, and Gene Patterson also deserve thanks for participating in the civil rights panel at the Florida ACLU's 2003 Nelson Poynter Award Banquet held in St. Petersburg. Thanks also to Maurice Jackson for bringing down the house with a medley of Freedom Rider and other freedom songs at the banquet. I am also grateful to Gordon Carey, Connie Curry, Pat and John Due, Walter Fauntroy, Robert Hayling, Stetson Kennedy, Bernard Lafayette, Fred Shuttlesworth, and a host of other veteran activists for participating in the June 2004 conference on the Civil Rights Movement in Florida, held at the University of South Florida, St. Petersburg.

Sincere thanks to Glenn Feldman for including an early version of chapter 1 in his anthology *Before Brown: Civil Rights and White Backlash in the Modern South*, and to Samuel C. Hyde Jr. for including a preliminary version of chapter 2 in *Sunbelt Revolution: The Historical Progression of the Civil Rights Struggle in the Gulf South, 1866–2000*. Thanks also to Bob Bickel for publishing chapter 1 in the Winter 2005 issue of the *Stetson Law Review*, and to Barbara O'Reilley and the Florida Humanities Council for including a portion of chapter 8 in the spring 2004 issue of *Forum*.

I want to acknowledge the generous support of the University of South Florida Publications Council, which helped fund the reproduction and acquisition of photographs for the book. I am also grateful for the long-standing support of the University of South Florida, St. Petersburg, which granted me a sabbatical leave during the fall of 2002. Over the past twenty-five years I have developed a deep affection for this unique institution and the community of scholars, students, and staff that have made it such a special place to teach. My life and career have been enriched by the genuine collegiality of a long line of supportive campus administrators, including John Hinz, Bill Garrett, Lowell Davis, Karen Spear, Sam Fustukjian, Bill Heller, Winston Bridges, Ralph Wilcox, Mark Durand, Lisa Starks, Jim Malek, Vivian Fueyo, and Karen White. In one way or another, all of these individuals helped make it possible for me to devote much of my time to research and writing, and I want to thank them for their many kindnesses and indulgences. I have also benefited greatly from the wise counsel and encouragement offered by a number of other colleagues at USFSP. I owe special thanks to my history colleagues Gary Mormino, David Carr, James Kessenides, and Susan Fernandez. Thanks also to Bob Hall, Tim Reilly, Harriet Deer, Herb Karl, Ambe Njoh, Jerry Dreller, Rebecca Johns, Hugh LaFollette, Thomas Smith, Jay Sokolovsky, Julie Armstrong, Tom Hallock, Chris Meindl, Deanna Michael, Van Hilliard, Joy Clingman, Bob Fowler, Bob Dardenne, Mike Killenberg, Mark Pezzo, Sarah Partan, Jessica Cabness, Peter Kalliney, Judithann McLauchlan, Darryl Paulson, Dan Wells, and Regis Factor.

I would also like to express my appreciation to the many students who, over the course of three decades, have helped sustain and broaden my interest in the history of civil rights and the struggle for racial justice. I do not have room to note them all by name, but some deserve special mention: Glenda Alvin, Ellen Babb, Evan Bennett, Stephanie Chiariello, Tom Collins, Joe Cubine, Anita Cutting, Jack Davis, Sam Davis, Don Falls, Thom Foley, Kathie Gibson, Amy Goodden, Lee Irby, Jamel Jemni, Scholastica Kimani, Janice Law, Meeghan Kane, Earl Lewis, Gordon Mantler, David McCally, Clark Miller, Marissa Monroe, Tiffany Patterson, Loretta Pippin, Kim Rogers, Marc Rotenberg, Monica Rowland, Jim Schnur, Ragnar Sigurdsson, David Shedden, David Starr, Joe Trotter, Milly Vappie, Jake Vonk, David Seth Walker, Christian Warren, and Jon Wilson.

Several graduate assistants in the Florida Studies Program helped me at various stages of the book's progress, and I want to acknowledge their hard work and important contributions. I was very fortunate to draw upon the talents of Kelly Benjamin, Judy Koch, Steve Davis-Thompson, Nick Hansen, Lucy Jones, Meeghan Kane, Monica Rowland, Scott Lauinger, Allen Miller, Suzanne St. John, Nevin Sitler, Albert Vogt, Diane Wakeman, and Edward Woodward. Meeghan Kane and Monica Rowland shouldered an extraordinary set of burdens during the 2004 conference on the Civil Rights Movement in Florida, and Meeghan went on to devote most of the past year to the Freedom Rides. Her cheerful enthusiasm and selfless dedication to the completion of the book have been invaluable, and I cannot thank her enough for all that she has done.

I would also like to thank the irrepressible denizens of the Snell House for providing me with what is surely one of the best places in the world to work. I owe so much to the campus earth mother and Devil Rays maven Sudsy Tschiderer, Marti "Moneybags" Garratt, Danita Marie, Barbara Ness, Lisa Wharton Turner, and Greta Scheid-Wells. Special thanks to wonderful Greta for returning to the fold.

This book could not have been completed without the help of numerous librarians and archivists. Foremost among them are the talented and dedicated librarians at the Nelson Poynter Memorial Library at the University of South Florida, St. Petersburg. I am especially grateful to Dean Kathleen Hardee Arsenault; Director of Special Collections Jim Schnur, Jerry Notaro, Jackie Jackson, Tina Neville, Mika Nelson, Karilyn Jaap, Jackie Shewmaker, Deb Henry, Anita Lindsay, Tony Smith, Berrie Watson, Charlotte Barbour, Barbara Reynolds, and David Brodosi. I also want to thank Mark Greenberg, director of Special Collections and head of the Florida Studies Center at the University of South Florida, Tampa, Library. In Alabama, I received excellent assistance from Jim Baggett of the Birmingham Public Library; Tom Mullins of the Anniston-Calhoun County Public Library; and from Ed Bridges, director of the Alabama State Archives in Montgomery. In Atlanta, Georgia, the library staff at the Martin Luther King Jr.

Center for Nonviolent Social Change, went out of their way to be helpful. At the Mississippi Department of Archives and History, I received valuable assistance from Nancy Bounds and Anne Webster. I also owe a special debt to Jan Hillegas of Jackson, who was instrumental in helping me photocopy a large portion of the Mississippi State Sovereignty Commission's records. In Tennessee, several librarians and archivists were extremely helpful. Thanks to Kathryn Bennett, Andrea Blackman, and Beth Odle of the Nashville Public Library; David Dwiggins and Chantay Steptoe of the *Nashville Tennessean* photo archives; Jessie Carney Smith, the director of the John Hope and Aurelia E. Franklin Library at Fisk University; Glenda Alvin of the Tennessee State University Library; and Juanita Murray, director of Special Collections at the Vanderbilt University Library. Thanks also to Fred Romanski of the National Archives II in College Park, Maryland; Wilma Slate of the Wellesley College archives; Joellen El Bashir of the Moorland-Spingarn Research Center at Howard University; and the helpful librarians at the Swarthmore College Library, the John F. Kennedy Library in Boston, the Mugar Library at Boston University, and the Amistad Research Center at Tulane University.

I am also heavily indebted to the staff of Oxford University Press. Peter Ginna has been an exemplary editor, combining a firm hand with the patience of Job. He has shepherded this project from the beginning with great skill and good humor, even during the darkest moments when our common passion for the Red Sox produced severe anxiety and depression. I would also like to thank two talented and gracious assistant editors, Furaha Norton and Laura Stickney, who somehow managed to stay on top of all the deadlines and details, and Joellyn Ausanka, who guided the production of the book with unflappable steadiness. I also had the good fortune of working with India Cooper, an extraordinarily gifted copyeditor who improved the manuscript in numerous ways, and Jeffrey Ward, who added so much to the book by creating imaginative, informative, and beautiful maps. Contributing to the Pivotal Moments in American History series has been an honor and a privilege, and I want to thank co-editors David Hackett Fischer and Jim McPherson for creating such an innovative framework for historical writing. Meeting the high standards set by these remarkably gifted historians was a daunting challenge, but I will always be grateful for the opportunity to work with them on such an important project. I only hope that in some measure I have justified their confidence in me.

As always, no written acknowledgment can do justice to the contributions of my family. My parents, Oscar and Patricia Arsenault, my sister, Pam, my amazing daughters, Amelia and Anne, and my wonderful wife, Kathy, have given me more love and support than anyone deserves. Kathy, who was crazy enough to join me on our own freedom ride/elopement thirty-eight years ago, has borne the heaviest burden and made the greatest sacrifices. But through it all she has maintained an uncommon grace, an incorruptible intellectual honesty, and an acute sense of irony that has kept us rolling in the right direction. I owe her everything and more.

Finally, I would like to dedicate this book to John Hope Franklin. Our long friendship has been one of the joys of my life, and nothing I can say here can adequately express my respect and admiration for him. As noted on the dedication page, he is the original "freedom writer." A man of true wisdom and moral courage, he humbles us all.

Appendix:
Roster of Freedom Riders

Journey of Reconciliation — April 9–23, 1947

Name	Race	Sex	Age	Residence	Occupation or Status
ADAMS, LOUIS	W	M		Greensboro, NC	Methodist minister; FOR
BANKS, DENNIS[adf]	B	M	20	Chicago, IL	Jazz musician
BROMLEY, ERNEST[c]	W	M	35	Stonewall, NC	Methodist minister; FOR

Born March 14, 1912. In 1991 he and 4 others were arrested for illegal entry and aiding and abetting the destruction of public property after scaling the fence surrounding the White House and pouring red dye in a fountain to protest the U.S. military presence in the Persian Gulf. Died in Boston after a long battle with cancer on December 17, 1997, at the age of 85.

| FELMET, JOSEPH | W | M | 25 | Asheville, NC | Labor activist, Southern Workers Defense League |

Born in Asheville, NC, on May 31, 1921. Longtime labor journalist. Ran unsuccessfully for Congress (NC) in 1976 and for the U.S. Senate (NC) in 1978. Died in Winston-Salem, NC, on September 20, 1994, at the age of 73.

| HOUSER, GEORGE[dgij] | W | M | 31 | New York, NY | FOR activist; CORE executive secretary |

See chapters 1 and 2. Born in Cleveland, OH, on June 2, 1916. Co-founder of American Committee on Africa. Currently lives in Pomona, NY.

| JACK, HOMER[h] | W | M | 31 | Chicago, IL | Unitarian minister; CORE founder |

Co-founder and associate director of the American Committee on Africa (1959–1960); co-founder and executive director of the National Committee for Sane Nuclear Policy (1960–1964); secretary-general of the NY–based World Conference on Religion and Peace (1970–1983). Died on August 5, 1993, in Swarthmore, PA.

| JOHNSON, ANDREW S. | B | M | 21 | Cincinnati, OH | Law student, Univ. of Cincinnati |
| LYNN, CONRAD | B | M | 39 | New York, NY | Attorney |

Civil rights attorney who initiated a legal action to desegregate the U.S. armed forces. He later represented Puerto Rican nationalists, Vietnam War resisters, Robert Williams and the

Monroe, NC, NAACP, and H. Rap Brown of the Black Panthers, among other controversial clients. Practiced law until the age of 87. Died on November 16, 1995.

NELSON, WALLACE[gj]   B   M   38   Columbus, OH   FOR peace activist; lecturer

Born in Arkansas in 1909. Son of a minister. Jailed twice as a conscientious objector during World War II. CORE's first field secretary, but refused to follow CORE policy of banning suspected Communists from the organization. He and his wife, Juanita, later lived on an organic farm in Deerfield, MA, without a phone or electricity. Died after a long battle with cancer in May 2002, at the age of 93.

PECK, JAMES[bf]   W   M   32   Stamford, CT   Editor, *Workers Defense League News Bulletin*

See chapters 1–5 and epilogue. See also his three books: *We Who Would Not Kill*, *Freedom Ride*, and *Underdogs vs. Upperdogs*. Died July 12, 1993, at the age of 78.

RANDLE, WORTH[b]   W   M   31   Cincinnati, OH   Biologist

Born on December 2, 1915. Noted naturalist and ornithologist; author of *The Birds of Southwestern Ohio* (1953). Died in Watertown, NY, in June 1968, at the age of 52.

ROODENKO, IGAL[e]   W   M   30   New York, NY   Printer; horticulturist

Born on February 8, 1917. Son of Ukranian Jewish immigrants. A lifelong pacifist who organized protests against U.S. military involvement in Vietnam as early as 1963. Following multiple arrests related to his anti-war stance, he was deported from Poland in 1987. Died of a heart attack on April 28, 1991, in New York City, at the age of 74.

RUSTIN, BAYARD   B   M   35   New York, NY   FOR and AFSC activist; CORE field secretary

See chapters 1 and 2 and D'Emilio, *Lost Prophet*. Died in New York City on August 24, 1987, at the age of 75.

STANLEY, EUGENE   B   M   30   Greensboro, NC   Agronomy instructor, North Carolina A&T College

Born in Ohio on November 3, 1916. Graduate of Ohio State Univ. (M.Ed, 1946). Leader of the Vanguard League, a Columbus, OH, civil rights organization that merged with CORE in the mid-1940s. Died on January 24, 1992, at the age of 75.

WORTHY, WILLIAM[cei]   B   M   25   New York, NY   Journalist; New York Council for a Permanent FEPC

Journalist and foreign correspondent for both the *Baltimore Afro-American* and CBS News. Worthy traveled to China in 1956–1957 despite a U.S. travel ban. After traveling to Cuba in 1961 without a passport, he received a prison sentence, but the decision was overturned in 1964. CBS correspondent in Iran in 1981. Currently a research fellow at Howard Univ. See also chapter 2.

WRIGHT, NATHAN[h]   B   M   23   Cincinnati, OH   Church social worker; Cincinnati CORE chairman

Episcopal minister and scholar. Chairman of the 1967 National Conference on Black Power and author of a number of books including *Black Power and Urban Unrest: Creative Possibilities* and *Ready to Riot*. Founding chairman of the African and Afro-American Studies Department at SUNY, Albany. Served on presidential task forces during the Nixon and Reagan adminstrations. Officiated wedding of close friend Louis Farrakhan. Died on February 22, 2005, at the age of 81.

CORE Freedom Ride, Washington, DC, to New Orleans, LA, May 4–17, 1961

Name	Race	Sex	Age	Residence	Occupation or Status
Bergman, Frances	W	F	57	Detroit, MI	Retired elementary school teacher and administrator

See epilogue and Kaufman, *The First Freedom Ride*. Died in 1979, at the age of 75.

Name	Race	Sex	Age	Residence	Occupation or Status
Bergman, Walter	W	M	61	Detroit, MI	Retired professor, Wayne State Univ. and Univ. of Michigan

See epilogue and Kaufman, *The First Freedom Ride*. Died on September 29, 1999, at the age of 100.

Name	Race	Sex	Age	Residence	Occupation or Status
Bigelow, Albert	W	M	55	Cos Cob, CT	Retired naval officer; architect; housing administrator; peace activist

See chapter 3. Born May 1, 1906. Designed buildings for 1939 World's Fair. Senior judge for U.S. Yacht Racing Union for ten years. Completed two trans-Atlantic crossings with close friend and novelist Ernest K. Gann. Died in Walpole, MA, on October 6, 1993, at the age of 87.

Name	Race	Sex	Age	Residence	Occupation or Status
Blankenheim, Edward	W	M	27	Tucson, AZ	Carpenter; student, Univ. of Arizona (Tucson)

See chapter 3. Born March 16, 1934. Carpenter and CORE activist in Chicago during 1960s. Moved to Hawaii in the 1970s and later to San Francisco, where he was arrested in 2000 while advocating the rights of handicapped bus riders. Died in San Francisco on September 26, 2004, at the age of 70.

Name	Race	Sex	Age	Residence	Occupation or Status
Cox, Benjamin Elton[m]	B	M	29	High Point, NC	Minister, Pilgrim Congregational Church; former youth secretary, NAACP

See chapters 3, 5, and 9. Longtime civil rights activist arrested thirty-eight times. Chaplain in VA Hospital in Urbana, IL. Recently retired from position as middle school counselor in Jackson,TN.

Name	Race	Sex	Age	Residence	Occupation or Status
Farmer, James	B	M	41	New York, NY	National director, CORE

See chapter 1, epilogue, and his autobiography *Lay Bare the Heart*. Born January 12, 1920. Awarded the Presidential Medal of Freedom in 1998. Died on July 9, 1999, in Fredricksburg, VA, at the age of 79.

Name	Race	Sex	Age	Residence	Occupation or Status
Griffin, Robert G. (Gus)[k]	B	M	20	Tampa, FL	Student, Johnson C. Smith Univ. (Charlotte, NC)

Born and raised in Tampa, FL.

Name	Race	Sex	Age	Residence	Occupation or Status
Harris, Herman K.[l]	B	M	21	Englewood, NJ	Student, Morris College (Sumter, SC)

See chapters 3 and 8. Born in Heath Springs, SC. Attended Friendship Jr. College (Rock Hill, SC) (1959–60). Graduate of Morris College (BA, 1964) and Univ. of California, Berkeley (MA, English). Taught poetry and English literature and coached basketball at Friendship Jr. College (early 1970s–1982). Pastor of Chestnut Grove AME Zion Church in Rock Hill (1982–88). Died in 1988.

Name	Race	Sex	Age	Residence	Occupation or Status
Hughes, Genevieve	W	F	28	Washington, DC	CORE field secretary

See chapters 3 and 8.

LEWIS, JOHN ROBERT[m] B   M   21   Troy, AL   Student, American Baptist
                                                          Theological Seminary
                                                          (Nashville, TN)

See chapter 3, epilogue, and Lewis, *Walking with the Wind.*

McDONALD, JIMMY   B   M   29   New York, NY   Folk singer; CORE activist

See chapter 3. Born June 4, 1931. NAACP activist in Yonkers, NY (1970–2000). Host of
two television programs, *Black Journal* and *Black Perspective on the News.* Executive
director of the Yonkers Human Rights Commission. Manager for pianist Cecil Taylor. Died
in Bronxville, NY, on July 11, 2000, at the age of 69.

MOORE, IVOR[l] (JERRY)   B   M   19   Bronx, NY   Student, Morris College

Born in Jamestown, NY, on September 21, 1941. Son of the Rev. Dr. Ivor Moore, pastor of
Walker Memorial Baptist Church in the Bronx. Graduate of Morris College (B.A., history,
1964). Folk and rock musician in Greenwich Village, NY City (1964–1967). Co-created
(with poet Dudley Randall) and performed "Ballad of Birmingham" following 1963 church
bombing. Member of "Children of God" rock group (1967–1971) and recording artist living
in Woodstock, NY (1967–1980). Moved to Los Angeles in 1980. Conducted street ministry
for drug addicts and homeless in South Central LA. Computer skills instructor, youth
recreation supervisor, and church outreach coordinator (1990s–present).

MOULTRIE, MAE   B   W   24   Sumter, SC   Student, Morris College
FRANCES[l]

Born in Dillon, SC. Moved to Philadelphia in October 1961 to attend Cheyney State
College. Later received M.S. in education at Temple Univ. Taught school in Wilmington,
DE (1964–1990). Missionary in Liberia, Mexico, and Canada. Currently teaches Christian
education at Sanctuary Christian Academy in Philadelphia. Current name: the Reverend
Mae Frances Howard.

PECK, JAMES   W   M   46   New York, NY   Editor, *CORE-lator*

See Journey of Reconciliation.

PERKINS, JOSEPH   B   M   27   Owensboro, KY   CORE field secretary

See chapter 3.

PERSON, CHARLES   B   M   18   Atlanta, GA   Student, Morehouse College
                                                      (Atlanta, GA)

See chapter 3. Born in Atlanta. Joined U.S. Marines in late 1961, retiring in 1981 after
twenty years of active service. Lived in Cuba 1981–1984 before returning to Atlanta, where
he currently works as an electronics technician for Atlanta's public schools.

REYNOLDS, ISAAC   B   M   27   Detroit, MI   CORE field secretary; student,
(IKE)[l]   Wayne State Univ.

See chapter 3. Born November 23, 1933. Attended Detroit Business Institute and the Univ.
of Maryland. Later affiliated with SCLC and the National Association of Black Social
Workers. Involved in 1963 Birmingham demonstrations. Later worked as an assistant clerk
for Orleans Parish Municipal Court in New Orleans. Died in New Orleans on February 22,
1998, at the age of 64.

THOMAS, HENRY   B   M   19   Elton, FL   Student, Howard Univ.
(HANK)   (Washington, DC); NAG activist

See chapter 3 and epilogue. Served in Vietnam, returning home in 1966 after being
wounded. Moved to Atlanta, where he opened a laundromat before investing in a series of
fast-food franchises. Currently owns 2 McDonald's restaurants and 3 Marriott hotels.
Collector of African American art. Lives in Stone Mountain, GA.

Nashville, TN, via Birmingham, AL, to Montgomery, AL, May 17–21, 1961

Name	Race	Sex	Age	Residence	Occupation or Status
BARBEE, WILLIAM[no]	B	M	19	Nashville, TN	Student, Tennessee State Univ.

Born and raised in Nashville, TN. Active in the Nashville sit-in movement, 1961–1964. Injuries suffered in the Montgomery anti–Freedom Rider riot led to an early death. Died in Nashville in the early 1980s.

Name	Race	Sex	Age	Residence	Occupation or Status
BROOKS, PAUL[o]	B	M	22	East St. Louis, IL	Student, American Baptist Theological Seminary

Born on February 28, 1939, in East St. Louis, IL. Parents from De Kalb, MS. Married Freedom Rider Catherine Burks in Monroe, NC, in August 1961; separated in 1985. SNCC and SCLC activist and editor of *Mississippi Free Press* in Jackson 1962–1963. Raised funds for the movement in Chicago, 1964. Returned to ABT in 1964 but did not finish. After moving to Detroit in 1965, he invented the Afro-pick comb and later opened a successful comb factory. During the 1970s he lived in Nassau, Bahamas, with frequent commutes to Detroit. Died in 1989 at the age of 50. See chapter 10.

Name	Race	Sex	Age	Residence	Occupation or Status
BURKS, CATHERINE[o]	B	F	21	Birmingham, AL	Student, Tennessee State Univ.

Born near Selma, AL, and raised in Birmingham. Married Freedom Rider Paul Brooks. Active in Mississippi movement and co-editor of *Mississippi Free Press*, 1962–1963. Taught elementary school in Chicago, 1964. Worked as social worker in Detroit, 1965–1966. Later ran successful Afro boutique specializing in African jewelry and clothing. Lived in Bahamas in 1970s before moving to Birmingham in 1979. District sales manager for Avon cosmetics, 1982–1998. Currently a substitute schoolteacher in Birmingham.

Name	Race	Sex	Age	Residence	Occupation or Status
BUSH, CARL	B	M	19	Nashville, TN	Student, Tennessee State Univ.
BUTLER, CHARLES[n]	B	M	20	Charleston, SC	Student, Tennessee State Univ.

Grew up in Charleston, SC.

Name	Race	Sex	Age	Residence	Occupation or Status
CARTER, JOSEPH	B	M	22	Brooklyn, NY	Student, American Baptist Theological Seminary

Formed the Nashville Quartet along with James Bevel, Bernard Lafayette, and Samuel Collier to write and perform freedom songs.

Name	Race	Sex	Age	Residence	Occupation or Status
CASON, ALLEN, JR.[o]	B	M	19	Orlando, FL	Student, Tennessee State Univ.

Born and raised in Orlando, FL.

Name	Race	Sex	Age	Residence	Occupation or Status
COLLINS, LUCRETIA[o]	B	F	21	El Paso, TX	Student, Tennessee State Univ.

Born and raised in Augusta, GA. Lived in El Paso, TX, where her stepfather was serving in the army. Graduate of Tennessee State Univ. (B.A., 1961). Lived in NY City (1961–1963) before spending 6 years abroad (1963-1969) in Africa and Italy, where she worked as an actress. Lived in NY City since 1969, working as a stage actress. Affiliated with ACRES, a NY-based organization that conducts civil rights educational tours. Married name: Lucretia Collins Gray.

Name	Race	Sex	Age	Residence	Occupation or Status
GRAHAM, RUDOLPH	B	M	20	Chattanooga, TN	Student, Tennessee State Univ.

Grew up in Chattanooga, TN.

Name	Race	Sex	Age	Residence	Occupation or Status
HARBOUR, WILLIAM[o]	B	M	19	Piedmont, AL	Student, Tennessee State Univ.

See epilogue. Born in Piedmont, AL. Oldest of eight children. Taught school in Blakely, GA, 1964. Moved to Atlanta in 1969. Longtime federal employee, first with the Community Relations Service and later as a civilian employee of the U.S. Army specializing in base closings. Active in Tennessee State alumni affairs. Unofficial archivist of Freedom Rider movement. Currently lives in retirement in Atlanta.

| HERMANN, SUSAN | W | F | 20 | Whittier, CA | Exchange student, Fisk Univ. (Nashville, TN); student, Whittier College |

See chapters 5 and 6.

| JENKINS, PATRICIA | B | F | 18 | Nashville, TN | Student, Tennessee State Univ. |

| LAFAYETTE, BERNARD, JR. | B | M | 20 | Tampa, FL | Student, American Baptist Theological Seminary |

See chapter 3 and epilogue. Born July 29, 1940. Longtime activist affiliated with SNCC and SCLC. Involved in voting rights and Poor People's campaigns, 1962–1965. After completing his doctorate at Harvard, he taught peace studies at Gustavus Adolphus Univ. in Minnesota. Later college administrator and president of ABT. Currently conducts international nonviolence projects as director of peace studies and scholar in residence at the Univ. of Rhode Island.

| LEONARD, FREDERICK | B | M | 18 | Chattanooga, TN | Student, Tennessee State Univ. |

Active in the Nashville sit-in movement, 1961–1964. Married Freedom Rider Joy Reagon. Appeared in episode 3 of *Eyes on the Prize I.*

| LEWIS, JOHN ROBERT[o] | B | M | 21 | Troy, AL | Student, American Baptist Theological Seminary |

See May 4–17 Ride.

| McCOLLUM, SALYNN[p] | W | F | 21 | Snyder, NY | Student, George Peabody College (Nashville, TN) |

See chapters 5 and 11. SNCC staff member, 1962–1963. Earned master's degree in education at CCNY. Career as teacher and school administrator. Currently director of the Woodmont Christian Pre-School in Nashville.

| MITCHELL, WILLIAM B., JR. | B | M | 18 | Oklahoma City, OK | Student, Tennessee State Univ. |

| SIMPSON, ETTA | B | F | 19 | Nashville, TN | Student, Tennessee State Univ. |

| SMITH, RUBY DORIS[q] | B | F | 19 | Atlanta, GA | Student, Spelman College (Atlanta, GA) |

See Fleming, *Soon We Will Not Cry.* Influential SNCC activist. Married Clifford Robinson in 1964. Died of cancer in 1965.

| WILBUR, SUSAN | W | F | 18 | Nashville, TN | Student, George Peabody College |

See chapters 5 and 6. Affiliated with the St. Petersburg, FL–based African Peoples' Socialist Party in the 1980s.

| WRIGHT, CLARENCE M. | B | M | 19 | Nashville, TN | Student, Tennessee State Univ. |

| ZWERG, JIM[o] | W | M | 21 | Appleton, WI | Exchange student, Fisk Univ.; Student, Beloit College (Beloit, WI) |

See chapters 6 and 7, epilogue, and Blake, *Children of the Movement.* United Church of Christ minister until 1975. Later worked as a personnel manager for IBM (1979–1993) and at a hospice in Tucson, AZ, where he currently lives in retirement.

Montgomery, AL, to Jackson, MS
(Trailways), May 24, 1961

Name	Race	Sex	Age	Residence	Occupation or Status
AARON, JULIA	B	F	20	New Orleans, LA	Student, Southern Univ. (New Orleans, LA)

Currently lives in Stone Mountain, GA. Married name: Julia Aaron Humbles.

| ANDERSON, ALEXANDER M. | B | M | 33 | Nashville, TN | AME minister |

Born and raised in Waycross, GA. Graduate of Morehouse College. Pastor of AME church near Fisk Univ. campus.

| ANDREWS, HAROLD | B | M | 23 | Atlanta, GA | Student, Morehouse College |

Member of the Committee on Appeal for Human Rights.

| BEVEL, JAMES L. | B | M | 24 | Itta Bena, MS | Student, American Baptist Theological Seminary |

See epilogue and Blake, *Children of the Movement*. Born on October 19, 1936, in Itta Bena, MS. Married Diane Nash in late 1961. SCLC activist in Mississippi and Alabama, 1962–1964. Currently pastor of the Hebrew, Christian, Islamic Assembly and an advisor and instructor at the Univ. of Civilization in Chicago.

| CARTER, JOSEPH | B | M | 22 | Brooklyn, NY | Student, American Baptist Theological Seminary |

See May 17–21 Ride.

| DENNIS, DAVID J. | B | M | 20 | Shreveport, LA | Student, Dillard Univ. (New Orleans, LA) |

See epilogue. After several years as a CORE field secretary in Louisiana and Mississippi, Dennis earned a law degree and became a successful attorney in New Orleans. He currently works alongside fellow activist Bob Moses as director and CEO of the Southern Initiative Algebra Project.

| DIETRICH, PAUL DAVID | W | M | 29 | Washington, DC | Office worker; restaurant owner; NAG activist |

Born in Albany, NY, in November 1931. Son of a Lutheran minister. Attended Wagner College, CCNY, Univ. of Virginia, and George Washington Univ. Founding member of NAG and active in SNCC until mid-1960s. Later active in anti-war movement and Angela Davis defense committee. Owned and operated Jazzland nightclub in Washinton until the club was burned down in a 1968 riot. Later worked as a bartender in New York City and Islamorada, FL. Converted to Islam in 1984. Returned to Washington in 1989. Worked with antipoverty activist Mitch Snyder for six years.

| LAFAYETTE, BERNARD, JR. | B | M | 20 | Tampa, FL | Student, American Baptist Theological Seminary |

See May 17–21 Ride.

| LAWSON, JAMES MORRIS, JR. | B | M | 32 | Nashville, TN | Methodist minister; SCLC and FOR activist |

See chapters 2, 5, and 11. Chairman of the strike committee for sanitation workers in Memphis in 1968. At his request, Martin Luther King spoke to the strikers the day before his assassination. Currently the pastor emeritus of the Holman United Methodist Church in Los Angeles, he remains actively involved in various human rights campaigns, including the immigrants' rights movement and nonviolent opposition to war and militarism.

THOMPSON, JEAN CATHERINE	B	F	19	New Orleans, LA	Unemployed

Daughter of forklift operator who was fired because of his daughters' civil rights activities. Later worked with the Freedom Highways Project and other CORE projects in the mid-1960s. Currently lives in Amherst, MA, where she works with developmentally disabled adults, including her autistic son Daniel. Converted to B'hai faith. Sister of Freedom Riders Alice and Shirley Thompson.

VIVIAN, CORDY T. (C. T.)	B	M	36	Chattanooga, TN	Baptist minister, NCLC board member

Born in Howard, MO, and raised in Macomb, IL, where he attended Western Illinois Univ. Graduate of American Baptist Theological Seminary. SCLC leader since 1961. Named director of SCLC affiliates in 1963. Author of *Black Power and the American Myth* (1970). Later founded and led several civil rights organizations, including Vision, the National Anti-Klan Network, the Center for Democratic Renewal, and Black Action Strategies and Information Center (BASIC). Currently lives in Atlanta.

WALKER, MATTHEW, JR.	B	M	19	Nashville, TN	Student, Fisk Univ.

His father, Matthew Walker Sr., was an active NCLC supporter and a prominent Nashville physician on the faculty of Meharry Medical School. After three years in the army in the mid-1960s, Matthew Walker Jr. became a labor organizer for the AFL-CIO in Newark, NJ. He returned to Nashville in 1975.

Montgomery, AL, to Jackson, MS (Greyhound), May 24, 1961

Name	Race	Sex	Age	Residence	Occupation or Status
ACKERBERG, PETER M.	W	M	22	Brooklyn, NY	Student, Antioch College (Yellow Springs, OH)

Born in NY City on April 19, 1939. Graduate of Antioch College (B.A., 1963), Columbia Univ. (M.A., Journalism, 1964), and Univ. of Minnesota (J.D., 1981). Newspaper reporter in Minneapolis (1965–1981). Lawyer with Minnesota Attorney General's office (1984–2000). Since 2001 has been working on a class-action discrimination suit by black farmers against the U.S. Dept. of Agriculture. Currently lives in Minneapolis.

CASTLE, DORIS JEAN	B	F	18	New Orleans, LA	CORE activist

A lifelong New Orleans resident and activist who helped to desegregate the city's buses and lunch counters and who worked tirelessly for equal employment opportunities and black voter registration. Employed as an admissions technician and supervisor at Charity Hospital in New Orleans from 1980 until her death in April 1998, at the age of 55.

COLLINS, LUCRETIA R.	B	F	21	El Paso, TX	Student, Tennessee State Univ.

See May 17–21 Ride.

COPELAND, JOHN LEE	B	M	44	Nashville, TN	Baptist minister

Born in Tennessee in April 1917. NCLC activist who often often allowed ABT students to preach at his church, which was near the ABT campus. Died in Nashville in May 1987, at the age of 70.

DIAMOND, DION TYRONE	B	M	19	Petersburg, VA	Student, Howard Univ.

See epilogue. Born on July 2, 1941, in Petersburg, VA. His father was a mail carrier, and his mother was a nurse. Founding member of NAG and SNCC field secretary in Louisiana and

Mississippi in 1962–1963. Studied physics at Howard Univ. (1959–1961) and later majored in history and sociology at Univ. of Wisconsin (1963–1966). Worked with DC Community Action Project (1966–1968) before earning M.Ed at Harvard Univ. in 1970. Long career as civil servant and consultant in Washington, DC, specializing in housing, social services, and employment issues.

DONALD, GRADY H.   B   M   31   Nashville, TN   Minister

Born in South Carolina in June 1929. NCLC activist. Pastor in the Bronx, NY, in the 1990s. Died in the Bronx in November 2002, at the age of 73.

FARMER, JAMES L.   B   M   41   New York, NY   National director, CORE

See May 4–17 Ride.

HOLLOWAY,   B   M   22   Atlanta, GA   Student, Morehouse College
FRANK GEORGE

Attended Delaware State College. Member of the Committee on Appeal for Human Rights. SNCC voter registration worker in Selma, AL, in the mid-1960s. Currently lives in Riverdale, GA. His son Jabari Holloway, a star football player and computer engineering major at Notre Dame in the 1990s, currently plays tight end for the Washington Redskins in the National Football League.

LEWIS, JOHN ROBERT   B   M   21   Troy, AL   Student, American Baptist
                                                       Theological Seminary

See May 17–21 Ride.

MOODY, JOHN H., JR.   B   M   30   Philadelphia, PA   Student, Howard Univ.

See chapters 3 and 7. Founding member of NAG. Longtime federal employee. Worked on anti-poverty projects at Community Services Administration, at the Defense Dept.'s Preparedness Office at Olney, MD, and at the Office of Human Rights during the 1970s. A work-related injury led to disability and early retirement in 1980. Currently lives in Greenbelt, MD.

PATTON, ERNEST,   B   M   21   Nashville, TN   Student, Tennessee State Univ.
JR. (RIP)

Later worked as a truck driver transporting automobiles. Currently lives in Nashville.

SMITH, JEROME H.   B   M   22   New Orleans, LA   Longshoreman; CORE activist;
                                                          former student, Southern Univ.
                                                          (Baton Rouge)

Lifelong civil rights activist and community organizer. Founded Tamburine and Fan, a New Orleans community empowerment group. Currently lives in New Orleans. See chapter 11.

THOMAS, CLARENCE   B   M   20   Champaign, IL   Student, American Baptist
LLOYD   Theological Seminary

Currently a minister living in Jackson, MS.

THOMAS, HENRY   B   M   19   Elton, FL   Student, Howard Univ.
J. (HANK)

See May 4–17 Ride.

WRIGHT, LEROY   B   M   19   Nashville, TN   Student, Fisk Univ.
GLENN

Atlanta, GA, to Montgomery, AL
(Greyhound), May 24–25, 1961

Name	Race	Sex	Age	Residence	Occupation or Status
CARTER, CLYDE	B	M	23	Charlotte, NC	Student, Johnson C. Smith Univ.; SNCC activist

Graduate of Johnson C. Smith Univ. Chaplain at Alcorn A&M in Mississippi in mid-1960s. Later attended Miles College in Birmingham. Chaplain at Birmingham VA hospital, 1972–1997. Copper bas-relief artist whose works include representations of Rosa Parks, Fred Shuttlesworth, and Martin Luther King. Recently commissioned to do nine pieces on the 1963 Sixteenth Street Church bombing. Currently interim pastor of Westminster Presbyterian Church in Birmingham.

Name	Race	Sex	Age	Residence	Occupation or Status
COFFIN, WILLIAM SLOANE JR.	W	M	36	New Haven, CT	Yale Univ. chaplain

See chapter 7 and Goldstein, *William Sloane Coffin.* Born in New York City. Became prominent anti-war activist in the late 1960s and co-founded Clergy and Laity Concerned About Vietnam (CALCAV). Traveled to Iran in 1979 to hold Christmas services for hostages there. Became president of SANE/FREEZE (later named Peace Action) in 1987. Currently lives in Strafford, VT.

Name	Race	Sex	Age	Residence	Occupation or Status
JONES, JOSEPH CHARLES	B	M	23	Charlotte, NC	Student, Johnson C. Smith Univ.; SNCC activist

See chapters 10 and 11 and epilogue. Born in Chester, SC. Son and grandson of Presbyterian ministers and nephew of Johnson C. Smith seminary dean. SNCC leader during the 1961–1962 Albany campaign. Graduate of Howard Univ. School of Law (J.D., 1966). Assistant District Attorney in Charlotte, NC (late 1970s). Law practice in Charlotte since 1980.

Name	Race	Sex	Age	Residence	Occupation or Status
MAGUIRE, JOHN	W	M	28	Middletown, CT	Professor of religion, Wesleyan Univ. (Middletown, CT)

Native of Montgomery, AL. Roommate of Martin Luther King at Crozer Seminary in 1951. Founding board chairman of MLK Center for Nonviolent Social Change (1968). College president at SUNY, Old Westbury (1970–1981) and the Claremont Graduate Univ. and Claremont Univ. Consortium (1981–1998). Founded the Institute for Democratic Renewal in 1998, which merged with Project Change in 2002. See chapter 7 and epilogue.

Name	Race	Sex	Age	Residence	Occupation or Status
NOYCE, GAYLORD	W	M	34	New Haven, CT	Professor of religion, Yale Univ.

Graduate of Yale Divinity School (M.Div.), where he taught for four decades. Author of *Pastoral Ethics* (1988) and *Minister as Moral Counselor* (1989). Currently professor emeritus of pastoral theology living in Hamden, CT.

Name	Race	Sex	Age	Residence	Occupation or Status
SMITH, GEORGE B.	B	M	24	New Haven, CT	Law student, Yale Univ.

Born in New Orleans, LA, in 1937. Graduate of Phillips Academy (1955), Yale Univ. (B.A., 1959, LL.B., 1962), NYU (M.A., pol. science, 1967; Ph.D., government, 1974), and the Univ. of Virginia (M. Judicial Process, 2001). A distinguished NY jurist who served on Civil Court of NY City (1975–1979), the Supreme Court in Manhattan (1979–1987), and the State Supreme Court, Appellate Div., First Dept. (1987–1992) before being appointed to the NY Court of Appeals by Gov. Mario Cuomo in 1992. Currently an Assoc. Justice of the Court of Appeals.

Name	Race	Sex	Age	Residence	Occupation or Status
SWIFT, DAVID E.	W	M	47	Middletown, CT	Professor of religion, Wesleyan Univ.

Taught at Wesleyan for nearly thirty years. Published two books: *Joseph John Gurney: Banker, Reformer, and Quaker* and *Black Prophets of Justice: Activist Clergy Before the Civil War.* Died on October 14, 2002, in Kennet Square, PA, at the age of 87.

Montgomery, AL
(Trailways terminal), May 25, 1961

Name	Race	Sex	Age	Residence	Occupation or Status
ABERNATHY, RALPH	B	M	35	Montgomery, AL	Baptist minister; SCLC leader

See Abernathy, *And the Walls Came Tumbling Down.* Died April 18, 1990, at the age of 65.

Name	Race	Sex	Age	Residence	Occupation or Status
LEE, BERNARD	B	M	22	Atlanta, GA	SCLC staff; former student, Alabama State College (Montgomery)

Lee remained on the SCLC staff for many years. After the Senate Secret Intelligence Committee judged FBI surveillance of Martin Luther King to be harassment, Lee spearheaded an SCLC civil suit against the U.S. government asking for monetary compensation and the destruction of the surveillance tapes and files. In 1977 a judge declined to award monetary damages but ordered the King files to be sealed for fifty years in the National Archives. Worked for the EPA in the late 1970s. Deputy campaign manager for the Carter-Mondale ticket in Mississippi in 1980. Died of a heart attack on February 10, 1991, at the age of 51.

Name	Race	Sex	Age	Residence	Occupation or Status
SHUTTLESWORTH, FRED	B	M	39	Birmingham, AL	Baptist minister; ACMHR and SCLC leader

See epilogue and Manis, *A Fire You Can't Put Out.* Born on March 18, 1922, in Mt. Meigs, AL. Ordained as baptist minister in 1948. Pastor of First Baptist Church in Selma, AL, 1949–1952. Pastor of Bethel Baptist Church in Birmingham, 1953–1961. Pastor of Revelation Baptist Church (1961–1966) and Greater New Light Baptist Church (1966–presently pastor emeritus) in Cincinnati, OH. Acting SCLC head, 2004. Currently lives in Cincinnati.

Name	Race	Sex	Age	Residence	Occupation or Status
WALKER, WYATT TEE	B	M	31	Atlanta, GA	SCLC executive director; Baptist minister

See chapters 3 and 10 and Fairclough, *To Redeem the Soul of America.* Born in Brockton, MA. Currently lives in New York City.

Nashville, TN, via Memphis, TN, to Jackson, MS
(Greyhound), May 28, 1961

Name	Race	Sex	Age	Residence	Occupation or Status
BURKS, CATHERINE	B	F	21	Birmingham, AL	Student, Tennessee State Univ.

See May 17–21 Ride.

Name	Race	Sex	Age	Residence	Occupation or Status
HARBOUR, WILLIAM E.	B	M	19	Piedmont, AL	Student, Tennessee State Univ.

See May 17–21 Ride.

Name	Race	Sex	Age	Residence	Occupation or Status
LEONARD, FREDERICK	B	M	18	Chattanooga, TN	Student, Tennessee State Univ.

See May 17–21 Ride.

Name	Race	Sex	Age	Residence	Occupation or Status
McKINNIE, LESTER G.	B	M	21	St. Bolivar, TN	Student, Tennessee State Univ.

SNCC field secretary in Mississippi in 1962. Later changed name to El Senzengakulu Zulu and founded an independent African (K–12) school, Ujamma, in Washington, DC, in 1968. The school has hosted a number of black nationalist leaders, including Minister Louis Farrakhan. Currently lives in Washington.

MITCHELL, WILLIAM B., JR.	B	M	18	Oklahoma City, OK	Student, Tennessee State Univ.
SIMPSON, ETTA	B	F	19	Nashville, TN	Student, Tennessee State Univ.
SMITH, MARY J.	B	F	19	Nashville, TN	Student, Tennessee State Univ.
WILSON, FRANCES L.	B	F	23	Nashville, TN	Student, Tennessee State Univ.
WRIGHT, CLARENCE M.	B	M	19	Nashville, TN	Student, Tennessee State Univ.

Nashville, TN, via Montgomery, AL, to Jackson, MS (Trailways), May 28, 1961

Name	Race	Sex	Age	Residence	Occupation or Status
CASON, ALLEN, JR.	B	M	19	Orlando, FL	Student, Tennessee State Univ.

See May 17–21 Ride.

| DUNN, ALBERT LEE | B | M | 26 | Fort Worth, TX | Minister at Clarkston AME Church (Clarkston, GA) |

Involved in 1962 Albany campaign and a 1964 Atlanta sit-in at Pickrick Restaurant that prompted a lawsuit against owner Lester Maddox.

| FANKHAUSER, DAVID B.[r] | W | M | 19 | Cincinnati, OH | Student, Central State College (Wilberforce, OH) |

Currently a professor of biology and chemistry at Univ. of Cincinnati, Clermont College, in Batavia, OH.

| HUNT, FRANKLIN W.[r] | B | M | 22 | Washington, DC | Student, Tennessee State Univ. |

Staff correspondent for *Baltimore Afro-American* in 1961.

| HUNTER, LARRY FRED | B | M | 18 | Atlanta, GA | Student, Tennessee State Univ. |

Moved to Canada in the 1960s to avoid imprisonment for draft evasion. Recently pardoned, he currently lives in Atlanta.

| KNIGHT, PAULINE EDYTHE | B | F | 20 | Nashville, TN | Student, Tennessee State Univ. |

See chapter 11. Expelled from Tennessee State. Currently lives in Fairfield, GA.

| MAHONEY, WILLIAM CARL[r] | B | M | 19 | Washington, DC | Student, Howard Univ.; NAG activist |

Author of the novel *Black Jacob* (1969), a dramatization of schisms within the civil rights movement.

| MYERS, CHARLES DAVID[r] | W | M | 21 | Noblesville, IN | Student, Central State College (Wilberforce, OH) |

Son of Indiana farm family. Attended Central State on a track scholarship. Married Winonah Beamer in April 1962. Worked as a photographer at Central State (1962–1965), as a newspaper photographer in Xenia, OH (1965–1968), and Waterloo, IA (1968–1970), and as Central State's sports information director (1970-73) before spending twenty-nine years (1973-2002) as a photographer, editor, and reporter at WHIO-TV in Dayton, OH. Currently lives in a mobile home park in Ellenton, FL.

New Orleans, LA, to Jackson, MS
(Illinois Central RR), May 30, 1961

Name	Race	Sex	Age	Residence	Occupation or Status
DAVIS, JAMES KEET, JR.	B	M	21	Florence, SC	Student, Claflin Univ. (Orangeburg, SC)

Son of a prominent Florence, SC, Methodist minister. Star lineman on Claflin Univ. football team. Married Freedom Rider Glenda Gaither in 1965. Worked as a Josten class-ring salesman until he was hired as a minority recruiter for Georgia Power Company in 1972. Retired from the company as a senior vice president in 2003. Currently lives in Atlanta.

GAITHER, GLENDA JEAN	B	F	18	Great Falls, SC	Student, Claflin Univ.

Born in Great Falls, SC. Sister of CORE field secretary Thomas Gaither. Married to James Keet Davis since 1965. Worked as job placement director at Spelman College.

GREEN, PAUL S.	W	M	22	Ithaca, NY	Student, Cornell Univ. (Ithaca, NY)

Currently a professor of mathematics at the Univ. of Maryland, College Park.

GRIFFITH, JOE HENRY	W	M	26	Ithaca, NY	Graduate student, Cornell Univ.

Born in Oklahoma City, OK, on November 11, 1934. Graduate of SMU (B.S., chemistry and biology, 1956) and Cornell Univ. (Ph.D., phys. chem., 1967). Participated in Route 40 campaign (1962), March on Washington (1963), and voter registration drives in Fayette, MS (1964). Active in anti-war movement (late 1960s). Teacher (1967–1971) and principal (1971–1988) in MA. Worked with Smithsonian's Nat. Acad. of Science (1988–1992) and Nat. Museum of Am. History (1992–1994), and NASA's educational outreach program (1998–2003). Currently lives in Durango, CO.

HAYNIE, CHARLES A.	W	M	25	Ithaca, NY	Graduate student, Cornell Univ.

Began teaching experimental courses at the Univ. of Buffalo in 1969. A leader of the political left on campus, he organized demonstrations against racism and nuclear power plants. A lecturer in the Social Sciences Interdisciplinary Program and affiliated with the Environment and Society Institute, he retired in 2000 and died a year later at the age of 65 following a three-year battle with cancer.

HELLER, ROBERT LAWRENCE	W	M	19	New York, NY	Student, Tulane Univ. (New Orleans, LA)

Born and raised at Rockville Center on NY's Long Island. Active in New Orleans CORE. Spent nineteen days in Hinds County Jail before bailing out. Economics major at Tulane. Returned to Tulane in 1962 but did not graduate. After working as a TV cameraman and announcer in New Orleans (1963–1964), he became a producer and director of commercials, industrial films, and documentaries in New York City (1965–1986), where he currently lives. Semiretired since 1986.

NIXON, SANDRA MARIE	B	M	19	New Orleans, LA	Student, Southern Univ. (New Orleans, LA)

Chair of New Orleans CORE membership committee in 1961. Her mother worked for New Orleans restauranteur Dukey Chase, who provided meals for the New Orleans Freedom Riders. Currently lives in New Orleans. Married name: Sandra Nixon Thomas.

STERLING, PETER	W	M	20	Rye, NY	Student, Cornell Univ.

Son of prominent writers Philip and Dorothy Sterling. Dorothy Sterling was the author of several well-known children's books, including *Mary Jane*, the story of a young black girl's experiences at an integrated school.

Montgomery, AL, to Jackson, MS
(Trailways), June 2, 1961

Name	Race	Sex	Age	Residence	Occupation or Status
BUTLER, CHARLES	B	M	18	Charleston, SC	Student, Tennessee State Univ.

See May 17–21 Ride.

| CHATHAM, PRICE | W | M | 29 | Rockaway, NY | Story analyst, 20th Century Fox and Paramount Pictures |

See chapter 9. Born in a sulphur-mining community in Texas. Attended Tulane Univ., where he was beaten by police during a racially integrated Henry Wallace campaign rally in 1948. A radical activist affiliated with the Committee for the Abolition of the House Un-American Activities Committee.

| McDONALD, JOSEPH JOHN MICHAEL | W | M | 20 | Oceanside, NY | Unemployed |

Currently lives in Oceanside, NY.

| REAGON, MERYLE JOY | B | F | 19 | Nashville, TN | Student, Tennessee State Univ. |

Sister of SNCC activist and Freedom Rider Cordell Reagon. Married Freedom Rider Fred Leonard. Currently lives in Nashville.

| SHILMAN, KENNETH MARTIN | W | M | 18 | Oceanside, NY | Unemployed |

Born on August 16, 1942, in New York City. Hospital workers union organizer in Brooklyn (1962). Active member of the Socialist Workers Party. Attacked outside SWP's New York headquarters in 1973. Died on September 7, 1989, at the age of 47.

| SMITH, RUBY DORIS | B | F | 19 | Atlanta, GA | Student, Spelman College |

See May 17–21 Ride.

Montgomery, AL, to Jackson, MS
(Trailways), June 2, 1961

Name	Race	Sex	Age	Residence	Occupation or Status
FERTIG, RALPH[s]	W	M	31	Chicago, Il	Social worker

Graduate of Univ. of Chicago (B.A., 1950), Columbia Univ. (M.A., 1952), and UCLA (J.D., 1979). Ran a settlement house in Washington, DC, before the Freedom Rides. Served as a federal administrative judge and taught law part-time at UCLA, USC, Georgetown, and the Universities of Illinois, Indiana, Maryland, and the District of Columbia. Currently president of the Humanitarian Law Project and a board member of Americans for Peace Now and the Progressive Jewish Alliance. Author of *Love and Liberation: When the Jews Tore Down the Ghetto Walls* (2001).

| GLEASON, RICHARD LEROY | W | M | 24 | Chicago, IL | Minister, Bible Witness Mission |

See chapter 8.

| HARRIS, JESSE J. | B | M | 24 | Atlanta, GA | Student, Howard Univ. |

| REAGON, CORDELL HULL | B | M | 18 | Nashville, TN | Student, Tennessee State Univ. |

See Chapter 11 and epilogue. Brother of Freedom Rider Meryle Joy Reagon. SNCC activist in Albany and southwestern Georgia, 1961-63. Helped organize the Albany Freedom Singers. Married Freedom Singer Bernice Johnson in 1963. The marriage produced two children, Kwan and Toshi, but ended in divorce in 1967. Murdered at his Berkeley, CA, apartment in 1996, at the age of 53.

| REED, CAROLYN YVONNE | B | F | 21 | Nashville, TN | Nurse's aide, Meharry Hospital |

| SINGER, FELIX JACQUES | W | M | 32 | Chicago, IL | Writer |

Author of *These Seventeen: Sixteen Stories and One Essay* (1959).

| WORD, LESLIE | B | M | 28 | Corinth, MS | Laborer, odd jobs |

| WYCKOFF, ELIZABETH PORTER | W | F | 45 | New York, NY | Freelance writer; former professor of Greek |

See chapter 9. Born on June 16, 1915. Her mother was a prominent women's magazine editor, and her father was dean of the NYU Medical School. Graduate of Bryn Mawr College (B.A.,1936; Ph.D., 1941) and Cambridge University (B.A., 1938). Taught Greek and classics at Bryn Mawr (1939–1941), Vassar (1942–1943), Wells (1943–1950), and Mt. Holyoke (1950–1959). Published translations of works by Sophocles and Euripides in the 1950s. Involved in 1962 Albany campaign. Lived in New York for many years and entered a Bronx nursing home in the 1980s. Died there on July 29, 1994, at the age of 79.

New Orleans, LA, to Jackson, MS (Trailways), June 6, 1961

Name	Race	Sex	Age	Residence	Occupation or Status
ASHFORD, JOHNNY FRANK	B	M	22	Chicago, IL	Student, Marion College (Chicago)
BASSFORD, ABRAHAM IV	W	M	24	Brooklyn, NY	Student, Wagner Lutheran College (Staten Island, NY); pipefitter's apprentice

Born in NY City on October 16, 1936. Named for an ancestral Civil War Union General. Pacifist and social activist. Member of CORE and Young People's Socialist League in 1961. Graduate of Wagner Lutheran College (B.A., 1965). Attended NY Theological Seminary (1966–1967). Anti-war protestor affiliated with Student Peace Union (1963–1968). Nat. secretary of Socialist Party (1973–1975). Attended Garrett Theological Sem. (1977–1981) in Evanston, IL. Varied career as psychiatric social worker, custodian, letter carrier, and advocate for the homeless. Currently lives in Chicago, IL.

| McDONOUGH, JAMES THOMAS | W | M | 22 | Huntington, NY | Student, Univ. of Toronto (Toronto, Ontario) |
| SULLIVAN, TERRY JOHN | W | M | 23 | Chicago, IL | Editor of *Awareness* (monthly paper) |

See chapter 8. Active in the Catholic workers' movement.

| THOMPSON, SHIRLEY | B | F | 18 | New Orleans, LA | Student, Carver High School |

See chapter 7. Born in Louisiana in April 1942. Sister of Alice and Jean Thompson. Died in Baton Rouge, LA, in January 1999, at the age of 56.

| WAHLSTROM, JAMES ROBERT | W | M | 22 | Madison, WI | Psychology student, Univ. of Wisconsin, Madison |

See chapters 8 and 9. Involved in the Fair Play for Cuba movement, 1960–1961. Worked in the primate lab at the Univ. of Wisconsin.

| WEBER, ERNEST NEWELL | W | M | 52 | Orange, NJ | Photographer (self-employed) |

Born on April 23, 1909. Died in Greensboro, NC, on April 15, 2003, at the age of 83.

Nashville, TN, via Memphis, TN, to Jackson, MS (Trailways), June 7, 1961

Name	Race	Sex	Age	Residence	Occupation or Status
GAGER, JOHN W GOODRICH, JR.	W	M	23	New Haven, CT	Student, Yale Divinity School

Graduate of Phillips Exeter Academy, Yale Univ. (B.A.,1959; M.Div., 1962), and Harvard Univ. (Ph.D). Has taught at Princeton Univ. since 1968; currently the William H. Danforth Professor of Religion. Author of *Moses in Greco-Roman Paganism* (1972), *The Origins of Anti-Semitism* (1983), and *Curse Tablets and Binding Spells from the Ancient World* (1992). Avid mountain climber and outdoorsman.

| GREEN, REGINALD MALCOM | B | M | 21 | Washington, DC | Student, Virginia Union Univ. (Richmond, VA) |

Born in Washington, DC, on June 17, 1939. Earned B.A. and M.Div. degrees at Virginia Union. One of the first students arrested in the 1960 Richmond sit-ins. Pastor of Springfield Baptist Church in Henrico County, VA, 1964–1966; pastor of Walker Memorial Baptist Church in Washington since 1966. Served as housing administrator for the DC Dept. of Housing and Community Development for twenty-seven years. Awarded Winston Churchill travel fellowship in 1980 to study Britain's affordable housing policies. Currently board secretary of the African American Freedom Fund Foundation, which established a memorial to black Civil War veterans.

| KALE, EDWARD W. | W | M | 24 | Grangeville, ID | Student, Yale Divinity School |

See chapter 10. Participated in Monroe, NC, Freedom Ride. Born in Idaho in 1937. Attended Univ. of Idaho. Graduate of Univ. of Denver (1959) and Yale Divinity School. Active in the Methodist student movement. Ordained minister and college chaplain. Retired from campus ministry. Owns a kayak company in Duluth, MN.

| RANDOLPH, RAYMOND B., JR. | B | M | 21 | New Haven, CT | Student, Virginia Union Univ. |

Arrested at a sit-in demonstration in Richmond, VA, in February 1960. His case went to the Supreme Court of Appeals, and the conviction was upheld. Chief Justice John W. Eggleston claimed that a proprietor of a business had the right to refuse service to anyone for personal reasons.

| SILVER, CAROL RUTH | W | F | 22 | New York, NY | Secretary and clerk, United Nations |

Born and raised in Massachusetts. After graduating from the Univ. of Chicago and law school, Silver worked with the California Office of Opportunity's legal aid programs, assisted the organizing efforts of Cesar Chavez's United Farmworkers, and later dedicated her legal services to the rights of jail inmates, Native Americans, women, and gays. Served three terms as a San Francisco supervisor (1978–1989). President of the board of governors regulating the Golden Gate Bridge Highway and Transportation District (1988–1989). Ran unsuccessfuly for Congress in 1996 and organized 40th Freedom Rider reunion in 2001. See chapter 9 and epilogue.

SIMMS, OBADIAH LEE   B   M   21   Pittsburgh, PA   Student, Virginia Union Univ.

Born in Richmond, VA, on December 12, 1939. Oldest of 8 children, son of a Baptist minister. Graduate of Va. Union Univ. (B.A., sociology) and Univ. of Chicago (M.S.W.). Organized community action groups to combat steel-mill pollution in Gary, IN, during the 1970s. Social worker with Manchester House and later with Saul Alinsky's Institute of Human Change in Chicago. Ran recycling business in NY City in 1990s. Avid sports fisherman. Died in July 1999, at the age of 59.

Jackson, MS
(Greyhound terminal), June 7, 1961

Name	Race	Sex	Age	Residence	Occupation or Status
AUDAIN, MICHAEL JAMES	W	M	23	Vancouver, B.C.	Political science student, Univ. of British Columbia (Vancouver, BC)

See chapter 7. Returned to Vancouver following the Freedom Rides and worked as a social worker for twenty years. Also taught at the Univ. of British Columbia's School of Community and Regional Planning. Later career as developer, home builder, and chairman of Polygon Homes, Ltd., in Vancouver, BC. Art patron and president of the Vancouver Art Gallery. Recipient of the 2004 Edmund C. Bovey Award for Leadership Support of the Arts.

St. Louis, MO, to Jackson, MS
(airport), June 7, 1961

Name	Race	Sex	Age	Residence	Occupation or Status
JENKINS, GWENDOLYN C.	B	F	21	St. Louis, MO	Receptionist for attorney James Bell
JENKINS, ROBERT L.	B	M	27	St. Louis, MO	Student, St. Louis Univ.
WASHINGTON, RALPH EDWARD	B	M	24	Webster Grove, MO	Pathology attendant, St. Louis County Hospital

Montgomery, AL, to Jackson, MS
(airport), June 8, 1961

Name	Race	Sex	Age	Residence	Occupation or Status
LANE, MARK	W	M	34	New York, NY	New York state legislator

High-profile attorney who volunteered to defend Lee Harvey Oswald after John F. Kennedy's assassination. Later wrote several books and screenplays about Kennedy's assassination, Oswald's innocence, and the CIA's complicity in the murder. After Martin Luther King's assassination, Lane defended James Earl Ray and later wrote the book *Murder in Memphis.*

SUTTON, PERCY	B	M	40	Springfield Gardens, NY	Attorney; New York NAACP branch president

Long career as New York City politician and NAACP leader. Manhattan borough president and leader of the Martin Luther King, Jr., Democratic Club. Chairman of Inner City Broadcasting. Produced the television program *Showtime at the Apollo* for fifteen years.

New Orleans, LA, to Jackson, MS
(Illinois Central RR), June 8, 1961

Name	Race	Sex	Age	Residence	Occupation or Status
BRITT, TRAVIS O.	B	M	27	Brooklyn, NY	Cafeteria worker; NAG activist (Washington, DC)

See chapter 11. Active in McComb voter registration movement, fall 1961. Married Freedom Rider Gwendolyn Greene. In 1976 he and his two sons walked from his home in Riverdale, MD, to Plains, GA, in support of Jimmy Carter's presidential campaign; later given White House tour by President Carter. In 2001 he was president of Potpourri Productions, a Mt. Rainer, MD, video and media services company. Graduated from Bowie State Univ. in 2003 with a degree in political science.

CARMICHAEL, STOKELY	B	M	19	Bronx, NY	Student, Howard Univ.

See Carmichael, *Ready for Revolution*. Became SNCC chairman in 1966 and honorary prime minister of Black Panther Party in 1967. Moved to Guinea in West Africa in 1969, changed his name to Kwame Ture in honor of African leaders Kwame Nkruma and Sekou Toure, and later traveled the globe as a proponent of the All African Peoples Revolutionary Party. Died in Conakry, Guinea, on November 15, 1998, at the age of 57.

GREENE, GWENDOLYN T.	B	F	19	Washington, DC	Student, Howard Univ.

Born on November 19, 1941. NAG activist. Married Freedom Rider Travis Britt. Elected to the Maryland state senate in 2002 as a representative of Prince George's County. Graduated from Bowie State Univ. in 2004 with a degree in political science.

PERLMAN, TERI SUSAN	W	F	19	Bronx, NY	Student, CCNY
ROSETT, JANE ELLEN	W	F	18	Washington, DC	Prospective student, Reed College (Portland, OR)

Founding member of the People With AIDS Coalition. A prominent AIDS activist, she has both curated and contributed her photography to art exhibits encouraging AIDS awareness.

TRIGGS, JAN LEIGHTON	B	M	19	New Rochelle, NY	Student, Howard Univ.

NAG activist.

TRUMPAUER, JOAN HARRIS	W	F	19	Washington, DC	Secretary for Rep. Claire Engle of California

Born in Washington, DC, on September 14, 1941. Raised in Arlington, VA. Daughter of a Washington bureaucrat (Depts. of Labor and State). Mother's family from rural Georgia, near Macon. Attended Duke University. NAG activist who left her conservative husband because he opposed desegregation. Tougaloo College student (1961–1964). Freedom Summer organizer, 1964. Later worked at the Smithsonian, with the Community Relations Service, and at the Depts. of Commerce and Justice. Currently teaches English as a second language at an elementary school in Arlington. Married name: Joan Mulholland.

WESBY, ROBERT	B	M	33	Aurora, IL	Baptist minister

Worked with Jesse Jackson as one of the leaders of Operation PUSH in he Chicago area during the 1970s and 1980s. Died on July 22, 1988, at the age of 61. Found beaten to death near the altar of the Progressive Baptist Church, which he had founded in Aurora, IL, in 1963.

WILSON, HELENE DOROTHY	W	F	26	Washington, DC	Housewife

Born on March 24, 1935. NAG and Washington CORE activist. After her release on bail, she helped organize a major Freedom Rider fund-raising rally in Washington featuring novelist James Baldwin.

Nashville, TN, to Jackson, MS
(Illinois Central RR), June 9, 1961

Name	Race	Sex	Age	Residence	Occupation or Status
BEAMER, MARGARET WINONAH	W	F	19	Dayton, OH	Student, Central State College

Born in Cleveland, OH. Only Freedom Rider to serve full six-month sentence in Mississippi jails. Released from Parchman on Christmas Day 1961. Married Freedom Rider Charles David Myers in April 1962. Graduated from Central State in 1966. Worked for seventeen years (1978–1995) with the Montgomery, OH, Board of Mental Rehabilitation as a teacher of profoundly retarded adults. Currently lives in Ellenton, FL.

BROMBERG, EDWARD J.	W	M	27	Chestnut Hill, MA	Student, Columbia Univ. (New York, NY)

See chapter 10. Born in Massachusetts on August 31, 1933. Participated in Monroe, NC, Freedom Ride. Died in New York City on October 10, 2001, at the age of 68.

BRYANT, PATRICIA ELAINE	B	F	20	Elmira, NY	Student, Central State College
GREENBLATT, DEL	W	F	21	Brooklyn, NY	Student, Cornell Univ.

Studied medieval history at Cornell. Served on the Board of Elections in Sunnyside, Queens (NY), in the mid-1960s.

RUSH, HEATH CLIFF	W	M	20	Concord, NH	Student, Central State College

See chapter 10. Participated in Monroe, NC, Freedom Ride.

Nashville, TN, to Jackson, MS
(Greyhound), June 10, 1961

Name	Race	Sex	Age	Residence	Occupation or Status
BERMAN, LEORA	W	F	18	Chicago, IL	Student

Born in Chicago in January 1943.

GREEN, STEPHEN JOHN	W	M	21	Rye, NY	Student, Middlebury College (Middlebury, VT)

See chapter 9 and epilogue. Born in Muncie, IN, in May 1940. Worked as a journalist with the *Christian Science Monitor*. Later worked with UNICEF. Employed by United Nations World Food Program for eleven years organizing emergency operations in war zones.

GRISWOLD, RICHARD P.	W	M	34	Brooklyn, NY	Social worker

See chapter 10. Born in Summerhill, NY, in August 1926. Participated in Monroe, NC, Freedom Ride.

HORNE, LEON DANIEL	B	M	24	Chicago, IL	Waiter and student, William Junior College (Chicago, IL).

Born in Tougaloo, MS, in June 1936. See chapter 8.

PLEUNE, KATHERINE A.	W	F	21	Chicago, IL	Mimeograph operator

See chapter 8. Born in Newark, NJ, in February 1940. Sister of Freedom Rider Joan Pleune. Involved with Fair Play for Cuba movement, 1960–1961.

WOODS, LOWELL A., JR.	B	M	34	Chicago, IL	Police reporter for *Crusader News*

Born in Chicago in August 1926. Died on June 11, 1998, at the age of 71.

Nashville, TN, to Jackson, MS (Greyhound), June 11, 1961

Name	Race	Sex	Age	Residence	Occupation or Status
AELONY, ZEV	W	M	23	St. Paul, MN	CORE activist (Palo Alto, CA)

See chapter 8 and epilogue. CORE voting rights activist in Florida and Georgia (1962–1963). He and his wife currently own a company that represents computer manufacturing firms.

BAUM, ROBERT M.	W	M	19	Excelsior, MN	Student, Univ. of Minnesota (Minneapolis, MN)

See chapter 8. Long career as a bus driver at the Univ. of Minnesota.

DAVIDOV, MARVIN ALLEN	W	M	29	Minneapolis, MN	Art dealer

See chapter 8. Currently lives in Minneapolis, where he remains a leading anti-war and human rights activist.

MORTON, DAVID KERR	W	M	21	Jackson, WY	Folk singer; freelance writer

See chapters 8 and 10. Born in Minnesota. Participant in the Monroe, NC, Freedom Ride.

O'CONNOR, CLAIRE	W	F	22	St. Paul, MN	Nurse and student, Univ. of Minnesota

See chapter 8 and epilogue. Currently the executive director of a teen health clinic in Minneapolis.

THOMPSON, DANIEL RAY	W	M	26	Cleveland, OH	Student

See chapter 10. Born in Indiana on April 21, 1935. Participated in Monroe, NC, Freedom Ride. A human rights advocate particularly supportive of Cleveland's homeless community. Performed his poetry for more than forty years, compiled two books of poetry, *Famous in the Neighborhood* and *Even the Broken Letters of the Heart Spell Earth*, and donated his poems to publications dedicated to helping the homeless. Named Cuyahoga County's poet laureate in 1992. Died of leukemia on May 6, 2004, at the age of 64.

UPHOFF, EUGENE JOHN	W	M	19	Minneapolis, MN	Student, Univ. of Minnesota

See chapter 8. One of four students chosen by the National Student Association to go on a sponsored tour of Africa and the Middle East in 1964. Became a prominent socially conscious physician and leading proponent of Oregon's "Death with Dignity" Act.

Interfaith Freedom Ride: Washington, DC, to Tallahassee, FL, June 13–16, 1961

Name	Race	Sex	Age	Residence	Occupation or Status
ALSTORK, C. DONALD	B	M	41	Saratoga, NY	Minister, Dyer Phelps AME Zion Church (Saratoga, NY)

Born in Mobile, AL. Graduate of CCNY and Hood Seminary at Livingstone College (Salisbury, NC). NAACP activist and Little Rock NAACP branch board chairman (1956–1958).

Brown, Robert   W   M   41   New York, NY   Minister; theologian
McAfee

Distinguished career as theologian and human rights activist. Protested the Vietnam War and went on hunger strikes to protest U.S. weapons policies. Author of over twenty-five books, including a biography of Holocaust survivor Elie Weisel. See his autobiography *Reflections over the Long Haul: A Memoir*. Died on September 4, 2001, at the age of 81.

Collier, John W. P.   B   M   46   Newark, NJ   Minister, Israel Memorial AME
                                                        Church (Newark, NJ)

Born in Plainfield, NJ, on October 3, 1914. Graduate of Wilberforce Univ. (B.A., 1936, B.D., 1938). Later attended Drew Univ. AME pastor in Buffalo, NY (1948–1950), and Newark, NJ (1950–1964). Temporarily traded pulpits with fellow Freedom Rider Israel Dresner in late 1961. In the 1960s he was president of the Newark Coordinating Council, a civil rights organization advocating equal employment rights. Involved in the Albany campaign in 1962. Secretary of missions for the AME Church (1969–1984). Staff member for AME Bishop Frank Cummings (1984–1989 in Philadelphia, 1995–2000 in Jacksonville, FL). Currently lives in Atlanta, where he and his second wife, Jacquelyn Grant, co-edit the AME *Voice of Missions*, and where he still delivers guest sermons at age 90.

Dresner, Israel (Si)   W   M   31   Springfield, NJ   Rabbi, Temple Sharey Shalom
                                                        (Springfield, NJ)

Born in Brooklyn. Son of a delicatessen owner. Graduate of the Univ. of Chicago (1950) and Hebrew Union College–Jewish Institute of Theology. Long career as a reform Jewish rabbi and human rights advocate in northern New Jersey. Continued civil rights activism throughout 1960s and participated in Albany (1962), St. Augustine (1964), and 1965 Selma-to-Montgomery march. Retired in 1996. Currently lives in Wayne, NJ.

Evans, Malcolm   W   M   36   Brooklyn, NY   Minister, Church of the
                                                        Crossroads (Brooklyn, NY)

Prominent social gospel advocate in New York. Associate pastor of the multilingual Presbyterian Church of the Crossroads (1959). A leading anti-poverty crusader in Brooklyn and greater New York for more than four decades. President of the Council for a Better East New York (1990).

Freedman, Martin   W   M   34   Paterson, NJ   Rabbi

Friend and associate of Bayard Rustin. Longtime rabbi of Barnert Temple in Franklin Lakes, NJ, New Jersey's oldest reform synagogue (founded 1847). Currently a rabbi emeritus living in Wayne, NJ.

Hardge, Arthur L.   B   M   34   New Britain, CT   AME Zion minister

Born in Indianapolis, IN, on April 8, 1927. Son of the Rev. Elias Hardge. Became pastor of Hood Memorial AME Zion Church in Rhode Island in 1968. First chairman of Rhode Island CORE. Executive secretary of Rhode Island Commission Against Discrimination (1965–1968). The first African American appointed to a cabinet position in Rhode Island (1968): director of Dept. of Community Affairs. Died of heart disease in October 1983, at the age of 56.

Hartmire, Wayne   W   M   29   New York, NY   Minister to youth, East Harlem
"Chris" Clyde, Jr.   Protestant Parish

Directed the California Migrant Ministry for several years before becoming an assistant to United Farm Workers leader Cesar Chavez. Consultant for the National Farm Workers Ministry. Currently part-time executive director of Clean and Sober, an organization designed to help the homeless.

Leake, George   B   M   31   Buffalo, NY   Minister

Active in the civil rights struggle in Charlotte, NC, in the mid-1960s.

LEVINE, ALLAN   W   M   28   Bradford, PA   Rabbi

A native of Montreal, Quebec. Emigrated to the U.S. in 1953. At Jim Farmer's request, he participated in July 1961 Freedom Ride from San Francisco Bay area to Jackson, MS. COFO volunteer during 1964 Freedom Summer. In 1970 he moved to Israel, where he currently resides in the city of Rehovot. Attended 2001 Freedom Rider reunion in Jackson, MS.

McKINNEY, PETTY   B   M   40   Springfield, MA   Minister, Eliza Ann Gardner
                                             AME Zion Church (Springfield,
                                             MA)

Graduate of Livingstone College (Salisbury, NC) and NYU (1942). World War II veteran (Marine Corps, 1943–1945). NAACP activist. Picketed segregated Woolworth's stores in Springfield (1961). Currently lives in Silver Spring, MD.

PLAUT, WALTER   W   M   41   Great Neck, NY   Rabbi

Fled Nazi Germany with his brother Jonas in 1937. Ordained in 1947, he served as a rabbi in Fargo, ND, Cedar Rapids, IA, and Great Neck, NY, before participating in the Freedom Rides. Died in 1964, at the age of 44.

PROCTOR, HENRY   B   M   53   Syracuse, NY   Minister

Born on November 24, 1907. Died in Arkansas in April 1965, at the age of 57.

ROY, RALPH LORD   W   M   32   New York, NY   Minister, Grace Methodist
                                             Church (New York City);
                                             writer

Friend and associate of George Houser. CORE activist in late 1940s. Graduate of Swarthmore College (1950). Long career as United Methodist minister, civil rights activist, and freelance writer. Author of *Communism and the Churches* (1960). Preached in Albany, GA, in 1962 at Martin Luther King's request. Currently lives in Southington, CT.

SMITH, PERRY A. III   B   M   27   Washington, DC   Minister, First Baptist Church
                                             of North Brentwood
                                             (MD)

Graduate of Howard Univ. Longtime minister and civil rights activist in suburban Prince George's County, MD. Began ministry at North Brentwood in 1958. Unsuccessful candidate for County Council (1970) and Congress (1982). Ran as a Republican.

STOŃE, ROBERT J.   W   M   41   New York, NY   Minister

Born August 10, 1919. Associate director of the Presbyterian Commission on Religion and Race in the 1960s. Arrested for protesting nuclear weapons and later arrested again protesting cruise missles. Member of the board of the Presbyterian Peace Fellowship that worked to ban land mines and to close down the military School of the Americas. Worked to bring refugees to the U.S. during the war in El Salvador. Died on January 1, 1999, in Pasadena, CA, at the age of 79.

WARNER, A.   W   M   41   New York, NY   Minister
   McRAVEN (MACK)

Executive secretary of the Manhattan Division of the Protestant Council of New York City in 1962. Faced anti-Communist protests in March 1962 when he tried to speak at a CORE rally in Scarsdale, NY.

WHITE, EDWARD   W   M   29   New York, NY   Minister

Washington, DC, to St. Petersburg, FL,
June 13–16, 1961

Name	Race	Sex	Age	Residence	Occupation or Status
BOBROW, JERALD	W	M	32	Port Washington, NY	Rabbi

Born January 10, 1929. Veteran of 1948 Israeli-Arab War. Lived on an Israeli kibbutz for several years in the 1950s. Died in March 1986, at the age of 57.

Name	Race	Sex	Age	Residence	Occupation or Status
CALLENDER, HERBERT	B	M	27	Bronx, NY	Union official, UAW

Became head of the Bronx CORE chapter, initiating job discrimination protests against the White Castle restaurant chain and threatening to disrupt the 1964 World's Fair with a stall-in. Arrested and committed to a psychiatric ward after trying to make a citizen's arrest of Mayor Robert F. Wagner for funding projects that allowed racial discrimination. Changed name to Makaza Kumanyika. Graduated from Cornell in 1977 and continued his activism heading groups such as the Federation of Southern Cooperatives, East Orange's Clean and Green Center, and Urban Center for Public/Private Parnerships. Died of cancer in East Orange, NJ, on September 22, 1993, at the age of 60.

Name	Race	Sex	Age	Residence	Occupation or Status
DIAMOND, RALPH	B	M	36	South Ozone, NY	Union official, UAW

Born July 9, 1924. Vice president and international trustee of United Auto Workers Local 259 from 1958 until his retirement in 1995. Died in Far Rockaway, NY, on December 4, 1996, at the age of 72.

Name	Race	Sex	Age	Residence	Occupation or Status
LEBOWITZ, JOYCE	W	F	26	New York, NY	Editor, Harvard University Press
MASSAQUOI, SHEREE	B	F	27	Brooklyn, NY	Sculptor
MORTON, EDWARD	B	M	32	Albany, NY	Minister

Former professional middleweight boxer (1947–1948) and judo trainer.

Name	Race	Sex	Age	Residence	Occupation or Status
NEGEN, GORDON	W	M	29	New York, NY	Pastor, First Christian Reformed Church (New York City)

Born in Wisconsin. Graduate of Calvin College (B.A., 1954), Calvin Seminary (B.A., 1957; M.Div., 1965), and Union Theological Seminary (M.Div., 1963). Pastor of Manhattan Christian Reform Church in Harlem (1959–1968). Helped to establish programs for drug rehabilitation and halfway houses in Harlem (1964). Worked on low-income housing issues in Denver (1968–1974). Headed Evangelical Concern, an organization designed to help churches focus on social issues (late 1970s). Currently lives in the Granville, MI, area, where he is pastor of the Granville-Jensen Congregational Church.

Name	Race	Sex	Age	Residence	Occupation or Status
O'CONNOR, JAMES	W	M	31	New York, NY	Economics Instructor, Barnard College (New York City)

Born on April 20, 1930. Graduate of Columbia Univ. (B.S., 1956, Ph.D., 1964). Taught economics at Barnard (1958–1962), Washington Univ. (1964–1966), San Jose State Univ. (1966–1976), and Univ. of California, Santa Cruz (1976–1993). Author of *Fiscal Crisis of the State* (1973) and *Natural Causes: Essays in Ecological Marxism* (1997). Ed. of journal *Capitalism, Nature, Socialism* (1988–2004). Currently lives in Santa Cruz, CA.

Name	Race	Sex	Age	Residence	Occupation or Status
RANDALL, FRANCIS B.	W	M	29	New York, NY	History instructor, Columbia Univ.

Graduate of Amherst College (Amherst, MA) (B.A.), and Columbia Univ. (M.A., Ph.D.). Specialist in Russian intellectual history. Taught at Sarah Lawrence College from the mid-1960s until his retirement in 2000. Currently lives in New York City. Husband of Laura Randall.

Name	Race	Sex	Age	Residence	Occupation or Status
RANDALL, LAURA	W	F	25	New York, NY	Graduate student in economics, Columbia Univ.

Graduate of Barnard College (B.A.), Univ. of Massachusetts (M.A.), and Columbia Univ. (Ph.D., 1962). An economist for the Federal Reserve Bank of New York. Lectured at Baruch

College and Columbia University and taught at Queens College before joining the Economics Department at Hunter College in 1968. Wrote and edited several books on Latin American economics. Retired in 2000. Currently lives in New York City with her husband, Francis B. Randall.

SMITH, LESLIE   B   M   35   Albany, NY   AME Zion minister

Born in Jamaica. Risked pending U.S. citizenship status by becoming Freedom Rider.

STERN, DANIEL N.   W   M   26   New York, NY   Doctor

Intern at Bellevue Hospital (New York City) in 1961.

WHITE, DUPREE   B   M   40   South Ozone, NY   Union official, UAW

NAACP activist. Died in March 1965.

WINSTON, BENNY   B   M   42   New York, NY   Union official, UAW

Nashville, TN, to Jackson, MS (Greyhound), June 16, 1961

Name	Race	Sex	Age	Residence	Occupation or Status
ADLER, ELIZABETH S.	W	F	21	Brooklyn, NY	Student, Univ. of Wisconsin, Madison
FILNER, ROBERT EARL	W	M	18	Forest Hills, NY	Student, Cornell University

See chapter 8 and epilogue. Born in Pittsburgh and raised in NY City. Graduate of Cornell Univ. (B.A., 1963; Ph.D., 1973) and the Univ. of Delaware (M.A., 1969). Moved to San Diego in 1970. Taught history of science at San Diego State Univ. (1970–1992). Member of San Diego School Board (1979–1983) and San Diego City Council (1987–1992). Elected to Congress as a liberal Democrat in 1992; has been reelected six times.

HIRSCHFELD, ELIZABETH SLADE	W	F	24	Ithaca, NY	Laboratory technician, Atomic Energy Com.

Born in Detroit in 1937. Graduated from Cornell Univ. in 1958. Longtime activist involvement with Michigan-based Friends of the South, United Farmworkers, Ralph Nader's Citizen Action Group, and various lesbian, feminist, and Jewish community groups. Lobbied for the Mississippi Freedom Democratic Party in 1964. Mother of four children.

KYTLE, KAREN ELIZABETH	W	F	18	Stillwater, OK	Student, Hills Business College (Oklahoma City, OK)

Went by nickname Kay. Joined other former Freedom Riders in Chicago in July 1961.

RICE, LEON N.	B	M	24	Chicago, IL	Student, Univ. of Chicago

Jackson, MS (Greyhound Terminal), June 19, 1961

Name	Race	Sex	Age	Residence	Occupation or Status
LEVINE, EUGENE	W	M	34	Stillwater, OK	English instructor, Oklahoma State Univ. (Stillwater, OK)

New Orleans, LA, to Jackson, MS
(Illinois Central RR), June 20, 1961

Name	Race	Sex	Age	Residence	Occupation or Status
CARTER, RITA J.	B	F	18	Berkeley, CA	Student, Oakland City College (Oakland, CA)
KERR, MARGARET ANN	W	F	26	Berkeley, CA	Student, Univ. of California, Berkeley
MARTINSON, ROBERT MAGNUS	W	M	34	Berkeley, CA	Student, Univ. of California, Berkeley
McCONNELL, PAUL DUNCAN	W	M	27	Castro Valley, CA	Student, Alameda State College (Alameda, CA); former student, Univ. of Mississippi (Oxford, MS)
MUNTEAN, FREDERICK DEAN	W	M	22	Sharon, PA	Student, Youngstown Univ. (Youngstown, OH)
MUSE, GRANT HARLAND, JR.	W	M	35	Berkeley, CA	Priest at the Good Shepherd Episcopal Church

Graduate of the Univ. of New Mexico. Studied theology at Mirfield, England, and the Church Divinity School of the Pacific.

Name	Race	Sex	Age	Residence	Occupation or Status
PETERSON, LESTRA ALENE	W	F	23	Berkeley, CA	Student, Oakland City College
PLEUNE, JOAN FRANCES	W	F	22	Berkeley, CA	Student, Univ. of California, Berkeley

Sister of Freedom Rider Katherine Pleune.

Name	Race	Sex	Age	Residence	Occupation or Status
PRATT, JOSEPH MARION	W	M	19	Durham, NC	Student, San Francisco State College (San Francisco, CA)
SIEGEL, JORGIA B. YVONNE	W	F	19	Berkeley, CA	Student, Univ. of California, Berkeley

Roomed with fellow Freedom Rider Pat Kovner at the University of California. Later worked in the CORE office in New York. Received her nursing degree at Brooklyn College. Currently lives in Santa Barbara, CA, where she is a nurse and conducts Lamaze childbirth classes. Married name: Jorgia Bordofsky.

Name	Race	Sex	Age	Residence	Occupation or Status
TEALE, BUREN LEWIS	W	M	32	Albany, CA	Machinist
TRISS, LAWRENCE, JR.	B	M	28	Berkeley, CA	Student, Univ. of California, Berkeley
VAN ROLAND, THOMAS	W	M	24	Berkeley, CA	Chemist

Montgomery, AL, to Jackson, MS
(Trailways), June 21, 1961

Name	Race	Sex	Age	Residence	Occupation or Status
FEINGOLD, MIRIAM (MIMI)	W	F	20	Brooklyn, NY	Student, Swarthmore College (Swarthmore, PA)

Born in Brooklyn in May 1941. Daughter of left-wing Jewish teachers fired by Brooklyn Board of Education. Helped organize Swarthmore College Cambridge, MD, project in 1963 and worked with Cambridge civil rights leader Gloria Richardson. CORE voting rights activist in Louisiana in late 1963. Involved in draft resistance and women's movement in California. Pioneering work in oral history documentation of the 1960s civil rights and SDS movements. Currently directs a Hebrew day school in Marin County, CA. See Hogan, *Many Minds, One Heart;* and Fairclough, *Race and Democracy.*

| FRIEZE, JUDITH ANN | W | F | 22 | Waban, MA | Student, Smith College (Northampton, MA) |

Born in Boston in March 1939. Graduate of Smith College (B.A., 1961). Her grandmother was a radical activist who clashed with HUAC in the 1950s. Member of the NAACP. Picketed Woolworth's in Northampton, MA, prior to Freedom Rides. Helped organize the Boston contingent in the 1963 March on Washington. After graduate work at Boston Univ. and a 1964 marriage, she and her husband participated in Freedom Summer and lived in Meridian, MS (1964–1965). Later involvement in the anti-war movement as a draft counselor and in the women's movement. Worked with the AIDS Action Committee since the early 1990s. Married name: Judith Wright.

| LEONARD, MARGARET BURR | W | F | 19 | Atlanta, GA | Student, Sophie Newcomb College (New Orleans, LA) |

See chapter 8. Born in Louisville, KY. *St. Petersburg Times* reporter (1973–1976). Lived in Austin, TX (1976–1980). After returning to Florida, she worked as an editor for the *Palm Beach Post, Miami Herald,* and *Tallahassee Democrat.* Currently edits the *Florida State Times* at Florida State University in Tallahassee.

| NASH, SAMUEL TIMOTHY | B | M | 24 | Chicago, IL | Part-time employee, U.S. Postal Service |

Born in Charleston, WV, in February 1937.

| SCHWARZSCHILD, HENRY | W | M | 35 | Highland Park, IL | Religious official, Congregation Solen |

Born in Wiesbaden, Germany. Moved to the U.S. as a refugee from Nazi Germany in 1939. Executive director of the Lawyer's Constitutional Defense Committee (1964–1972). Headed the Capital Punishment Project of the ACLU until he retired in 1990. Died of cancer on June 1, 1996, at the age of 70.

| SMITH, LEON FELTON, JR. | B | M | 31 | Cleveland, OH | Assistant pastor, Holiness Church of God |

Born in Cleveland, OH, in May 1930.

| WALKER, THERESA EDWARDS | B | F | 33 | Atlanta, GA | Housewife |

Born in Freehold, NJ, in February 1928. Wife of Wyatt Tee Walker.

| WALKER, WYATT TEE | B | M | 31 | Atlanta, GA | SCLC executive director; Baptist minister |

See May 25 ride. Husband of Theresa Walker.

| WHITE, MELVIN LORENZO | B | M | 19 | Talladega, AL | Unemployed |

Born in Montgomery, AL, in February 1942.

Jackson, MS (Trailways terminal), June 23, 1961

Name	Race	Sex	Age	Residence	Occupation or Status
ARMSTRONG, THOMAS MADISON III	B	M	19	Silver Creek, MS	Student, Tougaloo College

Born in Silver Creek, MS, on 1941. Student activist affiliated with CORE, SNCC, and the NAACP in 1961. Graduate of Tougaloo College (B.A., biology, 1964). Voter registration worker in Mississippi in the mid-1960s. Currently lives in Naperville, IL. Contract specialist with the U.S. Postal Service.

Name	Race	Sex	Age	Residence	Occupation or Status
HARRISON, MARY MAGDALENE	A	F	21	San Antonio, TX	Student, Tougaloo College

Raised in an Asian-American military family in Germany, France, the Philippines, and Ft. Riley, KS. Recently retired from the Jackson, MS, school system. Married name: Mary Harrison Lee.

Name	Race	Sex	Age	Residence	Occupation or Status
PRICE, ELNORA R.	B	F	26	Raymond, MS	No occupation given
ROSS, JOSEPH LEE	B	M	25	Nashville, TN	Student, Tennessee State Univ.

New Orleans, LA, to Jackson, MS (Illinois Central RR), June 25, 1961

Name	Race	Sex	Age	Residence	Occupation or Status
BLEVINS, GEORGE MARION	W	M	21	Los Angeles, CA	Student, Chouinard Institute (Los Angeles, CA)

Worked with New Orleans CORE in the summer of 1961.

Name	Race	Sex	Age	Residence	Occupation or Status
BOUKNIGHT, GLORIA LEEVARE-DEE	B	F	20	Columbia, SC	Legal secretary
BROOKS, ARTHUR, JR.	B	M	22	Los Angeles, CA	Student, Los Angeles City College
DOLAN, JOHN LUTHER	W	M	20	Berkeley, CA	Student, Univ. of California, Berkeley

Born in San Francisco, CA, on April 11, 1941. Graduate of Univ. of California, Berkeley (B.A., 1962) and the Univ. of California, San Francisco (M.D., 1968). Member of Berkeley CORE until 1963. Worked with New Orleans CORE in summer of 1961. Social worker in Alameda County (1962–1963). Interned under black NAACP activist Dr. Nathaniel Burbridge. Worked in medical clinics for farm workers (1970–1971). Long career in emergency medicine (1968–1998), mostly in Richmond, CA. Recently earned an M.A. degree in history and humanities at Sacramento State Univ., completing a thesis on the history of science in China. Currently lives in Emeryville, CA, and Ashland, OR, and works part-time at VA clinic in Oakland.

Name	Race	Sex	Age	Residence	Occupation or Status
HAMILTON, MARY LUCILLE	B	F	25	Los Angeles, CA	Teacher, Ascension Grammar School

Born in Cedar Rapids, IA, in October 1935. Raised in Denver. Graduate of Briarcliff College (B.A.) and Manhattanville College (M.A.). Member of CORE staff (1961–1964). CORE's Southern regional director before marriage to Walter Young, brother of SCLC leader Andrew Young. Following divorce and second marriage, she taught high school English in Ossining, NY, for a number of years. After retiring, she tutored Spanish students. Died of ovarian cancer on November 11, 2002, at the age of 67.

Harris, Gordon Lau	W	M	23	Rochester, NY	Student, Univ. of Rochester
Inghram, Louise Jean	W	F	26	Los Angeles, CA	Housewife
Johnson, Frank	B	M	21	Tucson, AZ	Student, Univ. of Arizona
Kendall, Marian Alice	W	F	35	San Leandro, CA	Social worker

Born in California on March 7, 1926. Died on December 15, 2002, at the age of 76.

Libson, Norma	W	F	27	Philadelphia, PA	Payroll clerk, Penn Wax Works

Born and raised in Philadelphia, PA. Fund-raiser for CORE after the Freedom Rides. Received her B.A. in urban studies from Temple Univ. and also completed coursework for an M.A. in Urban Studies at Temple in 1977. Wrote grant proposals for government and other nonprofit organizations, assisting with and establishing programs for economic development in inner cities and independent living for the developmentally disabled and emotionally handicapped. Retired in 2000 at age 66. Currently lives in Claymont, DE.

Liggins, Claude Albert	B	M	20	Los Angeles, CA	Student, Los Angeles City College

Born and raised in Lake Charles, LA. Oldest of 11 children. Moved to Los Angeles in August 1959 to be a dancer. Active in LA CORE (fund-raising and finance chairman) in mid-1960s. Volunteer with Watts Summer Festival and Nat. Council of Negro Women in late 1960s. Self-employed since 1968, manufacturing greeting cards and operating a printing and paper goods company. Currently lives in Los Angeles.

Manning, Eddora Mae	B	F	19	Los Angeles, CA	Student, Los Angeles City College
Mason, Robert William	B	M	17	Los Angeles, CA	Student, Fremont High School
Nelson, Frank Arthur	W	M	22	Brooklyn, NY	Civil engineer

Born in the Bronx, NY, on July 14, 1938. Graduate of Cooper Union (B.S., civil engineering, 1959). Married New Orleans CORE activist Patricia Smith. Active in NY CORE and the Freedom Highways Project, 1962–1963. Jailed in North Carolina in 1962 but released after hunger strike. Anti-war activist in Los Angeles (mid-1960s). Lived on Oregon commune (late 1960s–early 1970s). Worked as engineer, carpenter, and surveyor. Active in Committee in Solidarity with the People of El Salvador (1984–1994). Currently lives in San Francisco, CA, where he is active in Not in Our Name anti-war group.

Rogers, Janice Louise	W	F	25	Los Angeles, CA	Secretary and model (unemployed at the time)

Married to John Copeland Rogers. See chapter 9. Identified herself as black to MS officials in 1961.

Rogers, John Copeland	B	M	30	Los Angeles, CA	Boxer

Married to Janice Rogers.

Rosenbaum, Marcia Arlene	W	F	23	Los Angeles, CA	Painter

Born in Newark, NJ. Moved to Sacramento, CA, at age of 11. Attended LA City College, Univ. of California, Santa Barbara, and Sacramento State College. Active in New Orleans CORE (1961–1963) and Los Angeles CORE (mid-1960s). Peace Corps volunteer in Dominican Republic and Haiti (1971). Worked for Save the Children and trained Peace Corps volunteers in Costa Rica and Guatemala (1970s). Founded CREAR, an organization dedicated to rural development and education in Dominican Republic, in late 1970s.

Taught independent living skills to the disabled in New Mexico (1990s). Currently lives in Las Vegas. Current name: Chela Lightchild.

Name	Race	Sex	Age	Residence	Occupation or Status
TAYLOR, WAYNE LESLIE	B	M	23	Los Angeles, CA	No occupation given
THORNE, RICHARD	B	M	24	Berkeley, CA	Freelance fiction writer
TOOMBS, CLAIRE DREW	W	F	18	Silver Springs, MD	Salesperson, women's sports store (Chevy Chase, MD)

Montgomery, AL, to Jackson, MS (Trailways), July 2, 1961

Name	Race	Sex	Age	Residence	Occupation or Status
KAY, BARBARA JANE	B	F	35	Englewood, NJ	Housewife

Wife of noted musician and composer Ulysses Kay. Teacher in Chicago (1940s) and Harlem (1950s). Active in civil rights (1960s–1970s), working on school desegregation and organizing freedom schools. Participated in 1966 Meredith March, along with her daughter Virginia. Died in 1997, at the age of 71.

Name	Race	Sex	Age	Residence	Occupation or Status
MILLER, ROBERT ALLEN	W	M	22	Warren, MI	Student, Wayne State Univ.
PRITCHARD, MICHAEL LEON	W	M	18	New York, NY	Student, San Francisco City College
STONER, PETER HARRY	W	M	22	Chicago, IL	Student, Univ. of Chicago

Born and raised on a small farm in western Pennsylvania. Currently lives in Jackson, MS, where he owns an automobile repair shop.

Name	Race	Sex	Age	Residence	Occupation or Status
THORNTON, LEOTIS	B	M	23	San Jose, CA	Student, San Jose State College (San Jose, CA); working in public relations

Born in Kentucky on December 17, 1937. Died in August 1976 at the age of 38.

Jackson, MS (Trailways terminal), July 5, 1961

Name	Race	Sex	Age	Residence	Occupation or Status
BASS, ROBERT EARL	B	M	18	Jackson, MS	Student, Lanier High School

Father was a porter. Mother was a maid.

Name	Race	Sex	Age	Residence	Occupation or Status
FLOYD, RALPH	B	M	18	Jackson, MS	Student, Lanier High School

Father was a construction worker.

Name	Race	Sex	Age	Residence	Occupation or Status
LEE, EUGENE	B	M	18	Jackson, MS	Student, Lanier High School

Father was a construction worker. Mother owned a beauty shop.

Jackson, MS (Trailways terminal), July 5, 1961

Name	Race	Sex	Age	Residence	Occupation or Status
BENNETT, MARSHALL	B	M	18	Jackson, MS	Employed at the Vogue
GREEN, MILLER G., JR.	B	M	18	Jackson, MS	Employed at the Dollar Store
GREEN, ROBERT LEE	B	M	18	Jackson, MS	Student, Lanier High School

Father worked for a neon sign company.

HARRIS, JESSE L.	B	M	18	Jackson, MS	Caddy at a "Negro" golf course

See Carmichael, *Ready for Revolution*. Father was a brick mason. Mother was a maid. SNCC organizer in McComb, MS. Later a Nation of Islam minister in Jackson, MS.

JOHNSON, PERCY LEE	B	M	18	Jackson, MS	Student, Lanier High School
JONES, JAMES WILSON	B	M	18	Jackson, MS	Employed at Jitney Jungle

Jackson, MS (Illinois Central RR terminal), July 6, 1961

Name	Race	Sex	Age	Residence	Occupation or Status
CASTON, FRANK	B	M	18	Jackson, MS	Yard worker

Parents were cotton farmers in Raymond, MS.

GRIFFIN, FRANKIE LEE	B	M	21	Jackson, MS	Unemployed

Father worked for a lumber company. Mother worked at the Mississippi State Hospital in Whitfield.

PALMER, ALPHA ZARA	B	M	19	Jackson, MS	Student, Mississippi Vocational School (Itta Bena, MS)

Born in Mississippi on January 11, 1942. Father worked at Storkline. Mother was a school maid. Died in Chicago on November 7, 2003, at the age of 61.

PHILLIPS, WEST DAVIS	B	M	19	Jackson, MS	Mechanic, Tipton's Garage

He was married with two children in 1961. His stepfather owned Tipton's Garage.

WATTS, TOMMIE, JR.	B	M	17	Jackson, MS	Student, Brinkley High School
WELLS, MACK CHARLES	B	M	20	Jackson, MS	Unemployed

Jackson, MS (Greyhound terminal), July 6, 1961

Name	Race	Sex	Age	Residence	Occupation or Status
DENSON, ALFONZO, JR.	B	M	18	Jackson, MS	Student, James Hill High School
GIVENS, SAMUEL	B	M	16	Jackson, MS	Student, James Hill High School

One of nine children. Father worked at Dixie Cookie Co.

MCNAIR, LANDY, JR.	B	M	18	Jackson, MS	Student, Lanier High School

Born on October 29, 1943. Parents worked at a laundry. Field secretary for SNCC. Active in voter registration in Mississippi (1963–1964). Arrested at a Greenwood, MS, protest with comedian Dick Gregory. Arrested and jailed as a "Freedom Walker" in 1963 retracing slain activist William Moore's steps.

VANCE, EARL, JR.	B	M	19	Jackson, MS	Employed by Midwest Ice Cream Co.

WATKINS, HEZEKIAH	B	M	13	Jackson, MS	Student, Rowan Junior High School

Graduated from Lanier High School in 1965 and attended Utica Junior College until he was drafted into the military in 1966, Served two years in Vietnam and Korea. Owns a store in Jackson, MS, named Corner Food Market and Deli. Remains active as a community volunteer and local events organizer.

YOUNG, PAUL EDWARD	B	M	16	Jackson, MS	Student, James Hill High School

Montgomery, AL, to Jackson, MS (Trailways), July 7, 1961

Name	Race	Sex	Age	Residence	Occupation or Status
BIGGERS, CHARLES	B	M	21	Lamar, CO	Student, Univ. of Colorado (Boulder, CO)

Born in Waggoner, OK, in May 1939.

BROWN, ELMER L.	B	M	20	Akron, OH	Engineering student, Univ. of Akron

Born in Akron, OH, in November 1940.

HANSEN, WILLIAM WALTER, JR.	W	M	21	Cincinnati, OH	Student, Xavier Univ. (Cincinnati, OH)

Born in Cincinnati, OH, in July 1939. SNCC field secretary in Arkansas (1962).

LOWRY, JOHN	W	M	20	New York, NY	Student, Queens College (New York, NY); sales trainer

See chapter 10. Born in New York City in April 1941. Served three years in the army. Participant in Monroe, NC, Freedom Ride.

MATZKIN, NORMA	W	M	27	New York, NY	Elementary school teacher, New York City public schools

Born in New York City in November 1933. Union activist affiliated with United Federation of Teachers. Ended her career as a librarian at John F. Kennedy High School in the Bronx, NY.

REYNOLDS, ISAAC, JR. (IKE)	B	M	27	Detroit, MI	Student, Wayne State Univ.; CORE field secretary.

See May 17–21 Ride.

STEVENS, DANIEL	W	M	19	Saginaw, MI	Student, Wilmington College (Wilmington, OH)

Born in Ohio in May 1942.

THOMAS, WILLIE JAMES	B	M	20	Cincinnati, OH	Student, Ohio State Univ. (Columbus, OH)

Born in Cincinnati, OH, in July 1940.

Jackson, MS (Illinois Central RR terminal), July 7, 1961

Name	Race	Sex	Age	Residence	Occupation or Status
SLATER, MORTON BRUCE	W	M	18	New York, NY	Student, CCNY

Born in New York City in April 1943. In 1986 he co-founded Gateway, a program dedicated to preparing low-income and minority students in New York City public schools for careers in medicine, engineering, or other science-related fields.

New Orleans, LA, to Jackson, MS (Illinois Central RR), July 9, 1961

Name	Race	Sex	Age	Residence	Occupation or Status
BASKERVILLE, PATRICIA DALE	B	F	18	Tucson, AZ	Nurse's aide

Born in Tucson, AZ, in June 1943.

Name	Race	Sex	Age	Residence	Occupation or Status
BELL, LARRY	B	M	19	Los Angeles, CA	Plasterer

Born in Monroe, GA, in March 1942.

Name	Race	Sex	Age	Residence	Occupation or Status
BRASHEAR, TOMMIE ELDRIDGE	B	M	19	Los Angeles, CA	Maintenance worker

Born in New Iberia, LA, in September 1941.

Name	Race	Sex	Age	Residence	Occupation or Status
DALBERT, EDMOND, JR.	B	M	25	Los Angeles, CA	Postal clerk

Born in Hamlin, TX, in January 1936. Attended LA City College.

Name	Race	Sex	Age	Residence	Occupation or Status
JACKSON, REGINALD	B	M	21	Los Angeles, CA	Costume designer

Born in Houston, TX, in June 1940.

Name	Race	Sex	Age	Residence	Occupation or Status
JOHNSON, EDWARD B.	B	M	19	Los Angeles, CA	Student, Univ. of Texas (Austin, TX)

Born in Houston, TX, in October 1941.

Name	Race	Sex	Age	Residence	Occupation or Status
PERKINS, PHILIP JONATHAN	W	M	20	College Park, MD	Student, Ohio Wesleyan Univ. (Delaware, OH)

Born in Washington, DC, in October 1940.

Name	Race	Sex	Age	Residence	Occupation or Status
RAND, ROENA	B	F	29	Los Angeles, CA	Internal Revenue clerk

Born in Cleveland, OH, in March 1932. Member of CORE and the NAACP. Currently lives in Washington, DC.

Name	Race	Sex	Age	Residence	Occupation or Status
TAYLOR, JOHN CHARLES, JR.	B	M	26	Berkeley, CA	Pharmacy clerk

Born in Houston in June 1935. Moved to Oakland, CA, in 1940. Father worked at Naval Supply Center. Mother was a nurse. Attended San Francisco City College and San Francisco State Univ. (B.A.). Active in San Francisco Bay area sit-ins. Berkeley CORE chair. Long career as a lobbyist for black professional organizations, primarily in DC, California, Michigan, and New York. Currently lives in Hercules, CA.

Montgomery, AL, to Jackson, MS (Trailways), July 9, 1961

Name	Race	Sex	Age	Residence	Occupation or Status
BURKHOLDER, DANIEL E.	W	M	29	Chicago, IL	Businessman for CORE; lecturer

Born in Chicago in February 1932. Member of CORE and the NAACP.

| GOLDBART, LIONEL | W | M | 27 | Brooklyn, NY | Laborer, odd jobs, poet |

Born in Brooklyn, NY, in May 1934. Attended Brooklyn College. A self-styled beatnik, poet, mathematician, and onetime talk show host. In the 1980s he appeared on the television trivia show *Jeopardy!* three times, winning over $30,000. He remains a poet and activist in Miami, FL.

| GORDON, ALBERT FORREST | W | M | 27 | New York, NY | History teacher, Tilden High School (Brooklyn, NY) |

Born in Belgium in June 1934. Graduate of the Univ. of Paris. Also attended CCNY and Columbia Univ. Organized labor unions for teachers and hospital workers and protested the Vietnam War in the early 1960s. Operated Tribal Arts Gallery in Manhattan and later became a nationally prominent wholesaler of African art. Served in the Peace Corps in West Africa. Political activist; published the *Peace Dividend* newsletter. Currently co-owner of Origins Gallery in Stockbridge, MA.

| GREENSTEIN, STEPHEN | W | M | 22 | Brooklyn, NY | Student, Brooklyn College |

Born in Brooklyn, NY, in November 1938.

| HERRICK, JEANNE H. | W | F | 28 | Chicago, IL | Housewife |

Born in Indianapolis, IN, in July 1933. Attended Vassar College, Indiana Univ., and the Univ. of Chicago.

| MANFIELD, SAUL BERNARD | W | M | 34 | Chicago, IL | Television factory worker |

Born in St. Paul, MN, on April 8, 1927. Died in Chicago on February 11, 2005, at the age of 77.

| ROGERS, RALPH ROBERT | W | M | 32 | New York, NY | English instructor, Douglas College, Rutgers University (New Brunswick, NJ) |

Born in Milwaukee, WI, in October 1928. Graduate of Columbia Univ. (M.A., Ph.D.).

| WHITE, LULA MAE | B | F | 22 | Chicago, IL | Teacher, James Ward School |

Born in Eufaula, AL, in December 1938. Graduate of Univ. of Chicago.

Jackson, MS (Trailways station), July 9, 1961

Name	Race	Sex	Age	Residence	Occupation or Status
BLUE, LEO VONE	B	M	14	Jackson, MS	High school student

Born in Jackson, MS, in September 1946. Died December 1988 in New Haven, CT, at the age of 42.

BLUE, MILDRED JUANITA	B	F	16	Jackson, MS	Student, Lanier High School

Born in Hinds County, MS, on April 23, 1945. Died December 25, 1993, in Waterbury, CT, at the age of 48.

CLARK, FRED DOUGLAS	B	M	18	Jackson, MS	Student, Lanier High School

Born in Birmingham in May 1943. Attended Jackson State Univ. (B.A. and grad. work). Eclectic work career includes stints as a golf caddy, construction worker, educator, security guard, park ranger, deputized U.S. marshal, and assistant prison policeman. Currently lives in Jackson, MS, where he remains active in church, community, and political affairs.

DAVIS, JESSIE JAMES	B	M	19	Jackson, MS	Unemployed

Born in Jackson, MS, in August 1941. Graduate of Lanier High School. Active as a SNCC organizer in the mid-1960s. Currently lives in Fishkill, NY.

HAYES, GAINNEL	B	F	15	Jackson, MS	Student, Rowan Junior High School

Born in Jackson, MS, in March 1946.

HORNE, ANDREW, JR.	B	M	15	Jackson, MS	Student, Lanier High School

Born in Jackson, MS, in September 1945.

HORNE, ERMA LEE	B	F	16	Jackson, MS	Student, Holy Ghost High School

Born in Jackson, MS, in October 1944.

LYNCH, DELORES WILLIAMS	B	M	15	Jackson, MS	Student, Lanier High School

Born in Hinds County, MS, in February 1946. Deceased.

ROSELL, HENRY	B	M	18	Jackson, MS	Student

Born in Hinds County, MS, in February 1943.

VANCE, ONEAL	B	M	17	Jackson, MS	Employed by Holiday Inn restaurant

Born in Flora, MS, in March 1944.

WATTS, JOE, JR.	B	M	18	Jackson, MS	Student, Lanier High School

Born in Forest, MS, in July 1943. Died in Jackson, MS, on November 25, 2003, at the age of 60.

St. Louis, MO, via Little Rock, AR, to New Orleans, LA, July 8–15, 1961

Name	Race	Sex	Age	Residence	Occupation or Status
COX, BENJAMIN ELTON	B	M	30	High Point, NC	Minister, Pilgrim Congregational Church; CORE field secretary

See May 4–17 Ride.

LUMPKIN, ANNIE	B	F	18	St. Louis, MO	Student

MALONE, BLISS ANNE	B	F	23	St. Louis, MO	Public school teacher

RAINES, JOHN CURTIS	W	M	27	Long Island, NY	Pastor, Setauket Methodist Church (Long Island, NY)

Graduate of Carleton College, Northfield, MN (B.A., 1955) and Union Theological Seminary (B.D., 1959, Ph.D., 1967). Published *Attack on Privacy* (1974), *Illusion of Success* (1975), and *Marx on Religion* (2002). Long career as a professor of religion at Temple Univ. in Philadelphia. Research and teaching specialties include globalization, social justice, and Islam and the West.

REINITZ, JANET	W	F	23	New York, NY	Artist, homemaker

Attended Connecticut College. Rochester CORE chair. Worked at national CORE office in 1961–1962. Painter and muralist in New York City. In the late 1980s she painted the mural *An Interracial Journey,* based on experiences of slain civil rights workers Goodman, Schwerner, and Chaney.

New York, NY, via Chattanooga, TN, to Little Rock, AR, July 13–24, 1961

Name	Race	Sex	Age	Residence	Occupation or Status
HARVARD, JOHN C.	B	M	39	Elizabeth, NJ	Psychologist

Born September 8, 1921. Graduate of Howard Univ., where he was class president. During the 1950s and early 1960s, he was an active member of the Elizabeth, NJ, Area Council on Housing, the Elizabeth Good Neighbor Council, the Board of Directors for the New Jersey Committee Against Discrimination in Housing, the Rutgers University Committe on Human Relations, and the Howard University Alumni Assoc. Died in Elizabeth, NJ, in January 1986, at the age of 64.

SHANKEN, SIDNEY	W	M	39	Cranford, NJ	Rabbi; graduate student, Jewish Theological Seminary of New York

Born in St. Louis, MO, on May 1, 1922. Moved to San Antonio, TX, at age 7 and later attended Univ. of Texas. Served in army air corps as B-25 navigator, 1942–1945. Severely wounded at Anzio, Italy. Graduate of NYU (B.A., 1949) and Jewish Institute of Religion (M. Hebrew Lit., 1949). Long career as conservative rabbi, primarily at Temple Beth El in Cranford, NJ (1957–1982). Participated in Selma to Montgomery march and served on Mayor's Council on Housing in Cranford. Lived in Israel (1982–1984). Rabbi in Pottstown, PA (1984–1994). Currently active in Volunteers for Israel and lives in Boynton Beach, FL.

SMITH, WOOLLCOTT	W	M	20	Vineyard Haven, MA	Student, Michigan State Univ. (East Lansing, MI)

Son of Michigan State Univ. psychology professor. Nephew of historian Francis Jennings. Currently professor of statistics at Temple Univ. Senior fellow in the Marine Policy Center at the Woods Hole Oceanographic Institution. Co-authored *The Cartoon Guide to Statistics* with cartoonist Larry Gonick.

STERN, HERMAN (CHAIM) S.	W	M	30	River Edge, NJ	Rabbi, Temple Shalom; Hebrew instructor, Hebrew Union College, School of Sacred Music

Graduate of City College of New York (B.A., 1952), and Hebrew Union College (M.A., 1958). Edited and authored numerous Judaic prayer books used by American Reform Movement congregations. President Bill Clinton quoted one of Stern's contrition passages during the Monica Lewinsky sex scandal. Served as senior rabbi at Temple Beth El of Northern Westchester in Chappaqua, NY, for thirty-three years. Retired to Miami. Died in 2001 of a malignant brain tumor at the age of 71.

THOMAS, HENRY (HANK)	B	M	19	Elton, FL	Student, Howard Univ.; CORE staff

See May 4–17 Ride.

New Orleans, LA, to Jackson, MS (Greyhound), July 15, 1961

Name	Race	Sex	Age	Residence	Occupation or Status
BARBER, CARROLL GARY	W	M	36	Los Angeles, CA	Research associate, UCLA

Born in Geneva, IL, in August 1924. Graduate of the Univ. of Arizona (M.A.). Co-author of *Bilingualism in the Southwest* (1973). Died May 1999 in Tucson, AZ, at the age of 75.

BOOTH, CHARLES HENRY	B	M	18	Los Angeles, CA	Unemployed

Born in Little Rock, AR, in May 1943.

COOPER, RAY ALLEN	W	M	19	Spokane, WA	Artist

Born in Seattle in January 1942.

EISENBERG, MARILYN IRENE	W	F	18	Van Nuys, CA	Student, UCLA

Born in Philadelphia in August 1942.

OWENS, ROBERT LEWIS	B	M	23	Los Angeles, CA	Unemployed hospital orderly

Born in Springfield, IL, in May 1938.

PESTANA, JEAN ESTIL KIDWELL	W	F	43	Los Angeles, CA	Attorney

Born in San Francisco in August 1917. In 1969 she represented two members of Friends of the Black Panther Party accused of buying hand grenades for the Black Panthers' use. On other occasions she served as part of the Black Panthers' legal defense team. Active member of the U.S.–China Peoples' Friendship Association (USCPFA). Died in Los Angeles in September 1997, at the age of 80.

RICHARDS, DAVID LERING	W	M	22	Reseda, CA	Carpenter

Born in New York City in June 1939. Attended Pierce College (Woodland Hills, CA).

ROSENBERG, ROSE SCHORR	W	F	56	Los Angeles, CA	Attorney

Born in Hungary in September 1905.

RUSS, LEON, JR.	B	M	23	Los Angeles, CA	Unemployed

Born in Shreveport, LA, in June 1938. Attended Frank Wiggins Trade School (Los Angeles, CA).

WASHINGTON, LEO VERNON   B   M   24   New Orleans, LA   Student, Southern Univ. (New Orleans, LA)

Born in New Orleans in January 1937.

WILLIAMS, DOUGLAS ALBERT   B   M   38   Los Angeles, CA   Minister

Born in Cincinnati, OH, in September 1922. Attended College of Religion (Los Angeles, CA). Died in Los Angeles in May 1979, at the age of 56.

WOLFSON, JACK MIKHAIL   W   M   17   Los Angeles, CA   Student, UCLA

Born in Chicago, IL, on July 20, 1943. Moved to Los Angeles, CA, at the age of 9. Grew up in integrated neighborhoods with a radical family—both his mother and stepfather were members of the Communist Party. His sister Charlene was a member of the Central Committee of the CPUSA and was in Russia at the time of the Freedom Rides. Graduate of UCLA (B.S., chemistry, 1966) and Univ. of California, Riverside (Ph.D., chemistry, 1974). Worked with the Harvard School of Public Health since 1974 researching the relationship between air pollution and human health.

Nashville, TN, to Jackson, MS (Greyhound), July 16, 1961

Name	Race	Sex	Age	Residence	Occupation or Status
DENNIS, JAMES EMERSON[t]	B	M	25	Los Angeles, CA	Student, Los Angeles State College

Born in Hammond, TX, in October 1935. Graduate of Los Angeles State College (B.A., 1961) and California State Univ., Northridge (M.A., 1977). Member of CORE national board (1967–1972). Professor of pan-African studies at California State, Northridge (1969–2003). Currently lives in Lake View Terrace, CA.

FREELON, MARY	W	F	42	Telford, PA	Unemployed teacher

Born in Bensenville, IL, on April 2, 1919. Attended Northern Illinois State Teachers College. Died in Bensenville in July 1982, at the age of 63.

HAVEY, PHILLIP JAY	W	M	31	Staten Island, NY	Political editor, *The Catholic Worker*

Born in New Rochelle, NY, in June 1930. Graduate of Iona College (New Rochelle, NY).

MITARITONNA, RUDOLPH	W	M	50	Bronx, NY	Mortuary caretaker, New York City Dept. of Hospitals; municipal union member

Born in Argentina in October 1910. Member of the NAACP. Died in Queens, NY, in 1980, at the age of 79.

SMITH, SHIRLEY B.	W	F	34	New York, NY	Committee director

Born in Detroit in January 1927. Graduate of George Washington Univ. Attended Boston Univ.

SVANOE, WILLARD HOOKER	W	F	23	New York, NY	Graduate Student, Univ. of Minnesota

Born in Wilmington, DE, on January 16, 1938. Graduate of Oberlin College (B.F.A., 1959). Attended Univ. of Minnesota as a grad. student in economics (1960–1961). Folk singer, songwriter, and member of the folk trio The Rooftop Singers (1962–1969). Performed at the

1963 Newport Folk Festival and recorded the hit single "Walk Right In" the same year. Active in anti-war movement in late 1960s. Later career as a screenwriter, playwright, and producer. Television and movie credits include *Six Million Dollar Man, Waltz Across Texas,* and *Fatal Beauty.* Currently lives in Carboro, NC, as an adjunct prof. of dramatic arts at UNC, Chapel Hill.

WARREN, JAMES EDWARD	B	M	28	Philadelphia, PA	Baptist minister

Born in Cincinnati, OH, in November 1932. Graduate of Florida Normal College.

ZUCHMAN, LEWIS RICHARD	W	M	19	Forest Hills, NY	Student, Univ. of Bridgeport (Bridgeport, CT)

Born in the Bronx, NY, in March 1942. Founder of Bridgeport, CT, CORE. Social worker and founder of the Lenox Hill Neighborhood Association. Advocate for low-income residents in New York City. Currently executive director of Supportive Children's Advocacy Network (SCAN), a group of community-based family and children's centers in East Harlem, the South Bronx, and Morrisania.

Jackson, MS (airport), July 21, 1961

Name	Race	Sex	Age	Residence	Occupation or Status
CAREY, JAMES T.	W	M	35	Berkeley, CA	President, Catholic Interracial Council

Born in Chicago in August 1925. Graduate of the Univ. of Illinois and Columbia Univ.

GEDDES, FRANCIS L.	W	M	38	San Francisco, CA	Minister

Born in Oakland, CA, in July 1923. Graduate of Stanford Univ. Helped to rebuild a burned church in Mississippi in 1964 and participated in the Selma-to-Montgomery march in 1965. As a United Church of Christ minister, he served congregations in the San Francisco Bay area from the 1960s until his retirement in 1995. Currently provides spiritual direction for students at the Theological Seminary in San Anselmo, CA.

GUMBINER, JOSEPH HENRY	W	M	54	Orinda, CA	Rabbi, Hillel Foundation at the Univ. of California, Berkeley

Born in Pittsfield, IL, on September 4, 1906. Attended Univ. of Cincinnati, Univ. of Arizona, Yale Univ., and Hebrew Univ. in Jerusalem. Author of *Leaders of Our People* (1963). Died in Reseda, CA, on March 24, 1993, at the age of 86.

JORGENSEN, MARY L.	W	F	45	Berkeley, CA	Member of the American Friends Service Committee

Born in Bippus, IN, in July 1916. Graduate of Manchester College (Manchester, IN), and Pacific School of Religion (Berkeley, CA). Committed Quaker activist and frequent speaker and coordinator for the Friends Committee on Legislation, a group she and her husband, Russell, helped found in the early 1950s. Lives in Monan's Rill, an intentional community in northern California created in the 1970s by and for social theorists and activists.

JORGENSEN, RUSSELL F.	W	M	44	Berkeley, CA	Member of the American Friends Service Committee

Born in Racine, WI, in June 1917. Graduate of Univ. of Wisconsin and Pacific School of Religion. See also Mary Jorgensen bio.

LEVINE, ALLAN	W	M	28	Bradford, PA	Rabbi

See Interfaith Freedom Ride, June 13–16.

LUSTER, ORVILLE B. B M 36 Daly City, CA Member of the American Friends Service Committee

Born in Oklahoma City, OK, in May 1925. World War II veteran. Graduate of San Francisco State College (B.A., 1953). Began social work career as first African American counselor at Log Cabin Ranch in San Francisco (1956). Executive director of Youth for Service (1959–1973, 1994–2005), a San Francisco Bay area organization that helps students and disadvantaged young people develop career and vocational skills. Became chairman of Luster CM, a construction management firm, in 1990. In 1997, on the 40th anniversary of Youth for Service, San Francisco mayor Willie Brown presided at a banquet honoring Luster's contributions to the city's youth. Died in San Francisco on June 27, 2005, at the age of 80.

SELLERS, CHARLES W M 28 Berkeley, CA Professor of history, Univ. of
G., JR. California, Berkeley

Born in Charlotte, NC, in September 1923. Graduate of Harvard Univ. and Univ. of North Carolina (Ph.D.). Distinguished career as professor of Southern history at the Univ. of California, Berkeley. Editor of *The Southerner as American* and author of *Market Revolution: Jacksonian America, 1815–1846*, among other books. Currently lives in Berkeley, CA.

WASHINGTON, B M 32 San Francisco, CA Minister
JOHN R.

Born in Pittsburgh, PA, in September 1928. Graduate of the Univ. of Pittsburgh and Andover-Newton Seminary. Longtime pastor of the Claremont United Church of Christ in Claremont, CA. Currently in retirement in Claremont.

Nashville, TN, via Memphis, TN, to Jackson, MS (Greyhound), July 21, 1961

Name	Race	Sex	Age	Residence	Occupation or Status
BREINES, PAUL	W	M	20	Scarsdale, NY	Student and member of the Student Council on Civil Rights, Univ. of Wiconsin, Madison

Born in New York City in April 1941. Graduate of the Univ. of Wisconsin (B.A., 1963; Ph.D., 1972). Currently professor of history at Boston College. Author of *Tough Jews: Political Fantasies and the Moral Dilemma of American Jewry* (1990) and *Without Impact: A History of Ideas Whose Time Never Came* (2005).

| GARDE, DONNA SAGE | W | F | 25 | New York, NY | Public school teacher |

Born in Middletown, CT, in December 1935. Graduate of Syracuse Univ.

| GREENBERG, JOEL BEN | W | M | 22 | Baltimore, MD | Student, Loyola College (Baltimore, MD) |

Born in Baltimore in February 1939. Attended St. John's College (Annapolis, MD).

| MOSKOWITZ, RUTH ESTHER | W | F | 25 | Brooklyn, NY | Sociology researcher, New York Univ. (New York City) |

Born in New York City in May 1936. Graduate of Brooklyn College (B.A., 1957). Volunteered for the New York Committee Against Discrimination in Housing (1959). Attended Univ. of Connecticut and New York Univ. Appointed to the Brooklyn Supreme Court in 1982. During a high-profile 1988 case involving parking-meter collector fraud, she admonished New York City mayor Edward Koch for trying to bring attention to the proceedings for political reasons. A popular judge, she was reelected in November 1996 despite her recent death. Died of scleroderma on November 2, 1996, at the age of 60.

Nashville, TN, via Memphis, TN,
to Jackson, MS (Trailways), July 23, 1961

Name	Race	Sex	Age	Residence	Occupation or Status
HUDDLESTON, ALBERT ROY	W	M	32	San Francisco, CA	

Born in Avoca, PA, in June 1929. Jewish.

| IHRA, MARGARET | W | F | 22 | New York, NY | Student, City College of New York |

Born in Darby, PA, in October 1938. Married Freedom Rider Alexander Weiss.

| LALL, CANDIDA | W | F | 18 | Larkspur, CA | Student, Long Beach State College (Long Beach, CA) |

Born in San Francisco in November 1942.

| LINDER, MORTON G. | W | M | 23 | San Francisco, CA | Student, Univ. of Pennsylvania (Philadelphia) |

Born in Philadelphia, PA, on January 30, 1938. Graduate of Penn State Univ. (B.A., 1959) and Univ. of PA (Veterinary Medicine, 1961). Received notification that he had passed the California veterinary exam while he was in Parchman prison. CORE fund-raiser 1961–1962. Veterinary practice in San Francisco and Berkeley, CA, 1961–1969. Lived in Europe, 1972–1975. Varied career as a part-time veterinarian and bicycle repairman, 1982–1991. Currently a fabricator of custom bicycle wheels living in Point Reyes Station, CA.

| POWELL, MICHAEL HARRY | W | M | 20 | San Jose, CA | Student, San Jose State College (San Jose, CA) |

Born in Sacramento, CA in October 1940. Attended U. S. Maritime Academy (Kings Point, NY).

| WEISS, ALEXANDER | W | M | 25 | Daly City, CA | Student, San Francisco State College (San Francisco, CA) |

Born in Vienna, Austria, in May 1936. Migrated to America in 1940. Married Freedom Rider Margaret Ihra. California state park ranger for 17 years. In 1970, he spearheaded a movement to preserve the Angel Island Immigration Station (now a National Historic Landmark) in San Francisco.

| WILLIAMS, RALPH ALAN | W | M | 26 | San Francisco, CA | Artist |

Born in San Francisco, CA, on August 4, 1924. Attended California College of Arts and Crafts (Oakland). A lifelong civil rights and civil liberties activist. In a documentary on HUAC, he appears as a protester being dragged down the steps of San Francisco's City Hall. Advocate for the homeless. Active member of the San Francisco African American Historical Cultural Society. Died in San Francisco on July 1, 1995, at the age of 70.

Montgomery, AL, to Jackson, MS (airport), July 24, 1961

Name	Race	Sex	Age	Residence	Occupation or Status
PETWAY, ALPHONSO KELLY	B	M	16	Montgomery, AL	Student, Washington High School (Pensacola, FL)

Born in Pensacola, FL, in January 1945. Son of Reverend Matthew Petway and brother of Kredelle Petway. Post–Freedom Ride involvement in sit-ins in Alabama and Kentucky. Currently pastor of Asbury Chapel AME Zion Church in Pascagoula, MS.

Name	Race	Sex	Age	Residence	Occupation or Status
PETWAY, KREDELLE	B	F	20	Montgomery, AL	Student, Florida A & M University (Tallahassee)

Born in Camden, AL, on June 9, 1941. Daughter of Rev. Matthew Petway and sister of Alphonso Petway. Member of the MIA and active in both Montgomery and Tallahassee sit-ins (early 1960s). Graduate of Florida A & M Univ. (B.A., mathematics, 1972). Worked for the Louisville Urban League (1973–1974), U.S. Dept. of the Treasury (1975–1979), and the U.S. Dept. of Veterans Affairs (1967–1973, 1979–1986). Promoted equal opportunity employment practices. Retired on December 31, 1999. Currently lives in St. Petersburg, FL.

Name	Race	Sex	Age	Residence	Occupation or Status
PETWAY, MATTHEW	B	M	46	Montgomery, AL	AME Zion minister

Born in Camden, AL, in July 1915. Father of Alphonso and Kredelle Petway. Graduate of Alabama State College (Montgomery). NAACP activist. Died in Louisville, KY, in July 1972, at the age of 57.

Name	Race	Sex	Age	Residence	Occupation or Status
THOMAS, CECIL A.	W	M	44	Albany, CA	YMCA secretary (Berkeley, CA)

Born in Frankfort, OH, on June 14, 1917. Attended Cedarville (Cedarville, OH), Ohio State Univ. (Columbus, OH), Northwestern Univ. (Evanston, IL), and Fisk Univ. (Nashville). Died in August 1969, at the age of 52.

Nashville, TN, to Jackson, MS (Greyhound), July 29, 1961

Name	Race	Sex	Age	Residence	Occupation or Status
BAER, BYRON MARK	W	M	31	Englewood, NJ	Motion picture technician

Born in Pittsburgh, PA, in October 1929. Attended Cornell Univ. (Ithaca, NY). New Jersey state representative (1972–1993) and state senator (1994–2005). Member of state Martin Luther King, Jr., Commission (2002–2004). Senate leader ex officio and chair of senate commerce committee (2004–2005). Currently lives in Hackensack, NJ.

Name	Race	Sex	Age	Residence	Occupation or Status
PABEL, HILMAR EHRENFRIED	W	M	50	Munich, Germany	Journalist, *Quick* magazine

Born in Rawitsch, Germany, in September 1910. Attended Univ. of Berlin. Worked as independent photo-journalist for *Life*, *Paris Match*, *Epoca*, *Stern*, and *Quick* magazines. Photographed a number of important historical events, including Soviet tanks rolling into Prague in 1968 and "boat people" leaving Vietnam in the 1970s. Died in Germany on November 6, 2000, at the age of 90.

Name	Race	Sex	Age	Residence	Occupation or Status
PRENSKY, CATHERINE JO	W	F	18	New Rochelle, NY	Student, Univ. of Wisconsin, Madison

Born in New York City in June 1943. Jewish.

ROWLEY, SALLY JANE   W   F   29   New York City, NY   Secretary, Merrill Sharpe Co.

Born in Trenton, NJ, in October 1931. Attended Stevens College (Columbia, MO).

SCROGGINS, JUDITH   B   F   18   Cincinnati, OH   Secretary, NAACP branch office
NORENE

Born in Middleton, OH, in October 1942. Attended Xavier Univ. (Cincinnati, OH). Misidentified as a white Freedom Rider by Mississippi officials. Currently lives in Whitakers, NC. Married name: Judith Thomas.

SHEVIAKOV, RICK   W   M   18   Berkeley, CA   Student, San Francisco State
STANLEY   Univ.

Born in Chicago, IL, in February 1943. Raised in Berkeley, CA. Participated with the American Friends Service Committee protesting housing discrimination (1950s). Graduate of Univ. of Wisconsin (B.S., M.S., Ph.D. in school psychology). Psychologist for the Marin Country, CA, public school system. Currently lives in San Anselmo, CA.

SMITH, WOOLLCOTT   W   M   20   East Lansing,MI   Student, Michigan State Univ.

See July 13–29 Ride.

TJOKROADISUNATTO,   A   M   24   Seattle, WA   Student, Univ. of Washington
WIDJONAIKO   (Seattle)

See chapter 9. Son of Indonesian diplomat. Currently chief executive of PT Ramashinta Citra Kreasi and chairman of the Indonesian Toys Industry Association.

WAGNER, NORMA   W   F   44   Rochester, NY   Blind activist

See chapter 9.

ZISKIND, ELLEN LEE   W   F   21   New York, NY   Student, Columbia Univ.

Born in Lowell, MA, on September 5, 1939. Raised in a Conservative Jewish family. Attended Cambridge School of Weston, MA, and Antioch College (Yellow Springs, OH) (1957–1960). Graduate of Columbia Univ. (B.A., English, 1962), Harvard Univ. (M.Ed., 1966), and Simmons College (M.S.W., 1977). Worked with black journalist Louis Lomax on Freedom Rider benefit concert in June 1961. Worked at WBAI radio in NY City (1962–1964) and studied at Mass. General dyslexic clinic (1966–1967). Psych. social worker at Quincy, MA, community mental health clinics (1977–1986) and later in a private practice devoted to group therapy and adult trauma. Currently lives in Brookline, MA.

New Orleans, LA, to Jackson, MS
(Illinois Central RR), July 30, 1961

Name	Race	Sex	Age	Residence	Occupation or Status
BAROUGH, ALBERT	W	M	21	Los Angeles, CA	Student, UCLA

Born in New York City in June 1940. Died in a TWA plane crash near Chicago on September 1, 1961.

FULLER, WINSTON	W	M	24	Los Angeles, CA	Graduate student, UCLA

Born in Los Angeles in July 1937. Graduate of UCLA (B.A., 1961) and the Univ. of Colorado (M.A., 1965). Accomplished poet and author of *Twelve Poems* (1972). Currently professor of English and creative writing at West Virginia University (Morgantown), where he has taught since 1965.

GERBAC, JOSEPH   W   M   21   Los Angeles, CA   Student, UCLA
EDWARD

Born in Chicago, IL, in October 1939. Moved to Los Angeles, CA, at the age of 12. Father was a Croatian immigrant and member of the Communist Party. Graduate of UCLA (B.A., history, 1962) and UCLA Law School (J.D., 1965). Worked as an attorney in Los Angeles (late 1960s–early 1980s) and later in northern Santa Barbara County (late 1980s–2005). Currently lives in Lompoc, CA.

GRUBBS, MICHAEL R.   B   M   25   Los Angeles, CA   Student, UCLA

Born in Coffeeville, KS, on October 23, 1935. Son of longtime black women's and YWCA activist Darnell Medlock Grubbs. Member of the Urban League and NAACP. Studied psychology at UCLA. Remained involved in politics through his wife Thelma Jones's activism in PUSH and women's rights. Career in business consulting, real estate, and private business. Cousin of noted historian John Hope Franklin. Currently retired and living in Los Angeles.

KAUFMAN, ALAN   W   M   21   Berkeley, CA   Student, Univ. of California
                                                    (Berkeley, CA)

Born in Riverside, CA, in July 1940.

LEONS, WILLIAM   W   M   26   Los Angeles, CA   Graduate student, UCLA

Born in Rotterdam, Netherlands, in August 1935. Currently a professor of anthropology at the University of Toledo (Toledo, OH). Specialist in Latin American, peasant, immigrant, and Southeast Asian studies.

MANN, HERBERT S.   W   M   35   Los Angeles, CA   Postal worker

Born in Steinbach Connersberg, Germany, in August 1925. Attended Los Angeles City College. Spokesman for CORE in Los Angeles. Led protests against housing discrimination in Los Angeles in the mid-1960s. Died in Pasadena, CA, on June 5, 2003, at the age of 77.

PAVESIC, MAX   W   M   21   Los Angeles, CA   Student, UCLA
GREGORY

Born in Chicago, IL, in August 1939. Raised in Los Angeles, Graduate of Los Angeles City College (A.A., 1959), UCLA (B.A., 1962), and Univ. of Colorado (M.A., 1966, and Ph.D., 1971). Taught anthropology at Idaho State (1967–1971) and Boise State Univ. (1978–2001). Author of *Backtracking: Ancient Art of Southern Idaho* (1993) and co-editor of *Stone Tool Analysis: Essays in Honor of Don E. Crabtree.* Currently serves as chair of the Idaho State Historical Society's Board of Trustees and president of the Great Basin Anthropological Assoc.

POSNER, PHILIP M.   W   M   22   Los Angeles, CA   Student, Hebrew Union College
                                                    (Hollywood, CA)

Born in Tucson, AZ, in December 1938. Grew up in Southern California. Graduate of UCLA (B.A., history, 1962) and Hebrew Union College (1968). Worked as an assistant to Rabbi Jack Rothschild in Atlanta (1968–1971). Spent most of his career as a rabbi at Temple Beth El in Riverside, CA, before moving to the Mizpah Congregation in Chattanooga, TN (1997–2002). Retired in 2002 and currently works as a part-time rabbi near Guadalajara, Mexico, spending his summers in San Antonio, TX.

SINGLETON, HELEN   B   F   28   Los Angeles, CA   Student, Santa Monica City
IRENE   College

See epilogue. Born in Philadelphia, PA, in November 1932. Wife of Freedom Rider Robert Singleton. Graduate of Moore Inst. of Art and Loyola Marymont Univ. (M. Arts Admin.). Artist and director of Los Angeles art gallery.

SINGLETON, ROBERT   B   M   25   Los Angeles, CA   Graduate Student, UCLA

See chapter 9 and epilogue. Born in Philadelphia, PA, in January 1936. Graduate of Reed College (Portland, OR, B.A.) and UCLA (Ph.D.). Husband of Freedom Rider Helen Singleton. Currently professor of economics and chairman of the Economics Dept. at Loyola Marymount Univ. (Los Angeles).

STEWARD, RICHARD C.   B   M   21   New Orleans, LA   Student, Dillard Univ. (New Orleans, LA)

Born in New Orleans in December 1939. Currently lives in Los Angeles.

THURMAN, LONNIE   B   M   34   Los Angeles, CA   Teacher

Born in Montgomery, AL, in December 1926. Graduate of Alabama State College (Montgomery).

TOWNSEND, SAM JOE   W   M   27   Los Angeles, CA   Graduate student, UCLA

Born in San Angelo, TX, on August 11, 1933. Graduate of UCLA (B.A.). Died in October 1971, at the age of 38.

WREN, TANYA   W   F   22   Los Angeles, CA   Student, Los Angeles City College

Born in Los Angeles in June 1939.

Jackson, MS (Greyhound terminal), July 31, 1961

Name	Race	Sex	Age	Residence	Occupation or Status
WAHLSTROM, JAMES ROBERT	W	M	22	Madison, WI	Former student, Univ. of Wisconsin, Madison

See June 6 Ride.

Shreveport, LA (Trailways terminal), August 4, 1961

Name	Race	Sex	Age	Residence	Occupation or Status
BETHUNE, HAROLD L.	B	M	34	Shreveport, LA	CORE activist

Born April 10, 1927. Exec. Sec. of Shreveport NAACP in 1963. Gubernatorial candidate in the 1971 Democratic primary in Louisiana. Died in September 1973, at the age of 46.

BLAKE, HARRY	B	M	26	Shreveport, LA	CORE, SCLC, and NAACP activist

Graduate of Bishop College (Dallas, TX). SCLC field secretary and president of Shreveport NAACP in early 1960s. Suffered several arrests and beatings in 1962–1963. Pastor of Mount Canaan Missionary Baptist Church in Shreveport since 1966. Organized community development projects, such as Canaan Village Apartments, Canaan Towers, Project Uplift House, and the Mount Canaan Baptist Church and Family Life Center.

DENNIS, DAVID J.	B	M	20	Shreveport, LA	CORE field secretary

See May 24 Ride.

McGinnie, Delores	B	F	Shreveport, LA	CORE activist
McGinnie, Marie	B	F	Shreveport, LA	CORE activist
Taylor, Levert H.	B	M 20	Shreveport, LA	CORE activist

Along with Dave Dennis and Joseph Russell, he was the primary organizer of the Shreveport CORE chapter. See also *Taylor v. Louisiana,* 370 U.S. 154 (1962).

Nashville, TN, via Memphis, TN, to Jackson, MS (Trailways terminal), August 5, 1961

Name	Race Sex Age	Residence	Occupation or Status
Bohannon, Earl C.	B M 21	Chicago, IL	Student
Wagner, Norma	W F 44	Rochester, NY	Blind activist

See July 29 Ride.

Houston, TX (Union Railway Station), August 9–11, 1961

Name	Race Sex Age	Residence	Occupation or Status
Berrard, Charles	B M 21	Los Angeles, CA	Student, Los Angeles State College

Born in Houston, TX, on February 12, 1940. Moved to California in 1952. Attended LA City College, LA State College, and LA Trade Tech School. Member of Ind. Student Union at LA City College and Youth for Peace and Socialism (1960–1963). Building contractor in California (1980–2005). Currently an artist living in Santa Cruz, CA.

Dunson, Marjorie	B F 30	Los Angeles, CA	

Jamaican citizen at the time of the Freedom Rides.

Farrell, Robert	B M 23	Los Angeles, CA	Graduate Student, UCLA

Born in Natchez, MS, on October 1, 1936. Lived in New Orleans, LA, and Newark, NJ, before moving to Los Angeles in 1952. Served in U.S. Navy (1954–1956) and attended UCLA (B.A., Near Eastern Studies, 1961) on an NROTC scholarship. Active member of UCLA NAACP and CORE, and helped found Catholics United for Racial Equality (CURE) in 1959. Reporter for the *California Eagle* and *LA Sentinel* and did graduate work in journalism at UCLA (1961–1963). Aide to LA City Councilman Billy Mills (1964–1973) and Mayor Tom Bradley (1973–1974). Served on LA City Council (1974–1991). Active as board member of Pacifica Radio Foundation, Trans-Africa, and other non-profit organizations since 1991. Recently active as political consultant in Belize and Guyana.

Hamilton, Herbert	B M 20	Houston, TX	Student, Texas Southern Univ.; First vice president of the Progressive Youth Assoc, Inc.

Born in Jasper County, TX, on September 20, 1940. Leader of Progressive Youth Assoc. demonstrations (early 1960s). Graduate of Texas Southern Univ. (B.A., mathematics and physics, 1964; M.A., mathematics, 1966). Completed doctoral coursework at Univ. of Houston (late 1960s). Mathematics instructor at Texas Southern Univ. (1966–1973) and Houston Community College (1973–present). Currently lives in Houston, where he has served as a Democratic precinct chairman since the mid-1990s.

| HANDY, WILLIE | B | M | 18 | Houston, TX | Student, Texas Southern Univ.; Progressive Youth Assoc. activist |

| HOGROBROOKS, HOLLY | B | M | 20 | Houston, TX | Student, Texas Southern Univ.; Progressive Youth Assoc. activist |

Born and raised in Houston, TX. Active in Houston civil rights movement. Graduate of Texas Southern Univ. (B.A., journalism, 1963). From 1963 to 1968, worked as a county clerk, wrote for black newspapers *The Informer* and *Forward Times,* and became active in politics. Worked for a public relations firm in the 1980s. Instructor of communications at Texas Southern Univ. (1968–1980, 1990–present). Currently lives in Houston.

| HUTCHINS, JOHN | B | M | 20 | Houston, TX | Student, Texas Southern Univ.; Progressive Youth Assoc. activist |

| JONES, EDDIE | B | M | 19 | Houston, TX | Student, Texas Southern Univ.; Progressive Youth Assoc. activist |

| JONES, ROBERT E. | B | M | 32 | Houston, TX | Progressive Youth Assoc. activist |

| KAUFMAN, ROBERT PAUL | W | M | 23 | Los Angeles, CA | US History Graduate Student, Univ. of California, Berkeley |

Born in California on January 27, 1938. A Communist-affiliated peace and justice activist and longtime columnist and staff reporter for the Berkeley, CA–based newspaper *People's World.* Died of cancer in Berkeley in July 1979, at the age of 41. Author of posthumously published *Selected Writings by Bob Kaufman* (1980).

| KLEINMAN, ELLEN | W | F | 19 | Los Angeles, CA | Student, Los Angeles City College |

Graduate of California State Univ., Los Angeles (B.A., 1967) and UCLA (M.S.W., 1979). Active in peace and women's movements. Social worker specializing in children's welfare. Worked with Child Protective Services and California Dept. of Social Services. Currently lives in Sacramento, CA, where she works with children with special needs. Active member of Grandmothers for Peace. Married name: Ellen Broms.

| KOVNER, PAT | W | F | 20 | Sherman Oaks, CA | Student, Univ. of California, Berkeley |

Founded a CORE chapter in Sherman Oaks, CA. Roommates at Univ. of California with fellow Freedom Rider Jorgia Seigel. Active in SLATE, a student political party in Berkeley. Participated in "Redwood Summer," an Earth First!–sponsored demonstration in 1990 organized to halt the logging of California's redwoods. Later served on the Green Party Council in Mendocino County. Currently an environmental activist promoting sustainability. Lives in rural Northern California on a self-sustaining farm.

| LA BOSTRIE, RONALD | B | M | 26 | Los Angeles, CA | Artist |

Born and raised in New Orleans, LA, in a Catholic family. Close friend of Robert Farrell's in 1961. During the late 1950s and early 1960s, he was an active member of Catholics United for Racial Equality (CURE), an organization devoted to the liberalization of the Los Angeles diocese. A painter and graphic artist who sometimes worked as a draftsman. Long involvement with California counter-culture. Deceased.

| McNICHOLS, STEVEN | W | M | 22 | Los Angeles, CA | Student, recent UCLA graduate |

Born in NY City in 1939. Graduate of UCLA (B.A., 1961), Univ. of Texas (M.A., economics, 1977), and Hastings College of Law (J.D., 1983). Served as civil rights director for the National Student Assoc. Worked for Los Angeles mayor's office in community development (mid-1970s), where he exposed corruption as a whistleblower. Later a San Francisco public sector employment attorney. Currently writing *The Last Freedom Ride: Life in the Tank,* a memoir of the California-to-Houston Ride.

| MOODY, MARIAN | B | F | 19 | Houston, TX | Membership chairman of the Progressive Youth Assoc. |

RADCLIFFE, BEVERLY W F 23 Los Angeles, CA Student, Los Angeles City College, X-ray technologist

Born in Edmonton, Alberta, Canada, in 1938. Attended Univ. of New Brunswick, St. John, LA City College, and San Francisco State. Member of the Ind. Student Union and CORE in Los Angeles. Active in organizing demonstrations for civil rights and peace movements. Subpoenaed and labeled a Communist by HUAC in 1961. Worked as an X-ray technologist until her retirement in 2004. Currently lives in Nelson, British Columbia, where she founded a chapter of the Raging Grannies, an activist group promoting global peace and social justice. Married name: Beverly Mill.

SANFIELD, STEVEN W M 24 Los Angeles, CA Night manager, Larry Edmonds Bookstore; writer.

Born in Cambridge, MA, on August 3, 1937. Raised in Lynn, MA, in a politically active left-wing family. Graduate of Univ. of Massachusetts (B.A., 1958). Worked for CBS Radio before employment at bookstore in 1961. Lived in Greece and the Mediterranean region for several years. Became a Buddhist and spent three years as a Zen monk in California. Long career as a poet, folklorist, and children's writer. Author of ten children's books—including *A Natural Man: The True Story of John Henry* (1986) and *The Adventures of High John the Conqueror* (1989), the story of a slave trickster—and a recent collection of poems, *The Rain Begins Below* (2005). Currently lives near Nevada City, CA.

STEVENSON, JOSEPH McCLENDON W M 18 Los Angeles, CA Student

Currently lives in Astoria, OR, where he has enjoyed a long career as a nurse practitioner involved with hospice.

Jackson, MS (Trailways terminal), August 13, 1961

Name	Race	Sex	Age	Residence	Occupation or Status
RAYMOND, GEORGE	B	M	18	New Orleans, LA	CORE activist

Born in Louisiana on January 1, 1943. Active in 1964 Freedom Summer voter registration drives. Worked closely with David Dennis in Sunflower County. Instrumental in Fannie Lou Hamer's early involvement in the movement. Suffered a severe beating in Canton, MS, in 1964. Died of a heart attack in March 1973, at the age of 30.

| SIMS, PAULINE K. | W | F | 22 | Putney, England | CORE activist |

In early December 1961, Sims testified at the trial of Anthony Thomas Davis, a black disc jockey in Dallas who she claimed had raped her in a hotel room there on September 28. After spending thirty days in a Jackson jail, she had met Davis in a café and had asked him to help her raise funds for CORE. Davis admitted that he had consensual relations with Sims but pled not guilty to the rape charge. He was acquitted on December 8.

Monroe, NC, August 17–September 1, 1961

Name	Race	Sex	Age	Residence	Occupation or Status
BAUM, ROBERT M.	W	M	19	Excelsior, MN	Student, Univ. of Minnesota

See June 11 Ride.

| BROMBERG, EDWARD J. | W | M | 27 | Chestnut Hill, MA | Student, Columbia Univ. |

See June 9 Ride.

BROOKS, PAUL	B	M	22	East St. Louis, IL	Student, American Baptist Theological Seminary

See May 17–21 Ride.

BUTLER, CHARLES	B	M	20	Charleston, SC	Student, Tennessee State Univ.

See May 17–21 Ride.

CHATHAM, PRICE	W	M	29	Rockaway, NY	Story analyst, 20th Century Fox and Paramount Pictures

See June 2 Ride.

DIETRICH, PAUL DAVID	W	M	29	Washington, DC	Office worker; restaurant owner; NAG activist

See May 24 Ride.

FORMAN, JAMES	B	M	32	Atlanta, GA	SNCC executive director

See Forman, *Making of Black Revolutionaries,* and chapter 10. Born October 4, 1928. An advocate of black reparations, he moved to Washington, DC, in 1981 to begin an African American news service. Published *Self-Determination: An Examination of the Question and Its Application to the African American People* in 1984. Active involvement in the Democratic Party during his later years. Attended 2004 Democratic national convention in Boston despite declining health. Died in Washington, DC, on January 10, 2005, at the age of 76.

GRISWOLD, RICHARD P.	W	M	34	Brooklyn, NY	Social worker

See June 10 Ride.

HUNTER, LARRY FRED	B	M	18	Atlanta, GA	Student, Tennessee State Univ.

See May 28 Ride.

KALE, EDWARD W.	W	M	24	Grangeville, ID	Student, Yale Divinity School

See June 7 Ride.

LEONARD, FREDERICK	B	M	18	Chattanooga, TN	Student, Tennessee State Univ.

See May 17–21 Ride.

LOWRY, JOHN	W	M	20	New York, NY	Student, Queens College (New York City)

See July 7 Ride.

MAHONEY, WILLIAM CARL	B	M	19	Washington, DC	Student, Howard Univ.; NAG activist

See May 28 Ride.

MCDONALD, JOSEPH JOHN MICHAEL	W	M	20	Oceanside, NY	Unemployed

See June 2 Ride.

MORTON, DAVID KERR	W	M	21	Jackson, WY	Folk singer, freelance writer

See June 11 Ride.

RUSH, HEATH CLIFF	W	M	20	Concord, NH	Student, Central State College
See June 9 Ride.					

SHILMAN, KENNETH MARTIN	W	M	18	Oceanside, NY	Unemployed
See June 2 Ride.					

THOMPSON, DANIEL RAY	W	M	26	Cleveland, OH	Student
See June 11 Ride.					

WRIGHT, LEROY GLENN	B	M	19	Nashville, TN	Student, Fisk Univ.
See May 24 Ride.					

Prayer Pilgrimage, New Orleans, LA, to Jackson, MS (Trailways), September 13, 1961

Name	Race	Sex	Age	Residence	Occupation or Status
AVERY, GILBERT S., III	W	M	30	Roxbury, MA	Episcopal priest, St. John's Episcopal Church (Roxbury, MA)

Born in May 1931. Episcopal Community Services director in the early 1990s in Philadelphia, PA.

BLOY, MYRON B., JR	W	M	35	Newton, MA	Episcopal chaplain, MIT (Cambridge, MA)

Born in Detroit on March 28, 1926. Published several books, including *The Crisis of Cultural Change: A Christian Viewpoint* (1965) and *Christian Identity on Campus* (1971). Died in January 1985, at the age of 58.

BREEDEN, JAMES PLEASANT	B	M	26	Boston, MA	Episcopal priest, St. James Church (Roxbury, MA)

Born in Minneapolis in October 1934. Director of the Commission on Church and Race of the Massachusetts Council of Churches in 1967 during the race riots in Boston. Recently retired as dean of the Tucker Foundation at Dartmouth College (Hanover, NH).

CROCKER, JOHN, JR.	W	M	37	Providence, RI	Episcopal priest, Cathedral of St. John's

Born in Oxford, England, in October 1923. Became rector of the Trinity Episcopal Church in Princeton, NJ, in 1977.

EVANS, JAMES WALKER	W	M	31	St. Clair, MO	Episcopal priest, St. James Episcopal Church (St. Clair, MO)

Born in Kirkwood, MO, in August 1930.

EVANS, JOHN MARVIN	B	M	36	Toledo, OH	Episcopal priest, All Saints Episcopal Church (Toledo, OH)

Born in Cincinnati, OH, in September 1925.

GORDON, QUINLAND REEVES	B	M	45	Washington, DC	Episcopal priest, Church of the Atonement (Washington, DC)

Born in Greenwich, CT, in June 1915. Died in Atlanta on January 3, 1990, at the age of 74.

JONES, JAMES GARRARD	W	M	34	Chicago, IL	Episcopal priest, St. Leonard's House (Chicago, IL)

Born in Oak Park, IL, in January 1927.

MORRIS, JOHN BURNETT	W	M	31	Atlanta, GA	Episcopal priest; secretary of the Episcopal Society for Cultural and Racial Unity

Born in Brunswick, GA, in February 1930.

PIERSON, ROBERT LAUGHLIN	W	M	35	New York, NY	Episcopal priest

Born in Chicago in March 1926. He and his wife, Ann Clark Rockefeller, daughter of Governor Nelson Rockefeller of New York, supported a myriad of social causes, from civil and women's rights to the welfare of migrant laborers. Subsidized African American dance and theater and participated in a citizens' exchange project with the Soviet Union in 1965. Died in St. Petersburg, FL, on April 13, 1997, at the age of 71.

SIMPSON, GEOFFREY SEDGEWICK	W	M	29	Pewaukee, WI	Episcopal priest, St. Bartholomew's Church (Pewaukee, WI)

Born in South Milwaukee, WI, in August 1932.

TAYLOR, ROBERT PAGE	W	M	29	Chicago, IL	Episcopal priest, St. Leonard's House (Chicago, IL)

Born in Norfolk, VA, in December 1931.

WENDT, WILLIAM ANDREW	W	M	41	Washington, DC	Episcopal priest, St. Stephen's Church (Washington, DC)

Born in Mitchell, SD, in January 1920. Became an advocate for gay rights and an anti-war activist within the Episcopal Church. St. Stephen's became a center for political activity. In 1967, the church sponsored a controversial speech by H. Rap Brown. In 1975 Wendt was censured by the church for allowing a woman to serve communion. He also founded the St. Francis Burial and Counseling Society, Inc., in 1975 and earned a reputation as a pioneer in talking about and dealing with death and dying. A counseling center was named in his honor in 1999. He died of cancer on July 8, 2001, at the age of 81.

WOODWARD, VERNON P.	W	M	27	Cincinnati, OH	Episcopal priest, Church of the Advent (Cincinnati, OH)

Born in Cincinnati, OH, in May 1934.

YOUNG, MERRILL ORNE	W	M	31	Boston, MA	Episcopal priest, Harvard Univ. Divinity School

Born in Brooklyn, NY, in June 1930. Currently resides in Surrey, VA.

Atlanta, GA (Trailways station), November 1, 1961

Name	Race	Sex	Age	Residence	Occupation or Status
Bevel, James L.	B	M	24	Itta Bena, MS	SNCC activist
See May 24 Ride.					
Forman, James	B	M	33	Atlanta, GA	SNCC executive director
See Monroe, NC, Ride, August 17–September 1.					
Jones, Joseph Charles	B	M	23	Charlotte, NC	Student, Johnson C. Smith Univ.; SNCC activist
See May 24 Ride.					
Lafayette, Bernard, Jr.	B	M	20	Tampa, FL	SNCC activist
See May 17–21 Ride.					

Atlanta, GA, to Albany, GA (Trailways), November 1, 1961

Name	Race	Sex	Age	Residence	Occupation or Status
McCollum, Salynn[v]	W	F	21	Snyder, NY	Student, George Peabody College; SNCC activist
See May 17–21 Ride.					
Reagon, Cordell Hull	B	M	18	Nashville, TN	Student, Tennessee State Univ.; SNCC activist.
See June 2 Ride.					
Sherrod, Charles	B	M	22	Richmond, VA	SNCC field secretary

Born and raised in Petersburg, VA. Graduate of Virginia Union College (Richmond, VA) and Union Theological Seminary (New York City) (M.Th., 1967). Director of the Southwest Georgia Project for Community Education (1967–1987) and New Communities, Inc., a cooperative farming project (1969–1985). Member of Albany City Commission (1976–1990). Ran unsuccessfully for Georgia state senate in 1996. Currently works in Homerville, GA, as a chaplain at the Georgia State Prison.

Jackson, MS (Trailways station), November 1, 1961

Name	Race	Sex	Age	Residence	Occupation or Status
Jackson, Glenda	B	F	22	Shreveport, LA	CORE activist
Jones, Rev. Charles A.	B	M		Jackson, MS	Dean of religion, Campbell Junior College (Jackson, MS)
Longtime activist and leader of the Jackson, MS, branch of the NAACP.					
Taylor, Levert H.	B	M	20	Shreveport, LA	CORE activist
See August 4 Ride.					

Albany, GA (Trailways station), November 22, 1961

Name	Race	Sex	Age	Residence	Occupation or Status
CARSWELL, JULIAN	B	M		Albany, GA	High school student; NAACP Youth Council
GOBER, BERTHA	B	F		Atlanta, GA	Student, Albany State College (Albany, GA)

Movement songwriter and celebrated member of the Albany Freedom Singers. She can be heard on the Smithsonian recording *Voices of the Civil Rights Movement: Black American Freedom Songs, 1960–1966.*

HALL, BLANTON	B	M	23	Athens, GA	Student, Albany State College
TONEY, EVELYN	B	F		Albany, GA	High school student; NAACP Youth Council
WILSON, EDDIE	B	M		Albany, GA	High school student; NAACP Youth Council

New Orleans, LA, to McComb, MS (Greyhound), November 29, 1961

Name	Race	Sex	Age	Residence	Occupation or Status
RAYMOND, GEORGE	B	M	18	New Orleans, LA	CORE activist

See August 13 Ride.

SMITH, DORATHA	B	F	18	New Orleans, LA	CORE activist

Born in Benton, MS. Moved to New Orleans at the age of 2. Began work at Preservation Hall in 1965 and later helped organize the New Orleans Jazz and Heritage Festival. Currently lives in New Orleans. Married name: Doratha Smith-Simmons.

SMITH, JEROME H.	B	M	22	New Orleans, LA	Longshoreman; New Orleans CORE chairman

See May 24 Ride.

THOMPSON, ALICE	B	F	22	New Orleans, LA	CORE activist

Sister of Jean and Shirley Thompson. Long career as a social worker in New Orleans, where she currently lives in retirement.

VALENTINE, THOMAS	B	M	23	New Orleans, LA	CORE activist

Deceased.

Baton Rouge, LA, to McComb, MS (Greyhound), December 1, 1961

Name	Race	Sex	Age	Residence	Occupation or Status
BRADFORD, WILLIE	B	M		New Orleans, LA	CORE activist

PEETE, THOMAS	B	M		Shreveport, LA	CORE activist
RAYMOND, GEORGE	B	M	18	New Orleans, LA	CORE activist

See August 13 Ride.

REESE, CLAUDE	B	M		New Orleans, LA	CORE activist
TATE, PATRICIA	B	F		Baton Rouge, LA	Student, Southern Univ. (Baton Rouge, LA); CORE activist

Along with fellow Southern Univ. students Ronnie Moore and Weldon Rougeau, she helped found the Baton Rouge CORE chapter in October 1961. In 1962 she was arrested for defaming a grand jury that indicted Ben Cox for defamation and disturbing the peace.

THOMPSON, JEAN	B	F	19	New Orleans, LA	CORE activist

See May 24 Ride.

Jackson, MS, to McComb, MS (Greyhound), December 2, 1961

Name	Race	Sex	Age	Residence	Occupation or Status
BURNHAM, JAMES	B	M		McComb, MS	Ex–Burgland High School student, attending Campbell Junior College
BYRD, JEROME	B	M		McComb, MS	Ex–Burgland High School student, attending Campbell Junior College
COTTON, MACARTHUR[u]	B	M		Kosciusko, MS	Student, Tougaloo College (Jackson, MS); SNCC activist
GAITHER, THOMAS[u]	B	M	23	Jackson, MS	CORE field secretary

See chapters 2 and 3 and epilogue. Currently a professor of biology at Slippery Rock University (Slippery Rock, PA).

LEWIS, JOE	B	M		McComb, MS	Ex–Burgland High School student, attending Campbell Junior College

Atlanta, GA, to Albany, GA (Central Georgia Railroad), December 10, 1961

Name	Race	Sex	Age	Residence	Occupation or Status
BROWNING, JOAN	W	F	19	Atlanta, GA	Former student, Georgia State College for Women (Milledgeville); SNCC activist.

Born in Wheeler County, GA, in 1941. Raised on a small farm before attending Georgia State College for Women (Milledgeville), from which she was expelled in 1961 after worshipping at a black church. Later active in civil rights and anti-poverty campaigns during the 1970s. Organizer for the Federation of Southern Cooperatives. Graduate of West Virginia State College (B.A., 1994). Currently lives in Greenbrier County, WV, where she is a freelance writer, lecturer, and member of the West Virginia Human Rights Commission. See Curry et al., *Deep in Our Hearts*.

COLLINS, NORMA F.   B   F   20   Atlanta, GA   SNCC office manager

Born in Baltimore, MD, on March 30, 1941. Attended Morris Brown College (Atlanta, GA) in 1963 and Community College of Baltimore in 1964. Worked as a congressional office manager on Capitol Hill since 1981 for a series of representatives: Harold Washington (IL), Charles Hayes (IL), and Albert Wynn (MD).

FORMAN, JAMES   B   M   33   Atlanta, GA   SNCC executive director

See November 1 Ride.

HAYDEN, SANDRA[v]   W   F   23   Royal Oak, MI   National Student YWCA project
CASON "CASEY"   worker; SDS and SNCC activist.

Born in Victoria, TX, in 1937. Graduate of Univ. of Texas (Austin) (B.A., 1959). Involved in National Student YWCA and Austin sit-ins in 1960. Influential activist with SNCC and SDS during the 1960s. Married Tom Hayden in 1961. Involved in a wide range of counter-cultural activities since 1971, including alternative press, yoga institutes, and Buddhism. Currently married to Episcopal priest and community organizer Paul Buckwalter and living in Tucson, AZ.

HAYDEN, TOM   W   M   22   Royal Oak, MI   College journalist; SNCC and
                                                         SDS activist

Graduate of Univ. of Michigan (B.A., 1961). Leading anti-war activist affiliated with Students for a Democratic Society (SDS) in the 1960s. Elected to California state assembly in 1982 and the state senate in 1992. Major legislative efforts on behalf of African Americans, women, Latinos, Holocaust survivors, and sweatshop laborers. Currently a professor at Occidental College and social science advisor for Animoo public school consortium of Venice, Inglewood, Lenox, South Central, and Boyle Heights, CA. See Hayden, *Reunion: A Memoir.*

LAURSEN, PER   W   M   25   New York, NY   Journalist

Born in Copenhagen, Denmark.

LEE, BERNARD   B   M   22   Atlanta, GA   SCLC staff; former student,
                                                         Alabama State College

See May 24–25 Ride.

TAITT, LENORA   B   F   23   Atlanta, GA   SNCC activist; graduate student,
                                                         Atlanta Univ.

Born in NY City. Graduate of Spelman College (B.A.), Atlanta Univ. School of Social Work (M.S.W.), and Columbia Univ. Teachers College (Ed.D). Social Work and Education Officer for the UN High Commissioner for Refugees in Zambia. Exec. director of the NY Chapter of the Nat. Assoc. of Social Workers. Currently director of Bronx Preventative Services for Steinway Child and Family Services in NY City. Lives in NY City and South Africa. Married name: Lenora Taitt Magubane.

ZELLNER, ROBERT   W   M   22   Montgomery, AL   SNCC field secretary

See chapters 6 and 11. Born April 5, 1939. Currently completing a Ph.D. in history at Tulane University. Recently taught a course on the history of activism at Southampton College of Long Island University in the Friends World Program. His dissertation, tentatively entitled "Memories of a White Southerner in the Civil Rights Movement," describes his experiences as SNCC's first white field secretary.

Explanatory Note: The Roster of Freedom Riders does not include those who participated in the Little Freedom Ride of April 1961 or (with the exception of the well-documented Atlanta, Albany, and McComb test rides of November and December 1961) those who participated in the many test rides that followed the November 1, 1961, ICC transit desegregation order.

[a]Weaversville, NC, to Lynchburg, VA, April 19–21, by Greyhound.
[b]Charlottesville, VA, to Washington, DC, April 23, by Trailways.
[c]Roanoke, VA, to Washington, DC, April 20, by railroad.
[d]Roanoke, VA, to Lynchburg, VA, April 21, by Greyhound.
[e]Knoxville, TN, to Lexington, KY, April 18, by Greyhound.
[f]Bristol, VA, to Roanoke, VA, April 19–20, by Greyhound.
[g]Lynchburg, VA, to Amherst, VA, April 22, by Greyhound.
[h]Nashville, TN, to Lexington, KY, April 19, by railroad.
[i]Cincinnati, OH, to Roanoke, VA, April 19, by railroad.
[j]Amherst, VA, to Washington, DC, April 22, by railroad.
[k]Charlotte, NC, to Rock Hill, SC, May 9, by bus.
[l]Sumter, SC, to Birmingham, AL, May 11–14, by bus.
[m]Left Freedom Ride in South Carolina on May 10, rejoined Ride in Birmingham, AL.
[n]Traveled as an advance scout by car from Birmingham, AL, to Montgomery, AL.
[o]Nashville, TN, to Birmingham, AL, May 17, by bus.
[p]Pulaski, TN, to Birmingham, AL, May 17, by bus; left Freedom Ride in Birmingham.
[q]Joined the Freedom Ride in Birmingham, AL, May 19.
[r]Joined the Freedom Ride in Montgomery, AL, May 28.
[s]Montgomery, AL to Selma, AL where he was arrested and jailed on June 2.
[t]Traveled alone from New Orleans, LA, to Jackson, MS by rail; arrested at Illinois Central terminal.
[u]Arrested as observers.
[v]Designated observer.

FREEDOM RIDERS OF 1961:
ROSTER SUMMARY[1]

	Number	Percent
Total:	436	100.0
By Region:		
Born in the South[2]	196	45.0
Born outside the South	240	55.0
By Race:		
Black	230	52.7
White	204	46.8
Asian	2	00.5
By Gender:		
Male	326	74.8
Female	110	25.2
By Age:		
Under 20	111	25.5
20–29	221	50.7
30 and over	104	23.8

[1]Excludes participants in 1947 Journey of Reconciliation.
[2]Includes border states of Delaware, Kentucky, Maryland, Missouri, Oklahoma, and Washington, DC.

Note: Although they did not participate in any of the actual Rides, Diane Nash and Gordon Carey acted as the principal coordinators of the Freedom Rides. For biographical information on Nash and Carey, see especially chapters 3 through 8.

Notes

Abbreviations Used in Notes

APRP	A. Philip Randolph Papers, Library of Congress, Washington, DC
ARC	Amistad Research Center, Tulane University, New Orleans, LA
BCP	Theophilus Eugene "Bull" Connor Papers, Department of Archives and Manuscripts, Birmingham Public Library, Birmingham, AL
BMP	Burke Marshall Papers, John F. Kennedy Library, Boston, MA
BPL	Department of Archives and Manuscripts, Birmingham Public Library, Birmingham, AL
BRP	Bayard Rustin Papers (microfilm)
BSCPP	Brotherhood of Sleeping Car Porters Papers, Library of Congress, Washington, DC
CCHP	Clarie Collins Harvey Papers, Amistad Research Center, Tulane University, New Orleans, LA
COREC	Congress of Racial Equality Collection, Swarthmore College Peace Collection, Swarthmore, PA
COREP	Congress of Racial Equality Papers (microfilm)
COREPA	Congress of Racial Equality Papers, Addendum, 1944–1968 (microfilm)
CUOHC	Columbia University Oral History Collection, New York, NY
FBI-FRI	FBI Case Files, Freedom Rider Investigation, Department of Archives and Manuscripts, Birmingham Public Library, Birmingham, AL
FORP	Fellowship of Reconciliation Papers, Swarthmore College Peace Collection, Swarthmore, PA
FUSC	Fisk University Special Collections, Nashville, TN
ICCR	Interstate Commerce Commission Records, Record Group 134, U.S. National Archives II, College Park, MD
JFKL	John F. Kennedy Library, Boston, MA
KMSP	Kelly Miller Smith Papers, Vanderbilt University, Nashville, TN
KPA	Martin Luther King, Jr. Papers, the Martin Luther King, Jr., Center for Nonviolent Social Change, Atlanta, GA
MLKP	Martin Luther King, Jr., Papers, Mugar Library, Boston University, Boston, MA
MSCP	Mississippi State Sovereignty Commission Papers, Mississippi Department of Archives and History, Jackson, MS
NAACPP	National Association for the Advancement of Colored People Papers, Library of Congress, Washington, DC
NTP	Norman Thomas Papers, New York Public Library, New York, NY
RBOHC	Ralph Bunche Oral History Collection, Moorland-Spingarn Research Center, Howard University, Washington, DC

RFKP	Robert F. Kennedy Papers, John F. Kennedy Library, Boston, MA
RRLR	*Race Relations Law Reporter*
SCLCP	Southern Christian Leadership Conference Papers (microfilm)
SCPC	Swarthmore College Peace Collection, Swarthmore, PA
SNCCP	Student Nonviolent Coordinating Committee Papers, the Martin Luther King, Jr. Center for Nonviolent Social Change, Atlanta, GA
SRCP	Southern Regional Council Papers (microfilm)
TIRRCF	Tuskegee Institute Race Relations Clipping File (microfilm)
UMFRC	Freedom Rider Collection, University of Mississippi, Oxford, MS
USDJ/CRD	United States Department of Justice, Civil Rights Division Records, Record Group 60, U.S. National Archives II, College Park, MD
WHC	Wiliam Harbour Freedom Rider Collection, in possession of William Harbour, Atlanta, GA
WRLP	War Resisters League Papers, Swarthmore College Peace Collection, Swarthmore, PA

Introduction

1. Stokely Carmichael with Ekwueme Michael Thelwell, *Ready for Revolution: The Life and Struggles of Stokely Carmichael (Kwame Ture)* (New York: Scribner, 2003), 178.
2. Founded by ex-slaves in 1867, the First Baptist Church (Colored) of Montgomery boasted the largest black congregation in the United States during the 1910s. Following a devastating fire in 1910, the church was rebuilt under the leadership of the Reverend Andrew Jackson Stokes, who asked parishioners who could not afford to contribute to the rebuilding fund to contribute a brick every Sunday. Known locally as the "Brick-a-Day Church," First Baptist was the Reverend Ralph Abernathy's church from 1950 to 1961. See Barbara Carter, "A Brick Every Sunday," *Reporter* 26 (September 20, 1961): 39–40; First Baptist Church, *'Tis a Glorious Church: The Brick-a-Day Church* (Montgomery: First Baptist Church, 2001); Taylor Branch, *Parting the Waters: America in the King Years, 1954–63* (New York: Simon and Schuster, 1988), 1–4; and Ralph David Abernathy, *And the Walls Came Tumbling Down: An Autobiography* (New York: Harper and Row, 1989), 82–83, 101–102, 118–119, 185–188. The organizers of the Freedom Rides never offered any public explanation for their choice of terminology, other than a brief comment in James Farmer, *Lay Bare the Heart: An Autobiography of the Civil Rights Movement* (New York: New American Library, 1985), 196. For an exposition of the evolving concept of "freedom" in American history, see David Hackett Fischer, *Liberty and Freedom* (New York: Oxford University Press, 2004); and Eric Foner, *The Story of American Freedom* (New York: Norton, 1998). On freedom's connection to the civil rights movement, see Richard H. King, *Civil Rights and the Idea of Freedom* (New York: Oxford University Press, 1992). *Morgan v. Virginia*, 328 U.S. 373 (1946); *Boynton v. Virginia*, 364 U.S. 454 (1960).
3. On the philosophical, religious, and psychological motivations of nonviolent civil rights activists during the 1960s, see King, *Civil Rights and the Idea of Freedom*; James H. Laue, *Direct Action and Desegregation, 1960–1962: Toward a Theory of the Rationalization of Protest* (Brooklyn: Carlson, 1989); and David L. Chappell, *A Stone of Hope: Prophetic Religion and the Death of Jim Crow* (Chapel Hill: University of North Carolina Press, 2004). On the Freedom Riders' moral and religious values, see David J. Mussatt, "Journey for Justice: A Religious Analysis of the Ethics of the 1961 Albany Freedom Ride" (Ph.D. thesis, Temple University, 2001); and Henry Louis Gerner, "A Study of the Freedom Riders with Particular Emphasis upon Three Dimensions, Dogmatism, Value-Orientation, Religiosity" (Th.D. thesis, Pacific School of Religion, 1963).
4. Michael Belknap, *Federal Law and Southern Order: Racial Violence and Constitutional Conflict in the Post-Brown South* (Athens: University of Georgia Press, 1987), 77–78. For a brief but insightful summary of the civil rights struggle and massive resistance during the period 1954–1961, see C. Vann Woodward, *The Strange Career of Jim Crow* (New York: Oxford University Press, 2002), 149–173.
5. The phrase "with all deliberate speed" first appeared in the May 1955 school desegregation implementation ruling known as *Brown II*. See Richard Kluger, *Simple Justice: The History of Brown v. Board of Education and Black America's Struggle for Equality* (New York: Random House, 1975), 714–747; James T. Patterson, *Brown v. Board of Education: A Civil Rights Milestone and Its Troubled Legacy* (New York: Oxford University Press, 2001), 82–85; Michael J. Klarman, *From Jim Crow to Civil Rights: The Supreme Court and the Struggle for Racial Equality* (New York: Oxford University Press, 2004), 256–258, 312–320; and Charles J. Ogletree Jr., *All Deliberate Speed: Reflections on the First Half Century of Brown v. Board of Education* (New York: Norton, 2004). Theodore H. White, *The Making of the President 1960* (New York: Atheneum, 1961); Richard Reeves, *President Kennedy: Profile of Power* (New York: Simon and Schuster, 1993), 36 (quotation), 58–64; Carl M. Brauer, *John F. Kennedy and the Second Reconstruction* (New York: Columbia University Press, 1977), 35–36, 39, 75, 94–97, 126–127; Robert Dallek, *An Unfinished Life: John F. Kennedy, 1917–1963* (Boston: Little, Brown, 2003), 373–388; James W. Hilty, *Robert Kennedy: Brother Protector* (Philadelphia: Temple University Press, 1997), 133–134, 151, 170–176, 289–306.
6. Reeves, *President Kennedy*, 63 (first quotation), 60 (second quotation). On Hesburgh and the U.S. Civil Rights Commission, see Theodore Hesburgh, *God, Country, Notre Dame* (New York: Doubleday,

1990); and Foster Rhea Dulles, *The Civil Rights Commission, 1957–1965* (East Lansing: Michigan State University Press, 1968).

7. Henry Hampton and Steve Fayer, *Voices of Freedom: An Oral History of the Civil Rights Movement from the 1950s through the 1980s* (New York: Vintage, 1990), 75 (quotation).

8. On McCarthyism and anti-Communist hysteria during the 1950s, see Richard H. Rovere, *Senator Joe McCarthy* (New York: Harcourt, Brace, 1959); David M. Oshinsky, *A Conspiracy So Immense: The World of Joe McCarthy* (New York: Free Press, 1983); Ellen Schrecker, *Many Are the Crimes: McCarthyism in America* (Princeton: Princeton University Press, 1998); Stephen J. Whitfield, *The Culture of the Cold War* (Baltimore: Johns Hopkins University Press, 1991); Richard M. Fried, *Nightmare in Red: The McCarthy Era in Perspective* (New York: Oxford University Press, 1990); and David Caute, *The Great Fear: The Anti-Communist Purge Under Truman and Eisenhower* (New York: Simon and Schuster, 1978). On the Cold War's impact on the American civil rights struggle, see Mary L. Dudziak, *Cold War Civil Rights: Race and the Image of American Democracy* (Princeton: Princeton University Press, 2000); Thomas Borstelmann, *The Cold War and the Color Line: American Race Relations in the Global Arena* (Cambridge: Harvard University Press, 2001); Jeff Woods, *Black Struggle, Red Scare: Segregation and Anti-Communism in the South, 1948–1968* (Baton Rouge: Louisiana State University Press, 2004); George Lewis, *The White South and the Red Menace: Segregationists, Anticommunism, and Massive Resistance, 1945–1965* (Gainesville: University Press of Florida, 2004); Gilbert Jonas, *Freedom's Sword* (New York: Routledge, 2005), 135–149; and Manfred Berg, *"The Ticket to Freedom"* (Gainesville: University Press of Florida, 2005), 116–139.

9. George H. Gallup, *The Gallup Poll: Public Opinion, 1935–1971* (New York: Random House, 1971), vol. 3, 1723–1724.

10. Robert Cook, "From Shiloh to Selma: The Impact of the Civil War Centennial on the Black Freedom Struggle in the United States, 1961–65," in *The Making of Martin Luther King and the Civil Rights Movement,* ed. Brian Ward and Tony Badger (New York: New York University Press, 1996), 131–146. On the South's "siege mentality," see Sheldon Hackney, "Southern Violence," *American Historical Review* 74 (February 1969): 924–925. On the mythology of the "tragic era," see Kenneth M. Stampp, "The Tragic Legend of Reconstruction," in *Reconstruction: An Anthology of Revisionist Writings,* ed. Kenneth M. Stampp and Leon F. Litwack (Baton Rouge: Louisiana State University Press, 1969), 3–21. On the concept of the Second Reconstruction, see Woodward, *Strange Career of Jim Crow,* 8–10, 122–147, 209–210; and Manning Marable, *Race, Reform, and Rebellion: The Second Reconstruction in Black America, 1945–1982* (Jackson: University Press of Mississippi, 1984). Roy Wilkins with Tom Mathews, *Standing Fast: The Autobiography of Roy Wilkins* (New York: Viking Penguin, 1982), 283 (first quotation); Jonas, *Freedom's Sword,* 170–178; Berg, *"The Ticket to Freedom,"* 166–177; Leslie Dunbar, interview by author, October 25, 2003 (second quotation); John Lewis with Michael D'Orso, *Walking with the Wind: A Memoir of the Movement* (New York: Simon and Schuster, 1998), 113–114, 135.

11. See Appendix: Roster of Freedom Riders.

12. Brief accounts of the Freedom Rides written by academic historians include Howard Zinn, *SNCC: The New Abolitionists* (Boston: Beacon Press, 1965), 40–61; Brauer, *John F. Kennedy and the Second Reconstruction,* 98–112; August Meier and Elliott Rudwick, *CORE: A Study in the Civil Rights Movement* (Urbana: University of Illinois Press, 1975), 135–158; Clayborne Carson, *In Struggle: SNCC and the Black Awakening of the 1960s* (Cambridge: Harvard University Press, 1981), 31–44; Harvard Sitkoff, *The Struggle for Black Equality, 1954–1980* (New York: Hill and Wang, 1981), 97–114; Catherine A. Barnes, *Journey from Jim Crow: The Desegregation of Southern Transit* (New York: Columbia University Press, 1983), 157–175; Kenneth O'Reilly, *"Racial Matters": The FBI's Secret File on Black America, 1960–1972* (New York: Free Press, 1989), 81–97; Robert Weisbrot, *Freedom Bound: A History of America's Civil Rights Movement* (New York: Norton, 1990), 55–63; David R. Goldfield, *Black, White, and Southern: Race Relations and Southern Culture, 1940 to the Present* (Baton Rouge: Louisiana State University Press, 1990), 124–130; Steven F. Lawson, *Running for Freedom: Civil Rights and Black Politics in America Since 1941* (New York: McGraw-Hill, 1991), 80–81; John Dittmer, *Local People: The Struggle for Civil Rights in Mississippi* (Urbana: University of Illinois Press, 1994), 90–99; John Morton Blum, *Years of Discord: American Politics and Society, 1961–1974* (New York: Norton, 1991), 69–71; David Farber, *The Age of Great Dreams: America in the 1960s* (New York: Hill and Wang, 1994), 79–82; Numan V. Bartley, *The New South 1945–1980* (Baton Rouge: Louisiana State University Press, 1995), 306–312; Terry H. Anderson, *The Movement and the Sixties: Protest in America from Greensboro to Wounded Knee* (New York: Oxford University Press, 1995), 51–56; James T. Patterson, *Grand Expectations: The United States, 1945–1974* (New York: Oxford University Press, 1996), 468–475; Glenn T. Eskew, *But for Birmingham: The Local and National Movements in the Civil Rights Struggle* (Chapel Hill: University of North Carolina Press, 1997), 153–165; John A. Salmond, *"My Mind Set on Freedom": A History of the Civil Rights Movement, 1954–1968* (Chicago: Ivan R. Dee, 1997), 87–94; Steven F. Lawson and Charles Payne, *Debating the Civil Rights Movement, 1945–1968* (Lanham, MD: Rowman and Littlefield, 1998), 20–22; Timothy B. Tyson, *Radio Free Dixie: Robert F. Williams and the Roots of Black Power* (Chapel Hill: University of North Carolina Press, 1999), 244–249, 262–275; Andrew M. Manis, *A Fire You Can't Put Out: The Civil Rights Life of Birmingham's Reverend Fred Shuttlesworth* (Tuscaloosa: University of Alabama Press, 1999), 262–280; John Hope Franklin and Alfred A. Moss Jr., *From Slavery to Freedom: A History of African Americans,* 8th ed. (New York: Knopf, 2000), 530–531; Maurice Isserman and Michael Kazin, *America Divided: The Civil War of the 1960s* (New York: Oxford University Press, 2000), 34–36; Adam Fairclough, *Better Day Coming: Blacks and Equality, 1890–2000* (New York: Penguin, 2001), 252–256; James Oliver Horton and Lois E. Horton, *Hard Road to Freedom: A History of African America* (New Brunswick: Rutgers University Press, 2001), 286–287, 290–291; J. Mills Thornton III, *Dividing Lines: Municipal Politics and the Struggle for Civil Rights in Montgomery, Birmingham, and Selma* (Tuscaloosa: University of Alabama Press, 2002), 239–253 and passim; and Dallek, *An Unfinished Life,* 383–388. See also the recently

completed and unpublished dissertation, Derek Catsam, " 'A Brave and Wonderful Thing': The Freedom Rides and the Desegregation of Interstate Transport, 1941–1965" (Ph.D. thesis, Ohio University, 2003). Accounts by political scientists, sociologists, or legal scholars include Doug McAdam, *Political Process and the Development of Black Insurgency, 1930–1970* (Chicago: University of Chicago Press, 1982), 152, 165, 170–171, 176–177, 187–188; David J. Garrow, *Bearing the Cross: Martin Luther King, Jr., and the Southern Christian Leadership Conference* (New York: William Morrow, 1986), 154–180; Todd Gitlin, *The Sixties: Years of Hope, Days of Rage* (New York: Bantam, 1987), 136–142; Mark Stern, *Calculating Visions: Kennedy, Johnson, and Civil Rights* (New Brunswick: Rutgers University Press, 1992), 58–62; Edward P. Morgan, *The Sixties Experience: Hard Lessons About Modern America* (Philadelphia: Temple University Press, 1991), 51–55; Aldon D. Morris, *The Origins of the Civil Rights Movement: Black Communities Organizing for Change* (New York: Free Press, 1984), 231–236; Rhonda Lois Blumberg, *Civil Rights: The 1960s Freedom Struggle* (Boston: Twayne, 1984), 73–81; and Belknap, *Federal Law and Southern Order*, 77–88. The only extant book-length study of the Freedom Rides written by a social scientist is David Niven, *The Politics of Injustice: The Kennedys, the Freedom Rides, and the Electoral Consequences of a Moral Compromise* (Knoxville: University of Tennessee Press, 2003), a provocative indictment of the Kennedy administration's reluctance to support the Riders' constitutional rights.

13. Branch, *Parting the Waters*; David Halberstam, *The Children* (New York: Random House, 1998); Diane McWhorter, *Carry Me Home: Birmingham, Alabama: The Climactic Battle of the Civil Rights Revolution* (New York: Simon and Schuster, 2001). Other journalistic accounts include Anthony Lewis and *The New York Times*, *Portrait of a Decade: The Second American Revolution* (New York: Random House, 1964), 87–93; Milton Viorst, *Fire in the Streets: America in the 1960s* (New York: Simon and Schuster, 1979), 140–160; Fred Powledge, *Free at Last? The Civil Rights Movement and the People Who Made It* (Boston: Little, Brown, 1991), 253–308; Harry S. Ashmore, *Civil Rights and Wrongs: A Memoir of Race and Politics, 1944–1994* (New York: Pantheon, 1994), 146–148; Townsend Davis, *Weary Feet, Rested Souls: A Guided History of the Civil Rights Movement* (New York: Norton, 1998), 42–44, 58–60, 193–195, 213–215; Evan Thomas, *Robert Kennedy, His Life* (New York: Simon and Schuster, 2000), 128–132; and Frye Gaillard, *Cradle of Freedom: Alabama and the Movement That Changed America* (Tuscaloosa: University of Alabama Press, 2004), 73–112 and passim.

14. On the 1960s as a turbulent era of protest, see Viorst, *Fire in the Streets*; Gitlin, *The Sixties*; Anderson, *The Movement and the Sixties* ; Blum, *Years of Discord*; Farber, *The Age of Great Dreams*; Isserman and Kazin, *America Divided*; Morgan, *The Sixties Experience*; Patterson, *Grand Expectations*, 442–745; Allen J. Matusow, *The Unraveling of America: A History of Liberalism in the 1960s* (New York: Harper Torchbooks, 1984); James Miller, *"Democracy Is in the Streets": From Port Huron to the Siege of Chicago* (New York: Simon and Schuster, 1987); Maurice Isserman, *If I Had a Hammer: The Death of the Old Left and the Birth of the New Left* (New York: Basic Books, 1987); Morris Dickstein, *Gates of Eden: American Culture in the Sixties* (New York: Basic Books, 1977); Barbara L. Tischler, ed., *Sights on the Sixties* (New Brunswick: Rutgers University Press, 1992); and Alexander Bloom and Wini Breines, eds., *"Takin' It to the Streets": A Sixties Reader* (New York: Oxford University Press, 1995).

15. On the colonial and nineteenth-century phases of what has become known as the "freedom struggle," see Franklin and Moss, *From Slavery to Freedom*; Horton and Horton, *Hard Road to Freedom*; Vincent Harding, *There Is a River: The Black Struggle for Freedom in America* (New York: Harcourt Brace, 1981); Alice Felt Tyler, *Freedom's Ferment* (New York: Harper and Row, 1962); James Brewer Stewart, *Holy Warriors: The Abolitionists and American Slavery* (New York: Hill and Wang, 1976); William McFeely, *Frederick Douglass* (New York: Simon and Schuster, 1991); James Oliver Horton and Lois E. Horton, *In Hope of Liberty: Culture, Community and Protest Among Northern Free Blacks, 1700–1860* (New York: Oxford University Press, 1997); Leon F. Litwack, *Been in the Storm So Long: The Aftermath of Slavery* (New York: Vintage, 1980; Eric Foner, *Reconstruction: America's Unfinished Revolution, 1863–1877* (New York: Harper and Row, 1988); James M. McPherson, *The Abolitionist Legacy: From Reconstruction to the NAACP* (Princeton: Princeton University Press, 1975); and Steven Hahn, *A Nation Beneath Our Feet: Black Political Struggles in the Rural South from Slavery to the Great Migration* (Cambridge: Harvard University Press, 2003). On the twentieth-century manifestations of the struggle prior to 1961, see Kluger, *Simple Justice*; Klarman, *From Jim Crow to Civil Rights*; Jonas, *Freedom's Sword*; Woodward, *The Strange Career of Jim Crow*; Barnes, *Journey from Jim Crow*; August Meier, Elliott Rudwick, and Francis L. Broderick, eds., *Black Protest Thought in the Twentieth Century* (Indianapolis: Bobbs-Merrill, 1971); August Meier and Elliott Rudwick, "The Boycott Movement Against Jim Crow Streetcars in the South, 1900–1906," *Journal of American History* 51 (March 1969): 756–775; Fairclough, *Better Day Coming*, 23–248; Robert J. Norrell, *The House I Live In: Race and the American Century* (New York: Oxford University Press, 2005), xi–186; Herbert Shapiro, *White Violence and Black Response: From Reconstruction to Montgomery* (Amherst: University of Massachusetts Press, 1988); James Tracy, *Direct Action: Radical Pacifism from the Union Eight to the Chicago Seven* (Chicago: University of Chicago Press, 1996), 1–118; Randy Roberts, *Papa Jack: Jack Johnson and the Era of White Hopes* (New York: Free Press, 1983); David Levering Lewis, *W.E.B. DuBois: Biography of a Race, 1919–1963* (New York: Henry Holt, 1993); David Levering Lewis, *W.E.B. DuBois: The Fight for Equality and the American Century, 1919–1963* (New York: Henry Holt, 2000); Martin B. Duberman, *Paul Robeson: A Biography* (New York: Knopf, 1988); Walter White, *A Man Called White* (New York: Viking, 1948); Raymond Wolters, *The New Negro on Campus: Black College Rebellions of the 1920s* (Princeton: Princeton University Press, 1975); James R. Grossman, *Land of Hope: Chicago, Black Southerners, and the Great Migration* (Chicago: University of Chicago Press, 1991); Harvard Sitkoff, *A New Deal for Blacks: The Emergence of Civil Rights as a National Issue* (New York: Oxford University Press, 1978); Vicki L. Crawford, Jacqueline Anne Rouse, and Barbara Woods, eds., *Women in the Civil*

Rights Movement: Trailblazers and Torchbearers, 1941–1965 (Bloomington: Indiana University Press, 1993); Lynne Olson, *Freedom's Daughters: The Unsung Heroines of the Civil Rights Movement from 1830 to 1970* (New York: Scribner, 2001); Linda O. McMurry, *To Keep the Waters Troubled: The Life of Ida B. Wells* (New York: Oxford University Press, 1999); Kevin Boyle, *Arc of Justice: A Saga of Race, Civil Rights, and Murder in the Jazz Age* (New York: Henry Holt, 2004); Dan Carter, *Scottsboro: A Tragedy of the American South* (Baton Rouge: Louisiana State University Press, 1979); Robin D. G. Kelley, *Hammer and Hoe: Alabama Communists During the Great Depression* (Chapel Hill: University of North Carolina Press, 1990); Barbara Ransby, *Ella Baker and the Black Freedom Movement: A Radical Democratic Vision* (Chapel Hill: University of North Carolina Press, 2003); Pauli Murray, *The Autobiography of a Black Activist, Feminist, Lawyer, Priest, and Poet* (Knoxville: University of Tennessee Press, 1987); Juan Williams, *Thurgood Marshall: American Revolutionary* (New York: Times Books/Random House, 1998); Denton L. Watson, *Lion in the Lobby: Clarence Mitchell Jr.'s Struggle for the Passage of Civil Rights Laws* (New York: Morrow, 1990); Genna Rae McNeil, *Groundwork: Charles Hamilton Houston and the Struggle for Civil Rights* (Philadelphia: University of Pennsylvania Press, 1983); Gilbert Ware, *William Hastie: Grace Under Pressure* (New York: Oxford University Press, 1984); Robert L. Zangrando, *The NAACP Crusade Against Lynching, 1909–1950* (Philadelphia: Temple University Press, 1980); Jacquelyn Dowd Hall, *Revolt Against Chivalry: Jesse Daniel Ames and the Southern Women's Campaign Against Lynching* (New York: Columbia University Press, 1979); Ben Green, *Before His Time: The Untold Story of Harry T. Moore* (New York: Free Press, 1999); Will Haygood, *King of the Cats: The Life and Times of Adam Clayton Powell* (Boston: Houghton Mifflin, 1993); Linda Reed, *Simple Decency and Common Sense: The Southern Conference Movement, 1938–1963* (Bloomington: Indiana University Press, 1991); Darlene Clark Hine, *Black Victory: The Rise and Fall of the White Primary in Texas* (Millwood, NJ: KTO Press, 1979); James Peck, *Freedom Ride* (New York: Simon and Schuster, 1962); Farmer, *Lay Bare the Heart;* Dorothy B. Kaufman, *The First Freedom Ride: The Walter Bergman Story* (Detroit: ACLU Fund Press, 1989); Paula F. Pfeffer, *A. Philip Randolph, Pioneer of the Civil Rights Movement* (Baton Rouge: Louisiana State University Press, 1990); Jervis A. Anderson, *A. Philip Randolph: A Biographical Portrait* (New York: Harcourt Brace Jovanovich, 1972); Herbert Garfinkel, *When Negroes March: The March on Washington Movement in the Organizational Politics for FEPC* (New York: Atheneum, 1969); John D'Emilio, *Lost Prophet: The Life and Times of Bayard Rustin* (New York: Free Press, 2003); Patricia Sullivan, *Days of Hope: Race and Democracy in the New Deal Era* (Chapel Hill: University of North Carolina Press, 1996); Michael K. Honey, *Southern Labor and Black Civil Rights: Organizing Memphis Workers* (Urbana: University of Illinois Press, 1993); Robert Rogers Korstad, *Civil Rights Unionism: Tobacco Workers and the Struggle for Democracy in the Mid-Twentieth-Century South* (Chapel Hill: University of North Carolina Press, 2003); Thomas Kreuger, *And Promises to Keep: The Southern Conference for Human Welfare, 1938–1948* (Nashville: Vanderbilt University Press, 1967); Frank Adams with Myles Horton, *Unearthing Seeds of Fire: The Idea of Highlander* (Winston-Salem: John F. Blair, 1975); John Egerton, *Speak Now Against the Day: The Generation Before the Civil Rights Movement in the South* (New York: Knopf, 1994); Gail W. O'Brien, *The Color of the Law: Race, Violence, and Justice in the Post–World War II South* (Chapel Hill: University of North Carolina Press, 1999): Glenn Feldman, ed., *Before Brown: Civil Rights and White Backlash in the Modern South* (Tuscaloosa: University of Alabama Press, 2004); and Martha Biondi, *To Stand and Fight: The Civil Rights Movement in Postwar New York City* (Cambridge: Harvard University Press, 2003). On Montgomery, see Martin Luther King Jr., *Stride Toward Freedom: The Montgomery Story* (New York: Harper and Row, 1958); Thornton, *Dividing Lines,* 1–140; Branch, *Parting the Waters,* 120–205; Garrow, *Bearing the Cross,* 11–90; and Stewart Burns, ed., *Daybreak of Freedom: The Montgomery Bus Boycott* (Chapel Hill: University of North Carolina Press, 1997). On Tallahassee, see Glenda Alice Rabby, *The Pain and the Promise: The Struggle for Civil Rights in Tallahassee, Florida* (Athens: University of Georgia Press, 1999), 1–80. On the sit-ins, see William Chafe, *Civilities and Civil Rights: Greensboro, North Carolina, and the Black Struggle for Freedom* (New York: Oxford University Press, 1980), 110–141; Morris, *Origins of the Civil Rights Movement,* 188–228; and Laue, *Direct Action and Desegregation.*

16. "The Significance of Emancipation in the West Indies," speech in Canandauga, New York, August 3, 1957, in John W. Blassingame, ed., *The Frederick Douglass Papers, Series One: Speeches, Debates, and Interviews,* vol. 3, *1855–63* (New Haven: Yale University Press, 1991), 204 (quotation).

Chapter 1: You Don't Have to Ride Jim Crow

1. Bayard Rustin Files, box 51, FORP. The lyrics for "You Don't Have to Ride Jim Crow" were co-written by Bayard Rustin, Johnny Carr, Donald Coan, Doreen Curtis, and A. C. Thompson at the FOR/CORE-sponsored Interracial Workshop in Washington, D.C., on July 7, 1947. The music was an adaptation of the traditional Negro spiritual "There's No Hidin' Place Down Here." The epigraph is the second stanza. See also the documentary film *You Don't Have to Ride JIM CROW!* (New Hampshire Public Television, 1995), produced and directed by Robin Washington.

2. *Baltimore Afro-American,* January 26, 1946; *New York People's Voice,* June 15, 1946; Aleah Bacquie (Irene Amos [Morgan] Kirkaldy's granddaughter), interview by author, October 9, 2003; Irene Amos [Morgan] Kirkaldy, interview by Sherwood Morgan, January 4, 2004; Sherwood Morgan, interview by author, January 3, 2004. Prior to emancipation in 1865, several generations of Irene Morgan's ancestors worked as slaves on the Tabb plantation in Gloucester County. Box II-B190, NAACPP,

contains numerous documents related to Irene Morgan and the 1946 Supreme Court decision *Morgan v. Virginia*. See especially "Opinion by Justice Herbert B. Gregory," typescript, June 6, 1945; "Argument in Irene Morgan Case," undated typescript; "Irene Morgan, Appellant vs. Commonwealth of Virginia—Brief of Appellee," undated typescript; and "Virginia Goes A'Courtin'," *Headlines and Pictures* (May 1946): 15. On the racial situation in Baltimore during the 1940s, see the papers of the Baltimore Branch of the NAACP, box C77, NAACPP; and the extensive coverage in the *Baltimore Afro-American*. For brief accounts of the Morgan incident, see Barnes, *Journey from Jim Crow*, 45; Kluger, *Simple Justice*, 237–238; Jack Greenberg, *Race Relations and American Law* (New York: Columbia University Press, 1959), 118–119; and Carol Morello, "The Freedom Rider a Nation Nearly Forgot," *Washington Post*, July 30, 2000, A1, A16. On Gloucester County, see Federal Writers' Project, *Virginia: A Guide to the Old Dominion* (New York: Oxford University Press, 1940), 455–459.

3. *Baltimore Afro-American*, January 26, 1946; Morello, "The Freedom Rider a Nation Nearly Forgot"; Bacquie, Kirkaldy, and Morgan interviews; Federal Writers' Project, *Virginia*, 453.

4. *Baltimore Afro-American*, January 26, 1946; *New York People's Voice*, June 15, 1946 (first quotation); Bacquie, Morgan, and Kirkaldy interviews; Morello, "The Freedom Rider a Nation Nearly Forgot" (second and third quotations). According to Morgan's brother-in-law, James Finney, Morgan's mother, Ethel Amos, was a key supporter of her daughter's fight for justice. "Irene's mother deserves a lot of credit in this . . . ," Finney told Virginia Gardner of the *People's Voice*. "Her mother got to work and raised the money to make bond for Irene when she decided to appeal her conviction in the lower court." Gardner added that "at the time the elderly woman took up the cudgel in her daughter's case, Irene had no attorney, no advisers." *New York People's Voice*, June 15, 1946.

5. "Opinion by Justice Herbert B. Gregory" and "Irene Morgan, Appellant, vs. Commonwealth of Virginia—Brief of Appellee," box II-B190, NAACPP; Morello, 'The Freedom Rider a Nation Nearly Forgot"; Kirkaldy and Morgan interviews. In Virginia the official name of the state supreme court is "the Supreme Court of Appeals of Virginia."

6. Barnes, *Journey from Jim Crow*, 3–4, 10, 14, 18, 44–47; Spottswood Robinson, "Memorandum Covering Transportation Cases," c. January 1945, box II-B190, NAACPP; Ray Stannard Baker, *Following the Color Line: American Negro Citizenship in the Progressive Era* (New York: Harper and Row, 1964), 31 (quotation); Gunnar Myrdal, *An American Dilemma: The Negro Problem and American Democracy* (New York: Harper and Brothers, 1944), 635 (quotation); Jules Tygiel, *Baseball's Great Experiment: Jackie Robinson and His Legacy* (New York: Oxford University Press, 1983), 59. The incident took place near Fort Hood, Texas, on July 6, 1944, ten days prior to Irene Morgan's arrest. Although the military police and the base provost marshal sided with the bus driver who ordered Robinson to move, a military court ruled in Robinson's favor in August 1944. On the special character of race relations and racial politics in mid-twentieth-century Virginia, see J. Douglas Smith, *Managing White Supremacy: Race, Politics, and Citizenship in Jim Crow Virginia* (Chapel Hill: University of North Carolina Press, 2003). For a sense of the frequency of confrontations related to Jim Crow transit during the early and mid-1940s, see reels 67, 73, 77, 81, 87, 91, 95–96, and 100, TIRRCF.

7. Barnes, *Journey from Jim Crow*, 16 (quotation), 2–19, 22–23; *Plessy v. Ferguson*, 163 U.S. 537 (1896); *Chiles v. Chesapeake and Ohio Railway Company*, 218 U.S. 71 (1910); *McCabe v. Atchison, Topeka and Santa Fe Railway Company*, 235 U.S. 151 (1914). For an excellent summary of the *Plessy* decision, see Kluger, *Simple Justice*, 73–83.

8. Barnes, *Journey from Jim Crow*, 1–2, 5–7, 14–44; Kluger, *Simple Justice*, 73, 77, 105–226, 238; "Argument in Irene Morgan Case," NAACPP; *Hall v. DeCuir*, 95 U.S. 485 (1878); *Mitchell v. United States*, 313 U.S. 80 (1941). See also Joseph R. Palmore, "The Not-So-Strange Career of Interstate Jim Crow: Race, Transportation, and the Dormant Commerce Clause, 1878–1946," *Virginia Law Review* 83 (November 1997): 1773–1817.

9. Spottswood W. Robinson III to Thurgood Marshall, January 11, 1945, and Thurgood Marshall to Spottswood W. Robinson III, January 15, 1945, folder 1, box II-B190, NAACPP; Robinson, "Memorandum Covering Transportation Cases"; Barnes, *Journey from Jim Crow*; Mark V. Tushnet, *Making Civil Rights Law: Thurgood Marshall and the Supreme Court, 1936–1961* (New York: Oxford University Press, 1994), 72–73; Carl T. Rowan, *Dream Makers, Dream Breakers: The World of Justice Thurgood Marshall* (Boston: Little, Brown, 1993), 106; Williams, *Thurgood Marshall*, 145.

10. *Irene Morgan v. Commonwealth of Virginia*, 184 Va. 24, in *Virginia Reports* 184 (Richmond, 1946), 39.

11. "Argument in Irene Morgan Case"; "Irene Morgan, Appellant, vs. Commonwealth of Virginia—Brief of Appellee"; Richard E. Westbrooks to Thurgood Marshall, June 15, 1945; Memorandum to Mr. Wilkins from Thurgood Marshall, November 28, 1945; Clifford Forster (ACLU) to Marian Perry, January 10, 1946; "Memorandum for Bulletin on Irene Morgan Case"; Earl B. Dickerson (National Bar Association) to Thurgood Marshall, February 5, 1946; "Virginia 'Jim-Crow' Law Argued Before Supreme Court: Decision Pending," *NAACP Bulletin*, March 28, 1946, all in box II-B190, NAACPP. See also Barnes, *Journey from Jim Crow*, 45–46; Tushnet, *Making Civil Rights Law*, 73–75; Kluger, *Simple Justice*, 238 (quotation); Williams, *Thurgood Marshall*, 145–146; Carter, *A Matter of Law*, 61; and Rowan, *Dream Makers, Dream Breakers*, 106.

12. *Smith v. Allwright*, 321 U.S. 649 (1944); Kluger, *Simple Justice*, 234–238, 237 (quotation); Tushnet, *Making Civil Rights Law*, 74–75, 99–115. On the Columbia, Tennessee, crisis, see O'Brien, *The Color of the Law*. On the significance of Jackie Robinson in the immediate postwar era, see Tygiel, *Baseball's Great Experiment*; Arnold Rampersad, *Jackie Robinson: A Biography* (New York: Knopf, 1997); and Randy Roberts and James Olson, *Winning Is the Only Thing: Sports in America Since 1945* (Baltimore: Johns Hopkins University Press, 1989), 25–45. For a perceptive analysis of the political context of the racial crosscurrents of the mid-1940s, see Sullivan, *Days of Hope*, 133–275; and Patricia Sullivan, "Southern

Reformers, the New Deal, and the Movement's Foundation," in *New Directions in Civil Rights Studies,* ed. Armistead L. Robinson (Charlottesville: University of Virginia Press, 1991), 81–104. See also Egerton, *Speak Now Against the Day,* 330–532; and Norrell, *The House I Live In,* 138–144.

13. *Morgan v. Virginia,* 328 U.S. 373 (1946); Kluger, *Simple Justice,* 236–238; Klarman, *From Jim Crow to Civil Rights,* 217, 220–224; "Question Ducked," *Time* 47 (June 10, 1946): 23. Barnes, *Journey from Jim Crow,* 47, notes that "Chief Justice Harlan Fiske Stone had been prepared to dissent in *Morgan.* Because he died on April 22, 1946, before the decision was handed down, his views were not made public, but in conference, the Chief Justice had maintained that racial seating on buses was a predominantly local matter which the states could regulate."

14. Folder 1, box II-B190, NAACPP, contains numerous clippings, press releases, and congratulatory telegrams related to the *Morgan* decision. See also the clippings in reel 96, TIRRCF; and the *Baltimore Afro-American,* June 8–July 27, 1946.

15. "National Leaders Hail Supreme Court Decision on Jim Crow Buses," press release, typescript, June 10, 1946; and Telegram, Adam Clayton Powell to Walter White, June 6, 1946 (quotation), both in folder 1, box II-B190, NAACPP; *Baltimore Afro-American,* June 15, 1946 (McGehee quotation). An editorial in the *Washington Post,* June 10, 1946, noted that Rep. Powell "had introduced a bill to abolish Jim Crow practices in interstate transportation a year and a half ago." In the wake of the *Brown* decision, billboards calling for Warren's impeachment were a common sight along the major highways of the Deep South.

16. Telegram, Walter White to a long list of political and civil rights leaders, June 5, 1946 (quotation), folder 1, box II-B190, NAACPP; *Chicago Defender,* June 15, 1946 (Winborne, Coleman, Sparks, and Bailey quotations); *Baton Rouge State-Times,* June 4, 1946; *Baltimore Afro-American,* June 15, 1946 (Talmadge quotation); Barnes, *Journey from Jim Crow,* 50–51. On Talmadge's racial demagoguery, see William Anderson, *The Wild Man from Sugar Creek: The Political Career of Eugene Talmadge* (Baton Rouge: Louisiana State University Press, 1975).

17. *Chicago Defender,* June 15, 1946; *Baltimore Afro-American,* June 15–July 27, 1946; Barnes, *Journey from Jim Crow,* 52–53, 62–65; Robert G. Dixon Jr., "Civil Rights in Transportation and the ICC," *George Washington Law Review* 31 (October 1962): 198–213.

18. Tushnet, *Making Civil Rights Law,* 75–76 (quotations); Barnes, *Journey from Jim Crow,* 62–65; Klarman, *From Jim Crow to Civil Rights,* 221–225. Robert L. Carter to Daniel E. Byrd, June 12, 1946, folder 1, box II-B190, NAACPP, expresses Carter's early suspicion that "the bus companies' rules and regulations requiring segregation, apart from state statutes, are not affected by the Morgan case. Where such rules are inaugurated, as we expect them to be, we will have to go to court in an attempt to have them set aside as being unreasonable and invalid." Robert L. Carter, interview by author, March 8, 2005.

19. Carter interview; *Baltimore Afro-American,* June 15, 1946 (quotation); "Virginia Goes A'Courtin' " claimed that Morgan was having "domestic problems" during the spring of 1946: "In April she left her service job and her husband who works as a maintenance man in one of Manhattan's less swanky apartment houses." *New York People's Voice,* June 15, 1946. At the time of the decision, she was employed "as a practical nurse for the children of Mr. and Mrs. Harold Wolff, writers, 70 Haven Ave." On Marshall's unshakable commitment to the NAACP's legal and constitutional civil rights strategy during the 1940s, see Tushnet, *Making Civil Rights Law,* 67–136; Williams, *Thurgood Marshall,* 145–166; and Kluger, *Simple Justice,* 214–314.

20. Williams, *Thurgood Marshall,* 167–169; Kluger, *Simple Justice,* 190–191; Wilkins, *Standing Fast,* 190, 205–206, 210–211; Carter interview. On the NAACP Youth Councils and other sources of direct action advocacy within the NAACP, see Ransby, *Ella Baker and the Black Freedom Movement,* 105–147; Joanne Grant, *Ella Baker: Freedom Bound* (New York: Wiley, 1998), 50–51, 93; and Adam Fairclough, *Race and Democracy: The Civil Rights Struggle in Louisiana, 1915–1972* (Athens: University of Georgia Press, 1995), xi–xx, 110–111, 272–283, 296, 407–408. On the NAACP and anti-Communism, see Wilson Record, *Race and Radicalism: The NAACP and the Communist Party in Conflict* (Ithaca: Cornell University Press, 1964); Woods, *Black Struggle, Red Scare,* 9, 49, 53, 61–62, 138, 156–157; Tushnet, *Making Civil Rights Law,* 44–47; Kenneth R. Janken, "From Colonial Liberation to Cold War Liberalism: Walter White, the NAACP, and Foreign Affairs, 1941–1955," *Ethnic and Racial Studies* 21 (1998): 1074–1095; and Carol Anderson, *Eyes off the Prize: The United Nations and the African American Struggle for Human Rights, 1944–1955* (Cambridge: Cambridge University Press, 2003).

21. While there is no comprehensive study of radical civil rights activism during the 1930s and 1940s, there are a number of monographs that discuss the activities of individual activists and specific organizations. See especially Meier and Rudwick, *CORE,* 3–40; Jervis Anderson, *Bayard Rustin: Troubles I've Seen* (New York: HarperCollins, 1997), 3–149; Daniel Levine, *Bayard Rustin and the Civil Rights Movement* (New Brunswick: Rutgers University Press, 2000); D'Emilio, *Lost Prophet*; Anderson, *A. Philip Randolph*; Pfeffer, *A. Philip Randolph*; Carter, *Scottsboro*; John A. Salmond, *A Southern Rebel: The Life and Times of Aubrey Williams, 1890–1965* (Chapel Hill: University of North Carolina Press, 1983); John A. Salmond, *Southern Struggles: The Southern Labor Movement and the Civil Rights Struggle* (Gainesville: University Press of Florida, 2004); Bruce Nelson, *Divided We Stand: American Workers and the Struggle for Black Equality* (Princeton: Princeton University Press, 2001); Frank T. Adams, *James A. Dombrowski: An American Heretic, 1897–1983* (Knoxville: University of Tennessee Press, 1992); Robert F. Martin, *Howard Kester and the Struggle for Social Justice in the South, 1904–1977* (Charlottesville: University of Virginia Press, 1991); Honey, *Southern Labor and Black Civil Rights*; Anthony P. Dunbar, *Against the Grain: Southern Radicals and Prophets, 1929–1959* (Charlottesville: University of Virginia Press, 1981); John M. Glen, *Highlander: No Ordinary School, 1932–1962* (Lexington: University of Kentucky Press, 1988); Kreuger, *And Promises to Keep*; H. L. Mitchell, *Mean Things Happening in This Land* (Montclair, NJ: Allanheld, Osmun, 1979); Nell Irvin Painter, *The*

Narrative of Hosea Hudson: His Life as a Negro Communist in the South (Cambridge: Harvard University Press, 1979); Kelley, *Hammer and Hoe*; Mark Naison, *Communists in Harlem During the Depression* (Urbana: University of Illinois Press, 1981); Anne C. Loveland, *Lillian Smith: A Southerner Confronting the South* (Baton Rouge: Louisiana State University Press, 1986); Patricia Sullivan, ed., *Freedom Writer: Virginia Foster Durr, Letters from the Civil Rights Years* (New York: Routledge, 2003); Sullivan, *Days of Hope*; and Egerton, *Speak Now Against the Day*. See also Jacquelyn Dowd Hall, "The Long Civil Rights Movement and the Political Uses of the Past," *Journal of American History* 91 (March 2005): 1233–1250; and Richard M. Dalfiume, "The 'Forgotten Years' of the Negro Revolution," *Journal of American History* 55 (June 1968): 90–106. On the evolution of nonviolence and the American peace movement, see Joseph Kip Kosek, "Richard Gregg, Mohandas Gandhi, and the Strategy of Nonviolence," *Journal of American History* 91 (March 2005): 1318–1348; Lawrence S. Wittner, *Rebels Against War: The American Peace Movement, 1941–1960* (New York: Columbia University Press, 1969); Tracy, *Direct Action*; Scott H. Bennett, *Radical Pacifism: The War Resisters League and Gandhian Nonviolence in America, 1915–1963* (Syracuse: Syracuse University Press, 2003); Charles Chatfield, *For Peace and Justice: Pacifism in America, 1914–1941* (Knoxville: University of Tennessee Press, 1971); Staughton Lynd, ed., *Nonviolence in America: A Documentary History* (Indianapolis: Bobbs-Merrill, 1966); and Jo Ann O. Robinson, *Abraham Went Out: A Biography of A. J. Muste* (Philadelphia: Temple University Press, 1981). On Gandhi, see Louis Fischer, *The Life of Mahatma Gandhi* (London: Jonathan Cape, 1951); Judith M. Brown, *Gandhi: Prisoner of Hope* (New Haven: Yale University Press, 1989); and Stanley Wolpert, *Gandhi's Passion: The Life and Legacy of Mahatma Gandhi* (New York: Oxford University Press, 2001). On Gandhian and nonviolent philosophy, see Joan V. Bondurant, *Conquest of Violence: The Gandhian Philosophy of Conflict* (Berkeley: University of California Press, 1965); Erik H. Erikson, *Gandhi's Truth: On the Origins of Militant Nonviolence* (New York: Norton, 1969); Richard B. Gregg, *The Power of Non-Violence* (Philadelphia: J. P. Lippincott, 1934); Mulford Q. Sibley, ed., *The Quiet Battle: Writings on the Theory and Practice of Non-Violent Resistance* (Garden City, NY: Anchor, 1963); and William Robert Miller, *Nonviolence: A Christian Interpretation* (New York: Schocken Books, 1966).

22. Robinson, *Abraham Went Out*, 3–118; Meier and Rudwick, *CORE*, 4–34; Anderson, *Bayard Rustin*, 61–77, 81–110; D'Emilio, *Lost Prophet*, 35–54; Farmer, *Lay Bare the Heart*, 70–161; Tracy, *Direct Action*, 20–29. See also Nat Hentoff, *Peace Agitator: The Story of A. J. Muste* (New York: Macmillan, 1963); Chatfield, *For Peace and Justice*; and Wittner, *Rebels Against War*, 1–181.

23. Anderson, *Bayard Rustin*, 114–124, 183–196, 224–235; D'Emilio, *Lost Prophet*, 133–140, 225–301, 319–325; Bayard Rustin, *Down the Line: The Collected Writings of Bayard Rustin* (Chicago: Quadrangle Books, 1971), ix–61; Raymond Arsenault, "Bayard Rustin and the 'Miracle in Montgomery,' " in *A History of the African American People*, ed. James O. Horton and Lois E. Horton (Detroit: Wayne State University Press, 1997), 156–157; Peck, *Freedom Ride*; Farmer, *Lay Bare the Heart*, 2–32, 101–116, 165–166, 195–291; Meier and Rudwick, *CORE*, 4–19, 131–417.

24. Anderson, *Bayard Rustin*, 6–95, 23 (first quotation); D'Emilio, *Lost Prophet*, 7–56; Levine, *Bayard Rustin and the Civil Rights Movement*, 1984–1987, CUOHC; Bayard Rustin interviews, 1984–1987, CUOHC; Charles Moritz, ed., *Current Biography Yearbook 1967* (New York: H. W. Wilson, 1967), 360; Branch, *Parting the Waters*, 168–171; Adam Fairclough, *To Redeem the Soul of America: The Southern Christian Leadership Conference and Martin Luther King, Jr.* (Athens: University of Georgia Press, 1987), 23–24; Robinson, *Abraham Went Out*, 111; Anderson, *A. Philip Randolph*, 249–274, 275 (second quotation), 280–281, 378–380; Pfeffer, *A. Philip Randolph*, 51–90; Viorst, *Fire in the Streets*, 200–208; Kosek, "Richard Gregg, Mohandas Gandhi, and the Strategy of Nonviolence," 1336–1343; Tracy, *Direct Action*, 28–29; Bayard Rustin, "The Negro and Non-Violence," *Fellowship* 8 (October 1942): 166–167 (third quotation); Rustin, *Down the Line*, ix–xv, 11. On Carl Rachlin, see Anderson, *Bayard Rustin*, 41–44, 157, 271; Meier and Rudwick, *CORE*, 143, 151, 168, 173, 180, 226, 271, 277, 283, 412; and *New York Times*, January 4, 2000 (obituary).

25. Rustin, *Down the Line*, 6–7; D'Emilio, *Lost Prophet*, 46–47; Levine, *Bayard Rustin and the Civil Rights Movement*, 32–33; Tracy, *Direct Action*, 30–31. On Mayor Ben West, see Halberstam, *The Children*, 111–114, 127, 179, 198, 200, 210–213, 230–234, 199; and "Ain't Scared of Your Jails," episode 3 of the documentary film series *Eyes on the Prize: America's Civil Rights Years* (Boston: Blackside, 1986).

26. Anderson, *Bayard Rustin*, 96–110, 111 (quotation); D'Emilio, *Lost Prophet*, 50–134; Levine, *Bayard Rustin and the Civil Rights Movement*, 27–28, 34–51; Moritz, *Current Biography Yearbook 1967*, 360–361; Rustin, *Down the Line*, ix–x, 5–52; Rustin interviews, CUOHC; Branch, *Parting the Waters*, 171–172; Fairclough, *To Redeem the Soul of America*, 24; Robinson, *Abraham Went Out*, 111–117; Viorst, *Fire in the Streets*, 208–210; Pfeffer, *A. Philip Randolph*, 62, 142, 150–168; Meier and Rudwick, *CORE*, 12–20, 34–50, 57, 64.

27. *New York Times*, July 13, 1993 (obituary); James Peck, *Underdogs vs. Upperdogs* (Canterbury, NJ: n.p., 1969); James Peck, *We Who Would Not Kill* (New York: Lyle Stuart, 1958); Peck, *Freedom Ride*, 15, 38–39 (quotations); Meier and Rudwick, *CORE*, 35; James Peck, interview by James Mosby Jr., February 19, 1970, RBOHC; Marvin Rich, interview by author, January 24, 2003, May 4, 2005; Gordon Carey, interview by author, November 24, December 11, 2002; Nancy L. Roberts, *American Peace Writers, Editors, and Periodicals: A Dictionary* (Westport, CT: Greenwood Press, 1991), 221–222; Tracy, *Direct Action*, 37. On the National Maritime Union, see Bruce Nelson, *Workers on the Waterfront: Seamen, Longshoremen, and Unionism in the 1930s* (Urbana: University of Illinois Press, 1988). On Baldwin and the ACLU, see Samuel Walker, *In Defense of American Liberties: A History of the ACLU* (New York: Oxford University Press, 1990); Diane Garey, *Defending Everybody: A History of the American Civil Liberties Union* (New York: TV Books, 1998); and Peggy Lamson, *Roger Baldwin: Founder of the American Civil Liberties Union* (Boston: Houghton Mifflin, 1976). On the activities of the War Resisters League, see Bennett, *Radical Pacifism*.

28. Farmer, *Lay Bare the Heart*, 33–65; James Farmer, interview by Ed Edwin, 1979, CUOHC.
29. Farmer, *Lay Bare the Heart*, 117–128, 129 (quotation); Farmer interview, CUOHC. In a 1970 interview, Jim Peck stated: "I feel that Mr. Farmer's only asset was that he was an effective public speaker. . . . Therefore we needed somebody like Marvin Rich to really do the brain work, strategy, and basic work required in running a national organization." Peck interview, RBOHC. Following Farmer's death in 1999, an Associated Press wire service story emphasized the strange power of his voice: "Diabetes stilled the legs that had walked treacherous miles on the roads of the hostile South during the Freedom Rides of the 1960s. But, oh, that voice! Right up to his final days, nothing had muted the mighty, flowing baritone that helped mold and inspire the civil rights movement for one generation, then brought it back to life for college students of a later time." *St. Petersburg Times*, July 11, 1999. See also Farmer's interview in the documentary "Ain't Scared of Your Jails."
30. Farmer, *Lay Bare the Heart*, 129–133; Sullivan, *Days of Hope*, 150; John B. Kirby, "Race, Class, and Politics: Ralph Bunche and Black Protest," in *Ralph Bunche: The Man and His Times*, ed. Benjamin Rivlin (New York: Holmes and Meier, 1990), 36–39; Pfeffer, *A. Philip Randolph*, 32–43; Anderson, *Bayard Rustin*, 58; *Official Proceedings of the Second National Negro Congress* (Philadelphia: October 15–17, 1937). See also Lawrence Wittner, "The National Negro Congress: A Reassessment," *American Quarterly* 22 (Fall 1970): 883–901.
31. Farmer, *Lay Bare the Heart*, 135 (first quotation), 71 (second quotation), 133–146; James Farmer, interview by John Britton, September 28, 1968, RBOHC; Farmer interview, CUOHC; Tracy, *Direct Action*, 22–23. On Howard Thurman, see Walter E. Fluker and Catherine Tumber, eds., *A Strange Freedom: The Best of Howard Thurman on Religious Experience and Public Life* (Boston: Beacon, 1998); Walter E. Fluker, *They Looked for a City: A Comparative Analysis of the Ideal of Community in the Thought of Howard Thurman and Martin Luther King, Jr.* (Lanham, MD: University Press of America, 1989); Luther E. Smith, *Howard Thurman: The Mystic as Prophet* (Richmond: Friends United Press, 1992); and Alton B. Pollard III, *Mysticism and Social Change: The Social Witness of Howard Thurman* (New York: Peter Lang, 1992).
32. Meier and Rudwick, *CORE*, 4–17, 18 (quotation); Farmer, *Lay Bare the Heart*, 67–116; Anderson, *Bayard Rustin*, 93; D'Emilio, *Lost Prophet*, 50–54; Tracy, *Direct Action*, 22–27; George Houser, interview by Katherine Shannon, September 11, 1967, RBOHC; Farmer interview, RBOHC; Farmer interview, CUOHC.
33. Farmer, *Lay Bare the Heart*, 116 (quotation), 115–116, 149–161; Meier and Rudwick, *CORE*, 19–25, 42–44; Robinson, *Abraham Went Out*, 111–117; D'Emilio, *Lost Prophet*, 62–63; Houser interview, RBOHC; Farmer interview, CUOHC; Rich interview; Anderson, *Bayard Rustin*, 93–95. On the difficulties and controversies surrounding the merger of pacifism, nonviolence, and civil rights activism during the 1940s and 1950s, see Kosek, "Richard Gregg, Mohandas Gandhi, and the Strategy of Nonviolence," 1318–1320, 1336–1348; and Tracy, *Direct Action*, 26–75.
34. Farmer, *Lay Bare the Heart*, 165–166; Farmer interview, CUOHC; Rich and Carey interviews.
35. Houser interview, RBOHC; George M. Houser, "A Personal Retrospective on the 1947 Journey of Reconciliation," typescript of a paper given at Bluffton College, September 1992, box 1, COREC; George M. Houser, " 'Thy Brother's Blood: Reminiscences of World War II," *Christian Century* 112 (August 16, 1995): 774; Meier and Rudwick, *CORE*, 5–6, 16–21, 29, 34; D'Emilio, *Lost Prophet*, 50–55, 62, 64, 67, 76, 119, 125–126, 128, 131–134; Tracy, *Direct Action*, 20–21, 26, 28, 32, 36, 53–55.
36. Houser, "A Personal Retrospective," 3–4 (quotations); Tracy, *Direct Action*, 54.
37. On the Isaac Woodard episode, see Egerton, *Speak Now Against the Day*, 362–363 (quotation); Barnes, *Journey from Jim Crow*, 62; Sullivan, *Days of Hope*, 219; *Crisis* 53 (September 1946): 276; and *Race Relations: A Monthly Summary of Events and Trends in Race Relations* 4 (August–September 1946): 6–7. The NAACP brought a civil suit against Atlantic Greyhound in an attempt to recover damages for Woodard, but in November 1947 a Charleston, West Virginia, jury issued a verdict in favor of the bus company. On Wilson Head's freedom ride, see Salmond, *"My Mind Set on Freedom,"* 3–4, 87, 149; John Hope Franklin, interview by author, February 9, 2005. The Richmond incident took place in July 1947, in the aftermath of the Journey of Reconciliation. Houser interview, RBOHC; Houser, "A Personal Retrospective," 2–6; Anderson, *Bayard Rustin*, 114–116; Meier and Rudwick, *CORE*, 20, 34; Peck, *Freedom Ride*, 14–15; Rustin, *Down the Line*, 13; D'Emilio, *Lost Prophet*, 133–134; Robinson, *Abraham Went Out*, 113–114.
38. Houser, "A Personal Retrospective," 5–6 (quotations); George M. Houser and Bayard Rustin, "Memorandum #2: Bus and Train Travel in the South," box 20, FORP; Peck, *Freedom Ride*, 16; Meier and Rudwick, *CORE*, 34; D'Emilio, *Lost Prophet*, 133–134; Tracy, *Direct Action*, 54–55; Grant, *Ella Baker*, 91–92; Marian B. Mollin, "The Limits of Egalitarianism: Radical Pacifism, Civil Rights, and the Journey of Reconciliation," *Radical History Review* 88 (Winter 2004): 113–138. See also Marian B. Mollin, "Actions Louder than Words: Gender and Political Activism in the American Radical Pacifist Movement, 1942–1972" (Ph.D. thesis, University of Massachusetts, 2000). Baker had already conducted her own "freedom rides" on several occasions. In December 1942 she and a second black passenger refused to relinquish their seats on a crowded Georgia bus; although they avoided arrest and violence, both were subjected to threats and verbal abuse. Six months later, on May 4, 1943, Baker successfully challenged Jim Crow dining car restrictions on a train from Mobile, Alabama, to Jacksonville, Florida. However, when she traveled from Jacksonville to New York City on May 29, a second challenge was foiled by two military policemen who drove her from the dining car, bruising one of her legs in the process. With Thurgood Marshall's help, she later filed a formal complaint against the railway company. See Ransby, *Ella Baker and the Black Freedom Movement*, 124–127.
39. Robert L. Carter to Daniel E. Byrd, June 12, 1946; George Houser to Marian Perry, October 9, 1946; W. A. C. Hughes to Thurgood Marshall, July 8, 1946; Robert L. Carter, Memos to Walter

White, July 26, September 26, 1946, all in box II-B190, NAACPP. *Baltimore Afro-American*, June 26, July 6, 27, November 2, 1946; *Los Angeles Tribune*, September 21, 1946; *Kansas City Plaindealer*, September 20, 1946; *Chicago Defender*, August 17, November 30, 1946; *Oklahoma City Black Dispatch*, December 9, 1946; *Memphis World*, November 15, 1946; *Atlanta Daily World*, November 27, 1946; Houser, "A Personal Retrospective," 6–8; Barnes, *Journey from Jim Crow*, 52–53, 62–63; Tushnet, *Making Civil Rights Law*, 74–76; Peck, *Freedom Ride*, 17; Meier and Rudwick, *CORE*, 34–35; Anderson, *Bayard Rustin*, 114–115. On the Fellowship of Southern Churchmen, see Robert F. Martin, "Critique of Southern Society and Vision of a New Order: The Fellowship of Southern Churchmen, 1934–1957," *Church History* 52 (March 1983): 66–80; and Martin, *Howard Kester and the Struggle for Social Justice in the South, 1904–1977*.

40. Thurgood Marshall to Dear Sir [members of NAACP Legal Committee], November 6, 1946, box II-B190, NAACPP; *New York Times*, November 23, 1946 (quotation); Anderson, *Bayard Rustin*, 114–115; Carter interview. According to Rustin and Houser, Roy Wilkins, the assistant secretary who worked under executive secretary Walter White, was the only national NAACP leader to respond favorably to the proposed Journey of Reconciliation. D'Emilio, *Lost Prophet*, 134.

41. Bayard Rustin, "Our Guest Column: Beyond the Courts," *Louisiana Weekly*, January 4, 1947; Anderson, *Bayard Rustin*, 115–116.

42. On Truman and the President's Committee on Civil Rights, see John Hope Franklin, "A Half-Century of Presidential Race Initiatives: Some Reflections," *Journal of Supreme Court History* 24 (1999): 227–230; William C. Berman, *The Politics of Civil Rights in the Truman Administration* (Columbus: Ohio State University Press, 1970); and Donald R. McCoy and Richard T. Ruetten, *Quest and Response: Minority Rights and the Truman Administration* (Lawrence: University Press of Kansas, 1973). See also President's Committee on Civil Rights, *To Secure These Rights: The Report of the President's Committee on Civil Rights* (Washington: GPO, 1947); and Steven Lawson, ed., *To Secure These Rights: The Report of Harry S. Truman's Committee on Civil Rights* (New York: Bedford, 2003).

43. Peck, *Freedom Ride*, 17; D'Emilio, *Lost Prophet*, 134–135; Houser, "A Personal Retrospective," 6–7 (quotation); Carter interview. Rustin and Houser traveled together to Washington, D.C.; Richmond and Petersburg, Virginia; and Chapel Hill, Greensboro, Winston-Salem, and Asheville, North Carolina. Houser traveled alone to Nashville and Knoxville, Tennessee, and Louisville, Kentucky. Rustin and Houser, "Memorandum #2: Bus and Train Travel in the South"; Houser interview, RBOHC. During the scouting trip, Rustin and Houser met Floyd McKissick, a young black attorney practicing in Durham, North Carolina. The first black graduate of the University of North Carolina Law School, McKissick would later serve as CORE's national chairman (1963–1966) and national director (1966–1968). On McKissick, see Meier and Rudwick, *CORE*, 293–294, 381, 396, 402–424.

44. Houser, "A Personal Retrospective," 7–8; Rustin and Houser, "Memorandum #2: Bus and Train Travel in the South."

45. Rustin, *Down the Line*, 13–14; Houser, "A Personal Retrospective," 7–8; Meier and Rudwick, *CORE*, 35; Anderson, *Bayard Rustin*, 116; D'Emilio, *Lost Prophet*, 135; Tracy, *Direct Action*, 55; *Boston Globe*, August 28, 1993, May 29, 2002; *New York Times*, November 18, 1995; *Los Angeles Times*, March 4, 2005.

46. Peck, *Freedom Ride*, 15–16 (quotations); Houser, "A Personal Retrospective," 8; Anderson, *Bayard Rustin*, 116; Meier and Rudwick, *CORE*, 35–36; Tracy, *Direct Action*, 55.

47. Bayard Rustin and George Houser, *You Don't Have to Ride Jim Crow* (Washington: Interracial Workshop, 1947). Copies of this pamphlet can be found in reel 25, COREP; and in the "George Houser Scrapbook—Journey of Reconciliation 1947," box 2, COREC.

48. Peck, *Freedom Ride*, 16.

49. Ibid., 18 (quotation); "Log—Journey of Reconciliation," April 9–23, 1947, typescript, Bayard Rustin Files, box 51, FORP. Wally Nelson maintained the log. Houser, "A Personal Retrospective," 9; *Pittsburgh Courier*, April 5, 19, 1947. When interviewed by historian John D'Emilio a half century later, Bromley recalled: "Nobody knew what was going to happen. Everybody on this thing went into it with apprehension because they knew what could occur and what had occurred. . . . I wouldn't say we were terror-stricken, but everybody was frightened." D'Emilio, *Lost Prophet*, 135.

50. "Log—Journey of Reconciliation," 1–2; Rustin and Houser, *You Don't Have to Ride Jim Crow*, 1 (quotation); Rustin, *Down the Line*, 14; Houser, "A Personal Retrospective," 9–10; Peck, *Freedom Ride*, 18; Anderson, *Bayard Rustin*, 117; D'Emilio, *Lost Prophet*, 136; Conrad Lynn, *There Is a Fountain* (Westport, CT: Lawrence Hill, 1979), 109 (quotation).

51. "Log—Journey of Reconciliation," 2; Rustin and Houser, *You Don't Have to Ride Jim Crow*, 1; Houser, "A Personal Retrospective," 10 (quotation); Rustin, *Down the Line*, 14-15, 16 (quotation).

52. Rustin, *Down the Line*, 15 (first and second quotations); "Log—Journey of Reconciliation," 2–4; Houser, "A Personal Retrospective," 10–11; Anderson, *Bayard Rustin*, 117; D'Emilio, *Lost Prophet*, 136–137; Lynn, *There Is a Fountain*, 109–110, 111 (third quotation).

53. Rustin, *Down the Line*, 16–17 (quotations); "Log—Journey of Reconciliation," 5–6; Peck, *Freedom Ride*, 18–20; Houser, "A Personal Retrospective," 11–12.

54. "Log—Journey of Reconciliation," 6–7; Houser, "A Personal Retrospective," 12–14; Houser interview, RBOHC; Peck, *Freedom Ride*, 20–21; *Chapel Hill Daily Tar Heel*, April 16–19, 1947; W. McKee Evans, interview by author, February 18, 2005; Anderson, *Bayard Rustin*, 118; D'Emilio, *Lost Prophet*, 137–138; Egerton, *Speak Now Against the Day*, 422–423, 556–559. The "George Houser Scrapbook—Journey of Reconciliation 1947," box 2, COREC, contains numerous clippings on the Chapel Hill incident. See especially *Greensboro Daily News*, April 15, 17–18, 1947; *Pittsburgh Courier*, April 19, 1947; and *Carolina Times*, April 26, 1947. On Frank Porter Graham, see Warren Ashby, *Frank Porter Graham: A Southern Liberal* (Winston-Salem: John F. Blair, 1980). On Nelle Morton and

the Fellowship of Southern Churchmen's role in the Journey of Reconciliation's visit to Chapel Hill, see John Salmond, " 'Flag-bearers for Integration and Justice': Local Civil Rights Groups in the South, 1940–1954," in Feldman, *Before Brown*, 227–235.

55. Houser, "A Personal Retrospective," 12 (quotation); Peck, *Freedom Ride*, 20–21; *Pittsburgh Courier*, April 19, 1947.

56. "Log—Journey of Reconciliation," 6 (quotations)–7; Houser interview, RBOHC; Peck, *Freedom Ride*, 21–22; Rustin, *Down the Line*, 17; Anderson, *Bayard Rustin*, 118; D'Emilio, *Lost Prophet*, 138; *New York Times*, April 14, 1947; *Chapel Hill Daily Tar Heel*, April 15–16, 1947.

57. Rustin, *Down the Line*, 17 (first quotation); Peck, *Freedom Ride*, 21 (second and third quotations); Houser interview, RBOHC; "Log—Journey of Reconciliation," 7; *Pittsburgh Courier*, April 19, 1947; *Chapel Hill Daily Tar Heel*, April 15–16, 1947; Evans interview; D'Emilio, *Lost Prophet*, 139.

58. Peck, *Freedom Ride*, 22 (quotation)–23; "Log—Journey of Reconciliation," 7; Rustin, *Down the Line*, 17; *Pittsburgh Courier*, April 19, 1947; *Chapel Hill Daily Tar Heel*, April 15–16, 1947; Evans interview; D'Emilio, *Lost Prophet*, 139; Anderson, *Bayard Rustin*, 119, offers a detailed but largely inaccurate account of the pursuit.

59. Peck, *Freedom Ride*, 23; *New York Times*, April 14, 1947; *Greensboro Daily News*, April 17, 1947 (first quotation); *Chicago Defender*, May 3, 1947 (second quotation); *Chapel Hill Daily Tar Heel*, April 15–18, 1947; Evans interview.

60. *Greensboro Daily News*, April 18, 1947 (Jones quotations); *Chapel Hill Daily Tar Heel*, April 17–May 1 (McGirt quotation), 1947; *Carolina Times*, April 26, 1947; Evans interview. Houser, "A Personal Retrospective," 13–14, notes: "I always had a guilt feeling about this incident because we left Charles Jones to face the wrath of the taxi drivers and others of their ilk in Chapel Hill. He was already a marked man in the community because he was always on the cutting edge of racial and social issues (such as union organization) which divided the community." Conservative editors and reporters in North Carolina often printed diatribes against Jones. See, for example, the editorial in the *Charlotte Textile Times*, April 15, 1947 (typescript copy in "George Houser Scrapbook—Journey of Reconciliation 1947"), which declared: "The town of Chapel Hill, N.C., has for several years been affiliated with a 'crank,' a Presbyterian preacher named Charles M. Jones, who was brought there from Tennessee. He is the type of minister who, like the Holy Rollers and the sect which handles live snakes, interprets the Bible to suit his own warped ideas and he seems to be hipped upon the subject of social equality with Negroes. When, during the war, a Negro band was sent to Chapel Hill to furnish music for Navy preflight trainees, Mr. Jones saw a great opportunity. He began to invite Negroes to his church for ice cream socials and encouraged white girls to attend and have dates with the Negro men. Encouraged by the success of that effort, Mr. Jones invited students and professors from a Negro college at Durham, N.C., to a breakfast at his church. Four students and a professor accepted and each was seated at breakfast beside a white girl. . . .There are always a few crack-pot students in a university or college, but it is unusual for them to have the encouragement and support which they receive at Chapel Hill." In 1953, conservative critics of Jones's civil rights activism prompted a Presbytery inquiry that led to his resignation from the Presbyterian ministry. See Ashby, *Frank Porter Graham*, 305–309; "Deplore Secrecy in the Jones Case," *Christian Century* 70 (March 4, 1953): 245; "Presbyterian U.S. Commission Fires Chapel Hill Pastor," *Christian Century* 70 (March 11, 1953): 277; Henry Ruark, "Orange Presbytery vs. Jones," *Christian Century* 70 (March 18, 1953): 319–320; and "Pastor vs. Presbytery," *Time* 61 (February 23, 1953): 53.

61. Peck, *Freedom Ride*, 23 (quotations); D'Emilio, *Lost Prophet*, 139. On Greensboro, see Federal Writers' Project, *North Carolina: A Guide to the Old North State* (Chapel Hill: University of North Carolina Press, 1939), 203–213.

62. Rustin, *Down the Line*, 18 (first and second quotations); "Log—Journey of Reconciliation," 8; Houser, "A Personal Retrospective," 14, 15 (third quotation).

63. Peck, *Freedom Ride*, 24–26 (quotations); Rustin, *Down the Line*, 18; Houser, "A Personal Retrospective," 16; *Asheville Citizen*, April 19, 1947; *Pittsburgh Courier*, April 26, 1947; *Baltimore Afro-American*, April 26, 1947; James Peck, "Not So Deep Are the Roots," *Crisis* 54 (September 1947): 274. On Felmet, see the Joe Felmet Papers, Southern Historical Collection, University of North Carolina, Chapel Hill; and the FBI files on Felmet in the Journey of Reconciliation folder, box 20, FORP.

64. Peck, *Freedom Ride*, 26 (quotations); Rustin, *Down the Line*, 18; Curtiss Todd to Thurgood Marshall, April 19, 1947, Robert L. Carter to Curtiss Todd, April 23, 1947, box II-B184, NAACPP.

65. Homer A. Jack, "Journey of Reconciliation," *Common Ground* 8 (Autumn 1947): 22, 23 (quotation); Houser, "A Personal Retrospective," 14–15; Houser interview, RBOHC.

66. Jack, "Journey of Reconciliation," 23–24 (quotations); Rustin, *Down the Line*, 19; Houser, "A Personal Retrospective," 15–16.

67. Rustin, *Down the Line*, 19; Houser, "A Personal Retrospective," 15–16. In 1961 Worthy told ICC investigators: "It has been my practice, started as far back as 1944, that whenever I am traveling in the Southern part of the United States, to deliberately go into the white waiting room." Typescript, March 21, 1961, RD 56, box 9, Investigative Report Case Files Relating to Complaints Against Motor Carriers in Interstate Commerce, 1961–70 (hereafter cited as Investigative Report Case Files), ICCR.

68. Jack, "Journey of Reconciliation," 24; Rustin, *Down the Line*, 19–21; Houser, "A Personal Retrospective," 16–17; Houser interview, RBOHC; Peck, "Not So Deep Are the Roots," 273, 274 (quotation); *Lynchburg News*, April 23–24, 28, 1947; *Lynchburg Advance*, April 29, 1947. "Log—Journey of Reconciliation," 9–11, provides a detailed summary of Houser's and Nelson's bus and train trip from Lynchburg, Virginia, to Washington, D.C.

69. Peck, *Freedom Ride*, 27 (quotation); "Log—Journey of Reconciliation," 11; Rustin, *Down the Line*, 14. For a sampling of the press reaction to the Journey of Reconciliation, see "George Houser Scrap-

book—Journey of Reconciliation 1947," box 2, COREC. On the public reaction to and press coverage of Jackie Robinson's first month as a Major League ballplayer, see Tygiel, *Baseball's Great Experiment*, 174–200, and reel 102, TIRRCF.

70. *Baltimore Afro-American*, April 26, 1947.
71. Rustin, *Down the Line*, 22–25; Jack, "Journey of Reconciliation," 26 (last quotation).
72. Rustin, *Down the Line*, 21–22; Peck, "Not So Deep Are the Roots," 282; Jack, "Journey of Reconciliation," 24; Houser, "A Personal Retrospective," 17; *Pittsburgh Courier*, May 3, 1947; *Knoxville News-Sentinel*, May 21, 1947; *Lynchburg Advance*, April 29, 1947; Workers Defense League, "Bus Companies Urged to Obey Supreme Court Ruling Outlawing Jimcrow," press release, typescript, May 6, 1947; "Group Finds Bus Companies Evading Supreme Court's Anti–Jim Crow Ruling," FOR press release, typescript, April 28, 1947, both in Bayard Rustin Files, box 51, FORP.
73. Peck, "Not So Deep Are the Roots," 274 (first quotation); *New York Times*, May 22, 1947; *Long Island Daily Press*, May 21, 1947; Anderson, *Bayard Rustin*, 122 (second quotation); D'Emilio, *Lost Prophet*, 168; "Chapel Hill Judge Sentences Rustin and Roodenko," *Fellowship* 13 (July 1947); C. Jerry Gates to Roy Wilkins, May 27, 1947, and C. Jerry Gates to Thurgood Marshall, May 27, 1947, box II-B184, NAACPP; *Call*, July 2, 1947 (third quotation).
74. *Durham Morning Herald*, March 18, 1948; *Chicago Defender*, March 27, 1948; *Pittsburgh Courier*, March 27, 1948; *Asheville Times*, December 14, 1948; *State of North Carolina v. Johnson et al.* (1949), Orange County, NC 723; "Carolina Journey Members Lose North Carolina Appeal," *Fellowship* 15 (February 1949): 20; "Background Statement on the North Carolina Case," typescript, February 1949, reel 3, BRP; Bayard Rustin to C. Jerry Gates, May 13, June 5, 1947, reel 44, COREP. C. Jerry Gates to Roy Wilkins, May 27, 1947; C. Jerry Gates to Robert L. Carter, June 16, 1947; Robert L. Carter to C. Jerry Gates, July 25, 1947; Robert L. Carter to George Houser, August 12, 1947, all in box II-B184, NAACPP. Robert L. Carter to George Houser, February 8, 1949, in "Journey of Reconciliation, 1949, Chapel Hill Case" folder, reel 44, COREP; Anderson, *Bayard Rustin*, 122, 123 (quotation); D'Emilio, *Lost Prophet*, 168–169. The Virginia Supreme Court later overturned Lee's conviction. See *Norvell Lee v. Commonwealth of Virginia* (1949), record 3558; and Martin A. Martin to George Houser, October 12, 1949, reel 44, COREP.
75. C. E. Boulware to George Houser, January 18, 1949; Robert L. Carter to George Houser, February 8, 1949; minutes of FOR/CORE Legal Committee meeting, February 11, 1949; George Houser to Nelle Norton, February 12, 1949; Conrad Lynn to Andrew Johnson, February 14, 1949; Andrew Johnson to George Houser, March 12, 1949 (first quotation); FOR press release, typescript, March 20, 1949, all in "Journey of Reconciliation, 1949, Chapel Hill Case" folder, reel 44, COREP. George Houser to Dear Fellows, November 13, 1948, and George Houser to Bayard Rustin, November 20, 1948, reel 3, BRP; Anderson, *Bayard Rustin*, 123, 130–134; D'Emilio, *Lost Prophet*, 164–165; "Negro Acclaimed at Home and Abroad Sentenced to North Carolina Road Gang," FOR/CORE press release, typescript, March 9, 1949, Bayard Rustin Files, box 51, FORP (second quotation); Carter interview.
76. Rustin, *Down the Line*, 26–49, 29 (quotation); Anderson, *Bayard Rustin*, 135–136; D'Emilio, *Lost Prophet*, 170; Levine, *Bayard Rustin and the Civil Rights Movement*, 61–65. See also the correspondence and clippings (including the *New York Post* series) in reel 3, BRP; and the reports and correspondence in the Roxboro Prison Report folders, Bayard Rustin Files, box 51, FORP.
77. Houser, "A Personal Retrospective," 17–21; Peck, *Freedom Ride*, 27; Bayard Rustin, "From Freedom Ride to Ballot Box: The Changing Strategies of Black Struggle," typescript of lecture delivered as part of the William Radner Lecture Series, Columbia University, October 9–11, 1973, section 31, reel 18, BRP; Anderson, *Bayard Rustin*, 123; Meier and Rudwick, *CORE*, 38–39; Barnes, *Journey from Jim Crow*, 60–65; Levine, *Bayard Rustin and the Civil Rights Movement*, 64–67; D'Emilio, *Lost Prophet*, 170; Tracy, *Direct Action*, 56.

Chapter 2: Beside the Weary Road

1. *The Hymnbook* (Atlanta: Presbyterian Church in the United States, 1955), 160.
2. In February 1948 the Council on Intolerance in America awarded two of its annual Thomas Jefferson Awards to Rustin and Houser. Rustin, *Down the Line*, 50 (quotation), 51–52; Anderson, *Bayard Rustin*, 123–124; Levine, *Bayard Rustin and the Civil Rights Movement*, 65–69; D'Emilio, *Lost Prophet*, 175–183; Meier and Rudwick, *CORE*, 38–71; Tracy, *Direct Action*, 56–75; Farmer, *Lay Bare the Heart*, 176; Robinson, *Abraham Went Out*, 116–117; "Discrimination in Interstate Transportation, April 1947–May 1955," folder 40, reel 10, COREP; *CORE-lator*, October 1947–November 1954, reel 49, COREP; Peck, *Freedom Ride*, 27, 42 (quotation). On the evolving relationship between the Cold War, decolonization, and the civil rights struggle, see Dudziak, *Cold War Civil Rights*; and Borstelmann, *The Cold War and the Color Line*.
3. Meier and Rudwick, *CORE*, 69–75; Morris, *Origins of the Civil Rights Movement*, 128–130. George M. Houser to Thurgood Marshall, March 10, 1954; James Peck to Maurice McCrackin, n.d.; Robert L. Carter to Billie Ames, October 22, 1954 (quotation); Ames to Carter, October 26, 1954, all in reel 10, COREP. *CORE-lator*, October–November 1954, February 1955, Spring 1955, Fall 1955, reel 49, COREP; Rich interview. On the broader evolution of the American nonviolent movement in the period 1952–1955, see Tracy, *Direct Action*, 77–90.
4. Meier and Rudwick, *CORE*, 75–76; Farmer, *Lay Bare the Heart*, 185–187; typescript by James R. Robinson, February 8, 1956, reel 30, COREP. For a brief biographical sketch of Carter, see John

McCormally, "Profile of a Man with a Job," *Hutchinson* (Kansas) *News-Herald*, July 29, 1956, clipping in reel 31, COREP. On the origins and early weeks of the Montgomery Bus Boycott, see Martin Luther King Jr., *Stride Toward Freedom* (New York: Harper and Row, 1958), 10–126; Jo Ann Robinson, *The Montgomery Bus Boycott and the Women Who Started It* (Knoxville: University of Tennessee Press, 1987); Rosa Parks, *My Story* (New York: Dial, 1992), 108–150; Thornton, *Dividing Lines*, 20–88; Garrow, *Bearing the Cross*, 11–65; Branch, *Parting the Waters*, 128–185; Burns, *Daybreak of Freedom*; Morris, *Origins of the Civil Rights Movement*, 40–63; and Charles Marsh, *The Beloved Community: How Faith Shapes Social Justice, from the Civil Rights Movement to Today* (New York: Basic Books, 2005), 20–38.

5. Meier and Rudwick, *CORE*, 76; Morris, *Origins of the Civil Rights Movement*, 135; *CORE-lator*, Spring 1956, reel 49 (quotations); typescript by James R. Robinson, August 20, 1956, reel 30; James Peck to Martin Luther King Jr., March 9, 1956 (first quotation); King to Peck, May 10, 1956, reel 39, all in COREP.

6. Glenn Smiley, "The Miracle of Montgomery," typescript, 1956, box 16, FORP; Farmer, *Lay Bare the Heart*, 186–188 (quotations); Morris, *Origins of the Civil Rights Movement*, 128–138; Barnes, *Journey from Jim Crow*, 161; Meier and Rudwick, *CORE*, 76, 78; *CORE-lator*, February 1957, Spring 1958, Fall 1958, February 1959, reel 49, COREP; Rich interview.

7. On the shifting nature of American politics and society in the 1950s, see Stephen J. Whitfield, *The Culture of the Cold War*: Charles C. Alexander, *Holding the Line: The Eisenhower Era, 1952–1961* (Bloomington: Indiana University Press, 1975); Eric F. Goldman, *The Crucial Decade—and After: America, 1945–1960* (New York: Vintage, 1960); John Patrick Diggins, *The Proud Decades: America in War and Peace, 1941–1960* (New York: Norton, 1988); William O'Neill, *American High: The Years of Confidence, 1945–1960* (New York: Free Press, 1986); David Halberstam, *The Fifties* (New York: Villard, 1993); Patterson, *Grand Expectations*; and Elaine Tyler May, *Homeward Bound: American Families in the Cold War Era* (New York: Basic Books, 1988). For a provocative interpretation of the South in the 1950s, see Pete Daniel, *Lost Revolutions: The South in the 1950s* (Chapel Hill: University of North Carolina Press, 2000).

8. John Swomley, interview by author, November 8, 1985; William Worthy, interview by author, May 10, 2001; D'Emilio, *Lost Prophet*, 67–71, 114–116, 170–224; Anderson, *Bayard Rustin*, 140–179; Levine, *Bayard Rustin and the Civil Rights Movement*, 70–75; Viorst, *Fire in the Streets*, 210; Branch, *Parting the Waters*, 168, 172–173; Garrow, *Bearing the Cross*, 66; Tracy, *Direct Action*, 81–82, 91; Kosek, "Richard Gregg, Mohandas Gandhi, and the Strategy of Nonviolence," 1343–1344. On the presumed connection between homosexuality and security risks during the 1950s and 1960s, see David K. Johnson, *The Lavender Scare: The Cold War Persecution of Gays and Lesbians in the Federal Government* (Chicago: University of Chicago Press, 2004).

9. On Lillian Smith, see Loveland, *Lillian Smith*; Margaret Rose Gladney, ed., *How Am I to Be Heard: The Letters of Lillian Smith* (Chapel Hill: University of North Carolina Press, 1993); and Lillian Smith, *Killers of the Dream* (New York: Norton, 1949). Howell Raines, *My Soul Is Rested: Movement Days in the Deep South Remembered* (New York: G. P. Putnam's Sons, 1977), 53; Swomley interview; John M. Swomley Jr. to Wilson Riles, February 21, 1956, box 16, FORP (first, second, and third quotations); Worthy interview; Garrow, *Bearing the Cross*, 66, 642 n46; Norman Thomas to Homer Jack, February 12, 1956, box 62, NTP (fourth quotation); Viorst, *Fire in the Streets*, 210–211 (fifth quotation); Anderson, *Bayard Rustin*, 183–186. Levine, *Bayard Rustin and the Civil Rights Movement*, 78–82, 263–265, n5–13, offers an alternative chronology and explanation of Rustin's mission to Montgomery. Based largely on an interview with James Farmer, Levine argues that the idea for the trip came from Randolph, that Farmer suggested that Rustin would be the best person for the mission, and that Rustin may have visited Montgomery as early as December 1955. While many of the details related to Rustin's trip to Montgomery are open to speculation, at this point Levine's account does not appear to rest on solid evidence. The date of Lillian Smith's correspondence with Rustin and King also remains a subject of speculation. See D'Emilio, *Lost Prophet*, 227, which concludes that Smith did not write to King until after Rustin's arrival in Montgomery in late February. See also Lillian Smith to Martin Luther King, March 10, 1956, in Gladney, *How Am I to Be Heard*, 94.

10. Swomley interview; John Swomley to Glenn Smiley, February 29, 1956, box 16, FORP; War Resisters League Executive Committee Minutes, February 20, 1956, Series B, box 1, WRLP; Farmer interview, CUOHC; Raines, *My Soul Is Rested*, 53–54; Anderson, *Bayard Rustin*, 187; Viorst, *Fire in the Streets*, 210–211; Farmer, *Lay Bare the Heart*, 186–187; Garrow, *Bearing the Cross*, 66–67; Robinson, *Abraham Went Out*, 117; Pfeffer, *A. Philip Randolph*, 173–174; Bayard Rustin, "Report on Montgomery, Alabama" (New York: War Resisters League, March 21, 1956), copy in Bayard Rustin Files, box 51, FORP; Fairclough, *To Redeem the Soul of America*, 24; Worthy interview. On Worthy, see Meier and Rudwick, *CORE*, 35, 40, 45–46; Pfeffer, *A. Philip Randolph*, 149–150, 155–156, 161, 166–167; Raines, *My Soul Is Rested*, 53; *Who's Who Among Black Americans, 1990–1991* (Detroit: Gale Research, 1991), 1408; and *New York Times*, July 8, 1950, June 23, 1955, September 9, December 26, 1956, February 4, April 30, 1957, September 21, 1960, October 12, 1962, March 4, November 22, 1964.

11. Bayard Rustin, "Montgomery Diary," *Liberation* 1 (April 1956): 7 (quotations); Worthy interview; Branch, *Parting the Waters*, 173–177; Garrow, *Bearing the Cross*, 67; Anderson, *Bayard Rustin*, 186; D'Emilio, *Lost Prophet*, 228–229.

12. Rustin, "Montgomery Diary," 7–10 (quotations); Rustin, "Report on Montgomery, Alabama"; Swomley interview; Glenn Smiley to John Swomley and Al Hassler, February 29, 1956, box 16, FORP; Branch, *Parting the Waters*, 177–180; Garrow, *Bearing the Cross*, 67–68; Raines, *My Soul Is Rested*, 52–57; Farmer, *Lay Bare the Heart*, 187; Fairclough, *To Redeem the Soul of America*, 23–24; David L. Lewis, *King: A Critical Biography* (New York: Praeger, 1970), 41–42, 72; Anderson, *Bayard Rustin*, 187; D'Emilio, *Lost Prophet*, 229-230. On the long-term relationship between Rustin and

King, see Anderson, *Bayard Rustin*, 197–308; D'Emilio, *Lost Prophet*, 235–241, 266–269, 298–300, 359, 365, 371–374, 394–396, 405–406, 453–460; and Viorst, *Fire in the Streets*, 210–231.

13. Rustin, "Montgomery Diary," 10; Swomley interview; Swomley to Riles, February 21, 1956, and Smiley to Swomley and Hassler, February 29, 1956, both in box 16, FORP; Branch, *Parting the Waters*, 179–180; Farmer, *Lay Bare the Heart*, 187; Fairclough, *To Redeem the Soul of America*, 24; Garrow, *Bearing the Cross*, 68–69; Raines, *My Soul Is Rested*, 55; Robinson, *Abraham Went Out*, 117; Anderson, *Bayard Rustin*, 189–193; D'Emilio, *Lost Prophet*, 231–232; Tracy, *Direct Action*, 91–92. In a letter written in Birmingham on March 8, Rustin explained the *Le Figaro* and *Manchester Guardian* statement to King: "For the record, at no time did I say that I was a correspondent for either of these papers. I did say that I was writing articles which were to be submitted to them, and this is now in the process of being done." Bayard Rustin to Martin Luther King Jr., March 8, 1956, box 5, MLKP. On the prevalence of anti-Communist hysteria in the South during the 1950s, see Woods, *Black Struggle, Red Scare*; and Lewis, *White South and the Red Menace*.

14. Swomley interview; Glenn Smiley, interview by Katherine M. Shannon, September 12, 1967, RBOHC; Frank Wilkinson, interview by author, March 23, 1993. "Data Sheet: Rev. Glenn E. Smiley," 1958 typescript; "Proposal for Race Relations Work in the South," typescript, February 13, 1956; Smiley, "Report from the South, Number 1," February 29, 1956; Al Hassler to Smiley, November 4, 1955; Smiley to Dear Friend, December 5, 1955; Swomley to To Whom it May Concern, February 8, 1956, all in box 16, FORP. D'Emilio, *Lost Prophet*, 40, 47–48, 174, 191, 200, 204, 226, 231–234, 245; Tracy, *Direct Action*, 88–92; Branch, *Parting the Waters*, 180; Garrow, *Bearing the Cross*, 68; Morris, *Origins of the Civil Rights Movement*, 62, 157, 159–160; David L. Chappell, *Inside Agitators: White Southerners in the Civil Rights Movement* (Baltimore: Johns Hopkins University Press, 1994), 58–59; Anderson, *Bayard Rustin*, 191.

15. Swomley interview; Smiley interview, RBOHC; Swomley to Smiley (two letters), February 29, 1956 (quotation), Swomley to Smiley, March 1, 1956, and Smiley to Swomley, March 2, 1956, all in box 16, FORP; Anderson, *Bayard Rustin*, 190–193; D'Emilio, *Lost Prophet*, 234–243; Branch, *Parting the Waters*, 179–180; Garrow, *Bearing the Cross*, 69, 642 n45; Farmer, *Lay Bare the Heart*, 187; Fairclough, *To Redeem the Soul of America*, 24; Robinson, *Abraham Went Out*, 117; Raines, *My Soul Is Rested*, 55; Tracy, *Direct Action*, 94. Chappell, *Inside Agitators*, 59, incorrectly states that Smiley arrived in Montgomery on February 14. During his interview with Katherine Shannon in 1967, Smiley himself incorrectly recalled his arrival date as February 14. See also Levine, *Bayard Rustin and the Civil Rights Movement*, 84, 264 n9. On the Autherine Lucy episode, see Gaillard, *Cradle of Freedom*, 38–42; and E. Culpepper Clark, *The Schoolhouse Door: Segregation's Last Stand at the University of Alabama* (New York: Oxford University Press, 1993), 19–21, 37–113.

16. Smiley, "Report from the South, Number 1"; Smiley interview, RBOHC; Swomley interview; Morris, *Origins of the Civil Rights Movement*, 157–162; Garrow, *Bearing the Cross*, 69–70, 72, 79; Branch, *Parting the Waters*, 180; Fairclough, *To Redeem the Soul of America*, 24–25; Chappell, *Inside Agitators*, 59–60; Anderson, *Bayard Rustin*, 191–192; Tracy, *Direct Action*, 94–95; Kosek, "Richard Gregg, Mohandas Gandhi, and the Strategy of Nonviolence," 1344.

17. Smiley to Swomley and Hassler, February 29, 1956, box 16, FORP; Tracy, *Direct Action*, 95.

18. Smiley to Swomley, March 2, 1956, box 16, FORP.

19. Smiley interview, RBOHC; Morris, *Origins of the Civil Rights Movement*, 159–162, 166; Branch, *Parting the Waters*, 180; Garrow, *Bearing the Cross*, 70, 72; Chappell, *Inside Agitators*, 59–60, 240–241 n. 24; William Miller, *Martin Luther King, Jr.: His Life, Martyrdom, and Meaning for the World* (New York: Avon, 1968), 57–58, 60, 63; *Washington Afro-American*, March 20, 1956; "Four Hundred Clergymen Express Support for Montgomery Pastors," typescript press release, March 18, 1956, reel 39, COREP (first and second quotations). Smiley, "Report from the South, Number 1"; Smiley, "Report from the South, Number 2," August 15, 1956; Smiley to the Editor of the *Lungerville* (Arizona) *News*, March 9, 1956; Smiley to George C. Hardin, April 6, 1956; Smiley, memorandum to Paul Macy et al., April 7, 1956; Smiley to John Swomley, April 7, 1956 (third quotation); Smiley to Swomley (2 letters), April 10, 1956; Smiley to Rev. Matthew M. McCollum, n.d.; Smiley to Swomley, April 12, 1956; "Proposal for Race Relations Work in the South"; Smiley, "The Miracle of Montgomery," typescript, 1956; Smiley to Martin Luther King Jr., April 13, 1956; Martin Luther King Jr. to Smiley, July 5, 1956; Robert Graetz to Alfred Hassler, May 15, 1957, all in box 16, FORP. Smiley to Martin Luther King Jr., June 1, 1956, box 5, MLKP. On Graetz's role in the boycott, see Robert S. Graetz, *A White Preacher's Memoir: The Montgomery Bus Boycott* (Montgomery: Black Belt Press, 1998); and Chappell, *Inside Agitators*, 56–58, 61.

20. Bayard Rustin, "Notes of a Conference . . . ," reel 3, BRP; Garrow, *Bearing the Cross*, 72–73; Robinson, *Abraham Went Out*, 117; Raines, *My Soul Is Rested*, 54–57; Viorst, *Fire in the Streets*, 211; Fairclough, *To Redeem the Soul of America*, 25–26; Martin Luther King Jr., "Our Struggle," *Liberation* 1 (April 1956), 3–6; Anderson, *Bayard Rustin*, 193–194; D'Emilio, *Lost Prophet*, 238–239.

21. Raines, *My Soul Is Rested*, 53 (Rustin quotations); Garrow, *Bearing the Cross*, 72–73 (first Smiley quotation); Fairclough, *To Redeem the Soul of America*, 25–26; Morris, *Origins of the Civil Rights Movement*, 159–160 (second Smiley quotation); Robinson, *Abraham Went Out*, 117; Anderson, *Bayard Rustin*, 187–188; D'Emilio, *Lost Prophet*, 230–231, 236–239, 245, 267, 395, 453; King, *Stride Toward Freedom*, 143, 150. See Keith D. Miller, *Voice of Deliverance: The Language of Martin Luther King, Jr., and Its Sources* (New York: Free Press, 1992), chapter 5, for a perceptive discussion of the origins and evolution of King's ideas on nonviolence. See also Greg Moses, *Revolution of Conscience: Martin Luther King, Jr., and the Philosophy of Nonviolence* (New York: Guilford Press, 1997); Marsh, *The Beloved Community*, 21–50; Chappell, *A Stone of Hope*, 44–63; Christopher B. Strain, *Pure Fire: Self-Defense as Activism in the Civil Rights Era* (Athens: University of Georgia Press, 2005), 33–48; Harris Wofford,

Of Kennedys and Kings: Making Sense of the Sixties (Pittsburgh: University of Pittsburgh Press, 1992), 103ff.; Lewis, *King*, 29–40, 72, 85–111; and Miller, *Martin Luther King, Jr.*, 29–31, 63, 82, 90, 298–299, and passim. King's own account of his "Pilgrimage to Nonviolence" in *Stride Toward Freedom*, 66–88, raises more questions than it answers and must be used with caution. Kosek, "Richard Gregg, Mohandas Gandhi, and the Strategy of Nonviolence," 1343–1348, notes the influence of Richard Gregg's classic study of Gandhian philosophy, *The Power of Non-Violence*, on King's evolving conception of nonviolent direct action. As Kosek points out, "Gregg's ideas and sometimes his language appear in King's own explanation of his philosophy. King stressed the militant, aggressive qualities of nonviolence, as Gregg had" (1345). On the diffusion of Gandhian ideas among black Americans, see Sudarshan Kapur, *Raising Up a Prophet: The African American Encounter with Gandhi* (Boston: Beacon Press, 1992). See also Charles Chatfield, ed., *The Americanization of Gandhi: Images of the Mahatma* (New York: Garland, 1976). On the desegregation of Montgomery's buses and the integrated bus ride of December 21, 1956, see King, *Stride Toward Freedom*, 147–151; Thornton, *Dividing Lines*, 93–96; and Chappell, *Inside Agitators*, 60–61.

22. Minutes of the Atlanta Conference, May 12, 1956 (quotations), and Smiley, "Report from the South, Number 2," 3, both in box 16, FORP; Robinson, *Abraham Went Out*, 109–118; King, *Stride Toward Freedom*, 77; Fairclough, *To Redeem the Soul of America*, 29; Garrow, *Bearing the Cross*, 75, 643 n50; Anderson, *Bayard Rustin*, 194; D'Emilio, *Lost Prophet*, 239.

23. Norman Thomas to Martin Luther King Jr., March 23, 1956 (quotation), and Thomas to Homer Jack, March 12, 1956, both in box 62, NTP; Garrow, *Bearing the Cross*, 69–70, 642 n45; Viorst, *Fire in the Streets*, 210–211; Fairclough, *To Redeem the Soul of America*, 32. Morris Milgrim to Daniel James, January 1, March 19, 1949; Norman Thomas to A. Philip Randolph, January 19, 1956; Randolph to Thomas, January 23, 1956, all in Corres. Box, APRP. Robinson, *Abraham Went Out*, 111–117, 131; Pfeffer, *A. Philip Randolph*, 66, 142, 150–152, 165–166, 203–205. Harris Wofford expressed similar concerns after he became involved with King in 1957: "If King had asked me to join him full-time I suspect I would have gone, but already he was being plagued by offers of assistance from people all over the world. Even the shrewd and intelligent help of Bayard Rustin verged on a kind of manipulation I disliked. Steeped in Gandhian lore, with extraordinary personal experience in nonviolent action, Rustin seemed ever-present with advice, and sometimes acted as if King were a precious puppet whose symbolic actions were to be planned by a Gandhian high command." Wofford, *Of Kennedys and Kings*, 115.

24. A. Philip Randolph to Martin Luther King Jr., November 19, 1958, Corres. Box, APRP; Pfeffer, *A. Philip Randolph*, 58 (first quotation), 62 (third quotation), 169–205; Thomas Sancton, "Something's Happened to the Negro," *New Republic* 108 (February 8, 1943): 177, quoted in ibid., 64; Anderson, *A. Philip Randolph*, 90, 105, 231, 250, 265–266, 279; Robinson, *Abraham Went Out*, 111–112; Branch, *Parting the Waters*, 170–171; A. Philip Randolph to Nathaniel Cooper, February 13, 1953, and Cooper to Randolph, January 30, 1953, February 14, 1953, all in Corres. Box, APRP. On the March on Washington Movement, see Pfeffer, *A. Philip Randolph*, 45–132; Anderson, *A. Philip Randolph*, 249–261, and Garfinkel, *When Negroes March*.

25. Pfeffer, *A. Philip Randolph*, 23, 88, 172–174; Anderson, *A. Philip Randolph*, 177; Branch, *Parting the Waters*, 121; Morris, *Origins of the Civil Rights Movement*, 158; Viorst, *Fire in the Streets*, 21–25, 30; A. Philip Randolph to Dr. George D. Cannon, June 21, 1956, Corres. Box, APRP; A. Philip Randolph to President Dwight D. Eisenhower, February 2, 1956, telegram, box 3, APRP; Warren Olney III to A. Philip Randolph, February 8, 1956, box 15, BSCPP; A. Philip Randolph to George Meany, March 5, 1956, box 19, BSCPP.

26. "Memo on In Friendship," February 17, 1956 (first quotation); Walter Petersen, "Proceedings of Conference on Aid to Race Terror Victims," January 5, 1956; Madison S. Jones to Roy Wilkins, January 9, 1956, all in box B-186, NAACP. A. Philip Randolph to Eleanor Roosevelt, January 31, 1956, box 24, BSCPP; Norman Thomas to Roy Wilkins, A. Philip Randolph, et al., January 12, 1956, Corres. Box, APRP; Norman Thomas to A. Philip Randolph, March 8, 1956, box 2, APRP; Fairclough, *To Redeem the Soul of America*, 29–32; Branch, *Parting the Waters*, 208–209, 231, 233, 330; Anderson, *Bayard Rustin*, 195; D'Emilio, *Lost Prophet*, 224–227; Garrow, *Bearing the Cross*, 84, 102–103; David J. Garrow, *The FBI and Martin Luther King, Jr.: From "Solo" to Memphis* (New York: Norton, 1981), 26, 40–44; Morris, *Origins of the Civil Rights Movement*, 83. For a discussion of Baker's remarkable career, see Ransby, *Ella Baker and the Black Freedom Movement*; Grant, *Ella Baker*; Olson, *Freedom's Daughters*, 132–150; Sharon Harley, "Ella Jo Baker," in *The Encyclopedia of Southern Culture*, ed. Charles Reagan Wilson and William Ferris (Chapel Hill: University of North Carolina Press, 1989), 1570–1571; Belinda Robnett, *How Long? How Long? African-American Women in the Struggle for Civil Rights* (New York: Oxford University Press, 1997), passim; Peggy Peterman, "A Leader in the Struggle," *St. Petersburg Times*, February 11, 1992 (second quotation); Viorst, *Fire in the Streets*, 119–124; Carson, *In Struggle*, 19–31, 41–42, 70–71; and Gerda Lerner, "Developing Community Leadership: Ella Baker," in *Black Women in White America: A Documentary History*, ed. Gerda Lerner (New York: Vintage Books, 1973), 352. See also the transcript of a June 19, 1968, interview with Baker, RBOHC. There is no general history of In Friendship, but see Eugene P. Walker, "A History of the Southern Christian Leadership Conference, 1955–1965: The Evolution of a Southern Strategy for Social Change" (Ph.D. thesis, Duke University, 1978); Ransby, *Ella Baker and the Black Freedom Movement*, 161–178, 195, 302; and "A Brief Digest of the Activities of 'In Friendship,' " March 6, 1957, box 2, APRP.

27. A. Philip Randolph to Dear Friend, February 17, 1956, box B-186, NAACPP (quotation); "A Brief Digest of the Activities of 'In Friendship.' "

28. A. Philip Randolph to Ella Baker, March 7, 1956; Randolph to Rabbi Edward E. Klein, March 15, 1956; "A Brief Digest of the Activities of 'In Friendship,' " all in box 2, APRP. *Chicago Defender,* June 2, 9, 1956 (quotation); Fairclough, *To Redeem the Soul of America,* 31–32; Garrow, *The FBI and Martin Luther King, Jr.,* 26; Anderson, *Bayard Rustin,* 195–196; D'Emilio, *Lost Prophet,* 240; Wilkins, *Standing Fast,* 235–236.

29. "A Brief Digest of the Activities of 'In Friendship' "; Ella Baker to A. Philip Randolph, August 29, 1956; In Friendship, minutes of executive committee meetings, June 20 and July 19, 1956, Ella Baker to Cornelius J. Drew, October 9, 1956; Ella Baker to A. Philip Randolph, memorandum, January 1, 1957, all in box 2, APRP. Norman Thomas to A. Philip Randolph, August 26, 1956, Corres. Box, APRP; Ella Baker to Dear Friend, June 2, 1956, and In Friendship, "We Believe," broadside, 1956 (quotation), both in box B-186, NAACPP; Ransby, *Ella Baker and the Black Freedom Movement,* 165–168; Garrow, *The FBI and Martin Luther King, Jr.,* 42; Garrow, *Bearing the Cross,* 103; Morris, *Origins of the Civil Rights Movement,* 116; Branch, *Parting the Waters,* 209, 216, 227, 231. The NAACP did provide strong support for the December 5 concert. See Cornelius Drew et al. to Mrs. Roy Wilkins, telegram, October 14, 1956; Ella Baker to Roy Wilkins, November 10, 1956; Roy Wilkins to Dear NAACP Member, November 23, 1956; Stanley Levison to Roy Wilkins, December 12, 1956, all in box B-186, NAACPP; and Fairclough, *To Redeem the Soul of America,* 32, which probably overstates the degree of cooperation between the two organizations.

30. Wilkins, *Standing Fast,* 237–238; Pfeffer, *A. Philip Randolph,* 174–176 (quotation); "Map, 'State of Race' Confab for D.C.," *Jet* 9 (April 19, 1956): 3; "73 Negro Leaders in D.C. Session Seek Immediate Meeting with Ike," *Jet* 9 (May 10, 1956): 4–5. A. Philip Randolph to President Dwight D. Eisenhower, May 8, 1956, box 3, APRP. On Randolph's complicated and often frustrating relationship with Wilkins, see Randolph to Wilkins, March 16, 1956; Wilkins to Randolph, September 22, 1958; Randolph to Wilkins, October 6, 1958, all in box 30, BSCPP; Anderson, *A. Philip Randolph,* 319–324, 348; Pfeffer, *A. Philip Randolph,* 190–205; and Wilkins, *Standing Fast,* passim. On the Dixie Manifesto, also known as the "Southern Manifesto" or "Declaration of Constitutional Principles," see Numan V. Bartley, *The Rise of Massive Resistance: Race and Politics in the South During the 1950s* (Baton Rouge: Louisiana State University Press, 1969), 116–117; *Congressional Record,* 84th Congress, 2d Session (March 12, 1956), 3948, 4004; Brooks Hays, *A Southern Moderate Speaks* (Chapel Hill: University of North Carolina Press, 1959), 89; Tony Badger, "The Forerunner of Our Opposition: Arkansas and the Southern Manifesto of 1956," *Arkansas Historical Quarterly* 56 (1999): 353–360; and Tony Badger, "The White Reaction to *Brown*: Arkansas, the Southern Manifesto, and Massive Resistance," in *Understanding the Little Rock Crisis,* ed. Elizabeth Jacoway and Fred C. Williams (Fayetteville: University of Arkansas Press, 1999), 83–97.

31. Barnes, *Journey from Jim Crow,* 121–131; King, *Stride Toward Freedom,* 157–180; Burns, *Daybreak of Freedom,* 270–273, 299–347; Thornton, *Dividing Lines,* 93; Klarman, *From Jim Crow to Civil Rights,* 266–267, 372, 377–378, 392; *Browder v. Gayle,* 142 F. Supp. 707 (M.D. Ala. 1956); *Browder v. Gayle,* 1 RRLR 678 (1956); *Gayle v. Browder,* 352 U.S. 903 (1956).

32. Branch, *Parting the Waters,* 199–206; Garrow, *Bearing the Cross,* 115–125; Miller, *Martin Luther King, Jr.,* 69–82; Halberstam, *The Children,* 26–27; Farmer, *Lay Bare the Heart,* 193; Fairclough, *To Redeem the Soul of America,* 35; Grant, *Ella Baker,* 102–103; Ransby, *Ella Baker and the Black Freedom Movement,* 170–230; King, *Stride Toward Freedom,* 158–201; Fred Shuttlesworth, interview by author, February 19, June 6, 2004. King begins his memoir of the boycott by describing the Alabama State Capitol, where "on February 18, on the steps of the portico, Jefferson Davis took his oath of office as President of the Confederate States. It is for this reason that Montgomery has been known across the years as the Cradle of the Confederacy." See ibid., 1–2. On Montgomery in the aftermath of the boycott, see Thornton, *Dividing Lines,* 96–118. On Shuttlesworth, the ACMHR, and the Birmingham movement during the 1950s, see Thornton, *Dividing Lines,* 170–238; Eskew, *But for Birmingham,* 53–151; Manis, *A Fire You Can't Put Out,* 68–252; McWhorter, *Carry Me Home,* 84–145; and Lewis W. Jones, "Fred L. Shuttlesworth, Indigenous Leader," in *Birmingham, Alabama, 1956–1963: The Black Struggle for Civil Rights,* ed. David J. Garrow (Brooklyn: Carlson, 1989), 115–150.

33. On the rise of massive resistance in the late 1950s, see Bartley, *The Rise of Massive Resistance,* 170–292; Francis M. Wilhoit, *The Politics of Massive Resistance* (New York: George Braziller, 1973); Neil R. McMillen, *The Citizens' Council: Organized Resistance to the Second Reconstruction, 1954–1964* (Urbana: University of Illinois Press, 1971); Belknap, *Federal Law and Southern Order,* 27–69 ; Patterson, *Brown v. Board of Education,* 86–117; Woods, *Black Struggle, Red Scare,* 49–142; Thornton, *Dividing Lines,* 96–118; John Bartlow Martin, *The Deep South Says "Never"* (New York: Ballantine Books, 1957); and Harry S. Ashmore, *An Epitaph for Dixie* (New York: Norton, 1958). See also the important collection of essays in Clive Webb, ed., *Massive Resistance: Southern Opposition to the Second Reconstruction* (New York: Oxford University Press, 2005). The term "massive resistance" originated in Virginia. See James W. Ely Jr., *The Crisis of Conservative Virginia: The Byrd Organization and the Politics of Massive Resistance* (Knoxville: University of Tennessee Press, 1976); and Benjamin Muse, *Virginia's Massive Resistance* (Bloomington: Indiana University Press, 1961).

34. On Eisenhower and civil rights during the late 1950s, see Robert F. Burk, *The Eisenhower Administration and Black Civil Rights* (Knoxville: University of Tennessee Press, 1984), 151–266; Kenneth O'Reilly, *Nixon's Piano: Presidents and Racial Politics from Washington to Clinton* (New York: Free Press, 1995), 165–187; Kluger, *Simple Justice,* 650–651, 657–665, 715, 726–727, 753–754, 774; J. W. Anderson, *Eisenhower, Brownell, and Congress: The Tangled Origins of the Civil Rights Bill of 1956–57* (University: University of Alabama Press, 1964); Herbert Brownell, *Advising Ike* (Lawrence: University Press of Kansas, 1993); Maxwell Rabb, interview by Steven Lawson, October 6, 1970, CUOHC; E. Frederic Morrow, *Black Man in the White House: A Diary of the Eisenhower Years by the Administrative Officer for*

Special Projects, the White House, 1955–1961 (New York: Coward-McCann, 1963); E. Frederic Morrow Diary Transcript, box 1, E. Frederic Morrow Papers, Dwight David Eisenhower Library, Abilene, KS; Belknap, *Federal Law and Southern Order*, 34–52; Branch, *Parting the Waters*, 180–183, 212–213, 223–224, 233–237; Garrow, *Bearing the Cross*, 119, 130; Wilkins, *Standing Fast*, 212–213, 229–269; and Brauer, *John F. Kennedy and the Second Reconstruction*, 1–8. On Eisenhower and the Little Rock crisis, see Bartley, *The Rise of Massive Resistance*, 251–269; Dudziak, *Cold War Civil Rights*, 115–151; Jacoway and Williams, *Understanding the Little Rock Crisis*; and John A. Kirk, *Redefining the Color Line: Black Activism in Little Rock, Arkansas, 1940–1970* (Gainesville: University Press of Florida, 2002), 106–138. On the 1957 Civil Rights Act, see Robert A. Caro, *Master of the Senate: The Years of Lyndon Johnson* (New York: Random House, 2002), 831–1012; and Anderson, *Eisenhower, Brownell, and Congress.*

35. Carter interview; Garrow, *Bearing the Cross*, 97–105, 121–124, 134–137; Branch, *Parting the Waters*, 186, 197–199, 297–298; Fairclough, *To Redeem the Soul of America*, 32–35, 64–65; Farmer, *Lay Bare the Heart*, 178, 188, 189 (first quotation), 190–193; Wilkins, *Standing Fast*, 228–229, 237 (second quotation), 238–271; Jonas, *Freedom's Sword*, 161–166; Ransby, *Ella Baker and the Black Freedom Movement*, 170–238; Robert Jerome Glennon, "The Role of Law in the Civil Rights Movement: The Montgomery Bus Boycott, 1955–1957," *Law and History Review* 9 (Spring 1991): 59–112. On NAACP fund-raising during the boycott, see Martin Luther King Jr. to Roy Wilkins, March 3, 1956; telegram, Roy Wilkins to NAACP Branches, February 23, 1956; memorandum, Gloster Current to NAACP Field Secretaries, February 23, 1956; Thurgood Marshall to Mr. Moon, February 23, 1956; Roy Wilkins to Martin Luther King Jr., March 8, 1956, all in box B-185, NAACPP; Ruby Hurley to Lucille Black, February 13, 1956, and "News and Action," April 1956, Southeast Regional Office of the NAACP, both in box H-213, NAACPP; "Mass Rally and Prayer Hour on Alabama Bus Boycott," 1956 Annual Report of the Chicago Branch, box H-108, NAACPP; Roy Wilkins to Martin Luther King Jr., March 8, April 12, May 4, 1956, box B-191, NAACPP; Morris, *Origins of the Civil Rights Movement*, 57; and Lewis, *King*, 71. On Marshall's attitude toward the bus boycott and direct action, see Tushnet, *Making Civil Rights Law*, 305–306; and Michael D. Davis and Hunter R. Clark, *Thurgood Marshall: Warrior at the Bar, Rebel on the Bench* (New York: Birch Lane Press, 1992), 201–206. See also Harris Wofford Jr. to Thurgood Marshall, January 9, 1958, box 78, MLKP. On the vulnerability of the NAACP's Southern branches, see Ruby Hurley, "1956—The Civil War of the 20th Century," Annual Report of the Southeast Regional Office, December 1956, box H-213, NAACPP; and Carter, *A Matter of Law*, 135–163. Even Hurley, perhaps the most passionate MIA supporter among NAACP officials, recognized that direct action had burdened the NAACP with unexpected and threatening complications. While she was "a bit encouraged by the emergence of the new Negro as evidenced in Montgomery," she feared that Southern blacks were about to reap the whirlwind. "There is reason to believe that Negroes . . . in the South have little patience left," she concluded, "and that after this storm has passed, the Fight for Freedom will be more easily won. In the meantime, we are convinced, unhappily, that things will be worse before they get better."

36. Fairclough, *To Redeem the Soul of America*, 32–55; Morris, *Origins of the Civil Rights Movement*, 174–178; Branch, *Parting the Waters*, 206–271; Garrow, *Bearing the Cross*, 83–125; Debbie Louis, *And We Are Not Saved: A History of the Movement as People* (Garden City, NY: Doubleday, 1970), 89–95; Laue, *Direct Action and Desegregation*, 71–74; Ransby, *Ella Baker and the Black Freedom Movement*, 170–189; Grant, *Ella Baker*, 102–107; Robnett, *How Long? How Long?* 88–89, 93–95; Anderson, *Bayard Rustin*, 197–212; Levine, *Bayard Rustin and the Civil Rights Movement*, 91–103; D'Emilio, *Lost Prophet*, 245–248, 262–277; Shuttlesworth interview. On C. K. Steele and the Tallahassee movement during the 1950s, see Rabby, *The Pain and the Promise*, 1–108; and Gregory B. Padgett, "The Tallahassee Bus Boycott," in Samuel C. Hyde Jr., *Sunbelt Revolution: The Historical Progression of the Civil Rights Movement in the Gulf South, 1866–2000* (Gainesville: University Press of Florida, 2003), 190–209. On Kelly Miller Smith and the founding and evolution of the NCLC, see Smith's fragmentary unpublished manuscript, "Pursuit of a Dream," folders 7 and 8, box 28; and the NCLC materials in boxes 74–76, all in KMSP.

37. On the national culture of violence in the United States, see Hugh Davis Graham and Ted Robert Gurr, *The History of Violence in America: Historical and Comparative Perspectives* (New York: Praeger, 1969); Richard Slotkin, *Regeneration Through Violence: The Myth of the American Frontier, 1600–1860* (Middletown, CT: Wesleyan University Press, 1973); and Richard Slotkin, *Gunfighter Nation: The Myth of the Frontier in Twentieth-Century America* (New York: Atheneum, 1992). On the South's special proclivity for violence, see Hackney, "Southern Violence," 906–925 (first quotation); H. C. Brearley, "The Pattern of Violence," in *Culture in the South*, ed. W. T. Couch (Chapel Hill: University of North Carolina Press, 1934), 678–692; Raymond Gastil, "Homicide and a Regional Culture of Violence," *American Sociological Review* 36 (June 1971): 412–427; John Hope Franklin, *The Militant South, 1800–1861* (Cambridge: Harvard University Press, 1956); Dickson D. Bruce, *Violence and Culture in the Antebellum South* (Austin: University of Texas Press, 1979); John Shelton Reed, *The Enduring South: Subcultural Persistence in Mass Society* (Lexington, MA: Heath, 1972), 45–55; Tyson, *Radio Free Dixie*, 1–89, 205 (second quotation); Timothy B. Tyson, *Blood Done Sign My Name: A True Story* (New York: Crown, 2004); and Ransby, *Ella Baker and the Black Freedom Movement*, 193–194, 211–212. On the historical connections between violence, self-defense, and civil rights activism prior to 1963, see Strain, *Pure Fire*, 1–77.

38. Tyson, *Radio Free Dixie*, 71–165, 122 (first quotation), 149 (second quotation); Strain, *Pure Fire*, 51–58. See also Robert F. Williams, *Negroes with Guns* (Chicago: Third World Press, 1973).

39. Tyson, *Radio Free Dixie*, 214–217 (quotations); *Liberation* 4 (September, October 1959); *Southern Patriot* 18 (January 1960): 3; Strain, *Pure Fire*, 58–64 . See also Clayborne Carson et al., eds., *The Eyes on the Prize Civil Rights Reader* (New York: Penguin, 1991), 110–113. On Braden, see Anne Braden, *The*

Wall Between (New York: Monthly Review Press, 1959); Catherine Fosl, *Subversive Southerner: Anne Braden and the Struggle for Racial Justice in the Cold War South* (New York: Palgrave, 2002); Olson, *Freedom's Daughters*, 173–181; and Ransby, *Ella Baker and the Black Freedom Movement*, 231–237.

40. Morris, *Origins of the Civil Rights Movement*, 188–196; Meier and Rudwick, *CORE*, 77–98; Sitkoff, *Struggle for Racial Equality*, 57–60; Peck, *Freedom Ride*, 61–71; Carey and Rich interviews; Patricia Stephens Due, interview by author, April 27, 2002; D'Emilio, *Lost Prophet*, 290. See also reels 31, 38, 39, 43, and the 1957–59 issues of *CORE-lator* in reel 49, COREP; and Kristin M. Anderson-Bricker, "Making a Movement: The Meaning of Community in the Congress of Racial Equality, 1958–1968" (Ph.D. thesis, Syracuse University, 1997). On Miami CORE, see Susan Bodan and James R. Robinson, *1959 Miami Interracial Action Institute: Summary and Evaluation* (New York: CORE, 1960), 1–11; Gordon R. Carey, "Action Institute Aids Miami CORE," *CORE-lator* 78 (Fall 1959): 1–3; Raymond A. Mohl, " 'South of the South?' Jews, Blacks, and the Civil Rights Movement in Miami, 1945–1960," *Journal of American Ethnic History* 18 (Winter 1999): 3–26; and Raymond A. Mohl, *South of the South: Jewish Activists and the Civil Rights Movement in Miami, 1945–1960* (Gainesville: University Press of Florida, 2004), 53–58, 147–194. On the formation and evolution of the CORE chapter in Tallahassee in 1959, see Rabby, *The Pain and the Promise*, 81–87; Tananarive Due and Patricia Stephens Due, *Freedom in the Family: A Mother-Daughter Memoir of the Fight for Civil Rights* (New York: Ballantine, 2003), 96–105; and reel 19, COREP. On the use of direct action as a means of advancing issues other than civil rights during these years, see Tracy, *Direct Action*, 99–117.

41. Meier and Rudwick, *CORE*, 49, 77–83; Carey and Rich interviews.

42. Chafe, *Civilities and Civil Rights*, 98–141; Miles Wolff, *Lunch at the Five and Ten: The Greensboro Sit-ins, a Contemporary History* (New York: Stein and Day, 1970); Morris, *Origins of the Civil Rights Movement*, 195–221; Sitkoff, *Struggle for Black Equality*, 61–83; Carson, *In Struggle*, 9–18; Meier and Rudwick, *CORE*, 98–106, 112; Peck, *Freedom Ride*, 61 (first quotation), 72–93, 117; Tracy, *Direct Action*, 117–118; Branch, *Parting the Waters*, 271–275; Farmer, *Lay Bare the Heart*, 191–192 (second quotation); Louis, *And We Are Not Saved*, 98–103; Laue, *Direct Action and Desegregation*, 75–95; Fairclough, *To Redeem the Soul of America*, 55; Wilkins, *Standing Fast*, 267–271; Zinn, *SNCC*, 1–17, 20–22; Carter interview.

43. Carey interview; Meier and Rudwick, *CORE*, 101–102, 103 (quotation)–106; Morris, *Origins of the Civil Rights Movement*, 213–214.

44. Miscellaneous materials on April 15–17, 1960, conference at Shaw University, folder 1, box 25, SNCCP; "1960 Nashville Sit-Ins," commemorative issue, *Tennessee Tribune*, February 12–18, 2004, 3D (first quotation); Matthew Walker Jr., interview by author, November 8, 2004; Carson, *In Struggle*, 19–22, 23 (second quotation); 24; Zinn, *SNCC*, 1–34; Cheryl Lynn Greenberg, ed., *A Circle of Trust: Remembering SNCC* (New Brunswick: Rutgers University Press, 1998), 18–38; Garrow, *Bearing the Cross*, 120–121, 131–134; Meier and Rudwick, *CORE*, 105; Fairclough, *To Redeem the Soul of America*, 58–64; Ransby, *Ella Baker and the Black Freedom Movement*, 239–247; Grant, *Ella Baker*, 105–131; Olson, *Freedom's Daughters*, 148–150; Lewis, *Walking with the Wind*, 114 (third quotation); Ella Baker, "Bigger than a Hamburger," *Southern Patriot* 18 (May 1960): 4; Constance Curry et al., *Deep in Our Hearts: Nine White Women in the Freedom Movement* (Athens: University of Georgia Press, 2000), 107, 345–346; Marsh, *The Beloved Community*, 88. On Lawson, see Halberstam, *The Children*, 11–106, 122–125, 214–226; Branch, *Parting the Waters*, 204–205, 259–299; Chappell, *A Stone of Hope*, 67–71; Greenberg, ed., *A Circle of Trust*, 19, 33–36, 47, 236; Morris, *Origins of the Civil Rights Movement*, 162–163; and Farmer, *Lay Bare the Heart*, 193. On the uproar surrounding Lawson's expulsion, see Paul Conkin, *Gone with the Ivy: A Biography of Vanderbilt University* (Knoxville: University of Tennessee Press, 1985), 547–580; *Nashville Tennessean*, March 3–June 6, 1960; Ray Waddle, "Days of Thunder: The Lawson Affair," *Vanderbilt Magazine* 83 (Fall 2002): 35–43; Morgan Jackson Wills, "Walking the Edge: Vanderbilt University and the Sit-In Crisis of 1960" (senior thesis, Princeton University, 1990); and the special sit-in edition of the Vanderbilt Divinity School student newspaper *Prospectus* 83 (March 16, 1960), the *Vanderbilt Hustler*, March 4, 11, and 25, 1960, and other materials in the Lawson Case vertical file, Vanderbilt University Special Collection. On the Nashville student movement and the sit-ins of 1960, see Halberstam, *The Children*, 90–234; Lewis, *Walking with the Wind*, 68–117; Linda T. Wynn, "The Dawning of a New Day: The Nashville Sit-Ins, February 13–May 10, 1960," *Tennessee Historical Quarterly* (Spring 1991): 42–54; Sandra A. Taylor, "The Nashville Sit-In Movement, 1960" (M.A. thesis, Fisk University, 1972); David Sumner, "The Local Press and the Nashville Student Movement" (Ph.D. thesis, University of Tennessee, 1989); Paul LaPrad, "Nashville: A Community Struggle," in Peck, *Freedom Ride*, 82–88; and the Nashville Community Relations Conference *Report* (1960), copy in Student Sit-In Movement vertical file, FUSC. See also the documentary films "Ain't Scared of Your Jails," episode 3 of *Eyes on the Prize I*; *Sit-In* (NBC White Paper, 1960); *Anatomy of a Demonstration* (CBS Television, 1960); and *Nashville: We Were Warriors* (excerpted from *A Force More Powerful: A Century of Nonviolent Conflict*, PBS television series, 2000), all available for viewing in the Civil Rights Room at the Nashville Public Library.

45. Carson, *In Struggle*, 25, 26 (quotation), 27–31; Grant, *Ella Baker*, 131–137; Farmer, *Lay Bare the Heart*, 192–193; Lewis, *Walking with the Wind*, 124–125; Zinn, *SNCC*, 1 (quotation), 34–35; Benjamin Elton Cox, interview by author, April 5–6, May 8, 2001, May 9, November 7, 2004. See also the first issue of the SNCC newspaper, *The Student Voice* (June 1960). On the rising tide of student activism in the early 1960s, see Gitlin, *The Sixties*; Miller, *Democracy Is in the Streets*; Isserman, *If I Had a Hammer*; Anderson, *The Movement and the Sixties*, 3–130; Irwin Unger, *The Movement: A History of the American New Left, 1959–1972* (New York: Harper and Row, 1974); and W. J. Rorabaugh, *Berkeley at War: The 1960s* (New York: Oxford University Press, 1989). On the earlier student movement of the 1930s, see Ralph S. Brax, *The First Student Movement: Student Activism in the United States*

During the 1930s (Port Washington, NY: Kennikat Press, 1981); and Robert Cohen, *When the Old Left Was Young: Student Radicals and America's First Mass Student Movement, 1929–1941* (New York: Oxford University Press, 1993).

46. Meier and Rudwick, *CORE*, 104–117, 107 (first quotation); Lewis, *Walking with the Wind*, 113 (second quotation); Patricia Stephens, "Tallahassee: Through Jail to Freedom," in Peck, *Freedom Ride*, 73–79; Due interview; Due and Due, *Freedom in the Family*, 4, 69–82, 94–98; Rabby, *The Pain and the Promise*, 5–6, 81–89, 105–106, 116–120, 133–139, 148, 183.

47. Peck, *Freedom Ride*, 94–95 (quotation), 96–113; Meier and Rudwick, *CORE*, 104, 113–119, 136; Branch, *Parting the Waters*, 392–393; Zinn, *SNCC*, 23–24, 38–39, 41; Tom Gaither, interview by author, November 9–11, 2001; James K. Davis and Glenda Gaither Davis, interview by author, May 12, 2001; Charles Jones, interview by author, May 12, 2001; J. Charles Jones, "Timeline–Rock Hill and Charlotte Sit-ins," 2 (www.crmvet.org/info/rockhill.htm); *Rock Hill Evening Herald*, February–March, 1961, January 29, 2001. See also Gaither's reports and correspondence in folder 249, reel 36, COREP.

48. Meier and Rudwick, *CORE*, 112 (quotation), 113–114; Bernard Lafayette, interview by author, April 6, May 11, 2001, June 9–10, 2004; Carey, Due, and Gaither interviews; Mohl, " 'South of the South?' " 21–22; Due and Due, *Freedom in the Family*, 98–99, 101–104. See also the correspondence related to the institute in reel 19, COREP; Joseph Perkins, "My 219 Days with CORE," August 24, 1961, section 260, reel 39, COREP; Richard Haley, interview by Robert Wright, August 12, 1969, RBOHC; Richard Haley, interview by Kim Lacy Rogers, April 25, May 9, 1979, ARC.

49. *New Orleans Times-Picayune*, September 10–12, 1960; *Atlanta Constitution*, October 20–29, 1960; Meier and Rudwick, *CORE*, 114–116; *CORE-lator*, Fall 1960, box 49, COREP; Dave Dennis, interview by author, May 11–12, 2001; Ed Blankenheim, interview by author, April 6, May 11, 2001, May 7, 2004; Gaither and Cox interviews; Branch, *Parting the Waters*, 345–350, 351 (second quotation), 352–361; Carson, *In Struggle*, 27–28, 29 (first quotation), 30; Anne Braden, "Student Protest Movement Taking Permanent Form," *Southern Patriot* 18 (October 1960): 4; Anne Braden, "Student Movement: New Phase," *Southern Patriot* 18 (November 1960): 4; "SNCC Conference," *Student Voice* (October 1960): 1; minutes, SNCC staff meeting, November 25–27, 1960, box 7, SNCCP; Zinn, *SNCC*, 18–19; Greenberg, *A Circle of Trust*, 4–5, 34–36, 39–40, 45–47, 68–70, 189, 257; Chuck McDew, interview by Katherine Shannon, August 24, 1967, RBOHC; Fairclough, *To Redeem the Soul of America*, 73; Arthur M. Schlesinger Jr., *Robert Kennedy and His Times* (Boston: Houghton Mifflin, 1978), 216.

50. Wofford, *Of Kennedys and Kings*, 11–28; *New York Times*, October 20–29, 1960; Branch, *Parting the Waters*, 306–308, 313–314, 318–319, 341–342, 345–360, 361 (quotation), 362–378; Brauer, *John F. Kennedy and the Second Reconstruction*, 35–59; Stern, *Calculating Visions*, 33–39; Lawson, *Running for Freedom*, 54–55, 75–79; Niven, *The Politics of Injustice*, 21–23; Dallek, *An Unfinished Life*, 268–269, 291–295; Hilty, *Robert Kennedy*, 169–175; Fairclough, *To Redeem the Soul of America*, 73–75; Halberstam, *The Children*, 252–254; Garrow, *Bearing the Cross*, 83–84, 113, 138–149; Carson, *In Struggle*, 29; Schlesinger, *Robert Kennedy and His Times*, 216–218; Reeves, *President Kennedy*, 62; Martin Luther King, Jr., interview by Berl Bernhard, March 9, 1964, JFKL; Harris Wofford, interview by Larry Hackman, May 22, 1968, February 3, 1969, JFKL. See also the transcripts of the 1988 interviews of Louis Martin, Parren Mitchell, Samuel D. Proctor, Sargent Shriver, Franklin Williams, and Harris Wofford, all by Anthony Shriver, filed under "Kennedy's Call to King," JFKL. Theodore C. Sorensen, *Kennedy* (New York: Harper and Row, 1965), 33, relates the story of "Kennedy's reaction to the news that Negro leader Martin Luther King's father had announced his support—after the Senator's phone call to Mrs. King—stating he had previously planned to vote against Kennedy on religious grounds": " 'That was a hell of an intolerant statement, wasn't it?' said Kennedy. 'Imagine Martin Luther King having a father like that.' Then a pause, a grin, and a final word: 'Well, we all have fathers, don't we?' "

51. Brauer, *John F. Kennedy and the Second Reconstruction*, 1–60; Stern, *Calculating Visions*, 9–39; O'Reilly, *Nixon's Piano*, 189–199; Branch, *Parting the Waters*, 379–384; Wilkins, *Standing Fast*, 272–282; Dudziak, *Cold War Civil Rights*, 152–157; Lewis, *Walking with the Wind*, 129; Fairclough, *To Redeem the Soul of America*, 76; Niven, *The Politics of Injustice*, 8–24, 16 (quotation); Dallek, *An Unfinished Life*, 330–332; John Doar, interview by author, June 8, 2005.

52. Farmer, *Lay Bare the Heart*, 193–195 (quotations); Meier and Rudwick, *CORE*, 127–131; Rich, Carey, and Carter interviews.

Chapter 3: Hallelujah! I'm a-Travelin'

1. Jerry Silverman, *Songs of Protest and Civil Rights* (New York: Chelsea House, 1992), 18–19. Composed by an anonymous "southern black farmer" in the immediate aftermath of the *Morgan v. Virginia* decision, "Hallelujah! I'm a-Travelin' " appeared in the magazine *People's Songs* in September 1946. In 1961 the Freedom Riders revived the song, adding six new verses: "In 1954 our Supreme Court said, 'Look a-here Mr. jim crow, it's time you were dead.'/ I'm paying my fare on the Greyhound Bus line, I'm riding the front seat to Montgomery this time./ In Nashville, Tennessee, I can order a coke, And the waitress at Woolworth's knows it's no joke./ In old Fayette County, set off and remote, The polls are now open for Negroes to vote./ I walked in Montgomery, I sat in Tennessee, And now I'm riding for equality./ I'm travelin' to Mississippi on the Greyhound Bus line, Hallelujah, I'm ridin' the front seat this time." James Farmer can be heard singing several of these lines during an interview included in "Ain't Scared of Your Jails," episode 3 of *Eyes on the Prize I*.

2. Farmer, *Lay Bare the Heart*, 195–196; Farmer interview, RBOHC; Raines, *My Soul Is Rested*, 109–110 (quotation); Carey and Rich interviews; Hampton and Fayer, *Voices of Freedom*, 74–75; *Baltimore Afro-American*, June 3, 10, 24, 1961; *Boynton v. Commonwealth of Virginia*, 364 U.S. 454 (1960); Barnes, *Journey from Jim Crow*, 145–151, 155–157; Branch, *Parting the Waters*, 390–391; Meier and Rudwick, *CORE*, 72, 135–136; Peck, *Freedom Ride*, 114–115; Lewis, *Walking with the Wind*, 137; McWhorter, *Carry Me Home*, 195; Olson, *Freedom's Daughters*, 339–342. Boynton was the son of Amelia and Sam Boynton, two well-known Selma civil rights leaders who had been active in the local voting rights movement since the 1930s. See Gaillard, *Cradle of Freedom*, 62–65, 222–223, 227, 230–231, 242–243, 245. On December 4, 1960, Gordon Carey discussed the implications of the *Boynton* decision in a memorandum that read: "This is a limited decision but it has wide implications. As in the past, CORE continues to urge all its members not to voluntarily accept segregation. This decision by the Supreme Court has not actually desegregated any restaurants. *The restaurants will only be desegregated when you use them.* Therefore, let it be the responsibility of every CORE member to enforce the decision of the Supreme Court. If you travel in an interracial group you should only use eating facilities in bus, train and airport terminals that are marked 'white only' if the terminal has any such signs. If you are Negro you should use only those facilities which are reserved for whites. If you are white you should only use those facilities which are reserved for Negroes. Only in this manner will the desegregation edict of the Supreme Court become a reality." Gordon R. Carey to Local CORE groups, etc., December 7, 1960, box 23, MLKP. On January 21, during Farmer's final week at the NAACP, the Savannah, Georgia, branch of the NAACP organized a series of "ride-ins" designed to challenge segregated seating practices on local buses. Although several white patrons objected to the "ride-ins"–including one man who threatened NAACP activist Carolyn Quilloin with a knife–there were no arrests. *Pittsburgh Courier*, February 4, 1961.

3. Thomas Gaither, Field Report from Rock Hill, September 29–October 1, 1960, and Thomas Gaither to Gordon Carey, January 20, 1961, both in reel 36, COREP; Gaither and Carey interviews; Thomas Gaither, *Jailed-In*, and James Farmer to Edward King, telegram, February 7, 1961, both in folder 3, box 8, SNCCP; Peck, *Freedom Ride*, 99–113; Meier and Rudwick, *CORE*, 117–119, 136; *Rock Hill Evening Herald*, January 31–February 21, 1961, January 29, March 18, 2001; *New York Times*, February 1–2, 13, 20–21, 1961; *Baltimore Afro-American*, February 21, 1961; Branch, *Parting the Waters*, 391–394; Jones interview; Raines, *My Soul is Rested*, 109 (quotation); Carson, *In Struggle*, 31–33, 39–40; Zinn, *SNCC*, 38–39; Cynthia Griggs Fleming, *Soon We Will Not Cry: The Liberation of Ruby Doris Smith Robinson* (London: Rowman and Littlefield, 1998), 72–77; Charles Sherrod, interview by Bret Eynon, May 12, 1985, CUOHC; Olson, *Freedom's Daughters*, 158, 160, 212; Halberstam, *The Children*, 267–268; Jones, "Timeline–Rock Hill and Charlotte Sit-ins," 4–5.

4. Minutes of CORE National Action Committee meeting, Lexington, KY, February 11–12, 1961, reel 16, COREP; Tracy, *Direct Action*, 75, 118. CORE's main policy-making body, the National Action Committee merged with the National Council to become the National Action Council in 1962. On Houser's interest in Africa, see George Houser, *No One Can Stop the Rain: Glimpses of Africa's Liberation Struggle* (New York: Pilgrim Press, 1989). On Rustin's exile from the American civil rights movement in 1960–62, see D'Emilio, *Lost Prophet*, 288–325. Farmer, *Lay Bare the Heart*, 197 (first quotation); Gaither, Carey, and Worthy interviews; Thomas Gaither, reports, March and April 1961, reel 36, COREP; minutes of SNCC meeting, April 21–23, 1961, and "SNCC Launches Drive Against Travel Bias," (second quotation) both in folder 2, box 7, SNCCP; *Student Voice* (April–May 1961): 44; Ed King to Chuck McDew, May 2, 1961, folder 7, box 8, SNCCP; Meier and Rudwick, *CORE*, 136 (third quotation); Peck, *Freedom Ride*, 115; Branch, *Parting the Waters*, 393, 417; *Baltimore Afro-American*, June 3, 1961 (fourth quotation). After the Freedom Riders were attacked in Montgomery, Worthy related his recent Alabama experiences in a letter to the *Afro-American*: "It could have been me, was my personal reaction to the savage beating of the 'Freedom Riders' in Montgomery. With shivers and shudders, my thoughts went back to January when I was traveling alone from Memphis to Tuskegee to Boston. . . . I promptly reported the episode to the indifferent local FBI offices and in the pages of the AFRO. A month and a half later, March 17, the FBI got around to interviewing me. No Federal action has resulted. Until this week, a realist would have expected none. On Feb. 1, I telephoned Arthur Schlesinger Jr., special White House assistant. On the basis of talks with colored and white integration leaders in both Birmingham and Montgomery, I warned him that the tensions there would explode at any moment. Mr. Schlesinger promised he would contact the Civil Rights Division of the Justice Department. But almost a month later when I spoke with the Civil Rights Division, there had been no call from the former professor." See also the documents on Worthy's Alabama experience in file RD 56, box 9, Investigative Report Case Files, ICCR; see especially Worthy's eighteen-page statement of March 21, 1961.

5. Carey and Rich interviews. On the "Little Freedom Ride," see *CORE-lator* 88 (April 1961): 4; and memorandum, Gordon Carey to CORE Groups, National Officers, May 1, 1961, box 52A, MLKP (quotation).

6. Farmer, *Lay Bare the Heart*, 196–197; Peck, *Freedom Ride*, 115; Meier and Rudwick, *CORE*, 114–116, 136–137; Lewis, *Walking with the Wind*, 133–134. See national CORE office memoranda and correspondence for March–April 1961 in reel 25, COREP, especially the sample Freedom Ride application forms and "Freedom Ride, 1961–Participants," April 26, 1961. See also *CORE-lator*, May 1961; and section 456, reel 44, COREP. Estimates of the total number of applications have varied widely. In an interview with Milton Viorst in the 1970s, Farmer "recalled receiving twenty-five or thirty applications." At the other extreme, Simeon Booker, the *Jet* reporter who accompanied the Freedom Riders, claimed that the Riders were "selected from a field of more than three hundred throughout the country." Farmer's estimate is almost certainly more reliable than Booker's. Viorst, *Fire in the*

Streets, 141; Simeon Booker, *Black Man's America* (Englewood Cliffs, NJ: Prentice-Hall, 1964), 199; Carey and Rich interviews. On Smith and Aaron, see Kim Lacy Rogers, *Righteous Lives: Narratives of the New Orleans Civil Rights Movement* (New York: New York University Press, 1993), 111–149, 184–186, 195, 205–206; Anderson-Bricker, "Making a Movement," 1–2, 262, 265–266, 269, 346–347; Freedom Rider applications, Julia Aaron and Jerome Smith, section 456, reel 44, COREP; section 268, reel 37, COREP; and Jerome Smith, interview by Kim Lacy Rogers, July 9, 26, 1988, ARC.

7. Freedom Rider application, Genevieve Hughes, section 456, reel 44, COREP; "Freedom Ride, 1961–Participants"; Blankenheim, Cox, and Rich interviews; Farmer, *Lay Bare the Heart*, 197; Lewis, *Walking with the Wind*, 137, 139 (first quotation); *Baltimore Afro-American*, May 20, 1961 (second quotation); *Denver Post*, October 30, 1961; Meier and Rudwick, *CORE*, 113, 136, 152, 164, 183, 186, 189, 207, 227, 229; Anderson-Bricker, "Making a Movement," 46–57. In late 1960 and early 1961 Hughes conducted CORE fieldwork in Ohio, New York, Kentucky, Pennsylvania, Maryland, the District of Columbia, and Virginia. She became CORE's Western field secretary in late 1961. By 1963 she was no longer a member of the CORE staff, but she remained an active participant in the Berkeley, California, CORE chapter. On Hughes's activities as a CORE field secretary, see sections 254–255, reel 36, COREP.

8. Freedom Rider application, Joseph P. Perkins Jr., section 456, reel 44, COREP; "Freedom Ride, 1961–Participants"; Meier and Rudwick, *CORE*, 113, 120–121, 136, 152; Blankenheim, Carey, Rich, and Lafayette interviews; Farmer, *Lay Bare the Heart*, 197; *Baltimore Afro-American*, May 20, 1961 (quotation). Lewis, *Walking with the Wind*, 137, misidentifies Perkins as a student at the University of Kentucky. On Perkins's activities as a CORE field secretary, see section 260, reel 37, COREP.

9. Freedom Rider application, Walter and Frances Bergman, section 456, reel 44, COREP; "Freedom Ride, 1961–Participants"; Kaufman, *The First Freedom Ride*, 10–83; *Baltimore Afro-American*, May 20, 1961; Meier and Rudwick, *CORE*, 137; Lewis, *Walking with the Wind*, 139; *New York Times*, October 10, 1999 (obituary); Howard Simon, interview by author, December 2, 1999; William Goodman, interview by author, June 13, 2005.

10. Freedom Rider application, Albert Bigelow, section 456, reel 44, COREP; "Freedom Ride, 1961–Participants"; Albert Bigelow, *The Voyage of the Golden Rule: An Experiment with Truth* (New York: Doubleday, 1959); Albert Bigelow, "Why I Am Sailing into the Pacific Bomb-Test Area," *Liberation* 2 (February 1958): 4–6; James Peck, "Jail Is Our Home Port," William Huntington, "If You Feel Like It," and A. J. Muste, "Follow the Golden Rule," all in *Liberation* 3 (June 1958): 4–8; Norman Cousins, "The Men of the Golden Rule," *Saturday Review* 41 (May 17, 1958): 24; Wittner, *Rebels Against War*, 246–250; Tracy, *Direct Action*, 99–105, 109; Hentoff, *Peace Agitator*, 151–155; Robinson, *Abraham Went Out*, 164; Peck, *Freedom Ride*, 119; Farmer, *Lay Bare the Heart*, 197, 203; Lewis, *Walking with the Wind*, 136; *Baltimore Afro-American*, May 20, 1961; Blankenheim and Carey interviews. For an obituary, see *New York Times*, October 8, 1993. On the CNVA, see Neil H. Katz, "Radical Pacifism and the Contemporary American Peace Movement: The Committee for Nonviolent Action, 1957–1967" (Ph.D. thesis, University of Maryland, 1974). Jim Peck participated in the *Golden Rule*'s voyage of June 4, 1958, but he did not serve time in jail because, unlike Bigelow and the rest of the crew, he was not a repeat offender with respect to violation of a federal injunction prohibiting the voyage. See Tracy, *Direct Action*, 103.

11. Freedom Rider application, Jimmy McDonald, section 456, reel 44, COREP; "Freedom Ride, 1961–Participants"; Jimmy McDonald, interview by James Mosby Jr., November 5, 1969, RBOHC (quotations); Jimmy McDonald, "A Freedom Rider Speaks His Mind," *Freedomways* 1 (Summer 1961): 158–162, rpt. in *Freedomways Reader: Prophets in Their Own Country*, ed. Esther Cooper Jackson (Boulder, CO: Westview Press, 2000), 59–64; *Baltimore Afro-American*, May 20, 1961; Lewis, *Walking with the Wind*, 137–138; Carey, Rich, and Blankenheim interviews; Peck, *Freedom Ride*, 120, refers to McDonald as "our group's chief singer." Although the details of his family background and early life are sketchy, McDonald sometimes identified himself as a onetime resident of Accomack County, Virginia. *Montgomery Advertiser*, May 5, 1961. For an obituary, see *Chicago Sun-Times*, July 16, 2000; and *Atlanta Constitution*, July 16, 2000.

12. Freedom Rider application, Edward Blankenheim, section 456, reel 44, COREP; "Freedom Ride, 1961–Participants"; Edward J. Blankenheim, "Freedom Ride," unpublished memoir in author's possession, 2001, 2 (quotation); Blankenheim interview; Ed Blankenheim, interview by Scott Simon, National Public Radio *Weekend Edition* broadcast, April 7, 2001; Cox interview; *Baltimore Afro-American*, May 20, 1961; Meier and Rudwick, *CORE*, 151; *San Francisco Chronicle*, October 3, 2004 (obituary); Hank Thomas, interview by author, April 5–6, 2001. According to Thomas, the affection for Blankenheim among the other Freedom Riders led to the quip "God sent us a carpenter from Arizona." The fact that Blankenheim was a secular activist added a touch of irony to this Jesus-related reference. On McReynolds, see "Background Information on David McReynolds," folder 8, box 23, SNCCP.

13. Freedom Rider application, John H. Moody Jr., section 456, reel 44, COREP; "Freedom Ride, 1961–Participants"; John Moody, interview by author, May 10–11, November 8–9, 2001; Hank Thomas and John Moody, interview by author, May 11, 2001; John Moody, remarks at "Ride to Freedom," 40th anniversary celebration, Atlanta Convention Center, Atlanta, GA, May 11, 2001; Doug Miller, "The Forgotten Freedom Rider," *Columbia Flier*, April 14, 1994; Halberstam, *The Children*, 249; Branch, *Parting the Waters*, 470. On NAG, see Zinn, *SNCC*, 56; Carson, *In Struggle*, 30, 72, 83–84, 103–104, 162–163, 252; and Anderson-Bricker, "Making a Movement," 48–50. The organization was formed in the spring of 1960. Jane Stembridge to Henry Thomas, August 29, 1960, folder 24, box 10, SNCCP; Joan Trumpauer Mulholland, interview by author, November 8–9, 2001; Paul Dietrich, interview by author, July 8, 2005; Dion Diamond, interview by author, July 13, 2005.

14. Freedom Rider application, Henry James Thomas, section 456, reel 44, COREP; Thomas interview; Thomas and Moody interview; Diamond and Dietrich interviews; *Washington Post*, May 5, 1961; *New Orleans Times-Picayune*, July 21, 1991, April 7, 2001; Baltimore *Afro-American*, May 20, 1961; *Atlanta Constitution*, May 10, 2001 (quotation); Hank Thomas profile, typescript, folder 24, box 10, SNCCP; Halberstam, *The Children*, 215–216, 249, 255, 574; Lewis, *Walking with the Wind*, 137; Carson, *In Struggle*, 33, 38; Peck, *Freedom Ride*, 121–122; Branch, *Parting the Waters*, 412; Farmer, *Lay Bare the Heart*, 24, 197, mistakenly describes Thomas as a senior.
15. Freedom Rider application, Charles Person, section 456, reel 44, COREP; "Freedom Ride, 1961– Participants"; Charles Person, interview by author, May 11–12, 2001; Charles Person, remarks at "Ride to Freedom," 40th anniversary celebration, Atlanta Convention Center, Atlanta, GA, May 11, 2001; *Washington Post*, May 5, 1961; *Baltimore Afro-American*, May 20, 1961; *Birmingham News*, May 18, 1961; Zinn, *SNCC*, 43; Branch, *Parting the Waters*, 419. The official color bar at Georgia Tech ended in May 1961 when the university offered admission to three black students. *Pittsburgh Courier*, May 20, 1961. Farmer, *Lay Bare the Heart*, 197, Lewis, *Walking with the Wind*, 137, and Branch, *Parting the Waters*, 412, omit Person from the list of original Freedom Riders. Because of this oversight, Hank Thomas and John Lewis are often mistakenly described as the youngest participants in the original Ride.
16. Freedom Rider application, B. Elton Cox, section 456, reel 44, COREP; "Freedom Ride 1961– Participants"; Cox interview; Benjamin Elton Cox, interview by Scott Simon, National Public Radio *Weekend Edition* broadcast, April 7, 2001; Thomas interview; Bernard Lafayette and Hank Thomas, interview by author, April 6, 2001; *Baltimore Afro-American*, May 20, 1961; Farmer, *Lay Bare the Heart*, 197, 200; Meier and Rudwick, *CORE*, 151–152; Lewis, *Walking with the Wind*, 137, 139. Cox served as a CORE field representative from the fall of 1961 to the summer of 1964. See section 244, reel 36, COREP. Cox stressed the religious implications of segregation in a statement to an Associated Press reporter just prior to leaving Washington on the Freedom Ride: "I believe we cannot expect to live in a segregated society, be buried by a segregated mortician in a segregated cemetery, and then live eternally in an integrated heaven." *Montgomery Advertiser*, May 5, 1961.
17. Freedom Rider application, John R. Lewis, section 456, reel 44, COREP; "Freedom Ride 1961– Participants"; John Lewis, interview by author, January 31, 2001; Lewis interview, RBOHC; Lewis, *Walking with the Wind*, 11–134, 90 (first quotation), 108 (second quotation); Halberstam, *The Children*, 66–72, 238–249; Meier and Rudwick, *CORE*, 116, 136 (third quotation); Peck, *Freedom Ride*, 119; Branch, *Parting the Waters*, 261–264, 278–280, 379–380, 394–395, 411–412; Carson, *In Struggle*, 21–24, 33; Raines, *My Soul Is Rested*, 71–74, 97–100; Zinn, *SNCC*, 5, 8, 19. On the early development of the Nashville student movement and its relationship with the NCLC, see the 1958–1960 NCLC meeting minutes in folders 22 and 23, box 76, KMSP. See especially Jim Lawson's comments on the relationship in the minutes for November 3, 1960. On the activities of Lewis and the Nashville student movement in early 1961, see the biweekly student newsletter *Voice of the Movement* 1, nos. 1– 7 (February–May 1961), copies in folder 8, box 76, KMSP.
18. Lewis, *Walking with the Wind*, 87–88, 96–97, 132 (first quotation), 133–136; Lafayette interview (second quotation); Halberstam, *The Children*, 246 (third quotation), 247–249; Gaillard, *Crucible of Freedom*, 75–76; Branch, *Parting the Waters*, 412; Lewis and Shuttlesworth interviews; Bernard Lafayette, remarks at "Ride to Freedom," 40th anniversary celebration, Atlanta Civic Center, Atlanta, GA, May 11, 2001. Lafayette's paternal grandfather was a French-speaking cigarworker who migrated to Tampa from Cuba in the 1880s. On Ybor City, see Gary R. Mormino and George Pozzetta, *The Immigrant World of Ybor City: Italians and Their Latin Neighbors in Tampa, 1885–1985* (Urbana: University of Illinois Press, 1987).
19. Lewis, *Walking with the Wind*, 138 (first quotation); Farmer, *Lay Bare the Heart*, 197–198 (second and third quotations); Rich, Blankenheim, and Cox interviews.
20. Farmer, *Lay Bare the Heart*, 198 (first quotation) ; Carey and Cox (second quotation) interviews; Lewis, *Walking with the Wind*, 138; Raines, *My Soul Is Rested*, 110–111; Viorst, *Fire in the Streets*, 141– 142; McDonald interview, RBOHC; Thomas and Moody interview.
21. Lewis, *Walking with the Wind*, 139–140 (first quotation); Farmer, *Lay Bare the Heart*, 198–199 (second quotation); Blankenheim, Carey, Cox (Wilkins quotation), Dietrich, Lewis, and Rich interviews; Raines, *My Soul Is Rested*, 111 (fourth quotation); Carmichael, *Ready for Revolution*, 182. On Chennault, see Martha Byrd, *Chennault: Giving Wings to the Tiger* (Tuscaloosa: University of Alabama Press, 1987); and Daniel Ford, *Flying Tigers: Claire Chennault and the American Volunteer Group* (Washington: Smithsonian Institution Press, 1991). The celebration of the fortieth anniversary of the Freedom Rides opened on May 10, 2001, with a commemorative Chinese buffet dinner at the Washington Court Hotel, a few blocks from the site of the "Last Supper" of 1961.
22. *Washington Evening Star*, May 4, 1961; *Washington Post*, May 5, 1961; Farmer, *Lay Bare the Heart*, 199; Raines, *My Soul Is Rested*, 110; Lewis, *Walking with the Wind*, 139–140; Viorst, *Fire in the Streets*, 142–143; Halberstam, *The Children*, 250–251; Branch, *Parting the Waters*, 412–413 (quotation); Wofford, *Of Kennedys and Kings*, 151; Schlesinger, *Robert Kennedy and His Times*, 295; Reeves, *President Kennedy*, 123–124; Gordon R. Carey to Paul Bennett (Chair, Washington CORE), March 16, 1961, and Frances and Walter Bergman to CORE friends (hereinafter cited as Bergman letter), May 9, 1961, both in reel 25, COREP; Gordon R. Carey to Edward Blankenheim, April 25, 1961, reel 44, COREP; James Farmer, interview by John F. Stewart, March 10, 1967, JFKL; John Seigenthaler, interview by Ronald J. Grele, February 21–23, 1966, JFKL; John Seigenthaler, interview by author, February 13, 2004; Burke Marshall, interview by Robert Wright, February 27, 1970, RBOHC; Theodore Gaffney, interview by author, October 12, 2004 (first and second quotations); Moses Newson, interview by author, March 2, 2002; Walter Fauntroy, interview by author, June 5, 2004;

Rich, Carey, Lewis, Cox, Blankenheim, and Thomas interviews; *Montgomery Advertiser*, May 5, 1961 (Farmer quotations). See also Simeon Booker, "How Atty.-Gen. Kennedy Plans to Aid Dixie Negroes," *Jet* 19 (April 20, 1961): 12–15; Simeon Booker and Theodore Gaffney, "Eyewitness Report on Dixie 'Freedom Ride'—Jet Team Braves Mob Action 4 Times Within 2-Day Period," *Jet* 19 (June 1, 1961): 14–21; and Booker, *Black Man's America*, 1–8, 199–201. On Devree, see Bill Mobley, "Writer on Bus Trip Tells of Her Escape," *Birmingham Post-Herald*, May 15, 1961; and Charlotte Devree, "The Young Negro Rebels," *Harper's* 223 (October 1961): 133–138. A graduate of Sarah Lawrence College, Devree had contributed articles to *Look* and the *New York Times Magazine*. Her husband, Howard Devree, was a noted New York art critic. For Newson's coverage of the second week of the Ride, see the *Washington Afro-American*, May 13, 1961; and the *Baltimore Afro-American*, May 20, 27, June 3, 1961.

23. Peck, *Freedom Ride*, 116; Jim Peck, "Freedom Ride," *CORE-lator* (May 1961): 2; Raines, *My Soul Is Rested*, 111; Lewis, *Walking with the Wind*, 140; Lewis and Person interviews; Farmer, *Lay Bare the Heart*, 199; Branch, *Parting the Waters*, 413; McDonald interview, RBOHC. Halberstam, *The Children*, 255, mistakenly claims that the Riders stopped in Charlottesville, Virginia, and that Person was arrested there for trying to desegregate a shoeshine stand. The Freedom Ride did not pass through Charlottesville, but an incident similar to the one described by Halberstam did occur several days later in Charlotte, North Carolina. On Fredericksburg, see Ronald E. Shibley, "Fredericksburg, Va.," in Roller and Twyman, *The Encyclopedia of Southern History*, 488; and Federal Writers' Project, *Virginia*, 216–226. Most of the Riders, especially those from the South, did not find the Jim Crow signs in Fredericksburg shocking, but at least two—Frances and Walter Bergman—were shaken by this blatant declaration of *de jure* segregation. "We were jolted out of our dream of a peaceful and beautiful world," they recalled several days later, "to find that even this close to the capital restrooms were labeled . . . *White Men, Colored Men*, etc." Bergman letter.

24. Lewis, *Walking with the Wind*, 140 (first quotation); Bergman letter; Lewis, Blankenheim, and Cox interviews; Peck, *Freedom Ride*, 116 (second quotation); Peck, "Freedom Ride," 2; Farmer, *Lay Bare the Heart*, 199; Perkins, "My 219 Days with CORE," 14; Meier and Rudwick, *CORE*, 136; Gaither, reports, March and April 1961, and "Freedom Ride Itinerary," typescript, April 24, 1961, both in reel 25, COREP; Larry A. Still, "A Bus Ride Through Mississippi," *Ebony* 16 (August 1961): 22; Charlotte Devree, "The Young Negro Rebels," 134 (third quotation); Sherrod interview, CUOHC; Federal Writers' Project, *Virginia*, 283–300.

25. Lewis, *Walking with the Wind*, 140–141 (quotation), mistakenly places Walker in Petersburg on May 5. Wyatt Tee Walker, interview by author, December 22, 2003; Wyatt Tee Walker, interview by John Britton, October 11, 1967, RBOHC; Grady Wilson Powell Sr., interview by author, December 17, 2003; Margaret Crowder, interview by author, December 17, 2003; Barnes, *Journey from Jim Crow*, 143–144; Lewis, Blankenheim, and Cox interviews; Thomas Gaither, field report from Petersburg, September 18–21, 1960, and memorandum to Gordon Carey on trip to Virginia, North Carolina, and South Carolina, c. December 1960, both in section 249, reel 36, COREP; Gordon Carey to Martin Luther King Jr., March 31, 1961, box 52A, MLKP; Meier and Rudwick, *CORE*, 86, 112; Branch, *Parting the Waters*, 285–286, 413; Garrow, *Bearing the Cross*, 124–125, 131, 136–137, 140–141; Fairclough, *To Redeem the Soul of America*, 67; "Freedom Rider Itinerary"; Still, "A Bus Ride Through Mississippi," 22; Perkins, "My 219 Days with CORE," 14. Petersburg hosted an SCLC "Institute on Nonviolence" in July 1960. See reel 3, SCLCP. In the spring and summer of 1961, the Reverend Milton A. Reid of Petersburg served as president of the Virginia Christian Leadership Conference. *Baltimore Afro-American*, June 3, 1961. On Petersburg, see U. S. Department of Commerce, *County and City Data Book 1956* (Washington: GPO, 1957), table 4; Roller and Twyman, *Encyclopedia of Southern History*, 970; Federal Writers' Project, *Virginia*, 273–282, and James G. Scott and Edward A. Wyatt, *Petersburg's Story* (Petersburg: Titmus Optical, 1960).

26. Peck, *Freedom Ride*, 116; Peck, "Freedom Ride," 2; Branch, *Parting the Waters*, 413; Lewis, *Walking with the Wind*, 141; Blankenheim and Cox interviews; James Schefter, *The Race: The Uncensored Story of How America Beat Russia to the Moon* (New York: Doubleday, 1999), 139–144; *New York Times*, May 5–12, 1961; Federal Writers' Project, *Virginia*, 398. On the civil rights struggle in Farmville and Prince Edward County, see Amy E. Murrell, "Standing Steady: Toward an Understanding of the Prince Edward School Crisis, 1959–1964" (MA thesis, University of Virginia, 1996; Barbara L. LaJaunie, "A Question of Legitimacy: the *Farmville Herald* and the *Brown* Decision" (Ph.D. thesis, University of Kentucky, 1998); Robert F. Pace, ed., *Two Hundred Years in the Heart of Virginia: Perspectives on Farmville's History* (Farmville: Longwood College Foundation, 1998); and Kluger, *Simple Justice* , 451–507.

27. Peck, *Freedom Ride*, 116–117 (first quotation); Peck, "Freedom Ride," 2; Perkins, "My 291 Days with CORE," 14; Bergman letter (second quotation); Cox (third quotation), Blankenheim, and Lewis interviews; Virgil Wood, interview by author, March 1, 2002; Meier and Rudwick, *CORE*, 119; U.S. Department of Commerce, *County and City Data Book 1956*, table 4. On the March 1961 SCLC "Institute on Nonviolence," see reel 3, SCLCP. On Lynchburg, see Roller and Twyman, *Encyclopedia of Southern History*, 762; P. L. Scruggs, *History of Lynchburg, 1786–1946* (Lynchburg: J. P. Bell, 1973); Darrell Laurant, *A City unto Itself: Lynchburg, Virginia in the Twentieth Century* (n.p.: D. Laurant, 1997); and Federal Writers' Project, *Virginia*, 264–272. On race and civil rights in Lynchburg, see Steven E. Tripp, *Yankee Town, Southern City: Race and Class Relations in Civil War Lynchburg* (New York: New York University Press, 1997); Henry W. Powell, *Witness to Civil Rights History: The Essays and Autobiography of Henry W. Powell* (Hastings, NY: Patrick Cooney, 2000); and Georgia R. W. Barksdale, *Lest We Forget: Remember the Pioneers, Lynchburg Early Civil Rights Movement, 1960–1963* (Lynchburg: privately printed, 1999).

28. Blankenheim interview; Blankenheim, "Freedom Ride," 3; Perkins, "My 291 Days with CORE," 14; *Baltimore Afro-American*, May 20, 1961; Peck, *Freedom Ride*, 117 (quotation); Peck, "Freedom Ride," 2; Branch, *Parting the Waters*, 413, 822, 834. On Danville, see Roller and Twyman, *Encyclopedia of Southern History*, 329; Federal Writers' Project, *Virginia*, 597–599; W. Thomas Mainwaring, "Community in Danville, Virginia, 1880–1963" (Ph.D. thesis, University of North Carolina, Chapel Hill, 1988); and Jane E. Dailey, "Deference and Violence in the Postbellum Urban South: Manners and Massacres in Danville, Virginia," *Journal of Southern History* 63 (August 1991): 554–590. Danville was the scene of major SCLC demonstrations in the summer and fall of 1963. See Fairclough, *To Redeem the Soul of America*, 145–147, 161; James W. Ely Jr., "Negro Demonstrations and the Law: Danville as a Test Case," *Vanderbilt Law Review* 25 (October 1974): 931–943; Sally Belfrage, "Danville on Trial," *New Republic* 49 (November 2, 1963): 11–12; and Peggy Thompson, "A Visit to Danville," *Progressive* 27 (November 1963): 28.

29. Peck, *Freedom Ride*, 117 (first and second quotations), 118; Peck, "Freedom Ride," 2; Perkins, "My 291 Days with CORE," 14; *Baltimore Afro-American*, May 20, 1961 ; *Greensboro Daily News*, May 7, 8 (Farmer quotations), 1961; *Winston-Salem Journal*, May 8, 1961; *Raleigh News and Observer*, May 7, 1961; Chafe, *Civilities and Civil Rights*, 57–141, 155–156; Meier and Rudwick, *CORE*, 136; Gaither reports, March and April 1961; Cox, Lewis, and Newson interviews.

30. Peck, *Freedom Ride*, 118; Peck, "Freedom Ride," 2; Twyman and Roller, *Encyclopedia of Southern History*, 1075–1076; Federal Writers' Project, *North Carolina*, 376–378; Cox interview. The local newspaper, the *Salisbury Evening Post*, ran Associated Press stories on the Freedom Ride on May 9, 10, and 11, but made no mention of the stop in Salisbury.

31. Federal Writers' Project, *North Carolina*, 158–168; Peck, *Freedom Ride*, 118 (first quotation); Peck, "Freedom Ride," 2; Perkins, "My 291 Days with CORE," 14–15; *Charlotte Observer*, May 9, 1961, May 6, 2001; *Charlotte News*, May 8–10, 1961; *Washington Afro-American*, May 13, 1961; *Baltimore Afro-American*, May 20, 27, 1961; *Salisbury Saturday Evening Post*, May 9, 1961; *Sumter Daily Item*, May 10–11, 1961; *Rock Hill Evening Herald*, May 10–11, 1961; Lewis, *Walking with the Wind*, 141; Halberstam, *The Children*, 255; Raines, ed., *My Soul Is Rested*, 111; Blankenheim, "Freedom Ride," 3 (second quotation); Person, Blankenheim, and Newson interviews; Simeon Booker, "Alabama Mob Ambush Bus, Beat Biracial Group and Burn Bus," *Jet* 20 (May 25, 1961): 14; Booker and Gaffney, "Eyewitness Report on Dixie 'Freedom Ride,' " 14; Jones, "Timeline—Rock Hill and Charlotte Sit-ins," 1–8. A decade later, Charlotte and surrounding Mecklenburg County became the backdrop of a precedent-setting legal struggle over the use of county-wide busing for the purpose of school desegregation. In *Swann v. Charlotte-Mecklenburg Board of Education*, 402 U.S. 1 (1971), the U.S. Supreme Court unanimously upheld federal district judge James B. McMillan's county-wide busing order. See Bernard Schwartz, *Swann's Way: The School Busing Case and the Supreme Court* (New York: Oxford University Press, 1986).

32. James Farmer, "Jail-Inners Resume Struggle," *CORE-lator* (April 1961): 3–4; Gaither reports, March and April 1961; Gaither interview; *Rock Hill Evening Herald*, May 10–11, 1961, January 29, March 18, 2001; *Baltimore Afro-American*, May 27, 1961; *Charlotte Observer*, May 6, 2001; Peck, *Freedom Ride*, 118; Peck, "Freedom Ride," 2; Perkins, "My 291 Days with CORE," 15; Lewis, *Walking with the Wind*, 141 (quotation); Jones, "Timeline—Rock Hill and Charlotte Sit-ins," 1–8. On Tillman, Blease, and Smith, see Francis Butler Simkins, *Pitchfork Ben Tillman: South Carolinian* (Baton Rouge: Louisiana State University Press, 1944); David Carlton, *Mill and Town in South Carolina, 1880–1920* (Baton Rouge: Louisiana State University Press, 1982); Stephen Kantrowitz, *Ben Tillman and the Reconstruction of White Supremacy* (Chapel Hill: University of North Carolina Press, 2000); Bryant Simon, *Fabric of Defeat: The Politics of South Carolina Millhands, 1910–1948* (Chapel Hill: University of North Carolina Press, 1998); Ronald D. Burnside, "The Governorship of Coleman L. Blease of South Carolina, 1911–1915" (Ph.D. thesis, Indiana University, 1963); and W. J. Cash, *The Mind of the South* (New York: Knopf, 1941), 250–259. On Rock Hill, see Federal Writers' Project, *South Carolina: A Guide to the Palmetto State* (New York: Oxford University Press, 1941), 253–257.

33. Lewis, *Walking with the Wind*, 142 (first and second quotations), 143–144; Lewis and Newson interviews; *Charlotte Observer*, May 10–11, 1961, May 6, 2001; *Rock Hill Evening Herald*, May 10, 1961; *Washington Afro-American*, May 13, 1961; *Baltimore Afro-American*, May 20, 1961; *Salisbury Evening Post*, May 10, 1961; *High Point Enterprise*, May 10, 1961; *Pittsburgh Courier*, May 20, 1961; Farmer, *Lay Bare the Heart*, 199; Peck, *Freedom Ride*, 118–120 (third and fourth quotations); Peck, "Freedom Ride," 2; Perkins, "My 291 Days with CORE," 15; Blankenheim, "Freedom Ride," 4; Branch, *Parting the Waters*, 415–416; Halberstam, *The Children*, 255–257; Raines, *My Soul Is Rested*, 111; Viorst, *Fire in the Streets*, 143–144; Still, "A Bus Ride Through Mississippi," 22; Federal Writers' Project, *South Carolina*, 315 (fifth quotation). See also the interviews of Moses Newson, James Farmer, Hank Thomas, and John Lewis in the documentary film *Down Freedom's Main Line* (Washington: George Washington University Institute for Historical Documentary Filmmaking, 1998).

34. Federal Writers' Project, *South Carolina*, 316–317; U.S. Department of Commerce, *County and City Data Book 1961* (Washington: GPO, 1961), table 4; *New York Times*, May 10–11, 1961; *Sumter Daily Item*, May 11–12, 1961; *Rock Hill Evening Herald*, May 11, 1961; *Charlotte Observer*, May 6, 2001; Peck, *Freedom Ride*, 120–122 (first and second quotations); Peck, "Freedom Ride," 2; Perkins, "My 291 Days with CORE," 15; *Baltimore Afro-American*, May 20, 1961 (third quotation); *Atlanta Constitution*, May 10, 2001 (fourth quotation); Blankenheim, "Freedom Ride," 4–5; Thomas interview. Halberstam, *The Children*, 257–258, provides a detailed description of Thomas's ordeal but mistakenly identifies the location as Rock Hill.

35. *Sumter Daily Item*, May 10–12, 1961; *Baltimore Afro-American*, May 20, 27, 1961; Cox, Blankenheim, and Newson interviews; Mae Frances Moultrie Howard, interview by author, April 28, 2005; James

Farmer to Mae Frances Moultrie, February 27, 1961, Edward B. King Jr. to Mae Moultrie, March 9, 1961, and Gordon Carey to Max Moultrie, April 4, 1961, letters in author's possession; Ivor Moore, interview by author, September 18, 2005. Peck, *Freedom Ride*, 122–123; Peck, "Freedom Ride," 2; Perkins, "My 291 Days with CORE," 15; "Freedom Ride Itinerary"; Freedom Rider applications, Mae Frances Moultrie, Ivor Moore, Herman K. Harris, and Isaac Reynolds, section 456, reel 44, COREP; Isaac Reynolds, interview by James Mosby Jr., November 5, 1969, RBOHC; *New Orleans Times-Picayune*, March 1, 1998 (Reynolds's obituary); Meier and Rudwick, *CORE*, 106, 116–117, 137, 219, 357; Powledge, *Free at Last?* 256; *Birmingham Post-Herald*, May 15, 1961; *Montgomery Advertiser*, May 15, 1961; Still, "A Bus Ride Through Mississippi," 23; *James T. McCain: A Quiet Hero* (Sumter: n.p., 2002), commemorative pamphlet in author's possession. On Sumter, see Federal Writers' Project, *South Carolina*, 265–267. On the legal tangle precipitated by the Morris College sit-ins, see *Charlotte Observer*, March 3, 1961.

36. *New York Times*, May 7 (Kennedy quotations), 10, 11, 1961; *Atlanta Constitution*, May 8, 1961 (McGill quotation); *Baltimore Afro-American*, May 20, 1961; *Pittsburgh Courier*, May 20, 1961; Edwin O. Guthman, *We Band of Brothers* (New York: Harper and Row, 1971), 159–165; Schlesinger, *Robert Kennedy and His Times*, 293–294; Thomas, *Robert Kennedy*, 127; Branch, *Parting the Waters*, 414–415; Wofford, *Of Kennedys and Kings*, 150–151 (NAACP quotation); Brauer, *John F. Kennedy and the Second Reconstruction*, 95–98; Seigenthaler interview; Eugene Patterson, interview by author, February 14, 2004. On Vandiver, see Harold P. Henderson, *Ernest Vandiver: Governor of Georgia* (Athens: University of Georgia Press, 2000). On Charlayne Hunter, who went on to become a successful public television commentator, see Charlayne Hunter-Gault, *In My Place* (New York: Farrar Straus Giroux, 1992); Calvin Trillin, *An Education in Georgia: The Integration of Charlayne Hunter and Hamilton Holmes* (New York: Viking, 1963); and Robert A. Pratt, *We Shall Not Be Moved: The Desegregation of the University of Georgia* (Athens: University of Georgia Press, 2002). See also Eugene Patterson, "The Long Road Back to Georgia," in *The Changing South of Gene Patterson: Journalism and Civil Rights, 1960–1968*, ed. Roy Peter Clark and Raymond Arsenault (Gainesville: University Press of Florida, 2002), 255–263.

37. On the political and social history of Edgefield, see Orville Vernon Burton, *In My Father's House Are Many Mansions: Family and Community in Edgefield, South Carolina* (Chapel Hill: University of North Carolina Press, 1985); Drew Gilpin Faust, *James Henry Hammond and the Old South: A Design for Mastery* (Baton Rouge: Louisiana State University Press, 1982); Fox Butterfield, *All God's Children: The Bosket Family and the American Tradition of Violence* (New York: Knopf, 1995); Simkins, *Pitchfork Ben Tillman*; Kantrowicz, *Ben Tillman and the Reconstruction of White Supremacy*; Nadine Cohodas, *Strom Thurmond and the Politics of Southern Change* (New York: Simon and Schuster, 1993); and Jack Bass, *Ol' Strom: An Unauthorized Biography of Strom Thurmond* (Atlanta: Longstreet, 1998).

38. Peck, *Freedom Ride*, 123 (quotations); Peck, "Freedom Ride," 2–3; Farmer, *Lay Bare the Heart*, 200; Blankenheim, "Freedom Ride," 5; *Augusta Chronicle*, May 6–13, 1961; *Pittsburgh Courier*, June 3, 1961; Still, "A Bus Ride Through Mississippi," 23; Eugene Patterson interview; Stephen G. N. Tuck, *Beyond Atlanta: The Struggle for Racial Equality in Georgia, 1940–1980* (Athens: University of Georgia Press, 2001), 30, 36, 39, 51–52, 65, 80, 85, 108–109, 145–147, 204, 210, 234–235. On Augusta, see Roller and Twyman, *The Encyclopedia of Southern History*, 90; Numan V. Bartley, *The Creation of Modern Georgia* (Athens: University of Georgia Press, 1983), 131–136, 162–163, 196; J. William Harris, *Plain Folk and Gentry in a Slave Society: White Liberty and Black Slavery in Augusta's Hinterlands* (Middletown, CT: Wesleyan University Press, 1985); Richard H. L. German, "The Queen City of the Savannah: Augusta, Georgia During the Urban Progressive Era, 1890–1917" (Ph.D. thesis, University of Florida, 1971); and Edward Cashin, *The Story of Augusta* (Augusta: Richmond County Board of Education, 1980). See also Donald L. Grant, *The Way It Was in the South: The Black Experience in Georgia* (Athens: University of Georgia Press, 2001); Paul Bolster, "Civil Rights Movement in Twentieth-Century Georgia" (Ph.D. thesis, University of Georgia, 1972); and Joseph Yates Garrison, "The Augusta Black Community Since World War II" (M.A. thesis, University of Miami, 1971).

39. Peck, *Freedom Ride*, 123–124 (quotations); Peck, "Freedom Ride," 3; Hunter-Gault, *In My Place*; Ralph McGill, *The South and the Southerner* (Boston: Little, Brown, 1963), 289–291; Harold H. Martin, *Ralph McGill, Reporter* (Boston: Little, Brown, 1973), 174–180; Fairclough, *To Redeem the Soul of America*, 73–75; Bartley, *The Creation of Modern Georgia*, 193–206; Barbara B. Clowse, *Ralph McGill: A Biography* (Macon: Mercer University Press, 1998); Leonard Ray Teel, *Ralph Emerson McGill: Voice of the Southern Conscience* (Knoxville: University of Tennessee Press, 2001); Jeff Roche, *Restructured Resistance: The Sibley Commission and the Politics of Desegregation in Georgia* (Athens: University of Georgia Press, 1998); Ronald Bayor, *Race and the Shaping of Twentieth-Century Atlanta* (Chapel Hill: University of North Carolina Press, 1996); Tuck, *Beyond Atlanta*; Grant, *The Way It Was in the South*; and Eugene Patterson interview. For a series of discussions on Atlanta's struggle with desegregation in 1960 and 1961, see the periodic editorials of publisher Ralph McGill and the daily columns of editor Eugene Patterson in the *Atlanta Constitution*, 1960–1961. For a sampling of Patterson's columns, see Clark and Arsenault, *The Changing South of Gene Patterson*, 46–87.

40. Gordon Carey to Martin Luther King Jr., March 31, 1961; Gordon Carey to Dora E. McDonald (King's secretary), April 18, 1961; Gordon Carey to Martin Luther King Jr., telegram, May 8, 1961, all in box 52A, MLKP. *Atlanta Constitution*, May 13–15, 1961; Farmer, *Lay Bare the Heart*, 200 (first quotation); Branch, *Parting the Waters*, 416–417 (second quotation); Raines, *My Soul Is Rested*, 111–112; Walker interview, RBOHC; Peck, *Freedom Ride*, 123–124; Garrow, *Bearing the Cross*, 155–156; Blankenheim, "Freedom Ride," 5; Fairclough, *To Redeem the Soul of America*, 77; Halberstam, *The Children*, 258–259; Lewis, *Walking with the Wind*, 144; Still, "A Bus Ride Through Mississippi," 23; Blankenheim, Carey, Newson, Person, Thomas, and Wyatt Tee Walker interviews.

41. Farmer, *Lay Bare the Heart*, 200 (quotations); Blankenheim, Newson, Person, and Thomas interviews.
42. Farmer, *Lay Bare the Heart*, 200–201 (quotations); Raines, *My Soul Is Rested*, 112; Blankenheim, Cox, Newson, Person, and Thomas interviews; Branch, *Parting the Waters*, 417; Viorst, *Fire in the Streets*, 144; Booker, "Alabama Mob Ambush Bus," 12; Perkins, "My 291 Days with CORE," 15.
43. Lewis, *Walking with the Wind*, 144 (quotation); Cox, Lafayette, and Lewis interviews; Diane Nash, interview by author, April 6–7, 2001; *Voice of the Movement* 1 (May 20, 1961): 1; Branch, *Parting the Waters*, 424–425. Halberstam, *The Children*, 265–266, mistakenly claims that Lewis was still in Philadelphia on Sunday, May 14.
44. Kaufman, *The First Freedom Ride*, 157–166 (quotations); Thornton, *Dividing Lines*, 167, 240–242; McWhorter, *Carry Me Home*, 131, 161–168, 177–198; O'Reilly, *"Racial Matters,"* 79–90; Gary Thomas Rowe Jr., *My Undercover Years with the Ku Klux Klan* (New York: Bantam, 1976), 1–40; Gary May, *The Informant: The FBI, the Ku Klux Klan, and the Murder of Viola Liuzzo* (New Haven: Yale University Press, 2005), 1–29; Eskew, *But for Birmingham*, 85–119, 156–157; William A. Nunnelley, *Bull Connor* (Tuscaloosa: University of Alabama Press, 1991), 85–108. See also the voluminous FBI correspondence in the following files available through the Freedom of Information Act: FBI–CORE Files; FBI–Walter and Frances Bergman Freedom Rider Files; and FBI–Alabama Freedom Rider Files. All are available at FBI-FRI (in the Birmingham Public Library). See especially Memoranda on Information from G. Thomas Rowe, April 24, and May 4, 10, 12, 1961; SAC Birmingham to FBI Director, April 19, 24, and May 5, 9, 10, 12, 1961; FBI Director to SAC Atlanta, April 24, 1961; FBI Director to SAC Birmingham, May 10, 1961, all in FBI-FRI. On Shelton and the competing Klan organizations of the early 1960s, see James Graham Cook, *The Segregationists* (New York: Appleton-Century-Crofts, 1962), 117–147.
45. Memoranda on Rowe, May 4, 10, 12, 1961; SAC Birmingham to FBI Director, May 5, 9, 10, 12, 13, 1961; FBI Director to SAC Birmingham, May 10, 1961; SAC Birmingham to FBI Director and SAC Mobile, May 14, 1961, all in FBI-FRI. Kaufman, *The First Freedom Ride*, 162–163 (quotations); Thornton, *Dividing Lines*, 243–245; McWhorter, *Carry Me Home*, 162, 194; O'Reilly, *"Racial Matters,"* 83, 89–90; Wofford, *Of Kennedys and Kings*, 151–152; Branch, *Parting the Waters*, 420; Halberstam, *The Children*, 321–322; May, *The Informant*, 29–31; Burke Marshall, interview in documentary "Ain't Scared of Your Jails"; Burton Hersh, interview by author, April 26, 2005. See also U.S. Department of Justice, *The FBI, the Department of Justice, and Gary Thomas Rowe, Jr.: Task Force Report on Gary Thomas Rowe, Jr.* (Washington: GPO, 1979), 54–55, for an evaluation of the FBI's failure to share information with other government agencies prior to the Klan assaults on Freedom Riders in Alabama.
46. Kaufman, *The First Freedom Ride*, 164 (quotations), 165–167; McWhorter, *Carry Me Home*, 194–199, 203; Thornton, *Dividing Lines*, 245–246, 643–644; May, *The Informant*, 28–29. SAC Birmingham to FBI Director, May 15–18, 20–21, 1961; SAC Birmingham to FBI Director and SAC Mobile, May 14–15, 1961; SA Barrett G. Kemp to SAC Thomas Jenkins, May 15, 17, 24, 1961, all in FBI-FRI.

Chapter 4: Alabama Bound

1. In 1964 Chuck Berry, one of America's most popular black rock 'n' roll stars, released "Promised Land," a song with lyrics that recalled the 1961 CORE Freedom Ride. In Berry's version, the trip to the "Promised Land" begins in Norfolk, Virginia, and ends in Los Angeles, California. While the song does not mention the Freedom Rides by name, the third stanza (the epigraph) provides a direct link to the Freedom Riders' troubles in Alabama. As the historian Brian Ward has written, "It is hard to imagine that Berry's black audience did not hear echoes of these incidents [the assaults on Freedom Riders in Anniston and Birmingham, Alabama]" in this stanza. The song also begins with two stanzas that describe a route roughly similar to the CORE Freedom Ride: "I left my home in Norfolk, Virginia,/ California on my mind./ Straddled that Greyhound,/ rode him past Raleigh,/ On across Caroline./ Stopped in Charlotte and bypassed Rock Hill,/ And we never was a minute late./ We was ninety miles out of Atlanta by sundown,/ Rollin' cross the Georgia state." Brian Ward, *Just My Soul Responding: Rhythm and Blues, Black Consciousness, and Race Relations* (Berkeley: University of California Press, 1998), 213–214. Berry wrote *Promised Land* in 1962, while he was living and working at a federal medical facility in Springfield, Missouri. Chuck Berry, *Chuck Berry: The Autobiography* (New York: Hammond Books, 1987), 216–217.
2. Farmer, *Lay Bare the Heart*, 201; Peck, *Freedom Ride*, 124; Shuttlesworth, Blankenheim, and Carey interviews; McWhorter, *Carry Me Home*, 202; Manis, *A Fire You Can't Put Out*, 262–263; Branch, *Parting the Waters*, 417, 420; Meier and Rudwick, *CORE*, 137. According to Powledge, *Free at Last?* 255: "Everybody was in good spirits except the highly conspicuous photographer from the Georgia Bureau of Investigation who always showed up on such occasions, trying unsuccessfully to assume the protective coloration of the press."
3. Genevieve Hughes, "Freedom Ride Report," May 15, 1961, section 116, reel 25, COREP; W. E. Jones (Greyhound Vice-President) to A. H. Walter (ICC), May 15, 1961, file RD 195, box 20, Investigative Report Case Files, ICCR; Perkins, "My 291 Days with CORE"; Blankenheim, Newson, and Thomas interviews; *Baltimore Afro-American*, May 27, 1961; *Birmingham Post-Herald*, May 15, 1961; *Birmingham News*, May 15, 1961; Kaufman, *The First Freedom Ride*, Appendix C, 152; Branch, *Parting the Waters*, 417. Halberstam, *The Children*, 258–260, 263, claims that there were also two FBI agents on board the bus, but there is no corroborating evidence of their presence; in all likelihood, the two "agents" described by Hank Thomas in a 1990s interview were actually Cowling and Sims. O'Reilly, *"Racial Matters,"* 83, notes that the FBI had advance information related to the attack in Anniston,

which it forwarded to the Anniston police on May 13. On the surveillance activities of Ell Cowling, see Powledge, *Free at Last?* 255, 269–270. On Anniston, see Roller and Twyman, *The Encyclopedia of Southern History*, 47; Gary S. Sprayberry, " 'Town Among the Trees': Paternalism, Class, and Civil Rights in Anniston, Alabama, 1872 to Present" (Ph.D. thesis, University of Alabama, 2003); Robert Entire, ed., *Anniston, Alabama, Centennial, 1883–1983* (Anniston: Higginbotham, 1983); Grace Hooten Gates, *The Model City of the New South: Anniston, Alabama, 1872–1900* (Tuscaloosa: University of Alabama Press, 1978); Kimberly O'Dell, *Anniston* (Charleston: Arcadia, 2000); Phil Noble, *Beyond the Burning Bus: The Civil Rights Revolution in a Southern Town* (Montgomery: New South Books, 2003); and Wayne Flynt, *Poor but Proud: Alabama's Poor Whites* (Tuscaloosa: University of Alabama Press, 1989), passim. See also the *Anniston Star*, May–June 1961. Anne Braden, the noted Louisville, Kentucky, civil rights activist, grew up in Anniston from the age of seven until adulthood (1931–1946). See Fosl, *Subversive Southerner*, 15–71.

4. Hughes, "Freedom Ride Report," 1 (quotation); Peck, *Freedom Ride*, 125; Sprayberry, " 'Town Among the Trees,' " 229–232; Thornton, *Dividing Lines*, 246; *Anniston Star*, May 15, 1961. See also folder 111.3.1.6.1, FBI-FRI.

5. Folder 111.3.1.6.1, FBI-FRI; Halberstam, *The Children*, 261 (quotation); Sprayberry, " 'Town Among the Trees,' " 232. Chappell owned an upholstery shop in Anniston. Southern Greyhound's semiofficial account of the Anniston episode contains no suggestion of O. T. Jones's complicity. See W. E. Jones to A. H. Walter, May 15 and 22, 1961, file RD 195, box 20, Investigative Report Case Files, ICCR.

6. Folders 111.3.1.6.1, 111.3.1.6.2, and 111.3.1.6.3, FBI-FRI; Sprayberry, " 'Town Among the Trees,' " 232–233 (first and second quotations); Hughes, "Freedom Ride Report," 1 (third quotation); Blankenheim and Newson interviews; Bill Mobley, "Writer on Bus Trip Tells of Her Escape," *Birmingham Post-Herald*, May 15, 1961; *Baltimore Afro-American*, May 27, 1961; *Anniston Star*, May 15, 1961; *Montgomery Advertiser*, May 15, 1961; Halberstam, *The Children*, 260–261; Branch, *Parting the Waters*, 417–418.

7. Hughes, "Freedom Ride Report," 1 (quotations); Mobley, "Writer on Bus Trip Tells of Her Escape"; Kaufman, *The First Freedom Ride*, 152–153; Peck, *Freedom Ride*, 125; Halberstam, *The Children*, 262; McWhorter, *Carry Me Home*, 203; Sprayberry, " 'Town Among the Trees,' " 234–236; *Anniston Star*, May 15, 1961; Folder 111.3.1.6.1, FBI-FRI.

8. Thomas interview; Peck, *Freedom Ride*, 125; Halberstam, *The Children*, 262–263 (quotations); folders 111.3.1.6.1, and 111.3.6.3, FBI-FRI; Gaillard, *Cradle of Freedom*, 81. See also Howell Raines's interview with Hank Thomas in Raines, *My Soul Is Rested*, 113–115.

9. Hughes, "Freedom Ride Report," 2; Blankenheim and Howard interviews; Blankenheim, "Freedom Ride," 6 (quotation); Perkins, "My 291 Days with CORE," 15; Halberstam, *The Children*, 264; Peck, *Freedom Ride*, 125–126; Powledge, *Free at Last?* 255, 269–270; McWhorter, *Carry Me Home*, 203; *Anniston Star*, May 15, 1961; *Nashville Tennessean*, May 15, 1961; folders 111.3.1.6.1, 111.3.1.6.3, and 111.3.1.7.2, FBI-FRI. In 1991 Janie Miller attended a Freedom Rider reunion in Jackson, Mississippi. *Atlanta Constitution*, July 21, 1991.

10. Hughes, "Freedom Ride Report," 2.

11. Halberstam, *The Children*, 264; Raines, *My Soul Is Rested*, 114–115; Sprayberry, " 'Town Among the Trees,' " 237–238; Blankenheim interview.

12. Hughes, "Freedom Ride Report," 2; Perkins, "My 291 Days with CORE," 15; Manis, *A Fire You Can't Put Out*, 264 (quotation); Fred Shuttlesworth, interview by James Mosby, September 1968, RBOHC; Raines, *My Soul Is Rested*, 115; Branch, *Parting the Waters*, 423; Blankenheim, Newson, and Shuttlesworth interviews; Gaillard, *Cradle of Freedom*, 82–84.

13. Hughes, "Freedom Ride Report," 2; Raines, *My Soul Is Rested*, 115; Blankenheim and Newson interviews; Gaillard, *Cradle of Freedom*, 83–84 (quotation).

14. Hughes, "Freedom Ride Report," 2; Blankenheim and Newson interviews.

15. Booker and Gaffney, "Eyewitness Report," 14 (quotation); Booker, *Black Man's America*, 1; Gaffney interview; Kaufman, *The First Freedom Ride*, 153–154.

16. Kaufman, *The First Freedom Ride*, 154.

17. Ibid.; Peck, *Freedom Ride*, 126; Booker, "Alabama Mob Ambush Bus," 13–14; Booker and Gaffney, "Eyewitness Report," 14 (quotation); Booker, *Black Man's America*, 1–2; John Olan Patterson, interview by FBI, May 17, 1961, FBI-FRI; Branch, *Parting the Waters*, 419; Thornton, *Dividing Lines*, 246–247; May, *The Informant*, 31–33.

18. Booker and Gaffney, "Eyewitness Report," 16 (quotations); Booker, "Alabama Mob Ambush Bus," 13–14; *Nashville Tennessean*, May 15, 1961; Booker, *Black Man's America*, 2–3; Kaufman, *The First Freedom Ride*, 154–155; Peck, *Freedom Ride*, 126; James Peck, Herman K. Harris, Isaac Reynolds, Charles A. Person, and Dr. Walter Bergman, interviews by FBI, May 18, 1961, FBI-FRI; Frances Bergman, interview by FBI, May 17, 1961, FBI-FRI; Branch, *Parting the Waters*, 419; May, *The Informant*, 33–34; Thornton, *Dividing Lines*, 247; McWhorter, *Carry Me Home*, 204. For a time, no one appreciated the severity of Bergman's injuries, but ten days after the attack, he suffered a stroke. Four months later, after entering the hospital for an appendectomy, he suffered a heart attack. At that point doctors discovered that he had incurred serious brain damage during the May beating. Confined to a wheelchair for the remainder of his life, he nonetheless lived to the age of one hundred. He died on September 29, 1999. In 1982, with the help of the Michigan affiliate of the ACLU, he filed a successful lawsuit against the FBI, which, according to Federal District Judge Richard A. Enslen, had advance information that could have prevented Bergman's beating. Although Bergman's lawyers asked for $2 million in damages, Judge Enslen restricted the award to $35,000, ruling that the appendectomy was, in all likelihood, partially responsible for Bergman's crippled condition. *New*

York Times, October 10, 1999; *Bergman v. U.S.*, 551 F. Supp. 407, 565 F. Supp. 1353, 579 F. Supp. 911; Kaufman, *The First Freedom Ride*, 146–203 (Appendix C); Simon and Goodman interviews. See also *Peck v. U.S.*, 470 F. Supp. 1003, 514 F. Supp. 210, 522 F. Supp. 245 (1979).

19. Booker and Gaffney, "Eyewitness Report," 16–18 (quotations); Booker, *Black Man's America*, 3; Kaufman, *The First Freedom Ride*, 155; Peck, *Freedom Ride*, 126–127; *Bergman v. U.S.*; Peck, Harris, Reynolds, Person, Patterson, Frances Bergman, and Walter Bergman interviews, FBI-FRI; Mary Spicer, interview by FBI, May 25, 1961, FBI-FRI; Branch, *Parting the Waters*, 419–420; Thornton, *Dividing Lines*, 247; McWhorter, *Carry Me Home*, 204; May, *The Informant*, 32–34.

20. Kaufman, *The First Freedom Ride*, 146–203 (Appendix C); O'Reilly, *"Racial Matters,"* 79–89; McWhorter, *Carry Me Home*, 190–194, 198, 201–205. Rowe, *My Undercover Years with the Ku Klux Klan*, 38–50; May, *The Informant*, 29–31. For the details of FBI operations related to the Freedom Rides, see the voluminous correspondence in FBI-FRI.

21. Kaufman, *The First Freedom Ride*, 155–170; O'Reilly, *"Racial Matters,"* 84–88; Thornton, *Dividing Lines*, 247; Branch, *Parting the Waters*, 420–421; Rowe, *My Undercover Years with the Ku Klux Klan*, 42 (quotation), 40–42. In his memoir Rowe claims that "nearly 1,000" men were running and walking toward the station, but all other accounts suggest that this number represents a gross exaggeration. The actual number was probably between one hundred and two hundred. Among others, William A. Nunnelley, a young reporter at the *Birmingham Post-Herald* in 1961 who later wrote a biography of Bull Connor, has questioned the overall reliability of Rowe's account. See Nunnelley, *Bull Connor*, 106–109.

22. Kaufman, *The First Freedom Ride*, 155–156 (second quotation); Rowe, *My Undercover Years with the Ku Klux Klan*, 41; SAC Birmingham to Director J. Edgar Hoover, May 15, 1961, FBI-FRI; Edward Fields File, box 3, and National States Rights Party File, box 7, Birmingham Police Surveillance Files, BPL. On the extremist activities of Fields, Stoner, and the National States Rights Party, which was founded in Jefferson, Indiana, in 1958, see Peter Applebome, *Dixie Rising: How the South Is Shaping American Values, Politics, and Culture* (San Diego: Harcourt Brace, 1996), 46–52, 112–113; Carter, *Politics of Rage*, 164–167; Raines, *My Soul Is Rested*, 167–171; and Cook, *The Segregationists*, 136–137, 167–186. See also Stoner's monthly newspaper, *The Thunderbolt: The White Man's Viewpoint* (1961–1963); and Melissa Fay Greene, *The Temple Bombing* (Reading, MA: Addison-Wesley, 1996). McWhorter, *Carry Me Home*, 200–203 (Cook quotation), 204–205; Manis, *A Fire You Can't Put Out*, 255, 263; Eskew, *But for Birmingham*, 150, 157; Harrison Salisbury, "Fear and Hatred Grip Birmingham," *New York Times*, April 12, 1960 (first quotation); Branch, *Parting the Waters*, 420; Jonathan Bass, *Blessed Are the Peacemakers: Martin Luther King Jr., Eight White Religious Leaders, and the "Letter from Birmingham Jail"* (Baton Rouge: Louisiana State University Press, 2001), 36–37, 92–94. Smith and his camera crew filmed Shuttlesworth and others during a May 13 mass meeting. See the transcript of *CBS Reports: Who Speaks for Birmingham?* May 18, 1961, BPL; Howard K. Smith, *Events Leading Up to My Death: The Life of a Twentieth-Century Reporter* (New York: St. Martin's, 1996). O'Reilly, *"Racial Matters,"* 87–88, claims that Fields "threatened to shoot any FBI agent he caught snooping around." Moore, with Connor's approval, spent Mother's Day 1961 in his hometown of Albertville, Alabama, where he attended a Decoration Day ceremony at the Alder Spring Cemetery. Nunnelley, *Bull Connor*, 98.

23. Nunnelley, *Bull Connor*, 93–99, 104–109; Kaufman, *The First Freedom Ride*, 160–167; McWhorter, *Carry Me Home*, 73–75, 129–141, 192–199, 205; Thornton, *Dividing Lines*, 179–186, 200–247; Gaillard, *Cradle of Freedom*, 91; Manis, *A Fire You Can't Put Out*, 246–255, 265–266; Eskew, *But for Birmingham*, 53–151; Branch, *Parting the Waters*, 420; O'Reilly, *"Racial Matters,"* 86, 88–89. See also *United States v. United States Klans, Knights of Ku Klux Klan, Inc., et al.*, 194 F. Supp. 897 (M. D. Ala 1961).

24. Peck interview, FBI-FRI (first quotation); Peck, *Freedom Ride*, 127–128 (second quotation); May, *The Informant*, 36; Branch, *Parting the Waters*, 421; McWhorter, *Carry Me Home*, 206; Person interview.

25. Peck, *Freedom Ride*, 128; Booker and Gaffney, "Eyewitness Report," 18; Booker, *Black Man's America*, 4–5; *Birmingham Post-Herald*, May 15, 1961; *Birmingham News*, May 15, 1961; Rowe, *My Undercover Years with the Ku Klux Klan*, 43 (first quotation); Smith, *Events Leading Up to My Death*, 271; May, *The Informant*, 36 (second quotation); Person and Peck interviews, FBI-FRI; Jesse Oliver Faggard, interview by FBI, May 16, 1961, and John H. Thompson, interview by FBI, May 26, 1962, both in FBI-FRI; McWhorter, *Carry Me Home*, 206–207; Thornton, *Dividing Lines*, 247–248; Nunnelley, *Bull Connor*, 97–98, 104.

26. Moore, Harris, Frances Bergman, and Walter Bergman interviews, FBI-FRI; Moore interview, Booker and Gaffney, "Eyewitness Report," 18–19; Booker, *Black Man's America*, 5; Kaufman, *The First Freedom Ride*, 4–5; Branch, *Parting the Waters*, 421–422; May, *The Informant*, 36–37.

27. Reynolds and Mary Spicer interviews, FBI-FRI; George E. Webb, interview by FBI, May 25, 1961, and John W. Bloomer, interview by FBI, May 19, 1961, both in FBI-FRI; Rowe, *My Undercover Years With the Ku Klux Klan*, 43 (quotation). In Rowe's memoir, Self is identified with the pseudonym Abe Turner. Gary Thomas Rowe folders, box 9, Birmingham Police Surveillance Files, BPL; May, *The Informant*, 36–41; McWhorter, *Carry Me Home*, 207, 614; Smith, *Events Leading Up to My Death*, 271. According to one deposition given by Rowe, Self yelled: "Your fifteen minutes is up. All goddamn hell is going to break loose. Get these guys out of here. The police are coming." On Self's role in the Trailways station riot, see Thornton, *Dividing Lines*, 247–248.

28. Rowe, *My Undercover Years with the Ku Klux Klan*, 43 (quotation), 44–50; May, *The Informant*, 38–47. Langston's photograph was later nominated for a Pulitzer Prize. *Birmingham Post-Herald*, May 15, 1961. SAC Birmingham to FBI Director, May 14, 17, 1961; Clancy Lake, interview by FBI, May 15, 1961; Thomas E. Langston, interview by FBI, May 21, 1961; Julian A. "Bud" Gordon, interview by FBI, May 16, 19, 1961; Thomas Lankford, interview by FBI, May 19, 20, 1961, all in FBI-FRI.

Freedom Riders folders, box 5, and Gary Thomas Rowe folders, box 9, Birmingham Police Surveillance Files, BPL; Brian Ward, *Radio and the Struggle for Civil Rights in the South* (Gainesville: University Press of Florida, 2004), 201; Peck, *Freedom Ride*, 128; Booker and Gaffney, "Eyewitness Report," 18; Booker, *Black Man's America*, 5; Branch, *Parting the Waters*, 422; McWhorter, *Carry Me Home*, 207–208; Thornton, *Dividing Lines*, 248–249; Eskew, *But for Birmingham*, 157.

29. Peck, *Freedom Ride*, 128–129; *Birmingham Post-Herald*, May 15, 1961; Rowe, *My Undercover Years with the Ku Klux Klan*, 43–44; Peck and Walter Bergman interviews, FBI-FRI; Thornton, *Dividing Lines*, 248; McWhorter, *Carry Me Home*, 207; May, *The Informant*, 37; Smith, *Events Leading Up to My Death*, 271–272 (quotations); McWhorter, *Carry Me Home*, 183–187, 207–209 (last quotation); Reynolds interview, FBI-FRI.

30. Smith, *Events Leading Up to My Death*, 272; McWhorter, *Carry Me Home*, 209 (first quotation); Peck, *Freedom Ride*, 128–129; Manis, *A Fire You Can't Put Out*, 264, 266 (quotations); Gaffney, Howard, Person, and Shuttlesworth interviews; Shuttlesworth interview, RBOHC; Branch, *Parting the Waters*, 422.

31. *Birmingham News*, May 15, 1961; Peck, *Freedom Ride*, 129–130; Manis, *A Fire You Can't Put Out*, 267; Branch, *Parting the Waters*, 423–424 (quotation).

32. *Montgomery Advertiser*, May 15, 1961; *Nashville Tennessean*, May 15, 1961; Booker and Gaffney, "Eyewitness Report," 19–20; Booker, *Black Man's America*, 5; Branch, *Parting the Waters*, 423; Manis, *A Fire You Can't Put Out*, 266–267 (quotations); "A Great Thing," *Southern Patriot* 19 (June 1961): 4; Shuttlesworth, Blankenheim, and Cox interviews.

33. Peck, *Freedom Ride*, 129–130; Shuttlesworth interview; Shuttlesworth interview, RBOHC; Police Report, J. E. LeGrand and M. A. Jones to Jamie Moore, May 16, 1961, folder 24, box 9, BCP; Manis, *A Fire You Can't Put Out*, 267 (quotation); Booker and Gaffney, "Eyewitness Report," 20, notes that "some Negro families hesitated to board the white members because of the increasing tension—and the Rev. Mr. Shuttlesworth kept four in his own home." Two of the white Riders spent the night at the home of Lola Hendricks, Shuttlesworth's secretary. Years later, she told the journalist Frye Gaillard: "They were white. I never did get their names. They were upset, terrified. They had no idea what was going to happen to them." Gaillard, *Cradle of Freedom*, 84.

34. Branch, *Parting the Waters*, 423; Cook, *The Segregationists*, 132 (quotation); Seigenthaler interview. Booker's account in *Black Man's America*, 5, does not mention the call to the Justice Department, but it does mention two other calls: "Once at the minister's home, I called the New York office of CORE and my home in Washington."

35. Wofford, *Of Kennedys and Kings*, 135 (quotation), 151; Seigenthaler interview; John Seigenthaler, interview by Robert Campbell, July 10, 1968, RBOHC; George E. Barrett, interview by author, November 8, 2004; Brauer, *John F. Kennedy and the Second Reconstruction*, 83, 277–278; Reeves, *President Kennedy*, 124; Stern, *Calculating Visions*, 35; Schlesinger, *Robert Kennedy and His Times*, 238, 240, 289–297; Thomas, *Robert Kennedy*, 84; Guthman, *We Band of Brothers*, 58, 70, 81–82, 100, 160. See also John Seigenthaler, "Civil Rights in the Trenches," in *The Kennedy Presidency: Seventeen Intimate Perspectives of John F. Kennedy*, ed. Kenneth W. Thompson (Portraits of American Presidents, vol. 4) (Lanham, MD: University Press of America, 1985); and the multiple interviews of Seigenthaler located at JFKL: by William A. Geohegan, July 22, 1964; by Larry J. Hackman (for the Robert F. Kennedy Oral History Program), June 5, July 1, 1970; by Ronald J. Grele, February 21–23, 1966.

36. Wofford, *Of Kennedy and Kings*, 153 (quotations), 134–177; Branch, *Parting the Waters*, 397–411; Niven, *The Politics of Injustice*, 24–38; Stern, *Calculating Visions*, 35, 40–62; Reeves, *President Kennedy*, 59–64; Dallek, *An Unfinished Life*, 382–384; Seigenthaler, "Civil Rights in the Trenches"; Brauer, *John F. Kennedy and the Second Reconstruction*, 1–98; Victor Navasky, *Kennedy Justice* (New York: Atheneum, 1971), 14–23; Schlesinger, *Robert Kennedy and His Times*, 286–367; Guthman, *We Band of Brothers*, 108–136; Belknap, *Federal Law and Southern Order*, 70–105; Burke Marshall, *Federalism and Civil Rights* (New York: Columbia University Press, 1964); Seigenthaler and Doar interviews; Farmer interview, JFKL, 1, 5–6; Lee C. White, interview by Milton Gwirtzman, May 26, 1964, JFKL, 66–67, 73–74; Martin Luther King Jr. interview, JFKL, 3–4, 15–17; Burke Marshall, interview by Larry J. Hackman, January 19–20, 1970, JFKL, 1–93; Burke Marshall, interview by Louis Oberdorfer, May 29, 1964, JFKL, 1–61, 86; Wofford interview, JFKL, 44, 51, 61, 66–67, 124, 134–135. See also May 1961 folder, box 1; folder 2, box 4; and Misc. Clippings 1961–62, box 14, BMP; and Civil Rights: Alabama folders, box 10, RFKP. On Doar, see John Doar Records, boxes 1 and 2, USDJ/CRD; and "Ubiquitous Rights Aide, John Michael Doar," *New York Times*, September 3, 1963.

37. Wofford, *Of Kennedy and Kings*, 152; O'Reilly, *"Racial Matters"*, 49–123; Kaufman, *The First Freedom Ride*, 159–202; Navasky, *Kennedy Justice*, 6–14, 23–29, 41–43, 96–101, 106–108; Reeves, *President Kennedy*, 127; Schlesinger, *Robert Kennedy and His Times*, 291–293; Thomas, *Robert Kennedy*, 109, 115–119; Guthman, *We Band of Brothers*, 104, 167; Branch, *Parting the Waters*, 413; Seigenthaler and Hersh interviews. Despite bureau denials, Rowe insisted that FBI agents were present at the Trailways station during the riot, and that some even captured what happened on movie film. McWhorter, *Carry Me Home*, 213–215.

38. Lewis, *Walking with the Wind*, 146 (first quotation); Wofford, *Of Kennedys and Kings*, 152 (second and third quotations); Smith, *Events Leading Up to My Death*, 271–272; *New York Times*, May 15, 1961; McWhorter, *Carry Me Home*, 183–187, 209.

39. On the public reaction to the Till murder, see Stephen J. Whitfield, *A Death in the Delta: The Story of Emmett Till* (New York: Free Press, 1988).

40. *New York Times*, May 15, 1961; *Washington Post*, May 15, 1961; Farmer, *Lay Bare the Heart*, 203 (quotation); Peck, *Freedom Ride*, 133–135; Branch, *Parting the Waters*, 418, 425. Part of Schakne's report can be seen in the documentary "Ain't Scared of Your Jails."

41. Carey, Cox, and Rich interviews; Raines, *My Soul Is Rested*, 112; Farmer, *Lay Bare the Heart*, 201; *Nashville Tennessean*, May 16, 1961. In his memoir Farmer makes no specific mention of a formal order or decision to cancel the remainder of the Freedom Ride; nor does he reveal when or how the decision, official or unofficial, was made. John Lewis (*Walking with the Wind*, 147) recalls that he and his SNCC colleagues in Nashville received word of Farmer's decision on Monday morning, May 15. All other sources, however, suggest that the decision was made later in the day, after the Freedom Riders arrived at the Birmingham Greyhound terminal and were stymied in their efforts to board a bus to Montgomery. According to Ed Blankenheim, the decision to end the Ride came during an emergency meeting held at the Birmingham airport on Monday evening. Blankenheim interview.

42. Peck, *Freedom Ride*, 130 (quotation); Blankenheim, Carey, Cox, Gaffney, Howard, Newson, and Shuttlesworth interviews; Baltimore *Afro-American*, May 27, 1961; Booker and Gaffney, "Eyewitness Report," 13; Perkins, "My 291 Days with CORE," 15. Suffering from smoke inhalation, Moultrie flew to Columbia, South Carolina, on May 15, and then went on to Sumter, where she spent several days in a small private clinic. During the summer of 1961 she returned home to Dillon but soon moved on to Philadelphia, Pennsylvania, where she found work as a nurse's aide at a Methodist hospital. In the fall of 1961 she joined the Philadelphia chapter of CORE and spoke to a radio audience and a local church congregation on her Freedom Rider experiences, but her active involvement with the Freedom Rides ended in Birmingham. She did not return to Morris College but did receive an education degree from Cheyney State University in Pennsylvania. She later earned a master's degree in education at Temple University and taught special education in the public schools of Wilmington, Delaware, for twenty-five years, retiring in 1990. Howard interview.

43. *Birmingham Post-Herald*, May 15, 1961 (quotation); Shuttlesworth and Blankenheim interviews; McWhorter, *Carry Me Home*, 213–215; Branch, *Parting the Waters*, 425. For an extended analysis of the rapidly evolving political climate in Birmingham in the early 1960s, see Eskew, *But for Birmingham*, 153–192; Thornton, *Dividing Lines*, 231–370; and McWhorter, *Carry Me Home*, 149–300.

44. Booker, *Black Man's America*, 200; Booker and Gaffney, "Eyewitness Report," 20 (first quotation); Seigenthaler and Shuttlesworth interviews; Seigenthaler and Shuttlesworth interviews; Police Intelligence Report, May 16, 1961, box 9, BCP; Manis, *A Fire You Can't Put Out*, 268; Branch, *Parting the Waters*, 426 (second quotation).

45. John Patterson, interview by John Stewart, May 26, 1967, JFKL; Seigenthaler interview; *Nashville Tennessean*, May 16, 1961; Branch, *Parting the Waters*, 426; McWhorter, *Carry Me Home*, 216; Raines, *My Soul Is Rested*, 114, 304–311; Wofford, *Of Kennedys and Kings*, 152–155; Reeves, *President Kennedy*, 124; Schlesinger, *Robert Kennedy and His Times*, 296. See also the documentary "Ain't Scared of Your Jails."

46. Shuttlesworth interview, RBOHC; Shuttlesworth, Carey, and Blankenheim interviews; *Montgomery Advertiser*, May 16, 1961 (quotation); Peck, *Freedom Ride*, 130; Booker, *Black Man's America*, 200; Booker and Gaffney, "Eyewitness Report," 20; Manis, *A Fire You Can't Put Out*, 268; Branch, *Parting the Waters*, 427.

47. *New York Times*, May 16, 1961; *Washington Post*, May 16, 1961; *Montgomery Advertiser*, May 16, 1961; *Nashville Tennessean*, May 16, 1961; Booker and Gaffney, "Eyewitness Report," 20; documentary "Ain't Scared of Your Jails"; Patterson interview, JFKL; Shuttlesworth interview; Shuttlesworth interview, RBOHC; Branch, *Parting the Waters*, 427; Manis, *A Fire You Can't Put Out*, 268, 269 (quotations).

48. Manis, *A Fire You Can't Put Out*, 269 (quotation); Shuttlesworth interview; Shuttlesworth interview, RBOHC; Booker and Gaffney, "Eyewitness Report," 20; Police Intelligence Report, May 16, 1961, BCP; "Kennedy's Call to B'ham" transcript, May 15, 1961, General Correspondence, box 10, RFKP; McWhorter, *Carry Me Home*, 216.

49. "Kennedy's Call to B'Ham" (quotations); Schlesinger, *Robert Kennedy and His Times*, 296; James Farmer and James Patterson statements, documentary "Ain't Scared of Your Jails"; W. E. Jones to A. H. Walter, May 15, 22, 1961, file RD 195, box 20, Investigative Report Case Files, ICCR; Branch, *Parting the Waters*, 426; Manis, *A Fire You Can't Put Out*, 269; McWhorter, *Carry Me Home*, 216.

50. *Birmingham News*, May 15, 1961 (quotation); Branch, *Parting the Waters*, 425–427; Manis, *A Fire You Can't Put Out*, 267–268. On Connor's periodic battles with the Birmingham business community prior to May 1961, see Nunnelley, *Bull Connor*, 13–85. Thornton, *Dividing Lines*, 156, argues persuasively that, despite the apparent conflicts between Connor and the Birmingham business community, from 1937 on "the source of Connor's subsequent political strength was in fact his ability to link white employers' and employees' fears into a single political response." For a general survey of the complex relationship between Southern business leaders and resistance to desegregation, see Elizabeth Jacoway and David Colburn, eds., *Southern Businessmen and Desegregation* (Baton Rouge: Louisiana State University Press, 1982). See especially the chapter by Robert Corley, "In Search of Racial Harmony: Birmingham Business Leaders and Desegregation, 1950–1963," 170–190.

51. Peck, *Freedom Ride*, 131; Peck, "Freedom Ride," 1–4; Booker and Gaffney, "Eyewitness Report," 20; Blankenheim, "Freedom Ride," 10–11; Blankenheim, Carey, Cox, Newson, Seigenthaler, and Shuttlesworth interviews; Seigenthaler interview, RBOHC; *Montgomery Advertiser*, May 16, 1961; *New York Times*, May 16, 1961; *Washington Post*, May 16, 1961; Branch, *Parting the Waters*, 427; Manis, *A Fire You Can't Put Out*, 269–270.

52. Booker and Gaffney, "Eyewitness Report," 20; Booker, *Black Man's America*, 201; Blankenheim, "Freedom Ride," 11–12; Blankenheim, Carey, Cox, Gaffney, Newson, and Shuttlesworth interviews; Reeves, *President Kennedy*, 124; Manis, *A Fire You Can't Put Out*, 270; Branch, *Parting the Waters*, 428; Peck, *Freedom Ride*, 131 (quotation); McWhorter, *Carry Me Home*, 217.

53. Seigenthaler interview; Seigenthaler interviews, JFKL; Seigenthaler interview, RBOHC; Reeves, *President Kennedy*, 124 (quotations); Branch, *Parting the Waters*, 428.

54. Police Intelligence Report, May 16, 1961, BCP; Shuttlesworth interview; Branch, *Parting the Waters*, 428–429; Manis, *A Fire You Can't Put Out*, 270; Eskew, *But for Birmingham*, 159–160.
55. Blankenheim, Carey, Cox, Gaffney, Newson, and Seigenthaler interviews; Seigenthaler interviews, JFKL; Seigenthaler interview, RBOHC; Peck, *Freedom Ride*, 132; Blankenheim, "Freedom Ride," 11–12 (first quotation); Booker and Gaffney, "Eyewitness Report," 20–21 (second quotation); Booker, *Black Man's America*, 201; *Nashville Tennessean*, May 16, 1961; Perkins, "My 291 Days with CORE," 15; Branch, *Parting the Waters*, 429; Halberstam, *The Children*, 285 (third quotation), 286; Gaillard, *Crucible of Freedom*, 85–86.
56. Seigenthaler interview by Grele, JFKL; Seigenthaler interview, RBOHC; Blankenheim, Carey, Cox, Newson, and Seigenthaler interviews; Peck, *Freedom Ride*, 132; Halberstam, *The Children*, 286; *New Orleans Times-Picayune*, May 16–17, 1961; Gaillard, *Crucible of Freedom*, 86. Schlesinger, *Robert Kennedy and His Times*, 295, notes that Seigenthaler "ran into Barry Goldwater" while disembarking at the New Orleans airport, prompting the conservative U.S. senator from Arizona to comment: "This is horrible. Just horrible. Never should have happened. I'm glad you're with them."

Chapter 5: Get on Board, Little Children

1. Silverman, *Songs of Protest and Civil Rights*, 58–59, presents this version of the chorus and fourth verse of the popular 1960s freedom song "Get on Board, Little Children," an adaptation of the antebellum Underground Railroad anthem "The Gospel Train." The chorus and best-known verse of the original spiritual is: "The Gospel train is coming, I hear it just at hand./ I hear the car wheels moving, And rumbling thro' the land./ Get on board, children, Get on board." James Haskins, *Black Music in America* (New York: HarperTrophy, 1987), 7.
2. Blankenheim, Carey, Cox, Rich, and Seigenthaler interviews; Sandra Nixon, interview by author, November 8, 2001; Farmer, *Lay Bare the Heart*, 203–204; Peck, *Freedom Ride*, 133–134; *New Orleans Times-Picayune*, May 17, 1961 (quotations); *New York Times*, May 16, 1961; Baltimore *Afro-American*, May 27, 1961. On New Orleans CORE, see Rogers, *Righteous Lives*; Anderson-Bricker, "Making a Movement," 226–420; and section 351, reel 39, COREP. On the Castles, see Rogers, *Righteous Lives*, 10, 68, 92–93, 110–117, 123–127, 130, 136–146, 170, 175–178, 205; Fairclough, *Race and Democracy*, 10, 272, 279, 289, 295–298; Meier and Rudwick, *CORE*, 116, 169, 344–345, 395, 401–402; Doris Jean Castle Scott, interview by Kim Lacy Rogers, January 19, 1989, ARC; Oretha Castle Haley, interview by James Mosby Jr., May 26, 1970, RBOHC; Oretha Castle Haley, interview by Kim Lacy Rogers, November 27, 1978, ARC; Richard Haley interview, RBOHC; and Richard Haley interview, ARC. Oretha Castle later married CORE field secretary Richard Haley. For an assessment of the strengths and weaknesses of American nonviolent direct action in the 1960s, see Tracy, *Direct Action*, 99–153.
3. Lewis, *Walking with the Wind*, 67–147; Halberstam, *The Children*, 11–266; Branch, *Parting the Waters*, 259–280; Robert Moses, "Foreword," in Ken Light, *Delta Time: Mississippi Photographs by Ken Light* (Washington: Smithsonian Institution Press, 1995), xiv (quotation). On nonviolence and the black student movement of the early 1960s, see Laue, *Direct Action and Desegregation*; Zinn, *SNCC*, 220–224; Carson, *In Struggle*, 2–33; Greenberg, *A Circle of Trust*, 4, 10, 19–24; Marsh, *The Beloved Community*, 87–124; and Chappell, *A Stone of Hope*, 67–86.
4. Nash, Lewis, and Lafayette interviews; Lewis, *Walking with the Wind*, 144–147; Branch, *Parting the Waters*, 424–425; Halberstam, *The Children*, 270; Olson, *Freedom's Daughters*, 184. Bevel was temporary chairman of the central committee, which rotated leaders every few weeks.
5. Lewis, *Walking with the Wind*, 147 (quotation); Branch, *Parting the Waters*, 425, 428; Lewis, Lafayette, and Nash interviews; Jim Zwerg, interview by author, September 12, 2004; Jim Zwerg, 1961 Nashville Movement log, May 15, 1961, in Zwerg's possession.
6. Lewis, *Walking with the Wind*, 70–71, 87, 91–92 (quotations), 149; Halberstam, *The Children*, 94–102, 435–443; Branch, *Parting the Waters*, 263–264; Olson, *Freedom's Daughters*, 151–160; Lafayette interview.
7. Olson, *Freedom's Daughters*, 151–161; Lafayette and Nash interviews; Diane Nash, remarks at "The Freedom Riders: A 40-Year Retrospective," Tulane–Cambridge Atlantic World Conference, Tulane University, New Orleans, Louisiana, April 7, 2001; Lewis, *Walking with the Wind*, 91–95, 110–111, 114–116, 142; Halberstam, *The Children*, 3–10, 59–63, 143–148, 234–237, 267–269; Branch, *Parting the Waters*, 279–280, 295, 345; *Nashville Banner*, November 3, 1960, April 13, 1961; *Nashville Tennessean*, February 9, 1961; NCLC minutes, March 11, April 5, May 3, 1961, folder 24, box 75, KMSP; *Voice of the Movement* 1:4–5 (April 14, 21, 1961).
8. Farmer, *Lay Bare the Heart*, 203 (quotations); Lewis, *Walking with the Wind*, 146, 148 (second quotation); Branch, *Parting the Waters*, 428; Olson, *Freedom's Daughters*, 184; Nash and Zwerg interviews; Halberstam, *The Children*, 282–283.
9. Lewis, *Walking with the Wind*, 147 (quotation), 149; Lafayette and Zwerg interviews; Zwerg, Nashville Movement log, May 15, 1961.
10. Seigenthaler and Barrett interviews; Seigenthaler interview, RBOHC; Branch, *Parting the Waters*, 429–430 (first quotation); Halberstam, *The Children*, 274–277, 286 (second quotation), 287; Lewis, *Walking with the Wind*, 149; Lafayette and Zwerg interviews; Olson, *Freedom's Daughters*, 185; Gaillard, *Crucible of Freedom*, 86–87, 90. Born a few days apart in 1927, Barrett and Seigenthaler were fellow Roman Catholics and high school classmates at a Nashville parochial school.
11. Seigenthaler, Barrett, Lafayette, and Zwerg interviews; Zwerg, Nashville Movement log, May 16, 1961; NCLC minutes, May 17–18, 1961, folder 24, box 75, KMSP; Branch, *Parting the Waters*, 430;

Halberstam, *The Children*, 274–278; Lewis, *Walking with the Wind*, 149 (first quotation); Gaillard, *Crucible of Freedom*, 90–91; Rip Patton, remarks delivered at the 40th Anniversary of the Freedom Rides commemorative luncheon, Atlanta, GA, May 11, 2001, (second quotation). On Vivian, see Halberstam, *The Children*, 51, 56–58, 162, 200, 212, 230; Hampton and Fayer, *Voices of Freedom*, 59–60, 65–66, 660; and Lewis, *Walking with the Wind*, 108, 115–116. See also C. T. Vivian, *Black Power and the American Myth* (Philadelphia: Fortress Press, 1970).

12. Branch, *Parting the Waters*, 430 (quotations); Olson, *Freedom's Daughters*, 184–185; Halberstam, *The Children*, 283; Shuttlesworth interview; Shuttlesworth interview, RBOHC; Eskew, *But for Birmingham*, 161; Manis, *A Fire You Can't Put Out*, 271; McWhorter, *Carry Me Home*, 220, claims that Nash first called Shuttlesworth on Monday night. Shuttlesworth, while unable to recall the exact number and timing of the calls from Nash, remembers the directness of her manner, noting: "She was as calculating as a butcher cutting meat." Shuttlesworth interview.

13. Lewis, *Walking with the Wind*, 149, lists the original ten Nashville Freedom Riders but misidentifies Charles Butler as Charles Butt; Roster of Freedom Riders Arrested in Jackson, Mississippi, Groups 1–6, May 24–June 2, 1961, MSCP; Lewis, Lafayette, and Zwerg interviews; William Harbour, interview by author, July 10, 2004; Catherine Burks Brooks, interview by author, May 11–12, 2001; Zwerg, Nashville Movement log, March–May 1961; Branch, *Parting the Waters*, 430–431; Halberstam, *The Children*, 278–282; Zinn, *SNCC*, 47–49, 127; James Forman, *The Making of Black Revolutionaries: A Personal Account* (New York: Macmillan, 1972), 147–157; John Blake, *Children of the Movement* (Chicago: Lawrence Hill Books, 2004), 3–14, 25–36.

14. Shuttlesworth interview, RBOHC; Shuttlesworth, Lafayette, Harbour, and Zwerg interviews; Zwerg, Nashville Movement log, May 15–16, 1961; McWhorter, *Carry Me Home*, 220 (first quotation); Halberstam, *The Children*, 283; Lewis, *Walking with the Wind*, 149 (second quotation); Manis, *A Fire You Can't Put Out*, 271; Branch, *Parting the Waters*, 431; Gaillard, *Crucible of Freedom*, 90–91; Olson, *Freedom's Daughters*, 185; Zinn, *SNCC*, 44–45; Carson, *In Struggle*, 34; Diane Nash, "Inside the Sit-ins and Freedom Rides: Testimony of a Southern Student," in *The New Negro*, ed. Mathew H. Ahmann (New York: Biblo and Tannen, 1969), 53 (third quotation); Forman, *The Making of Black Revolutionaries*, 151 (fourth quotation).

15. Lewis, *Walking with the Wind*, 151–153 (quotations); Nash, "Inside the Sit-ins and Freedom Rides," 53–54; Nash, "Inside the Sit-ins and Freedom Rides," 53–54; *Nashville Tennessean*, May 18, 1961; McWhorter, *Carry Me Home*, 220–221; Branch, *Parting the Waters*, 431–433; Gaillard, *Crucible of Freedom*, 91–93; Manis, *A Fire You Can't Put Out*, 271–272; Eskew, *But for Birmingham*, 161; Viorst, *Fire in the Streets*, 149–150; Nunnelley, *Bull Connor*, 101–102; Halberstam, *The Children*, 289–294, offers an unreliable account that incorrectly claims that Connor himself intercepted the bus at the city limits; Brooks, Shuttlesworth, Harbour, and Zwerg interviews; Lucretia Collins, interview by James Forman, June 1961, in *Southern Exposure* 9 (Spring 1981): 35; Forman, *The Making of Black Revolutionaries*, 150–151; *Birmingham News*, May 17 (Patterson quotation), 18, 1961; *Montgomery Advertiser*, May 17–18, 1961; *Baltimore Afro-American*, May 27, 1961; *New York Times*, May 17, 1961. Although some sources suggest that McCollum overslept, she actually woke up early enough to pick up Zwerg at Fisk and join him for breakfast before driving on to the terminal. Zwerg, Nashville Movement log, May 17, 1961; Zwerg interview. On the birth and early development of the Ku Klux Klan in Pulaski, see Allen W. Trelease, *White Terror: The Ku Klux Klan Conspiracy and Southern Reconstruction* (New York: Harper and Row, 1971), 3–35. On the Klansmen arrests and subsequent trials, see McWhorter, *Carry Me Home*, 218–220, 247; May, *The Informant*, 43–44, 46–47, and the various FBI interviews with the Faggards, Dove, and other beating suspects and witnesses conducted on May 17, 20, 23, and 26, 1961, FBI-FRI.

16. Carey, Blankenheim, Cox, and Newson interviews; Jerome Smith, interview by author, November 10, 2001; "Violence Follows the Freedom Riders in Alabama," CORE pamphlet, c. May 19, 1961, box 52A, MLKP; *Baltimore Afro-American*, May 27, 1961 (quotations); *New Orleans Times-Picayune*, May 18, 1961 (Cox quotation); Peck, *Freedom Ride*, 133. On May 18 Joe Perkins accompanied Genevieve Hughes to Washington, where she was admitted to Georgetown Hospital. Perkins, "My 291 Days with CORE," 15; Genevieve Hughes to Gordon Carey, May 31, 1961, section 254, reel 36, COREP. On Davis's long career as a civil rights activist, see Fairclough, *Race and Democracy*, 55–56, 65, 211–212, 272, 275, 281; Rogers, *Righteous Lives*, 10, 22, 39–40, 66–67, 78, 90–93, 109, 132, 155–156, 205; and Fairclough, *To Redeem the Soul of America*, 42. In 1958 Davis served as second vice president of SCLC before being replaced by the Reverend Joseph Lowery of Mobile, Alabama.

17. Louis Oberdorfer, interview by Roberta Greene, February 5, 12, 1970, JFKL; McWhorter, *Carry Me Home*, 221–222 (quotation); Guthman, *We Band of Brothers*, 168–169.

18. Marshall interview, JFKL; Patterson interview, JFKL; Seigenthaler interview; Seigenthaler interview, RBOHC; Halberstam, *The Children*, 293–294 (quotation); Branch, *Parting the Waters*, 433–436; Niven, *The Politics of Injustice*, 68–70; Guthman, *We Band of Brothers*, 168–169; Wofford, *Of Kennedys and Kings*, 153; Reeves, *President Kennedy*, 125–128. On Johnson, see Tinsley E. Yarbrough, *Judge Frank Johnson and Human Rights in Alabama* (University: University of Alabama Press, 1981); Robert F. Kennedy Jr., *Judge Frank M. Johnson, Jr.* (New York: G. P. Putnam's Sons, 1978); and Jack Bass, *Taming the Storm: The Life and Times of Frank M. Johnson and the South's Fight over Civil Rights* (New York: Doubleday, 1992). On the ironies of Kennedy's feud with his former ally John Patterson, see Drew Pearson's column, "Behind Mobs in Alabama," *Nashville Tennessean*, May 24, 1961. On the Kennedy administration's decision to use federal marshals in Alabama, see folder 1, "Montgomery–Use of Marshals–1961," box 1, files of W. Wilson White, assistant attorney general, Civil Rights Division, 1958–1959, USDJ/CRD.

19. *Birmingham News*, May 18, 1961 (first and third quotations), May 19, 1961; *Montgomery Advertiser*, May 19, 1961; McWhorter, *Carry Me Home*, 221, 225 (second quotation), 227; Manis, *A Fire You*

Can't Put Out, 272–273; Fairclough, *To Redeem the Soul of America*, 78–79; Shuttlesworth interview. On Wednesday, May 17, the NCLC executive board voted to send Rollins to Birmingham as an official observer. NCLC minutes, May 17 and 20, 1961, folder 24, box 75, KMSP. On Arthur Shores, see Raines, *My Soul Is Rested*, 348–351; and Eskew, *But for Birmingham*, 61–62, 324. On Joseph Lowery, see Raines, *My Soul Is Rested*, 66–70. Originally involved with CORE as a field secretary in Norfolk, Len Holt went on to handle several important civil rights cases in Danville, Virginia, and in Mississippi during the mid-1960s. See Zinn, *SNCC*, 34, 180; Meier and Rudwick, *CORE*, 120; and Len Holt, *The Summer That Didn't End* (London: Heinemann, 1966).

20. *Who Speaks for Birmingham?* May 18, 1961, transcript, *CBS Reports*, BPL (quotations); McWhorter, *Carry Me Home*, 223–226; *Montgomery Advertiser*, May 20, 1961; A. M. Sperber, *Murrow: His Life and Times* (New York: Freundlich, 1986), 615–618, 641–642. The flap over the Birmingham broadcast led to Smith's firing by CBS executives in the fall of 1961. See Robert Lewis Shayon, "Why Did Howard K. Smith Leave?" *Saturday Review* 44 (November 18, 1961): 37; and Smith, *Events Leading Up to My Death*, 268–276. On the ideological transformation of John Temple Graves, who died of heart failure during a pro-segregation luncheon speech in Mobile the day after the broadcast, see Egerton, *Speak Now Against the Day*, 465, 492–493, 499, 521; Richard H. King, *A Southern Renaissance: The Cultural Awakening of the American South, 1930–1955* (New York: Oxford University Press, 1980), 12–13, 150, 180, 243, 249; and William D. Barnard, *Dixiecrats and Democrats: Alabama Politics, 1942–1950* (University: University of Alabama Press, 1974), 34, 38–39, 42–47, 51, 55, 118.

21. *Birmingham News*, May 19, 1961 (first, second, fourth, and seventh quotations); *Montgomery Advertiser*, May 20, 1961; *Nashville Tennessean*, May 20, 1961; *Baltimore Afro-American*, May 27, 1961; Lewis, *Walking with the Wind*, 153–155 (third, sixth, and eighth quotations); Harbour, Brooks (fifth quotation), Lewis, and Zwerg interviews; Collins interview, *Southern Exposure*, 35; James Forman, Freedom Rider interview notes, folder 24, box 55, SNCCP; Manis, *A Fire You Can't Put Out*, 273; Viorst, *Fire in the Streets*, 150 (ninth, tenth, and eleventh quotations); Branch, *Parting the Waters*, 436–438; McWhorter, *Carry Me Home*, 225–226; Gaillard, *Crucible of Freedom*, 93–95; Raines, *My Soul Is Rested*, 117–119; Olson, *Freedom's Daughters*, 185; Nunnelley, *Bull Connor*, 102–103; Halberstam, *The Children*, 294–297; Powledge, *Free at Last?* 259–260.

22. Kwame Leo Lillard, interview by author, May 11, 2001. Lillard later spent four years (1991–1995) as a Nashville city councilman. Forman, Freedom Rider interview notes, SNCCP; Brooks, Lafayette, Harbour, and Zwerg interviews; Collins interview, *Southern Exposure*, 35–36; *Baltimore Afro-American*, May 27, 1961; Lewis, *Walking with the Wind*, 155 (quotation); Raines, *My Soul Is Rested*, 119; Nash, "Inside the Sit-ins and Freedom Rides," 53–54; Branch, *Parting the Waters*, 438–440; McWhorter, *Carry Me Home*, 226; Olson, *Freedom's Daughters*, 160, 185–186; Viorst, *Fire in the Streets*, 150–151; Halberstam, *The Children*, 297–298, 305; Powledge, *Free at Last?* 258–259. On Smith as a Freedom Rider, see Fleming, *Soon We Will Not Cry*, 72–85; and Zinn, *SNCC*, 44–46. The seven Tennessee State Riders in the second wave were Carl Bush, Rudolph Graham, Patricia Jenkins, Frederick Leonard, William Mitchell Jr., Etta Simpson, and Clarence M. Wright. *Nashville Tennessean*, May 20, 1961.

23. Seigenthaler interview; Seigenthaler interview, RBOHC; Patterson interview, JFKL; Marshall interview, JFKL; Collins interview, *Southern Exposure*, 36; *Baltimore Afro-American*, May 27, 1961; Raines, *My Soul Is Rested*, 304–311; Branch, *Parting the Waters*, 436; McWhorter, *Carry Me Home*, 225–226; Halberstam, *The Children*, 299; Gaillard, *Crucible of Freedom*, 93 (quotation). Centered in Cape Town and Johannesburg, the South African arrests began on May 18. The withdrawal from the Commonwealth was scheduled for May 31. *New York Times*, May 19, 1961; *Nashville Tennessean*, May 19, 1961. On the developing crisis in South Africa in 1961, see Nelson Mandela, *Long Walk to Freedom: The Autobiography of Nelson Mandela* (Boston: Little, Brown, 1994), 224–250.

24. Lewis, *Walking with the Wind*, 155–156 (quotations); *Birmingham News*, May 20, 1961; *Baltimore Afro-American*, May 27, 1961; *Montgomery Advertiser*, May 20, 1961; Lafayette, Harbour, Shuttlesworth, Zwerg, and Brooks interviews; Shuttlesworth interview, RBOHC; Collins interview, *Southern Exposure*, 36; Branch, *Parting the Waters*, 440; Gaillard, *Crucible of Freedom*, 95–96; McWhorter, *Carry Me Home*, 226–227; Manis, *A Fire You Can't Put Out*, 273; Nunnelley, *Bull Connor*, 103; Halberstam, *The Children*, 305–308; Powledge, *Free At Last?* 260–264.

25. Marshall interview, JFKL; Patterson interview, JFKL; Robert F. Kennedy and Burke Marshall, interview by Anthony Lewis, December 4, 1964, JFKL; *Montgomery Advertiser*, May 20, 1961; *Baltimore Afro-American*, May 27, 1961; Guthman, *We Band of Brothers*, 170; Branch, *Parting the Waters*, 441; Gaillard, *Crucible of Freedom*, 96; Niven, *The Politics of Injustice*, 70; Reeves, *President Kennedy*, 128; Navasky, *Kennedy Justice*, 21; Dallek, *An Unfinished Life*, 385.

26. Seigenthaler interview; Seigenthaler interview, RBOHC; Patterson interview, JFKL; Marshall interview, JFKL; Halberstam, *The Children*, 299–304; Gaillard, *Crucible of Freedom*, 96–97; Niven, *The Politics of Injustice*, 71–73; Branch, *Parting the Waters*, 441–442; Schlesinger, *Robert Kennedy and His Times*, 296; On Mann, see Powledge, *Free at Last?* 263, 267–271. Formerly Southeast Greyhound, Greenslit's division took the name of Southern Greyhound on January 1, 1961. File RD 34, box 6, Investigative Report Case Files, ICCR.

27. *Montgomery Advertiser*, June 2–5, 12, 1956, May 20, 1961; *Nashville Tennessean*, May 20, 1961; *Baltimore Afro-American*, May 27, 1961; Branch, *Parting the Waters*, 442–443; Powledge, *Free at Last?* 259. As state attorney general in 1956, Patterson asked Judge Jones to grant a temporary injunction outlawing the NAACP in Alabama. Jones complied, initiating years of legal wrangling over the state organization's right to exist. The temporary injunction remained in effect until December 1961, when Jones substituted a permanent injunction. The permanent injunction was finally vacated in October 1964. Thornton, *Dividing Lines*, 91, 120, 197, 608 n108; Carter, *A Matter of Law*, 149–155; Gaillard, *Crucible of Freedom*, 126.

28. Manis, *A Fire You Can't Put Out*, 273–274 (quotations); Shuttlesworth interview, RBOHC; Shuttlesworth and Seigenthaler interviews. See also phone logs for May 19, 1961, box 8, BMP; Powledge, *Free at Last?* 280–281, offers a slightly different version of the Shuttlesworth-Kennedy conversation. In his interview with Powledge, Shuttlesworth suggested that Kennedy had tried to convince him and the Freedom Riders to travel all the way to New Orleans by bus, without an overnight stop in Jackson, Mississippi.

29. Seigenthaler interview, RBOHC (second quotation); Seigenthaler, Doar, Shuttlesworth, Lafayette, Zwerg, Brooks, and Harbour interviews; Collins interview, *Southern Exposure*, 36–37; *New York Herald Tribune*, May 21, 1961; Grant, *Black Protest*, 318, 322–323. The dispatcher was J. T. Duncan, and the Teamsters official was Joe C. Morgan, president of Local 1314, Amalgamated Street, Electric Railway, and Motorcoach Employees of America. Both men accompanied the Freedom Riders to Montgomery. Powledge, *Free at Last?* 261; Branch, *Parting the Waters*, 443 (first quotation), 444; Raines, *My Soul Is Rested*, 119–120; Lewis, *Walking with the Wind*, 154; Viorst, *Fire in the Streets*, 151–152; Manis, *A Fire You Can't Put Out*, 273, 274 (third quotation), 275; Wofford, *Of Kennedys and Kings*, 154 (fourth quotation); Halberstam, *The Children*, 302, 306–308; Fleming, *Soon We Will Not Cry*, 82–83; Zinn, *SNCC*, 44–46; Schlesinger, *Robert Kennedy and His Times*, 296; Guthman, *We Band of Brothers*, 170; Kennedy and Marshall interview, JFKL; Marshall interview, JFKL; *Nashville Tennessean*, May 21, 1961. See also the materials in file RD 195, box 20, Investigative Report Case Files, ICCR. In an interview with Fred Powledge, Shuttlesworth advanced the theory that he was arrested because Robert Kennedy had asked Jamie Moore to do so. The reason, according to Shuttlesworth, was "to keep me from being killed." Powledge, *Free at Last?* 281. Many accounts–including those by Schlesinger, Branch, Lewis, and Guthman–confuse some of the events of May 20 with those of May 15. In particular, the famous phone conversation between Robert Kennedy and George Cruit, during which Kennedy refers to "Mr. Greyhound," took place on Monday afternoon, May 15, not on Saturday morning, May 20. One source of confusion was Cruit's testimony before Judge Frank Johnson on May 31, 1961. Although the hearing pertained to the events of May 20, Cruit, without ever expressly saying so, related details of his May 15 conversation with Robert Kennedy. See *Montgomery Advertiser*, June 1, 1961; *Birmingham Post-Herald*, June 1, 1961; "Kennedy's Call to B'ham," transcript, May 15, 1961, box 10, RFKP; and "Untold Story of the 'Freedom Rides,'" *U.S. News and World Report* 51 (October 23, 1961): 76–79.

Chapter 6: If You Miss Me from the Back of the Bus

1. Silverman, *Songs of Protest and Civil Rights*, 10–11. The second stanza of this popular freedom song was a slight but significant variation of the first: "If you miss me from the front of the bus, and you can't find me nowhere,/ Come on up to the driver's seat, I'll be drivin' up there./ I'll be drivin' up there, I'll be drivin' up there,/ Come on up to the driver's seat, I'll be drivin' up there."

2. Lewis, *Walking with the Wind*, 157–158 (quotations); Lewis interview, documentary, "Ain't Scared of Your Jails"; Hampton and Fayer, *Voices of Freedom*, 86, 88; *Baltimore Afro-American*, May 27, 1961; Collins interview, *Southern Exposure* , 37; Seigenthaler, Doar, Harbour, Lafayette, and Zwerg interviews; *Birmingham News*, May 21, 1961; *New York Herald Tribune*, May 21, 1961; Grant, *Black Protest*, 318–320; Branch, *Parting the Waters*, 444; McWhorter, *Carry Me Home*, 228; Halberstam, *The Children*, 308–309; Viorst, *Fire in the Streets*, 152; Fleming, *Soon We Will Not Cry*, 83.

3. Lewis, *Walking with the Wind*, 157–158 (quotations); Lewis interview, documentary, "Ain't Scared of Your Jails"; Seigenthaler interview, RBOHC; Seigenthaler interviews, JFKL; Seigenthaler, Doar, Lafayette, Harbour, and Brooks interviews; Patterson interview, JFKL; Marshall interview, JFKL; Collins interview, *Southern Exposure*, 37; Hampton and Fayer, *Voices of Freedom*, 87–89; *Nashville Tennessean*, May 21–22, 1961; *Baltimore Afro-American*, May 27, June 3, 1961; *Pittsburgh Courier*, May 27, 1961; *New York Times*, May 21, 1961; *New York Herald Tribune*, May 21, 1961; Grant, *Black Protest*, 318–321; *Birmingham News*, May 21, 29, June 1, 1961; *Montgomery Advertiser*, May 21, 1961; *Montgomery Alabama Journal*, May 20–21, 1961; Branch, *Parting the Waters*, 444–446; Halberstam, *The Children*, 309–311; McWhorter, *Carry Me Home*, 228; Guthman, *We Band of Brothers*, 170–171; Viorst, *Fire in the Streets*, 152; Powledge, *Free at Last?* 262, 267; Niven, *The Politics of Injustice*, 76–78; Garrow, *Bearing the Cross*, 157; Zinn, *SNCC*, 47; Fleming, *Soon We Will Not Cry*, 83. For an eyewitness account by Ritter, see *Life* 50 (May 26, 1961): 24–25. On the involvement of Montgomery Klansmen in the Birmingham riot, see SA Barrett Kemp to SA Thomas Jenkins, May 15, 1961, FBI-FRI. On Henley, see *Montgomery Advertiser*, June 3, 8, 1961; *Birmingham Post-Herald*, June 8, 1961; Thornton, *Dividing Lines*, 119, 503, 616–617; and *Lewis v. Greyhound Corporation*, 199 F. Supp. 210; and *U.S. v. U.S. Klans*, 194 F. Supp. 892. Sullivan's libel suit ultimately resulted in a landmark 1964 United States Supreme Court decision affirming the First Amendment right to criticize public officials in the press and belatedly closing the book on the 1798 Sedition Act. See Anthony Lewis, *Make No Law: The Sullivan Case and the First Amendment* (New York: Random House, 1991); and *New York Times v. Sullivan*, 376 U.S. 254.

4. *Birmingham News*, May 21, 29, 1961; *Montgomery Advertiser*, May 21, 30, 1961; *Baltimore Afro-American*, May 27, June 3, 1961; *Nashville Tennessean*, May 21–22, 1961; Frederick Leonard interview, documentary, "Ain't Scared of Your Jails"; Hampton and Fayer, *Voices of Freedom*, 87–88; Lafayette and Brooks interviews; Collins interview, *Southern Exposure*, 37–38; *New York Times*, May 21, 1961; Lewis, *Walking with the Wind*, 159; Zinn, *SNCC*, 47–48; Fleming, *Soon We Will Not Cry*, 83; Branch, *Parting the Waters*, 445–446; Halberstam, *The Children*, 311, 316; McWhorter, *Carry Me Home*, 228; Hollinger

Barnard, ed., *Outside the Magic Circle: The Autobiography of Virginia Foster Durr* (New York: Simon and Schuster, 1985), 297. On Wilbur and Hermann, see *Christian Science Monitor*, May 25, 1961; *Louisville Times*, May 22, 1961; and Susan Wilbur's personal account, "Waiting Crowd but No Police," *Nashville Tennessean*, May 22, 1961, 1–2.

5. Seigenthaler interview; Seigenthaler interviews, JFKL (quotations); Seigenthaler interview, RBOHC; Seigenthaler interview, documentary, "Ain't Scared of Your Jails"; Hampton and Fayer, *Voices of Freedom*, 87, 89–90; Patterson interview, JFKL; *Nashville Tennessean*, May 21–22, 1961; *New York Times*, May 21, 1961; *Montgomery Advertiser*, May 21, 1961; *Baltimore Afro-American*, June 3, 1961; Lewis, *Walking with the Wind*, 160; Halberstam, *The Children*, 316–317; Branch, *Parting the Waters*, 447–448; Guthman, *We Band of Brothers*, 171; Niven, *The Politics of Injustice*, 78–79; Navasky, *Kennedy Justice*, 22; O'Reilly, *"Racial Matters,"* 90–91.

6. *Birmingham News*, May 21, 1961 (first quotation); *Baltimore Afro-American*, May 27, June 3, 1961; *Pittsburgh Courier*, May 27, June 3, 1961; Hampton and Fayer, *Voices of Freedom*, 87–88 (second and sixth quotations); Collins interview, *Southern Exposure*, 38 (third quotation); Nash, "Inside the Sit-Ins and Freedom Rides," 58 (fourth quotation); Lewis, *Walking with the Wind*, 159–160 (fifth quotation); Lafayette (seventh quotation), Harbour, and Zwerg interviews; *Montgomery Advertiser*, May 21, 1961; *New York Times*, May 21, 1961; *New York Herald Tribune*, May 21, 1961; *Birmingham Post-Herald*, June 9, 1961; Branch, *Parting the Waters*, 448; Niven, *The Politics of Injustice*, 76–77, 80; Gaillard, *Crucible of Freedom*, 98–99; Thornton, *Dividing Lines*, 120, 616; Viorst, *Fire in the Streets*, 152; Halberstam, *The Children*, 311–312; Fleming, *Soon We Will Not Cry*, 83–84; Zinn, *SNCC*, 48. See also the trial transcripts of *Lewis v. Greyhound Corporation*, 199 F. Supp. 210; and *U.S. v. U.S. Klans*, 194 F. Supp 892, both located at Federal Records Center, East Point, GA.

7. *Birmingham News*, May 20 (quotations), 21, 1961; *Montgomery Advertiser*, May 21, 1961; *Baltimore Afro-American*, May 27, 1961; *Nashville Tennessean*, May 21, 1961; Patterson interview, JFKL; Halberstam, *The Children*, 312–313; Branch, *Parting the Waters*, 448; Lewis, *Walking with the Wind*, 160; Gaillard, *Crucible of Freedom*, 100; Barnard, *Outside the Magic Circle*, 298; Powledge, *Free at Last?*, 263, 267, 270; Hampton and Fayer, *Voices of Freedom*, 88–89; Nash, "Inside the Sit-Ins and Freedom Rides," 58. Atkins was the son-in-law of Charles Meriwether, a close friend of John Patterson's who had facilitated Patterson's political endorsement of John Kennedy in 1960. In early 1961 Kennedy acknowledged Patterson's support in the 1960 campaign by appointing Meriwether as a director of the Export-Import Bank. A political conservative and staunch segregationist, Meriwether received confirmation from the Senate over the strong objections of liberal senators such as William Proxmire of Wisconsin, Wayne Morse of Oregon, and Jacob Javits of New York. At Kennedy's request, Meriwether flew to Montgomery on May 19 to meet with Patterson in an effort to convince the governor to cooperate with federal officials during the Freedom Rider crisis. Meriwether spent several hours with Patterson on May 20 and 21 but reportedly made little progress. According to the syndicated columnist Drew Pearson, the Kennedys' relationship with Meriwether was laced with irony, considering Meriwether's long-standing connections to Robert Shelton and other Alabama Klansmen. In a May 24 column, Pearson described Meriwether as "the No. 1 politico of Alabama who used to walk through the Alabama capitol with his arm around Bob Shelton, imperial wizard of the Ku Klux Klan." *Nashville Tennessean*, May 24, 1961; Thornton, *Dividing Lines*, 120–123; Niven, *The Politics of Injustice*, 68–69; *New York Times*, May 24, 1961.

8. Guthman, *We Band of Brothers*, 171 (first quotation); Doar interview; Marshall interview, JFKL; Branch, *Parting the Waters*, 447; Powledge, *Free at Last?* 277; McWhorter, *Carry Me Home*, 230; O'Reilly, *"Racial Matters,"* 90–91; Virginia Durr to Burke Marshall, c. May 15, 1961, box 1, BMP (second quotation); Sullivan, *Freedom Writer*, 248–251, 264–265; Gaillard, *Crucible of Freedom*, 100–101; Barnard, *Outside the Magic Circle*, 296–299. On Clifford Durr, see John A. Salmond, *The Conscience of a Lawyer: Clifford J. Durr and American Civil Liberties, 1899–1975* (Tuscaloosa: University of Alabama Press, 1990). On Mitford's experiences in Montgomery, see Jessica Mitford, *Poison Penmanship: The Gentle Art of Muckraking* (New York: Vintage, 1980), 70–78. Zellner's father was a liberal Methodist minister who had once belonged to the Ku Klux Klan. Zellner himself had experienced a liberal transformation while writing a college term paper on the Montgomery Improvement Association. Marsh, *The Beloved Community*, 91, 98; Bob Zellner, "Notes of a Native Son," *Southern Exposure* 9 (Spring 1981): 48–49.

9. *Montgomery Advertiser*, May 21, June 1–2, 1961; *Nashville Tennessean*, May 21, 1961; *Birmingham News*, May 21, 1961 (quotation); *Pittsburgh Courier*, May 27, 1961; *Baltimore Afro-American*, May 27, 1961; *New York Times*, May 21, 1961; Barnard, *Outside the Magic Circle*, 296–299; Thornton, *Dividing Lines*, 121; Lewis, *Walking with the Wind*, 160–161; Halberstam, *The Children*, 319; Guthman, *We Band of Brothers*, 171; Branch, *Parting the Waters*, 448; McWhorter, *Carry Me Home*, 229; Zwerg interview. Clifford Durr later represented the Gaches in court. See Virginia Durr to Burke Marshall, June 4, 1961, box 1, BMP; Sullivan, *Freedom Writer*, 252, 256, 258–259; *Baltimore Afro-American*, June 10, 1961; and "Montgomery After the Mob," *Southern Patriot* 19 (September 1, 1961): 1, 4.

10. Brooks interview; *New York Times*, May 21, 1961; Collins interview, *Southern Exposure*, 38; Wilbur, "Waiting Crowd but No Police," 2; *Nashville Tennessean*, May 22, 1961; Branch, *Parting the Waters*, 449–450; Lewis, *Walking with the Wind*, 161; Niven, *The Politics of Injustice*, 80. Hazel Gregory, secretary of the Montgomery Improvement Association, and the Reverend H. T. Palmer, an MIA chaplain and associate pastor at First Baptist Church, were at the station and tried to help Barbee, Zwerg, and others escape from the mob. *Baltimore Afro-American*, May 27, June 3, 1961.

11. Lewis, *Walking with the Wind*, 161 (first quotation); *Birmingham News*, May 21, 1961 (second quotation); *New York Times*, May 21, 1961; *Montgomery Advertiser*, May 30, 1961; *Pittsburgh Courier*, May 27, June 3, 1961; *Baltimore Afro-American*, May 27, 1961; *Nashville Tennessean*, May 22, 1961;

Seigenthaler interview; Seigenthaler interview, RBOHC; Seigenthaler interviews, JFKL; Patterson interview, JFKL; *Life* 50 (May 26, 1961): 24–25; Halberstam, *The Children*, 320–321; Thornton, *Dividing Lines*, 121; Guthman, *We Band of Brothers*, 171; Branch, *Parting the Waters*, 449; Barnard, *Outside the Magic Circle*, 298 (third quotation); Powledge, *Free at Last?* 263, 267 (fourth quotation); Hampton and Fayer, *Voices of Freedom*, 90.

12. Seigenthaler interview; Seigenthaler interview, RBOHC (quotations); Seigenthaler interview, JFKL; Kennedy interview, JFKL: Marshall interview, JFKL; Patterson interview, JFKL; *New York Times*, May 21, 1961; *Montgomery Advertiser*, May 21, 1961; *Birmingham News*, May 21, 1961; *Nashville Tennessean*, May 22, 1961; Guthman, *We Band of Brothers*, 172; Branch, *Parting the Waters*, 451; Niven, *The Politics of Injustice*, 81–82; Halberstam, *The Children*, 321; McWhorter, *Carry Me Home*, 231; Schlesinger, *Robert Kennedy and His Times*, 297; Thomas, *Robert Kennedy*, 129–130; Hilty, *Robert Kennedy*, 323. On Seigenthaler's displeasure with the FBI agents who stood by and watched as he was being beaten, see O'Reilly, *"Racial Matters,"* 90–92. Two of Seigenthaler's Nashville friends, George Barrett and the Reverend Will Campbell, visited him in his hospital room on Sunday afternoon. They flew to Montgomery on a private plane and returned to Nashville before dark, unaware of the developing situation at the First Baptist Church. Barrett interview. On Mann's moderate views on civil rights and the Freedom Riders, see Powledge, *Free at Last?* 269–271.

13. Alabama split its eleven electoral votes in the 1960 presidential election. Five votes were cast for Kennedy, and the other six, cast by "unpledged" Democratic electors, went to Senator Harry Flood Byrd of Virginia, as did all eight of Mississippi's and one of Oklahoma's electoral votes. Richard M. Scammon, *America Votes 5: A Handbook of Contemporary American Election Statistics, 1962* (Pittsburgh: University of Pittsburgh Press, 1964), 17; *New York Times*, May 21, 1961 (quotations); *Pittsburgh Courier*, June 3, 1961; *Birmingham Post-Herald*, May 22, 1961; *Nashville Tennessean*, May 22, 1961; Marshall interview, JFKL; W. Wilson White files, folder 1, box 1, USDJ/CRD; Branch, *Parting the Waters*, 451; Halberstam, *The Children*, 314–319, 323–324; Thomas, *Robert Kennedy*, 129; Hilty, *Robert Kennedy*, 323; Niven, *The Politics of Injustice*, 83–84; Thornton, *Dividing Lines*, 121–122; Zinn, *SNCC*, 49–50.

14. Memorandum, summary of telephone conversation between Attorney General Robert Kennedy and Governor John Patterson, May 20, 1961, 7:30 P.M., box 10, RFKP (quotations); Marshall interview, JFKL; Patterson interview, JFKL; Raines, *My Soul Is Rested*, 309–311; Schlesinger, *Robert Kennedy and His Times*, 298; Brauer, *John F. Kennedy and the Second Reconstruction*, 102. See also Powledge, *Free at Last?* 266–271.

15. *New York Times*, May 21, 1961 (quotation); *Birmingham News*, May 21, 1961; *Montgomery Advertiser*, May 21, 1961; Patterson interview, JFKL; Manis, *A Fire You Can't Put Out*, 275. See also John Patterson to John F. Kennedy, May 21, 1961, box 10, RFKP.

16. *Birmingham News*, May 21, 1961 (quotations); *Birmingham Post-Herald*, May 22, 1961; *New York Times*, May 21–22, 1961; *Montgomery Advertiser*, May 21, 1961; Baltimore *Afro-American*, May 27, June 3, 1961; *Pittsburgh Courier*, June 3, 1961; Lafayette, Zwerg, Harbour, and Wyatt Tee Walker interviews; Wyatt Tee Walker interview, RBOHC; Collins interview, *Southern Exposure*, 38; Branch, *Parting the Waters*, 449–450; Lewis, *Walking with the Wind*, 161; Olson, *Freedom's Daughters*, 187–188.

17. Carey, Lafayette, Harbour, Lillard, Moody, Nash, Rich, and Thomas interviews; Nash, "Inside the Sit-Ins and Freedom Rides," 54–55; *Nashville Tennessean*, May 21–22, 1961; *Pittsburgh Courier*, June 3, 1961; Lewis, *Walking with the Wind*, 161; Branch, *Parting the Waters*, 450, 452; Manis, *A Fire You Can't Put Out*, 276; Powledge, *Free at Last?* 262; Halberstam, *The Children*, 325–326; Hampton and Fayer, *Voices of Freedom*, 82; Carmichael, *Ready for Revolution*, 186–187.

18. Farmer, *Lay Bare the Heart*, 204 (quotation); Carey, Rich, and Wyatt Tee Walker interviews; Wyatt Tee Walker interview, RBOHC; Branch, *Parting the Waters*, 452; Lewis, *Walking with the Wind*, 166; Halberstam, *The Children*, 327.

19. Viorst, *Fire in the Streets*, 153–154 (quotation); Marshall interview, JFKL; Wofford interview, JFKL; William H. Orrick Jr., interview by Larry Hackman, April 13, 1970, JFKL; Seigenthaler interview; *Montgomery Advertiser*, May 22, 1961; *Birmingham News*, May 21, 1961; *Birmingham Post-Herald*, May 22, 1961; *New York Times*, May 22, 1961, April 18, 2002; McWhorter, *Carry Me Home*, 231; Branch, *Parting the Waters*, 452; Thomas, *Robert Kennedy*, 129–130; Hilty, *Robert Kennedy*, 324; Raines, *My Soul Is Rested*, 309–310; Powledge, *Free at Last?* 267–268, 270; Reeves, *President Kennedy*, 129; Wofford, *Of Kennedys and Kings*, 63, 92–94, 154, 169; Niven, *The Politics of Injustice*, 83.

20. Marshall interview, JFKL; Doar interview; *Nashville Tennessean*, May 22, 1961; Hilty, *Robert Kennedy*, 323; Branch, *Parting the Waters*, 452; Bass, *Taming the Storm*, 179; Kennedy, *Judge Frank M. Johnson, Jr.*, 15. Doar wrote the introduction to Kennedy's biography of Johnson.

21. *Birmingham Post-Herald*, May 22, 1961 (quotations); *New York Times*, May 22, 1961; *Christian Science Monitor*, May 22, 1961; *Montgomery Advertiser*, May 22, 1961; *Nashville Tennessean*, May 22, 1961; Patterson interview, JFKL; McWhorter, *Carry Me Home*, 232; Branch, *Parting the Waters*, 453–454; Guthman, *We Band of Brothers*, 172–173; Schlesinger, *Robert Kennedy and His Times*, 297; Raines, *My Soul Is Rested*, 310; Powledge, *Free at Last?* 264–265.

22. Lewis, *Walking with the Wind*, 161–162; Nash, Lafayette, Harbour, Shuttlesworth, and Wyatt Tee Walker interviews; Patterson interview, JFKL; Collins interview, *Southern Exposure*, 38; Branch, *Parting the Waters*, 453–454. Both Barbee and Zwerg remained in the hospital for five days before returning to Nashville. At the request of Zwerg's parents, a minister and family friend flew to Montgomery to convince him to abandon his movement activities and return to Wisconsin. Despite heavy pressure and the knowledge that his father had suffered a mild heart attack in the aftermath of the Montgomery riot and that his mother was on the verge of a nervous breakdown, Zwerg returned to Fisk to take his final exams and planned to remain in Nashville as a movement volunteer during the summer.

However, his injuries–which included a concussion, three broken ribs, and lower vertebrate damage–proved to be more serious than he or the doctors in Montgomery realized, and he returned home to Appleton, Wisconsin, in early June. Despite his parents' misgivings, Zwerg was hailed as a local hero in Appleton, and the Beloit College faculty passed a resolution praising him as "a courageous witness in defense of Christian principles and basic human liberties." After his graduation from Beloit, Zwerg became a minister in the United Church of Christ. He left the ministry in 1975. Zwerg interview; Mary R. Zwerg to Robert F. Kennedy, May 20, 1961, box 10, RFKP; *Jet* 20 (June 8, 1961): 51; NCLC Minutes, July 15, 1961, folder 24, box 75, KMSP; Blake, *Children of the Movement*, 25–36; Dwight Lewis, "Rides Marked a Milestone in History of Hate," *Nashville Tennessean*, May 13, 2001, 21A. Barbee remained active in the Nashville Movement but never fully recovered from the head injuries he sustained during the Montgomery beating. In the spring of 1964 he participated in sit-ins at Morrison's Cafeteria in Nashville that provoked violent resistance from local white supremacists. Following the Morrison's sit-ins, he was arrested along with Fred Leonard, Lester McKinnie, and others. *Nashville Tennessean*, February 13, 2004. Harbour, Lafayette, and Lewis interviews.

23. "The South and the Freedom Riders: Crisis in Civil Rights," *Time* 77 (June 2, 1961): 14 (quotations); *Montgomery Advertiser*, May 22, 1961; Lewis, *Walking with the Wind*, 162; Branch, *Parting the Waters*, 454–456; Viorst, *Fire in the Streets*, 154; Powledge, *Free at Last?* 265, 267, 269–270; Reeves, *President Kennedy*, 129–130; Patterson interview, JFKL; Orrick interview, JFKL.

24. Lewis, *Walking with the Wind*, 162 (quotation); Moody, Lafayette, Harbour, and Shuttlesworth interviews; Collins interview, *Southern Exposure*, 38; *New York Times*, May 22, 1961; Halberstam, *The Children*, 326–327; Branch, *Parting the Waters*, 455–456; Garrow, *Bearing the Cross*, 157–158; Barnard, *Outside the Magic Circle*, 299–300; Mitford, *Poison Penmanship*, 73–76; Sullivan, *Freedom Writer*, 251.

25. Branch, *Parting the Waters*, 455, 457 (first quotation), 458; Viorst, *Fire in the Streets*, 154–155 (second quotation); Shuttlesworth and Lafayette interviews; Manis, *A Fire You Can't Put Out*, 276–277; Lewis, *Walking with the Wind*, 162–163; Farmer, *Lay Bare the Heart*, 204–205; Raines, *My Soul Is Rested*, 122–123; Hampton and Fayer, *Voices of Freedom*, 91; McWhorter, *Carry Me Home*, 232–233; Fairclough, *To Redeem the Soul of America*, 79.

26. Barnard, *Outside the Magic Circle*, 299–301 (first quotation). The original owner of the Buick was Aubrey Williams, the former director of the National Youth Administration and a close friend of the Durrs'. Branch, *Parting the Waters*, 458 (second quotation), 459; *New York Times*, May 22, 1961; *Pittsburgh Courier*, May 27, June 3, 1961; *Montgomery Advertiser*, May 22, 1961; *Birmingham Post-Herald*, May 22, 1961; Marshall interview, JFKL; Oberdorfer interview, JFKL; Guthman, *We Band of Brothers*, 173; McWhorter, *Carry Me Home*, 233; Manis, *A Fire You Can't Put Out*, 277–278; Garrow, *Bearing the Cross*, 158; Reeves, *President Kennedy*, 130; Thomas, *Robert Kennedy*, 130; Niven, *The Politics of Injustice*, 92–93.

27. *New York Times*, May 22, 1961 (first quotation); Lewis, *Walking with the Wind*, 163 (second quotation); *Christian Science Monitor*, May 22, 1961; Lafayette interview; Collins interview, *Southern Exposure*, 38; Hampton and Fayer, *Voices of Freedom*, 92; "The South and the Freedom Riders," 14; Halberstam, *The Children*, 329; Branch, *Parting the Waters*, 459; Manis, *A Fire You Can't Put Out*, 278. According to a *Pittsburgh Courier* correspondent on the scene, support for nonviolent restraint was waning among Montgomery blacks in 1961. See "Montgomery's Negroes 'Tired' of Being Kicked," *Pittsburgh Courier*, June 3, 1961.

28. Farmer, *Lay Bare the Heart*, 205 (first quotation); Branch, *Parting the Waters*, 459–460 (second and third quotations); Lewis, *Walking with the Wind*, 163; Marshall interview, JFKL; Kennedy and Marshall interview, JFKL; Schlesinger, *Robert Kennedy and His Times*, 297–298; Hilty, *Robert Kennedy*, 324–325; Thomas, *Robert Kennedy*, 130–131; Garrow, *Bearing the Cross*, 158; Olson, *Freedom's Daughters*, 188; Manis, *A Fire You Can't Put Out*, 278; Niven, *The Politics of Injustice*, 87; Telephone Log, May 15–25, 1961, box 10, RFKP. See also Fred Shuttlesworth's response to the suggested "cooling off" in Shuttlesworth, "Cool Off? . . . For What? The Mob Must Not Win," *Pittsburgh Courier*, June 3, 1961, 2.

29. Farmer, *Lay Bare the Heart*, 295–206 (quotations); Olson, *Freedom's Daughters*, 188–189; McWhorter, *Carry Me Home*, 233; Halberstam, *The Children*, 327–328; Lafayette, Nash, and Wyatt Tee Walker interviews.

30. Lewis, *Walking with the Wind*, 163 (quotation); *New York Times*, May 22, 1961; *Montgomery Advertiser*, May 22, 1961; Shuttlesworth and Lafayette interviews; Collins interview, *Southern Exposure*, 38; Branch, *Parting the Waters*, 460–461; Farmer, *Lay Bare the Heart*, 206; Niven, *The Politics of Injustice*, 88–90; Fleming, *Soon We Will Not Cry*, 84; Hampton and Fayer, *Voices of Freedom*, 92. "Asking for Trouble—and Getting It: The Ride for Rights," *Life* 50 (June 2, 1961): 48–49, includes several revealing photographs of the scene in the sanctuary. See also the newsreel footage used in "Ain't Scared of Your Jails."

31. *Birmingham Post-Herald*, May 22, 1961 (first quotation); typescript, Robert Kennedy statement called to UPI, May 21, 1961, box 10, RFKP; Robert F. Kennedy interviews, 1964–1967, JFKL; Marshall interview, JFKL; Doar interview; Branch, *Parting the Waters*, 461; Schlesinger, *Robert Kennedy and His Times*, 298; Reeves, *President Kennedy*, 130; Hilty, *Robert Kennedy*, 325; Powledge, *Free at Last?* 265, 269 (second quotation); *Birmingham News*, May 22, 1961; *Christian Science Monitor*, May 22, 1961.

32. Lafayette and Shuttlesworth interviews; Marshall interview, JFKL; Orrick interview, JFKL; *Montgomery Advertiser*, May 22, 1961; *Birmingham News*, May 22, 1961; Walker interview, RBOHC; Manis, *A Fire You Can't Put Out*, 278 (first quotation); Powledge, *Free at Last?* 269; Fairclough, *To Redeem the Soul of America*, 79–80; *New York Times*, May 22, 1961 (second quotation); Branch, *Parting the Waters*, 461–462; Halberstam, *The Children*, 329–330; Raines, *My Soul Is Rested*, 309–310; Viorst, *Fire in the Streets*, 155; Reeves, *President Kennedy*, 130; Thomas, *Robert Kennedy*, 131; Hilty, *Robert Kennedy*, 325.

33. A draft of the prepared text of King's May 21, 1961, speech is on file in the KPA. Nash, "Inside the Sit-Ins and Freedom Rides," 55 (first quotation); Garrow, *Bearing the Cross*, 157 (first and third King quotations), 158; Wofford, *Of Kennedys and Kings*, 154 (second King quotation); *Birmingham News*, May 22, 1961 (fourth King quotation); *New York Times*, May 22, 1961; *Montgomery Advertiser*, May 22, 1961; *Pittsburgh Courier*, May 27, June 3, 1961; Lafayette, Shuttlesworth, Harbour, Moody, and Lewis interviews; Lewis, *Walking with the Wind*, 164; Branch, *Parting the Waters*, 462–463; McWhorter, *Carry Me Home*, 234; Manis, *A Fire You Can't Put Out*, 278; documentary "Ain't Scared of Your Jails" (Shuttlesworth quotation); Farmer, *Lay Bare the Heart*, 206 (Farmer quotation); Collins interview, *Southern Exposure*, 38.

34. *Birmingham News*, May 22 (first quotation), June 3, 1961; Lewis, *Walking with the Wind*, 164 (second quotation); Telephone Log, May 15–25, 1961, box 10, RFKP; Marshall interview, JFKL; Orrick interview, JFKL; Lafayette and Shuttlesworth interviews; *Birmingham Post-Herald*, May 22, 1961; *New York Times*, May 22, 1961; *Montgomery Advertiser*, May 22, 1961; Edwin O. Guthman and Jeffrey Shulman, eds., *Robert Kennedy in His Own Words: The Unpublished Recollections of the Kennedy Years* (New York: Bantam, 1988), 89; Branch, *Parting the Waters*, 463–464; Abernathy, *And the Walls Came Tumbling Down*, 618; Guthman, *We Band of Brothers*, 173, 177–178 (third quotation); McWhorter, *Carry Me Home*, 234–235 (fourth quotation); Niven, *The Politics of Injustice*, 94; Reeves, *President Kennedy*, 130–131; Schlesinger, *Robert Kennedy and His Times*, 298; Hilty, *Robert Kennedy*, 325–326; Brauer, *John F. Kennedy and the Second Reconstruction*, 103; Wofford, *Of Kennedys and Kings*, 154. Thomas, *Robert Kennedy*, 131, notes that "Kennedy apparently garbled an obscure Boston Irish expression 'as tight as Kelsey's nuts,' meaning cheap."

35. Telephone Log, May 15–25, 1961, box 10, RFKP; Patterson interview, JFKL (first quotation); Marshall interview, JFKL; Guthman, *We Band of Brothers*, 178 (second and fourth quotations); Raines, *My Soul Is Rested*, 309 (third quotation); Schlesinger, *Robert Kennedy and His Times*, 297–298; Hilty, *Robert Kennedy*, 326.

36. Zinn, *SNCC*, 50 (first quotation); Barnard, *Outside the Magic Circle*, 301 (second quotation); Orrick interview, JFKL (Orrick and Graham quotations); *Montgomery Advertiser*, May 22, 1961; *Pittsburgh Courier*, June 3, 1961; Branch, *Parting the Waters*, 464–465; Lewis, *Walking with the Wind*, 164–165; Schlesinger, *Robert Kennedy and His Times*, 298–299; Guthman, *We Band of Brothers*, 175; Halberstam, *The Children*, 330; McWhorter, *Carry Me Home*, 235; Viorst, *Fire in the Streets*, 155; Garrow, *Bearing the Cross*, 158; Farmer, *Lay Bare the Heart*, 206; Lafayette, Lewis, and Shuttlesworth interviews. Manis, *A Fire You Can't Put Out*, 279, notes Shuttlesworth's wry comment to an ACHMR mass meeting on Monday evening, May 22: "When I left church this morning, Pat's marshals carried me home." During the evacuation of the church on Monday morning, SNCC leader Ed King told Baltimore *Afro-American* reporter Samuel Hoskins: 'It was a church meeting, but it appeared to me as if we were in a war.' *Baltimore Afro-American*, June 3, 1961. See also Edward B. King Jr. to Maurice C. Clifford, May 26, 1961, folder 7, box 8, SNCCP.

37. *New York Times*, May 22, 1961 (quotations); *New York Herald Tribune*, May 22, 1961; *Washington Post*, May 22, 1961; *Washington Evening Star*, May 22, 1961; *Chicago Tribune*, May 22, 1961; *Los Angeles Times*, May 22, 1961; *Boston Globe*, May 22, 1961; *Montgomery Advertiser*, May 22, 1961; *Birmingham Post-Herald*, May 22, 1961; *Atlanta Constitution*, May 22, 1961; *St. Petersburg Times*, May 22, 1961; *Miami Herald*, May 22, 1961; *New Orleans Times-Picayune*, May 22, 1961; *Nashville Tennessean*, May 22, 1961; Branch, *Parting the Waters*, 465; Brauer, *John F. Kennedy and the Second Reconstruction*, 103–104; Niven, *The Politics of Injustice*, 95–97; Hilty, *Robert Kennedy*, 326. See also the May 1961 press clippings in reels 189 and 190, TIRRCF.

38. *Montgomery Advertiser*, May 22–24, 1961 (quotations); *Montgomery Alabama Journal*, May 22–24, 1961; *Birmingham News*, May 22–23, 1961; *Birmingham Post-Herald*, May 23, 1961; Thornton, *Dividing Lines*, 123–127; Branch, *Parting the Waters*, 465–466; "Folsom Call," typescript, May 22, 1961, and Montgomery Chamber of Commerce to Robert F. Kennedy, May 22, 1961, both in box 10, RFKP.

39. *Montgomery Advertiser*, May 23, 1961 (quotations); *Birmingham Post-Herald*, May 23, 1961; *Birmingham News*, May 22, 1961.

40. *Birmingham Post-Herald*, May 23, 1961 (first quotation); *Montgomery Advertiser*, May 23, 1961; *Birmingham News*, May 23, 1961; Navasky, *Kennedy Justice*, 14, 20–24 (second quotation); Branch, *Parting the Waters*, 468–469; Powell, *Free at Last?* 277; McWhorter, *Carry Me Home*, 198, 212–213, 236–237 (third quotation); O'Reilly, *"Racial Matters,"* 84–93; Garrow, *The FBI and Martin Luther King, Jr.*, 23–25 and passim; May, *The Informant*, 49–53; Richard Gid Powers, *Secrecy and Power: The Life of J. Edgar Hoover* (New York: Free Press, 1987), 368–369; see also the voluminous correspondence related to FBI activities during the period May 14–22, 1961 in FBI-FRI.

41. Lewis, *Walking with the Wind*, 165–167 (quotations); Branch, *Parting the Waters*, 466–468; Raines, *My Soul Is Rested*, 123; Farmer, *Lay Bare the Heart*, 206–207; Lafayette, Harbour, Diamond, Dietrich, Lewis, Brooks, Moody, Nash, Thomas, Dennis, Wyatt Tee Walker, and Matthew Walker Jr. interviews; *Baltimore Afro-American*, May 27, 1961; Edward B. King Jr. to Henry Thomas, May 19, 1961, folder 7, box 8, SNCCP. Of the two Tennessee State students remaining in Montgomery, only Collins had participated in the Nashville-to-Montgomery Freedom Ride. The second Tennessee State student, Ernest "Rip" Patton, joined the Riders in Montgomery on May 23. Patton remarks, May 11, 2001. *Birmingham Post-Herald*, May 22, 1961; *Birmingham News*, May 22, 1961; *Nashville Tennessean*, May 20–22, 1961; McWhorter, *Carry Me Home*, 238; Fairclough, *To Redeem the Soul of America*, 98; Garrow, *Bearing the Cross*, 159; Viorst, *Fire in the Streets*, 156; Peter J. Ling, *Martin Luther King, Jr.* (London: Routledge, 2002), 80–81; Lewis, *King*, 133–134 (Williams quotation); Tyson, *Radio Free Dixie*, 246. Halberstam, *The Children*, 270–273, 325, 331–332, claims that Nash and Rodney

Powell, a black medical student at Nashville's Meharry College of Medicine, made a special trip to Atlanta to convince King to become a Freedom Rider. Based on an interview with Powell, Halberstam's account does not give the exact date of the trip to Atlanta but suggests that it took place over dinner at King's home on Sunday, "a few days" before the May 22 meeting at Harris's house. The only possible date for the trip is May 20, the day of the Montgomery bus station riot, but Nash recalls no such trip on that day. However, she does recall phone conversations earlier in the week during which she broached the idea of King becoming a Freedom Rider. Nash interview.

42. *Jackson Daily News*, May 23, 1961 (first quotation); *Jackson Clarion-Ledger*, May 24, 1961 (second quotation); Ross R. Barnett, interview by Dennis O'Brien, May 6, 1969, JFKL. On Barnett (1898–1988), see Dennis J. Mitchell, "Ross Barnett," in *The Encyclopedia of Southern Culture*, ed. Charles Reagan Wilson and William Ferris (Chapel Hill: University of North Carolina Press, 1989), 1182; Robert Sherrill, *Gothic Politics in the Deep South* (New York: Grossman,1968), 2–4, 174–186, 203–212; and Erle Johnston, *I Rolled With Ross: A Political Portrait* (Baton Rouge: Moran Publishing, 1980). Born in Standing Pine, Mississippi, in 1898, Barnett was the tenth and youngest child of a Civil War veteran.

43. Marshall interview, JFKL (first quotation); Niven, *Politics of Injustice*, 102–103; *Jackson Clarion-Ledger*, May 24, 1961; *Montgomery Advertiser*, May 24, 1961 (Patterson quotation).

44. *Atlanta Journal*, May 23, 1961; Branch, *Parting the Waters*, 468 (quotation); Lewis, *Walking with the Wind*, 167–168; Halberstam, *The Children*, 332; *Nashville Tennessean*, May 24, 1961; Diamond interview.

45. Branch, *Parting the Waters*, 470; Lewis, *Walking with the Wind*, 168; Dennis, Lafayette, Diamond, Dietrich, Moody, and Matthew Walker Jr. interviews; *Nashville Tennessean*, May 24, 1961 (quotation).

46. Lafayette, Thomas, Moody, and Dennis interviews; Lewis, *Walking with the Wind*, 167 (first quotation); Still, "A Bus Ride Through Mississippi," 21 (second quotation).

47. Ross Barnett to Robert F. Kennedy, May 23, 1961; telephone conversation between Ross Barnett and Robert F. Kennedy, typescript, May 23, 1961; and telephone conversation between Burke Marshall and Attorney General Patterson of Mississippi, typescript, May 22, 1961, all in box 10, RFKP. On the contacts between Marshall and Patterson, see also box 19, BMP. Branch, *Parting the Waters*, 470 (first quotation); *Jackson Daily News*, May 22, 1961 (second quotation); *New Orleans Times-Picayune*, June 11, 1961; Baltimore *Afro-American*, June 3, 1961; Niven, *Politics of Injustice*, 103–104; Hilty, *Robert Kennedy*, 326–327; Schlesinger, *Robert Kennedy and His Times*, 299 (third and fourth quotations); Marshall interview, JFKL (fifth quotation); Robert F. Kennedy interview, JFKL; Barnett interview, JFKL. On Eastland, see Sherrill, *Gothic Politics in the Deep South*, 174–215.

48. Marshall interview, JFKL; Robert F. Kennedy interview, JFKL; Doar and Seigenthaler interviews; Niven, *The Politics of Injustice*, 4–5, 104; Hilty, *Robert Kennedy*, 329; James M. McPherson, *Crossroads of Freedom: Antietam* (New York: Oxford University Press, 2002). On the Lincoln/Kennedy comparison, see "Compendium of Curious Coincidences; Parallels in the Lives and Deaths of Abraham Lincoln and John F. Kennedy," *Time* 84 (August 21, 1964): 19; Simeon Booker, "How JFK Surpassed Abraham Lincoln," *Ebony* 19 (February 1964): 25–28+; and M. Quigley, "Carl Sandburg Tells How He Thinks Great Emancipator Would Have Reacted to Today's Touchy Race Problems," *Ebony* 18 (September 1963): 158–159. On Lincoln as a moderate Republican, see David M. Potter, *The Impending Crisis, 1848–1861* (New York: Harper and Row, 1976), 421–447, 454, 526; Eric Foner, *Free Soil, Free Labor, Free Men: The Ideology of the Republican Party Before the Civil War* (New York: Oxford University Press, 1970), 205–225; David Herbert Donald, *Lincoln* (New York: Simon and Schuster, 1995), 207–209, 331–333, 342, 424–425, 633–634; T. Harry Williams, *Lincoln and the Radicals* (Madison: University of Wisconsin Press, 1941); Robert W. Johannsen, *Lincoln, the South, and Slavery: The Political Dimension* (Baton Rouge: Louisiana State University Press, 1991); Mark E. Neely Jr., *The Last Best Hope of Earth: Abraham Lincoln and the Promise of America* (Cambridge: Harvard University Press, 1993); and George M. Fredrickson, "A Man but Not a Brother: Abraham Lincoln and Racial Equality," *Journal of Southern History* 41 (February 1975): 39–58.

Chapter 7: Freedom's Coming and It Won't Be Long

1. First sung on May 24, 1961, the "calypso" freedom song was an adaptation of Harry Belafonte's popular hit "The Banana Boat Song." *New York Times*, May 25, 1961; Still, "A Bus Ride Through Mississippi," 23. A second stanza focused on May 14 and the original CORE Freedom Ride: "I took a trip down Alabama way./ Freedom's coming and it won't be long./ I met much trouble on Mother's Day./ Freedom's coming and it won't be long." *Boston Globe* , May 25, 1961; Niven, *The Politics of Injustice*, 236 n239. On Belafonte, see Genia Fogelson, *Harry Belafonte: Singer and Actor* (Belmont, CA: Wadsworth, 1996).

2. *Montgomery Advertiser*, May 25, 1961 (first quotation); *New York Times*, May 25, 1961; *Jackson Daily News*, May 24, 1961; Baltimore *Afro-American*, June 3, 1961; *Nashville Tennessean*, May 25, 1961; Lafayette, Dennis, Dietrich and Matthew Walker Jr. interviews; Still, "A Bus Ride Through Mississippi," 22; Lewis, *Walking with the Wind*, 168; Farmer, *Lay Bare the Heart*, 207; Branch, *Parting the Waters*, 470–471; Raines, *My Soul Is Rested*, 277 (second quotation); Garrow, *Bearing the Cross*, 159; Niven, *The Politics of Injustice*, 106; Rogers, *Righteous Lives*, 126, 129–130; Anderson-Bricker, "Making a Movement," 265–266, 283–284, 313–318; Roster of Freedom Riders Arrested in Mississippi Through July 31, 1961, Group 1, May 24, 1961, typescript, MSCP.

3. *New York Times*, May 25, 1961 (first quotation); *Birmingham Post-Herald*, May 25, 1961 (second quotation); *Boston Globe*, May 25, 1961; *Baltimore Afro-American*, June 3, 1961; Still, "A Bus Ride Through Mississippi," 23 (third, fourth, and fifth quotations); Larry A. Still, "Freedom Riders Gather from Across the Nation: Miss. Trip Brings More Arrests," *Jet* 20 (June 8, 1961): 12–17; *Birmingham News*, May 24, 1961; *Montgomery Advertiser*, May 25, 1961; Marshall interview, JFKL; Lafayette interview; Hampton and Fayer, *Voices of Freedom*, 92; Halberstam, *The Children*, 333–338; Guthman, *We Band of Brothers*, 176; Niven, *The Politics of Injustice*, 106; Branch, *Parting the Waters*, 471–472; Lewis, *Walking with the Wind*, 168; Viorst, *Fire in the Streets*, 157. On the Selma-to-Montgomery march and the voting rights controversy of 1965, see David J. Garrow, *Protest at Selma: Martin Luther King, Jr., and the Voting Rights Act of 1965* (New Haven: Yale University Press, 1978); Fairclough, *To Redeem the Soul of America*, 225–251; and Raines, *My Soul Is Rested*, 187–226. On the background to the march, see Taylor Branch, *Pillar of Fire: America in the King Years, 1963–65* (New York: Simon and Schuster, 1998), 513–600.
4. Branch, *Parting the Waters*, 472; *Nashville Tennessean*, May 25, 1961 (first quotation); *New York Times*, May 25, 196 (second quotation); Still, "A Bus Ride Through Mississippi," 26 (third quotation); Still, "Freedom Riders Gather," 14–15; *Baltimore Afro-American*, June 3, 1961; Lewis, *Walking with the Wind*, 169; Marshall interview, JFKL; Lafayette and Matthew Walker Jr. interviews; *Birmingham News*, May 24, 1961; Halberstam, *The Children*, 333–338, 349.
5. Branch, *Parting the Waters*, 472; Lewis, *Walking with the Wind*, 168–169; Farmer, *Lay Bare the Heart*, 1–6, 207 (Farmer quotations); Collins interview, *Southern Exposure*, 38–39 (Collins quotation); Diamond, Moody, and Thomas interviews, Roster of Freedom Riders, Group 2, May 24, 1961, MSCP; *New York Times*, May 25, 1961; *Montgomery Advertiser*, May 25, 1961; Frank Holloway, "Travel Notes from a Deep South Tourist," *New South* 16 (July/August 1961): 5–6; Hampton and Fayer, *Voices of Freedom*, 93 (lyrics); Niven, *The Politics of Injustice*, 107. On Collins, see Forman, *The Making of Black Revolutionaries*, 145, 150–157.
6. *New York Times*, May 25, 1961 (quotations); *Montgomery Advertiser*, May 25, 1961; *Nashville Tennessean*, May 25, 1961; Marshall interview, JFKL; Branch, *Parting the Waters*, 472; Niven, *Politics of Injustice*, 109; Hilty, *Robert Kennedy*, 327.
7. *New York Times*, May 25 (first quotation), 27 (second quotation), 1961; *Montgomery Advertiser*, May 25, 1961; *Jackson Daily News*, May 24–25, 1961; *Jackson Clarion-Ledger*, May 25, 1961; *Birmingham Post-Herald*, May 25, 1961; *Atlanta Constitution*, May 25, 1961; *Baltimore Afro-American*, June 3, 1961; *Nashville Tennessean*, May 25, 1961; Marshall interview, JFKL; Robert F. Kennedy interview, JFKL (third quotation); Niven, *Politics of Injustice*, 104; Branch, *Parting the Waters*, 473–474 (Abernathy quotation); Halberstam, *The Children*, 338–339, 349; Viorst, *Fire in the Streets*, 157; Wofford, *Of Kennedys and Kings*, 156; Hilty, *Robert Kennedy*, 328; McWhorter, *Carry Me Home*, 239; William Sloane Coffin Jr., interview by author, June 22, 2005; John Maguire, interview by author, June 21, 2005. Well known among members of the Northeastern intellectual establishment, Coffin went on to become a celebrated opponent of the Vietnam War. His personal celebrity was enhanced by his marriage to the daughter of the noted pianist Arthur Rubinstein. See William Sloane Coffin Jr., *Once to Every Man: A Memoir* (New York: Atheneum, 1977), 144–169; Warren Goldstein, *William Sloane Coffin, Jr.: A Holy Impatience* (New Haven: Yale University Press, 2004), 111–128; Coffin, "Why Yale Chaplain Rode: Christians Can't Be Outside," *Life* 50 (June 2, 1961): 54–55; and "The South and the Freedom Riders," 17. John Maguire went on to become a distinguished college president in Connecticut and California, retiring from the Claremont Colleges in 1998. During a Freedom Rider reunion in Jackson, in November 2001, he quipped: "It's taken me forty years to get here." John Maguire, remarks at the Freedom Riders' 40th reunion, Jackson, MS, November 10, 2001. See also John Maguire, interview by Susan Glisson, November 9, 1961, UMFRC.
8. *New York Times*, May 25, 1961 (first and second quotations); *Birmingham Post-Herald*, May 25, 1961 (third quotation); *Nashville Tennessean*, May 25, 1961; *Baltimore Afro-American*, June 3, 1961; Marshall interview, JFKL; Branch, *Parting the Waters*, 475; David Brinkley, *Brinkley's Beat: People, Places, and Events That Shaped My Time* (New York: Knopf, 2003), 70, 147–179.
9. Raines, *My Soul Is Rested*, 125 (first quotation); Farmer, *Lay Bare the Heart*, 6–7; Holloway, "Travel Notes from a Deep South Tourist," 6; Lewis, *Walking with the Wind*, 169 (second quotation); Marshall interview, JFKL; Telephone Log, May 24, 1961, box 10, RFKP; *Jackson Clarion-Ledger*, May 25, 196; Zinn, *SNCC*, 51–52; Thomas, *Robert Kennedy*, 131–132; Brauer, *John F. Kennedy and the Second Reconstruction*, 107. A partial transcript of the King-Kennedy telephone conversation appears in Guthman, *We Band of Brothers*, 154–155; Schlesinger, *Robert Kennedy and His Times*, 299–300; Wofford, *Of Kennedys and Kings*, 155; Branch, *Parting the Waters*, 475; Hilty, *Robert Kennedy*, 328; and Garrow, *Bearing the Cross*, 159–160.
10. Wofford, *Of Kennedys and Kings*, 156 (quotations); Branch, *Parting the Waters*, 475–476; Coffin, *Once to Every Man*, 157–160; Goldstein, *William Sloane Coffin, Jr.*, 118–119; Coffin and Maguire interviews; Maguire interview, UMFRC; Clyde Carter, interview by author and Meeghan Kane, August 10, 2005. Maguire had known King since 1951, when they had shared a room during a weekend seminar at Crozer Seminary in Philadelphia. *San Bernardino County Sun*, January 18, 1987.
11. Lawrence N. Powell, "When Hate Came to Town: New Orleans' Jews and George Lincoln Rockwell," *American Jewish History* 85 (December 1997): 394–419, 398 (first quotation); *Nashville Tennessean*, May 25, 1961 (second quotation); *New York Times*, May 25, 1961 (third quotation); *New Orleans Times-Picayune*, May 25, 1961; *Montgomery Advertiser*, May 25, 1961. On Rockwell, see George Lincoln Rockwell, *This Time the World* (n.p.: 1963); Leland V. Bell, *In Hitler's Shadow: The Anatomy of American Nazism* (Port Washington, NY: Associated Faculty Press, 1973); and "Death of a Storm Trooper," *New York Times*, August 27, 1967.

12. *New York Times*, May 25, 1961 (quotations). On Stennis's conservatism, see Brauer, *John F. Kennedy and the Second Reconstruction*, 55–56; Sherrill, *Gothic Politics in the Deep South*, 205–214; and Harry S. Ashmore, *Hearts and Minds: The Anatomy of Racism from Roosevelt to Reagan* (New York: McGraw-Hill, 1982), 369. On Javits's strong views on racial discrimination, see Jacob K. Javits, *On Discrimination* (New York: Harcourt, Brace, 1960); and *Javits: The Autobiography of a Public Man* (Boston: Houghton Mifflin, 1981). Though generally considered to be a political moderate, New Orleans mayor deLesseps Morrison lumped Freedom Riders and Nazis together as unwanted troublemakers. "Nazi storm troopers and freedom riders and other such groups," he told reporters, "mean nothing but trouble and are not welcome here." *Nashville Tennessean*, May 25, 1961.

13. Lewis, *Walking with the Wind*, 169 (first quotation); George Brown Tindall, *The Emergence of the New South, 1913–1945* (Baton Rouge: Louisiana State University Press, 1967), 234 (second quotation); U.S. Bureau of the Census, *18th Census of the United States, 1960, Population* (Washington: GPO, 1961). On Bevel's background, see Halberstam, *The Children*, 94–96, 350–355. On the folk culture of Mississippi blues music, see Alan Lomax, *The Land Where the Blues Began* (New York: Dell, 1993); and Elijah Wald, *Escaping the Delta: Robert Johnson and the Invention of the Blues* (New York: HarperCollins, 2004). On Mississippi's racial and white supremacist traditions, see Albert J. Kirwan, *Revolt of the Rednecks: Mississippi Politics, 1876–1925* (Lexington: University of Kentucky Press, 1951); William F. Holmes, *The White Chief: James Kimble Vardaman* (Baton Rouge: Louisiana State University Press, 1970); Neil R. McMillen, *Dark Journey: Black Mississippians in the Age of Jim Crow* (Urbana: University of Illinois Press, 1989); James W. Silver, *Mississippi: The Closed Society*, new enlarged ed. (New York: Harcourt, Brace, and World, 1966); James C. Cobb, *The Most Southern Place on Earth: The Mississippi Delta and the Roots of Regional Identity* (New York: Oxford University Press, 1992); John Dollard, *Caste and Class in a Southern Town* (New Haven: Yale University Press, 1937); Allison Davis, Burleigh B. Gardner, and Mary R. Gardner, *Deep South: A Social Anthropological Study of Caste and Class* (Chicago: University of Chicago Press, 1941); Hortense Powdermaker, *After Freedom: A Cultural Study in the Deep South* (New York: Viking Press, 1939) ; Richard Wright, *Black Boy* (New York: Harper and Brothers, 1945); Jack E. Davis, *Race Against Time: Culture and Separation in Natchez Since 1930* (Baton Rouge: Louisiana State University Press, 2001); Whitfield, *A Death in the Delta*; and Howard Smead, *Blood Justice: The Lynching of Mack Charles Parker* (New York: Oxford University Press, 1986). On the "Mississippi Plan," see Woodward, *The Strange Career of Jim Crow*, 83, 152.

14. *Jackson Clarion-Ledger*, May 23–26, 1961; *Jackson Daily News*, May 23–26, 1961; *Jackson State-Times*, May 26, 1961. On the White Citizens' Councils, see McMillen, *The Citizens' Council*; Hodding Carter, *The South Strikes Back* (Garden City, NY: Doubleday, 1959); and Bartley, *The Rise of Massive Resistance*, 82–107. On the Sunflower County roots of the Citizens' Councils, see J. Todd Moye, *Let the People Decide: Black Freedom and White Resistance Movements in Sunflower County, Mississippi, 1945–1986* (Chapel Hill: University of North Carolina Press, 2004), 64–86.

15. The New York reporter was Philip S. Cook of the *New York Herald Tribune* News Service. His story was reprinted in the *Birmingham Post-Herald*, May 28, 1961 (first quotation); Lafayette, Dietrich, and Moody interviews; Lafayette and Thomas interview; Holloway, "Travel Notes from a Deep South Tourist," 6; Farmer, *Lay Bare the Heart*, 7 (second and third quotations); Halberstam, *The Children*, 339–344; Lewis, *Walking with the Wind*, 169–170; *Nashville Tennessean*, May 25, 1961. See also Farmer's extended description of his Mississippi jail experiences in *Lay Bare the Heart*, 7–32; and Peck, *Freedom Ride*, 143–146.

16. UPI press release, Jerome Brazda, May 26, 1961, typescript, MSCP ; *Montgomery Advertiser*, May 26, 1961; *Birmingham Post-Herald*, May 26, 1961; *Birmingham News*, May 25, 1961 (first quotation); *New York Times*, May 26, 1961 (second quotation); Branch, *Parting the Waters*, 476; Maguire, Coffin, Jones, and Clyde Carter interviews; Maguire interview, UMFRC; Goldstein, *William Sloane Coffin, Jr.*, 119–121; Coffin, *Once to Every Man*, 160–162.

17. Written by James Clayton, the story in the May 25, 1961, issue of the *Washington Post* does not identify the speaker as Robert Kennedy, and Navasky, *Kennedy Justice*, 206, reprints the story without any attempt to identify the speaker. However, the conclusion of Branch, *Parting the Waters*, 476, that the unidentified Justice Department spokesman in the story was Kennedy is highly plausible. *Jackson Clarion-Ledger*, May 26, 1961; *New York Times*, May 26, 1961 (Eastland quotations). The *Times* story also quoted Peck, who, while speaking at a CORE rally at the Concord Baptist Church in Brooklyn, refuted Eastland's accusations: "I am opposed to all kinds of dictatorship, Communist or fascist." See also Peck, *Freedom Ride*, 136–137.

18. *New York Times*, May 26, 1961; Branch, *Parting the Waters*, 477–478 (first quotation); Reeves, *President Kennedy*, 135–140; Hilty, *Robert Kennedy*, 328–329. For the full text of the May 25, 1961 State of the Union address, see *Public Papers of the Presidents: John F. Kennedy, 1961–1963* (Washington: GPO, 1962), vol. 1, 396–405. The rabbi who questioned the president's priorities was Rabbi Edward E. Klein of the Stephen Wise Free Synagogue. *Baltimore Afro-American*, June 24, 1961.

19. *Jackson State-Times*, May 26, 1961 (first quotation); *New York Times*, May 26, 1961 (remaining quotations); *Baltimore Afro-American*, June 3, 1961; *Pittsburgh Courier*, June 10, 1961; Branch, *Parting the Waters*, 476–477; Meier and Rudwick, *CORE*, 139. The CORE office was flooded with Freedom Rider applications in the weeks following the initial Mississippi arrests. See sections 441–443, reel 43, COREP.

20. *Jackson Clarion-Ledger*, May 29, 1961 (first quotation). Peck also appeared on Mike Wallace's *PM East* television show, as well as other television and radio broadcasts. See Peck, *Freedom Ride*, 135. On the origins of the FRCC, see Gordon Carey, "Report of Meeting of the Freedom Ride Coordinating Committee," May 26, 1961, reel 25, COREP; Minutes, FRCC organizational meeting, May 26, 1961, box 10, KPA; minutes, SNCC meeting, Louisville, Kentucky, June 9–11, 1961, folder 2, box 7,

SNCCP; FRCC organizational summary, folder 11, box 75, KMSP; *Birmingham Post-Herald*, May 29, 1961; *Jackson State-Times*, May 28, 1961; Laue, *Direct Action and Desegregation*, 109–110; Branch, *Parting the Waters*, 477; and Meier and Rudwick, *CORE*, 139 (second quotation), 144.

21. *New York Times*, May 26, 1961 (quotations).
22. Clyde Carter, Coffin, and Maguire interviews; Maguire interview, UMFRC; Coffin, *Once to Every Man*, 161–162; Goldstein, *William Sloane Coffin, Jr.*, 120–121; Coffin, "Why Yale Chaplain Rode," 54 (quotation); *Montgomery Advertiser*, May 27, 1961 (quotations); *New York Times*, May 27–28, 1961; *Atlanta Constitution*, May 27, 1961; *Birmingham News*, May 28, 1961. The *Montgomery Advertiser* reported George Smith's claim that the hunger strike began when a guard denied Abernathy "permission to telephone his wife."
23. *New York Times*, May 27, 1961 (first, second, and third quotations); *Jackson Daily News*, May 27, 1961 (Spencer quotations); *Jackson Clarion-Ledger*, May 25, 27, 1961; *Baltimore Afro-American*, June 3, 1961 (Travis-Vivian exchange); *Montgomery Advertiser*, May 27, 1961; *Atlanta Constitution*, May 27, 1961; Lewis, *Walking with the Wind*, 170; Peck, *Freedom Ride*, 140; Holloway, "Travel Notes from a Deep South Tourist," 7. On Branton, who gained fame as an attorney for students attempting to desegregate Little Rock's schools in the late 1950s, see Kirk, *Redefining the Color Line*, 32, 58–62, 99–100, 118, 132–133, 161, 167; Wiley A. Branton, "Little Rock Revisited: Desegregation to Resegregation," *Journal of Negro Education* 52 (Summer 1983): 250–269; and Meier and Rudwick, *CORE*, 175, 177, 179, 259–260, 269. See also Tony Freyer, *The Little Rock Crisis: A Constitutional Interpretation* (Westport, CT: Greenwood Press, 1984); and Jacoway and Williams, *Understanding the Little Rock Crisis*.
24. *Jackson Daily News*, May 25, 27, 1961; *Jackson Clarion-Ledger*, May 28, 1961; *New York Times*, May 28, 1961; *Montgomery Advertiser*, May 27, 1961; Collins interview, *Southern Exposure*, 39. The speakers at the Jackson NAACP rally included Charles Darden of the NAACP's National Board of Directors; Julia Wright, an NAACP regional secretary based in Columbia, South Carolina; Medgar Evers, NAACP field secretary for Mississippi; the Reverend John D. Mangram, chaplain of Tougaloo Southern Christian College; and Ella Baker. *Baltimore Afro-American*, June 3, 1961.
25. "Sit-In Lull Won't Last, King Warns," unidentified clipping, May 28, 1961, MSCP (first quotation); *Jackson Clarion-Ledger*, May 28, 1961; *New York Times*, May 27 (Wilkins quotation), 29, 1961; *Nashville Tennessean*, May 25, 1961; NCLC minutes, June 3, 1961, folder 24, box 75, KMSP; *Jackson State-Times*, May 28, 1961 (Lillard and Ed King quotations); *Birmingham Post-Herald*, May 29, 1961; *Baltimore Afro-American*, June 10, 1961; *Pittsburgh Courier*, June 10, 1961; Walter L. Wallace to Dr. King, May 24, 1961, folder 8, and "Freedom Riders Call for Volunteers," press release, May 28, 1961, folder 7, both in box 8, SNCCP.
26. Roster of Freedom Riders, Groups 3 and 4, May 28, 1961, MSCP; Brooks and Harbour interviews; Charles David Myers, interview by author, June 23, 2005; *New York Times*, May 29, 1961 (first and second quotations); *Montgomery Advertiser*, May 29, 1961; *Nashville Tennessean*, May 29–30, 1961; *Jackson Daily News*, May 29, 1961; *Atlanta Journal*, May 29, 1961; *Baltimore Afro-American*, June 10, 1961; *Birmingham Post-Herald*, May 29, 1961; Hampton and Fayer, *Voices of Freedom*, 94 (third quotation); *Jackson Clarion-Ledger*, May 28, 29 (fourth quotation), 1961. See also Leonard's interview in the documentary "Ain't Scared of Your Jails."
27. *New York Times*, May 28 (first quotation), 29 (second quotation), 1961; *Baltimore Afro-American*, June 10, 1961; Reeves, *President Kennedy*, 143–144. See also the *Wall Street Journal* editorial reprinted in the *Jackson Daily News*, May 27, 1961. Sharply critical of the Kennedy administration, the editorial declared: "In this particular case the trouble was deliberately provoked. The so-called freedom riders went looking for trouble, in one of the most likely parts of the South, and they found it. The local and state authorities failed, in the beginning at least, in their duties to prevent violence and maintain law and order. That was said to require Federal intervention, and perhaps it did. But the present Administration sometimes seems almost as zealous in this matter as some of the agitators. It seems to believe that by fast, firm action it can clear up this whole question of segregation in the near future. If that is indeed the view at the Justice Department, we fear it is an illusion."
28. Raines, *My Soul is Rested*, 127 (first quotation); Farmer, *Lay Bare the Heart*, 17 (second quotation), 18–22; Zinn, *SNCC*, 52; *Jackson State-Times*, May 29, 1961 (Gilfoy quotations); *Jackson Clarion-Ledger*, May 30, 1961; *Jackson Daily News*, May 30, 1961; *Baltimore Afro-American*, June 10, 17, 1961; Lewis, *Walking with the Wind*, 170; Holloway, "Travel Notes from a Deep South Tourist," 7–8 (Holloway quotations); Dietrich interview.
29. *New York Times*, May 25, 30 (first quotation); *Montgomery Advertiser*, May 25, 30 (second and third quotations), 1961; *Birmingham Post-Herald*, May 29, 1961; *Birmingham News*, May 29, 1961; *Baltimore Afro-American*, June 10, 1961; McWhorter, *Carry Me Home*, 239–241; Bass, *Taming the Storm*, 181.
30. *New Orleans Times-Picayune*, May 29–June 2, 1961; *New York Times*, May 30, 1961; *Jackson Daily News*, May 29, 1961; *Jackson State-Times*, May 29, 1961; Powell, "When Hate Came to Town," 416; Meier and Rudwick, *CORE*, 138–140; Roster of Freedom Riders, Group 5, May 30, 1961, MSCP; *Jet* 20 (June 8, 1961): 42.
31. Marshall interview, JFKL; *New York Times*, May 27, 30 (first, second, and fourth quotations), 1961; *Montgomery Advertiser*, May 30, 1961; *Birmingham News*, May 26–27, 1961; *Baltimore Afro-American*, June 3, 10, 1961; Branch, *Parting the Waters*, 478; Guthman, *We Band of Brothers*, 175; "Freedom Riders Force a Test," *Newsweek* 57 (June 5, 1961): 22; Schlesinger, *Robert Kennedy and His Times*, 300; Barnes, *Journey from Jim Crow*, 86–107, 134–135 (third quotation), 137, 169–170; Viorst, *Fire in the Streets*, 158; Hilty, *Robert Kennedy*, 329; Doar interview; Dixon, "Civil Rights in Transportation and the ICC," 198–217. Lewis, *Portrait of a Decade*, 117–118, characterized the ICC as "centipedal." See also the booklet "Before the ICC . . ." and related documents in box 1, Records of Burke Marshall,

USDJ/CRD; Reverend Robert E. Hughes (Alabama Council on Human Relations executive director) to ICC, May 19, 1961, RD 195, box 20, Investigative Report Case Files, ICCR; and Robert W. Ginnane (Office of the General Counsel), memorandum to ICC Commissioners, June 16, 1961, box 1, Correspondence and Unnumbered Cases Relating to Complaints, 1961–69, ICCR.

32. *New York Times*, May 30–31 (quotations), 1961; Roster of Freedom Riders, Group 5, May 30, 1961, MSCP; Davis and Davis interview; Freedom Rider application, Glenda Gaither, section 441, reel 43, COREP; Freedom Rider application, James K. Davis, section 443, reel 43, COREP; Gaither, Nixon, and Lafayette interviews; Robert Heller, interview by author; November 8, 2001, June 23, 2005; Robert Heller, interview by Susan Glisson, November 9, 2001, UMFRC; Sandra Nixon, interview by Susan Glisson, November 10, 1961, UMFRC; *Baltimore Afro-American*, June 10, 1961; *Jackson Daily News*, May 31, 1961; *Jackson Clarion-Ledger*, May 31, 1961; *Jackson State-Times*, May 31, 1961; *Birmingham Post-Herald*, May 31, 1961; *Montgomery Advertiser*, May 31, 1961; Raines, *My Soul Is Rested*, 126–127; Peck, *Freedom Ride*, 143–146; Halberstam, *The Children*, 342–345; Viorst, *Fire in the Streets*, 158; Barnes, *Journey from Jim Crow*, 166; Holloway, "Travel Notes from a Deep South Tourist," 7 (last two quotations); Farmer, *Lay Bare the Heart*, 19–21. Betsy Wyckoff to Gordon Carey, June 15, 1961, Jesse Harris, typescript, June 24, 1961, and Gordon Harris to Dear Folks, June 26, 1961, all in section 448, reel 44, COREP.

33. Farmer, *Lay Bare the Heart*, 21 (first quotation); *New York Times*, May 31, 1961 (second and third quotations); Southern Regional Council, *The Freedom Ride* (Atlanta: Southern Regional Council, 1961); Leslie Dunbar, "The Freedom Ride," *New South* 16 (July/August 1961): 9–10; Dunbar interview. See also the documents on the Southern Regional Council's reaction to the Freedom Rides in reels 59, 111, and 112, SRCP.

34. *Montgomery Advertiser*, May 31, June 1, 1961; *New York Times*, May 31, June 1, 1961; *Birmingham Post-Herald*, May 31, June 1, 1961; *Birmingham News*, May 30 (first quotation), May 31, June 1, 1961; *Baltimore Afro-American*, June 10, 1961; "Kennedy's Call to B'ham," May 15, 1961, typescript, box 10, RFKP (second quotation); Bass, *Taming the Storm*, 181–182; McWhorter, *Carry Me Home*, 242; Schlesinger, *Robert Kennedy and His Times*, 296; Branch, *Parting the Waters*, 443–444; Doar interview; Marshall interview, JFKL; Kennedy and Marshall interview, JFKL.

35. *New York Times*, June 2, 1961 (quotations); *Montgomery Advertiser*, June 1–2, 1961; *Birmingham News*, June 1, 1961; *Birmingham Post-Herald*, June 2, 1961; *Jackson Daily News*, June 2, 1961; *Jackson Clarion-Ledger*, June 2, 1961; *Christian Science Monitor*, June 2, 1961; *Baltimore Afro-American*, June 10, 1961; *Pittsburgh Courier*, June 10, 1961; Manis, *A Fire You Can't Put Out*, 280–282. A twenty-year-old Cornell junior, Sterling was the son of two prominent New York writers, Philip and Dorothy Sterling. The latter was the author of several well-known children's books, including the novel *Mary Jane*, the story of a young black girl's experiences at an integrated school. *New York Times*, May 31, 1961; Freedom Rider application, Peter Sterling, section 441, reel 43, COREP.

36. *New York Times*, June 3, 1961 (quotations); *Montgomery Advertiser*, June 3, 1961; *Birmingham Post-Herald*, June 3, 1961; *Baltimore Afro-American*, June 10, 1961; Bass, *Taming the Storm*, 182–183; Yarbrough, *Judge Frank Johnson*, 81.

37. *Birmingham News*, June 3, 1961 (first quotation); *New York Times*, June 3, 1961 (all other quotations); *Montgomery Advertiser*, June 3, 1961.

38. *Birmingham News*, June 3, 1961 (first and third quotations); *Montgomery Advertiser*, June 3, 4 (second quotation), 6 (fourth quotation), 1961; *Birmingham Post-Herald*, June 3–5, 1961; Yarbrough, *Judge Frank Johnson*, 81–82.

39. *Birmingham Post-Herald*, June 3, 1961 (first quotation); *Atlanta Journal*, June 3, 1961 (second quotation); *New York Times*, June 3, 1961; *Montgomery Advertiser*, June 3, 1961; *Baltimore Afro-American*, June 10, 1961; *Birmingham News*, June 3, 1961.

40. *Montgomery Advertiser*, June 3, 1961; *Jackson Clarion-Ledger*, June 3, 1961; *Jackson Daily News*, June 1, 3, 1961; *Baltimore Afro-American*, June 10, 1961; Roster of Freedom Riders, Groups 6 and 7, June 2, 1961, MSCP; Fleming, *Soon We Will Not Cry*, 85–86. Fertig later allowed a number of Freedom Riders to use his Chicago home as an unofficial headquarters for fund-raising and other movement activities. On Cordell Reagon, see Branch, *Parting the Waters*, 513, 524–528, 531–537, 558; Carson, *In Struggle*, 56–58, 60; and Zinn, *SNCC*, 14, 123–127, 132–134.

41. *Birmingham News*, June 3, 1961; *New York Times*, June 3, 1961; *Baltimore Afro-American*, June 10, 1961; *Montgomery Advertiser*, June 4, 1961 (quotations); Marshall interview, JFKL; Doar interview. On the Little Rock case, see *Cooper v. Aaron*, 358 U. S. 1 (1958); Freyer, *The Little Rock Crisis*; and Patterson, *Brown v. Board of Education*, 112.

42. Wofford, *Of Kennedys and Kings*, 157; *Montgomery Advertiser*, June 3–6, 1961; *New York Times*, June 3–4, 1961 (Truman and Seligson quotations); *Baltimore Afro-American*, June 10, 17 (Barbee quotation), 1961; *CORE-lator* (June 1961): 3. In March 1960 Truman made similarly disparaging remarks about the sit-in movement, declaring: "If anybody came to my store and tried to stop business, I'd throw him out." *New York Times*, June 3, 1961. Rabbi Seligson was speaking to the Reform congregation at the Central Synagogue, located at Lexington Avenue and Fifty-first Street.

Chapter 8: Make Me a Captive, Lord

1. *The Hymnbook* (Atlanta: Presbyterian Church in the United States, 1955), 308. The lyrics of this traditional "nonviolent" hymn were written by George Matheson in 1890.

2. *New York Times,* June 5–6 (quotations), 1961; Peck, *Freedom Ride,* 154–156; *Philadelphia Inquirer,* June 5, 1961; *Baltimore Afro-American,* June 17, 1961; *Pittsburgh Courier,* June 17, 1961; *Jackson Advocate,* June 10, 1961. On the crucial role of the media in the civil rights struggle, see Richard Lentz, *Symbols, the News Magazines, and Martin Luther King* (Baton Rouge: Louisiana State University Press, 1990).

3. "The South and the Freedom Riders" (quotations). On the daily press coverage, see the *New York Times,* the *Washington Post,* and the *Atlanta Constitution* during the period June 1–15, 1961; the civil rights scrapbooks for 1961 at the Birmingham Public Library (BPL); and the voluminous clippings compiled by the Mississippi State Sovereignty Commission (MSCP). The latter two sources contain few clippings from newspapers outside of Mississippi and Alabama. For an analysis of magazine coverage of the Freedom Rides, see Lentz, *Symbols, the News Magazines, and Martin Luther King,* 50–60. Lentz focuses on *Time, Newsweek,* and *U.S. News and World Report.*

4. "Asking for Trouble—and Getting It," 49 (quotation). *Life*'s first story on the Freedom Rides, "Bloody Beatings, Burning Bus in the South," appeared in the May 26, 1961, issue (vol. 50, pp. 22–25).

5. Lentz, *Symbols, the News Magazines, and Martin Luther King,* 54–57; *Pittsburgh Courier,* June 10, 1961; *Jet* 20 (June 8, 1961): 20–21; "Label U.S. Racial Violence 'Shot Heard 'Round the World,' " *Jet* 20 (June 22, 1961): 16–17; "Uncle Sam, Get That Monkey off Your Back," *Jet* 20 (July 13, 1961): 8; "The Historic Image," and "The Test of Nonviolence," *Nation* 192 (June 3, 1961): 469–470; "Is South Headed for Race War?" *U.S. News and World Report* 50 (June 5, 1961): 42–48; "Let Us Try, at Least, to Understand," *National Review* 10 (June 3, 1961): 338; "Freedom Riders," *New Republic* 144 (June 5, 1961): 5; Gerald W. Johnson, "Who Turned the Bull Loose?" in ibid., 20; Helen Fuller, "We, the People of Alabama . . .," ibid., 21–23; "Freedom Riders Force a Test," 18–20, 21–23 (quotations). See also "Freedom Riders: Cracks in the Levee," *America* 105 (May 27, 1961): 358; "Violence in Alabama," *America* 105 (June 3, 1961): 388; "The Negro Tries Passive Resistance," *New York Times Magazine* (May 28, 1961): 12–13; "Days of Violence in the South," *Newsweek* 57 (May 29, 1961): 21–22; Booker and Gaffney, "Eyewitness Report"; Still, "Freedom Riders Gather"; "Seeking a Damper for Racial Strife," *Business Week* (June 3, 1961): 22–23; "Trouble in Alabama," *Time* 77 (May 26, 1961): 16–17; "Rolling On," *Time* 77 (June 9, 1961): 15–16; "Violence in Alabama," *Commonweal* 74 (June 2, 1961): 244; "A Question of Responsibility," *Commonweal* 74 (June 9, 1961): 267; W. D. Patterson, "The Calloused Conscience," *Saturday Review* 44 (June 10, 1961): 28; "Tensions and Justice," *Newsweek* 57 (June 12, 1961): 37–38; and "Race Tension and the Law," *U.S. News and World Report* 50 (June 12, 1961): 85.

6. Meier and Rudwick, *CORE,* 139–140; *New York Times,* May 31–June 6, 1961; *Pittsburgh Courier,* June 10, 1961; *Philadelphia Inquirer,* June 5, 1961; *Atlanta Journal,* June 3, 1961; *Jackson Clarion-Ledger,* June 2, 1961; *Baltimore Afro-American,* June 10, 24, July 1, 1961; *Jet* 20 (June 29, 1961): 49; Alex Poinsett, "Who Speaks for the Negro? Many Voices in Harmony as Freedom Struggle Mounts," *Jet* 20 (July 6, 1961): 14–23; *Jet* 20 (July 6, 1961): 30; *Voice of the Movement,* June 30, 1961, in folder 8, box 76, KMSP; Lillard and Gaither interviews. On the summit and John Kennedy's first presidential visit to Europe, see Reeves, *President Kennedy,* 143–174.

7. Lewis, *Walking with the Wind,* 169–170; Farmer, *Lay Bare the Heart,* 11–22; Carmichael, *Ready for Revolution,* 194–198; Carson, *In Struggle,* 38; Meier and Rudwick, *CORE,* 140; Robert Martinson, "Prison Notes of a Freedom Rider," *Nation* (January 6, 1962): 4; Holloway, "Travel Notes from a Deep South Tourist"; Gaither, Lafayette, and Thomas interviews; Haley interview, RBOHC; Marvin Rich, interview by James Mosby Jr., November 6, 1969, RBOHC; *New York Times,* June 6, 8, 1961; *Jackson State-Times,* June 1, 5 (quotations), 6, 8, 1961; *Jackson Daily News,* June 1, 8, 1961; *Jackson Clarion-Ledger,* June 4, 6 (fourth quotation), 1961; *Baltimore Afro-American,* June 24, 1961; *Pittsburgh Courier,* June 24, 1961; *Jet* 20 (June 22, 1961): 6–7, 42; *Jet* 20 (July 6, 1961): 30.

8. Roster of Freedom Riders, Group 8, June 6, 1961, MSCP; Rogers, *Righteous Lives,* 126, 129; Doratha Smith-Simmons, interview by author, June 27, 2005; Alice Thompson, interview by Kim Lacy Rogers, July 25, 1988, ARC; *Jackson Daily News,* June 1 (Gilfoy quotation), 6, 1961; Alex Poinsett, "Ten Biggest Lies About Freedom Riders," *Jet* 20 (June 22, 1961): 12–14; *Jet* 20 (June 22, 1961): 5; *New York Times,* June 6, 7 (Spencer quotation), 1961; *Jackson Clarion-Ledger,* June 1, 7, 1961. Weber served as the group leader. Abraham Bassford IV, interview by author, August 22, 2005.

9. Roster of Freedom Riders, Groups 9 and 10, June 7, 1961, MSCP; *New York Times,* June 6–7, 1961; *Jackson Clarion-Ledger,* June 5, 8, 1961; *Jackson Daily News,* June 9, 1961; Reginald Green, interview by author, August 11, 2005; Michael Audain, interview by Susan Glisson, November 9, 2001, UMFRC; Michael Audain, interview by author, November 10, 2001. Audain's father, who disapproved of the Freedom Rides, put up five hundred dollars in bail money to secure his son's release in early July. Deeply affected by his experiences in Mississippi, Audain worked as a social worker for twenty years and taught at the University of British Columbia's School of Communications and Regional Planning. He did not return to Mississippi until November 2001.

10. *Jackson Daily News,* June 8, 1961 (quotations); Farmer, *Lay Bare the Heart,* 12–14; Poinsett, "Who Speaks for the Negro?"; *Baltimore Afro-American,* July 1, 1961; *Pittsburgh Courier,* July 1, 1961.

11. Farmer, *Lay Bare the Heart,* 14–15 (quotations); *Baltimore Afro-American,* June 10, 17 (final quotation), 24, 1961; Carmichael, *Ready for Revolution,* 195–196. Set in the 1930s South, Lee's novel focuses on the interrelated experiences of a black man falsely accused of rape and a courageous white lawyer named Atticus Finch. In May and June 1961, it hovered near the top of the *New York Times* best-seller list. *New York Times,* May 21, 1961. In 1962 a Hollywood movie based on the novel and starring Gregory Peck as Finch became one of the first pro-civil-rights films to reach a mass audience. Horton Foote wrote the screenplay. Harper Lee, *To Kill a Mockingbird* (Philadelphia: J. P. Lippincott, 1960); *To Kill a Mockingbird* (University City, CA: MCA Videocassette, 1981).

12. Roster of Freedom Riders, Group 11, June 8, 1961, MSCP; Freedom Rider application, Gwendolyn Greene, section 441, reel 43, COREP; *New York Times*, June 8–9, 1961; *Jackson State-Times*, June 8, 1961 (quotation); *Jackson Daily News*, June 8, 1961; *Jackson Clarion-Ledger*, June 9, 1961; *Baltimore Afro-American*, June 17, 1961; *Pittsburgh Courier*, June 17, 24, 1961; Carmichael, *Ready for Revolution*, 192 (quotation), 193; *Washington Post*, August 4, 2004; Travis Britt, interview by James Mosby Jr., September 14, 1968, RBOHC; Mulholland interview; Joan Trumpauer Mulholland, interview by Susan Glisson, November 10, 1961, UMFRC.

13. Roster of Freedom Riders, Group 12, June 9, 1961, MSCP; *Jackson Daily News*, June 9–10, 1961 (quotations); *Jackson Clarion-Ledger*, June 10, 1961; *Pittsburgh Courier*, June 10, 17, 1961; *Baltimore Afro-American*, June 17, 1961; *Jet* 20 (June 22, 1961): 5; *Washington Evening Star*, June 9, 1961; Myers interview. On Motley's long and distinguished career with the NAACP Legal Defense Fund, see Constance Baker Motley, *Equal Justice Under Law: An Autobiography* (New York: Farrar, Straus, and Giroux, 1998). Derrick Bell later taught at Harvard Law School and wrote several influential books on the racial aspects of American culture. See Derrick A. Bell, *And We Are Not Saved: The Elusive Quest for Racial Justice* (New York: Basic Books, 1987); Bell, *Faces at the Bottom of the Well: The Permanence of Racism* (New York: Basic Books, 1992); and Bell, *Confronting Authority: Reflections of an Ardent Protester* (Boston: Beacon Press, 1994).

14. Roster of Freedom Riders, Groups 13 and 14, June 10–11, 1961, MSCP; *Jackson Daily News*, June 10–12, 14, 1961; *Jackson Clarion-Ledger*, June 12, 14 (Horne quotations), 1961; *Washington Evening Star*, June 11–12, 1961; *New York Times*, June 11–12, 1961; Steve Green, interview by author, November 9, 2001; Steve Green, interview by Susan Glisson, November 10, 2001, UMFRC; Steve Green, "Freedom Rider Diary: Forty Years Later" (2001, unpublished ms. in author's possession), 1–12, 2 (Coffin quotation).

15. Marv Davidov, interview by author, November 9, 2001; Marv Davidov, interview by Susan Glisson, November 9, 2001, UMFRC; Ed Felien, "The History of Honeywell as Seen from South Minneapolis," *Pulse of the Twin Cities* 3 (June 16–22, 1999): 3–5; Noam Chomsky to "whom it may concern," October 2, 1995, in author's possession; Marv Davidov, "Formal Education and Practical Experience in Nonviolent Social Change Movements" (November 2001, typescript in author's possession); Peck, *Freedom Ride*, 150–151. In 2001 Davidov served as the director of the Midwest Institute for Social Transformation, sponsored by the Meridel Leseur Center for Peace and Justice, in Minneapolis. Zev Aelony, interview by author, November 9, 2001; Zev Aelony, interview by Susan Glisson, November 9, 2001, UMFRC; Due and Due, *Freedom in the Family*, 41–43, 175–179; www.crmvet.org/vet/aelony.htm; G. McLeod Bryan, *These Few Also Paid a Price: Southern Whites Who Fought for Civil Rights* (Macon: Mercer University Press, 2001); Zev Aelony, "Back on the Road: Freedom Riders Return to the New South," *Pulse of the Twin Cities* 5 (December 19, 2001); Robert Baum, interview by author, November 9–10, 2001 (quotation); Robert Baum, interview by Susan Glisson, November 9, 2001, UMFRC; Dave Morton, interview by author, November 10, 2001; Claire O'Connor, interview by author, November 9, 2001 (quotation); Claire O'Connor, interview by Susan Glisson, November 10, 2001, UMFRC. On Tobias Simon, see Florence Morgenroth, "Organization and Activities of the American Civil Liberties Union in Miami, 1955–1966" (M.A. thesis, University of Miami, 1966).

16. *New York Times*, June 13, 1961; *Montgomery Advertiser*, June 13–15, 1961; *Jackson Clarion-Ledger*, June 15, 1961; *Jackson Daily News*, June 21, 1961; Gaither interview; Harold E. Fey, "Freedom Rides at N.C.C.," *Christian Century* 78 (June 21, 1961): 766–767.

17. Freedom Rider application, Danny Thompson, section 441, reel 43, COREP; *Jackson Daily News*, May 24, June 12–15, 1961; *Jackson Clarion-Ledger*, June 12, 13 (first quotation); *Washington Evening Star*, June 13, 1961; Farmer, *Lay Bare the Heart*, 22 (third quotation); Carmichael, *Ready for Revolution*, 198–202. On Parchman's gruesome history, see David M. Oshinsky, *"Worse than Slavery": Parchman Farm and the Ordeal of Jim Crow Justice* (New York: Free Press, 1996), especially pp. 233–236, which deal with the Freedom Riders' experiences. The facetious invitation, which appeared in the *Jackson Daily News* on June 24, 1961, is quoted in ibid., 233–234.

18. Freedom Rider applications, C. Donald Alstork, Israel Dresner, Martin Freedman, Petty McKinney, James O'Connor, et al., section 116, reel 25, COREP; Israel Dresner, interview by author, November 9–10, 1961; Martin Freedman, interview by author, November 8, 1961; Martin Freedman, interview by Susan Glisson, November 9, 2001, UMFRC; Ralph Roy, interview by author, November 9, 1961; Ralph Roy, interview by Susan Glisson, November 10, 2001, UMFRC; Ralph Roy, "A Freedom Rider's Report from Jail," *New York Amsterdam News*, June 24, 1961; Ralph Roy, "Freedom Ride" (2001, unpublished ms. in author's possession); Alan Levine, interview by Susan Glisson, November 10, 2001; Alan Levine, interview by author, November 8, 1961; Robert McAfee Brown, "I Was a Freedom Rider," *Presbyterian Life* (August 1, 1961): 10–11, 32–33; Robert McAfee Brown and Frank Randall, *The Freedom Riders: A Clergyman's View, an Historian's View* (New York: CORE, 1962), 1–9, rpt. from *Amherst College Alumni News* 14 (1961): 11–17; *New York Times*, June 13–15, 1961 (quotations); *Washington Evening Star*, June 13–15, 1961; *Baltimore Afro-American*, July 1, 1961; Francis and Laura Randall, "Freedom Riders' Diary" (1961, unpublished ms. in author's possession), 1–14.

19. Brown, "I Was a Freedom Rider," 11 (quotations); Dresner, Freedman, and Howard interviews; John W. Collier, interview by author, August 19, 2005; Roy, "A Freedom Rider's Report from Jail"; Roy, "Freedom Ride," 3; *Baltimore Afro-American*, June 24, 1961. On the Harris incident, see *Pittsburgh Courier*, June 10, 1961; Baltimore *Afro-American*, June 10, 1961; *Jet* 20 (June 1, 1961): 13; *Jet* 20 (June 15, 1961): 53; and *Washington Evening Star*, May 30, June 7 (first quotation), 1961. When the Interfaith Riders arrived in Sumter, Jim McCain was apparently in New Orleans recruiting and training prospective Freedom Riders. Meier and Rudwick, *CORE*, 139–140.

20. Brown, "I Was a Freedom Rider," 32; Roy, "Freedom Ride," 3–4; Dresner and Freedman interviews; *Washington Evening Star*, June 15, 1961; *New York Times*, June 15, 1961; *Baltimore Afro-American*, June 24, July 1, 1961; *Pittsburgh Courier*, June 24, 1961; *St. Petersburg Times*, June 15, 1961; Rabby, *The Pain and the Promise*, 135; RD 68, box 10, Investigative Report Case Files, ICCR. On Farris Bryant's opposition to desegregation, see David Colburn and Richard K. Scher, *Florida's Gubernatorial Politics in the Twentieth Century* (Tallahassee: University Presses of Florida, 1980), 78–80, 226–228, 232–235, 289.

21. Brown, "I Was a Freedom Rider," 10, 32–33; *New York Times*, June 16–17, 1961; *St. Petersburg Times*, June 16, 1961; *Tallahassee Democrat*, June 16–17, 1961; *Baltimore Afro-American*, June 24, July 1, 1961; Roy, "Freedom Ride," 1–8; Roy, Freedman, Dresner (quotation), Collier, and Levine interviews; Rabby, *The Pain and the Promise*, 135–138.

22. *New York Times*, June 12 (first quotation), 16–18, 1961; *St. Petersburg Times*, June 17–19, 1961; *Baltimore Afro-American*, June 24, 1961; Rabby, *The Pain and the Promise*, 136 (second quotation); Dresner, Collier, Freedman, and Roy interviews; Roy, "Freedom Ride," 5–6 (third quotation). On Poland, see RD 44, box 7, and RD 47 and 54, box 8, Investigative Report Case Files, ICCR.

23. Randall and Randall, "Freedom Riders' Diary," 14–20; Brown and Randall, *The Freedom Riders*, 6–9; Gordon Negen, "I Went on a Freedom Ride," *Reformed Journal* (July–Aug. 1961): 4–6. *St. Petersburg Times*, June 16, 17 (Diamond and Smith quotations), 18, 19, 1961; *Tampa Tribune*, June 16–18, 1961; *New York Times*, June 17–18, 1961, September 20, 1993; *Ocala Banner*, June 17, 1961; RD 62, box 9, and RD 141, box 17, Investigative Report Case Files, ICCR; Clark Bouwman, interview by author, May 28, 2005. On the racial history of St. Petersburg, see Raymond Arsenault, *St. Petersburg and the Florida Dream, 1888–1950* (Gainesville: University Press of Florida, 1996). On the spring training desegregation controversy, see Jack E. Davis, "Baseball's Reluctant Challenge: Desegregating Major League Spring Training Sites, 1961–1964," *Journal of Sport History* 19 (Summer 1992): 144–162.

24. *New York Times*, June 18, 1961; *St. Petersburg Times*, June 19, 1961; *Tallahassee Democrat*, June 17–22, 23 (quotations), 1961; *Jackson Daily News*, June 23, 1961; Rabby, *The Pain and the Promise*, 137–139; Collier, Dresner, Freedman, and Roy interviews. See also *Priscilla G. Stephens v. City of Tallahassee*, Law No. 10085 (1962); and *Israel Dresner et al. v. City of Tallahassee*, Law No. 10084 (Fla. 1961, 1962), and 375 U.S. 136 (1963).

25. Lewis, *Walking with the Wind*, 170 (first quotation); Farmer, *Lay Bare the Heart*, 22; Oshinsky, *"Worse than Slavery,"* 1, 234 (second and third quotations); Peck, *Freedom Ride*, 147–152; Carmichael, *Ready for Revolution*, 201–203; Meier and Rudwick, *CORE*, 141; Branch, *Parting the Waters*, 483; *Jackson Daily News*, June 14, 16, 18, 1961; *New York Times*, June 16, 1961; Lafayette interview. See also Zinn, *SNCC*, 54–57; and Farmer, *Lay Bare the Heart*, 22–32.

26. Lewis, *Walking with the Wind*, 171–172 (quotations); Peck, *Freedom Ride*, 147–148 (Sullivan quotation); Carmichael, *Ready for Revolution*, 201–203 (quotation); Branch, *Parting the Waters*, 483–484; Oshinsky, *"Worse than Slavery,"* 234–235; Farmer, *Lay Bare the Heart*, 22 (quotation), 23; *Baltimore Afro-American*, July 15, 1961; Freedom Rider application, Terry Sullivan, section 441, reel 43, COREP; Jesse Harris, typescript, June 24, 1961, section 116, reel 25, COREP.

27. *Jackson Clarion-Ledger*, June 16, 1961 (quotations); *Jackson Daily News*, June 16, 1961; *New York Times*, June 16, 1961; *Baltimore Afro-American*, June 24, 1961; Lewis, *Walking with the Wind*, 172; Farmer, *Lay Bare the Heart*, 25; Raines, *My Soul Is Rested*, 127–128; Oshinsky, *"Worse than Slavery,"* 235.

28. Reeves, *President Kennedy*, 178–182; *Jackson Daily News*, June 16, 1961; *Washington Post*, June 16–18, 1961; *Washington Evening Star*, June 16–18, 1961; Roster of Freedom Riders, Fifteenth Group, June 16, 1961, MSCP; Robert Filner, interview by author, November 9, 2001 (quotation); Robert Filner, interview by Susan Glisson, November 9, 2001, UMFRC; Larry Copeland, "Freedom Riders Go South Again," *USA Today*, November 8, 2001, 9D.

29. Branch, *Parting the Waters*, 479–480 (quotation); Lewis, *Walking with the Wind*, 180–181; Carson, *In Struggle*, 38–39; Zinn, *SNCC*, 58; *New York Times*, June 15, 17, 20, 1961; Burke Marshall interview, JFKL; Raines, *My Soul Is Rested*, 227–228, 230–231; Brauer, *John F. Kennedy and the Second Reconstruction*, 114–117; Carmichael, *Ready for Revolution*, 218–224; Schlesinger, *Robert Kennedy and His Times*, 302; Navasky, *Kennedy Justice*, 117–118, 121, 207; Charles M. Payne, *I've Got the Light of Freedom: The Organizing Tradition and the Mississippi Freedom Struggle* (Berkeley: University of California Press, 1995), 107–111; Belford Lawson III, interview by author, September 21, 2005.

30. *Jackson State-Times*, June 18, 1961 (quotation); Payne, *I've Got the Light of Freedom*, 107–111; Lewis, *Walking with the Wind*, 182; Brauer, *John F. Kennedy and the Second Reconstruction*, 112; Wofford, *Of Kennedys and Kings*, 159; *Pittsburgh Courier*, July 1, 1961; *Jet* 20 (July 6, 1961): 58–59.

31. Carson, *In Struggle*, 40; Branch, *Parting the Waters*, 481; Lewis, *Walking with the Wind*, 181; Meier and Rudwick, *CORE*, 127; Brauer, *John F. Kennedy and the Second Reconstruction*, 221; Thomas, *Robert Kennedy*, 179; Carmichael, *Ready for Revolution*, 222–224. See also Wofford, *Of Kennedys and Kings*, 125–126.

32. *Jackson Daily News*, June 20–21 (quotation); *Jackson Clarion-Ledger*, June 20–21, 1961; *Jackson State-Times*, June 18, 1961; *New York Times*, June 21, 1961; Roster of Freedom Riders, Groups 16–19, June 20–25, 1961, MSCP.

33. Roster of Freedom Riders, Group 17, June 21, 1961, MSCP; *New York Times*, June 21, 1961 (first quotation); *Jackson Daily News*, June 21–22, 1961; *Montgomery Advertiser*, June 20–22, 1961; Philip Frieze to Marvin Rich, June 27, 1961, and Marvin Rich to Philip Frieze, June 28, 1961, both in section 448, reel 44, COREP; Freedom Rider applications, Miriam Feingold and Judith Frieze, section 441, reel 43, COREP; Margaret Leonard, interview by author, November 9, 11, 2001; Margaret Leonard, interview by Susan Glisson, November 10, 2001; Mary Little-Vance, interview by author, November 9, 11, 2001 (second quotation); Mary Little-Vance, interview by Susan Glisson, November 10, 2001,

UMFRC; Eugene Patterson interview. Leonard later (1973–1994) worked as a reporter and editor at the *St. Petersburg Times*, the *Palm Beach Post*, the *Miami Herald*, and the *Tallahassee Democrat*.

34. *Jackson Daily News*, June 17, 20, 21 (quotation), July 13, 1961; *Jackson Clarion-Ledger*, June 17–18, 21–22, 25, 1961; Baltimore *Afro-American*, July 1, 8, 1961; *New York Times*, June 22, 1961; Zinn, *SNCC*, 55; Freedom Rider application, Elizabeth Wyckoff, section 441, reel 43, COREP; SNCC press release on Wyckoff case, folder 3, box 8, SNCCP. On Kunstler and the Freedom Riders, see David J. Langum, *William M. Kunstler: The Most Hated Lawyer in America* (New York: New York University Press, 1999), 56–62, 67–68, 75, 237; and William M. Kunstler with Sheila Isenberg, *My Life as a Radical Lawyer* (New York: Birch Lane Press, 1994), 101–107, 116, 118, 126, 189. Kunstler often served as a cooperating attorney for the American Civil Liberties Union. In 1956 he, along with Tobias Simon, helped the ACLU to represent William Worthy in the passport confiscation case. See ibid., 95–97, 102, 137.

35. *New York Times*, June 22, 1961 (quotations); *Jackson Daily News*, June 21, 1961; *Jackson Clarion-Ledger*, June 22, 1961; *Pittsburgh Courier*, July 8, 1961. On Judge Tuttle, see Raines, *My Soul Is Rested*, 343–347, 401–402; Jack Bass, *Unlikely Heroes* (New York: Simon and Schuster, 1981), 15–41; Bass, *Taming the Storm*, 132–133, 140–141, 154, 160, 272, 360, 406, 424, 461, 467; and J. W. Peltason, *Fifty-eight Lonely Men: Southern Federal Judges and School Desegregation* (Urbana: University of Illinois Press, 1971), 26. As a young lawyer in Atlanta during the 1930s, Tuttle helped handle the successful appellate case of Angelo Herndon, a black Communist organizer convicted of violating a Georgia insurrection statute. On the Herndon case, see Charles H. Martin, *The Angelo Herndon Case and Southern Justice* (Baton Rouge: Louisiana State University Press, 1976); Angelo Herndon, *Let Me Live* (New York: Random House, 1937); and David Entin, "Angelo Herndon" (M.A. thesis, University of North Carolina, 1963).

36. *New York Times*, June 24, 1961; *Jackson Daily News*, June 23, 1961; *Jackson Advocate*, June 10, 1961 (quotation); Thomas Armstrong III, interview by author, November 11, 2001; Thomas Armstrong, interview by Susan Glisson, November 9, 2001, UMFRC; Mary Harrison Lee, interview by Susan Glisson, November 10, 2001, UMFRC; Gaither interview; Minutes, NCLC Board meeting, June 14, 1961, folder 24, box 75, KMSP. On Percy Greene, see Dittmer, *Local People*, 74.

37. Payne, *I've Got the Light of Freedom*, 21–102; Dittmer, *Local People*, 29–89; Maryanne Vollers, *Ghosts of Mississippi: The Murder of Medgar Evers, the Trials of Byron De La Beckwith, and the Haunting of the New South* (Boston: Little, Brown, 1995), 8–80; Carmichael, *Ready for Revolution*, 200. See also Davis, *Race Against Time*; and David T. Beito and Linda Royster Beito, "T. R. M. Howard: Pragmatism over Strict Integrationist Ideology in the Mississippi Delta, 1942–1954," in Feldman, ed., *Before Brown*, 68–95. On the Parker lynching, see Smead, *Blood Justice*.

38. Dittmer, *Local People*, 85–89, 118, 120–121 (quotation); Vollers, *Ghosts of Mississippi*, 81–82; *Jackson Daily News*, May 2, 1961; *Jackson Clarion-Ledger*, June 18, 1961; Baltimore *Afro-American*, June 24, 1961; *Jet* 19 (June 1, 1961): 6–7. On Aaron Henry, see Payne, *I've Got the Light of Freedom*, 56–66, 130, 355–356; and Aaron Henry with Constance Curry, *Aaron Henry: The Fire Ever Burning* (Jackson: University Press of Mississippi, 2000). On the rise and fall of COFO, see ibid., 109, 115, 129–132, 137–139, 156–157, 162–163, 203, 211; Dittmer, *Local People*, 200–207, 236–237, 315–318, 343–344; Payne, *I've Got the Light of Freedom*, 62, 130–132, 157–168, 174–229, 239–255, 290–337, 375, 461–462; and Carson, *In Struggle*, 97–100, 111–121, 149–150, 171–173.

39. Dittmer, *Local People*, 98 (quotations), 99, 117–118; Peck, *Freedom Ride*, 153; George Alexander Sewell, *Mississippi Black History Makers* (Jackson: University Press of Mississippi, 1977), 267–275. For documents related to Harvey and Womanpower Unlimited, see boxes 70 and 85, CCHP. Educated at Spelman College (B.A. in economics, 1937) and Columbia University (M.A. in personnel administration, 1950), Harvey (1916–1989) was a trustee of Rust College (1953), served on the Mississippi State Advisory Committee to the U.S. Commission on Civil Rights (1964–1970) and on the board of the Southern Regional Council (1965), and acted as secretary of the Mississippi Ethics Commission (1980–1982). In 1972 she became the first black woman to serve on the board of trustees of the Tuskegee Institute, and in 1974 she became the first black trustee of Millsaps College. See also Tiyi Makeda Morris, "Black Women's Civil Rights Activism in Mississippi: The Story of Womanpower United" (Ph.D. thesis, Purdue University, 2002).

40. *New York Times*, June 18, 21, 1961; Baltimore *Afro-American*, June 24, July 8, 1961; *Jet* 20 (July 6, 1961): 4. On the Episcopal Society for Cultural and Racial Unity and its 1961 Prayer Pilgrimage, see box 52, Episcopal Society for Cultural and Racial Unity Records; and the correspondence in section 442, reel 43, COREP. Debra L. Schultz, *Going South: Jewish Women in the Civil Rights Movement* (New York: New York University Press, 2001), 36–43; Clive Webb, *Fight Against Fear: Southern Jews and Black Civil Rights* (Athens: University of Georgia, 2001), 184–188, 197. One notable exception to the anti–Freedom Rider position taken by Mississippi's Jewish leaders was the Canadian-born Rabbi Perry Nussbaum, who served as an unofficial chaplain to the Jewish Freedom Riders incarcerated at Parchman. On several occasions, he ministered to non-Jewish Riders. "It was in this spirit," Clive Webb writes (186), "that the rabbi conducted the first interracial services ever held in the state of Mississippi." During the late summer of 1961 Nussbaum persuaded Rabbi Irwin Schar of Clarksdale to make periodic visits to Parchman, but a more general effort to enlist other rabbis proved futile. Rabbi Charles Mantinband of Hattiesburg privately expressed some sympathy for the Riders, but he did not become a public supporter. See ibid., 172, 184–188. On Nussbaum and Martinband, see Gary Phillip Zola, "What Price Amos? Perry Nussbaum's Career in Jackson, Mississippi," and Clive Webb, "Big Struggle in a Small Town: Charles Martinband of Hattiesburg, Mississippi," both in *Quiet Voices: Southern Rabbis and Black Civil Rights, 1880s to 1990s*, ed. Mark Bauman and Berkley Kalin (Tuscaloosa: University of Alabama Press, 1998), 213–260.

41. *Pittsburgh Courier*, June 24, 1961; *Baltimore Afro-American*, June 10, 17, 24 (Reuther quotation), 1961; Poinsett, "Ten Biggest Lies About Freedom Riders," 12 (Rockefeller quotation); *Jet* 20 (July 6, 1961): 10; William Goldsmith, "The Cost of Freedom Rides," *Dissent* 4 (Autumn 1961): 499–502; Eric F. Goldman, "Progress–By Moderation *and* Agitation," *New York Times Magazine* (June 18, 1961): 5, 10–12 (quotations). The author of two highly acclaimed books, *Rendezvous with Destiny: A History of Modern American Reform* (New York: Knopf, 1952) and *The Crucial Decade–and After: America 1945–60* (New York: Knopf, 1960), Goldman served as special consultant to President Lyndon Johnson from 1963 to 1966. For several years during the 1960s he also acted as the moderator of the NBC public affairs television program *The Open Mind*. Goldman was not the only historian to offer a historical brief for the Freedom Riders. Leon Litwack, an assistant professor of history at the University of Wisconsin and the author of *North of Slavery* (Chicago: University of Chicago Press, 1961), wrote a widely syndicated newspaper article on the antebellum origins of direct action. In the *New York Times*, June 25, 1961, Litwack's article ran under the provocative headline "Negroes Fought Racism in North—'Freedom Rides' Produced Pre–Civil War Riots." Leon Litwack, interview by author, March 31, 2005. On religious leaders' attitudes toward the Freedom Rides, see *New York Times*, June 13–16,18, 21, 26, 1961; "Freedom Riders: Cracks in the Levee," 358; "Violence in Alabama," *America*, 388; "Violence in Alabama," *Commonweal*, 244; "A Question of Responsibility"; "All, Here and Now," *Christian Century* 78 (June 28, 1961): 787–788; Brown, "I Was a Freedom Rider"; George H. Dunne, "God Bless America!" *America* 105 (June 17, 1961): 442–443; Fey, "Freedom Rides at N.C.C."; "I.C.C. Should Act to Protect Travelers," *Christian Century* 78 (June 14, 1961): 732; "Injunctions and Freedoms," *Commonweal* 74 (June 16, 1961): 292; "Injustice Will Tire First," *Christian Century* 78 (July 26, 1961): 892; and "Our Friend in Jail," *America* 105 (July 1, 1961): 476.
42. Eugene V. Rostow, "The Freedom Riders and the Future," *Reporter* 24 (June 22, 1961): 18–21 (quotations). A member of the Peace Corps National Advisory Council, Rostow experienced a brief confrontation with President Kennedy during a May 19 meeting at the White House. When Rostow urged him to exert "moral leadership" in defense of the Freedom Riders, Kennedy became exercised. Later, as Rostow and the other council members were leaving the meeting, Kennedy complained to Harris Wofford: "What in the world does he think I should do? Doesn't he know I've done more for civil rights than any President in American history? How could any man have done more than I've done?" Reeves, *President Kennedy*, 131–132; Wofford, *Of Kennedys and Kings*, 125–126; *New York Times*, June 25, 1961 (Murrow quotation); *Jet* 20 (July 13, 1961): 8; *Baltimore Afro-American*, June 17 (Johnson quotation), 24 (Bunche quotation), July 8, 1961. In early June, Bunche praised the Freedom Riders during a commencement address at Loyola University in Baltimore. "I am all for them," he declared. "All of the non-white people are properly insisting on their rights to traverse the highways and byways of the world in equality with all other men, with dignity and self-respect, with their heads held high. . . . And they cannot fail in this, just as in America we must not fail to obtain full democracy for all of our citizens. The recent racial incidents in Alabama and Mississippi are deplorable. They could have been avoided, I believe, with a little common sense and tolerance, and were it not for the callous racial attitudes of some state and local authorities, who openly endorse bigotry. Such officials and the relatively few who form the mobs who savagely attack defenseless people are a discredit to a civilized society. They do, moreover, give much aid and comfort to our communist detractors." *Baltimore Afro-American*, June 17, 1961. On Bunche (1904–1971), see Benjamin Rivlin, ed., *Ralph Bunche: The Man and His Times* (New York: Holmes and Meier, 1990); Brian Urquhart, *Ralph Bunche: An American Life* (New York: Norton, 1993); Ben Keppel, *The Work of Democracy: Ralph Bunche, Kenneth B. Clark, Lorraine Hansberry, and the Cultural Politics of Race* (Cambridge: Harvard University Press, 1995); Jonathan Scott Holloway, *Confronting the Veil: Abram Harris, Jr., E. Franklin Frazier, and Ralph Bunche, 1919–1941* (Chapel Hill: University of North Carolina Press, 2002); and Peggy Mann, *Ralph Bunche: UN Peacemaker* (New York: Coward, McCann, and Geoghegan, 1975).
43. *New York Times*, June 23, 1961 (quotations); Eugene Patterson interview. On McGill's career as a liberal Southern journalist, see McGill, *The South and the Southerner*; Martin, *Ralph McGill, Reporter*; Teel, *Ralph Emerson McGill*; Raines, *My Soul Is Rested*, 367-368; and Clark and Raymond Arsenault, *The Changing South and Gene Patterson*, 3–24, 38–41, 291. Born in Tennessee in 1898, McGill worked as a reporter for the *Nashville Banner* before moving to the *Atlanta Constitution* in 1929. During his forty years as a *Constitution* reporter and editor, he championed educational and political reform, racial tolerance, and gradual social change. A founding member of the Southern Regional Council (1944), he won a Pulitzer Prize in 1959 for his editorials condemning the bombing of an Atlanta synagogue. He died in 1969. On the June 1961 Gallup Poll results, see Brauer, *John F. Kennedy and the Second Reconstruction*, 112; Hazel Gaudet Erskine, "The Polls: Race Relations," *Public Opinion Quarterly* 26 (Spring 1962): 145; Hazel Gaudet Erskine, "The Polls: Kennedy as President," *Public Opinion Quarterly* 28 (Summer 1964): 336; and *Jackson Clarion-Ledger*, June 28, 1961 (poll quotation). *Jet* 20 (June 22, 1961): 8. When asked "Do you believe that the non-violence and passive resistance movement is the best way to win civil rights in the SOUTH?" 73.4 percent of the *Jet* poll respondents said yes, 23.1 percent said no, and 3.5 percent had no opinion.
44. Carey interview; *New York Times*, June 25, 1961; *Pittsburgh Courier*, July 8, 1961; Poinsett, "Who Speaks for the Negro?"; *Baltimore Afro-American*, July 1, 1961; Eugene Patterson interview; McWhorter, *Carry Me Home*, 231–232, 238. On Sitton, see Raines, *My Soul Is Rested*, 378–381, 427.
45. Carey interview; *New York Times*, June 28, 1961 (quotations); *Jackson Daily News*, June 27–28, 1961; Jackson *Clarion-Ledger*, June 28, 1961; Ed King to Charles Sherrod, June 26, 1961, folder 8, box 8, SNCCP; minutes, SNCC meeting in Baltimore, July 14–16, 1961, folder 3, box 7, SNCCP.
46. Roster of Freedom Riders, Group 19, June 25, 1961, MSCP; Freedom Rider applications, John Dolan, Mary Hamilton, Marian Kendall, Claude Liggins, Janice Rogers, John Rogers, Marcia

Rosenbaum, Wayne Taylor, section 441, reel 43, COREP; *New York Times*, June 26, 1961; *Jackson Daily News*, June 26, 1961; *Jackson Clarion-Ledger*, June 26, 1961. John Dolan interview by author, August 31, 2005; Norma Libson, Chela Lightchild, and Claude Liggins, interviews by author and Meeghan Kane, August 11, 17, 22, 2005.

Chapter 9: Ain't Gonna Let No Jail House Turn Me 'Round

1. Silverman, *Songs of Protest and Civil Rights*, 56–57.
2. On the climate of fear in the 1950s and early 1960s, see Whitfield, *The Culture of the Cold War*; Schrecker, *Many Are the Crimes*; and Walter Goodman, *The Committee: The Extraordinary Career of the House Committee on Un-American Activities* (New York: Farrar, Straus, and Giroux, 1968). On the issue of race and the Cold War, see Borstelmann, *The Cold War and the Color Line*; Dudziak, *Cold War Civil Rights*; Woods, *Black Struggle, Red Scare*; and Lewis, *The White South and the Red Menace*.
3. *Jackson Daily News*, June 1, 6, 10, 16 (first Pegler quotation), 22 (second Pegler quotation), July 6, 1961; *Jackson Clarion-Ledger*, June 1–16, July 6, 16, 30, 1961. Myers was a high school and college track-and-field athlete attending Central State College on an athletic scholarship. One of the few white students at Central State, he was raised in a working-class family in Noblesville, Indiana. Myers interview. See also the voluminous records of surveillance and investigation for the year 1961 in MSCP.
4. *Jackson Daily News*, June 22 (quotations), July 2, 1961; *Jackson Clarion-Ledger*, June 23, 1961 (Dabney quotations).
5. Bartley, *The Rise of Massive Resistance*, 180 (quotation), 181–183, 222–224; *Jackson Daily News*, July 1, 1961. On the Mississippi State Sovereignty Commission, see Yatsuhiro Katagiri, *The Mississippi State Sovereignty Commission: Civil Rights and States' Rights* (Jackson: University Press of Mississippi, 2001); McMillen, *The Citizens' Council*, 253–254, 334–337, 347; Dittmer, *Local People*, 58–60, 80–83; Sarah Rowe-Simms, "The Mississippi State Sovereignty Commission: An Agency History," *Journal of Mississippi History* 61 (1999): 29–58; Gregory C. Crofton, "Defending Segregation: Mississippi State Sovereignty Commission and the Press" (M.A. thesis, University of Mississippi, 2000); Laura Ingram Moore, "The Mississippi State Sovereignty Commission: State-Supported Resistance to Desegregation" (M.A. thesis, Wake Forest University, 1997); Melissa Lynn Finley, "But I Was a Practical Segregationist: Erle Johnston and the Mississippi State Sovereignty Commission, 1960–1968" (M.A. thesis, University of Southern Mississippi, 2000); and Erle Johnston, *Mississippi's Defiant Years, 1953–1973: An Interpretive Documentary with Personal Experiences* (Forest, MS: Lake Harbor, 1990). On Florida's notorious Johns Committee, see James A. Schnur, "Cold Warriors in the Hot Sunshine: The Johns Committee's Assault on Civil Liberties in Florida, 1956–1965" (M.A. thesis, University of South Florida, 1995). The Johns Committee and the Mississippi State Sovereignty Commission shared information on the Freedom Riders. See the Florida Legislative Investigation Committee Records, Record Group 940, Series 1486, State Archives of Florida, Tallahassee.
6. *Birmingham News*, May 19–26, June 29, 1961; *Birmingham Post-Herald*, May 20–26, 1961; *Montgomery Advertiser*, May 28, June 9, 1961; *Jackson Daily News*, June 9, 16, 21, 24, 1961 (quotations); *Jackson Clarion-Ledger*, June 23, July 13, 1961; *New York Times*, June 15, 1961; *Citizens' Council*, June 1961; *New Orleans States-Item*, July 19, 1961.
7. *Jackson Daily News*, June 29 (first and second quotations), July 1, 16, 1961; *Jackson Clarion-Ledger*, June 30 (third through seventh quotations), July 2 (Richardson quotations), July 3, 1961; *New York Times*, June 30, 1961 (Carey quotation); *Jackson State-Times*, July 3, 1961; *Baltimore Afro-American*, July 15, 1961; Freedom Rider applications, Katherine Pleune and James Wahlstrom, section 441, reel 43, COREP; Carol Ruth Silver, "The Diary of a Freedom Rider," ms. in author's possession, 75–76; Carol Ruth Silver, interview by Susan Glisson, November 10, 2001, UMFRC; Carol Ruth Silver, interview by author, November 10, 2001, June 2, 2005.
8. *Citizens' Council*, June 1961 (quotations); *Jackson Clarion-Ledger*, July 4 (Winchell quotation), 13 (Patterson quotation), 1961; *New York Times*, May 31, June 1, 1961; *Jackson Daily News*, July 16, 1961. When hard evidence against Pleune and Wahlstrom failed to materialize, Birdsong tried to distance himself from the anti-Communist campaign against them. *Baltimore Afro-American*, July 15, 1961.
9. Lewis, *Walking with the Wind*, 172 (quotations), 173; Peck, *Freedom Ride*, 143–152; Farmer, *Lay Bare the Heart*, 23–30; Carmichael, *Ready for Revolution*, 202–210; Branch, *Parting the Waters*, 484–485; Oshinsky, "*Worse than Slavery*," 235–236; Halberstam, *The Children*, 345–347, 410–411; Lafayette, Lafayette and Thomas, Thomas, Silver, and Davis and Davis interviews; Silver, "Diary of a Freedom Rider," 59ff.; Green, "Freedom Rider Diary—Forty Years Later," 6–7 (quotation); *Jackson Daily News*, July 5, 1961; *Pittsburgh Courier*, July 15, 1961; *Louisiana Weekly*, September 30, 1961.
10. Davidov, Lafayette, and Lafayette and Thomas interviews; Lewis, *Walking with the Wind*, 173; Farmer, *Lay Bare the Heart*, 23–30; Carmichael, *Ready for Revolution*, 206–208; Peck, *Freedom Ride*, 149–152 (quotations); Silver, "Diary of a Freedom Rider"; Branch, *Parting the Waters*, 484–485; Green, "Freedom Rider Diary—Forty Years Later," 6–7. On Mahoney, see Zinn, *SNCC*, 55–57.
11. Lewis, *Walking with the Wind*, 173 (quotation); Silver, "Diary of a Freedom Rider"; Peck, *Freedom Ride*, 143–144; Lafayette, Lafayette and Thomas, and Davis and Davis interviews; Branch, *Parting the Waters*, 484–485; Green, "Freedom Rider Diary—Forty Years Later," 6–9; Halberstam, *The Children*, 347–348; Carmichael, *Ready for Revolution*, 202–210.
12. Green, "Freedom Rider Diary—Forty Years Later," 7 (quotations); Green interview.
13. Hampton and Fayer, *Voices of Freedom*, 94–95 (quotations); Farmer, *Lay Bare the Heart*, 27 (second part of Bevel quotation); Lewis, *Walking with the Wind*, 173; Peck, *Freedom Ride*, 149; Zinn, *SNCC*, 40, 54–57; Oshinsky, "*Worse than Slavery*," 235–236; Carmichael, *Ready for Revolution*, 199, 205; Branch,

Parting the Waters, 484–485; Lafayette interview; Jackson *Clarion-Ledger*, July 5, 1961. See also the interview with Fred Leonard in the documentary "Ain't Scared of Your Jails." Leonard later married fellow Freedom Rider Joy Reagon.

14. Farmer, *Lay Bare the Heart*, 27–28 (quotations); Lafayette interview; Halberstam, *The Children*, 410–411; Carmichael, *Ready for Revolution*, 205–206.

15. Farmer, *Lay Bare the Heart*, 29–30 (quotations); Carmichael, *Ready for Revolution*, 210; *Jackson Clarion-Ledger*, July 5, 1961.

16. Lafayette and Thomas, Lafayette, Davis and Davis, and Green interviews; Silver, "Diary of a Freedom Rider," passim; Green, "Freedom Rider Diary—Forty Years Later," 7; Farmer, *Lay Bare the Heart*, 24 (first quotation), 25, 29–30; Peck, *Freedom Ride*, 150, 152 (Mahoney quotation); Freedom Rider applications, Price Chatham and Ken Shilman, section 441, reel 43, COREP; Jesse Harris, typescript, June 24, 1961, section 116, reel 25, COREP; Carmichael, *Ready for Revolution*, 200–201, 208–210; Branch, *Parting the Waters*, 484; Lewis, *Walking with the Wind*, 169–170; *Baltimore Afro-American*, July 1, 1961; *Jackson Clarion-Ledger*, June 21, 26–27, July 12, 15, 1961; *Jackson Daily News*, June 21, July 13, 1961; *New York Times*, June 20–21, 1961; *Birmingham News*, June 27, 1961; *Montgomery Advertiser*, June 27, 1961.

17. *Montreal Gazette*, July 1, 1961 (first quotation); Audain and Mulholland interviews; Audain interview, UMFRC; *Jackson Clarion-Ledger*, July 5, 1961 (second and fourth quotations); *Jackson Daily News*, July 3 (third quotation), 5, 1961; Silver, "Diary of a Freedom Rider," passim; Farmer, *Lay Bare the Heart*, 30–31; *Pittsburgh Courier*, July 8, 1961.

18. *Jackson Clarion-Ledger*, July 4 (first quotation), 6, 7, 8 (third quotation), 9, 11, 1961; *Jackson Daily News*, July 3, 5, 6 (second quotation), 7, 10–11, 1961; *New York Times*, July 4, 7, 1961; Aelony, Baum, Davidov, Morton, and O'Connor interviews A complaint letter from O'Connor's parents to Minnesota attorney general Walter Mondale helped trigger the investigation, but O'Connor posted bond and returned to Minnesota just prior to Brooks's and Casey's arrival in Mississippi.

19. Oshinsky, *"Worse than Slavery,"* 162–168, 174–177, 247–250, 252; Green, "Freedom Rider Diary—Forty Years Later," 7–8; Green, Lafayette, Myers, Davidov, and Lafayette and Thomas interviews; Silver, "Diary of a Freedom Rider," passim.

20. Oshinsky, *"Worse than Slavery,"* 168–177; Langum, *William M. Kunstler*, 59 (quotations); Kunstler, with Sheila Isenberg, *My Life as a Radical Lawyer*, 104; Bass, *Unlikely Heroes*, 144; Silver, "Diary of a Freedom Rider," 23 (quotation)–101; Silver interview; Silver interview, UMFRC; Ellen Ziskind, interview by author, September 1, 2005; Schultz, *Going South*, 36–39; Anderson-Bricker, "Making a Movement," 318–320; Fleming, *Soon We Will Not Cry*, 87; Olson, *Freedom's Daughters*, 190–194; Mulholland, O'Connor, Davis and Davis, and Brooks interviews; Miriam Feingold to Ann Kendall, August 1, 1961, section 441, reel 43, COREP; *Baltimore Afro-American*, July 15, September 23, 1961; *Louisiana Weekly*, July 22, August 5, 1961; *Jackson Clarion-Ledger*, June 17, 1961; *Jackson Daily News*, June 23, 28–29, July 3, 1961; William Kunstler to Jim McCain, August 21, 1961, section 447, reel 44, COREP. For a broader discussion of gender, sexuality, and the experiences of women in the civil rights movement of the 1960s, see Sara Evans, *Personal Politics: The Roots of Women's Liberation in the Civil Rights Movement and the New Left* (New York: Knopf, 1978); Sara Evans, "Women's Consciousness and the Southern Black Movement," *Southern Exposure* 4 (1977): 10–18; Crawford, Rouse, and Woods, *Women in the Civil Rights Movement*; Robnett, *How Long? How Long?*; Anne Moody, *Coming of Age in Mississippi* (New York: Dial, 1968); Mary King, *Freedom Song: A Personal Story of the 1960s Civil Rights Movement* (New York: William Morrow, 1987); Kay Mills, *This Little Light of Mine: The Life of Fannie Lou Hamer* (New York: Dutton, 1993); Chana Kai Lee, *For Freedom's Sake: The Life of Fannie Lou Hamer* (Urbana: University of Illinois Press, 1999); Mamie E. Locke, "The Role of African-American Women in the Civil Rights and Women's Movements in Hinds County and Sunflower County, Mississippi," *Journal of Mississippi History* 53 (1991): 229–239; Curry et al., *Deep in Our Hearts*; Constance Curry, *Silver Rights* (Chapel Hill: Algonquin Books, 1995); Olson, *Freedom's Daughters*; Ransby, *Ella Baker and the Black Freedom Movement*; Due and Due, *Freedom in the Family*; and Alvin Poussaint, "The Stresses of the White Female Worker in the Civil Rights Movement in the South," *Journal of American Psychiatry* 123 (October 1966): 401–407.

21. Silver, "Diary of a Freedom Rider," 41–48 (quotations); Silver and Myers interviews; Schultz, *Going South*, 39–43; Pauline Knight, "Notes from Prison," *Southern Patriot* 19 (September 1961): 1; Hirschfeld online interview, Jewish Women's Archive.

22. Green, "Freedom Rider Diary–Forty Years Later," 6 (quotations); Green, Lafayette, and Lafayette and Thomas interviews; Carmichael, *Ready for Revolution*, 14–82, 204–205 (last quotation); Farmer, *Lay Bare the Heart*, 24–25, 30; Lewis, *Walking with the Wind*, 173, 178–179, 292, 296–297, 363–371; Fleming, *Soon We Will Not Cry*, 87; Branch, *Parting the Waters*, 484–485; Carson, *In Struggle*, 38, 209–228, 274–284, 292, 306; Meier and Rudwick, *CORE*, 140–142. On the unintended effects of Jim Crow, see Joel Williamson, *The Crucible of Race: Black-White Relations in the American South Since Emancipation* (New York: Oxford University Press, 1984); Leon F. Litwack, *Trouble in Mind: Black Southerners in the Age of Jim Crow* (New York: Knopf, 1998); McMillen, *Dark Journey*; and Nan E. Woodruff, *American Congo: The African American Freedom Struggle in the Delta* (Cambridge: Harvard University Press, 2003).

23. Goldsmith, "The Cost of Freedom Rides," 499–502; Meier and Rudwick, *CORE*, 142–144, 148–149; James Farmer to CORE Chapters and Officers, memorandum, August 2, 1961, and Evert Makinen to Steve Allen, July 27, 1961, both in section 116, reel 25, COREP; *CORE-lator*, June 1961; Rich and Carey interviews; Farmer, *Lay Bare the Heart*, 210–212; Lewis, *Walking with the Wind*, 174; *New York Times*, July 13, 1961; *Birmingham News*, June 20, 1961; *Jackson Daily News*, June 21, 26, July 13, 1961; *Citizens' Council*, June 1961.

24. Farmer, *Lay Bare the Heart*, 208 (quotations); Rich and Carey interviews. Farmer's decision to remain in Parchman brought him new respect among the student activists of SNCC. Jim Forman, Nashville notes, July 29, 1961, box 55, SNCCP.

25. Rich and Carey interviews; Goldsmith, "The Cost of Freedom Rides"; Meier and Rudwick, *CORE*, 142–144, 148–152. See the correspondence on fund-raising in section 116, reel 25, COREP.

26. Farmer, *Lay Bare the Heart*, 210–212; Rich and Carey interviews; *New York Times*, June 20, July 11, 1961; *Birmingham News*, June 14, 1961; "Before the ICC, Docket No. MC-C-3358 . . . ," box 1, Burke Marshall Records, USDJ/CRD; General File 1, folder 4, box 1, Investigative Report Case Files, ICCR; Chuck McDew to ICC Director, July 24, 1961, folder 9, box 8, SNCCP; "Injustice Will Tire First."

27. Kunstler, *My Life as a Radical Lawyer*, 103–105; Langum, *William M. Kunstler*, 58–60; Bass, *Unlikely Heroes*, 144–145; *New York Times*, June 22, 28, July 4, 13, 23, 27, 1961; *Jackson Daily News*, June 27–29, July 3–6, 13, 27, 1961; *Jackson Clarion-Ledger*, June 25, 28, July 4, 9, 13, 1961; *Birmingham Post-Herald*, June 27, 1961; *Christian Science Monitor*, July 26, 1961; *Montgomery Advertiser*, July 27, 1961; "CORE Asks U.S. Supreme Court Ruling on Mississippi Freedom Ride Arrests," SNCC press release, July 24, 1961, folder 3, box 8, SNCCP; Silver, "Diary of a Freedom Rider," passim, discusses Wyckoff's experiences at Parchman.

28. *New York Times*, June 12, 15, 20 (quotations), 27, 28, July 7, 12, 1961; *Birmingham News*, June 20, 1961; *Jackson Clarion-Ledger*, June 20, 1961; *Montgomery Advertiser*, June 27, 1961; *New Orleans Times-Picayune*, June 27, 1961; *Baltimore Afro-American*, July 8, 1961; "The Hostess Was Sorry," *Newsweek* 58 (July 10, 1961): 78. The NAACP filed a desegregation suit against the Mobile, Alabama, airport terminal on June 26. *New York Times*, June 27, 1961.

29. *New York Times*, July 11, 1961; Barnes, *Journey from Jim Crow*, 120–128; Doar interview.

30. *Jackson Daily News*, June 18, 26–27, July 3–6, 7 (quotations), 1961; *Jackson Clarion-Ledger*, June 15, July 5–8, 1961; *New York Times*, June 24, July 5, 23, 1961; *Baltimore Afro-American*, July 15, 1961; Rich and Gaither interviews; Hezekiah Watkins, interview by author, November 11, 2001; Freedom Riders Roster, Groups 21–24, July 5–6, 1961, MSCP; Dittmer, *Local People*, 116–118; Meier and Rudwick, *CORE*, 166.

31. *Jackson Daily News*, July 8–22, 1961; *Jackson Clarion-Ledger*, July 8–22, 1961; *New York Times*, July 18–20, 1961; Freedom Riders Roster, Groups 25–31, July 7, 9, 15, 16, 21, 1961, MSCP; Dittmer, *Local People*, 116–117; Meier and Rudwick, *CORE*, 166; Lafayette interview.

32. Dittmer, *Local People*, 117–118; Gaither interview.

33. *New York Times*, July 11 (quotations), 12–13, 14 (Sherrod quotation), 15, 16, 1961; Carter interview.

34. *New York Times*, July 1–2, 5, 9, 1961; Carter, Gaither, and Lafayette interviews.

35. Kirk, *Redefining the Color Line*, 146–150 (quotations); Cox interview; Janet Baum Reinitz, interview by author, November 10, 2001; Janet Baum Reinitz, interview by Susan Glisson, November 9, 2001, UMFRC; Freedom Rider applications, Janet Reinitz and John Raines, section 441, reel 43, COREP; *Little Rock Arkansas Gazette*, July 11–14, 1961; *New York Times*, July 12–15, 1961. On the Baton Rouge situation, see RD 107, box 15, Investigative Report Case Files, ICCR; and Fairclough, *Race and Democracy*, 287–288.

36. *New York Times*, July 14–16, 17 (quotation), 1961; *Chattanooga Times*, July 17, 1961; *Baltimore Afro-American*, July 27, 1961; Thomas interview; Woollcott Smith, interview by author, November 10, 2001; Woollcott Smith, interview by Susan Glisson, November 10, 2001, UMFRC; Genevieve Hughes to Woollcott Smith, July 8, 1961, section 453, reel 44, COREP; Freedom Rider application, Herman Stern, and John C. Harvard to CORE, both in section 441, reel 43, COREP; Sidney Shanken, interview by author, August 19, 2005.

37. *New York Times*, July 20, 23, 24 (quotation), 1961; *Jackson Daily News*, July 19–21, 1961; *Jackson Clarion-Ledger*, July 19–21, 1961. Thomas and the other four Riders ended their Freedom Ride in Little Rock on July 24, a little more than a week after Cox's group had been arrested. But the second group of Little Rock Freedom Riders encountered no resistance and ate without incident at both the Union bus terminal and the Little Rock airport restaurant before flying back to New York. The only negative incident in Arkansas occurred in Stuttgart, where they were denied service at a bus station lunch counter and where, according to Thomas, the bus driver "made a desperate attempt to leave us—we had to run out to catch it." "Core Riders Served in Little Rock," SNCC press release, July 24, 1961, folder 3, box 8, SNCCP; Thomas and Shanken interviews.

38. *Jackson Clarion-Ledger*, July 21, 1961; *Jackson Daily News*, July 13, 20, 1961; Memphis *Commercial Appeal*, July 22, 1961; *New Orleans States-Item*, July 21, 1961; *New Orleans Times-Picayune*, July 21, 1961; *New York Times*, July 21, 1961.

39. *New York Times*, July 20, 1961 (quotations).

40. *New York Times*, July 23 (quotation), 28, 1961. On Cox's appointment and controversial tenure as a federal judge, see Bass, *Unlikely Heroes*, 164–167; Navasky, *Kennedy Justice*, 245, 247–252; Wofford, *Of Kennedys and Kings*, 168–169; Niven, *The Politics of Injustice*, 10, 109, 213, 236; and Dallek, *An Unfinished Life*, 494–495. The former college roommate of Senator James Eastland, Cox reportedly received the appointment after the Kennedys and Eastland worked out a deal that facilitated Thurgood Marshall's appointment to a Federal judgeship. According to the journalist Robert Sherrill, Eastland approached Robert Kennedy in a Capitol corridor and said: "Tell your brother that if he will give me Harold Cox I will give him the nigger." Navasky, *Kennedy Justice*, 251–252. After considerable deliberation, John Kennedy appointed Marshall to the U.S. Second Circuit Court of Appeals in August 1961. According to biographer Juan Williams: "The nomination was carefully timed. The Kennedy brothers, anticipating opposition, nominated Marshall a week before the Senate Judiciary Committee was to go out of session for the rest of the year, not leaving the committee time to act. Thus the president was able to give Marshall a recess appointment, allowing the new judge to be in place until Congress could recon-

vene." Williams, *Thurgood Marshall*, 294; Baltimore *Afro-American*, September 23, 30, October 7, 1961. Marshall was sworn in on October 23, 1961, but he had to wait until September 11, 1962, for Senate confirmation. The vote to confirm was 54 to 16. Williams, *Thurgood Marshall*, 294–303.

41. *New York Times*, June 17, July 27 (Patterson quotations), 1961; Patterson and Marshall interviews, JFKL; *Montgomery Advertiser*, July 27, August 1 (Kennedy quotation), 1961; *Birmingham News*, June 29, July 21, 27, 1961; "Patterson Says 'Rides' Hurt Race Relations," *Southern School News* 8 (July 1961): 9; McWhorter, *Carry Me Home*, 237, 240, 246–247; O'Reilly, *"Racial Matters,"* 92–93; Thornton, *Dividing Lines*, 249–251; May, *The Informant*, 51–54. See also the voluminous correspondence among FBI agents and investigators in Alabama during the summer and fall of 1961 in FBI-FRI.

Chapter 10: Woke Up This Morning with My Mind on Freedom

1. Based on the traditional gospel song "I Woke Up This Morning with My Mind on Jesus," the words to "Woke Up This Morning with My Mind on Freedom" were written in the Hinds County Jail during the summer of 1961 by Robert Wesby, a thirty-three-year-old black minister from Aurora, Illinois. Wesby was arrested in Jackson on June 8. Roster of Freedom Riders, Group 11, June 8, 1961, MSCP. By late summer "Woke Up This Morning with My Mind on Freedom" was a popular movement song, especially in McComb, Mississippi, where it became the unofficial anthem of the local voter registration drive. Silverman, *Songs of Protest and Civil Rights*, 50–52. Later affiliated with the Reverend Jesse Jackson's Operation PUSH, Wesby was beaten to death in his church in July 1988. See *New York Times*, July 24, 1988.

2. *Jackson Daily News*, July 16, 1961 (quotations). In the *Daily News*, the Mulligan story ran under the headline "Non-Violent War—AP Story Tells Nation About Freedom Riders" and was preceded by the following explanation: "The Associated Press dispatch has been sent out to every (AP) member newspaper across the country for use in today's papers. It is the story of the Freedom Riders and Jackson as it will be told perhaps to more people than have read about the 'non-violent war' before." Despite this effort, press coverage of the Freedom Rides declined in July. See the July issues of the *New York Times*, the *Washington Post*, the *Washington Evening Star*, the *Chicago Tribune*, the *Atlanta Constitution*, and the *Los Angeles Times*. This was less true of black newspapers such as the *Chicago Defender*, the *Pittsburgh Courier*, and the *Baltimore Afro-American*.

3. Rich and Carey interviews; Meier and Rudwick, *CORE*, 142; Farmer, *Lay Bare the Heart*, 210–211; sections 445–449, reel 44, COREP; Alphonso Petway and Kredelle Petway, interview by author, November 9, 2001; Alphonso Petway and Kredelle Petway, interview by Susan Glisson, November 10, 2001, UMFRC; Monton G. Linder, interview by author and Meeghan Kane, August 23, 2005; Roster of Freedom Riders, Groups 33 and 34, July 23–24, 1961, MSCP; *Jackson Daily News*, July 23–25, 1961; *New York Times*, July 23–24, 1961.

4. Roster of Freedom Riders, Group 35, July 29, 1961, MSCP; Freedom Rider application, Byron Baer, section 441, reel 43, COREP; Woollcott Smith and Ziskind interviews; Wollcott Smith interview, UMFRC; *New Orleans States-Item*, July 21, 1961; *Jackson State-Times*, July 30, 1961 (second quotation); *McComb Enterprise-Journal*, July 31, 1961 (first and fourth quotation); *Jackson Clarion-Ledger*, July 30, 1961 (telegram quotation); *Jackson Daily News*, August 1, 3, 1961; *New Orleans Times-Picayune*, July 30, 1961; *New York Times*, July 30, August 1, 1961; Peck, *Freedom Ride*, 152–153.

5. Roster of Freedom Riders, Group 36, July 30, 1961, MSCP; Robert Singleton, interview by author, November 9, 2001; Robert Singleton, interview by Susan Glisson, November 10, 2001, UMFRC; Helen Singleton, interview by Susan Glisson, November 10, 2001, UMFRC; Philip Posner, Winston Fuller, Max Pavesic, Joe Gerbac, and Michael Grubbs, interviews by author and Meeghan Kane, August 18–19, 31, September 14–15, 2005; *New York Times*, July 31, 1961; *Jackson Daily News*, July 31, August 1, 1961; *Jackson Clarion-Ledger*, July 31, 1961. On Hodge and the evolution of Los Angeles CORE, see Meier and Rudwick, *CORE*, 49, 74, 96, 109–110, 127–128, 130; and the chapter correspondence in reels 18 and 39, COREP.

6. Franklin P. Hall to T. B. Birdsong, c. August 1961, section 448, reel 44, COREP; *Jackson Daily News*, June 29, July 21 (quotation), 1961; *Jackson Clarion-Ledger*, June 30, August 3, 1961; *New York Times*, August 2–15, 1961; Woods, *Black Struggle, Red Scare*, 150–152. On the Berlin crisis, see Reeves, *President Kennedy*, 185–220; and Honore M. Catudal, *Kennedy and the Berlin Wall Crisis: A Case-Study in U.S. Decision Making* (West Berlin: Berlin-Verlag, 1980). See also Wofford, *Of Kennedys and Kings*, 153; and Branch, *Parting the Waters*, 491.

7. Farmer, *Lay Bare the Heart*, 210–211 (quotations); Rich interview; Langum, *William M. Kunstler*, 58–61; Niven, *The Politics of Injustice*, 114–115; Goldsmith, "The Cost of Freedom Rides"; "Freedom Ride Costs," CORE memorandum, August 17, 1961, folder 3, box 8, SNCCP.

8. *Jackson Daily News*, August 9 (first quotation), 10, 1961; *Jackson Clarion-Ledger*, August 11, 1961 (second and third quotations); *New Orleans Times-Picayune*, August 11, 1961; *New York Times*, August 11, 1961; Branch, *Parting the Waters*, 490; Wyatt Tee Walker, Carey, and Rich interviews.

9. *Washington Evening Star*, August 6, 1961; *Memphis Commercial Appeal*, August 8, 1961; *New Orleans Times-Picayune*, August 8, 1961; *Jackson Clarion-Ledger*, August 8, 1961; *New York Times*, August 8, 12, 1961. In addition, on August 11 Judge Moore denied Kunstler's request for a release order for CORE field secretary Richard Haley, who had been charged with breach of peace while picketing the hotel where the Southern governors were housed during the July 19–20 conference in Jackson. "CORE Secretary Pickets Southern Governors: Arrested and Sentenced to Six Months in Jail," CORE press release, July 24, 1961, folder 3, box 8, SNCCP.

10. Farmer, *Lay Bare the Heart*, 211 (quotations); Rich, Carey, and Gaither interviews; James Farmer to CORE Chapters and Officers, August 2, 1961, reel 25, COREP. See the correspondence on the

returning Freedom Riders in sections 445–448, reel 44, COREP. "Farmer Requests Federal Marshals to Protect Riders in Jackson Trials" and "Six Field Secretaries," CORE press releases, August 4, 1961, and CORE press release on August 12 arrests in New Orleans, c. August 14, 1961, all in folder 3, box 8, SNCCP. On the New Orleans arrests, see *Louisiana Weekly*, August 19, 1961; and Anderson-Bricker, "Making a Movement," 320–324. On the Houston arrests, see *Houston Chronicle*, August 12, 1961; Steve McNichols, "The Last Freedom Ride: Life in the Tank," ms. in author's possession, 2005 (quotations); Steve McNichols, testimony, March 2002, webspinner@crmvet.org; John W. Hollie to Ed King, August 15, 1961, folder 10, box 8, SNCCP; John W. Hollie to Cyril Simon, August 14, 1961, and Information Gathered from John W. Hollie, typescript, August 14, 1961, both in section 447, reel 44, COREP; and John W. Hollie to Cyril Simon, August 15, 1961, section 456, reel 44, COREP. Pat Kovner, Ellen Broms, Steve Sanfield, Steve McNichols, Beverly Mill, Holly Hogrobrooks, Herbert Hamilton, Robert Farrell, and Charles Berrard, interviews by author and Meeghan Kane, July 19, August 12–13, 16, 19, 22–23, 25, 2005; "Back to Jackson," *Newsweek* 58 (August 28, 1961): 28; "Freedom Ride Round-Up," *Southern Patriot* 19 (September 1961): 1; Meier and Rudwick, *CORE*, 142; Barnes, *Journey from Jim Crow*, 173–174; Niven, *The Politics of Injustice*, 114; *Jackson Clarion-Ledger*, August 6, 1961; *Jackson Daily News*, August 9, 12–15, 1961; *New York Times*, August 12–15, 1961. Peck, *Freedom Ride*, 152–153, noted that Wagner and Bohannon were "the first and only Freedom Riders to date to be served at the Jackson terminal, thanks to human decency." On Wagner, see Norma Wagner to Gordon Carey, July 13, 1961, and Milton Wagner to Gordon Carey, July 13, 1961, both in section 441, reel 43, COREP; *CORE-lator* (August 1961); and *Louisiana Weekly*, August 12, 1961.

11. *Jackson Daily News*, August 13, 14 (quotations), 1961; *New York Times*, August 13–14, 1961; *Washington Evening Star*, August 13, 1961; Wyatt Tee Walker interview.

12. *Jackson Clarion-Ledger*, August 15 (quotations), 19, 1961; *Jackson Daily News*, August 14–16, 1961; *New Orleans Times-Picayune*, August 16, 1961; *New York Times*, August 15, 1961. One of the departing Freedom Riders, Leslie Word, was detained by the police in his home town of Corinth, Mississippi, after trying to use the telephone in the white waiting room of the Corinth bus station. He was released without being charged.

13. *New York Times*, August 14 (King quotations), 15, 16 (Barrett and Rachlin quotations), 1961; *Washington Evening Star*, August 14–15, 1961; *Nashville Banner*, August 15, 1961; "CORE Leader Says: 'End Segregation or End Interstate Transportation,'" CORE press release, August 17, 1961, folder 3, box 8, SNCCP; Wyatt Tee Walker, Rich, Carey, Fauntroy, and Dunbar interviews; Farmer, *Lay Bare the Heart*, 13–14, 211–212; Niven, *The Politics of Injustice*, 115–120; Barnes, *Journey from Jim Crow*, 168–170. See "Before the ICC . . . ," Burke Marshall Records, box 1, USDJ/CRD, which includes the results of an extensive government survey of segregated transit facilities in Southern cities. Appendix A provides a "Summary of Complaints"; Appendix B is a tabulation of an FBI survey of motor carrier terminals; and Appendix C contains a large number of FBI photographs of segregated transit facilities.

14. *New York Times*, August 16, 1961; Barnes, *Journey from Jim Crow*, 170–173; Niven, *The Politics of Injustice*, 119–120; Marshall interview, JFKL. "Meeting with Representatives of Various Bus Companies," memorandum, August 3, 1961; Burke Marshall to Dean Rusk, June 2, 1961; Robert F. Kennedy to Everett Hutchinson (ICC chairperson), August 25, 1961, and Burke Marshall to Clifford P. Cherry (Greyhound executive vice president), August 31, 1961, all in box 1, BMP. "Before the ICC . . . ," USDJ/CRD; General File 1, ICCR.

15. Renee Romano, "No Diplomatic Immunity: African Diplomats, the State Department, and Civil Rights, 1961–1964," *Journal of American History* 87 (September 2000): 546–574; Wofford interview, JFKL; *Washington Evening Star*, August 7–9, 1961; *Baltimore Afro-American*, September 23, 1961; John Anthony Lukas, "Trouble on Route Forty," *Reporter* 25 (October 26, 1961): 41; Niven, *The Politics of Injustice*, 192–193; Dudziak, *Cold War Civil Rights*, 152–153, 167–169; Borstelmann, *The Cold War and the Color Line*, 164–169; Meier and Rudwick, *CORE*, 162–163.

16. Marshall interview, JFKL; Dunbar interview; Wofford, *Of Kennedys and Kings*, 159; Carmichael, *Ready for Revolution*, 218–224; Zinn, *SNCC*, 58–66; Carson, *In Struggle*, 40–41, 45–47; Dittmer, *Local People*, 48, 58, 72–73, 99–103; Branch, *Parting the Waters*, 330–331, 345, 485–488, 492–494; Bob Moses, "Mississippi: 1961–1962," *Liberation* 14 (January 1970): 6–17; Eric Burner, *And Gently He Shall Lead Them: Robert Parris Moses and Civil Rights in Mississippi* (New York: New York University Press, 1994), 34–39; Forman, *The Making of Black Revolutionaries*, 224–225; Neil McMillen, "Black Enfranchisement in Mississippi: Federal Enforcement and Black Protest in the 1960s," *Journal of Southern History* 43 (August 1977): 355–360. On McComb and Pike County, see Federal Writers' Project, *Mississippi: A Guide to the Magnolia State* (New York: Viking Press, 1938), 396. A growing interest in voter registration was a movement-wide trend in August 1961. See James Farmer to Stephen Carrier (Taconic Foundation), August 17, 1961, folder 3, box 8, and Memorandum from the Southern Regional Council, August 23, 1961, folder 21, box 9, both in SNCCP.

17. Minutes of SNCC meeting, July 14–16, 1961, box 7, SNCCP; SNCC Executive Committee Office Report and Proposed Agenda, August 11–13, 1961, folder 4, box 6, SNCCP. Carson, *In Struggle*, 40; Zinn, *SNCC*, 58; Branch, *Parting the Waters*, 485–486.

18. Carson, *In Struggle*, 41 (first quotation); Forman, *The Making of Black Revolutionaries*, 159–160; Lewis, *Walking with the Wind*, 180–181 (fourth quotation); Carmichael, *Ready for Revolution*, 215–225, 217–218 (second quotation), 222 (third quotation); Raines, *My Soul Is Rested*, 227–231.

19. Glen, *Highlander*, 146–153; SNCC Executive Committee Office Report and Proposed Agenda, August 11–13, 1961, SNCCP; Ed King to SNCC Members, September 12, 1961, folder 11, box 8, SNCCP; Lewis, *Walking with the Wind*, 181–182; Carson, *In Struggle*, 41–42; Zinn, *SNCC*, 58–59; Branch, *Parting the Waters*, 486–487, 491; Dittmer, *Local People*, 107; Forman, *The Making of Black Revolutionaries*, 221–222; Ransby, *Ella Baker and the Black Freedom Movement*, 267–270. See also Greenberg, *A Circle of Trust*, 39–60.

20. Forman, *The Making of Black Revolutionaries*, 223–227; Moses, "Mississippi: 1961–1962," 7–10; Dittmer, *Local People*, 103–106; Zinn, *SNCC*, 62–67, 70; Janet Feagans, "Voting, Violence, and Walkout in McComb," *New South* 16 (October 1961): 3–4; Tom Hayden, *Revolution in Mississippi* (New York: Students for a Democratic Society, 1962), 1–5; Joanne Grant, ed., *Black Protest: History, Documents, and Analyses, 1619 to the Present* (New York: Fawcett, 1968), 304–306, 309; McMillen, "Black Enfranchisement in Mississippi," 360; Lewis, *Walking with the Wind*, 183; Carson, *In Struggle*, 46–47; Branch, *Parting the Waters*, 325–331, 492–496; Carmichael, *Ready for Revolution*, 240–242; Federal Writers' Project, *Mississippi*, 481–483; Robert Moses to John Doar, July 11, 1961, and John Doar to Robert Moses, July 17, 1961, box 1, John Doar Records, USDJ/CRD; Doar interview. On Moses's background, see Burner, *And Gently He Shall Lead Them*, 1–45; and Robert Penn Warren, *Who Speaks for the Negro?* (New York: Random House, 1964), 90–99. On August 25, 1960, Moses was rebuffed when he insisted on buying a ticket directly from a Trailways driver rather than going to the "colored" ticket window at the Jackson, Mississippi, Trailways terminal. Two weeks later he filed a discrimination complaint with the ICC. See RD 39, box 7, Investigative Report Case Files, ICCR.
21. Forman, *The Making of Black Revolutionaries*, 226–228; Zinn, *SNCC*, 68–69; Dittmer, *Local People*, 106–108; Burner, *And Gently He Shall Lead Them*, 45–55; Branch, *Parting the Waters*, 496–500; Carson, *In Struggle*, 47–48; Hollis Watkins, interview by Robert Wright, August 5, 1968, RBOHC; Moses, "Mississippi: 1961–1962," 10–14; Grant, *Black Protest*, 306–307; Ed King to Wyatt Tee Walker, August 28, 1961, folder 19, box 9, SNCCP.
22. Brooks interview; Forman, *The Making of Black Revolutionaries*, 3–148; Carson, *In Struggle*, 42–43; Zinn, *SNCC*, 60; Tyson, *Radio Free Dixie*, 246, 262; James Forman, interview by Susan Glisson, November 10, 2001, UMFRC.
23. Forman, *The Making of Black Revolutionaries*, 137–138 (quotation), 147–148; Forman notes, July 29, 1961, box 55, SNCCP; Tyson, *Radio Free Dixie*, 262; Strain, *Pure Fire*, 64; Brooks interview.
24. Forman, *The Making of Black Revolutionaries*, 158–159, 164–182; Tyson, *Radio Free Dixie*, 137–205 (first quotation), 243 (second quotation), 262; Williams, *Negroes with Guns*, 39–74; Strain, *Pure Fire*, 57–64; Brooks interview. Born and raised in Macon, Georgia, Mallory moved to Harlem as a young woman. She joined the Communist Party in the early 1950s but later left the Party and became a fervent black nationalist before discovering Williams. Tyson, *Radio Free Dixie*, 189–190.
25. Forman, *The Making of Black Revolutionaries*, 159–161 (quotations), 162; Forman "Nashville" notes, July 29, 1961, box 55, SNCCP; King to SNCC Members, September 12, 1961, box 8, SNCCP; Tyson, *Radio Free Dixie*, 262; Carmichael, *Ready for Revolution*, 224–225.
26. Forman, *The Making of Black Revolutionaries*, 162 (first and second quotations), 163, 178, 183–185 (third quotation), 186 (fourth quotation); Tyson, *Radio Free Dixie*, 264; Williams, *Negroes with Guns*, 77–78. See also Carmichael, *Ready for Revolution*, 225–234.
27. *Charlotte Observer*, August 16–18, 1961; Harry Boyte Jr., interview by author, December 1, 1977; Williams, *Negroes with Guns*, 78–80; Tyson, *Radio Free Dixie*, 264–266 (quotation), 267; Forman, *The Making of Black Revolutionaries*, 186–188; Strain, *Pure Fire*, 64–68; Carmichael, *Ready for Revolution*, 225. Harry Boyte Sr. later served as an SCLC staff member and played an influential role in the effort to desegregate St. Augustine, Florida, in 1964. On the Boytes, see Janet Boyte, "White Rebel of SCLC," 1963 typescript, box 26, Boyte Family Papers, Special Collections, Perkins Library, Duke University, Durham, NC; Ed Clayton, "The Men Behind Martin Luther King," *Ebony* 20 (June 1965): 170; Fairclough, *To Redeem the Soul of America*, 176, 182, 185, 207–208, 221, 335; Branch, *Pillar of Fire*, 324–325; and David Colburn, *Racial Change and Community Crisis: St. Augustine, Florida, 1877–1980* (Gainesville: University of Florida Press, 1991), 83, 86–87, 93, 144, 180. The seventeen Freedom Riders who joined Brooks and Forman in Monroe were Robert Baum, Ed Bromberg, Charles Butler, Price Chatham, Paul Dietrich, Richard Griswold, Larry Hunter, Ed Kale, Frederick Leonard, John Lowry, William Mahoney, Joe McDonald, David Morton, LeRoy Wright, Heath Rush, Ken Shilman, and Danny Thompson. Baum, Dietrich, and Morton interviews; Baum interview, UMFRC; Edward Kale, interview by Susan Glisson, November 9, 2001, UMFRC.
28. Tyson, *Radio Free Dixie*, 268–269 (quotations); Williams, *Negroes with Guns*, 79–80; Forman, *The Making of Black Revolutionaries*, 187–190, 194; John Lowry, "Should Violence Be Met with Violence?" *Realist* 32 (March 1962): 7–9; Constance Lever, "Monroe Doctrine," *Spectator* (September 15, 1961): 346; Dietrich interview.
29. Forman, *The Making of Black Revolutionaries*, 190–191 (first three quotations), 192–193; Tyson, *Radio Free Dixie*, 269–271 (fourth quotation); Lowry, "Should Violence Be Met with Violence?" 8; Williams, *Negroes with Guns*, 80–82.
30. Tyson, *Radio Free Dixie*, 271–272 (first and second quotations), 273 (third quotation), 274; Forman, *The Making of Black Revolutionaries*, 192–196 (fourth and fifth quotations), 197–202; Lowry, "Should Violence Be Met with Violence?" 8; Lever, "Monroe Doctrine," 346; Williams, *Negroes with Guns*, 83–84.
31. Tyson, *Radio Free Dixie*, 147, 204–205, 223, 269, 275–283 (quotations); Williams, *Negroes with Guns*, 84–90; Forman, *The Making of Black Revolutionaries*, 189–190, 201, 206–207; Strain, *Pure Fire*, 68; *New York Times*, August 29–30, 1961; *Charlotte Observer*, August 29, 1961; *Raleigh News and Observer*, August 29, 1961; *Monroe Enquirer*, August 31, 1961; Lowry, "Should Violence Be Met with Violence?" 9. See also Julian Mayfield, "Challenge to Negro Leadership: The Case of Robert Williams," *Commentary* 31 (April 1961): 297–305; *Baltimore Afro-American*, July 22, October 7, 14, 21, 1961; and Truman Nelson, *People with Strength: The Story of Monroe, N.C.* (New York: Marzani and Munsell, 1962).
32. *New York Times*, August 29, 1961 (quotations); *Charlotte Observer*, August 29, 1961; *Monroe Enquirer*, August 31, 1961; Carey and Boyte interviews; Tyson, *Radio Free Dixie*, 283–284; Williams, *Negroes with Guns*, 89–93; Strain, *Pure Fire*, 68–69.

33. Forman, *The Making of Black Revolutionaries*, 202–206; Wyatt Tee Walker and Dietrich interviews; *New York Times*, August 29 (quotation), 30, 1961.
34. Forman, *The Making of Black Revolutionaries*, 206 (first quotation), 207–210 (second quotation); Williams, *Negroes with Guns*, 93–100; *New York Times*, August 30, 1961; Wyatt Tee Walker interview; Kunstler, *My Life as a Radical Lawyer*, 107; Langum, *William M. Kunstler*, 61–62 (third quotation).
35. Meier and Rudwick, *CORE*, 202–203; Lowry, "Should Violence Be Met with Violence?" 7–9; Langum, *William M. Kunstler*, 62, 66, 68; Morton, Baum, Dietrich, and Wyatt Tee Walker interviews; Williams, *Negroes with Guns*, 94–95; Strain, *Pure Fire*, 68–69, 73. On CORE's involvement with the CAMD, see the correspondence in section 19, reel 1, COREP. On Williams's relationships with Lynn and Worthy, see Tyson, *Radio Free Dixie*, 112–135, 222–223, 231–237, 242, 244, 266, 283, 287–288, 291, 294; and *Baltimore Afro-American*, October 7, 14, 1961.
36. *Baltimore Afro-American*, October 7, 14, 21, 1961; Tyson, *Radio Free Dixie*, 283–307 (quotation); Strain, *Pure Fire*, 69–75, 184–190; Williams, *Negroes with Guns*, 101–124; Carmichael, *Ready for Revolution*, 594. Parks moved to Detroit in 1957. Parks, *Rosa Parks: My Story*, 161–175; Douglas Brinkley, *Rosa Parks* (New York: Viking Penguin, 2000), 174–178.
37. *Jackson Clarion-Ledger*, August 20, 1961 (quotations); *Jackson State-Times*, August 20, 1961; Langum, *William M. Kunstler*, 60, 69; Niven, *The Politics of Injustice*, 10, 109; Meier and Rudwick, *CORE*, 180; Stern, *Calculating Visions*, 48; Navasky, *Kennedy Justice*, 48, 133, 244–252.
38. *New York Times*, August 22–23, 1961; Fairclough, *Race and Democracy*, 287–289. On the 1968 anti-war trial of Philip Berrigan, his brother Daniel, and seven other members of the "Catonsville Nine," see Kunstler, *My Life as a Radical Lawyer*, 188–193; Mangum, *William H. Kunstler*, 224–228; Rosemary S. Brannan, *Law, Morality, and Vietnam: The Peace Militants and the Courts* (Bloomington: Indiana University Press, 1974), 124–150; and Steven E. Barkan, *Protesters on Trial: Criminal Justice in the Southern Civil Rights and Vietnam Antiwar Movements* (New Brunswick: Rutgers University Press, 1985), 87–93, 121–148.
39. *Jackson Clarion-Ledger*, August 22, 1961; *Jackson Daily News*, August 23, 1961 (quotations); *New York Times*, August 23, 1961; Lafayette and Thomas interview; Gaither interview.
40. *Jackson Clarion-Ledger*, August 24, 1961 (first and second quotations); *Jackson Daily News*, August 23, 1961; *New York Times*, August 24, 1961 (third quotation); *Montgomery Advertiser*, August 24, 1961.
41. *New York Times*, August 25, 1961; Peck, *Freedom Ride*, 142 (first quotation); Memphis *Commercial Appeal*, August 25, 1961 (second quotation); *Jackson Clarion-Ledger*, August 24, 25 (third quotation), 1961; Lafayette and Thomas interview; Gaither interview; "Two CORE Freedom Riders Convicted in Mississippi: United States Supreme Court Appeal Planned," CORE press release, August 28, 1961, folder 3, box 8, SNCCP. See also untitled typescript of trial report prepared for *Jubilee* magazine, c. August 1961, section 457, reel 44, COREP.
42. *Jackson Daily News*, August 26, 1961 (quotations); *New York Times*, August 26, 1961; Gaither, Rich, and Blankenheim interviews; Fairclough, *Race and Democracy*, 289; Farmer, *Lay Bare the Heart*, 211–212.
43. *Memphis Commercial Appeal*, August 27, 1961 (quotations); *Jackson Clarion-Ledger*, August 27, 1961; *New York Times*, August 27, 1961.
44. *Jackson Clarion-Ledger*, August 29, 1961 (quotation); Gaither, Moody, and Matthew Walker Jr. interviews; Moody interview, UMFRC.
45. On the payment of fines and the controversies related to appeals and bonds, see sections 445 and 450, reel 44, COREP. *Jackson State-Times*, August 31, 1961 (quotations); *Memphis Commercial Appeal*, August 31, 1961; *New York Times*, August 29–30, 1961; *Jackson Daily News*, September 1, 1961; Rich and Gaither interviews; Haley interview, RBOHC. No stranger to adversity, Haley had lost his position as a music professor at Florida A&M University in Tallahassee in 1960 after university officials became aware of his activities with the local CORE chapter. See Due and Due, *Freedom in the Family*, 45, 101–104, 135; and Rabby, *The Pain and the Promise*, 121–122. On the Freedom Rider trials in Jackson, see sections 450 and 454, reel 44, COREP.

Chapter 11: Oh, Freedom

1. Silverman, *Songs of Protest and Civil Rights*, 44–45. The song was adapted from the traditional spiritual "Oh, Freedom."
2. *New York Times*, September 2, 1961 (quotations); *Memphis Commercial Appeal*, September 2, 1961; *Washington Evening Star*, September 1, 1961; *Baltimore Afro-American*, September 16, 1961; Rich and Gaither interviews; Meier and Rudwick, *CORE*, 142–143, 153; Farmer, *Lay Bare the Heart*, 211–214.
3. *Birmingham News*, September 2, 1961 (quotation); *Birmingham Post-Herald*, September 2, 1961; *Anniston Star*, September 1–3, 1961; *New York Times*, September 2, 1961; *Washington Evening-Star*, September 1, 1961; Thornton, *Dividing Lines*, 246, 249; Sprayberry, " 'Town Among the Trees,' " 248–254.
4. Meier and Rudwick, *CORE*, 153; 1961 CORE Convention, memoranda and correspondence, section 1, reel 16, COREP; Farmer, *Lay Bare the Heart*, 213–214; Rich and Carey interviews; *Jackson Daily News*, September 5, 1961 (quotation); *Jackson Clarion-Ledger*, September 5, 1961; *Washington Evening Star*, September 5, 1961; *New York Times*, September 5, 1961; *Baltimore Afro-American*, September 16, 1961.
5. *Jackson Clarion-Ledger*, September 5, 1961 (first quotation); *Jackson Daily News*, September 6, 1961 (second quotation); *Baltimore Afro-American*, September 16, 23, 1961.

6. Dittmer, *Local People*, 108; Zinn, *SNCC*, 69–70 (quotation); Forman, *The Making of Black Revolution-aries*, 229–230; Branch, *Parting the Waters*, 501–504; Carson, *In Struggle*, 48; *Kansas City Star*, September 7, 1961; *Jet* 20 (September 21, 1961); Britt interview, RBOHC.

7. *Jackson Clarion-Ledger*, September 6–8, 1961; *Jackson Daily News*, September 5–8, 1961; *Baltimore Afro-American*, September 16, 23, 1961; Aelony interview; Aelony interview, UMFRC; Armstrong interview; Armstrong interview, UMFRC; section 441, reel 43, COREP.

8. Zinn, *SNCC*, 70–71 (first quotation); Forman, *The Making of Black Revolutionaries*, 230 (second quotation); Dittmer, *Local People*, 108–109, 458 n. 37; Branch, *Parting the Waters*, 503–504, 507–508; Carson, *In Struggle*, 48; Burner, *And Gently He Shall Lead Them*, 55–56; Bass, *Unlikely Heroes*, 216; Doar interview; Marshall interview, JFKL; John Doar and Dorothy Landsberg, "The Performance of the FBI in Investigating Violations of Federal Laws Protecting the Right to Vote, 1960–1967," 1971 essay, copy in JFKL, 28; *U.S. v. Wood*, 295 F. 2d 772; Grant, *Black Protest*, 307–311; Feagans, "Voting, Violence, and Walkout in McComb," 3; *Baltimore Afro-American*, September 30, October 7, November 11, 1961; Barbara Carter, "The Fifteenth Amendment Comes to Mississippi," *Reporter* 28 (January 17, 1963): 22.

9. Meier and Rudwick, *CORE*, 150–152; Barnes, *Journey from Jim Crow*, 168; memoranda and correspondence, sections 244, 249, 254–255, 260, 270, reels 36–37, sections 456–457, reel 44, COREP; "Farmer Announces CORE Expansion to Establish 5 Regional Offices," July 28, 1961, folder 3, box 8, SNCCP; Blankenheim, Cox, Brooks, Gaither, Harbour, Rich, and Carey interviews; *New York Times*, September 9, 1961; *Nashville Tennessean*, September 12, 1961; *Voice of the Movement*, September 9, 1961, copy in folder 8, box 76, KMSP; Peck, *Freedom Ride*, 158. Walter Bergman was involved in recruiting and fund-raising activities until an emergency appendectomy left him in critical condition in September. *Baltimore Afro-American*, September 30, 1961; Kaufman, *The First Freedom Ride*, 84–91.

10. Martin Luther King Jr., " 'The Time for Freedom Has Come,' " *New York Times Magazine* (September 10, 1961): 25, 118–119.

11. Arraignment correspondence (August 15–October 10, 1961), section 445, reel 44, COREP; *New York Times*, September 12, 1961; *Jackson Clarion-Ledger*, September 12, 1961; *Birmingham News*, September 13, 1961 (quotation); *Baltimore Afro-American*, September 16, 1961.

12. *Jackson Daily News*, September 14, 1961.

13. Roster of Freedom Riders, Group 37, September 13, 1961, MSCP; *Jackson Clarion-Ledger*, September 14, 1961 (first quotation); *Birmingham News*, September 14, 1961 (telegram quotation); *Birmingham Post-Herald*, September 15–16, 20, 1961; *Jackson Daily News*, September 16, 1961 (third quotation); *New York Times*, September 14, 17 (fourth quotation), 1961; *Memphis Commercial Appeal*, September 16, 1961 (fifth and sixth quotations); *Christian Science Monitor*, September 16, 1961; *Montgomery Advertiser*, October 10, 1961; Baltimore *Afro-American*, September 23, October 7, 1961; Scott Bates, interview by author, February 18, 2005. On Belford, see Peck, *Freedom Ride*, 141–142. For miscellaneous correspondence and other materials on the September 1961 Prayer Pilgrimage, see box 52, Episcopal Society for Cultural and Racial Unity Records. Malcolm Boyd later became a best-selling author. See Malcolm Boyd, *Are You Running with Me, Jesus? Prayers* (New York: Avon, 1967); Malcolm Boyd, *As I Live and Breathe: Stages of an Autobiography* (New York: Random House, 1970); and Malcolm Boyd, *Half Laughing/Half Crying: Songs of My Life* (New York: St. Martin's, 1986).

14. *Montgomery Advertiser*, September 17, 1961; *Birmingham News*, September 16, 1961 (quotation); *New York Times*, September 16, 1961; Shuttlesworth, Coffin, Maguire, and Wyatt Tee Walker interviews; Maguire interview, UMFRC; Manis, *A Fire You Can't Put Out*, 287; Coffin, *Once to Every Man*, 169.

15. Manis, *A Fire You Can't Put Out*, 240–245, 241 (quotations); "Delinquency—Alabama Style," *Southern Patriot* 8 (October 1960): 2–4; *Birmingham Post-Herald*, September 17, 1960; *Birmingham News*, September 7, 1960; Shuttlesworth interview; RD 34, box 6, Investigative Report Cases Files, ICCR. See also Ellen Levine, ed., *Freedom's Children: Young Civil Rights Activists Tell Their Own Stories* (New York: G. P. Putnam's Sons, 1993), 67–68, for a personal account by Ricky Shuttlesworth Bester.

16. On Shuttlesworth's consistent militancy from 1960 to 1962, see Manis, *A Fire You Can't Put Out*, 236–317; Eskew, *But for Birmingham*, 27, 32–33, 158–160, 205, 208; McWhorter, *Carry Me Home*, 151–154, 159–160, 174–177, 180–181, 243–244, 266–267; and Thornton, *Dividing Lines*, 259–289. On the mixed signals coming out of the Kennedy administration, see Niven, *The Politics of Injustice*, 118–123; and Peck, *Freedom Ride*, 156–158. *Jackson Daily News*, July 18, 1961 (quotations); *Baltimore Afro-American*, September 23, 1961.

17. *New York Times*, September 20, 1961 (quotations); *Memphis Commercial Appeal*, September 19, 1961; *Jackson Clarion-Ledger*, September 20, 1961; *Jackson Daily News*, September 19, 1961.

18. Farmer, *Lay Bare the Heart*, 211–212 (quotations); Meier and Rudwick, *CORE*, 142–143; Barnes, *Journey from Jim Crow*, 174; Rich interview; minutes of National Action Committee meetings, September 8, October 27, 1961, section 5, reel 16, COREP; "NAACP Legal Defense Fund to Defend Jackson Riders," NAACP press release, November 2, 1961, folder 19, box 77, KMSP. On the burden of the bond payments, see the memoranda and documents in sections 444 and 450, reel 44, COREP. In the weeks preceding and following Marshall's departure from the NAACP Legal and Educational Defense Fund, the organization was racked with controversy over the choice of his successor. When Marshall made sure that the position went to the white attorney Jack Greenberg instead of Robert Carter or Constance Baker Motley, there were hard feelings. See Williams, *Thurgood Marshall*, 294–295; and Carter, *A Matter of Law*, 136–170.

19. *New York Times*, September 23, 1961 (first quotation); Meier and Rudwick, *CORE*, 143 (second quotation); Carey interview; "Washington Project" memorandum, September 1961, reel 47, COREP;

CORE press release, September 5, 1961, reel 31, COREP; Barnes, *Journey from Jim Crow*, 175 (third quotation).

20. *New York Times*, September 23, 1961 (quotations); Barnes, *Journey from Jim Crow*, 176–177; ICC Order No. MC-C-3358 (Part 180A), September 22, 1961, copy in box 1, Correspondence and Un-numbered Cases, ICCR.

21. Marshall interview, JFKL (quotation); Niven, *The Politics of Injustice*, 120; Navasky, *Kennedy Justice*, 21, 445; Wofford, *Of Kennedys and Kings*, 157; Barnes, *Journey from Jim Crow*, 177, 265. "Before the ICC . . .," Burke Marshall Records, box 1, USDJ/CRD. In addition to William H. Tucker, the 1961 ICC included John W. Bush, Howard G. Freas, Abe McGregor Goff, Clyde E. Herring, Everett Hutchinson, Donald P. McPherson, Rupert L. Murphy, Kenneth H. Tuggle, Lawrence K. Walrath, and Charles Webb.

22. *New York Times*, September 24, 1961 (first quotation). Reporters and editors for the three white newspapers published in Jackson, Mississippi–the *Daily News*, the *Clarion-Ledger*, and the *State-Times*–made only passing mention of the ICC order during the week following the ruling. On September 23 the *Birmingham News* ran a story under the headline "State Officials Flay Mix Edict," and the *Montgomery Advertiser* carried a front-page story with the title "ICC Orders Interstate Bus, Terminal Mixing." But neither paper offered much in the way of editorial comment on the order. For a limited survey of the black press reaction to the order, see the various clippings in reel 191, TIRRCF. *Baltimore Afro-American*, September 30, October 7, 1961; Farmer, *Lay Bare the Heart*, 213 (quotations).

23. Rich and Carey interviews; Farmer, *Lay Bear the Heart*, 213; Niven, *The Politics of Injustice*, 120–121; Wofford, *Of Kennedys and Kings*, 157. On CORE's dealings with the ICC, see the correspondence and testing forms in section 497, reel 46, COREP.

24. Moses, "Mississippi: 1961–1962," 12–13; Branch, *Parting the Waters*, 508–511 (quotations), 520–522; Dittmer, *Local People*, 109–110, 114, 131–132; Carson, *In Struggle*, 48–49; Zinn, *SNCC*, 72–74; Doar and Landsberg, "The Performance of the FBI," 32–39; Forman, *The Making of Black Revolutionaries*, 231; *Baltimore Afro-American*, October 7, 14, 1961; Julian Bond, "Death of a Quiet Man—A Mississippi Postscript," *Rights and Reviews* (Winter 1967): 15–17; Carter, "The Fifteenth Amendment Comes to Mississippi," 21. More than two years after Lee's murder, on January 31, 1964, Louis Allen was shot and killed by an unknown gunman. Burner, *And Gently He Shall Lead Them*, 56–59, 236; Doar interview.

25. *Jackson Clarion-Ledger*, September 25, 26 (quotation), 1961; *Baltimore Afro-American*, October 7, 1961. On Rives, see Bass, *Unlikely Heroes*, 69–83. On Motley, see Motley, *Equal Justice Under Law*.

26. *Jackson Daily News*, September 26, 1961 (first quotation); *Jackson Clarion-Ledger*, September 27, 1961 (second quotation).

27. *Jackson Daily News*, September 26, 1961 (first and second quotations); *Jackson Clarion-Ledger*, September 28, 1961 (third, fourth, and fifth quotations).

28. *Jackson State-Times*, September 28, 1961 (first quotation); *Jackson Daily News*, September 28, 1961; *Jackson Clarion-Ledger*, September 29, 1961 (second quotation); *Baltimore Afro-American*, October 7, 1961.

29. *New York Times*, September 26 (quotations), 29, 30, 1961; *Baltimore Afro-American*, October 7, 1961; *Pittsburgh Courier*, October 7, 1961; Final Report on Belafonte Concert, September 27, 1961, folder 10, box 74, KMSP; SCLC board meeting minutes, September 27, 1961, folder 1, box 29, KPA; Branch, *Parting the Waters*, 514–515; Garrow, *Bearing the Cross*, 167–169; Brooks, Harbour, and Wyatt Tee Walker interviews.

30. Garrow, *Bearing the Cross*, 168 (quotation), 169; Branch, *Parting the Waters*, 514–515; Carson, *In Struggle*, 54; Chappell, *Stone of Hope*, 67–71; James Lawson, "Eve of Nonviolent Revolution," *Southern Patriot* 19 (November 1961): 1; Wyatt Tee Walker and Lafayette interviews.

31. Forman, *The Making of Black Revolutionaries*, 221–223, 234 (first quotation), 235–240 (third quotation), 249. Forman states that MOM stood for "March on Mississippi," but earlier in the summer the Nashville faction of SNCC had formulated a program called "Move on Mississippi." The two phrases were later used interchangeably. Dittmer, *Local People*, 107; Branch, *Parting the Waters*, 510 (second quotation), 518–519; Carson, *In Struggle*, 42–43, 50–55; Burner, *And Gently He Shall Lead Them*, 61–62; "New Spirit Moves in Mississippi," *Southern Patriot* 19 (November 1961): 1.

32. Dittmer, *Local People*, 110–113; Branch, *Parting the Waters*, 512–514; Zinn, *SNCC*, 74–76, 167–171; Burner, *And Gently He Shall Lead Them*, 60–62; Carson, *In Struggle*, 49; Forman, *The Making of Black Revolutionaries*, 231–232; Robert Zellner to Ed King, August 8, 1961, and Ed King to Robert Zellner, August 17, 1961, folder 10, box 8, SNCCP; Moses, "Mississippi, 1961–1962," 14; Hampton and Fayer, *Voices of Freedom*, 146; Grant, *Black Protest*, 307–308; Hayden, *Revolution in Mississippi*, 1–5; Adams, *James A. Dombrowski*, 256; Fosl, *Subversive Southerner*, 275–278; *McComb Enterprise Journal*, October 5–6, 1961; *New York Times*, October 5, 7, 12, 21, 24, 27, November 1, 1961; *Baltimore Afro-American*, October 14, 1961; McDew interview, RBOHC; Diamond interview. On Hayden, see Tom Hayden, *Reunion: A Memoir* (New York: Random House, 1988), 43–66; and Curry et al., *Deep in Our Hearts*, 340–344, 347–350.

33. Burner, *And Gently He Shall Lead* Them, 62 (first quotation), 63–68; Zinn, *SNCC*, 76–79 (second quotation); Moses, "Mississippi," 14–15 (third and fourth quotations); Carson, *In Struggle*, 49–50 (fifth quotation); Grant, *Black Protest*, 303; Hayden, *Revolution in Mississippi*, 1–2; Branch, *Parting the Waters*, 522, 560; Dittmer, *Local People*, 113–114; Forman, *The Making of Black Revolutionaries*, 233; Fosl, *Subversive Southerner*, 278; Adams, *James A. Dombrowski*, 256; SNCC press release on McComb, typescript draft, December 6, 1961, box 99, SNCCP.

34. Dittmer, *Local People*, 114–115; Branch, *Parting the Waters*, 524–528; Garrow, *Bearing the Cross*, 173–177; Lewis, *King*, 140–144; Michael Chalfen, "Rev. Samuel B. Wells and Black Protest in Albany, 1945–1965," *Journal of Southwest Georgia History* 9 (Fall 1994): 37–64; Fairclough, *To Redeem the Soul of America*, 85–88; Zinn, *SNCC*, 123–127; Howard Zinn, "Albany," typescript of Southern Regional Council Report No. 22, January 8, 1962, folder 14, box 20, SNCCP, 8–10; Cordell Reagon, "Report from Deep South," November 18–29, 1961, folder 24, box 19, SNCCP; Charles Sherrod, field report on Albany, folder 31, box 95, SNCCP; Forman, *The Making of Black Revolutionaries*, 240, 248–250, 251 (first quotation); Carson, *In Struggle*, 56–57, 58 (second quotation); Vernon Jordan with Annette Gordon-Reed, *Vernon Can Read: A Memoir* (New York: Public Affairs, 2001), 151–163; RD 128, box 16, and James Forman statement, RD 89, box 12, both in Investigative Report Case Files, ICCR; James Forman statement, folder 30, box 95, SNCCP; SNCC memorandum, November 10, 1961, folder 3, box 7, SNCCP.

35. Meier and Rudwick, *CORE*, 143; Carey and Rich interviews; *CORE-lator* (December 1961): 1–2; CORE testing forms and related documents, section 497, reel 46, COREP. See especially the November 7 memorandum from CORE to the Justice Department and the ICC, "Preliminary Report: Compliance with ICC Regulations," and the "Confidential Report: Bus Terminal Survey," issued November 6. See also the scattered material on the tests in sections 448, 450–452, reel 44, COREP. *New York Times*, November 1, 5 (quotations), 12, 1961; *Atlanta Constitution*, November 2, 1961; *Memphis Commercial Appeal*, November 1–2, 1961; *Baltimore Afro-American*, November 4, 11, 1961; Farmer, *Lay Bare the Heart*, 209–210, 213; Peck, *Freedom Ride*, 159; Barnes, *Journey from Jim Crow*, 179–180; Forman statement, folder 30, box 95, SNCCP; RD 89, box 12, Investigative Report Case Files, ICCR; Lafayette interview; "Signs Down," *Newsweek* 58 (November 13, 1961): 22–24. Branch, *Parting the Waters*, 527, estimates that CORE mobilized as many as seven hundred testers in November 1961. Carson, *In Struggle*, 37, 58; Niven, *The Politics of Injustice*, 121; Forman, *The Making of Black Revolutionaries*, 250; Garrow, *Bearing the Cross*, 172, 175. See also the investigative case files in boxes 12, 14–17, Investigative Report Case Files, ICCR. See especially cases RD 89, RD 105, RD 106, RD 110, RD 116, RD 119, RD 120, RD 122, RD 132, RD 135, RD 136, and RD 140.

36. *Montgomery Advertiser*, November 2, 1961 (quotation); *Birmingham News*, November 3–10, 1961; *Birmingham Post-Herald*, November 7, 9, 1961; *New York Times*, November 2, 5, 12, 1961; *Baltimore Afro-American*, November 4, 11, 1961; *Anniston Star*, November 1–4, 1961; Sprayberry, " 'Town Among the Trees,' " 259; "Preliminary Report: Compliance with ICC Regulations"; "Confidential Report: Bus Terminal Survey"; Lafayette interview; Thornton, *Dividing Lines*, 209; Nunnelley, *Bull Connor*, 118–120; Yarbrough, *Judge Frank Johnson and Human Rights in Alabama*, 83; Barnes, *Journey from Jim Crow*, 180, 267; RD 110, box 16, Investigative Report Case Files, ICCR. See also files 144-104-1-1 and 144-101-1-10, USDJ/CRD.

37. "Preliminary Report: Compliance with ICC Regulations"; "Confidential Report: Bus Terminal Survey"; *New York Times*, November 5, 12 (first quotation), 1961; *Baltimore Afro-American*, November 11, 1961; *Memphis Commercial Appeal*, November 2, 1961; *New Orleans Times-Picayune*, November 2, 1961 (second quotation); *Jackson Daily News*, November 4, 1961; Barnes, *Journey from Jim Crow*, 180. See the list of ICC actions in folder 1, box 1, Investigative Report Case Files, ICCR. See also files 144-01-40-10 (Grenada), 144-101-41-36 (Meridian), 144-101-41-28 (Vicksburg), and 144-01-41-22 (Jackson), USDJ/CRD.

38. Rich and Carey interviews; *New York Times*, November 3, 5, 1961; *Birmingham News*, November 9, 11, 1961; *Baltimore Afro-American*, November 11, 1961. The reporter was James Free, Washington correspondent for the *Birmingham News*. Barnes, *Journey from Jim Crow*, 180, 267. By the end of 1961 the Justice Department had filed seven requests for court orders to enjoin noncompliance. The seven communities involved were Greenwood and McComb, Mississippi; Alexandria, Baton Rouge, Monroe, and Rushton, Louisiana; and Birmingham, Alabama. See folder 1, box 1, and RD 110, box 15, Investigative Report Cases Files, ICCR; and files 144-101-33-4 (Monroe), 144-101-33-5 (Alexandria), 144-101-33-8 (Rushton), 144-101-32-10 (Baton Rouge), 144-101-40-5 (Greenwood), 144-101-41-20 (McComb), and 144-101-1-10 (Birmingham), USDJ/CRD.

39. Romano, "No Diplomatic Immunity," 568–574, 571 (quotation); *Baltimore Sun*, October 20, 1961; *Washington Evening Star*, October 20, 1961; *New York Times*, October 29, November 9, 11, 1961; *Baltimore Afro-American*, October 28, November 4, 11, 1961; "Halfway Home to Equality on Highway 40," *Life* 51 (November 16, 1961): 6; Route 40 Campaign correspondence and test results, sections 496–497, Reel 46, COREP. On the activities of Baltimore CORE in 1961, see sections 48–49, reel 21, COREP. Meier and Rudwick, *CORE*, 162, point out that student activists in Baltimore, organized as the Baltimore Civic Interest Group "felt that CORE had sold out by accepting even this compromise." To fend off such criticism, "CORE hastily redirected the manpower which had been mobilized for the Freedom Ride to 'Project Baltimore.' For three successive Saturdays in November and December, hundreds of demonstrators, mainly northeastern college students, tested and picketed Baltimore restaurants—all to no avail." On Hobson and Washington CORE, see section 24, reel 19, COREP; and Anderson-Bricker, "Making a Movement," 23–202.

40. On the relationship between the Kennedy brothers, Robert Kennedy's policies on civil rights enforcement, and the political pressures exerted on the Justice Department during the Kennedy administration, see Navasky, *Kennedy Justice*; Niven, *The Politics of Injustice*; Hilty, *Robert Kennedy*; Schlesinger, *Robert Kennedy and His Times*, 239–391, 584–602; Thomas, *Robert Kennedy*, 109–280; Wofford, *Of Kennedys and Kings*, 124–151, 160–177; Guthman, *We Band of Brothers*, 88–90, 95–107, 176–182; Russell L. Riley, *The Presidency and the Politics of Racial Inequality* (New York: Columbia University Press, 1999), 207–219; and Sorensen, *Kennedy*, 267–269. Marshall and Robert Kennedy

interviews, JFKL; Doar and Seigenthaler interviews; *Jackson Daily News*, November 18–20, 1961; *New York Times*, November 3, 18 (quotation), 21–23, 1961; *Bailey v. Patterson*, 199 F. Supp. 595 (S.D. Miss. 1961); Barnes, *Journey from Jim Crow*, 167; folder 1, box 1, Investigative Report Case Files, ICCR. Three days after the disappointing ruling in Jackson, on November 20, Alabama Circuit Judge Eugene Carter summarily rejected the appeals of William Sloane Coffin, Wyatt Tee Walker, and ten other Freedom Riders arrested in Montgomery on May 25. *Birmingham News*, November 20–21, 1961.

41. *New York Times*, November 22, 28–30, December 1, December 3, 1961 (quotations); *New York Post*, November 30, 1961; *New Orleans Times-Picayune*, December 2, 1961; *Louisiana Weekly*, December 9, 1961; *McComb Enterprise-Journal*, December 2, 6, 1961; *Jackson State-Times*, November 30, 1961; Doar and Gaither interviews; Doratha Smith-Simmons, interview by author, June 27, 2005; Jerome Smith, Doratha Smith-Simmons, and Alice Thompson interviews, ARC; George Raymond, interview by Robert Wright, September 28, 1968, RBOHC; *Jet* 21 (December 14, 1961): 4; *Jet* 21 (December 21, 1961): 6; *Time* 58 (December 8, 1961): 25; "Bus Stop," *Newsweek* (December 11, 1961): 31–32; Branch, *Parting the Waters*, 559; Dittmer, *Local People*, 114; Anderson-Bricker, "Making a Movement," 328–330; Rogers, *Righteous Lives*, 130–143. See also *U.S. v. Mayor and Selectmen of McComb*, 6 RRLR 1169 (1961); and RD 132, box 17, Investigative Report Case Files, ICCR.

42. *New York Times*, December 4 (first and second quotations), 5, 7, 10, 23, 1961; Doar and Gaither interviews; Dittmer, *Local People*, 66; Branch, *Parting the Waters*, 560 (third quotation); Niven, *The Politics of Injustice*, 121; Hayden, *Reunion*, 61.

43. Fairclough, *To Redeem the Soul of America*, 85–88 (first quotation); *New York Times*, December 11, 13, 14 (second quotation), 15 (third quotation), 1961; *Atlanta Constitution*, December 13–16, 1961; *Albany Herald*, November 22–December 16, 1961; Zinn, "Albany," 11–16; Reagon, "Report from the Deep South"; Sherrod, field report on Albany; Blanton Hall statement, November 11, 1961, and Bernice Johnson statement, December 13, 1961, both in folder 30, box 95, SNCCP; Zinn, *SNCC*, 123–130; Branch, *Parting the Waters*, 529–538; Lewis, *King*, 143–147; Garrow, *Bearing the Cross*, 173–182; Forman, *The Making of Black Revolutionaries*, 251–255; Carson, *In Struggle*, 56–60; Morris, *The Origins of the Civil Rights Movement*, 239–242; William G. Anderson, "Reflections on the Origins of the Albany Movement," *Journal of Southwest Georgia History* 9 (Fall 1994): 1–14; Barnes, *Journey from Jim Crow*, 190–191; Hayden, *Reunion*, 67–74; Pat Watters, *Down to Now: Reflections on the Civil Rights Movement* (New York: Random House, 1971), 158–163; Mussatt, "Journey for Justice," 40–48, 69–80, 89–92, 115–131, 143–145, 177–181, 195–198; Curry et al., *Deep in Our Hearts*, 66–71, 74, 344–347; Norma Collins, interview by author and Kelly Benjamin, June 25, 2005; Joan Browning, interview by author, November 10, 2001, July 9, 2004, June 11, 2005; Joan Browning, "Who, What, When, Where?—Success or Failure? Conflicting Memories of the Albany Freedom Ride and Albany Movement," unpublished paper presented at the annual meeting of the Georgia Association of Historians, Albany, GA, April 15, 2000. On the evolution of railway desegregation in late 1961 and the Justice Department's efforts to bring the railways into line with the ICC order, see Barnes, *Journey from Jim Crow*, 177–178, 182, 265–266; "On the Railroad," *Newsweek* 58 (October 30, 1961): 19; and *Baltimore Afro-American*, October 28, 1961.

44. *New York Times*, December 15 (first quotation),16 (third quotation), 1961; *Albany Herald*, December 15–17, 1961; *Atlanta Constitution*, December 15–16, 1961; Branch, *Parting the Waters*, 540–541, 542 (second quotation), 543–545, 546 (fifth quotation), 547–550, 551 (fourth quotation), 552 (sixth quotation), 553–560; Fairclough, *To Redeem the Soul of America*, 88–91; Garrow, *Bearing the Cross*, 181–188; Lewis, *King*, 147–155; Forman, *The Making of Black Revolutionaries*, 255–262; Lewis, *Walking with the Wind*, 186–187; Zinn, "Albany," 16–34; Zinn, *SNCC*, 130–133; Sherrod, field report on Albany; Morris, *Origins of the Civil Rights Movement*, 242–245; Watters, *Down to Now*, 163–165; Carson, *In Struggle*, 60; Abernathy, *And the Walls Came Tumbling Down*, 154–155; Marshall interview, JFKL; Wyatt Tee Walker interview, RBOHC; Carey and Wyatt Tee Walker interviews; New York *Herald Tribune*, December 19, 1961 (seventh quotation). On *Georgia v. U.S. and ICC* (No. 963) (1961), see the motion to affirm in folder 3, box 1, Correspondence and Unnumbered Cases, ICCR; and case file 144-101-19-6, USDJ/CRD. On the complexities of King's involvement in Albany, see the three essays published in the *Journal of Southwest Georgia History* 2 (Fall 1984) under the general title "The Civil Rights Struggle in Southwest Georgia: Three Perspectives": John A. Ricks III, " 'De Lawd' Descends and Is Crucified: Martin Luther King, Jr., in Albany, Georgia," 3–14; Clayborne Carson, "SNCC and the Albany Movement," 15–25; and Stephen B. Oates, "The Albany Movement: A Chapter in the Life of Martin Luther King, Jr.," 26–39.

45. *New York Times*, December 3 (Lewis quotation), 17, 1961; Meier and Rudwick, *CORE*, 162–163; Lee Hamalian, "Life Begins on Route 40," *Nation* 194 (January 27, 1962): 71–73; Romano, "No Diplomatic Immunity," 573; Julius Hobson, memorandum, section 35, reel 13, COREP; Wofford, *Of Kennedys and Kings*, 126–128. See also section 495, reel 46, COREP. Nunnelley, *Bull Connor*, 120; Thornton, *Dividing Lines*, 204–205, 209–210; *Birmingham World*, December 20, 1961; *Birmingham Post-Herald*, December 20, 29, 1961, January 6, 1962; *Birmingham News*, December 15, 20, 1961, January 9, 1962; *Montgomery Advertiser*, December 15, 17, 20, 29, 1961; Barnes, *Journey from Jim Crow*, 189; *Boman v. Morgan*, 7 RRLR 569 (1962); files 144-104-1-1, and 144-101-1-10, USDJ/CRD.

46. *Jackson Daily News*, December 6, 17–20, 1961; *Jackson Clarion-Ledger*, December 15 (first quotation), 17, 19, 1961; *New York Times*, December 17, 19, 23 (second quotation), 1961. On the continuing effort to enforce the ICC order in Jackson, see folder 1, box 1, Investigative Report Case Files, ICCR; and the legal briefs for *U.S. and ICC v. City of Jackson and Mayor Allen Thompson* (No. 19,794, Fifth Circuit Court of Appeals), folder 3, box 1, Correspondence and Unnumbered Cases, ICCR.

Epilogue: Glory Bound

1. This often-quoted verse became a Freedom Rider anthem in 1961. Freedom Rides exhibit text, National Civil Rights Museum, Memphis, Tennessee.
2. McWhorter, *Carry Me Home*, 236.
3. Jackson trial correspondence, reel 44, COREP; Meier and Rudwick, *CORE*, 143; Barnes, *Journey from Jim Crow*, 180–184; *Memphis Commercial Appeal*, January 11, 1962; *Jackson Clarion-Ledger*, February 1, April 9–12, 1962; *Jackson Daily News*, January 17, 1962; *New York Times*, January 25, February 27 (quotation)–28, March 22, 1962; *Bailey v. Patterson*, 369 U.S. 31 (1962); RD 97, box 13, RD 108, box 15, RD 132, RD 140, RD 142, RD 145, box 17, RD 153, RD 157, box 18, RD 171, box 19, Investigative Report Case Files, ICCR; Bureau of Inquiry and Compliance, memorandum to Chairman Walrath, August 7, 1963, box 1, Correspondence and Unnumbered Cases, ICCR; folders 2–4, box 1, Burke Marshall Records, USDJ/CRD. See also the Mississippi case files in 144–101, 144–103, and 144–104, USDJ/CRD.
4. *Jackson Clarion-Ledger*, January–June 1962; *Jackson Daily News*, January–June 1962; Dittmer, *Local People*, 123; Moye, *Let the People Decide*, 89–90; file 144-41-450, USDJ/CRD.
5. Dittmer, *Local People*, 122–124; Meier and Rudwick, *CORE*, 144, 166; Branch, *Parting the Waters*, 578, 633–638; Zinn, *SNCC*, 79–80; Payne, *I've Got the Light of Freedom*, 128–131; Carson, *In Struggle*, 79–80; Garrow, *Bearing the Cross*, 194; Gaither and Lafayette interviews.
6. Payne, *I've Got the Light of Freedom*, 130–153, 146 (second quotation); Zinn, *SNCC*, 79–102; Dittmer, *Local People*, 117–136, 150 (third quotation), 180–183; Branch, *Parting the Waters*, 633–639; Meier and Rudwick, *CORE*, 178–180, 185; Carson, *In Struggle*, 77–81; Moye, *Let the People Decide*, 89–110; Fairclough, *To Redeem the Soul of America*, 91; Lewis, *Walking with the Wind*, 187; *Jackson Advocate*, May 12, 1962; *Student Voice* (April 1962); RD 164, box 19, Investigative Report Case Files, ICCR; *New York Times*, April 22, 2000.
7. SNCC press release, April 30, 1962, box 38, SNCCP (quotation); SCEF press release, May 21, 1962, box 10, SNCCP; *Student Voice*, June 1962; *Jackson Advocate*, May 12, 1962; Garrow, *Bearing the Cross*, 197, 202; Branch, *Parting the Waters*, 634–639; Zinn, *SNCC*, 80–81; Dittmer, *Local People*, 123–124.
8. Barnes, *Journey from Jim Crow*, 181–184; Dittmer, *Local People*, 183–142 (quotation), 183; Branch, *Parting the Waters*, 633–672; Moye, *Let the People Decide*, 104–105; William Doyle, *An American Insurrection: The Battle of Oxford, Mississippi, 1962* (New York: Doubleday, 2001); Powledge, *Free at Last?* 421–445; Motley, *Equal Justice Under Law*, 162–192; Silver, *Mississippi*; James Meredith, *Three Years in Mississippi* (Bloomington: Indiana University Press, 1966); James Meredith, *James Meredith vs. Ole Miss* (Jackson: Meredith Publishing, 1995); James Meredith, *Me and My Kind: An Oral History* (Jackson: Meredith Publishing, 1995).
9. Barnes, *Journey from Jim Crow*, 181–192, 183 (quotation); U.S. Department of Justice, Attorney General, *Annual Report of the Attorney General of the United States for the Fiscal Year Ended June 30, 1963* (Washington: GPO, 1964), 188; RD 97, box 13, Investigative Report Case Files, ICCR; Meier and Rudwick, *CORE*, 143; Jackson *Clarion-Ledger*, December 29, 1964. See also the legal and other correspondence related to the Freedom Rider cases in reels 25 and 44, COREP; and the bail bond material in reel 10, COREPA.
10. Fairclough, *Race and Democracy*, 280–296; Meier and Rudwick, *CORE*, 166–169, 176–177; Willie Burton, *On the Black Side of Shreveport* (Shreveport, 1983), 81–108; Barnes, *Journey from Jim Crow*, 181, 183; Garrow, *Bearing the Cross*, 200; Powledge, *Free at Last?* 367–368; Dennis, Diamond, and Cox interviews; *Student Voice*, January 1, 1962; *Student Voice*, April 1962; SNCC press releases, March 28, 1962 (quotations), April 6, 1962, SNCCP; *New York Times*, June 5, 1962; memorandum to Chairman Walrath, August 7, 1963; RD 95, RD 100, box 13, RD 107, RD 109, box 15, RD 122, box 16, RD 137, box 17, RD 157, box 18, RD 170, box 19, RD 187, box 20, Investigative Report Case Files, ICCR. On the 1953 Baton Rouge bus boycott, see Morris, *Origins of the Civil Rights Movement*, 17–25.
11. Fairclough, *Race and Democracy*, 199–200, 235–264, 278–279; Rogers, *Righteous Lives*, 49–76; Glen Jeansonne, *Leander Perez: Boss of the Delta* (Baton Rouge: Louisiana State University Press, 1977); Sherrill, *Gothic Politics in the Deep South*, 5–38; *New York Times*, April 25, 27–29, 1962; Clive Webb, " 'A Cheap Trafficking in Human Misery': The Reverse Freedom Rides of 1962," *Journal of American Studies* 38 (2004): 251, 253 (second quotation), 254–255 (first quotation), 256–258; *Newsweek* (May 7, 1962): 30; *New York Herald Tribune*, April 25, 1962; *New York Times*, April 25, 28, 1962; McMillen, *The Citizens' Council*, 230–233.
12. Webb, " 'A Cheap Trafficking in Human Misery,' " 256–271; *New York Times*, April 25 (quotations), 27–29, May 19, 30, June 9, 11–12, 19, 1962; *Washington Star*, May 10, 1962 (Kennedy quotation); *Montgomery Advertiser*, June 10, 1962; *Charleston News and Courier*, June 10, 1962; *New Orleans Times-Picayune*, April 24, 1962; *Jackson Clarion-Ledger*, April 25, 28, 1962.
13. Webb, " 'A Cheap Trafficking in Human Misery,' "257 (first quotation), 258, 259 (third quotation), 260 (second quotation), 261–271; *New York Times*, April 28, May 11, 13, 22, 28, 30–31, June 5, 19, 1962; *Birmingham News*, May 25, 1962; *Montgomery Advertiser*, June 10, 17, 1962; *Louisville Courier-Journal*, May 25, 1962; *Pittsburgh Courier*, May 12, June 9, 1962.
14. Webb, " 'A Cheap Trafficking in Human Misery,' "256; *New York Times*, June 15, 1962; RD 64, box 10, RD 91, box 12, RD 116, RD 127, box 16, RD 165, box 19, RD 190, box 20, Investigative Report Case Files, ICCR; Bartley, *The Creation of Modern Georgia*, 199–207; Numan V. Bartley, *From Thurmond to Wallace: Political Tendencies in Georgia, 1948–1968* (Baltimore: Johns Hopkins University Press, 1970); Jack Bass and Walter DeVries, *The Transformation of Southern Politics: Social Change and Political Consequences Since 1945* (New York: Basic Books, 1976), 136–144; Tuck, *Beyond Atlanta*, 114–147;

Jimmy Carter, *Turning Point: A Candidate, a State, and a Nation Come of Age* (New York: Times Books, 1992); Clark and Arsenault, *The Changing South of Gene Patterson*; Roche, *Restructured Resistance*; Ivan Allen Jr., *Mayor: Notes on the Sixties* (New York: Simon and Schuster, 1971); Sherrill, *Gothic Politics in the Deep South*, 65–78, 277–301; Bruce Galphin, *The Riddle of Lester Maddox* (Atlanta: Camelot, 1968); McGill, *The South and the Southerner*; Charles Weltner, *Southerner* (Philadelphia: J. B. Lippincott, 1966).

15. *New York Times*, January 6, March 27, July 27, 1962; Lewis *Portrait of a Decade*, 141–146; Zinn, *SNCC*, 133–139; Garrow, *Bearing the Cross*, 190–198; Lewis, *King*, 155–160; Fairclough, *To Redeem the Soul of America*, 91–100; Carson, *In Struggle*, 60; Branch, *Parting the Waters*, 620 (quotation), 630, 636–640; Pat Watters, *Down to Now: Reflections on the Southern Civil Rights Movement* (New York: Pantheon, 1971), 164–168; Powledge, *Free at Last?* 373–376; Tuck, *Beyond Atlanta*, 165–166; *Student Voice*, April 1962; SNCC press releases, March 22, June 26, 1962, box 34, SNCCP; Charles Jones statement, typescript, January 18, 1962, box 95, SNCCP; RD 128, box 16, Investigative Report Case Files, ICCR.

16. Branch, *Parting the Waters*, 601–632; Powledge, *Free at Last?* 376–420; Carson, *In Struggle*, 61–65; Garrow, *Bearing the Cross*, 202–219; Fairclough, *To Redeem the Soul of America*, 92, 101–108; Zinn, *SNCC*, 134–146; Tuck, *Beyond Atlanta*, 158–191; Lewis, *Walking with the Wind*, 191–192; Lewis, *King*, 160–170; Hayden, *Reunion*, 72.

17. *New York Times*, January 10, 17, February 1 (first quotation)13, 1962; *Birmingham News*, January 9, 16–17, February 1–13, 1962; *Birmingham Post-Herald*, January 8–10, 16–18, 1962; SCLC to Southern Civil Rights Organizations, memoranda, January 19, 26, 1962, and Southern Civil Rights Organizations to Attorney General Robert Kennedy, telegram, January 26, 1962, box 20, SNCCP; Manis, *A Fire You Can't Put Out*, 289–299, 315; Thornton, *Dividing Lines*, 259–268; McWhorter, *Carry Me Home*, 259–265; Branch, *Parting the Waters*, 570–572 (second quotation); Nunnelley, *Bull Connor*, 112–121; Gaillard, *Cradle of Freedom*, 129–133, 186–187; Eskew, *But for Birmingham*, 165; Meier and Rudwick, *CORE*, 165–166; Harbour and Thomas interviews; RD 110, box 15, RD 136, box 17, RD 147, RD 148, RD 152, box 18, Investigative Report Case Files, ICCR.

18. Shuttlesworth interview; Manis, *A Fire You Can't Put Out*, 299 (first quotation), 304–315, 307 (fourth quotation), 310 (second, third, and sixth quotations), 314 (fifth quotation); Branch, *Parting the Waters*, 572–573; *Jet* 21 (March 22, 1962): 24; SCLC press release, March 1, 1962, SCLCP; SCEF press release, April 3, 1962, and Anne Braden to Julian Bond, April 15, 1962, box 20, SNCCP; Eskew, *But for Birmingham*, 196–201; Thornton, *Dividing Lines*, 264–270; McWhorter, *Carry Me Home*, 265–268; Fairclough, *To Redeem the Soul of America*, 113; Garrow, *Bearing the Cross*, 199; Fosl, *Subversive Southerner*, 283–284; Nunnelley, *Bull Connor*, 121–122.

19. *Birmingham News*, May 5–9, 1962; *Montgomery Advertiser*, May 2–9, 1962; Dan T. Carter, *The Politics of Rage: George Wallace, the Origins of the New Conservatism, and the Transformation of American Politics* (Baton Rouge: Louisiana State University Press, 2000), 90–96 (second quotation), 105 (first quotation)–108; Nunnelley, *Bull Connor*, 123–125; McWhorter, *Carry Me Home*, 268–271; Manis, *A Fire You Can't Put Out*, 315–316; Gaillard, *Cradle of Freedom*, 112–117; Marshall Frady, *Wallace* (New York: New American Library, 1976), 122–135.

20. Manis, *A Fire You Can't Put Out*, 292 (first quotation), 315; Nunnelley, *Bull Connor*, 123–125 (second and fourth quotations); Carter, *The Politics of Rage*, 110 (third quotation). On the relationship between Wallace and Johnson, see Bass, *Taming the Storm*, 3, 49–50, 195, 214–217, 261, 266, 353, 461–462. On Wallace and the 1962–1963 University of Alabama desegregation crisis, see Clark, *The Schoolhouse Door*. *Student Voice*, April and June 1962; SNCC press releases, April 10, 30, 1962, box 34, SNCCP; Harry Harvey, interview by author, June 4, 2005. On Talladega College, a black college founded in 1867 by Northern white Congregationalists and affiliated with the United Church of Christ, see Maxine D. Jones and Joe D. Richardson, *Talladega College: The First Century* (Tuscaloosa: University of Alabama Press, 1990).

21. Manis, *A Fire You Can't Put Out*, 290, 317–326; Garrow, *Bearing the Cross*, 220–230; Eskew, *But for Birmingham*, 181–187; Fairclough, *To Redeem the Soul of America*, 113–114; Thornton, *Dividing Lines*, 271–290; McWhorter, *Carry Me Home*, 275–322; Branch, *Parting the Waters*, 693–707; Nunnelley, *Bull Connor*, 125–133, 137; Gaillard, *Cradle of Freedom*, 131–133, 135–139; Powledge, *Free at Last?* 480–495.

22. McWhorter, *Carry Me Home*, 323–454; Branch, *Parting the Waters*, 703–802; Fairclough, *To Redeem the Soul of America*, 114–140; Lewis, *King*, 171–209; Garrow, *Bearing the Cross*, 231–271; Eskew, *But for Birmingham*, 210–340; Thornton, *Dividing Lines*, 290–379; Powledge, *Free at Last?* 496–519. On King's Birmingham jail letter, see Bass, *Blessed Are the Peacemakers*.

23. Mary Stanton, *Freedom Walk: Mississippi or Bust* (Jackson: University Press of Mississippi, 2003), xiii–90, 211–218, 3 (first quotation), 54 (second quotation), 69 (third quotation); *New York Times*, April 24–29, 1963; *New York Post*, April 24–25, 30, 1963; *Washington Post*, April 30, 1963; *Baltimore Evening Sun*, April 24, 1963; *Birmingham Post-Herald*, April 25–26, 29–30, 1963; *Birmingham News*, April 25–26, 1963; *Pittsburgh Courier*, April 25, 1963; *Jet* 23 (May 9, 1963): 14–19; Murray Kempton, "Pilgrimage to Jackson," *New Republic* 148 (May 11, 1963): 15; Meier and Rudwick, *CORE*, 215; Zinn, *SNCC*, 174–175; Branch, *Parting the Waters*, 748–750, 754; McWhorter, *Carry Me Home*, 358–359. See also the correspondence and documents in section 236, box 35, COREP.

24. Stanton, *Freedom Walk*, 93–95, 99–222, 109 (second quotation), 95 (third quotation), 122 (fourth and fifth quotations); Branch, *Parting the Waters*, 750–751, 754–755, 764–765; Zinn, *SNCC*, 175–180, 183, 193; Meier and Rudwick, *CORE*, 215–216; McWhorter, *Carry Me Home*, 364, 370, 373; Gaillard, *Cradle of Freedom*, 157–163; Forman, *The Making of Black Revolutionaries*, 308–110; Adams, *James A. Dombrowski*, 259–260; *New York Times*, April 27 (Nashville march quotations), 28, May 1–5, June 21,

1963; *New York Post*, April 30, 1963; *Montgomery Advertiser*, May 1, 1963; *Birmingham News*, April 29–May 4, 1963; *Baltimore Afro-American*, June 29, 1963; Richard Haley to Dear Friend, c. May 1, 1963, box 12, SNCCP; CORE steering committee minutes, April 26, 1963, section 5, box 16, and misc. correspondence, section 236, box 35, COREP.

25. Harbour interview (quotation); Brooks, Lewis, and Maguire interviews.
26. Barnes, *Journey from Jim Crow*, 179–184; Department of Justice, Attorney General, *Annual Report for 1963*, 188. See the correspondence and test results in sections 495–497, reel 46, COREP. See also RD 66, box 10, RD 73–RD 87, box 11, RD 90–RD 93A, box 12, RD 98, RD 101, RD 102, box 13, RD 119, box 16, RD 160, RD 166, box 18, RD 179, box 19, RD 191, box 20, Investigative Report Case Files, ICCR. The political and cultural gap between the border and Rim South states and the Deep South became increasingly obvious during the early and mid-1960s. See especially the essays in John C. McKinney, ed., *The South in Continuity and Change* (Durham: Duke University Press, 1963); Allen P. Sindler, ed., *Change in the Contemporary South* (Durham: Duke University Press, 1964); and Willie Morris, ed., *The South Today: One Hundred Years After Appomattox* (New York: Harper and Row, 1965). On the political and socio-economic transformation of the border and Rim South states, see Bass and DeVries, *The Transformation of Southern Politics*, 3–40, 87–135, 284–368; William C. Havard, ed., *The Changing Politics of the South* (Baton Rouge: Louisiana State University, 1972), 3–293, 366–423; Neal Peirce, *The Border South States: People, Politics, and Power in the Five Border South States* (New York: Norton, 1975); Alexander P. Lamis, *The Two-Party South* (New York: Oxford University Press, 1984); and Earl Black and Merle Black, *Politics and Society in the South* (Cambridge: Harvard University Press, 1987). For an overview of regional realignment and the emergence of the Sunbelt, see John Egerton, *The Americanization of Dixie: The Southernization of America* (New York: Harper's Magazine Press, 1974); Kirkpatrick Sale, *Power Shift: The Rise of the Southern Rim and Its Challenge to the Eastern Establishment* (New York: Random House, 1975); Joel Garreau, *The Nine Nations of North America* (Boston: Houghton Mifflin, 1981); Randall M. Miller and George E. Pozzetta, eds., *Shades of the Sunbelt: Essays on Race, Ethnicity and the Urban South* (Westport, CT: Greenwood Press, 1988); Raymond Mohl, ed., *Searching for the Sunbelt: Historical Perspectives on a Region* (Knoxville: University of Tennessee Press, 1990); Bartley, *The New South, 1945–1980*, 417–454; and Applebome, *Dixie Rising*. On South Carolina in the 1960s, see Bass and DeVries, *The Transformation of Southern Politics*, 248–283; and Havard, *The Changing Politics of the South*, 588–636. Meier and Rudwick, *CORE*, 176, 217; sections 96–98, reel 24, and section 258, reel 37, COREP; James T. McCain, *The Right to Vote* (New York: CORE, 1962), copy in section 17, reel 40, COREP; section 133, reel 22, COREPA.
27. Meier and Rudwick, *CORE*, 170–171 (quotations), 172; Jim Peck, "A Carolina City—15 Years Later," *CORE-lator*, November 1962; Cox and Blankenheim interviews; *Student Voice* (June 1962); RD 90, box 12, RD 133, RD 136, RD144, box 17, RD 162, RD 163, box 18, Investigative Report Case Files, ICCR. On the Freedom Highways project, see the correspondence in section 37, reel 3, COREP; and Anderson-Bricker, "Making a Movement," 81–84. On the activities of North Carolina CORE chapters, see sections 81–84, reel 23, and sections 390–395, reel 42, COREP. On Statesville, see the pamphlet by Gordon Carey, *The City of Progress* (New York: CORE, 1962), copy in section 6, reel 49, COREP. On the situation in Monroe in 1962, see section 19, reel 1, and section 394, reel 42, COREP; and Committee to Aid the Monroe Defendants, Information Bulletin 4, April 4, 1962, box 12, SNCCP. On the general expansion of civil rights activity in North Carolina in the early 1960s, see Capus M. Waynick, John C. Brooks, and Elsie W. Pitts, eds., *North Carolina and the Negro* (Raleigh: North Carolina Mayors' Co-operating Committee, 1964).
28. Bass and Devries, *The Transformation of Southern Politics*, 284–304; Havard, *The Changing Politics of the South*, 165–200; Charles L. Fontenay, *Estes Kefauver: A Biography* (Knoxville: University of Tennessee Press, 1980); Joseph Bruce Gorman, *Kefauver: A Political Biography* (New York: Oxford University Press, 1971); Kyle Longley, *Senator Albert Gore, Sr.: A Tennessee Maverick* (Baton Rouge: Louisiana State University Press, 2004); Barrett, Harbour, Lafayette, Lewis, Lillard, and Matthew Walker Jr., interviews; Lewis, *Walking with the Wind*, 183–185, 190–192 (quotation), 193–201, 429–456; Halberstam, *The Children*, 396–468; Powledge, *Free at Last?* 449–452; *New York Times*, January 3, March 27, 1962; *Student Voice*, June 1962; SNCC press release, May 16, 1962, box 34, SNCCP; RD 124, box 16, RD 146, box 18, RD 176, box 19, RD 186, box 20, Investigative Report Case Files, ICCR. On Lebanon, see Meier and Rudwick, *CORE*, 169–170, and section 419, reel 42, section 100, reel 24, COREP. On Fayette and Haywood counties, see section 515, reel 47, and section 99, reel 24, COREP; Lewis, *Portrait of a Decade*, 137–140; and Robert Hamburger, *Our Portion of Hell: Fayette County, Tennessee, An Oral History of the Struggle for Civil Rights* (New York: Links Books, 1973), 1–82. New Orleans CORE, also a source of regional leaders, suffered much the same fate as the Nashville Movement. See Anderson-Bricker, "Making a Movement," 377–389.
29. Marshall and Robert Kennedy interviews, JFKL; Doar and Seigenthaler interviews; "Progress in the Field of Civil Rights, a Summary, January 20 to November 20, 1961," typescript, November 22, 1961, box 14, BMP (first quotation); Niven, *The Politics of Injustice*, 116–123 (second quotation); Brauer, *John F. Kennedy and the Second Reconstruction*, 109–112, 126–127.
30. For a sharp and persuasive critique of the Kennedy Administration's political rationale for caution on civil rights matters, see Niven, *The Politics of Injustice*. Brauer, *John F. Kennedy and the Second Reconstruction*, 126–204; Meier and Rudwick, *CORE*, 180–181; Stern, *Calculating Visions*, 63–77; Wofford, *Of Kennedys and Kings*, 160–169; Guthman, *We Band of Brothers*, 179–207; Riley, *The Presidency and the Politics of Racial Inequality*, 207–219, 228, 235–274; Doar interview.
31. Niven, *The Politics of Injustice*, 5, 6 (quotations), 36–38, 205–206; Sitkoff, *Struggle for Black Equality*, 106 (quotation); Dittmer, *Local People*, 169 (quotation); Marshall and Robert Kennedy interviews,

JFKL; Doar interview; Thomas, *Robert Kennedy*, 240–253; Brauer, *John F. Kennedy and the Second Reconstruction*, 230–320; Branch, *Parting the Waters*, 562–600; O'Reilly, *"Racial Matters,"* 96–123; Navasky, *Kennedy Justice*, 96–155; Garrow, *The FBI and Martin Luther King, Jr.*, 43–100; Garrow, *Bearing the Cross*, 194–201; Fairclough, *To Redeem the Soul of America*, 98–99.

32. Meier and Rudwick, *CORE*, 168–169, 180 (quotations), 181; Brauer, *John F. Kennedy and the Second Reconstruction*, 156–157. See also the materials in section 474, reel 45, section 3, reel 17, and section 40, reel 7, COREP; and the May 1962 correspondence in box 16, BMP. Despite the administration's inability to guarantee the safety of civil rights workers in the Deep South, John Doar and other representatives of the Civil Rights Division were increasingly active as civil rights violations investigators in 1962. Doar, in particular, developed a close relationship with Bob Moses and several other SNCC activists whom he came to admire as "the true heroes" of the Southern civil rights struggle. Doar interview. See also Doar and Landsberg, "The Performance of the FBI."

33. Meier and Rudwick, *CORE*, 144–210, 213; Laue, *Direct Action and Desegregation*, 106–111; Barnes, *Journey from Jim Crow*, 188–189; Farmer, *Lay Bare the Heart*, 210–221; Phil Ochs, "Freedom Riders" (1962). The song was not recorded as part of an album in 1962 but was later included in *The Best of Broadside, 1962–1988: Anthems of the American Underground from the Pages of Broadside Magazine* (Smithsonian Folkways SFW40130, 2000). Ochs also paid tribute to William Worthy and the Journey of Reconciliation in a companion folk song called "Ballad of William Worthy." See Ward, *Just My Soul Responding*, 213–214, 309. Branch, *Parting the Waters*, 452; Sitkoff, *The Struggle for Black Equality*, 100–103; Louis, *And We Are Not Saved*, 116–126; Lewis, *Walking with the Wind*, 194, 249; Blankenheim, Carey, Cox, Gaither, and Rich interviews. See also the 1962 issues of *CORE-lator*, which chronicle the expanding influence of CORE in the wake of the Freedom Rides.

34. Carson, *In Struggle*, 37, 66–82; Zinn, *SNCC*, 79–275; Lewis, *Walking with the Wind*, 187–189 (quotation), 190–200; Forman, *The Making of Black Revolutionaries*, 262–307; Carmichael, *Ready for Revolution*, 216–322; Fleming, *Soon We Will Not Cry*, 92–100; Greenberg, *A Circle of Trust*, 5–8, 39–60, 200–219; King, *Freedom Song*; Dittmer, *Local People*, 128–193; Payne, *I've Got the Light of Freedom*, 100–206; Powledge, *Free at Last?* 352–372, 400–420, 462–479; Laue, *Direct Action and Desegregation*, 113–132; Sitkoff, *The Struggle for Black Equality*, 103–117; *Student Voice*, April 1962; SNCC press releases, April 6, 14, May 4, 1962, box 34, SNCCP; Lafayette and Lewis interviews.

35. Garrow, *Bearing the Cross*, 189–230; Fairclough, *To Redeem the Soul of America*, 91–109; Branch, *Parting the Waters*, 562–707; Lewis, *King*, 156–170; Ling, *Martin Luther King, Jr.*, 93–105; Lewis, *Walking with the Wind*, 184, 187, 190; Manis, *A Fire You Can't Put Out*, 321, 326, 330; Edward T. Clayton, ed., *The SCLC Story* (Atlanta: SCLC, 1964); Martin Luther King Jr., *Strength to Love* (New York: Harper and Row, 1963); Martin Luther King Jr., *Why We Can't Wait* (New York: New American Library, 1964); Fauntroy, Shuttlesworth, and Wyatt Tee Walker interviews.

36. Wilkins, *Standing Fast*, 285–294; Klarman, *From Jim Crow to Civil Rights*, 374–384; Motley, *Equal Justice Under Law*, 148–158; Jonas, *Freedom's Sword*, 169–201; Berg, *"The Ticket to Freeom,"* 166–249; Carter interview. See Waynick, Brooks, and Pitts, *The North Carolina Negro*, on how the NAACP branches in one state expanded their protest activities following the Freedom Rides.

37. *Baltimore Afro-American*, November 11, 1961 (quotation). On the South African pass laws, see Mandela, *Long Walk to Freedom*, 49, 83, 191–194, 205–207, 370; and Joseph Lelyveld, *Move Your Shadow: South Africa, Black and White* (New York: Times Books, 1985), 7–8, 22, 36, 39, 189, 355, 319–327. Ronald Anderson, interview by author, November 1999; Charles Perkins, *A Bastard Like Me* (Sydney: Ure Smith, 1975); Ann Curthoys, *Freedom Ride: A Freedom Rider Remembers* (Crows Nest, NSW: Allen and Unwin, 2003); http://freedomride.net; Kim Bullimore, "The Aboriginal Struggle for Justice and Land Rights," *Green Left Weekly* (2001), available online at www.greenleft.org.au/back/2001; *Sydney Daily Telegraph*, May 20, 1997; *Melbourne Herald Sun*, September 15, 2002. Perkins died on October 18, 2000. *London Independent*, October 20, 2000; *Adelaide Advertiser*, October 19, 21, 2000; *Queensland Courier Mail*, October 19, 2000; *Sydney Australian*, October 20, 2000.

38. On the persistent but unfulfilled ideal of the beloved community, see Marsh, *The Beloved Community*. On the "rights revolution," see John D. Skrentny, *The Minority Rights Revolution* (Cambridge: Harvard University Press, 2002); Louis Henken, *The Age of Rights* (New York: Columbia University Press, 1990); Cass R. Sunstein, *After the Rights Revolution: Reconceiving the Regulatory State* (Cambridge: Harvard University Press, 1990); Ronald Dworkin, *Taking Rights Seriously* (Cambridge: Harvard University Press, 1977); Charles R. Epp, *The Rights Revolution: Lawyers, Activists, and Supreme Courts in Comparative Perspective* (Chicago: University of Chicago Press, 1998); Judith N. Sklar, *American Citizenship: The Quest for Inclusion* (Cambridge: Harvard University Press, 1991); Lawrence H. Fuchs, *American Kaleidoscope: Race, Ethnicity, and the Civic Culture* (Hanover, NH: Wesleyan University Press, 1990); Alan Wolfe, *One Nation, After All* (New York: Viking, 1998); John D'Emilio, William B. Turner, and Urvashi Vaid, eds., *Creating Change: Sexuality, Public Policy, and Civil Rights* (New York: St. Martin's, 2000); Margaret Cruikshank, *The Gay and Lesbian Liberation Movement* (New York: Routledge, 1992); Richard K. Scotch, *From Good Will to Civil Rights: Transforming Federal Disability Policy* (Philadelphia: Temple University Press, 1984); Stephen L. Percy, *Disability, Civil Rights, and Public Policy* (Tuscaloosa: University of Alabama Press, 1989); and Paul L. Murphy, "Balancing Acts: The Supreme Court and the Bill of Rights, 1965–1991," in *Crucible of Liberty: 200 Years of the Bill of Rights*, ed. Raymond Arsenault (New York: Free Press, 1991), 96–107. Malcolm Gladwell, *The Tipping Point: How Little Things Can Make a Big Difference* (Boston: Little, Brown, 2000), 7–14; Carmichael, *Ready for Revolution*, 178 (quotation).

39. Laue, *Direct Action and Desegregation*, 107–108 (quotations); Viorst, *Fire in the Streets*, 159 (quotation). On the implementation and impact of the VEP, see Lawson, *Running for Freedom*, 81–84, 116–117; Steven F. Lawson, *Black Ballots: Voting Rights in the South, 1944–1969* (New York: Columbia

University Press, 1976), 261–265, 276–277, 283–285, 332; Garrow, *Bearing the Cross*, 161–163, 168, 189, 194, 197, 216, 223, 233, 322; Payne, *I've Got the Light of Freedom*, 108–109, 141–172; and Forman, *The Making of Black Revolutionaries*, 265–269, 273. On the 1965 Voting Rights Act, see David Garrow, *Protest at Selma: Martin Luther King and the Voting Rights Act of 1965* (New Haven: Yale University Press, 1978); and Lawson, *Black Ballots*, 307–352. See also Pat Watters and Reese Cleghorn, *Climbing Jacob's Ladder: The Arrival of Negroes in Southern Politics* (New York: Harcourt, Brace, and World, 1967). For a broad survey of the evolution of federal civil rights policies during the 1960s and early 1970s, see Hugh Davis Graham, *The Civil Rights Era: Origins and Development of National Policy* (New York: Oxford University Press, 1990). For illuminating discussions of the complex relationships between moral suasion, movement culture, social change, and governmental policy during the modern civil rights era, see Lawson and Payne, *Debating the Civil Rights Movement*, 3–42, 99–136; Sara M. Evans and Harry C. Boyte, *Free Spaces: The Sources of Democratic Change in America* (New York: Harper and Row, 1986), 50–68, 182–202; Norrell, *The House I Live In*, xi–xvii, 365–371, and passim; Chappell, *A Stone of Hope*; and Marsh, *The Beloved Community*.

40. Laue, *Direct Action and Desegregation*, 109–111, and Appendices A–E (275–328), which present a long list of activists interviewed by Laue in 1960 and 1962, the questions asked during the interviews, and a tabulation of results. John Lewis, remarks at the 40th Anniversary of the Freedom Rides luncheon, Atlanta, Georgia, May 11, 2001 (first quotation); Lewis, remarks at the Birmingham Civil Rights Institute, Birmingham, Alabama, May 12, 2001 (second quotation).

41. On Freedom Summer, see Dittmer, *Local People*, 242–285; Branch, *Pillar of Fire*, 341–509; Doug McAdam, *Freedom Summer* (New York: Oxford University Press, 1988); Sally Belfrage, *Freedom Summer* (New York: Viking Press, 1965); Mary Aickin Rothschild, *A Case of Black and White: Northern Volunteers and Southern Freedom Summers* (Westport, CT: Greenwood Press, 1982); Seth Cagin and Philip Dray, *We Are Not Afraid: The Story of Goodman, Schwerner, and Chaney and the Civil Rights Campaign for Mississippi* (New York: Macmillan, 1988); and Nicolaus Mills, *Like a Holy Crusade: Mississippi 1964—The Turning Point of the Civil Rights Movement in America* (Chicago: Ivan R. Dee, 1992).

42. *New York Times*, August 15, 2001 (Clinton quotation); *Los Angeles Times*, August 15, 2001. Vice President Al Gore repeated Clinton's identification of Lieberman as a "Freedom Rider." *Houston Chronicle*, August 17, 2000. *Ladykillers* (2004), Touchstone Pictures (Buena Vista Home Video DVD), directed by Ethan and Joel Coen.

43. Blankenheim, Brooks, Carey, Cox, Davidov, Dolan, Dresner, Farrell, Gaither, Harbour, Lafayette, Lewis, Sanfield, Thomas, Rich, and Ziskind interviews; Jim Peck, "Fifteen Years After the Freedom Rides," *War Resisters League News* (January–February 1977): 6; Halberstam, *The Children*, 523–719; Carmichael, *Ready for Revolution*, 263–264, 507–590; Stokely Carmichael and Charles V. Hamilton, *Black Power: The Politics of Liberation in America* (New York: Random House, 1967); Carson, *In Struggle*, 215–244; Farmer, *Lay Bare the Heart*, 315–346; *Atlanta Constitution*, May 8, 1981; *Jackson Clarion-Ledger*, May 9, 1981 (quotations); *New York Times*, May 10, 1981.

44. Lafayette interview; *Jackson Daily News*, July 21, 1981 (quotation); *Jackson Clarion-Ledger*, July 22, 1981; Beverly Keel, "A Mission of Nonviolence," *American Profile* (January 11–17, 2004): 6, 8; *St. Petersburg Times*, May 7, 2003. On the Philadelphia murders, see Cagin and Dray, *We Are Not Afraid*; and William Bradford Huie, *Three Lives for Mississippi* (New York: WCC Books, 1965).

45. Kaufman, *The First Freedom Ride*, ii–iv, 92–125, 146–203 (Douglass quotation); Powledge, *Free at Last?* 272–275; *New York Times*, January 23, June 1, 1983, February 8, 1984, July 13, 1993, October 10, 1999 (Enslen and Simon quotations); Simon interview; Goodman interview; American Civil Liberties Union of Michigan, *Civil Liberties Newsletter* 4 (Spring 1983): 1–3; Walter and Pat Bergman, New Year's Day 1986 letter to friends, in author's possession; Smith, *Events Leading Up to My Death*, 408; *Bergman v. U.S.*, 565 F. Supp 1353 W.D. Mich. (1983); *Bergman v. U.S.*, 579 F. Supp. 911 W.D. Mich. (1984); *Bergman v. U.S.*, 844 F. 2d 353 (1988); *Peck v. U.S.*, 470 F. Supp. 1003 S.D. N.Y. (1979); May, *The Informant*, 322–324, 364. *Undercover with the KKK* (Columbia Pictures, 1979); *Washington Post*, July 12, 30, 1978, October 23, 1979; *Birmingham Post-Herald*, July 13, 1978; *Detroit Free Press*, October 23, 1979. On Liuzzo, see May, *The Informant*; and Mary Stanton, *From Selma to Sorrow: The Life and Death of Viola Liuzzo* (Athens: University of Georgia Press, 1998).

46. "Ain't Scared of Your Jails," documentary; Halberstam, *The Children*, 701–702; *Milwaukee Journal Sentinel*, June 17, 1999; and the documentary "Skin Deep, The Fight Against Legislated Racism," episode of *People's Century* (PBS, 1999). See also the interview with Zwerg and his daughter, Mary Brown, in Blake, *Children of the Movement*, 25–36. Zwerg left the ministry in 1975 and later worked as a lobbyist for the Chamber of Commerce, an IBM executive, and a business manager for a local hospice before retiring in 1999. Prior to the 1980s, he rarely mentioned his Freedom Rider experiences, and his daughter was sixteen years old before she heard him discuss the details of his beating in Montgomery. Zwerg interview. The twenty-fifth anniversary of the Rides was also commemorated by a "Freedom Ride" from New York to Alabama led by the Reverend Dr. Benjamin F. Chavis, the head of the United Church of Christ's Commission for Racial Justice. Departing from New York on February 28, Chavis, accompanied by a busload of students and other supporters, announced that his group hoped "to lift the veil of fear and intimidation now being imposed on the western Alabama black belt by the Reagan Administration and other forces of racial oppression." *New York Times*, March 1, 1986. While some former Freedom Riders applauded Chavis's initiative, others resented his unauthorized appropriation of the Freedom Rider label. Cox and Blankenheim interviews.

47. *Jackson Clarion-Ledger*, May 25 (Farmer quotations), June 19, July 20–21 (first quotation), 1991. The Farmer statements originated in an interview two months before the reunion, but he reportedly used virtually the same words in July. *Jackson Advocate*, May 30, June 5, July 25 (second quotation); *Hattiesburg American*, June 19, 1991; *Clarksdale Press Register*, July 22, 1991; *Atlanta Constitution*, July

21, 1991; "The Freedom Rides: A Thirty-Year Perspective," program typescript, June 19, 1991, MSCP.

48. The groundbreaking for the National Civil Rights Museum in Memphis took place in 1987, and the museum opened in September 1991. The Birmingham Civil Rights Institute opened in November 1992. See www.bcri.org and www.civilrights.org. John Lewis, "Freedom Riders of 2003," *Washington Post*, October 1, 2003, A23 (quotation); Ellie Hidalgo, "Freedom Rides for Immigrant Workers," *Tidings* (Los Angeles), September 26, 2003.

49. Sean Wilentz, "The Last Integrationist," *New Republic* 215 (July 1, 1996): 19–26, 20 (first quotation), 5 (second quotation); Lewis, Filner, and Franklin interviews; *New York Times*, June 15, September 28, 1997; John Hope Franklin, "A Half-Century of Presidential Race Initiatives: Some Reflections," *Journal of Supreme Court History* 24 (1999): 226–238; John Hope Franklin, interview by author, March 3, 2005, to be published in *Public Historian* (Winter 2006); *Boston Globe*, August 28, 1993.

50. The documentary filmmaker was Robin Washington, the managing editor of the *Bay State Banner*; narrated by Judge A. Leon Higginbotham, *You Don't Have to Ride JIM CROW!* was shown on New Hampshire Public Television in 1995. James Haskins, *The Freedom Rides: Journey for Justice* (New York: Hyperion Books for Children, 1995); Deborah Kent, *The Freedom Riders* (Chicago: Children's Press, 1993). See also Ann Bausum, *Freedom Riders: John Lewis and Jim Zwerg on the Front Lines of the Civil Rights Movement* (Washington: National Geographic Children's Books, 2005). Vicki Covington, *The Last Hotel for Women* (New York: Simon and Schuster, 1993). For plays based on the Freedom Rides, see *Chicago Sun-Times*, September 6, 1998, January 15, 2004; *Washington Post*, April 25, 2003; and *Minneapolis Star Tribune*, February 11, 2004. In 2005, Angela Madeiros, a children's author and playwright living in Austin, Texas, wrote a musical based on Carol Ruth Silver's Parchman diary; Silver interview. *On Wisconsin* (Spring 2004): 6, 8.

51. Gary Younge, *No Place Like Home: A Black Briton's Journey Through the American South* (London: Picador, 1999), 36 (quotation).

52. "Evening Glory," *People* (April 6, 1998): 134 (quotation); *New York Times*, August 25, 1987, July 13, 1993, July 10, 1999; *Washington Post*, August 25, 1987, January 16, 1998; July 10, 1999; *St. Petersburg Times*, July 10–11, 1999; Senator Charles Robb and Congressman John Lewis, "A Tribute to an American Freedom Fighter," January 16, 1998, and Senator Charles S. Robb, "Honoring James Farmer," floor statement, U.S. Senate, February 25, 1998, both texts in author's possession; William Hansen, interview by author, May 10, 2001; Ransby, *Ella Baker and the Black Freedom Movement*, 10–12; D'Emilio, *Lost Prophet*, 492–494.

53. *The 40th Anniversary Ride to Freedom, 1961–2001*, program in author's possession; John Lewis, remarks at the Birmingham Civil Rights Institute, May 12, 2001 (quotation); John Lewis, Hank Thomas remarks, May 10, 2001, Washington Court Hotel, Washington, DC; Freedom Rider remarks, May 11, 2001, Atlanta Civic Center, Atlanta, GA; *Atlanta Journal-Constitution*, May 10, 2001; *Boston Globe*, May 22, 2001; Brooks, Davis and Davis, Lewis, Lillard, Moody, Thomas, and Zwerg interviews; Blake, *Children of the Movement*, 36; Niven, *The Politics of Injustice*, 207–208. The two historians conducting interviews were the author and Clayborne Carson of Stanford University. On the evolution and persistence of the "beloved community" ideal, see Marsh, *The Beloved Community*, a generally insightful analysis but one that curiously overlooks the Freedom Rides and significant individuals such as James Lawson, James Bevel, Bernard Lafayette, and Bayard Rustin.

54. Copeland, "Freedom Riders Go South Again"; www.FreedomRidersFoundation.org; "Governor Musgrove Declares: Freedom Riders Day in Mississippi," *Newsletter of the Freedom Riders 40th Reunion* 1 (November 10, 2001): 1 (quotations); Gaither, Green, Maguire, O'Connor, Silver, and Singleton interviews; Green, "Freedom Rider Diary: Forty Years Later"; *San Bernardino County Sun*, January 18, 1987; *Los Angeles Times*, January 18, 1989; Green, Maguire, O'Connor, Silver, Bob Singleton, and Helen Singleton interviews, UMFRC. The interviews and materials collected during the reunion are on file at the William Winter Institute for Racial Reconciliation, University of Mississippi, Oxford, MS. Born in Tocowa, Mississippi, in 1956, David Ronald "Ronnie" Musgrove served in the state senate and as lieutenant governor before defeating Republican Mike Parker for the governorship in 1999. A liberal by Mississippi standards, Musgrove advocated the adoption of a new state flag to replace the traditional design featuring the Confederate battle flag. But the design was rejected by a margin of two to one in an April 2001 referendum. This and other setbacks hampered his bid for reelection, and he was defeated by Republican Haley Barbour in November 2003. *New York Times*, October 17, 2003; *Jackson Clarion-Ledger*, October–November 2003.

55. The film was *You Don't Have to Ride JIM CROW! Boston Globe*, August 28, 1993; Morello, "The Freedom Rider a Nation Nearly Forgot"; Morgan and Bacquie interviews; *Washington Post*, January 9, 2001; www.citizensmedal.com/2001Recipients.htm (quotation). In October 2001, the Society of Adventist Communicators established the Irene Morgan Award for Courage and Integrity.

Bibliography

Manuscript and Archival Collections

Amistad Research Center, Tulane University, New Orleans, LA (ARC)
    Clarie Collins Harvie Papers (CCHP)
    Bayard Rustin Papers (microfilm) (BRP)
Department of Archives and Manuscripts, Birmingham Public Library, Birmingham, AL (BPL)
    Birmingham Police Department Surveillance Files
    Centers of Southern Struggle: FBI Files on Montgomery, Albany, St. Augustine, Selma, and Memphis (microfilm)
    Civil Rights Scrapbooks
    FBI Case Files, Freedom Rider Investigation (FBI-FRI)
    George C. Wallace Scrapbooks
    Theophilus Eugene "Bull" Connor Papers (BCP)
Dwight David Eisenhower Presidential Library, Abilene, KS
    E. Frederic Morrow Papers
Fisk University Library, Nashville, TN
    Vertical File, Special Collections (FUSC)
John F. Kennedy Library, Boston, MA (JFKL)
    Burke Marshall Papers (BMP)
    Robert F. Kennedy Papers (RFKP)
Library of Congress, Washington, DC
    A. Philip Randolph Papers (APRP)
    Brotherhood of Sleeping Car Porters Papers (BSCPP)
    National Association for the Advancement of Colored People Papers (NAACPP)
    National Urban League Papers
The Martin Luther King, Jr. Center for Nonviolent Social Change, Atlanta, GA
    Albany City Records, 1960–1963
    Episcopal Society for Cultural and Racial Unity Records
    Fred Gray Files
    William Hansen Papers (microfilm)
    Martin Luther King, Jr. Papers (KPA)
    Charles Sherrod Papers
    Fred L. Shuttlesworth Papers
    Student Nonviolent Coordinating Committee Papers (SNCCP)
    Southern Christian Leadership Conference Papers (microfilm) (SCLCP)
Mississippi Department of Archives and History, Jackson, MS
    Mississippi State Sovereignty Commission Papers (MSCP)
Mugar Library, Boston University, Boston, MA
    Martin Luther King, Jr. Papers (MLKP)
Nashville Public Library, Nashville, TN
    Southern Regional Council Papers (microfilm) (SRCP)
New York Public Library, New York, NY
    Norman Thomas Papers (NTP)

Swarthmore College Peace Collection, Swarthmore College, Swarthmore, PA
    Congress of Racial Equality Collection (COREC)
    Fellowship of Reconciliation Papers (FORP)
    War Resisters League Papers (WRLP)
U.S. National Archives II, College Park, MD
    United States Department of Justice, Civil Rights Division Records, Record Group 60 (USDJ/CRD)
    Interstate Commerce Commission Records, Record Group 134 (ICCR)
University of Mississippi Library, Oxford, MS
    Freedom Rider Collection (UMFRC)
University of South Florida Libraries, Tampa and St. Petersburg, FL
    American Civil Liberties Union Papers (microfilm)
    Congress of Racial Equality Papers (microfilm) (COREP)
    Congress of Racial Equality Papers, Addendum, 1944–1968 (microfilm) (COREPA)
    Tuskegee Institute Race Relations Clipping File (microfilm) (TIRRCF)
Vanderbilt University Library, Nashville, TN
    Kelly Miller Smith Papers (KMSP)
William Harbour, Atlanta, GA
    William Harbour Freedom Rider Collection (WHC)

Court Decisions

Bailey v. Patterson, 199 F. Supp. 595 (S.D. Miss. 1961).
Bergman v. U.S., 551 F. Supp. 407 (1983), 565 F. Supp. 1353 (1984), 579 F. Supp. 911 (1988).
Boman v. Morgan, 7 RRLR 569 (1962).
Boynton v. Commonwealth of Virginia, 364 U.S. 454 (1960).
Browder v. Gayle, 142 F. Supp. 707 (M.D. ALA. 1956).
Chiles v. Chesapeake and Ohio Railway Company, 218 U.S. 71 (1910).
Cooper v. Aaron, 358 U.S. 1 (1958).
Gayle v. Browder, 352 U.S. 903 (1956).
Georgia v. U.S., 371 U.S. 9 (1962).
Hall v. DeCuir, 95 U.S. 485 (1878).
Irene Morgan v. Commonwealth of Virginia, 184 Va. 24 (1946).
Israel Dresner et al. v. City of Tallahassee, Law No. 10084 (Fla. 1961, 1962), 375 U.S. 136 (1963).
Lewis v. Greyhound Corporation, 199 F. Supp. 210 (1961).
McCabe v. Atchison, Topeka and Santa Fe Railway Company, 235 U.S. 151 (1914).
Mississippi v. Farmer, 6 RRLR 544 (1961).
Mitchell v. United States, 313 U.S. 80 (1941).
Morgan v. Virginia, 328 U.S. 373 (1946).
Norvell Lee v. Commonwealth of Virginia, record 3558 (1949).
New York Times v. Sullivan 376 U.S. 254 (1961).
Peck v. U.S., 470 F. Supp. 1003, 514 F. Supp. 210, 522 F. Supp. 245 (1979).
Plessy v. Ferguson, 163 U.S. 537 (1896).
Priscilla G. Stephens v. City of Tallahassee, Law No. 10085 (1962).
Smith v. Allwright, 321 U.S. 649 (1944).
State of North Carolina v. Johnson, et al., Orange County, NC, NC 723 (1949).
Swann v. Charlotte-Mecklenburg Board of Education, 402 U.S. 1 (1971).
Thomas v. Mississippi, 380 U.S. 524 (1965).
United States v. United States Klans, Knights of Ku Klux Klan, Inc., et al., 194 F. Supp. 897 (M.D. Ala. 1961).
U.S. v. Mayor and Selectman of McComb, 6 RRLR 1169 (1961).
U.S. v. Wood, 295 F. 2d 772 (1961).

Government Publications

Alabama Department of Public Safety, Investigative and Identification Division. *Individuals Active in Civil Disturbances*. 2 vols. Montgomery: Alabama Department of Public Safety, c. 1965.
Public Papers of the Presidents of the United States. John F. Kennedy (1961), vol. 1. Washington, DC: GPO, 1962.
U.S. Bureau of the Census. *Eighteenth Census of the United States, 1960, Population*. Wahington: GPO, 1961.
U.S. Department of Commerce. *County and City Data Book 1956*. Washington: GPO, 1957.
———. *County and City Data Book 1961*. Washington: GPO, 1961.
U.S. Department of Justice. *The FBI, the Department of Justice, and Gary Thomas Rowe, Jr.: Task Force Report on Gary Thomas Rowe, Jr.* Washington: GPO, 1979.
———, Attorney General. *Annual Report of the Attorney General of the United States for the Fiscal Year Ended June 30, 1962*. Washington: GPO, 1963.
———. *Annual Report of the Attorney General of the United States for the Fiscal Year Ended June 30, 1963*. Washington: GPO, 1964.

Interviews

Ackerberg, Peter. Interview by author and Meeghan Kane, August 25, 2005.
Aelony, Zev. Interview by author, November 9, 2001.
Aelony, Zev. Interview by Susan Glisson, November 9, 2001, UMFRC.
Anderson, Ronald. Interview by author, November 1999.
Armstrong, Thomas, III. Interview by author, November 11, 2001, August 23, 2005.
Armstrong, Thomas, III. Interview by Susan Glisson, November 9, 2001, UMFRC.
Audain, Michael. Interview by author, November 10, 2001.
Audain, Michael. Interview by Susan Glisson, November 9, 2001, UMFRC.
Bacquie, Aleah. Interview by author, October 9, 2003.
Baker, Ella. Interview by John Britoon, June 19, 1968, RBOHC.
Barnett, Ross R. Interview by Dennis O'Brien, May 6, 1969, JFKL.
Barrett, George. Interview by author, November 8, 2004.
Bassford, Abraham. Interview by author, August 22, 2005.
Bates, Scott. Interview by author, February 18, 2005.
Baum, Robert. Interview by author, November 9, 2001.
Baum, Robert. Interview by Susan Glisson, November 9, 2001, UMFRC.
Berrard, Charles. Interview by author and Meeghan Kane, August 25, 2005.
Blankenheim, Edward. Interview by author, April 6, May 11, 2001, May 7, 2004.
Blankenheim, Edward. Interview by Scott Simon, National Public Radio *Weekend Edition* broadcast,
    April 7, 2001.
Bordofsky, Jorgia Siegel. Interview by author and Meeghan Kane, June 27, 2005.
Bouwman, Clark. Interview by author, May 28, 2005.
Boyte, Harry, Jr. Interview by author, December 1, 1977.
Britt, Travis. Interview by James Mosby Jr., September 14, 1968, RBOHC.
Broms, Ellen. Interview by author and Meeghan Kane, August 12, 2005.
Brooks, Catherine Burks. Interview by author, May 11–12, 2001.
Browning, Joan. Interview by author, November 10, 2001, July 9, 2004, June 11, 2005.
Browning, Joan. Interview by Susan Glisson, November 9, 2001, UMFRC.
Carey, Gordon. Interview by author, November 24, December 11, 2002.
Carter, Clyde. Interview by author and Meeghan Kane, August 10, 2005.
Carter, Robert L. Interview by author, March 8, 2005.
Coffin, William Sloane, Jr. Interview by author, June 22, 2005.
Collier, John. Interview by author, August 19, 2005.
Collins, Lucretia. Interview by author, September 22, 2005.
Collins, Lucretia. Interview by James Forman, June 1961, in *Southern Exposure* 9 (Spring 1981): 35–39.
Collins, Norma. Interview by author and Kelly Benjamin, June 25, 2005.
Cox, Benjamin Elton. Interview by author, April 5–6, May 8, 2001, May 9, November 7, 2004.
Cox, Benjamin Elton. Interview by Scott Simon, National Public Radio *Weekend Edition* broadcast,
    7 April 2001.
Crowder, Margaret. Interview by author, December 17, 2003.
Davidov, Marv. Interview by author, November 9, 2001.
Davidov, Marv. Interview by Susan Glisson, November 9, 2001, UMFRC.
Davis, James K., and Glenda Gaither Davis. Interview by author, May 12, 2001.
Dennis, David J. Interview by author, May 11–12, 2001.
Dennis, James Emerson. Interview by author, June 27, 29, 2005.
Diamond, Dion. Interview by author, July 13, 2005.
Dietrich, Paul Abdullah. Interview by author, July 8, 2005.
Doar, John. Interview by author, June 8, 2005.
Dolan, John. Interview by author, August 31, 2005.
Dolan, John. Interview by Susan Glisson, November 9, 2001, UMFRC.
Dresner, Israel. Interview by author, November 9–10, 2001, June 5, 2004.
Due, Patricia Stephens. Interview by author, April 27, 2002, June 5, 2004.
Dunbar, Leslie. Interview by author, October 25, 2003.
Evans, W. McKee. Interview by author, February 18, 2005.
Farmer, James. Interview by John F. Stewart, March 10, 1967, JFKL.
Farmer, James. Interview by John Britton, September 28, 1968, RBOHC.
Farmer, James. Interview by Ed Edwin, 1979, CUOHC.
Farrell, Robert. Interview by author, August 23, 2005.
Fauntroy, Walter. Interview by author, June 5, 2004.
Filner, Robert. Interview by author, November 9, 2001.
Filner, Robert. Interview by Susan Glisson, November 9, 2001, UMFRC.
Forman, James. Interview by Susan Glisson, November 10, 2001, UMFRC.
Franklin, John Hope. Interview by author, February 9, March 3, 2005.
Freedman, Martin. Interview by author, November 8, 2001.
Freedman, Martin. Interview by Susan Glisson, November 9, 2001, UMFRC.
Fuller, Winston. Interview by author and Meeghan Kane, August 19, 2005.
Gaffney, Theodore. Interview by author, October 12, 2004.
Gaither, Thomas. Interview by author, November 9–11, 2001.
Gaither, Thomas. Interview by Susan Glisson, November 9, 2001, UMFRC.

Gerbac, Joe. Interview by author and Meeghan Kane, September 14, 2005.
Goodman, William. Interview by author, June 13, 2005.
Grant, Jacquelyn. Interview by author, June 27, 2005.
Green, Reginald. Interview by author, August 11, 2005.
Green, Steve. Interview by author, November 9, 2001, January 16, 2003.
Green, Steve. Interview by Susan Glisson, November 9, 2001, UMFRC.
Griffith, Joe. Interview by author and Meeghan Kane, September 9, 2005.
Grubbs, Michael. Interview by author and Meeghan Kane, September 14–15, 2005.
Haley, Oretha Castle. Interview by James Mosby Jr., May 26, 1970, RBOHC.
Haley, Oretha Castle. Interview by Kim Lacy Rogers, November 27, 1978, ARC.
Haley, Richard. Interview by Robert Wright, August 12, 1969, RBOHC.
Haley, Richard. Interview by Kim Lacy Rogers, April 25, May 9, 1979, ARC.
Hansen, William. Interview by author, May 10, 2001.
Harbour, William. Interview by author, July 10, 2004, April 6, 2005.
Hartmire, Wayne. Interview by Susan Glisson, November 9, 2001, UMFRC.
Harvey, Harry. Interview by author, June 4, 2005.
Heller, Robert. Interview by author, November 8, 2001, June 23, 2005.
Heller, Robert. Interview by Susan Glisson, November 9, 2001, UMFRC.
Hersh, Burton. Interview by author, April 26, 2005.
Hogrobrooks, Holly. Interview by author and Meeghan Kane, August 19, 22, 2005.
Houser, George. Interview by Katherine Shannon, September 11, 1967, RBOHC.
Howard, Mae Frances Moultrie. Interview by author, April 28, 2005.
Jones, Charles. Interview by author, May 12, 2001.
Kale, Edward. Interview by Susan Glisson, November 9, 2001, UMFRC.
Kennedy, Robert F. Interviews, 1964, 1965, 1967, JFKL.
Kennedy, Robert F., and Burke Marshall. Interview by Anthony Lewis, December 4, 1964, JFKL.
Kennedy's Call to King. (Louis Martin, Sargent Shriver, et al.) Interviews by Anthony Shriver, 1988, JFKL.
King, Martin Luther, Jr. Interview by Berl Bernhard, March 9, 1964, JFKL.
Kirkaldy, Irene Amos (Morgan). Interview by Sherwood Morgan, January 4, 2004.
Kovner, Pat. Interview by author and Meeghan Kane, July 19, 2005.
Lafayette, Bernard. Interview by author, April 6, May 11, 2001, June 9–10, 2004.
Lafayette, Bernard, and Hank Thomas. Interview by author, April 6, 2001.
Lawrence, Barbara. Interview by author and Meeghan Kane, September 26, 2005.
Lawson, Belford III. Interview by author, September 21, 2005.
Lee, Mary Harrison. Interview by Susan Glisson, November 10, 2001, UMFRC.
Leonard, Margaret. Interview by author, November 9, 11, 2001.
Leonard, Margaret. Interview by Susan Glisson, November 10, 2001, UMFRC.
Levine, Alan. Interview by author, November 8, 2001.
Levine, Alan. Interview by Susan Glisson, November 10, 2001, UMFRC.
Lewis, John. Interview by author, January 31, 2001.
Lewis, John. Interview by Katherine Shannon, August 22, 1967, RBOHC.
Libson, Norma. Interview by author and Meeghan Kane, August 11, 2005.
Liggins, Claude. Interview by author and Meeghan Kane, August 22, 2005.
Lightchild, Chela. Interview by author and Meeghan Kane, August 17, 2005.
Lillard, Kwame Leo. Interview by author, May 11, 2001.
Linder, Morton G. Interview by author and Meeghan Kane, August 23, 2005.
Little-Vance, Mary. Interview by author, November 9, 11, 2001.
Little-Vance, Mary. Interview by Susan Glisson, November 10, 2001, UMFRC.
Litwack, Leon. Interview by author, March 31, 2005.
Lombard, Rudy. Interview by author, September 21, 2005.
Magubane, Lenora Taitt, Interview by author and Meeghan Kane, September 5, 2005.
Maguire, John. Interview by author, June 21, 2005.
Maguire, John. Interview by Susan Glisson, November 10, 2001, UMFRC.
Marshall, Burke. Interview by Louis Oberdorfer, May 29, 1964, JFKL. (Cited in notes as "Marshall inter-
     view, JFKL.")
Marshall, Burke. Interview by Larry J. Hackman, January 19–20, 1970, JFKL.
Marshall, Burke. Interview by Robert Wright, February 27, 1970, RBOHC.
McCollum, Salynn. Interview by author and Kelly Benjamin, June 25, 2005.
McCray, Mikki. Interview by author and Meeghan Kane, August 29, 2005.
McDew, Chuck. Interview by Katherine Shannon, August 24, 1967, RBOHC.
McDonald, Jimmy. Interview by James Mosby Jr., November 5, 1969, RBOHC.
McNichols, Steven. Interview by author and Meeghan Kane, August 16, 2005.
Mill, Beverly Radcliffe. Interview by author and Meeghan Kane, August 18, 2005.
Moody, John. Interview by author, May 10–11, November 8–9, 2001, July 19, 2005.
Moody, John. Interview by Susan Glisson, November 10, 2001, UMFRC.
Moore, Ivor "Jerry," Jr. Interview by author, September 19–20, 2005.
Morgan, Sherwood. Interview by author, January 3, 2004.
Morton, Dave. Interview by author, November 9–10, 2001.
Mulholland, Joan Trumpauer. Interview by author, November 8–9, 2001.
Mulholland, Joan Trumpauer. Interview by Susan Glisson, November 10, 2001, UMFRC.
Myers, Charles David. Interview by author, June 23, 2005.
Nash, Diane. Interview by author, April 6–7, 2001.

Negen, Gordon. Interview by author and Meeghan Kane, August 16, 2005.

Newson, Moses. Interview by author, March 2, 2002.

Nelson, Frank. Interview by author, September 18, 2005.

Nelson, Juanita. Interview by author, August 12, 2005.

Nixon, Sandra. Interview by author, November 8, 2001.

Nixon, Sandra, Interview by Susan Glisson, November 9, 2001, UMFRC.

Oberdorfer, Louis. Interview by Roberta Greene (for the Robert F. Kennedy Oral History Program), February 5, 12, 1970, JFKL.

O'Connor, Claire. Interview by author, November 9, 2001.

O'Connor, Claire. Interview by Susan Glisson, November 10, 2001, UMFRC.

Orrick, William H., Jr. Interview by Larry Hackman, April 13, 1970, JFKL.

Patterson, Eugene. Interview by author, December 10, 2001, November 4, 2002, February 14, 2004.

Patterson, John. Interview by John Stewart, May 26, 1967, JFKL.

Pavesic, Max. Interview by author and Meeghan Kane, August 31, 2005.

Peck, James. Interview by James Mosby Jr., February 19, 1970, RBOHC.

Person, Charles. Interview by author, May 11–12, 2001.

Person, Charles. Interview by Susan Glisson, November 10, 2001, UMFRC.

Petway, Alphonso, and Kredelle Petway. Interview by author, November 9, 2001.

Petway, Alphonso, and Kredelle Petway. Interview by Susan Glisson, November 10, 2001, UMFRC.

Posner, Philip. Interview by author and Meeghan Kane, August 18, 2005.

Powell, Grady Wilson, Sr. Interview by author, December 17, 2003.

Rabb, Maxwell. Interview by Steven Lawson, October 6, 1970, CUOHC.

Randall, Laura. Interview by author, June 28, 2005.

Raymond, George. Interview by Robert Wright, September 28, 1968, RBOHC.

Reinitz, Janet B. Interview by author, November 10, 2001.

Reinitz, Janet B. Interview by Susan Glisson, November 9, 2001, UMFRC.

Reynolds, Isaac. Interview by James Mosby Jr., November 5, 1969, RBOHC.

Rich, Marvin. Interview by author, January 24, 2003, May 4, 2005.

Rich, Marvin. Interview by James Mosby Jr., November 6, 1969, RBOHC.

Roy, Ralph. Interview by author, November 9, 2001.

Roy, Ralph. Interview by Susan Glisson, November 10, 2001, UMFRC.

Sanfield, Steve. Interview by author, August 13, 2005.

Scott, Doris Jean Castle. Interview by Kim Lacy Rogers, January 19, 1989, ARC.

Seigenthaler, John. Interview by author, February 13, 2004.

Seigenthaler, John. Interview by William A. Geohegan, July 22, 1964, JFKL.

Seigenthaler, John. Interview by Ronald J. Grele, February 21–23, 1966, JFKL.

Seigenthaler, John. Interview by Robert Campbell, July 10, 1968, RBOHC.

Seigenthaler, John. Interview by Larry J. Hackman (for the Robert F. Kennedy Oral History Program), June 5, July 1, 1970, JFKL.

Shanken, Sidney. Interview by author, August 19, 2005.

Sherrod, Charles. Interview by Bret Eynon, May 12, 1985, CUOHC.

Sheviakov, Rick. Interview by author and Diane Wakeman, September 14, 2005.

Shuttlesworth, Fred. Interview by author, February 19, June 6, 2004.

Shuttlesworth, Fred. Interview by James Mosby Jr., September 1968, RBOHC.

Silver, Carol Ruth. Interview by author, November 10, 2001, June 2, 2005.

Silver, Carol Ruth. Interview by Susan Glisson, November 10, 2001, UMFRC.

Simms, Benjamin. Interview by author and Meeghan Kane, August 30, 2005.

Simon, Howard. Interview by author, December 9, 1998, December 2, 1999.

Singleton, Helen. Interview by Susan Glisson, November 10, 2001, UMFRC.

Singleton, Robert. Interview by author, November 9, 2001.

Singleton, Robert. Interview by Susan Glisson, November 10, 2001, UMFRC.

Smiley, Glenn. Interview by Katherine M. Shannon, September 12, 1967, RBOHC.

Smith, Jerome. Interview by author, November 10, 2001.

Smith, Jerome. Interview by Kim Lacy Rogers, July 8, 26, 1988, ARC.

Smith-Simmons, Doratha. Interview by author, June 27, 2005.

Smith-Simmons, Doratha. Interview by Kim Lacy Rogers, July 27, 1988, ARC.

Smith, Wollcott. Interview by author, November 10, 2001.

Smith, Wollcott. Interview by Susan Glisson, November 10, 2001, UMFRC.

Stoner, Peter. Interview by Susan Glisson, November 10, 2001, UMFRC.

Svanoe, Bill. Interview by author and Meeghan Kane, September 8, 2005.

Swomley, John. Interview by author, November 8, 1985.

Taylor, John. Interview by author, August 20, 2001, July 19, 2005.

Thomas, Hank. Interview by author, April 5–6, May 11, 2001.

Thomas, Hank, and John Moody. Interview by author, May 11, 2001.

Thompson, Alice. Interview by Kim Lacy Rogers, July 25, 1988, ARC.

Uphoff, Eugene. Interview by author, October 17, 2005.

Vivian, C. T. Interview by author and Meeghan Kane, August 10, 2005.

Walker, Matthew, Jr. Interview by author, November 8, 2004.

Walker, Wyatt Tee. Interview by author, December 22, 2003.

Walker, Wyatt Tee. Interview by John Britton, October 11, 1967, RBOHC.

Watkins, Hezekiah. Interview by author, November 11, 2001.

Watkins, Hollis. Interview by Robert Wright, August 5, 1968, RBOHC.
White, Lee C. Interview by Milton Gwirtzman, May 26, 1964, JFKL.
Wilkinson, Frank. Interview by author, March 23, 1993.
Wofford, Harris. Interview by Berl Bernhard, November 29, 1965, JFKL.
Wofford, Harris. Interview by Larry Hackman, May 22, 1968, February 3, 1969, JFKL.
Wolfson, J. Mikhail. Interview by author and Meeghan Kane, September 12, 2005.
Wood, Virgil. Interview by author, March 1, 2002.
Worthy, William. Interview by author, May 10, 2001.
Ziskind, Ellen. Interview by author, September 1, 2005.
Zuchman, Lewis. Interview by author and Meeghan Kane, August 23, 2005.
Zwerg, Jim. Interview by author, March 2, 2001, September 12, 2004.

Unpublished Memoirs

Berrard, Charles. "Notes on a 1961 Freedom Ride to Houston." Ms. in author's possession, 2005.
Blankenheim, Edward J. "Freedom Ride." Ms. in author's possession, 2001.
Browning, Joan. "Who, What, When, Where?—Success or Failure? Conflicting Memories of the Albany Freedom Ride and Albany Movement." Paper presented at the annual meeting of the Georgia Association of Historians, Albany, GA, April 15, 2000.
Davidov, Marv. "Formal Education and Practical Experience in Nonviolent Social Change Movements." Ms. in author's possession, 2001.
Doar, John, and Dorothy Landsberg. "The Performance of the FBI in Investigating Violations of Federal Laws Protecting the Right to Vote—1960–1967." 1971 essay, copy in JFKL.
Green, Steve. "Freedom Rider Diary—Forty Years Later." Ms. in author's possession, 2001.
McNichols, Steven. "The Last Freedom Ride: Life in the Tank." Ms. in author's possession, 2005.
Randall, Francis, and Laura Randall. "Freedom Riders' Diary." Ms. in author's possession, 1961
Roy, Ralph. "Freedom Ride." Ms. in author's possession, 2001.
Sheviakov, Rick. "Freedom Rider Report, with Addendum." Ms. in author's possession, 1962, 2005.
Silver, Carol Ruth. "The Diary of a Freedom Rider." Ms. in author's possession, 1961.
Smith, Kelly Miller. "Pursuit of a Dream (The Nashville Story)." Folder 7, box 28, KMSP.

Newspapers

Adelaide Advertiser (Australia)
Albany Herald
Amsterdam News (New York City)
Anniston Star
Asheville Citizen
Asheville Times
Atlanta Constitution
Atlanta Daily World
Atlanta Journal
Augusta Chronicle
Baltimore Afro-American
Baltimore Sun
Baton Rouge State-Times
Birmingham News
Birmingham Post-Herald
Birmingham World
Boston Globe
Carolina Times
Chapel Hill Daily Tar Heel
Charlotte News
Charlotte Observer
Charlotte Textile Times
Chattanooga Times
Chicago Defender
Chicago Sun-Times
Chicago Tribune
Christian Science Monitor
Citizens' Council
Civil Liberties Newsletter
Clarksdale Press Register
Columbia (MD) *Flyer*
Columbia Owl (Columbia University)

Daily Worker (NY)
Denver Post
Detroit Free Press
Durham Morning Herald
Le Figaro (France)
Greensboro Daily News
Hattiesburg American
High Point Enterprise (NC)
Houston Chronicle
Hutchinson (KS) *News-Herald*
Kalamazoo Gazette
Kansas City Plaindealer
Kansas City Star
Knoxville News-Sentinel
Jackson Clarion-Ledger
Jackson Daily News
Jackson State-Times
Lancaster News
Little Rock Arkansas Gazette
London Independent (UK)
London Times (UK)
Long Island Daily Press
Los Angeles Times
Los Angeles Tribune
Louisiana Weekly
Lungerville News (AZ)
Lynchburg Advance
Lynchburg News
Manchester Guardian (UK)
McComb Enterprise-Journal
Melbourne Herald Sun (Australia)
Memphis Commercial Appeal

Memphis World
Miami Herald
Milwaukee Journal Sentinel
Monroe Enquirer
Montgomery Advertiser
Montgomery Alabama Journal
Montreal Gazette (Canada)
Nashville Banner
Nashville Tennessean
New Orleans States-Item
New Orleans Times-Picayune
New York Herald Tribune
New York People's Voice
New York Post
New York Times
Ocala Banner
Oklahoma City Black Dispatch
Palm Beach Post
Philadelphia Inquirer
Pittsburgh Courier
Queensland Courier Mail (Australia)
Raleigh News and Observer
Rock Hill Evening Herald

St. Petersburg Times
San Bernardino County Sun
San Fernando Valley Sun
Salisbury Evening Post
Salisbury Saturday Evening Post
Student Voice (Atlanta, GA)
Sumter Daily Item
Sydney Australian (Australia)
Sydney Daily Telegraph (Australia)
Tallahassee Democrat
Tampa Tribune
Thunderbolt (National States Rights Party)
USA Today
Vanderbilt Divinity School Prospectus
Vanderbilt Hustler
Voice of the Movement (Nashville, TN)
Wall Street Journal
Washington Afro-American
Washington Evening Star
Washington Post
Winston-Salem Journal

Books and Pamphlets

Abernathy, Ralph David. *And the Walls Came Tumbling Down: An Autobiography.* New York: Harper and Row, 1989.

Adams, Frank T. *James A. Dombrowski: An American Heretic, 1897–1983.* Knoxville: University of Tennessee Press, 1992.

Adams, Frank, with Myles Horton. *Unearthing Seeds of Fire: The Idea of Highlander.* Winston-Salem: John F. Blair, 1975.

Ahmann, Mathew H., ed. *The New Negro.* New York: Biblo and Tannen, 1969.

Albert, Peter J., and Ronald Hoffman, eds. *We Shall Overcome: Martin Luther King, Jr., and the Black Freedom Struggle.* New York: Da Capo Press, 1993.

Alexander, Charles C. *Holding the Line: The Eisenhower Era, 1952–1961.* Bloomington: Indiana University Press, 1975.

Allen, Ivan, Jr. *Mayor: Notes on the Sixties.* New York: Simon and Schuster, 1971.

Anderson, Carol. *Eyes off the Prize: The United Nations and the African American Struggle for Human Rights, 1944–1955.* Cambridge: Cambridge University Press, 2003.

Anderson, J. W. *Eisenhower, Brownell, and Congress: The Tangled Origins of the Civil Rights Bill of 1956–57.* University: University of Alabama Press, 1964.

Anderson, Jervis. *A. Philip Randolph: A Biographical Portrait.* New York: Harcourt Brace Jovanovich, 1973.

———. *Bayard Rustin: Troubles I've Seen.* New York: HarperCollins, 1997.

Anderson, Terry H. *The Movement and the Sixties: Protest in America from Greensboro to Wounded Knee.* New York: Oxford University Press, 1995.

Anderson, William. *The Wild Man from Sugar Creek: The Political Career of Eugene Talmadge.* Baton Rouge: Louisiana State University Press, 1975.

Applebome, Peter. *Dixie Rising: How the South Is Shaping American Values, Politics, and Culture.* San Diego: Harcourt Brace, 1996.

Arsenault, Raymond. *St. Petersburg and the Florida Dream, 1888–1950.* Gainesville: University Press of Florida, 1996.

———, ed. *Crucible of Liberty: 200 Years of the Bill of Rights.* New York: Free Press, 1991.

Ashby, Warren. *Frank Porter Graham: A Southern Liberal.* Winston-Salem: John F. Blair, 1980.

Ashmore, Harry S. *Civil Rights and Wrongs: A Memoir of Race and Politics, 1944–1994.* New York: Pantheon, 1994.

———. *An Epitaph for Dixie.* New York: Norton, 1958.

———. *Hearts and Minds: The Anatomy of Racism from Roosevelt to Reagan.* New York: McGraw-Hill, 1982.

Baker, Ray Stannard. *Following the Color Line: American Negro Citizenship in the Progressive Era.* New York: Harper and Row, 1964.

Barkan, Steven E. *Protesters on Trial: Criminal Justice in the Southern Civil Rights and Vietnam Antiwar Movements.* New Brunswick: Rutgers University Press, 1985.

Barksdale, Georgia R. W. *Lest We Forget: Remember the Pioneers, Lynchburg Early Civil Rights Movement, 1960–1963.* Lynchburg: privately printed, 1999.

Barnard, Hollinger, ed. *Outside the Magic Circle: The Autobiography of Virginia Foster Durr.* New York: Simon and Schuster, 1985.

Barnard, William D. *Dixiecrats and Democrats: Alabama Politics, 1942–1950.* University: University of Alabama Press, 1974.

Barnes, Catherine A. *Journey from Jim Crow: The Desegregation of Southern Transit*. New York: Columbia University Press, 1983.
Bartley, Numan V. *The Creation of Modern Georgia*. Athens: University of Georgia Press, 1983.
———. *From Thurmond to Wallace: Political Tendencies in Georgia, 1948–1968*. Baltimore: Johns Hopkins University Press, 1970.
———. *The New South 1945–1980*. Baton Rouge: Louisiana State University Press, 1995.
———. *The Rise of Massive Resistance: Race and Politics in the South During the 1950s*. Baton Rouge: Louisiana State University Press, 1969.
Bass, Jack. *Ol' Strom: An Unauthorized Biography of Strom Thurmond*. Atlanta: Longstreet, 1998.
———. *Taming the Storm: The Life and Times of Frank M. Johnson and the South's Fight over Civil Rights*. New York: Doubleday, 1992.
———. *Unlikely Heroes*. New York: Simon and Schuster, 1981.
Bass, Jack, and Walter DeVries. *The Transformation of Southern Politics: Social Change and Political Consequences Since 1945*. New York: Basic Books, 1976.
Bass, Jonathan. *Blessed Are the Peacemakers: Martin Luther King Jr., Eight White Religious Leaders, and the "Letter from Birmingham Jail."* Baton Rouge: Louisiana State University Press, 2001.
Bauman, Mark, and Berkley Kalin, eds. *Quiet Voices: Southern Rabbis and Black Civil Rights, 1880s to 1990s*. Tuscaloosa: University of Alabama Press, 1998.
Bayor, Ronald. *Race and the Shaping of Twentieth-Century Atlanta*. Chapel Hill: University of North Carolina Press, 1996.
Belfrage, Sally. *Freedom Summer*. New York: Viking Press, 1965.
Belknap, Michael R. *Federal Law and Southern Order: Racial Violence and Constitutional Conflict in the Post-Brown South*. Athens: University of Georgia Press, 1987.
Bell, Derrick A. *And We Are Not Saved: The Elusive Quest for Racial Justice*. New York: Basic Books, 1987.
———. *Confronting Authority: Reflections of an Ardent Protester*. Boston: Beacon Press, 1994.
———. *Faces at the Bottom of the Well: The Permanence of Racism*. New York: Basic Books, 1992.
Bell, Inge Powell. *CORE and the Strategy of Nonviolence*. New York: Random House, 1968.
Bell, Leland V. *In Hitler's Shadow: The Anatomy of American Nazism*. Port Washington, NY: Associated Faculty Press, 1973.
Bennett, Leone. *What Manner of Man*. New York: Pocket Books, 1964.
Bennett, Scott H. *Radical Pacifism: The War Resisters League and Gandhian Nonviolence in America, 1915–1963*. Syracuse: Syracuse University Press, 2003.
Berg, Manfred. *"The Ticket to Freedom": The NAACP and the Struggle for Black Political Integration*. Gainesville University Press of Florida, 2005.
Berman, William C. *The Politics of Civil Rights in the Truman Administration*. Columbus: Ohio State University Press, 1970.
Berry, Chuck. *Chuck Berry: The Autobiography*. New York: Hammond Books, 1987.
Bigelow, Albert. *The Voyage of the Golden Rule: An Experiment with Truth*. New York: Doubleday, 1959.
Biondi, Martha. *To Stand and Fight: The Civil Rights Movement in Postwar New York City*. Cambridge: Harvard University Press, 2003.
Black, Earl, and Merle Black. *Politics and Society in the South*. Cambridge: Harvard University Press, 1987.
Blake, John. *Children of the Movement: The Sons and Daughters of Martin Luther King, Jr., Malcolm X, Elijah Muhammad, George Wallace, Andrew Young, Julian Bond, Stokely Carmichael, Bob Moses, James Chaney, Elaine Brown, and Others Reveal How the Civil Rights Movement Tested and Transformed Their Families*. Chicago: Lawrence Hill Books, 2004.
Bloom, Alex, and Wini Breines, eds. *"Takin' It to the Streets": A Sixties Reader*. New York: Oxford University Press, 1995.
Blum, John Morton. *Years of Discord: American Politics and Society, 1961–1974*. New York: Norton, 1991.
Blumberg, Rhonda Lois. *Civil Rights: The 1960s Freedom Struggle*. Boston: Twayne, 1984.
Bodan, Susan, and James R. Robinson. *1959 Miami Interracial Action Institute: Summary and Evaluation*. New York: CORE, 1960.
Bondurant, Joan V. *Conquest of Violence: The Gandhian Philosophy of Conflict*. Berkeley: University of California Press, 1965.
Booker, Simeon. *Black Man's America*. Englewood Cliffs, NJ: Prentice-Hall, 1964.
Borstelmann, Thomas. *The Cold War and the Color Line: American Race Relations in the Global Arena*. Cambridge: Harvard University Press, 2001.
Boyd, Malcolm. *Are You Running with Me, Jesus? Prayers*. New York: Avon, 1967.
———. *As I Live and Breathe: Stages of an Autobiography*. New York: Random House, 1970.
———. *Half Laughing/Half Crying: Songs of My Life*. New York: St. Martin's, 1986.
Boyle, Kevin. *Arc of Justice: A Saga of Race, Civil Rights, and Murder in the Jazz Age*. New York: Henry Holt, 2004.
Braden, Anne. *The Wall Between*. New York: Monthly Review Press, 1959.
Branch, Taylor. *Parting the Waters: America in the King Years, 1954–63*. New York: Simon and Schuster, 1988.
———. *Pillar of Fire: America in the King Years, 1963–65*. New York: Simon and Schuster, 1998.
Brannan, Rosemary S. *Law, Morality, and Vietnam: The Peace Militants and the Courts*. Bloomington: Indiana University Press, 1974.
Brauer, Carl M. *John F. Kennedy and the Second Reconstruction*. New York: Columbia University Press, 1977.
Brax, Ralph S. *The First Student Movement: Student Activism in the United States During the 1930s*. Port Washington, NY: Kennikat Press, 1981.

Brearley, H. C. "The Pattern of Violence." In *Culture in the South*, ed. W. T. Couch. Chapel Hill: University of North Carolina Press, 1934.

Brinkley, David. *Brinkley's Beat: People, Places, and Events That Shaped My Time*. New York: Knopf, 2003.

Brinkley, Douglas. *Rosa Parks*. New York: Viking Penguin, 2000.

Brown, Judith M. *Gandhi: Prisoner of Hope*. New Haven: Yale University Press, 1989.

Brown, Robert McAfee, and Frank Randall. *The Freedom Riders: A Clergyman's View, an Historian's View*. New York: CORE, 1962. Rpt. from *Amherst College Alumni News* 14 (1961): 11–17.

Brownell, Herbert. *Advising Ike*. Lawrence: University Press of Kansas, 1993.

Bruce, Dickson D. *Violence and Culture in the Antebellum South*. Austin: University of Texas Press, 1979.

Bryan, G. McLeod. *These Few Also Paid a Price: Southern Whites Who Fought for Civil Rights*. Macon: Mercer University Press, 2001.

Burk, Robert F. *The Eisenhower Administration and Black Civil Rights*. Knoxville: University of Tennessee Press, 1984.

Burner, Eric. *And Gently He Shall Lead Them: Robert Parris Moses and Civil Rights in Mississippi*. New York: New York University Press, 1994.

Burns, Stewart, ed. *Daybreak of Freedom: The Montgomery Bus Boycott*. Chapel Hill: University of North Carolina Press, 1997.

Burton, Orville Vernon. *In My Father's House Are Many Mansions: Family and Community in Edgefield, South Carolina*. Chapel Hill: University of North Carolina Press, 1985.

Burton, Willie. *On the Black Side of Shreveport: A History*. Shreveport: privately printed, 1983.

Butterfield, Fox. *All God's Children: The Bosket Family and the American Tradition of Violence*. New York: Knopf, 1995.

Byrd, Martha. *Chennault: Giving Wings to the Tiger*. Tuscaloosa: University of Alabama Press, 1987.

Cagin, Seth, and Philip Dray. *We Are Not Afraid: The Story of Goodman, Schwerner, and Chaney and the Civil Rights Campaign for Mississippi*. New York: Macmillan, 1988.

Calvert, Robert E., ed. *"The Constitution of the People": Reflections on Citizens and Civil Society*. Lawrence: University of Kansas Press, 1991.

Carey, Gordon. *The City of Progress*. New York: CORE, 1962.

Carlton, David. *Mill and Town in South Carolina, 1880–1920*. Baton Rouge: Louisiana State University Press, 1982.

Carmichael, Stokely, and Charles V. Hamilton. *Black Power: The Politics of Liberation in America*. New York: Random House, 1967.

Carmichael, Stokely, with Ekwueme Michael Thelwell. *Ready for Revolution: The Life and Struggles of Stokely Carmichael (Kwame Ture)*. New York: Scribner, 2003.

Caro, Robert A. *Master of the Senate: The Years of Lyndon Johnson*. New York: Random House, 2002.

Carson, Clayborne. *In Struggle: SNCC and the Black Awakening of the 1960s*. Cambridge: Harvard University Press, 1981.

Carson, Clayborne, et al., eds. *The Eyes on the Prize Civil Rights Reader*. New York: Penguin, 1991.

———. *The Papers of Martin Luther King, Jr.* 5 vols. Berkeley: University of California Press, 1992–2004.

Carter, Dan T. *The Politics of Rage: George Wallace, the Origins of the New Conservatism, and the Transformation of American Politics*. Baton Rouge: Louisiana State University Press, 2000.

———. *Scottsboro: A Tragedy of the American South*. Baton Rouge: Louisiana State University Press, 1969.

Carter, Hodding. *The South Strikes Back*. Garden City, NY: Doubleday, 1959.

Carter, Jimmy. *Turning Point: A Candidate, a State, and a Nation Comes of Age*. New York: Times Books, 1992.

Carter, Robert J. *A Matter of Law: A Memoir of Struggle in the Cause of Equal Rights*. New York: New Press, 2005.

Cash, W. J. *The Mind of the South*. New York: Knopf, 1941.

Cashin, Edward. *The Story of Augusta*. Augusta: Richmond County Board of Education, 1980.

Catudal, Honore M. *Kennedy and the Berlin Wall Crisis: A Case-Study in U.S. Decision Making*. West Berlin: Berlin-Verlag, 1980.

Caute, David. *The Great Fear: The Anti-Communist Purge Under Truman and Eisenhower*. New York: Simon and Schuster, 1978.

Chafe, William. *Civilities and Civil Rights: Greensboro, North Carolina, and the Black Struggle for Freedom*. New York: Oxford University Press, 1980.

Chappell, David L. *Inside Agitators: White Southerners in the Civil Rights Movement*. Baltimore: Johns Hopkins University Press, 1994.

———. *A Stone of Hope: Prophetic Religion and the Death of Jim Crow*. Chapel Hill: University of North Carolina Press, 2004.

Chatfield, Charles. *For Peace and Justice: Pacifism in America, 1914–1941*. Knoxville: University of Tennessee Press, 1971.

———, ed. *The Americanization of Gandhi: Images of the Mahatma*. New York: Garland, 1976.

Clark, E. Culpepper. *The Schoolhouse Door: Segregation's Last Stand at the University of Alabama*. New York: Oxford University Press, 1993.

Clark, Roy Peter, and Raymond Arsenault, eds. *The Changing South of Gene Patterson: Journalism and Civil Rights, 1960–1968*. Gainesville: University Press of Florida, 2002.

Clayton, Edward T., ed. *The SCLC Story*. Atlanta: SCLC, 1964.

Clowse, Barbara B. *Ralph McGill: A Biography*. Macon: Mercer University Press, 1998.

Cobb, James C. *The Most Southern Place on Earth: The Mississippi Delta and the Roots of Regional Identity*. New York: Oxford University Press, 1992.

Coffin, William Sloane, Jr. *Once to Every Man: A Memoir*. New York: Atheneum, 1977.

Cohen, Robert. *When the Old Left Was Young: Student Radicals and America's First Mass Student Movement, 1929–1941*. New York: Oxford University Press, 1993.

Cohodas, Nadine. *Strom Thurmond and the Politics of Southern Change*. New York: Simon and Schuster, 1993.

Colburn, David. *Racial Change and Community Crisis: St. Augustine, Florida, 1877–1980*. Gainesville: University Press of Florida, 1991.

Colburn, David, and Richard K. Scher. *Florida's Gubernatorial Politics in the Twentieth Century*. Tallahassee: University Presses of Florida, 1980.

Collier-Thomas, Bettye, and V. P. Franklin, eds. *Sisters in the Struggle: African American Women in the Civil Rights–Black Power Movement*. New York: New York University Press, 2001.

Conkin, Paul. *Gone with the Ivy: A Biography of Vanderbilt University*. Knoxville: University of Tennessee Press, 1985.

Cook, James Graham. *The Segregationists*. New York: Appleton-Century-Crofts, 1962.

Couch, W. T., ed. *Culture in the South*. Chapel Hill: University of North Carolina Press, 1934.

Covington, Vicki. *The Last Hotel for Women: A Novel*. New York: Simon and Schuster, 1996.

Crawford, Vicki L., Jacqueline Anne Rouse, and Barbara Woods, eds. *Women in the Civil Rights Movement: Trailblazers and Torchbearers, 1941–1965*. Bloomington: Indiana University Press, 1993.

Cruikshank, Margaret. *The Gay and Lesbian Liberation Movement*. New York: Routledge, 1992.

Curry, Constance. *Silver Rights*. Chapel Hill: Algonquin Books, 1995.

Curry, Constance, et al. *Deep in Our Hearts: Nine White Women in the Freedom Movement*. Athens: University of Georgia Press, 2000.

Curthoys, Ann. *Freedom Ride: A Freedom Rider Remembers*. Crows Nest, NSW: Allen and Unwin, 2002.

Dailey, Jane, et al., eds. *Jumpin' Jim Crow: Southern History from Civil War to Civil Rights*. Princeton: Princeton University Press, 2000.

Dalfiume, Richard M. *Desegregation of the U.S. Armed Forces: Fighting on Two Fronts, 1939–1953*. Columbia: University of Missouri Press, 1969.

Dallek, Robert. *An Unfinished Life: John F. Kennedy, 1917–1963*. Boston: Little, Brown, 2003.

Daniel, Pete. *Lost Revolutions: The South in the 1950s*. Chapel Hill: University of North Carolina Press, 2000.

Davis, Allison, Burleigh B. Gardner, and Mary R. Gardner. *Deep South: A Social Anthropological Study of Caste and Class*. Chicago: University of Chicago Press, 1941.

Davis, Jack E. *Race Against Time: Culture and Separation in Natchez Since 1930*. Baton Rouge: Louisiana State University Press, 2001.

Davis, Michael D., and Hunter R. Clark. *Thurgood Marshall: Warrior at the Bar, Rebel on the Bench*. New York: Birch Lane Press, 1992.

Davis, Townsend. *Weary Feet, Rested Souls: A Guided History of the Civil Rights Movement*. New York: Norton, 1998.

D'Emilio, John. *Lost Prophet: The Life and Times of Bayard Rustin*. New York: Free Press, 2003.

D'Emilio, John, William B. Turner, and Urvashi Vaid, eds. *Creating Change: Sexuality, Public Policy, and Civil Rights*. New York: St. Martin's, 2000.

Devree, Charlotte, ed. *Justice?* New York: CORE, 1962.

Dickstein, Morris. *Gates of Eden: American Culture in the Sixties*. New York: Basic Books, 1977.

Diggins, John Patrick. *The Proud Decades: America in War and Peace, 1941–1960*. New York: Norton, 1988.

Dittmer, John. *Local People: The Struggle for Civil Rights in Mississippi*. Urbana: University of Illinois Press, 1994.

Dollard, John. *Caste and Class in a Southern Town*. New Haven: Yale University Press, 1937.

Donald, David Herbert. *Lincoln*. New York: Simon and Schuster, 1995.

Dorsen, Norman. *The Evolving Constitution*. Middletown, CT: Wesleyan University Press, 1987.

Doyle, William. *An American Insurrection: The Battle of Oxford, Mississippi, 1962*. New York: Doubleday, 2001.

Duberman, Martin B. *Paul Robeson: A Biography*. New York: Knopf, 1988.

Dudziak, Mary L. *Cold War Civil Rights: Race and the Image of American Democracy*. Princeton: Princeton University Press, 2000.

Due, Tananarive, and Patricia Stephens Due. *Freedom in the Family: A Mother-Daughter Memoir of the Fight for Civil Rights*. New York: Ballantine, 2003.

Dulles, Foster Rhea. *The Civil Rights Commission, 1957–1965*. East Lansing: Michigan State University Press, 1968.

Dunbar, Anthony P. *Against the Grain: Southern Radicals and Prophets, 1929–1959*. Charlottesville: University of Virginia Press, 1981.

Dunn, Marvin. *Black Miami in the Twentieth Century*. Gainesville: University Press of Florida, 1997.

Dworkin, Ronald. *Taking Rights Seriously*. Cambridge: Harvard University Press, 1977.

Edmonds, Randolph. *Earth and Stars*. Tallahassee, FL: n.p., 1961.

Egerton, John. *The Americanization of Dixie: The Southernization of America*. New York: Harper's Magazine Press, 1974.

———. *Speak Now Against the Day: The Generation Before the Civil Rights Movement in the South*. New York: Knopf, 1994.

Ely, James W., Jr. *The Crisis of Conservative Virginia: The Byrd Organization and the Politics of Massive Resistance*. Knoxville: University of Tennessee Press, 1976.

Entire, Robert, ed. *Anniston, Alabama, Centennial, 1883–1983*. Anniston: Higginbotham, 1983.

Epp, Charles R. *The Rights Revolution: Lawyers, Activists, and Supreme Courts in Comparative Perspective*. Chicago: University of Chicago Press, 1998.

Erikson, Erik H. *Gandhi's Truth: On the Origins of Militant Nonviolence*. New York: Norton, 1969.

Eskew, Glenn T. *But for Birmingham: The Local and National Movements in the Civil Rights Struggle*. Chapel Hill: University of North Carolina Press, 1997.

Estes, Steve. *I Am a Man! Race, Manhood, and the Civil Rights Movement*. Chapel Hill: University of North Carolina Press, 2005.

Evans, Sara. *Personal Politics: The Roots of Women's Liberation in the Civil Rights Movement and the New Left*. New York: Knopf, 1978.

Evans, Sara M., and Harry C. Boyte. *Free Spaces: The Sources of Democratic Change in America*. New York: Harper and Row, 1986.

Fairclough, Adam. *Better Day Coming: Blacks and Equality, 1890–2000*. New York: Penguin, 2001.

———. *Race and Democracy: The Civil Rights Struggle in Louisiana, 1915–1972*. Athens: University of Georgia Press, 1995.

———. *To Redeem the Soul of America: The Southern Christian Leadership Conference and Martin Luther King, Jr.* Athens: University of Georgia Press, 1987.

Farber, David. *The Age of Great Dreams: America in the 1960s*. New York: Hill and Wang, 1994.

Farmer, James. *Lay Bare the Heart: An Autobiography of the Civil Rights Movement*. New York: New American Library, 1985.

Faust, Drew Gilpin. *James Henry Hammond and the Old South: A Design for Mastery*. Baton Rouge: Louisiana State University Press, 1982.

Federal Writers' Project. *Alabama: A Guide to the Deep South*. New York: R. R. Smith, 1941.

———. *Mississippi: A Guide to the Magnolia State*. New York: Viking Press, 1938.

———. *North Carolina: A Guide to the Old North State*. Chapel Hill: University of North Carolina Press, 1939.

———. *South Carolina: A Guide to the Palmetto State*. New York: Oxford University Press, 1941.

———. *Virginia: A Guide to the Old Dominion*. New York: Oxford University Press, 1940.

Feldman, Glenn, ed. *Before Brown: Civil Rights and White Backlash in the Modern South*. Tuscaloosa: University of Alabama Press, 2004.

Findlay, James F. *Church People in the Struggle: The National Council of Churches and the Black Freedom Movement, 1950–1970*. New York: Oxford University Press, 1977.

First Baptist Church. *'Tis a Glorious Church: The Brick-a-Day Church*. Montgomery: First Baptist Church, 2001.

Fischer, David Hackett. *Liberty and Freedom*. New York: Oxford University Press, 2004.

Fischer, Louis. *The Life of Mahatma Gandhi*. London: Jonathan Cape, 1951.

Fleming, Cynthia Griggs. *Soon We Will Not Cry: The Liberation of Ruby Doris Smith Robinson*. London: Rowman and Littlefield, 1998.

Fluker, Walter E. *They Looked for a City: A Comparative Analysis of the Ideal of Community in the Thought of Howard Thurman and Martin Luther King, Jr.* Lanham, MD: University Press of America, 1989.

Fluker, Walter E., and Catherine Tumber, eds. *A Strange Freedom: The Best of Howard Thurman on Religious Experience and Public Life*. Boston: Beacon, 1998.

Flynt, Wayne. *Alabama in the Twentieth Century*. Tuscaloosa: University of Alabama Press, 2004.

———. *Montgomery: An Illustrated History*. Woodland Hills, CA: Windsor, 1980.

———. *Poor but Proud: Alabama's Poor Whites*. Tuscaloosa: University of Alabama Press, 1989.

Fogelson, Genia. *Harry Belafonte: Singer and Actor*. Belmont, CA: Wadsworth, 1996.

Foner, Eric. *Free Soil, Free Labor, Free Men: The Ideology of the Republican Party Before the Civil War*. New York: Oxford University Press, 1970.

———. *Reconstruction: America's Unfinished Revolution, 1863–1877*. New York: Harper and Row, 1988.

———. *The Story of American Freedom*. New York: Norton, 1998.

Fontenay, Charles L. *Estes Kefauver: A Biography*. Knoxville: University of Tennessee Press, 1980.

Ford, Daniel. *Flying Tigers: Claire Chennault and the American Volunteer Group*. Washington: Smithsonian Institution Press, 1991.

Forman, James. *The Making of Black Revolutionaries: A Personal Account*. New York: Macmillan, 1972.

Fosl, Catherine. *Subversive Southerner: Anne Braden and the Struggle for Racial Justice in the Cold War South*. New York: Palgrave, 2002.

Frady, Marshall. *Martin Luther King, Jr.* New York: Viking, 2002.

———. *Wallace*. New York: New American Library, 1976.

Franklin, John Hope. *The Militant South, 1800–1861*. Cambridge: Harvard University Press, 1956.

Franklin, John Hope, and Alfred A. Moss, Jr. *From Slavery to Freedom: A History of African Americans*. 8th ed. New York: Knopf, 2000.

Freyer, Tony. *The Little Rock Crisis: A Constitutional Interpretation*. Westport, CT: Greenwood Press, 1984.

Fried, Richard M. *Nightmare in Red: The McCarthy Era in Perspective*. New York: Oxford University Press, 1990.

Fuchs, Lawrence H. *American Kaleidoscope: Race, Ethnicity, and the Civic Culture*. Middletown, CT: Wesleyan University Press, 1990.

Gaillard, Frye. *Cradle of Freedom: Alabama and the Movement That Changed America*. Tuscaloosa: University of Alabama Press, 2004.

Gallup, George H. *The Gallup Poll: Public Opinion, 1935–1971*. New York: Random House, 1971.

Galphin, Bruce. *The Riddle of Lester Maddox*. Atlanta: Camelot, 1968.

Garey, Diane. *Defending Everybody: A History of the American Civil Liberties Union*. New York: TV Books, 1998.

Garfinkel, Herbert. *When Negroes March: The March on Washington Movement in the Organizational Politics for FEPC*. New York: Atheneum, 1969.

Garreau, Joel. *The Nine Nations of North America*. Boston: Houghton Mifflin, 1981.

Garrow, David J. *Bearing the Cross: Martin Luther King, Jr., and the Southern Christian Leadership Conference*. New York: William Morrow, 1986.

———. *The FBI and Martin Luther King, Jr.: From "Solo" to Memphis*. New York: W. W. Norton, 1981.

———. *Protest at Selma: Martin Luther King and the Voting Rights Act of 1965*. New Haven: Yale University Press, 1978.

———, ed. *Birmingham, Alabama, 1956–1963: The Black Struggle for Civil Rights*. Brooklyn: Carlson, 1989.

Garrow, David J., Bill Kovatch, and Carol Polsgrove, eds. *Reporting Civil Rights*, part 1, *American Journalism, 1941–1963*. New York: Library of America, 2003.

Gates, Grace Hooten. *The Model City of the New South: Anniston, Alabama, 1872–1900*. Tuscaloosa: University of Alabama Press, 1978.

Gentry, Curt. *J. Edgar Hoover: The Man and the Secrets*. New York: Norton, 1991.

Gitlin, Todd. *The Sixties: Years of Hope, Days of Rage*. New York: Bantam, 1989.

Gladney, Margaret Rose, ed. *How Am I to Be Heard: The Letters of Lillian Smith*. Chapel Hill: University of North Carolina Press, 1993.

Gladwell, Malcolm. *The Tipping Point: How Little Things Can Make a Big Difference*. Boston: Little, Brown, 2000.

Glen, John M. *Highlander: No Ordinary School, 1932–1962*. Lexington: University of Kentucky Press, 1988.

Goldfield, David R. *Black, White, and Southern: Race Relations and Southern Culture, 1940 to the Present*. Baton Rouge: Louisiana State University Press, 1990.

Goldman, Eric F. *The Crucial Decade—and After: America, 1945–1960*. New York: Vintage, 1960.

———. *Rendezvous with Destiny: A History of Modern American Reform*. New York: Knopf, 1952.

Goldstein, Warren. *William Sloane Coffin, Jr.: A Holy Impatience*. New Haven: Yale University Press, 2004.

Goodman, Walter. *The Committee: The Extraordinary Career of the House Committee on Un-American Activities*. New York: Farrar, Straus, and Giroux, 1968.

Gorman, Joseph Bruce. *Kefauver: A Political Biography*. New York: Oxford University Press, 1971.

Graetz, Robert S. *A White Preacher's Memoir: The Montgomery Bus Boycott*. Montgomery: Black Belt Press, 1998.

Graham, Hugh Davis. *The Civil Rights Era: Origins and Development of National Policy*. New York: Oxford University Press, 1990.

Graham, Hugh Davis, and Ted Robert Gurr. *The History of Violence in America: Historical and Comparative Perspectives*. New York: Praeger, 1969.

Grant, Donald L. *The Way It Was in the South: The Black Experience in Georgia*. Athens: University of Georgia Press, 2001.

Grant, Joanne. *Ella Baker: Freedom Bound*. New York: Wiley, 1998.

———, ed. *Black Protest: History, Documents, and Analyses, 1619 to the Present*. New York: St. Martin's Press, 1970.

Gray, Fred. *Bus Ride to Justice*. Montgomery: Black Belt Press, 1995.

Green, Ben. *Before His Time: The Untold Story of Harry T. Moore*. New York: Free Press, 1999.

Greenberg, Cheryl Lynn, ed. *A Circle of Trust: Remembering SNCC*. New Brunswick: Rutgers University Press, 1998.

Greenberg, Jack. *Race Relations and American Law*. New York: Columbia University Press, 1959.

Greene, Melissa Fay. *The Temple Bombing*. Reading, MA: Addison-Wesley, 1996.

Gregg, Richard B. *The Power of Non-Violence*. Philadelphia: J. P. Lippincott, 1934.

Grossman, James R. *Land of Hope: Chicago, Black Southerners, and the Great Migration*. Chicago: University of Chicago Press, 1991.

Guthman, Edwin O. *We Band of Brothers*. New York: Harper and Row, 1971.

Guthman, Edwin O., and Jeffrey Shulman, eds. *Robert Kennedy in His Own Words: The Unpublished Recollections of the Kennedy Years*. New York: Bantam, 1988.

Hahn, Steven. *A Nation Under Our Feet: Black Political Struggles in the Rural South from Slavery to the Great Migration*. Cambridge: Harvard University Press, 2003.

Halberstam, David. *The Children*. New York: Random House, 1998.

———. *The Fifties*. New York: Villard, 1993.

Hall, Jacquelyn Dowd. *Revolt Against Chivalry: Jesse Daniel Ames and the Southern Women's Campaign Against Lynching*. New York: Columbia University Press, 1979.

Hamburger, Robert. *Our Portion of Hell: Fayette County, Tennessee, an Oral History of the Struggle for Civil Rights*. New York: Links Books, 1973.

Hamilton, Mary. *Freedom Riders Speak for Themselves*. Detroit: News and Letters, 1961.

Hampton, Henry, and Steve Fayer. *Voices of Freedom: An Oral History of the Civil Rights Movement from the 1950s through the 1980s*. New York: Vintage, 1990.

Harding, Vincent. *There Is a River: The Black Struggle for Freedom in America*. New York: Harcourt Brace Jovanovich, 1981.

Harrington, Michael. *Decade of Decision: The Crisis of the American System*. New York: Simon and Schuster, 1980.

Harris, J. William. *Plain Folk and Gentry in a Slave Society: White Liberty and Black Slavery in Augusta's Hinterlands*. Middletown, CT: Wesleyan University Press, 1985.

Haskins, James. *Black Music in America*. New York: HarperTrophy, 1987.

———. *The Freedom Rides: Journey for Justice*. New York: Hyperion Books for Children, 1995.

Havard, William C., ed. *The Changing Politics of the South*. Baton Rouge: Louisiana State University, 1972.

Hayden, Tom. *Revolution in Mississippi*. New York: Students for a Democratic Society, 1962.

———. *Reunion: A Memoir*. New York: Random House, 1988.

Haygood, Will. *King of the Cats: The Life and Times of Adam Clayton Powell*. Boston: Houghton Mifflin, 1993.

Hays, Brooks. *A Southern Moderate Speaks*. Chapel Hill: University of North Carolina Press, 1959.

Henderson, Harold P. *Ernest Vandiver: Governor of Georgia*. Athens: University of Georgia Press, 2000.

Henken, Louis. *The Age of Rights*. New York: Columbia University Press, 1990.

Henry, Aaron, with Constance Curry. *Aaron Henry: The Fire Ever Burning*. Jackson: University Press of Mississippi, 2000.

Hentoff, Nat. *Peace Agitator: The Story of A. J. Muste*. New York: Macmillan, 1963.

Herndon, Angelo. *Let Me Live*. New York: Random House, 1937.

Hersh, Seymour M. *The Dark Side of Camelot*. Boston: Little, Brown, 1997.

Hesburgh, Theodore M. *God, Country, Notre Dame*. New York: Doubleday, 1990.

Hickock, Eugene W., Jr. *The Bill of Rights: Original Meaning and Current Understanding*. Charlottesvile: University of Virginia Press, 1991.

Hilty, James W. *Robert Kennedy: Brother Protector*. Philadelphia: Temple University Press, 1997.

Hine, Darlene Clark. *Black Victory: The Rise and Fall of the White Primary in Texas*. Milkwood, NJ: KTO Press, 1979.

Hoffer, Peter Charles. *The Law's Conscience: Equitable Constitutionalism in America*. Chapel Hill: University of North Carolina Press, 1990.

Hogan, Wesley. *Many Minds, One Heart*. Chapel Hill: University of North Carolina Press, forthcoming 2006.

Holloway, Jonathan Scott. *Confronting the Veil: Abram Harris, Jr., E. Franklin Frazier, and Ralph Bunche, 1919–1941*. Chapel Hill: University of North Carolina Press, 2002.

Holmes, William F. *The White Chief: James Kimble Vardaman*. Baton Rouge: Louisiana State University Press, 1970.

Holt, Len. *The Summer That Didn't End*. London: Heinemann, 1966.

Honey, Michael K. *Southern Labor and Black Civil Rights: Organizing Memphis Workers*. Urbana: University of Illinois Press, 1993.

Horton, James Oliver, and Lois E. Horton. *Hard Road to Freedom: A History of African America*. New Brunswick: Rutgers University Press, 2001.

———. *In Hope of Liberty: Culture, Community and Protest Among Northern Free Blacks, 1700–1860*. New York: Oxford University Press, 1997.

———, eds. *A History of the African American People*. Detroit: Wayne State University Press, 1997.

Houser, George. *No One Can Stop the Rain: Glimpses of Africa's Liberation Struggle*. New York: Pilgrim Press, 1989.

Huie, William Bradford. *Three Lives for Mississippi*. New York: WCC Books, 1965.

Hunter-Gault, Charlayne. *In My Place*. New York: Farrar Straus Giroux, 1992.

Hyde, Samuel C., Jr., ed. *Sunbelt Revolution: The Historical Progression of the Civil Rights Struggle in the Gulf South, 1866–2000*. Gainesville: University Press of Florida, 2003.

The Hymnbook. Atlanta: Presbyterian Church in the United States, 1955.

Israel, Fred L., ed. *The State of the Union Messages of the Presidents, 1790–1966*, vol. 3. New York: Chelsea House, 1967.

Isserman, Maurice. *If I Had a Hammer: The Death of the Old Left and the Birth of the New Left*. New York: Basic Books, 1987.

Isserman, Maurice, and Michael Kazin. *America Divided: The Civil War of the 1960s*. New York: Oxford University Press, 2000.

Jackson, Esther Cooper, ed. *Freedomways Reader: Prophets in Their Own Country*. Boulder, CO: Westview Press,, 2000

Jacoway, Elizabeth, and David Colburn, eds. *Southern Businessmen and Desegregation*. Baton Rouge: Louisiana State University Press, 1982.

Jacoway, Elizabeth, and C. Fred Williams, eds. *Understanding the Little Rock Crisis: An Exercise in Remembrance and Reconciliation*. Fayetteville: University of Arkansas Press, 1999.

Jakoubek, Robert E. *James Farmer and the Freedom Rides*. Brookfield, CT: Millbrook Press, 1994.

James T. McCain: A Quiet Hero. Sumter, SC: n.p., 2002.

Javits, Jacob K. *Javits: The Autobiography of a Public Man*. Boston: Houghton Mifflin, 1981.

———. *On Discrimination*. New York: Harcourt, Brace, 1960.

Jeansonne, Glen. *Leander Perez: Boss of the Delta*. Baton Rouge: Louisiana State University Press, 1977.

Johannsen, Robert W. *Lincoln, the South, and Slavery: The Political Dimension*. Baton Rouge: Louisiana State University Press, 1991.

Johnson, David K. *The Lavender Scare: The Cold War Persecution of Gays and Lesbians in the Federal Government*. Chicago: University of Chicago Press, 2004.

Johnston, Erle. *I Rolled With Ross: A Political Portrait*. Baton Rouge: Moran Publishing, 1980.

———. *Mississippi's Defiant Years, 1953–1973: An Interpretive Documentary with Personal Experiences*. Forest, MS: Lake Harbor, 1990.

Jonas, Gilbert. *Freedom's Sword: The NAACP and the Struggle Against Racism in America, 1909-1969*. New York: Routledge, 2005.

Jones, Maxine D., and Joe D. Richardson. *Talladega College: The First Century*. Tuscaloosa: University of Alabama Press, 1990.

Jordan, Vernon, with Annette Gordon-Reed. *Vernon Can Read: A Memoir*. New York: Public Affairs, 2001.

Kantrowitz, Stephen. *Ben Tillman and the Reconstruction of White Supremacy*. Chapel Hill: University of North Carolina Press, 2000.

Kapur, Sudarshan. *Raising Up a Prophet: The African-American Encounter with Gandhi*. Boston: Beacon Press, 1992.

Karst, Kenneth L. *Belonging to America: Equal Citizenship and the Constitution*. New Haven: Yale University Press, 1989.

Katagiri, Yatsuhiro. *The Mississippi State Sovereignty Commission: Civil Rights and States' Rights*. Jackson: University Press of Mississippi, 2001.

Kaufman, Dorothy B. *The First Freedom Ride: The Walter Bergman Story*. Detroit: ACLU Fund Press, 1989.

Kelley, Robin D. G. *Hammer and Hoe: Alabama Communists During the Great Depression*. Chapel Hill: University of North Carolina Press, 1990.

Kennedy, Robert. *Robert Kennedy in His Own Words*. New York: Bantam, 1988.

Kennedy, Robert F., Jr. *Judge Frank M. Johnson, Jr.* New York: G. P. Putnam's Sons, 1978.

Kent, Deborah. *The Freedom Riders*. Chicago: Children's Press, 1993.

Keppel, Ben. *The Work of Democracy: Raph Bunche, Kenneth B. Clark, Lorraine Hansberry, and the Cultural Politics of Race*. Cambridge: Harvard University Press, 1995.

King, Martin Luther, Jr. *Strength to Love*. New York: Harper and Row, 1963.

———. *Stride Toward Freedom: The Montgomery Story*. New York: Harper and Row, 1958.

———. *Why We Can't Wait*. New York: New American Library, 1964.

King, Mary. *Freedom Song: A Personal Story of the 1960s Civil Rights Movement*. New York: William Morrow, 1987.

King, Richard H. *Civil Rights and the Idea of Freedom*. New York: Oxford University Press, 1992.

———. *Race, Culture, and the Intellectuals, 1940–1970*. Baltimore: Johns Hopkins University Press, 2004.

———. *A Southern Renaissance: The Cultural Awakening of the American South, 1930–1955*. New York: Oxford University Press, 1980.

Kirk, John A. *Redefining the Color Line: Black Activism in Little Rock, Arkansas, 1940–1970*. Gainesville: University Press of Florida, 2002.

Kirwan, Albert J. *Revolt of the Rednecks: Mississippi Politics, 1876–1925*. Lexington: University of Kentucky Press, 1951.

Klarman, Michael J. *From Jim Crow to Civil Rights: The Supreme Court and the Struggle for Racial Equality*. New York: Oxford University Press, 2004.

Klibaner, Irwin. *Conscience of a Troubled South: The Southern Conference Educational Fund, 1946–1966*. Brooklyn: Carlson, 1988.

Klinkner, Philip A., and Rogers M. Smith. *The Unsteady March: The Rise and Decline of Racial Equality in America*. Chicago: University of Chicago Press, 1999.

Kluger, Richard. *Simple Justice: The History of Brown v. Board of Education and Black America's Struggle for Equality*. New York: Random House, 1975.

Kneebone, John T. *Southern Liberal Journalists and the Issue of Race*. Chapel Hill: University of North Carolina Press, 1985.

Korstad, Robert Rogers. *Civil Rights Unionism: Tobacco Workers and the Struggle for Democracy in the Mid-Twentieth-Century South*. Chapel Hill: University of North Carolina Press, 2003.

Kotz, Nick. *Judgment Days: Lyndon Baines Johnson, Martin Luther King Jr., and the Laws That Changed America*. Boston: Houghton Mifflin, 2005.

Kreuger, Thomas A. *And Promises to Keep: The Southern Conference for Human Welfare, 1938–1948*. Nashville: Vanderbilt University Press, 1967.

Kunstler, William M., with Sheila Isenberg. *My Life as a Radical Lawyer*. New York: Birch Lane Press, 1994.

Lamis, Alexander P. *The Two-Party South*. New York: Oxford University Press, 1984.

Lamson, Peggy. *Roger Baldwin: Founder of the American Civil Liberties Union*. Boston: Houghton Mifflin, 1976.

Langum, David J. *William M. Kunstler: The Most Hated Lawyer in America*. New York: New York University Press, 1999.

Laue, James H. *Direct Action and Desegregation, 1960–1962: Toward a Theory of the Rationalization of Protest*. Brooklyn: Carlson Publishing, 1989.

Laurant, Darrell. *A City unto Itself: Lynchburg, Virginia in the Twentieth Century*. N.p.: D. Laurant, 1997.

Lawson, Steven F. *Black Ballots: Voting Rights in the South, 1944–1969*. New York: Columbia University Press, 1976.

———. *Running for Freedom: Civil Rights and Black Politics in America Since 1941*. New York: McGraw-Hill, 1991.

———, ed. *To Secure These Rights: The Report of Harry S. Truman's Committee on Civil Rights*. New York: Bedford, 2003.

Lawson, Steven F., and Charles Payne. *Debating the Civil Rights Movement, 1945–1968*. Lanham, MD: Rowman and Littlefield, 1998.

Layton, Azza. *International Politics and Civil Rights Policies in the United States, 1941–1960*. New York: Cambridge University Press, 2000.

Lee, Chana Kai. *For Freedom's Sake: The Life of Fannie Lou Hamer*. Urbana: University of Illinois Press, 1999.

Lee, Harper. *To Kill a Mockingbird*. Philadelphia: J. P. Lippincott, 1960.

Lelyveld, Joseph. *Move Your Shadow: South Africa, Black and White*. New York: Times Books, 1985.

Lemann, Nicholas. *The Promised Land: The Great Black Migration and How It Changed America*. New York: Knopf, 1991.

Lentz, Richard. *Symbols, the News Magazines, and Martin Luther King*. Baton Rouge: Louisiana State University Press, 1990.

Lerner, Gerda, ed. *Black Women in White America: A Documentary History*. New York: Vintage Books, 1973.

Levine, Daniel. *Bayard Rustin and the Civil Rights Movement*. New Brunswick: Rutgers University Press, 2000.

Levine, Ellen, ed. *Freedom's Children: Young Civil Rights Activists Tell Their Own Stories*. New York: G. P. Putnam's Sons, 1993.

Lewis, Anthony. *Make No Law: The Sullivan Case and the First Amendment*. New York: Random House, 1991.

Lewis, Anthony, and *The New York Times*. *Portrait of a Decade: The Second American Revolution*. New York: Random House, 1964.

Lewis, David Levering. *King: A Critical Biography*. New York: Praeger, 1970.

———. *W.E.B. DuBois: Biography of a Race, 1919–1963*. New York: Henry Holt, 1993.

———. *W.E.B. DuBois: The Fight for Equality and the American Century, 1919–1963*. New York: Henry Holt, 2000.

Lewis, George. *The White South and the Red Menace: Segregationists, Anticommunism, and Massive Resistance, 1945–1965*. Gainesville: University Press of Florida, 2004.

Lewis, John, with Michael D'Orso. *Walking with the Wind: A Memoir of the Movement*. New York: Simon and Schuster, 1998.

Light, Ken. *Delta Time: Mississippi Photographs by Ken Light*. Washington: Smithsonian Institution Press, 1995.

Ling, Peter J. *Martin Luther King, Jr.* London: Routledge, 2002.

Litwack, Leon F. *Been in the Storm So Long: The Aftermath of Slavery*. New York: Vintage, 1980.

———. *North of Slavery*. Chicago: University of Chicago Press, 1961.

———. *Trouble in Mind: Black Southerners in the Age of Jim Crow*. New York: Knopf, 1998.

Lomax, Alan. *The Land Where the Blues Began*. New York: Dell, 1993.

Lomax, Louis E. *The Negro Revolt*. New York: Harper and Row, 1962.

Longley, Kyle. *Senator Albert Gore, Sr.: A Tennessee Maverick*. Baton Rouge: Louisiana State University Press, 2004.

Louis, Debbie. *And We Are Not Saved: A History of the Movement as People*. Garden City, NY: Doubleday, 1970.

Loveland, Anne C. *Lillian Smith: A Southerner Confronting the South*. Baton Rouge: Louisiana State University Press, 1986.

Lynd, Staughton, ed. *Nonviolence in America: A Documentary History*. Indianapolis: Bobbs-Merrill, 1960.

Lynn, Conrad. *There Is a Fountain*. Westport, CT: Lawrence Hill, 1979.

Mandela, Nelson. *Long Walk to Freedom: The Autobiography of Nelson Mandela*. Boston: Little, Brown, 1994.

Manis, Andrew M. *A Fire You Can't Put Out: The Civil Rights Life of Birmingham's Reverend Fred Shuttlesworth*. Tuscaloosa: University of Alabama Press, 1999.

Mann, Peggy. *Ralph Bunche: UN Peacemaker*. New York: Coward, McCann, and Geoghegan, 1975.

Marable, Manning. *Race, Reform, and Rebellion: The Second Reconstruction in Black America, 1945–1982*. Jackson: University Press of Mississippi, 1984.

Marsh, Charles. *The Beloved Community: How Faith Shapes Social Justice, from the Civil Rights Movement to Today*. New York: Basic Books, 2005.

———. *God's Long Summer: Stories of Faith and Civil Rights*. Princeton: Princeton University Press, 1997.

Marshall, Burke. *Federalism and Civil Rights*. New York: Columbia University Press, 1964.

Martin, Charles H. *The Angelo Herndon Case and Southern Justice*. Baton Rouge: Louisiana State University Press, 1976.

Martin, Harold H. *Ralph McGill, Reporter*. Boston: Little, Brown, 1973.

Martin, John Bartlow. *The Deep South Says "Never."* New York: Ballantine Books, 1957.

Martin, Robert F. *Howard Kester and the Struggle for Social Justice in the South, 1904–1977*. Charlottesville: University of Virginia Press, 1991.

Matusow, Allen J. *The Unraveling of America: A History of Liberalism in the 1960s*. New York: Harper Torchbooks, 1984.

May, Elaine Tyler. *Homeward Bound: American Families in the Cold War Era*. New York: Basic Books, 1988.

May, Gary. *The Informant: The FBI, the Ku Klux Klan, and the Murder of Viola Liuzzo*. New Haven: Yale University Press, 2005.

Mayer, Jeremy D. *Running on Race: Racial Politics in Presidential Campaigns, 1960–2000*. New York: Random House, 2002.

McAdam, Doug. *Freedom Summer*. New York: Oxford University Press, 1988.

———. *Political Process and the Development of Black Insurgency, 1930–1970*. Chicago: University of Chicago Press, 1982.

McCain, James T. *The Right to Vote*. New York: CORE, 1962.

McCoy, Donald R., and Richard T. Ruetten. *Quest and Response: Minority Rights and the Truman Administration*. Lawrence: University Press of Kansas, 1973.

McFeely William. *Frederick Douglass*. New York: Simon and Schuster, 1991.

McGill, Ralph. *The South and the Southerner*. Boston: Little, Brown, 1963.

McKinney, John C., ed. *The South in Continuity and Change*. Durham: Duke University Press, 1963.

McMillen, Neil R. *The Citizens' Council: Organized Resistance to the Second Reconstruction, 1954–1964*. Urbana: University of Illinois Press, 1971.

———. *Dark Journey: Black Mississippians in the Age of Jim Crow*. Urbana: University of Illinois Press, 1989.

McMurry, Linda O. *To Keep the Waters Troubled: The Life of Ida B. Wells*. New York: Oxford University Press, 1999.

McNeill, Genna Rae. *Groundwork: Charles Hamilton Houston and the Struggle for Civil Rights*. Philadelphia: University of Pennsylvania Press, 1983.

McPherson, James M. *The Abolitionist Legacy: From Reconstruction to the NAACP*. Princeton: Princeton University Press, 1975.

———. *Crossroads of Freedom: Antietam*. New York: Oxford University Press, 2002.

McWhorter, Diane. *Carry Me Home: Birmingham, Alabama: The Climactic Battle of the Civil Rights Revolution*. New York: Simon and Schuster, 2001.

Meier, August, and Elliott Rudwick. *CORE: A Study in the Civil Rights Movement*. Urbana: University of Illinois Press, 1975.

Meier, August, Elliott Rudwick, and Francis Broderick, eds. *Black Protest Thought in the Twentieth Century*. Indianapolis: Bobbs-Merrill, 1971.

Meredith, James. *James Meredith vs. Ole Miss*. Jackson: Meredith Publishing, 1995.

———. *Me and My Kind: An Oral History*. Jackson: Meredith Publishing, 1995.

———. *Three Years in Mississippi*. Bloomington: Indiana University Press, 1966.

Miller, James. *"Democracy Is in the Streets": From Port Huron to the Siege of Chicago*. New York: Simon and Schuster, 1987.

Miller, Keith D. *Voice of Deliverance: The Language of Martin Luther King, Jr., and Its Sources*. New York: Free Press, 1992.

Miller, Randall M., and George E. Pozzetta, eds. *Shades of the Sunbelt: Essays on Race, Ethnicity, and the Urban South*. Westport, CT: Greenwood Press, 1988.

Miller, Robert. *Nonviolence: A Christian Interpretation*. New York: Schocken Books, 1966.

Miller, William. *Martin Luther King, Jr.: His Life, Martyrdom, and Meaning for the World*. New York: Avon, 1968.

Mills, Kay. *This Little Light of Mine: The Life of Fannie Lou Hamer*. New York: Dutton, 1993.

Mills, Nicolaus. *Like a Holy Crusade: Mississippi 1964—The Turning Point of the Civil Rights Movement in America*. Chicago: Ivan R. Dee, 1992.

Miroff, Bruce. *Pragmatic Illusions: The Presidential Politics of John F. Kennedy*. New York: Longman, 1976.

Mitchell, H. L. *Mean Things Happening in This Land*. Montclair, NJ: Allanheld, Osmun, 1979.

Mitford, Jessica. *Poison Penmanship: The Gentle Art of Muckraking*. New York: Vintage, 1980.

Mohl, Raymond A. *South of the South: Jewish Activists and the Civil Rights Movement in Miami, 1945–1960*. Gainesville: University Press of Florida, 2004.

———, ed. *Searching for the Sunbelt: Historical Perspectives on a Region*. Knoxville: University of Tennessee Press, 1990.

Moody, Anne. *Coming of Age in Mississippi*. New York: Dial, 1968.

Morgan, Edward P. *The 60s Experience: Hard Lessons About Modern America*. Philadelphia: Temple University Press, 1991.

Moritz, Charles, ed. *Current Biography Yearbook 1967*. New York: H. W. Wilson, 1967.

Mormino, Gary R., and George Pozzetta. *The Immigrant World of Ybor City: Italians and Their Latin Neighbors in Tampa, 1885–1985*. Urbana: University of Illinois Press, 1987.

Morris, Aldon D. *The Origins of the Civil Rights Movement: Black Communities Organizing for Change*. New York: Free Press, 1984.

Morris, Willie, ed. *The South Today: One Hundred Years After Appomattox*. New York: Harper and Row, 1965.

Morrow, E. Frederic. *Black Man in the White House: A Diary of the Eisenhower Years by the Administrative Officer for Special Projects, the White House, 1955–1961*. New York: Coward-McCann, 1963.

Moses, Greg. *Revolution of Conscience: Martin Luther King, Jr., and the Philosophy of Nonviolence*. New York: Guilford Press, 1997.

Motley, Constance Baker. *Equal Justice Under Law: An Autobiography*. New York: Farrar, Straus, and Giroux, 1998.

Moye, Todd J. *Let the People Decide: Black Freedom and White Resistance Movements in Sunflower County, Mississippi, 1945–1986*. Chapel Hill: University of North Carolina Press, 2004.

Murray, Pauli. *The Autobiography of a Black Activist, Feminist, Lawyer, Priest, and Poet*. Knoxville: University of Tennessee Press, 1987.

Muse, Benjamin. *Virginia's Massive Resistance*. Bloomington: Indiana University Press, 1961.

Myrdal, Gunnar. *An American Dilemma: The Negro Problem and American Democracy*. New York: Harper and Brothers, 1944.

Naison, Mark. *Communists in Harlem During the Depression*. Urbana: University of Illinois Press, 1981.

Navasky, Victor. *Kennedy Justice*. New York: Atheneum, 1971.

Neely, Mark E., Jr. *The Last Best Hope of Earth: Abraham Lincoln and the Promise of America*. Cambridge: Harvard University Press, 1993.

Nelson, Bruce. *Divided We Stand: American Workers and the Struggle for Black Equality*. Princeton: Princeton University Press, 2001.

———. *Workers on the Waterfront: Seamen, Longshoremen, and Unionism in the 1930s*. Urbana: University of Illinois Press, 1988.

Nelson, Truman. *People with Strength: The Story of Monroe, N.C*. New York: Marzani and Munsell, 1962.

Niven, David. *The Politics of Injustice: The Kennedys, the Freedom Rides, and the Electoral Consequences of a Moral Compromise*. Knoxville: University of Tennessee Press, 2003.

Nivola, Pietro S., ed. *Comparative Disadvantage: Social Regulations and the Global Economy*. Washington: Brookings Institution, 1997.

Noble, Phil. *Beyond the Burning Bus: The Civil Rights Revolution in a Southern Town*. Montgomery: New South Books, 2003.

Norrell, Robert J. *The House I Live In: Race in the American Century.* New York: Oxford University Press, 2005.

Nunnelley, William A. *Bull Connor.* Tuscaloosa: University of Alabama Press, 1991.

O'Brien, Gail. *The Color of the Law: Race, Violence, and Justice in the Post–World War II South.* Chapel Hill: University of North Carolina Press, 1999.

O'Dell, Kimberly. *Anniston, Alabama.* Charleston, SC: Arcadia, 2000.

Odum, Howard. *Race and Rumors of Race.* Chapel Hill: University of North Carolina Press, 1943.

Official Proceedings of the Second National Negro Congress. Philadelphia: October 15–17, 1937.

Ogletree, Charles J., Jr. *All Deliberate Speed: Reflections on the First Half Century of Brown v. Board of Education.* New York: Norton, 2004.

Olson, Lynne. *Freedom's Daughters: The Unsung Heroines of the Civil Rights Movement from 1830 to 1970.* New York: Scribner, 2001.

O'Neill, William. *American High: The Years of Confidence, 1945–1960.* New York: Free Press, 1986.

O'Reilly, Kenneth. *Nixon's Piano: Presidents and Racial Politics from Washington to Clinton.* New York: Free Press, 1995

———. *"Racial Matters": The FBI's Secret File on Black America, 1960–1972.* New York: Free Press, 1989.

Oshinsky, David M. *A Conspiracy So Immense: The World of Joe McCarthy.* New York: Free Press, 1983.

———. *"Worse than Slavery": Parchman Farm and the Ordeal of Jim Crow Justice.* New York: Free Press, 1996.

Ownby, Ted, ed. *The Role of Ideas in the Civil Rights South.* Jackson: University Press of Mississippi, 2002.

Pace, Robert F., ed. *Two Hundred Years in the Heart of Virginia: Perspectives on Farmville's History.* Farmville: Longwood College Foundation, 1998.

Painter, Nell Irvin. *The Narrative of Hosea Hudson: His Life as a Negro Communist in the South.* Cambridge: Harvard University Press, 1979.

Parks, Rosa, with James Haskins. *My Story.* New York: Dial, 1992.

Patterson, James T. *Brown v. Board of Education: A Civil Rights Milestone and Its Troubled Legacy.* New York: Oxford University Press, 2001.

———. *Grand Expectations: The United States, 1945–1974.* New York: Oxford University Press, 1996.

Payne, Charles M. *I've Got the Light of Freedom: The Organizing Tradition and the Mississippi Freedom Struggle.* Berkeley: University of California Press, 1995.

Peck, James. *Freedom Ride.* New York: Simon and Schuster, 1962.

———. *Underdogs vs. Upperdogs.* Canterbury, NJ: n.p., 1969.

———. *We Who Would Not Kill.* New York: Lyle Stuart, 1958.

Peirce, Neal. *The Border South States: People, Politics, and Power in the Five Border South States.* New York: Norton, 1975.

Peltason, J. W. *Fifty-eight Lonely Men: Southern Federal Judges and School Desegregation.* Urbana: University of Illinois Press, 1971.

Percy, Stephen L. *Disability, Civil Rights, and Public Policy.* Tuscaloosa: University of Alabama Press, 1989

Perkins, Charles. *A Bastard Like Me.* Sydney: Ure Smith, 1975.

Pfeffer, Paula F. *A. Philip Randolph, Pioneer of the Civil Rights Movement.* Baton Rouge: Louisiana State University Press, 1990.

Pleasants, Julian, and Augustus M. Burns. *Frank Porter Graham and the 1950 Senate Race in North Carolina.* Chapel Hill: University of North Carolina Press, 1990.

Plummer, Brenda Gayle, ed. *Window on Freedom: Race, Civil Rights, and Foreign Affairs, 1945–1968.* Chapel Hill: University of North Carolina Press, 2003.

Poinsett, Alex. *Walking with Presidents: Louis Martin and the Rise of Black Political Power.* Lanham, MD: Madison Books, 1997.

Pollard, Alton B., III. *Mysticism and Social Change: The Social Witness of Howard Thurman.* New York: Peter Lang, 1992.

Polsgrove, Carol. *Divided Minds: Intellectuals and the Civil Rights Movement.* New York: Norton, 2001.

Potter, David M. *The Impending Crisis, 1848–1861.* New York: Harper and Row, 1976.

Powdermaker, Hortense. *After Freedom: A Cultural Study in the Deep South.* New York: Viking Press, 1939.

Powell, Henry W. *Witness to Civil Rights History: The Essays and Autobiography of Henry W. Powell.* Hastings, NY: Patrick Cooney, 2000.

Powers, Richard Gid. *Secrecy and Power: The Life of J. Edgar Hoover.* New York: Free Press, 1987.

Powledge, Fred. *Free at Last? The Civil Rights Movement and the People Who Made It.* Boston: Little, Brown, 1991.

Pratt, Robert A. *We Shall Not Be Moved: The Desegregation of the University of Georgia.* Athens: University of Georgia Press, 2002.

President's Committee on Civil Rights. *To Secure These Rights: The Report of the President's Committee on Civil Rights.* Washington: GPO, 1947.

Rabby, Glenda Alice. *The Pain and the Promise: The Struggle for Civil Rights in Tallahassee, Florida.* Athens: University of Georgia Press, 1999.

Raines, Howell, ed. *My Soul Is Rested: Movement Days in the Deep South Remembered.* New York: G. P. Putnam's Sons, 1977.

Rampersad, Arnold. *Jackie Robinson: A Biography.* New York: Knopf, 1997.

Ransby, Barbara. *Ella Baker and the Black Freedom Movement: A Radical Democratic Vision.* Chapel Hill: University of North Carolina Press, 2003.

Record, Wilson. *Race and Radicalism: The NAACP and the Communist Party in Conflict.* Ithaca: Cornell University Press, 1964.

Reddick, Lawrence. *Crusader Without Violence: A Biography of Martin Luther King, Jr.*. New York: Harper and Brothers, 1959.

Reed, John Shelton. *The EnDuring South: Subcultural Persistence in Mass Society*. Lexington, MA: D. C. Heath, 1972.

Reed, Linda. *Simple Decency and Common Sense: The Southern Conference Movement, 1938–1963*. Bloomington: Indiana University Press, 1991.

Reeves, Richard. *President Kennedy: Profile of Power*. New York: Simon and Schuster, 1993.

Riley, Russell L. *The Presidency and the Politics of Racial Inequality*. New York: Columbia University Press, 1999.

Ringer, Benjamin B. *We the People and Others: Duality and America's Treatment of Racial Minorities*. New York: Routledge, 1983.

Rivlin, Benjamin, ed. *Ralph Bunche: The Man and His Times*. New York: Holmes and Meier, 1990.

Roberts, Nancy L. *American Peace Writers, Editors, and Periodicals: A Dictionary*. Westport, CT: Greenwood Press, 1991.

Roberts, Randy. *Papa Jack: Jack Johnson and the Era of White Hopes*. New York: Free Press, 1983.

Roberts, Randy, and James Olson. *Winning Is the Only Thing: Sports in America Since 1945*. Baltimore: Johns Hopkins University Press, 1989.

Robinson, Armistead L., and Patricia Sullivan, eds. *New Directions in Civil Rights Studies*. Charlottesville: University of Virginia Press, 1991.

Robinson, Jo Ann Gibson. *The Montgomery Bus Boycott and the Women Who Started It*. Knoxville: University of Tennessee Press, 1987.

Robinson, Jo Ann Ooiman. *Abraham Went Out: A Biography of A. J. Muste*. Philadelphia: Temple University Press, 1981.

Robnett, Belinda. *How Long? How Long? African-American Women in the Struggle for Civil Rights*. New York: Oxford University Press, 1997.

Roche, Jeff. *Restructured Resistance: The Sibley Commission and the Politics of Desegregation in Georgia*. Athens: University of Georgia Press, 1998.

Rockwell, George Lincoln. *This Time the World*. N.p.: 1963.

Roediger, David R. *The Wages of Whiteness: Race and the Making of an American Working Class*. London: Verso, 1991.

Rogers, Kim Lacy. *Righteous Lives: Narratives of the New Orleans Civil Rights Movement*. Athens: University of Georgia Press, 1995.

Roller, David C., and Robert W. Twyman, eds. *The Encyclopedia of Southern History*. Baton Rouge: Louisiana State University Press, 1979.

Rorabaugh, W. J. *Berkeley at War: The 1960s*. New York: Oxford University Press, 1989.

Rosenberg, Jonathan, and Zachary Karabell. *Kennedy, Johnson, and the Quest for Justice: The Civil Rights Tapes*. New York: Norton, 2003.

Rothschild, Mary Aickin. *A Case of Black and White: Northern Volunteers and Southern Freedom Summers*. Westport, CT: Greenwood Press, 1982.

Rovere, Richard H. *Senator Joe McCarthy*. New York: Harcourt, Brace, 1959.

Rowan, Carl T. *Breaking Barriers*. Boston: Little, Brown, 1991.

———. *Dream Makers, Dream Breakers: The World of Justice Thurgood Marshall*. Boston: Little, Brown, 1993.

Rowe, Gary Thomas, Jr. *My Undercover Years with the Ku Klux Klan*. New York: Bantam, 1976.

Rural Organizing and Cultural Center. *Minds Stayed on Freedom: The Civil Rights Struggle in the Rural South: An Oral History*. Boulder, CO: Westview Press, 1991.

Rustin, Bayard. *Down the Line: The Collected Writings of Bayard Rustin*. Chicago: Quadrangle Books, 1971.

Rustin, Bayard, and George Houser. *You Don't Have to Ride Jim Crow*. Washington: Interracial Workshop, 1947.

Sale, Kirkpatrick. *Power Shift: The Rise of the Southern Rim and Its Challenge to the Eastern Establishment*. New York: Random House, 1975.

Salmond, John A. *Conscience of a Lawyer: Clifford J. Durr and American Civil Liberties, 1899–1975*. Tuscaloosa: University of Alabama Press, 1990.

———. *"My Mind Set on Freedom": A History of the Civil Rights Movement, 1954–1968*. Chicago: Ivan R. Dee, 1997.

———. *A Southern Rebel: The Life and Times of Aubrey Williams, 1890–1965*. Chapel Hill: University of North Carolina Press, 1983.

———. *Southern Struggles: The Southern Labor Movement and the Civil Rights Struggle*. Gainesville: University Press of Florida, 2004.

Schefter, James. *The Race: The Uncensored Story of How America Beat Russia to the Moon*. New York: Doubleday, 1999.

Schlesinger, Arthur M., Jr. *Robert Kennedy and His Times*. Boston: Houghton Mifflin, 1978.

Schrecker, Ellen. *Many Are the Crimes: McCarthyism in America*. Princeton: Princeton University Press, 1998.

Schulke, Flip, ed. *Martin Luther King, Jr.: A Documentary . . . Montgomery to Memphis*. New York: Norton, 1976.

Schultz, Debra L. *Going South: Jewish Women in the Civil Rights Movement*. New York: New York University Press, 2001.

Schwartz, Bernard. *Swann's Way: The School Busing Case and the Supreme Court*. New York: Oxford University Press, 1986.

Scotch, Richard K. *From Good Will to Civil Rights: Transforming Federal Disability Policy*. Philadelphia: Temple University Press, 1984.

Scott, James G., and Edward A. Wyatt. *Petersburg's Story*. Petersburg, VA: Titmus Optical, 1960.

Scruggs, Phillip L. *Lynchburg, Virginia*. Lynchburg: J. P. Bell, 1973.

Sellers, Cleveland. *The River of No Return: The Autobiography of a Black Militant and the Life and Death of SNCC*. New York: William Morrow, 1973.

Sewell, George Alexander. *Mississippi Black History Makers*. Jackson: University Press of Mississippi, 1977.

Shapiro, Herbert. *White Violence and Black Response: From Reconstruction to Montgomery*. Amherst: University of Massachusetts Press, 1987.

Sherrill, Robert. *Gothic Politics in the Deep South*. New York: Grossman,1968.

Sibley, Mulford Q., ed. *The Quiet Battle: Writings on the Theory and Practice of Non-Violent Resistance*. Garden City, NY: Anchor, 1963.

Silver, James W. *Mississippi: The Closed Society*. New enlarged ed. New York: Harcourt, Brace, and World, 1966.

Silverman, Jerry. *Songs of Protest and Civil Rights*. New York: Chelsea House, 1992.

Simkins, Francis Butler. *Pitchfork Ben Tillman: South Carolinian*. Baton Rouge: Louisiana State University Press, 1944.

Simon, Bryant. *Fabric of Defeat: The Politics of South Carolina Millhands, 1910–1948*. Chapel Hill: University of North Carolina Press, 1998.

Sindler, Allen P., ed. *Change in the Contemporary South*. Durham: Duke University Press, 1964.

Sitkoff, Harvard. *A New Deal for Blacks: The Emergence of Civil Rights as a National Issue*. New York: Oxford University Press, 1978.

———. *The Struggle for Black Equality, 1954–1980*. New York: Hill and Wang, 1981.

Sklar, Judith N. *American Citizenship: The Quest for Inclusion*. Cambridge: Harvard University Press, 1991.

Skrentny, John D. *The Minority Rights Revolution*. Cambridge: Harvard University Press, 2002.

Slotkin, Richard. *Gunfighter Nation: The Myth of the Frontier in Twentieth-Century America*. New York: Atheneum, 1992.

———. *Regeneration Through Violence: The Myth of the American Frontier, 1600–1860*. Middletown, CT: Wesleyan University Press, 1973.

Smead, Howard. *Blood Justice: The Lynching of Mack Charles Parker*. New York: Oxford University Press, 1986.

Smith, J. Douglas. *Managing White Supremacy: Race, Politics, and Citizenship in Jim Crow Virginia*. Chapel Hill: University of North Carolina Press, 2003.

Smith, Howard K. *Events Leading Up to My Death: The Life of a Twentieth-Century Reporter*. New York: St. Martin's, 1996.

Smith, Lillian. *Killers of the Dream*. New York: Norton, 1949).

Smith, Luther E. *Howard Thurman: The Mystic as Prophet*. Richmond: Friends United Press, 1992.

Sorensen, Theodore C. *Kennedy*. New York: Harper and Row, 1965.

Sosna, Morton P. *In Search of the Silent South: Southern Liberals and the Race Issue*. New York: Columbia University Press, 1977.

Southern Regional Council. *The Freedom Ride*. Atlanta: Southern Regional Council, 1961.

Sperber, A. M. *Murrow: His Life and Times*. New York: Freundlich, 1986.

Stampp, Kenneth M., and Leon F. Litwack, eds. *Reconstruction: An Anthology of Revisionist Writings*. Baton Rouge: Louisiana State University Press, 1969.

Stanton, Mary. *Freedom Walk: Mississippi or Bust*. Jackson: University Press of Mississippi, 2003.

———. *From Selma to Sorrow: The Life and Death of Viola Liuzzo*. Athens: University of Georgia Press, 1998.

Stern, Mark. *Calculating Visions: Kennedy, Johnson, and Civil Rights*. New Brunswick: Rutgers University Press, 1992.

Stewart, James Brewer. *Holy Warriors: The Abolitionists and American Slavery*. New York: Hill and Wang, 1976.

Strain, Christopher B. *Pure Fire: Self-Defense as Activism in the Civil Rights Era*. Athens: University of Georgia, 2005.

Sugarman, Tracy. *Stranger at the Gates: A Summer in Mississippi*. New York: Hill and Wang, 1966.

Sullivan, Patricia. *Days of Hope: Race and Democracy in the New Deal Era*. Chapel Hill: University of North Carolina Press, 1996.

———, ed. *Freedom Writer: Virginia Foster Durr, Letters from the Civil Rights Years*. New York: Routledge, 2003.

Sunnemark, Fredrik. *Ring Out Freedom: The Voice of Martin Luther King Jr. and the Making of the Civil Rights Movement*. Bloomington: Indiana University Press, 2004.

Sunstein, Cass R. *After the Rights Revolution: Reconceiving the Regulatory State*. Cambridge: Harvard University Press, 1990.

Teel, Leonard Ray. *Ralph Emerson McGill: Voice of the Southern Conscience*. Knoxville: University of Tennessee Press, 2001.

Thomas, Evan. *Robert Kennedy, His Life*. New York: Simon and Schuster, 2000.

Thompson, Kenneth W., ed. *The Kennedy Presidency: Seventeen Intimate Perspectives of John F. Kennedy*. Portraits of American Presidents, vol. 4. Lanham, MD: University Press of America, 1985.

Thornton, J. Mills, III. *Dividing Lines: Municipal Politics and the Struggle for Civil Rights in Montgomery, Birmingham, and Selma*. Tuscaloosa: University of Alabama Press, 2002.

Tindall, George Brown. *The Emergence of the New South, 1913–1945*. Baton Rouge: Louisiana State University Press, 1967.

Tischler, Barbara L, ed. *Sights on the Sixties*. New Brunswick: Rutgers University Press, 1992.

Tracy, James. *Direct Action: Radical Pacifism from the Union Eight to the Chicago Seven*. Chicago: University of Chicago Press, 1996.

Trelease, Allen W. *White Terror: The Ku Klux Klan Conspiracy and Southern Reconstruction*. New York: Harper and Row, 1971.

Trillin, Calvin. *An Education in Georgia: The Integration of Charlayne Hunter and Hamilton Holmes*. New York: Viking, 1963.

Tripp, Steven E. *Yankee Town, Southern City: Race and Class Relations in Civil War Lynchburg*. New York: New York University Press, 1997.

Tuck, Stephen G. N. *Beyond Atlanta: The Struggle for Racial Equality in Georgia, 1940–1980*. Athens: University of Georgia Press, 2001.

Tushnet, Mark V. *Making Civil Rights Law: Thurgood Marshall and the Supreme Court, 1936–1961*. New York: Oxford University Press, 1994.

Tygiel, Jules. *Baseball's Great Experiment: Jackie Robinson and His Legacy*. New York: Oxford University Press, 1983.

Tyler, Alice Felt. *Freedom's Ferment*. New York: Harper and Row, 1962.

Tyson, Timothy B. *Blood Done Sign My Name: A True Story*. New York: Crown, 2004.

———. *Radio Free Dixie: Robert F. Williams and the Roots of Black Power*. Chapel Hill: University of North Carolina Press, 1999.

Unger, Irwin. *The Movement: A History of the American New Left, 1959–1972*. New York: Harper and Row, 1974.

Urquhart, Brian. *Ralph Bunche: An American Life*. New York: Norton, 1993.

Van Deburg, William L. *New Day in Babylon: The Black Power Movement and American Culture, 1965–1975*. Chicago: University of Chicago Press, 1992.

Viorst, Milton. *Fire in the Streets: America in the 1960s*. New York: Simon and Schuster, 1979.

Vivian, C. T. *Black Power and the American Myth*. Philadelphia: Fortress Press, 1970.

Vollers, Maryanne. *Ghosts of Mississippi: The Murder of Medgar Evers, the Trials of Byron De La Beckwith, and the Haunting of the New South*. Boston: Little, Brown, 1995.

Wald, Elijah. *Escaping the Delta: Robert Johnson and the Invention of the Blues*. New York:HarperCollins, 2004.

Walker, Samuel. *In Defense of American Liberties: A History of the ACLU*. New York: Oxford University Press, 1990.

Walton, Hanes, Jr. *When the Marching Stopped: The Politics of the Civil Rights Regulatory Agencies*. Albany: State University of New York Press, 1988.

Ward, Brian. *Just My Soul Responding: Rhythm and Blues, Black Consciousness, and Race Relations*. Berkeley: University of California Press, 1998.

———. *Radio and the Struggle for Civil Rights in the South*. Gainesville: University Press of Florida, 2004.

Ward, Brian and Tony Badger, eds. *The Making of Martin Luther King and the Civil Rights Movement*. New York: New York University Press, 1996.

Ware, Gilbert. *William Hastie: Grace Under Pressure*. New York: Oxford University Press, 1984.

Warren, Robert Penn. *Segregation: The Inner Conflict in the South*. New York: Vintage, 1956.

———. *Who Speaks for the Negro?*. New York: Random House, 1965.

Watson, Denton L. *Lion in the Lobby: Clarence Mitchell Jr.'s Struggle for the Passage of Civil Rights Laws*. New York: Morrow, 1990.

Watters, Pat. *Down to Now: Reflections on the Civil Rights Movement*. New York: Random House, 1971.

Watters, Pat, and Reese Cleghorn. *Climbing Jacob's Ladder: The Arrival of Negroes in Southern Politics*. New York: Harcourt, Brace, and World, 1967.

Waynick, Capus M., John C. Brooks, and Elsie W. Pitts, eds. *North Carolina and the Negro*. Raleigh: North Carolina Mayors' Co-operating Committee, 1964.

Webb, Clive. *Fight Against Fear: Southern Jews and Black Civil Rights*. Athens: University of Georgia Press, 2001.

———, ed. *Massive Resistance: Southern Opposition to the Second Reconstruction*. New York: Oxford University Press, 2005.

Weiss, Nancy J. *Whitney M. Young Jr. and the Struggle for Civil Rights*. Princeton: Princeton University Press, 1989.

Weisbrot, Robert. *Freedom Bound: A History of America's Civil Rights Movement*. New York: Norton, 1990.

Weltner, Charles. *Southerner*. Philadelphia: J. B. Lippincott, 1966.

Werner, Craig. *A Change Is Gonna Come: Music, Race, and the Soul of America*. New York: Penguin, 1999.

Wexler, Sanford. *The Civil Rights Movement: An Eyewitness History*. New York: Facts on File, 1993.

White, Theodore H. *The Making of the President 1960*. New York: Atheneum, 1961.

White, Walter. *A Man Called White*. New York: Viking, 1948.

Whitfield, Stephen J. *The Culture of the Cold War*. Baltimore: Johns Hopkins University Press, 1991.

———. *A Death in the Delta: The Story of Emmett Till*. Baltimore: Johns Hopkins University Press, 1991.

Who's Who Among Black Americans, 1990–1991. Detroit: Gale Research, 1991.

Wilhoit, Francis M. *The Politics of Massive Resistance*. New York: George Braziller, 1973.

Wilkins, Roy with Tom Mathews. *Standing Fast: The Autobiography of Roy Wilkins*. New York: Viking Penguin, 1982.

Williams, Juan. *Eyes on the Prize: America's Civil Rights Years, 1954–1965*. New York: Viking, 1987.

———. *Thurgood Marshall: American Revolutionary*. New York: Times Books/Random House, 1998.

————, ed. *My Soul Looks Back in Wonder*. New York: AARP/Sterling, 2004.

Williams, Robert F. *Negroes with Guns*. Chicago: Third World Press, 1973.

Williams, T. Harry. *Lincoln and the Radicals*. Madison: University of Wisconsin Press, 1941.

Williamson, Joel. *The Crucible of Race: Black-White Relations in the American South Since Emancipation*. New York: Oxford University Press, 1984.

Wilson, Charles Reagon, and William Ferris, eds. *The Encyclopedia of Southern Culture*. Chapel Hill: University of North Carolina Press, 1989.

Wittner, Lawrence S. *Rebels Against War: The American Peace Movement, 1941–1960*. New York: Columbia University Press, 1969.

Wofford, Harris. *Of Kennedys and Kings: Making Sense of the Sixties*. Pittsburgh: University of Pittsburgh Press, 1992.

Wolfe, Alan. *One Nation, After All*. New York: Viking, 1998.

Wolff, Miles. *Lunch at the Five and Ten: The Greensboro Sit-ins, a Contemporary History*. New York: Stein and Day, 1970.

Wolpert, Stanley. *Gandhi's Passion: The Life and Legacy of Mahatma Gandhi*. New York: Oxford University Press, 2001.

Wolters, Raymond. *The New Negro on Campus: Black College Rebellions of the 1920s*. Princeton: Princeton University Press, 1975.

Woodruff, Nan E. *American Congo: The African American Freedom Struggle in the Delta*. Cambridge: Harvard University Press, 2003.

Woods, Jeff. *Black Struggle, Red Scare: Segregation and Anti-Communism in the South, 1948–1968*. Baton Rouge: Louisiana State University Press, 2004.

Woodward, C. Vann. *The Strange Career of Jim Crow*. Commemorative Edition. New York: Oxford University Press, 2002.

Wright, Richard. *Black Boy*. New York: Harper and Brothers, 1945.

Wyatt, Edward A. *Petersburg's Story*. Petersburg, VA: Titmus Optical, 1960.

Wynn, Neil A. *The Afro-American and the Second World War*. New York: Holmes and Meier, 1976.

Yarbrough, Tinsley E. *Judge Frank Johnson and Human Rights in Alabama*. University: University of Alabama Press, 1981.

Young, Andrew. *An Easy Burden: The Civil Rights Movement and the Transformation of America*. New York: HarperCollins, 1996.

Younge, Gary. *No Place Like Home: A Black Briton's Journey Through the American South*. London: Picador, 1999.

Zangrando, Robert L. *The NAACP Crusade Against Lynching, 1909–1950*. Philadelphia: Temple University Press, 1980.

Zinn, Howard. *SNCC: The New Abolitionists*. Boston: Beacon Press, 1965.

Articles and Chapters

Aelony, Zev. "Back on the Road: Freedom Riders Return to the New South." *Pulse of the Twin Cities*, December 19, 2001.

"All, Here and Now." *Christian Century* 78 (June 28, 1961): 787–788.

Anderson, William G. "Reflections on the Origins of the Albany Movement." *Journal of Southwest Georgia History* 9 (Fall 1994): 1–14.

Arsenault, Raymond. "Bayard Rustin and the 'Miracle in Montgomery.' " In *A History of the African American People*, ed. James O. Horton and Lois E. Horton, 156–157. Detroit: Wayne State University Press, 1997.

————. "Civil Rights." In *The Columbia Companion to American History on Film: How the Movies Have Portrayed the American Past*, ed. Peter C. Rollins, 331–343. New York: Columbia University Press, 2003.

————. "The Folklore of Southern Demagoguery." In *Is There a Southern Political Tradition?* ed. Charles Eagles, 79–132. Jackson: University Press of Mississippi, 1996.

————. "One Brick at a Time: The Montgomery Bus Boycott, Nonviolent Direct Action, and the Development of a National Civil Rights Movement." In *Sunbelt Revolution: The Historical Progression of the Civil Rights Struggle in the Gulf South, 1866–2000*, ed. Samuel C. Hyde Jr., 153–189. Gainesville: University Press of Florida, 2003.

————. "Taking the Road to Freedom." *Forum* 28 (Spring 2004): 31–35.

————. " 'You Don't Have to Ride Jim Crow': CORE and the 1947 Journey of Reconciliation." In *Before Brown: Civil Rights and White Backlash in the Modern South*, ed. Glenn Feldman, 21–67. Tuscaloosa: University of Alabama Press, 2004.

"Asking for Trouble—and Getting It: The Ride for Rights." *Life* 50 (June 2, 1961): 46–53.

"Back to Jackson." *Newsweek* 58 (August 28, 1961): 28–29.

Badger, Tony. "The Forerunner of Our Opposition: Arkansas and the Southern Manifesto of 1956." *Arkansas Historical Quarterly* 56 (1999): 353–360.

————. "The White Reaction to *Brown*: Arkansas, the Southern Manifesto, and Massive Resistance." In *Understanding the Little Rock Crisis: An Exercise in Remembrance and Reconciliation*, ed. Elizabeth Jacoway and Fred C. Williams, 83–97. Fayetteville: University of Arkansas Press, 1999.

Baker, Ella. "Bigger than a Hamburger." *Southern Patriot* 18 (May 1960): 4.

Beito, David T., and Linda Royster Beito. "T.R.M. Howard: Pragmatism over Strict Integrationist Ideology in the Mississippi Delta, 1942–1954." In *Before* Brown: *Civil Rights and White Backlash in the Modern South*, ed. Glenn Feldman, 68–95.

Belfrage, Sally. "Danville on Trial." *New Republic* 149 (November 2, 1963): 11–12.

Bigelow, Albert. "Why I Am Sailing into the Pacific Bomb-Test Area." *Liberation* 2 (February 1958): 4–6.

"Bloody Beatings, Burning Bus in the South." *Life* 50 (May 26, 1961): 22–25.

Bond, Julian. "Death of a Quiet Man—A Mississippi Postscript." *Rights and Reviews* (Winter 1967): 15–17.

Booker, Simeon. "Alabama Mob Ambush Bus, Beat Biracial Group and Burn Bus." *Jet* 20 (May 25, 1961): 12–15.

———. "How Atty.-Gen. Kennedy Plans to Aid Dixie Negroes." *Jet* 19 (April 20, 1961): 12–15.

———. "How JFK Surpassed Abraham Lincoln." *Ebony* 19 (February 1964): 25–28+.

Booker, Simeon, and Theodore Gaffney. "Eyewitness Report on Dixie 'Freedom Ride'–*Jet* Team Braves Mob Action 4 Times Within 2-Day Period." *Jet* 19 (June 1, 1961): 14–21.

Braden, Anne. "Student Movement: New Phase." *Southern Patriot* 18 (November 1960): 4.

———. "Student Protest Movement Taking Permanent Form." *Southern Patriot* 18 (October 1960): 4.

Branton, Wiley A. "Little Rock Revisited: Desegregation to Resegregation." *Journal of Negro Education* 52 (Summer 1983): 250–269.

Brearley, H. C. "The Pattern of Violence." In *Culture in the South*, ed. W. T. Couch, 678–692. Chapel Hill: University of North Carolina Press, 1934.

Brown, Robert McAfee. "The Freedom Riders: A Clergyman's View." *Amherst Alumni Magazine* 14 (Fall 1961): 11–14.

———. "I Was a Freedom Rider." *Presbyterian Life* (August 1, 1961): 10–11, 32–33.

Bullimore, Kim. "The Aboriginal Struggle for Justice and Land Rights," *Green Left Weekly.* http://www.greenleft.org.au/back/2001/433/433p16.htm.

Burke, Thomas F. "On the Rights Track: The Americans with Disabilities Act." In *Comparative Disadvantage: Social Regulations and the Global Economy*, ed. Pietro S. Nivola, 242–318. Washington: Brookings Institution, 1997.

"Bus Stop." *Newsweek* 58 (December 11, 1961): 30–32.

Carey, Gordon R. "Action Institute Aids Miami CORE." *CORE-lator* (Fall 1959): 1–3.

"Carolina Journey Members Lose North Carolina Appeal." *Fellowship* 15 (February 1949).

Carson, Clayborne. "SNCC and the Albany Movement." *Journal of Southwest Georgia History* 2 (Fall 1984): 15–25.

Carter, Barbara. "A Brick Every Sunday." *Reporter* 26 (September 20, 1961): 39–40.

———. "The Fifteenth Amendment Comes to Mississippi," *Reporter* 28 (January 17, 1963): 20–24.

Chalfen, Michael. "Rev. Samuel B. Wells and Black Protest in Albany, 1945–1965." *Journal of Southwest Georgia History* 9 (Fall 1994): 37–64.

"Chapel Hill Judge Sentences Rustin and Roodenko." *Fellowship* 13 (July 1947).

Clayton, Ed. "The Men Behind Martin Luther King." *Ebony* 20 (June 1965): 170.

Coffin, William Sloane, Jr. "Why Yale Chaplain Rode: Christians Can't Be Outside." *Life* 50 (June 2, 1961): 54–55.

"Compendium of Curious Coincidences: Parallels in the Lives and Deaths of Abraham Lincoln and John F. Kennedy." *Time* 84 (August 21, 1964): 19.

Cook, Robert. "From Shiloh to Selma: The Impact of the Civil War Centennial on the Black Freedom Struggle in the United States, 1961–1965." In *The Making of Martin Luther King and the Civil Rights Movement*, ed. Brian Ward and Tony Badger, 131–146. New York: New York University Press, 1996.

Copeland, Larry. "Freedom Riders Go South Again." *USA Today*, November 8, 2001, 9D.

Corley, Robert. "In Search of Racial Harmony: Birmingham Business Leaders and Desegregation, 1950–1963." In *Southern Businessmen and Desegregation*, ed. Elizabeth Jacoway and David Colburn, 170–190. Baton Rouge: Louisiana State University Press, 1982.

Cousins, Norman. "The Men of the Golden Rule." *Saturday Review* 41 (May 17, 1958): 24.

"Crisis in Civil Rights." *Time* 77 (June 2, 1961): 14–18.

Dailey, Jane E. "Deference and Violence in the Postbellum Urban South: Manners and Massacres in Danville, Virginia." *Journal of Southern History* 63 (August 1991): 554–590.

Dalfiume, Richard M. "The 'Forgotten Years' of the Negro Revolution." *Journal of American History* 55 (June 1968): 90–106.

Davis, Jack E. "Baseball's Reluctant Challenge: Desegregating Major League Spring Training Sites, 1961–1964." *Journal of Sport History* 19 (Summer 1992): 144–162.

"Days of Violence in the South." *Newsweek* 57 (May 29, 1961): 21–22.

"Delinquency—Alabama Style." *Southern Patriot* 8 (October 1960): 2–4.

"Deplore Secrecy in the Jones Case." *Christian Century* 70 (March 4, 1953): 245.

Devree, Charlotte. "The Young Negro Rebels." *Harper's* 223 (October 1961): 133–138.

Dixon, Robert G., Jr. "Civil Rights in Transportation and the ICC." *George Washington Law Review* 31 (October 1962): 198–241.

Dunbar, Leslie. "The Freedom Ride." *New South* 16 (July/August 1961): 9–10.

Dunne, George H. "God Bless America!" *America* 105 (June 17, 1961): 442–443.

Eagles, Charles W. "Toward New Histories of the Civil Rights Era." *Journal of Southern History* 66 (November 2000): 815–848.

Ely, James W., Jr. "Negro Demonstrations and the Law: Danville as a Test Case." *Vanderbilt Law Review* 25 (October 1974): 931–943.

Erskine, Hazel Gaudet. "The Polls: Kennedy as President." *Public Opinion Quarterly* 28 (Summer 1964): 334–342.

———. "The Polls: Race Relations." *Public Opinion Quarterly* 26 (Spring 1962): 137–148.

Evans, Sara. "Women's Consciousness and the Southern Black Movement." *Southern Exposure* 4 (1977): 10–18.

"Evening Glory: Forgotten Civil Rights Pioneer James Farmer Finally Gets His Medal." *People* (April 6, 1998): 133–134.

Farmer, James. "Jail-Inners Resume Struggle." *CORE-lator* (April 1961): 3–4.

Feagans, Janet. "Voting, Violence, and Walkout in McComb." *New South* 16 (October 1961): 3–4.

Felien, Ed. "The History of Honeywell as Seen from South Minneapolis." *Pulse of the Twin Cities*, June 16–22, 1999.

Fey, Harold E. "Freedom Rides at N.C.C." *Christian Century* 78 (June 21, 1961): 766–767.

Fifty Members of Montgomery Ministerial Association. "Prevent Future Incidents of Mob Action, Bloodshed." *New South* 16 (June 1961): 13–15.

"Four Freedom Riders." *Time* 77 (June 2, 1961): 17.

Franklin, John Hope. "A Half-Century of Presidential Race Initiatives: Some Reflections." *Journal of Supreme Court History* 24 (1999): 226–238.

Fredrickson, George M. "A Man but Not a Brother: Abraham Lincoln and Racial Equality." *Journal of Southern History* 41 (February 1975): 39–58.

"Freedom Ride Round-Up." *Southern Patriot* 19 (September 1961): 1.

"Freedom Riders." *New Republic* 144 (June 5, 1961): 5.

"Freedom Riders: Cracks in the Levee." *America* 105 (May 27, 1961): 358.

"Freedom Riders Force a Test." *Newsweek* 57 (June 5, 1961): 18–20, 22.

Fuller, Helen. "We, the People of Alabama. . . ." *New Republic* 144 (June 5, 1961): 21–23.

Gastil, Raymond. "Homicide and a Regional Culture of Violence." *American Sociological Review* 36 (June 1971): 412–427.

Glennon, Robert Jerome. "The Role of Law in the Civil Rights Movement: The Montgomery Bus Boycott, 1955–1957." *Law and History Review* 9 (Spring 1991): 59–112.

Goldman, Eric F. "Progress—By Moderation *and* Agitation." *New York Times Magazine* (June 18, 1961): 5, 10–12.

Goldsmith, William. "The Cost of Freedom Rides." *Dissent* 4 (Autumn 1961): 499–502.

"A Great Thing." *Southern Patriot* 19 (June 1961): 4.

Hackney, Sheldon. "Southern Violence." *American Historical Review* 74 (February 1969): 906–925.

Halberstam, David. "The Kids Take Over." *Reporter* 24 (June 22, 1961): 22–23.

"Halfway Home to Equality on Highway 40." *Life* 51 (November 16, 1961): 6.

Hall, Jacquelyn Dowd. "The Long Civil Rights Movement and the Political Uses of the Past." *Journal of American History* 91 (March 2005): 1233–1250.

Hamalian, Lee. "Life Begins on Route 40." *Nation* 194 (January 27, 1962): 71–73.

Harley, Sharon. "Ella Jo Baker." In *The Encyclopedia of Southern Culture*, ed. Charles Reagan Wilson and William Ferris, 1570–1571. Chapel Hill: University of North Carolina Press, 1989.

Hidalgo, Ellie. "Freedom Rides for Immigrant Workers." *Tidings* (Los Angeles), September 26, 2003.

"The Historic Image." *Nation* 192 (June 3, 1961): 469–470.

Holloway, Frank. "Travel Notes from a Deep South Tourist." *New South* 16 (July/August 1961): 3–8.

"The Hostess Was Sorry." *Newsweek* 58 (July 10, 1961): 28–29.

Houser, George M. " 'Thy Brother's Blood': Reminiscences of World War II." *Christian Century* 112 (August 16, 1995): 772–781.

Huntington, William. "If You Feel Like It." *Liberation* 3 (June 1958): 5–6.

"I.C.C. Should Act to Protect Travelers." *Christian Century* 78 (June 14, 1961): 732.

"Injunctions and Freedoms." *Commonweal* 74 (June 16, 1961): 292.

"Injustice Will Tire First." *Christian Century* 78 (July 26, 1961): 892.

"Is South Headed for Race War?" *U.S. News and World Report* 50 (June 5, 1961): 42–48.

Jack, Homer A. "Journey of Reconciliation." *Common Ground* 8 (Autumn 1947): 21–26.

Janken, Kenneth R. "From Colonial Liberation to Cold War Liberalism: Walter White, the NAACP, and Foreign Affairs, 1941–1955." *Ethnic and Racial Studies* 21 (1998): 1074–1095.

Johnson, Gerald W. "Who Turned the Bull Loose?" *New Republic* 144 (June 5, 1961): 20.

Johnson, Suzanne. "The Stand." *Tulanian* 72 (Summer 2001): 14–17.

Jones, Lewis W. "Fred L. Shuttlesworth, Indigenous Leader." In *Birmingham, Alabama, 1956–1963: The Black Struggle for Civil Rights*, ed. David J. Garrow, 115–150. Brooklyn: Carlson, 1989.

Joseph, Peniel E. "Black Liberation Without Apology: Reconceptualizing the Black Power Movement." *Black Scholar* 31 (Fall/Winter 2001): 2–19.

Keel, Beverly. "A Mission of Nonviolence." *American Profile* (January 11–17, 2004): 6, 8.

Kelley, Robin D. G. "Freedom Riders (The Sequel): The Politics of Busing Has Taken Another Wrong Turn." *Nation* 262 (February 6, 1996): 18.

Kempton, Murray. "Pilgrimage to Jackson." *New Republic* 148 (May 11, 1963): 15.

King, Martin Luther, Jr. "Our Struggle." *Liberation* 1 (April 1956): 3–6.

———. " 'The Time for Freedom Has Come.' " *New York Times Magazine* (September 10, 1961): 25, 118–119.

Kirby, John B. "Race, Class, and Politics: Ralph Bunche and Black Protest." In *Ralph Bunche: The Man and His Times*, ed. Benjamin Rivlin, 28–49. New York: Holmes and Meier, 1990.

Knight, Pauline. "Notes from Prison." *Southern Patriot* 19 (September 1961): 1.

Korstad, Robert, and Nelson Lichtenstein. "Opportunities Lost: Labor, Radicals, and the Early Civil Rights Movement." *Journal of American History* 75 (December 1988): 786–811.

Kosek, Joseph Kip. "Richard Gregg, Mohandas Gandhi, and the Strategy of Nonviolence." *Journal of American History* 91 (March 2005): 1318–1348.

"Label U.S. Racial Violence 'Shot Heard 'Round World." *Jet* 19 (June 22, 1961): 16–17.

LaPrad, Paul. "Nashville: A Community Struggle." In James Peck, *Freedom Ride*, 82–88. New York: Harper and Row, 1962.

Lawson, James. "Eve of Nonviolent Revolution." *Southern Patriot* 19 (November 1961): 1.

Lerner, Gerda. "Developing Community Leadership: Ella Baker." In *Black Women in White America: A Documentary History*, ed. Gerda Lerner, 352. New York: Vintage Books, 1973.

"Let Us Try, at Least, to Understand." *National Review* 10 (June 3, 1961): 338.

Lever, Constance. "Monroe Doctrine." *Spectator* (September 15, 1961): 346.

Lewis, John. "Freedom Riders of 2003." *Washington Post*, October 1, 2003.

Locke, Mamie E. "The Role of African-American Women in the Civil Rights and Women's Movements in Hinds County and Sunflower County, Mississippi." *Journal of Mississippi History* 53 (1991): 229–239.

Lowry, John. "Should Violence Be Met with Violence?" *Realist* 32 (March 1962): 7–9.

Lukas, John Anthony. "Trouble on Route Forty." *Reporter* 25 (October 26, 1961): 41.

"Map, 'State of Race' Confab for D.C." *Jet* 9 (April 19, 1956): 3.

Martin, Robert F. "Critique of Southern Society and Vision of a New Order: The Fellowship of Southern Churchmen, 1934–1957." *Church History* 52 (March 1983): 66–80.

Martinson, Robert. "Prison Notes of a Freedom Rider." *Nation* 194 (January 6, 1962): 4.

Mayfield, Julian. "Challenge to Negro Leadership: The Case of Robert Williams." *Commentary* 31 (April 1961): 297–305.

McDonald, Jimmy. "A Freedom Rider Speaks His Mind." *Freedomways* 1 (Summer 1961): 158–162. Rpt. in *Freedomways Reader: Prophets in Their Own Country*, ed. Esther Cooper Jackson, 59–64. Boulder, CO: Westview Press,, 2000.

McMillen, Neil R. "Black Enfranchisement in Mississippi: Federal Enforcement and Black Protest in the 1960s." *Journal of Southern History* 43 (August 1977): 351–372.

Meier, August, and Elliott Rudwick. "The Boycott Movement Against Jim Crow Streetcars in the South, 1900–1906." *Journal of American History* 51 (March 1969): 756–775.

Miller, Doug. "The Forgotten Freedom Rider." *Columbia Flier*, April 14, 1994.

Mitchell, Dennis J. "Ross Barnett." In *The Encyclopedia of Southern Culture*, ed. Charles Reagan Wilson and William Ferris, 1182. Chapel Hill: University of North Carolina Press, 1989.

Mohl, Raymond A. " 'South of the South?' Jews, Blacks, and the Civil Rights Movement in Miami, 1945–1960." *Journal of American Ethnic History* 18 (Winter 1999): 3–26.

Mollin, Marian B. "The Limits of Egalitarianism: Radical Pacifism, Civil Rights, and the Journey of Reconciliation." *Radical History Review* 88 (Winter 2004): 113–138.

"Montgomery After the Mob." *Southern Patriot* 19 (September 1, 1961): 1, 4.

"More Momentum." *Newsweek* 57 (June 19, 1961): 27–28.

Morello, Carol. "The Freedom Rider a Nation Nearly Forgot." *Washington Post*, July 30, 2000, A1, A16.

Moses, Bob. "Foreword." In Ken Light. *Delta Time: Mississippi Photographs by Ken Light*, xi–xiv. Washington: Smithsonian Institution Press, 1995.

———. "Mississippi: 1961–1962." *Liberation* 14 (January 1970): 6–17.

Murphy, Paul L. "Balancing Acts: The Supreme Court and the Bill of Rights: 1965–1991." In *Crucible of Liberty: 200 Years of the Bill of Rights*, ed. Raymond Arsenault, 96–107. New York: Free Press, 1991.

Murray, Hugh, Jr. "The Struggle for Civil Rights in New Orleans in 1960: Reflections and Recollections." *Journal of Ethnic Studies* 6 (Spring 1978): 25–41.

Murray, Pauli. "A Blueprint for Full Citizenship." *Crisis* 51 (November 1944): 358–359.

Muste, A. J. "Follow the Golden Rule." *Liberation* 3 (June 1958): 7–8.

Nash, Diane. "Inside the Sit-ins and Freedom Rides: Testimony of a Southern Student." in *The New Negro*, ed. Mathew H. Ahmann, 42–60. New York: Biblo and Tannen, 1969.

Nasstrom, Kathryn. "Down to Now: Memory, Narrative, and Women's Leadership in the Civil Rights Movement in Atlanta, Georgia." *Gender and History* 11 (April 1999): 113–144.

Negen, Gordon. "I Went on a Freedom Ride." *Reformed Journal* (July-August 1961): 4-6.

"Negro Transit Jobs Spread in South." *New South* 16 (November 1961): 11.

"The Negro Tries Passive Resistance." *New York Times Magazine* (May 28, 1961): 12–13.

"A New Breed: The Militant Negro in the South." *Newsweek* 57 (June 5, 1961): 21.

"New Spirit Moves in Mississippi." *Southern Patriot* 19 (November 1961): 1.

Oates, Stephen B. "The Albany Movement: A Chapter in the Life of Martin Luther King, Jr." *Journal of Southwest Georgia History* 2 (Fall 1984): 26–39.

"On the Railroad." *Newsweek* 58 (October 30, 1961): 19.

"Our Friend in Jail." *America* 105 (July 1, 1961): 476.

Padgett, Gregory. "The Tallahassee Bus Boycott." In *Sunbelt Revolution: The Historical Progression of the Civil Rights Struggle in the Gulf South, 1866–2000*, ed. Samuel C. Hyde Jr., 190–209. Gainesville: University Press of Florida, 2003.

Palmore, Joseph R. "The Not-So-Strange Career of Interstate Jim Crow: Race, Transportation, and the Dormant Commerce Clause, 1878–1946." *Virginia Law Review* 83 (November 1997): 1773–1817.

"Pastor vs. Presbytery." *Time* 61 (February 23, 1953):53.

Patterson, Eugene. "The Long Road Back to Georgia." In *The Changing South of Gene Patterson: Journalism and Civil Rights, 1960–1968*, ed. Roy Peter Clark and Raymond Arsenault, 255–263. Gainesville: University Press of Florida, 2002.

Patterson, W. D. "The Calloused Conscience." *Saturday Review* 44 (June 10, 1961): 28.

"Patterson Says 'Rides' Hurt Race Relations." *Southern School News* 8 (July 1961): 9.

Payne, Charles. "Ella Baker and Models of Social Change." *Signs* 14 (Summer 1989): 885–899.

Peck, Jim. "A Carolina City—Fifteen Years Later." *CORE-lator* (November 1962): 2.

———. "Fifteen Years After the Freedom Rides." *War Resisters League News* (January–February 1977): 6.

———. "Freedom Ride." *CORE-lator* (May 1961): 1–4.

———. "Jail Is Our Home Port." *Liberation* 3 (June 1958): 4–5.

———. "Not So Deep Are the Roots." *Crisis* (September 1947): 273–274, 282–283.

Poinsett, Alex. "Ten Biggest Lies About Freedom Riders." *Jet* 20 (June 22, 1961): 12–14.

———. "Who Speaks for the Negro? Many Voices in Harmony as Freedom Struggle Mounts." *Jet* 20 (July 6, 1961): 14–23.

Poussaint, Alvin. "The Stresses of the White Female Worker in the Civil Rights Movement in the South." *Journal of American Psychiatry* 123 (October 1966): 401–407.

Powell, Lawrence N. "When Hate Came to Town: New Orleans' Jews and George Lincoln Rockwell." *American Jewish History* 85 (December 1997): 394–419.

"Presbyterian U.S. Commission Fires Chapel Hill Pastor." *Christian Century* 70 (March 11, 1953): 277.

"Question Ducked." *Time* 47 (June 10, 1946): 23.

"A Question of Responsibility." *Commonweal* 74 (June 9, 1961): 267.

Quigley, M. "Carl Sandburg Tells How He Thinks Great Emancipator Would Have Reacted to Today's Touchy Race Problems." *Ebony* 18 (September 1963): 158–159.

"Race Tension and the Law." *U.S. News and World Report* 50 (June 12, 1961): 85.

Randall, Frank. "The Freedom Riders: An Historian's View." *Amherst Alumni Magazine* 14 (Fall 1961): 15–17.

Ricks, John A., III. " 'De Lawd' Descends and Is Crucified: Martin Luther King, Jr., in Albany, Georgia." *Journal of Southwest Georgia History* 2 (Fall 1984): 3–14.

"Rolling On." *Time* 77 (June 9, 1961): 15–16.

Romano, Renee. "No Diplomatic Immunity: African Diplomats, the State Department, and Civil Rights, 1961–1964." *Journal of American History* 87 (September 2000): 546–574.

Rostow, Eugene V. "The Freedom Riders and the Future." *Reporter* 24 (June 22, 1961): 18–21.

Rowe-Simms, Sarah. "The Mississippi State Sovereignty Commission: An Agency History." *Journal of Mississippi History* 61 (1999): 29–58.

Ruark, Henry. "Orange Presbytery vs. Jones." *Christian Century* 170 (March 18, 1953): 319–320.

Rustin, Bayard. "Montgomery Diary." *Liberation* 1 (April 1956), 7–19.

———. "The Negro and Non-Violence." *Fellowship* 8 (October 1942).

———. "Our Guest Column: Beyond the Courts." *Louisiana Weekly*, January 4, 1947.

Salmond, John. " 'Flag-bearers for Integration and Justice': Local Civil Rights Groups in the South, 1940–1954." In *Before Brown: Civil Rights and White Backlash in the Modern South*, ed. Glenn Feldman, 222–237. Tuscaloosa: University of Alabama Press, 2004.

Sancton, Thomas. "Something's Happened to the Negro." *New Republic* 108 (February 8, 1943): 175–179.

"Seeking a Damper for Racial Strife." *Business Week* (June 3, 1961): 22–23.

Seigenthaler, John. "Civil Rights in the Trenches." In *The Kennedy Presidency: Seventeen Intimate Perspectives of John F. Kennedy*, ed. Kenneth W. Thompson, 101–126. Portraits of American Presidents, vol. 4. Lanham, MD: University Press of America, 1985.

"73 Negro Leaders in D.C. Session Seek Immediate Meeting with Ike." *Jet* 9 (May 10, 1956): 4–5.

Shayon, Robert Lewis. "Why Did Howard K. Smith Leave?" *Saturday Review* 44 (November 18, 1961): 37.

Shibley, Ronald E. "Fredericksburg, Va.." In *The Encyclopedia of Southern History*, ed. David C. Roller and Robert W. Twyman, 488. Baton Rouge: Louisiana State University Press, 1979.

"Signs Down." *Newsweek* 58 (November 13, 1961): 22–24.

"Silent Majority." *Ebony* 16 (July 1961): 76.

Sitkoff, Harvard. "Racial Militancy and Interracial Violence During the Second World War." *Journal of American History* 58 (June 1971): 663–683.

"Small Success." *Time* (December 8, 1961): 25.

"SNCC Conference." *Student Voice* 1 (October 1960): 1.

"The South and the Freedom Riders: Crisis in Civil Rights." *Time* 77 (June 2, 1961): 14–18.

"Southern Schrecklichkeit: The Isaac Woodard Case." *Crisis* 51 (September 1946): 276.

Stampp, Kenneth M. "The Tragic Legend of Reconstruction." In *Reconstruction: An Anthology of Revisionist Writings*, ed. Kenneth M. Stampp and Leon F. Litwack, 3–21. Baton Rouge: Louisiana State University Press, 1969.

Stephens, Patricia. "Tallahassee: Through Jail to Freedom." In James Peck, *Freedom Ride*, 73–79. New York: Harper and Row, 1962.

Still, Larry A. "A Bus Ride Through Mississippi." *Ebony* 16 (August 1961): 21–28.

———. "Freedom Riders Gather from Across the Nation: Miss. Trip Brings More Arrests." *Jet* 20 (June 8, 1961): 12–19.

Sullivan, Patricia. "Southern Reformers, the New Deal, and the Movement's Foundation." In *New Directions in Civil Rights Studies*, ed. Armistead L. Robinson and Patricia Sullivan, 81–104. Charlottesville: University of Virginia Press, 1991.

"Tensions and Justice." *Newsweek* 57 (June 12, 1961): 37–38.

"The Test of Nonviolence." *Nation* 192 (June 3, 1961): 469–470.

"Thirty-Year Reunion: Triumphant Freedom Riders Return to Mississippi." *Ebony* 46 (October 1991): 120–124.

Thompson, Peggy. "A Visit to Danville." *Progressive* 27 (November 1963): 28.

"Three Questions of the Law." *Time* 77 (June 2, 1961): 16.

"Trouble in Alabama." *Time* 77 (May 26, 1961): 16–17.

Umoja, Akinyele K. "Ballots and Bullets: A Comparative Analysis of Armed Resistance in the Civil Rights Movement." *Journal of Black Studies* 29 (March 1999): 558–578.

"Uncle Sam, Get That Monkey off Your Back." *Jet* 20 (July 13, 1961): 8.

"Untold Story of the 'Freedom Rides.' " *U.S. News and World Report* 51 (October 23, 1961): 76–79.

"Virginia Goes A'Courtin'." *Headlines and Pictures* (May 1946): 15.

"Violence in Alabama." *America* 105 (June 3, 1961): 388.

"Violence in Alabama." *Commonweal* 74 (June 2, 1961): 244.

Waddle, Ray. "Days of Thunder: The Lawson Affair." *Vanderbilt Magazine* 83 (Fall 2002): 35–43.

Webb, Clive. "'A Cheap Trafficking in Human Misery': The Reverse Freedom Rides of 1962." *Journal of American Studies* 38 (2004): 249–271.

———. "Big Struggle in a Small Town: Charles Martinband of Hattiesburg, Mississippi." In *Quiet Voices: Southern Rabbis and Black Civil Rights, 1880s to 1990s*, ed. Mark Bauman and Berkley Kalin, 213–229. Tuscaloosa: University of Alabama Press, 1998.

Wilentz, Sean. "The Last Integrationist." *New Republic* 215 (July 1, 1996): 19–26.

Wittner, Lawrence. "The National Negro Congress: A Reassessment." *American Quarterly* 22 (Fall 1970): 883–901.

"World Press Views Freedom Rides and the United States." *New South* 16 (July/August 1961): 11–15.

Wynn, Linda T. "The Dawning of a New Day: The Nashville Sit-Ins, February 13–May 10, 1960." *Tennessee Historical Quarterly* (Spring 1991): 42–54.

Zellner, Bob. "Notes of a Native Son." *Southern Exposure* 9 (Spring 1981): 48–49.

Zola, Gary Phillip. "What Price Amos? Perry Nussbaum's Career in Jackson, Mississippi." In *Quiet Voices: Southern Rabbis and Black Civil Rights, 1880s to 1990s*, ed. Mark Bauman and Berkley Kalin, 230–260. Tuscaloosa: University of Alabama Press, 1998.

Unpublished Theses

Anderson-Bricker, Kristin M. "Making a Movement: The Meaning of Community in the Congress of Racial Equality, 1958–1968." Ph.D. thesis, Syracuse University, 1997.

Bolster, Paul. "Civil Rights Movement in Twentieth-Century Georgia." Ph.D. thesis, University of Georgia, 1972.

Burnside, Ronald D. "The Governorship of Coleman L. Blease of South Carolina, 1911–1915." Ph.D. thesis, Indiana University, 1963.

Catsam, Derek, " 'A Brave and Wonderful Thing': The Freedom Rides and the Integration of Interstate Transport, 1941–1965." Ph.D. thesis, Ohio University, 2003.

Clark, Benjamin Franklin, Sr. "The Editorial Reaction of Selected Southern Black Newspapers to the Civil Rights Movement, 1954–1968." Ph.D. thesis, Howard University, 1989.

Crofton, Gregory C. "Defending Segregation: Mississippi State Sovereignty Commission and the Press." M.A. thesis, University of Mississippi, 2000.

Entin, David. "Angelo Herndon." M.A. thesis, University of North Carolina, 1963.

Finley, Melissa Lynn. "But I Was a Practical Segregationist: Erle Johnston and the Mississippi State Sovereignty Commission, 1960–1968." M.A. thesis, University of Southern Mississippi, 2000.

German, Richard H. L. "The Queen City of the Savannah: Augusta, Georgia, During the Urban Progressive Era, 1890–1917." Ph.D. thesis, University of Florida, 1971.

Gerner, Henry L. "A Study of the Freedom Riders with Particular Emphasis upon Three Dimensions, Dogmatism, Value-Orientation, Religiosity." Th.D. thesis, Pacific School of Religion, 1963.

Katz, Neil H. "Radical Pacifism and the Contemporary American Peace Movement: The Committee for Nonviolent Action, 1957–1967." Ph.D. thesis, University of Maryland, 1974.

LaJaunie, Barbara L. "A Question of Legitimacy: The *Farmville Herald* and the *Brown* Decision." Ph.D. thesis, University of Kentucky, 1998.

Mainwaring, W. Thomas. "Community in Danville, Virginia, 1880–1963." Ph.D. thesis, University of North Carolina, Chapel Hill, 1988

Mollin, Marian B. "Actions Louder than Words: Gender and Political Activism in the American Radical Pacifist Movement, 1942–1972." Ph.D. thesis, University of Massachusetts, 2000.

Moore, Laura Ingram. "The Mississippi State Sovereignty Commission: State-Supported Resistance to Desegregation." M.A. thesis, Wake Forest University, 1997.

Morgenroth, Florence. "Organization and Activities of the American Civil Liberties Union in Miami 1955–1966." M.A. thesis, University of Miami, 1966.

Morris, Tiyi Makeda. "Black Women's Civil Rights Activism in Mississippi: The Story of Womanpower Unlimited." Ph.D. thesis, Purdue University, 2002.

Murrell, Amy E. "Standing Steady: Toward an Understanding of the Prince Edward School Crisis, 1959–1964." M.A. thesis, University of Virginia, 1996.

Mussatt, David J. "Journey for Justice: A Religious Analysis of the Ethics of the 1961 Albany Freedom Ride." Ph.D. thesis, Temple University, 2001.

Schneidler, Emilie. "Shapings Ideas and Action: CORE, SCLC, and SNCC in the Struggle for Equality, 1960–1966." Ph.D. thesis, University of Michigan, 1980.

Schnur, James A. "Cold Warriors in the Hot Sunshine: The Johns Committee's Assault on Civil Liberties in Florida, 1956–1965." M.A. thesis, University of South Florida, 1995.

Secrest, A. M. "In Black and White: Press Opinion and Race Relations in South Carolina, 1954–1964." Ph.D. thesis, Duke University, 1971.

Sprayberry, Gary S. " 'Town Among the Trees': Paternalism, Class, and Civil Rights in Anniston, Alabama, 1872 to Present." Ph.D. thesis, University of Alabama, 2003.

Sumner, David. "The Local Press and the Nashville Student Movement." Ph.D. thesis, University of Tennessee, 1989.

Taylor, Sandra A. "The Nashville Sit-In Movement, 1960." M.A. thesis, Fisk University, 1972.

Walker, Eugene P. "A History of the Southern Christian Leadership Conference, 1955–1965: The Evolution of a Southern Strategy for Social Change." Ph.D. thesis, Duke University, 1978.

White, Robert M. "The Tallahassee Sit-ins and CORE: A Nonviolent Revolutionary Submovement." Ph.D. thesis, Florida State University, 1965.

Wills, Morgan Jackson. "Walking the Edge: Vanderbilt University and the Sit-in Crisis of 1960." Senior thesis, Princeton University, 1990.

Films, Documentaries, Sound Recordings, and Television Videos

"Ain't Scared of Your Jails." Episode 3 of the documentary film series *Eyes on the Prize: America's Civil Rights Years*. Boston: Blackside, 1986.

Anatomy of a Demonstration. New York: CBS Television, 1960.

Down Freedom's Main Line. Washington, DC: George Washington University Institute for Historical Documentary Filmmaking, 1998.

The Fabulous Sixties, 1961. Oak Forest, IL: MPI Home Video, 1970.

Freedom Rider Arrests, May–June 1961. Video footage, WJBT television, Jackson, MS.

Freedom Song. Atlanta: TNT Productions, 2000.

Fundi: The Story of Ella Baker. New York: First Run Features, 1981.

I Am on the Battlefield. Albany, GA: Rutha Harris, 2004. Albany Civil Rights Museum Freedom Singers recording.

James McCain: The Quest for Civil Rights. Columbia: University of South Carolina Instructional Services Center, 1980.

Ladykillers. Buena Vista Home Video DVD, 2004.

Nashville: We Were Warriors. Excerpted from *A Force More Powerful: A Century of Nonviolent Conflict*. New York: PBS, 2000. Copy available at Nashville Public Library.

Promised Land (Chuck Berry). Tristan Music, 1963.

Robert F. Kennedy: The American Experience. New York: PBS, 2004.

Sing for Freedom: The Story of the Civil Rights Movement Through Its Songs. Washington, DC: Smithsonian Folkways Records, 1990.

Sit-in (NBC White Paper). New York: NBC Television, 1960.

Sit-in Songs, Songs of the Freedom Riders. New York: Dauntless Records, 1962.

"Skin Deep: The Fight Against Legislated Racism." Episode of *People's Century*. New York: PBS, 1999.

Tales of Cape Cod Freedom Riders. Boston: C3TV, 1962. Copy in Margaret Mosely Papers, Schlesinger Library, Harvard University, Cambridge, MA.

To Kill a Mockingbird. University City, CA: MCA Videocassette, 1981.

We Shall Overcome: Songs of the Freedom Riders and the Sit-ins. Washington, DC: Smithsonian Folkways Records, 1991.

Who Speaks for Birmingham? New York: CBS Reports, May 18, 1961. Transcript available at BPL.

You Don't Have to Ride JIM CROW! Durham, NH: New Hampshire Public Television, 1995.

Websites

Civil Rights Movement Veterans. www.crmvet.org

Congress of Racial Equality (CORE). http://www.core-online.org

Footsoldiers: The Fight for Civil Rights. http://www.footsoldiers.org

Freedom Rides in Australia 1965. http://freedomride.net

The Immigrant Workers Freedom Ride. http://www.iwfr.org

Jewish Women's Archive. http://www.jwa.org

McCain Library, University of Southern Mississippi. *Civil Rights in Mississippi Digital Archive*. http://www.lib.usm.edu/~spcol/crda

Nashville Public Library—Civil Rights Room. http://www.library.nashville.org/Newsevents/Civil%20Rights%20Room/civilrightsroom.htm

1961 Freedom Riders' 40th Reunion. www.freedomridersfoundation.com

Social Security Death Index. http://ssdi.genealogy.rootsweb.com

Voices of Civil Rights: Ordinary People. Extraordinary Stories. www.voicesofcivilrights.org

You Don't Have to Ride Jim Crow. http://www/robinwashington.com/jimcrow/1_home.html

Index

Note: Page numbers in *italics* refer to illustrations.